Quantitative Management of Bond Portfolios

ADVANCES IN FINANCIAL ENGINEERING

Andrew Lo, Editor

Quantitative Management of Bond Portfolios, by Lev Dynkin, Anthony Gould, Jay Hyman, Vadim Konstantinovsky, and Bruce Phelps

Quantitative Management of Bond Portfolios

LEV DYNKIN

ANTHONY GOULD

JAY HYMAN

VADIM KONSTANTINOVSKY

BRUCE PHELPS

PRINCETON UNIVERSITY PRESS

Princeton and Oxford

Library of Congress Cataloging-in-Publication Data

Quantitative management of bond portfolios / by Lev Dynkin . . . [et al.].
   p.   cm. — (Advances in financial engineering)
   Includes bibliographical references and index.
   ISBN-13: 978-0-691-12831-3 (hardcover : alk. paper)
   ISBN-10: 0-691-12831-6 (hardcover : alk. paper)
   1. Bonds.   2. Portfolio management.   I. Dynkin, Lev, 1957–   II. Series.
   HG4651.Q36 2006
   332.63′23—dc22   2006016995

British Library Cataloging-in-Publication Data is available

This book has been composed in Minion Pro and Syntax by Princeton Editorial Associates, Inc., Scottsdale, Arizona

Printed on acid-free paper. ∞

pup.princeton.edu

Printed in the United States of America

10 9 8 7 6 5 4 3 2

To my dear parents David and Tsivya—

my friends, teachers, and

supporters in everything I do.

LD

CONTENTS

FOREWORD

Twenty-five years ago, a book with this title would have been thought of as a somewhat odd duck. Now the adjective "quantitative" when applied to bond portfolios seems quaint if not redundant. After all, how else is one to manage a fixed-income portfolio? Indeed, the management of bond portfolios—from the choice of objectives through the models for interest-rate processes and credit evaluation and on to the variety of implementation technologies—is now a center-piece of the modern arsenal of financial tools. In the same time period, the chasm that once divided the academic world from the "street" has been transformed into a four-lane expressway. Seemingly instantaneously, research in academic finance finds its way into practice. Conversely, researchers on the street are actively en-gaged in work that is of great interest to academics. Moreover, the two ends of the expressway collaborate and innovate together. In some areas, such as the employ-ment of optimization and numerical analytic techniques, the street has pioneered and the academy has followed.

It is this environment that makes this work such a wonderful and unique addi-tion to my bookshelf. Here one of the most talented and experienced groups of "quants" on the street explains how to put theory into practice to manage bond portfolios. This transition requires a host of practical compromises with empirical estimation, the reality of market instruments, and trading and implementation. It is this reality that makes this book far more than the usual excursion into the thicket of equations of neoclassical fixed-income finance that often seem naked without an institutional context. Here the reader will learn about the different objectives of the host of institutions and individuals that operate in the markets, from the chief investment officer of a financial management organization to the strategist for a central bank. Here, too, the reader will learn how to use theory to design strategies to fit objectives and how to implement those strategies in the markets. Perhaps most innovative, though, is the recognition that institutions in-vest within a hierarchical structure that requires strategies that fit not only with objectives, but also with the performance capabilities of the organization. Wearing my academic hat, this is a fascinating excursion into relatively virgin territory—the melding of agency considerations, portfolio and performance analysis, and organizational incentives.

By their focus on the practical and empirical, tempered and disciplined by a steadfast allegiance to the substantial body of theory in fixed-income finance, the authors have attained that most elusive of goals. While by no means a light read, this book is accessible to the newly minted portfolio manager and simultaneously offers up nuggets all along the way for even the most experienced. It is one thing to discover that the research on the street is the equal of that in the universities; it is somewhat more humbling to find that the pedagogy is also at the highest level. I thoroughly enjoyed this book, I learned much from it, and I will now have the pleasant task of reading it again to find the stuff I missed the first time. For those just starting out, pleasant trekking.

Steve Ross
Franco Modigliani Professor of Financial Economics,
MIT Sloan School of Management
Cambridge, Massachusetts

ACKNOWLEDGMENTS

The authors thank the following individuals, who all share credit for this book: Ravi Mattu, for his prescience about the bright future of quantitative research on Wall Street and for his long-term support of our group; Jack Malvey, for his encouragement and guidance of our research efforts; Michael Gelband and Bart McDade, for their continued commitment to fund our activity; Tom Humphrey, for tirelessly promoting our research to investors; Bob Fuhrman and Ivan Gruhl, for their confidence in our work during the early days when doubts were plentiful; Steve Berkley and Nick Gendron, for the high-quality index data that helped ground our studies in reality; Prof. Andrew Lo, for the inspiration behind this book; Prof. Frank Fabozzi, for his interest in our work over many, many years; and Peter Dougherty, director of Princeton University Press, and Seth Ditchik, editor, for their professionalism and patience, and for making the experience of publishing this book as pleasant as possible.

. . . .

We thank our families, for their patience and for the meaning they lend to all our endeavors.

NOTE ON AUTHORSHIP

The following members of the Quantitative Portfolio Strategies group played important roles in the effort of writing this book:

Arik Ben Dor contributed to the chapters on empirical duration of credit securities, the DTS measure of spread risk, and central bank reserve management. He was also of great help with the manuscript preparation.

Albert Desclée contributed to the chapters on risk modeling, replicating global benchmarks, optimal risk budget allocation, and global integration of credit markets.

Yang Chen participated in studies underlying several chapters of this book.

Michael Ng and Anthony Marenghi developed analytics and produced data that made our empirical research possible.

Jeremy Rosten contributed to the chapters on risk modeling, replicating global benchmarks, and global integration of credit markets.

• • • • • • • • • • • • • • • • • •

Our colleagues from other parts of Lehman Brothers Fixed-Income Research made the following contributions:

Dev Joneja managed the development of the global risk model and contributed to the chapters on risk modeling and swap indices.

Anthony Lazanas managed the development of the performance attribution model and contributed to the corresponding chapter.

Dick Kazarian, Marco Naldi, and Antonio Silva contributed to the chapter on risk modeling.

Vasant Naik and Minh Trinh authored the chapter on hedging debt with equity.

Lakshman Easwaran reviewed the entire manuscript and made a number of useful suggestions.

• • • • • • • • • • • • • • • • • •

Patrick Houweling, Erik van Leewen, and Olaf Penninga of the Robeco Group participated in the study of the spread-based measure of credit risk; Philippe Richer (with Credit Lyonnais at the time) contributed to the study of the value of skill in macro strategies.

....

Other current or former Lehman Brothers researchers who, at some point over the past decade, participated in studies discussed in this book include: Srivaths Balakrishnan, Jonathan Carmel, Yuri Greenfield, Peter Lindner, Bill Lu, Jordan Mann, Sandeep Mody, Saurav Sen, Philip Weissman, and Wei Wu.

INTRODUCTION

In 1998, shortly before the launch of the European Monetary Union, a European asset management company asked us how the EMU might change the management of credit portfolios. The credit markets in Europe, fragmented and dominated by high-quality financial issuers in multiple currencies, were about to be transformed into a single-currency market expected to increase in size, sector diversity, and issuer breadth. The questions this institution posed to us were both deep and challenging. Does a credit portfolio benefit from a "bottom-up" management style with all the associated costly fundamental analysis of individual issuers in the market? Or can a manager achieve comparable results at a lower cost by timing duration or credit sector allocation while diversifying away issuer risk?

This investor was not looking for any subjective opinion or intuition, but rather for empirical evidence of the relative merits of the "top-down" vs. "bottom-up" styles of portfolio management. This evidence would form the basis for structuring its credit portfolio team and allocation of budget. In response to this query, we carried out an empirical study that simulated the historical performance of different strategies, including security selection as well as several macro strategies. We simulated the performance of each strategy under different assumptions about the manager's skill. Our results showed that, for a given level of skill, security selection outperforms macro-allocation strategies on a risk-adjusted (information ratio) basis. We attributed the advantage of the security selection strategy to the high number of independent decisions it employed, and showed the results to be much closer across strategies on a "per decision" basis. Analysis of practical strategies by information ratio they produce in a historical simulation showed security selection on top by a wide margin, followed by the timing of sectors or credit ratings, with duration timing coming last. If the results of the simulation were adjusted by the number of independent decision involved in each strategy, the order was reversed. This confirmed the opinion of many portfolio managers that duration timing is the *single* most important decision in a portfolio.

This study, which is included in the first chapter of this book, bears the hallmark characteristics of our work: driven by investor inquiry, grounded in empirical research, and offering practical guidance to portfolio managers. Most of the research herein has been motivated by the same goal: to provide objective, practical answers to investors' questions.

The book is the result of more than a decade of such interaction between the Quantitative Portfolio Strategies Group, which is part of Lehman Brothers Fixed-Income Research, and institutional bond market investors around the globe. We feel privileged to have received investor inquiries across a broad spectrum of portfolio management issues that lend themselves to quantitative solutions. The queries have ranged from benchmark customization to empirical durations of credit securities, studies of investment style, diversification requirements, risk budgeting, and other strategic and tactical issues investors face in managing their portfolios.

Despite a wide range of topics, one common theme runs through all of them: investors expect us to give them objective quantitative solutions and methodologies for portfolio construction. Our choice of inquiries to focus on implicitly assumes that the formation of market views is a portfolio manager's job. Of course, quantitative models for alpha generation are being developed and may provide useful guidance or serve as filters for security selection, but market calls are, ultimately, subjective. The situation is very different when it comes to the *implementation* of a manager's views in an optimal portfolio structure—the main focus of this book. We see this "portfolio engineering" part of fund management as driven mostly, if not entirely, by quantitative analysis, empirical evidence, and a rigorous decision-making framework. In fact, subjectivity in the implementation of the manager's market views may lead to unwarranted or insufficient risk, suboptimal portfolio structure, and, in the end, may adversely impact performance.

Many investors concentrate their resources on identifying the best opportunities to generate alpha. Investment banks vie with each other to offer their clients the best trade ideas. Alpha-generation strategies are self-limiting in nature: acceptance by even a few institutions can lead to the disappearance of the relative value opportunity. Substantially less effort is devoted to translating the best ideas into an actual portfolio. Yet, assembling a portfolio is a critical component of the investment process. Without this step, the portfolio will simply be a collection of separate trades, which may or may not be correlated with each other. In the portfolio construction process, the relationship among various trades and their contributions to portfolio risk and return should be analyzed and then reflected in the optimal solution.

Research presented here relies on high-quality historical data that backs Lehman Brothers bond market indices and is supported by state-of-the-art security analytics. The former provided a source of security pricing and return information, and the latter enabled access to a full range of risk sensitivities across a broad spectrum of fixed-income assets. Together they formed the basis for empirical studies and calibration of portfolio optimization models.

All the material herein is original. Most of our findings have appeared in some form in Lehman Brothers publications delivered to the firm's clients; some were published in professional and academic journals and handbooks. This book has all this information under one cover for the first time, for the benefit of chief investment officers, bond portfolio managers and investors, risk managers, fixed-income research analysts, and finance students interested in the issues that confront industry practitioners. Much care has been taken to preserve the quantitative rigor of the original research, yet avoid complex mathematics, so as to make the book accessible to a wide audience. In our view, the studies and models we have selected retain lasting methodological value even when they are calibrated to historical data that is a year or two old.

The book consists of two parts. Part I offers a selection of empirical studies that concern benchmark customization and replication, analysis of investment style and constraints, optimal diversification in credit portfolios and navigating stressful credit markets, and managing portfolios of mortgage-backed securities. Part II focuses on portfolio management tools aimed primarily at the evaluation and optimization of portfolio risk and performance. Among them are models for optimal risk budgeting, bottom-up risk optimization, performance attribution, and analytical measures of risk sensitivities.

Our work has always focused on methodologies for answering practical portfolio management questions. For example:

- What is the "cost" of investment constraints imposed on a portfolio manager in terms of performance degradation?

- Can returns of broad market indices be successfully replicated with a few cash securities or liquid derivatives?

- How should a fair benchmark reflect nondiscretionary constraints under which many specialty managers operate? Examples of such constraints include caps on issuer exposure, presence of liability targets, and book-accounting-based performance evaluation.

- How many bonds must be included in a credit portfolio to make it "sufficiently diversified"? At what point does diversification become excessive?

- Are empirical durations of MBS securities more predictive of realized returns than prepayment model durations?

- What should the framework for benchmark selection be in a reserve port-folio of a central bank? How should a duration target and asset mix be established for a reserve portfolio?

Performance benchmarks are central to our work. Because Lehman Brothers is a major provider of bond market indices, most of the inquiries we receive are from investors benchmarked to various Lehman indices. Throughout this book, we refer to "indices" and "benchmarks" interchangeably. In the strict sense, an index is a market-weighted set of security returns and risk characteristics. The benchmark, on the other hand, is any yardstick used for measuring portfolio performance, which can be funding cost, peer group performance, or a reweighted (away from market weights) set of security returns. However, most fixed-income investors use market-weighted indices as their benchmarks.

The concept of a benchmark may differ significantly among various categories of investors. For institutional asset managers, a benchmark defines the opportunity set and market returns (beta) to be outperformed by value-added decisions (alpha). They may hold a subset of securities in the benchmark (core strategies) or products not included in the benchmark (core-plus strategies). For a central bank, a benchmark may define a risk target and strict investment guidelines to control deviation from that target. For an issuer, a benchmark may be the cost of funding under a "naïve" strategy of issuance structure and timing, to be improved upon by the treasurer's office. For a commercial bank, a benchmark may be the funding cost.

Establishing an appropriate benchmark and a process for portfolio comparison is important for both "passive" investors engaged in index replication strategies and active managers with a high alpha target. The latter have to be sure that they are taking enough ex ante risk to achieve their alpha target, verify that their risk budget is allocated optimally and that the portfolio does not contain any unintentional exposures, and attribute the actual performance to the ex ante risks taken. Regardless of whether a benchmark is formally required, the concept is present explicitly or implicitly in most investment processes. A significant part of the book deals with various benchmark-related issues, such as selection, construction, and customization of benchmarks, as well as investment constraints and risk optimization relative to a benchmark, at both macro and issuer levels.

A fixed-income portfolio is an ultimate product of a complex interplay between market- and issuer-level views of a manager, portfolio constraints and risk limits imposed by investment mandates, alpha targets, selective hedging of risk exposures, correlations among active strategies, and a great many other considerations. A bond portfolio has many "moving parts," all of which have to be managed as one. The manager cannot afford to focus on any one of them ignoring its relationships with all the others. Picking credit securities on the basis of fundamental analysis has to be done with an eye on the issuer concentration risk as well as the risk of diluting alpha by excessive diversification. Views in the mortgage pass-through market cannot be implemented without reliable duration measures and a full understanding of the risk factors that drive return volatility. A correct view of a U.S. manager on the direction of the euro government curve may be rendered totally ineffective by an incorrect duration hedge between Bunds and U.S. Treasuries, and the list goes on.

The important conclusion is that to fully realize their skill in generating alpha, portfolio managers need a rigorous and comprehensive analysis and decision-making framework, which should consist of knowledge-based and quantitative tools, methodologies, and models. In our work, we have been engaged in building this framework, not from a preset blueprint, but rather guided by a dynamic dialogue with investors. The book reflects this effort. Some chapters are, no doubt, more relevant to some investors than others. We took great care to make every chapter readable on its own. While one central theme ties all the chapters together, the book is organized in such a way that the reader can proceed to any chapter without necessarily having to read all the preceding ones. We know that some important components of the portfolio management framework we set out to build are still missing, which suggests that our work is far from completed. We hope that the reader will find this book thought provoking and practical, and, above all, will share our enthusiasm for the quantitative approach to fixed-income portfolio management.

PART I

··

Empirical Studies of Portfolio Strategies and Benchmark Design

EVALUATING INVESTMENT STYLE

The investment management process is the means by which an asset manager (investor) translates the objectives and constraints of the portfolio's owner(s) into a portfolio. Although investors typically devote much time and significant resources to the formulation of investment views, many of them spend remarkably little time on the construction of the portfolio itself. A fixed-income investor is faced with a multitude of investment choices. Through these choices he can achieve desired country, currency, yield curve, sector, or issuer exposures. Investment departments are structured in order to identify the most attractive risk exposures. But in many cases, portfolios are simply collections of trades. Managers may be highly skilled in predicting the directionality of certain market factors, but may not have a well-defined process for sizing exposures and combining them into a portfolio in a way that allows for their interaction.

Investment style is a very broad term. At a high level, it is sometimes used to delineate active from passive management (which is discussed in the section on Index Replication). It also serves to describe the difference between managing portfolios for total return vs. for book yield. It is commonly applied in fixed-income portfolio management to delineate the main sources of risk that are intentionally taken by the manager. For example, the active portfolio risk of a "top-down" macro manager derives largely from duration or sector exposures, whereas that of a "bottom-up" manager comes primarily from issuer-specific exposures. But style can also describe: (1) the degree of diversification typically employed by a manager, (2) the length of time horizon of a typical exposure, (3) the implementation of investment views, and (4) the way in which out-of-benchmark sectors are utilized.

Some managers may take relatively concentrated "bets" in their portfolios, expressing either macro or issuer-specific views, while other managers deal with much more diverse portfolios. In this section we consider how macro views can be sized and reflected in an optimal asset allocation. Some managers trade frequently in their portfolios, looking to add alpha from a large number of relatively low-return strategies, whereas others trade less frequently looking for higher-return opportunities. This style choice has important implications for the way in which manager skill translates into risk-adjusted returns.

Many managers are constrained by their investment guidelines as to how investment views can be implemented. For example, if only cash instruments are permitted and no leverage is allowed, pure directional interest-rate views are difficult to separate from views on the shape of the yield curve. If portfolio guidelines do permit derivatives, some managers make active use of them in implementing investment views. For example, portfolio credit derivatives are used to take views on the direction of credit spreads or futures to implement interest-rate views. Some managers make active use of nonbenchmark sectors, employing a so-called core-plus style, which may include exposure to high yield, emerging market debt, currencies, and foreign bond markets and opt for a variety of styles in including those exposures in portfolios. If the manager expects that over time the portfolio's strategic allocation will outperform its benchmark, some exposures will be tactical, short-term exposures, whereas others may be strategic longer-term allocations.

Over the years, we have been asked by many investors to assist with these issues. The chapters in this section provide answers to some real-life problems posed, for example, by a chief investment officer concerned not with theoretical discussions, but with practical, implementable solutions.

Mean-variance optimization has been with us for 50 years, but, though a useful framework, it is built upon certain assumptions that do not reflect the real world—for example, that all investors have identical sets of investment expectations, objectives, time horizons, and constraints. How should decisions be made in a world in which investment expectations are not uniform, where investors have different skill sets and are faced with, in some cases, very restrictive constraints? How should investors allocate their scarce research resources among the various dimensions of active management? Should investors concentrate on those active strategies where they possess the most skill, or should they allocate their risk budget across different strategies in which they possess varying degrees of skill? Do some kinds of investment strategies have more attractive risk/return profiles than others? How can investors incorporate uncertainty of their own directional views into asset allocation? How should risk positions be sized in a portfolio? What framework should be used to justify allocations to core-plus strategies and to determine their size?

To answer these questions, we needed a model that reflected the fact that, based on their skill levels, investors have varying abilities to generate outperformance from different exposures. The "imperfect foresight" approach, described in detail in Chapter 1, allows us to model skill directly. We assume that managers choose trades neither entirely at random nor with perfect foresight. With hindsight, we can simulate performance of a skilled manager by tilting the investment choices in a specific strategy toward the outperforming ones more often than randomly. This model allows us to compare the performance of different investment styles by simulating historically the investment results that an active manager might have been expected to achieve in a given strategy with various skill levels. We apply this model in Chapter 1, where we try to answer an investor's question triggered by the changing nature of the European credit markets brought about by European Monetary Union (EMU): Does security selection offer higher risk-adjusted returns than sector rotation or other investment styles?

The finding that security selection is a more attractive investment style is shown to reflect the greater number of independent decisions that can be made compared to other approaches. For example, a duration manager can go long or short and perhaps express a view on the steepness or flatness of the yield curve. A sector rotator can select an asset class sector (e.g., corporates and mortgages) or an industry × rating cell (e.g., A-rated financials to Baa-rated telecoms). But a bottom-up security selector can choose among hundreds of issuers and engage in such choices many times. This perhaps explains why comparatively few investors are engaged in "pure duration" management and many more in security selection.

Many managers choose to combine various investment styles in their portfolios, combining security selection with duration management and sector rotation. So-called core-plus managers typically also add tactical exposures such as foreign exchange or high yield. Which of these strategies are optimal? In a world of scarce resources, but ever increasing complexity, no manager is able to monitor the entire opportunity set of fixed-income investments, so what proportions of their resources should they commit to each of these styles?

In Chapter 2, we examine these questions from the perspective of a global fixed-income manager, who is faced with a large array of potential trade opportunities. The motivation for this study was provided by an asset manager who wished to know where his research effort could be deployed most efficiently. But this study is relevant for all managers who are considering blending more than one strategy or style in a portfolio. In addition to finding the answer to our question, we also demonstrated the primary importance of skill (rather than style) in determining risk-adjusted performance, examined the impact of combining disparate strategies, and empirically calculated the impact of investment constraints on performance.

If markets are moderately efficient over longer periods of time, we would expect that risk premia are similar across different kinds of risk exposures. Therefore, the main determinant of risk-adjusted performance for a single pure strategy should not be the choice of the strategy, but rather the skill the manager brings to it, a conclusion that is empirically demonstrated by our study. A more subtle finding, however, is that while skill is paramount in determining risk-adjusted performance, an optimal portfolio may include certain strategies in which the manager possesses less skill than in other strategies. Or put another way, there is great value in strategy diversification. This has very important implications not just for portfolio construction but also for the structuring of an investment department. For example, a manager who is skilled in sector-rotation strategies or duration management may be better advised allocating additional resources to new strategies (such as foreign exchange), rather than further improving skill at the existing ones. This finding likely will hold true even if the additional strategy has lower risk-adjusted returns than the existing one.

The breadth of strategies is therefore of critical importance in achieving high risk-adjusted returns. Breadth of strategies reflects not only the number of exposures taken in a portfolio, but the diversification across strategies. For example, adding high yield exposure to a portfolio already overweighted in investment-grade credit may add alpha, but will probably also add appreciably to portfolio risk. Risk-adjusted returns are highest when relatively independent positive-alpha strategies are combined. This sounds sensible in theory, but is it workable in practice?

Many kinds of risk exposures in a portfolio can be highly correlated. For example, a portfolio that is benchmarked to a U.S. Government-Corporate Index, with an overweight to investment-grade credit, an allocation to high yield, a short-duration exposure, and positioned for a flattening yield curve is a portfolio with performance closely linked to a single economic factor—the strength of the U.S. economy. Some investors have centralized committees that may develop top-down macro views for the global economy and capital markets. Money managers that are employed by third parties may be pressured to construct portfolios that reflect a coherent overarching theme. Yet if this single view is incorporated into every portfolio overweight, then the result is a portfolio full of highly correlated exposures. The alternative, building a portfolio of either independent views or negatively correlated exposures, can deliver higher risk-adjusted returns, but may also be criticized for containing inconsistent views (e.g., long duration and long credit). Of course, even in a more decentralized policy setting, risk exposures may be inadvertently correlated.[1]

Most investors operate under a set of investment constraints, placed upon them either by their clients or by regulatory or risk capital considerations. The most common is the long-only constraint. In Chapter 2, we investigate the impact of this constraint on portfolio performance by comparing core strategies to core-

---

1. The great advantage of a risk model is that it can gauge the impact on total portfolio risk of combining different kinds of exposures (see Chapter 26).

plus strategies. In the presence of a long-only constraint, an investment-grade benchmarked manager is able effectively to go long-and-short various kinds of core exposures that are in their benchmark by simply underweighting them. But the manager can only express long positions in the "plus" exposures that are not in their benchmark (e.g., high yield). Since there are fewer opportunities to add value with the plus strategies, one would expect them to have less desirable risk-return characteristics, a hypothesis that is confirmed by our empirical analysis. In a portfolio context, it may still be desirable to include core-plus strategies. The risk-adjusted performance of the portfolio is stronger with core-plus strategies, though not as strong as in the absence of the long-only constraint. This also helps explain the popularity of hedge funds in recent years. Many hedge funds use long-short strategies across a wide range of exposures, so that they generally display considerably greater breadth than more conventional, long-only, strategies. Greater breadth leads to higher risk-adjusted returns.

Another constraint typically faced by a long-only manager is the inability to use leverage in the portfolio, a strategy that is strongly favored by hedge funds. This constraint reduces the attractiveness of certain low-risk/low-return strategies and limits the kinds of strategies that a long-only manager can employ. This is particularly true for certain yield curve strategies, which we explore in Chapter 3. We show that a Treasury portfolio manager constrained to long-only cash securities and prohibited from buying futures can be expected to lose 20% of the portfolio's risk-adjusted performance.

There are some practical steps that managers can implement in light of the conclusions presented in this section. First, in constructing a portfolio of exposures, managers must take into account their skill in forming market views for a given strategy, as well as the relationships among strategies. In the first section of Part II, we describe our ORBS (optimal risk budgeting with skill) methodology for achieving the maximum alpha from a combination of different strategies and skill levels. Second, in the presence of a long-only constraint, the best benchmark for a manager to follow is the broadest possible one. As an example, an investor with a U.S. Treasury benchmark can express only long sectoral views in his portfolio, whereas a Global Aggregate-benchmarked investor can express long and short views on sectors, currencies, global durations, and so on. Third, there is a cost in performance to imposition of portfolio constraints. A long-only portfolio manager who is compared by his client to an unrestricted hedge fund is facing an unfair comparison. Portfolio managers should therefore encourage alpha-seeking clients to relax investment constraints.

1. Value of Security Selection vs. Asset Allocation in Credit Markets

In the late 1990s, several new groups of investors started adding credit securities to their debt portfolios. First, the European Monetary Union served as a catalyst for increasing the size and liquidity of the European credit markets, which, in turn, spurred greater demand for credit products from European portfolio managers. Second, a fall in outstanding U.S. Treasury securities prompted central banks to look for alternative ways to invest their reserve portfolios. Especially in Europe, with the European Central Bank providing the first line of reserves in support of the euro, the national central banks switched to maximization of total return as an objective for their portfolios. Over a long investment horizon, this favors credit securities over government bonds.

As they began the process of credit investing, portfolio managers started asking some fundamental philosophical questions. If an investor's objective is maximization of risk-adjusted return, what style of portfolio management holds the most promise? Is it yield curve timing, sector rotation, or security selection? Can one develop an intuition to understand the relative merits of each style? Can this be quantified?

To address these questions, this study evaluates investment styles using an "imperfect foresight" approach. Rather than choosing the single best allocation decision each month, we incorporate the notion that even well-informed investment decisions sometimes result in losses or underperformance. We do not assume that the simulated manager of this study will call the market correctly every month. He will position the portfolio to be neutral to the benchmark in every dimension but one, and in this selected dimension will express a view, which may be right or wrong. This view leads to the risk of performance differences between the portfolio and the benchmark, which is known as tracking error. If the position

Based on research first published by Lehman Brothers in 2000.

is chosen purely at random, there should be no mean outperformance of the benchmark to justify this risk. If the manager is skilled at this task, he will choose correctly more often than not, and on average the portfolio will outperform.

We simulate the performance of various investment strategies using historical data from the Lehman Brothers U.S. Investment-Grade Corporate Bond Index, and we use information ratios to evaluate performance.[1] Managerial skill is modeled as follows: in the unskilled case (0% skill), each decision made by a manager involves a random selection from among a discrete set of possibilities, with equal probabilities assigned to each. In the perfect foresight case (100% skill), the manager always makes a correct decision, which leads to outperformance (as determined by future results). We investigate two different approaches to defining a "correct" decision in this context: one in which only the single best decision is considered correct and another in which any decision that outperforms the index is included. In either case, for skill levels between 0 and 100%, the selection probabilities for all choices are linearly interpolated between these two extremes.

A similar definition of skill was used by Steven Fox to simulate manager performance in tactical allocation between stocks and bonds.[2] This simulation-based approach was applied by Mary Fjelstad to duration allocation and sector allocation in fixed-income portfolios.[3] In both of these studies the allocation along each dimension was limited to a binary decision (long or short duration, overweight or underweight corporates relative to governments). Security selection was not addressed. Eric Sorenson et al.[4] simulated manager skill at security selection for equity portfolios and addressed the implications for allocation of funds among managers of different classes.[5]

We explore a set of reasonable investment strategies that isolate one investment style at a time. As the outcome of a particular strategy in a given month is not deterministic, the risk and return of each strategy are evaluated on a prob-

---

1. The information ratio is the mean annual outperformance of an investment strategy divided by the annualized standard deviation of the outperformance. Both risk and return are measured vs. the benchmark. The Sharpe ratio can be considered the special case of an information ratio with a riskless asset (cash) as the benchmark.

2. Steven M. Fox, "Assessing TAA Manager Performance," *Journal of Portfolio Management,* Fall 1999, pp. 40–49.

3. Mary Fjelstad, "Modeling the Performance of Active Managers in the Euroland Bond Market," *Journal of Fixed Income,* June 1999, pp. 32–45.

4. Eric H. Sorenson, Keith L. Miller, and Vele Samak, "Allocating between Active and Passive Management," *Financial Analysts Journal,* September/October 1998, pp. 18–31.

5. All of these studies consider the unskilled case to correspond to a skill of 50%, where skill is defined as the probability of a correct decision. A skill level of 60% according to this convention corresponds to 20% skill by our definition.

abilistic basis. The measurement of portfolio/benchmark performance deviation across all possible allocation decisions and over time allows an accurate assessment of the risk of a given strategy. Expected returns are evaluated as a function of manager skill for each investment style by a combination of closed-form calculations and simulation. All of the strategies are based on a foresight horizon of 1 month and monthly rebalancing.

STRATEGY DESIGN

The investment strategies were designed to focus on just one form of risk at a time. Thus, our sector allocation strategy is designed to take no risk vs. the index in term-structure allocation, quality allocation, or security selection. To control risk in all but the single dimension in which the strategy expresses a view, we begin with a detailed analysis of index composition.

Cell Definitions

The investment universe consists of all bonds in the Lehman Brothers Corporate Bond Index. The index is divided into cells along three dimensions: duration, sector, and quality. As shown in Figure 1-1, we use three duration cells, four broadly defined sectors, and three quality cells for a total of 36 cells. The index is characterized by the percentage of market capitalization and the average duration of the bonds within each of these cells.

The marginal sums of this three-dimensional market view can provide a similar two-dimensional view along any two of these axes. The rightmost column of Figure 1-1 gives the index composition by sector and quality. The subtotals at the bottom of each credit quality level give the breakdown by quality and duration. The two-dimensional profile by duration and sector is given in Figure 1-2.

To isolate the effect of only one type of investment decision, we constrain each portfolio to exactly match the index according to one of the views just shown. Our security selection strategy is constrained to match the index weights and durations in each cell illustrated in Figure 1-1, but does so by selecting a small number of the bonds in each cell. Our asset allocation strategies all match the index along two out of three dimensions, but vary the allocations along the third. For instance, our quality allocation strategy matches the index view shown in Figure 1-2, but achieves the desired allocation to each duration × sector cell by adjusting the weights of the three qualities within the cell. This ensures that the returns of our quality allocation strategy are not colored by inadvertent secondary exposures to duration or sector.

Figure 1-1. Corporate Index Profile by Duration, Sector, and Quality
July 1, 1999

Duration	Percent of Market Value			
	0 to 4	4 to 7	More than 7	Total
Aaa and Aa				
Industrials	1.6	1.1	2.5	5.2
Utilities	0.1	0.2	0.2	0.5
Finance	4.9	2.9	1.7	9.5
Yankees	4.5	3.4	2.3	10.2
Total Aaa–Aa	11.1	7.6	6.7	25.4
A				
Industrials	4.6	5.5	8.7	18.8
Utilities	0.7	0.8	1.0	2.5
Finance	6.6	5.7	3.1	15.4
Yankees	1.4	2.2	2.8	6.4
Total A	13.3	14.2	15.6	43.1
Baa				
Industrials	4.5	6.9	7.5	18.9
Utilities	1.2	1.4	1.2	3.8
Finance	1.8	1.3	0.3	3.4
Yankees	1.7	2.9	0.8	5.4
Total Baa	9.2	12.5	9.8	31.5
Corporate Index	33.6	34.3	32.1	100.0

Building Duration-Neutral Strategies

We remove duration bias by matching cell durations as well as percentages to those of the index. To accomplish this, each market cell shown in Figure 1-1 is further divided by duration. An appropriate blend of the long and the short half of any cell can then match the required duration. For example, Figure 1-3 shows a detailed view of short A-rated corporates. This cell, as shown in Figure 1-1, accounts for 13.3% of the index and has an average duration of 2.61. If we had chosen to represent this cell in our portfolio by purchasing a single sector according to its market composition, we would be short duration had we chosen industrials and long had we chosen any other sector. By adjusting the market weights to the long and short halves of the cell, we can create a set of single-sector investments

Figure 1-2. Corporate Index Composition by Duration and Sector
July 1, 1999

Duration	Percent of Market Value			
	0 to 4	4 to 7	More than 7	Total
Industrials	10.7	13.5	18.7	42.9
Utilities	2.0	2.4	2.4	6.8
Finance	13.3	9.9	5.1	28.3
Yankees	7.6	8.5	5.9	22.0
Totals	33.6	34.3	32.1	100.0

that matches the 2.61 duration of the index for the cell. If the short and long halves of the cell have durations of D_S and D_L, respectively, then the weights needed to match a benchmark duration of D_B are obtained by solving the set of Equations (1-1),

$$x_s + x_L = 1$$
$$x_S D_S + x_L D_L = D_B, \qquad (1\text{-}1)$$

to obtain $x_L = (D_B - D_S)/(D_L - D_S)$. Figure 1-3 shows that for industrials such a position would be composed by blending 44.2% of the 0–2.5 duration cell with 55.8% of the 2.5–4.0 duration cell, overweighting the longer cell relative to the index. A similar position in short single-A utilities would require 42.9% of the 0–2.5 duration cell and 57.1% of the 2.5–4.0 duration cell, overweighting the shorter cell.[6] The sector allocation strategy chooses one of these duration-neutral single-sector investments within each quality × duration cell, ensuring against any incidental curve exposure owing to duration differences between sectors. The technique illustrated here for the sector allocation strategy is utilized for quality allocation as well. A very similar approach is used to match cell duration in our security selection strategy, as explained later.

---

6. Other mechanisms could be used to match duration and market value within each cell. One alternative method that does not require subdividing the cell is to blend the selected portion of the cell (e.g., short single-A utilities) with a cash position. Equation (1-1) could be re-interpreted to provide the necessary weights for bonds and cash, with the cash duration D_s set to zero. This procedure has the advantage of maintaining the relative weights of each security within a cell. However, when the duration of the selected sector in a given cell is shorter than the target duration, this method requires leveraging the portfolio with a negative cash position. The method used in our study never requires such leveraging.

Figure 1-3. Construction of Duration-Neutral Sector Allocation Strategy

Short Single-A Corporates, July 1999

Sector	Duration	Short Single-A Corporate Index Composition			Duration-Matched Sector Selection Strategy		
		0.0–2.5	2.5–4.0	Total	0.0–2.5	2.5–4.0	Total
Industrials	Number of bonds	81	86	167			
	Market value ($ millions)	25,773	25,336	51,109			
	Percent of short A	17.5	17.2	34.7			
	Percent of A corporates	5.4	5.3	10.7			
	Percent of cell	50.4	49.6	100.0	44.2	55.8	
	Duration	1.70	3.33	2.51			2.61
	Total return (%)	0.24	–0.10	0.07			0.05
Utilities	Number of bonds	13	24	37			
	Market value ($ millions)	2,759	5,079	7,838			
	Percent of short A	1.9	3.4	5.3			
	Percent of A corporates	0.6	1.1	1.7			
	Percent of cell	35.2	64.8	100.0	42.9	57.1	
	Duration	1.60	3.37	2.75			2.61
	Total return (%)	0.00	0.22	0.14			0.13

Finance

Number of bonds	105	130	235		
Market value ($ millions)	31,222	41,757	72,979		
Percent of short A	21.2	28.3	49.5		
Percent of A corporates	6.6	8.8	15.3		
Percent of cell	42.8	57.2	100.0	45.9	54.1
Duration	1.82	3.28	2.66		2.61
Total return (%)	0.07	-0.39	-0.19		-0.18

Yankees

Number of bonds	18	29	47		
Market value ($ millions)	5,304	10,193	15,497		
Percent of short A	3.6	6.9	10.5		
Percent of A corporates	1.1	2.1	3.3		
Percent of cell	34.2	65.8	100.0	39.7	60.3
Duration	1.64	3.25	2.70		2.61
Total return (%)	0.35	-0.16	0.01		0.04

Total

Number of bonds	217	269	486
Market value ($ millions)	65,058	82,366	147,424
Percent of short A	44.1	55.9	100.0
Percent of A corporates	13.7	17.3	31.0
Percent of cell	44.1	55.9	100.0
Duration	1.75	3.29	2.61
Total return (%)	0.16	-0.23	-0.06

Bet Size

Every allocation strategy consists of two parts. First a manager forms a view favoring one market segment over another; then the portfolio is constructed by overweighting the selected segment. More or less risk (and potential for excess return) can be assumed by accepting larger or smaller deviations from the benchmark.

All of the allocation strategies in the next section are presented in their purest form, with an extreme application of manager views to portfolio composition. Once a decision is made to favor a particular market segment (either on a cell-by-cell basis or for the portfolio as a whole), we shift the entire portfolio to reflect this view. We do not imply that this is a realistic approach to sector allocation. Rather, we assume that managers take more moderate stances to implement their views, and we can approximate their performance by blending the extreme approach with an investment in the benchmark.

To achieve more moderate levels of risk, the strategy can be applied to only a portion of the portfolio assets. Thus, for a bet size b, we can invest a percentage b in one of the strategies described earlier, leaving a percentage $1 - b$ invested in the benchmark. Applying any of the above strategies in this way reduces both the mean outperformance and the tracking error by the factor b, leaving the information ratio unchanged. (The proof of this result is given in Appendix A.) With this approach, we can apply any of the following strategies at any desired level of risk.

ASSET ALLOCATION STRATEGIES

To define asset allocation strategies, we first assign probabilities to each allocation decision. The probabilities are a function of a skill parameter that controls the likelihood of a correct decision. The probability distribution of strategy performance can then be evaluated directly from these decision probabilities. To illustrate the strategy formulation and the calculation of the performance statistics, we take the sector allocation strategy as an example. Starting with an explanation of how the strategy works in a single cell in a single month, we then extend the calculation to cover the entire portfolio and its evolution over time.

Setting the Allocation Probabilities

The construction of a duration-neutral position in a single sector, as shown in Figure 1-3, forms the basis for our sector selection strategy. The index return within this cell, short single-A corporates, is –0.06%, which represents the benchmark for the strategy's performance within the cell. The rightmost column of this figure shows the returns that would have resulted from an implementation of this strategy in July 1999. We can see that had we placed our short single-A allocation entirely in the financial sector, the resulting return (−0.18%) would have underperformed by 0.12%. Had we selected any other sector, we would have outperformed this portion of the index. Because our sector allocation strategy matches index weights by quality and duration, overall strategy outperformance of the Corporate Index can be expressed as a weighted sum of such cell-by-cell outperformance numbers.

We view the strategy outperformance of the index within each cell as a random variable. Each month, the strategy chooses one of the four sectors within each cell. If we assume that many portfolio managers are carrying out the same strategy (by making one of the four possible sector choices), we find that the distribution of results consists of just four possible events, weighted by the probabilities of selection. The success of the strategy may be measured by the mean outperformance $\bar{r}$ and the standard deviation of outperformance σ. If r_i represents the outperformance of the duration-neutral strategy using sector i and p_i is the probability of a manager choosing sector i, then the mean and variance of the outperformance are given by[7]

$$\bar{r} = \sum_{s=1}^{4} p_i r_i$$

$$\sigma^2 = \sum_{s=1}^{4} p_i (r_i - \bar{r})^2. \tag{1-2}$$

Figure 1-4 illustrates this calculation under three different sets of sector selection probabilities, corresponding to different assumptions about manager skill.

BY RANDOM SELECTION

In the simplest case, we assume that the strategy chooses one sector at random, with equal probabilities for all sectors. If there are n possibilities, the selection probabilities are given simply by

$$p_i^{\text{random}} = 1/n. \tag{1-3}$$

For the sector allocation problem at hand, in which the strategy selects one of four sectors, this random selection rule gives $p_i = 25\%$. As shown in Figure 1-4, this "no skill" strategy outperforms the index by an average of 6.8 bp this month, with a standard deviation of 11.4 bp.

---

7. The quantities defined in Equation (1-2) are actually the conditional mean and variance of the strategy given a particular market outcome. A more formal treatment is given in Appendix B.

Figure 1-4. Imperfect Foresight: Representing Skill by Manipulating Sector Selection Probabilities
Single-Cell Example, Short Single-A Corporates, July 1999

Sector	Index			Strategy		Sector Selection Probabilities by Skill Level		
	Percent	Duration	Return (%)	Return (%)	Outperformance (%)	Random Selection (no skill)	20% Choose Any Winner	20% Choose Best
Industrials	34.7	2.51	0.07	0.05	0.11	25	27	20
Utilities	5.3	2.75	0.14	0.13	0.18	25	27	40
Finance	49.5	2.66	-0.19	-0.18	-0.12	25	20	20
Yankees	10.5	2.70	0.01	0.04	0.10	25	27	20
Index totals	100.0	2.61	-0.06					
Mean strategy outperformance (%)						0.068	0.080	0.091
Standard deviation of strategy outperformance (%)						0.114	0.106	0.112

The reason that this random selection outperforms the index on average is clear. The index return is heavily influenced by the negative return in the finance sector, which accounts for 49.5% of the index in this cell. As the assumed selection probability for finance in our equally weighted strategy is much lower than this, on average the strategy outperforms. In months in which a single large sector significantly outperforms the others, thereby bringing up the index return, this strategy tends to underperform. All in all, we expect this strategy to outperform in some months and underperform in others, but over time it should perform roughly similarly to the index.[8]

Note that even in a month such as this, where the strategy outperforms on the whole, there is certainly a possibility of underperformance. The 25% of managers who choose to purchase only finance bonds in this cell will underperform the index by 12 bp. The 11.4 bp standard deviation shown here represents the variation across different managers implementing the same strategy. This measure provides a fair assessment of strategy risk, as it reflects the losses that the strategy will incur if the view that is implemented turns out to be incorrect.

BY SKILL AT CHOOSING ANY WINNING SECTOR

What is skill? It is not our purpose here to philosophize on what abilities, personality traits, or organizational factors contribute to the success of a particular manager. A manager who consistently outperforms the index is considered skillful. From this result-oriented viewpoint, skill can be defined as the ability to make correct decisions more frequently than not. The views of a successful manager are not always borne out to be correct, but they are correct more often than under random selection.

Our imperfect foresight technique uses knowledge of future returns to determine which sector allocation decisions are the right ones, but does not assume that the manager always chooses the best possible sector. Rather, we simulate the effect of skill by shifting the selection probabilities between the two extremes of random selection and perfect foresight. We have explored two slightly different interpretations of manager skill. A particular decision may be deemed "correct" as long as it outperforms the index or only if it is the best of the available choices. By leaving the number of correct decisions as a variable, the same set of equations can be used to define the selection probabilities for both of these approaches.

---

8. An alternative for the base case ("no skill") assumption would be to use index weights as the sector selection probabilities. This would have the advantage that the mean outperformance of the strategy would be close to zero every month. However, this would imply a connection between sector views and market weights. We prefer to carefully match the index along two dimensions, but to leave the manager free from indexation constraints in the dimension in which a view is to be expressed.

For a selection among n choices, where n_W represents correct decisions, or "winners," and $n_L = n - n_W$ are incorrect decisions ("losers"), the probabilities under perfect foresight are

$$p_i^{\text{perfect}} = \begin{cases} 1/n_W & \text{if } i \text{ is a correct decision} \\ 0 & \text{otherwise.} \end{cases} \tag{1-4}$$

If more than one decision is deemed correct in a given month, then the strategy assigns equal probabilities to each of the correct decisions.

For a manager with skill s, we assume that the selection probabilities $p_i(s)$ are scaled between random selection and perfect foresight, and are given by

$$\begin{aligned} p_i(s) &= (1 - s)p_i^{\text{random}} + sp_i^{\text{perfect}} \\ &= \begin{cases} (n_W + sn_L)/n_W(n_W + n_L) & \text{if } i \text{ is a correct decision} \\ (1 - s)/(n_W + n_L) & \text{otherwise.} \end{cases} \end{aligned} \tag{1-5}$$

As there are n_W correct decisions, the overall probability of selecting a winning sector is $(n_W - sn_L)/(n_W - n_L)$, which converges to $n_W/(n_W - n_L)$ for the unskilled case ($s = 0$) and to 1 for the perfect foresight case ($s = 100\%$).

In the first approach, skill represents the ability to find a sector that outperforms the index, but not necessarily the best one. At 100% skill, this approach assumes a weakened form of perfect foresight, in which the manager has equal probabilities of choosing from among all of the outperforming sectors. For lower skill levels, the selection probabilities are scaled between random selection and this weakened form of perfect foresight, with increased probabilities for sectors that outperform the index and decreased probabilities for underperforming sectors.

In the example illustrated in Figure 1-4, there are three sectors that outperform the index (industrials, utilities, and Yankees); only one sector (financial) underperforms. Evaluating Equation (1-5) at 20% skill with $n_W = 3$ and $n_L = 1$ gives a probability $p_i(20\%) = 3.2/12 \approx 27\%$ of choosing any of the winning sectors and a probability of $0.8/4 = 20\%$ of choosing the underperforming financial sector. The mean and standard deviation of the strategy results within this cell for this month are calculated according to Equation (1-2). Figure 1-4 shows that under this more favorable set of selection probabilities, the standard deviation of strategy performance is almost identical to that under purely random selection, but that the mean return has increased from 6.8 to 8.0 bp.

BY SKILL AT CHOOSING THE BEST SECTOR

The second approach interprets skill as the ability to choose the best-performing sector. According to this interpretation 100% skill corresponds to perfect foresight. In the example of Figure 1-4, a manager with perfect foresight would choose utilities and outperform the index by 18 bp. Our imperfect foresight technique similarly uses knowledge of future returns to determine which sector allocation decisions are the right ones, but does not assume that the manager always chooses the best possible sector. Rather, we simulate the effect of skill by shifting the selection probabilities between the two extremes of random selection and perfect foresight. These probabilities are given by Equations (1-4) and (1-5) for the special case in which only the single best sector is considered "correct" and we always have $n_W = 1$.

The probability of choosing the best sector is 25% with no skill and 100% with perfect foresight. For a manager with 20% skill, the linear interpolation rule of Equation (1-5) gives a 40% probability of choosing the best sector ($n_W = 1$). The probability of choosing any of the other sectors is reduced to 20%. This set of probabilities leads to even better performance. Once again, the standard deviation of strategy performance changes very little, but mean outperformance is increased to 9.1 bp.

For all of the strategies considered, the performance numbers shown are for the extreme case in which the portfolio is invested entirely in the selected sector within each cell. At a bet size of 25%, both the mean outperformance and the standard deviation would be scaled down accordingly. Within the cell shown in Figure 1-4, the standard deviation of outperformance would be about 2.8 bp, with the mean outperformance ranging from 1.7 bp in the random case to 2.3 bp for 20% skill at choosing the best sector.

Calculating Mean and Variance of Overall Portfolio Outperformance

The portfolio is constructed by investing in each cell a percentage w_j corresponding to the percentage of the market capitalization of the index in that cell. The sector allocation scheme described earlier is applied independently in each quality × duration cell. The overall portfolio performance is then the weighted sum of the cell-by-cell results. That is, if the random variable r_j represents the strategy outperformance of the index within a particular cell j, characterized by a mean $\bar{r}_j$ and a standard deviation σ_j, then the index outperformance of the overall portfolio is given by

$$r = \sum_j w_j r_j,$$ (1-6)

and the mean and standard deviation of r are given by

$$\bar{r} = \sum_j w_j \bar{r}_j.$$
$$\sigma^2 = \sum_j w_j^2 \sigma_j^2.$$ (1-7)

This calculation is illustrated in Figure 1-5 for the sector allocation strategy with 20% skill at choosing any winning sector in July 1999. As we saw in Figure 1-4, this strategy achieved a mean return of about 0.08% with a standard deviation of 0.11% in the short (0 to 4 years duration) single-A cell. This cell accounts for 13.3% of the index and, hence, of the portfolio. In other cells (such as Baa over 7 years), this strategy gives a mean return below that of the index for this particular month. On the whole, the strategy produces a mean outperformance of 0.02% with a standard deviation of 0.05%, which represents the distribution across a population of managers of equivalent skill all pursuing the same strategy in this month. (If we take the strategy outlined earlier and simulate the results obtained for this month at this skill level many times, the mean and standard deviation converge to these values. Simulation is not necessary for this case, as the calculation shown in Figures 1-4 and 1-5 is both more precise and computationally more efficient.)

Of course, strategy results vary over time. The mean outperformance in a given month might be more or less than the 2 bp observed in Figure 1-5 for this strategy (we will see that the long-term average is 5 bp/month), and the standard deviation across sectors (and hence across managers) will be larger in more volatile months and smaller during calm periods. After calculating the mean and variance of strategy performance as in Figure 1-5 for each month of available data, overall strategy performance is obtained by analyzing the time series of results. The mean outperformance is given by the average of the monthly means. The variance of strategy outperformance is measured in two ways. First, we calculate the time average of the variance across managers in a given month (as in Figure 1-5). This represents the risk of choosing wrong and is related to the magnitude of the performance difference between the best and worst sectors. Second, we measure the variance of the mean strategy outperformance over time. This gives the risk owing to the fact that changing market conditions make the strategy more effective in some months than in others. The sum of these two variance terms gives the overall variance of strategy outperformance. A proof of this assertion and a more precise formulation of this calculation in terms of conditional probabilities are given in Appendix B.

Sector Allocation Results

Figure 1-6 shows the results of the sector allocation strategy over time for different levels of manager skill. For the 20% skill case, the strategy outperforms the index by an average of 60.6 bp/year, with a standard deviation (or tracking error) of 45.3 bp/year. Dividing the mean outperformance by the tracking error, we obtain an information ratio of 1.34. Of the 45.3 bp of tracking error, we find that 40.7 bp is due to the variance across managers (or the risk of choosing the wrong sector for a given month), and 19.9 bp is due to the volatility of the spread markets over time.

We see that for reasonable levels of skill, the tracking error is fairly stable, at about 40 to 50 bp/year. Mean outperformance improves steadily with increasing

Figure 1-5. Sector Allocation Example: Calculating the Mean and Variance of Strategy Outperformance
July 1999, 20% Skill, Choosing Winning Sectors in Each Cell

Quality Cell	Duration Cell	Percent	Index Return (%)	Strategy Return (%)	Strategy Outperformance (%)	Variance Outperformance (%)	Standard Deviation Outperformance (%)
Aaa and Aa	0 to 4	11.0	-0.10	-0.05	0.05	0.01	0.09
Aaa and Aa	4 to 7	7.6	-0.75	-0.73	0.02	0.00	0.06
Aaa and Aa	More than 7	6.8	-1.17	-1.09	0.08	0.03	0.18
A	0 to 4	13.3	-0.06	0.02	0.08	0.01	0.11
A	4 to 7	14.2	-0.56	-0.49	0.07	0.02	0.13
A	More than 7	15.4	-1.06	-1.12	-0.06	0.03	0.17
Baa	0 to 4	9.3	-0.04	-0.01	0.03	0.00	0.07
Baa	4 to 7	12.6	-0.40	-0.41	-0.01	0.03	0.17
Baa	More than 7	9.9	-1.04	-1.27	-0.13	0.03	0.18
Total		100.0	-0.55	-0.53	0.02	0.0023	0.05

Figure 1-6. Sector Allocation: Historical Performance at Different Skill Levels

August 1988–July 1999, by Skill at Choosing Best Sectors in Each Cell

Skill (%)	Mean Outperformance (bp/year)	Standard Deviation over Managers (bp/year)	Standard Deviation over Time (bp/year)	Overall Tracking Error (bp/year)	Information Ratio
0	−6.6	39.8	15.9	42.9	−0.15
10	27.0	40.6	16.7	43.9	0.62
20	60.6	40.7	19.9	45.3	1.34
40	127.9	39.2	30.2	49.5	2.58
60	195.2	34.9	42.5	55.0	3.55
80	262.5	26.6	55.4	61.4	4.27
100	329.7	0.0	68.6	68.6	4.81

skill, from near zero for the random selection case (0% skill) to 329.7 bp/year for 100% skill. The results shown here are for the "choosing the best sector" variant of the strategy.

The distinction between the two types of variance displayed in Figure 1-6 is a subtle one. For a single manager, with a single time series of returns, an information ratio is calculated based on the mean and standard deviation of this return series. Although both sources of volatility come into play (better decisions are made in some months than in others and market volatility levels change over time), it is not easy to separate the two effects. The attribution of volatility to these two sources is shown in Figure 1-6 to illustrate that skill has two distinct and opposing effects on the volatility of strategy performance. As skill increases, the risk of incorrect decisions decreases, but the exposure to market volatility becomes greater.

One concern regarding our results was that the true risk of the strategy might be understated owing to the one-sided nature of the results at high skill levels, when the strategy outperforms its benchmark every month and the tracking error is merely the standard deviation of this outperformance. This measure does not reflect the risk of underperformance owing to wrong decisions. The use of these numbers to calculate information ratios implied that this standard deviation of outperformance could be used as a rough estimate of the risk such a strategy would entail without perfect foresight. Figure 1-6 demonstrates that this does not in fact cause risk to be underestimated. It is true that under 100% skill, the risk owing to variance of results across managers is reduced to zero (from a maximum level of 40.7 bp/year), but this effect is more than counterbalanced by an increase in the variance over time (from 15.9 to 68.6 bp/year). The increased skill level leads to extreme results in months with large market swings, thus causing a far greater variance of outperformance than would be observed at more realistic skill levels.

Figure 1-7a compares the results achieved by our two definitions of skill. At all positive skill levels, choosing the best sector in each cell predictably gives higher mean returns. Choosing any of the outperforming cells produces lower variance of outperformance, but significantly lower mean outperformance as well, for a lower information ratio. However, it is misleading to compare these two approaches at equal skill levels, since choosing any winner is an easier task than choosing the best. A manager who is capable of choosing the best sector with 10% skill is likely to have higher skill at choosing any winning sector.

Making Fewer Sector Decisions

The strategy previously outlined makes nine independent sector decisions, one for each duration × quality cell, which allows the portfolio to add value when different sectors outperform in different quality groups. It also leads to diversification

Figure 1-7a. Sector Allocation Results, Choosing One Sector per Quality × Duration Cell
By Skill Level

	Sector Allocation					
	Any Winner per Cell			Best per Cell		
Skill (%)	Mean (bp/year)	Standard Deviation (bp/year)	Information Ratio	Mean (bp/year)	Standard Deviation (bp/year)	Information Ratio
0	−6.4	42.9	−0.15	−6.6	42.9	−0.15
10	17.9	42.7	0.42	27.0	43.9	0.62
20	42.3	42.8	0.99	60.6	45.3	1.34
40	91.0	44.1	2.07	127.9	49.5	2.58
60	139.7	46.6	3.00	195.2	55.0	3.55
80	188.4	50.2	3.76	262.5	61.4	4.27
100	237.0	54.6	4.34	329.7	68.6	4.81

Figure 1-7b. Sector Allocation Results for Different Number of Decisions
By Skill Level, Choosing Any Outperforming Sector

| | Sector Allocation | | | | | | | | |
| | One Decision per Cell | | | One Decision per Quality | | | One Decision Overall | | |
Skill (%)	Mean (bp/year)	Standard Deviation (bp/year)	Information Ratio	Mean (bp/year)	Standard Deviation (bp/year)	Information Ratio	Mean (bp/year)	Standard Deviation (bp/year)	Information Ratio
0	-6.4	42.9	-0.15	-6.6	58.0	-0.11	-6.6	79.9	-0.08
10	17.9	42.7	0.42	14.5	57.8	0.25	12.5	80.1	0.16
20	42.3	42.8	0.99	35.6	57.6	0.62	31.6	80.0	0.40
40	91.0	44.1	2.07	77.8	57.3	1.36	69.8	78.5	0.89
60	139.7	46.6	3.00	120.0	57.0	2.10	108.1	75.5	1.43
80	188.4	50.2	3.76	162.2	56.9	2.85	146.3	70.6	2.07
100	237.0	54.6	4.34	204.3	56.9	3.59	184.5	63.4	2.91

of the portfolio sector exposures, helping to keep down the tracking errors vs. the index, but we do not know of anyone who manages a portfolio this way. Sector views for long and short single-A corporates are rarely if ever different and are certainly not independent.

Consider a strategy in which the entire portfolio is placed in a single sector across all quality and duration cells. As before, we construct four single-sector duration-matched portfolios within each quality × duration cell. These are then combined with index weights to form four single-sector portfolios that match the index in quality × duration composition. The skill setting determines the probability of choosing a sector for which this portfolio outperforms the index. In an intermediate version of the strategy, independent sector allocation decisions are made for each of the three quality groups and enforced across all duration cells.

Results for these constrained versions of the strategy are shown in Figure 1-7b. The definition of skill in each case involves choosing any outperforming sector—for the portfolio overall (one decision), within each quality (three decisions), or within each quality × duration cell (nine decisions). We see that when we limit the strategy to a single overall sector allocation decision, the mean outperformance decreases somewhat and the risk increases significantly. At a skill level of 20%, for example, the tracking error is nearly twice as large as for the cell-by-cell allocation. As a result, the information ratio for choosing a single sector with 20% skill is only 0.40, similar to the results for choosing a winning sector within each cell at a skill level of 10%. The three-decision scheme in which we choose one sector within each quality group gives results between those of the cell-by-cell strategy and the single-decision strategy. Of course, it is harder to maintain a high level of skill when making a greater number of finer-grained sector calls.

Quality Allocation Results

The quality allocation strategy is analogous to that used for sector allocation. Within each of the twelve sector × duration cells, the portfolio is concentrated into a single credit quality level, matching the cell's index weight and duration. The skill setting determines the probability of choosing any winning quality, or the best quality, within the cell. The results, shown in Figure 1-8, are largely similar to those obtained for sector allocation. For the most part, both mean outperformance and tracking error are somewhat smaller than for sector allocation at similar skill levels. As the differences in tracking errors are more pronounced than the differences in mean outperformance, the information ratios are generally better for quality than for sector allocation.

We also consider the single-decision case, in which a single quality level is chosen for the entire portfolio. Once again, risk is nearly double that of the cell-by-

Figure 1-8. Quality Allocation Results
By Skill Level, Choosing Any Outperforming Sector

	Quality Allocation								
	One Decision per Cell			One Decision per Sector			One Decision Overall		
Skill (%)	Mean (bp/year)	Standard Deviation (bp/year)	Information Ratio	Mean (bp/year)	Standard Deviation (bp/year)	Information Ratio	Mean (bp/year)	Standard Deviation (bp/year)	Information Ratio
0	-2.5	33.1	-0.08	-2.8	45.0	-0.06	-2.0	62.0	-0.03
10	17.1	33.0	0.52	14.2	44.9	0.32	12.1	62.2	0.19
20	36.8	33.2	1.11	31.1	44.8	0.69	26.1	62.1	0.42
40	76.1	34.6	2.20	65.0	44.9	1.45	54.2	61.2	0.89
60	115.4	37.1	3.12	98.9	45.0	2.20	82.2	59.1	1.39
80	154.8	40.4	3.83	132.8	45.3	2.93	110.3	55.8	1.98
100	194.1	44.4	4.37	166.7	45.8	3.64	138.4	51.1	2.71

cell allocation scheme and returns are lower, leading to much lower information ratios. Compared to the single-sector case, both mean outperformance and tracking error are lower by about the same amount. The resulting information ratios are roughly equivalent at similar levels of skill.

Yield Curve Allocation

The third type of allocation decision considered here is placement along the yield curve. The entire portfolio is placed in one of the three duration cells. Each sector × quality cell is divided into three by duration, and the appropriate portion of each of these twelve cells is combined with index weights to obtain three possible portfolios (short, medium, and long duration), each matching the sector × quality composition of the index by market value.

In simulating this strategy, the choice of duration cell is assumed to be based on projections of Treasury yield curve movement. When adjusting the probability of selecting a given cell based on the skill level, the definition of an outperforming duration cell is based on the analysis of the Treasury Index. Nonetheless, it is assumed that the portfolio remains entirely in corporates and that the duration view is implemented as an overweight to the appropriate duration cells relative to the Corporate Index.[9]

The performance achieved by this strategy at different skill levels is shown in Figure 1-9. Compared to the duration-neutral strategies considered earlier, this strategy entails much more risk, but promises greater potential for returns. At 20% skill, the strategy achieves a mean annual outperformance of 119.8 bp and a tracking error of 226.4 bp/year, for an information ratio of 0.53. This information ratio is not as good as those obtained for the cell-by-cell versions of sector and quality allocation at this skill level, but is better than the results for the strategies that commit the portfolio to a single sector or quality.[10]

---

9. This implementation of a duration view in an all-corporate portfolio carries with it an implicit spread view as well. Although the portfolio matches benchmark allocations to each sector by percentage of market value, a position that is long-duration in this way will be long-spread duration as well. This does not bias the results, however, since the implementation of skill is based solely on Treasury Index returns, offering no information on the direction of spread movement.

10. The information ratio of 0.29 shown in Figure 1-9 for duration allocation at 10% skill agrees perfectly with the results of Fjelstad (see Note 3). For the task of choosing one of two duration cells to overweight, with a 55% probability of choosing correctly, she reports a mean outperformance and tracking error that correspond to an information ratio of 0.29.

Figure 1-9. Duration Allocation Results
By Skill Level, Choosing Any Winning Cell

Skill (%)	Duration Allocation		
	Mean (bp/year)	Standard Deviation (bp/year)	Information Ratio
0	11.0	226.1	0.05
10	65.4	226.8	0.29
20	119.8	226.4	0.53
40	228.6	222.4	1.03
60	337.4	213.7	1.58
80	446.1	199.8	2.23
100	554.9	179.4	3.09

SECURITY SELECTION STRATEGY

In our security selection strategy, the portfolio allocates funds along the three-dimensional grid described earlier to exactly match the percentage of index capitalization and the average index duration in each cell. There is no attempt to outperform the index based on systematic duration differences or sector exposures. Rather, the manager's skill at security selection within each cell is the key to strategy performance.

Unlike the allocation strategies, for which we were able to calculate exact statistics by summing across the entire distribution of possible results each month, the performance of the security selection strategy requires simulation. The simulation procedure detailed in what follows was used to generate 10,000 portfolios each month for each set of parameters.

Number of Securities

The most important determinant of the risk of this strategy is the number of bonds in the portfolio. Clearly, the larger the exposure of the portfolio to any single security or issuer, the greater the nonsystematic risk. As more securities are purchased, diversification reduces this risk, and the portfolio behaves more like the index. In our simulations, we express the size of the portfolio as a percentage of the number of bonds in the index. Within a given cell, the number of bonds that the portfolio purchases is computed by taking this percentage of the number of index bonds in the cell.

Duration Matching

To ensure that the bonds selected for the portfolio in a given cell match the duration of the index in that cell, we split each cell into two before selecting bonds. We choose one set of bonds from those with duration above the average and another from the set below it. An appropriate mix of these two portfolios can always be found to match the index duration for the cell as a whole. To make this possible, we always choose a minimum of one bond from each half-cell, regardless of the targeted number of bonds based on the percentage of the index.

Selection Criterion: Excess Return

The measures of future performance ("foresight") used to select bonds, sectors, and qualities shift the relevant selection probabilities away from purely random. For sector and quality allocation, we use total returns, with duration neutrality ensured by the method described previously. For security selection, however, the selection process occurs before the duration correction. We use our skill to select the best-performing bonds within each half-cell and then blend the results. Security selection based on total returns during a yield curve rally would then show a bias toward the longer securities in each half-cell, which would need to be corrected during the weighting phase by weighting the shorter half-cell more heavily. To avoid this anomaly, we use excess returns as the basis for security selection.

Skill Implementation

Within each half-cell, the following procedure is used to simulate the selection of securities at a certain level of skill. The number of bonds we have to select is determined in advance, based on the desired percentage of index bonds. Using our foresight of excess returns, we calculate the market-weighted average performance of all index bonds in the cell and divide those bonds by which perform better than the average (which we call "winners") and which do worse ("losers"). The probability of selecting each security is calculated according to Equation (1-5), based on manager skill and the numbers of winners and losers available. Bonds are selected in a sequential fashion to avoid selecting the same bond twice in a given month. After each bond is selected, it is removed from the pool of available securities. The numbers of winners and losers remaining in the pool are updated, and the selection probabilities are once again interpolated between random selection and perfect foresight using Equation (1-5). This procedure is repeated until the desired number of securities has been selected.

Figure 1-10. Security Selection: Historical Performance at Different Skill Levels
August 1988–July 1999, Choosing 5% of Index Bonds

Skill (%)	Mean Outperformance (bp/year)	Overall Tracking Error (bp/year)	Information Ratio (annualized)
0	3.4	28.4	0.12
10	56.3	29.2	1.93
20	109.4	31.1	3.52
40	215.2	37.4	5.75
60	320.8	46.0	6.98
80	426.4	55.8	7.64
100	532.0	66.2	8.03

Equal Weighting vs. Market Weighting

Once the required number of bonds is chosen within each half-cell, we have to set the amounts of each security to be purchased in the portfolio. We consider two weighting schemes. In market weighting, the selected securities are weighted by the ratios of their overall market capitalizations. Larger issues are given a bigger share of the portfolio. This helps to make the portfolio more similar to the index, which is similarly market weighted, especially when many securities are selected. In equal weighting, we purchase the same market value of each security selected within a half-cell, which avoids overly large exposures to any single issuer. Unless otherwise noted, the results reported for our security selection strategies use market weighting within each cell to generate portfolios.

Results

Figure 1-10 shows the results of the security selection strategy, selecting 5% of the bonds in the index. With a tracking error of about 30 bp/year, this strategy generates a mean outperformance of 56.3 bp/year, for an information ratio of 1.93, at a skill level of only 10%. At 20% skill, the information ratio rises to 3.52. The information ratios that can be achieved by security selection greatly exceed those that are obtained by any of the asset allocation strategies.

Figure 1-11a shows the dependence of these results on the size of the portfolio at 10% skill. We see that as more securities are selected, the main result is a continued decrease in tracking error as a result of increased diversification. Although

Figure 1-11a. Security Selection: Historical Performance for Different Portfolio Sizes
August 1988–July 1999, Skill 10%, by Portfolio Size

Percent of Index Bonds	Mean Outperformance (bp/year)	Overall Tracking Error (bp/year)	Information Ratio (annualized)
2.5	57.7	39.3	1.47
5.0	56.3	29.2	1.93
7.5	54.5	23.3	2.34
10.0	53.4	19.8	2.70
15.0	51.3	15.9	3.22
20.0	49.5	13.5	3.68
25.0	47.9	11.9	4.03

mean outperformance declines slightly as more securities are chosen,[11] the information ratio increases steadily with the number of bonds. In Figure 1-11b, we see that the same effect holds at 20% skill, regardless of whether the bonds selected within each cell are purchased in equal market values or weighted according to

---

11. This effect may be understood based on the fact that several bonds are chosen sequentially from each cell without replacement. At each stage, as described above, the probability of choosing a winner at a skill level s is $(n_W - sn_L)/(n_W - n_L)$. When choosing with skill has increased the chances of picking winners in the early rounds, the remaining pool of securities has a higher concentration of losers, limiting the potential outperformance. Consider a cell with four bonds, two winners and two losers. On the first pick, the unskilled manager has a 50% chance of selecting a winner. If he has picked a winner, his probability of choosing another on the next pick has decreased to 1/3. If the first pick was a loser, the probability of selecting a winner on the second try is 2/3. So the four possible outcomes of choosing two bonds from the four are given by:

$$P_{ww} = \frac{1}{2}\frac{1}{3}, \quad P_{wl} = \frac{1}{2}\frac{2}{3}, \quad P_{lw} = \frac{1}{2}\frac{2}{3}, \quad P_{ll} = \frac{1}{2}\frac{1}{3}.$$

The resulting probability of choosing two winners is 1/6, and the probability of choosing one winner sums to 2/3. The mean number of winners out of the two bonds is thus exactly one, and the mean performance of the strategy in the unskilled case is exactly the same for choosing two bonds as it is for choosing a single bond. The probability of choosing a winner at the second pick is never the same as it was on the first, but the lack of skill on the first pick makes it equally likely that the probability of picking a winner on the second pick is higher or lower. In the skilled case, because the probability of choosing a winner on the first pick is higher, the overall probability of choosing a winner on the second pick is lower. For example, for 20% skill, we have

$$P_{ww} = \left(\frac{2 + 0.2 \times 2}{2 + 2}\right)\left(\frac{1 + 0.2 \times 2}{1 + 2}\right) = \frac{2.4}{4}\frac{1.4}{3}, \quad P_{wl} = \frac{2.4}{4}\frac{1.6}{3}, \quad P_{lw} = \frac{1.6}{4}\frac{2.2}{3}, \quad P_{ll} = \frac{1.6}{4}\frac{0.8}{3}.$$

In this case, the probability of choosing two winners is 28%, the probability of choosing one winner is 61%, and the mean number of winners selected out of the two bonds is 1.17. The mean performance is somewhat lower than that of a strategy that picks one bond at 20% skill, with 0.6 winners on average.

Figure 1-11b. Security Selection: Market Weighted vs. Equal Weighted within Each Cell
Skill 20%, by Portfolio Size

Percent of Index Bonds	Market Weighted			Equal Weighted		
	Mean Outperformance (bp/year)	Overall Track Error (bp/year)	Information Ratio	Mean Outperformance (bp/year)	Overall Track Error (bp/year)	Information Ratio
2.5	111.0	40.6	2.73	111.1	40.9	2.72
5.0	109.4	31.1	3.52	109.9	31.3	3.52
7.5	107.0	25.7	4.16	108.2	26.6	4.07
10.0	105.3	22.5	4.69	106.9	23.9	4.47
15.0	102.1	18.9	5.39	104.2	21.1	4.95
20.0	99.1	16.8	5.91	101.4	19.3	5.25
25.0	96.1	15.3	6.27	98.5	18.3	5.38

Figure 1-12. Security Selection Results
By Skill Level and Portfolio Size

	2.5% of Index			5% of Index		
Skill (%)	Mean (bp/year)	Tracking Error (bp/year)	Information Ratio	Mean (bp/year)	Tracking Error (bp/year)	Information Ratio
0	4.6	38.7	0.12	3.4	28.4	0.12
10	57.7	39.3	1.47	56.3	29.2	1.93
20	111.0	40.6	2.73	109.4	31.1	3.52
40	217.2	45.3	4.80	215.2	37.4	5.75
60	323.2	52.1	6.21	320.8	46.0	6.98
80	429.0	60.1	7.14	426.4	55.8	7.64
100	534.9	69.1	7.74	532.0	66.2	8.03

	15% of Index			20% of Index		
Skill (%)	Mean (bp/year)	Tracking Error (bp/year)	Information Ratio	Mean (bp/year)	Tracking Error (bp/year)	Information Ratio
0	0.9	14.7	0.06	0.5	12.2	0.04
10	51.3	15.9	3.22	49.5	13.5	3.68
20	102.1	18.9	5.39	99.1	16.8	5.91
40	204.5	28.1	7.27	199.6	26.3	7.58
60	308.3	39.1	7.88	302.6	37.6	8.05
80	413.9	51.1	8.1	408	49.7	8.21
100	521.5	63.6	8.2	515.7	62.4	8.26

their market capitalization. When dealing with a small number of bonds, there is little performance difference between these two schemes. (In cells in which only a single bond is chosen, the two are identical.) As more bonds are included in the strategy, the information ratio of the market-weighted scheme increases faster, owing to a smaller tracking error relative to the market-weighted index. For this reason, we have chosen to concentrate on the market-weighted version of the strategy, and all of our subsequent results come through this approach.

Figure 1-12 provides the results of the security selection strategy across a wide range of skill levels and portfolio sizes.

7.5% of Index			10% of Index		
Mean (bp/year)	Tracking Error (bp/year)	Information Ratio	Mean (bp/year)	Tracking Error (bp/year)	Information Ratio
2.0	22.4	0.09	1.7	18.7	0.09
54.5	23.3	2.34	53.4	19.8	2.70
107.0	25.7	4.16	105.3	22.5	4.69
212.1	33.3	6.37	209.3	30.7	6.82
317.3	42.8	7.41	313.8	41.0	7.66
422.6	53.5	7.90	418.9	52.2	8.03
528.3	64.8	8.15	524.8	64.0	8.20

25% of Index		
Mean (bp/year)	Tracking Error (bp/year)	Information Ratio
0.3	10.5	0.03
47.9	11.9	4.03
96.1	15.3	6.27
195	25.2	7.75
296.8	36.5	8.13
401.5	48.6	8.26
508.3	60.9	8.35

ANALYSIS OF RESULTS

What is the most appropriate way to compare the results of these very different investment strategies? One approach is simply to examine the results of all the strategies at the same skill level. Figure 1-13 shows that at 20% skill, the strategies span a wide range of mean outperformance, tracking error, and information ratios. The information ratios of the security selection strategies far surpass all those of the allocation strategies. Cell-by-cell sector and quality allocation outperform the duration allocation scheme, which in turn surpasses the single-sector and single-quality strategies.

Figure 1-13. Performance of Different Investment Styles with Imperfect Foresight
August 1988–July 1999, Skill 20%

Strategy	Mean Outperformance (bp/year)	Overall Tracking Error (bp/year)	Information Ratio
Duration	119.8	226.4	0.53
Quality (best per cell)	43.5	34.2	1.27
Quality (any winner per cell)	36.8	33.2	1.11
Quality (one per sector)	31.1	44.8	0.69
Quality (one decision)	26.1	62.1	0.42
Sector (best per cell)	60.6	45.3	1.34
Sector (any winner per cell)	42.3	42.8	0.99
Sector (one per quality)	35.6	57.6	0.62
Sector (one decision)	31.6	80.0	0.40
Security (5% of bonds)	109.4	31.1	3.52
Security (10% of bonds)	105.3	22.5	4.69
Security (25% of bonds)	96.1	15.3	6.27

A slightly different way of looking at the relative performance of the different strategies is to compare the mean outperformance that can be achieved at a given level of risk. Let us define the intrinsic risk of a given strategy as the tracking error achieved by that strategy at the 0% skill level. For the security selection strategy using 5% of index securities, the intrinsic risk is 28.4 bp/year. By choosing an appropriate bet size, as described earlier, any of the allocation strategies can be implemented so as to have the same level of intrinsic risk. For example, the intrinsic risk of the duration allocation strategy, which is 226.1 bp at a bet size of 100%, can be reduced to 28.4 bp by using a bet size of 13%. This strategy at a skill level of 20% achieves a mean outperformance of 13% × 119.8 bp, or about 15 bp. In Figure 1-14, we compare the strategies (only the "any winner" variants are plotted), with all bet sizes adjusted to achieve an intrinsic risk of 28.4 bp/year. Mean outperformance is plotted as a function of skill for each strategy.

The results of Figure 1-14 are clearly divided into three tiers. Security selection earns far and away the greatest return for a given skill level, followed by sector and quality allocation within each cell, followed by the three allocation schemes that make a single decision (duration cell, sector, or quality) for the entire portfolio.

To interpret this graph properly, we must recognize that the skill levels assumed for different strategies are not directly comparable. One can achieve the unlikely result of 50 bp of mean annual outperformance for this amount of risk by

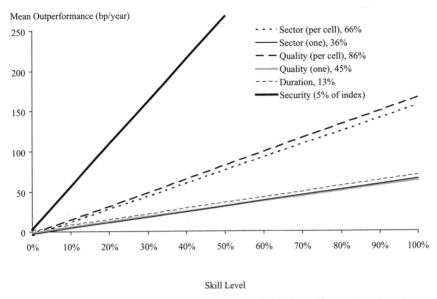

Figure 1-14. Mean Outperformance as a Function of Skill for Different Investment Styles, with Bet Sizes Chosen to Achieve Equivalent Levels of Risk

applying security selection with 10% skill, sector or quality allocation per cell with about 35% skill, or one of the single-decision allocation methods with 75% skill. However, it is not clear which of these is the hardest to achieve.

The clear tiering effect shown in Figure 1-14 suggests that the number of independent decisions required to implement a strategy is a major determinant of risk-adjusted performance. The security selection method, in which the number of decisions is equal to the number of securities in the portfolio (for 5% of the index, this averaged 178 securities), is by far the best performer. The quality allocation strategy with twelve decisions (one per sector × duration cell) and the sector allocation strategy with nine decisions (one per quality × duration cell) make up the next performance tier. When viewed in this manner, the three single-decision allocation strategies have the lowest information ratios for a given skill level.

The cause of this effect is clear. In the performance comparison of Figure 1-14, the bet sizes have been chosen to achieve the same level of risk for each strategy. When an investment strategy is the result of many independent decisions, each month's performance is a combination of successful and unsuccessful bets. The diversification of the risks decreases the overall risk of the strategy without reducing the expected return, which allows the strategies with better diversification of risk to take larger positions and achieve greater outperformance.

Value of a Single Decision

To create a simplified model of this effect, let us assume that each strategy (at any given skill level) can be viewed as an equally weighted sum of n subcomponents reflecting the individual decisions taken. Let r_i be the outperformance owing to a single decision i taken alone, and let the overall portfolio outperformance be the average of n such terms:

$$r = \frac{1}{n}\sum_{i=1}^{n} r_i, \tag{1-8}$$

where all of the r_i are independent and identically distributed random variables with mean $\mu_{decision}$ and standard deviation $\sigma_{decision}$. The outperformance of the overall strategy then has a mean $\mu_{strategy} = \mu_{decision}$ and a standard deviation $\sigma_{strategy} = \sigma_{decision}/\sqrt{n}$.

For example, in the sector allocation strategy, the r_i could represent the return difference between the portfolio and index components within each of the $n = 9$ quality × duration cells. This model would be precise if: (1) all of the cells had equal weights in the index, (2) the distribution of strategy outperformance at a given skill was the same in each cell, and (3) the results in each cell were independent of one another. Although these conditions do not necessarily hold, it is interesting to look at the per-decision tracking errors $\sigma_{decision}$ implied by this model for each strategy. While not directly observable, we can back them out of our observations by multiplying the tracking error $\sigma_{strategy}$ by $\sqrt{n}$. Information ratios at the per-decision level can be computed as $\mu_{decision}/\sigma_{decision}$.

Figure 1-15 revisits the performance data of Figure 1-13 in light of this analysis. We calculate the implied per-decision tracking errors as described earlier to reflect the number of independent decisions involved in each strategy. Comparing the resulting per-decision information ratios, we find that the results for the different strategies are close in magnitude. The highest per-decision information ratio is achieved by the duration decision, with the next highest being the single-decision versions of sector and quality allocation. The cell-by-cell sector and quality decisions come next, closely followed by security selection.

How do we reconcile these two diametrically opposed points of view? Which better represents the truth—Figure 1-13 or Figure 1-15? Is security selection the most important or the least important portfolio strategy?

The answer, of course, is both. Figure 1-15 confirms the commonly held notion that the most important single decision is the duration call, but Figure 1-13 emphasizes the power of diversification in reducing risk. When portfolio managers attempt to enhance portfolio return by taking several independent risk exposures instead of one large one, tracking error is reduced. The information ratio

Figure 1-15. Performance of Different Investment Styles, with Risk Adjusted for Number of Independent Decisions

August 1988–July 1999, Skill 20%

Strategy	Mean Outperformance (bp/year)	Overall Tracking Error (bp/year)	Number of Independent Decisions	Tracking Error per Decision (bp/year)	Information Ratio per Decision
Duration	119.8	226.4	1	226.4	0.53
Quality (best per cell)	43.5	34.2	12	118.6	0.37
Quality (any winner per cell)	36.8	33.2	12	115.1	0.32
Quality (one per sector)	31.1	44.8	4	89.7	0.35
Quality (one decision)	26.1	62.1	1	62.1	0.42
Sector (best per cell)	60.6	45.3	9	136.0	0.45
Sector (any winner per cell)	42.3	42.8	9	128.4	0.33
Sector (one per quality)	35.6	57.6	3	99.7	0.36
Sector (one decision)	31.6	80.0	1	80.0	0.40
Security (5% of bonds)	109.4	31.1	178	414.9	0.26
Security (10% of bonds)	105.3	22.5	369	432.2	0.24
Security (25% of bonds)	96.1	15.3	961	474.3	0.20

is increased as a result, provided that the same level of skill (and hence outperformance) can be maintained across the greater number of decisions.

It is clear from Figure 1-15 that the model of n independent sources of risk as implied by Equation (1-8) does not provide a perfect adjustment for the number of decisions. In particular, once we have made our adjustment, we should expect to see the information ratio per security selection decision to be independent of the number of bonds selected. Instead, we seem to have adjusted by too much. This is consistent with the situation in which there are positive correlations among the various decisions (e.g., correlations between bonds of the same issuer or industry group). When dividing risk among n positively correlated decisions, the risk is decreased by less than $\sqrt{n}$, and our adjustment overstates the benefit of diversification. This effect can also explain why the information ratios per decision seem to be lower for the sector and quality allocation strategies that make separate decisions in each cell. The best sector allocation for single-A bonds may not always be the same as for Baa-rated bonds, but there is certainly a positive correlation between the two. The adjusted numbers in Figure 1-15 should thus be viewed only as a crude approximation.

The presentation of results according to a constant skill level is possibly misleading in another way as well. The strategies requiring many decisions (e.g., sector allocation in twelve cells, selection of 961 bonds) are compared to similar strategies requiring many fewer decisions (e.g., single-decision quality allocation, selection of 178 bonds) at the same skill level. This is where the greatest challenge lies. A sector rotation specialist may always have a view favoring one sector or another on a macro basis, but if asked to choose his favorite sector in each of nine quality × duration cells separately, would he be equally confident of each of these views? It would seem to be much harder to maintain the same skill level across this expanded set of decisions. A similar argument can be advanced regarding security selection. Although an analyst may have an excellent track record concerning the performance results of his top picks, it is difficult to maintain the same skill level when it becomes necessary to select a greater number of securities. Clearly, for a fixed number of bonds, even a very small increase in the skill level of the security selection process can have a marked effect on overall performance. To help decide how to allocate a fixed research budget, it might be more interesting to compare the trade-off between skill and the number of decisions. For instance, we see in Figure 1-12 that security selection using 5% of the index with 20% skill achieves an information ratio of 3.52, whereas using 20% of the index with 10% skill achieves an information ratio of 3.68.

Are there specific sectors in which security selection is most important? Figure 1-16 gives a detailed breakdown of our results for the security selection strategy using 5% of the bonds in the index at a 10% skill level by sector × quality ×

duration cells. Comparing the tracking errors achieved by the strategy in different cells, we find that certain trends hold in general, but not in every case. Within a given sector and quality cell, longer-duration cells tend to have greater risk than their shorter-duration counterparts. Similarly, lower-quality cells tend to have greater tracking errors than those of higher quality, and further, cells with greater tracking errors tend to offer a skilled manager more opportunity for outperformance. Nevertheless, the information ratios cover a fairly wide range, from 0.17 for Baa short Yankees to 0.56 for A short financials. It is noteworthy that these are also the smallest and largest cells in the index, respectively. Strategy risk in the larger cells is reduced by the additional diversification owing to choosing more securities. Once again, we divide the information ratio by the square root of the average number of bonds in the portfolio to obtain an information ratio per decision. These numbers have a much tighter distribution, ranging from 0.09 to 0.24.

Diversification of Risk among Different Strategies

We have emphasized the role played by the number of independent decisions within a given strategy in reducing risk and improving risk-adjusted return. The same effect is achieved by combining strategies that express independent views in different dimensions.

Consider a strategy that takes risk in four dimensions simultaneously, at approximately equal levels of tracking error. Specifically, we allocate 13% of the portfolio to the duration allocation strategy, 36% to the sector allocation strategy, and 46% to the quality allocation strategy (one decision each). (These weights correspond to the bet sizes used in Figure 1-14 to obtain equivalent risk levels.) The remaining 5% of the portfolio is neutral to the benchmark. The combination of these strategies is used to set the portfolio allocations to sector × quality × duration cells. We further assume that the portfolio is composed of only 5% of index securities and is thus subject to the nonsystematic tracking error that we observed in our security selection strategy. Assuming independence of the results for the different strategies, we can calculate the mean outperformance and tracking error of this blended strategy using Equation (1-7). This blended strategy has a tracking error of 55.7 bp/year.

Figure 1-17 shows the performance of this strategy as a function of the skill levels for each management task. In the unskilled case (all skill levels at 0%), the strategy does no better than the index on average. When the skill level for any one of the allocation strategies is raised to 10%, we see a modest gain of about 8 bp/year for any of the three, with information ratios of about 0.14. If the skill at all three allocation tasks is raised to 10%, the gains combine to an expected outperformance of 21.1 bp/year, for an information ratio of 0.38. Comparing these

Figure 1-16. Performance of Security Selection Strategy by Cell
Choosing 5% of Bonds, Skill 10%

Quality	Duration Cell	Sector	Average Number of Bonds in Cell	Average Percent of Index Market Value	Average Cell Duration
Aaa-Aa	Short	Industrial	62.2	1.8	2.44
Aaa-Aa	Medium	Industrial	57.7	1.8	5.49
Aaa-Aa	Long	Industrial	48.5	1.7	9.45
Aaa-Aa	Short	Utility	78.7	1.3	2.51
Aaa-Aa	Medium	Utility	174.5	2.7	5.67
Aaa-Aa	Long	Utility	121.5	2.4	8.82
Aaa-Aa	Short	Finance	156.3	4.2	2.29
Aaa-Aa	Medium	Finance	78.1	2.1	5.38
Aaa-Aa	Long	Finance	43.1	0.9	9.46
Aaa-Aa	Short	Yankees	91.1	3.1	2.56
Aaa-Aa	Medium	Yankees	94.7	4.3	5.54
Aaa-Aa	Long	Yankees	69.6	2.0	9.46
A	Short	Industrial	187.1	4.9	2.49
A	Medium	Industrial	216.7	5.8	5.49
A	Long	Industrial	207.3	6.2	9.32
A	Short	Utility	110.5	1.8	2.45
A	Medium	Utility	214.1	3.3	5.62
A	Long	Utility	103.3	2.3	8.44
A	Short	Finance	304.7	7.6	2.41
A	Medium	Finance	217.6	5.8	5.40
A	Long	Finance	75.6	2.2	8.79
A	Short	Yankees	38.3	1.1	2.56
A	Medium	Yankees	60.3	2.5	5.62
A	Long	Yankees	53.0	2.5	9.71
Baa	Short	Industrial	130.0	3.6	2.53
Baa	Medium	Industrial	170.8	4.9	5.49
Baa	Long	Industrial	128.1	4.2	8.89
Baa	Short	Utility	118.4	2.2	2.46
Baa	Medium	Utility	196.9	3.2	5.58
Baa	Long	Utility	79.0	1.9	8.54
Baa	Short	Finance	85.7	1.9	2.40
Baa	Medium	Finance	86.3	1.9	5.41
Baa	Long	Finance	20.8	0.5	8.66
Baa	Short	Yankees	13.5	0.4	2.49
Baa	Medium	Yankees	28.4	0.9	5.64
Baa	Long	Yankees	20.4	0.5	9.24

Average Cell Return (%/month)	Average Number of Bonds in Portfolio	Mean Outperformance (bp/year)	Tracking Error (bp/year)	Information Ratio	Information Ratio per Decision
0.62	2.4	29.4	106.7	0.28	0.18
0.74	2.1	49.7	151.4	0.33	0.23
0.82	2.1	119.7	369.5	0.32	0.22
0.59	3.4	55.3	153.7	0.36	0.19
0.75	7.8	68.9	154.2	0.45	0.16
0.83	5.4	68.5	161.3	0.42	0.18
0.64	7.0	30.5	65.0	0.47	0.18
0.74	3.3	56.1	129.3	0.43	0.24
0.82	2.1	109.0	357.2	0.31	0.21
0.63	3.7	27.2	88.0	0.31	0.16
0.76	3.8	43.4	163.2	0.27	0.14
0.85	2.7	66.4	214.9	0.31	0.19
0.64	8.3	27.4	71.1	0.39	0.13
0.75	9.9	50.8	90.6	0.56	0.18
0.84	9.4	69.2	123.7	0.56	0.18
0.61	4.8	45.0	122.7	0.37	0.17
0.76	9.8	64.5	120.8	0.53	0.17
0.84	4.4	74.2	265.5	0.28	0.13
0.65	14.3	22.5	40.4	0.56	0.15
0.75	9.9	44.9	101.3	0.44	0.14
0.82	3.3	96.3	248.2	0.39	0.21
0.62	2.0	52.6	196.0	0.27	0.19
0.73	2.6	60.4	200.5	0.30	0.19
0.85	2.7	47.5	164.4	0.29	0.17
0.67	5.6	47.7	227.3	0.21	0.09
0.73	7.6	98.8	264.5	0.37	0.14
0.82	5.7	87.3	380.3	0.23	0.10
0.64	5.0	48.2	140.6	0.34	0.15
0.79	8.9	72.8	175.5	0.41	0.14
0.86	3.3	59.4	282.4	0.21	0.12
0.68	3.4	48.2	196.6	0.24	0.13
0.75	3.3	106.0	355.1	0.30	0.16
0.81	2.0	108.2	456.8	0.24	0.17
0.68	2.0	58.4	353.0	0.17	0.12
0.71	2.2	115.3	345.0	0.33	0.23
0.85	1.9	89.0	394.7	0.23	0.16

Figure 1-17. Performance of a Blended Investment Strategy at Different Skill Levels for Each Style

	Skill Level (%)			Performance		
				Mean Outperformance	Tracking Error	Information
Duration	Sector	Quality	Security	(bp/year)	(bp/year)	Ratio
0	0	0	0	1.5	55.7	0.03
10	0	0	0	8.1	55.7	0.14
0	10	0	0	8.2	55.7	0.15
0	0	10	0	7.8	55.7	0.14
0	0	0	2	12.1	55.8	0.22
0	0	0	4	22.7	55.9	0.41
10	10	10	0	21.1	55.8	0.38
20	10	10	0	27.6	55.8	0.49
10	20	10	0	27.7	55.8	0.50
10	10	20	0	27.4	55.8	0.49
10	10	10	2	31.6	55.9	0.57
10	10	10	4	42.2	56.0	0.75
20	20	20	0	40.6	55.8	0.73

results to those in Figures 1-7 through 1-9, we see that even though we have increased our risk estimate to include the effect of security risk, we achieve a higher information ratio than with 10% skill at any of these three single-decision allocation strategies alone. The effect of a small increase in skill at security selection is even more striking. Increasing the security selection skill from 0 to 2% provides more outperformance than 10% skill at any single allocation dimension; at 4% it outperforms 10% skill at each of the three allocation strategies. A similar effect is observed if we look at the incremental effect of raising allocation skills from 10 to 20%.

CONCLUSION

At equivalent skill levels, the security selection strategy gives the highest information ratios of the strategies considered. We have seen that this is true in large part because of the diversification of risk among the many independent decisions involved in selecting each security in the portfolio. This observation provides a clear message for all portfolio managers, including the purest of asset allocators: the single most important element in achieving a high information ratio is diversification of risk among several independent return-enhancing strategies.

Concerning security selection, we are left with the question of what skill level is reasonable to expect across a wide range of securities. Nevertheless, we have unequivocally demonstrated the importance of security selection skill. Any systematic improvement in the selection process undoubtedly gives a significant boost to portfolio performance.

This study was conducted on a single asset class (corporate bonds) in a single market (U.S. fixed-income) over a single decade. Care should be taken when generalizing these results to other asset classes (such as mortgages), other markets (e.g., Europe), or other time periods. Several interesting issues remain for further study. We did not use either a model for transaction costs or a mechanism for reducing turnover. What levels of skill are required to produce steady outperformance once transaction costs are considered? How will the performance achievable at a given skill level be affected by constraints on portfolio turnover? How will the conclusions change if the foresight horizon is not matched to the average holding period? In future research to explore these issues, we will apply the imperfect foresight approach to foresight horizons longer than 1 month.

The conclusions of this study should be of particular interest to new investors in the credit markets, such as European credit portfolio managers and central banks, who are in the process of establishing their investment style.

We do not offer a quantitative model for building views on market sectors or individual credits. As such, none of the strategies studied can be implemented directly. However, interpretation of these results can impact portfolio management practice in several different ways. First, it can help guide the formation of an investment style and an associated research program. In particular, our results underscore the importance of skill at security selection. More generally, they highlight the importance of diversifying the portfolio views among several independent sources of risk. This should encourage risk-conscious managers to pursue multiple avenues of research simultaneously.

Second, the results of such simulation studies can be used to help evaluate manager performance. Steven Fox and Mary Fjelstad analyzed the observed performance distributions for managers with known investment styles,[12] and showed that the manager's skill can be estimated by simulating distributions with various skill and bet size parameters and finding the one that matches the observed performance most closely.

The comparison of information ratios between simulated strategies and actual manager track records provides another interesting interpretation. Thomas Goodwin reported empirically observed information ratios for institutional money

12. See Notes 2 and 3.

managers benchmarked against the Lehman Brothers Aggregate Index.[13] Only 20.5% of the managers in this sample achieve information ratios of more than 0.5, and only 2.6% reach 1.0 or better. Our results show that, at least when transaction costs are neglected, such results can be achieved even at fairly low levels of skill, where correct views are established only slightly more often than with random selection.

APPENDIX A. INDEPENDENCE OF INFORMATION RATIO FROM BET SIZE

Denote the return of a given strategy by R_S and that of the benchmark by R_B. The mean μ_S and variance σ_S^2 of the strategy outperformance are given by

$$\mu_S = E(R_s - R_B)$$
$$\sigma_S^2 = \text{Var}(R_S - R_B).$$

Now consider an investment scheme in which only a portion b of portfolio assets is committed to the strategy, with the remainder invested in the benchmark. The return on this investment is given by

$$R_{S,b} = bR_S + (1 - b)R_B = R_B + b(R_S - R_B).$$

We can easily see that the mean and variance of outperformance of the strategy at bet size b are given by

$$\mu_{S,b} = E(R_{S,b} - R_B) = E(b(R_S - R_B)) = bE(R_S - R_B) = b\mu_s$$
$$\sigma_{S,b}^2 = \text{Var}(R_{S,b} - R_B) = \text{Var}(b(R_S - R_B)) = b^2\text{Var}(R_S - R_B) = b^2\sigma_S^2.$$

Turning our attention to the strategy information ratio

$$IR_S = \frac{\mu_S}{\sigma_S},$$

we find it to be independent of bet size:

$$IR_{S,b} = \frac{\mu_{S,b}}{\sigma_{S,b}} = \frac{b\mu_S}{b\sigma_S} = \frac{\mu_S}{\sigma_S} = IR_S.$$

13. Thomas H. Goodwin, "The Information Ratio," *Financial Analysts Journal*, 1998, vol. 39, no. 1, pp. 34–43.

APPENDIX B. DECOMPOSING THE VARIANCE
OF STRATEGY OUTPERFORMANCE

In this appendix, we characterize the strategy outperformance by a conditional random distribution. We develop expressions for the unconditional mean and variance of the distribution and show that the variance of outperformance can be viewed as the sum of two terms: the variance of performance across managers and the variance of performance over time.

Let us represent the outperformance of each deterministic strategy considered by a set of N random variables $x_1, x_2, \ldots, x_N$. Using sector allocation as an example, we have $N = 4$, and the x_i are the outperformance of the four different sectors in our duration-neutral and quality-neutral strategy. We use a vector $\mathbf{x}$ to represent them.

We assume that the vector random variable $\mathbf{x}$ has a probability distribution function (pdf) $f(\mathbf{x})$, and that each month of historical observation corresponds to a single outcome of this random variable.

Let the random variable y denote the outperformance of the portfolio strategy. The process of using imperfect foresight to alter the probabilities of choosing the different sectors makes the distribution of the strategy outperformance y conditional on the outcome of the sector return vector $\mathbf{x}$. The strategy outperformance y is thus a Bayesian process and follows a conditional random distribution.

Let us denote the conditional pdf of y for given $\mathbf{x}$ by $p(y \mid \mathbf{x})$. This represents the probability of any particular outcome of the strategy given our weighted probabilities for choosing each sector. Figure 1-4 shows explicitly the conditional pdf for one particular cell for a given month.

The distributions $p(y \mid \mathbf{x})$ are in discrete form, owing to the finite number of sectors from which one may choose. Nevertheless, in this discussion we use a continuous representation. By using the Dirac function $\delta(x)$, which has the properties that $\delta(x) = 0$ when $x \neq 0$ and $\int \delta(x) dx = 1$, we can use the continuous form of pdf to express a discrete distribution $p(y \mid \mathbf{x})$ in terms of the sum of different Dirac functions centered at different points appropriately weighted. We can thus use the continuous representation with no loss of generality.

Bayesian statistics or conditional probability theory states that if event $\mathbf{x}$ has an unconditional distribution $f(\mathbf{x})$, and event y has a conditional pdf $p(y \mid \mathbf{x})$, then the joint pdf of $\mathbf{x}$ and y is $p(y \mid \mathbf{x}) \cdot f(\mathbf{x})$, and the unconditional pdf for y is then given by $g(y) = \int p(y \mid \mathbf{x}) \cdot f(\mathbf{x}) d\mathbf{x}$.

The conditional mean and variance are defined as

$$E(y \mid \mathbf{x}) = \int y p(y \mid \mathbf{x}) dy$$
$$\mathrm{Var}(y \mid \mathbf{x}) = E((y - E(y \mid \mathbf{x}))^2 \mid \mathbf{x}) = E(y^2 \mid \mathbf{x}) - [E(y \mid \mathbf{x})]^2$$
$$= \int y^2 p(y \mid \mathbf{x}) dy - (\int y p(y \mid \mathbf{x}) dy)^2,$$

where the notation $E(x)$ denotes the expectation of a random variable x under its pdf. The conditional mean and variance of strategy outperformance is exactly what we have calculated for each month of historical data considered in our study. Figure 1-5 shows the details of this calculation conditioned on x_{jul99}, the performance vector of individual sectors in July 1999.

When we consider the overall performance of a strategy over time, two different measures of variance are of interest. The first considers the variance of the expected strategy performance over time, $\text{Var}(E(y \mid x))$. If a strategy has a small positive expected return every month, it is less risky in some sense than one that has a large positive expected return under some market outcomes and a large negative expected return in others. The second considers the conditional variance of the strategy performance within each month. This is the variance that we see across a population of managers implementing the same strategy independently under a given market outcome. Taking the average $E(\text{Var}(y \mid x))$ of this conditional variance gives us another (very different) measure of the long-term variance of strategy outperformance. We conjecture that the overall variance of strategy outperformance is equal to the sum of these two terms and that the unconditional mean is equal to the expectation of the conditional means:

$$E(y) = E(E(y \mid x)), \tag{1-9}$$

$$\text{Var}(y) = \text{Var}(E(y \mid x)) + E(\text{Var}(y \mid x)). \tag{1-10}$$

Equation (1-9) is almost obvious:

$$\begin{aligned}E(y) &= \int yg(y)dy = \iint yp(y \mid x)f(x)dxdy = \int(\int yp(y \mid x)dy)f(x)dx \\ &= \int E(y \mid x)f(x)dx = E(E(y \mid x)).\end{aligned}$$

To prove Equation (1-10), we first expand each term separately:

$$\begin{aligned}\text{Var}(y) &= E(y^2) - (E(y))^2 = \int y^2 g(y)dy - (\int yg(y)dy)^2 \\ &= \iint y^2 p(y \mid x)f(x)dxdy - (\iint yp(y \mid x)f(x)dxdy)^2,\end{aligned} \tag{1-11}$$

$$\begin{aligned}\text{Var}(E(y \mid x)) &= \int(E(y \mid x))^2 f(x)dx - (\int E(y \mid x)f(x)dx)^2 \\ &= \int(\int yp(y \mid x)dy)^2 f(x)dx - (\iint yp(y \mid x)f(x)dydx)^2,\end{aligned} \tag{1-12}$$

$$\begin{aligned}E(\text{Var}(y \mid x)) &= \int \text{Var}(y \mid x)f(x)dx = \int(\int y^2 p(y \mid x)dy) - (\int yp(y \mid x)dy)^2)f(x)dx \\ &= \iint y^2 p(y \mid x)f(x)dydx - \int(\int yp(y \mid x)dy)^2 f(x)dx.\end{aligned} \tag{1-13}$$

We can see that the first term of Equation (1-12) and the second term of Equation (1-13) are the same. So when we add Equations (1-12) and (1-13), these terms cancel out, and we have

$$\text{Var}(E(y \mid \mathbf{x})) + E(\text{Var}(y \mid \mathbf{x})) = \iint y^2 p(y \mid \mathbf{x}) f(\mathbf{x}) dy \mathbf{dx}$$
$$- \left(\iint y p(y \mid \mathbf{x}) f(\mathbf{x}) dy \mathbf{dx} \right)^2. \tag{1-14}$$

The right-hand sides of Equations (1-11) and (1-14) are the same, and we have proven our conjecture [Equation (1-10)].

2. Value of Skill in Macro Strategies for Global Fixed-Income Investing

Global fixed-income investors have recently experienced a major shift in the landscape. Five years ago, global fixed-income mandates were almost universally benchmarked against indices of global government debt, but there were many opportunities for astute managers to add value. A manager might have considered his views on a dozen different currencies and yield curves before setting the portfolio's allocation. In the period leading up to European Monetary Union, convergence trades provided a consistent source of alpha for believers.

With monetary union a reality, global bond portfolio managers suddenly found themselves with a much smaller opportunity set for generating outperformance within the investment universe. There are now just a handful of currencies and yield curves on which to form views. To make matters worse, the increasing globalization of the world economy has caused even those few remaining currencies to be more closely linked to one another. In particular, interest-rate movements in the United States and in Europe are more highly correlated than before.

In response to this loss of diversification within the global government debt universe, investors have sought to expand their efforts to new horizons. The most natural step is the inclusion of investment-grade credit and collateralized debt. The rapid rise of the Lehman Brothers Global Aggregate Index, which now serves as a benchmark for debt portfolios totaling over $300 billion, attests to the strength of this trend. The search for higher returns and greater diversification has even prompted investors to look beyond investment grade. Over $65 billion is currently benchmarked to the Global Universal Index, which combines the Global Aggregate with high yield and emerging market debt. In many cases, even for portfolios still benchmarked against all-government indices, these additional asset classes may be used as out-of-index investments.

Based on research first published by Lehman Brothers in 2003.

Building active management capabilities for all subsets of the Global Aggregate Index within a domestic boutique is likely to entail massive new investment to develop security selection skills and solve complex implementation issues. As an alternative way to maintain significant excess returns and attractive information ratios, many global fixed-income managers adapt an investment framework based on macro-level asset allocation. This approach entails much lower entry cost and can be implemented inexpensively and efficiently if derivatives are allowed. Many of these managers invest in nonindex asset classes such as high yield, credit, emerging market debt, and inflation-linked securities. The use of asset classes outside of the benchmark is often referred to as a "core-plus" strategy.

With the inclusion of all of these additional asset classes in the investment set, managers now have many choices as to how to position their portfolios, from the macro to the micro level. The main question, of course, is where to focus the research effort. Of all the macro strategies available, will the best risk-adjusted returns be achieved by skilled timing of exposures to yield curves, foreign exchange rates, credit sectors, or core-plus asset classes? This study addresses that issue using the "imperfect foresight" methodology[1] to simulate skill in a broad set of macro strategies for global investing.

We include a fairly broad set of classical strategies based on yields and FX rates within the global government market. The first level is a global duration call, in which the portfolio chooses whether to go long or short duration on a global basis, with exposures taken in the same direction in all currencies. Next is a market duration strategy, in which a duration overweight in one currency is offset by an underweight in another. Yield curve twist strategies (steepening or flattening) are implemented on a single-currency basis in each of the G3 currencies. The currency allocation is viewed as an independent decision that is layered on top of whatever bond positions are selected by cross-hedging to achieve the desired set of FX exposures.

We also investigate a number of strategies based on allocations to additional market segments. The sectors covered are investment-grade credit, high yield credit, emerging markets, and inflation-linked securities. Although conceptually these are global strategies, we show sample implementations of each one in a single-currency framework. We look at euro-denominated investment-grade credits on an excess return basis vs. euro Treasuries, U.S. Treasury inflation-protected securities (TIPS) relative to U.S. Treasuries, and USD-denominated high yield and emerging market debt.

1. *Combining Strategies.* It is well known that risk-adjusted performance can be improved by diversifying the portfolio risk exposures among several different

---

1. See Chapter 1.

alpha-generation strategies. However, to get the full benefit of this diversification, it is important for the investment decisions in the various strategies to be made independently. In practice, this independence of decisions can be very hard to achieve.

For example, suppose a senior partner in an investment management firm makes an interest-rate call. The managers of the corporate and core-plus portions of the portfolio are very likely to reflect this view not only in their curve positioning, but also by overweighting market segments that are likely to outperform on a spread basis under the expected scenario. While this could further leverage the value of a correct interest-rate call, it reduces the level of strategy diversification. We explore the effect of combining strategies under different correlation assumptions.

2. *Risk Budgeting by Investment Committees.* In our simulation of the various yield curve and foreign exchange strategies, we have included a simple model of a risk-budgeting process. We recognize that ex ante risk analysis has become an intrinsic part of the portfolio management process. Before a particular strategy is implemented, the tracking error incurred is projected based on the asset class volatilities and correlations observed to date.[2] This allows a manager to scale the position sizes for each strategy to achieve a targeted amount of risk. In practice, risk budgeting may be used to allot the total amount of risk among the various dimensions (or decision makers). For the purposes of this study, the procedure allows us to compare the performance of different strategies operating under the same ex ante risk constraints, as opposed to simply analyzing the results on a risk-adjusted basis after the fact. It has been claimed that the use of risk budgeting in this way can improve risk-adjusted performance by both increasing mean return and decreasing its volatility.[3]

3. *Effect of Constraints.* Portfolio managers often operate under mandates that include constraints of various types. Some may be unavoidable owing to regulatory or operational requirements; others protect investors against certain types of risk. When they curtail the ability of a manager to fully implement his views, such constraints can reduce performance.

We investigate the effect on performance of two relatively common types of constraints. The first is the long-only constraint that often governs the use of

---

2. Tracking error is the standard deviation of the performance difference between a portfolio and its benchmark. For a detailed discussion of the calculation of tracking error and risk model applications, see Chapter 26. In this study, tracking error is not calculated using a multifactor model, but rather with a simpler approach involving the covariance of asset class returns. However, the risk-budgeting techniques we discuss could be implemented using a multifactor model as well.

3. Mark Lundin, "Risk Budgeting in Investment Management," *Journal of Performance Measurement,* Summer 2002.

core-plus assets in a portfolio. Many global aggregate mandates allow (limited) long positions in high yield or emerging market assets, but no short positions. As the index has zero weight in these assets, a manager is allowed to overweight these sectors but not to underweight them. When research results in a negative view on these assets, this view cannot be used to enhance portfolio performance.

The second type of constraint we consider is a related one that is often applied even within government bond markets—the "no leverage" or "cash" constraint— under which a portfolio may consist only of long positions in cash and securities. If such a portfolio is positioned passively with respect to an index and the manager wishes to introduce a long-duration view, he may not use a long futures position or buy additional bonds on a leveraged basis. Rather, he must sell shorter-dated securities and buy longer ones. In addition to the desired duration view, this introduces an unanticipated exposure to changes in the shape of the curve. We investigate the performance impact of this effect.[4]

DETAILED DESCRIPTION OF STRATEGIES AND METHODOLOGY

Historical Data

The study covers five currencies: EUR (DEM before 1999), USD, JPY, GBP, and CAD. For each currency, we gathered the following monthly data for January 1, 1987, through May 31, 2002: (1) exchange rates, (2) 1-month deposit rates, (3) Treasury Bond Index.

The Treasury Index data were obtained from the components of the Lehman Brothers Global Treasury Index corresponding to the five selected currencies. Each currency's Treasury Index was divided into four maturity cells: 1–3, 3–7, 7–10, and more than 10 years. For each maturity cell in each currency, we obtained a monthly time series of market value, duration, and total return. Market values and returns for each index are expressed in its local currency (i.e., no currency returns are included in the Bond Index data).

These were processed to obtain the following return series:

1. Returns on cash in each currency, with base currency EUR (DEM). This return includes both the return on cash and the FX return.

2. For each maturity cell in each market, the excess return of that cell over cash in its local currency.

---

4. We address this topic using a combination of bonds and futures in the U.S. Treasury market in Chapter 3.

To compare one type of macro investment strategy to another, it is important to ensure that the performance of each strategy is a pure reflection of the result of implementing a particular type of view. Thus, the monthly return on an FX strategy that shifts cash from one currency to another includes both the interest-rate differential between the two currencies and the change in the exchange rate over the course of the month. All other strategies (yield curve, credit, core-plus) are assumed to be carried out on a fully hedged basis, and performance is measured in terms of excess return over cash in each local currency.

The returns on cash are used to measure the performance of FX strategies. The excess returns over cash in each currency are used to measure the performance of all yield curve strategies. These numbers are an idealization of the hedged returns over base currency cash, assuming perfect hedging. For example, consider a euro-based investor who goes long the 1- to 3-year sector of the U.S. Treasury Index. To hedge the FX exposure of this transaction, he effectively goes long euro cash and short USD cash. The difference between the return of this hedged index exposure and that of a pure euro cash investment is thus approximately the difference between the USD returns on the index and on USD cash. By taking this approximation, we make our results essentially independent of the base currency selected.

Historical index data are not available for the nongovernment asset classes for the full time period of the study. For each asset class, we have gathered index data going as far back as possible, as follows. For the Emerging Markets Index of dollar-denominated emerging market debt, we retrieved total returns in USD terms beginning in January 1993 and use these to calculate excess returns over USD cash. For U.S. high yield, we have data back to August 1988. Here, too, we subtract the returns on cash to obtain a time series of excess returns over USD cash. For euro-denominated investment-grade credit, our index data are available back to September 1998. For this asset class, investment decisions are guided by views on return relative to euro Treasuries, and any investment comes at the expense of the euro Treasury allocation. The return measure we use is therefore excess returns over duration-matched euro Treasuries. The final asset class we study is U.S. TIPS. For a customized index of TIPS with maturities of 7–10 years, we obtained total returns (in USD terms) and real durations since February 1997. These were used to construct a series of excess returns for a hedged TIPS position relative to nominal U.S. Treasuries, as described later.

Risk-Budgeting Approach

All of the investment strategies studied are expressed in terms of allocations to the asset classes described earlier. As a result, the historical returns of these asset classes can be used to form a simple ex ante risk estimate for any strategy. At the start of each month, we compute the covariance matrix among all of the different asset returns using historical return data up to that time. This covariance matrix is then used to estimate the tracking error volatility (TEV) of each of the macro strategies to be considered. The position used to implement the strategy can then be scaled up or down so that the position taken each month is equal to a desired amount of risk—set here to 50 bp/year. This provides a realistic way of comparing different strategies on a risk-equivalent basis.

To study a strategy based on ex ante risk estimation, we have to use some of the data to form the first covariance matrix before we begin strategy simulation. We have chosen to use 3 years of monthly return data for this purpose. As a result, although our data series begin in January 1987, our studies of strategy performance begin in January 1990. For the core-plus strategies, the available return histories are even shorter. (For euro corporates, for example, we have little more than 3 years of history altogether.) In addition, there are mathematical complications involved in building a covariance matrix from asset return series of different lengths. Consequently, we have used this risk-budgeting technique only for the four conventional strategies (global duration, market duration, curve twist, and FX). For the core-plus strategies, we simply choose a constant position size of 5% of the portfolio and go long or short (neutral if shorts are not allowed) by this amount each month. We measure the statistics of this return series and obtain a risk-adjusted comparison with our other strategies by using information ratios.

Formulation of the Various Strategies

1. *Global Duration Exposure.* In the global duration timing strategy, a single decision is made each month to go long or short duration on a global basis. Duration is increased by the same amount in every currency, on a currency-hedged basis, with the amount selected to match a targeted amount of risk (e.g., 50 bp/year TEV). Within each local currency, duration is increased by going long the entire market on a financed basis. That is, the active exposure to each maturity cell will be proportional to that cell's weight in the index. The strategy will choose each month between two positions: long all markets, as described above, and short all markets, which is exactly the negative of that position.

In practice, this strategy might be implemented using futures contracts to replicate the interest risk of the index in each currency. For the purposes of this study, we assume that the portfolio borrows cash at the deposit rate to buy the index. Performance is measured using index return over cash in each currency.

2. *Regional Duration Exposure.* The regional duration strategy reflects skill at relative interest-rate calls. A decision is made to increase duration in one currency and decrease it in another. The positions are offsetting in terms of contributions

to duration, so that the net effect on global duration is zero. The magnitudes of the exposures are set to always match the risk target. As described earlier, duration positioning within each local currency is implemented by taking a leveraged position in the entire market proportional to index weights. In our simulation with five currencies, we consider twenty possible positions each month for this investment style: for each of the five currencies in which one can go long, there are four possibilities in which to go short. To represent a group of managers who each implement one of these twenty positions each month, we assign a selection probability to each position, as described later.

3. *Curve Twist Exposures.* The curve twist strategy reflects skill at selecting steepening/flattening positions in each local currency on a duration-neutral basis. In each of the three major currencies (USD, EUR, JPY), we consider an exposure to a twist in the yield curve, which is to be implemented by going long one-half of the local market and short the other on a duration-neutral basis. For instance, to implement a steepening trade, we overweight the short end of the curve and underweight the long end. To make this position duration neutral, the contributions to duration of these two exposures have to offset each other. This means that the overweight at the short end has a higher market value than the underweight at the long end, and we have to borrow cash to make up the difference. The flattening trade is exactly the opposite: the underweight to the short end of the curve frees up enough cash to overweight the long end and remain with a positive cash position.

Unlike our treatment of market duration risk, we do not assume that a steepening play in one currency has to be offset by a flattener in another. Instead, we treat the curve play in each currency as a separate strategy with two choices. We analyze the effectiveness of skilled curve twist timing separately in each currency. Later on, we also investigate a combined strategy that independently implements views on curve shape in the three currencies.

4. *Foreign Exchange Exposure.* In this macro approach to portfolio management, the decision on which foreign exchange exposures to take on is totally independent of the interest-rate view. A manager bullish on U.S. interest rates but not on the dollar can overweight the U.S. component of the index but short the currency in the FX markets. In this investment strategy, we isolate the FX component by assuming that the bond composition of the portfolio exactly matches the benchmark and that the entire difference between the two is an FX overlay that changes the allocations to the three main currencies. We look at two different types of positions in the three currencies, for a total of six positions: (1) long 1 short 2—long one currency by a certain percentage of market value, short each of the other two currencies by half this amount; (2) the symmetric positions of short one currency and long two.

In each month of our simulation, the manager in this style is faced with a choice among six strategies: he may go long (or short) any one of the three currencies vs. the other two. In each case, the magnitude of the position is set so that the ex ante estimate of tracking error volatility matches the targeted 50 bp/year.

The returns on these overlay positions consist of two components: a pure "currency" return based on the change in exchange rates and an "income" return based on the deposit rate differentials.

5. *Emerging Markets Exposure.* This is a market timing strategy based on skill at determining when to take on exposure to emerging markets as a core-plus asset. The return earned for going long this market is the excess return of the U.S. dollar-denominated Lehman Brothers Emerging Market Index over USD cash. (Any currency risk is assumed to be completely hedged.) At first we investigate a long-only strategy in which the portfolio may either go long the market or stay neutral to it. In the sequel, we remove the no-shorts constraint and investigate the performance when either long or short positions are permitted.

6. *High Yield Exposure.* As in the emerging markets strategy, we measure the performance of a strategy that market times an exposure to the excess return of the Lehman Brothers U.S. High Yield Index over USD cash. We consider both a long-only strategy and a long-short variation.

7. *Euro Credit Exposure.* The decision is made each month whether to overweight euro-denominated credit. This allocation, when made, is assumed to be based on a view of credit relative to euro governments. As such, the performance of the strategy is measured by the excess return of the credit component of the Lehman Brothers Euro-Aggregate Index over duration-equivalent euro Treasuries. Once again, no currency risk is assumed with this strategy, and both long-only and long-short versions are investigated.

8. *Inflation-Protection Exposure.* A view on inflation may be reflected by taking a position in inflation-linked bonds. As a proxy for a long position in global inflation-linked treasuries, we consider an allocation to U.S. TIPS, relative to U.S. Treasuries. The strategy goes long 7- to 10-year TIPS and short the 7- to 10-year portion of the Lehman Brothers Treasury Index on a duration-neutral basis. As this is not necessarily a cash-neutral trade, the performance of this strategy is computed after adjusting for cash. That is, if the market value of the TIPS position is greater than that of the nominal treasuries, the financing cost on the difference is subtracted from the TIPS return. Like all the other core-plus strategies, we consider both the long-only and the long-short cases.

Figure 2-1 shows a sample of strategies scaled to achieve the same estimated tracking error volatility of 50 bp/year. It can be seen that correlations play a major role in determining which position sizes fall within risk limits for a given strategy. For example, the EUR-USD market duration strategy, which offsets a long-

Figure 2-1. Sample Strategies Scaled to a Target Tracking Error Volatility of 50 bp/year
May 31, 2002

Asset	Global Duration (%)	Market Duration Strategies			Curve Twist Strategies			Long FX Strategies		
		GBP-JPY (%)	JPY-EUR (%)	EUR-USD (%)	JPY Curve (%)	EUR Curve (%)	USD Curve (%)	JPY (%)	EUR (%)	USD (%)
GBP1-3	0.4	1.4								
GBP3-7	0.6	2.0								
GBP7-10	0.4	1.3								
GBP10+	0.9	3.0								
JPY1-3	0.7	-2.2	2.7		14.7					
JPY3-7	1.2	-3.9	4.6		25.7					
JPY7-10	0.7	-2.4	2.8		-10.8					
JPY10+	0.3	-1.0	1.1		-4.4					
CAD1-3	0.8									
CAD3-7	0.8									
CAD7-10	0.4									
CAD10+	0.8									
EUR1-3	0.9		-3.4	3.7		18.0				
EUR3-7	1.1		-4.3	4.5		22.4				
EUR7+	1.1		-4.4	4.7		-13.7				
USD1-3	0.9			-3.7			24.3			
USD3-7	0.6			-2.7			17.6			
USD7-10	0.3			-1.2			-2.6			

USD10+		1.0	-4.0	-8.5			
GBPcash							
JPYcash					4.5	-2.7	-2.4
CADcash							
EURcash					-2.3	5.4	-2.4
USDcash					-2.3	-2.7	4.9
Estimated tracking error volatility (bp/year)	50	50	50	50	50	50	50

Strategy Descriptions

Global duration: Long market exposure (and short cash) in each currency with equal contributions to duration. No FX exposure. Total (leveraged) long market exposure: 13.9% of portfolio value.

Market duration: Directional calls on interest rates with no net global duration exposure. Long the market (and short cash) in one currency; short the market (and long cash) with same duration contribution in another. Total market weights of leveraged long and short positions (yield curve exposures) in example strategies:

Long	Short
7.7% GBP	-9.5% JPY
11.3% JPY	-12.1% EUR
12.9% EUR	-11.7% USD

Curve twist strategies: Steepening or flattening positions within a single currency. No net duration or FX exposure. (1) Steepener: long position in the short end of the curve vs. a short position in the long end (and cash). (2) Example strategy: long 49% at the short end and of the U.S. curve vs. short -11.1% at the long end, for TEV = 50 bp/year. Even though this trade is the largest magnitude of those shown, the risks are largely offsetting, and TEV is the same.

FX strategy: Long one of the G3 currencies, short the other two in equal amounts.

duration exposure on the EUR curve with a short-duration exposure in USD, is allowed to take larger position sizes (in market value terms, shown here, as well as in dollar duration terms) than the similar GBP-JPY strategy. The higher correlations between EUR and USD interest rates make the offsetting exposures more effective at reducing risk. Similarly, the yield curve twist exposures are larger still in terms of market value exposures because long and short yields within a single currency are much more highly correlated than yields of different currencies.

In Figure 2-2, we illustrate how the risk-budgeting technique is used to determine the strategy positions. First, the shape of a given position is specified in terms of a scaling variable x. In the FX allocation example shown here, the position "long JPY" is defined as going long x% in JPY, and short $(x/2)$% in both USD and EUR. A starting value is selected (here 5% is the base scale), and the risk can then be calculated. The resulting estimated tracking error volatility of 55 bp/year is greater than our target of 50 bp/year, so we must reduce the position size. The ratio of the targeted risk budget to the risk of the base scale position is used as a scaling factor, which is multiplied by the base scale to obtain the scale of the position to be implemented, here 4.5%. The same base scale and the same approach are applied to all three currencies; differences in the historical volatilities of the different currencies cause us to increase the size of the "long EUR" position and decrease the other two to achieve the same risk of 50 bp/year. With this risk normalization technique, the value used for the base scale does not have any effect on the final scale of the position; starting with a larger base scale merely results in a smaller scaling factor.

Simulation of Skill

What is management skill? In terms of results, one could say simply that a skillful manager outperforms more frequently than not. To do so, such a manager may gather information of many different types, process it using some combination of quantitative methods and intuition, and forecast various types of market behavior.

To evaluate the performance of a skilled duration timer vs. that of an FX expert or a core-plus allocator, we do not attempt to model any of these complex decision-making processes. Rather, we simulate management skill based on results, using the imperfect foresight approach. If a manager is faced with two choices (such as to go long or short global duration), we can label these as "good" and "bad" based on our knowledge of the eventual outcome. The skill in selecting the winning strategy (the good choice) is assumed to range from 0 to 100%. At 0% skill, the manager has a 50% chance of selecting the winning strategy. At 100% skill, the manager makes the winning choice with certainty. Probabilities at intermediate skill levels are prorated. For example, at a 40% skill level, the probability of

Figure 2-2. Illustration of Risk Budgeting, FX Allocation Strategy
May 31, 2002

Strategy	Base Scale	Currency Allocations (base scale)			Tracking Error Volatility (bp/year)	Scaling Factor	New Scale	Currency Allocations (rescaled for risk budget)			Tracking Error Volatility (bp/year)
		JPY (%)	EUR (%)	USD (%)				JPY (%)	EUR (%)	USD (%)	
Long JPY	5.0	5.0	-2.5	-2.5	55.0	90.9	4.5	4.5	-2.3	-2.3	50.0
Long EUR	5.0	-2.5	5.0	-2.5	46.7	107.1	5.4	-2.7	5.4	-2.7	50.0
Long USD	5.0	-2.5	-2.5	5.0	51.4	97.2	4.9	-2.4	-2.4	4.9	50.0

Figure 2-3. Probability of the Right Choice as a Function of Skill Level

Skill Level (%)	Two Choices (%)		Six Choices (FX) (%)		Twenty Choices (market duration) (%)	
	Right	Wrong	Right	Wrong	Right	Wrong
0	50.0	50.0	16.7	16.7	5.0	5.0
5	52.5	47.5	17.5	15.8	5.3	4.8
10	55.0	45.0	18.3	15.0	5.5	4.5
15	57.5	42.5	19.2	14.2	5.8	4.3
20	60.0	40.0	20.0	13.3	6.0	4.0
40	70.0	30.0	23.3	10.0	7.0	3.0
60	80.0	20.0	26.7	6.7	8.0	2.0
80	90.0	10.0	30.0	3.3	9.0	1.0
100	100.0	0.0	33.3	0.0	10.0	0.0

making the good choice is $0.5 + 0.5 \times 0.4 = 0.70$. Correspondingly, the probability of making the bad choice is 0.30.

For a decision in which the manager has more than two possible choices, we divide the choices into two groups based on the outcomes and continue along the same lines. For example, as discussed earlier, there are twenty different choices considered in our market duration strategy. However, ten of these positions are the negatives of the other ten. For example, the position "long USD duration, short EUR duration" is the exact opposite of "long EUR duration, short USD duration," so that in every month, one of these strategies will be a winner and the other a loser. At 0% skill, each of the twenty choices will be chosen with an equal probability of 5%. At 100% skill, we will assign a 10% probability to each of the ten winning strategies and 0% to each of the ten losing ones.[5] At 40% skill, the probability of making each of the winning choices will be $(5\%) + (5\% \times 40\%) = 7\%$. Figure 2-3 shows the probabilities assigned to each of the winning and losing choices, as a function of skill level, for strategies with different numbers of available choices.

The imperfect foresight methodology is illustrated in Figure 2-4 using the FX allocation task as an example. The six positions considered by our strategy are shown in the six rightmost columns of the figure. Each shows an overweight or

---

5. In Chapter 1, we model skill in two different ways: skill at picking any winning strategy and skill at picking the best strategy. Here, we use skill at picking any winning strategy. In the other model, increasing skill would increase the probability of the single best choice to 100%, while decreasing the probabilities of all other choices.

Figure 2–4. Strategy Simulation Example: FX Allocation
20% Skill, May 2002

Asset	Return (bp)	Long JPY (%)	Long EUR (%)	Long USD (%)	Short JPY (%)	Short EUR (%)	Short USD (%)
JPYcash	−24.5	4.5	−2.7	−2.4	−4.5	2.7	2.4
EURcash	27.7	−2.3	5.4	−2.4	2.3	−5.4	2.4
USDcash	−340.3	−2.3	−2.7	4.9	2.3	2.7	−4.9
Overall strategy return (bp)		6.0	11.3	−16.6	−6.0	−11.3	16.6
Selection probabilities for:							
0% skill		16.7%	16.7%	16.7%	16.7%	16.7%	16.7%
100% skill		33.3%	33.3%	0.0%	0.0%	0.0%	33.3%
20% skill		20.0%	20.0%	13.3%	13.3%	13.3%	20.0%
R^2		13.9	80.9	356.5	68.1	182.5	206.4
Mean return		2.3					
Variance		141.2					
Volatility		11.9					

underweight of approximately 5% to one of the currencies, with an equal and op-posite weight split between the other two. (The differences in position sizes are due to the risk-budgeting process—bets that have been historically more risky are taken in smaller sizes.) In the unskilled case, we assume that a manager may choose any one of these positions with a probability of 1/6. For the month shown (May 2002), it turns out that the big story was a depreciation of the U.S. dollar vs. the other two currencies, which caused all three strategies that were overweight the dollar to underperform and the three that were underweight the dollar to outperform. The performance that would have been achieved by each strategy is shown beneath the column. In the 100% skill case, we assume that a manager def-initely chose one of the winning positions, and we assign a probability of 1/3 to each of these and 0 to the losers. To simulate a manager with 20% skill, we inter-polate between these two extremes to obtain the probabilities shown. The per-formance of such a manager for this month can thus be considered as a random variable following the discrete distribution given by these six returns and proba-bilities. We calculate the mean and standard deviation of this distribution. We re-peat this procedure for each month and aggregate the results over time. A similar procedure is followed for every strategy.

Time Period Studied

To be fair, performance comparisons among different strategies should be carried out over the same time period. However, this study spans a broad range of asset classes, and the time period for which data are available is different for each. For the four strategies based on multicurrency yield curve and FX data (global dura-tion, market duration, curve twist, and FX), we have assembled historical data from January 1987 through May 2002. We required at least three years of data for building the covariance matrix used in risk budgeting, so that studies of strategy performance begin with January 1990.

In addition to analyzing results over the entire period, we analyze performance over two subperiods, before and after European Monetary Union (EMU) on Jan-uary 1, 1999. There have been important structural changes in the markets since that time, and we seek to identify their implications for global fixed-income management.

RESULTS FOR INDIVIDUAL STRATEGIES

The performance of the core strategies is summarized in Figure 2-5. For each strategy, at each skill level, we show both the mean outperformance and the over-all standard deviation of outperformance on an annualized basis. In addition, we show the ratio between these two quantities, known as the information ratio, the standard measure of risk-adjusted performance.

The first thing we check is whether the risk-budgeting procedure has succeeded in keeping tracking error close to the ex ante target of 50 bp/year. It can be seen that the realized standard deviations of outperformance (tracking error) are generally close to their targets. For several strategies, though, the realized tracking errors are smaller than the targets. This is true for the global duration and regional duration strategies and for the curve twist strategy in EUR and JPY. Historical volatility is not always a good predictor of future volatility, and in these cases volatility seems to have been overestimated, causing the positions to be smaller than they might have been. In the FX overlay strategy, the realized tracking error is a bit higher than the target, indicating that our historical volatility estimates were a bit low.

In general, we find that the mean outperformance of a given strategy increases linearly with skill. Moreover, the volatility of outperformance tends to decrease at high skill levels. As a result, the increases in information ratios with greater skill are more than linear.

To understand this decrease in volatility with increasing skill, we can decompose the volatility of outperformance into two components: volatility across managers and volatility over time. The first is the volatility across a population of managers implementing the same strategy at the same level of skill and represents the risk of making the wrong decision. The second is the volatility over time of the mean strategy return, reflecting the fact that some months offer more opportunity than others for a given strategy. These two components are shown in Figure 2-6 for the market duration strategy. The volatility over time tends to increase with skill. At high skills, the manager is able to exploit nearly every market opportunity, this component of strategy outperformance mirrors market volatility. Yet the overall strategy volatility declines at high skills, owing to the dramatic drop in the volatility over managers. The major risk in any allocation strategy is making the wrong decision. When this becomes highly unlikely, the risk is reduced accordingly.

In terms of information ratios, we find that the various strategies provide nearly identical performance for a given level of skill. For example, Figure 2-5 shows that 10% skill produces information ratios ranging from 0.26 to 0.28. At 20% skill, results range from 0.51 through 0.56. All of the strategies show an information ratio of exactly 0.0 at 0% skill. This is due to the method of implementation, in which 0% skill means we choose with equal weights from two symmetrical groups of positions. In each month for each strategy, there is an equal probability of going long and short each position, so the mean strategy outperformance is zero.

The performance of the core-plus strategies is similarly summarized in Figure 2-7. Two cases are shown. In the first, the core-plus strategies are implemented

Figure 2-5. Performance Summary for Core Strategies
January 1990–December 2002

Skill Level (%)	Global Duration			Market Duration			FX Overlay in G3 Currencies		
	Mean Outperformance (bp/year)	Volatility (bp/year)	Information Ratio	Mean Outperformance (bp/year)	Volatility (bp/year)	Information Ratio	Mean Outperformance (bp/year)	Volatility (bp/year)	Information Ratio
0	0.0	44.9	0.00	0.0	44.7	0.00	0.0	52.5	0.00
5	6.2	44.8	0.14	6.0	44.7	0.13	6.8	52.5	0.13
10	12.3	44.7	0.28	12.0	44.6	0.27	13.6	52.3	0.26
15	18.5	44.6	0.41	18.0	44.4	0.41	20.4	52.2	0.39
20	24.6	44.3	0.56	24.0	44.2	0.54	27.2	51.9	0.52
40	49.3	42.6	1.16	48.0	42.5	1.13	54.4	50.1	1.09
60	73.9	39.5	1.87	72.0	39.6	1.82	81.6	46.9	1.74
80	98.5	34.8	2.83	96.0	35.1	2.73	108.9	42.1	2.59
100	123.2	27.5	4.48	120.0	28.3	4.23	136.1	34.9	3.90

Skill Level (%)	EUR Curve Twist			USD Curve Twist			JPY Curve Twist		
	Mean Outperformance (bp/year)	Volatility (bp/year)	Information Ratio	Mean Outperformance (bp/year)	Volatility (bp/year)	Information Ratio	Mean Outperformance (bp/year)	Volatility (bp/year)	Information Ratio
0	0.0	42.6	0.00	0.0	52.8	0.00	0.0	39.8	0.00
5	5.7	42.6	0.13	6.7	52.8	0.13	5.4	39.8	0.14
10	11.3	42.5	0.27	13.4	52.6	0.26	10.9	39.7	0.27
15	17.0	42.3	0.40	20.1	52.5	0.38	16.3	39.5	0.41
20	22.7	42.1	0.54	26.9	52.2	0.51	21.7	39.3	0.55
40	45.4	40.6	1.12	53.7	50.5	1.06	43.5	37.8	1.15
60	68.0	37.8	1.80	80.6	47.4	1.70	65.2	35.1	1.86
80	90.7	33.7	2.69	107.4	42.8	2.51	86.9	31.0	2.81
100	113.4	27.4	4.14	134.3	35.9	3.74	108.7	24.6	4.41

Figure 2-6. Decomposition of Volatility of Market Duration Strategy
January 1990–December 2002

Skill Level (%)	Mean Outperformance (bp/year)	Volatility Managers (bp/year)	Volatility Time (bp/year)	Volatility Total (bp/year)	Information Ratio
0	0.0	44.7	0.0	44.7	0.00
5	6.0	44.7	0.8	44.7	0.13
10	12.0	44.6	1.6	44.6	0.27
15	18.0	44.4	2.4	44.4	0.41
20	24.0	44.1	3.2	44.2	0.54
40	48.0	42.0	6.4	42.5	1.13
60	72.0	38.4	9.6	39.6	1.82
80	96.0	32.7	12.8	35.1	2.73
100	120.0	23.4	16.0	28.3	4.23

with a long-only constraint, which corresponds to the way these strategies are commonly used in portfolios. In the second case, the long-only constraint is relaxed and short positions (underweights) are allowed in all assets.

The first set of results shown in Figure 2-7 corresponds to the long-only constraint. If the manager has a positive view on the asset class, he includes a 5% overweight to that asset class in his portfolio. If the view is negative, the asset class is excluded from the portfolio. The results therefore look very different from those of Figure 2-5. The lack of symmetry means that the 0% skill case no longer gives zero outperformance on average. Instead, each strategy has a mean return (and an information ratio) that partially reflects the performance of a long position in the selected asset class over the time period studied. As this bias is not indicative of either future performance or manager skill, and especially because the different strategies cover different time periods, we have elected to remove it from the analysis. In the second set of results, the mean outperformance column is "demeaned" by subtracting the mean outperformance at 0% skill from that at all skill levels. If we compare the resulting information ratios with those in Figure 2-5, it is clear that all of the core-plus strategies have much lower information ratios than the core strategies at the same skill levels.

In the third set of results in Figure 2-7, the long-only constraint has been relaxed and short positions are allowed. This could correspond to the use of derivatives to implement a short position or to the case in which these assets are included in the benchmark, thus making it possible to underweight the assets without actually shorting any securities. In the long-short case, the information ratios achieved are in line with those of the core strategies, with the exception of the euro credit strategy, which is implemented only over a relatively short time period.

The fact that all of these different strategies achieve nearly identical information ratios when applied with the same degree of skill is not surprising. In our previous work, we found that a critical determinant of a strategy's information ratio is the number of independent decisions involved. In each of the core-plus strategies, there is just a single decision made each month. Although the decision is made from among different numbers of alternatives in the various strategies, the portfolio risk is concentrated in just one of them at a time.

This idea has been formalized by Grinold and Kahn as the "fundamental law of active management."[6] They show that the information ratio IR is a function of the information coefficient IC and the strategy breadth BR, given by

$$IR = IC \cdot \sqrt{BR}. \tag{2-1}$$

The breadth is the number of independent decisions made each year, and the information coefficient is a measure of skill, defined as the correlation between forecasts and actual outcomes.

If we assume for a moment that our skill parameter is equivalent to Grinold and Kahn's IC, then this fundamental law can easily be applied to obtain a theoretical information ratio for a given skill level. As all of the strategies implemented here consist of a single decision made on a monthly basis, the strategy breadth on an annual basis is 12, and the fundamental law predicts a maximum information ratio of $IR = \text{skill} \cdot \sqrt{12}$. In Figure 2-8, we plot the achieved information ratios as a function of skill against the theoretical maximum. Not only do all the strategies achieve similar information ratios when implemented with equal skill, but the observed values are very close to the theoretical ones.

Why do the observed information ratios not match the Grinold and Kahn results even more precisely? For low values of skill the observed results are somewhat below the theoretical limit, whereas for higher values the observed results can exceed the theoretical value. There are two distinct causes for these phenomena. The first is related to the difference in the way skill is represented in our work and in theirs. Grinold and Kahn assume that investment decisions are built upon an explicit forecast of asset returns, and the information coefficient is defined as

6. Richard C. Grinold and Ronald N. Kahn, *Active Portfolio Management,* McGraw-Hill, 1999.

Figure 2-7. Performance Summary for Core-Plus Strategies

Long-Only Results

U.S. Credit
Aug 1988–Dec 2002

Skill Level (%)	Mean Outperformance (bp/year)	Volatility (bp/year)	Information Ratio
0	0.1	7.0	0.02
5	0.7	7.0	0.09
10	1.2	6.9	0.17
15	1.7	6.9	0.25
20	2.2	6.9	0.32
40	4.3	6.7	0.65
60	6.4	6.4	1.00
80	8.5	6.1	1.40
100	10.6	5.7	1.87

Long-Only Results (De-Meaned)

U.S. Credit
Aug 1988–Dec 2002

Skill Level (%)	Mean Outperformance (bp/year)	Volatility (bp/year)	Information Ratio
0	0.0	7.0	0.00
5	0.5	7.0	0.08
10	1.0	6.9	0.15
15	1.6	6.9	0.23
20	2.1	6.9	0.31
40	4.2	6.7	0.63
60	6.3	6.4	0.98
80	8.4	6.1	1.38
100	10.5	5.7	1.84

Long/Short Results

U.S. Credit
Aug 1988–Dec 2002

Skill Level (%)	Mean Outperformance (bp/year)	Volatility (bp/year)	Information Ratio
0	0.0	9.9	0.00
5	1.0	9.9	0.11
10	2.1	9.9	0.21
15	3.1	9.8	0.32
20	4.2	9.8	0.43
40	8.4	9.6	0.87
60	12.6	9.2	1.37
80	16.8	8.6	1.94
100	21.0	7.8	2.68

Euro Credit Jan 1999–Dec 2002			Emerging Markets Jan 1993–Dec 2002		
Mean Outperformance (bp/year)	Volatility (bp/year)	Information Ratio	Mean Outperformance (bp/year)	Volatility (bp/year)	Information Ratio
0.2	3.4	0.07	18.8	53.4	0.35
0.5	3.4	0.15	23.6	53.1	0.44
0.8	3.4	0.23	28.3	52.8	0.54
1.1	3.4	0.32	33.0	52.4	0.63
1.4	3.4	0.41	37.8	51.9	0.73
2.5	3.3	0.77	56.7	49.7	1.14
3.6	3.1	1.17	75.6	46.8	1.61
4.8	2.9	1.63	94.6	43.1	2.19
5.9	2.7	2.18	113.5	38.2	2.97

Euro Credit Jan 1999–Dec 2002			Emerging Markets Jan 1993–Dec 2002		
Mean Outperformance (bp/year)	Volatility (bp/year)	Information Ratio	Mean Outperformance (bp/year)	Volatility (bp/year)	Information Ratio
0.0	3.4	0.00	0.0	53.4	0.00
0.3	3.4	0.08	4.7	53.1	0.09
0.6	3.4	0.17	9.5	52.8	0.18
0.9	3.4	0.25	14.2	52.4	0.27
1.1	3.4	0.34	18.9	51.9	0.36
2.3	3.3	0.70	37.9	49.7	0.76
3.4	3.1	1.09	56.8	46.8	1.21
4.6	2.9	1.55	75.7	43.1	1.76
5.7	2.7	2.10	94.7	38.2	2.48

Euro Credit Jan 1999–Dec 2002			Emerging Markets Jan 1993–Dec 2002		
Mean Outperformance (bp/year)	Volatility (bp/year)	Information Ratio	Mean Outperformance (bp/year)	Volatility (bp/year)	Information Ratio
0.0	4.8	0.00	0.0	75.8	0.00
0.6	4.8	0.12	9.5	75.8	0.12
1.1	4.8	0.24	18.9	75.6	0.25
1.7	4.8	0.36	28.4	75.4	0.38
2.3	4.8	0.48	37.9	75.0	0.50
4.6	4.6	0.98	75.7	72.6	1.04
6.8	4.4	1.55	113.6	68.4	1.66
9.1	4.1	2.24	151.5	62.1	2.44
11.4	3.6	3.19	189.3	52.8	3.59

(*continued*)

Figure 2-7. (continued)

Long-Only Results	U.S. High Yield Aug 1988–Dec 2002		
Skill Level (%)	Mean Outperformance (bp/year)	Volatility (bp/year)	Information Ratio
0	6.4	25.4	0.25
5	8.6	25.4	0.34
10	10.8	25.3	0.43
15	12.9	25.2	0.51
20	15.1	25.1	0.60
40	23.9	24.5	0.97
60	32.6	23.7	1.38
80	41.3	22.5	1.84
100	50.1	20.9	2.39

Long-Only Results (De-Meaned)	U.S. High Yield Aug 1988–Dec 2002		
Skill Level (%)	Mean Outperformance (bp/year)	Volatility (bp/year)	Information Ratio
0	0.0	25.4	0.00
5	2.2	25.4	0.09
10	4.4	25.3	0.17
15	6.6	25.2	0.26
20	8.7	25.1	0.35
40	17.5	24.5	0.71
60	26.2	23.7	1.11
80	35.0	22.5	1.55
100	43.7	20.9	2.09

Long/Short Results	U.S. High Yield Aug 1988–Dec 2002		
Skill Level (%)	Mean Outperformance (bp/year)	Volatility (bp/year)	Information Ratio
0	0.0	36.0	0.00
5	4.4	36.0	0.12
10	8.7	35.9	0.24
15	13.1	35.8	0.37
20	17.5	35.6	0.49
40	35.0	34.6	1.01
60	52.4	32.7	1.60
80	69.9	29.8	2.34
100	87.4	25.7	3.39

USD Inflation Protection
Feb 1997–Dec 2002

Mean Outperformance (bp/year)	Volatility (bp/year)	Information Ratio
−4.1	14.6	−0.28
−2.7	14.6	−0.18
−1.3	14.6	−0.09
0.1	14.5	0.01
1.5	14.5	0.10
7.0	14.1	0.49
12.5	13.6	0.92
18.0	12.9	1.40
23.6	11.9	1.98

USD Inflation Protection
Feb 1997–Dec 2002

Mean Outperformance (bp/year)	Volatility (bp/year)	Information Ratio
0.0	14.6	0.00
1.4	14.6	0.09
2.8	14.6	0.19
4.1	14.5	0.29
5.5	14.5	0.38
11.1	14.1	0.78
16.6	13.6	1.22
22.1	12.9	1.72
27.6	11.9	2.32

USD Inflation Protection
Feb 1997–Dec 2002

Mean Outperformance (bp/year)	Volatility (bp/year)	Information Ratio
0.0	20.7	0.00
2.8	20.6	0.13
5.5	20.6	0.27
8.3	20.5	0.40
11.1	20.4	0.54
22.1	19.7	1.12
33.2	18.3	1.81
44.2	16.3	2.72
55.3	13.2	4.18

Information Ratio

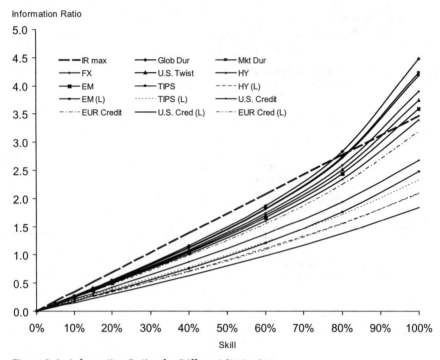

Figure 2-8. Information Ratios for Different Strategies
As a Function of Skill, Compared with Theoretical Limit

the correlation between the forecast and realized returns.[7] Furthermore, the information ratios produced by the fundamental law assume that the manager follows an optimal management policy in which the amount of risk taken in a given month depends on the return forecast. In our study, by contrast, the skill coefficient is used to model the investment decision directly, and the amount of risk is held to a constant each month by our risk-budgeting process.

Grinold and Kahn discuss a special case in which only the directionality of returns is forecast. In this case, both the forecast and the realized returns are modeled by variables that take on only the values of ±1. For this simple case, it can be shown that our definition of skill is equivalent to their information coefficient. To test the agreement of our results with the fundamental law, we recalculated the information ratios for our global duration strategy by replacing the time series of realized strategy returns with the sign of those returns. The results are

---

7. The notion that skill is essentially the ability to process all available information to produce a successful forecast has led Grinold and Kahn to use the term "information coefficient" (IC) to denote their measure of manager skill.

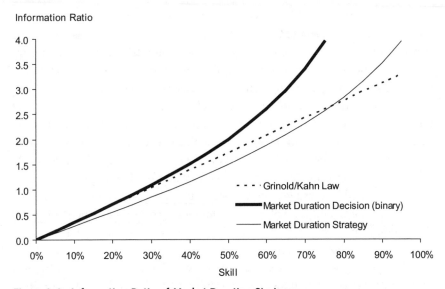

Figure 2-9. Information Ratio of Market Duration Strategy
Based on Actual Returns and on Binary Results Only, Compared with Theoretical Limit

shown in Figure 2-9. For low values of skill, the "decision information ratios" measured using this binary method exactly match the theoretical results.

Although it shows agreement at low skill levels, Figure 2-9 accentuates the mismatch at high skill levels. The graphs of observed information ratios follow a concave upward pattern, whereas the Grinold and Kahn equation is linear with respect to IC because, by the authors' own admission, the equation is only an approximation meant for use at low skill levels. It reflects the increase in outperformance that comes from increased skill, but not the decrease in volatility discussed earlier. While it may look dramatic in the figure, this nonlinear effect is not particularly significant, as it appears only at unrealistically high levels of skill.

EFFECT OF CONSTRAINTS

In order for a skilled manager to generate outperformance, he not only has to forecast the direction of the market successfully, but also has to be able to take positions that capitalize on his views. A recent paper by Clarke et al. generalizes the work of Grinold and Kahn to include the effect of portfolio constraints.[8] In addition to the

8. Roger Clarke, Harindra de Silva, and Steven Thorley, "Portfolio Constraints and the Fundamental Law of Active Management," *Financial Analysts Journal*, September/October 2002, pp. 48–56.

information coefficient (IC), which relates to allocation skill, the authors intro-duce a transfer coefficient (TC), which reflects the extent to which manager views may be implemented in the portfolio. Constraints lower the TC and hence the in-formation ratio. While our methodology does not allow the direct calculation of a transfer coefficient,[9] we investigate the performance impact of certain constraints.

The results shown previously for core-plus strategies illustrate the effect of portfolio management constraints on performance. An investment policy that disallows short positions in out-of-benchmark assets decreases the information ratios that can be achieved because it allows the manager to express views in only one direction. For example, Figure 2-7 shows that if the U.S. high yield strategy could be carried out using long and short positions with 20% skill, it could achieve an information ratio of 0.49. The long-only constraint reduces this (after de-meaning) to 0.35 for the same skill level. Similar results are obtained for all of the strategies shown in Figure 2-7.

When dealing with core asset classes, the situation is different. Even though short positions may be disallowed, most views can be expressed in either direction in a benchmarked portfolio, as the active position is always constructed relative to the benchmark. A portfolio can go short duration relative to the benchmark or underweight a particular asset class without actually shorting any securities.

However, the imposition of a "no leverage" constraint limits the way in which a duration view can be implemented. In the strategies investigated earlier, we were careful to separate the duration view from the yield curve twist view. As shown in Figure 2-1, the long duration view is achieved by going long the entire govern-ment bond market in a given currency, on a financed basis, according to index weights. This strategy would be disallowed under a "no leverage" constraint. In-stead, one would have to increase duration by overweighting longer-duration assets vs. shorter ones. This method creates an unintended exposure to yield curve twist along with the duration exposure.

In reality this unintentional twist exposure generally reduces the value of the duration timing call. Going long duration is accompanied by an unintended flat-tening position. There is strong evidence that most yield curve rallies are accom-panied by curve steepening.[10]

To simplify the analysis of this effect, we investigate the performance implica-tions of such a constraint on a single-currency basis. In Figure 2-10, we show the

9. The transfer coefficient (TC) is defined as the correlation between the forecast residual returns on a set of assets and the portfolio weights in those assets. As our formulation of skill does not involve an explicit forecast, we cannot directly measure TC, but we can directly mea-sure strategy performance with and without a given constraint.

10. See Chapter 3.

results of a single-currency duration timing strategy in each of three currencies using two different strategies. In the pure duration strategy we follow the method used until now. The duration view is implemented by going long or short the index as a whole, on a leveraged basis when necessary. In the cash-neutral strategy, the same amount of ex ante tracking error is assumed, using a position that goes long or short duration by overweighting (or underweighting) the long half of the index vs. the short half. In both cases, the skill level is assumed to refer to skill at making a pure duration call—that is, predicting the success or failure of the pure duration strategy. In this case, the unanticipated exposure to yield curve twist brings extra volatility, which reduces the information ratio.

In a second experiment, we look at the performance using skill to predict both the shift and the twist in the curve. Skill at predicting the pure yield curve movement is first used to decide whether to go long or short; then skill at predicting the twist is used to decide whether to take a pure duration bet or add on a steepener or a flattener. There is thus a total of six positions that can be selected: pure long, long flattener, long steepener, pure short, short flattener, and short steepener. Each of the six positions is scaled to achieve the same ex ante risk; therefore, the three variants of the long-duration view typically entail different amounts of duration extension. The construction of the combined positions is described in more detail in the following section.

The long flattener used in this combination is precisely the same as the cash-neutral duration strategy described earlier. It achieves the long duration by overweighting the long end relative to the short. In the cash-constrained case, this is the only long position that the portfolio can take. (The long steepener is even more leveraged than the pure duration trade.) However, the short-duration position is easy to achieve under the cash constraint by simply shifting assets out of the entire index and into cash. This cash cushion allows the freedom to implement either a flattener or a steepener on top of the duration position if desired. As a result, the cash-constrained case can use four of the six positions available: either the long flattener or any of the three short-duration positions. We compare the unconstrained and constrained version of this strategy in Figure 2-11. Once again, we see that the no leverage constraint results in a decrease in information ratio.

COMBINING STRATEGIES

A cursory reading of the results presented in the foregoing could easily lead to erroneous conclusions. We showed that the main determinant of strategy performance is skill, with all strategies achieving similar information ratios for a given skill level. From this, one might draw the conclusion that a manager should focus all his energy on the single strategy at which he has the most skill. Similarly,

Figure 2-10. Performance of Single-Currency Duration Timing in G3 Currencies
With and without Cash Constraint, January 1990–December 2002

Pure Duration	EUR		
Skill Level (%)	Mean Outperformance (bp/year)	Volatility (bp/year)	Information Ratio
0	0.0	51.3	0.00
5	7.2	51.3	0.14
10	14.5	51.1	0.28
15	21.7	50.9	0.43
20	28.9	50.6	0.57
40	57.9	48.5	1.19
60	86.8	44.8	1.94
80	115.7	39.0	2.97
100	144.6	29.9	4.84

Cash-Neutral Duration	EUR		
Skill Level (%)	Mean Outperformance (bp/year)	Volatility (bp/year)	Information Ratio
0	0.0	53.4	0.00
5	6.5	53.4	0.12
10	13.0	53.3	0.24
15	19.4	53.1	0.37
20	25.9	52.9	0.49
40	51.8	51.3	1.01
60	77.8	48.5	1.60
80	103.7	44.3	2.34
100	129.6	38.3	3.39

our demonstration that the long-only constraint puts core-plus strategies at a disadvantage might seem to indicate that this investment style is suboptimal and should never be used. Neither of these conclusions is correct.

In each of the strategies just discussed, the portfolio takes on just a single active risk exposure each month. Whenever a wrong decision is made, the portfolio underperforms. Clearly, if several strategies are available that offer similar risk/

USD			JPY		
Mean Outperformance (bp/year)	Volatility (bp/year)	Information Ratio	Mean Outperformance (bp/year)	Volatility (bp/year)	Information Ratio
0.0	46.0	0.00	0.0	42.3	0.00
6.4	46.0	0.14	5.6	42.3	0.13
12.7	45.8	0.28	11.1	42.2	0.26
19.1	45.7	0.42	16.7	42.0	0.40
25.5	45.4	0.56	22.3	41.8	0.53
51.0	43.6	1.17	44.6	40.3	1.11
76.4	40.4	1.89	66.9	37.7	1.78
101.9	35.4	2.88	89.2	33.6	2.65
127.4	27.7	4.60	111.5	27.6	4.04

USD			JPY		
Mean Outperformance (bp/year)	Volatility (bp/year)	Information Ratio	Mean Outperformance (bp/year)	Volatility (bp/year)	Information Ratio
0.0	48.1	0.00	0.0	41.9	0.00
6.0	48.1	0.12	4.9	41.9	0.12
12.0	48.0	0.25	9.8	41.8	0.23
18.0	47.8	0.38	14.7	41.7	0.35
24.0	47.6	0.50	19.6	41.5	0.47
48.0	46.1	1.04	39.2	40.4	0.97
72.0	43.5	1.66	58.8	38.4	1.53
96.0	39.4	2.43	78.4	35.4	2.22
119.9	33.5	3.58	98.0	31.1	3.15

reward profiles (i.e., if they can be carried out at the same skill), it would be advantageous to diversify the risk by taking several smaller exposures instead of one big one. In this way, a loss from one exposure can often be offset by a gain from another within the same month, leading to a much less volatile return series for a given level of outperformance. If the portfolio is being managed with a certain risk budget in mind, this reduction of risk owing to strategy diversification can allow

Figure 2-11. **Performance of Combination Shift/Twist Strategy**
With and without Cash Constraint, January 1990–December 2002

Unconstrained	EUR Combined Shift/Twist		
Skill Level (%)	Mean Outperformance (bp/year)	Volatility (bp/year)	Information Ratio
0	–0.0	50.5	–0.00
5	9.8	50.4	0.20
10	19.7	50.3	0.39
15	29.4	50.2	0.59
20	39.2	49.9	0.79
40	78.0	48.0	1.62
60	116.4	44.8	2.60
80	154.4	39.9	3.87
100	192.0	32.8	5.86

Cash-Constrained	EUR Combined Shift/Twist		
Skill Level (%)	Mean Outperformance (bp/year)	Volatility (bp/year)	Information Ratio
0	–3.3	52.0	–0.06
5	4.9	51.8	0.09
10	13.0	51.6	0.25
15	21.1	51.3	0.41
20	29.1	51.0	0.57
40	60.7	49.0	1.24
60	91.4	45.8	2.00
80	121.4	41.5	2.93
100	150.5	35.7	4.22

the manager to scale up the size of the combined strategy and boost the long-term outperformance.

In this section, we explore the improvement in performance that can be achieved by combining strategies. We begin with a brief review of the basic theory—how much of an improvement in information ratio should one expect by combining strategies and how do correlations affect this relationship? We then describe how

USD Combined Shift/Twist			JPY Combined Shift/Twist		
Mean Outperformance (bp/year)	Volatility (bp/year)	Information Ratio	Mean Outperformance (bp/year)	Volatility (bp/year)	Information Ratio
0.0	46.7	0.00	0.0	42.6	0.00
8.3	46.7	0.18	7.8	42.6	0.18
16.6	46.6	0.36	15.5	42.5	0.36
24.9	46.4	0.54	23.2	42.4	0.55
33.2	46.2	0.72	30.9	42.3	0.73
66.3	44.4	1.49	61.7	41.1	1.50
99.2	41.2	2.41	92.2	39.1	2.36
132.1	36.4	3.63	122.6	36.1	3.39
164.8	29.0	5.69	152.7	32.0	4.78

USD Combined Shift/Twist			JPY Combined Shift/Twist		
Mean Outperformance (bp/year)	Volatility (bp/year)	Information Ratio	Mean Outperformance (bp/year)	Volatility (bp/year)	Information Ratio
−4.3	47.4	−0.09	−3.4	42.2	−0.08
2.9	47.3	0.06	3.0	42.1	0.07
10.0	47.2	0.21	9.3	42.0	0.22
17.1	47.0	0.36	15.5	41.8	0.37
24.2	46.7	0.52	21.7	41.6	0.52
52.2	44.9	1.16	46.2	40.3	1.14
79.9	42.0	1.90	70.0	38.4	1.82
107.1	37.7	2.84	93.2	35.7	2.61
133.9	31.7	4.22	115.7	32.4	3.57

we implement combined strategies in our risk-budgeting framework and explore several practical issues with numeric examples. If one's skill is highest at one particular type of allocation, to what extent should one allocate risk to strategies with lower skills for the sake of diversification? Do core-plus strategies with a long-only constraint have a place in a combined strategy even though they do not look attractive on a stand-alone basis?

Theory of Combining Strategies: A Brief Review

Grinold and Kahn, in discussing their fundamental law, point out that it is additive in the squared information ratios. That is, if strategies 1 through n could achieve information ratios IR_1 through IR_n if each was implemented on its own, then a combination of all n strategies can achieve an information ratio of

$$IR_{combined} = \sqrt{IR_1^2 + IR_2^2 + \ldots + IR_n^2}. \tag{2-2}$$

If the n strategies all have the same information ratios, we can see that the combination of n strategies increases the information ratio by a factor of $\sqrt{n}$. This is closely related to the basic form of the fundamental law as expressed in Equation (2-1). The combination of n strategies is equivalent to multiplying the breadth of the strategy by a factor n.

It is important to note that Equation (2-2) is valid only if all of the n strategies are uncorrelated. The advantage offered by strategy diversification can be diminished by correlations among strategies. For example, if two strategies have the same information ratios, but have a correlation ρ between them, then the information ratio is improved by a factor of $\sqrt{2/(1 + \rho)}$. If the two strategies are uncorrelated ($\rho = 0$), then according to Equation (2-2) we obtain an improvement of $\sqrt{2}$. However, as ρ increases, this gain is reduced. In the limit of perfect correlation ($\rho = 1$), the two strategies are identical and combining them does not add anything.[11] For a combination of more than two strategies, the math is a bit more complex, but the idea remains the same. Adding an additional strategy to the mix is effective only to the extent that it is uncorrelated to other strategies already included.

Combining Strategies in a Risk-Budgeting Framework

Say we have decided to combine two different strategies. For each, we have decided what position we would take to implement it and have scaled it so that the risk taken is estimated to equal our overall target of 50 bp/year. How should we construct a blend of these two positions?

One interpretation of risk budgeting is that the total available risk is allocated in an additive manner. For example, we can scale each of our two positions by 0.5 such that each strategy gets a risk budget of 25 bp/year. This conservative approach

---

11. Grinold and Kahn actually present this relationship in the context of the information coefficient, showing that the combination of two correlated information sources with the same level of skill improves the information coefficient (and hence the information ratio) by this amount.

ensures that even if the two strategies are perfectly correlated, the overall risk of the position equals the target.[12] However, if the correlation between the two strategies is relatively low, the risk of the combined strategy can be significantly lower than the target (by a factor of $\sqrt{2}$ in the uncorrelated case). If we recall that outperformance is proportional to the amount of risk taken, we see that this constrains the portfolio from achieving its potential outperformance.

A more aggressive approach is to assign risk budgets for each strategy using an assumption of independence. For example, if two independent strategies are used, each could be assigned a risk budget of 35 bp/year ($50/\sqrt{2} \cong 35$). Such an approach could be justified if the strategies in question have a proven track record of uncorrelated historical behavior and/or if a manager is convinced by fundamentals that the two strategies are independent. The danger of this strategy is that if indeed the two strategies are correlated in the future, the strategy will have exceeded the risk budget and could suffer from unacceptably high return volatility.

In our risk management framework, we can construct a combination of strategies that gives a desired set of weights to the various strategies and has no more or no less than the targeted amount of risk. We use a simple four-step construction method:

1. For each strategy, construct a position that reflects the current view and scale it such that its risk is equal to the full targeted amount as described earlier (e.g., 50 bp/year).

2. Apply a desired set of weights to the various strategies such that all the weights sum to one and scale each strategy by the appropriate weight. Up to here, this is equivalent to the additive approach to risk budgeting.

3. Calculate the risk of the combined position using the covariance matrix (or a risk model of your choice).

4. Scale the combined position linearly so that its risk equals the risk target for the portfolio.

The method is illustrated in Figure 2-12 for a blend of the global duration and high yield strategies. In step 1, we find the position that would be needed to achieve an estimated tracking error of 50 bp/year for each strategy. For the global duration strategy, the position consists of going long each asset class in index proportions. The position shown carries a global duration overweight of 0.83, with contributions evenly split across five markets, and the total position size represents

---

12. This approach is similar in spirit to the traditional requirements for risk-based capital.

Figure 2-12. Building Combination Strategies Using the Four-Step Construction Method

75% Global Duration, 25% High Yield, November 30, 2002

| Asset | Step 1: Individual Strategies Scaled to 50 bp/year Tracking Error Volatility | | Step 2: Form Blend of Strategies with Desired Weights (75/25) | | Step 4: Rescale Each Blended Position to Hit Risk Target | |
	Global Duration (scaled, %)	High Yield (scaled, %)	Long/Long (weighted, %)	Long/Short (weighted, %)	Long/Long (scaled, %)	Long/Short (scaled, %)
GBP1-3	0.29	0.00	0.22	0.22	0.26	0.30
GBP3-7	0.60	0.00	0.45	0.45	0.54	0.61
GBP7-10	0.39	0.00	0.29	0.29	0.35	0.39
GBP10+	0.98	0.00	0.74	0.74	0.88	1.00
JPY1-3	0.70	0.00	0.53	0.53	0.63	0.71
JPY3-7	1.19	0.00	0.89	0.89	1.06	1.21
JPY7-10	0.71	0.00	0.54	0.54	0.64	0.73
JPY10+	0.31	0.00	0.23	0.23	0.27	0.31
CAD1-3	0.79	0.00	0.59	0.59	0.70	0.80
CAD3-7	0.81	0.00	0.60	0.60	0.72	0.82
CAD7-10	0.47	0.00	0.35	0.35	0.42	0.47

CAD10+	0.76	0.00	0.57	0.57	0.68	0.78
EUR1-3	0.85	0.00	0.64	0.64	0.76	0.86
EUR3-7	1.06	0.00	0.79	0.79	0.95	1.08
EUR7+	1.14	0.00	0.85	0.85	1.01	1.15
USD1-3	0.96	0.00	0.72	0.72	0.86	0.97
USD3-7	0.66	0.00	0.50	0.50	0.59	0.67
USD7-10	0.27	0.00	0.20	0.20	0.24	0.27
USD10+	0.96	0.00	0.72	0.72	0.85	0.97
GBPcash	0	0.00	0.00	0.00	0.00	0.00
JPYcash	0	0.00	0.00	0.00	0.00	0.00
CADcash	0	0.00	0.00	0.00	0.00	0.00
EURcash	0	0.00	0.00	0.00	0.00	0.00
USDcash	0	0.00	0.00	0.00	0.00	0.00
USHY	0	7.12	1.78	-1.78	2.12	-2.41

Step 3: Calculate Risk for Each Position Vector Using Covariance Matrix

Tracking error volatility (bp/year)	50.0	50.0	42.0	37.0	50.0	50.0

13.9% of the portfolio market value. For the high yield strategy, a leveraged position of 7.12% of portfolio market value is determined to have the same risk.[13]

In step 2, we blend the strategies by taking a weighted sum. In this case, we
have used a blend of 75% of the global duration strategy and 25% of the high yield
strategy.[14] Four different positions are considered: long both strategies (long/
long), long global duration and short high yield (long/short), short/long, and
short/short, but as short/long and short/short are simply the negatives of the first
two, they are not shown in the figure. The positions shown in this step are the
ones that would be implemented if one used the most conservative form of additive risk budgeting shown earlier. The global duration part of the position carries
a tracking error volatility (TEV) of 37.5 bp, and the high yield part treated alone
would exhibit a TEV of 12.5 bp.

Step 3 is to apply the covariance matrix to calculate the projected risk of these
combined positions. Because the two strategies are not highly correlated, we find
that the risk of the combined positions is significantly lower than 50 bp, which allows us to scale up the positions to take advantage of strategy diversification. This
scaling is applied separately to each position. The TEV measured for the long/long
position is 42.0 bp, whereas that measured for the long/short position is 37.0. This
reflects a small positive correlation between the two strategies, which increases the
risk of going long in both (or short in both) relative to the uncorrelated case and
decreases the risk of taking opposite positions.

In step 4, we scale the positions up such that the TEV of each is equal to the risk
target. As a result of the different risk estimates for the two positions shown, they
are scaled by different amounts, and the position magnitudes for the long/short
position are somewhat larger than those of the long/long position.

There are several advantages to this method. When combining correlated
strategies, the resulting position does not take either too much or too little risk.
In addition, it does not require any explicit assessment of the correlations among
strategies, as this is implicitly provided by the use of the risk model.

One drawback to this method is that it does not offer the clean separation of
responsibilities implied by the phrase "risk budgeting." The portfolio management process is often carried out hierarchically, with capital allocated at the top

13. For this example, we have extended the covariance matrix to include the high yield asset
class as well.

14. We shall see later that this allocation of risk budget is optimal for a particular mix of
skills. Note that the absolute values of these initial weights do not affect the position that is ultimately selected; nor is it critical that the common risk level set in step 1 should equal the total
risk budget. The critical element is the ratios of the risk levels of the positions to be combined.
Had we instead taken here 300% of the global duration strategy and 100% of the high yield strategy, the normalization in step 4 would yield the same results.

level to different groups that then manage the different parts independently. In the risk-budgeting paradigm, one may think of assigning a certain amount of risk to the teams implementing the various strategies and then giving each team the freedom to apply that risk as it sees fit, independently of all the others. The framework outlined here calls for a more centralized management style, or at least for a more cooperative one, with more interaction among the various management teams. In our example, the decisions to go short or long global duration can be made entirely independently of the decision to go short or long high yield. Each team suggests the position that represents its views, but then an analysis of the overall portfolio position is carried out to obtain the final scaling.

Pure Tilt Strategies

Before we proceed to more detailed applications of combination strategies, we digress briefly to study the historical behavior of the individual strategies considered—or, more precisely, the positions from which these strategies were constructed. Our study has focused on the performance of various timing strategies. For each strategy considered, we use a skilled short-term forecast to adjust the position each month by choosing from a fixed menu of possible positions. In situations where a longer-term trend is anticipated, it might be more appropriate to choose a single position and leave it in place for an extended period of time. Such a strategy, in which a portfolio takes a constant long-term exposure, is often referred to as a "tilt" strategy. This approach would clearly incur lower transaction costs than a timing strategy and could be quite successful in a consistent long-term trend.

As a control on our studies of performance with skill, we report the performance of the pure tilt strategies from which our skilled strategies were derived: that is, what performance would have been achieved by taking the long global duration position each month, instead of choosing between long and short in a skilled manner? How would one have performed by having the same yield curve positioning month after month—for example, long-duration in USD and short-duration in JPY? In market dimensions that experienced significant trends over the study period, it is interesting to see what skill levels would have been required for a market timer to outperform a pure tilt. In addition, the correlations among the pure tilt strategies can be very instructive in helping to form effective combination strategies.

The results of the pure tilt positions for all of the core strategies are shown in Figure 2-13. In many cases, we find information ratios close to zero, indicating that gains and losses canceled out over the time period, leaving a small mean return relative to the volatility. However, in some cases, long-term trends over the course

Figure 2-13. Performance Summary of Various Pure Tilt Strategies over Different Time Periods

Strategy	Entire Time Period (1990–2002)			Before EMU (1990–1998)			Since EMU (1999–2002)		
	Mean (bp)	Standard Deviation (bp)	Information Ratio	Mean (bp)	Standard Deviation (bp)	Information Ratio	Mean (bp)	Standard Deviation (bp)	Information Ratio
Market Duration Strategies									
Global duration	37.5	43.7	0.9*	42.7	45.1	0.9*	26.1	40.6	0.6*
GBP-JPY	-8.5	52.6	-0.2	1.7	55.8	0.0	-31.6	44.4	-0.7
GBP-CAD	-10.1	41.3	-0.2	-6.2	45.7	-0.1	-18.8	29.2	-0.6
GBP-EUR	4.7	44.2	0.1	14.3	46.6	0.3	-16.8	37.7	-0.4
GBP-USD	-5.4	38.1	-0.1	5.0	40.5	0.1	-28.6	31.4	-0.9
JPY-GBP	8.5	52.6	0.2	-1.7	55.8	-0.0	31.6	44.4	0.7*
JPY-CAD	-1.5	46.5	-0.0	-8.0	49.3	-0.2	13.1	39.4	0.3
JPY-EUR	16.3	44.2	0.4	13.0	49.7	0.3	23.7	28.3	0.8*
JPY-USD	3.7	46.8	0.1	2.6	45.8	0.1	6.3	49.4	0.1
CAD-GBP	10.1	41.3	0.2	6.2	45.7	0.1	18.8	29.2	0.6*
CAD-JPY	1.5	46.5	0.0	8.0	49.3	0.2	-13.1	39.4	-0.3
CAD-EUR	15.7	43.2	0.4	19.9	48.5	0.4	6.3	28.0	0.2
CAD-USD	5.1	48.5	0.1	12.8	54.4	0.2	-12.1	31.7	-0.4

EUR-GBP	-4.7	44.2	-0.1	-14.3	46.6	-0.3	16.8	37.7	0.4
EUR-JPY	-16.3	44.2	-0.4	-13.0	49.7	-0.3	-23.7	28.3	-0.8
EUR-CAD	-15.7	43.2	-0.4	-19.9	48.5	-0.4	-6.3	28.0	-0.2
EUR-USD	-12.6	40.7	-0.3	-10.2	40.8	-0.2	-18.0	40.9	-0.4
USD-GBP	5.4	38.1	0.1	-5.0	40.5	-0.1	28.6	31.4	0.9*
USD-JPY	-3.7	46.8	-0.1	-2.6	45.8	-0.1	-6.3	49.4	-0.1
USD-CAD	-5.1	48.5	-0.1	-12.8	54.4	-0.2	12.1	31.7	0.4
USD-EUR	12.6	40.7	0.3	10.2	40.8	0.2	18.0	40.9	0.4
Twist Strategies									
JPY Twist	17.8	39.6	0.4	27.1	43.5	0.6*	-3.1	28.4	-0.1
EUR Twist	17.3	42.5	0.4	14.1	41.5	0.3	24.5	44.8	0.5*
USD Twist	38.1	51.8	0.7*	27.8	47.6	0.6*	61.1	60.1	1.0*
All Twists	42.2	48.1	0.9*	39.8	45.7	0.9*	47.6	53.5	0.9*
FX Strategies									
Long JPY	-2.5	58.1	0.0	3.1	62.6	0.0	-15.2	46.7	-0.3
Long EUR	-4.3	53.3	-0.1	-0.4	54.4	0.0	-13.2	51.4	-0.3
Long USD	6.9	45.8	0.2	-1.9	47.8	0.0	26.8	40.6	0.7*
Short JPY	2.5	58.1	0.0	-3.1	62.6	0.0	15.2	46.7	0.3
Short EUR	4.3	53.3	0.1	0.4	54.4	0.0	13.2	51.4	0.3
Short USD	-6.9	45.8	-0.2	1.9	47.8	0.0	-26.8	40.6	-0.7

of the study period allowed certain pure tilt strategies to perform admirably. When we separate the time period into the subperiods before and after EMU, we find most of these trends to be very different in the two periods. All of the pure tilt strategies with information ratios greater than 0.5 are marked with asterisks. An overweight to JPY duration vs. GBP or EUR duration produced an IR of 0.7 or 0.8 since EMU, but much less in the earlier period. The only pure tilt strategies that achieved information ratios above 0.5 in both halves of the study were the USD steepener, the all twists strategy combining steepeners in all three G3 yield curves,[15] and the pure long global duration position, which produced an information ratio of 0.9 in the pre-EMU period and 0.6 post-EMU.

Figure 2-13 can also serve as a check on how well the realized tracking errors of the tilt strategies correspond to the ex ante limits placed upon them in strategy construction. Recall that each strategy was designed to achieve a tracking error of 50 bp/year. In the period before EMU, the realized tracking errors were reasonably close to this target for most strategies, with the largest realized TEV going to the FX strategies going long or short JPY. In the post-EMU period, many of the realized tracking errors were significantly smaller, owing to the fact that our covariance matrix was constructed each month using equally weighted data over a growing time window. At the start of 1990, the matrix was constructed using 36 months of data from 1987 through 1989. At the start of 1999, the matrix was constructed using 144 months of data from 1987 through 1998. This indicates that the volatility associated with many of these strategies has decreased over the past few years.

The question of how much historical data should be used when projecting risk is not a simple one, and various approaches have been taken. To avoid using out-of-date estimates, many market practitioners put greater emphasis on more recent data. This can be done via exponential weighting or by using a smaller time window. The danger of this approach is that after a quiet period in the market, risk estimates may be too low when volatility next flares up. To investigate how our results might change, we repeated our study using a rolling 3-year historical time window to calculate the covariance matrix. We found that the realized tracking errors were indeed closer to the target. However, when evaluated in terms of information ratios, there was very little difference in the performance of the skilled strategies.

It is also interesting to look at the correlations among the historical outcomes of the pure tilt strategies. We calculated the correlations between each pair of pure

---

15. The three twist positions used in this combination were scaled to the smaller limit of 29 bp/year in each currency ($50/\sqrt{3}$) so that the combination of all three twists would hit the 50-bp limit. This is similar to the combination strategy discussed in the next section, except that for this tilt strategy the positions in the three currencies were always in the same direction.

tilt strategies over the entire time period and the two subperiods. As the resulting matrices are quite large, we have selected a sampling of such correlations to display in Figure 2-14.

The market duration strategies experienced a major paradigm shift between one period and the other. For example, the correlation between the EUR-JPY strategy (long EUR duration and short JPY duration) and the EUR-USD strategy was 0.29 before EMU and then changed sign to –0.55 after EMU. The correlations of the main market duration strategies (EUR-USD, USD-JPY, EUR-JPY) with the global duration strategy changed dramatically as well. This is because Japanese interest rates have remained remarkably stable in the post-EMU period, linking the results of the global duration strategy more closely to rate changes in the USD and EUR markets. Large negative correlations between the long global duration tilt and several of the market duration strategies persist throughout the entire time period. It therefore appears that strategy diversification between the global duration strategy and the market duration strategy may not offer the best results in terms of risk-adjusted performance.

By contrast, we find that the correlations involving FX strategies have remained relatively stable over the time period studied. The strategies that go long the three major currencies have negative correlations with each other, as each strategy goes long one currency and short the other two. More importantly, the FX strategies tend to have relatively low correlations with both the global duration strategy and the market duration strategies. This shows that the FX allocation strategy is insensitive to interest-rate movements and offers good diversifying value.

The yield curve twist strategies also seem to offer good diversification of risk. While the changes in the slopes of the USD and EUR curves have been fairly highly correlated in the post-EMU period, these strategies tend to have low to moderate correlations with FX strategies, global duration, and market duration.

Finally, among the core-plus strategies, we find that both the emerging markets and high yield asset classes have low correlations with global duration and are good candidates for strategy diversification. However, it must be noted that there is a fairly high positive correlation between the two. The USD inflation strategy shows large negative correlations with the global duration tilt (and with USD-EUR) that persist throughout the entire time period and thus seems to offer less diversification potential. (Note that the sign of the correlation is not significant here—a high negative correlation is just as undesirable as a high positive correlation. The long position in the USD inflation strategy is positively correlated with a short position in global duration, so these two strategies share a common risk exposure. Ideally, we seek to combine strategies with correlations near zero.)

Excess returns of investment-grade credit exhibit fairly high positive correlations with total returns on high yield credit and moderate negative correlations with

Figure 2-14. Pairwise Performance Correlations among Pure Tilt Strategies over Different Time Periods

		Pre-EMU	Post-EMU	Overall
Market Duration Pairs				
EUR-JPY	EUR-USD	0.29	−0.55	0.12
EUR-JPY	EUR-GBP	0.10	−0.57	−0.01
EUR-GBP	EUR-USD	0.33	0.53	0.37
EUR-CAD	EUR-USD	0.61	0.72	0.61
USD-JPY	USD-GBP	0.25	0.45	0.30
Long global duration	EUR-JPY	−0.32	0.47	−0.17
Long global duration	EUR-USD	−0.51	−0.81	−0.59
Long global duration	EUR-GBP	−0.66	−0.64	−0.66
Long global duration	USD-JPY	0.13	0.75	0.31
Long global duration	USD-GBP	−0.20	0.32	−0.09
FX Pairs				
Long JPY FX	Long EUR FX	−0.55	−0.64	−0.56
Long JPY FX	Long USD FX	−0.63	−0.50	−0.60
Long USD FX	Long EUR FX	−0.30	−0.35	−0.32
Long JPY FX	Long global duration	0.07	0.04	0.06
Long EUR FX	Long global duration	−0.07	0.17	0.00
Long USD FX	Long global duration	0.01	−0.23	−0.05
Long JPY FX	JPY-EUR	−0.11	−0.08	−0.11
Long EUR FX	EUR-USD	−0.23	−0.18	−0.22
Long USD FX	USD-EUR	−0.17	−0.34	−0.21
Twist Pairs				
EUR steepener	USD steepener	0.04	0.53	0.23
EUR steepener	JPY steepener	0.09	−0.12	0.04
USD steepener	JPY steepener	−0.03	−0.12	−0.06
USD steepener	USD-EUR	0.32	0.28	0.30
All three steepeners	Long global duration	0.10	0.23	0.14
EUR steepener	Long EUR FX	−0.22	0.14	−0.11
USD steepener	Long USD FX	−0.38	−0.28	−0.33
JPY steepener	Long JPY FX	0.00	−0.05	−0.01
Core-Plus Pairs				
Emerging markets	Long global duration	0.24	−0.05	0.15
High yield	Long global duration	0.33	−0.08	0.18
Euro credit	Long global duration	−1.00	−0.31	−0.31
USD inflation	Long global duration	−0.82	−0.78	−0.79
USD inflation	USD-EUR	−0.82	−0.78	−0.75
Euro credit	EUR steepener	N/A	−0.38	−0.38
High yield	USD steepener	0.10	−0.28	−0.08
Emerging markets	USD steepener	0.01	−0.22	−0.07
Emerging markets	High yield	0.63	0.51	0.49
U.S. credit	Long global duration	−0.09	−0.35	−0.18
U.S. credit	High yield	0.55	0.77	0.67
U.S. credit	Euro credit	N/A	0.85	0.85
U.S. credit	Long USD FX	0.31	0.20	0.24
U.S. credit	USD-EUR	−0.19	−0.47	−0.30
U.S. credit	USD steepener	−0.26	−0.32	−0.29

global duration, USD-EUR market duration, and USD twist. While the numeric values of these correlations may change over time, their direction and relative magnitudes seem to be quite stable.

Practical Applications: Examples of Combined Strategies

It is very important to understand correlations because they play a major role in determining the performance of combined strategies. The fundamental law states that information ratios are additive in their squares—but only if all of the strategies are carried out independently. To the extent that two strategies (or two information sources) are correlated, the benefits of strategy diversification are reduced.

We now take a look at some examples of combination strategies using different approaches. First, we look at a combination of the yield curve twist strategies in the G3 currencies, in which we assume that the strategies are independent and assign a risk budget of 29 bp/year ($50/\sqrt{3} \cong 29$) to each. Second, we examine the combination of yield curve shift and twist in each currency using our risk-budgeting framework to match separately the overall risk target for each combination. Third, we use this method to analyze a blend of the global duration and high yield strategies and address the issue of how to set the allocations to strategies with lower information ratios that are the result of lower skill or implementation constraints.

EXAMPLE 1: COMBINATION YIELD CURVE TWIST STRATEGY

In our first combination strategy, we implement the yield curve twist strategy in all three G3 currencies simultaneously. Each month, a separate decision is made to put on either a steepener or a flattener in each currency. In this case, we assume that the strategies are independent and assign a risk budget of 29 bp/year ($50/\sqrt{3} \cong 29$) to each one. The results are shown in Figure 2-15. The results for each single-currency twist strategy are simply scaled versions of those shown in Figure 2-5 with a risk budget of 50 bp. The mean and standard deviation of strategy returns are both divided by $\sqrt{3}$, and the information ratios for each skill level are therefore identical to those in Figure 2-5. The combination strategy diversifies among all three of these strategies at identical skill levels and, as a result, achieves information ratios that are better than any single strategy by a factor of about $\sqrt{3}$, as predicted by Equation (2-2). We further find that the realized standard deviation of outperformance falls within our target of 50 bp/year.

EXAMPLE 2: COMBINATION SHIFT AND TWIST STRATEGY

For our second example, we revisit the combination shift/twist strategy discussed previously (Figure 2-11) in which we use skill to predict both the shift and the

Figure 2-15. Performance of Individual Curve Twist Strategies (Scaled)
and Their Combination

| Skill Level (%) | EUR Curve Twist | | |
	Mean Outperformance (bp/year)	Volatility (bp/year)	Information Ratio
0	0.0	24.6	0.00
5	3.3	24.6	0.13
10	6.5	24.5	0.27
15	9.8	24.4	0.40
20	13.1	24.3	0.54
40	26.2	23.4	1.12
60	39.3	21.8	1.80
80	52.4	19.4	2.69
100	65.5	15.8	4.14

| Skill Level (%) | G3 Combined Twists | | |
	Mean Outperformance (bp/year)	Volatility (bp/year)	Information Ratio
0	0.0	45.4	0.00
5	10.3	45.4	0.23
10	20.6	45.3	0.45
15	30.9	45.1	0.68
20	41.1	44.9	0.92
40	82.3	43.4	1.90
60	123.4	40.8	3.03
80	164.6	36.8	4.47
100	205.7	30.9	6.66

twist in the curve in a single-currency setting. In our earlier presentation, our focus was on the performance effects of the cash constraint. We now turn our attention to the construction of the strategy itself. In fact, the positions were defined using the four-step construction technique described earlier. In this strategy, we choose from a total of six positions: pure long, long flattener, long steepener, pure short, short flattener, and short steepener.

The construction begins by creating the previously described cash-constrained long duration position by overweighting the long-duration half of the index and

USD Curve Twist			JPY Curve Twist		
Mean Outperformance (bp/year)	Volatility (bp/year)	Information Ratio	Mean Outperformance (bp/year)	Volatility (bp/year)	Information Ratio
0.0	30.5	0.00	0.0	23.0	0.00
3.9	30.5	0.13	3.1	23.0	0.14
7.8	30.4	0.26	6.3	22.9	0.27
11.6	30.3	0.38	9.4	22.8	0.41
15.5	30.1	0.51	12.5	22.7	0.55
31.0	29.1	1.06	25.1	21.8	1.15
46.5	27.4	1.70	37.6	20.3	1.86
62.0	24.7	2.51	50.2	17.9	2.81
77.5	20.8	3.74	62.7	14.2	4.41

underweighting the shorter half by the same market value. This position is the long flattener in our combined strategy. We then decompose this position into two parts: a pure duration trade that goes long the entire index on a leveraged basis to achieve the same duration exposure and a flattening trade that plays the long end against the short end on a duration-neutral basis. The long steepener is defined by combining the pure duration component of this decomposition with the equal and opposite twist exposure—so we now overweight the short end of the curve. For the pure long view, we omit the twist component of the trade entirely. We then estimate the tracking errors of each combination and scale the positions to all have the same tracking error of 50 bp/year. As a result, the three variants of the long-duration view typically entail different amounts of duration extension. The three possible short-duration positions are each the negative of one of the long-duration positions. In Figure 2-16, to highlight the advantage offered by this combination, we summarize the information ratios of the single-currency pure duration strategies from Figure 2-10, the pure twist strategies from Figure 2-5, and the unconstrained shift/twist combination strategies from Figure 2-11. As expected, combining these two largely independent strategies with equal skill gives a performance improvement of approximately $\sqrt{2}$ relative to either strategy on its own.

EXAMPLE 3: BLEND OF GLOBAL DURATION AND HIGH YIELD STRATEGIES
In our third example, we analyze the combination of the global duration and high yield strategies. The high yield strategy was shown in Figure 2-14 to have low

Figure 2-16. Performance Comparison of Shift/Twist Combination with Its Two Component Strategies

Skill Level (%)	Information Ratios								
	EUR			USD			JPY		
	Shift	Twist	Combo	Shift	Twist	Combo	Shift	Twist	Combo
0	0.00	0.00	0.00	0.00	0.00	0.00	0.00	0.00	0.00
5	0.14	0.13	0.20	0.14	0.13	0.18	0.13	0.14	0.18
10	0.28	0.27	0.39	0.28	0.26	0.36	0.26	0.27	0.36
15	0.43	0.40	0.59	0.42	0.38	0.54	0.40	0.41	0.55
20	0.57	0.54	0.79	0.56	0.51	0.72	0.53	0.55	0.73
40	1.19	1.12	1.62	1.17	1.06	1.49	1.11	1.15	1.50
60	1.94	1.80	2.60	1.89	1.70	2.41	1.78	1.86	2.36
80	2.97	2.69	3.87	2.88	2.51	3.63	2.65	2.81	3.39
100	4.84	4.14	5.86	4.60	3.74	5.69	4.04	4.41	4.78

correlation with the global duration strategy and thus seems like a good candidate for strategy diversification. In this context we investigate the role of the weights used to combine the two strategies and find the optimal weights for a two-strategy blend when the skills of the two strategies are unequal. Is it helpful to shift assets away from a more skilled strategy and into a less skilled one simply for the diversification benefit?

The detailed construction of the positions used in this strategy was illustrated in Figure 2-12 for a blend of 75% global duration and 25% high yield. We simulated the results using our imperfect foresight framework with various blends of the two strategies and various skill levels at the two decisions. In Figure 2-17, we show the strategy results for this 75/25 mix, using 20% skill at global duration and only 10% skill at high yield. (In this example we have not included the long-only constraint for high yield; we make the assumption that we are allowed to short the High Yield Index.) By including a 25% allocation to the high yield strategy, the combined strategy achieves an information ratio of 0.599, compared to 0.553 for the global duration strategy alone. Diversification can help improve risk-adjusted performance even when skill in the secondary strategy is not as high as in the primary one. These results are quite consistent with Equation (2-2), which would predict an information ratio of $\sqrt{(0.553)^2 + (0.240)^2} = 0.603$ if the two strategies were independent.

Figure 2-18 shows the dependence of strategy performance on the relative skill of the two strategies and the percentage of risk budget allocated to each. In each

Figure 2-17. Performance of a 75/25 Combination of Global Duration and High Yield Strategies with Unequal Skills

Strategy	Mean Outperformance (bp/year)	Volatility (bp/year)	Information Ratio
Global duration (20% skill)	25.6	46.3	0.553
High yield (10% skill)	14.6	60.9	0.240
Blend (75% global duration, 25% high yield)	28.6	47.8	0.599

case, we assume 20% skill at global duration allocation. The skill at high yield is varied from 0 to 20%, and the allocation to the high yield strategy is varied from 0 to 50%. When the high yield strategy is carried out at 0% skill (purely random decisions), its inclusion merely increases volatility without providing any outperformance, thus decreasing the information ratio; the optimal allocation in this case is clearly zero. For nonzero skill at high yield timing, we find that as we increase the

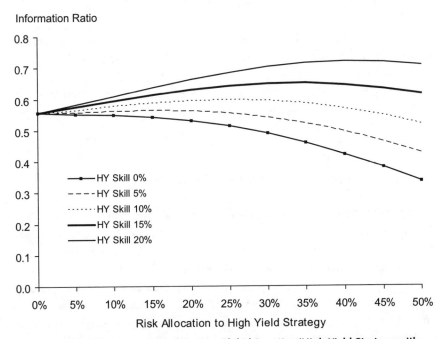

Figure 2-18. Performance of Combination Global Duration/High Yield Strategy with 20% Skill at Global Duration Timing and Several Skill Levels for High Yield Allocation
As a Function of High Yield Weight

allocation to high yield, the information ratio rises to a maximum and then decreases. As the skill level increases, so does the optimal allocation to high yield.

We can find the optimum allocation for any such blend of two strategies analytically. Assume that strategies 1 and 2 are expected to outperform by α_1 and α_2, respectively, with tracking error volatilities of σ_1 and σ_2, and that the correlation between the strategies is ρ. A blend of the two strategies with weights w_1 and w_2 has an expected outperformance α, and tracking error volatility σ given by

$$
\begin{aligned}
\alpha &= w_1\alpha_1 - w_2\alpha_2 \\
\sigma^2 &= w_1^2 VAR_1 + 2w_1 w_2 COV + w_2^2 VAR_2 \\
&= w_1^2\sigma_1^2 + 2w_1 w_2 \rho\sigma_1\sigma_2 + w_2^2\sigma_2^2 .
\end{aligned}
\tag{2-3}
$$

where the two weights are assumed to sum to one. We can express the information ratio as a function of these quantities and use this to find the blend of the two strategies that maximizes the information ratio. If we take the derivative of the information ratio $IR = \alpha/\sigma$ with respect to w_1 and set it to zero, we can show that the optimal weight for strategy 1 is given by

$$
w_1^* = \frac{\alpha_1 VAR_2 - \alpha_2 COV}{(\alpha_1 VAR_2 - \alpha_2 COV) + (\alpha_2 VAR_1 - \alpha_1 COV)} .
\tag{2-4}
$$

If we make use of the fundamental law to express the expected outperformance in terms of the skill level and the strategy breadth of 12 ($IR_i = s_i\sqrt{12} \Rightarrow \alpha_i = s_i\sqrt{12}\sigma_i$), we can reformulate this equation in terms of the strategy skills, volatilities, and correlation. Furthermore, if we assume that both of the individual strategies start with the same volatility, then this cancels out as well, leaving us with the simplified form:

$$
w_1^* = \frac{s_1 - \rho s_2}{(s_1 - \rho s_2) + (s_2 - \rho s_1)} = \frac{s_1}{s_1 + s_2} + \frac{\rho}{1 - \rho}\frac{s_1 - s_2}{s_1 + s_2} .
\tag{2-5}
$$

When the strategies are uncorrelated, the optimal allocation to a given strategy is proportional to skill. As correlations are increased, the weight of the more skilled strategy is increased. This makes sense, as the allocation to a less skilled strategy is only justifiable to the extent that it provides diversification of risk.

In order to apply this technique to find the optimal blend, one needs to have estimates for all of the quantities in Equation (2-3). In practice, the parameters most difficult to estimate are the skill parameters or, equivalently, the alphas for each strategy. In our example, we have specified them from the outset, so that the only parameter that is not clearly defined is the correlation. We can actually use

Equation (2-3) to back out the correlation ρ implied by the risk model. If we refer back to Figure 2-12, we see that the long/long position with a 75/25 weighting had a 42.0 bp/year tracking error before rescaling. If we set $w_i = 75\%$, $w_2 = 25\%$, $\sigma_1 = \sigma_2 = 50.0$, and $\sigma = 42.0$ in Equation (2-3), we can solve for ρ and find that it is 0.215. Using this value in Equation (2-5), we find that the optimal blend of these two strategies at these skill levels is 75.8% in global duration timing and 24.2% in high yield timing. This is consistent with the pattern shown in Figure 2-18.

We have to address one more point concerning the inclusion of high yield and other core-plus strategies. We have thus far analyzed the inclusion of high yield on a long-short basis. However, as discussed at length, many managers can include high yield and other core-plus strategies as an overweight, but may not take short positions. When we analyzed these strategies on a stand-alone basis, we found that this limitation leads to a significant drag on performance because under the long-only constraint, the manager is unable to take advantage of a negative view. Not only does this waste some of his skill, but in months where the view is negative, the risk budget is not used at all—that is, the portfolio remains completely passive.

In a combined strategy, it may still be true that there is no way to act directly upon a negative view on a core-plus asset class. However, such a view does not have to result in underutilization of the risk budget. For instance, in our combination of global duration and high yield, in months where the outlook on high yield is negative, the portfolio would not stand idle, but would implement the pure global duration strategy at a risk level of 50 bp/year. In terms of Figure 2-12, the position taken to implement the long/short decision at the far right would now be the pure long global duration position at the far left, and a short/short decision would no longer correspond to the negative of long/long, but rather to the negative of the pure long global duration position (i.e., pure short global duration). We simulated the performance of this strategy and found that the information ratios were even higher than for the long-short case, owing to the fact that the long-only high yield strategy has a positive bias over the time period of the study, as we saw in Figure 2-7. The interaction among the long-only constraint, the blending of the strategies, and the risk scaling produces uncertainty as to how one can properly adjust for this bias.

The effect of the long-only constraint within one portion of a combined strategy is illustrated in Figure 2-19, using a different combination of strategies as an example. In a single-currency setting (USD), we combine views on duration and credit with different levels of skill. In the two top panels, we assume that the portfolio can go either long or short in both duration and credit. This might be an appropriate assumption for a portfolio benchmarked against the Lehman Aggregate Index, where a negative view on credit can be expressed as an underweight.

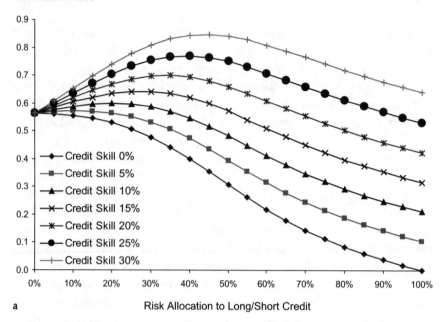

a

Risk Allocation to Long/Short Credit

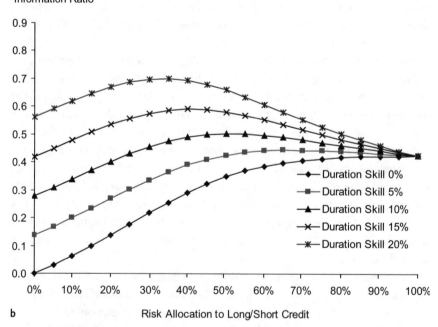

b

Risk Allocation to Long/Short Credit

Figure 2-19. Information Ratios for a Combination of U.S. Duration Timing and U.S. Credit

August 1991–December 2002: (a) Long/Short Credit, Fixed 20% Duration Skill, Varying Credit Skill; (b) Long/Short Credit, Fixed 20% Credit Skill, Varying Duration Skill; (c) Long-Only Credit, Fixed 20% Duration Skill, Varying Credit Skill; (d) Long-Only Credit, Fixed 20% Credit Skill, Varying Duration Skill

Information Ratio

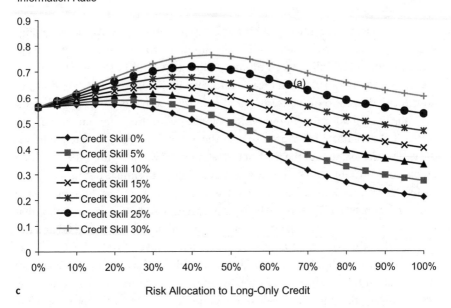

c   Risk Allocation to Long-Only Credit

Information Ratio

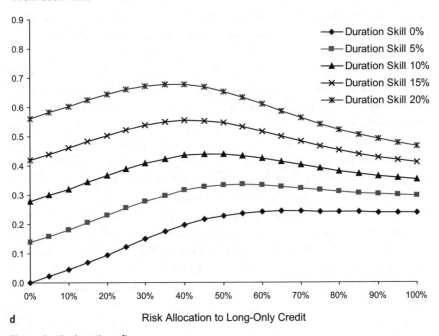

d   Risk Allocation to Long-Only Credit

Figure 2-19. (continued)

In this case, we see much the same effect as in Figure 2-18. At the left of Figure 2-19a, all of the risk is allocated to the duration strategy, and performance is independent of the skill at credit timing. At the right, with 100% allocation to the credit strategy, performance increases linearly with credit skill and goes down to an information ratio of 0.0 for 0% credit skill. For any nonzero level of credit skill, the overall information ratio is increased by allocating some amount of risk to credit. As credit skill increases, so does the optimal risk allocation to credit, indicated by the location of the peak of the relevant curve. In Figure 2-19b, we hold credit skill constant at 20% and vary duration skill, with similar results.

In Figure 2-19c and d, we treat credit as a core-plus asset class and impose the long-only constraint. This would be an appropriate assumption for portfolios that incorporate credit against an all-government benchmark. Comparing (c) and (a), we find that the constraint affects performance in several ways. First of all, as expected, the overall information ratios achievable by the combined strategy are lower than in the unconstrained case. Second, the much narrower spread of the results toward the right-hand side of the graph indicates that the overall performance is less sensitive to credit skill. Third, even at 100% allocation to credit, the 0% credit skill case achieves a positive information ratio. A fourth effect can be found in (d), where we find that the results for the 100% allocation to credit do not converge to a single point, but remain sensitive to the skill at duration timing.

All of these phenomena stem from the same root cause. In the method we use to construct our combination strategies, we do not allow the long-only constraint to cause us to regularly undershoot our risk target. Instead, whenever the constraint disallows a short credit position to implement a negative view on credit, the risk-budgeting algorithm scales up the duration position accordingly. The actual risk allocation of the combination strategy is thus not perfectly reflected in Figure 2-19c and d. In fact, a combination strategy with a nominal credit risk allocation of 50% is constructed as follows: when the credit view is positive, it allocates the risk evenly between a long credit position and either a long- or short-duration position; when the credit view is negative, however, 100% of the risk budget is allocated to the implementation of the duration view. This explains the reduced role of credit skill in determining the performance of the combined strategy, as well as the dependence on duration skill even when the risk allocation to credit is nominally 100%.

The incorporation of core-plus strategies in this manner greatly mitigates the performance effect of the long-only constraint. Whereas a combination of duration and long-only credit may underperform its long-short counterpart, it should outperform a pure duration strategy. The major performance penalty that we saw in the single-strategy results in Figure 2-7 was due to underutilization of the risk budget, which is avoided in our combined strategies.

INTERPRETING A STRATEGY'S INFORMATION RATIO

In our tables of strategy performance, such as Figure 2-5, we show the information ratio for a given strategy at a given skill level. How should these numbers be understood? In particular, how do they relate to the ex post information ratios recorded by actual managers in the real world?

For example, Figure 2-5 tells us that the market duration strategy, with 20% skill, recorded a mean outperformance of 24.0 bp/year with a tracking error volatility of 44.2 bp/year, for an annualized information ratio of 0.54. However, this does not mean that every manager with this level of skill will record exactly these results if he uses this strategy. Rather, this ex ante information ratio represents the expected value of the information ratio that will be realized by any given manager. The realized IR can be higher or lower. The distribution of the realized information ratios has a standard deviation that depends on the length of time over which it is observed, and is approximately equal to $\sqrt{12/n}$, where n is the number of months of observed performance.

We tested this result using Monte Carlo simulation of 10,000 managers using the market duration strategy with 20% skill over the 149 months from January 1990 through May 2002. As indicated earlier, we know that the ex ante information ratio is 0.54, and we expect the realized information ratio to be distributed around this mean with a standard deviation of $\sqrt{12/149} = 0.283$. In our simulation, we indeed found that the realized information ratios averaged 0.55 and that their standard deviation was 0.29. The values ranged from a minimum of –0.51 to a maximum of 1.64. Of the 10,000 managers, there were 293 that had negative information ratios. (This is in very good agreement with the normal distribution, which would give a probability of 2.96% to negative outcomes given the above mean and standard deviation.)

The wide range of information ratios that can be realized by managers with the same degree of skill makes it difficult to back out an implied skill level from a realized information ratio. The best we can do is back out a range of reasonable values. Referring again to Figure 2-5, we suppose that a manager realized an ex post information ratio of 0.55 over the 149-month sample period using the market duration strategy. It is certainly possible that this manager has 20% skill and achieved the expected IR. Yet it is also possible to have generated this result by starting with a much lower skill level (about 10%) with an ex ante IR of 0.27, one standard deviation below the mean, or a much higher one (about 30%) with an ex ante IR of 0.83. This rule of thumb of plus/minus one standard deviation thus defines an approximate skill range between 10 and 30%.

Repeating this analysis over a shorter observation period would give a wider window on skill. Say the manager achieved a realized information ratio of 0.55

over a 5-year period. In this case, the standard deviation of realized IR is $\sqrt{12/60}$ = 0.45, and this could have been a reasonable outcome for a manager having an ex ante IR ranging anywhere from 0.1 to 1.0 or having a skill range from 4 to 35%.

The information ratio is closely related to the t-statistic, a common measure of statistical significance. For a given excess return history, we can ask whether there is a reasonable chance that this performance was achieved by a manager with 0% skill totally by chance. A statistical test of this possibility is carried out by calculating the t-statistic, the ratio of the average excess return to its standard error. If the t-statistic is greater than some critical value, then the excess returns are deemed statistically significant, with less than a 5% possibility that they could have been generated by chance. Goodwin has shown[16] that the t-statistic is related to the information ratio by t-statistic = $\sqrt{T} \cdot IR$, where T is the number of return periods included in the analysis. He points out that a realized annualized information ratio of 0.5 achieved over nine years has a t-statistic of 1.5 and is not statistically significant, but that the same information ratio maintained over 21 years has a t-statistic of 2.29, which is significant. He does, however, downplay the role of statistical significance, saying that its importance "should not be overstated." That said, we offer the following table of realized information ratios that a manager would have to achieve over a given period of time to convince a skeptical scientist that the results cannot possibly be explained by luck. To prove that a 3-year track record is no fluke, the annualized IR would need to be 0.98. Over a 10-year time frame, a sustained IR of 0.52 would suffice. These numbers are not meant to be used as a litmus test for evaluating realized performance. They simply offer another illustration of the commonsense idea that a given IR is a surer sign of manager skill when it can be maintained for the long term.

Annualized (monthly observations) information ratios required to prove statistical significance are as follows:

Number of Years	Information Ratio
2	1.21
3	0.98
5	0.75
10	0.52
15	0.43
20	0.37

16. Thomas H. Goodwin, "The Information Ratio," *Financial Analysts Journal,* July/August 1998, pp. 34–43.

CONCLUSION

We have outlined the essential components of an investment management process that uses macro strategies to outperform a global fixed-income benchmark. First, we define a set of investment strategies that isolates different types of market views. Second, we establish a risk-budgeting process by which we can control the amount of risk to be assigned to each strategy. We have shown how strategies can be combined within this framework to achieve the best performance while adhering to a targeted tracking error.

We have explored the skilled implementation of a diverse set of pure strategies and confirmed that in each case a given level of skill produces approximately the same information ratio. An open question remains: in which dimension is it easiest to achieve a given level of skill?

Another axiom that we have confirmed is that the constraints included in an investment policy have a direct impact on the information ratios that a skilled manager can achieve. We have seen that a long-only constraint can result in a skilled core-plus manager achieving lower information ratios than he might in a long-short setting. This may argue for the selection of benchmarks that include all asset classes that may be used in the portfolio, thus allowing the portfolio to underweight as well as overweight each asset class.

Similarly, we found that a no-leverage constraint could cause a significant drag on the performance of duration-timing strategies, owing to the forced inclusion of an unintended twist exposure with the implementation of a duration view. This evidence may encourage plan sponsors to allow the use of derivatives to enable more flexible expression of yield curve views.

The key to risk-adjusted performance is strategy diversification. One needs to spread the risk over multiple strategies, developing as high a skill level as possible in each. The big challenge is to keep the decision-making processes independent of each other. Correlations among the various macro strategies may form a limiting factor in determining just how much outperformance can be added by combining different macro strategies.

The need to maintain independence of decisions presents a dilemma for many managers. For example, suppose that there is a well-established negative correlation between Treasury yields and corporate spreads or that certain industry groups are expected to outperform in a market rally. Should the managers of these sectors key their decisions on the direction of their yield curve view? In practice, many often do. But if this occurs, the benefit of diversifying the active bets among many different strategies can be greatly diminished. The result of such activity will be positive correlation among the strategies, leading to higher volatility and lower information ratios.

Here, we have focused only on the systematic risks at the macro level. We have assumed the ability to earn the return on any index component when desired and to go in and out of these positions at will. These simplifications have helped us focus our attention on the core topic of macro strategies, but in the process we have skirted some other important issues. In reality, every investment strategy entails some amount of nonsystematic risk along with the desired macro exposure. This can affect the decision process in several ways. To minimize nonsystematic risk, it can be helpful to select strategies involving indices that are easy to replicate. It also may help to use different types of instruments to replicate different portions of the market, in order to avoid correlations among the replication errors of different markets.[17] Of course, the decision as to which specific instruments are to be used to implement a particular view is more than just a source of nonsystematic risk. If security selection is carried out skillfully, it has the potential to generate higher information ratios than any macro strategy, as it can incorporate a large number of independent decisions.[18]

One also must consider the transaction costs and liquidity risks that are incurred in implementing a particular strategy. Macro positions in the liquid global government and currency markets can be modified with ease and at low cost under almost all market conditions. In spread sectors, and especially in core-plus markets, modifying macro positions is more complex. Not only is there greater nonsystematic risk in replicating these indices, but the higher transaction costs and liquidity risks typically require making strategy adjustments only over a longer time horizon.

What is the best mix of strategies for a global manager to develop? There is no single answer to this question. The goal is to develop high skill levels at several strategies that are not highly correlated. For a manager working under a fixed research budget, this elusive goal involves different types of trade-offs. In many cases, a manager brings to the table expertise in a single type of strategy, and the cost of developing similar skills in other strategies will be much higher. This leans heavily toward a "play to your strength" strategy. However, we have demonstrated the benefits of allocating resources to a diversifying strategy, even with lower skill. How much of an investment is required to build enough skill to justify allocating a significant portion of the risk budget? In the case of core-plus strategies, in addition to these considerations, the advantage of low correlations with other strategies has to be considered against the disadvantage of the long-only constraint.

---

17. See Chapter 5 for a detailed discussion of this topic. It is shown there that a combination of Treasury futures, money market futures, and swaps can track the returns of various indices much better than Treasury futures alone, largely owing to correlations among replication errors.

18. Chapter 1 presents evidence of much higher potential performance in security selection, and traces this advantage to the much greater number of independent decisions.

3. Cost of the No-Leverage Constraint in Duration Timing

In many portfolio settings, investment policy forbids the use of leverage. This undoubtedly serves to prevent portfolio managers from engaging in certain extremely risky strategies. However, the no-leverage constraint can also have an unintended effect on portfolio performance by limiting the types of views that can be implemented.

In particular, a portfolio manager operating under a no-leverage constraint cannot easily implement a purely bullish view on interest rates. A typical method of adding duration to such a portfolio is to underweight the short-duration part of the market and overweight the long-duration part. However, such a position is clearly not a pure duration play, but carries with it an exposure to changes in the slope of the curve. The no-leverage constraint essentially forces the combination of a bullish view on duration with an unintended flattener. Historically, this combination has not been a very effective one. Figure 3-1 shows a scatter plot of changes in the level and slope of the curve (par yield vs. 2–30 slope). The graph shows a clear bias toward the top-left quadrant (bullish steepening, 30 out of 104 observations) and the bottom-right quadrant (bearish flattening, observed in 33 months). The bottom-left quadrant shows only 23 months with bullish flattening, and even these tend to show only mild flattening. At the top right, we find 18 months with bearish steepening. The correlation between the level and slope over this time period is –25.6%. Decreases in the level of rates have historically been accompanied by steepening of the curve. Shifting portfolio exposure from the short end of the curve to the long end should therefore lead to performance reduction, compared with a pure duration strategy that increases exposure all along the curve by using leverage.

To quantify the cost of the no-leverage constraint on portfolio performance, we investigate several different mechanisms for implementing a view on duration

Based on research first published by Lehman Brothers in 2002.

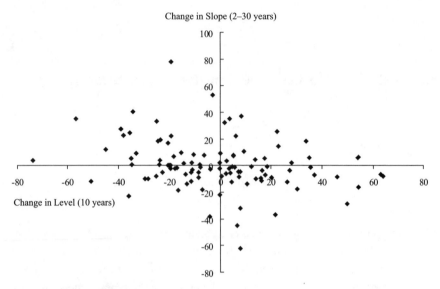

Figure 3-1. Historically Observed Yield Curve Changes
December 1993–July 2002

and simulate their historical performance using "perfect foresight" for predicting the direction of interest rates. In each strategy, the portfolio duration is reset at the start of each month to be either 1 year longer than the benchmark or 1 year shorter, depending on the direction of the signal. Several different signals are explored. Although the returns obtained using the perfect foresight assumption are unrealistically high, the comparison of the results of the different strategies should carry over to any setting in which a manager exhibits skill at duration timing.

A manager who wishes to extend the portfolio's duration can do so in any number of ways. Positioning a portfolio entails not only deciding what the duration exposure should be, but also where it should lie along the curve. Steepening or flattening exposures assumed in the process of extending duration may well be intentional, based on detailed analyses of curve dynamics and relative value. In this study, we investigate a simple, idealized version of the investment process. The duration view is assumed to be purely directional, and any steepening or flattening exposure is considered to be incidental. Further, the means of extending duration are limited to a small set of specific strategies. The no-leverage constraint may thus have a milder effect on performance in the more general portfolio context than in the simplified setting studied here.

STRATEGIES CONSIDERED

In this study, we consider the performance of six portfolios benchmarked against the Lehman Brothers Treasury Index from December 1993 through July 2002. All six use duration timing strategies that go either long- or short-duration by 1 year vs. the index according to a signal. Three are all-cash strategies, in which the duration view is implemented by overweighting and underweighting different parts of the index; the other three use overlays of Treasury futures.

The strategies are as follows:

1. *Scaled-Index.* The portfolio either overweights or underweights the entire index to achieve the desired duration exposure. This is a purely directional view on the index, but may involve leverage. When the portfolio takes the bearish view, duration is shortened by selling bonds and leaving the proceeds in cash. To implement a bullish view, the portfolio lengthens duration by borrowing cash to buy more of each index security. In practice, strategies of this type can be implemented in the repo market.

2. *Cash-Neutral.* The portfolio always remains fully invested in bonds, but shifts assets between the long-duration and the short-duration halves of the index to achieve the desired duration exposure. When bullish, there is an overweight to the long-duration half and an underweight to the short-duration half. This position is reversed to implement a bearish view. This strategy satisfies the no-leverage constraint, but always contains an unintended exposure to curve slope (most likely in the wrong direction) as it alternates between a bullish flattener and a bearish steepener.

3. *Mixed.* This is an asymmetric combination of the cash-neutral and scaled index strategies. For a bullish view, where the scaled-index strategy would violate the no-leverage rule, we use the cash-neutral strategy to go long duration. When a bearish view is indicated, it is implemented using the scaled-index strategy, spreading the underweight across the whole index to avoid the performance dilution that would occur if the curve flattened as rates rose (as is often the case). This strategy satisfies the no-leverage constraint and alternates between a bullish flattener and a purely bearish position.

4. *10-Year Futures.* In this strategy (as in the next two), we assume that the portfolio is constructed around a core bond position that is completely passive to the index. The active position consists entirely of a

futures position that is layered above the bond portfolio to implement the desired duration view. In this strategy the entire duration exposure is implemented using a long or short position in 10-year Treasury note futures.

5. *Bond Futures.* This is the same as 10-year futures, but using the Treasury bond futures contracts.

6. *Futures Replication.* The active duration bet of 1 year is implemented using a combination of four futures contracts (2- , 5- , and 10-year Treasury note futures, and bond futures) selected to best match the duration profile of the index, using a simple matching of duration buckets with futures contracts. This strategy is very closely related to the scaled-index strategy, except that the monthly changes in the position involve transactions on four futures contracts instead of all of the bonds in the index.

Figure 3-2 illustrates how the various strategies would have implemented a bullish duration exposure of 1 year longer than the index as of June 30, 2002. The Treasury index is divided into four duration cells, which correspond roughly to the four futures contracts used in the replication strategy. The cash-neutral strategy overweights the two longer-duration cells and underweights the two shorter-duration cells, matching the index distribution between the two cells in each half of the index. It can be seen that this strategy has a large allocation (and by far the largest duration contribution) in the longest index cell—a duration of more than 7.5 years. The scaled-index strategy overweights the four index cells proportionally to their index weights, and the futures replication strategy approximates this distribution using the four U.S. Treasury futures contracts. At the bottom of Figure 3-2, we show the effective cash position of each strategy as a percentage of portfolio market value. The negative numbers shown for all but the cash-neutral strategy indicate leveraged positions. For the futures strategy, the negative cash positions shown are those implied by treating the contracts as leveraged positions in Treasury bonds and notes.

PERFECT FORESIGHT USING DIFFERENT SIGNALS

To simulate the performance of each strategy historically, we just have to fill in the sequence of duration calls made each month—bullish or bearish. We investigate the unrealizable upper limits of performance by utilizing a perfect foresight assumption—the duration decision at the start of each month is based on advance knowledge of what will happen as that month unfolds. In other words, the strategy

Figure 3-2. Illustration of Strategies for Implementing Bullish 1-Year Duration View
As of June 30, 2002

Asset	Duration	Treasury Index (%)	Active Positions to Achieve a Duration Overweight of +1 Year				
			Cash Neutral (%)	Scaled Index (%)	10-Year Futures (%)	30-Year Futures (%)	Futures Replication (%)
Treasury Index, duration 0–3	1.76	35.8	−8.9	6.2			
Treasury Index, duration 3–5	3.82	18.6	−4.6	3.2			
Treasury Index, duration 5–7.5	6.07	12.3	3.7	2.1			
Treasury Index, duration 7.5+	11.22	33.2	9.9	5.7			
2-year futures	1.93						5.6
5-year futures	4.19						2.9
10-year futures	6.55				15.3		2.0
30-year futures	12.29					8.1	5.2
Total duration		5.82	1.00	1.00	1.00	1.00	1.00
Effective cash position (percentage of portfolio value)			0.0	−17.2	−15.3	−8.1	−15.7

always makes the "right" duration call. Interestingly enough, there is some ambiguity in determining which is the right duration call even after the fact. We have run the simulation using four different signals: (1) 10-year yield—the strategy is bullish during months in which the fitted 10-year par yield falls and bearish when it rises; (2) average yield—the strategy is bullish during months in which there is a decline in the average of the fitted par yields at four points on the curve: 2, 5, 10, and 30 years; (3) index vs. cash—the strategy is bullish during months in which the Treasury Index earns a positive excess return over cash; (4) index slope—the strategy is bullish during months in which the long-duration half of the Treasury Index earns a greater total return than the short-duration half of the index.

This menu of signals corresponds to different ways of looking at interest rates. The 10-year yield is quite commonly used as a very simple barometer of the level of interest rates. The average yield, which spreads out the exposure along the curve, is somewhat more indicative of the yield change experienced by the index. The two strategies based on index returns are designed to produce the "right" duration call for specific implementations of the duration view. The index-vs.-cash indicator should always give the best result for the scaled-index strategy, and the index slope indicator should always give the best result for the cash-neutral strategy.

These four signals are usually in sync with one another. A downward parallel shift in rates should result in a bullish signal by all four indicators; an upward parallel shift should give four bearish signals. The different indicators are most likely to give different signals in months where there is no noticeable parallel shift, but the curve changes shape. Nonparallel yield curve changes could make the 10-year yield move in the opposite direction from the average yield. When the dominant change in the yield curve is a change in slope, the index slope indicator is likely to give a different result than the others. In a steep yield curve environment, when any duration extension earns a pickup in yield, the bullish view may be a winning one even when rates back up slightly. This could cause the index-vs.-cash indicators to be different from the yield change signals.

RESULTS

We simulated each of our six strategies using the four indicators from December 1993 through July 2002. For each of the twenty-four combinations, we calculated the mean monthly outperformance, the tracking error volatility, and the annualized information ratio. The results are shown in Figure 3-3.

In our view, average yield is the fairest indicator for duration timing in an index context, as it most closely corresponds to a parallel shift in the yield curve. Using this signal, we see that the highest information ratio (4.32) is obtained using the scaled-index strategy. As expected, the futures replication strategy turns in

Figure 3-3. Summary of Perfect Foresight Results for Duration Timing Using Different Strategies and Indicator Signals
December 1993–July 2002

	Scaled-Index	Cash-Neutral	Mixed	10-Year Futures	30-Year Futures	Futures Replication
Indicator: 10-Year Yield (Change in 10-Year Par Yield)						
Mean outperformance (bp/month)	18.5	16.8	17.2	21.4	17.8	19.4
Tracking error volatility (bp/month)	14.9	14.9	14.7	18.3	14.7	15.7
Information ratio (annualized)	4.3	3.9	4.1	4.0	4.2	4.3
Indicator: Average Yield (Average of Changes in 2-, 5-, 10-, and 30-Year Par Yield)						
Mean outperformance (bp/month)	18.5	15.6	16.6	21.6	17.1	19.5
Tracking error volatility (bp/month)	14.9	16.2	15.3	18.1	15.5	15.7
Information ratio (annualized)	4.3	3.3	3.7	4.1	3.8	4.3
Indicator: Index vs. Cash (Excess Return of Treasury Index over Cash Earning GC Rate)						
Mean outperformance (bp/month)	18.8	16.9	17.3	21.8	17.9	19.8
Tracking error volatility (bp/month)	14.5	14.9	14.5	17.8	14.6	15.3
Information ratio (annualized)	4.5	3.9	4.1	4.2	4.3	4.5
Indicator: Index Slope (Difference in Returns of Long-Duration and Short-Duration Halves of Treasury Index)						
Mean outperformance (bp/month)	17.5	18.3	17.4	19.7	18.5	18.6
Tracking error volatility (bp/month)	16.1	13.0	14.6	20.1	13.9	16.7
Information ratio (annualized)	3.8	4.9	4.1	3.4	4.6	3.9

a very similar performance, with an information ratio of 4.30.[1] Comparing the cash-neutral strategy to the scaled-index strategy, we see that the average monthly outperformance is 16% lower (15.6 vs. 18.5 bp), whereas the tracking error volatility is 9% higher (16.2 vs. 14.9 bp), making the annualized information ratio 23% lower (3.33 vs. 4.32). The mixed strategy, as a blend of the scaled-index and cash-neutral strategies, falls between the other two: its average outperformance of 16.6 bp is 11% less than that of the scaled-index strategy and its information ratio (3.74) is 13% lower.

If the duration timing signal is based on the 10-year yield indicator, the results are largely unchanged for the scaled-index and futures replication strategies, but the cash-neutral and mixed strategies fare much better, owing to the fact that the implementation of the duration view in the cash-neutral strategy places the exposure mostly on the 10- to 30-year part of the curve. In this case, the scaled-index strategy achieves an information ratio of 4.31, the cash-neutral strategy is 9% lower at 3.91, and the mixed strategy is 6% lower at 4.06.

The improved performance of the cash-neutral strategy using the 10-year signal raises an interesting point. Within the framework of this study, duration extension was conceived as a view on the direction of a parallel shift in rates. We included the 10-year signal as a simple, commonly cited measure of the level of interest rates, but did not expect it to be a good measure of parallel shift. The improved performance of the cash-neutral strategy using this signal is due to the fact that the 10-year yield change just happens to coincide with the part of the curve to which this strategy is most sensitive. The general message for investors who use a variant of this cash-neutral strategy is that a duration extension of this type should not be considered as a view on a parallel shift in rates, but rather as a view on a single point on the yield curve where the strategy has the greatest duration exposure.

One surprise in the results concerns the use of the 10-year futures contract alone to implement the duration view. One might have expected that this would be the most effective strategy, especially when the signal was the change in 10-year yields. In fact, regardless of which indicator was used, the 10-year futures strategy achieved the highest mean outperformance, but also had the highest tracking error volatility. As a result, its information ratio is lower than that of the more

---

1. The futures replication strategy achieves slightly higher mean outperformance than the scaled-index strategy regardless of which indicator is used. This can be attributed to changes in the futures basis over the period studied. It does not directly pertain to the phenomenon we are studying and cannot necessarily be expected to persist in the future. For this reason, when comparing the mean outperformance of different strategies, we compare the cash-neutral strategy to the scaled-index strategy, and not to the futures replication results.

balanced futures replication strategy in every case. The replication strategy, by diversifying the basis risk across four different contracts, reduces the tracking error volatility. The 10-year strategy exhibits particularly high volatility because high demand by convexity hedgers and the hedging of new corporate issues in the 10-year part of the curve cause many issues in that part of the curve to achieve above-average returns.

The two additional index-based indicators are not the best representations of a pure duration view. Rather, each is designed to take the "perfect foresight" approach to the limit and give the best possible results for one particular strategy. The index-vs.-cash indicator should always signal the winning direction for the scaled-index strategy. Indeed, the performance of that strategy using perfect foresight on this indicator gives the highest outperformance, the lowest volatility, and the highest information ratio across the four signals. Similarly, the index slope indicator should always signal whether it is better to go long or short duration using the cash-neutral strategy—and it achieves its best performance using this signal. The information ratio of 4.87 achieved in this case shows that the cash-neutral strategy can certainly generate a good risk-adjusted performance. The caveat is that skill at using this strategy involves more than a directional view on interest rates. The perfect foresight simulated in this case is more complex and involves a simultaneous prediction of the changes in the level and shape of the curve.

The information ratios obtained here are all unrealistically high, owing to the use of the perfect foresight assumption for generating the duration timing signal. (Generally speaking, an information ratio of 1.0 or better is considered to indicate excellent risk-adjusted performance.) However, we believe that the effect shown here can be applied proportionally to an actual portfolio management context. Figure 3-4 summarizes the proportional reduction in performance achieved by the cash-neutral and mixed strategies relative to the scaled-index strategy, in terms of both mean outperformance and information ratio. We show the results using both the average yield signal, which corresponds to a view on parallel shift, and the 10-year yield signal, which matches more closely the true yield exposure of this strategy. To the extent that a skilled manager can generate outperformance by pure duration timing calls, the no-leverage constraint may be expected to reduce the risk-adjusted outperformance by anywhere from 6 to 23%.

To ensure that these results are robust, we calculated the information ratios over rolling 3-year time windows in addition to the single calculation over the entire time period. Figure 3-5 compares the information ratios of the cash-neutral strategy with those of the futures replication strategy, using the average yield indicator. We see that the futures replication strategy achieves a higher information ratio over every 3-year window in our data sample.

Figure 3-4. Summary of Underperformance of Cash-Neutral and Mixed
Strategies Relative to the Scaled-Index Strategy

Signal	Strategy	Mean (%)	Information Ratio (%)
Average yield	Cash-neutral	−16	−23
	Mixed	−11	−13
10-year yield	Cash-neutral	−9	−9
	Mixed	−7	−6

CONCLUSION

The no-leverage constraint can impair a portfolio manager's ability to implement
a pure directional view on interest rates in a risk-efficient manner. When a pure
view on rates is implemented using the cash-neutral strategy, it entails an exposure to the slope of the curve as well and, thus, additional risk. Moreover, his-

Figure 3-5. Annualized Information Ratios for Cash-Neutral and Futures Replication
Strategies over Rolling 3-Year Windows
Using an Average Yield Indicator

torical correlations between changes in curve level and slope show that this slope exposure is usually in the wrong direction. A manager who expects rates to rally is forced into a flattening trade, even though the curve tends to steepen as rates drop. In our observations, this reduced the achieved information ratio by 6 to 23%.

One clear conclusion of this study is that plan sponsors should consider this cost of the no-leverage constraint before imposing it on their portfolios. If possible, managers should be allowed to employ futures, swaps, or financed bond purchases on at least a limited basis to enable the risk-efficient implementation of yield curve views.[2] Additional risk constraints, for example, on the maximum duration deviation from the index, could be put into place to prevent the misuse of these instruments. Utilization of derivatives for curve trades might also entail advantages with respect to the ease and cost of trade execution.

For managers who have to operate under the no-leverage constraint, this study suggests several mechanisms for mitigating the concomitant adverse effects. First, we observe that the mixed strategy holds a clear performance advantage over the cash-neutral strategy. Even though the no-leverage constraint may force all bullish trades to be flatteners, there is no reason to also require all bearish trades to be steepeners. Rather than overweighting the short half of the index to reflect a bearish view, one can reduce exposure across the curve. Second, we note that the problem is not so much with the inclusion of a slope exposure per se, but the inclusion of an *unintended* slope exposure. If the duration-positioning decision can be made to include skilled consideration of the slope exposure implications as well, the problem can be avoided. Third, in the case of a pure view on directionality of rates, a manager using the cash-neutral strategy should focus specifically on predicting changes in the 10-year rate rather than on predicting the direction of parallel shift across the curve.

2. Similar effects can be accomplished with structured notes that are designed to reward specific types of yield curve movements. The use of structured notes allows managers to express any view on the curve they desire. The cost of the constraint in this case may be simply the increased cost of customized structured notes rather than standard derivatives like futures.

INDEX REPLICATION

Investors use benchmarks almost universally to communicate to managers the desired risk characteristics of a portfolio and to measure its performance. The widespread acceptance of modern portfolio theory increased the desire for broad-based passive strategies to capture the "market portfolio," which in turn increased demand for indexation strategies.[1] While some investors complain about the "tyranny of the benchmark," many others recognize that portfolios constructed to perform in line with a benchmark have some advantages. Such portfolios offer diversification through exposure to multiple sectors, low issuer-specific risk, consistency of returns vs. the benchmark, and the possibility for investors to increase their focus on asset allocation. However, much of the recent interest in tracking benchmark returns has arisen to meet a number of different objectives for which replication rather than passive indexation is a more appropriate strategy.

Indexation and index replication differ in both objectives and implementation:

Investment Style	Objectives	Instruments	Methodology
Passive indexation	Very low tracking error	Cash securities	Stratified sampling and/or tracking error minimization
Index replication within a broader strategy	Low tracking error Low transaction costs High liquidity	Cash securities Derivative instruments	Exposure matching

---

1. In a strict sense, the market portfolio comprises all (fixed-income) instruments, whereas the most widely used indices do not capture all fixed-income instruments. The Lehman Universal Index is the most comprehensive index of U.S. dollar-denominated instruments, covering high yield and emerging market instruments in addition to U.S. investment-grade fixed-income securities, while the Lehman Multiverse is a similarly comprehensive index of global fixed-income securities.

A passive manager strives to minimize tracking error (expected return deviation) against the chosen benchmark. Passive managers typically build portfolios of hundreds or even thousands of securities to track the performance of their benchmark as closely as possible. An index manager may use a variety of techniques to track the index, including stratified sampling (or "cell matching"), cash-flow matching, and tracking error minimization (or optimization). An exposure-matching approach aims to achieve a match between risk factor exposures of the portfolio and the benchmark (e.g., changes in yield curve level and shape, changes in implied volatilities, and credit spread fluctuations). Indexation is most appropriate for longer-term allocations to an asset class. Over a long period of time, the benefits of low tracking errors vs. the benchmark will be greater than the costs of assembling a portfolio of many cash bonds, some of which may be less liquid and carry higher transaction costs.

The aim of index replication is not to match exactly the performance of a given index, but rather to generate returns close to those of the index. The focus is on delivering low tracking error with minimal trading costs, using instruments with a high degree of liquidity. An indexation strategy comprises many securities, almost all of which are constituents of the index in question. A replication strategy typically comprises relatively few instruments, which may or may not be index constituents. Replication strategies can be formed using either cash or derivatives securities or a combination of the two. The choice is typically determined by the rationale for doing the replication and investor constraints; the latter may prohibit the use of some (or all) derivatives. In particular, interest-rate swaps, though a very liquid bond market instrument, require that counterparties execute legal agreements known as ISDAs,[2] which may encourage investors to use futures instead.

Apart from indexation and replication, there is an additional way to get exposure to fixed-income indices—through the use of total return index swaps. Under a total return swap, the investor is guaranteed to receive the total return on the index selected and pays the counterparty floating-rate LIBOR plus a spread to compensate the dealer for the risk in hedging the index exposure. Typically a total return swap on the Aggregate will trade only very infrequently and usually at sizes well below US$100 million. Accordingly, owing to their limited liquidity and higher transaction costs, total return swaps are appropriate for investors with a high degree of risk aversion or relatively long (6 months and longer) time horizons.

---

2. The International Swaps and Derivatives Association publishes a standard agreement for all swap transactions. The annexes to the agreements, which deal with collateral arrangements and events of default, are negotiated.

In many cases the particular purpose of the replication determines the choice of replication methodology. In the chapters in this section we describe approaches for replicating various indices, some with cash instruments and others with derivatives. The following table summarizes the various uses of replication strategies and the optimal choices of replication approach for each strategy:

Objective	Key Characteristics	Preferred Replication Strategy
Portable alpha	Use cash for alpha strategy Higher tolerance for tracking error	Derivatives
Manage a multisector portfolio	Alpha from <100% of portfolio's cash Alpha from 100% of portfolio's cash Constraints, or low risk tolerance	Cash securities Derivatives Cash securities
Tactical asset allocation	Preserve existing allocation to sectoral or regional managers	Derivatives
Transition management	Minimize transaction costs Minimize market impact	Derivatives
Management of inflows and outflows	Short time horizon Lag between trade/settlement date	Derivatives

PORTABLE ALPHA

Ironically, the recent substantial increase in demand for replication strategies has come largely from investors who are interested in risk taking rather than risk reduction. As yields have fallen in fixed-income markets and equity returns have moderated following the outsized gains of the 1990s, the search for alpha has become ever more critical. In particular, pension fund sponsors have become more interested in strategies that allow them to achieve twin objectives: increase fixed-income exposure (to better match pension liabilities) and generate returns in excess of the growth rate of liabilities. In many cases, pension funds have the Lehman Aggregate as their benchmark, so their sponsors may look to portable alpha strategies as a way of adding high excess returns to their fixed-income allocation.

Alpha can be defined as the return earned in excess of that generated from taking market exposure. The challenge for many investors who allocate assets to multiple active portfolio managers is to seek out managers who can consistently generate alpha. The manager who opportunistically allocates to high yield may generate outperformance that is positively correlated with, for example, an active equity manager. Performance of managers who generate "true" alpha should not be correlated. Then, owing to the diversification among managers, the investor can construct a portfolio that generates alpha with moderate active risk.

In the traditional asset management setting, an asset allocation target is established and one or more managers are selected for each asset class. However, many plan sponsors have discovered over the years that in some asset classes it is more difficult to find managers who can generate alpha. The more efficient the market, the more difficult it is to generate alpha. Therefore, some investors have begun to look for ways to separate the asset allocation decision from the manager selection. Since it is much more difficult to obtain alpha than beta (market exposure), it seems more sensible to start the asset management process by first finding alpha sources and worrying about the market exposure afterward, reversing the "traditional" approach. Imagine a pension plan sponsor who needs to have an allocation to fixed income but at the same time found an equity manager capable of generating alpha of 200 bp/year over the S&P 500. By selling S&P 500 stock index futures and buying some fixed-income derivative instruments, the plan sponsor can preserve the alpha but transform the market exposure from equity to fixed income, in a classic example of portable alpha.

A recent popular application of portable alpha is in the realm of hedge funds and fund-of-funds (henceforth "hedge funds"). Market-neutral hedge funds are often constructed to minimize market exposure. If they succeed, their returns are defined as "pure alpha." By transporting this alpha to a fixed-income target index, an investor can attain fixed-income returns plus hedge fund alpha. For some investors, this can be an attractive strategy compared to the alternative of hiring an active fixed-income manager.

How does an investor know whether a hedge fund return is alpha or beta? This question is particularly important when the hedge fund exposure is part of a broader portable alpha strategy, because if its return is highly correlated with the beta exposure, the overall market exposure may rise above the desired level. The minimal disclosure typically provided by hedge funds, coupled with investment mandates that allow leverage, short selling, derivatives, and illiquid securities make it challenging for investors to quantify market exposure. Style analysis, originally developed by William Sharpe[3] to analyze mutual funds, provides a solution.

Style analysis examines historical returns of a strategy by regressing them against a set of observable market risk factors (e.g., returns on small-cap U.S. equities) to determine which of these factors have been the main contributors to the returns. In

---

3. William Sharpe, "Determining a Fund's Effective Asset Mix," *Investment Management Review,* December 1988, pp. 59–69.

a separate study,[4] we suggested some modifications to Sharpe's original approach to account for the specific nature of hedge funds. For example, the short-selling constraint was relaxed and some market factors were added, including realized-vs.-implied volatility. Applying style analysis to hedge funds presents challenges: survivorship bias in the data, relatively short return time series, and a wide variety of market factors to consider in explaining funds' returns. We were able to find solutions to these problems and to decompose hedge fund returns into three elements: pure alpha, core market beta (exposure to factors specific to each group of funds), and market timing. All three elements were found to be statistically significant contributors to nonarbitrage hedge funds' returns.

For an investment advisory firm, a replication strategy can be valuable in that it allows it to offer a product where there is perceived to be a market need, but in which the manager lacks expertise. For example, a fixed-income manager may see rising demand for U.S. equity managers who can consistently outperform market indices with low levels of risk. By selling a replicating portfolio of derivatives (to eliminate the fixed-income beta) and buying, for example, stock index futures, the manager can create an equity product with a track record of outperformance from managing fixed-income portfolios.

In most portable alpha strategies, the desired market exposure (beta) is achieved using derivatives replication, in order to allow the cash to be utilized in the alpha strategy. So, for example, if a $100 million allocation is made to a hedge fund portable alpha strategy, $100 million is invested into the hedge fund and a derivatives portfolio is created to generate $100 million exposure to a desired fixed-income index. Tracking errors for derivatives replication strategies are typically higher than for cash replication strategies. Nevertheless, they are at sufficiently low levels compared to the alphas and volatilities of hedge funds.

INDEXING SOME SECTORS IN A MULTISECTOR PORTFOLIO

In the United States, the Lehman Aggregate Index has become the most popular benchmark for fixed-income portfolios. For fixed-income managers who specialize in one sector of the fixed-income markets (e.g., U.S. credit), replicating other sectors can allow them to offer a product benchmarked to the Lehman Aggregate Index. As broader indices have become more widely used (witness the increasing use of the Global Aggregate Index in preference to global government indices), investors have become more interested in replicating some components of these

---

4. "The Nature of Hedge Funds Alpha," in *Global Relative Value*, Lehman Brothers, March 20, 2006.

indices so that they can concentrate on generating alpha from sectors in their field of expertise.

In these cases, either a cash or a derivatives portfolio could be utilized. The choice of strategy will depend upon three main factors. First, the proportion of the overall mandate that is represented by the replicated index may dictate the tolerance for tracking error in the replication. The higher this proportion the lower the tolerance for risk. Second, the effectiveness of a derivatives replication strategy for that index may also determine the choice. Credit is the most difficult sector to replicate, and if it represents a sizable proportion of the index, it may be best to replicate it with cash instruments. Finally, investment constraints may simply prohibit the use of derivatives.

Why replicate a sector of a larger index with derivatives rather than cash instruments? An active manager is paid to generate outperformance. If cash instruments are used to replicate a given sector, it leaves less cash available for the alpha strategy. A sector can instead be replicated using derivatives, leaving 100% of the portfolio to be used for alpha generation, essentially a portable alpha strategy.

TACTICAL ASSET ALLOCATION

A replicating portfolio can also be employed effectively in asset allocation. A manager can express views on sectors most efficiently and cheaply using replication overlay strategies. A U.S. aggregate manager may wish to underweight credit given a medium-term bearish outlook for corporate bonds. The manager can express a negative view on credit more efficiently and cheaply by selling a portfolio of derivatives that replicate the credit index than by selling individual bond positions that may have taken months to accumulate. Moreover, the manager preserves the ability to generate alpha from name selection within the corporate bond portfolio.

Frequently, different teams of managers are responsible for regional components of the Global Aggregate Index, whereas a global investment committee is responsible for setting the allocations across regions. When this committee changes its regional allocations, it can upset the sector allocations within regions. For example, if an allocation is made from U.S. Treasuries to Bunds (in futures or cash instruments), it upsets the regional sectoral composition of the U.S. and euro portfolios. Using a derivatives replication overlay strategy (to short the U.S. Aggregate vs. the Euro Aggregate) preserves the separation between global and regional decisions.

TRANSITION MANAGEMENT

Another application of replication to asset allocation is its use in the management of transitions. A plan sponsor that has made a decision to reallocate assets from one asset class to another may have to wait weeks until the cash is first raised by the existing (legacy) manager and then fully invested by the new (target) manager. Thus, for various institutional and practical reasons, the period between the asset allocation decision and its execution can give rise to "implementation shortfall." If the managers involved are external, and the asset reallocation is significant, then one or more managers will likely be terminated. Investment advisory contracts typically specify a minimum notice period, perhaps 30 to 60 days. Over this period, the manager will be less concerned with the portfolio's performance than with its liquidation. Furthermore, the new manager will likely take some time to fully invest the portfolio. Therefore, the performance of the overall fund may suffer owing to the performance differences between the old and new asset classes (opportunity cost), underperformance of the portfolios vs. their benchmarks, and transaction costs.

Opportunity cost is frequently the largest cost in a "traditional" transition and one that can most easily be minimized. The period between the asset allocation decision and the execution of that decision can give rise to a substantial investment shortfall. As an example, the investment committee of a pension fund decides to make an allocation from U.S. equities (benchmarked to the S&P 500) to U.S. fixed-income (benchmarked to the Lehman Aggregate). If the reallocation does not occur for 60 days, the fund will be overexposed to equities and underexposed to bonds compared to its new desired asset allocation, which could give rise to a substantial opportunity cost.

In recent years, transition management has been a popular method for reducing implementation shortfall. A transition manager is hired to liquidate the legacy portfolio and purchase the target portfolio to minimize the overall costs of the transition. In order to reduce opportunity costs, either the sponsor or the transition manager can use replication strategies. In our example of a pension plan making an allocation from equities to fixed income, the plan sponsor could execute (or ask a transition manager to execute) a series of transactions designed to achieve the desired asset reallocation quickly and cheaply. This would be done by selling S&P 500 stock index futures and buying a replicating portfolio designed to track the Lehman Aggregate. As the legacy manager liquidates the equity portfolio and the target manager assembles the fixed-income portfolio, the derivatives positions are unwound. In this way, the plan sponsor's asset allocation can be changed as soon as the investment committee has made its decision, rather than being delayed by the transition process.

In a transition, the focus is on minimizing the overall implementation shortfall. Opportunity cost is an important component of the shortfall, but market impact costs can also be significant. In particular, for a large transition, managers must consider the trade-off between minimizing opportunity costs (by trading as quickly as possible) and spreading the trade over hours or days (to reduce market impact cost). It is possible to optimize this trade-off in order to minimize implementation shortfall.

Transitions will typically be largely complete within 1 week. During this time a replicating portfolio will be purchased and then sold; therefore, low-cost derivatives will be preferred to cash instruments. In many cases, cash is unavailable during much of the transition pending settlement of trades, so derivative instruments are the only choice. Finally, in the case of large transitions, using liquid derivatives minimizes market impact.

MANAGEMENT OF INFLOWS AND OUTFLOWS

Asset managers frequently have to deal with cash inflows and outflows in their portfolios, which can have a sizable impact on performance. For example, a pending large portfolio outflow may require that a manager liquidate some holdings a few days in advance of the actual outflow to allow for the settlement of transactions. If the liquidations are relatively large, the manager may wish to spread these over a period of days. During this period effective exposure to corporates and Treasuries is reduced, increasing the risk relative to the benchmark. A derivatives replication strategy allows the manager to retain market exposure in the portfolio between the date of notification and the settlement date of the cash outflow. As soon as the cash outflow occurs, the replication strategy is unwound. This process enables the investor to retain market exposure throughout the cash-generating process.

Cash inflows may be too small to deploy into cash securities, for example, in a credit portfolio. The manager could put these inflows into a short-term investment vehicle and structure a basket of derivatives (interest-rate swaps and CDX baskets) to gain synthetic exposure to the target index and maintain this exposure until there are enough cash inflows to consider buying credit securities. Alternatively, it may take some time to deploy cash inflows into desired credit issues, and a replicating basket can be used to maintain market exposure.

With the short time horizon and, in the case of outflows the gap between the trade and settlement dates, a derivatives replication strategy is preferred to cash replication.

REPLICATION WITH DERIVATIVE INSTRUMENTS

For all replication strategies, the most difficult exposure to replicate is the one to credit. In a Global Aggregate portfolio interest-rate swaps and/or futures can largely eliminate sources of term-structure risk, while mortgages purchased for future delivery (TBAs) can largely reduce mortgage spread risk. This still leaves exposure to movements in other sector spreads, the most volatile of which are credit spreads. The recent development of portfolio CDS instruments in the United States (CDX) and Europe (iTraxx) provides efficient, highly liquid instruments that can be used to gain exposure to credit spreads.

The chapters in this section present strategies for replicating the U.S. Aggregate Index (Chapter 4) and the Global Aggregate Index (Chapter 5) with derivative instruments and the High Yield Index (Chapter 7) and the Commercial Mortgage-Backed Securities Index (Chapter 8) with cash instruments. It is no accident that the broader indices are replicated with derivatives and the sector indices with cash instruments. For example, derivatives replication of the U.S. Credit Index generates monthly tracking error volatility above 20 bp/month. Therefore, a manager replicating that index by itself may prefer to use a proxy portfolio of cash instruments, which might generate lower tracking errors. In replicating a broader index, the tracking errors of the components of broad indices are often uncorrelated (and sometimes negatively correlated), which dampens the contribution of the Credit Index replication tracking error to the overall portfolio tracking error.

In replicating the U.S. Aggregate and the Global Aggregate indices, we examine the performance of various replication strategies using liquid derivatives and, in some cases, mortgage-backed securities for future delivery (replication of the MBS Index is explored in greater detail in Chapter 6). In both cases, tracking errors are acceptably low for most investors, which should reduce the concern that some managers have as they move toward embracing broader benchmarks. If they have little confidence in their ability to manage a given portion of a broad index, tracking one part of that index can certainly be accomplished without adding appreciably to active portfolio risk.

The replicating portfolios are constructed by matching the portfolio and benchmark risk factor. In order to be able to match the risk exposures exactly, it is necessary to have at least as many instruments as there are risk exposures. In this sense, interest-rate swaps are preferred to bond futures as hedging instruments, because one can select swaps along the whole maturity spectrum instead of being limited to the maturities of listed futures. Exposures to credit sectors are matched using spread duration.[5] When matching exposures, it is critical that the investor have analytics systems capable of computing accurately the sensitivities of both the

---

5. As an alternate methodology, we could have matched instead the duration times spread (DTS) measure, described in Chapter 34. While DTS is indeed a better measure of spread risk than spread duration, our empirical analysis suggests that its use does not significantly improve the performance of replicating portfolios over the study period.

index and the instruments in the replicating portfolio. This is particularly important for instruments with embedded optionality such as mortgage-backed securities (MBS) and futures.

For many global managers based outside the United States the inclusion of U.S. MBS in the Global Aggregate can make this broader index a somewhat daunting benchmark against which to manage. However, as we show in Chapter 6, it is straightforward to build a portfolio that can track the MBS index closely, with highly liquid instruments and without having to deal with all of the back-office work involved in processing principal prepayments. Indeed this strategy has proven very popular with European investors in particular.

REPLICATION WITH CASH INSTRUMENTS

For narrower indices, a derivatives replication strategy may not deliver acceptably low tracking errors. This may be due either to the nature of the asset class or to an investor's risk preferences. Cash replication may also be preferable owing to the existence of investment constraints or simply because cash is available for investment over a long time horizon. Here we present replication strategies for the U.S. High Yield and CMBS indices, but the same approaches can also be used to replicate broader indices.

Derivatives strategies work well when a high proportion of the volatility of a given asset class is explained by market risk, since derivatives portfolios can be constructed to match market exposures. However, in the case of high yield, idiosyncratic (issuer and issue-specific) risk is a substantial component of overall risk and cannot easily be replicated with derivatives. While high yield CDX instruments exist, the distribution of issuers and their concentrations is very different compared to the High Yield Index. There is also substantial volatility in the spread basis between high yield cash and CDS instruments. Together these factors make it impossible for a derivatives-only replication strategy to track the indices effectively. Therefore, an investor who wishes to replicate the High Yield Index with moderate tracking error will have to build a portfolio of cash bonds.

The rationale for replicating the CMBS Index with cash instruments is somewhat different. CMBS represents 3.6% of the U.S. Aggregate Index, too large to ignore, but perhaps, in the eyes of many managers, too small to warrant meaningful deployment of research resources. Interest-rate swaps may be used to replicate the index adequately when spreads are stable. At other times, or when investment guidelines prohibit derivatives, cash replication will be preferable.

Replicating portfolios of cash instruments can be generated using various methods. The approach we use in the cash replications presented here is stratified sampling. This sorts each issue in the index into "cells" according to various characteristics that are believed to impact returns of the relevant index. For credit, these might be sector and rating. At least one bond is then chosen from each "cell" and weighted (by market value or spread duration contribution)[6] in the portfolio to match the cell's weight in the index. To create a liquid, tradable "proxy portfolio," we choose the larger issues in any given cell. The more granular the "bucketing" of the index, the more issues will be chosen for the replicating portfolio, which could ultimately lead to a full indexation with hundreds or thousands of holdings. The advantage of this approach is its simplicity and flexibility. The disadvantage is that it ignores the correlations among cells. For example, an overweight in the A-rated banking sector may be offset by an underweight in A-rated insurance or BBB-rated telecoms. In the former case, the impact on risk is minimal, but in the latter, it could be substantial. A stratified sampling approach is "blind" to the relationships among cells, but this can be remedied by complementing a stratified sampling approach with the use of an optimizer (which accounts for such correlations), which is the approach taken in the MBS replication (Chapter 6).

More broadly, cells into which a portfolio manager partitions an index for sampling represent this manager's view of common risk factors affecting a given market. In Chapter 26 we introduce a multifactor risk model that uses a predetermined set of risk factors within each asset class and fully accounts for correlations among them based on historical calibration. It projects tracking error volatility (TEV)—return deviation between a portfolio and an index. To achieve index replication a manager would have to minimize the expected TEV by selecting a certain number of securities in the replicating portfolio. Practitioners generally use stratified sampling techniques with cells of their choice and risk model optimizations together. This combination allows them to consider the correlations among cells or risk factors and yet avoid blind reliance on them.

The widespread use of broad domestic and global indices presents challenges for investors who must allocate their scarce research resources across multiple sectors. The use of replication strategies allows investors to neutralize their active risk exposures to one or more sectors and concentrate their resources in those sectors in which they possess the greatest expertise. Alternatively, the use of proxy portfolios allows a manager to begin with an indexed portfolio and change only a small number of holdings. This strategy can be of great benefit to a manager

---

6. Matching market value or spread duration exposure of a given cell is the traditional approach used in stratified sampling. In Chapter 34 we advocate matching cell contributions to DTS when sampling securities for credit index replication.

overseeing credit portfolios with limited resources. Finally, replication strategies allow investors to transform alphas from multiple sources to create fixed-income exposures.

In the two chapters that follow we describe approaches to replicating the U.S. Aggregate and Global Aggregate bond indices. To avoid unnecessary repetition, the general description of replication techniques and derivative instruments these techniques use is provided only in the first chapter.

4. Replicating the Lehman Brothers U.S. Aggregate Index with Liquid Instruments

There are various methods for replicating the U.S. Aggregate Index and its sub-indices. In this chapter, we present the outcomes of historical simulation of different approaches and quantify the risk of each. In a real-life situation, the method of choice will not necessarily be the one promising the lowest tracking error vs. the index. Other factors and constraints will influence the decision.

SOURCES OF RISK IN THE LEHMAN BROTHERS U.S. AGGREGATE INDEX

In considering the merits of various replication strategies, we start with an examination of the sources of volatility in the U.S. Aggregate Index. Figure 4-1 shows output from the Lehman Brothers risk model, which breaks down the sources of risk for the Lehman Brothers Aggregate Index and various subcomponents.[1]

The Lehman Brothers multifactor risk model quantifies the ex ante tracking error volatility (the expected volatility of the return deviation) of a portfolio vs. its benchmark or the absolute volatility of a portfolio or index. The model is based on the historical returns of individual securities in the Lehman Brothers bond indices, in many instances dating back over more than a decade. The model derives historical magnitudes of different market risk factors and the relationships among them. It then measures current mismatches between the portfolio and benchmark sensitivities to these risks and multiplies these mismatches by historical volatilities and correlations ("covariance matrix") to produce its output.

Although tracking error volatility (TEV) is a measure of volatility, it can also be used (with caution) to make forecasts of the likely distribution of future relative

Based on research first published by Lehman Brothers in 2004.
  1. A detailed description of the Lehman Brothers risk model is provided in Chapter 26.

Figure 4-1. Sources of Risk in the Lehman Brothers Indices
As of July 2004

Global Risk Factor	U.S. Aggregate (bp/month)	U.S. Treasury (bp/month)	U.S. MBS (bp/month)	U.S. Credit (bp/month)
Yield curve	150.03	141.78	77.65	150.91
Swap spreads	19.73		18.01	33.88
Volatility	7.34	0.06	10.33	0.3
Investment-grade spreads	19.02	7.4	22.01	57.01
Treasury spreads	0.79	7.4		
Credit and agency spreads	15.76			57.01
MBS/securitized	7.81		22.01	
CMBS/ABS	0.89			
Systematic risk	146.79	139.36	80.43	145.75
Idiosyncratic risk	2.74	0.61	2.83	7.89
Total risk (bp/month)	146.81	139.36	80.48	145.96

returns. For example, assuming that returns are normally distributed, a portfolio with a TEV of 25 bp/month would be expected to have a return within ±25 bp/month around the expected return difference between the portfolio and benchmark approximately two-thirds of the time (and underperformance of worse than –25 bp relative to the expected return difference one-sixth of the time).

The total volatility of a given index reflects the risk owing to exposure to various risk factors and correlations among risk factors. Accordingly, the volatilities are not additive. The expected volatility of a given index can be expressed as a function of its exposures to risk factors and the volatility of those factors. The Credit Index (or an individual credit security) will be exposed to term structure risk, swap spread risk, credit spread risk (together, "systematic risk"), and idiosyncratic risk.

The risk characteristics of a given index determine which instruments can best replicate it. For all U.S. investment-grade fixed-income indices, term structure is by far the dominant source of risk. Therefore, a portfolio of Treasury futures, matched as closely as possible to the duration characteristics of the relevant index, should be able to attain a reasonable replication "result." For mortgage-backed securities, swap spread risk is almost as important as MBS spread risk. Therefore, we would expect that receiving fixed on interest-rate swaps would achieve a better replication result than using Treasury futures. For credit, while swaps would also be expected to achieve improved replication, additional instruments would be

**Figure 4-2. Decisions in Forming
a Replication Strategy with
Derivative Instruments**

Instruments
- Bond futures
- Interest-rate futures
- Interest-rate swaps
- Mortgage TBAs
- Credit default swaps

Replication Techniques
- Stratified sampling (cell matching)
- Key-rate duration matching
- Minimum variance hedge

needed to reduce credit spread risk in order to achieve replication results closer to those of other sectors.

FORMING A DERIVATIVES REPLICATION STRATEGY

Our examination of the sources of risk in various indices suggests that a replicating portfolio that matches the systematic exposure of these indices would achieve reasonable results in delivering acceptably low levels of tracking error. However, we have two categories of choices in building such a portfolio: a choice of instruments (pick any or all) and a choice of replication technique (pick one), as shown in Figure 4-2.

There are three main approaches to replication:

- The *stratified sampling* approach divides the index into duration cells. A derivative instrument is selected for each cell in an amount to match the duration exposure of that cell.

- The *key-rate duration* (KRD) approach matches the key-rate duration profile of the index. KRDs measure sensitivities to shifts at specific "key-rate" points along the yield curve (and can therefore measure the effect of non-parallel yield curve shifts). In contrast, a "conventional" duration measures sensitivity to parallel shifts.

- The *minimum-variance hedge* approach, with the help of a risk model, seeks to minimize the predicted tracking error of a replicating portfolio

Figure 4-3. Key-Rate Durations of Treasury Futures Contracts
As of August 31, 20004

Contract	6-Month KRD	2-Year KRD	5-Year KRD	10-Year KRD	20-Year KRD	30-Year KRD
2-year	−0.07	1.97	0.06	0.00	0.00	0.00
5-year	0.00	0.70	3.55	0.00	0.00	0.00
10-year	0.01	0.05	3.41	2.85	0.00	0.00
Long bond	0.01	0.05	0.23	2.65	8.16	0.61

against its index. Therefore, the replicating portfolio reflects the correlations between sectors and instruments in the portfolio and index, for example, between corporate and government bonds.

In the past, we used the stratified sampling approach in our replication studies. However, since 2001, we have been computing KRDs, which we found provide a modest improvement in tracking errors relative to stratified sampling. The regression hedge approach is more model-driven and less transparent than the other two; furthermore, it relies on the relationships among different risk factors—for example, between term structure movements and credit spread changes, which change over time. Accordingly, in this chapter, we examine the performance of various replication strategies using the KRD-matching approach.

The Lehman Brothers yield curve model includes six key rates (Figure 4-3). In some cases, however, we have fewer than six instruments available for our replication (e.g., replication with Treasury futures, for which we have only four separate instruments). Accordingly, it is not possible to match all six key-rate durations.

REPLICATION STRATEGIES

Replication with Treasury Futures

The number of bond futures contracts available—the 2-year, 5-year, 10-year, and long contracts—is not sufficient to achieve a perfect match of the six KRDs in the Lehman Brothers yield curve model. We consider two possible choices in dealing with this issue.

First, an optimization can be established to minimize the sum of the squared differences between the respective index and the replicating portfolio KRDs. However, we choose a second method—reducing the number of key rates to equal the number of available instruments by combining the 6-month and 2-year and the 20- and 30-year KRDs in order to achieve a perfect match. As Figure 4-3 demonstrates, the KRD exposure of the bond futures contracts is minimal for the 6-month rate, while only the long bond contract has any exposure to the 20- or 30-year rate. Nevertheless, there will still be an unavoidable mismatch between the duration exposure of the futures-replicating portfolio and the Aggregate Index. We can match the sum of the KRDs of the 20- and 30-year vertices with a single instrument, but we cannot match the KRD exposure of the two vertices separately.

Replication with Interest Rate Swaps

The fixed-rate leg of an interest-rate swap represents the average of forward rates, which reflect the credit quality of the panel of banks that set the LIBOR rates. Therefore, the pricing of interest-rate swaps reflects a credit risk premium and their spread to Treasuries also reflects a liquidity premium. Accordingly, receiving the fixed component of an interest-rate swap would be expected to provide a better alternative to replicating the returns of non-Treasury components of the Aggregate Index. In addition, since the swap curve is effectively continuous, we can select six instruments to match exactly the KRD profile of the Aggregate Index.

The historical relationships between yields on various indices and on portfolios of duration-matched interest-rate swaps can be examined using the Lehman Brothers Mirror Swap indices.[2] Moreover, for investors who do not wish to enter into several interest-rate swaps, Lehman Brothers offers a total-return swap on various Mirror Swap indices. This also eliminates the need to rebalance the portfolio to bring duration exposures back into line as the index changes from month to month and swap instruments age.

Replication with Futures and Interest Rate Swaps

An obvious extension of the futures and swaps replication is to use Treasury futures to replicate the Treasury sector and swaps to replicate the non-Treasury sectors. In this strategy, we eliminate the term-structure replication error of the Treasury component using swaps (see earlier).

Replication of the MBS Index with TBAs

Mortgage-backed securities (MBS) represent a large component of the Aggregate Index. The availability of liquid instruments to replicate the index and a

---

2. The Mirror Swap Index is a portfolio of interest-rate swaps (receiving fixed) constructed to match the key-rate duration profiles of various Lehman Brothers indices. For more details, see Chapter 11.

straightforward method for doing so suggest that such an approach should not greatly increase the complexity relative to a futures-only or swaps-only replication. Although futures and swaps can replicate the yield curve exposures of the MBS Index, they leave exposure to MBS spread, prepayment, and volatility effects. Using a mortgage product can improve the replication considerably by hedging these exposures as well. TBAs offer two key advantages over MBS pools in replication strategies: (1) they are suitable for an unfunded strategy without cash outlays because a TBA is simply rolled from month to month prior to settlement; and (2) the back-office aspects of investing in mortgages are much simpler for TBAs than for pools because monthly interest payments and principal paydowns are avoided. The remaining risk in a TBA replication is essentially due to the difference in risk characteristics between new and seasoned mortgages (see Chapter 6).

Replication of the Credit Index with CDS and Interest-Rate Swaps

Interest-rate swap spreads are at times highly correlated with credit spreads, but there have been extended periods during which this relationship has broken down. In such periods, LIBOR spreads have typically remained quite stable, whereas credit spreads have been quite volatile. For example, Figure 4-4 shows that 2002 was a period of great volatility for credit spreads, whereas swap spreads, as measured by the Mirror Swap Credit Index, were relatively stable.

Portfolio credit default swap (CDS) baskets now provide a very liquid instrument that investors can use to take a long (or short) position in credit. Credit yields can be broken down into two constituents: the swap yield and a credit spread to swaps. Accordingly, we can match the exposure of credit to movements in swap yields using interest-rate swaps and the exposure to movements in LIBOR credit spreads by using CDS. The widely traded CDX.IG products are baskets of 125 equally weighted CDS available in 5- and 10-year maturities. In our analysis, we combine 5- and 10-year CDX in proportions sufficient to match the spread duration and yield of the Credit Index.[3]

Since these instruments have been available only since October 2003, a period of stable credit spreads, we cannot easily gauge the benefits of including them in a credit index replication strategy. Therefore, we supplemented the CDX data by valuing portfolios of CDS instruments constructed from the issuers that composed the CDX basket as of October 2003 for the period June 2002 to September 2003.

---

3. Various alternative weighting schemes could have been used for CDX instruments, including matching the spread of the combined CDX portfolio to the LIBOR spread of the Credit Index or matching the duration times spread or DTS (see Chapter 34 for details), but, over the study period, both schemes lead to much more unstable allocations between CDX instruments and, in some cases, short positions.

Option-Adjusted Spread

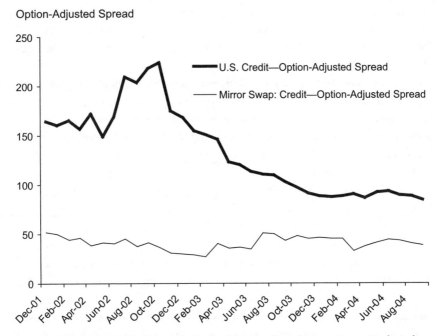

Figure 4-4. Option-Adjusted Spreads for the U.S. Credit and Mirror Swap Credit Index

We would caution that this introduces a look-forward bias. CDX.IG by construction comprises investment-grade-only issuers. In constructing a basket in October 2003 valued back to July 2002, we are certain to avoid some issuers that may have been included in a basket actually constructed in 2002 and were downgraded since. The large number of names in the basket (125) should mitigate this risk.[4] The period under review was admittedly one in which there were very few "fallen angels." We note that in addition to the basis risk that exists between CDS and credit, there is an additional basis between CDX and the underlying CDS that is not modeled in our supplemental study, but we do not believe that its presence materially altered the outcome.

PERFORMANCE SUMMARY OF REPLICATION STRATEGIES

The key metric by which we measure the performance of various replication strategies is realized TEV. This is preferable to using average outperformance and

---

4. During the period, EP and AHOLD were investment-grade issuers that were downgraded to high yield but might have been included in a CDS basket. They represented 0.4 and 0.1% of the Credit Index, respectively, in the month prior to downgrade.

underperformance for several reasons. The volatility of returns tends to be much more persistent than the returns themselves; that is, history is a much better guide for predicting volatility than for predicting return. It is also not likely that a period of substantial underperformance of a given replication strategy will persist, since this would imply a secular cheapening in a group of highly liquid derivative instruments or a secular trend in credit or MBS spreads. Finally, the objective of any replication strategy is to replicate the index, not outperform. Outperformance is what active managers are paid for. Nevertheless, we report mean outperformance of each replicating strategy to give a flavor for the degrees of out- and underperformance.

Figure 4-5 shows the results of replicating the Lehman Brothers Aggregate Index and selected subindices using the approaches outlined above. The replication of the Treasury Index with Treasury futures achieves an acceptable TEV of 10.4 bp/month. We find that over this period, the futures portfolio outperformed the Treasury Index. Interestingly, this is consistent with prior studies that found mean outperformance of 3.1 bp/month over three separate time periods.[5] This reflects two effects. We assume in our replication that cash is invested at LIBOR, which over the past 2 years has had a 1.8 bp/month higher yield than Treasury bills. The residual outperformance suggests that the premium that long futures positions enjoy for being short the cash bond delivery option has been "too large" over these periods (see later for more discussion of the delivery option).

As expected, Treasury futures fare less well as instruments with which to replicate the MBS and Credit indices. Term structure risk is reduced, but spread risk remains. In prior studies, we found that interest-rate swaps delivered measurable reductions in tracking error volatility compared with Treasury futures when replicating the MBS and Credit indices. In the most recent period, however, we note that while swaps deliver lower TEV against the Credit Index, they have a higher TEV for replication of the MBS Index compared with Treasury futures.

Figure 4-6 shows that there has been a close relationship between mortgage spreads and swap spreads, so it might seem that swaps should have performed better than futures. The replication results suggest, however, that other factors are responsible for this effect. In recent years, swaps have been a favored tool for the convexity hedging[6] of MBS securities, so swap spreads have tended to behave

---

5. See Lev Dynkin, Jay Hyman, and Peter Lindner, "Hedging and Replication of Fixed Income Portfolios," *Journal of Fixed Income,* March 2002.

6. To hedge the interest-rate sensitivity of a fixed-income security, investors sell hedging instruments, for example, Treasury futures or swaps. The interest-rate sensitivity of negatively convex securities such as MBS typically moves faster than that of a hedging instrument and in the opposite direction. Convexity hedging refers to rather aggressive (and more expensive) hedge

Figure 4-5. Index Replication Results

August 2002–September 2004

Replication Method	Mean Outperformance (bp/month)	Tracking Error Volatility (bp/month)	R^2
U.S. Treasury Index Replication			
Treasury futures	4.5	10.4	0.997
U.S. MBS Index Replication			
Treasury futures	1.2	35.3	0.811
Interest-rate swaps	−1.8	38.5	0.775
TBAs	0.3	4.3	0.997
U.S. Credit Index Replication			
Treasury futures	−25.1	62.7	0.878
Interest-rate swaps	−26.9	57.8	0.896
Interest-rate swaps+ CDX	2.5	29.1	0.974
U.S Aggregate Index Replication			
Treasury futures	−5.2	22.7	0.972
Interest-rate swaps	−7.4	17.5	0.983
Futures + swaps	−7.1	17.3	0.983
Futures + swaps + TBAs	−6.1	16.9	0.984
Futures + swaps + CDX	0.7	10.9	0.994
Futures + swaps + TBAs + CDX	1.6	9.4	0.995

directionally, tightening as Treasury yields fall and widening as they rise. Therefore, using swaps in a replication in place of Treasury futures may increase the effective duration mismatch of the replication strategy. An additional factor is the optionality of MBS and futures. A buyer of futures is short a delivery option.[7] The seller has the option to deliver one of a basket of cash securities to the buyer. Therefore, the futures buyer is short interest-rate volatility, as is the MBS buyer. A combination of swaps and swaptions would benefit from the correlation of swaps

---

adjustments that necessitate selling more of a hedging instrument when prices are falling while buying more of it when prices are rising.

7. There are actually several delivery options and the value of all of them is positively affected by interest-rate volatility. A detailed exposition of the various delivery options is beyond the scope of this chapter.

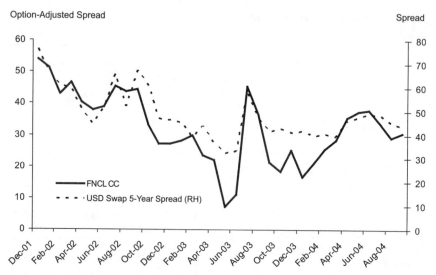

Figure 4-6. Option-Adjusted Spread of Current Coupon FNMA 30-Year MBS vs. 5-Year Swap Spread

with MBS, as well as the exposure to interest-rate volatility, but that discussion is beyond the scope of this chapter.

Interest-rate swaps improve upon the replication of the Credit Index with futures given the credit exposure embedded in interest-rate swaps. Figure 4-4 shows that swap spreads have been relatively stable during a period of volatility in credit spreads. The sharp contraction in credit spreads caused significant underperformance in return terms of futures and swaps replications relative to the Credit Index. While swap spreads and credit spreads have been relatively stable since the fourth quarter of 2003, the period prior to that was far from stable.

The use of CDX in the replication, not surprisingly, improves upon the replication with swaps alone. As Figure 4-7 shows, CDS spreads tracked credit spreads closely over this period. We also see that the relative advantage of CDS, compared to swaps alone, was much greater during the earlier period of volatility.

Figure 4-8 demonstrates that the tracking error of the swaps-only strategy was more than twice as large as that of the swaps-plus-CDS strategy during the period of greater spread volatility. An additional benefit of CDS is the greater carry earned by the portfolio. In return for accepting default risk (which is also present in the Credit Index), the investor earns that incremental carry. As long as CDS spreads are sufficient to offset default losses, CDS will increase expected return and reduce risk.

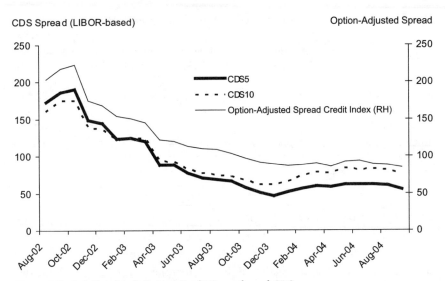

Figure 4-7. Relationship between Credit Spreads and CDS

Bringing together all of the various replication strategies in Figure 4-5d, we can see how the tracking error of the Aggregate Index improves as we add more replicating instruments. The most notable improvement would seem to be adding CDS, which reduced the volatility by 6.5–7.3 bp. Intriguingly, while TBAs are greatly superior to other methods in replicating the MBS Index by itself (4.3 bp TEV vs. 35.3 bp for replication with futures), TBAs do not greatly improve the replication of the Aggregate Index. Figure 4-9 gives us some insight into this result.

Comparing the first two lines in the correlation matrix, we find a substantial negative correlation between the MBS replication with swaps and the Treasury replication with futures. There is a smaller, positive correlation between the MBS replication with TBAs and the futures replication. This reflects the volatility effect highlighted earlier. In an environment of rising interest-rate volatility, futures would be expected to underperform cash Treasuries and swaps would

Figure 4-8. Credit Index Replication Tracking Error Volatility in Two Different Subperiods

	Tracking Error Volatility (bp/month)		
	8/02–9/03	10/03–9/04	Total Period
Swaps only	75.9	22.6	57.8
Swaps + CDS	34.7	19.0	29.1

Figure 4-9. Correlations of Realized Return Differentials of Replicating Strategies

	Swaps for MBS	TBAs for MBS	Futures for UST	Swaps for Credit
Swaps for MBS	1.000	−0.533	−0.732	−0.268
TBAs for MBS	−0.533	1.000	0.343	0.156
Futures for UST	−0.732	0.343	1.000	0.364
Swaps for credit	−0.268	0.156	0.364	1.000

outperform MBS (i.e., strong negative correlation). In that same environment, TBAs would tend to underperform the MBS Index (i.e., weak positive correlation) as TBAs tend to have higher-volatility exposures than the more seasoned issues in the index. The correlation of the credit replication strategy with the two MBS replication strategies is also notably different. Rising interest-rate volatility causes swaps to outperform MBS, whereas convexity hedging causes them to underperform credit, demonstrating a negative correlation between the MBS-with-swaps replication and the credit-with-swaps replication.

An example of this can be seen in Figure 4-10a, which plots the return difference to benchmark of various replication strategies. In July 2003, the Aggregate Index fell by 3.36%, as yields rose 94 bp. Swap spreads widened, causing swaps to underperform duration-matched Treasuries, although they outperformed MBS. Swaps replicating portfolios for both the Credit and Aggregate indices substantially underperformed, so we see a negative correlation between these replication strategies and the MBS replication-with-swaps strategy. During this same month, the TBA replication strategy also underperformed, a positive correlation with the non-MBS replication strategies. Thus, a swaps replication strategy for MBS, while notably inferior for replicating mortgages in isolation, is little different from TBA replication as part of an Aggregate Index replication strategy.

Figure 4-10b demonstrates that the return differential of the full aggregate replication strategy is driven by the performance of the Credit Index replication. Indeed, 91% of the volatility of the aggregate replication strategy over this period can be explained by the Credit Index replication (as measured by R^2).

In some cases the replication errors of various strategies can be explained by the presence of a risk factor in the index that is not reflected in the replicating portfolio. For example, the futures replication of the Aggregate Index attempts to replicate its term structure exposure, but cannot replicate its credit exposure. Not surprisingly, as Figure 4-11 shows, the realized return differential of the futures portfolio to the Aggregate Index is highly correlated with changes in credit spreads.

Return Difference (bp)

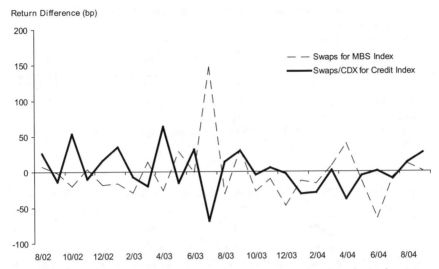

Figure 4-10a. Realized Return Differences of MBS Replication and Credit Replication

On the other hand, the return differential of the "full replication" strategy is not correlated with credit spreads.

These findings have important implications for the choice of replication strategy. Considered in isolation and given investor risk preferences, the choice of strategy may be clear. However, if this replication strategy is part of a larger port-folio, the relationship between the return difference of a given replication strategy

Return Difference (bp)

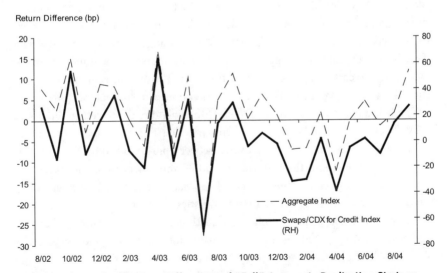

Figure 4-10b. Realized Return Differences of "Full" Aggregate Replication Strategy

Figure 4-11. Correlation of Selected Aggregate Replication Strategies with Credit Spreads and Equities

	Futures Replication	"Full" Replication[a]
Correlation with change in OAS Credit Index	−0.847	0.065
Correlation with change in S&P 500 Index	−0.505	0.047

[a]Replication with futures, swaps, TBAs, and CDX.

and the returns of other portfolio assets must be considered. For example, an investor with sizable equity exposure may prefer a fixed-income replication strategy using only futures, given the negative correlation with equity returns shown in Figure 4-11. Falling equity prices have been correlated with rising credit spreads and, therefore, with excess returns to a credit replication strategy with bond futures (and swaps).

USING A RISK MODEL TO FORECAST REPLICATION RISK

While an empirical analysis is valuable in forecasting the likely tracking errors of various replication strategies, there are some drawbacks to this approach. Most important, the weightings and characteristics of the sectors within the Lehman Aggregate Index change over time, which affects the relative success of each index replication strategy. Figure 4-12 shows that the sectoral distribution of the Aggregate Index has changed markedly over time. We have previously seen that credit spreads are the dominant source of risk in replication strategies. Accordingly, we would expect that replication performance would change depending on the weight of credit instruments in the aggregate. There may, therefore, be some bias introduced into forecasts of aggregate replication TEV by differences in the characteristics of the index over time. The use of a risk model can eliminate such biases.

The Lehman global risk model forecasts the volatility of the return difference (TEV) between a portfolio and its benchmark. The TEV uses the current index weights and the current relative exposures between portfolio and benchmark (e.g., key-rate durations) and the historic volatilities and correlations of risk factors (e.g., yield changes). Hence, the risk model approach generates a TEV forecast that is independent of changes in index characteristics over time.

Figure 4-13 looks at three replicating portfolios created to track the Lehman Aggregate for August 2004, using only Treasury futures; futures and swaps; and a combination of futures, swaps, and TBAs. In each case, the forecast TEV is within 1–2 bp of the empirically achieved result. The risk model covariance matrix is

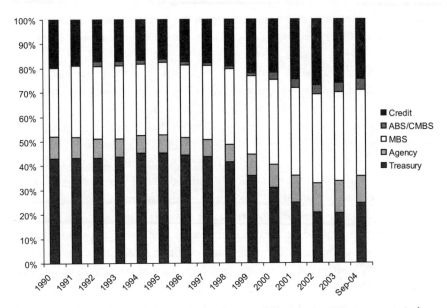

Figure 4-12. Changes in the Sectoral Distribution of the Lehman U.S. Aggregate Index over Time

Figure 4-13. Sources of Risk (Factor Volatilities) in the Lehman Aggregate and Replicating Strategies
Exponentially Weighted Covariance Matrix

Risk Factor	Sources of Tracking Error Volatility (bp/month)			
	Lehman Aggregate	Treasury Futures	Futures + Swaps	Futures + Swaps + TBAs
Yield curve	150.0	3.2	6.0	2.7
Swap spreads	19.7	19.7	1.8	0.8
Volatility	7.3	7.3	7.3	0.4
Investment-grade spreads	19.0	19.0	19.0	16.5
Treasury spreads	0.8	0.8	0.8	0.8
Credit and agency spreads	15.8	15.8	15.8	15.8
MBS/securitized	7.8	7.8	7.8	0.9
CMBS/ABS	0.9	0.9	0.9	0.9
Systematic risk	146.8	23.1	19.3	16.0
Idiosyncratic risk	2.7	6.4	3.1	3.3
Total risk	146.8	24.0	19.6	16.3
Empirically derived risk	N/A	22.7	17.3	16.9

constructed from many months of data, which greatly increases the confidence in the forecast TEV suggested by our empirical results, accumulated over 25 monthly observations.

The risk model output is also valuable for the insight into the risks that are reduced through various replication strategies, as well as quantifying the exposures and risk factor volatilities that remain. In Figure 4-13, we see the importance of yield curve risk as part of the overall volatility of the Lehman Aggregate. Each replication strategy largely eliminates this source of risk, leaving other risk exposures. The risk of the futures replication strategy is, not surprisingly, dominated by credit and agency spread risk, while MBS spread risk and volatility risk (which largely reflects the optionality of MBS) are also significant. Interestingly, using futures introduces idiosyncratic risk, reflecting the basis risk between cash and futures instruments. Spread risk factors are expressed relative to swaps, with the exception of Treasuries. Therefore, replicating credit or MBS using swaps reduces the forecast TEV attributable to swaps spreads, but leaves the TEV attributable to credit and MBS spreads unchanged.

Compared to using swaps, the risk model forecasts a reduction in TEV of 3.3 bp when using TBAs to replicate the MBS portion of the Aggregate. Our empirical analysis showed a reduction of only 0.4 bp, however, which indicates the closer correlation between swaps and MBS during the past 2 years than over the longer period to which the risk model was calibrated. This increased correlation caused swaps to "perform" almost as well as TBAs over the period of our empirical study. Using both empirical analysis and a risk model to forecast replication tracking errors allows investors to view the effect of changes in correlations between instruments.[8]

The replication with futures, swaps, and TBAs is dominated by credit spread risk. Therefore, CDS improve the replication, as is indicated by our empirical results.

RBI^{SM} BASKETS

The establishment of a replication strategy requires sophisticated analytics to compute the correct quantities of each derivative instrument. The replicating portfolio has to be rebalanced regularly to continue to track the target benchmark. Whereas some investors are willing to do it themselves, many more would prefer to get synthetic index exposure without having to manage a full-blown replicating

---

8. Using an exponentially weighted or a simple-weighted covariance matrix for ex ante tracking errors can also allow for the impact of changing correlations on TEV.

portfolio (implying a lengthy list of derivative trades). It is for that reason that Replicating Bond Index (RBI)[9] baskets were created.

RBI baskets are portfolios of derivative instruments, designed to track a fixed-income index. A set of predefined rules is applied at the beginning of each month to create an RBI basket, in much the same way that portfolios of derivatives were created in our historical simulations. RBI baskets can be created for published Lehman indices[10] or for custom indices and may use a variety of replicating instruments (interest-rate swaps, Treasury futures, currency forwards, CDX, or iTraxx baskets of credit default swaps). For example, U.S. Aggregate RBI basket Series 1 includes both interest-rate swaps and CDX, while RBI basket Series 2 does not include CDX.

An investor can enter into a total return swap on an RBI basket, where the receiver earns the basket total return[11] (dollar return depends on the swap's notional value) and pays LIBOR plus or minus a spread. Thus the investor receives the return on a replication strategy without having to manage the replication portfolio.

Traders can hedge RBI swaps easily with liquid derivatives. As a result, there are virtually no limitations on size and tenor of an RBI swap while difficult-to-hedge index total return swaps are offered only in limited sizes and for just a few tenors. For investors seeking synthetic exposure to an index and willing to tolerate modest deviations from the index returns, RBI baskets offer an attractive alternative.

MINIMIZING THE CARRY DRAG OF REPLICATION STRATEGIES

Entering into a receiver RBI swap does not deliver the exact Aggregate Index performance. First, the RBI basket may outperform or underperform the Aggregate because of an imperfect match in their risk exposures. Second, the other side of the RBI swap involves paying LIBOR plus or minus a spread. This spread can be a performance drag for the replication strategy. For example, if the spread is quoted at LIBOR + 15 bp, the investor would have to earn extra LIBOR + 15 bp to match the Aggregate's total return, even if the RBI basket's return exactly matches the Aggregate's return.

Consequently, combining a receiver RBI swap with a cash investment in LIBOR (LIBID) is a strategy that is unlikely to outperform the Aggregate. In this section we consider a realistic strategy long used by MBS investors who roll TBA positions

---

9. RBI is a service mark of Lehman Brothers, patent pending.

10. There are RBI baskets for such Lehman indices as Global Aggregate, Global Aggregate ex-USD, Euro Aggregate, Pan-Euro Aggregate, Euro Corporate, and Yen Aggregate.

11. The *Quantitative Portfolio Strategies Group* page on *LehmanLive* website maintains performance monitors for various RBI baskets. The site also provides daily data for the RBI series back to April 1, 2005.

to reduce the performance drag of the replication strategy: invest cash in floating-rate notes (FRN) to earn an ex ante spread above LIBOR. Specifically, we examine how well a receiver RBI swap plus a cash investment in a credit FRN[12] portfolio could have performed relative to the Aggregate Index.

Constructing the RBI Swap + FRN Replicating Portfolio

We assume that at inception an investor has $100 million to invest. He can choose to invest in the cash Aggregate Index. Alternatively, he can enter into a receiver swap on the Lehman U.S. Aggregate RBI basket return and pay 3-month LIBOR + 15 bp while investing the $100 million equity in a cash portfolio of credit FRN.[13] To increase the realism of this strategy, we assume that the investor buys a portfolio, rather than an entire index, of FRN. For comparison we consider a cash investment strategy of investing in LIBID, which we model as LIBOR − 12 bp and label as the LIBID strategy.

We construct FRN portfolios at the beginning of each month. Cash in the FRN portfolio is invested corresponding to the inception month of the replication strategy. Any subsequent cash flow generated by the FRN or swap is reinvested in the contemporaneous FRN portfolio corresponding to the month the cash flow is received.

Each month, we construct three separate FRN portfolios for different quality ratings (Aaa-Aa, A, and Baa). For the FRN portfolio of each rating we select up to ten bonds from the Lehman FRN Index.[14] Consequently, using the A-rating quality as an example, we have an October 2003 A-FRN portfolio, a November 2003 A FRN portfolio, and so on. The bonds selected for each portfolio must satisfy the following criteria to reflect what a portfolio manager might reasonably require:

1. Issued within one year.

2. Maximum remaining maturity of 3 years.

---

12. The too brief history of the Lehman ABS Floating Rate Index prevents us from analyzing the ABS variant of this strategy.

13. We ignore any costs or fees that the investor would incur on the cash Aggregate Index investment. Balancing this assumption, in part, is the assumption that the investor purchases cash FRN at the bid side as this is the pricing assumption for Lehman indices.

14. Lehman introduced the Credit FRN Index in October 2003. It includes both corporate and noncorporate sectors. The corporate sectors include financial institutions that constitute more than 60% of the total market value of the credit FRN Index, as well as industrials and utilities. The noncorporate sector includes sovereigns (such as Mexico and Chile). ABS floaters are excluded from the Credit FRN Index (Lehman introduced a separate ABS Floating Rate Index in January 2005).

3. Quarterly coupon reset based on 3-month LIBOR.

4. Coupon reset in the current month or the next month to match the LIBOR reset of the RBI swap more closely.

5. Clean price greater than 98 (avoid buying distressed bonds whose rating has not yet changed).

6. No zero-coupon FRN.

7. Minimum discount margin (DM) of 5 bp.[15]

If, in a given month, there are more than ten FRN that satisfy the foregoing criteria, we select the ten most recently issued FRN. Each FRN portfolio is equally weighted. This helps, but does not guarantee, issuer diversification. Since the Baa-rated portion of the FRN Index contains very few issuers (mainly auto issuers), these selection criteria produce Baa-rated FRN portfolios that also have very few issuers from only one or two credit sectors. Consequently, the Baa-rated FRN portfolio exposes the strategy to significant systematic sector risk and idiosyncratic issuer risk.

A case in point: our selection criteria produced a 10/31/2003 Baa-rated FRN portfolio that consisted of only three issuers: GM, Ford, and HAL. Most portfolio managers would not choose (certainly not in retrospect!) such a highly issuer-concentrated portfolio. So, we also construct "capped" Baa-rated FRN portfolios using the same selection criteria but imposing a maximum of one bond per issuer in each equally weighted portfolio.

Finally, we require that an FRN downgraded below its initial quality rating is sold from the portfolio at the end of its downgrade month and that the proceeds are reinvested in the contemporaneous FRN portfolio.

When an investor initiates the strategy he buys and holds the FRN portfolio constructed in that month. Any subsequent monthly cash flows generated by this portfolio (plus any net payments on the swap and proceeds from any FRN that mature or are downgraded below their initial credit quality) are reinvested in the contemporaneous FRN portfolio.

RBI Swap + FRN Portfolio Performance

We examined the monthly historical performance of various RBI swap + FRN portfolio combinations from October 2003 through February 2006, corresponding

---

15. We use this DM filter to avoid buying FRN that trade overly rich for their rating quality.

to the period for which we have historical data for both the RBI basket and the FRN Index.[16]

Figure 4-14 summarizes the portfolio returns for the four FRN strategies and the LIBID strategy. We assume the spread on the LIBOR side of the RBI swap is set at 15 bp (annualized) throughout the study period. We also show the Aggregate Index return. During this time period, the Aggregate returned 29.9 bp/month with a monthly volatility of 95.8 bp. By comparison, the RBI swap + LIBID strategy returned 26.3 bp/month with a monthly volatility of 98.9 bp. Overall, the RBI swap + LIBID strategy underperformed the Aggregate by approximately 3.6 bp/month. The total return underperformance arises from two sources. First, the investor is earning LIBID, which is approximately 27 bp (or 2.3 bp/month) less than the LIBOR + 15 bp that he must pay on the RBI swap. Second, over the period the RBI basket underperformed the Aggregate Index by 1.4 bp/month.

The volatility of the monthly return difference (i.e., realized tracking error volatility or TEV) between the RBI swap + LIBID portfolio and the Aggregate Index was 6.5 bp. This is close to the TEV of the RBI basket return vs. the Aggregate return since we define LIBID as a rate fixed at 12 bp below LIBOR.

As Figure 4-14 shows, the RBI swap + Aaa-Aa FRN strategy produced an average monthly return of 29.2 bp, which is only 0.7 bp/month lower than that of the Aggregate, with a monthly volatility of 99.0 bp. The realized monthly TEV was 6.4 bp, which can be decomposed into 6.5 bp of TEV between the RBI basket and the Aggregate and 1.6 bp TEV between LIBOR and the Aaa-Aa FRN monthly return. The correlation between the RBI basket—Aggregate return difference and the FRN—(LIBOR + 15 bp) return difference was 0.13, indicating some diversification benefit offered by the FRN portfolio during this period.

For the four FRN strategies, we can decompose the return difference between the RBI swap + FRN portfolio and the Aggregate into its two components: the monthly RBI basket—Aggregate return and the FRN—(LIBOR + 15 bp) return. The sum of the two in a given month equals the total return difference between the RBI swap + FRN portfolio and the Aggregate. As shown in Figure 4-14 the Aaa-Aa FRN portfolio adds little to the strategy's overall TEV vs. the Aggregate Index.

The investor can try to improve performance by reducing the quality of the FRN portfolio. The RBI swap + A FRN portfolio produced an average monthly return of 29.9 bp, which equals the Aggregate's return, with a monthly volatility of 98.7 bp, which still exceeds the Aggregate's monthly volatility of 95.8 bp. The

---

16. In this example, we use RBI basket Series 1. For any given index, there may be multiple RBI baskets, each reflecting a different methodology for index replication. For example, for the U.S. Aggregate, there are currently two baskets: Series 1 that includes CDX and interest rate swaps and Series 2 that does not include CDX.

Figure 4-14. Summary Monthly Statistics of Different Replication Strategies and the Aggregate Index
October 31, 2003–February 28, 2006

Portfolio	Average FRN OAD at Inception (bp/month)	Avergage FRN OASD at Inception (bp/month)	Monthly Average Return (bp/month)	Monthly Return Volatility (bp/month)	Monthly Return Difference (RBI Swap +FRN) – Aggregate (bp/month)		Monthly Return Difference RBI Basket – Aggregate (bp/month)		Monthly Return Difference FRN – LIBOR (bp/month)	
					Average	Volatility	Average	Volatility	Average	Volatility
RBI + Aaa/Aa FRN	0.08	2.59	29.24	99.04	−0.66	6.44	−1.37	6.48	0.72	1.61
RBI + A FRN	0.15	2.21	29.94	98.74	0.04	6.48	−1.37	6.48	1.39	2.80
RBI + Baa FRN	0.17	1.65	32.65	101.92	2.75	27.03	−1.37	6.48	4.24	28.91
RBI + Cap Baa FRN	0.21	1.86	34.78	99.52	4.88	20.46	−1.37	6.48	6.41	22.55
RBI + LIBID			26.26	98.87	−3.63	6.46	−1.37	6.48	−2.27	0.06
Aggregate			29.9	95.80						

Cumulative Return Difference (bp)

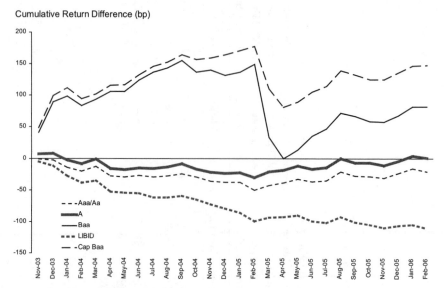

Figure 4-15. Cumulative Return Differences between Various RBI Swap + FRN Portfolios and the Aggregate Index
October 31, 2003–February 28, 2006

A FRN strategy outperformed the Aaa-Aa FRN strategy by 0.7 bp/month with a comparable realized monthly TEV of 6.5 bp.

The RBI swap + Baa FRN portfolio outperformed the Aggregate by 2.7 bp/ month (32.6 vs. 29.9 bp), with a monthly volatility of 101.9 bp. While this strong showing for the Baa FRN strategy no doubt owes much to the robust credit environment during the sample period, the Baa FRN portfolio was not immune to credit event risk.

We also constructed an issuer capped Baa FRN portfolio to reduce sector and idiosyncratic risk in the FRN portion of the replication strategy. The RBI swap + cap Baa FRN portfolio outperformed the Aggregate by a larger margin (4.9 bp/ month) and with lower volatility (99.5 bp) compared to the no-cap Baa FRN port-folio. The realized TEV (20.5 bp/month) was also considerably less than that of the no-cap Baa FRN portfolio. These results indicate that the Baa-rated FRN sec-tor has both high systematic and idiosyncratic risk and that issuer diversification helped to reduce these risks.

To summarize the time series performance of the replication strategies, Fig-ure 4-15 shows the monthly cumulative performance difference between various RBI swap + FRN portfolios and the Aggregate. Again, the cumulative return dif-ference for the RBI swap + LIBID portfolio can be viewed as a benchmark.

The monthly cumulative performance difference for the RBI swap + Aaa-Aa and RBI swap + A FRN portfolios moved roughly in parallel fashion and both steadily outperformed the RBI swap + LIBID benchmark. Over the entire period, the RBI swap + A FRN strategy outperformed the Aggregate by 0.3 bp, while the RBI swap + Aaa-Aa FRN strategy underperformed by 21 bp. Over the same period the RBI swap + LIBID strategy underperformed the Aggregate by 110.5 bp.

In contrast, the RBI swap + no-cap Baa FRN strategy outperformed the Aggregate (despite the GM and F downgrades!) by a whopping 80 bp, but with quite a bit of volatility (27.0 bp) owing to the Baa-quality FRN portfolio.

While investing in Baa-rated FRN outperformed the Aggregate, it suffered from considerable TEV. However, for investors (e.g., hedge funds or credit specialty cash investors) with sufficient credit expertise, using RBI swaps with opportunistic credit selection can produce top quartile performance.

When replicating the U.S. Aggregate using an RBI swap, a carry drag arises when the investor earns less on cash than the floating-rate side of the swap, which is LIBOR plus a spread. We have shown that one way to reduce this performance drag is to invest in a small portfolio of credit floating-rate notes. However, other cash investment strategies are also possible: ABS floaters and asset swaps on fixed rate bonds.

REPLICATION DETAILS

A sample U.S. Aggregate replication portfolio as of July 31, 2004, is provided in Appendix C for a portfolio with a notional size of $1 billion.

In our empirical studies, we assume that all positions are rebalanced monthly. In practice, most investors make small adjustments to positions monthly to allow for the changing characteristics of the index and the aging of derivatives positions. On a quarterly basis, futures are rolled to prevent the exercise of the delivery option and swaps are rolled into the "on-the-run" maturities. TBAs are rolled monthly to avoid pool delivery. New CDX instruments are created semiannually, and we assume in our studies that a roll into the new instrument is executed with the same frequency.

During the period preceding the creation of the next CDX series, an issuer may be downgraded and removed from the Credit Index (but remain in CDX). During this period, the investor may be subject to tracking error, as the performance of the fallen angel may not match that of the investment-grade credits. Based on an analysis of the historic performance of fallen angels, in the months following a fall below investment grade and the credit ratings of CDX, we estimate this risk to be

**Figure 4-16. Transactions Costs of Different
Replication Strategies**

Replication Strategy	Cost (bp/month)
Futures	0.5
Swaps	0.3
Futures + swaps	0.3
Futures + swaps + TBAs	0.9
Futures + swaps + TBAs + CDX	1.0

7 bp/month for the Credit Index.[17] However, this risk can be largely eliminated if the investor buys single-name default protection for the downgraded issuer.

An all-derivatives portfolio, by definition, does not require cash, apart from what is needed to meet the variation margin for futures or mark-to-market collateral calls for swaps. We assume in our study that cash is invested in 1-month LIBOR. In practice, investors are required to deposit initial margin with the clearing firm, which, for an Aggregate Index replicating portfolio, currently averages 1.3% of the notional portfolio amount.[18] However, both this and any variation margin can be posted in the form of Treasury bills, so, in practice, only a small portion of funds will be invested below LIBOR.

Transaction costs depend upon the choice of strategy and the frequency of rebalancing. Figure 4-16 displays estimated transaction costs, assuming monthly rebalancing.

CONCLUSION

There are various considerations in choosing the appropriate replication strategy. Portfolio constraints may ultimately determine the choice of strategy, perhaps restricting the investor to a futures-only strategy or a combination not considered herein (e.g., futures plus TBAs). In the absence of client constraints, the investor's risk "utility function" (i.e., cost per unit of risk reduction) determines the choice of strategy. If the degree of risk aversion is high, a total return swap may prove to be a desirable choice. However, for large replicating portfolios (e.g., above $300 million), there may not be sufficient liquidity to permit the use of an index swap for the entire portfolio.

17. For an analysis of the performance of distressed bonds see Chapter 15.

18. As of October 2004, CBOT initial margin requirements for 2-year, 5-year, 10-year, and long bond futures are $743, $810, $1,350, and $2,025 per contract, respectively.

The choice of replication method should not be considered in isolation but rather in combination with the overall strategy. It is not necessarily the case that the lowest-TEV strategy is always preferable. For example, if the replication is part of a portable alpha strategy, the relationship of the expected return deviations from benchmark of various replication strategies should be considered relative to the expected alpha of the strategy. A replication strategy for the Aggregate Index using Treasury futures will outperform during times of widening spreads and underperform in the opposite environment. The correlation of this performance pattern to the alpha strategy may actually make this a more attractive option than a replication strategy that, by itself, has a lower tracking error. The choice of replication strategy to be used for the MBS Index will depend upon whether the entire Aggregate Index is being replicated or just the mortgage component.

The data we possess for credit default swaps limit the period over which we have been able to conduct this study. Nevertheless, the sample size is large enough to give statistical significance to the key findings of this chapter. As more data from the credit default swaps market become available, further investigation may yield new insights into the relative merits of various replication strategies and the diversification benefits that arise from combining them.

An investor who wishes to receive the return on a replicating portfolio can either establish a replication strategy and manage it himself or achieve the same exposure using RBI swaps.

APPENDIX A. THE LEHMAN U.S. AGGREGATE INDEX

The U.S. Aggregate Index contains U.S. dollar-denominated securities that qualify under the index's rules for inclusion (see below). Inclusion is based on the currency of the issue and not the domicile of the issuer. The principal asset classes in the index are government, credit (including corporate issues), and securitized bonds. Securities in the index roll up to the U.S. Universal and Global Aggregate indices. The U.S. Aggregate Index was launched on January 1, 1976.

PRICING AND RELATED ISSUES

- Frequency: Daily, on a $T + 1$ basis. If the last business day of the month is a holiday in the U.S. market, then prices from the previous business day are used.

- Timing: 3:00 PM New York time.

- Bid/Offer: Outstanding issues are priced on the bid side. New issues enter the index on the offer side.

- Sources: Lehman trading desks.

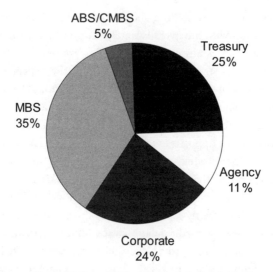

Figure 4-A1. Composition of Lehman U.S. Aggregate Index by Sector
August 31, 2005

- Methodology: Multicontributor verification—the Lehman price for each
  security is checked against a blend of alternative valuations by our quality
  control group. Variations are analyzed and corrected as necessary.

- Reinvestment: Index cash flows are reinvested at the start of the month
  following their receipt. There is no return on cash held intramonth.

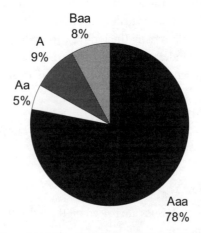

Figure 4-A2. Composition of Lehman U.S. Aggregate Index by Quality
August 31, 2005

RULES FOR INCLUSION

- Amount Outstanding: $250 million as of July 1, 2004.

- Quality: A minimum bond level rating of Baa3 from Moody's Investors Service or BBB-from Standard & Poor's ratings group. The lower of the two agencies' ratings is applied for qualification purposes. Where a rating from only one agency is available, that rating is used to determine the bond's index rating. Unrated securities are included if an issuer rating is applicable. Unrated subordinated securities are included if a subordinated issuer rating is applicable.

- Maturity: One-year minimum to final maturity on dated bonds, regardless of put or call features. Undated securities are included in the index provided their coupons switch from fixed to variable rate. These are included until 1 year before their first call dates, providing they meet all other index criteria.

- Debt Seniority: Senior and subordinated issues are included. Undated securities are included provided their coupons switch from fixed to variable rate. Fixed to variable rate security structures also qualify for the index if the holder has the option of forcing the issuer to issue preference shares post the call date or if there are other economic incentives for the issuer to call the issue, such as the removal of tax benefits after the first call date. Fixed-rate perpetual capital securities that remain fixed rate following their first call dates and do not provide economic incentives to call the bonds are excluded.

- Currency of Issue: U.S. dollars.

- Market of Issue: U.S. public debt market.

- Security Types: The index includes all fixed-rate bullets, putable and callable bonds, and soft bullets. Excluded are bonds with equity-type features (e.g., warrants, convertibility to equity), private placements and floating-rate issues.

REBALANCING RULES

- Frequency: Statistics (projected) universe: daily. Returns universe: monthly, on the last business day of the month.

- Methodology: During the month, all indicative changes to securities are reflected in both the statistics (projected) universe and returns universe on a daily basis. These include changes to ratings, amounts outstanding, or sector. These changes affect the qualification of securities in the statistics (projected) universe on a daily basis, but only affect the qualification of bonds for the returns universe at the end of the month.

• Timing: Qualifying securities issued, but not necessarily settled, on or before the month-end rebalancing date qualify for inclusion in the following month's returns universe.

APPENDIX B. CREDIT DEFAULT SWAPS

The primary purpose of credit derivatives is to enable the efficient transfer and repackaging of credit risk. Our definition of credit risk encompasses all credit-related events ranging from a spread widening, through a ratings downgrade, all the way to default. In their simplest form, credit derivatives provide an efficient way to replicate the credit risk that exists in a standard cash instrument. A standard credit default swap can be replicated using a cash bond and the repo market. Alternatively, a cash credit instrument can be replicated by combining a credit default swap with the fixed receipt of an interest-rate swap.

A default swap is a bilateral contract that enables an investor to buy protection against the risk of default of an asset issued by a specified reference entity. Following a defined credit event, the buyer of protection receives a payment intended to compensate against the loss on the investment. This is shown in Figure 4-A3. In return, the protection buyer pays a fee. Usually, the fee is paid over the life of the transaction in the form of a regular accruing cash flow. The contract is typically specified using the confirmation document and legal definitions produced by the International Swap and Derivatives Association (ISDA).

Some default swaps define the triggering of a credit event using a reference asset. The main purpose of the reference asset is to specify exactly the capital structure seniority of the debt that is covered. The reference asset is also important in the determination of the recovery value should the default swap be cash settled. In many cases, following a default, the protection buyer delivers a defaulted security for which he receives par from the protection seller. Moreover, the maturity of the default swap need not be the same as the maturity of the reference asset. It is common to specify a reference asset with a longer maturity than the default swap.

CDX.NA.IG is a static portfolio of 125 equally weighted credit default swaps on 125 North American reference entities that are rated investment grade and available in a range of maturities. Every 6 months a new set of CDX instruments is created, though existing instruments continue to trade. Like individual CDS instruments, they are unfunded. A credit event triggered by a reference asset will be settled by the physical delivery of a deliverable defaulted security in exchange for par. By combining CDX with a portfolio of interest-rates swaps (receiving fixed), it is possible to replicate, in unfunded form, the exposures of a portfolio of cash credit instruments.

Between trade initiation and the default or maturity, protection buyer makes regular payments of default swap spread to protection seller.

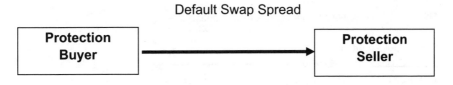

Following the credit event one of the following will take place:

Cash Settlement

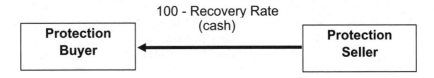

Physical Settlement

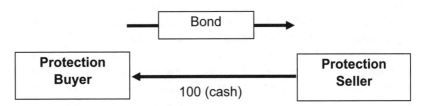

Figure 4-A3. Mechanics of a Default Swap

APPENDIX C. REPLICATING PORTFOLIO AS OF JULY 31, 2004

Identifier	Position	Description	Coupon/Maturity
Cash			
USD	$1,000,000,000	Cash—U.S. dollar	
Futures (four positions)			
TUU4:CBT	$98,800,000	2-year Treasury notes	
FVU4:CBT	–$1,800,000	5-year Treasury notes	
TYU4:CBT	$75,800,000	10-year Treasury notes	
USU4:CBT	$42,700,000	30-year Treasury bonds	
Interest Rate Swaps (six positions)			
IRD_9327	$72,227,000	IRSwap USD 1.965 LIBOR 6M	1/31/2005
IRD_9332	$144,781,000	IRSwap USD 3.087 LIBOR 2Y	7/31/2006
IRD_9335	$135,037,000	IRSwap USD 4.199 LIBOR 5Y	7/30/2009
IRD_9338	$67,731,000	IRSwap USD 4.99 LIBOR 10Y	7/30/2014
IRD_9341	$21,536,000	IRSwap USD 5.535 LIBOR 20Y	7/30/2024
IRD_9344	$16,971,000	IRSwap USD 3.0 LIBOR 30Y	7/30/2034
Mortgages (thirteen positions)			
FNC044QG	$43,608,833	FNMA conventional 15 years	4.5
FNC050QG	$39,688,972	FNMA conventional 15 years	5
FNC054QG	$13,946,931	FNMA conventional 15 years	5.5
FNC060QG	$18,488,638	FNMA conventional 15 years	6
FNA054QG	$42,630,967	FNMA conventional 30 years	5.5
FNA060QG	$38,007,295	FNMA conventional 30 years	6
FNA064QG	$54,389,948	FNMA conventional 30 years	6.5
FGB050QG	$31,962,198	FHLM gold guarantee single-family 30 years	5
FGB054QG	$27,945,910	FHLM gold guarantee single-family 30 years	5.5
GNA064QG	$22,404,484	GNMA I single-family 30 years	6.5
GNA060QG	$13,129,784	GNMA I single-family 30 years	6
GNA054QG	$1,961,961	GNMA I single-family 30 years	5.5
GNA050QG	$10,934,080	GNMA I single-family 30 years	5
Credit Default Swaps (two positions)			
CDX.IG 2/09	$167,429,000	CDX investment grade 5 years #2	9/20/2009
CDX.IG 2/14	$76,671,000	CDX investment grade 10 years #2	9/20/2014

5. Replicating the Lehman Brothers Global Aggregate Index with Liquid Instruments

The Lehman Brothers Global Aggregate Bond Index is the most widely used index for benchmarking global bond portfolios. Part of the reason for its extensive acceptance is that it fairly represents the broad investable universe of investment-grade fixed-income securities, including government bonds, credit instruments, and securitized assets. The breadth of the index, comprising more than 10,000 securities denominated in 24[1] different currencies, can make it a challenging benchmark for investors, but that breadth is actually an advantage when it comes to designing strategies to replicate it. The multiple exposures contained within the Global Aggregate Index help diversify its overall risk (and diversify the tracking errors of replication strategies).

This chapter describes strategies for replicating the Global Aggregate Index, as well as its largest regional components (U.S. Aggregate and Dollar Bloc, Euro and Pan-European Aggregate, and Asia-Pacific Aggregate). We are mindful that, in many cases, the objective of a replication strategy is not to build a passive portfolio with thousands of securities that needs constant rebalancing, but rather to achieve acceptably low tracking errors using a relatively small number of highly liquid instruments. This reflects the various uses made of replicating portfolios by investors: (1) as part of a portable alpha strategy, (2) to "fill out" an existing portfolio, (3) for tactical asset allocation, (4) for asset allocation transitions, and (5) for management of inflows and outflows.

Since the Global Aggregate Index is fast becoming the benchmark of choice for many sponsors, managers whose expertise is focused on a specific market will have

Based on research first published by Lehman Brothers in 2005.

1. On January 1, 2006, two new currencies, Taiwan dollar and Malaysian ringgit, were added to the Global Aggregate Index. Because the study in this chapter was completed in May 2005, all figures reflect the 22-currency index composition. However, the weights of the two new currencies are extremely small and would not affect the results.

to forgo participating in much of the growth in global fixed-income assignments. A strategy of replicating segments of the Global Aggregate as a way of filling out an existing fixed-income product allows managers to offer a Global Aggregate service. In particular, European investors have been interested in techniques to replicate the U.S. portion of the Global Aggregate or just the mortgage component.

Global Aggregate managers frequently divide portions of their portfolios among various teams, so, for example, the U.S. portion is managed by U.S. fixed-income managers. When a country allocation shift is made, it can upset the sector allocations within each regional portfolio. For example, a 5% portfolio shift from Treasuries to Bunds may represent 15% of the U.S. fixed-income portfolio, possibly completely eliminating the U.S. Treasury exposure. By selling a U.S. replicating portfolio of derivatives and buying a euro-replicating portfolio, the trade can be executed more cheaply than using cash instruments and with no disruption to the underlying portfolio.

Alternatively, a replicating strategy can be used to express a negative view on a given segment of the Global Aggregate. For example, a bearish view on the euro credit market may cause managers to reduce their cash bond holdings, which may have taken months to accumulate. By selling a replicating portfolio of derivatives, they can reduce market exposure but retain the ability to generate outperformance from security selection.

SOURCES OF RISK IN THE LEHMAN BROTHERS GLOBAL AGGREGATE INDEX

The Global Aggregate Index comprises 24 currencies (Figure 5-1), of which just four, U.S. dollar, euro, yen, and sterling, make up 94% of the index market value. This suggests that a portfolio comprising only those four currencies may do an adequate job of replicating the Global Aggregate, simplifying the replication greatly. Almost 50% of the Global Aggregate is represented by non-Treasury securities (Figure 5-2), dominated by credit and collateralized securities (with the inclusion of U.S. mortgages). Approximately 90% of the credit component is in the United States or Europe.

The sources of volatility in the underlying index can give valuable insights into the likely success of any replication strategy. The Lehman Brothers global multifactor risk model quantifies the ex ante tracking error volatility (the expected volatility of the return deviation) of a portfolio vs. a benchmark or the absolute volatility of a portfolio or index. Figure 5-3 shows the model's analysis of the absolute volatility of the Global Aggregate Index. The model is based on the historical returns of individual securities in the Lehman Brothers bond indices, in many instances dating back more than a decade, and derives historical magni-

Figure 5-1. Global Aggregate Composition by Currency

May 31, 2005

Currency	Issues	Market Value (%)	Cumulative Market Value (%)
United States dollar	4,378	38.71	38.71
European euro	2,461	31.50	70.21
Japanese yen	1,479	18.76	88.97
United Kingdom pounds sterling	687	4.97	93.94
Canadian dollar	265	2.00	95.94
Korean won	108	1.13	97.08
Australian dollar	95	0.46	97.53
South African rand	40	0.30	97.83
Danish krone	36	0.55	98.38
Swedish krona	31	0.53	98.91
Thai baht	24	0.10	99.01
Singapore dollar	18	0.14	99.15
Hungarian forint	16	0.11	99.26
Mexican peso	15	0.16	99.42
Polish zloty	15	0.26	99.68
Czech koruna	11	0.08	99.76
Norwegian krone	9	0.12	99.88
New Zealand dollar	9	0.07	99.95
Slovakian koruna	7	0.02	99.98
Chilean peso	6	0.01	99.99
Hong Kong dollar	2	0.00	100.00
Slovenian tolar	2	0.00	100.00
Total	9,714	100.00	

tudes of different market risk factors and the relationships among them. It then measures current mismatches between the portfolio and benchmark sensitivities to these risks and multiplies these mismatches by historical volatilities and correlations ("covariance matrix") to produce its output.

Figure 5-3 suggests that in order to replicate the unhedged Global Aggregate, it is important to manage currency exposure, which represents almost 75% of the variance of the index. In the model, swap spread factors are disaggregated from those of investment grade and globally are a more significant source of risk. We note, however, that the relative importance of spread factors varies by currency bloc. For example, within the dollar bloc, investment-grade spreads (particularly credit/agency and MBS spreads) are a larger source of risk than swap spreads, whereas in the European bloc, swap spread risk is more than double that

Figure 5-2. Global Aggregate Composition by Sector and Major Currencies
May 31, 2005

| | Market Value (%) | Global Aggregate Composition (%) | | | | | | |
		Treasury	Agency	Credit	MBS	ABS/CMBS	Collateralized	Others
Total	100.00	50.23	10.01	20.67	13.25	1.44	4.34	0.06
U.S. dollar	38.71	9.73	4.07	10.52	13.25	1.14		
Euro	31.50	18.95	2.59	5.86		0.09	4.00	
Yen	18.76	14.82	2.13	1.81		0.01		
Sterling	4.97	2.48	0.10	2.09		0.20	0.04	0.06
Others	6.06	4.26	1.12	0.39		0.00	0.30	

Figure 5-3. Sources of Risk in Lehman Global Aggregate

Global Risk Factor	Isolated Tracking Error Volatility (bp/month)	Percentage of Tracking Error Variance
Global		
Currency	144.27	73.95
Yield curve	83.71	27.29
Swap spreads	9.52	0.46
Volatility	1.13	−0.15
Investment-grade spreads	8.29	−1.47
Treasury spreads	1.96	−0.12
Credit and agency spreads	6.61	−0.96
MBS/securitized	2.75	−0.33
CMBS/ABS	0.27	−0.06
Emerging markets spread	0.47	−0.08
Systematic risk	172.03	99.99
Idiosyncratic risk	1.11	0.00
Credit default risk	0.53	0.00
Total risk		100
Portfolio volatility (bp/month)		172.03
Dollar Bloc (USD + CAD + AUD + NZD)		
Yield curve	45.71	
Swap spreads	6.47	
Volatility	1.13	
Investment-grade spreads	7.15	
Treasury spreads	0.81	
Credit and agency spreads	5.60	
MBS	2.73	
CMBS/ABS	0.27	
Emerging markets spread	0.43	
Cumulative	43.85	
European Bloc (EUR + CHF + DKK + NOK + SEK)		
Yield curve	37.09	
Swap spreads	4.43	
Volatility	0.00	
Investment-grade spreads	2.11	
Treasury spreads	1.48	
Credit and agency spreads	1.23	
Securitized	0.24	
Emerging markets spread	0.03	
Cumulative	36.61	

(*continued*)

Figure 5-3. (continued)

Global Risk Factor	Isolated Tracking Error Volatility (bp/month)	Percentage of Tracking Error Variance
U.K. Pound Sterling Bloc		
Yield curve	8.65	
Swap spreads	1.45	
Volatility	0	
Investment-grade spreads	1.22	
Credit and agency spreads	1.19	
Securitized	0.11	
Cumulative	8.53	
Japanese Yen Bloc		
Yield curve	12.02	
Swap spreads	0.57	
Investment-grade spreads	0.85	
Treasury spreads	0.75	
Credit and agency spreads	0.37	
Emerging markets spread	0.01	
Cumulative	12.35	

of investment grade. This suggests that interest-rate swaps are likely to replicate European investment-grade sectors more effectively than U.S. investment grade. We also note that in the yen bloc, credit and agency spread risk is not significant.

FORMING A DERIVATIVES REPLICATION STRATEGY

The aim of this chapter is to assess various practical approaches to replicating the Global Aggregate and its major subindices. Most investors would not wish to trade 24 different currencies and alter their positions in line with index changes on a monthly basis. A more acceptable strategy (subject to achieving a reasonable tracking error) would be to use instruments from the four largest constituent currencies (USD, EUR, JPY, GBP), which together make up 94% of the Global Aggregate. In each region, as detailed in Figure 5-4, we map each component of the Global Aggregate to a currency and a set of instruments. For example, Canadian dollar-denominated credit is replicated by a variety of U.S. derivative instruments, depending upon the strategy chosen, which may include futures, swaps, or swaps

Figure 5-4. Replication Currency/Instruments Mapping Table

Index Currency	Percentage of Currency Bloc	Replicating Currency	Instruments
United States dollar	93.5	U.S. dollar	Futures, Swaps, CDX, TBA
Australian dollar	1.1		
Canadian dollar	4.8		
Chilean peso	0.0		
Mexican peso	0.4		
New Zealand dollar	0.2		
Euro	94.1	Euro	Futures, Swaps, iTraxx
Czech koruna	0.2		
Danish krone	1.6		
Hungarian forint	0.3		
Norwegian krone	0.4		
Polish zloty	0.8		
Slovakian koruna	0.1		
Slovenian tolar	0.0		
South African rand	0.9		
Swedish krona	1.6		
United Kingdom pounds sterling	100.0	U.K. pounds sterling	Futures, swaps, iTraxx
Japanese yen	93.2	Japanese yen	Futures, swaps
Hong Kong dollar	0.0		
Korean won	5.6		
Singapore dollar	0.7		
Thai baht	0.5		

+ CDX. For replicating the unhedged index, the weight of the Canadian dollar in the Global Aggregate is represented by U.S. dollar cash.

In all replication strategies, we examine various portfolios of derivative instruments, constructed to match the interest-rate profile of the relevant index. Interest-rate swaps are an excellent choice for a replication strategy, since they are available in a broad range of maturities and currencies. Embedded in the pricing of interest-rate swaps are a credit risk premium and a liquidity premium, which can be expected to help in replicating the returns of non-Treasury components of the Global Aggregate. Moreover, since the swap curve is effectively continuous, we can select six instruments to match exactly the key-rate duration profile of the index.

Replication of the U.S. Dollar Bloc

The details on techniques and derivative instruments used in replicating the U.S. Aggregate Index can be found in Chapter 4. Although the approach remains basically the same, the USD bloc in the Global Aggregate index is not identical to the U.S. Aggregate Index. Most importantly, several other currencies in addition to USD are included in the bloc and are replicated with USD derivatives. Furthermore, there are structural differences. For example, while the U.S. Aggregate includes only publicly issued securities (as well as 144A securities with registration rights and Reg-S securities), the U.S. portion of the Global Aggregate also includes eurodollar securities. Furthermore, the minimum issue size for inclusion is $250 million in the U.S. Aggregate and $300 million in the Global Aggregate.

Replication of the Pan-European and Euro Aggregate

The European portion of the Global Aggregate Index can be split into three parts: the Euro Aggregate Index, a very popular benchmark for euro-based investors; the Sterling Aggregate Index; and the other small markets that together account for 4% of the Pan-European Aggregate and 1.6% of the Global Index.

Swaps replicate the Euro Aggregate Index returns much more accurately than futures contracts. Indeed, euro swap spreads are generally tighter and less volatile than in the U.S. market, a reflection of the diversity of Treasury issuers in the euro zone. Many sectors of the euro market, including collateralized, credit, and some Treasury markets, are priced off the swap curve. This reflects the importance of floating-rate buyers (e.g., banks) in the European fixed-income markets. In replicating portfolios that are allowed to hold both swaps and futures contracts, there is no reason to use futures, since swaps generate lower tracking errors.

For replicating the credit portion of the Euro and Sterling Aggregate indices, we use iTraxx Europe 5-year, a portfolio of 125 equally weighted credit default swaps, to match DTS (spread duration times spread) of the indices.[2] Although other maturities are available, they offer only limited liquidity and are not included in this chapter. Including a position in the portfolio CDS improves the tracking error vs. the Euro Aggregate Index only marginally, though we see a clearer bene-

---

2. While we have endeavored to synthesize the iTraxx contract to allow us to extend our analysis to points in history further back than the launch of the contract (see results in Figure 5-5a for Euro and Pan-Euro Aggregate indices), the process of synthesis makes various assumptions that affect reported results. The iTraxx contract does not behave precisely as the sum of its parts and, in addition, 125 names were not generally available, especially further back in the past. Results based on observed prices for the contract after its launch carry more authority, although any results will reflect the short period over which such data are available.

fit in recent months as spread volatility has risen. Credit represents only 16% of the index; therefore, the risk reduction associated with iTraxx inclusion is more visible when replicating the Euro Corporate Index.

Although much smaller, the Sterling Aggregate Index cannot be replicated as accurately as its euro counterpart. A portfolio holding only the 10-year Gilt contract leaves substantial curve and spread risk unmatched, while the swap replication is less efficient because swap spreads are substantially more volatile in sterling than in the euro market. There is no sterling equivalent for iTraxx or CDX, so we proxy the credit spread exposure of the sterling market with iTraxx Europe 5-year. This should also be expected to add some tracking error, given the longer maturity of the sterling spread market compared with that of the iTraxx contract used, which is composed of 5-year CDS.

Replication of the Asia-Pacific Aggregate

The Asia-Pacific Aggregate Index is dominated by Japan, so we use yen instruments, with two exceptions, to replicate the Asia-Pacific Aggregate. The Australian and New Zealand currencies and bond markets have higher correlations with U.S. dollar instruments than with yen instruments and are better replicated with U.S. instruments. The only widely traded bond future in Japan is the 10-year future, with a deliverable basket of bonds with maturities between 7 and 11 years. Therefore, for the Asia-Pacific ex-AUD, ex-NZD replication, we use interest-rate swaps in order to achieve a better match of yield curve exposure than can be achieved with a single bond instrument.

PERFORMANCE SUMMARY OF REPLICATION STRATEGIES

The performance of various replication strategies is measured using tracking error volatility (TEV), which is preferable to using average out- or underperformance.[3] Figure 5-5 presents two sets of results. Figure 5-5a illustrates the period during which we have data for CDX and iTraxx, and Figure 5-5b shows results for a longer period and excludes portfolio CDS. The differences in tracking errors are striking, largely because credit spreads were much more volatile prior to August 2002 than after that month. Figure 5-6 shows that excess return volatility of credit was substantially greater in earlier periods.

In Europe, where volatilities have been consistently lower, the benefit of adding iTraxx to the replicating portfolio has manifested itself only recently. In the past 12 months, adding iTraxx to a swap portfolio meant to replicate the Euro

---

3. See Chapter 4 for a discussion of the proper metric.

Figure 5-5a. Replication Results for the Global Aggregate Index
August 2002–May 2005

	Unhedged		Hedged	
	Mean Outperformance (bp/month)	Tracking Error Volatility (bp/month)	Mean Outperformance (bp/month)	Tracking Error Volatility (bp/month)
Dollar Bloc				
Swaps	–11.3	21.9	–7.1	17.4
Swaps + futures	–10.7	21.9	–6.6	16.6
Swaps + futures + TBA	–9.1	20.1	–5.0	17.4
Swaps + futures + CDX	–4.9	15.2	–0.7	10.9
Swaps + futures + CDX + TBA	–3.2	12.1	0.9	11.8
Swaps + CDX	–5.4	16.3	–1.3	13.5
Swaps + CDX + TBA	–3.8	14.6	0.4	15.3
U.S. Aggregate				
Swaps	–7.3	16.8	–	–
Swaps + futures	–6.7	16.7	–	–
Swaps + futures + CDX	–0.7	10.7	–	–
Swaps + futures + CDX + TBA	1.0	8.8	–	–
Swaps + CDX	–1.3	12.2	–	–
Swaps + CDX + TBA	0.4	11.9	–	–

Pan-Euro Bloc				
Swaps	-1.5	8.9	0.2	7.8
Swaps + iTraxx	1.6	8.6	3.3	8.0
Euro Aggregate				
Swaps	-1.8	6.0	-1.8	6.0
Swaps + iTraxx	0.7	6.1	0.7	6.0
Yen Bloc				
Swaps	-6.8	15.1	-5.2	11.5
Total Global Aggregate				
Swaps	-7.0	11.0	-4.1	8.1
Swaps + futures	-6.7	11.2	-3.9	8.2
Swaps + futures + TBA	-6.1	10.9	-3.2	8.8
Swaps + futures + CDX/iTraxx	-2.9	7.5	-0.1	5.3
Swaps + futures + CDX/iTraxx + TBA	-2.2	6.9	0.6	5.7
Swaps + CDX/iTraxx	-3.1	8.0	-0.3	6.1
Swaps + CDX/iTraxx + TBA	-2.5	7.8	0.4	7.0

Figure 5-5b. Replication Results for the Global Aggregate Index
September 2000–May 2005

	Unhedged		Hedged	
	Mean Outperformance (bp/month)	Tracking Error Volatility (bp/month)	Mean Outperformance (bp/month)	Tracking Error Volatility (bp/month)
Dollar Bloc				
Swaps	1.5	35.1	3.6	31.4
Swaps + futures	–1.0	30.0	1.2	25.5
Swaps + futures + TBA	–1.5	26.1	0.6	22.6
Pan-Euro Bloc				
Swaps	3.0	11.5	3.8	9.9
Euro Aggregate				
Swaps	1.2	8.5	1.1	8.5
Yen Bloc				
Swaps	–4.7	17.9	–2.8	16.2
Total Global Aggregate				
Swaps	0.8	19.3	2.4	16.7
Swaps + futures	–0.4	17.0	1.3	14.0
Swaps + futures + TBA	–0.7	15.3	1.0	12.5

Figure 5-5c. Replication Results for Selected Credit Indices
August 2002–May 2005

	Mean Outperformance (bp/month)	Tracking Error Volatility (bp/month)
U.S. Credit		
Swaps	−20.7	55.2
Swaps + CDX	1.8	26.4
Euro Corporate		
Swaps	−11.3	20.8
Swaps + iTraxx	2.7	16.0
Sterling Corporate		
Swaps	−12.0	53.7
Swaps + iTraxx	15.4	47.9

Corporate Index would have led to a tracking error reduction from 19.7 to 8.8 bp/month (Figure 5-7b). This reflects the lower correlation between changes in credit spreads and changes in swap spreads over the most recent period. Similarly, Sterling Corporate Index replication would have been improved from 46.7 to 30.3 bp/month by adding the iTraxx Europe 5-year contract to a sterling swap portfolio.

Figure 5-6. Excess Return and Return Volatility in Two Subperiods

	Average Return (bp/month)	
	November 2002–May 2005	August 2002–May 2005
U.S. Credit	−13.3	23.0
Euro Credit	1.1	9.9
Yen Credit	1.1	3.2
Global Credit	−1.1	6.0

	Monthly Return Volatility (bp/month)	
	November 2002–May 2005	August 2002–May 2005
U.S. Credit	95.8	56.9
Euro Credit	33.4	24.0
Yen Credit	8.7	4.6
Global Credit	16.2	12.5

Figure 5-7a. Replication Details for Pan-European Aggregate
Tracking Errors and Returns for Selected Indices, November 2002–May 2005 (futures data begin May 2002)

Index	Swaps Only		Swaps + iTraxx		Futures	
	Tracking Error Volatility (bp/month)	Return (bp/month)	Tracking Error Volatility (bp/month)	Return (bp/month)	Tracking Error Volatility (bp/month)	Return (bp/month)
Pan-Euro Aggregate (hedged into euros)	7.5	0.0	7.6	-2.7	17.6	-1.3
Pan-Euro Aggregate (unhedged base euros)	8.8	1.7	8.4	-1.0		
Euro Aggregate	5.4	-2.1	5.7	0.0	17.7	-1.5
Euro Corporate	20.8	-11.3	16.0	2.7		
Euro Treasury					18.5	1.7
Sterling Aggregate	28.7	-1.6	29.6	5.6	41.5	1.7
Sterling Corporate	53.7	-12.0	47.9	15.4		
Sterling Non-Gilt	38.9	-7.0	37.5	8.6		
Sterling Gilt	27.2	2.78			33.3	3.8

Figure 5-7b. Replication Details for Pan-European Aggregate

Tracking Errors for Selected European Corporate Indices, Period Ending May 2005

Number of Months	Euro Corporate Index		Sterling Corporate Index	
	Swaps	Swaps + iTraxx	Swaps	Swaps + iTraxx
12	19.7	8.8	53.7	47.9
18	16.7	13.3	44.2	41.6
24	17.2	16.2	41.4	34.8
30	20.8	16.0	46.7	30.3

When tracking either the Euro Treasury or Euro Aggregate Index, duration-matched portfolios of the three German contracts (2-, 5-, and 10-year) display tracking errors on the order of 17 bp/month, substantially higher than the 5 bp/month associated with Mirror Swap Index replication. This is due both to the better yield curve match that can be achieved with six interest-rate swaps rather than three bond futures and to the better tracking of non-German markets offered by swaps. Adding iTraxx brings only small benefits to a Euro Aggregate portfolio. This can be explained by the relatively small share of corporate bonds in the Euro Aggregate Index, currently 15%. iTraxx brings more tangible benefits when replicating the Euro Corporate Index.

It appears that sterling indices are more difficult to track than their euro equivalent. The 10-year Gilt futures contract displayed tracking errors of 33 bp/month with respect to the Gilt Index and 42 bp/month (Figure 5-7a) with respect to the Sterling Aggregate Index. Similarly, swaps or combinations of swaps and iTraxx—there is no CDS basket trading in the sterling market—display larger tracking errors with respect to the Sterling Aggregate or Corporate indices than to equivalent euro indices. Nevertheless, iTraxx exposure helps reduce tracking error volatility when hedging exposure to the Sterling Corporate Index—from 47 to 30 bp/month over the most recent 12 months.

The tracking errors for the Euro-Aggregate replications are lower than for the U.S. Aggregate replication. This reflects differences both in the sectoral composition of the two indices and in the relative volatilities of credit spreads in both regions. Treasury securities represent 25% of the U.S. Aggregate and 60% of the Euro Aggregate. Additionally, the compositions of the credit indices are very different, as shown in Figure 5-8. The Euro Credit Index is of higher credit quality, with a greater proportion weighted in financial issuers. Both characteristics suggest that credit spreads would track swap spreads (which in part reflect the credit quality of the financial system) more closely in Europe than in the United States. These

Figure 5-8. U.S. and Euro Credit Index: Market Value by Sector and Rating

	Market Value (%)				
	Total	Aaa	Aa	A	Baa
U.S. Credit	100.00	11.55	11.69	39.86	36.90
Euro Credit	100.00	19.58	17.37	39.21	23.84
Government-Related					
U.S. Credit	18.02	7.52	4.50	2.32	3.66
Euro Credit	19.14	12.33	1.14	2.60	3.08
Corporate Industrial					
U.S. Credit	40.52	0.95	2.66	13.73	23.18
Euro Credit	30.89	0.63	2.79	11.10	16.37
Corporate Utility					
U.S. Credit	7.08	0.01		1.67	5.40
Euro Credit	7.54		1.26	4.71	1.58
Corporate Financial Institutions					
U.S. Credit	34.38	3.06	4.51	22.14	4.66
Euro Credit	42.42	6.62	12.19	20.80	2.81

differences are reflected in the tracking error volatility of the U.S. Credit and European Credit indices, reported in Figure 5-5c.

For the Global Aggregate replications, portfolio CDS is clearly beneficial in reducing tracking errors—by 3.0 to 3.5 bp/month. To the extent that CDS gave exposure to credit spreads, they increased returns in the replicating portfolio because of higher carry and spread contraction. TBAs also reduce tracking errors, by 0.5 to 1.5 bp/month, depending on the period, though in the shorter period, TBAs did not reduce risk for the hedged index. Overall, a strategy that makes use of all available hedging instruments considered here would seem likely to deliver the lowest tracking errors.

Since non-Treasury instruments represent a larger proportion of the U.S. market than of the non-U.S. markets, it is not surprising that the tracking error for the dollar bloc is higher than for the other blocs. Overall, the results for the Global Aggregate demonstrate the power of diversification. The tracking error volatility of the "full replication" strategy is lower than that of any of the constituents. Figure 5-9 displays the diversification achieved by combining replication strategies for

Figure 5-9. Correlations of Realized Return Differentials among the Blocs within the Global Aggregate Index

August 2002–May 2005; Swaps + Futures + CDX/iTraxx + TBA

	Unhedged				Hedged			
	Dollar Bloc	Pan-Euro Bloc	Yen Bloc	Global Aggregate	Dollar Bloc	Pan-Euro Bloc	Yen Bloc	Global Aggregate
Tracking error volatility (bp/month)	12.1	8.6	15.1	6.9	11.8	8.0	11.5	5.7
Dollar bloc	1.00	0.05	0.05	0.83	1.00	0.24	-0.54	0.84
Pan-Euro bloc	0.05	1.00	-0.13	0.42	0.24	1.00	-0.22	0.62
Yen bloc	0.05	-0.13	1.00	0.40	-0.54	-0.22	1.00	-0.23
Global Aggregate	0.83	0.42	0.40	1.00	0.84	0.62	-0.23	1.00

different regions by examining the correlations of the return differences of the regional replication strategies with their respective indices. The unhedged replication strategies are essentially uncorrelated. For the hedged replication strategies, we actually see negative correlations with the yen bloc replication.

The relatively small difference in the risk profiles of the hedged and unhedged replications suggests that the currency risk derived from using only four currencies to track the performance of 24 currencies is limited, but could be reduced somewhat by increasing the number of currencies held.

We have focused on tracking error volatility, not return. While tracking errors can change over different time periods, volatilities are much more stable than returns, particularly in relative terms. For example, we can confidently say that over a given period, a replication that includes swaps, futures, and portfolio CDS will deliver significantly lower tracking error volatility than one that includes just swaps, but we cannot make the same prediction for returns. In Figure 5-6, we saw that monthly excess returns for credit have varied greatly between two different periods, whereas the variation in return volatilities is substantially less.

USING A RISK MODEL TO FORECAST REPLICATION RISK

Figure 5-10 presents a risk analysis of the currency-hedged replicating portfolio shown in Appendix B, which uses interest-rate swaps, U.S. Treasury futures, TBAs, CDX, and iTraxx. The predicted TEV is somewhat higher than that shown in our empirical analysis. In part, this reflects the changes in the composition of the Global Aggregate. It also reflects the fact that in the period prior to our empirical analysis, volatility was somewhat higher (reflected in the covariance matrix used in the risk model). The model provides a risk attribution, giving us insight into the remaining sources of risk in the replication strategy. Most of the risk comes from term-structure exposures, a reflection of the fact that while most of the risk can be eliminated by using swaps in four currencies, there is still a term-structure mismatch from, for example, using U.S. interest-rate swaps to hedge Canadian interest-rate risk.

A comparison with the overall volatility of the Global Aggregate is also instructive. Exposure to almost all of the risk factors has been reduced in the replicating portfolio. The exceptions are high yield spreads and credit default risk through exposure to some credits in CDX/iTraxx; idiosyncratic (issue or issuer-specific) risk, which primarily reflects differences between the issuer weightings in the Credit Index (market-weighted) and the portfolio CDS (equal-weighted); and CDS basis risk, which is the risk between CDS and cash bond prices. CDX/iTraxx clearly reduces credit spread risk, but adds basis risk.

Figure 5-10. Sources of Risk in the Replication of the Lehman Global Aggregate (hedged), with U.S. Futures, Swaps, TBAs, CDX, and iTraxx
Exponentially Weighted Covariance Matrix

Global Risk Factor	Isolated Total Volatility (bp/month)	Isolated Tracking Error Volatility (bp/month)	Percentage of Tracking Error Variance
Yield curve	83.05	6.06	55.38
Swap spreads	7.27	2.58	11.72
Volatility	1.41	0.20	−0.83
Investment-grade spreads	7.10	2.86	5.02
Treasury spreads	1.16	1.19	−0.92
Credit and agency spreads	6.26	2.15	6.14
MBS/securitized spreads	2.18	0.65	0.06
CMBS/ABS spreads	0.25	0.25	−0.25
High yield spreads	—	1.00	2.65
Emerging markets spread	0.61	0.62	1.34
CDS basis	—	3.10	11.99
Systematic risk	80.73	6.47	87.26
Idiosyncratic risk	1.03	1.59	5.29
Credit default risk	0.62	1.89	7.45
Total risk	80.74	6.93	
Empirically derived risk		5.70	

IMPROVING THE PERFORMANCE OF REPLICATION STRATEGIES

There are additional ways to lower the tracking error volatility of a replication strategy. The trade-off is between the cost and complexity of the strategy and its TEV. Investors with high risk aversion try to reduce TEV by adding more replicating instruments. For the unhedged Global Aggregate Index, the easiest way to reduce TEV is to add additional currency exposures instead of mapping them to one of the G4 currencies. For example, Canadian dollar exposure can be added via 1-month forward foreign exchange contracts. The high correlation between changes in U.S. and Canadian bond yields suggests that adding Canadian interest-rate exposure would be less beneficial. To further reduce TEV, exposures to the Australian dollar, South African rand, and Korean won can be added. The addition of these currencies to the unhedged Global Aggregate replication with futures, swaps, and TBAs would have reduced the monthly TEV over the period September 2000–May 2005 from 15.3 to 13.3 bp, improving the relative return from –0.7 to 0.5 bp/month.

Additional strategies can be implemented to reduce other risk exposures. For example, in the replication of the Japanese Aggregate Index, interest-rate swaps achieve a better term structure match than the 10-year futures contract alone (the only liquid futures contract in the JGB market). However, the use of swaps exposes the replication to the fluctuations in the yen swap spreads. By buying the futures contract and paying the fixed leg of an interest-rate swap of equivalent duration, this exposure could largely be eliminated. One caveat is that the total notional amount of derivatives in this case would be substantially larger than that of the replication target, which may present a problem for some investors. Over the period September 2000–May 2005, this approach would have reduced the monthly TEV of the yen replication strategy from 14.6 bp (with interest-rate swaps only) to 6.7 bp, improving the relative return from –0.1 to +1.4 bp/month.

CONCLUSION

The scope of the Global Aggregate Index, which today comprises more than 10,000 securities, actually makes it easier to replicate than single-country indices, owing to the low or negative correlations among the replication errors of the currency bloc components of the index. The advent of portfolio CDS has had an important effect on the success of replication strategies, and it is now reasonable to expect them to produce tracking error volatilities of less than 10 bp/month. This relatively low level of volatility makes a derivatives replication strategy suitable for a variety of needs, from portable alpha to asset allocation shifts. At the margin, replication results could be improved by adding more markets. The availability of total return swaps on RBI baskets (portfolios of derivatives constructed to track a given index, described in Chapter 4) means that investors can choose either to manage the replication strategy themselves or receive the return on the replication strategy directly without establishing a replicating portfolio.

APPENDIX A. THE LEHMAN BROTHERS GLOBAL AGGREGATE INDEX

The Global Aggregate Index contains three major components: the U.S. Aggregate Index, the Pan-European Aggregate Index, and the Asian-Pacific Aggregate Index. In addition to securities from these three benchmarks, the Global Aggregate Index includes eurodollar and euroyen corporate bonds; Canadian government, agency, and corporate securities; and U.S. dollar-denominated investment-grade 144A securities. The index was launched on January 1, 1999.

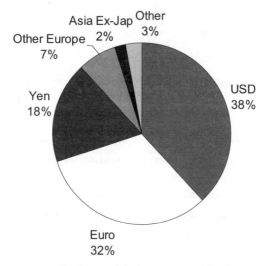

Figure 5-A1. Composition of Lehman Global Aggregate Index by Currency
August 31, 2005

- Frequency: Daily, on a $T + 1$ basis. If the last business day of the month is a holiday in the U.S. market, then prices from the previous business day are used.

- Timing: European currency bonds: 4:15 PM London time; American currency bonds: 3:00 PM New York time; Asian currency bonds: each at own market's close.

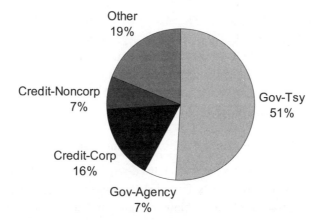

Figure 5-A2. Composition of Lehman Global Aggregate Index by Sector
August 31, 2005

- Bid/Offer: Outstanding issues are priced on the bid side. New issues enter the index on the offer side.

- Sources: Lehman trading desks in most cases.

- Methodology: Multicontributor verification—the Lehman price for each security is checked against a blend of alternative valuations by our quality control group. Variations are analyzed and corrected as necessary.

- Reinvestment: Index cash flows are reinvested at the start of the month following their receipt. There is no return on cash held intramonth.

RULES FOR INCLUSION
- Amount Outstanding: U.S. and Canadian dollar-denominated securities must have a par amount outstanding of at least USD300 million. Pan-European securities must have a par amount outstanding of EUR300 million currency equivalent. Securities denominated in GBP must have a par amount outstanding of GBP200 million currency equivalent. Asian-Pacific securities must have a par amount outstanding of JPY35 billion currency equivalent.

- Quality: Only bonds from investment-grade-rated countries are included.

- Maturity: One year minimum to final maturity on dated bonds, regardless of put or call features.

- Debt Seniority: Senior and subordinated issues are included. Undated securities are included provided their coupons switch from fixed to variable rate.

- Currency of Issue: As included in the regional aggregate indices—Pan-Euro Aggregate: EUR, GBP, CZK, DKK, HUF, NKK, PLN, SIT, SKK, SEK; U.S. Aggregate—USD; Asian-Pacific Aggregate—JPY, AUD, HKD, KRW, NZD, SGD, THB, TWD, MYR; other currencies—CAD, CLP, MXN, ZAR.

The list of eligible currencies is reviewed once a year:

- Market of Issue: Publicly issued in the global and regional markets.

- Security Types: The index includes all fixed-rate bullets, putable and callable bonds, and soft bullets. Excluded are bonds with equity-type features (e.g., warrants, convertibility to equity), private placements, floating rate issues, and strips.

REBALANCING RULES

- Frequency: Statistic (projected) universe—daily. Returns universe—monthly, on the last business day of the month.

- Methodology: During the month, all indicative changes to securities are reflected in both the statistics (projected) and returns universes on a daily basis and include changes to ratings, amounts outstanding, or sector. These changes affect the qualification of securities in the statistics (projected) universe on a daily basis, but only affect the qualification of bonds for the returns universe at the end of the month.

- Timing: Qualifying securities issued, but not necessarily settled, on or before the month-end rebalancing date qualify for inclusion in the following month's returns universe.

APPENDIX B. REPLICATING PORTFOLIO AS OF MARCH 31, 2005

Identifier	Classification— Broad	Position Amount	Description	Coupon
Currency: USD (twenty-three positions)				
Sector—Broad: Futures (four positions)				
TUU5:CBT	Futures	6,650,000	2-year Treasury notes	
FVU5:CBT	Futures	41,700,000	5-year Treasury notes	
TYU5:CBT	Futures	−9,500,000	10-year Treasury notes	
USU5:CBT	Futures	39,200,000	30-year U.S. Treasury bonds	
Sector—Broad: FHLMC (two positions)				
02R05064	FHLMC	9,962,845	FHLM gold guaranteed single-family 30 years	5.00
02R05264	FHLMC	10,640,920	FHLM gold guaranteed single-family 30 years	5.50
Sector—Broad: FNMA (eight positions)				
01F04244	FNMA	13,315,625	FNMA conventional 15 years	4.50
01F05044	FNMA	12,476,403	FNMA conventional 15 years	5.00
01F05244	FNMA	12,697,340	FNMA conventional 15 years	5.50
01F06044	FNMA	6,499,237	FNMA conventional 15 years	6.00

(continued)

Identifier	Classification— Broad	Position Amount	Description	Coupon
01F04264	FNMA	5,431,175	FNMA conventional 30 years	4.50
01F05264	FNMA	23,353,581	FNMA conventional 30 years	5.50
01F06064	FNMA	11,633,364	FNMA conventional 30 years	6.00
01F06264	FNMA	8,673,428	FNMA conventional 30 years	

Sector—Broad: GNMA (three positions)

01N05064	GNMA	3,905,677	GNMA I single-family 30 years	5.00
01N06064	GNMA	6,123,912	GNMA I single-family 30 years	6.00
01N06264	GNMA	6,460,258	GNMA I single-family 30 years	6.50

Sector—Broad: Interest-Rate Swaps (six positions)

SWCXX006	Treasury	28,546,000	SW CURR 006-MO	3.43
SWCXX024	Treasury	61,347,000	SW CURR 024-MO	4.21
SWCXX060	Treasury	59,123,000	SW CURR 060-MO	4.62
SWCXX120	Treasury	29,449,000	SW CURR 120-MO	4.95
SWCXX240	Treasury	10,220,000	SW CURR 240-MO	5.22
SWCXX360	Treasury	7,615,000	SW CURR 360-MO	5.27

Sector—Broad: Portfolio Default Swaps (two positions)

CDX.IG3	Portfolio CDS	74,570,000	SW CURR 006-MO	0.50
CDX.IG3.10Y	Portfolio CDS	35,371,000	SW CURR 024-MO	0.75

Currency: JPY (six positions)
Sector—Broad: Interest-Rate Swaps (six positions)

SWCJP006	Treasury	3,378,000,000	SW CURR 006-MO	0.07
SWCJP024	Treasury	8,194,000,000	SW CURR 024-MO	0.19
SWCJP060	Treasury	7,779,000,000	SW CURR 060-MO	0.62
SWCJP120	Treasury	3,883,000,000	SW CURR 120-MO	1.38
SWCJP240	Treasury	1,023,000,000	SW CURR 240-MO	2.07
SWCJP360	Treasury	222,000,000	SW CURR 360-MO	2.29

Identifier	Classification— Broad	Position Amount	Description	Coupon
Currency: GBP (six positions)				
Sector—Broad: Interest-Rate Swaps (six positions)				
SWCGB006	Treasury	1,453,000	SW CURR 006-MO	5.04
SWCGB024	Treasury	5,574,000	SW CURR 024-MO	5.04
SWCGB060	Treasury	6,198,000	SW CURR 060-MO	5.03
SWCGB120	Treasury	7,230,000	SW CURR 120-MO	5.00
SWCGB240	Treasury	5,395,000	SW CURR 240-MO	4.91
SWCGB360	Treasury	3,132,000	SW CURR 360-MO	4.81
Currency: EUR (six positions)				
Sector—Broad: Interest-Rate Swaps (six positions)				
SWCEU006	Treasury	32,165,000	SW CURR 006-MO	2.23
SWCEU024	Treasury	92,187,000	SW CURR 024-MO	2.63
SWCEU060	Treasury	96,800,000	SW CURR 060-MO	3.16
SWCEU120	Treasury	48,336,000	SW CURR 120-MO	3.72
SWCEU240	Treasury	19,891,000	SW CURR 240-MO	4.14
SWCEU360	Treasury	6,107,000	SW CURR 360-MO	4.23
Sector—Broad: Portfolio Default Swaps (one position)				
ITRX.EUR.3	Portfolio CDS	58,100,000	iTraxx3 5-year	0.35

6. Tradable Proxy Portfolios for the Lehman Brothers MBS Index

....

Mortgage-backed securities (MBS) constitute a significant portion of the Lehman Brothers Aggregate Index and the Lehman Global Aggregate Index (35.0 and 16.5%, respectively, as of May 31, 2001). To track these indices, one must take exposure to the U.S. mortgage market. To some investors, the U.S. mortgage market is enigmatic and intimidating because of its arcane terminology and highly variable cash flows. However, while achieving outperformance in this market indeed requires considerable knowledge and experience, the MBS Index is surprisingly easy to track. The purpose of this study is to investigate how investors with limited MBS knowledge can replicate the MBS Index. We design and evaluate two relatively simple replication strategies that invest in highly tradable and liquid MBS securities and do not require detailed knowledge of the U.S. mortgage market.

Why would knowledge of the MBS market be necessary for index replication? After all, replication means tracking the index, not outperforming it. Investors who want to replicate an index can use sampling and optimization techniques to identify a set of index securities that track the index with an expected tracking error. Such an exercise does not require detailed knowledge of the market. Investors simply buy the selected set with the expectation that its performance will, with some degree of error, track the performance of the overall index.

However, in the case of the MBS Index, going from identifying a set of securities to actually buying the set is not trivial. Unlike most other indices, the MBS Index contains only nontraded annual aggregates (their creation is discussed later). The first step in the replication process selects these index generics to form a tracking proxy portfolio. Then a second step is necessary: one or more tradable securities must be purchased for each generic to form the tradable proxy port-

Based on research first published by Lehman Brothers in 2001.

folio. Suppose the replication strategy selects the 1997 GNMA 8% index generic. There are many 1997 GNMA 8% pools to choose from, and there is no assurance that a particular pool selected for the tradable proxy portfolio will perform identically to the generic suggested by the replication technique. This additional layer of decision making (i.e., pool selection) and the potential for added tracking error from performance mismatch can make investors who are new to the MBS market uneasy about replicating the MBS Index.

We propose the following solution to this problem. First, we identify MBS securities that are likely to track their respective index generics. Next, we discuss which of these MBS securities are "tradable," that is, bought and sold easily. Finally, we constrain the replication strategy to select only from among those generics for which there are tradable securities likely to track their performance. This approach improves the chances that the tradable proxy portfolio will track the performance of the generics proxy portfolio constructed by the replication technique. We measure the empirical success of this approach in replicating the MBS Index. It is our belief that the results should convince investors with little mortgage market knowledge that they can replicate the MBS Index without too much concern about pool selection.

We develop and evaluate two replication strategies that use this approach. The first involves only TBA (to-be-announced) contracts. Holding only TBAs simplifies the back-office operational aspects of investing in mortgages because it avoids taking physical delivery of MBS pools. However, the TBAs-only strategy replicates just the recently originated part of the MBS market. The risk is that the seasoned portion of the MBS Index may behave differently, leading to tracking error. Better tracking of the index is achieved by the second replication strategy, which uses only large MBS pools and, over time, represents the seasoned part of the index, as well as new issuance.

As demonstrated later, both replication strategies use only MBS securities that are sufficiently liquid to make the replication feasible and practical. Both strategies are also easy to implement and maintain, and neither presupposes that the investor has detailed knowledge of the MBS market. Both strategies deliver fairly low tracking errors relative to the index, while reducing the risk of additional tracking error owing to pool selection.

GENERICS, POOLS, AND TBA CONTRACTS

Index generics are composites of tradable MBS securities (pools) defined by three characteristics: agency/program (e.g., 30-year Fannie Mae [FNMA] conventional); origination year of the underlying mortgages (e.g., 1996); and coupon (e.g., 7.5%).[1] Pools are mapped to a generic according to these characteristics. For example, pool FN #512677 is a FNMA 7.5% pass-through security containing 30-year mortgage loans originated in 1999. This pool is mapped to the 1999 30-year FNMA 7.5% index generic. If an annual aggregate satisfies the liquidity constraint of Lehman's Global Family of Indices (currently at $150 million remaining outstanding balance), it is included in the MBS Index. Currently, there are hundreds of thousands of pools, but only about 3200 annual aggregates. Out of these, 533 formed the MBS Index as of May 31, 2001.

To replicate the MBS Index, the investor must buy either specific pools or TBA contracts. The buyer of an MBS pool is entitled to the monthly interest and principal paydowns. The magnitude of these monthly payments depends on the prepayment behavior of the individual mortgages underlying the pool.

In lieu of buying a pool, an investor can buy a TBA contract that is a forward contract to buy MBS pools of a given agency/program and coupon. The specific pools that the investor is buying are unknown until 2 days before settlement. Because it is a forward contract, no cash outlay is required until settlement. For example, in December 2000, an investor could agree to buy a 30-year FNMA 7.5% TBA for delivery and settlement on January 16, 2001.[2] On the trade date, the TBA buyer does not know the origination year, originator, WAM, or WAC[3] (and many other attributes) of the pool(s) he will receive. The seller has an option to deliver any mortgage pool(s) to satisfy a TBA contract and usually delivers the least attractive pool(s) he can find.[4]

Generally, but not always, the seller delivers pools containing recently originated mortgages, as these often have the worst prepayment characteristics. If mortgage rates fall, it is relatively easy and inexpensive for a homeowner to refinance a recently originated mortgage compared with a seasoned mortgage. On the other

---

1. For a detailed discussion of the construction, pricing, and return calculations for Lehman Brothers MBS Index generics, refer to "Managing Against the Lehman Brothers MBS Index: MBS Index Prices" and "Managing Against the Lehman Brothers MBS Index: MBS Index Returns," *Handbook of Mortgage-Backed Securities,* 6th edition, Frank J. Fabozzi, editor, McGraw-Hill, 2006.

2. Delivery dates are specified at the time of purchase. Most follow dates set by the Bond Market Association (formerly called the PSA).

3. A pool may contain loans from a single originator or multiple originators. GNMA I pools contain loans from only a single originator. WAM is the weighted average of the remaining terms to maturity of the mortgage loans underlying the pool, using the balance of each mortgage as the weighting factor. WAC is the weighted average of the gross interest rates of the loans underlying the pool. WAM and WAC are important determinants of a pool's proclivity to prepay in various interest rate environments.

4. This is why a mortgage pool of a given agency/program and coupon will not trade at a price less than the TBA price.

Figure 6-1. The Lehman Brothers MBS Index: Composition by Market Value
April 1, 2001

	30-Year Conventional	30-Year GNMA	15-Year and Balloons	Total
Priced at TBA level (%)	25.6	10.5	4.8	41.0
Non-TBA or seasoned (%)	33.5	12.3	13.2	59.0
Total (%)	59.2	22.8	18.0	100.0

hand, if mortgage rates rise, homeowners with new mortgages might be less likely to move and prepay the loans compared with homeowners with seasoned mortgages who have lived in their houses for some time. Moreover, because there is little prepayment history on new mortgages, market participants may discount them a bit more until their prepayment behavior is better understood. Because a TBA seller will likely deliver pools containing recently originated mortgages, TBA contracts and same-coupon pools of recently originated mortgages usually have the same price. Pools that trade at TBA prices are referred to as "TBA pools," and pools that trade at a higher price are referred to as "seasoned" or "non-TBA pools." As of April 1, 2001, the MBS Index was divided between TBA and seasoned issues (by percentage of market value) as shown in Figure 6-1.

A pool may trade at the TBA level for a period and then trade at a "payup" to the TBA price. For example, a 30-year FNMA 6.5% pool containing mortgages originated in 1999 currently trades at a payup of 7/32 to TBA 30-year FNMA 6.5%. A pool may trade back at the TBA level after trading at a payup for a period of time. Pools trade at a payup as they age, or if they have other valuable attributes that are different from the new pool production. Depending on the market environment, the percentage of the MBS market that trades as TBAs varies over time, as does the payup level for seasoned pools. Consequently, TBA contracts and TBA pools may not track the performance of many index generics, particularly seasoned ones.

TBA contract buyers can postpone accepting pool delivery by "rolling" their TBA positions month to month. Rolling works as follows. Before the upcoming settlement, the TBA buyer contacts the seller and asks for the "drop" in price to delay settlement 1 month.[5] If agreeable, the buyer and seller "offset" the upcoming

---

5. Settlement can be delayed for more than 1 month, but usually not more than 3 months. The drop is usually positive, as mortgage yields are generally greater than 1-month rates. However, mortgage rolls can occur at negative drops.

sale and enter into a new purchase/sale contract for the next month at the (lower) price determined by the drop. The advantage of rolling is that it simplifies the buyer's operations requirements, as there are no monthly interest and principal payments from pools to be collected and reconciled. In addition, because no cash is required in the TBA purchase until settlement, some TBA buyers may invest cash in high-yielding short-term instruments to earn additional return.

Identifying Tradable MBS Securities Likely to Track Index Generics

Irrespective of the replication technique (e.g., optimization or stratified sampling, discussed later), the investor must hold some combination of MBS pools and TBA contracts to track the MBS Index. Unfortunately, there is no guarantee that these tradable MBS instruments will track their respective index generics. Potential performance differences between pools and TBA contracts and their generics should be taken into account when evaluating the tracking error of any replication strategy.

As an example, consider how a specific pool can differ from its index generic. MBS pricing services generally price all MBS pools of a given agency/program, coupon, and origination year at the same level. However, the timing of their cash flows may be very different, depending on the prepayments of the mortgage loans underlying each pool. Of course, even similar pools are unlikely to have identical prepayments, but the difference in prepayments owing purely to random noise averages out over time. However, pools belonging to the same index generic can have materially different characteristics (e.g., WAC, weighted average loan age [WALA], geography, originator, and average loan balance). Prepayment differences resulting from these could persist. Consider the following two 1997 30-year GNMA 8% pools that are mapped to the same 1997 30-year GNMA 8% index generic (Figure 6-2).

As the pools are priced identically, the large difference in performance (60 bp) is due to differences in prepayments. For the 12-month period shown, pool #435461 had faster prepayments than pool #436112. The difference was probably due to an originator's aggressive buyout activity.[6] Because the latter pool is a premium security, faster prepayments were a drag on total returns. Even though buyouts may not persist, the potential for additional tracking error is clear.

---

6. Mortgage servicers have the option to purchase, at par, loans from a GNMA mortgage pool once the loans have become 3 months delinquent. These purchases tend to occur in pools trading above par and show up as prepayments. It is profitable for servicers to purchase these loans at par, cure the delinquencies, and then resell the reperforming loans as another pool at a higher price.

●

Figure 6-2. Comparison of Two 30-Year GNMA 8% Pools Mapped to the Same Index Generic (GNA08097)[a]

December 1, 2000

	Pool GN #436112	Pool GN #435461	GNA08097
Coupon (%)	8	8	8
WAC (%)	8.5	8.5	8.5
WALA (months)	37	35	41
3-month CPR (%)	0.0	60.5	16.5
6-month CPR (%)	0.0	48.6	14.7
12-month CPR (%)	3.1	31.2	14.2
Original balance ($millions)	2.53	2.02	12,830
Geography	44% OH; 11% FL	50% MI; 24% OH	N/A
Total return (12/99–11/00) (%)	8.73	8.13	8.58

[a] GNA08097 refers to the 1997 30-year GNMA 8% index generic. For a complete description of MBS Index notation, refer to the publication in footnote 1.

Other reasons for noticeable prepayment differences among pools would be: (1) geographic differences (one part of the country has faster housing turnover than another), (2) loan size (smaller loans are less likely to be refinanced than larger ones because of the fixed costs involved in refinancing), and (3) pool-level diversification (a small pool with fewer loans may be more prone to idiosyncratic prepayment behavior than a large pool).

As discussed earlier, an index generic is a composite of all its mapped tradable MBS pools. Compare these two pools with their index generic. Prepayments (and total returns) for the generic were somewhere between those for the two pools. Not only can similar pools perform differently from each other; they can perform differently from their index generic. This fact makes MBS Index replication some-what challenging because there is no assurance that a tradable MBS instrument will perform according to its index generic. Nevertheless, might there be some tradable MBS instruments that are likely to track their index generics? If so, we can have more confidence in the use of replication techniques to create efficient tradable proxy portfolios.

Using Pools to Track Index Generics

The GNMA 8% example referred to earlier may give investors pause as pools in their tradable proxy portfolio may not track the performance of the generic as-sumed by the replication technique. So, which pools might reasonably be expected

1-Year CPR (%)

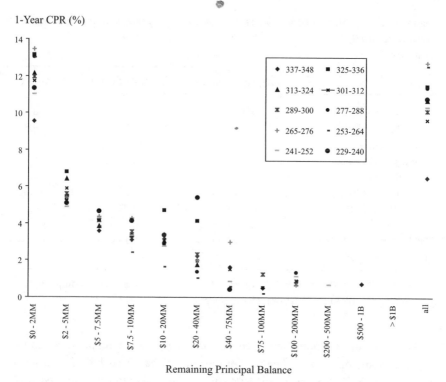

Remaining Principal Balance

Figure 6-3. The Standard Deviation of 1-Year CPR for Different WAM Ranges
December 1, 2000

to track their generic? Pricing is usually not the issue because pools of a given vintage are priced the same as the generic.[7] The main issue is the timing of cash flows owing to prepayments. If the pool size is large enough, will it behave like the "average"? Will a $50 million pool track the performance of its generic more closely than a $5 million pool? As a pool contains a sample of mortgages drawn from the population of mortgages of a given coupon range, it seems reasonable to expect that increasing the pool (i.e., sample) size increases the chance that the pool will track the generic (i.e., population) closely.

How well do large pools track their generics? We examine the 1-year CPRs across all of the more than 35,000 30-year FNMA 7.5% pools as of December 1, 2000. We present the standard deviations of 1-year CPR percentages across pools,

7. This may not always remain so. The market does distinguish between low-WAC and high-WAC and low-loan-balance and high-loan-balance pools of a given vintage. Pricing services may follow.

Mean 1-Year CPR (%)

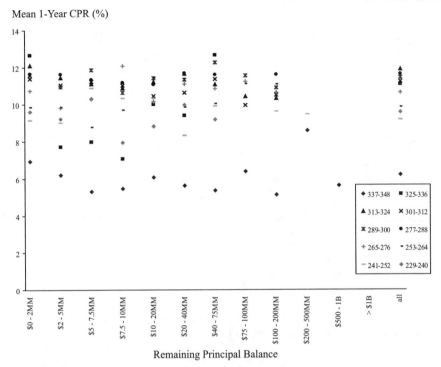

Figure 6-4. The Mean 1-Year CPR for Different WAM Ranges
December 1, 2000

sorted by WAM group and current pool balance. As can be seen in Figure 6-3, the standard deviation declines as pool size increases. Figure 6-4 demonstrates that the mean 1-year CPR is roughly constant for each WAM irrespective of the pool size. Finally, Figure 6-5 shows that the range of 1-year CPR declines as the pool size increases. For a given WAM group, the range shows the 1-year CPR difference between the pool with the greatest 1-year CPR and the pool with the smallest one.

If large pools (both seasoned and recently issued) tend to track the "average" (i.e., generic) pool closely, then a strategy of buying pieces of large pools may be an effective way to build a tradable proxy portfolio. While large pools are a small percentage of the total number of pools, they are well represented as a percentage of the total remaining principal balance. As shown in Figure 6-6, for example, in the WAM range of 337–348 months, the $500 million–$1 billion bucket accounts for 14.2% of the total principal balance but is represented by just six pools, or 0.2% of the total number. Consequently, buying large pools to replicate index generics is a viable strategy.

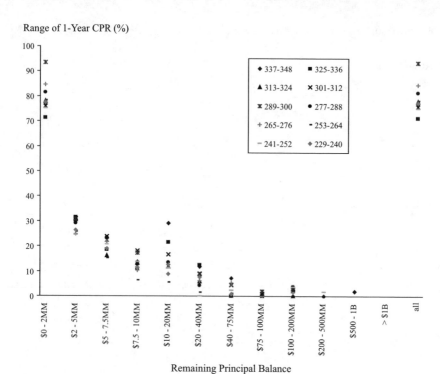

Figure 6-5. The Range of 1-Year CPR for Different WAM Ranges
December 1, 2000

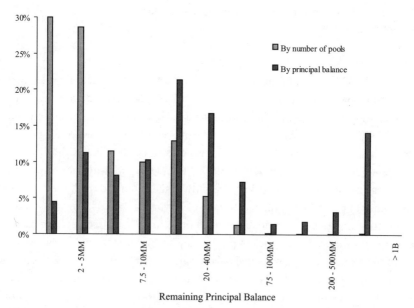

Figure 6-6. Percentage of Total Pools and Total Remaining Principal Balance by Pool Size for the 337-348 WAM Range
December 1, 2000

Another advantage of this strategy is that a considerable portion of the index is composed of seasoned generics, as shown in Figure 6-1. In theory, large seasoned pools could be used to track the seasoned generic component of the index, which would help reduce the proxy portfolio's overall tracking error. In practice, however, large seasoned pools are often difficult to find in the marketplace. Consequently, buying pieces of large pools to replicate seasoned index generics is a difficult strategy to implement, and any proposed replication strategy using large pools must account for this difficulty.

USING TBA CONTRACTS TO TRACK INDEX GENERICS

The TBA Roll: Background

The TBA roll offers the potential for additional returns that can enhance the performance of a TBA mortgage portfolio. This advantage arises from imbalances in the current month's supply and demand for a particular mortgage coupon. Mortgage originators often sell their current production to broker/dealers a month or two in advance (which reflects the time between the mortgage commitment and the mortgage closing). Consequently, broker/dealers are usually long current production coupon MBS in the forward months. To entice MBS buyers to defer taking delivery until a forward month in which the broker/dealer has more supply, the level of the drop adjusts to offer a roll advantage. As a result of these supply and demand dynamics, a roll advantage often exists only for current production coupons. At other times, there is no roll advantage at all. Even if there appears to be a roll advantage, care must be taken to verify that the implied financing rate was correctly estimated and interpreted.

First, the implied financing rate may be less than the current short-term rates because the market is expecting rate reductions (e.g., Federal Reserve actions). The implied financing rate of the mortgage roll applies for the period between two PSA settlement dates. Investors usually agree to roll well before this period begins. Consequently, to measure the roll advantage, investors must compare the implied rate with the proper forward short-term investment rate.

Second, in addition to the drop level, estimating the implied financing rate requires assumptions about prepayments, reinvestment rate, and the type of MBS pool likely to be delivered at the termination of the roll. As discussed earlier, it is typically assumed that the TBA deliverable is the same at the beginning and at the end of the roll. In other words, the MBS security in the hold strategy is comparable to the underlying TBA deliverable in the roll strategy. This last component of the implied financing rate calculation is sometimes overlooked. The underlying characteristics of pools likely to be delivered against a TBA contract change over time. For example, the FNMA 6% deliverable into the TBA contract in January 2001 may be very different from the FNMA 6% deliverable in April 2001 because there was much new production of FNMA 6% pools during the first calendar quarter of 2001. New production FNMA 6% pools have significantly higher WACs and WAMs (i.e., worse convexity characteristics), which make them less valuable than older production. As the market fluctuates, the assumption as to which type of MBS pool will likely be delivered changes and is reflected in the dollar roll market. In fact, the original TBA seller may temporarily offer a particularly attractive roll level just to ensure that TBA holders continue rolling at least until the new (less desirable) supply becomes available. Consequently, any roll advantage has to be adjusted, if appropriate, for the expected change in the quality of the pool deliverable. A reported roll advantage may just be fair compensation for rolling into a less valuable TBA deliverable.

The roll advantage can, at times, offer significant added return, but we do not calculate and add a roll advantage to the TBA proxy portfolio returns in this study. Our focus is on the tracking error of the proxy portfolio to the MBS Index. Any roll advantage will produce primarily an improved mean return for the proxy, not an improved tracking error. Furthermore, many investors try to enhance the roll advantage by assuming additional credit and option risk in their short-term cash investments. While this strategy often has merit, it deviates from the pure index replication strategies we focus on.

Off-market TBA contracts occur when there have been large changes in mortgage interest rates. For example, suppose that several years ago, 9% coupon mortgages were current production. Subsequently, interest rates declined and no new 9% coupon mortgages have been originated since. Today, an investor might still be able to buy a 9% TBA contract and expect the contract to track the respective 9% index annual aggregate for the most recent year of issuance. However, as we argue later, off-market TBA contracts are less likely to track their respective index generic than current-coupon TBA contracts.

Off-market-coupon TBA contracts have their own price dynamics, which depend on expectations of future mortgage supply, the trading positions of the TBA seller, and technical conditions in the marketplace. By definition, there is little or no new pool production for off-market coupons. However, sellers of off-market TBA contracts must be prepared for the possibility that the TBA buyer who is currently rolling his contracts may decide to take delivery. As there is no new pool production, the seller runs the risk of having difficulty finding pools to satisfy the TBA contract. The possibility of being caught short can make broker/dealers reluctant to continue rolling off-market TBA contracts. In fact, in response to this risk, there might come a time when the TBA seller may want to encourage the investor to take delivery by offering an unattractive drop level. He may also do this because he has received or located some off-market pools that have unattractive prepayment characteristics that he would like to deliver. Given the availability of prepayment history and the likelihood that the more desirable pools may be locked up in other portfolios, the off-market coupon pools available for delivery will probably be those least attractive to hold, with potentially high idiosyncratic risk compared with the relevant index generic. If the TBA buyer takes delivery because the roll advantage is no longer positive, the pools he receives may not track the relevant index annual aggregate.

Another problem with off-market TBA contracts is that the underlying deliverable can change more dramatically. If the investor bought and rolled an off-market TBA contract and interest rates subsequently changed so that market participants began to anticipate future production of the coupon, the TBA contract would begin to track the characteristics of anticipated future production. Depending on how long ago the coupon was last produced and the structural changes in the mortgage market, the differences between the old and new production for the coupon could be substantial. In addition, depending on movements in mortgage rates, this change can come about relatively suddenly. Consequently, investors must monitor the characteristics of anticipated mortgage production and compare them with the assumptions underlying their off-market TBA contracts. They must also be prepared to re-examine the structure of the proxy portfolio, as the TBA position may no longer track the index generic assumed by their replication techniques.

Generally, buyers and sellers of TBA contracts on current production mortgage coupons implicitly assume average attributes (e.g., WAC and average loan size) of the pools likely to be delivered. In other words, a TBA contract corresponds to a large pool of recently issued loans or a current production index generic. Because there is ample supply of new production to deliver against the TBA contract and little prepayment history to help identify pools with potentially highly idiosyncratic prepayment behavior, it is likely that a TBA contract will closely track its corresponding current production index generic.[8]

Although prices for TBA contracts and their corresponding recently originated index generics are usually identical, one potential source of performance difference between them is the TBA roll. At times, TBA holders are able to pick up additional return by rolling the settlement of TBA contracts at an "implied financing rate" from one month to the next and investing the unused cash in a higher-yielding short-term asset. The implied financing rate is essentially what the rolling TBA holder (also known as the roll "seller") pays to entice someone else to use capital to take delivery this month and allow the roll seller to postpone delivery. One can derive the implied financing rate using an arbitrage argument. The holder of a TBA contract can either take delivery or roll the TBA position to the next month. If the holder takes delivery, he uses cash to settle the trade and receives MBS pools and the monthly cash flows (coupon, principal prepayments, and any reinvestment income) from these pools. The monthly rate of return expected by the pool holder is determined by these cash flows and next month's TBA price (which reflects the roll drop).

Alternatively, by rolling the TBA position to the following month, holders agree to settle the trade at the next month's TBA price (including the drop) and will hold onto the cash. If the TBA buyer rolls, then someone else takes pool delivery. The monthly rate of return earned by the pool holder is the implied financing rate that the roller of the TBA position forgoes, or "pays," for deferring settlement. This implied financing rate is essentially the no-arbitrage rate that must be earned on cash to make the TBA buyer indifferent in regard to taking delivery or rolling the position. If the rate actually earned on cash is greater than the implied rate, then the roll offers a return advantage.

It is important to note that an investor using TBA contracts to replicate the MBS Index is affected by any change in the prepayment quality of the TBA deliverable, even if the investor never takes delivery. As the market fluctuates, there may be a change in the assumed TBA deliverable, and the new deliverable underlying the TBA in the proxy might have different convexity properties than the old one. Perhaps the old TBA deliverable was a good tradable proxy security for re-

---

8. It is still possible for TBAs to diverge from the current index generic. The TBA contract more accurately reflects what is likely to be delivered in the near future. Over the course of a year, some characteristics of the TBA deliverable might change (e.g., WAC and average loan balance) as changes occur in mortgage originations. The current annual generic, on the other hand, reflects the year's cumulative production. Nevertheless, buying a TBA contract and rolling it from month to month is likely to track its corresponding current production index generic quite well.

cent production generics in the index, but the new deliverable may not be. To the extent that the characteristics of the TBA deliverable depart from recent production generics used in the replication, the proxy portfolio's ex post (realized) tracking error may exceed the ex ante (expected) tracking error. In particular, this problem is most likely to arise with "off-market" TBA contracts.

To keep the replication strategy simple and less dependent on detailed MBS market knowledge, we assume that a TBA contract tracks its corresponding relevant recent origination index generic used by the replication technique. While off-market TBA contracts may also track their generics, they are disqualified from the tradable proxy portfolio because they require more detailed MBS market knowledge than assumed by these replication techniques. Consequently, a replication strategy using TBA contracts produces a tradable proxy portfolio containing only TBAs on current production mortgage coupons.

TWO TRADABLE MBS REPLICATION STRATEGIES: DESIGN, CONSTRUCTION, AND EMPIRICAL PERFORMANCE

Two tradable MBS instruments are likely to track index generics: large pools and TBA contracts, and these can be used in a tradable proxy portfolio to track the MBS Index. Unfortunately, there are limitations to this approach. First, large seasoned pools are often not available in the marketplace and, thus, cannot initially be part of a realistic tradable proxy portfolio. Second, TBAs adequately track only recently originated generics. With these limitations in mind, we consider two strategies for constructing proxy portfolios. We then compare the historically simulated empirical performance of these strategies with the MBS Index.

While there are several key differences between the two strategies, some of the mechanics of constructing proxy portfolios are the same. At the end of each calendar quarter, a mortgage proxy portfolio is constructed using the Lehman Brothers multifactor risk model and its portfolio optimizer.[9] (There are other ways to construct proxy portfolios. Stratified sampling can be applied to divide the index into orthogonal buckets, and securities can be selected using linear programming techniques so as to match the curve, convexity, and sector risk of the index. Another technique is to purchase total-return swaps on the Lehman MBS Index.)

The optimization process begins with the creation of a "seed" portfolio that contains just one manually selected generic (theoretically, the seed may be anything, but careful selection of the first security makes the optimization path more straightforward). Next, an investable set, that is, a set of securities acceptable for

9. For a detailed description of the model, refer to Chapter 26.

inclusion in the portfolio, is chosen. Once this set is selected, the optimizer begins an iterative process, known as gradient descent, searching for market value-neutral, one-for-one swap transactions that will minimize the expected tracking error. The securities in the swap pool are ranked in terms of reduction in tracking error per unit of each security purchased. The model indicates which bond, if purchased, will lead to the steepest decline in tracking error, but leaves the choice of the trade to the investor. Once a bond has been selected for purchase, the optimizer offers a list of recommended candidates to sell (with the optimal transaction size for each pair of bonds), sorted in order of achievable reduction in tracking error. Investors are free to adjust the model's recommendations, either selecting different bonds to sell or adjusting recommended trade amounts.

As a result, at each rebalancing, the optimizer selects index generics from a specified available set to form a proxy portfolio with the minimum possible expected tracking error vs. the Lehman MBS Index. The resulting proxy portfolio is held for the next 3 months, and its monthly total returns are compared with the returns on the index. At the end of the next calendar quarter, the proxy portfolio is rebalanced (i.e., "reoptimized") by selling issues in the old proxy and buying new issues in the current available set to produce a new proxy that minimizes the expected tracking error. The optimizer uses risk sensitivities, historical variances, and correlations of risk factors available at the time of rebalancing. The rebalancing process is constrained to allow additions to existing holdings only if they are included in the current available set. This constraint ensures that the two strategies are replicable by the investor.

TBAs-Only Strategy

The first strategy builds a proxy portfolio of recently issued generics. The investor can then buy a tradable proxy portfolio of corresponding TBAs with the expectation that the TBAs will track the performance of the generics. As the composition of the new issue mortgage market changes over time, this strategy adjusts its holdings of TBA contracts so as always to reflect the most recent and active portion of the mortgage market. For example, if 2 years ago, high-coupon mortgages were issued predominantly, then, at that time the tradable proxy portfolio would contain TBAs on high coupons. If low-coupon issuance dominates today, the replication process will have gradually led to the replacement of high-coupon TBAs with low-coupon TBAs.

The basket of recently issued generics is optimized to minimize the expected tracking error relative to the MBS Index. Specifically, the available set for the TBAs-only strategy is defined as the set of index generics with at least $2.5 billion outstanding and a WAM of at least 348 months (for the 15-year product, the constraints are $1 billion outstanding and a WAM of at least 168 months). Motivation for these constraints is explained later. Every 3 months, at each rebalancing period, the optimizer considers recently originated index generics in the available set for the proxy portfolio. Index generics for coupons not recently issued in sufficient volume are ineligible. Under this replication strategy, the tradable proxy contains only actively traded TBA contracts. Once a year, the existing proxy portfolio is purged and an entirely new proxy portfolio of index generics is constructed. If, as is likely, some of the generics in the old proxy remain in the available set, then the new proxy may contain generics that had been purged. This annual purging simply ensures that the proxy portfolio contains only recently issued generics. The corresponding tradable proxy portfolio will, therefore, contain TBA contracts that are likely to track the performance of the generics assumed by the optimizer.

Large-Pools-Only Strategy

The second strategy builds a proxy portfolio of generics, both seasoned and of recent origination. The investor then buys portions of large MBS pools for the tradable proxy portfolio with the expectation that large pools will track the performance of the generics. In practice, however, tradable large seasoned pools are difficult to find, so we assume that they can be bought initially only as new originations. Consequently, the proxy portfolio for this strategy initially contains only recently issued generics and a portion of these holdings remains in the portfolio and seasons over time.

Specifically, the available set for the large-pools-only (LP-only) strategy is defined as the set of index generics with at least $5 billion outstanding and a WAM of at least 336 months (for the 15-year product, a WAM of at least 156 months). The large amount outstanding and recent WAM requirements ensure that an investor is able to obtain large pools for the proxy portfolio.[10]

---

10. How can investors obtain large current production pools? There are many ways. First, investors can ask broker/dealers for their inventory of pools and then select pools (or a portfolio of pools) that are likely to behave close to the "average" pool. For example, each month, there is usually a FNMA "major" pool (or the FHLMC "auction" pool) that is the largest FNMA pool for a given coupon created that month. Broker/dealers may have a piece of this pool in inventory. Second, investors could combine many small pools into a single large pool (sometimes called a "mega" or "giant" pool). This is a straightforward process that occurs regularly as firms try to reduce operations costs. Third, when buying TBA contracts with the intention to take delivery, buyers can make "stipulations." For example, when buying 30-year FNMA 7.5% pools, buyers could stipulate that they wish to receive pools that have a remaining principal balance of $20 million or more. Fourth, investors could stipulate that they wish to receive no fewer than x pools

Initially, the LP-only proxy portfolio contains generics selected from among all agency/programs and coupons of recent origination, which is similar to the TBAs-only strategy. By the next rebalancing, the proxy generics will have aged, but because the tradable proxy pools are large and track their generics as they both season, the seasoned generics remain eligible for the rebalanced proxy portfolio. This is in contrast to the TBAs-only strategy, which purges its proxy portfolio once a year. The new LP-only proxy is chosen from among the existing generics, as well as recent originations (as was done initially). Additions to an already-held issue are still allowed, but only if that issue is in the current available set. This strategy allows large, diverse, and seasoned pools to remain in the proxy portfolio while minimizing pool-specific risk. At each rebalancing, new large pools are added to keep up with new additions to the index. A drawback of this approach is that the proxy portfolio initially tracks the index only as well as the TBAs-only strategy presented earlier. It takes time for positions in large seasoned pools to reduce tracking error further.

The Available Sets

A key difference between the two replication strategies is the definition of their available sets. The criteria for the respective available sets differ so that each strategy's tradable proxy portfolio contains securities likely to track generic performance assumed by the replication technique.

The available set for the TBAs-only replication strategy consists of index annual aggregates with a WAM of 348 or higher and an amount outstanding of at least $2.5 billion.[11] The magnitudes of these constraints guide the replication technique to select only those index generics for which there are current-coupon TBA contracts. The $2.5 billion amount-outstanding restriction prevents the replication technique from selecting an index annual aggregate for which there is very little new tradable production. Figure 6-7 shows that as of December 31, 2000, the 6.5 and 9.0% 30-year FNMA index generics with a WAM of 348 or higher had small amounts outstanding. Although TBA contracts on FNMA 6.5 and 9.0% coupons were available in the market, the TBAs-only strategy considers them off-market coupons and thus less likely to track their index generic. The $2.5 billion restriction keeps the optimizer from selecting such off-market generics for the

---

in an effort to get overall pool diversification. One drawback of this approach is the increased operations effort compared with receiving a portion of a single very large pool. Not surprisingly, such "stips" often require a modest payup to TBA. It is not always the case, though, especially not for recent origination, to which we constrained the optimization.

11. For brevity, we discuss in detail only the constraints on 30-year FNMA generics.

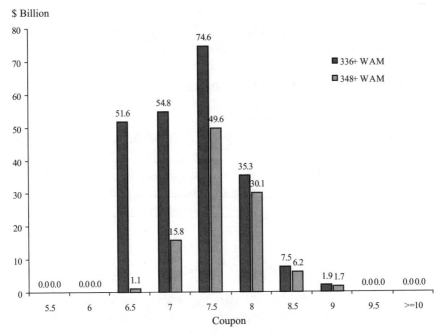

Figure 6-7. Distribution of Amount Outstanding by Coupon
December 31, 2000

proxy portfolio. If, during the quarter, production increases in these two coupons, then they may become part of the available set the following quarter. As can be seen in Figure 6-7, given the magnitude of new production by coupon, the $2.5 billion constraint is not very restrictive.

The TBAs-only strategy also has a WAM restriction of 348 or higher. As with the $2.5 billion liquidity constraint, the WAM restriction ensures that the replication technique selects only current-production index generics so that the TBA contracts in the tradable proxy portfolio will track their performance. In reality, the TBA market may track shorter WAM generics from time to time, so the 348+ WAM constraint in the replication might be too conservative. However, over the past few years, the mortgage market seems to treat even moderately seasoned product differently than TBAs.

The available set for the LP-only strategy differs from that of TBAs-only in both WAM and amount outstanding. For the former, the goal is to have the optimizer select only those index generics for which it is possible to obtain large pools. While large pools of seasoned product are hard but not impossible to find, the LP-only strategy conservatively assumes that an investor can consistently only find large pools with a WAM of 336 or higher. This strategy could have used the higher WAM constraint in the TBAs-only strategy with little impact on the over-all results. As it allows pools to season in the proxy portfolio, initially buying pools with a 348+ WAM rather than a 336+ WAM would make little difference in the tracking error performance of the strategy over time. The larger amount-outstanding constraint of $5 billion is imposed so that there is sufficient produc-tion of the 336+ WAM generics to make it likely that large pools are available. As Figure 6-7 shows, the 30-year FNMA 9.0% index generic with a 336+ WAM had an amount outstanding of less than $5 billion. To be conservative, the LP-only strategy assumes that an investor would be unlikely to find large pools for this coupon. Overall, the WAM and amount-outstanding constraints ensure that the tradable MBS proxy portfolio contains securities likely to track generic perform-ance. Of course, whenever an investor is able to find large pools of shorter WAMs, the tracking error of the LP-only strategy improves faster.

Construction of Proxy Portfolios

For the historical evaluation of both strategies, the proxy portfolios remain un-changed for 3 months after construction/rebalancing. In practice, the proxy port-folio can be rebalanced more frequently (e.g., once a month). Monthly rebalanc-ing would likely improve tracking, especially in such tumultuous periods as early 1994. When the proxy portfolio is rebalanced, issues in the old proxy are sold and new issues in the current available set are purchased to generate a new proxy that minimizes expected tracking error.

As mentioned earlier, there is a difference in the rebalancing process between the two strategies. The LP-only strategy rebalances once a quarter, as described. For the TBAs-only strategy, however, in addition to quarterly rebalancing, once a year (at the end of March), the proxy portfolio is purged and a completely new one is selected from the current available set. Many of the generics selected for the new proxy may be the same as those that were purged. The purpose of purging the TBAs-only proxy is to prevent the accumulation of seasoned generics because there are no TBA contracts that will track their performance.

A TBAs-only proxy portfolio always contains a limited number of issues be-cause it is designed to hold only recently issued generics, enforced by the annual purging. Over the period from December 1993 to December 2000, the TBAs-only proxy held an average of eleven generics. The number of generics in the proxy fluctuates as new generics emerge that mirror changes in mortgage rates.

The number of generics in the LP-only proxy tends to increase steadily as por-tions of seasoned generics are permitted to remain while new generics are added. By December 2000, the LP-only proxy contained seventy-seven generics, having

Figure 6-8. Performance Summary for the Replication Strategies
January 1994–May 2001

	Monthly Return Difference (portfolio vs. the index, bp)	
	TBAs Only	Large Pools Only
Average	−1.2	0.2
Standard deviation (realized tracking error)	6.0	4.4
Minimum	−18.7	−9.2
Maximum	17.6	23.6
Realized tracking error (annualized)	20.9	15.2

started with ten in December 1993. (Later we discuss a variation on the LP-only strategy to limit the number of generics in the proxy portfolio.)

Empirical Performance of Replication Strategies

For both strategies, we examine the realized tracking errors from January 1994 through May 2001. We calculate the actual monthly returns for the proxy portfolio and compare them with the returns on the MBS Index. The results for both strategies are summarized in Figure 6-8. We chose to begin the historical simulation on December 31, 1993, which marked the beginning of a major directional change in interest rates and stress in the mortgage market. Including this period allows readers to examine the performance of the two strategies in a wider range of market environments.

Not surprisingly, the LP-only strategy had a lower annualized tracking error than the TBAs-only strategy (15 vs. 21 bp). Graphs of the monthly performance differences vs. the MBS Index for each strategy are presented in Figures 6-9 and 6-10. Both strategies experienced relatively large tracking errors in the first few months of the period, from January 1994 through March 1994. This was a period of tumult in the mortgage market, as the Federal Reserve reversed course and began a dramatic tightening of short-term interest rates. Once this period passed, the tracking error for both strategies improved. Moreover, as of December 1993, the MBS part of the covariance matrix underlying the risk model was calibrated with only three years of historical data, which was too short a period to prepare it for the sudden market shift in early 1994. This probably explains the relatively large performance differences between the proxy portfolios and the index during that period. Now the risk model has almost a hundred months of history, covering

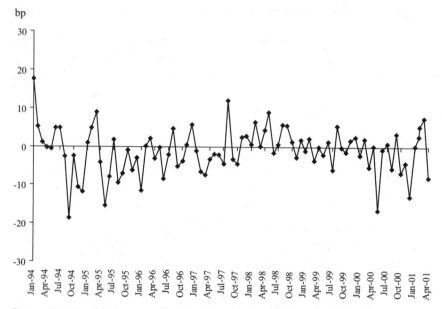

Figure 6-9. Monthly Return Difference: TBAs-Only Strategy vs. the MBS Index
January 1994–May 2001

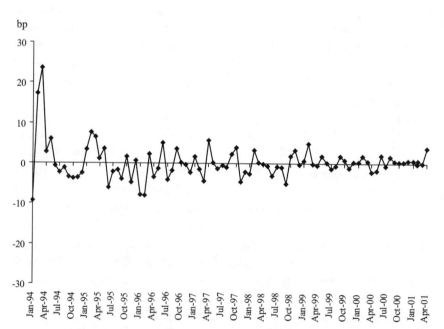

Figure 6-10. Monthly Return Difference: Large-Pools-Only Strategy vs. the MBS Index
January 1994–May 2001

Number of Holdings

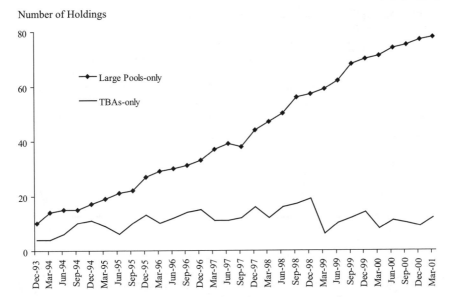

Figure 6-11. Number of Holdings in the Proxy Portfolio: TBAs-Only Strategy vs. Large-Pools-Only
December 1993–May 2001

a variety of market environments. Investors using the model today to construct replicating portfolios are unlikely to experience this phenomenon.

The variability in the monthly return differences for the LP-only strategy tends to dampen over time. This is not surprising because this proxy portfolio looks more and more like the underlying index as the proxy holdings season. Furthermore, the initial return deviation for this strategy is probably the worst-case result. Tracking could be improved if large seasoned pools were purchased at the outset of the replication strategy, as opposed to waiting for proxy securities to season. For example, if an investor commenced the strategy today and if a large pool of 1993 30-year GNMA 7%s became available, it could immediately be added to the proxy portfolio to improve tracking error. However, to be conservative, we measured historical performance assuming that seasoned large pools are not available at the commencement of the strategy.

Overall, the LP-only strategy has an annual realized tracking error that is 6 bp lower than that of the TBAs-only strategy. This difference in tracking error is not surprising, as the two proxies gradually become very different. The LP-only proxy can hold large seasoned pools, and the number of bonds in the portfolio increases over time (Figure 6-11).

Figure 6-12. Realized Tracking Error vs. the Lehman MBS Index
2-Year Overlapping Intervals, January 1994–May 2001

	TBAs Only		Large Pools Only	
Period	Tracking Error (bp/year)	Average Number of Holdings	Tracking Error (bp/year)	Average Number of Holdings
Jan 94–Dec 95	28.0	8	25.1	17
Jan 95–Dec 96	20.2	11	14.7	25
Jan 96–Dec 97	17.4	12	12.5	33
Jan 97–Dec 98	16.8	14	9.5	43
Jan 98–Dec 99	12.2	14	7.3	55
Jan 99–May 01	18.3	11	5.1	69

In contrast, the number of bonds in the TBAs-only proxy remains relatively constant, containing twelve bonds by May 2001. The number of issues in the TBAs-only proxy tends to drop each March as its proxy portfolio begins from scratch. The number of issues tends to increase as the mortgage current coupon changes and new actively traded TBA coupons become available. However, because the TBAs-only strategy periodically culls off-market coupons, the number of issues in the proxy portfolio remains limited.

A more significant performance difference between the two strategies becomes apparent when the sample period is divided into 2-year overlapping windows. Figure 6-12 presents these results.

Upon closer inspection, the relative performance of the two strategies becomes clearer. For the first 2-year period, the realized tracking errors for the two strategies were comparable. This result is reasonable because the LP-only strategy has had relatively little time to add seasoned generics to the proxy portfolio. Thereafter, however, the realized tracking error of the LP-only strategy steadily improves relative to that for the TBAs-only, as the former proxy becomes more and more similar to the index. The performance of the latter remains relatively constant as it tracks the recently issued portion of the index. For the final period, from January 1999 to May 2001, the LP-only strategy had a realized tracking error of only 5.1 bp, compared with 18.3 bp for the TBAs-only strategy.

In the historical simulation of the two replication strategies, we chose not to limit portfolio turnover. Yet even in the absence of any restrictions, the LP-only strategy required, on average, a modest 7.5% turnover per quarter. The TBAs-only strategy assumes rolling the whole position each month without ever taking delivery of pools, so there is really no comparable turnover measure.

Figure 6-13. Performance Summary for Large-Pools-Only Replication Strategies
January 1994–May 2001

	Monthly Return Difference (portfolio vs. the index, bp)	
	Max12 Large-Pools Only	Large-Pools Only
Average	0.6	0.2
Standard deviation (realized tracking error)	4.4	4.4
Minimum	−9.2	−9.2
Maximum	24.4	23.6
Realized tracking error (annualized)	15.2	15.2

Strategy Refinements ("Max12 Large-Pools-Only" Strategy)

The number of issues in the LP-only proxy portfolio increases over time, whereas the number of issues in the TBAs-only proxy is relatively static. For the period from January 1994 through May 2001, the LP-only proxy held, on average, forty-four issues, whereas the TBAs-only proxy held only eleven. Is the better tracking error performance of the LP-only strategy due mostly to the larger number of issues in the proxy portfolio or to the inclusion of seasoned pools in the proxy that better track the seasoned generics in the index?

To investigate the relative importance of having a larger number of issues vs. including seasoned issues, we re-examined the LP-only strategy and limited the number of issues in the proxy to twelve. This strategy is labeled "Max12 LP-only." The proxy construction methodology and the available set of generics from which the optimizer selects are unchanged.

Performance results for the Max12 LP-only strategy are presented in Figure 6-13 (and compared with the initial unconstrained variant). Realized tracking error for the Max12 LP-only strategy is remarkably similar to that of the unrestricted LP-only strategy. This indicates that the better relative tracking error performance of the LP-only strategy over the TBAs-only strategy is due primarily to the presence of seasoned issues in the proxy portfolio and not to the much larger number of issues.

The two proxies have similar tracking errors for the entire period. However, there is a modest difference between the two strategies when the sample period is divided into 2-year overlapping windows. These results are presented in Figure 6-14. As mentioned earlier, realized tracking errors for the LP-only strategy steadily decrease as the strategy ages. This pattern was expected because the portfolio

Figure 6-14. Realized Tracking Error vs. the Lehman MBS Index
2-Year Overlapping Intervals, January 1994–May 2001

Period	Max12 Large Pools Only		Large Pools Only	
	Tracking Error (bp/year)	Average Number of Holdings	Tracking Error (bp/year)	Average Number of Holdings
Jan 94–Dec 95	26.2	12	25.1	17
Jan 95–Dec 96	13.8	12	14.7	25
Jan 96–Dec 97	9.5	12	12.5	33
Jan 97–Dec 98	7.2	12	9.5	43
Jan 98–Dec 99	8.6	12	7.3	55
Jan 99–May 01	7.7	12	5.1	69

begins to look more like the MBS Index over time. In contrast, while the realized tracking errors for the Max12 LP-only strategy also decline, they do so more unevenly and do not decline as far as the unconstrained strategy. Limiting the number of issues in the proxy portfolio seems to limit how low realized tracking error can go. While both strategies get the early and sustained benefit from the presence of seasoned issues in the proxy compared with the TBAs-only strategy, the unconstrained LP-only strategy continues to benefit as the number of issues increases.

MBS INDEX REPLICATION: CHALLENGES FOR THE FUTURE

As discussed earlier, an investor replicating the MBS Index faces the added difficulty of finding tradable MBS securities that track their respective index generic securities. We argue that TBAs and large pools are likely to track their respective index generics and present several replication strategies that historically would have offered low tracking errors vs. the MBS Index. However, as with all financial markets, the behavior and structure of the MBS market continually evolves, and replication strategies must constantly be re-evaluated.

As an example, consider the following potential pattern emerging in the MBS market. As more loan-level detail and historical performance become available, investors have begun to examine mortgage loans more closely, looking for characteristics that may make them more valuable. For example, the data may show that mortgage loans with particularly low average loan balances are relatively slow to refinance when the opportunity arises compared with loans with high average loan balances. As investors begin to identify the mortgage loan characteristics (e.g., WAC, geography, originator, and average loan balance) that make some loans less susceptible to prepayments, they will seek out those loans for their portfolios.

How can investors obtain these loans? One way is to stipulate those desirable characteristics when buying pools from a broker/dealer. Another way is for investors to approach mortgage originators directly for loans having desirable attributes. Having purchased the loans for their portfolios, these investors may subsequently securitize the loans into agency pools, either for liquidity or for regulatory capital reasons. As a result of this securitization activity, these pools may become part of index generics. However, as these pools are locked up in portfolios, they are not available to other investors.

If this "skimming and securitization" activity picks up, the performance of many pools available in the market may diverge increasingly from their respective index generic. This divergence may take the form of systematic prepayment differences, and certain current production pools will likely trade at a payup to TBA. This would complicate the replication process, especially for the TBAs-only strategy, because the underlying characteristics of the TBA deliverable will diverge from the current production index generics. In particular, the TBA position may be priced at an increasing discount to the respective index generic. In addition, the TBA position may become more negatively convex than assumed by the replication techniques that use generics. Both of these outcomes could cause a long-term TBAs-only strategy to underperform the index and to have greater realized tracking error than what was expected from the replication technique.

The efficacy of the LP-only strategy will also be affected because large pools will be delivered from a reduced supply of available pools. Consequently, the large pools' characteristics will also diverge from their generics. However, the situation may be less problematic for the LP-only strategy compared with the TBAs-only strategy. The large pool size will continue to offer diversification advantages, especially if the large pool contains loans from multiple originators. The idiosyncratic risk of a small pool could be greater than before if the available supply of pools has less desirable characteristics than the index generics. Another mitigating effect is that the LP-only strategy allows pools to season. To the extent that the prevalence of skimming gradually increases, the LP-only strategy will have the advantage of retaining seasoned pools acquired at the time when the skimming effect was less pronounced.

This potential change in the structure of the MBS market, as well as others that we may not foresee today, means that replication strategies cannot remain static but must continually adjust to remain relevant.

CONCLUSION

Replicating the Lehman MBS Index requires not only identifying the subset of generics that will track the index closely, but also choosing tradable MBS securities for the proxy portfolio that will, in turn, track their generics closely. This additional layer of decision making and required market knowledge has a potential for creating additional tracking error and has deterred some investors from replicating the index on their own.

We presented two strategies for the MBS Index replication: TBAs-only and LP-only. The genesis for both strategies was the search for MBS securities likely to track their generics so as to reduce the contribution of pool selection to tracking error. TBAs track recently originated generics almost by definition, because a TBA implicitly assumes average attributes of pools likely to be delivered. Unfortunately, the TBA market is limited to recently issued coupons. Consequently, while TBAs track current coupons well, they exhibit some tracking error when used to track the seasoned portion of the MBS Index. Yet, over all, the TBAs-only strategy (which also has limited back-office requirements) produces a relatively low realized tracking error of less than 21 bp/year.

The other strategy uses large-sized pools that tend to track their generics. While large pools for recent coupons are relatively easy to obtain, large seasoned pools are hard to find. Consequently, buying both large current- and seasoned-coupon pools is infeasible at the outset of a replication program. Instead, the LP-only strategy uses large pools for current coupons initially to replicate the index (similar to the TBAs-only strategy). However, these pools are allowed to remain in the proxy and season, leading to increasingly closer tracking of the seasoned component of the index. Over time, this strategy tracks the index with less and less tracking error.

One potential drawback of the LP-only strategy is the steadily increasing number of pools in the proxy portfolio. However, the Max12 LP-only strategy demonstrates that the improved tracking performance of the LP-only strategy is due primarily to the presence of seasoned issues in the proxy and not to a larger number of issues compared with the TBA strategy. Consequently, the Max12 strategy can be used if one wants to limit the number of issues in the proxy portfolio.

The chief merit of both strategies is that investors can effectively replicate the MBS Index without having detailed pool-level knowledge of the mortgage market. The relative simplicity of the two strategies may encourage some investors to attempt MBS Index replication on their own, rather than use an external manager.

7. High Yield Index Replication

....

For years, fixed-income managers have invested outside the U.S. Aggregate benchmark in search of additional risk-adjusted returns. Over time, many plan sponsors have grown comfortable with these out-of-index investments and have begun to evaluate fixed-income managers vs. a broader USD-denominated fixed-income investment universe. Consequently, plan sponsors are increasingly turning to the U.S. Universal Index as an appropriate benchmark. The U.S. Universal Index includes the U.S. Aggregate Index (87.1% of the total market value, as of January 31, 2001) plus five other indices: the Corporate High Yield (4.3%), Eurodollar (4.2%), Emerging Markets (2.7%), 144A (1.2%), and High Yield and non-ERISA CMBS (0.5%).

For some investors, a Universal Index mandate may raise certain management issues. Managers with a good record of outperforming the Aggregate Index may have limited experience in some of the other markets that make up the Universal Index. Managers run the risk of missing mandates if they wait while building expertise in the Universal Index sectors new to them. On the other hand, if a mandate is granted before the necessary expertise is in place and the manager is ready to trade actively vs. the index, there is a risk of increased tracking error.

Not all managers choose to develop in-house expertise in every sector of the Universal Index. Some sectors may be deemed too small to justify the cost of mastering markets that are brand new to the manager. However, if the investment mandate specifies the Universal Index as the benchmark, the manager has to allocate an appropriate share of the assets to all sectors. While active management with its search for outperformance may not be the goal in a particular small sector of the index, the manager needs a safe way to track this sector with an acceptable

Based on research first published by Lehman Brothers in 2001.

tracking error. This need is especially important because some of the small additions to the Aggregate Index are very volatile and can affect the overall portfolio risk in spite of their low market value share.

Of the five additional indices in the Universal Index, replication of the Eurodollar and 144A indices is relatively straightforward, as their behavior is similar to the Aggregate Index itself. The CMBS Index is comparatively small and can be replicated with stratified sampling.[1] The two remaining indices, the Emerging Markets Index and the High Yield Index, pose a challenge, as they make up a significant part of the Universal Index and their returns are volatile, behaving very differently from the returns of the Aggregate Index. Here, we focus on replication of the High Yield Index.

At first glance, the High Yield Index might seem to be a difficult index to replicate. From January 1993 through December 2000, the monthly mean excess (curve-adjusted) return over Treasuries was –0.3 bp, with a monthly standard deviation of 162 bp. In contrast, over the same period, the U.S. Credit Index had a monthly mean excess return of –1.2 bp and a monthly standard deviation of 48 bp. The relatively high excess return volatility of the High Yield Index gives a hint of the potential difficulty in creating a replicating portfolio with a relatively low tracking error.

Total returns of the two indices are similar. From January 1993 through December 2000, monthly mean total returns were 57 and 59 bp for the High Yield and Credit indices, respectively. The poor high yield performance in 2000 brought down the average for the entire 8-year period. The monthly standard deviations of total returns were 149 and 139 bp for the High Yield and Credit indices, respectively. Although the excess returns for high yield are more volatile, they tend to be negatively correlated with the term structure returns. As a result, the volatility of total returns for the High Yield Index is similar in magnitude to that of the Credit Index. These numbers show that most of the total-return volatility in the Credit Index is due to Treasury volatility. Stripping Treasury volatility from the 139 bp of total volatility leaves excess-returns volatility of only 48 bp. In stark contrast, stripping Treasury volatility from the High Yield Index total volatility of 149 bp leaves 162 bp.

We present three strategies for replicating the High Yield Index. First, we describe each strategy, and then we compare the strategies' empirical performance simulated historically over the period of 8 years from January 1993 through December 2000.

---

1. See Chapter 8 for a detailed description.

STRATEGIES

Issuer Strategy

The first replication strategy is simple. It selects securities for the replicating proxy portfolio from the list of the largest issuers in the index. The proxy portfolio is constructed as follows:

- Step 1. Compute each issuer's market value percentage in the index.

- Step 2. For each of the largest N issuers (N is a strategy parameter), choose the largest bond from each issuer. This step produces N bonds eligible for inclusion in the proxy portfolio.

- Step 3. The percentage of the proxy's market value allocated to each of the N bonds is determined so that the allocation ratio of any two bonds in the proxy equals the market value ratio of the two issuers in the index. For example, if issuers A and B account for 1.5 and 1% of the index, respectively, then the ratio between market values allocated to these issuers' largest bonds is 1.5:1.

The issuer strategy assumes that idiosyncratic risk is a key component of returns in the high yield market. The strategy does not explicitly control for Treasury duration. As a result, the duration of the proxy may not equal that of the index. On average, over the period studied, the Treasury duration of the proxy differed from the index by 0.25 year, which should not be viewed as a serious drawback. As we showed before, most total-return volatility for high yield is not due to term structure volatility. As a result, the issuer strategy is motivated by the view that idiosyncratic risk is a key component of returns in the high yield market, and matching issuer exposures should be a key feature of a successful replication strategy.

Structure Strategy

Another approach is a structure replication strategy that divides the High Yield Index into industry and credit "buckets" and then selects eligible bonds to populate each bucket. The strategy first computes the market value weight and the contribution to dollar spread duration for each bucket. Then, the replicating proxy portfolio is constructed so that in each bucket, the market weights and contributions to spread duration match those of the index. This procedure ensures that the proxy portfolio's overall spread duration matches that of the index. This strategy also matches the Treasury duration of the index. Finally, not only the duration but also the convexity of the proxy portfolio matches that of the index.

Because idiosyncratic risk is a large factor in a high yield bond's return variability (compared with investment-grade bonds), the strategy imposes a demanding set of eligibility criteria (described later) in an attempt to avoid bonds with a potential for high returns volatility. The number of bonds placed in each bucket (a diversification constraint) is also based on the bucket's historical behavior. This requirement helps to further diversify idiosyncratic risk.

The structure replication strategy works as follows. It defines fifteen buckets, of which ten are industry buckets and five are quality buckets. Each bond in the replicating proxy portfolio belongs to only one industry bucket and only one quality bucket.

The ten industry buckets are:

1. Utilities

2. Financial

3. Telecommunications-B (quality B3 or better)

4. Telecommunications-C (quality less than B3)

5. Media

6. Cyclical

7. Industrial

8. Sovereign

9. Foreign Agency

10. Foreign Corporation

The five quality buckets are:

1. Greater than B1

2. B1

3. B2

4. B3

5. Less than B3

Except for subdividing the telecommunications sector based on quality, the structure strategy does not create buckets defined in terms of *both* industry and quality as is common with some replication strategies for the Credit Index. In other words, it does not define a utilities bucket with a quality of B3. We found that dividing the High Yield Index into a larger number of smaller buckets (division along both industry and quality would result in fifty buckets) does not improve tracking error.

Because the sovereign, foreign agency, and foreign corporation buckets combined represent less than 1% of the market value of the High Yield Index, the proxy portfolio is not required to match those buckets in terms of market value percentage or contribution to spread duration.

Not all bonds in the index are eligible for inclusion in the proxy. As mentioned before, we exclude bonds that have the potential for wild swings in returns and might result in high tracking errors for the proxy portfolio. To be eligible for inclusion in the proxy portfolio a bond must meet the following inclusion criteria:

- Return Volatility. The bond's excess return for the previous month must be within three standard deviations of the bond's industry bucket mean return (provided that the bucket contains at least ten bonds).

- Age: The bond must be at least 1 month old.

- Distress Status: If the bond pays a coupon, its full price must be at least 60% of par, and, for all bonds, the yield to worst cannot be more than 1000 bp greater than the average yield to worst for its quality bucket.[2]

To ensure diversification within the proxy portfolio, we place an upper limit on the percentage of the proxy's market value contributed by each bond. Unlike the issuer replication strategy, this strategy looks at *bond* rather than *issuer* diversification. This upper limit varies from bond to bond and is set as the minimum of: (1) the global upper limit that applies to all bonds, for example, 2%; (2) the upper limit for the bond's quality bucket; and (3) the upper limit for the bond's industry bucket.

The last two upper limits depend on how important it is to have bond diversification in a particular bucket. For example, if the B3 bucket has a high standard deviation of total returns across all bonds in the bucket, then we require a lower upper limit for that quality bucket. By requiring a lower upper limit, we force the proxy portfolio to hold more bonds from that quality bucket in order to match

---

2. Excluding distressed bonds from the proxy portfolio significantly improves the proxy portfolio's tracking error. Since the proxy contains many fewer bonds than the index, the presence of distressed bonds in the proxy overemphasizes the variability of their returns.

the bucket's market weight. This method increases diversification in those buckets in which it is most needed.[3]

Securities for the proxy portfolio are selected from among all eligible bonds using linear optimization. The objective function is to maximize the amount outstanding (i.e., liquidity) of the proxy portfolio subject to the constraints outlined previously.

The expectation was that the structure strategy might perform better than the issuer strategy because it explicitly takes into account the industry and quality structure of the High Yield Index when constructing the proxy portfolio. As we show later, it actually does *not* perform better, indicating that issuer diversification must remain an integral part of the proxy portfolio construction. This result led us to the third replication strategy.

Structured-Issuer Strategy

The third replication strategy is similar to the second, except that it filters the list of eligible bonds further. The final list contains no more than one bond (the one with the largest market value) from every issuer in the index, to force more issuer diversification. Otherwise, this strategy follows the same methodology as the structure strategy. The added filtering also turns the upper limits on individual bonds (as in the second replication strategy) into upper limits on individual issuers (as in the first replication strategy), thus increasing diversification.

This strategy combines the emphasis on issuer diversification of the first strategy with the emphasis on index structure matching of the second, with the result that the tracking error it produced was the lowest of the three.

REPLICATION RESULTS

We examined the performance of all three replication strategies for the period from January 1993 through December 2000. For the issuer strategy, five simulations were conducted. Each simulation used a different number of issuers (N) in the proxy portfolio. The values of N examined were 20, 40, 60, 80, and 100. For both the structure and the structured-issuer strategies, two historical simulations

---

3. Consider the following example. The standard deviation of returns within the B1 quality bucket was 487 bp, while the standard deviation within the less-than-B3 bucket was 1058 bp. Therefore, the upper limit on the market value allocated to any bond from the B1 bucket was 3.23%, while the upper allocation limit in the less-than-B3 bucket was 0.68%. Details of the method for computing the upper limits for the industry and quality buckets can be provided upon request.

Figure 7-1. Performance Comparison of the Three Replication Strategies vs. the High Yield Index

January 1993–December 2000

Number of Issues	Monthly Mean Outperformance (bp/month)	Monthly Tracking Error (bp/month)	Percent of Variance Explained
Issuer Strategy			
20	18.8	90.4	63.4
40	11.4	68.6	78.9
60	8.3	58.0	84.9
80	8.5	50.9	88.4
100	8.1	46.2	90.4
Structure Strategy			
46	4.6	67.4	79.6
78	2.3	52.6	87.6
Structured-Issuer Strategy			
46	4.7	46.1	90.5
78	0.8	37.9	93.6

were conducted. The first had a global upper limit of 2% (which produced an average portfolio size of seventy-eight bonds for both strategies). The second used a global upper limit of 4% (which produced an average portfolio size of forty-six bonds for both strategies). Figure 7-1 presents the tracking errors obtained in every case.

For proxy portfolios with a similar number of issues, the issuer strategy is somewhat better than the structure strategy. The high monthly mean outperformance values for the issuer strategies with relatively few issues may be due to the fact that, owing to their liquidity advantage, bonds from the largest issuers performed best during the periods of market stress in the last few years. For example, with a forty-issue proxy portfolio, the issuer strategy produces an average monthly tracking error of 69 bp (explaining 79% of the variability of the index), compared with 67 bp for the structure strategy containing forty-six issues. However, the structured-issuer strategy produces the lowest tracking error of all three strategies: for example, for proxy portfolios of eighty issues, 38 vs. 51 bp for the issuer strategy. A summary graph of these results is presented in Figure 7-2.

There are several reasons why the issuer strategy, which does not explicitly match industry, quality, duration, and other characteristics of the index, performed better than the simple structure strategy. First, the idiosyncratic (issuer) risk of high

Tracking Error (bp/month)

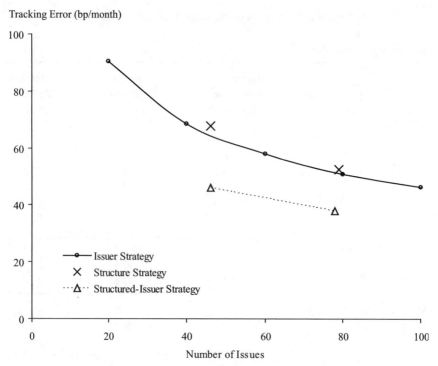

Figure 7-2. Performance Comparison of the Three Replication Strategies: Tracking Error vs. Number of Issues
January 1993–December 2000

yield bonds is much greater than that of investment-grade bonds. This makes is-suer diversification at least as important as market risk factor matching, especially in a small to medium-sized portfolio. Second, in recent years, the highly liquid (i.e., large issue size) component of the High Yield Index has had a composition similar to that of the index as a whole in terms of duration, industry, and quality exposures. Consequently, the issuer strategy produced a proxy portfolio with a composition similar to that of the index. Third, when constructing a small proxy portfolio using the structure strategy, we may pick multiple bonds from the same issuer and suffer higher tracking error owing to poor issuer diversification. In addition, we may be forced to select one or two relatively small issuers in order to match all the constraints. Given the small number of bonds in the portfolio, this may cause significant issuer mismatches and relatively high levels of idiosyn-cratic risk.

Another way to look at the performance results is to plot tracking error vs. the number of *issuers* in the proxy portfolio (Figure 7-3). Some investors may feel that the number of issuers in the proxy portfolio is a better measure of the cost

Tracking Error (bp/month)

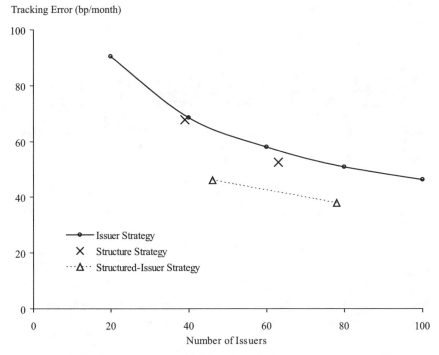

Number of Issuers

Figure 7-3. Performance Comparison of the Three Replication Strategies: Tracking Error vs. Number of Issuers
January 1993–December 2000

of monitoring the portfolio than the number of issues. Recall that the structure strategy forces diversification at the bond level, whereas the other two strategies force diversification at the issuer level, which is more stringent. Figure 7-3 shows that the structure strategy now performs a bit better than the issuer strategy. For example, the structure strategy with a global upper limit of 2% holds seventy-eight bonds, but only sixty-three issuer names.

Overall, the structured-issuer strategy with a global upper limit per bond of 2% proved the most successful. This strategy considers both issuer diversification and market risk factor matching. If at some point in the future liquid (i.e., top market value) bonds in the high yield market become concentrated in a particular industry or quality, the structured-issuer strategy should continue to work reasonably well, whereas the issuer strategy may be exposed to significant sector and market factor risk.

Figure 7-4 shows the actual performance of the structured-issuer strategy with a global upper limit per bond of 2% and the High Yield Index for January 1993 through December 2000.

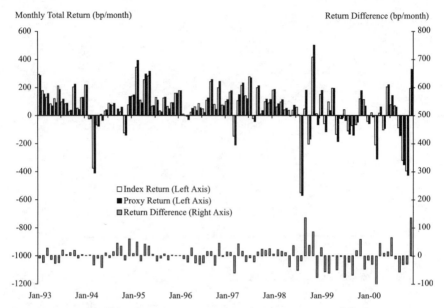

Figure 7-4. High Yield Index Return vs. Structured-Issuer Proxy Portfolio Return
January 1993–December 2000 (seventy-eight-issue portfolio)

CONCLUSION

We have presented three replication strategies for the High Yield Index and have
examined their empirical performance from January 1993 through December 2000.
Based on these results, we have learned that matching issuer exposures is a key
feature of a successful replication strategy, as is matching the industry and quality
structure of the index. Consequently, we recommend the structured-issuer strategy as the best replication technique. As a result of this work, several investors are
now exploring this approach to track the High Yield Index passively.

8. CMBS Index Replication

In January 1999, Lehman Brothers introduced the CMBS Investment-Grade Index as a subcomponent of the Lehman U.S. Aggregate Index, and as of February 2002, it accounted for 2.2% of the market value of the Aggregate Index. Although the CMBS market is relatively small, the asset class has been growing and has attracted attention for its relative stability and desirable convexity properties.

As the CMBS market grows, investment managers evaluated against the Aggregate Index are increasingly asking whether to dedicate analyst and management resources to this asset class. An alternative is to track the CMBS Index passively while continuing to manage the other asset classes actively. Some investors have asked how they can construct a replicating proxy portfolio that will track the CMBS Index with minimal tracking error.

Unfortunately, as CMBS risk factors are not yet modeled,[1] investors cannot effectively use Lehman's U.S. risk model to construct proxy portfolios containing CMBS. For investors who wish to construct such proxy portfolios this poses an efficiency problem, as they cannot use the risk model to analytically offset CMBS exposures with other portfolio positions. Consequently, these investors often construct stand-alone CMBS proxy portfolios using other replication techniques. While this strategy is effective, it is less efficient. Even for investors who wish to replicate the CMBS Index alone, the lack of a risk model also makes replication less efficient, as there is no opportunity to take advantage of correlations among CMBS risk factors.

Nevertheless, investors can easily construct CMBS proxy portfolios using straightforward sampling techniques. We propose to replicate the Lehman CMBS

Based on research first published by Lehman Brothers in 2002.
    1. CMBS are now part of the Lehman global risk model (see Chapter 26). However, the replication methodology described here remains relevant for investors desiring to replicate the CMBS market without the use of a multifactor risk model.

Index using a technique called "stratified sampling." The first step is to stratify, or sort, the issues in the index into "buckets" according to various issue characteristics. Issues for the proxy portfolio are then selected from each of the buckets so that the exposure of the proxy portfolio to a particular characteristic matches the index's exposure within prespecified tolerance bounds. For example, for the Credit Index, stratified sampling typically sorts the index into buckets defined by quality, sector, and duration. These characteristics are chosen because they are important factors driving the pricing of credit issues. A credit proxy portfolio is then selected so that the market value and contribution to spread duration of A-rated industrials with a modified duration between 2 and 5 years, for example, match those of the Credit Index within a few basis points. Selecting bonds for the proxy from each bucket is often facilitated using a linear optimizer. The optimizer can be set to maximize the liquidity (i.e., amount outstanding) of the proxy portfolio while satisfying all of the bucket constraints.

What are the important pricing characteristics of CMBS issues? Issues in the CMBS Index are priced by traders who use a matrix of nominal spreads to the swap curve.[2] The pricing matrix has three dimensions: quality grade (Aaa, Aa, A, Baa1 and Baa2, and Baa3), average life (e.g., 0–3, 3–5, 5–7, 7–9, 9–10, 10–12, 12–15, and 15–30 years) and dollar price (<90 and >112, with steps of 2 in between). Loan and property characteristics are not factored into the matrix. Depending on the quality grade, there may be more or fewer average life buckets. Overall, there are 564 pricing buckets. Issues in the index are then mapped to one and only one bucket in the pricing matrix. Many buckets in the pricing matrix have no bonds mapped to them. In addition, some CMBS issues having unusual characteristics are manually priced.

The CMBS pricing matrix generally reflects current market practice. Over the past few years, as the CMBS market has matured, the U.S. real estate market has been very strong. The good commercial real estate environment and diversity of collateral underlying CMBS issues have produced few large differences in spreads among issues in the same quality-average life-dollar price bucket. A CMBS proxy portfolio that matches the index across these three characteristics will most likely track the index closely. Back-testing this replication methodology produces excellent historical tracking results, as the CMBS pricing methodology has been based on the same three characteristics.

Going forward, however, there is no guarantee that the CMBS market will continue to price issues as reflected in the current pricing matrix. CMBS data quality

---

2. The pricing matrix also assumes that bonds' base case prepayment expectation is 0% CPR and default expectation is 0% CDR.

and analytics continue to improve. In addition, some investors are beginning to specialize in the CMBS asset class. As data, models, and expertise improve, and as the real estate market experiences more typical cyclical behavior, CMBS issues may show more varied pricing dynamics than are currently reflected in the pricing matrix. If the market's pricing conventions change and index pricing follows, then the performance of a proxy portfolio constructed to match only the quality-average life-dollar price characteristics of the index may experience increased tracking error. For example, issues with a relatively high weighting in California properties are not priced at a premium or discount to issues with a low (or "neutral") weighting. However, it is possible to imagine a market environment where issues with a high California weighting are priced at a differential to the matrix. Investors intuitively understand this and would feel uncomfortable with a replicating CMBS portfolio that had a weighting in California properties that was significantly different from that of the index.

The challenge for CMBS replication is to define issue characteristics that may drive CMBS pricing in the future. Matching the proxy to the index across these characteristics helps to keep tracking error low even as the market environment changes. In the next section, we identify those CMBS issue characteristics likely to have greater influence in CMBS pricing in the future. We then use stratified sampling to construct a proxy portfolio that closely matches the index across this broader set of characteristics. We then show that a replication strategy using this stratification would have closely tracked the index in the past. This result indicates that, even if the market's pricing methodology does not change, the replication methodology we propose should nevertheless continue to track the index well. However, if the pricing methodology does change, then the proposed replication methodology should keep tracking error low.

REPLICATION STRATEGY

A CMBS deal is backed by a pool of commercial mortgage loans and each CMBS deal is divided into various issues (i.e., tranches). Generally, each deal is collateralized by a diversified loan pool containing loans on properties of various types, geographic locations, and borrowers. We define a CMBS issue's exposure to a particular characteristic by calculating the deal's original principal balance weighted average of loans having that characteristic. For example, a deal's exposure to office properties would be the total original principal balances of all of the deal's loans on office properties divided by the total original principal balances of all the loans in the deal. This office percentage would then be assigned to each issue of that deal.

We choose to stratify issues in the CMBS Index across the following eight characteristics:

1. *Property Type.* We identify four property-type buckets (office, retail-anchored, multifamily, and hotel) that are prominent property types serving as collateral for commercial loans. Through the use of stratified sampling, the proxy portfolio has exposures to these four property types similar to those of the index. These four property types span the major sectors of the real estate market and often have different sensitivities to the economic cycle. Currently, these four account for 74% of the loans underlying the issues in the CMBS Index.

2. *Geography.* We identify the underlying property location for each loan backing CMBS deals in the index and calculate the total amount of loans by state. We then select the four largest states—California, New York, Texas, and Florida—as the four geography buckets. These four states are also located in different regions of the country, which helps ensure regional diversification as well. Different states and regions can be in different phases of an economic cycle and experience different legislative, environmental, and random real estate shocks. Currently, these four states account for 41% of the loans underlying the issues in the CMBS Index. The next four largest states account for 13%.

3. *Performance (Delinquencies).* We choose two performance buckets: (1) current and late less than 1 month and (2) late more than 1 month. If the market became concerned about the performance of commercial loans, then we would want the proxy portfolio to have a delinquency profile similar to that of the index.

4. *Prepayment Protection.* Commercial loans have varying amounts of prepayment risk depending on the type of prepayment protection provided. The market's valuation of different types of prepayment protection can vary depending on the general interest rate and property market environment. We specify three prepayment protection buckets (currently locked out, in the yield maintenance period, and in the fixed penalty period) and we require that the proxy portfolio closely match the CMBS Index with regard to these three prepayment protection types.

5. *Deal Type.* There are three general types of CMBS deals: conduit, fusion, and large loan. (Single-property and single-borrower deals are

not part of the CMBS Index.) At times the marketplace may put different valuations on these different deal types. Consequently, we require that the proxy portfolio have a deal-type profile similar to that of the index.

We also stratify issues in the CMBS Index according to the following three characteristics currently used by the market and the index pricing matrix:

6. *Dollar Price.* We define four dollar price buckets: discount (price < 98); par (price between 98 and 102); premium (price between 102 and 108); and super premium (price > 108).

7. *Average Life.* We define three average life buckets: less than 4 years; between 4 and 8 years; and greater than 8 years.

8. *Quality Grade.* We define four quality buckets: Aaa, Aa, A, and Baa.

Our bucketing strategy does not create multidimensional buckets defined in terms of more than one characteristic (e.g., Aa-hotel-current). Instead, each bucket is one dimensional, reducing the total number of buckets to twenty-seven. However, an issue can belong to more than one bucket of a given characteristic. For example, the property-type characteristic has four buckets. A given CMBS issue has its original principal balance weighted percentage allocated across the four buckets, though some of the issue's weight is not allocated to any of those buckets if it contains loans on less common types of properties, such as self-storage facilities.

There are other issue characteristics that might have been selected for use in stratification. For example, we could have controlled for tenant concentrations. However, it is difficult to measure tenant exposure in a commercial loan, as an underlying property often has many tenants. In addition, tenant concentrations are generally very low. Other possible characteristics are: deal trustee, deal special servicer, leasehold vs. fee simple, origination year, delinquencies at 60+ days, debt service coverage ratio, loan-to-value ratio, and loan originator. The CMBS replication software we have developed can be modified to incorporate these characteristics, if desired.

For each of these twenty-seven buckets, we require that the proxy portfolio match the market value percentage within a tolerance level of 0.03 and that the contribution to spread duration be within a tolerance level of 0.10. We also impose some additional constraints:

1. The overall duration of the proxy portfolio must be within 0.03 of the index.

2. We force diversification in the proxy portfolio by requiring that the maximum market value position size vary by credit quality. This latter feature stems from our work on sufficient diversification in a credit portfolio.[3] Lower-rated credit securities have a greater risk of downgrades than higher-rated securities. Furthermore, the impact of a downgrade can be particularly large for Baa securities. Since a proxy portfolio holds only a small subset of index bonds, the market value of any Baa bond in the proxy is likely to be much greater than the bond's weight in the index. Consequently, the impact of the Baa bond's downgrade would have a magnified impact on the proxy portfolio compared to the index. To reduce the tracking error risk owing to downgrades, we force diversification in the lower-quality buckets. Specifically, we follow the "7:3:1 rule" and vary the maximum market value position size of an issue in the proxy as follows:

Quality	Maximum Market Value Position Size per Issue (%)
Aaa	7
Aa	7
A	3
Baa1 and Baa2	1
Baa3	0

The index contains approximately 4% in issues rated Baa1 and Baa2. Consequently, the issue size constraint forces the replication to select at least four issues from these credit categories. The index contains less than 2% in the Baa3 quality category and we require that the proxy select no bonds rated Baa3. Given their small weight in the index and their potential to cause significant tracking error havoc in case of a credit event, we disallow Baa3 securities in the proxy portfolio. In lieu of Baa3 issues, the proxy contains a heavier weight in Baa1 and Baa2 issues so that the overall weight and contribution to spread duration of Baa issues in the proxy is within the tolerance limits.

3. We also restrict from the proxy portfolio any issues from CMBS deals identified as credit tenant lease (CTL) deals. CTLs, which are loans that are underwritten based primarily on the quality of the tenant and the lease agreement, rather than on the property, are a relatively small part of the index and are often treated differently by investors. Given their small weight in the index, and the potential for high idiosyncratic risk owing to non-real-estate events affecting the tenant, we exclude issues coming from CTL deals from the proxy.

3. See Chapter 14.

REPLICATION RESULTS

We examine the performance of the replication strategy from December 1999 through February 2002. To keep turnover low, we make the following two adjustments:

1. *Quarterly Rebalancing.* A proxy portfolio is created each calendar quarter (at the end of the month prior to the last month in the quarter). The proxy portfolio remains unchanged until the following quarter.

2. *Penalize Turnover.* We use an optimizer to select bonds for the proxy in such a way as to satisfy the constraints. Within the constraints, the optimizer puts as much of the proxy's market value as possible into issues with the most market value outstanding. By directing the optimizer to select issues with a relatively large market value, we aim to generate a proxy portfolio that will have relatively high liquidity. To help limit turnover, we adjust the market values of issues already in the proxy upward so that the optimizer is given an incentive to retain issues already in the portfolio.

Results from our replication are shown in Figure 8-1. Monthly return differences are presented in Figure 8-2. These figures show that the proposed replication methodology has tracked the CMBS Index closely. Over the 27-month period, the average monthly return difference equals 0 bp, with a monthly tracking error of 4 bp.

To measure turnover from this strategy, we calculate the market value of new issues added to the proxy at each quarterly rebalancing plus the market value of any "add-on" positions. We then divide this sum by the market value of the entire proxy portfolio to arrive at our turnover measure. As Figure 8-3 shows, turnover is very low.

OUTPERFORMING THE CMBS INDEX

A CMBS proxy portfolio can serve as a useful starting point for strategies that try to outperform the CMBS Index. There are numerous nuances to CMBS deals that savvy investors can exploit in order to outperform the index. These investors can first construct a replicating proxy portfolio and then selectively substitute issues with similar characteristics but the potential to outperform owing to some technical feature.

There has been extensive research on the potential value to bond investors of receiving yield maintenance penalties. Such penalties are designed to compensate

Figure 8-1. CMBS Replication: Proxy and Index Statistics and Returns
December 1999–February 2002

	Proxy Portfolio Return (%)	Number of Bonds in Proxy	CMBS Index Return (%)	Return Difference (bp)
Dec-99	−0.48	28	−0.46	−2
Jan-00	−0.79		−0.79	0
Feb-00	0.93		0.95	−2
Mar-00	1.38	27	1.44	−6
Apr-00	−0.10		−0.14	4
May-00	−0.44		−0.45	2
Jun-00	2.84	25	2.82	2
Jul-00	0.73		0.75	−2
Aug-00	1.82		1.85	−2
Sep-00	1.35	26	1.40	−4
Oct-00	0.83		0.79	4
Nov-00	1.86		1.92	−6
Dec-00	2.68	28	2.69	−1
Jan-01	1.69		1.69	0
Feb-01	1.15		1.15	0
Mar-01	0.28	24	0.28	0
Apr-01	−0.20		−0.26	6
May-01	0.39		0.43	−5
Jun-01	0.10	25	0.11	0
Jul-01	2.75		2.79	−5
Aug-01	1.54		1.57	−3
Sep-01	1.89	28	1.95	−6
Oct-01	2.03		2.02	1
Nov-01	−1.73		−1.76	2
Dec-01	−0.78	25	−0.78	0
Jan-02	1.22		1.15	8
Feb-02	1.66		1.62	5
Average monthly outperformance				0
Monthly tracking error				4
Annualized tracking error				13

bond holders for lost yield in the event of a loan prepayment. A prepaying borrower is obligated to pay a yield maintenance penalty that roughly equals the present value of the bond holder's lost cash flows. However, the discount rate used is typically the U.S. Treasury rate flat, not the yield of the bond, which produces a potential windfall for the bond holder.

Monthly Return Difference (bp)

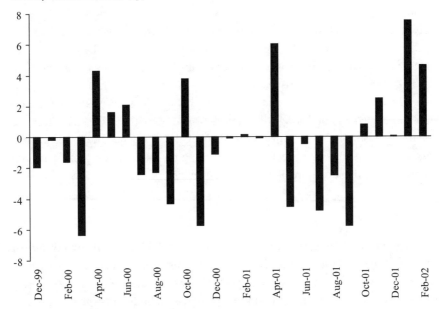

Figure 8-2. CMBS Replication: Monthly Return Differences
CMBS Index vs. the CMBS Proxy Portfolio, December 1999–February 2002

Figure 8-3. CMBS Replication: Turnover Statistics
December 1999–December 2001

	Number of Bonds	Number of New Bonds at Rebalancing	Number of Add-On Positions at Rebalancing	Quarterly Turnover (%)
Dec-99	28			
Mar-00	27	0	16	21
Jun-00	25	1	20	16
Sep-00	26	5	5	13
Dec-00	28	5	8	18
Mar-01	24	1	8	10
Jun-01	25	2	16	15
Sep-01	28	6	7	18
Dec-01	25	0	8	10

Why would the borrower prepay and pay such a yield maintenance penalty? Commercial borrowers often prepay to extract equity appreciation in their property. This additional equity can then be redeployed in the acquisition of additional properties. The value of the yield maintenance penalty is usually of secondary concern compared to the prospect of monetizing additional equity in a property.

The ability to identify issues likely to pay yield maintenance can be put to use in trying to outperform the CMBS Index. Like the market, the replication methodology does not distinguish between two bonds with similar characteristics even if one is more likely to pay a valuable penalty. Consequently, investors can outperform the index by selectively substituting for issues in the proxy portfolio similar issues that are more likely to pay a penalty.

SUMMARY

We have presented a replication strategy for the CMBS Index and have examined its empirical performance from December 1999 through February 2002. Based on these results we find that the proxy portfolio has tracked the index very closely with very low turnover. In addition, the proxy portfolio is constructed in such a way as to anticipate future changes in CMBS pricing methodology, which should help keep tracking error low.

BENCHMARK CUSTOMIZATION

Apart from modern portfolio theory, benchmarks have done more for investor welfare than any other twentieth-century investment innovation, and today it is hard to imagine investment management without benchmarks. Although a benchmark is simply a set of nondiscretionary portfolio rules, substantial benefits flow from its simplicity.

A benchmark allows an investor to measure the value of his manager's discretionary actions. Not only can a manager's performance be compared to the benchmark, but it can as well be evaluated relative to that of other managers. In other words, benchmarks permit comparison shopping for investment talent and provide a basis for determining the price for portfolio management services.

Benchmarks help investors in other ways besides performance measurement. With a benchmark, managers know what type of performance is expected of them and that performance deviations will be questioned. In other words, investors can use benchmarks as a control tool. Since managers typically manage to their benchmarks with relatively small deviations, investors can, with a sufficiently high degree of confidence, classify managers by their investment style. Knowing that a manager's performance will likely track the benchmark permits investors to use quantitative techniques and historical benchmark data to select managers across various asset classes in a way that maximizes investor welfare.

Benchmark construction requires a set of rules to determine which bonds to include or exclude, an infrastructure that can identify such a set of bonds, and an ability to price the bonds on a regular basis. Consequently, the first fixed-income benchmarks, such as indices of government bonds, were relatively simple. However, as technology has improved and the fixed-income market has broadened, so too have benchmarks. Today, there are benchmarks for virtually all fixed-income asset classes in all major currencies. These indices have one element in common: the underlying rules are not specific to a particular investor.

The performance measurement and monitoring function of benchmarks is so widely appreciated that investors now want benchmarks designed specifically for their own investment circumstances. For example, a bank treasurer may wish to monitor the performance of the bank's investment team by constructing a benchmark that reflects the bank's proprietary investment rules and would prefer one custom-designed around the bank's investment rules, rather than one "off-the-shelf."

Demand for a custom benchmark can arise from many circumstances. To satisfy the criterion of "objectivity," indices are typically constructed based on a set of predefined rules that are designed to make the index representative of the sector(s) it tracks. These construction rules ultimately dictate the issuer concentration of the index, as well as its overall characteristics (e.g., average duration, average credit quality). However, if the risk profile of the index does not coincide with an investor's risk preferences, that investor may create a customized benchmark to better reflect his investment objectives. Sometimes, investors want to deviate from the market weights of various parts of the index to create a benchmark with a particular duration or average quality.

Periodic outbreaks of idiosyncratic credit risk also drive customized benchmarks. As investors seek additional return, credit is a dominant portfolio risk that has prompted reconsideration of portfolio risk management. Managers and investors scrutinize the idiosyncratic risks embedded in benchmarks. Plan sponsors ask: "Should our plan have a 2% exposure to name XYZ via the benchmark?"[1] Although the manager may be neutral to the name vis-à-vis the benchmark, the plan remains exposed to the absolute idiosyncratic risk of the name.

The goal of many customizations is to reduce idiosyncratic risk within the benchmark. For example, an issuer-capped benchmark imposes a maximum issuer market value weight. In the simplest case, a market value cap (e.g., 1%) can be imposed and every issuer is checked against this ceiling. Any market value in excess of the cap is "shaved off" and redistributed to all other issuers in the index in proportion to their market values. In some cases, the caps are chosen to be different for various credit ratings, reflecting the differences in issuer-specific risk between higher- and lower-credit qualities. While issuer-capped benchmarks seem straightforward, the particular cap level and redistribution rule can significantly impact the benchmark's risk and return performance. In Chapter 13 we analyze how some redistribution rules can limit the benefits of issuer capping by inadvertently introducing unfavorable sector-quality risk exposures relative to the uncapped index.

---

1. Idiosyncratic risk can be substantial in a benchmark. For example, as of August 2005, the top ten issuers (predominantly financial) in the U.S. Corporate Index had a total market value weight of 22.1%.

Other investors have addressed idiosyncratic risk in benchmarks from a completely different angle: design a custom benchmark with zero idiosyncratic risk! For example, Treasuries have little, if any, idiosyncratic risk. One advantage of a Treasury benchmark is that a portfolio manager must justify any percentage holding of a credit asset. In stark contrast, a manager benchmarked against a credit index with one large issuer accounting for 2% of the market value will have to allocate the same 2% to that issuer to be neutral. The trouble with a Treasury benchmark built to avoid security-specific risk is that it does not offer any long-run spread advantage and does not challenge the investment manager to demonstrate skill in choosing credits.[2] The investment manager's relative performance is not penalized as it should be if he avoids making credit decisions.

However, a benchmark of interest-rate swaps has little security-specific risk and requires an investment manger to demonstrate credit selection skill. Swaps offer tremendous liquidity, limited "headline" or event risk, and an opportunity for plan sponsors to capture some of the long-run spread advantage of investing in non-Treasury product. A manager who has a swap index as a benchmark (Chapter 11) is completely free to hold only those credits that he thinks will outperform and avoid credits expected to underperform. If the manager has a neutral or no view, he can hold a zero market value weight with a swap benchmark. Custom swap benchmarks are also suitable for banks and insurance companies that manage credit portfolios internally and fund themselves close to LIBOR.

An important attribute of a benchmark is its replicability. In other words, can the portfolio manager produce benchmark returns if desired? If not, then the benchmark is not as meaningful a performance measurement tool. Periods of stressful credit markets sometimes raise the issue of the replicability of credit indices. Many high-grade credit benchmarks have rules that remove bonds downgraded below investment grade at the end of the downgrade month, at a price that reflects where they can be sold at the margin, not where all outstanding amounts of the bonds can be sold. In contrast, a portfolio manager must find willing buyers and often has little choice but to hold the bonds for at least several months. As a result, some investors believed that credit indices suffer from a "survivorship bias" that makes it extremely difficult for portfolio managers to outperform the benchmark.

In response to this issue some plan sponsors and investors have expressed interest in custom "downgrade-tolerant" indices that allow downgraded bonds to remain in the benchmark for a period of time following downgrade. In Chapter 13 we describe a methodology for measuring survivorship bias and have recently

---

2. Please refer to Chapter 22 for a discussion of the long-run advantage of moving to an Aggregate-type benchmark from a Treasury-only benchmark.

found that the bias is typically small, but not negligible. In addition, the bias is volatile and can, at times, be positive or negative. The bias is generally a decreasing function of the "tolerance period" or the length of time a downgraded issue is allowed to remain in the benchmark. For example, the bias is largest if the portfolio manager holds on to fallen angels for 3 months or less, but it disappears and turns negative at the 6-month tolerance period, reflecting the general recovery of fallen angels. The lesson learned during the study of downgrade-tolerant indices is that if plan sponsors are willing to give managers time to work out of downgraded issues, then they should give them at least 6 months to do so. In practice, however, most plan sponsors give their investment managers much less time.

Custom benchmarks are also sought for asset classes or investment strategies that have no established benchmark. For example, many credit investors buy only floating-rate credit assets or fixed-rate bonds on an asset-swapped basis. Such assets allow the portfolio manager to keep term-structure duration very short while using credit selection skill to profit from an overweight to credit-spread duration. Floating-rate indices are scarce and those that exist may not reflect the broader asset swap market. For example, the sponsor may want to benchmark the manager to the same set of diversified systematic spread sector risks (i.e., credit quality and sector exposures) as are embedded in a broad-based credit index, while simultaneously limiting term-structure risk to the 6-month Treasury rate. The challenge is to design a custom benchmark with a short Treasury duration that reflects the normal allocation to the overall credit sector with its diversified systematic credit spread sector risks.

To benchmark an asset-swapped portfolio effectively, the benchmark must represent a "neutral" spread sector portfolio so that a manager's deviations from neutral will have the potential to appear as outperforming the benchmark. Using 3-month swaps as a benchmark is inadequate in this situation because it reflects only a single credit (i.e., swap spreads) and does not represent the wide array of spread sector decisions available to the manager. An ideal benchmark design for an asset-swapped manager is a floating-rate benchmark that reflects his normal spread asset allocation. We have detailed a methodology for constructing floating-rate benchmarks for asset-swapped portfolios that uses mirror swap indices (Chapter 12) to construct asset swap indices.

Most custom benchmarks are total return benchmarks, but investors are applying the concept in "nonmarket" situations. For example, some portfolio managers operate under numerous constraints (e.g., cannot sell assets) or have their performance measured using book value accounting, not market value (Chapter 9). For these managers, a total return benchmark that assumes that the manager is unconstrained is not relevant. Instead, these portfolio managers prefer custom benchmarks that incorporate any nondiscretionary actions that they must obey.

For example, if a manager is required to raise cash without generating a book income gain or loss, then so too must the benchmark. The advantage of these custom indices is that they allow an impartial evaluation of the portfolio manager's performance while fully incorporating the imposed constraints.

The idea behind many of these nonmarket custom benchmarks is to mimic an investor passively investing in an index as if it were a portfolio. The composition of this "benchmark" portfolio is then fixed (except for future cash reinvestment) and the benchmark's book yield, book income, and book return are calculated and compared to the investor's actual portfolio. This allows portfolio managers to demonstrate their value added correctly. Because the book accounting performance of such an index depends on the timing and amounts of cash inflows and outflows preceding the current performance month, no two investors are likely to have the same book index even if their underlying market index is the same. By its very nature, a book index is the ultimate in a custom benchmark.

Some investment managers operate under a different set of constraints. For example, a plan's assets may be "dedicated" to satisfying a well-defined liability schedule and assets must be managed to satisfy those liabilities. In such cases, the sponsor specifies the universe of bonds in which the manager may invest and the liability schedule that must be satisfied. Often the investable universe is defined as a market-based index but usually has a term structure that is very different from the liability schedule (e.g., the liability schedule may have a longer duration than the market index). The manager now has two goals: produce added returns to help the plan achieve its long-term investment goals and, simultaneously, keep the portfolio's term structure aligned with the liability schedule. How does the sponsor evaluate the manager's performance? If the manager underperformed the market index, was it due to the a poor sector and security selection or because of the (correct) structuring of the portfolio to satisfy the liability term structure? What is needed is a custom benchmark that reflects both of the plan sponsor's goals.

A custom liability-based benchmark (Chapter 10) gives the sponsor and manager a performance yardstick incorporating both the term-structure constraints imposed by the liability schedule and the investment restrictions imposed by the sponsor's risk preferences. Sponsors can be confident that if their managers hold positions underlying the liability benchmark, they will meet their liability schedules while satisfying their investment restrictions.

Benchmark customization allows investors to better define their objectives and enables portfolio managers to better demonstrate their skill. Given the emphasis on pay for performance, both parties will continue to press for further benchmark customization.

9. Evaluating Performance of Long-Horizon Portfolios

Long-horizon investors, who are predominantly concerned with book yield and risk-adjusted book returns, can benefit from performance benchmarks that also use book accounting. The idea behind building such a benchmark is that a manager passively invests in an index (say, the Aggregate, Municipal, or an investor's own customized index) as if it were a portfolio. The composition of this portfolio is then fixed (except for future cash reinvestment), and the portfolio's book yield, book income, and book return are calculated and compared to the manager's own portfolio. The performance of a manager's book accounting benchmark reflects what the manager could have achieved (in book accounting terms) by passively investing in the underlying index and allows him to quantify the value of active portfolio management more accurately.

Book accounting performance of an index depends on the timing and amounts of cash inflows and outflows (and the particular rules for handling such cash flows) preceding the current performance month, so no two investors are likely to have the same book benchmark even if their underlying index is the same. By its very nature, a book benchmark must be customized for each investor to allow individuals to input their own historical "vector" of cash inflows and outflows (including rules) so as to produce proper book accounting values in the current month.

The benchmark's book yield and book income are indications of what could be achieved if the manager follows a passive strategy. However, a manager naturally tries to do better by adjusting the asset allocation mix, overweighting (underweighting) sectors that appear cheap (rich), and adding issues of a given peer group that trade at a wider spread given their credit outlook. Often, the manager's book yield exceeds that of his benchmark. But at what risk to future book income? We

Based on research first published by Lehman Brothers in 2006.

241

discuss how portfolio analytics tools can be used to assess whether a book manager is adding value on a risk-adjusted basis.

Finally, a book benchmark permits quantitative empirical studies on various portfolio strategies. For example, a manager who uses book accounting may wish to consider whether it would be better to have a portfolio's assets managed by a traditional book accounting manager (who buys and holds with a spread overweight) or a traditional total return manager (who trades actively to generate outperformance, or alpha). We examine how the performance of these two managers compares on both a book accounting and a market accounting basis.

BOOK ACCOUNTING AND MARKET ACCOUNTING

While many investors (e.g., a typical total return asset manager) use mark-to-market accounting to value assets and calculate periodic returns, there are other substantial investors (e.g., insurance companies and banks) who use book accounting. Book accounting values a bond at historical cost with smooth periodic adjustments to amortize any premium or discount to par by the time of the bond's anticipated maturity.[1] Discrete adjustments are made to a bond's book value when there is a change in the bond's anticipated maturity or par value owing, for example, to prepayments or credit impairment.

A bond's book yield is based on its yield at purchase and, barring any credit impairment (or prepayment recalculation in the case of prepaying securities), it is relatively static until maturity, irrespective of changes in market yields. A bond's book value is based on the bond's market (clean) price at purchase, adjusted over time for the difference between its stated interest (coupon) and its book yield. Typically, it gradually moves to par as the bond approaches maturity.

We define a bond's monthly book return as the bond's monthly book income, which includes the book yield earned over the period (and any adjustments to book income arising from a change in the assumed amortization schedule or any book gains or losses), divided by its beginning-of-the-period book value. Since book income is generally insensitive to market movements, a bond's book return is also much more stable over time compared to its market return.

If there is little turnover, changes in a portfolio's book yield and book return are also muted compared to the portfolio's market yields and returns. Consequently, it is not meaningful to compare a portfolio's book return against a market return benchmark (such as the Lehman Aggregate) as a measure of the portfolio's

---

1. Investors typically use book accounting when their liabilities are difficult to price at market and are instead carried at historical value. To better match the valuation of assets and liabilities, book accounting is used for both.

Monthly Return (%)

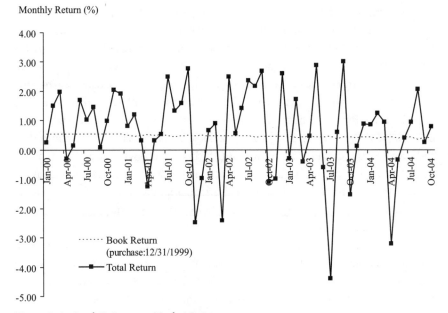

Figure 9-1. Book Return vs. Market Return

A Portfolio of the Lehman U.S. Treasury Index, Purchased on December 31, 1999

performance. For example, Figure 9-1 shows monthly book and market returns for an investment in the U.S. Treasury Index in December 1999. Any portfolio cash flows are reinvested in the contemporaneous Treasury Index. The portfolio's book returns are remarkably stable, drifting down slowly over time, reflecting the decline in market yields. In contrast, market returns are very volatile. In a given month, a manager using book accounting would have difficulty comparing performance against a market return benchmark.

Trading activity may further confuse relative performance vs. a market benchmark. When a bond is sold, book accounting marks the bond to market and recognizes any difference between book value and market value as a book gain or loss. If a bond's market price is up in a particular month (i.e., a positive market return) and the bond is sold, its book return depends on its book value relative to its market price and may be positive or negative.

How does one measure a manager's performance contribution to a portfolio that uses book accounting? Usually, a manager's quality is measured by his alpha, which is the portfolio's return vs. a benchmark's return. As discussed earlier, a book manager cannot use a traditional market index (e.g., the Lehman Aggregate) as a performance benchmark as the returns are too dissimilar, but there are other reasons as well.

The composition of a market index changes monthly as new issues become eligible for inclusion. Traditional active money managers can freely alter their portfolios in reaction to changes in index composition, whereas book investors are often more constrained in portfolio rebalancing. Over time, today's composition of a traditional market index may not closely reflect the index in existence when the portfolio was constructed, which makes comparison with a market index less meaningful. Moreover, book managers are often required to undertake nondiscretionary transactions. For example, a book manager may be required to raise cash from portfolio sales in such a way as to be book gain/loss neutral. This requirement forces him to sell certain bonds that may not have been his unconstrained choice. Again, comparing the book manager to a market index return implicitly assumes that the manager has full discretion regarding buy and sell decisions.

Alpha for a book manager can be measured by comparing the income realized by the manager's portfolio at maturity against the income generated by a passive buy-and-hold investment in the market portfolio corresponding to the date the manager initially purchased the assets. The difficulty with this alpha measure is the need to wait for the portfolio to mature before it can be calculated.

Alpha for an individual book manager is particularly difficult to measure. Given their long-horizon nature, book portfolios usually contain many "legacy" assets acquired long before a particular manager assumed portfolio responsibility. Unlike a traditional market accounting manager, a new book manager typically does not have the liberty to rebalance the portfolio to match her views completely. Alpha at an institutional level that spans the tenure of multiple managers is also difficult to measure. A portfolio's alpha can be measured by comparing the income generated by the portfolio—but only at maturity—with the income generated by a market-neutral passive portfolio that makes simultaneous investments as the institution's portfolio and is subject to the same nondiscretionary investment decisions. A market-neutral passive portfolio, in this context, refers to a set of all bonds (a market portfolio) eligible for inclusion in the book portfolio with no managerial decision as to which bonds to select.

An alternative, widely cited, measure of book portfolio performance is a comparison of a portfolio's book yield to a passive buy-and-hold portfolio's yield. Is the portfolio "out-yielding" a passively managed portfolio? This measure has its uses, but also has some limitations. Essentially, book yield is a measure of a portfolio's income-generating capability and, as such, often has little to say about past performance. In an environment of downgrades, defaults, and other prepayments, a portfolio's current book yield may not reflect earlier poor performance. A book portfolio may have a higher book yield than a passive portfolio but is clearly underperforming. If market yields are rising, a manager who experiences book losses from downgrades, defaults, and prepayments has more opportunities to invest new cash at higher yields. In contrast, if the passive portfolio experiences fewer prepayment events and book losses, its book yield may be lower. However, the passive portfolio's cumulative book income generation is likely to be superior compared to the manager's portfolio. As a result, while it is difficult to measure a portfolio's relative performance with a single number, we can make some progress by constructing a market-neutral passive portfolio as a performance benchmark and comparing its cumulative book income and book yield against the manager's portfolio. The next section describes the method for constructing such a book accounting benchmark.

CONSTRUCTING PERFORMANCE BENCHMARKS FOR BOOK MANAGERS

Imagine a book manager who has a new client and an initial cash inflow to invest. He selects specific bonds that constitute the portfolio. As the portfolio generates cash flow, he chooses assets in the marketplace to reinvest this cash at current market yields. The portfolio's performance is calculated according to specific book accounting guidelines: when to recognize a credit impairment, when to update prepayment realizations and expectations, how to handle callables, and so on. Moreover, from time to time the manager may receive additional client cash inflows to invest, and, again, selects assets in the marketplace in which to reinvest this cash at current market yields. Finally, the manager may be called on to raise cash from the portfolio, perhaps receiving nondiscretionary instructions as to how that cash is to be generated (e.g., gain/loss neutral).

Now imagine a passive manager with the same client and initial cash inflow. By the term "passive" we mean simply a manager who makes no investment decisions (e.g., timing, sector, and security selection). When cash must be put to work the manager simply buys the market. The passive manager also follows the same guidelines and rules as established by the client. By comparing the performance of the passive manager with the actual manager, we are implicitly giving the client a choice: invest in a portfolio that follows a passive investment strategy or in one wherein the manager has some scope to make active decisions. The performance difference (book yield and cumulative income) between the two represents the book manager's value added.

To construct a passive book portfolio, the following must be established at the outset:

1. What is the underlying investment (and reinvestment) universe? When the passive manager receives a client investment inflow what must the manager buy? For example, the client may instruct the manager to invest only in the Aggregate, in which case the passive investment rule for the manager is to buy the composition

of the Aggregate when the client makes an investment. In other words, as noted earlier, the passive manager does not make any investment decisions. In practice, the underlying index is likely to be a custom index (say, 70% U.S. Credit Index and 30% MBS Index). In fact, clients have very detailed and customized passive investment rules (e.g., 63% A+-rated or better bonds in the Credit Index that were issued in the last 5 years with at least $500 million outstanding and with an issuer cap of 2%; 25% current-coupon MBS Index; 10% AAA-rated Municipal Index with a remaining time to maturity of 10 years or less; and 2% 3-month LIBOR). Usually, but not always, a client's reinvestment universe is the same as the initial investment universe.

2. What is the passive strategy? Suppose the passive manager receives an investment inflow and buys the Aggregate (or any other index). Next month the Aggregate will have changed (new bonds coming in and some existing bonds dropping out). What strategy should the passive manager follow? Some of the possibilities are as follows:

(a) Follow a buy-and hold strategy. Once assets are purchased, continue to hold them even if they fall out of the underlying Aggregate Index (say, because maturity falls below 1 year).

(b) Follow a modified buy-and-hold strategy. Once assets are purchased, continue to hold them even if they fall out of the underlying Aggregate Index (say, because maturity falls below 1 year), except if they fall out of the index for some other specified reason (say, because they are downgraded below investment grade).

(c) Continually match the Aggregate. If necessary, sell bonds that are leaving the Aggregate and buy bonds that are entering. If more bonds are entering than leaving, sell a pro rata portion of existing holdings to be able to acquire new bonds in proportion.

(d) Track an external target variable, such as maintaining a certain OAD or asset allocation. For example, the initial investment may produce an OAD of 4.0. The passive strategy is to continually keep the passive portfolio's OAD equal to 4.0 irrespective of what happens to the Aggregate's OAD. Such a strategy involves buying and selling of bonds in the benchmark to meet the target.[2]

---

2. Alternatively, some investors may ask that no assets be sold to reach a target. Instead, the passive strategy will do its best to track the external target variable by using any available cash flow generated by the portfolio to "nudge" the portfolio toward the external variable.

3. How to handle cash outflows? From time to time a client may request that the book manager raise cash from the portfolio. Generally the client gives the manager specific (i.e., nondiscretionary) instructions as to how to raise the cash. The passive benchmark is constructed in such a way that it, too, follows the same nondiscretionary instructions. For example, the client may request:

(a) Raise $X in cash but be gain/loss neutral.

(b) Generate $Y in book gains (losses) and reinvest the cash generated in the passive benchmark by buying bonds in the current investment universe. Even within this category there may be directions given to the manager (e.g., generate as much cash to meet the gain/loss target or generate as little cash as possible).

(c) Raise $X in cash with no gain/loss goal and do so by selling previous investments on a pro rata basis.

(d) Raise $X in cash with no gain/loss goal but maximize the subsequent book yield on the portfolio.

Many other instructions are also possible. The important issue is that the passive manager must follow the same nondiscretionary rules as the book manager. For the construction of the book index performance benchmark, each client's cash outflow can follow its own particular rule. This reflects the reality for the book manager.

4. Specify the book accounting rules. Finally, the book index performance benchmark must follow the same book accounting conventions as the book manager. Specifically, it follows standard book accounting treatment and carries assets at their book value unless an asset becomes impaired, amortizes differently than expected at purchase, or is sold.[3] How does book accounting work? Generally speaking, when an investor buys a bond, he records its purchase (clean) price and yield, which is the bond's book yield. For each month thereafter, the investor records book income for the bond based on this book yield at purchase. The difference between a bond's monthly stated income (based on the bond's coupon) and its book income equals the monthly amortization amount to adjust the bond's book value. The accounting rules chosen will affect the following values:

---

3. However, some book indices may follow accounting rules different from others. For example, banks under GAAP have a book accounting treatment for callables that differs from the statutory accounting treatment followed by many insurance companies. Book indices must be customized according to the client's accounting conventions.

- Book Yield. A bond's book yield equals its bond-equivalent yield at the
  time of purchase. For book accounting indices, the time of purchase is defined as the beginning of the vintage month. Thus the book yield reported
  for the JAN04 Aggregate book accounting index equals the book value-
  weighted book yield for all the bonds in the Aggregate at the beginning
  of January 2004.

- Book Value. A bond's book value equals its market (clean) price at the time
  of purchase. Over time, the bond's book value may change. For bonds purchased at a premium, the premium amount must be amortized over the
  bond's life. Consequently, the bond's book value declines over time (declining each month by the amortization amount) until it equals par at maturity. Similarly, for bonds purchased at a discount (below par), the discount
  amount must be amortized over the bond's life so that at maturity the book
  value will also equal par. Generally, a bond's book value changes very gradually if at all. However, there are some special cases when it (and its book
  yield) can change significantly from month to month. These events are usually associated with a change in the prepayment assumption for prepaying
  securities (e.g., MBS) and with a credit impairment for credit-risky bonds.

- Book Income. Book income generally equals the bond's book yield for the
  performance month multiplied by the bond's prior month book value,
  plus any adjustments (if needed) to the prior month's book income (some
  special cases are discussed later) plus any final adjustments to a bond's
  final book value.

There are several special cases and we highlight two in particular: prepaying
securities and impaired credit securities.[4] When an MBS or another prepaying security is purchased, its book yield is calculated assuming a prepayment vector. If
the actual prepayment experience and/or forecast of prepayments differ from that
assumed in the initial month, the book yield must be recalculated (i.e., the retrospective yield method).[5] The recalculated book yield produces a revised book income each month following the initial month. Although prior book income values
are not restated, the book yield in the current performance month is adjusted to
reflect adjustments required for all of the prior months.

---

4. Other special cases are callable and putable (non-MBS) bonds. There are a couple of possible accounting treatments for such bonds.

5. A good summary of the retrospective yield method is: "Had I known at purchase what I
now know about the bond's actual and expected cash flows, then this is what I would have used
as its book yield."

Another special case is the handling of "impaired" credit bonds. Many book investors define an impaired bond as one that is downgraded below investment grade.[6] An impaired bond is sold from the book index at the end of the month that the bond is impaired. When the bond is sold the proceeds are recognized as the final cash flow. As with MBS, we go back to the purchase date and recalculate the bond's book yield, following the rule "If I knew then what I know now . . ."; recalculate the amortization schedule; and calculate book income in the downgrade month (t_{DG}): book income$_{tDG}$ = book yield$_{tDG}$ × book value$_{tDG-1}$ + the write-down owing to the impairment.

- Book Return. Book return (not a strict accounting term) equals the bond's book income for the performance month divided by its book value at the beginning of the month.

Book Accounting Indices

To be a relevant performance benchmark, a book accounting benchmark (sometimes called an "index") must be replicable by a portfolio manager. A book index mimics a passive investment in an index (say, the Aggregate or an investor's custom index) as if it were a portfolio. (A book index associated with the Aggregate is referred to as an "Aggregate book index." Note that the composition of a book index is identical to its corresponding index only at the time of the initial investment.) The composition of this portfolio is then fixed and its book yield, book income, and book return are calculated.[7] Any subsequent cash flow generated by the book index (coupon, prepayments, or proceeds from maturities) is reinvested in the corresponding index that is contemporaneous with the cash flow. Over time the portfolio, which originally was identical to the underlying index, becomes a conglomeration of the remaining initial investment in the index plus smaller investments in subsequent indices.

The interpretation of an investor's book index performance reflects what the investor could have achieved by being passively invested in the index. The performance of the book index (in book accounting terms) is then compared to the investor's portfolio.

A fundamental difference between a book index and a traditional market index is that the performance of the former during a given month, called the

---

6. Some investors may follow a different definition of impairment.

7. Other portfolio values are reported as well, including: book gains/losses and amortization, as well as market-related values, including market value, duration, convexity, credit quality, OAS, and sector distributions.

"performance month," depends on its "vintage month," that is, the month in which it was established. There are several reasons for this:

1. A book index is relatively static and its composition is not rebalanced every month as is a traditional market index based on the latter's inclusion rules. Once a bond enters a book index, it stays there until it matures, is called, or is downgraded. Therefore, the underlying index that constitutes the initial book index continues to represent the bulk of it for a long time.

2. The book index takes all the cash flows received in a particular month (say, month N) and reinvests them in the underlying index of month $N + 1$. Since the JAN00 book index and the FEB00 book index on the same underlying index differ in month N, they receive different amounts of cash flows in month N and therefore reinvest different amounts in the underlying index of month $N + 1$.

Figure 9-2 illustrates the changing composition of a given vintage book index over time. Suppose that the investor receives an investment contribution at the beginning of JAN00 and that the underlying index is the Aggregate. Assume also that there are no further investment contributions. The investor's book accounting benchmark is the JAN00 Aggregate book index. Figure 9-2 shows that the investor's JAN00 book index is 100% invested in the Aggregate as of the beginning of January 2000.

Suppose that in January the JAN00 book index generates some cash flow (e.g., coupon payments and prepayments). For illustration purposes suppose that the cash flow amounts to 10% of the February 2000 book value of the JAN00 book index. This 10% is then invested in the FEB00 Aggregate book index, so that by the beginning of February 2000, the JAN00 book index is a composite with 10% invested in the FEB00 book index and 90% invested in whatever remains of the original JAN00 book index.

The next cash flows for the JAN00 book index will likely occur during February 2000. These cash flows are generated both from the 10% of the portfolio invested in the FEB00 book index and the 90% invested in the original JAN00 book index. For illustration purposes only, suppose that the cash flow amounts to 10% of the March 2000 book value of the JAN00 book index. This February 2000 cash flow is then invested in the MAR00 Aggregate book index. Thus in March 2000, the JAN00 book index has approximately 10% invested in the MAR00 book index, 9% in whatever remains of the original FEB00 book index, and 81% in whatever remains of the original JAN00 book index. And so on. Figure 9-2 illustrates how the composition of the JAN00 book index changes over time.

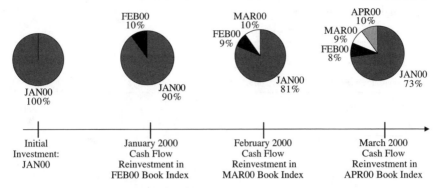

Figure 9-2. JAN00 Vintage Book Index
Changing Composition over Time

It is important to note that book accounting values (e.g., income and yield) of each bond position in a performance month depend on the month in which the position was acquired. Therefore, even if the JAN00 and FEB00 book indices both contain the same bond, they may not handle that bond in the same way. The JAN00 book index may have purchased the bond at the beginning of January and that position may earn a different book yield and income than if the bond was acquired in February 2000. This is the key difference between a book index and a market index: a book index must always keep track of each bond and the date it was added to the index, whereas a market index only needs to know the beginning-of-the-month price of each bond.

Since the performance of a book index in a given performance month depends on its vintage month, results are presented in a two-dimensional table (vintage month by performance month). Sample book yields and book returns for MBS book indices are shown in Figure 9-3.

Measuring Performance Using Book Accounting Benchmarks

How does a book accounting investor use a book accounting benchmark for performance measurement? Again, a book accounting benchmark represents a passive strategy for the investor: buying and holding all the bonds in the underlying index at the beginning of the month that the assets are invested. Any cash flows generated by the passive portfolio would be reinvested in the underlying index contemporaneous with the cash flow. If the investor makes only a single initial investment, the performance benchmark is simply the book index whose vintage month corresponds to the initial investment month. However, an investor's portfolio is likely to be much more complicated, with numerous investment inflows and cash outflows.

Figure 9-3. MBS Book Indices
Various Vintage Months

	Monthly Book Yields (%)				
Performance Month	11/30/2003	12/31/2003	1/31/2004	2/29/2004	3/31/2004
11/30/2003	5.1079	5.0601	5.0222	4.9764	4.9393
12/31/2003		4.9196	4.8790	4.8250	4.7794
1/31/2004			4.8364	4.7818	4.7329
2/29/2004				4.6754	4.6327
3/31/2004					4.6317
4/30/2004					
5/31/2004					
6/30/2004					
7/31/2004					
8/31/2004					
9/30/2004					
10/31/2004					
11/30/2004					

Vintage Month (row label)

	Monthly Book Returns (%)				
Performance Month	11/30/2003	12/31/2003	1/31/2004	2/29/2004	3/31/2004
11/30/2003		0.4016	0.3928	0.3894	0.4496
12/31/2003			0.3844	0.3789	0.4318
1/31/2004				0.3792	0.4173
2/29/2004					0.3989
3/31/2004					
4/30/2004					
5/31/2004					
6/30/2004					
7/31/2004					
8/31/2004					
9/30/2004					
10/31/2004					

Vintage Month (row label)

Suppose the investor makes an initial investment (say, January 2001) and subsequently (say, April 2001) makes another one. Until April 2001, his performance benchmark is the JAN01 book index (for the investor's underlying index). Beginning in April 2001, however, the investor has two vintage book index investments: the JAN01 book index and now the APR01 book index. The weights for this "composite" book index are the current book value weights of the two investments. For example, if the initial JAN01 investment was $1,050,000, the book value of that investment as of the beginning of APR01 was $1,000,000, and the investment at

4/30/2004	5/31/2004	6/30/2004	7/31/2004	8/31/2004	9/30/2004	10/31/2004	11/30/2004
5.0588	5.0797	5.0583	5.0287	4.9641	4.9591	4.9235	4.9537
4.9169	4.9363	4.9150	4.8805	4.8039	4.7973	4.7536	4.7891
4.8763	4.8939	4.8738	4.8375	4.7565	4.7491	4.7019	4.7394
4.7875	4.8026	4.7838	4.7443	4.6555	4.6469	4.5939	4.6349
4.7874	4.7991	4.7822	4.7427	4.6541	4.6450	4.5911	4.6319
5.2248	5.2499	5.2298	5.2054	5.1511	5.1474	5.1181	5.1442
	5.3854	5.3730	5.3537	5.3118	5.3094	5.2905	5.3082
		5.2860	5.2669	5.2177	5.2144	5.1914	5.2117
			5.1813	5.1289	5.1242	5.0958	5.1189
				4.8979	4.8933	4.8503	4.8831
					4.9502	4.9112	4.9432
						4.8245	4.8656
							5.0011

4/30/2004	5/31/2004	6/30/2004	7/31/2004	8/31/2004	9/30/2004	10/31/2004	11/30/2004
0.4158	0.3885	0.3815	0.3458	0.3938	0.3583	0.4330	0.3577
0.4020	0.3800	0.3709	0.3333	0.3808	0.3427	0.4214	0.3407
0.3963	0.3796	0.3707	0.3361	0.3777	0.3417	0.4151	0.3386
0.3871	0.3750	0.3661	0.3335	0.3701	0.3352	0.4054	0.3308
0.3852	0.3773	0.3702	0.3429	0.3711	0.3407	0.4009	0.3357
	0.4134	0.4128	0.3997	0.4139	0.3989	0.4293	0.3963
		0.4275	0.4202	0.4280	0.4197	0.4365	0.4168
			0.4162	0.4208	0.4130	0.4281	0.4088
				0.4142	0.4070	0.4198	0.4020
					0.3889	0.4007	0.3820
						0.4028	0.3906
							0.3869

the beginning of APR01 was $500,000, then the two weights for the performance months beginning in APR01 are 0.67 and 0.33, respectively. Outflows add further complexity. In which months do outflows occur? Which rules must be followed when raising cash (e.g., maximize loss or gain/loss neutral)?

As we noted earlier, since the performance of a book benchmark depends on the timing and amount of cash inflow and outflow (and the particular rules followed) preceding the current performance month, no two investors are likely to have the same book benchmark even if their underlying index is the same. By its very nature, each book index must be customized for each investor to allow him to input his own historical "vector" of cash inflows and outflows (including rules) so as to produce book accounting values in the current month. A custom book benchmark produces book accounting values (book yield, book income, book value, book return, and so on) as well as numerous market-based values (e.g., market value, OA duration, OA convexity).[8]

MANAGING AGAINST A BOOK ACCOUNTING INDEX: "A BOOK YIELD ADVANTAGE, BUT AT WHAT RISK?"

A manager of a book accounting portfolio is likely to follow different portfolio strategies than if he were managing a marked-to-market portfolio. One observation is that book managers tend to trade less actively compared to their total return counterparts. While a book manager at a listed company may be able to profitably trade the portfolio, any gains are reported as "trading gains" and may be heavily discounted by equity analysts as a dependable source of earnings. Consequently, the manager may demonstrate skill more effectively by identifying assets for purchase that will supply a reliably large book income advantage over time. This is why book managers may place relatively more emphasis on correctly estimating default probabilities over the life of a bond as opposed to the bond's short-term price volatility.

Furthermore, since total return managers are measured vs. their total return benchmark on a monthly basis, persistent monthly underperformance or high monthly tracking error casts the total return manager in a poor light. As a result, he must successfully anticipate monthly valuation changes in both the portfolio and benchmark. For example, both the book and total return manager may identify a bond as an attractive long-term income-producing asset. However, the total return manager will be tempted to temporarily underweight or overweight the bond in the portfolio in anticipation of short-term changes in market price, and such a focus generally leads to more portfolio trading activity.[9] Barring a credit or prepayment event, a portfolio's book income and book yield are relatively imper-

---

8. A book index may also provide a breakdown of why the benchmark's book yield is changing from month to month: change in prepayment estimates for prepaying securities; impact of impaired credit bonds; impact of bonds being called; impact of reinvestment of cash flows at significantly different book yields; and matured bonds leaving the book index.

9. Another reason a book manager may follow a buy-and-hold strategy is that the manager may have limited scope for trading and must anticipate having to hold an asset for long periods. Many book managers are part of larger institutions with many profit and loss centers. Owing to circumstances in other parts of the institution, the book manager may be constrained from trading as it may produce an undesired book gain or loss. Consequently, a book manager may be

vious to spread changes in the market. Thus, a book manager may buy a wide-spread credit asset to produce a steady book yield and book income advantage over the benchmark. He continues to enjoy this advantage even if the bond's spread widens, as long as the bond does not become credit impaired or prepays unexpectedly. In contrast, a total return manager buying the same asset would be penalized as soon as the asset's market performance begins to deteriorate.

Overall, the book manager typically strives more to identify assets that will produce relatively high book income (book yield) with a high degree of confidence (i.e., low default or prepayment risk) and less to anticipate monthly spread changes. This focus on book yield can often work to his advantage. To the extent that a portion of a bond's yield reflects a risk premium to compensate total return managers for spread volatility unrelated to default risk, the book manager can garner that additional spread because spread volatility does not affect the manager's performance.[10]

However, the book manager's long-horizon holding period means that he faces a very asymmetrical portfolio return profile. Asymmetrical returns increase as the investment horizon expands.[11] For credit assets in particular, long-horizon returns are very asymmetrical as a bond either earns a narrow spread over Treasuries with high probability or loses a large fraction of its value with low probability.[12] Consequently, long-horizon investors typically try to maximize a bond's expected yield (or spread over funding cost) while minimizing the probability of experiencing a large loss (sometimes referred to as "tail risk"). Risk for a book manager is the possibility that a bond will fail to produce its promised book yield (or spread) because defaults (or prepayments) over the holding period exceeded the rate anticipated at purchase, producing lower than expected income (or spread). As discussed later, not only must the long-horizon investor worry whether overall default rates are greater than expected, but also whether issuer defaults in the portfolio are correlated. While the realized overall default rate in the market may equal the expected rate, the portfolio's default rate may exceed that of the market if defaults in the portfolio are correlated.

A book accounting benchmark allows a manager to directly compare the portfolio's historical book income with that of a passive portfolio. Has the manager

---

reluctant to buy a bond for a short-term trade if there is a chance that he may face constraints on selling it subsequently.

10. For a discussion of this topic and how monthly spread volatility might affect a long-horizon manager's portfolio structuring, see Chapter 16.

11. For a discussion on how the excess return distribution becomes more asymmetrical as the investor's holding period increases see Chapter 17.

12. For securities that amortize depending on market movements, the comparable risk is that a premium amortizes faster or a discount amortizes slower than expected at purchase.

been able to add additional book income? In addition, is his portfolio likely to supply greater book income going forward as measured by the excess of the portfolio's book yield over that of the benchmark? Book accounting managers are constantly striving to add book yield to their portfolios. The benchmark's book yield and book income are indications of what could be achieved if the manager followed a passive strategy. He will surely try to do better by adjusting the asset allocation mix, overweighting (underweighting) sectors that appear cheap (rich), and by adding issues of a given peer group that trade at a wider spread given their credit outlook. Often, his book yield will exceed that of the benchmark. But at what risk to future book income? Specifically, he must manage the risk that too much is lost through defaults and prepayments to erase any initial book yield advantage to the portfolio.

A book manager enjoying a book yield advantage over the benchmark may be taking risks that may not manifest themselves—in book accounting terms—for some time. What are these risks and how can they be quantified? To discuss this issue, consider the following hypothetical credit portfolio of a book accounting manager. We assume that this manager received the following client investment inflows and there were no client outflows:[13]

| December 31, 2003: | $2,136,938,000 |
| December 31, 2004: | $1,069,948,000 |

The client has chosen to evaluate the manager against a book accounting benchmark based on the Credit Index. In other words, the client will evaluate our manager vs. a hypothetical one who passively invests in the Credit Index. Although the client has given the manager discretion to hold on to bonds that leave the index owing to downgrade, the manager's book benchmark follows index rules and removes downgraded bonds (sells at the market closing price and recognizes any book gain/loss) from the book benchmark. A comparison of his portfolio and book index at various dates since December 31, 2003, is presented in Figure 9-4, which shows that he put the client's initial investment into a portfolio of investment-grade credits that produced a higher book yield (4.48%) vs. the JAN04 Credit Book Index (i.e., Credit Index) book yield (4.32%). How did he accomplish this initial book yield advantage?

---

13. The client may give the manager discretion to invest outside the investment-grade index that is assumed in this example. In addition, the client may give the manager discretion as to when to invest the client's investment inflows (i.e., the manager may wait for higher book yields).

Figure 9-4. Comparison of Manager and Book Benchmark

	Manager	Book Benchmark	Lehman Credit Index
December 31, 2003			
Book yield (%)[a]	4.48	4.32	4.32
Book value ($)	2,110,723,000	2,105,059,186	
Cumulative book income ($)[b]	0	0	
OAD[c]	5.97	5.78	
Expected shortfall (1%)	14.2%	10.2%	
December 31, 2004			
Book yield (%)	4.51	4.42	4.58
Book value ($)	3,251,719,000	3,247,537,699	
Cumulative book income ($)	85,016,000	88,828,082	
March 31, 2005			
Book yield (%)	4.52	4.48	5.14
Book value ($)	3,283,428,000	3,288,578,870	
Cumulative book income ($)	121,637,000	123,857,381	
Expected shortfall (1%)	11.4%		

[a]Calculated using book value weights.

[b]Cumulative book income equals the sum of monthly book income to date. Book income includes any gain or loss arising from any bonds sold out of the index if they fail to satisfy index inclusion rules (e.g., due to downgrade). We assume the manager chooses not to sell any downgraded bonds.

[c]Calculated using market value weights.

To investigate, we load both the manager's portfolio and the book benchmark into a portfolio analytics system and use a global risk model to analyze the port-folio against its book benchmark.[14] Why use the risk model, which measures normal monthly return volatility, to evaluate the manager? As discussed earlier, the manager's risk is not the relatively symmetrical risk arising from short-term yield and spread volatility—as measured by the risk model—but the very asym-metrical credit risk arising from the probability of credit default. Although monthly volatility is not the best risk measure for a book manager, the risk model does help

14. A book accounting index should allow the manager to generate a list of CUSIPs and pars that comprise the book accounting benchmark, which can be quickly imported into a portfolio analytics system. For details on the Lehman global risk model, interpretations of its various reports, and portfolio applications, refer to Chapter 26.

Figure 9-5. Portfolio–Book Benchmark Comparison
December 31, 2003

Parameter	Manager's Portfolio	Book Benchmark	Difference
Positions	33	3482	
Issuers	27	673	
Market value ($)	2,136,938	2,149,935,298	
Yield-to-worst (%)	4.48	4.34	0.14
OAS (bp)	105	89	16
OAD	5.97	5.78	0.20
OA spread duration	5.81	5.64	0.17
Total volatility (bp/month)	154.0	144.5	
Systematic volatility (bp/month)	148.6	143.4	
Nonsystematic volatility (bp/month)	33.9	9.6	
Default volatility (bp/month)	23.9	15.3	

to identify the relative exposures in the portfolio vs. the book benchmark. Moreover, we observe that many book managers prefer to monitor market portfolio returns vs. the benchmark on a monthly basis for an early signal of potential problems. Although the portfolio's book returns may be relatively stable vs. the benchmark, the portfolio may begin to underperform on a market return basis. Persistent underperformance may foreshadow problems that will only appear after some time when reported on a book accounting basis.

Figure 9-5 presents a comparison between the portfolio and book benchmark. The manager initially invests in thirty-three issues from twenty-seven different issuers. The portfolio is moderately longer in duration (and spread duration) which, given the steepness of the term structure at the time, accounts for some of the manager's book yield advantage. The duration difference is probably of little concern for the client as long as any duration difference remains within tolerance limits (which we assume in this example). Figure 9-5 also shows the estimated monthly total return volatility of both the manager's portfolio and book benchmark—as well as the components of that volatility. As seen, the manager's portfolio is expected to have more monthly return volatility than the benchmark.

To get a clearer picture of the manager's credit decisions we first examine a simple market structure report (Figure 9-6). At a high level, we see that the manager chose to purchase a modest overweight to Baa/Ba bonds relative to the market, specifically bonds with longer duration and relatively higher book yields. For the higher qualities, the manager chose to hold shorter-duration bonds with relatively

Figure 9-6. Market Structure

	Manager			Book Benchmark		
	MV (%)	OAD	Yield (%)	MV (%)	OAD	Yield (%)
Total	100.0	6.0	4.5	100.0	5.8	4.3
Aaa	13.6	3.3	2.9	10.4	4.4	3.2
Aa	5.9	2.2	2.4	8.6	5.2	3.5
A	33.2	6.1	4.0	38.1	5.8	4.1
Baa	44.3	7.4	5.6	42.8	6.3	4.9
Ba	2.9	2.7	4.2			

lower yields. He is clearly making credit decisions to produce a higher portfolio book yield. What decisions did he make within each rating category? We can identify these decisions by examining the relative risk exposures between the portfolio and benchmark (Figure 9-7).

Figure 9-7 shows that the manager has some strong credit views. The portfolio has large net exposures (as measured by contribution to OA spread duration) to the Baa-rated cyclical and communication sectors as well as an overweight to the A-rated communication sector. These sectors were characterized at the time by high yields relative to other sectors of similar ratings. The manager has chosen to underweight higher-rated credits as well as sectors that have relatively lower yields (e.g., financials, foreign corporates, and energy). Moreover, he is overweight the corporate liquidity factor indicating that, as is common with many long-horizon investors, he is overweight bonds that trade at wider spreads relative to bonds belonging to the same peer group. Furthermore, he has an overweight to the corporate spread slope risk factor, which shows that he was moving out the curve to pick up additional yield.

Not only does the manager's portfolio contain significant systematic sector views, but the portfolio is also concentrated in relatively few names (Figure 9-8). While this is unrealistic for most long-horizon investors, it highlights the advantages of using a book accounting benchmark to evaluate the manager's performance. Figure 9-8 shows that the manager has significant Baa-rated issuer exposures: F, GM, T, and MEX.

Figure 9-9 completes the monthly volatility risk picture by calculating the overall monthly tracking error (43 bp/month) of the portfolio vs. the book accounting benchmark. This report incorporates the correlations among the various risk exposures. The report also decomposes tracking error into systematic (and its various

Figure 9-7. Portfolio–Book Index Tracking Error

Excerpts, December 31, 2003

	Book Portfolio Exposure (OASD)	Benchmark Exposure (OASD)	Net Exposure (OASD)	Factor Volatility (bp)	Tracking Error Impact[a] (bp)	Percentage of Tracking Error Variance
Credit Investment-Grade Spread						
Banking A	1.03	0.74	0.29	9.51	−2.76	2.53
Basic industry A	0.00	0.18	−0.18	7.64	1.35	−0.85
Basic industry Baa	0.10	0.27	−0.17	10.12	1.76	−1.46
Cyclical Baa	1.04	0.55	0.49	22.29	−10.97	12.67
Communication A	0.73	0.31	0.42	9.64	−4.02	3.87
Communication Baa	0.89	0.48	0.41	16.44	−6.76	7.67
Energy Baa	0.00	0.33	−0.33	10.42	3.43	−2.67
Financial Aaa–Aa	0.29	0.15	0.14	7.80	−1.11	0.89
Financial A	0.18	0.26	−0.07	10.60	0.76	−0.68
Financial Baa	0.00	0.15	−0.15	13.34	1.96	−1.21
Noncyclical A	0.00	0.22	−0.22	7.10	1.59	−0.87
Noncyclical Baa	0.13	0.20	−0.07	9.28	0.65	−0.43

Noncorporate Aaa–Aa	0.22	0.45	-0.23	5.66	1.31	-0.39
Noncorporate A	0.00	0.13	-0.13	8.22	1.06	-0.82
Utility A	0.05	0.12	-0.08	8.38	0.65	-0.49
Utility Baa	0.41	0.34	0.07	15.20	-1.10	1.05
Corporate spread slope	47.27	42.13	5.14	0.22	-1.14	-0.29
Corporate liquidity	1.38	0.79	0.59	7.66	-4.49	5.20
Foreign corporates A	0.00	0.37	-0.37	4.37	1.63	0.92
Foreign corporates Baa	0.00	0.36	-0.36	6.02	2.14	0.80
Credit High Yield Spread						
High yield utility	0.08	0.00	0.08	78.04	-6.20	6.56
High yield spread slope	-0.36	0.00	-0.36	0.54	0.19	0.15
High yield liquidity	-0.07	0.00	-0.07	8.04	0.53	-0.48
Emerging Market Spread						
Emerging market investment grade	0.61	0.17	0.43	39.49	-17.14	22.11
Emerging market nondistressed slope	4.44	1.30	3.14	1.50	-4.70	-2.94
Emerging market nondistressed liquidity	0.19	0.04	0.15	14.83	-2.21	2.48

[a]Tracking error impact of an isolated 1 standard deviation up change (bp).

Figure 9-8. Credit Tickers Report
Excerpts

Ticker	Name	Sector	Rating	Number of Issues	Weight (%)
F	Ford Capital	Transportation	Baa3 Baa2	2	9.1
GM	GMAC	Automotive	Baa2	2	9.0
GE	General Electric	Multiple	Aaa A3	2	6.8
VZ	Chesapeake + Potomac	Wirelines	A1 A3 A2 Baa1	2	6.3
C	Associates Corporation	Noncaptive consumer	Aa3 A1 A2 A3	2	5.8
MEX	UMS	Sovereigns	Baa3	1	4.7
NI	Columbia Energy	Electric	Baa2 Baa3	2	4.0
KFW	KFW	Foreign agencies	Aaa	1	3.8
T	AT&T Corporation	Wirelines	Baa2	1	3.3
WFC	Norwest Corporation	Noncaptive consumer	Aa3 A1 A2	1	3.2
PEMEX	PEMEX	Sovereigns	Baa3 Baa1 Aaa	1	3.2
IBRD	IBRD	Supranationals	Aaa	1	3.0

Figure 9-9. Portfolio–Book Index Tracking Error
December 31, 2003

Risk Factor	Isolated Tracking Error Volatility (bp)	Cumulative Tracking Error Volatility (bp)	Percentage of Tracking Error Variance
Yield curve	4.6	4.6	1.8
Swap spreads	3.0	5.3	0.6
Volatility	0.5	5.4	−0.1
Investment-grade spreads	16.5	17.6	21.4
High yield spreads	6.0	20.8	6.2
Emerging markets spread	16.6	31.1	21.7
Systematic risk	31.1	31.1	51.7
Idiosyncratic risk	27.1	41.2	39.4
Credit default risk	13.0	43.2	9.0
Tracking error volatility		43.2	100.0
Portfolio volatility (bp/month)			154.0
Benchmark volatility (bp/month)			144.5

subcomponents), idiosyncratic, and credit default components. As shown, the portfolio has relatively little duration risk as the yield curve risk factors account for only 1.8% of the total tracking error variance. Instead, the portfolio displays strong credit views at both the sector (systematic) and issuer (idiosyncratic) levels. We see that there are some very active exposures within the investment-grade sector (21% of the total tracking error variance), high yield sector (6% of total variance, arising from a holding of a split-rated utility bond), and emerging markets (22% of total variance, arising from investment-grade holdings in UMS and PEMEX). Finally, Figure 9-9 shows that the portfolio, given the relatively few issuers, has relatively high idiosyncratic risk (39% of total) contributing to tracking error volatility, as well as default risk (9% of total).[15]

As discussed earlier, risk for book investors is not monthly tracking volatility vs. a benchmark. Rather, the risk is that portfolio assets will fail to produce their

15. The tracking error volatility owing to default risk arises from the portfolio's particular exposure (net of the benchmark) to Baa-rated bonds, as well as its holding of the split-rated utility bond. Note that default tracking error volatility measures the expected monthly tracking error volatility that may arise owing to the probability of defaults. It is not a measure of the extreme losses that may occur in the portfolio relative to the benchmark in the event of defaults.

promised income owing to default or prepayment. In other words, will a portfolio of corporate bonds deliver their promised yield adjusted by the expected
default and recovery rates at time of purchase? Or will actual (correlated) defaults
over the holding period exceed the anticipated rate, producing a lower realized
yield?

Long-horizon investors typically try to maximize expected book yield (or
spread) while minimizing the probability of large portfolio losses, or tail risk. Tail
risk can be measured in several ways. One popular measure is "value-at-risk," or
VaR, which is a level of losses from defaults expected to occur less often than a
specified percentage of time. For example, a 1% VaR of 500 bp means that there is
a 1% probability that losses in a portfolio will exceed 500 bp. Another measure of
tail risk is "expected shortfall," which is the average of all losses in the tail beyond
the specified VaR level.[16]

To measure a portfolio's probability of loss owing to defaults, including the
possibility of correlated defaults, we use Lehman's portfolio tool, COMPASS,
which works as follows.[17] The investor supplies a list of credit bonds in the portfolio (e.g., CUSIPs and par weights) and specifies an investment horizon (e.g., 5
years). Each issue in the portfolio is mapped to its issuer, and each issuer, in turn,
is assigned to a market sector (e.g., industrial or consumer cyclical) and to a country (e.g., Japan or United States). Each issuer is also assigned a default rate depending on its credit rating, which can be an historical cumulative default rate
for the investment horizon, given the rating, as periodically published by the rating agencies or it could be independently specified by the investor. If the issuers
were assumed to default independently of each other, COMPASS would have
enough information to simulate (via Monte Carlo methods) the default loss distribution for the portfolio. However, as discussed earlier, not only does the investor run the risk that default rates may be higher than anticipated, but issuers
may default in a correlated fashion. If so, the possibility of large losses increases
compared to the case where the default rate is the same, but defaults are uncorrelated. A key feature of COMPASS is the explicit incorporation of the possibility of
correlated defaults in the simulation of portfolio losses.

16. To encourage diversification in portfolios, investors typically try to minimize expected
shortfall, rather than VaR, for a given level of yield (or spread).

17. Investors have used COMPASS to analyze portfolios containing not just credit but also
ABS and CMBS assets. COMPASS also includes an optimizer. Consequently, the investor can
specify a yield (or spread) target, a set of eligible bonds, various portfolio constraints (e.g., an issuer cap of 1.5%), and COMPASS then optimizes the portfolio by rebalancing bond positions,
subject to the constraints, to minimize the portfolio's expected shortfall while satisfying the yield
target.

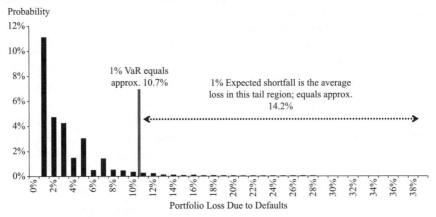

Figure 9-10. Example of Portfolio Loss Distribution from Defaults
COMPASS Simulation

COMPASS uses estimated historical equity market return correlations for the various sector-country pairs as estimators for default correlations between issuers from various sectors and countries.[18] Using default rates,[19] estimated default correlations, and assumed recovery rates, COMPASS generates an expected loss distribution for the portfolio.

Figure 9-10 shows the simulated distribution of losses owing to defaults for the manager's portfolio over a 5-year horizon. The bulk of the portfolio's loss distribution lies between 1 and 7%, indicating that this is a moderate-quality investment-grade portfolio. Some 11% of the time the portfolio will experience a loss owing to defaults over the horizon totaling 1% or less. The 1% VaR is approximately 10.7%, which indicates that 1% of the time the portfolio is expected to experience losses owing to defaults that exceed 10.7% of the portfolio's book value. The expected

18. Empirical evidence suggests that asset market returns (as well as other financial market returns) demonstrate "fat joint tails." In other words, the possibility of joint extreme realizations is empirically more likely than the probability implied by a joint normal distribution. The implication of fat joint tails is that if defaults were assumed to be joint normally distributed then the tail risk for the portfolio loss distribution would be understated. COMPASS includes a feature that allows the investor to specify a Student-t distribution (with user-specified degrees of freedom) when simulating the portfolio loss distribution to better fit the observed empirical pattern of fat joint tails. We assume a t-distribution with twelve degrees of freedom.

19. The assumed default rates are based on Moody's 5-year cumulative corporate default rates over the 1983–2003 period. The assumed recovery rate is fixed at 35%. It is also possible to use COMPASS with downgrade probabilities in lieu of default probabilities.

shortfall is the average of the losses that occur beyond this 1% VaR value of 10.7%. For this portfolio, the expected shortfall is approximately 14.2%.[20]

As a comparison, we ran the manager's book benchmark and measured its expected shortfall (1% tail) at 10.2%—substantially less than the manager's portfolio. Although the manager has a book yield advantage, there is also added risk, which is measured by the portfolio's expected shortfall relative to that of the benchmark. One possible risk-adjusted measure is to calculate how much book yield is generated per unit of tail risk. For the manager's portfolio we obtain 0.315 (= 4.48%/14.2%), which compares unfavorably with the book benchmark value of 0.424 (= 4.32%/10.2%). On a risk-adjusted basis the manager is not adding value.

The risk model reports indicated that the portfolio was probably earning the higher book yield as a fair return for the added monthly total return volatility that the manager shouldered relative to the benchmark. To the extent that the assets' added yield reflects additional return demanded by managers as compensation for the systematic spread volatility, and not for the default risk, the book manager earns this book yield advantage over time (via higher book income each period). However, as we saw from COMPASS, the manager was exposed to much greater risk of default than the benchmark, so his book yield advantage had to be scaled down to reflect this risk.

How did the manager perform? Over the next 1.5 years, none of the manager's assets defaulted. However, there was a downgrade below investment grade (AT&T) in July 2004. The downgrade prompted the manager to sell the bond, which, in turn, required recognizing a book loss equal to the difference between the bond's book value and its market value at the end of July 2004. The book loss significantly reduced book income for the month. In addition, the manager redeployed the proceeds into another asset that had a lower book yield. The book benchmark suffered the downgrade as well (in addition to others), but the benchmark had lower exposure to such bonds. As a result, the benchmark suffered proportionally smaller book losses. The effect of the downgrade caused the portfolio's cumulative book income by year end 2004 to be less than that of the book benchmark despite having the higher book yield at the outset. Although not shown, the manager's book yield decreased about 2 bp.

At year end 2004 the manager received another client investment inflow ($1,069,948,000). Although the details are not presented here he deployed the cash conservatively and added seventy-two new positions that had a book yield of 4.59%, which was comparable to the credit market yield available (4.58%). After adding the new client investment to the portfolio and updating the book bench-

---

20. This is the average loss conditional on the portfolio experiencing a loss in the 1% tail region.

mark, by March 31, 2005, the manager's book yield advantage had diminished to 4 bp. However, he also reduced the tail risk of the portfolio to 11.4%—producing a greatly improved yield per unit of tail risk of 0.396 (= 4.52%/11.4%).

Using Book Accounting Benchmarks: Performance Comparison of Book and Total Return Managers

Another advantage of having book benchmarks is the ability to conduct quantitative empirical studies on various portfolio strategies. For example, suppose a book accounting client wishes to consider whether to have its assets managed by a traditional book accounting manager or a traditional total return manager. We make the following assumptions (which, of course, can be changed as desired):

1. The traditional book accounting manager follows a strategy of a relatively heavy concentration in spread product with relatively little trading activity. Alpha (vs. a standard market benchmark) is generated over time from the spread product overweight and careful credit/prepayment selection that minimizes losses from credit events and prepayment shocks.

2. The traditional total return manager follows a strategy of active asset allocation, security selection, and yield curve timing. Correspondingly, the manager may trade actively. Alpha is generated from these active portfolio decisions.

How does the performance of these two managers compare on both a book accounting and marked-to-market accounting basis? To answer this question meaningfully, it is important that we model both managers in a way that permits a fair comparison of their performance. In other words, the durations of both portfolios should be comparable over time. Moreover, the book manager's portfolio should have a constant relative overweight (in percentage terms) to spread product over time. For example, if spread product currently makes up 60% of the Aggregate and the book manager's portfolio holds 72%, this 20% overweight should be maintained over time. Thus, if 10 years ago, the Aggregate contained 40% spread product, we assume that the book manager held 48% of the portfolio in spread assets. We assume that:

1. Both managers initialized their portfolios on December 31, 1994, with an investment of $100 million. As a point of reference, the option-adjusted spread (OAS) for the Credit Index was 78 bp on December 31, 1994, vs. 85 bp as of October 31, 2005. The 10-year U.S. Treasury yield

was 7.82 and 4.55% on December 31, 1994, and October 31, 2005, respectively.

2. The book manager buys a portfolio that has an overweight to spread product but is initially duration-matched to the Aggregate. Along with the initial spread product overweight, the book manager is somewhat of a passive investor, just reinvesting cash generated by the portfolio so as to maintain duration neutrality (if possible) and a constant spread product overweight.

3. The total return manager buys the Aggregate (i.e., no spread product overweight). However, he makes active decisions each month that produce outperformance vs. the Aggregate. We assume that he holds the Aggregate with an overlay that produces an additional realized book gain/loss each month as a result of a variable performance alpha. To make the contrast between a book and total return manager more realistic, we assume that the total return manager turns over the portfolio x% per year. For this report we assume an annual turnover rate of 50%, or 4.2% per month (= 50% ÷ 12). Any turnover cost is covered by the manager's alpha.

4. No external investment inflows/outflows occur after the initial date. Neither manager is asked to sell assets to generate an outflow or to realize a gain or loss. Each manager's portfolio is rebalanced (as discussed later) at the end of every month.

5. All cash flows generated by either portfolio are reinvested at contemporaneous yields.

6. Assets that are downgraded below investment grade are sold (at market) out of both portfolios on the earliest possible rebalancing date (i.e., at the end of the month in which they are downgraded). Although there are some book and total return managers who hold downgraded bonds, we assume that both managers follow index conventions.

TRADITIONAL BOOK ACCOUNTING MANAGER

Every month, the book manager calculates target allocations to these five asset classes: Treasuries, ABS & CMBS, Credit, MBS, and agencies. The target allocations are designed to maintain the manager's relative overweight to spread product over time. Within the allocation to spread product, the allocation across the four spread asset sectors is constant over time.

We assume that the book manager never sells assets for the purpose of meeting target allocations, so the target allocations may not always be exactly met. How-

Figure 9-11. Book Manager's Allocation to Spread Product
December 31, 1994

Asset Class	OAD	YTW (%)[a]	OAS (bp)	Aggregate (%)	Book Manager (%)
ABS[b]	2.4	8.2	50.2	1.2	7.1
Credit	5.6	8.7	77.8	16.0	28.2
MBS	4.4	8.7	62.9	28.9	21.2
Agency	4.8	8.1	28.5	6.8	7.1
Spread sector (index)	4.8	8.6	62.7	53.0	
Spread sector ("book" manager)	4.7	8.6	64.3		63.5
Index		33.2			
Book manager portfolio		40.8			

[a] Yield-to-worst values presented in this report are book value-weighted, whereas OAD and OAS values are market value-weighted.
[b] There were no CMBS in the Aggregate as of this date.

ever, as any cash flow becomes available, he always moves the portfolio's allocation as close as possible to the target allocation.

We assume there is always a target overweight of 19.7% to the four spread product classes relative to the Aggregate. For example, as of December 31, 1994, spread sectors comprised 53.0% of the Aggregate. So the book manager's total target allocation to spread product is 53.0% + (19.7% × 53.0%) = 63.5%. The target overweight is set to 19.7% so that the allocation to Treasuries will be exactly 10% as of January 31, 2005 (a recent month picked at random), based on the assumption that a book manager would probably hold about 10% Treasuries in a portfolio as of that month. Since the percentage of spread product in the Aggregate has changed so much over time, this method ensures that the book manager is making the same relative magnitude spread overweight decision throughout the period of the study. The target allocation to each of the four spread product classes is always a fixed fraction of the total allocation to spread product as follows: ABS + CMBS: 1/9, Credit: 4/9, MBS: 1/3, and Agency: 1/9.

Figure 9-11 shows the book manager's allocation to spread product as of December 31, 1994. Note that his portfolio, despite the overweight to spread product in general, has an underweight to MBS (21.2 vs. 28.9%) and an overweight to credit (28.2% vs. 16.0%) relative to the Aggregate, which seems fairly typical of book managers. There is also a large overweight to ABS (the Aggregate did not yet contain CMBS) and a smaller overweight to agency product.

As discussed earlier, the book manager has a 19.7% overweight to spread product (63.51%/53.06% = 1.197). It is interesting to note that although he has an

Figure 9-12. Book Manager's Allocation to Spread Product
December 31, 2004

Asset Class	OAD	YTW (%)	OAS (bp)	Aggregate (%)	Book Manager (%)
ABS + CMBS	4.0	4.2	64.0	4.4	10.0
Credit	5.7	4.6	75.0	24.8	40.1
MBS	2.9	4.9	24.1	35.1	30.1
Agency	3.8	3.8	30.7	11.0	10.0
Spread sector (index)	4.0	4.6	42.2	75.3	
Spread sector ("book" manager)	4.4	4.6	51.9		90.2
Index			33.3		
Book manager portfolio			46.8		

overweight to spread assets, the yield-to-worst on the spread portfolio is slightly less than the yield for the spread sector of the index. This is due to the relative weighting scheme within spread product (i.e., overweight credit and underweight MBS). Consequently, it is possible that the overall yield on his portfolio may be close to or less than that for the index (which is indeed the case), but this is a consequence of the yield calculation for MBS, which does not take into account the optionality of the MBS security. As most managers use OAS as opposed to yield to measure the potential spread contribution of MBS, we report the spread sector OAS for both the index and the book manager. As shown earlier, the book manager definitely has a spread overweight vs. the index (i.e., 41 bp vs. 33 bp).

To illustrate that we are carefully maintaining a constant spread overweight strategy for the book manager, Figure 9-12 shows the same information as Figure 9-11 but as of December 31, 2004. Again, note the overweight to credit (40.1% vs. 24.8%), the underweight to MBS (30.1% vs. 35.1%) and the higher OAS of the book manager's portfolio as compared to the Aggregate's (47 bp vs. 33 bp).

How does the book manager adjust the portfolio's allocation each month? At month-end, the portfolio's market value equals the market value of all the bonds in the portfolio plus the amount of cash earned by the portfolio in the past month. An asset class's target market value equals the portfolio market value multiplied by the class's target allocation. If the class's target market value exceeds its current market value, the manager uses some of the cash earned by the portfolio in the past month to purchase, on a market-weighted basis, all bonds in the Aggregate as of that date that belong to the asset class.

For example, suppose that on January 31, 2000, the total market value of the portfolio's existing assets is $99.5 million and the portfolio generated $500,000 in cash flows during January 2000, so the portfolio market value is $100 million.

Suppose also that the market value of agencies currently in the portfolio is $8.2 million. If the target allocation to agencies on this date is 9%, the target market value for agencies is $9 million and the manager will use some of the $500,000 to buy the agencies currently in the Aggregate on a market-value-weighted basis (although in this example he will clearly not be able to reach the target market value of $9 million). If, however, the target allocation to agencies is 8%, the target market value is less than the market value of the existing agencies and he neither buys nor sells agencies.

There may or may not be enough cash available to bring all the asset classes to their target market values. If there is insufficient available cash, it is allocated to the assets requiring an increase in market value on a pro rata basis, based on the size of the desired increases. In the previous example, if the target allocation for agencies is 9%, the agencies are $800,000 shy of their target market value before rebalancing. If the only other asset requiring an increase is MBS and it is $200,000 short of its target market value, then of the $500,000 in available cash, $400,000 will go toward agencies and $100,000 toward MBS.

If new Treasuries are bought for the portfolio, the set of Treasuries in the Aggregate as of that date is divided evenly into a long set and a short set, and a mix of the long and short sets is purchased with the goal of making the overall portfolio duration as close as possible to the duration of the Aggregate as of that date. (This is important because it is assumed that the total return manager will match the Aggregate's duration as well. To permit an accurate market value performance comparison of the book and total return managers, we must constantly adjust the book manager's duration to track the Aggregate closely.) The long and short sets are constructed by examining the durations of every Treasury in the Aggregate and using the median of those durations as the dividing line between the two sets. We assume that the book manager will not sell assets for the purpose of meeting the duration target even if no Treasuries are being purchased or it is impossible to meet the duration target with a combination of the long and short Treasuries.

TRADITIONAL TOTAL RETURN MANAGER

The total return manager rebalances the portfolio every month so that its holdings exactly match those of the Aggregate. (His alpha generation will be factored in later.) Unlike the book manager, the total return manager will sell assets if necessary to achieve the portfolio's allocation goals. The amount that must be sold is determined so that the proceeds of the sale, combined with cash generated by the portfolio in the previous month (including cash generated by redemptions and sales of existing issues), will be enough to buy a position in the new issues in the Aggregate that will make the portfolio match the Aggregate exactly (in terms of percentage of market value allocated to each security).

When selling existing assets, the total return manager sells a portion of each prior purchase lot on a pro rata basis. Suppose, for example, that as of February 28, 1995, his investment in the 12/31/1994 Aggregate is now worth $98.5 million, his investment in the 1/31/1995 *new issues* is now worth $0.5 million, and the investment in the 1/31/1995 *full index* is now worth $1 million, so the portfolio's holdings are worth $100 million. Suppose also that he needs to sell $100,000 worth of assets in order to have enough money to put into new issues. We assume that he sells $98,500 worth of the 12/31/1994 Aggregate (which constitutes 98.5% of the portfolio's existing holdings), $500 worth of the 1/31/1995 new issues (which constitutes 0.5% of existing holdings), and $1,000 worth of the 1/31/1995 full index (which constitutes 1% of existing holdings).

If turnover is not assumed (see later), and enough cash was generated in the previous month to acquire a sufficiently large position in the index's new issues without selling any existing holdings, no existing holdings are sold. The manager takes the proceeds of the sale (if any) and the cash generated in the previous month and buys a position in the new issues in the Aggregate that makes the portfolio match the Aggregate exactly. If there is any cash left over, he invests it in the full underlying index at current market yields.

To make for a more realistic comparison of book and total return managers, we assume that the total return manager produces turnover of $x\%$ per year (initially set at 50%, equivalent to 4.2% per month). This turnover amount is in addition to any turnover required to rebalance the portfolio to match the underlying index. Turnover involves selling a pro rata portion of all holdings and reinvesting the proceeds in the current underlying index at current market yields, so that the composition of the portfolio is unchanged. Turnover affects the book yield and book income of the portfolio relative to the book manager. Results are presented with and without this turnover feature.

Once the total return manager's analytics have been calculated based on this strict index-tracking method, we incorporate his volatile alpha. We model the alpha as follows. Each month a random alpha value (say, 4 bp/month) is generated based on the assumed mean and standard deviation of the normally distributed alpha variable. That alpha is then multiplied by the prior month-end's portfolio book value. This produces a dollar amount that we treat as a realized book gain/loss generated by the total return manager in the current month. We treat this gain as an exogenous realized book gain/loss that is then reinvested into the portfolio at current market yields. Consequently, the total return manager's ending book value, total book income, and ending book yield are affected by the realized alpha value. A total return manager with a normally distributed alpha (with an expected value of A and a standard deviation of B) who has an $x\%$ annual turnover rate is labeled the "$N(A, B) - x\%$" manager. For our exercise, we assume that the manager has an expected alpha of 30 bp/year, a standard deviation of 60 bp/year (for a very respectable information ratio of 0.5), and a 50% turnover rate (i.e., a $N(30, 60)$ – 50% manager).

RESULTS

We now examine the historical relative performance of the two managers over the period January 1995 through October 2005 in both book and mark-to-market terms. While these results depend on the chosen portfolio parameter values and the time period, they highlight the various trade-offs faced by book accounting clients who have a choice among various investment strategies.

Figure 9-13 shows that in terms of ending market value, the $N(30, 60)$ – 50% total return manager clearly outperformed the book manager (i.e., $219,894,502 vs. $215,899,443).[21] The former's relative annual outperformance equaled approximately 16.8 bp [= 12 × (61.4 bp/month – 60.0 bp/month)]. While this outperformance is substantially greater than zero, it is considerably less than the manager's realized average annual alpha of 32.3 bp.[22] In other words, the constant spread overweight of the book manager offset approximately one-half of the active manager's alpha.

To evaluate the difference between a strategy of constantly tracking the underlying index vs. constantly overweighting spread product—without the influence of alpha and turnover—Figure 9-13 also reports the market value performance of other total return managers with different parameter settings, including a constant zero alpha total return manager with no turnover, that is, a $N(0, 0)$ – 0% manager. In terms of ending market value, the $N(0, 0)$ – 0% manager underperformed the book manager, who maintained a constant spread sector overweight (i.e., $212,524,343 vs. $215,899,443), indicating that a constant spread overweight strategy produced some incremental market return over a passive index strategy.

In terms of monthly total return volatility, the $N(30, 60)$ – 50% manager was slightly more volatile than the book manager (i.e., 110.2 bp vs. 108.0 bp). However, his higher monthly market return volatility was not due to his volatile alpha

---

21. This result is also influenced by any duration mismatch between the two strategies. Recall that the spread overweight book manager tries as much as possible to always match the index duration without having to sell bonds. However, the manager does not always match the index duration exactly. The portfolio OAD is typically within ±0.2 of the index OAD. The maximum OAD deviation in a single month is 0.40.

22. The total return manager's realized alpha in our simulation was 32.3 bp, with a standard deviation of 59.7 bp.

Figure 9-13. Relative Manager Performance
January 1995–October 2005

Performance Measure	Book Manager	N(30, 60) – 50%	N(0, 0) – 50%	N(30, 60) – 0%	N(0, 0) – 0%
Beginning Portfolio (12/31/94)					
Book value ($)	98,520,714	98,520,714	98,520,714	98,520,714	98,520,714
Market value ($)	100,000,000	100,000,000	100,000,000	100,000,000	100,000,000
Book yield (%)	8.27	8.21	8.21	8.21	8.21
Ending Portfolio (10/31/05)					
Book value ($)	206,383,405	221,236,713	213,838,821	216,192,207	209,050,657
Market value ($)	215,899,443	219,894,502	212,529,056	219,763,745	212,524,343
Book yield (%)	5.49	4.69	4.69	5.05	5.05
Monthly Total Return					
Average (bp)	60.0	61.4	58.8	61.4	58.8
Standard deviation (bp)	108.0	110.2	110.2	110.2	110.2
Mean/standard deviation	0.55	0.56	0.53	0.56	0.53

Monthly Book Return					
Average (bp)	57.9	62.4	59.7	60.6	57.9
Standard deviation (bp)	8.0	24.2	15.7	20.8	9.1
Mean/standard deviation	7.26	2.58	3.79	2.91	6.3
Monthly Total Book Income					
Average ($)	842,243	942,363	885,156	903,400	848,173
Standard deviation ($)	93,105	311,286	171,021	279,890	105,854
Cumulative ($)	109,491,635	122,507,157	115,070,270	117,441,967	110,262,446
Monthly Ordinary Book Income					
Average ($)	853,909	798,514	772,613	841,980	815,255
Standard deviation ($)	89,738	82,022	71,122	86,948	74,590
Cumulative ($)	111,008,107	103,806,823	100,439,651	109,457,350	105,983,101
Monthly Realized Book Gain/Loss from Turnover					
Average ($)	−11,665	143,849	112,543	61,420	32,918
Standard deviation ($)	56,996	310,008	166,417	276,050	76,406
Cumulative ($)	−1,516,472	18,700,333	14,630,618	7,984,617	4,279,345

because the $N(0, 0)$ – 50% manager (i.e., a manager with the same turnover but with a constant zero alpha—not a desirable manager!) had a similar standard deviation of market return (i.e., 110.2 bp). This is not surprising as alpha has a much lower monthly standard deviation than monthly market returns and is modeled as independent of the market return. The book manager's spread overweight produced a slightly lower standard deviation of monthly market returns compared to the $N(30, 60)$ – 50% manager as spreads tend to move inversely to changes in interest rates. Overall, on a simple monthly total return risk-adjusted basis (mean divided by standard deviation), the book manager and the $N(30, 60)$ – 50% manager performed similarly (0.55 vs. 0.56).

What was the relative performance of the two managers in book accounting terms: book income and book value? We separate total book income into two components because some investors may attach more importance to one source of book income over the other. The first component is labeled "ordinary" book income and is calculated from the portfolio's book yield and book value at the beginning of the month. The second component is labeled realized book gains/ losses, which arise from "natural" portfolio turnover (e.g., to match the index or the spread overweight target over time), alpha (modeled as a monthly realized book gain/loss), and turnover associated with generating alpha. Figure 9-13 shows that the $N(30, 60)$ – 50% manager produced $13.0 million more total book income over the period ($122,507,157) compared to the book manager ($109,491,635). This is also evident by looking at the ending book values: $221,236,713 for the $N(30, 60)$ – 50% manager vs. $206,383,405 for the book manager. Note also the sharp difference in the volatility of monthly book returns (i.e., total book income divided by beginning-of-the-month book value). The $N(30, 60)$ – 50% manager had a monthly book return volatility of 24 bp compared to only 8 bp for the book manager.

Much of the relative total book value gain (and book return volatility) for the $N(30,60)$ – 50% manager was due to $20.2 million more realized book gains (i.e., $18,700,333 vs. –$1,516,472 for the book manager) arising from the manager's positive alpha and from the constant selling of appreciating bonds in a general environment of declining interest rates. For example, if yields fall and the total return manager sells a bond whose market value exceeds its book value, the manager recognizes a book gain that increases book value. However, the proceeds are now reinvested at lower book yields so his book income will be lower and book value will increase more slowly, going forward. A reverse pattern would occur in a rising-interest-rate environment. Note that the ending book yield for the $N(30, 60)$ – 50% manager is 4.69%, which is 80 bp lower than the book manager's ending book yield of 5.49%. Realized book gains/losses also occur owing to unexpected redemptions or downgrades when the manager must sell bonds at market prices that differ from book prices. The book manager experienced net negative realized book losses primarily from selling bonds downgraded below investment grade without a book gain offset of constantly turning over the portfolio in the declining-interest-rate environment that was experienced by the total return manager.

Over the period, the total return manager produced an average monthly book gain/loss of $143,849 with a standard deviation of $310,008, compared to the book manager, who has average gain/loss of –$11,665 with a standard deviation of only $56,996. While the total return manager produces considerably more book gains than the book manager (and they could have been book losses if interest rates had risen), these gains (or losses) can be very volatile from month to month, which produces much greater total book income volatility for the former.

Offsetting the $20.2 million advantage in realized gains, the $N(30, 60)$ – 50% manager had $7.2 million less ordinary book income than the book manager. Over the period, the $N(30, 60)$ – 50% manager produced cumulative ordinary book income of $103,806,823 (averaging $798,514 per month with a standard deviation of $82,022). In contrast, the book manager produced cumulative ordinary book income of $111,008,107 (averaging $853,909 per month with a standard deviation of $89,738). The total return manager's cumulative ordinary book income underperformance of approximately $7.2 million is due in large part to the effect of turnover in an interest-rate environment that is generally declining. The total return manager's book yield fell 352 bp over the period compared to a decline of 278 bp for the book manager. To measure the effect of turnover on cumulative book income we examine the cumulative ordinary book income for the $N(30, 60)$ – 0% manager. This zero-turnover manager would have produced cumulative ordinary book income of $109,457,350 (averaging $841,980 per month with a standard deviation of $86,948), indicating that turnover by itself caused cumulative ordinary book income to be approximately $5.6 million (out of the $7.2 million total) lower for the $N(30, 60)$ – 50% manager.

The remaining $1.6 million difference in cumulative ordinary book income underperformance by the $N(30, 60)$ – 50% manager is explained by two other factors. First, the total return manager earned additional book income from income earned on earlier realized alpha. We can get an approximate measure of this effect by comparing the cumulative ordinary book income for the $N(30, 60)$ – 0% and $N(0, 0)$ – 0% managers. The positive alpha manager earned approximately $3.5 million more in ordinary book income as income on earlier realized alpha. Consequently, the book manager should have outperformed by a cumulative sum of approximately $5.0 million (i.e., $1.6 million + $3.5 million). This leaves a net $5.0 million of book income underperformance to be explained.

The second reason for the relative outperformance of the book vs. total return cumulative ordinary book income arose from the difference in the underlying strategies: index-matching vs. the book manager's spread overweight. We can approximately measure this effect by comparing the cumulative ordinary book income for the $N(0, 0)$ – 0% and book managers. As shown in Figure 9-13 the latter earned approximately $5.0 million more in ordinary book income. In summary, the book manager earned a total of $7.2 million more ordinary book income, of which $5.6 was due to having less turnover than the active manager in a declining-interest-rate environment; $5.0 million was due to having a spread overweight strategy; and –$3.5 million was due to the income on the realized positive alpha of the total return manager.

To better evaluate the relative volatility of monthly book income from the two strategies, we first de-trend them because book income tends to increase as income compounds over time. To de-trend each manager's monthly book income we subtract the corresponding book income from a passive investment in the U.S. Agency Index.[23] The Agency Index might be considered a proxy for the funding cost of some typical book accounting investors (e.g., banks and insurance companies). Subtracting monthly total agency book income produces a *net* monthly book income (i.e., a "net margin") time series for both the total return and book managers (Figure 9-14).

As Figure 9-14 shows, a book accounting investor using either a total return manager or a spread overweight book manager experienced some monthly net book income volatility. However, there was a significant difference between the two managers. While the $N(30, 60)$ – 50% manager produced an average net book income of almost $147,000, it had a standard deviation of $304,000. In addition, in 32 of the 130 total months of the study period, the net book income was negative with an average during these months of –$253,141. In contrast to the total return manager, the spread overweight manager produced an average net book income of $46,000 with a standard deviation of $67,000. While the book manager had 24 months of negative net book income, the average value during those months was much lower at –$31,547.

Investors are often sensitive to book income volatility and the possibility of reporting negative book income even for short periods of time. For total return managers, net book income volatility is driven by both turnover and alpha volatility and net income shortfall is affected by turnover, alpha volatility, and the expected level of alpha. When considering active management, the book accounting client has a trade-off between possibly improved cumulative net book income (from alpha), book income volatility, and the possibility of negative net income

---

23. Bullet issues only. Book income for this index is very stable (there are no downgrades or unexpected changes in amortization schedules) except for a trend factor reflecting reinvestment of income.

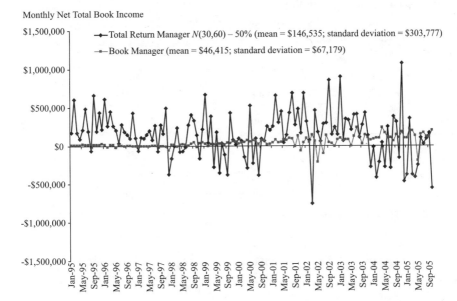

Monthly Net Total Book Income

Figure 9-14. Monthly Net Total Book Income
Total Return Manager vs. Book Manager, January 1995–October 2005

(i.e., shortfall). As shown in Figure 9-15, given a level of turnover, a higher expected alpha—holding alpha volatility constant—increases average net book income and reduces shortfall risk. Conversely, a higher alpha volatility—holding expected alpha and turnover constant—increases both the volatility and shortfall risk of book income. For example, assuming a turnover level of 50%, the $N(30, 0)$ – 50% manager has approximately the same shortfall risk as the $N(60, 30)$ – 50% manager—the higher expected alpha offsets the higher volatility to keep shortfall risk unchanged.

Figure 9-15 also shows the effect of turnover for total return managers. For a given level of expected alpha and alpha volatility, increasing turnover from 50 to 100% increases the volatility of book income and shortfall risk. So, both alpha volatility and turnover increase book income volatility and shortfall risk.[24] Note the contrast between a book accounting and marked-to-market investor. Return volatility for the latter is unaffected by the level of turnover in the portfolio (ignoring transactions costs). In contrast, return (i.e., book return) volatility for the

24. Over the study period, 50% turnover produced a book income time series that had a volatility comparable to the volatility of the book income time series produced by an alpha with a standard deviation of 30 bp. The book income volatility from 100% turnover was comparable to the volatility produced by an alpha with a standard deviation of 60 bp.

Figure 9-15. Monthly Net Total Book Income Statistics for Total Return Manager
Various Alpha Parameters and Turnover Levels, January 1995–October 2005
[(1) Average Monthly Net Book Income; (2) Standard Deviation of Monthly Net Book Income; (3) Number of Negative Net Book Income Months; (4) Average $ Loss in Negative Net Book Income Months]

			Turnover = 50%: Alpha Standard Deviation			
			0 bp	30 bp	60 bp	90 bp
	0 bp	(1)	$ 89,328			
		(2)	$155,872			
		(3)	34			
		(4)	−$111,533			
	30 bp	(1)	$142,239	$144,462	$146,535	$148,456
		(2)	$159,435	$197,831	$303,777	$432,164
		(3)	24	25	32	38
		(4)	−$99,610	−$147,881	−$253,141	−$360,387
Expected alpha	60 bp	(1)	$196,835	$199,127	$201,265	$203,247
		(2)	$165,151	$201,109	$307,533	$437,794
		(3)	15	22	29	34
		(4)	−$98,897	−$104,967	−$226,246	−$351,662
	90 bp	(1)	$253,162	$255,529	$257,736	$257,781
		(2)	$173,235	$206,232	$312,447	$444,250
		(3)	12	14	25	30
		(4)	−$72,315	−$86,383	−$200,576	−$343,585

			Turnover = 100%: Alpha Standard Deviation			
			0 bp	30 bp	60 bp	90 bp
	0 bp	(1)	$93,707			
		(2)	$271,113			
		(3)	47			
		(4)	−$197,027			
	30 bp	(1)	$147,082	$149,378	$151,521	$153,508
		(2)	$274,707	$296,027	$373,785	$483,397
		(3)	39	39	42	42
		(4)	−$184,517	−$197,224	−$264,981	−$376,277
Expected alpha	60 bp	(1)	$202,162	$204,531	$206,742	$208,793
		(2)	$279,571	$299,613	$377,964	$489,351
		(3)	31	34	39	38
		(4)	−$176,222	−$170,847	−$230,476	−$364,548
	90 bp	(1)	$259,000	$261,445	$263,726	$265,843
		(2)	$285,902	$304,444	$383,082	$496,042
		(3)	23	24	29	34
		(4)	−$180,078	−$175,998	−$246,935	−$353,853

former is very sensitive to the level of turnover. Interestingly, however, the effect of turnover is much more pronounced for managers with low alpha volatility. For example, the net book income volatility and shortfall risk for an $N(60, 30)$ manager increased from \$201,109 and –\$104,967, respectively, to \$299,613 and –\$170,847 as turnover increased from 50 to 100%. In addition, the number of shortfall months increased from 22 to 34. In contrast, the numbers for a $N(60, 90)$ manager increased from \$437,794 and –\$351,662, respectively, to only \$489,351 and –\$364,548 as turnover doubled. The number of shortfall months increased only from 34 to 38. Since fluctuations in alpha are independent from gains/losses from turnover, they tend to have little additional effect on book income volatility once the level of alpha volatility generates book income volatility similar to that produced by turnover. In other words, for total return managers with high alpha volatility, the relative level of turnover has less of an effect on book income volatility. However, for managers with low alpha volatility, relative levels of turnover have a significant effect on relative book income volatility.

Obviously, the results presented above depend heavily on the underlying assumptions. However, the example shows that while the alpha from total return management improves the level of book income, the volatility of the alpha and portfolio turnover are important determinants of net book income volatility and shortfall risk. This example may help book accounting clients better understand the potential volatility associated with various total return management styles. The client's willingness to trade off book income volatility and shortfall risk against additional book income determines the type of portfolio manager to hire.

CONCLUSION

The large class of book accounting–based investors can now benefit from having a performance benchmark that reflects their particular investment constraints and timing of cash inflows and outflows. We discuss how to construct such book accounting benchmarks and how such a benchmark reflects what the investor could have achieved (in book accounting terms) by passively investing in the underlying index. Consequently, a book accounting benchmark allows book accounting–based investors to quantify the value of their portfolio decisions over time. We also demonstrate how book benchmarks can be used in combination with portfolio analytics to measure portfolio risk relative to its benchmark.

The availability of book accounting benchmarks also permits investors to perform quantitative empirical studies to examine the historical book accounting performance of various investment strategies. We examine the relative performance of two such strategies: a constant spread overweight strategy often used by book investors and an active total return strategy that generates a variable alpha with portfolio turnover. We show that a modest spread overweight strategy produced additional book income with very little book income volatility and shortfall risk. An active total return manager with a modest expected alpha of 30 bp/year with a standard deviation of 60 bp can produce more book income. However, owing to the total return manager's volatile alpha and portfolio turnover, he produces a much more volatile book income and has considerably more shortfall risk. The book accounting–based investor can use the results of this section to help determine the type of investment management style that best meets his book income risk-return objectives.

10. Liability-Based Benchmarks: An Example

A liability-based benchmark combines the desirable attributes of a market-based index while matching the sponsor's liability term-structure and investment constraints (e.g., quality requirements). Consequently, a liability benchmark is "neutral," allowing the sponsor to evaluate directly an investment manager's performance and the manager to monitor actively investment risk and opportunities.

Two types of liability benchmarks are *composite benchmarks* (using market-based indices) and *portfolio benchmarks* (using a fixed portfolio of bonds). Portfolio benchmarks have two advantages: less frequent rebalancing and reduced risk of introducing unintended biases into the benchmark, but care must be taken to minimize idiosyncratic risk by holding many different issuer names in the portfolio. We discuss our method for constructing portfolio benchmarks and present an example.

Plan sponsors and investment managers are well acquainted with market-based fixed-income indices (e.g., the Lehman Government/Credit Index). These indices are defined as a set of well-publicized rules that govern which bonds are added and deleted. When a market-based index reflects the risk preferences of the plan sponsor and the investment opportunities facing the investment manager, the index serves as a useful tool for performance evaluation and risk analysis. In other words, the index is a neutral benchmark, and the manager is evaluated based on performance vs. the index. While the sponsor may impose some additional investment constraints (e.g., credit and issuer concentration and limits on deviations from the index), he otherwise wants the manager to be unfettered within the confines of the index in the search for added returns.

However, some investment managers operate in a more constrained environment. A plan's assets may be "dedicated" to satisfying a well-defined liability

Based on research first published by Lehman Brothers in 2001.

schedule and assets must be managed to satisfy those liabilities.[1] In such cases, the sponsor specifies, based on risk preferences, the universe of bonds in which the manager may invest and the liability schedule that must be satisfied. Often the investable universe is defined as a market-based index. However, the index usually has a term-structure that is very different from the liability schedule (e.g., the liability schedule may have a longer duration than the market index).

The manager now has two goals: produce added returns to help the plan achieve its long-term investment goals and, simultaneously, keep the portfolio's term-structure aligned with the liability schedule. How does the sponsor evaluate the manager's performance? If the manager underperformed the market index, was it because of poor sector and security selection or simply structuring the portfolio to match the liability term-structure? What is needed is a neutral benchmark that reflects both of the plan sponsor's goals. The manager's performance can then be properly compared with the return on the neutral benchmark.

A liability-based benchmark gives the sponsor and manager a performance yardstick incorporating both the term-structure constraints imposed by the liability schedule and the investment restrictions imposed by the sponsor's risk preferences. Sponsors can be confident that if they hold the positions underlying the liability benchmark, they will meet their liability schedules while satisfying their investment restrictions. This makes the liability benchmark a neutral one.

A liability-based benchmark can also retain many of the desirable attributes of a market-based index: benchmark returns are calculated using market prices, the investment manager can replicate the benchmark, and the benchmark is well defined so that the sponsor and manager can actively monitor and evaluate its risk and performance. Furthermore, if the liability benchmark contains published market-based indices or marketable securities, its performance can be calculated and published by third-party index or market data providers.

Because the liability benchmark reflects the sponsor's liability schedule and investment restrictions, a manager can directly evaluate an investment portfolio against the benchmark. Using standard portfolio analytics, he can estimate tracking error, perform scenario analyses, and evaluate individual security swaps. Moreover, since the liability benchmark is neutral, its performance can be compared directly with the manager's performance. This greatly facilitates sponsor-manager communication.

---

1. A dedicated portfolio refers to a portfolio of marketable securities that services a prescribed set of liabilities. There are various ways to construct a dedicated portfolio: cash matched, immunization, horizon matched, and contingent immunization. For an analysis of these various approaches see "Duration, Immunization and Dedication," Pt. IIID, in *Investing: The Collected Works of Martin L. Leibowitz*, Probus, 1992.

TYPES OF LIABILITY-BASED BENCHMARKS

A liability-based benchmark reflects the term-structure of the liability schedule and the investment restrictions of the plan sponsor. There are two possible ways to construct a liability benchmark of cash instruments.

1. Use market-based indices that reflect the sponsor's investment restrictions to construct a *composite benchmark* that reflects the liability term-structure. For example, if the liability schedule is longer-duration than the Lehman Aggregate Index, a composite index of the Credit and Aggregate indices and a custom long Treasury strips index could be created matching the duration of the liability schedule and the sponsor's investment restrictions.[2]

More complicated composite indices may contain several indices weighted so as to achieve various diversification goals and duration, convexity, and yield targets. Despite matching a targeted duration, however, composite benchmarks may still have cash flow distributions that differ significantly from the liability schedule. Consequently, the composite benchmark and the liability schedule may diverge owing to nonparallel shifts in the yield curve. Furthermore, as the underlying market indices are sets of rules rather than fixed sets of bonds, the characteristics of the indices change over time, which may require frequent rebalancing. Care must be taken in using composite benchmarks. Suppose the liability schedule is concentrated in the near-term years. The temptation may be to use a short-credit index as one of the indices in the composite. However, the short-credit index may introduce an unintended bias into the composite benchmark. For example, the industrial sector accounts for 37% of the 0–4 duration bucket of the Credit Index, whereas it accounts for 45.5% in the overall index. Consequently, using the 0–4 duration credit subindex in the composite may inadvertently underweight industrial paper in the composite benchmark.

2. Create a *portfolio benchmark* by selecting bonds from the investable universe such that the portfolio's cash flows closely match the liability schedule and the overall portfolio satisfies the sponsor's investment restrictions. As bonds in a portfolio benchmark are selected so that their overall characteristics match the investment restrictions, the risk described earlier of unintended biases with composite benchmarks is eliminated.

Unlike a composite benchmark that consists of indices and their sets of rules, a portfolio benchmark consists of a set of bonds and, by design, it is explicitly structured to track a given liability schedule over time, reducing the need for

2. For more on the construction of liability-based composite benchmarks see Boyce I. Greer, "Market-Oriented Benchmarks for Immunized Portfolios," *Journal of Portfolio Management*, vol. 18, no. 3, Spring 1992, pp. 26–35.

rebalancing. However, the relatively few bonds in the portfolio benchmark (compared with the many in the indices underlying a composite benchmark) make it susceptible to idiosyncratic risk, so in sectors in which there is significant event risk (e.g., corporates), great care must be taken to reduce idiosyncratic risk by holding many different issuers.[3]

BUILDING A LIABILITY-BASED PORTFOLIO BENCHMARK

The traditional dedication approach is to minimize the cost of a portfolio that funds a liability schedule subject to constraints such as requiring that the duration and convexity of the portfolio match those of the liabilities. Other constraints such as sector weights and a sufficient number of issuers in the portfolio ensure portfolio diversification. Overall, these optimization constraints help keep the portfolio's cash flows "matched" with the liabilities, while also adhering to the sponsor's investment guidelines. This approach is a linear optimization problem, as the objective function and constraints are linear equations.

A different approach is used to construct a liability-based portfolio benchmark. The idea is to create a portfolio such that its cash flows mimic as closely as possible the cash flows of the liability schedule subject to the portfolio investment constraints. In other words, the objective is to minimize the absolute value of the difference between each liability cash flow and the cash flow available from the portfolio at that time.

Since portfolio benchmark cash flows are unlikely to fall on the exact date of the liability cash flows, they are either reinvested forward or, if permitted, discounted back to a liability cash flow date. Consequently, a portfolio's available cash flow at each liability cash flow date is the amount of portfolio cash that can be delivered to that date. To illustrate, consider a liability cash flow L_t that occurs at time t (Figure 10-1). There are several cash flows (assume, for simplicity, that they are zero coupon bonds) available that might meet this liability cash flow. Two of these, P_1 and P_2, occur before and another one, P_3, occurs after the liability cash flow. However, depending on the assumptions allowed in the portfolio construction process, all three (if purchased in sufficient quantity) could satisfy L_t.

Consider cash flow P_1, which occurs before L_t. If the reinvestment rate, r, is assumed to equal zero, then a face amount of cash flow P_1 equal to L_t can be pur-

---

3. Chapter 14 discusses a methodology for constructing replicating credit portfolios that minimizes event risk. For example, the Lehman Credit Index can be replicated with a 100-bond portfolio such that it will not underperform the index by more than 35 bp with 95% confidence. The key is to hold most of the 100 issues in the Baa category: using sixty-two Baa bonds to replicate the Baa quality sector having a 31% market weight in the Credit Index.

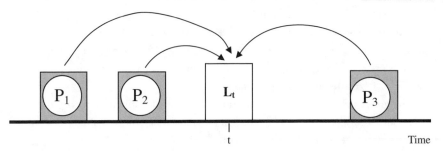

Figure 10-1. Borrowing and Lending to Fund a Liability

chased today. When P_1 is received at maturity, it can be held until time t and would be sufficient to satisfy L_t. If the reinvestment rate is greater than zero, then less P_1 is needed today to satisfy L_t. However, both P_1 and P_2 can be carried forward to time t to satisfy the liability requirement completely.

Now consider cash flow P_3, which is received after the liability cash flow requirement. If borrowing is not allowed, then P_3 cannot satisfy L_t. However, if borrowing is permitted, then, at time t, cash can be borrowed against P_3 (at the assumed borrowing rate) in order to satisfy L_t.

In the more general case, there are many liability cash flows of varying amounts and many feasible bonds, each with its many cash flows comprising periodic coupon payments and return of principal at maturity (Figure 10-2). To create a portfolio benchmark, our job is to select a set of bonds whose combined available cash flows at each liability payment date (given the reinvestment and borrowing rate assumptions) most closely match the liability cash flows. The portfolio benchmark is the solution to this optimization problem.

To set up the optimization problem, the liability schedule is first defined according to the amount of cash flow required at each time period. A feasible set of bonds is then identified as a candidate for the benchmark. For example, if bonds must be rated Aa2 or better, then the feasible set would be constrained to contain bonds rated only Aa2 or better. Then further investment restrictions are specified

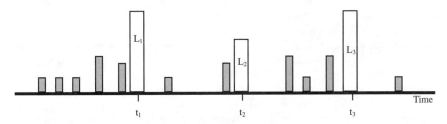

Figure 10-2. More General Case of Borrowing and Lending to Fund a Liability

that constrain the selection for the benchmark. For example, the benchmark may be required to have an asset mix of 60% governments and 40% corporates, with no single corporate issuer with more than 2% weight in the benchmark portfolio. Finally, a reinvestment rate, r, is specified (it may be zero), and borrowing is either denied or permitted at a specified rate, b.[4]

The goal of the optimization program is to select bonds for a portfolio benchmark such that the cash flows are as "close as possible" to the liability cash flow.[5] In other words, the program minimizes

$$\sum_{t=1}^{n} \frac{|\, CF_t(L) - CF_t(P)\,|}{(1 + IRR)^t} \qquad\qquad (10\text{-}1)$$

subject to the specified constraints. $CF_t(L)$ represents the nominal liability cash flow at time t. $CF_t(P)$ is the nominal amount of portfolio cash flow that can be made available at time t either from a cash flow that occurs exactly at time t or earlier cash flows reinvested forward to time t and, if permitted, later cash flows discounted back to time t.

Mechanically, the program works as follows. All available portfolio cash flows that occur before each liability cash flow at time t are reinvested forward to time t at rate r. If borrowing is allowed, then all available portfolio cash flows that occur after time t are discounted back to time t. The program then selects the portfolio of bonds whose cash flows minimize the sum of the absolute values of the cash flow differences across all time periods in which a liability cash flow occurs.

To build intuition for the optimization program, consider the case of two equal liability cash flows, L_1 and L_2. There are two possible bonds, P_1 and P_2. Bond P_1 has one cash flow that occurs before L_1, whose nominal value equals $L_1 + L_2$. Bond P_2 has two equal cash flows with one occurring before L_1 and the other after L_1 but before L_2. Each cash flow's nominal value equals L_1 (and L_2). (Fig-

---

4. To be conservative and ensure that all liability payments have sufficient cash, the sponsor could assume that the reinvestment rate equals zero and prohibit borrowing.

5. To achieve the closest match, we would like to minimize the "distance" between the portfolio cash flows and those of the liabilities. This could be expressed using the least-mean-squares approach, in which we minimize the sum of the squared differences, or by the absolute value approach shown earlier. Neither of these objective functions is linear. We have chosen to work with the formulation based on absolute values because it can be converted to a linear program. To accomplish this, the problem variables, which represent the cash flow carryovers from one vertex to the next (which can be positive or negative), are each split into two nonnegative variables, one representing a reinvestment and the other a loan. A linear program is used to minimize the weighted sum of all of these variables, using weights that make the problem equivalent to the absolute value minimization shown earlier.

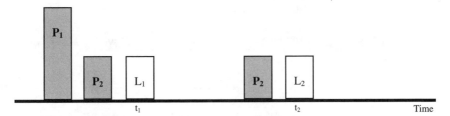

Figure 10-3. Portfolio Benchmark Approach Selects Bond P_2 over Bond P_1

ure 10-3 illustrates the cash flows.) Further, assume that the reinvestment rate is zero and that borrowing is not allowed. Finally, the market value of bond P_1 is 95 and the market value of bond P_2 is 100.

Both bonds would fully satisfy the liability schedule. However, P_1 would do so at a lower cost than P_2. Which bond does the optimizer select? The sum of the differences in cash flow between each liability cash flow and the available cash flow is less for P_2 than for P_1. Why is this? Both P_1 and P_2 exactly fund the liability cash flow at t_2, but P_1 must do this by overfunding the liability cash flow at time t_1. In other words, P_2 matches the liability schedule more closely than does P_1, so the optimizer selects bond P_2 and not bond P_1. This example indicates that the portfolio benchmark approach selects the best-matching portfolio and not necessarily the least expensive one, even if the latter also satisfies the liability schedule.

The term $(1 + IRR)^t$ in the denominator of Equation (10-1) is an additional discount factor for which IRR is the internal rate of return on the benchmark portfolio. This discount term essentially says that the optimization program cares more about minimizing near-term cash flow mismatches than more distant mismatches.

The solution of this optimization program is a liability-based benchmark portfolio of marketable securities whose cash flows are as close as possible to the liability cash flows. Note that this approach does not minimize the cost of the benchmark portfolio, as is the case for other dedication programs. Here, the goal is to create a portfolio benchmark whose cash flows closely mimic the liability schedule and meet investment constraints: a neutral benchmark.

EXAMPLE: CREATING COMPOSITE AND PORTFOLIO BENCHMARKS

Recently, a fund manager working with a plan sponsor decided to create a benchmark for a fixed liability stream (Figure 10-4) with a duration of 12.5. The sponsor's investment restrictions required that the benchmark have an asset mix of 50% government, 40% corporate, and 10% CMBS. The minimum credit quality allowed was A3.

Figure 10-4. Liability Schedule

Year	Amount ($)	Year	Amount ($)
1–8	0	20	5,550,285
9	36,631,879	21	5,550,285
10	24,236,243	22	4,625,237
11	20,351,044	23	4,625,237
12	15,355,787	24	3,700,190
13	15,355,787	25	3,700,190
14	8,325,427	26	2,775,142
15	8,325,427	27	2,775,142
16	7,400,380	28	1,850,095
17	7,400,380	29	1,850,095
18	6,475,332	30	925,047
19	6,475,332	31	925,047

To create a composite benchmark, at least three different subindices are needed, one for each asset class. A fourth subindex is also required so that the composite index matches the duration target of 12.5. A long corporate index containing only quality A3 and higher is 40% of the composite benchmark, the CMBS index is 10%, and the remaining 50% is split between the Long Government Index and a custom Treasury strips index containing strips of 18 years and longer. The weights of these two government indices, 23.1 and 26.9%, are such that they add up to 50% and produce an overall composite benchmark duration of 12.5. The weights are shown in Figure 10-5.

Figure 10-6 compares the cash flows of the composite benchmark with those of the liability schedule. Note that while the duration of the composite benchmark matches that of the liability schedule, there are considerable mismatches in the timing of cash flows. It is likely that cash flows could be more closely matched if additional subindices, appropriately weighted, were added to the composite benchmark.

Figure 10-5. Composite Benchmark Weights

Index	Weight (%)
Long corporate (A3 and higher)	40.0
CMBS	10.0
Long government	23.1
Treasury strip (18 years+)	26.9

Percentage of Total Cash Flow

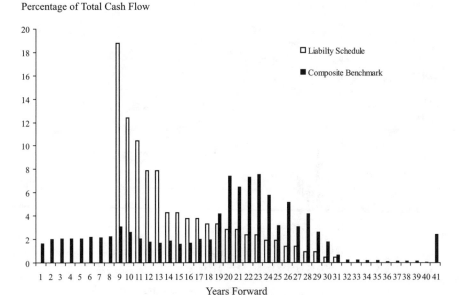

Years Forward

Figure 10-6. Cash Flow Comparison: Composite Benchmark vs. Liability Schedule

To create a portfolio benchmark, about 1000 bonds were chosen to make up the feasible set from which the optimizer can select bonds for the portfolio. Only bullet corporate and agency bonds were considered (so the cash flows would not fluctuate with interest rates) and only strips represented the Treasury sector. The bulk of the feasible set is corporate bonds, with good representation in all corporate sectors. This is desirable, as the portfolio benchmark must contain many corporate names for appropriate diversification.

The optimization problem was set up with constraints that reflect the investment restrictions: an asset mix of 50% government, 40% corporate, and 10% CMBS and a minimum credit quality of A3 for all issues. In addition, the 40% of the portfolio in corporates was further constrained to have the same proportional industry and quality breakdown as the Credit Index. No credit sector and no issuer was allowed to make up more than 22 and 1%, respectively, of the overall benchmark. (If desired, separate diversification constraints can be imposed by sector or by quality to reflect varying levels of protection from event risk.) As a result, the portfolio benchmark that was created consisted of approximately 100 securities.

Figure 10-7 compares the cash flows of the portfolio benchmark with those of the liability schedule. Overall, the portfolio benchmark cash flows closely match the liability cash flows. Note, however, that the first liability cash flow (year 9) is

Percentage of Total Cash Flow

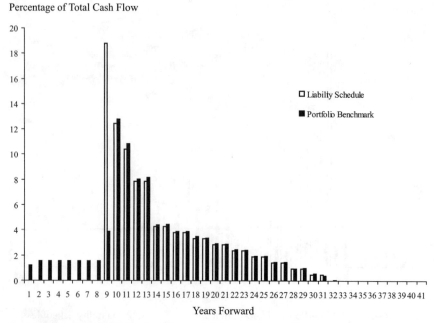

Figure 10-7. Cash Flow Comparison: Portfolio Benchmark vs. Liability Schedule

mostly prefunded by the portfolio. This is to be expected given the investment constraints, as 40% of the portfolio must be invested in corporates that predominantly pay a coupon. Consequently, the portfolio benchmark receives coupon payments in the first 8 years, which must be reinvested to meet the first liability cash flow in year 9.

As the portfolio benchmark reflects the liability structure and the investment constraints, the sponsor and investment manager can use it as a neutral benchmark: the manager can construct a portfolio with the benchmark as his bogey, and the sponsor can evaluate the manager's performance relative to the benchmark. The manager can also use it to identify the sources of risk in the investment portfolio relative to the benchmark and, therefore, relative to the liability structure. This is accomplished using the Lehman Brothers global risk model, which identifies sources of risk (i.e., tracking error) and suggests trades from a manager-selected list of bonds in order to reduce both systematic and security-specific risk. The risk model also suggests trades to move the portfolio toward matching the portfolio benchmark in yield curve, sector, and quality exposures. In general, if the manager wishes to deviate from the neutral benchmark, the risk model can estimate the potential tracking error.

CONCLUSION

A liability-based benchmark retains many of the desirable attributes of a market-based index while simultaneously matching the sponsor's liability term-structure more closely. A liability benchmark is a neutral one, which allows the sponsor to evaluate the manager's performance appropriately and permits the manager to actively monitor investment risk and opportunities.

This chapter deals with fixed, not inflation-linked, liabilities. However, the methodology can be adapted to build an inflation-protected liability benchmark in either of two very different ways. The first would require no changes to the methodology described here, except that the universe of securities from which the benchmark is constructed would contain only inflation-linked bonds. The main drawback of this approach is the relatively limited selection of bonds available in this category, which will both hamper our ability to match arbitrary cash flow streams and restrict benchmark diversification. Another limitation is that it only addresses inflation linked to a CPI-type inflation index, not to a wage inflation index, which is sometimes used to adjust future nominal liabilities. A second approach would be to match the liability cash flow stream using a benchmark composed of nominal bonds, as described here. An overlay portfolio of inflation swaps (either CPI or wage index-linked) could then be used to swap the cash flows of this bond portfolio for an inflation-linked cash flow stream. The main limitation here is the heavy reliance on inflation swaps, which is an emerging market. This may raise questions of liquidity and price transparency and may not be allowed in some portfolios.

Whether liabilities are fixed or inflation-linked, plan sponsors and managers are increasingly adopting the portfolio approach to liability benchmark construction and utilizing fixed-income quantitative portfolio management tools to implement this strategy.

Pension assets are increasingly managed against liability-based benchmarks. While this chapter has dealt with specific examples of benchmarks built from fixed-income securities, these can also be built by discounting liability cash flows using a spot curve, such as a zero-coupon swap curve, or by fitting a zero-coupon corporate curve. Ultimately the choice of an appropriate benchmark will depend on regulatory and/or accounting considerations.

11. Swap Indices

. . . .

Since the mid-1990s, interest-rate swaps have emerged as one of the primary benchmarks for pricing, valuation, and hedging of other fixed-income securities. This is particularly true for the investment-grade sectors, such as agencies, mortgages, and investment-grade corporates, which comprise 11.4, 35.0, and 26.3%, respectively, of the Lehman U.S. Aggregate Index. To help investors evaluate, price, and hedge their portfolios, Lehman Brothers is introducing the following two families of total return indices based on swaps:

1. Bellwether swap indices provide total returns of bellwether swaps ranging in maturity from 3 months to 30 years. For example, the 10-year Swap Index measures the total return of investing in 10-year par swaps over time. In addition to the bellwether swap indices, the Swap Total Return Index serves as a single performance measure for the swaps market as a whole. This index tracks total returns of an equally weighted portfolio of bellwether swaps with maturities ranging from 1 to 30 years. The Swap Index does not include swaps shorter than 1 year, in accordance with the Lehman index convention of not including short-maturity instruments in major indices. The 3- and 6-month swap indices are published separately and are already used by some investors as a benchmark of money market returns.

2. Mirror swap indices provide total returns of a portfolio of swaps constructed to match the key-rate durations of major Lehman bond indices. For example, the Mortgage-Mirror Swap Index uses a portfolio of swaps that matches key-rate exposures of the Mortgage Index and would be used to hedge it. A comparison with the total return of the

Based on research first published by Lehman Brothers in 2002.

Mortgage-Mirror Swap Index provides an easy way to measure the excess return of the Mortgage Index to a duration-matched portfolio of swaps.

Similar swap indices will be introduced for the euro, the British pound, the Japanese yen, and, possibly, several other currencies at a later time.

Since their arrival on the scene in the early 1980s, swaps have grown in importance as a result of several developments in the bond market. Traditionally, investors accounted for the following four factors in analyzing fixed-income securities: default-free interest rate, credit spread, liquidity premium, and idiosyncratic risk. The U.S. Treasury curve was regarded as a default-free interest-rate curve, whereas a security's spread to a particular Treasury rate was considered to represent its credit risk, liquidity premium, and idiosyncratic behavior. Implicit in this framework was the assumption that Treasuries did not pose any significant liquidity or idiosyncratic risk of their own.

This assumption came into question in recent years. The Russian default in August 1998 resulted in a spread sector crash and a dramatic increase in the liquidity premium commanded by Treasuries. The U.S. Treasury introduced a further complication in 2000 by beginning to buy back large amounts of its outstanding debt. Most recently, the Treasury suspended issuance of 30-year bonds in November 2001, sparking another strong rally in the 10- and 30-year sectors. It is now clear that a strong idiosyncratic component in the behavior of long-maturity Treasuries will not go away. In light of these changes in the market, the role of Treasuries as a sole benchmark for fixed-income securities, especially longer-dated ones, came under increased scrutiny.

In response to these developments, investors have been searching for an alternative benchmark. A detailed study carried out in late 2000 was devoted to finding an alternative proxy for default-free interest rates from among the following market sectors: agencies, swaps, and corporates.[1] The study used the framework of decomposing yields of fixed-income securities into the risk-free rate and three additional variables representing liquidity, credit, and idiosyncratic risks. A sophisticated econometric technique was employed to extract an unobservable variable representing the risk-free rate. The results confirmed that the crisis of 1998 and Treasury buybacks of 2000 were marked by a dramatic increase in the idiosyncratic risk of Treasuries.

More importantly, the statistical framework developed in the study allowed the measurement of common market risk shared by all credit sectors. It was shown

---

1. A. Kocic, C. Quintos, and F. Yared, *Identifying the Benchmark Security in a Multifactor Spread Environment*, Lehman Brothers, September 2000.

that of the instruments considered, swaps represented this common risk best. In other words, of the four components that determine pricing of fixed-income securities, *swaps represent the default-free interest rate, generic credit, and liquidity common to all investment-grade sectors*. The residual risk specific to a particular sector or security can be characterized in terms of spread to swaps or, equivalently, spread to LIBOR. In light of these findings, the study concluded that swaps work best for hedging products in the spread sector.

It is worth noting that agencies and MBS are already priced relative to swaps and quoted in terms of spreads to LIBOR. As we show later, the relationship between spreads to Treasuries of swaps, agencies, and MBS has been consistently strong since they emerged during the crisis of 1998. On the other hand, although swap spreads and corporate spreads are usually highly correlated, this relationship breaks down under stressful market conditions, such as those observed in the aftermath of September 2001 events. As markets calm down, the correlation between swaps and corporates tends to rise again. In any case, while swaps are evidently an appropriate proxy for agencies and MBS, many investors are likely to continue using Treasuries as a benchmark for corporate debt. With the U.S. Treasury moving back to deficits for at least 3 years, the supply of Treasuries should be adequate for hedging purposes in the near term.

FIXED-INCOME BENCHMARKS: U.S. TREASURIES AND SWAPS

The main advantage of swaps is that they are not funding instruments, but over-the-counter (OTC) contracts used to hedge interest-rate risk. For this reason, the supply of swaps is unlimited and is not determined exclusively by issuance. Though hedging a new bond issue is often the reason to enter into a swap, it is not the only reason. Many swap users are money managers hedging their existing bond portfolios and hedge funds taking positions with respect to interest rates. In recent years, the swap market has come to rival Treasuries with respect to size, liquidity, range of available maturities, and convenience. An item-by-item comparison of Treasuries and swaps is given in Figure 11-1.

In contrast to swaps, the Treasury market is dominated by a single issuer with changing funding needs. There is a similar problem with the agency market, which is effectively driven by only two issuers: Fannie Mae (FNMA) and Freddie Mac (FHLMC). Having such a small number of issuers causes shocks to supplies in the market, ultimately resulting in high levels of idiosyncratic risk. The swaps market, on the other hand, is affected by many participants and thus enjoys a substantial degree of diversification and less idiosyncratic risk. In other words, if a security's spread to Treasuries changes, it may reflect an event specific to the Treasury sector itself rather than the security in question. A change in a security's spread to

Figure 11-1. Fixed-Income Benchmarks: U.S. Treasuries and Swaps as of September 2001

	U.S. Treasuries	U.S. Interest-Rate Swaps
Total outstanding notional value	$2.8 trillion	$15 trillion
Daily volume	$200 billion	$50 billion
Bid/ask spread for a $50 million trade	0.25 bp running	0.5 bp running
Dominant market participant	U.S. Treasury	None
Available maturities	1 month to 30 years	1 month to 30 years
Origination	U.S. Treasury auction	Over-the-counter transaction
Supply	Determined by U.S. Treasury issuance	Unlimited
Risk of short squeeze	Substantial	None
Counterparty risk	None	Limited by collateral management, termination provisions, and other credit enhancements

swaps is much more likely to be caused by developments related to the security or its credit sector.

Having recognized this advantage offered by swaps, investors now use them widely for hedging market risk of spread products. It is a natural next step for them to compare such securities to swaps with respect to performance as well. We introduce bellwether swap indices to track returns of generic fixed-coupon bonds of a given maturity. Mirror swap indices serve the purpose of making duration-adjusted comparisons between swaps and other spread sectors, as represented by their respective indices. As mirror swap indices are simply portfolios of individual swaps, bellwether swap indices are essential ingredients for constructing the mirror indices. To the extent that other credit sectors are compared with swaps using a uniform methodology of mirror indices, swaps can effectively be used for performance comparison.

WHY USE TOTAL RETURN INDICES BASED ON SWAPS?

Total return indices based on swaps are helpful to investors in many contexts.

1. *Efficient Index Replication.* Many portfolio managers are interested in a realistic low-cost strategy for replicating popular indices. In general, this is accomplished by assembling a portfolio of relatively few liquid instruments, for example, Treasury futures, such that its duration profile matches that of the index to be replicated. Since most indices contain a substantial spread component, the quality of replication can be greatly improved by using swaps in addition to Treasury futures to capture the effect of changing credit spreads. Total return indices for swaps included in the replicating portfolio are necessary in order to calculate returns of the replicating portfolio.

A typical methodology for constructing a portfolio of derivatives to replicate a bond index is as follows. Initially, all bonds in the index are divided into four cells based on their modified duration, for example, from 0 to 3 years, from 3 to 5 years, from 5 to 7.5 years, and more than 7.5 years. For callable bonds, the modified duration is adjusted using an options-pricing model. Each cell is then replicated using one swap or Treasury futures contract of similar duration, for example, 2-year swap for the first cell, 5-year swap for the second, 10-year swap for the third, and 30-year swap for the last. The hedge ratio for each cell is calculated to match the total dollar duration of the cell with that of the respective derivative contract.

Figure 11-2 shows average monthly tracking errors of replicating the U.S. Aggregate Index with Treasury futures, swaps, and a combination of the two instruments. Not surprisingly, Treasury futures work well for the Treasury portion of the index, whereas swaps do better in replicating the spread sector. Most importantly, a portfolio of swaps and futures used together shows an average tracking error of

Figure 11-2. Monthly Tracking Errors of Replicating the U.S. Aggregate Index with Swaps and Treasury Futures

Component of the U.S. Aggregate Index	Treasury Futures (bp)	Interest Rate Swaps (bp)	Swaps and Futures (bp)
Treasuries	11.9	55.5	N/A
MBS, Agency, Credit	46.4	21.3	N/A
Full index	33.2	26.3	16.0

just 16 bp/month, which is less than half the error of replicating the index with Treasury futures alone. Even better results were obtained for the Global Aggregate Index, which enjoys diversification across several currencies.[2] The tracking error of replicating the index with Treasury futures, money market futures, and swaps in four major currencies was 10 bp/month. It can be further reduced to as little as 5 bp/month if the most liquid bonds from all sectors in the index are used in addition to swaps and futures.

2. *Security Selection Decisions and Performance Attribution.* As we mentioned at the end of the introductory section, a security's spread to swaps effectively represents the residual risk of holding that security after the common risk of spread products is stripped out. For structured securities with embedded options, the spread is calculated using a term-structure model for the entire yield curve. The resulting option-adjusted spread (OAS) measures returns from a security's yield net of the common factor driving the overall market. Money managers use the OAS framework for security selection and relative value analysis. Option-adjusted spreads were historically calculated with respect to the Treasury curve. However, since 1998, investors have increasingly used the OAS to the swap curve, effectively stripping out the liquidity and idiosyncratic components of Treasury yields. The swaps indices help facilitate this process by allowing easy computation of returns relative to swaps.

3. *Asset Allocation Decisions.* Excess returns to swaps play an important role in asset allocation. To understand the benefits of diversification in a portfolio, investors frequently focus on the correlation of security returns in excess of risk-free interest rates. When this is done using excess returns to Treasuries, the correlations are artificially high owing to the systematic inclusion of investment-grade credit spreads and the liquidity premium of Treasuries. By using excess returns to swaps, this common factor is stripped out, leading to improved evaluation of sector allocations.

2. See Chapter 5.

Figure 11-3. Correlation of Excess Returns to Treasuries and Swaps

	ABS (%)	Agencies (%)	Finance (%)	MBS (%)	Credit (%)
Treasuries					
ABS	—	58	74	44	67
Agencies	58	—	55	46	54
Finance	74	55	—	45	94
MBS	44	46	45	—	52
Credit	67	54	94	52	—
Swaps					
ABS	—	43	70	34	59
Agencies	43	—	29	36	42
Finance	70	29	—	37	91
MBS	34	36	37	—	46
Credit	59	42	91	46	—

The correlation matrix of excess returns, shown in Figure 11-3, is based on a 10-year time series of monthly returns from August 1992 through August 2001. In all cases shown, excess returns to swaps exhibit a lower correlation than the corresponding excess returns to Treasuries. In some cases, the difference can be substantial. For example, for agencies vs. finance companies, the correlation of excess returns to swaps is only 29%, compared with a 55% correlation of excess returns to Treasuries.

For total return investors who are benchmarked to one of the Lehman indices, the corresponding mirror swap index provides an easy mechanism for stripping out the effect of "pure" (i.e., free of liquidity premium and idiosyncratic risk) interest-rate movement and isolating the relative performance of a particular credit sector.

4. *Benchmark for Money Management.* For institutions such as commercial banks trying to outperform their funding costs, which track LIBOR rates rather than Treasury rates, short-maturity (6 months to 2 years) bellwether swap indices could be used as performance benchmarks. The same is true for money managers with funds invested in commercial paper and other money market instruments.

Pension funds and asset managers looking for very-long-duration investments with low risk face a different problem. The reduced issuance and continuing buybacks of 30-year Treasury bonds make the long end of the Treasury curve inadequate as a benchmark. Long high-grade corporates are not an alternative, owing to insufficient issuance and idiosyncratic "name" risk. The long agency market also has idiosyncratic risk to the two major issuers that dominate the sector. The swap market, on the other hand, with rates and supply determined by many competing market participants, provides the only viable benchmark for this part of the curve. As a result, the long-maturity bellwether swap indices would be of interest to this group.

5. *New Tools for Risk Management and Excess Returns.* The swap indices also allow us to create new contracts that have several advantages as risk management vehicles. For example, the duration of the CMBS Index is 5.1 years. Owing to prepayment lockouts and constant replenishment with new issues, this number is quite stable and corresponds to the duration of a 6-year swap. Investors who own a portfolio of CMBS bonds and pay total returns of the 6-year Bellwether Swap Index are isolating their exposure to the excess returns of CMBS over swaps. This can be further fine-tuned by paying the total returns of the CMBS Mirror Swap Index. This strategy can have several advantages over direct usage of swaps for hedging. The hedge is automatically rebalanced every month without having to engage in new transactions. The full value of the hedge is realized every month as a cash flow instead of just a mark-to-market gain. Finally, the transaction is marked to zero each month, thereby reducing counterparty risk without the use of collateral.

SWAPS AS A HEDGING INSTRUMENT

The primary use of swaps is to manage the interest-rate risk of securities with interest payments tied to LIBOR. For example, a floating-rate borrower paying LIBOR is exposed to rising interest rates. In order to hedge this risk, the borrower can enter into a payer swap, that is, make fixed-rate coupon payments and receive LIBOR on the notional equal to the amount of debt. Thus, any increase in interest payments that the borrower makes to the lender are offset by a matching increase in floating payments that the borrower receives on the swap. The net result is that the borrower effectively makes fixed-coupon payments on the amount owed. In other words, the swap enables the borrower to convert floating-rate debt into fixed-rate debt.

Paying fixed (and receiving floating) on an interest-rate swap has an interest-rate exposure similar to issuing a fixed-coupon bond. Receiving fixed rate on a swap has the opposite exposure, similar to being long a fixed-coupon bond. A floating-rate-note investor can obtain protection from falling rates by entering into a receiver swap. Asset managers who own fixed-coupon bonds and are worried about rising interest rates would enter into a payer swap, thereby converting their bonds from fixed to floating.

The universe of market participants using swaps to hedge interest-rate risk is large and diverse, and includes issuers of fixed-income securities, both corporate and financial, seeking to minimize or limit their funding costs. Bond investors, such as insurance companies, mutual funds, and mortgage lenders, use swaps to protect their fixed-coupon investments in a rising-interest-rate environment. Finally, many hedge funds view swaps as a large liquid market offering opportunities to make money by taking speculative positions and exploiting market volatility. The existence of many active market participants with opposite interest-rate objectives ensures enough liquidity for any one of them to take either side of a swap.

SWAPS AS A CREDIT SECTOR

As we mentioned earlier, LIBOR is an index of interbank lending rates offered by major banks to each other. The average credit rating of these banks tends to be around Aa1-Aa2.[3] Hence, LIBOR can be interpreted as the short-term funding rate of a generic highly rated financial company. The floating leg of an interest-rate swap, together with the principal cash flow at maturity, is effectively a floating-rate note (FRN) issued by such an entity. Since swaps are initiated at zero cost, the fixed leg of the swap together with the principal cash flow at maturity must be an economically equivalent borrowing arrangement for this company. Thus, the swap rate can be viewed as a fixed coupon that the company would pay on fixed-rate debt of the same maturity as the swap.

The interest-rate curve consisting of par swap rates, called the *swap curve*, plays an important role in fixed-income markets by virtue of being specifically defined, universally accepted, and highly liquid. Companies that issue fixed-rate debt at yields close to the corresponding swap rates are often referred to as "LIBOR-flat" issuers. Since the U.S. Treasury represents the best credit in the market, swaps trade at a positive spread to Treasuries known as the *swap spread*. Most swap market participants are investment-grade entities that are closer in credit quality to LIBOR-flat than to the U.S. Treasury. For this reason, the swap curve is a more natural choice for discounting their cash flows than the Treasury curve.

While swap spreads to Treasuries reflect the difference in credit quality between LIBOR-flat issuers and the U.S. Treasury, they bear no connection to counterparty risk of swaps. The counterparty risk is effectively eliminated through mutual collateral management and other credit enhancements. The sole reason for the existence of swap spreads is that floating payments are based on LIBOR, which is an index reflecting short-term funding costs of a generic investment-grade credit. If the floating side of a standard swap were instead tied to the 3-month

---

3. The official list of contributing banks for major currencies is available on the British Bankers Association website at http://www.bba.org.uk.

Treasury yield, the swap rates would not show any spread to Treasuries. Given the actual interest-rate swap structure, however, today's swap rate reflects the market's expectation of future values of LIBOR, rather than the 3-month Treasury yield, which is a higher number.

Since swap rates can be viewed as equivalent long-term fixed rates available to LIBOR-flat issuers, one may interpret the swap curve as a generic yield curve for highly rated issuers, such as banks that contribute lending rates to LIBOR. In reality, few bonds trade at exactly LIBOR-flat, and when they do, it is probably coincidental. At the end of October 2001, companies with zero option-adjusted spreads to swaps included the Inter-American Development Bank, the Alberta Province of Canada, Austrian Kontrollbank, Florida Power & Light, and Wal-Mart. On the other hand, most banks whose lending rates are used to calculate LIBOR recorded OAS to swaps in the range of 30 to 70 bp. The existence of spread to swaps for such banks is due in part to idiosyncratic risk of individual names. Moreover, if one of these banks is downgraded, it is replaced by another higher-rated bank for the sampling done by the BBA to set the LIBOR rate. More importantly, swap rates are determined by supply and demand in the swap market and are therefore a function of hedging activity.

As we pointed out in the previous section, swaps are used by many different types of market participants to hedge interest-rate risk. Their motivation is frequently unrelated to debt issuance by highly rated banks. In other words, swaps and high-grade bonds belong to different credit sectors that are linked more symbolically than through a clear market relationship. This gives rise to the following questions: Is there any connection between swaps and other spread products? If so, how stable is the relationship? To what extent do swaps reflect the behavior of the spread sector as a whole? In the next section, we use historical data to look for answers to these questions and explain some potentially puzzling relationships.

SWAPS VS. OTHER SPREAD PRODUCTS

Initial evidence of a strong relationship between swaps and high-grade securities emerged in the aftermath of Russian default in 1998. Figure 11-4 shows the history of spreads to Treasuries for 5-year swaps, agencies, MBS, and Aa-rated industrials. As evident from the figure, all spreads were relatively stable for several years, then widened together once the crisis erupted. The spread widening was mostly the result of a major flight to quality and an increase in the liquidity premium of Treasuries. Notably, in spite of high spread volatility, swaps continued to move in tandem with other sectors until September 2001. Following the terrorist attacks, agencies and MBS still moved with swaps, whereas investment-grade corporates decoupled from them.

Spread to Treasuries (bp)

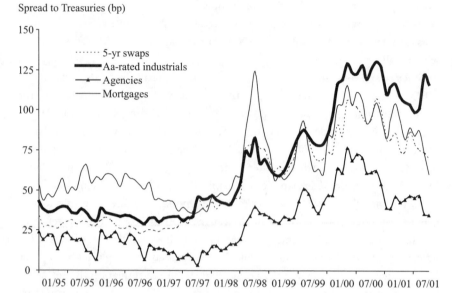

Figure 11-4. Spreads of Various Credit Sectors to Treasuries

Specifically, for the period from 1995 through October 2001, the correlation between monthly spread changes of the Agency Index and the 5-year swap is 63%. For the MBS Index vs. 5-year swaps, the same correlation is 65%. Both numbers are insensitive to the inclusion of September and October of 2001 in the data series. On the other hand, the correlation of spread changes for Aa-rated industrials vs. 7-year swaps is 53%, but it would be as high as 67% if the 2 months after the attack were excluded from the data series. These results indicate that swap spreads are a strong explanatory factor for agency and MBS spreads, but the relationship between swaps and corporates is less stable, particularly during crises.

The reason for a strong relationship among swap, MBS, and agency spreads is that the MBS market is dominated by several large buyers of mortgages. These institutions tend to take advantage of any substantial differences between mortgage yields and their own funding costs as reflected by the agency yields. As a result of their activity in the mortgage market, such discrepancies tend to disappear quickly, forcing the MBS and agency spreads to move together. On other hand, the agencies issue both fixed and floating debt and actively manage their interest-rate risk using swaps. For example, if swap rates were to decline, the agencies would seek to lower their funding costs by issuing more floating debt and swapping it to fixed. Thus, the relative supply of their fixed-rate obligations would decline, causing their spreads to Treasuries to come down in line with the swap spreads. Thus,

Trailing Correlation

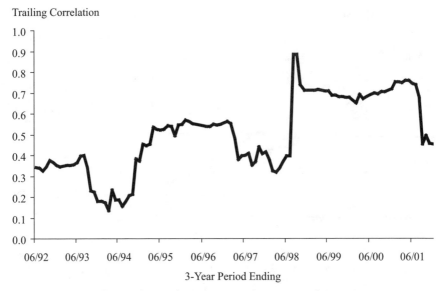

3-Year Period Ending

Figure 11-5. Correlation of Spreads to Treasuries for Swaps and Corporates

spreads to Treasuries of the MBS, agencies, and swaps are strongly interrelated and move together.

The relationship between swap and corporate spreads requires further investigation. Figure 11-5 shows the history of the 3-year trailing correlation between monthly spread changes of a portfolio of 5- and 7-year swaps and 5- to 10-year bullet corporates. The correlation rose sharply in the aftermath of the crisis of 1998, going from around 35 to 70%. It remained high for almost 3 years before collapsing to 45% following the attacks in September 2001. A recent drop in correlation was observed for corporates of all credit qualities, from Aa down to Baa, as seen in Figure 11-6. The effect was more pronounced for lower-quality bonds, indicating a greater extent of their decoupling from swaps.

The following explanation has been proposed. Following the attacks, the Fed repeatedly cut the interest rate in an attempt to bolster the economy, causing the yield curve to steepen dramatically. Since most corporate issuers carry long-term debt at fixed interest rates, they moved aggressively to convert their debt from fixed to floating and reduce funding costs by entering into receiver swaps. A significant drop in the overall level of interest rates also caused a wave of mortgage refinancing activity, shortening the duration of mortgage portfolios. In response, MBS investors hedged with receiver swaps to extend the duration of their holdings. These two major sources of demand for receiver swaps caused swap rates to decline substantially. Over the same period, corporate yields were relatively little changed.

Trailing Correlation

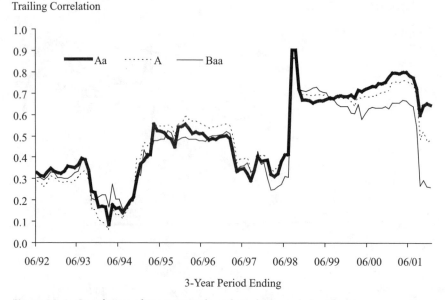

3-Year Period Ending

Figure 11-6. Correlation of Swap Spreads and Credit Spreads by Quality

In general, credit quality is the main factor setting lower-rated corporates apart from the agencies, which enjoy the highest credit rating. The funding costs are essentially tied to the level of credit spreads for the former but to the level of interest rates for the latter. The agencies also enjoy easier access to the swap market, where counterparty risk is an issue. As a result, they are in a better position to manage their funding costs using swaps than most corporates. In light of our discussion earlier in this section, the agency spreads are related to the swap spreads more closely than corporate spreads. Thus, market developments of several months following the September 2001 attacks confirmed that swaps retain their explanatory power for the agencies and MBS spreads, even as they decoupled from corporates.

Although it is hard to predict the future of the relationship between swap and corporate spreads, it seems reasonable to expect that when the yield curve flattens as the economy recovers, the widening of the credit-swap spread will likely stop and reverse. Once this occurs, the correlation between corporate and swap spreads will likely revert to approximately 70%. Stressful environments strain many market relationships, even those that are normally very close. Once the crises subside, however, the relationships often return to their previous levels. This should be the case for credit and swap spreads. In any case, the events of late 2001 show that the idiosyncratic risk embedded in Treasuries is not going away. Thus, swaps are likely to remain the instrument of choice for hedging market risk.

SWAPS AS A PERFORMANCE BENCHMARK

An investment-grade portfolio hedged with swaps retains exposure to the residual risk of specific sectors or securities contained in the portfolio. At the same time, most of the generic risk associated with default-free interest rates and investment-grade credit spreads is stripped out. Therefore, the net effect of hedging a portfolio with swaps is a relative value position betting that the portfolio will outperform the broad investment-grade universe, as represented by swaps.

Looking at hedging from this perspective suggests another natural application of swaps: as a total return benchmark for investment-grade securities. Total return indices based on swaps initially appeal to institutions whose funding costs closely track LIBOR, such as commercial banks. Money market investors holding very-short-duration instruments are also likely to be interested. On the other hand, managers of very-long-duration portfolios may also see swaps as a useful performance benchmark, given the shortage of longer-dated Treasuries.

Throughout this chapter, we have argued that swaps are closer in nature to investment-grade securities than are Treasuries. For this reason, swaps are a better hedge for the market risk of such securities, and they also have an advantage as a performance benchmark. For example, during the crisis of 1998 and the buybacks of 2000, any portfolio with a substantial credit component would have substantially underperformed Treasuries owing to spread widening. However, this relatively poor performance would not be a fair reflection of a manager's ability to pick the right securities from within the investment-grade universe. In order to assess performance of a portfolio properly, one has to compare it with a well-defined proxy of similar credit quality. Swaps are simply a good proxy for most investment-grade securities.

Since swaps are not funding instruments, we have to define what it means to invest in swaps and measure their performance. So far, we have treated swaps as a proxy for investment-grade securities in the sense that the fixed leg of a swap with the principal paid at maturity behaves as a generic fixed-coupon par bond. The next section addresses the issue of how one can effectively invest in such a bond and construct the relevant total return indices.

THE LEHMAN SWAP INDICES

We view each swap of a given maturity as a fixed-coupon par bond of the same maturity, and we construct a total return index for the swap. This is done for all swaps with maturities that are considered bellwethers, giving rise to bellwether swap indices. Very simply, these indices provide answers to questions of the form: What are historical total returns for 10-year swaps?

In addition to individual bellwether indices, we introduce the flagship Swap Index to represent the performance of swaps collectively as a market sector. The Lehman Swap Index tracks total returns of an equally weighted portfolio of thirty swaps with the following maturities: 1 year, 2 years, and annual increments thereafter out to 30 years.

An important benefit of creating bellwether swap indices is the ability to measure the performance of other credit sectors with respect to swaps. For a particular existing index, for example, the Agency Index, the corresponding mirror swap index tracks a portfolio of six specific bellwether swaps. The notional amounts of these swaps are chosen to match the key-rate durations of the original index. In other words, the mirror index is a portfolio of swaps that would be used to hedge market risk of the original index. The excess return of the index relative to swaps can then be calculated as the difference between the original index and its mirror swap index.

Bellwether Swap Indices

In the U.S. market, interest-rate swaps with certain maturities, such as 2, 3, 5, 10, 20, and 30 years, are considered bellwethers with easily observable market and liquid trading. For each of these swaps, we produce a time series of monthly total returns that would result from investing in a hypothetical generic bond with a coupon equal to the fixed rate of the swap and paying the principal at maturity.

The following are the only features that distinguish a receiver swap and a corresponding fixed-coupon bond:

- The swap is effectively a long position in a fixed-coupon bond, plus a short in the floating leg (with principal).

- At inception and on all quarterly payment dates, the floating leg is worth exactly par because it represents borrowing at the prevailing market rate.

- The swap is initiated at zero cost, whereas the bond must be worth par because the value of the fixed leg initially equals that of the floating leg.

As we explained earlier, a swap is economically equivalent to buying a generic fixed-coupon bond and funding it at LIBOR on a rolling basis. An investor wishing to buy the bond outright with available cash does not need the funding. To obtain an equivalent position using swaps, the investor could enter into a swap and use cash to offset the funding aspect of the swap by investing it at 3-month LIBOR. Over the first 3 months of the swap, this strategy can be summarized by the following equation:

Fixed Coupon Par Bond = Par Swap + 3-Month LIBOR Cash Investment.

At the end of the first quarterly period, the floating leg of the swap would again be worth par and pay interest at the LIBOR rate observed at the inception of the swap. That is exactly the case with our proposed cash investment at 3-month LIBOR as well. Thus, the cash investment offsets the floating leg of the swap perfectly over the first 3 months and every 3-month period thereafter. In light of this analysis, we define the total return of a swap to be the return on a portfolio consisting of the swap and cash investment at LIBOR. The total return of this portfolio is exactly the same as the total return of the fixed leg of the swap treated as a bond.

One must note that LIBOR published by the British Bankers Association (BBA) represents the average *offer* rate at which leading banks are willing to *lend* to each other. The average rate at which the same banks are willing to borrow money, that is, the bid side of the lending market, is lower and is known as the LIBID. Typically, a bank's bid rate is around 12 bp lower than its corresponding offered rate. To account for this factor, 1 bp/month or, equivalently, 12 bp/year, is subtracted from the total return of all swap indices.

The rules for calculating total returns on the bellwether swap indices are as follows:

- Securities. Swaps have the following maturities: 3 months, 6 months, 1 year, and annual maturity increments thereafter out to 30 years, for a total of thirty-two swaps.

- Rebalancing. In accordance with the current Lehman index policy of keeping the total return universe fixed during each calendar month, we assume that the proposed portfolio consisting of a par swap and a cash investment is created on the last business day of each month. The portfolio gets liquidated on the last business day of the following month and is replaced by a new trade of a par swap and a cash investment. On the unwind date (which defines the total return for the swap for that month) the swap is 1 month shorter than at inception.

- Coupon. New swaps are initiated on the last calendar day of the month at par. The coupon on the swap is the par coupon as obtained from the closing midmarket marks for swap rates from the most recent business day. Note that a consequence of this rebalancing approach is that the coupon, duration, and convexity of the swap would experience a small jump every month.

- Mark-to-Market. The total returns calculated on any day are based on the closing midmarket swap curve for that day.

- Settlement. For the purpose of calculating total returns, we assume that settlement on swaps is in 1 calendar day. This contrasts with standard settlement in the United States, which is in 2 business days. We use this convention to conform to other indices, allowing direct comparison of swap total returns with the other indices.

The Swap Index

We view swaps as a benchmark for the broad high-gráde bond market. With the objective of representing this market with a single variable, we introduce the Swap Index, tracking a portfolio of swaps with a wide range of maturities. Specifically, the portfolio is assumed to contain *equal notional values* of each of the bellwether swaps with maturities of 1 year, 2 years, and so forth up to 30 years in annual increments. As with individual bellwether swaps, we rebalance the portfolio at the end of each month. At that time, all swaps contained in the portfolio are unwound and a new portfolio of thirty current par swaps is composed and tracked over the next month.

Annual total returns for selected bellwether swaps, the main Swap Total Return Index, and a number of popular sector indices are shown in Figure 11-7.

The Mirror Swap Indices

The purpose of mirror indices is to track the performance of high-grade indices relative to swaps. We construct a separate mirror swap index for each of the following established indices:

1. Aggregate

2. Government/Credit

3. Credit

4. Agency

5. MBS

Each mirror index reflects the performance of a weighted portfolio of bellwether swaps with the following maturities: 6 months, 2, 5, 10, 20, and 30 years. The mechanics of investing in a particular swap in the portfolio is identical to the one described for bellwether swaps in the previous section. The appropriate notional amount of each swap is chosen to produce the same key-rate exposure profile for the mirror index portfolio as for the particular index with which it is

Figure 11-7. Total Returns of Bellwether Swaps, the Swap Total Return Index, and Major Lehman Sector Indices (percent)

	Bellwether Swaps				Swap Total Return Index	U.S. Treasuries	U.S. Agencies	MBS Fixed Rate	U.S. Credit
	2-Year	5-Year	10-Year	30-Year					
1993	6.1	10.9	14.7	18.1	15.0	10.7	10.5	6.8	12.2
1994	0.0	-4.2	-7.0	-8.3	-6.9	-3.4	-3.3	-1.6	-3.9
1995	12.4	18.8	25.8	37.9	28.4	18.4	18.3	16.8	22.2
1996	5.2	3.3	1.1	-1.7	0.6	2.7	3.3	5.4	3.3
1997	6.7	8.4	11.3	16.7	12.8	9.6	9.7	9.5	10.2
1998	7.4	9.7	12.3	14.5	12.3	10.0	8.8	7.0	8.6
1999	3.2	-1.1	-6.2	-12.8	-7.6	-2.6	-0.9	1.9	-2.0
2000	9.1	12.1	16.0	21.7	17.3	13.5	12.2	11.2	9.4
2001	10.0	10.2	9.0	8.0	8.6	6.7	8.3	8.2	10.4
Mean	6.7	7.6	8.6	10.5	9.0	7.3	7.4	7.2	7.8
Standard deviation	3.7	7.1	10.8	16.0	11.7	7.2	6.7	5.3	7.9
Duration as of Dec 2001	1.9	4.4	7.7	13.6	9.2	5.9	4.3	3.1	5.5

Figure 11-8. Excess Returns of Major Lehman Indices over Swaps (percent)
January–December 2001

	Lehman Index				
	Aggregate	Government/ Credit	Credit	Agency	MBS
January	−0.17	−0.16	0.82	−0.22	−0.19
February	−0.24	−0.21	−0.39	−0.14	−0.32
March	0.03	0.13	0.24	−0.01	−0.12
April	0.00	−0.05	0.34	−0.07	0.06
May	0.09	0.09	0.45	−0.13	0.10
June	0.24	0.37	0.43	0.14	0.01
July	−0.38	−0.41	−0.35	−0.34	−0.36
August	−0.16	−0.20	−0.17	−0.21	−0.11
September	−1.40	−1.85	−3.06	−0.44	−0.67
October	0.11	0.17	0.15	0.25	0.04
November	0.17	0.63	1.43	−0.05	−0.64
December	0.15	0.24	0.41	0.08	−0.03

compared. Figure 11-8 shows monthly excess returns of major Lehman indices over swaps for 2001. As we mentioned earlier, excess returns are calculated as the difference between an index and its respective mirror swap index.

Figure 11-9 gives an example of constructing the Agency-Mirror Swap Index at the end of October 2001. The six key-rate durations of the Agency Index are computed for the maturities listed earlier. The key-rate duration of a security is defined as the sensitivity of the value of the security to a change in the key maturity swap rate divided by the value of the security.[4] The key-rate duration of a portfolio, such as the Agency Index, is the weighted average of key-rate durations of individual securities in the index weighed by their respective market values.

---

4. Historically, key-rate durations of Lehman indices have been calculated with respect to the U.S. Treasury curve rather than the swap curve. To maintain consistency, we calculate sensitivities of the mirror portfolio to changes in Treasury yields subject to constant swap spreads. Since our analysis calls for using the swap curve rather than the Treasury curve, all key-rate durations should be calculated based on perturbations of swap rates. This would also make calculations used for construction of the mirror index portfolio straightforward. Though we intend to use the swap curve in the long term, the numerical difference between these two approaches is insignificant.

Figure 11-9. Construction of the Agency-Mirror Swap Index for November 2001

The Lehman Agency Index Market Value: $808,328,359

Par Maturity	Agency Index Key-Rate Durations	Swap Duration	Hedge Ratio (%)	Swap Notional ($)	Swap Total Return (%)
6 months	0.13	0.49	27.38	221,351,531	0.2184
2 years	0.72	1.94	37.18	300,575,619	−0.4757
5 years	1.12	4.54	24.79	200,344,688	−1.9893
10 years	1.15	8.05	14.33	115,861,235	−3.6965
20 years	0.74	12.47	5.97	48,232,292	−5.4380
30 years	0.61	14.69	4.15	33,568,472	−5.8717
Cash			−13.81	−111,605,477	0.1739
Index return	−1.79%				
Mirror return	−1.73%				

We next determine the hedge ratios for the six swaps in the mirror portfolio by dividing the key-rate durations by their respective swap durations. In order to ensure that the Agency Index and its mirror swap index have exactly the same sensitivity to a change in the key swap rate, the notional amount of each swap is taken to be the product of the Agency Index market value and the respective swap hedge ratio. Since the total investment in the mirror swap index must equal the market value of the Agency Index, any residual capital left over from swaps is invested in cash. In other words, the hedge ratios for the six swaps and cash add up to one. The amount invested in cash may be negative, as is the case in our example.

Similarly to other Lehman indices, mirror swap indices are rebalanced on the last business day of each month. At that time, all swaps in the mirror portfolio are unwound and the total return is calculated as the notional-weighted average of returns for six bellwether swaps. Next, the key-rate exposures of the index are recalculated, and a new mirror portfolio is assembled. Monthly rebalancing ensures that swaps in the mirror index are close to par and thus reflect the actively traded portion of the market. Since interest-rate risk profiles of the index and its mirror swap index are similar, it is reasonable to define the excess return to swaps as the difference between the original index and its mirror swap index. In the example shown in Figure 11-9, in November 2001 swaps outperformed agencies by 6 bp.

For a particular index, excess returns to Treasuries or swaps can also be interpreted as a tracking error of replicating the index with these respective instruments. The smaller the tracking error, the lower the basis risk of hedging the index using

Figure 11-10. Standard Deviations of Excess Returns to
Treasuries and Swaps

Index	Period[a]	Standard Deviation of Monthly Excess Returns to (bp)	
		Treasuries	Swaps
Aggregate	Precrisis	13	13
	Postcrisis	25	15
Agency	Precrisis	10	15
	Postcrisis	29	17
MBS	Precrisis	36	35
	Postcrisis	34	22
Credit	Precrisis	22	24
	Postcrisis	57	45

[a] The precrisis period covers 1992 through July 1998. The postcrisis period is January 1999 through August 2001.

Treasuries or swaps. Figure 11-10 shows average tracking errors—calculated as a standard deviation of monthly excess returns—that result from replicating several popular indices. The mirror portfolios of Treasuries and swaps used in this analysis were composed to match the overall duration of the index in question, rather than its key-rate durations. This enabled us to produce time series of excess returns going back to 1992.

As is evident from Figure 11-10, prior to the crisis of 1998, Treasuries tracked spread products better than swaps. This reflects the relative stability of spreads to Treasuries, which allowed investors to hedge their interest-rate risk with Treasuries and led the markets to quote prices in terms of spreads to Treasuries. In the aftermath of the crisis, spread products decoupled from Treasuries and were tracked better by swaps until September 2001. Over that period, investors largely switched from Treasuries to swaps as a hedging instrument of choice, and prices were increasingly quoted in terms of spreads to swaps. One should note, however, that though swaps exhibit a lower tracking error than Treasuries, the postcrisis numbers are substantially higher than the precrisis numbers for both of them.

REPLICATION OF SWAP INDICES

Once investors start actively using swap indices as a performance benchmark, they will need an easy and cost-efficient way of replicating their returns by trading real securities and derivative contracts. Our proposed strategy of investing the principal at 3-month LIBOR and entering into a receiver swap gives rise to several technical issues.

1. What are the transaction costs of doing swaps? The bid-ask spread on a standard interest-rate swap is about 0.5 bp running (i.e., per annum for the life of the swap). For a 10-year swap with duration of approximately 7 years, this cost amounts to 8 years × 0.5 bp/year = 4 bp up front to put the trade on and unwind it later. If swaps are initiated and unwound monthly as the index prescribes, the total cost of replicating the 10-year bellwether swap would be around 12 months × 4 bp/month = 48 bp/year, which is obviously extremely high. The cost of replicating the main Swap Index with average duration of 9½ years would be even higher, at 57 bp/year.

2. What are the alternatives to earning the LIBID? An investor seeking to earn the 3-month LIBOR rather than the lower LIBID could turn to the short-maturity asset-backed commercial paper (ABCP) market. The size of the market for high-rated ABCP in late 2001 was around $675 billion, and the yields ranged from around LIBOR − 8 bp for the most liquid issues up to LIBOR + 8 bp for the less liquid ones. The exact levels depend on the program, size, seasoning, and other factors. However, any commercial paper is subject to idiosyncratic risk of a particular issuer and, hence, possible spread widening and liquidity constraints. Investors who can take slightly more spread risk can get somewhat better returns in 1- to 2-year Aaa asset-backed floaters.

3. Are there cost-effective ways to closely replicate a swap index? It is possible to reduce transaction costs substantially by rebalancing the portfolio quarterly rather than monthly. In doing so, one would never have to unwind the cash investment, and the transaction costs on swaps would be reduced substantially. Each monthly roll amounts to replacing a swap with a very similar swap of a slightly longer maturity. Moreover, if an investor enters into a quarterly program roll with a dealer, the resulting transaction discount reduces costs to as little as 5 bp/year. Another possibility is to use swaps with payment dates on the floating side matching the IMM dates of the eurodollar futures. Such swaps have risk characteristics that are very similar to those of standard swaps, yet they can be hedged cheaply using the eurodollar futures at a cost of 0.5 bp per contract. Since contracts expire and get replaced only once a quarter, the total cost of hedging such swaps is only about 2 bp/year.

Whatever replication strategy one chooses introduces a small tracking error. For example, if the portfolio mimicking the 10-year bellwether swap is rebalanced quarterly rather than monthly, the resulting tracking error comes out to around 3 bp/month. Similar results can be expected in the case of replication with eurodollar futures.

CONCLUSION

The main purpose of the swap indices is to track performance of a key fixed-income market segment. Investors will also find the swap indices helpful in replicating the existing sector indices using swaps as well as in asset allocation decisions and relative value analysis. The swap indices provide an important new standard for fixed-income markets, enabling investors to look at various securities and credit sectors from a new perspective.

Over time, as swaps continue to grow in popularity with the investor community, the swap indices may be used as a performance benchmark for money managers focused on investment-grade securities. A number of low-cost strategies are available to investors seeking to replicate the swap indices with a small tracking error, and they can expect transaction costs to be as low as 5 bp annually.

Finally, in the near future we will be launching swap indices similar to the ones published for the U.S. dollar for three other major currencies: the euro, the British pound, and the Japanese yen.

12. Benchmarks for Asset-Swapped Portfolios

Many investors are permitted to take credit positions but are required to match their interest-rate exposure to their funding source (say, 3-month LIBOR). For example, some bank and insurance investment managers are required to manage their portfolio to a short-duration target for reasons of asset-liability management, but are free to exercise their credit skills by selecting assets likely to perform well. Moreover, leveraged investors (e.g., hedge funds) often concentrate on credit exposure but minimize interest-rate exposure by managing their portfolio duration to that of their 3-month LIBOR funding.

One way these managers can exercise credit selection skills while minimizing term-structure exposure is to buy credit product on an "asset swap" basis. Asset swaps are synthetic financial instruments that allow an investor to own a fixed-rate bond (and its credit exposure) and swap the fixed rate for floating-rate coupons. In essence, asset swaps give an investor the opportunity to take credit exposure with little term-structure risk. In the current environment of relatively wide credit spreads (and calls for tightening spreads) and low interest-rate levels (and calls for rising rates), asset swaps are poised to become more popular, as they permit an investor to take positions directly targeted to these market views.

A problem for asset swap investors is how to benchmark their performance so that it will potentially recognize their credit selection skill. Presently, there is no index of asset swap performance. Using 3-month LIBOR as a benchmark is inadequate because it reflects only a single credit (i.e., swap spreads) and does not represent the wide array of credit decisions available to the investment manager. To be able to highlight a manager's credit selection skill, the benchmark must represent a "neutral" credit portfolio so that a manager's deviations from neutral have the potential to outperform the benchmark.

Based on research first published by Lehman Brothers in 2002.

A benchmark for asset-swapped portfolios would offer a couple of advantages. First, the availability of such a benchmark might make investment managers more willing to engage in asset swaps, as their expertise could be quantified. Second, the publication of asset swap benchmarks and their performance might attract the attention of senior bank management and plan sponsors who might be more willing to give investment authority for such trades, as there is a systematic way to monitor performance.

We suggest a way to construct a performance benchmark for investors who buy spread product on an asset swap basis. The recent introduction of the Lehman swap indices offers an opportunity to construct a benchmark for asset swappers using information they now make available.[1] While the proposed benchmark does not always precisely replicate an asset-swapped portfolio, its close approximation and easy construction may entice managers to begin benchmarking the performance of their asset-swapped portfolios.

First, an asset swap is defined and its value and return are calculated. Second, we show how the bellwether swap indices can be used to approximate the performance of an asset swap position. Next, we suggest a way to construct a benchmark for an asset-swapped portfolio. Finally, we present performance data for various asset swap benchmarks using this methodology.

ASSET SWAPS

In a typical asset swap, the asset swap buyer buys a bond from the asset swap seller and pays a price of par irrespective of the current full price of the bond. Simultaneously, the asset swap buyer enters into a swap to pay the bond's fixed coupons in return for payments based on LIBOR plus the asset swap spread, A. The swap has the same maturity as the bond. The value of A (a constant) is set so that the net value of the swap plus the bond equals 100. To see this structure more clearly, let $L_j(t_i)$ be the value at time j of 3-month LIBOR set at time $i - 1$; C the coupon on the fixed-rate bond in the asset swap; P_0 the full price of the bond at time 0; A the asset swap spread; and $z_j(t_i)$ the discount factor from the par swap curve at time j for cash flow to be received at time i.

At the initiation of the asset swap, the buyer pays 100 in return for the bond plus an interest-rate swap wherein the buyer pays the bond's coupon in return for 3-month LIBOR plus the asset swap spread A. Consequently, the value of A is determined by the following equation (assuming, for simplicity, no differences in payment frequencies):

1. See Chapter 11.

$$100 = P_0 + \sum_{i=1\ldots N} [L_0(t_i) + A]z_0(t_i) - \sum_{i=1\ldots N} Cz_0(t_i).$$

If the full market price of the bond at the initiation of the asset swap is par, then the swap portion has no initial value. However, to the extent that the full price of the bond exceeds (is less than) par, the swap must have negative (positive) initial value. If the bond's full price is par ($P_0 = 100$) then the value of A represents the asset's spread over the LIBOR curve and is equivalent to a floating-rate note from the same issuer for the same term. However, if the price is greater than par, then A will be lower to reflect the fact that the asset swapper obtains the bond at a discounted price and pays for this discount with a lower value of A over the life of the swap. If the price of the bond is less than par, then A will be higher to compensate the buyer, over time, for paying an initial premium.

The asset swap buyer assumes full credit exposure to the bond. If the bond defaults, the asset swap buyer remains responsible for the fixed side of the interest-rate swap and suffers to the extent that any recovery is less than par.

Consider the investor buying a bond on an asset swap basis. The initial (time 0) value of the position is

$$V_{A,0} = P_0 + \sum_{i=1\ldots N} [L_0(t_i) + A - C]z_0(t_i) = 100. \tag{12-1}$$

Assuming that the relationship

$$[1 + L_j(t_i)/100] = [z_j(t_{i-1})/z_j(t_i)]$$

holds, we can rewrite $V_{A,0}$ as

$$V_{A,0} = P_0 + (A - C)\sum_{i=1\ldots N} z_0(t_i) + L_0(t_1)z_0(t_1) + 100[z_0(t_1) - z_0(t_N)].$$

The value of the position at time T is

$$V_{A,T} = P_T + (A - C)\sum_{i=1\ldots N} z_T(t_i) + L_0(t_1)z_T(t_1) + 100[z_T(t_1) - z_T(t_N)].$$

If we define the bond's price as $P_t = \sum_{i=1,N} Cv_t(t_i) + 100v_t(t_N)$, where $v_t(t_i)$ reflects the issuer's discount curve, which is a function of the benchmark (e.g., U.S. Treasury) discount curve and an issuer spread, then the change in the value of the asset swap position is given by

$$V_{A,T} - V_{A,0} = \left\{ \sum_{i=1\ldots N} C[\Delta v(t_i) - \Delta z(t_i)] + 100[\Delta v(t_N) - \Delta z(t_N)] \right\}$$
$$+ \left\{ \sum_{i=1\ldots N} A\Delta z(t_i) + L_0(t_1)\Delta z(t_1) + 100\Delta z(t_1) \right\}, \tag{12-2}$$

where $\Delta z(t_i) = z_T(t_i) - z_0(t_i)$, and so on.

The change in the value of the position can be broken into two components. The first (in curly brackets) reflects the exposure of the bond's cash flows to movements in the issuer discount curve, $\Delta v(t_i)$, relative to the LIBOR curve $\Delta z(t_i)$; the second (in curly brackets) reflects the return on a LIBOR-based floating-rate asset. Note that if the bond's spread tightens, holding everything else constant, then the position benefits, and vice versa. Note also that the return on the asset swap is not exposed directly to changes in the level of long-term interest rates, but only to relative movements between long issuer discount rates and long LIBOR discount rates. Overall, a bond bought on an asset swap basis gives the investor a position with relatively long-spread duration but relatively short-interest-rate duration.

USING BELLWETHER SWAP INDICES TO REPLICATE AN ASSET SWAP

Published Lehman index data can be used to approximate an asset swap position. Specifically, we replicate such a position by combining a position in the underlying fixed-rate bond with others in various bellwether swap indices. We show that such a combination closely replicates an asset swap and can be used to construct asset swap performance benchmarks.

A bellwether swap index is defined as the fixed-leg of a par interest-rate swap. Consequently, a bellwether par swap index of term N has the following value at time 0:

$$S_0 = \sum_{i=1\ldots N} SR_0(t_N)z_0(t_i) + 100z_0(t_N) = 0,$$

where $SR_j(t_N)$ is the par swap rate at time j for a par swap of term N.

Suppose an investor pays the full value, P_0, for a bond, goes short the bellwether swap index with the same maturity, and goes long the 3-month bellwether swap index.[2] The initial value, $V_{B+S,0}$, of this bond-plus-bellwether swap combination position is

$$V_{B+S,0} = P_0 + L_0(t_1)z_0(t_1) + 100z_0(t_1) - \sum_{i=1\ldots N} SR_0(t_N)z_0(t_i) \\ - 100z_0(t_N). \tag{12-3}$$

2. The bellwether swap indices are constructed to look like a fixed-rate bond by adding a 3-month LIBOR investment to offset the floating-rate leg of a par interest rate swap. Here, to transform the asset swap investor's position from fixed rate to floating, we have to subtract the 3-month LIBOR investment from the N-maturity bellwether swap index.

The difference between the initial value of the asset swap, $V_{A,0}$, and the bond-plus-bellwether swap combination, $V_{B+S,0}$, is given by

$$D_0 = V_{A,0} - V_{B+S,0} = \sum_{i=1\ldots N} [A - C + SR_0(t_N)] z_0(t_i).$$

In the special case that $P_0 = 100$, it can be shown that $D_0 = 0$. In general, however, the difference D_0 is relatively small. $A - C$ reflects the (negative) term LIBOR curve (adjusted for the difference between 100 and P_0) at the initiation of the asset swap. The term $SR_0(t_N)$ also reflects the term LIBOR curve at the initiation of the asset swap. Consequently, the difference between $(A - C)$ and $SR_0(t_N)$ is likely to be relatively small. At time T, the difference in value between the asset swap and the bond-plus-swap combination is

$$D_T = V_{A,T} - V_{B+S,T} = \sum_{i=1\ldots N} [A - C + SR_0(t_N)] z_T(t_i).$$

The change in the value difference is given by

$$\Delta D = \sum_{i=1\ldots N} [A - C + SR_0(t_N)] \Delta z(t_i), \qquad (12\text{-}4)$$

which is likely to remain small as it reflects the change in the present value of the difference between 100 and P_0 at the initiation of the asset swap. Consequently, we approximate an asset swap as a combination of the bond plus two swap indices, which is how we propose to construct performance benchmarks for asset-swapped portfolios.

CONSTRUCTION OF AN ASSET SWAP PERFORMANCE BENCHMARK

Because the asset swap buyer assumes the credit exposure of the bond he asset swaps, a performance benchmark must be able to recognize his credit selection skill. If the investor were not required to have term-structure exposure equal to that of, say, 3-month LIBOR, the asset swapper's natural benchmark would be a traditional index for the class of fixed-income spread product that he normally buys. Consequently, the index of the investor's normal asset class (e.g., the Lehman Credit Index) must be a component of the asset swap performance benchmark. However, the fixed-rate bond index alone would be inappropriate for the asset swapper who chooses to assume only the risk of 3-month LIBOR plus the spread over LIBOR. Ideally, his benchmark would be an index of all bonds in the index held on an asset-swapped basis. For example, if a manager can asset swap any bond in the Intermediate Lehman Credit Index, then a neutral position would be for the manager to asset swap all bonds in the index. The comparison of the

**Figure 12-1. Mirror Swap Index for the
Intermediate Credit Index**
December 2001

Bellwether Swap Index	Weight (%)
0.5-year	15
2-year	38
5-year	42
10-year	19
20-year	0
30-year	0
Cash	−15
	100

manager's actual asset-swapped portfolio with this benchmark would reflect his credit (and sector) selection skill.

Theoretically, we could construct a bond-plus-bellwether swap combination for each bond in the index and then weight each combination by the bond's market value in the index. However, to simplify the exercise, we make use of the Lehman Mirror Swap indices.

The Mirror Swap indices are portfolios of six bellwether swap indices plus cash.[3] The mirror portfolio weights are chosen so that the mirror swap index has the same key-rate duration profile as the index it is trying to mirror. For example, Figure 12-1 shows the weights for the component bellwether swap indices in the December 2001 Mirror Swap Index for the Intermediate Credit Index. Mirror swap indices can be constructed for any standard or custom fixed-rate index.

To construct a performance benchmark for asset swaps, we create a custom index combining the appropriate fixed-income index, a short position in the index's mirror swap index, and a long position in the 3-month bellwether swap index:

Asset swap performance benchmark = Fixed-rate bond index

− Index's mirror swap index

+ 3-month bellwether swap index.

For example, suppose the asset swapper can buy any corporate bond rated A or higher in the Lehman U.S. Credit Index on an asset-swapped basis. In this case, his asset swap performance benchmark is defined as

3. For details, refer to Chapter 11.

Figure 12-2. Various Asset Swap Performance Benchmarks, Monthly Performance
January 2001–December 2001

	Intermediate Credit				Intermediate Corporate Baa			
	Fixed-Rate Index Return (%)	− Mirror Swap Index Return (%)	+ 3-month Bellwether Swap (%)	= Synthetic Asset Swap Index Return (%)	Fixed-Rate Index Return (%)	− Mirror Swap Index Return (%)	+ 3-month Bellwether Swap (%)	= Synthetic Asset Swap Index Return (%)
Jan-01	2.12	1.95	0.68	0.85	2.35	1.97	0.68	1.06
Feb-01	0.98	1.08	0.48	0.39	1.06	1.10	0.48	0.44
Mar-01	0.83	0.68	0.45	0.59	0.78	0.66	0.45	0.57
Apr-01	−0.19	−0.30	0.48	0.59	−0.34	−0.37	0.48	0.51
May-01	0.76	0.50	0.42	0.69	0.75	0.47	0.42	0.70
Jun-01	0.44	0.09	0.36	0.72	0.52	0.06	0.36	0.82
Jul-01	2.34	2.52	0.35	0.17	2.57	2.67	0.35	0.25
Aug-01	1.14	1.23	0.35	0.27	1.13	1.29	0.35	0.19
Sep-01	0.62	2.84	0.44	−1.77	−0.37	2.96	0.44	−2.89
Oct-01	1.78	1.84	0.26	0.20	1.82	1.94	0.26	0.14
Nov-01	−0.77	−1.69	0.19	1.11	−1.12	−1.88	0.19	0.96
Dec-01	−0.64	−0.80	0.19	0.35	−0.78	−0.93	0.19	0.35

(continued)

Figure 12-2. (continued)

	High Yield Ba				ABS			
	Fixed-Rate Index Return (%)	− Mirror Swap Index Return (%)	+ 3-month Bellwether Swap (%)	= Synthetic Asset Swap Index Return (%)	Fixed-Rate Index Return (%)	− Mirror Swap Index Return (%)	+ 3-month Bellwether Swap (%)	= Synthetic Asset Swap Index Return (%)
Jan-01	3.83	1.97	0.68	2.54	1.66	1.80	0.68	0.54
Feb-01	1.52	1.15	0.48	0.85	0.98	0.95	0.48	0.52
Mar-01	0.39	0.59	0.45	0.25	0.64	0.73	0.45	0.35
Apr-01	1.02	-0.46	0.48	1.96	0.08	-0.01	0.48	0.56
May-01	1.78	0.47	0.42	1.73	0.68	0.56	0.42	0.54
Jun-01	-0.48	0.05	0.36	-0.18	0.32	0.20	0.36	0.48
Jul-01	1.69	2.76	0.35	-0.72	1.97	2.00	0.35	0.32
Aug-01	1.35	1.34	0.35	0.36	1.13	1.04	0.35	0.44
Sep-01	-4.95	2.92	0.44	-7.43	1.99	2.39	0.44	0.04
Oct-01	2.71	2.02	0.26	0.95	1.41	1.59	0.26	0.08
Nov-01	2.90	-1.96	0.19	5.05	-1.03	-1.19	0.19	0.36
Dec-01	-0.18	-0.94	0.19	0.96	-0.38	-0.43	0.19	0.24

| | CMBS | | | | MBS | | | |
	Fixed-Rate Index Return (%)	− Mirror Swap Index Return (%)	+ 3-month Bellwether Swap (%)	= Synthetic Asset Swap Index Return (%)	Fixed-Rate Index Return (%)	− Mirror Swap Index Return (%)	+ 3-month Bellwether Swap (%)	= Synthetic Asset Swap Index Return (%)
Jan-01	1.70	2.10	0.68	0.28	1.70	2.10	0.68	0.28
Feb-01	1.15	1.28	0.48	0.36	1.15	1.28	0.48	0.36
Mar-01	0.28	0.55	0.45	0.18	0.28	0.55	0.45	0.18
Apr-01	−0.26	−0.67	0.48	0.89	−0.26	−0.67	0.48	0.89
May-01	0.43	0.41	0.42	0.45	0.43	0.41	0.42	0.45
Jun-01	0.11	−0.04	0.36	0.51	0.11	−0.04	0.36	0.51
Jul-01	2.80	3.06	0.35	0.08	2.80	3.06	0.35	0.08
Aug-01	1.57	1.44	0.35	0.48	1.57	1.44	0.35	0.48
Sep-01	1.95	3.30	0.44	−0.91	1.95	3.30	0.44	−0.91
Oct-01	2.02	2.13	0.26	0.15	2.02	2.13	0.26	0.15
Nov-01	−1.76	−2.26	0.19	0.70	−1.76	−2.26	0.19	0.70
Dec-01	−0.79	−1.17	0.19	0.58	−0.38	−0.34	0.19	0.15

Credit Index (A-rated or better) − Mirror swap index for this index
+ 3-month bellwether swap index.

Instead of the 3-month bellwether swap index, the investor could substitute another short-term asset (e.g., 1-month LIBOR) as his long position. This might
be appropriate if the investor has a different funding requirement than 3-month
LIBOR.

Figure 12-2 presents monthly asset swap benchmark performance numbers
for various fixed-rate bond classes that are often bought on an asset-swapped
basis. These performance numbers highlight the credit exposure of asset swaps as
they performed poorly during the September 2001 credit spread widening. However, they rebounded substantially in November–December 2001 as credit spreads
tightened, even though interest rates rose substantially.

Asset swap performance indices can also be customized to suit a portfolio manager's investment guidelines. For example, if a manager can hold half the portfolio in A-rated intermediate corporates and the other half in Aaa-rated CMBS,
then the two asset swap performance indices can be weighted accordingly and
combined to produce an asset swap benchmark directly relevant for the manager.

CONCLUSION

A large number of investors have authority to take views on the spread markets
but must match a short-duration target (usually 3-month LIBOR). Unfortunately,
there is no performance benchmark available for these investors that would highlight their portfolio management skills. The lack of a performance benchmark
also hinders expansion of asset swap activity as supervisors and plan sponsors
have difficulty objectively evaluating the performance of their asset swap investment managers.

Investors who buy spread product on an asset-swapped basis can combine the
traditional fixed-income indices with the swap indices to produce an appropriate
asset swap performance benchmark.

13. Issuer-Capped and Downgrade-Tolerant U.S. Corporate Indices

. . . .

The years 2001 and 2002 witnessed a sharp increase in idiosyncratic credit risk—the so-called "credit torpedoes" that played havoc with investor portfolios. Unlike previous episodes of credit market turmoil, usually involving smaller and lower-quality names, this time the center of the credit storm included some large and high-quality issuers whose bonds were widely held. Not unexpectedly, the tremendous spread volatility was accompanied by serious liquidity problems.

For portfolio managers benchmarked against a credit index, the stressful credit markets forced a reconsideration of their approaches to risk management and portfolio construction. In addition, plan sponsors increased their involvement in the risk management of their plans' assets. Investors adopted a more disciplined approach to diversifying security-specific risk and also re-examined the design of their benchmark, the relevance of their investment policies, and the capabilities of their analytical tools. This chapter focuses on two topics of interest to portfolio managers in this context: credit benchmark design and investment strategy.

Excessive exposure to individual issuers is not an issue only for portfolio managers. Plan sponsors now scrutinize their benchmarks for high issuer concentrations. Sponsors ask: "Does it make sense for our organization to have a 2% exposure to name XYZ?" The high level of absolute issuer name risk has led to the demand for issuer-capped benchmarks. In the simplest case, a market value cap (e.g., 2%) can be imposed and every issuer capitalization is checked against this ceiling. The market value in excess of the cap is "shaved off" and distributed to all other issuers in the index in proportion to their market values. In some cases, the caps are chosen to be different for various credit ratings, reflecting the differences in issuer-specific risk between higher- and lower-credit qualities.

Based on research first published by Lehman Brothers in 2003.

Constructing an issuer-capped index requires two decisions. First, how low should the cap be? Second, how is the "excess" market value weight to be redistributed to other issuers in the index? The first part of this chapter examines the risk and return behavior of various issuer-capped indices using various cap levels and redistribution rules.

Another benchmark issue that both managers and sponsors face is whether the Corporate Index is replicable when a large number of issues are downgraded below investment grade (i.e., so-called "fallen angels"). The Corporate Index simply removes fallen angels at the end of the downgrade month, but a portfolio manager must find a willing buyer. This is particularly problematic for large fallen angels. Since the high yield market is much smaller than the investment-grade credit market, when a large investment-grade issue is downgraded investors must locate and entice high yield investors to buy a relatively very large holding in a new credit. The Corporate Index prices fallen angel issues at the end of their downgrade month at levels that reflect where bonds can be sold at the margin. However, this price is unlikely to reflect where all outstanding bonds of the issuer could be sold. In fact, the prices for fallen angel issues often continue to fall after the downgrade month as the high yield market is further encouraged to absorb the full supply of the fallen angel's debt.[1]

While some portfolio managers are required to sell fallen angels immediately at whatever price they can find, other investment-grade portfolio managers have discretion to hold the bonds (perhaps with increased monitoring requirements). As a practical matter, managers may have little choice but to hold on to fallen angels for at least several months until willing buyers can be located and the price stabilizes. Some investment-grade investors suspect that their inability to sell downgraded bonds immediately gives the Corporate Index an inherent performance advantage, a "survivorship bias," since the index can "sell" bonds immediately without suffering through the painful task of finding buyers. These investors are considering a custom index that is "downgrade-tolerant," allowing fallen angel issues to remain in the index for a fixed period of time after downgrade. The second part of this chapter investigates whether a downgrade-tolerant index might be a more replicable performance benchmark for investment managers. Of course, a key decision is how long a fallen angel issue should remain in the index.

---

1. Some high yield managers have adopted customized high yield indices that exclude fallen angels debt for some of the following reasons: the managers' lack of familiarity with new fallen angels inhibits discovery of an equilibrium price; the fallen angels are so large that they dominate the high yield indices; they have volatile prices which add to the volatility of the index.

ISSUER-CAPPED CREDIT BENCHMARKS

The Lehman indices are rules-based: issues are added to and removed from an index according to a published set of rules. In addition, in standard Lehman indices, individual securities contribute to index averages in proportion to their market value weight. Given the advancements in Lehman's index technology, investors can now request a wide array of made-to-order indices that follow a customized set of rules. In reaction to the recent credit market dynamics, many investors have examined adding two customized rules: imposing an issuer cap and having a more flexible quality requirement that allows downgraded bonds to remain in the index for a period of time. This chapter examines the implications of these suggested rules for the return performance of the Corporate Index.

Two important Lehman U.S. Corporate Index rules are the liquidity constraint and the quality requirement. The liquidity constraint states that a bond must have a minimum current par amount outstanding to be index eligible. For the Lehman U.S. Corporate Index the liquidity constraint is currently $250 million. There is no maximum issue size limit. In addition, there is no issuer-level minimum or maximum. In other words, the Lehman Corporate Index is uncapped. The liquidity constraint ensures that the index only contains issues that are large enough for investors to obtain. Obviously, it is not realistic for all investors to buy a given index issue. However, an index issue is typically large enough to be actively traded and, more importantly, to allow Lehman to obtain a market price for index calculations.

The absence of a minimum issuer-level constraint helps ensure that the Corporate Index is a well-diversified index of issuers. As of January 31, 2003, the U.S. Corporate Index contained 668 issuers, with over 500 of them having a weight of less than 0.2% in the index. This high level of diversification facilitates security selection (i.e., it is easy to overweight and underweight many different names), which is a potentially rewarding portfolio management activity.[2] Figure 13-1 shows a histogram of the issuer weights in the Corporate Index at the end of January 2003 and in the previous 2 years under the same liquidity constraint.

The absence of a minimum or maximum issuer-level constraint is also important, as it allows the index to adapt automatically to changes in the corporate marketplace. In other words, the composition of the Corporate Index reflects what is reasonably available in the marketplace and the performance of the index accurately captures the overall performance of the credit market.

The last few years have served as a painful reminder of the presence of idiosyncratic risk in the credit markets, as some of the largest issuers have been among

---

2. Chapter 1 examines the importance of security selection as an outperformance strategy.

Number of Issuers

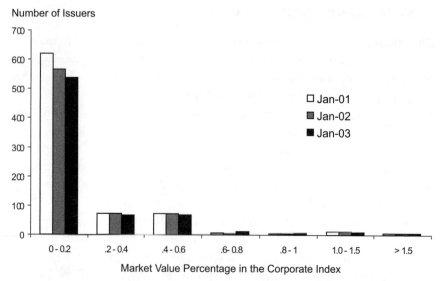

Market Value Percentage in the Corporate Index

Figure 13-1. Histogram of Issuer Market Value Weights in the Corporate Index
As of January 31, 2001, 2002, and 2003

the biggest relative underperformers. Figure 13-2 shows the cumulative excess returns (unannualized) of the top decile (by market value) of the Corporate Index,
the remaining 90% of the Corporate Index, and the Corporate Index itself.[3] It is
clear from the figure that the top decile was a severe relative underperformer during much of 2002.

Given the sharp underperformance of a few large issuers, some investors (e.g.,
plan sponsors and insurance companies) have raised questions about "uncapped
indices," that is, indices without a per-issuer maximum, as benchmarks. They are
asking whether it is appropriate from a risk management perspective for a plan's
assets to have, for example, a 2% exposure to a particular issuer due to the plan's
exposure to the benchmark. As a result, some investors are considering adopting
customized "issuer-capped" indices as benchmarks to limit any issuer's total return impact on the index. Although investors have often capped holdings in their
portfolios, the novel and strong interest in adopting capped benchmarks was a
direct response to the stressful credit markets of 2001 and 2002.

---

3. The top decile is identified as follows: The issuers are listed in market value order. We include in the top decile as many of the issuers from the top of the list as we can without exceeding
10% of the market value of the index. For example, if the top five issuers have a combined market value of 9.5% of the index market value, but the top six have a combined market value of
10.4%, then the top decile consists of the top five issuers. All remaining issuers belong to the
bottom 90%. Over this period, the top decile contained an average of four issuers.

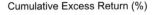

Cumulative Excess Return (%)

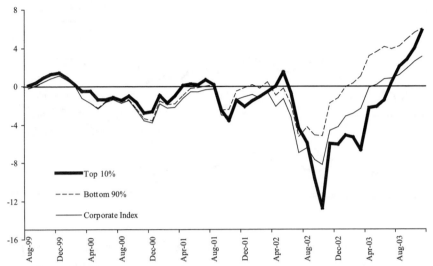

Figure 13-2. Cumulative Excess Returns
Top 10% and Bottom 90% by Percentage of Market Value Composition of Corporate
Index, August 1999–November 2003

Next, we examine the risk and return behavior of issuer-capped indices. Do
they accomplish their objective of having lower volatility and better information
ratios? To answer these questions we examine the performance of various issuer-
capped indices over the past several years.

Issuer Concentration in the Lehman U.S. Corporate Index

What is the degree of issuer concentration in the U.S. Corporate Index? Figure
13-3 shows that there are only a handful of issuers in the index that have relatively
large market value weights. As of the end of November 2003, the four largest
issuers each had a market value weight that exceeded 2% of the index's market
value. The largest issuer was Ford with a weight of 3.46%. Ford's weight exceeded
4% in early 2001 and then declined as the issuer increased its reliance on the asset-
backed market for financing in response to the difficult credit markets.[4]

4. The issuer concentration charts begin in August 1999, when the Lehman index database
adopted tickers to identify issuers. For large issuers, the market value percentage weights likely
jumped upward in July 1999 when the liquidity constraint increased from $100 million to
$150 million. Of course, large issuers may also lose issues from the index owing to the increased
liquidity constraint. However, the larger issuers typically have issue sizes that easily exceed the

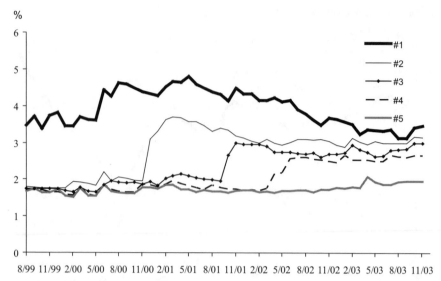

Figure 13-3. Percentage of Corporate Index Market Value Represented by the Top Five Issuers
August 1999–November 2003

Figure 13-4 presents the market value weights for the sixth through tenth largest issuers. As of the end of November 2003, the sixth through tenth largest issuers, BAC, VZ, MWD, DCX, and GS all had market value weights of approximately 1.5%.

Figure 13-5 shows that as of November 2003 the market value weight of the top ten issuers as a group was approximately 21%, near the high of its range over the previous 3.5 years. Figure 13-5 also shows that the weight of the ten largest issuers increased sharply at the end of 2000, owing primarily to the acquisition of Associates by Citicorp.

Constructing Issuer-Capped Indices

An issuer-capped benchmark imposes a maximum on the market value weight that an issuer can have in the index. For example, it might impose a requirement that an issuer's weight not exceed 1% of the index. The motivation for capping is to limit the index's exposure to the idiosyncratic risk of the issuer. Given the large

---

constraint. Interestingly, while most discussions regarding raising the liquidity constraint typically revolve around the impact of a large number of smaller issues excluded from the index, less attention is paid to the potential impact on issuer concentration.

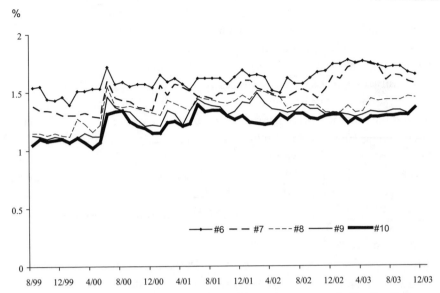

Figure 13-4. Percentage of Corporate Index Market Value Represented by the Sixth through the Tenth Largest Issuers

August 1999–November 2003

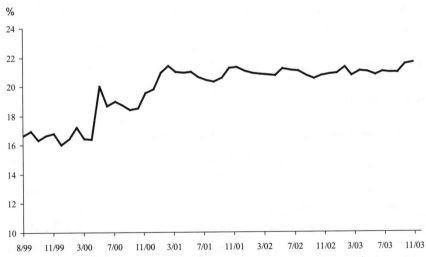

Figure 13-5. Percentage of Market Value Weighting of Top Ten Issuers as a Group in the Corporate Index

August 1999–November 2003

negative excess returns experienced by large issuers in recent years, an issuer-capped benchmark presumably would have higher excess returns and lower excess return volatility than an uncapped index. This section describes what the behavior of issuer-capped indices would have been in recent years.

Constructing an issuer-capped index requires two decisions. First, how low should the cap be? The answer depends on setting a cap level that is low enough to limit the impact of idiosyncratic risk on the index, but not so low that many issues will be capped. Keep in mind that limiting the size of a large issuer in the index is equivalent to boosting the size of all the others so that the large issuer becomes a smaller percentage of the whole. If too many large issuers are capped, the weights of very small issuers increase disproportionately to their availability in the marketplace, making the index less investable. To be practical, this section analyzes issuer cap levels that are greater than or equal to 1%.

An issuer cap works as follows. Suppose the cap level is set at 3% and the market value of a single issuer exceeds 3% by 0.5%. The issuer's market value is reduced 0.5% by shaving off a sufficient pro rata share from each of the issuer's issues in the index so that the shavings add up to 0.5% of the Corporate Index. In other words, if the issuer had two issues outstanding, one with a market value weight of 2% and the other 1.5%, then the weight of the first issue would be reduced approximately 0.29% to 1.71% and the second by 0.21% to 1.29%. How is the 0.5% excess market value reassigned to the other issues in the Corporate Index? To answer this question, we have to make a second decision on what *redistribution rule* to use.

We analyze two redistribution rules: "index-wide" redistribution and "quality-sector-neutral" redistribution. Index-wide redistribution takes any excess market value and distributes it across all issues of noncapped issuers in proportion to their weights in the index. In the preceding example, the large issuer under consideration originally constituted 3.5% of the index. Suppose that all the other issuers, which together constitute 96.5% of the index, do not need to be capped, and the 0.5% we shaved off the large issuer must therefore be divided among all of them. If one of the other issuers constitutes 2% of the index, then it will receive 0.0104% = 0.5% × 2% ÷ 96.5% of the weight of the index as a result of the redistribution of the large issuer's weight.

The quality-sector-neutral redistribution rule works as follows. The entire index is divided into sector-quality buckets. When a large issuer is capped, we look at each of the issuer's bonds to determine which bucket it belongs in. The weight shaved off that bond is redistributed among bonds in the same bucket issued by other issuers. In the previous example, one of the large issuer's bonds, which we call issue A, was reduced by 28.6 bp. Suppose that no other issuers need to be capped and that the sum of the weights of all bonds in the same bucket as A but from other issuers is 15%. Suppose, too, that issue B is in the same bucket as A, but from a different issuer and constitutes 0.5% of the index. Then the amount of index weight added to B as a result of the redistribution is 0.95 bp = 28.6 bp × 0.5% ÷ 15%. This redistribution rule has the effect of preserving the market value weights of each quality-sector combination in the Corporate Index. As we show next, both the choice of the cap level and the redistribution rule have important implications for the relative performance of an issuer-capped index vs. the uncapped index.[5]

Either redistribution rule may require several iterations until all issuers satisfy the cap level. In the first iteration, all issuers exceeding the cap are identified and their excess market value is then redistributed, depending on the redistribution rule, across all remaining issues. As a result of the redistribution, issuers that were below the cap before may be above the cap now, requiring another round of redistributions. The capping procedure is applied repetitively until all issuers satisfy the issuer cap.

Risk and Return Performance of Issuer-Capped Indices

We first examine the impact of the cap level assuming we follow the index-wide redistribution rule. Figure 13-6 shows the impact of various issuer cap levels, beginning at 1%, on the annualized excess return performance of the Corporate Index for the period from August 1999 through December 2002. These dates cover a period of intense idiosyncratic risk in the credit markets, especially for large issuers. If issuer caps were to influence the excess returns of the Corporate Index, their impact would likely appear during this period. Figure 13-6 shows that the impact on the average excess return is negligible for issuer cap levels down to approximately 1.5%, less than 3 bp/year. However, once the issuer cap is reduced below 1.5%, the average excess return increases more rapidly. For an issuer cap of 1.0%, the average annual excess return is approximately 7 bp higher (–0.98 vs. –1.05%). Nevertheless, this result is surprising and very disappointing. Given the very negative excess returns of large issuers, it is remarkable that a 1% issuer cap only improves annualized excess returns by 7 bp/year.

Another motivation for issuer caps is to reduce the excess return volatility of the benchmark. By removing the potential impact of idiosyncratic events affecting large issuers, an issuer-capped index should be expected to have less excess return

---

5. While an issuer-capped index can use a variety of redistribution rules (e.g., keep subsector weights unchanged) it is important to remember that the redistribution rule must be such that there are sufficient small issues remaining in each peer group so that the excess weight can be fully redistributed.

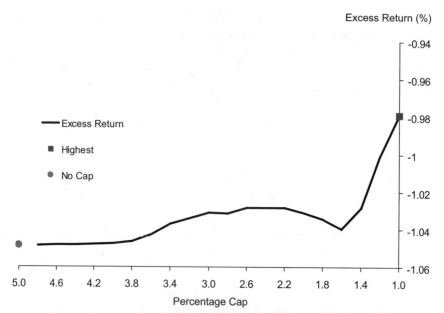

Figure 13-6. Average Excess Return of the Corporate Index as a Function of Cap
August 1999–December 2002, Annualized, Index-Wide Redistribution of Excess Weight

volatility. Figure 13-7 shows the excess return volatility of the Corporate Index for various issuer cap levels using index-wide redistribution: an issuer cap level of 1% reduces excess return volatility by only 4 bp compared to the uncapped Corporate Index. Again, this result is both surprising and disappointing. Issuer-capped indices, even at very reasonable cap levels, do not seem to provide much improvement in risk and return performance compared to uncapped indices.

Why do we observe only a very modest improvement in the risk and return characteristics of the issuer-capped index vs. the uncapped Corporate Index? As discussed at the outset, issuer-capped benchmarks require a decision on how to redistribute the excess market value weight. The results in Figures 13-6 and 13-7 are based on the redistribution rule that spreads the excess equally across all un-capped issues in the index. However, as we will see, such a rule can produce an index that has very different, and probably unintentional, sector and quality exposures than the uncapped index. For example, if the large issuers in the uncapped index are A-rated financials, then a 1% issuer cap using the index-wide redistri-bution rule may unintentionally produce a capped index having a higher weighting to Baa-rated industrials than the uncapped Corporate Index. In fact, this is ex-actly what happens. For the period from August 1999 through December 2002, we calculated the average sector and quality exposures of the 1% issuer-capped index

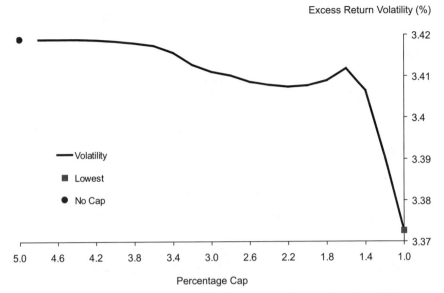

Figure 13-7. Excess Return Volatility of the Corporate Index as a Function of Cap
August 1999–December 2002, Annualized, Index-Wide Redistribution of Excess Weight

(with index-wide redistribution) and the Corporate Index. Figure 13-8 shows that the 1% issuer-capped index had a higher weighting in Baa-rated and industrial issues than the Corporate Index and a significant underweight to financials.

During the historical period under consideration, Baa-rated and industrial issues generally had lower excess returns and higher excess return volatility while financials outperformed other sectors.[6] Consequently, a 1% issuer-capped (with index-wide redistribution) index may not show much improvement vs. the

6. Average annualized excess returns and annualized excess return volatility for various sectors for the period August 1999 through December 2002 were:

Quality/Sector	Average Excess Return (%)	Excess Return Volatility (%)
Industrial	−1.35	3.97
Utility	−4.31	6.88
Financial	0.38	2.61
Aaa-rated	0.09	1.67
Aa-rated	0.80	1.97
A-rated	−0.62	3.14
Baa-rated	−2.55	4.94
Corporate Index	−1.05	3.42

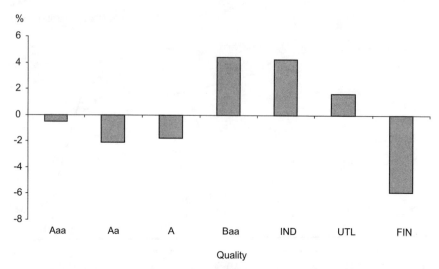

Figure 13-8. Average Sector and Quality Exposures of 1%-Capped Index vs. Corporate Index

August 1999–December 2002, Index-Wide Redistribution of Excess Weight

Corporate Index, as the increased exposure to Baa-rated and industrial issues off-sets much of the reduction in idiosyncratic risk that is due to the cap. The lesson learned here is that the redistribution rule can undo much of the benefit of an is-suer cap. Investors who seek issuer caps most likely do not wish their issuer-capped indices to have different quality and sector weightings from the Corporate Index. Investors want to reduce the impact of large issuers but not necessarily change their market value exposures to the various quality and sector buckets in the credit marketplace.

As noted earlier, the quality-sector-neutral redistribution rule avoids introduc-ing any unintended quality-sector biases as a result of the issuer-capping process. Figure 13-9 shows that using a quality-sector redistribution rule significantly improves the average excess return of the issuer-capped index relative to the uncapped index. Specifically, the average excess return of the 1% issuer-capped index (quality-sector neutral) is approximately 24 bp better than the uncapped Cor-porate Index.

The benefits of issuer-capped indices using the quality-sector-neutral redistribu-tion rule are also apparent in terms of excess return volatility (see Figure 13-10). At a 1% cap, the annualized excess return volatility of the issuer-capped index is approximately 3.24%, compared to 3.42% for the Corporate Index.

We also examined the performance of another sector-quality-neutral variant in which we impose lower caps on lower-quality issuers than on higher-quality ones.

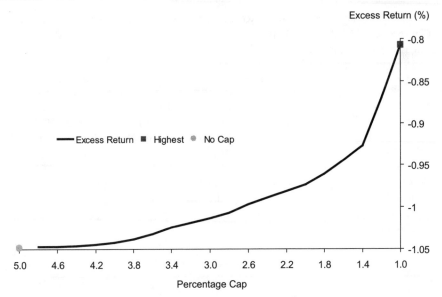

Figure 13-9. Average Excess Return as a Function of Cap

August 1999–December 2002, Annualized, Quality-Sector-Neutral Redistribution

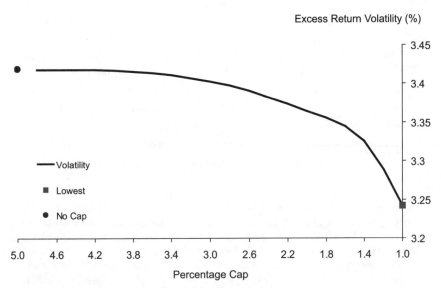

Figure 13-10. Excess Return Volatility as a Function of Cap

August 1999–December 2002, Annualized, Quality-Sector-Neutral Redistribution

Figure 13-11. Annualized Average Excess Return and Volatility as a Function of Issuer Cap Level and Redistribution Rule
August 1999–December 2002

	Difference from Corporate Index			
	Average Excess Return (%)	Excess Return Volatility (%)	Average Excess Return (bp)	Excess Return Volatility (bp)
Corporate Index	−1.05	3.42	–	–
1% issuer cap (index-wide)	−0.98	3.37	7	−5
1% issuer cap (sector-quality neutral)	−0.81	3.24	24	−18
2.5%/1%/0.5% issuer-caps (sector-quality-neutral) (cap varies with quality)	−0.89	3.20	16	−22

Adjusting the issuer cap level according to the quality of the issuer is in keeping with the principle that lower-quality issuers are subject to greater idiosyncratic risk than those of higher quality and therefore require greater diversification.[7] Specifically, we examined a sector-quality-neutral capping of the Corporate Index that imposes a 2.5% cap on Aaa-Aa issuers, a 1% cap on single-A issuers, and a 0.5% cap on Baa issuers.[8] Over the period August 1999 to December 2002, this index had an average annualized excess return 15 bp better than that of the unconstrained index and an annualized volatility of excess returns 22 bp lower than that of the unconstrained index. Figure 13-11 provides a summary of the results.

To further examine the potential benefits of issuer capping and different methods of redistribution, we looked at what would happen to the Corporate Index and its issuer-capped variants in the event of default by a major issuer. To simulate such an event, we examined these indices during the period from August 1999 until Enron's bankruptcy in November 2001 and "imagined" what the returns of these indices would have been during this time if the amounts outstand-

---

7. For an analysis on how the idiosyncratic risk varies with quality, see Chapter 14.

8. Another difference between this index and the 1% sector-quality-neutral index is related to the handling of issuers that have issues in more than one sector-quality bucket. The 1% index considers all the issuer's bonds, regardless of which buckets they are in, when deciding whether the issuer exceeds the cap or not. In contrast, this index effectively treats the issuer's bonds in two different buckets as belonging to two separate issuers, and applies the appropriate caps separately to the issuer's bonds in each bucket.

Figure 13-12. Performance of Corporate Index with and without 1% Caps

With Enron Amounts Outstanding Multiplied by 10, August 1999–November 2001

		1% Cap	
	Corporate Index	Index-Wide	Sector-Quality Neutral
Average excess return (annualized) (%)	−1.39	−1.12	−0.99
Excess return volatility (annualized) (%)	2.63	2.71	2.65

ing of all of Enron's bonds had been ten times larger than they were. This would have given Enron up to a 3.76% market value weight in the Corporate Index in some months, making Enron one of the largest issuers but still not the largest. The results, shown in Figure 13-12, indicate that imposing a 1% cap on the Corporate Index would have boosted annualized average excess return significantly at the expense of a slight increase in excess return volatility and that sector-quality-neutral redistribution would have been somewhat better than index-wide redistribution in this regard.

"Sloshing"

While issuer-capped indices do reduce the market value weight of the largest issuers, the flip-side of such indices is that the market value weight of the smaller issuers is increased, often dramatically so. This shift of market value weight from the large issuers to the small ones, which we call "sloshing," may make it difficult for the portfolio manager to replicate the index. Recall that an advantage of "uncapped" indices is that the index reflects what is available in the marketplace. However, a capped index increases the market value weight of small issuers in the index above their market value weight in the marketplace. Consequently, a pertinent question arises: Is there enough supply in the marketplace to enable an investor to replicate the issuer-capped index?

To give a sense of the amount of sloshing that an issuer-capped benchmark can produce we first calculate, as of May 2003, how much market value is moved among issues in a 1% capped index that uses a quality-sector-neutral redistribution rule. For each sector bucket we find all of the issues that increased in market value as a result of the capping and add up the dollar amounts of all the increases. This gives us a dollar amount of sloshing per bucket. (Equivalently, we could find

Figure 13-13. Sloshing

As a Percentage of Bucket Market Value, Based on May 2003 Corporate
Index Composition and a 1% Issuer-Capped Index with Quality-Sector-
Neutral Redistribution

	Industrial (%)	Utilities (%)	Finance (%)
Aa+	7.0	0.0	32.4
A	5.4	0.0	22.0
Baa	4.1	0.0	0.0

all the issues that decreased in market value and add up the dollar amounts of
their decreases.) To express sloshing as a percentage, we take the dollar amount
of sloshing and divide by the market value of the bucket. These results are presented in Figure 13-13. Note that some buckets experience a large amount of
sloshing. For example, the Aa+-FIN sector has over 32% of its market value re-
allocated across different issues within the bucket. On the other hand, none of the
utilities buckets experiences any sloshing.

The Aa+-FIN bucket experiences a great deal of sloshing because it contains
some large issuers that greatly exceed the 1% cap. In a further illustration of the
degree of sloshing in the Aa+-FIN bucket, Figure 13-14 presents the "scale factors" by which issuers in the bucket are adjusted as a result of the 1% cap with
quality-sector-neutral redistribution. The scale factor is the amount by which
an issuer's initial market value (across all of its issues in the bucket) is multiplied
to arrive at its market value in the capped index. For example, the market value
of Northern Trust in the Aa+-FIN bucket in the uncapped index is $166 million.
As a result of the 1% cap, a large amount of market value from other, larger,
issuers must be redistributed to Northern Trust. In fact, the market value weight
of Northern Trust in the capped index is approximately five times its weight in
the uncapped index ($834 million vs. $166 million). Some investors may have difficulty locating bonds for a relatively small issuer whose market value weight in
the benchmark has been artificially raised owing to issuer capping. Figure 13-14
highlights one of the potential risks of issuer-capped indices—the index may become uninvestable.

Note that many issuers in the Aa+-FIN bucket have the same scale factor of
5.03. These are relatively small issuers with few, if any, issues in other buckets
(e.g., A-FIN bucket). The market value weight for all these issuers is scaled up by
the same factor to preserve their relative weights. However, some other issuers
have different scale factors. Those issuers with scale factors less than 1.0 were

Figure 13-14. Sloshing–Scale Factors

1% Issuer-Capped Index with Quality-Sector-Neutral Redistribution, May 2003

Issuer	Uncapped Market Value ($ thousand)	1% Capped Market Value ($ thousand)	Scale Factor
American General Financial Corporation	2,092,880	2,494,155	1.19
American Express Company	262,879	1,321,529	5.03
Bank of America Corporation	32,138,680	18,359,337	0.57
Bank of New York	1,051,487	5,285,975	5.03
Barclays Bank PLC	495,595	2,491,429	5.03
BBV International Finance (Cayman)	392,256	1,971,925	5.03
Banque Paribas NY	1,549,277	7,788,437	5.03
CalEnergy Company Inc.	376,041	1,486,020	3.95
CIBC Capital Funding LP	381,604	1,918,380	5.03
Citigroup Inc.	48,567,674	18,359,336	0.38
Credit Suisse USA Inc.	15,546,949	18,359,336	1.18
Fifth Third Bancorp	520,515	2,616,701	5.03
General Electric Capital	48,738,154	16,018,374	0.33
Goldman Sachs Group	20,802,031	18,359,335	0.88
Household Finance	1,745,528	889,884	0.51
ING Group NV	1,728,152	8,687,670	5.03
JP Morgan Chase	11,767,761	10,967,533	0.93
Marshall & Ilsley Bank	313,630	1,576,662	5.03
MBIA Inc	357,659	1,798,005	5.03
Mercantile Safe Deposit & Trust	224,234	1,127,257	5.03
Merrill Lynch & Company	15,357,059	18,359,335	1.20
Morgan Stanley Dean Witter	26,422,956	18,359,335	0.69
National City Corporation	1,034,855	4,158,743	4.02
Natwest PLC	3,044,474	15,305,005	5.03
Northern Trust	165,953	834,269	5.03
Pitney Bowes Inc.	581,959	2,925,589	5.03
Santander Central Hispano	214,401	835,657	3.90
State Street Corporation	174,681	878,147	5.03
Suntrust Bank–Atlanta	2,936,688	11,608,971	3.95
Svenska Handelsbanken	442,156	2,222,779	5.03
Toyota Motor Credit	1,554,789	7,816,149	5.03
Union Bank Switzerland–NY	4,598,877	18,359,336	3.99
US Bank	8,706,905	14,296,938	1.64
Wachovia Corporation	10,521,786	10,635,846	1.01
Wells Fargo	22,814,509	18,359,336	0.80

subject to the 1% cap owing to their initial market value weight in the index. For example, Wells Fargo has a scale factor of 0.80 as its uncapped market value of $22,814,509,000 fell to $18,359,336,300 in the 1% capped index.

Other issuers have scale factors of 1.00–5.03, having had initial market value weights less than 1%. However, as a result of redistribution, their weights reached 1% and they became ineligible for any further redistribution. Hence, their scale factors were less than the maximum of 5.03. Finally, note that the market values of some issuers in the bucket are reduced by the capping process to an amount well below the cap limit ($18,359,336,300), for example, Bank One with an un-capped market value of $11,767,761 and a 1% capped market value of $10,967,533. Why was it necessary to reduce its market value to a level below the 1% limit? (Moreover, in the case of Bank One, which was below the 1% limit to begin with, why was it necessary to lower its market value at all?) The answer is that the cap operates at the index level, not the bucket level. Bank One has index issues in other buckets that cause its overall weight in the uncapped index to exceed 1%. Consequently, its weight in every bucket, including the Aa+-FIN bucket, must be reduced. Its overall weight in the capped index is 1%, or $18,359,336,300, but only a portion of that amount is in the Aa+-FIN bucket.

In summary, the Lehman Corporate Index is composed of issues that conform to certain rules, of which the two most important are the liquidity constraint and the quality requirement. However, credit events over the last few years have caused investors to re-evaluate the Corporate Index rules. In particular, they have sought to impose a cap on the maximum weight that any one issuer may have in the Corporate Index.

In this section, we have examined the risk and return behavior of indices with issuer caps. We saw that imposing a 1% cap on the market value weight that an issuer may have in the Corporate Index would have improved the index's average excess return and excess return volatility over the past few years. It would also have improved average excess returns, at the expense of a slight increase in excess return volatility, in the event of a default by a major issuer (such as Enron). The magnitude of these improvements, however, depends on the rules used for redistributing index weight from large issuers to small ones. The index-wide redistribution rule tends to lessen the benefits of capping by introducing unfavorable sector-quality exposures relative to the uncapped index. The sector-quality-neutral redistribution rule, which preserves the sector and quality weights of the index, achieves much better results.

The next section discusses the second key index rule: the quality requirement. What would be the risk and performance effect on the Corporate Index if the quality requirement were relaxed to allow downgraded bonds to remain in the index for a period of time subsequent to downgrade?

DOWNGRADE-TOLERANT CREDIT BENCHMARKS

Compounding the poor performance of large issuers in the index has been the recent downgrading of some large issuers below investment grade. This downgrade event invokes another key index rule, the quality requirement, which states that an issue must be rated investment grade to be index eligible. If at some point during the month an index issue is subsequently rated below investment grade, it is removed from the index at the end of that month. The quality requirement ensures that the index maintains a certain minimum quality level over time. Consistency in index quality is very important for plan sponsors who make strategic asset allocation decisions and select indices as their benchmarks.

When a large issuer is dropped from the index owing to downgrade, a portfolio manager must sell the issuer's bonds at the end of the month to be neutral to the index with respect to the issuer. In practice, some managers feel that they have no practical alternative but to hold a downgraded issue for several months after the downgrade as they try to find buyers in the smaller high yield market.

Bonds downgraded below investment grade are often referred to as "fallen angels." For purposes of this study we define a fallen angel as a bond in the Corporate Index downgraded below investment grade and removed from the index. We consider the fallen angel to be outstanding until it matures, is called, goes into default, or is bought back by the issuer.

Figure 13-15 shows the number and total market value as a percentage of the Corporate Index market value of all the fallen angel issues that dropped out of the Corporate Index after January 1990 and were still outstanding as of the end of the month in question. As of the end of September 2003, there were 618 such issues outstanding, and their combined market value was 10.1% of the market value of the Corporate Index on that date.

When a fallen angel is dropped from the Corporate Index at the end of its downgrade month, the index prices it at levels that reflect where it can be sold at the margin. However, this price is unlikely to reflect where all outstanding bonds of the downgraded issuer can be sold. In fact, the prices for fallen angel issues often continue to fall after the downgrade month as the high yield market needs an incentive to absorb the full supply of the fallen angel's debt.[9]

9. Some high yield managers have adopted customized high yield indices that exclude fallen angels for some period of time following downgrade. They worry that immediately adding fallen angels to the High Yield Index would cause the index to perform poorly. The concern is that fallen angels will continue to decline in price following downgrade owing to both a lack of familiarity with new fallen angels and because some fallen angels are very large relative to the high yield market. Some managers also seek to exclude new fallen angels because they feel that such

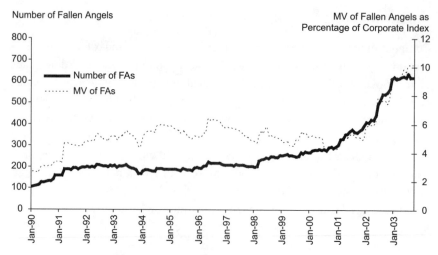

Figure 13-15. Total Number and Market Value of Fallen Angel Issues Outstanding
January 1990–September 2003

Some investment-grade investors suspect that their inability to sell down-graded bonds immediately gives the Corporate Index an inherent performance advantage, a "survivorship bias," since the index "sells" the bonds immediately without suffering through the painful task of finding buyers. These investors are considering a custom index that is "downgrade-tolerant," allowing fallen angel issues to remain in the index for a fixed period of time after downgrade. A downgrade-tolerant index might be a more replicable performance benchmark for investment managers. Of course, a key decision is how long a fallen angel issue should remain in such an index.

Constructing a Downgrade-Tolerant Corporate Index

To measure the performance of a downgrade-tolerant corporate index we first construct an index consisting only of fallen angels (market value weighted). A key parameter of the fallen angel index is the "tolerance period"—the period of time that a fallen angel is permitted to remain in the index. For example, a fallen angel index with a 1-month tolerance period contains only issues that left the Corporate Index owing to downgrade at the prior month end. Consequently, the monthly returns series for such an index is the average monthly return for a portfolio of fallen angels during the first month after their downgrade month.

---

bonds have volatile prices for a period of time after downgrade. Immediately adding such bonds to a high yield index would increase the volatility of the index.

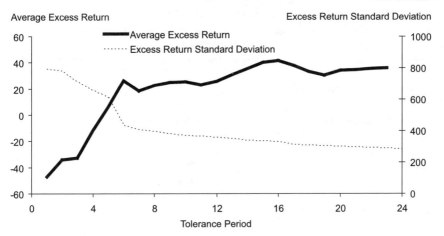

Figure 13-16. Performance of Fallen Angel Indices as a Function of the Tolerance Period
January 1990–September 2003

We then examine tolerance periods of 2 months, 3 months, and so on out to 24 months. For example, a fallen angel index with a 6-month tolerance period contains issues that were dropped from the Corporate Index owing to downgrade in any of the 6 months prior to the current month. In other words, the June 2002 monthly return for the 6-month-tolerant fallen angels index is the average June 2002 return for issues that were downgraded during the months of December 2001 through May 2002. Another way of looking at the fallen angel index is that an issue downgraded during the month of January 2002 will be included in the 6-month-tolerant fallen angel index beginning in February 2002 through July 2002.

Finally, we define a fallen angel index with an "unconstrained" tolerance period, which allows fallen angels to remain in the index until they are no longer outstanding. The monthly returns series for such an index is the average return for a portfolio of all outstanding fallen angels.

Figure 13-16 presents the average monthly excess returns for the fallen angel indices of various tolerance periods and shows that an index of fallen angels that were downgraded in the prior month (i.e., an index with a 1-month tolerance period) had an average monthly excess return of –47 bp for the period from January 1990 through September 2003. However, the volatility of this excess return (792 bp) was more than sixteen times the mean excess return, indicating that monthly returns vary considerably from the mean. An index of issues that were downgraded in the prior 3 months had a better average monthly excess return of –33 bp (and a standard deviation of 710 bp) over the same period. The unconstrained

Figure 13-17. Excess Returns: Means and Standard Deviations

Unconstrained Fallen Angels Index and Corporate Index, January 1990–September 2003

Period	Unconstrained Fallen Angels	Corporate Index
January 1990–September 2003		
Mean (bp)	27.4	2.8
Standard deviation (bp)	218.0	63.1
January 1990–July 1998		
Mean (bp)	36.4	4.7
Standard deviation(bp)	143.6	30.1
August 1998–September 2003		
Mean (bp)	12.5	−0.4
Standard deviation (bp)	304.9	95.7

fallen angel index had an average monthly excess return of 27 bp with a considerable amount of volatility (218 bp).

Figure 13-16 shows that the average monthly excess return generally increases as the tolerance period lengthens. Allowing downgraded bonds to remain in the index longer improves the performance of the fallen angels index. This result also suggests that seasoned fallen angels tend to perform better than those that are unseasoned. We use the various fallen angel indices described in Figure 13-16 as a first step toward determining what the characteristics of the Corporate Index would have been had fallen angels been allowed to remain in the index for a given tolerance period.

Not unexpectedly, fallen angel issues performed very differently from corporates over the period. Figure 13-17 presents the mean monthly excess return and standard deviation for both the unconstrained fallen angel index and the Corporate Index. For the period from January 1990 to September 2003, the unconstrained fallen angel index had an average monthly excess return of 27.4 bp compared to 2.8 bp for the Corporate Index. The standard deviations of the monthly excess returns were 218.0 and 63.1 bp, respectively, for the unconstrained fallen angel index and the Corporate Index. Figure 13-17 also subdivides the period, using July 1998 as the break point, and presents the same statistics for the subperiods. The performance of both the fallen angels and Corporate indices was much worse in the latter subperiod, but the fallen angel index outperformed the Corporate Index in both subperiods.

Figure 13-18. Average Monthly Excess Returns and Survivorship Bias

Corporate Index and Unconstrained Downgrade-Tolerant Index, January 1990–September 2003

Period	Unconstrained Downgrade-Tolerant Index	Corporate Index	Survivorship Bias
January 1990–September 2003			
Mean (bp/month)	4.0	2.8	–1.2
January 1990–July 1998			
Mean (bp/month)	6.2	4.7	–1.5
August 1998–September 2003			
Mean (bp/month)	0.4	–0.4	–0.8

Measuring the Survivorship Bias in the Lehman Corporate Index

The purpose of introducing fallen angel indices is to estimate what the performance of the Corporate Index would have been if downgraded bonds had been allowed to remain within it for the specified tolerance period. What is the value of this exercise? Currently, the Corporate Index removes bonds at the end of their downgrade month. However, portfolio managers may only be able to remove such bonds from their portfolio after some delay (say, 3 months). If fallen angel issues continue to underperform over the next 3 months, then the manager will underperform the index even if his goal at the outset was to replicate it. The difference between the index return and the manager's return is the survivorship bias, which is due to the fact that the Corporate Index can jettison fallen angels immediately, whereas the manager cannot.

To measure the survivorship bias we construct a market value–weighted combination of the fallen angels index for a given tolerance period and the Corporate Index and define this combination as the downgrade-tolerant Corporate Index for the given tolerance period. We then define the survivorship bias as the difference in excess returns between the Corporate Index and the downgrade-tolerant Corporate Index. If the performance of the Corporate Index is higher, then the fact that the Corporate Index immediately discards fallen angel issues produces a survivorship bias in its favor.

First, we show in Figure 13-18 the performance of the downgrade-tolerant Corporate Index assuming an unconstrained tolerance period. This downgrade-

Excess Return Difference (bp)

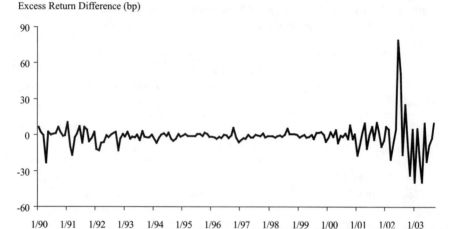

Figure 13-19. Excess Return Differential between the Corporate Index and the Unconstrained Downgrade-Tolerant Index
Monthly between January 1990 and September 2003

tolerant index outperforms the Corporate Index by 1.2 bp/month, indicating that there is actually no survivorship bias against the unconstrained downgrade-tolerant index.

Figure 13-19 presents the monthly excess return difference between the Corporate Index and the unconstrained downgrade-tolerant index from January 1990 through September 2003. As illustrated, since the latter half of 1999, the bias has been quite volatile, exhibiting a peak in June of 2002 with the downgrade of WorldCom. Figures 13-18 and 13-19 show that while the survivorship bias is negative for the period as a whole, there are periods when the survivorship bias is positive. These figures only display data for the unconstrained downgrade-tolerant index. Figure 13-20 shows the magnitude of the survivorship bias for the other downgrade-tolerant indices as a function of the tolerance period.

Figure 13-20 illustrates that the magnitude of survivorship bias is small but not negligible. If portfolio managers were unable to sell downgraded bonds for a month after they left the Corporate Index, then they underperformed their benchmark by 0.3 bp/month over the past 14 years or so. Figure 13-20 also shows that the survivorship bias is generally a decreasing function of the tolerance period.[10] If fallen

10. Figure 13-20 is not necessarily the mirror image of Figure 13-16 and does not necessarily rise when Figure 13-16 falls or vice versa. As we lengthen the tolerance period, the market value of the fallen angels index increases (i.e., there are more fallen angel issues in the index), which increases its relative weight in the downgrade-tolerant corporate index. Thus the fluctuations in

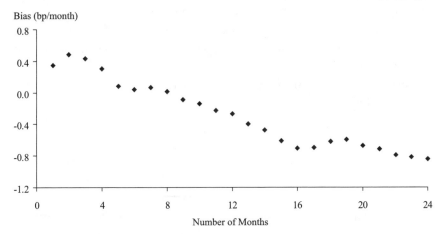

Figure 13-20. Average Survivorship Bias as a Function of the Tolerance Period
January 1990–September 2003

angels are permitted to remain in the Corporate Index for a longer period of time, then their general partial recovery helps to reverse the survivorship bias. If downgraded bonds are allowed to remain in the Corporate Index for 6 months, then the survivorship bias is effectively zero, and if they are allowed to stay in the index longer the bias becomes negative. An important lesson from these results for plan sponsors who want to use the Corporate Index as a benchmark is that they should consider using a downgrade-tolerant index in order to eliminate the survivorship bias against the manager.

In summary, the quality requirement of the Lehman Corporate Index puts managers at a disadvantage because they cannot sell their positions in fallen angel issues as soon as those bonds leave the index. We examined relaxing the index's quality requirement by first constructing a fallen angels index. Our results indicate that as the tolerance period for the fallen angels index is extended, the average monthly return performance improves up to the sixth month, with less dramatic improvement afterward. Furthermore, by combining the fallen angel indices (with various tolerance periods) with the Corporate Index, we are able to create the corresponding downgrade-tolerant Corporate indices. We then measure the survivorship bias that may be inherent in the Corporate Index vs. downgrade-

---

Figure 13-20 are caused not only by the fluctuation in the performance of the set of fallen angels as we increase the tolerance period but also by the change in their weight in the full downgrade-tolerant index.

tolerant corporate indices. The results indicate that the survivorship bias is particularly acute when the tolerance period is 3 months or less. Beyond this point the bias diminishes and eventually turns negative, demonstrating the recovery of fallen angels over this lengthening tolerance period. Our evidence suggests that plan sponsors should consider a time horizon of at least 6 months to allow managers to unwind their positions of fallen angel debt.

MANAGING CREDIT PORTFOLIOS

Credit investors are a nervous and cautious lot—for good reason. MBS investors, while confident of ultimately receiving principal and interest, are only vulnerable to relatively modest changes in anticipated principal repayment dates. Credit investors, however, cannot be certain that their principal will ever be returned! One bad credit pick and a year's hard work can vanish in a day. This is another way of saying that credit investors face a very asymmetrical return potential. The credit investor has a very high probability of receiving a modest return advantage relative to government securities with a very low probability of losing most of his investment (referred to as security-selection or "idiosyncratic" risk). In the face of low-probability but catastrophic events, logic often yields to emotion. Periods of calm seem deceptively risk-free, causing investors to lower their guard and hold credit assets at narrow spreads, while periods of chaos seem interminable, causing them to shun the asset class despite very wide spreads. In such a context, quantitative bond portfolio management techniques have much to offer credit investors.

Much of the effort in quantitative fixed-income management has been targeted at helping credit investors manage idiosyncratic risk. Many sections of this book—index replication, benchmark customization, risk modeling, and portfolio and index analytics—address the particularly nettlesome idiosyncratic risk problems faced by credit managers. In general, quantitative portfolio management has approached the problem of controlling idiosyncratic risk from two directions: *benchmarks* and *portfolios*.

Several chapters in the preceding section on Benchmark Customization dealt with the issue of managing idiosyncratic risk embedded in benchmarks. This topic gained prominence during the stressful credit markets of 2001–2002, which, unlike several previous episodes of credit market turmoil, produced downgrades of many large and highly rated issuers whose bonds were widely held. The credit shocks were compounded by severe market illiquidity, as many investors simultaneously rushed to reduce large exposures to troubled names. As credit event risk began to dominate overall portfolio risk, plan sponsors revisited benchmark design and examined their benchmarks closely for large single-issuer concentrations. Sponsors asked: "Does it make sense for our organization to have a 2% exposure to issuer X even if our investment manager is completely neutral to the benchmark?" Sponsors reacted to the high level of idiosyncratic risk in their benchmarks by adopting issuer-capped and downgrade-tolerant benchmarks (Chapter 13) as well as swap-based benchmarks (Chapter 11).

OPTIMAL DIVERSIFICATION

Managing idiosyncratic risk in portfolios has always been a key consideration for credit managers. The credit shocks of 2001–2002 brought this issue to the fore and led portfolio managers to embrace a more disciplined and quantitative approach to managing portfolio credit risk. While managers have long known that event risk is higher in lower-credit qualities, the optimal levels of diversification across qualities in a credit portfolio were not at all obvious. Moreover, diversification cannot be pursued willy-nilly because thoughtless and uncontrolled diversification not only increases research and transaction costs, but also dilutes the value of credit research, as the portfolio may begin to include bonds not recommended by the analyst. Credit managers have long sought a methodology to quantify idiosyncratic risk so as to permit rational analysis of the trade-off between the alpha potential of name selection and the risk of name concentration.

We present such a methodology in Chapter 14, which deals with the security-specific risk of downgrades in investment-grade portfolios. We develop a model of downgrade risk based on the observed historical underperformance of downgraded bonds and transition probabilities published by rating agencies. We also take into account the volatility of spreads not caused by rating transitions (so-called "natural" volatility), which is relatively more significant for higher-quality issuers. To minimize tracking error owing to both natural volatility and downgrade risk, the model recommends uneven diversification in various credit ratings in the ratio 5:3:1.[1] In other words, the optimal position size in Baa-rated bonds is one-fifth the position size of Aaa/Aa-rated bonds and one-third the position size of A-rated bonds. While investors may not precisely follow these ratios, and the ratio may fluctuate depending on changes in transition probabilities and spreads, many investors have embraced the lessons of the methodology and now follow a more disciplined diversification strategy in the lower-credit qualities.

---

1. This empirical ratio depends, of course, on the study period. However, the optimal position size is likely to be found highly uneven across qualities over any time frame.

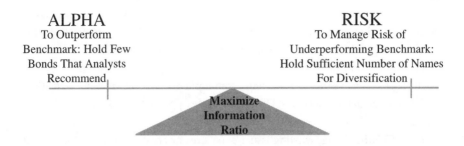

ALPHA	RISK
To Outperform	To Manage Risk of
Benchmark: Hold Few	Underperforming Benchmark:
Bonds That Analysts	Hold Sufficient Number of Names
Recommend	For Diversification

This methodology has broad applicability, as it can be extended to analyze a variety of issues facing the head of a credit research team. For example, an investment advisor can combine this work with our research on measuring the value of credit analyst security selection (Chapter 1) to help build a credit analysis structure for maximizing risk-adjusted performance. Depending on the analyst's skill, we can calculate the mean and standard deviation of the excess return contribution by an analyst from either recommending bonds that will outperform or avoiding bonds that are likely to be downgraded. However, following the analyst's recommendations comes at a potential cost of high-concentration (idiosyncratic) risk in the portfolio. As shown in Chapter 14, the consequences of a bad credit pick (e.g., a downgraded bond) are very severe, especially in Baa-rated securities. As the accompanying figure illustrates, the key issue for the chief investment officer is how to structure the portfolio to reap the benefits of the analyst's skill through name concentration while controlling the potential harm caused by an inevitable bad call.

The optimal amount of diversification depends on the trade-off between the cost of diversification (i.e., the decrease in expected portfolio outperformance from adding bonds the analyst may not like and the increase in the cost of credit analysis) against the benefit of diversification (i.e., the continued decline in tracking error volatility). Given a level of analyst skill, the chief investment officer can use the methodology explained in this book to answer two important questions: "How much of the market should research cover?" and "Given the analyst's recommendations, how many of his picks should be added to the portfolio to manage expected risk-adjusted returns?"

NEW INVESTMENT PRODUCTS AND STRATEGIES

The market continues to come up with new credit products to help investors manage portfolio idiosyncratic risk better. One new type of cash credit instrument is the basket of liquid corporate bonds traded as *one security*. These securities contain about twenty-five corporate bonds and are issued in several maturities, different currency markets (e.g., dollar and euro), and for different subsectors of the credit market (e.g., investment grade and high yield). In a single trade, an investor can achieve credit market spread exposure with a reasonable degree of credit diversification.

The past several years have also witnessed rapid growth in the credit derivatives market. Credit default swaps (CDS), credit index products (CDX), and tranches of indices have found a permanent place in the portfolios of credit managers, helping them to either hedge existing issuer exposures or create new diversified credit exposures that they could not create otherwise. In fact, the growth of the credit derivatives market now makes it possible to replicate efficiently broad aggregate indices with very little expected tracking error volatility (Chapters 4 and 5).

In contrast to the excitement of new product innovation, one of the cheerless aspects of the stressful credit markets of 2001–2002 was working with investors who found their investment-grade credit portfolios suddenly chock-a-block with many investment-grade bonds trading at distressed levels. Many of these investors were forced to re-examine the question of whether it made sense to sell these bonds. Some felt that it was better to sell as soon as an issuer became distressed because it was unlikely that the issuer would ever recover. Others believed it was better to hold on as credit market shocks tend to produce vicious crises of confidence that cause investors to disregard credit fundamentals. In such an environment, the market displays its dysfunction as bonds decline further in price simply because they had declined in price. Surely the market will eventually come to its senses, and then distressed bonds should recover.

To help investors grapple with this issue, we offer a dispassionate historical perspective on the performance of investment-grade bonds after distress. Chapter 15 shows that, in fact, distressed investment-grade bonds have performed well, as a group, subsequent to their distress month vs. Treasuries and quality- and duration-matched corporates. However, this outperformance takes time—over a year. This finding was reassuring to many investors and formed the basis for their portfolio strategy for managing through the credit crisis.

Many credit managers believed the degree of distress in the 2001–2002 investment-grade markets was much worse than in previous credit crises. "This time it's different!" In particular, investors felt that distressed issues fell more sharply in price in the month after a credit event than they had ever done before. Moreover, investors believed that the threshold price level below which a bond was unlikely to recover (the so-called "knife-edge" price) had moved up from prior crises. In other words, if a bond's price fell below $Z\%$ in the month after distress, then the bond was unlikely ever to recover and there was no good reason to continue holding it.

Although the number of distressed investment-grade issues in 2001–2002 was certainly greater than in any period since 1990, both in absolute and percentage terms, we found many similarities with earlier credit episodes. In particular, the average price of distressed issues at the end of their distress month changed very little: 73.26% for prior-2001 distressed issues vs. 72.04% for post-2001 issues. Furthermore, the knife-edge price remained at approximately $50 for both pre- and post-2001 distressed bond vintages. While many investors believed that the 2001–2002 credit markets were unprecedented, in actuality we found many similarities with earlier episodes such as 1990–1991 and 1997–1998. One indicator of the mystery of investor psychology is the fact that of the 330 issues that became distressed in 2001 or later, 249 were no longer distressed by September 2003. Yet, while investors can easily rattle off a list of issuers that became distressed, many are often hard-pressed to list issuers that subsequently recovered!

Another strategy that credit investors can use to manage portfolio idiosyncratic risk is to use interest-rate swaps as a substitute for credit exposure. Interest-rate swaps have long been used for tactical (e.g., hedging) purposes by banks and other portfolio investors, but it is only recently that they have been receiving attention as a strategic asset class. Swap rates represent an average of forward LIBOR rates and are influenced by market factors that move credit spreads such as changes in credit risk premia and relative supply and demand for spread assets.

However, there are some key differences between swaps and other credit spread markets. First, swaps trade with remarkable liquidity compared to other spread markets. Second, and more importantly, in contrast to individual spread assets, swaps have little idiosyncratic default risk because the LIBOR setting is tied to the credit performance of a group of banks and not to a single issuer name. As a result, the correlation between changes in swap spreads and similar-duration credit spreads is not very stable, especially for lower-rated credit classes. The correlation tends to break down during periods of perceived very high credit-event risk outside of the highly rated financial sector. Thus, although swaps may not be a good hedge for much of the credit sector, perhaps they are an attractive asset class that offers credit spread exposure without much idiosyncratic risk. Indeed, swaps have offered total returns comparable to those of other spread asset categories and can provide useful portfolio diversification benefits as well.[2] Since 1992, swaps have outperformed Treasuries, MBS, and agencies and have modestly underperformed credit and ABS. In particular, they performed well relative to credit during the stressful credit period of 2001–2002, as they avoided the large idiosyncratic credit shocks.

---

2. The Lehman Brothers swap indices, whose total return replicates a receive-fixed swap position and a cash investment in 3-month LIBOR, provide market participants with a high-quality source for swaps pricing, returns, and analytics. See Chapter 11 for details.

NEW PORTFOLIO MANAGEMENT TOOLS

Credit managers have long used risk models to measure how much of their tracking error risk is coming from market (systematic) factors and security-specific (idiosyncratic) risk factors. However, in response to heightened security-specific event risk, investors have sought better quantitative credit analysis tools to measure portfolio risk. In the 2001–2002 period, many credit portfolios experienced deviations from the benchmark that exceeded five times the standard deviation predicted by multifactor risk models. These deviations were driven almost entirely by security-specific events. The risk model's estimate of portfolio risk, based on the long-term historical volatility of residuals in the credit market, was an inadequate predictor in a marketplace with heightened and fast-moving security-specific risk.

In response to these events, we enhanced the risk model (Chapter 26) to allow a portfolio manager to give recent historical observations more weight in the estimation of idiosyncratic risk. The weighting scheme is exponential time decay, an option that lets the risk model adjust to idiosyncratic shocks much faster if the portfolio manager so chooses. As a result, tracking errors predicted by the model for undiversified portfolios increased significantly. In the months following the change, the realized performance of most credit portfolios fell into line with predicted tracking errors.[3]

We continue to examine our modeling of a bond's idiosyncratic risk. We find that the correlation between spread changes of two bonds of the same issuer, denominated in the same or different currencies, increases as the bond's spread level increases (Chapter 18). In other words, for high-spread issuers, a long position in a name offsets much of the risk of a short position in the same name, irrespective of the currency of denomination. This implies that for high-spread issuers much of the bond-level idiosyncratic volatility is *issuer*-specific. In contrast, for low-spread issuers a long position in a name does not offset much of the risk of a short position in the same name, implying that idiosyncratic volatility is *issue*-specific. As a result, for modeling purposes we take into account an issuer's spread level when estimating idiosyncratic tracking error between a portfolio and its benchmark.

---

3. Users of the risk model should give careful consideration as to whether to use time decay. It is not necessarily always the best and "most conservative" option. Indeed, if a user had chosen time decay prior to the 1998 crisis, he would have severely underestimated the tracking error, as the experience of the 1990 recession would have been significantly underweighted. In general, one should not use time decay after a period of calm. When, at some point, the current high idiosyncratic volatility comes to an end, managers looking for conservative estimates of risk should switch back to the equal weighting scheme. The risk model will soon start reporting tail risk measures such at VaR and expected shortfall.

These results also have implications for global credit management. Managers of portfolios denominated in different currencies should coordinate their respective holdings of high-spread issuers, as there is little cross-currency idiosyncratic risk diversification and the global portfolio's risk exposure to a name could be unacceptably high. Moreover, investors may wish to consider using these results for forming relative value judgments. Since issue-level idiosyncratic risk is relatively low for high-spread issuers, differential spread movements between two issues from the same issuer, which might be more likely if the bonds are denominated in different currencies, may present an opportunity for a long-short strategy as the differential spread move is subsequently reversed.

As we explain in Chapter 26, the multifactor risk model measures "normal" monthly volatility. It was not designed to measure volatility arising from low-probability extreme events such as defaults (so-called "tail risk"). Over a monthly horizon, the probability of an investment-grade issuer defaulting is indeed very low. However, the events of 2001–2002 caused investors to try to estimate tail risk, including the risk that issuer defaults could be correlated. In response, many new quantitative tools have been developed both inside and outside the multifactor risk model framework to measure both the "value-at-risk" (VaR) and expected shortfall (ExpS) of a credit portfolio. The interpretation of the value-at-risk is: you can be 95% confident that the result you obtain will be the VaR or better. The interpretation of the expected shortfall is the average of all the possible outcomes that go beyond the VaR. (One could imagine two different distributions with the same VaR, but with one having a much worse ExpS than the other.) While many of these tools are more appropriate to credit investors who intend to hold assets for long horizons (as we discuss shortly), all investors now measure the tail risk of their portfolios.[4]

4. A Lehman Brothers portfolio tool for measuring the tail risk in credit portfolios, known as COMPASS, works roughly as follows. Individual asset default rates are mapped to historical default rates based on the asset's credit rating. (Alternatively, the investor can use his own default rate assumptions.) Using equity returns, COMPASS models the default correlations of various assets in a credit portfolio. This correlation matrix is updated monthly using market data. With this information, COMPASS uses Monte Carlo techniques to simulate the correlated defaults for assets (including structured credit assets such as ABS and CMBS) in a portfolio. With this information and applying a model of recovery rates (which may, in turn, be correlated with default rates), COMPASS can generate a loss distribution for a portfolio. For a given level of expected return, COMPASS generates the various possible portfolio loss distributions using a given set of available assets as identified by the investor as inputs. COMPASS then identifies the single portfolio with the lowest tail risk measure (e.g., expected shortfall) given the level of expected return. This optimal portfolio can either be purchased outright or can be used to determine buys and sells for an existing credit portfolio. COMPASS can also generate an "efficient frontier" and show the investor how the optimal portfolio risk exposure changes as the investor strives for different levels of expected portfolio return.

LONG VS. SHORT INVESTMENT HORIZONS

There are many credit investors, often called "buy-and-hold" or "long-horizon" investors, who, for various reasons, hold credit assets until their maturity.[5] Long-horizon credit investors face the trade-off between risk and return from a very different viewpoint than short-horizon investors. Especially in credit, the longer horizon carries with it a much more asymmetric return distribution because the maximum return is the (relatively modest) yield earned and the maximum loss is represented by default. Furthermore, long-horizon investors face the risk of correlated defaults in their portfolios. Although the market default rate may be as anticipated, the investor's default experience may be much worse than expected if the investor happened to pick credits that tend to default together. Correlation of issuer defaults reduces the benefit of diversification and creates a systematic component of undiversifiable default risk. Consequently, the standard tools used by short-horizon total return portfolio managers for top-down asset allocation (e.g., mean-variance optimization) and bottom-up security selection (e.g., multifactor risk models) do not meet the needs of long-horizon investors.

Chapter 17 demonstrates that the return profile of credit assets changes as the investment horizon changes. Specifically, tail risk increases even for relatively modest increases in the investor's holding period. To show this, we gather the monthly and quarterly excess returns for a variety of subindices of the Lehman Brothers Credit Index. For each index, we measure the negative tail of each distribution by calculating the average excess return for both the worst and best 5% of excess returns. For example, for the Corporate Energy Index, the average *monthly* excess return from 1994–2003 was –1.89% in the negative tail and +1.67% in the positive tail. However, for the same period, the average *quarterly* excess return was –3.66 and 2.10%, respectively, suggesting that the excess return distribution is more negatively skewed for the longer holding period.

In contrast to short-horizon investors who trade off expected short-term return against short-term return volatility, long-horizon investors trade off yield to maturity (i.e., income) against the risk of default losses. This difference in perspective may create superior long-term investment opportunities for long-horizon investors to the extent that they can garner any spread risk premium demanded by short-horizon investors as compensation for bearing short-term spread volatility. This trade-off of yield vs. default risk also raises new questions regarding asset allocation and how to analyze a portfolio in terms of exposures to individual issuers.

---

5. Chapter 9 discusses why some investors are buy-and-hold.

How should a long-horizon investor approach the problem of allocating credit assets across the various credit qualities? Chapter 16 presents our asset allocation methodology for long-horizon credit investors. We develop a model at the credit quality level (e.g., A and Baa) that requires a small set of assumptions about the spread, expected default rate, and correlations for typical issuers within each quality class. With this information we can then calculate (or simulate) the portfolio's tail risk (value-at-risk and expected shortfall) at a given confidence level for various percentage portfolio allocations to the different credit qualities classes. Depending on the underlying assumptions, the investor can select the portfolio quality allocation that meets the portfolio's expected return goals and risk targets.

Rather than providing specific point-in-time recommendations, this methodology offers investors an opportunity to produce customized asset allocation solutions given each investor's individual situation: the types of assets used and their spreads, views on expected default probabilities and correlations, and the precise formulation of the constraint on default risk. The solution is the investor's optimal portfolio allocation across the various credit qualities. However, the investor must then choose which particular bonds to buy to fill each quality allocation. Fortunately, there are other tools that help investors construct actual bond-level optimized credit portfolios that will maximize expected portfolio returns while minimizing a specified portfolio tail risk measure subject to various constraints.[6] With such tools, long-horizon investors can now objectively improve the performance efficiency of their credit portfolios.

Quantitative techniques have much to offer the credit investor. While such analyses and tools cannot prevent the credit event risk that so vexes the portfolio manager, they can help him better understand, measure, and hedge undesired credit risks. Although quantitative techniques are relatively new to credit managers, they have the potential to profoundly change the nature and structure of the credit management process.

6. COMPASS is one such tool. See note 4.

14. Sufficient Diversification in Credit Portfolios

How many different issuers should an investor have in a credit portfolio? This question, in one form or another, has long occupied the minds of portfolio managers around the globe, but it has taken on a new urgency for credit market veterans, as well as for relative newcomers to the debt asset management business. Two main factors motivate this wave of interest in credit risk and diversification: asset shifts to credit markets and a marked increase in spread volatility.

Global demand for credit securities is rising for several reasons. In Europe, where many bond investors traditionally bought only government bonds, the monetary union in 1999 created a much more homogeneous government bond market. This transformation leaves less opportunity for portfolio managers to outperform strictly by varying their country/currency mix, which has prompted many asset managers to consider extending their investment set to other asset classes, including credit product. A growing number of investors now switch from all-government benchmarks to those including credit products as well, such as the Lehman Brothers Euro-Aggregate and Global Aggregate indices.

The unified market and a greater appetite for credit have led to a large increase in issuance. The European corporate bond market, previously dominated by highly rated financial issuers, has given a warm reception to issues by lower-rated corporations that had previously been forced to rely exclusively on bank financing. Moreover, the single-currency market provides better support for larger issue sizes. For investors, the greater credit diversity and higher liquidity make the European credit market much more attractive.

In the United States, where credit product has always been a prominent part of debt portfolios, the changes are less dramatic. Yet, the momentum for credit has been increasing in the United States as well. Globally, some investors who have

Based on research first published by Lehman Brothers in 2002.

traditionally relied on Treasuries, such as central banks, are now investigating opportunities in other asset classes. U.S. agency issues, and particularly their benchmark programs, have been the primary beneficiaries, but the search for extra spread has spilled over into the corporate market as well. Some large Asian investors are among those who view corporates as a possible alternative to Treasuries.

However, as the demand for credit product increased, the credit markets encountered several difficult years. Spreads widened suddenly in the liquidity crisis of 1998 and then again in 2000. In both 2000 and 2001, a slew of "credit bombs" painfully illustrated the dangers inherent in credit investing.

The credit market volatility of 1997–2001 has increased the caution of investors approaching credit for the first time. As such investors redesign their processes to include credit, they seek a complete understanding of the diversification needed to protect their portfolios from the risks of downgrades and defaults. Even long-time credit managers should revisit this issue in this high-spread-volatility environment. For managers of structured credit products such as CDOs and CLOs, diversification is a critical concern.

We establish a quantitative framework to address the issues of credit risk and diversification, with an emphasis on the implications for portfolio structure. We build a model for portfolio credit risk using rating transition probabilities from the major rating agencies (Moody's and Standard & Poor's) and historical return data from the Lehman Brothers U.S. Investment-Grade Credit Index. With this model, we explore how portfolios should be structured to meet various investment goals. Among the problems we address are the following:

- For a portfolio of N bonds, how many should be purchased from each credit quality to minimize exposure to downgrade risk?

- How many securities should be held in a credit portfolio to bring the impact of downgrade risk below a given threshold?

- With the assumption of a simple model for the expected outperformance owing to credit research, what number of bonds maximizes the information ratio?

- What percentage of the market should be covered by credit research?

SYSTEMATIC RISK, NONSYSTEMATIC RISK, AND DOWNGRADE RISK

Managers of credit portfolios face many different risks. Systematic risks include interest-rate movements, changes in market volatility, and across-the-board changes in credit spreads, either for the market as a whole or for a particular industry or quality. Nonsystematic risk reflects developments that affect specific issuers or securities but not the broader market.[1]

The decisions as to how much of a portfolio to allocate to the credit markets or how to allocate the portfolio among different industries and qualities are tied closely to the study of systematic risk. This risk results from differences between portfolio and benchmark exposures to systematic risk factors such as changes in interest rates and sector spreads. A manager might overweight a sector if its expected outperformance over the market as a whole compensates sufficiently for the added risk. More simply, current spreads (or excess returns) are judged against their historical volatility.

This type of analysis, while important, is not the subject of this study. Our emphasis is on nonsystematic risk, which is created by differences between portfolio and benchmark exposures to specific issuers and securities. Large allocations to particular issuers make a portfolio vulnerable to credit events at these issuers, while their impact on the highly diversified index is much smaller. Nonsystematic risk is often called *diversifiable* risk, that is, reducible by diversification.

The most extreme form of credit event is default, but the risk of immediate default for an investment-grade bond is extremely small. Developments that increase the market's perception of the probability of downgrade or default are far more typical in the investment-grade market. Examples include disappointing earnings, a large equity buyback, a planned change in financial leverage, a merger announcement, or a rating action.

We have chosen to focus on changes in ratings as the credit events of interest in the U.S. investment-grade market. Our index database contains monthly data on all securities in the Lehman Brothers U.S. Investment-Grade Credit Index since 1988, with credit ratings from both Moody's and Standard & Poor's along with prices, durations, and returns. The downgrade data offer a fairly complete view of all serious credit events affecting index securities. Defaults directly from investment grade are rare, but any degradation in an issuer's credit worthiness almost inevitably results first in its market underperformance and then in its eventual downgrade.

First, we develop an approach for estimating the risk of downgrades in a credit portfolio. The analysis proceeds from the risk of a single security to the absolute risk of a portfolio and finally to tracking error relative to a benchmark. Some simplifying assumptions are made to facilitate analytical treatment. Next, we show

---

1. For a detailed discussion of the Lehman Brothers Risk Model and its applications, see the Chapter 26.

how this model can be used to answer the questions raised previously concerning optimal portfolio structuring. Simple models of the utility of credit research are introduced to study the trade-off between two effects of increasing diversification: decreased risk and decreased expected outperformance.

MODELING DOWNGRADE RISK IN A SINGLE BOND

Historical Approach: Observed Returns of Downgraded Bonds

Rating agencies provide data on the historical frequency of corporate upgrades and downgrades. The data on performance consequences of downgrades are not as readily available. The sequential nature of downgrade announcement complicates measurement of the return impact of downgrades. The rating agencies typically watchlist an issuer in advance of rating changes; the fundamental financial information that can trigger a ratings action is usually available to market participants well before the downgrade. As a result, there is often no apparent negative effect on performance during the month of the actual downgrade; rather underperformance may be spread over the course of several preceding months. To quantify this effect, we conducted a study of all the bonds in the Lehman Brothers U.S. Investment-Grade Credit Index that were downgraded from August 1988 through December 2001.[2] For each downgraded security, we measured performance relative to its peer group over the course of the four quarters preceding the downgrade. For the purposes of this analysis, we partitioned the U.S. investment-grade credit market by quality, sector, and duration. To ensure adequate sample sizes, the credit-quality grid was rather coarse with three levels: Aaa-Aa, A, and Baa.[3] There were four sectors: industrial, financial, utilities, and non-U.S issuers. Finally, there were three duration groups: under 4 years, 4–7 years, and more than 7 years.

For each security in the index in a given month, we calculated excess return over duration-equivalent U.S. Treasuries. We then averaged these excess returns over all the bonds in each of the thirty-six cells of the quality × sector × duration partition.

---

2. While a return time series for this index, originally called the Corporate Bond Index, extends back to 1973, our archives have detailed analytics beginning only in August 1988.

3. Our index database lists ratings from Moody's when available. For bonds not rated by Moody's, we use the S&P rating. If neither Moody's nor S&P rates the bond, then we use ratings from Fitch or Duff and Phelps. For simplicity, a single notation denotes the roughly equivalent rating classes from different providers. Thus, Baa is used to denote bonds rated Baa1 through Baa3 by Moody's or BBB+ through BBB– by S&P. The Aaa and Aa ratings have been grouped together, because there are relatively few Aaa credits.

For each bond, the cell it belonged to became its peer group. We proceeded to measure each bond's outperformance relative to its peer group, defined as the difference between the bond's excess return and the peer group's average excess return.

We defined a downgrade as a transition from one of our three coarse rating levels to a lower one. A downgrade from one subclass of single-A to another, for example, was not counted. (This is consistent with the granularity at which the rating agencies publish rating transition matrices.) For each downgrade, we examined the performance of the bond relative to its peer group during the month of the downgrade and over the preceding 11 months. We checked that the bond's rating was unchanged over this 11-month period. Downgrades following on the heels of prior downgrades were excluded because of the difficulty of separating the effects of the two events.

Figure 14-1 summarizes our findings. Not surprisingly, we see that most of the impact from a downgrade is absorbed in the final few months before the event. The largest underperformance comes in the month of the downgrade and the 2 months preceding it. As we look further back in time, we find that there is noticeable underperformance 3–5 months before a downgrade and that the effect can be felt as far back as 8 months before, but 9 or more months before a downgrade, bonds do not significantly underperform their peer groups.

For example, securities downgraded from Baa experienced an average underperformance of −12.92% compared to their peer group during the year leading up to the downgrade. This amount gathers unevenly through the year. The average quarterly underperformance was −8.59% in the quarter immediately preceding a downgrade, but only −2.80 and −1.50%, respectively, in the previous two quarters. The t-statistic shows all of these numbers to be statistically significant; no significant underperformance is seen 9–11 months prior to the downgrade.

Severe return consequences are usually limited to downgrades from lower-rated credits. The most drastic underperformance is found when bonds are downgraded from Baa to below investment grade. The crossing of the investment-grade boundary can create major price dislocations because many portfolios (e.g., forced by the investment policy) must sell into a falling market. For bonds downgraded from single-A, the resulting underperformance in the two to three quarters preceding the event is roughly one-fourth of the losses in the Baa sector. The time distribution of these losses roughly mirrors the Baa pattern. For securities rated Aaa and Aa, we did not detect any statistically significant underperformance owing to downgrades.

In all cases, the standard deviation of underperformance exceeds the mean underperformance, which indicates that a downgraded bond could very well do

Figure 14-1. Average Underperformance Owing to Downgrades
August 1988–December 2001

Months Prior to Downgrade	Initial Quality	Number of Observations	Underperformance (%)				
			Monthly		Quarterly		
			Mean	Standard Deviation	Mean	Standard Deviation	t-Statistic
0–2	Aaa-Aa	716	-0.08	1.07	-0.23	1.85	-3.4
	A	974	-0.72	3.28	-2.15	5.67	-11.8
	Baa	523	-2.86	13.34	-8.59	23.10	-8.5
3–5	Aaa-Aa	716	-0.01	0.70	-0.02	1.21	-0.5
	A	974	-0.20	1.40	-0.61	2.43	-7.9
	Baa	523	-0.93	4.40	-2.80	7.61	-8.4
6–8	Aaa-Aa	716	-0.00	0.67	-0.01	1.17	-0.2
	A	974	-0.06	0.94	-0.19	1.62	-3.7
	Baa	523	-0.50	2.71	-1.50	4.70	-7.3
9–11	Aaa-Aa	716	-0.01	0.70	-0.03	1.21	-0.7
	A	974	0.04	0.90	0.11	1.56	2.3
	Baa	523	-0.01	1.66	-0.03	2.87	-0.2
Full year	Aaa-Aa	716	-0.02	0.74	-0.30	2.55	-3.1
	A	974	-0.24	1.90	-2.84	6.58	-13.5
	Baa	523	-1.08	6.54	-12.92	22.65	-13.0

much worse than the average. In fact, several bonds downgraded from Baa lost more than half of their value during the year preceding the downgrade.

Figure 14-2 highlights the extent to which these results vary over time by breaking down the results by the year in which the downgrade took place. Both the mean peer group underperformance and its standard deviation across all downgraded bonds vary quite a bit from year to year. Interestingly, the peak downgrade losses occur at different times for different credit qualities. This supports the common wisdom that the main source of credit risk in higher qualities is related to specific credit events, whereas in the lower qualities it is driven mainly by recessions. Accordingly, in the Baa sector, the worst years were 2000 and 2001, whereas the worst single year for single-A was 1997, the inception year of the "Asian Contagion" and the year of the South Korea downgrade.

As apparent from Figure 14-2, the years 2000 and 2001 brought extremely large downgrade losses, in terms of both the average loss and its standard deviation, especially in the Baa sector. A number of bonds deteriorated rapidly from investment grade toward default, suffering losses as great as 40% in a month.

In addition to the losses observed on downgraded bonds, the modeling of downgrade risk requires one more crucial set of input data—the probabilities of various types of downgrades. The major rating agencies regularly publish annual transition matrices with the probability distribution of a bond's rating at the end of a given year, based on its rating at the start of that year. Our study dealt with the total probability of a downgrade, which is obtained as a sum of transition probabilities to all rating categories lower than the initial rating. In Figure 14-3 we show the total probability of a downgrade from each initial rating group, according to both Standard & Poor's (1981–2001) and Moody's (1970–2001). These probabilities are compared to the downgrade frequencies observed for the issuers in the Lehman Brothers U.S. Investment-Grade Credit Index from 1990 through 2001.

As noted previously, bonds downgraded during 2000 and 2001 suffered unusually big losses. The severity of the credit events in those 2 years led Moody's to publish additional 2000- and 2001-only transition matrices. Figure 14-3 includes results from these matrices as well. But the severity of 2000 and 2001 is not in the downgrade probabilities (both of which are actually lower than the long-term averages), but exclusively in the magnitude of the losses, as shown in Figure 14-2.

A Simple Model of Downgrade Risk

Using the performance results and downgrade probabilities presented previously, we constructed a simple model for the losses bondholders may suffer from downgrades. These losses can be characterized by a two-stage random process. First,

Figure 14-2. Average Underperformance Owing to Downgrades by Year
1989–2001

Year	Number of Issues (Issuers)			Average (%/month)			Standard Deviation (%/month)		
	Aaa-Aa	A	Baa	Aaa-Aa	A	Baa	Aaa-Aa	A	Baa
1989	16 (7)	32 (15)	18 (8)	-0.28	-0.17	-0.35	1.47	0.86	1.71
1990	132 (27)	90 (34)	30 (16)	0.01	-0.23	-1.16	0.42	1.43	6.66
1991	138 (18)	86 (20)	54 (13)	-0.03	-0.08	-0.70	0.54	0.90	2.53
1992	84 (26)	130 (17)	30 (11)	-0.01	-0.10	-0.31	0.89	0.65	1.62
1993	66 (21)	14 (9)	35 (13)	0.03	0.04	-0.25	0.72	0.64	1.39
1994	15 (11)	38 (10)	16 (4)	-0.04	-0.08	-0.31	0.31	1.00	1.84
1995	56 (23)	54 (19)	26 (8)	0.05	-0.08	-0.43	0.95	1.27	1.46
1996	33 (11)	59 (12)	35 (11)	0.02	-0.05	-0.47	0.23	0.47	3.16
1997	6 (7)	107 (31)	10 (5)	-0.05	-0.62	-0.28	0.42	3.28	1.99
1998	50 (16)	70 (29)	46 (16)	-0.08	-0.27	-0.51	0.51	1.31	3.35
1999	42 (15)	64 (30)	54 (14)	0.00	-0.12	-0.71	0.49	0.77	3.58
2000	48 (10)	94 (25)	57 (16)	-0.04	-0.34	-2.65	0.50	2.20	7.80
2001	30 (25)	136 (57)	112 (30)	-0.25	-0.37	-1.94	1.48	2.62	10.08
Totals	716 (217)	974 (308)	523 (165)	-0.02	-0.24	-1.08	0.74	1.90	6.54

Figure 14-3. Total 1-Year Downgrade Probabilities
By Initial Rating, Estimated from Different Sources

Agency	Time Period	Probability (%)		
		Aaa-Aa	A	Baa
Moody's	1970–2001	8.13	5.49	5.70
	2000 only	6.52	4.95	4.18
	2001 only	3.28	7.64	5.62
Standard & Poor's	1981–2001	7.24	5.99	5.69
Lehman Brothers	1990–2001	8.00	7.66	5.15

there is a probability that a bond will be downgraded; second, there is a fairly wide distribution of losses among downgraded bonds. Our model captures both of these sources of randomness and projects the standard deviation of the resulting loss distribution.

Assume that a bond has a probability p of being downgraded over the coming year. If it does suffer a downgrade, the conditional distribution of peer group underperformance is assumed to have mean μ and standard deviation σ. Parameters p, μ, and σ are all functions of the current credit rating; to reduce clutter, we omit the subscripts as we develop the equations for bonds of a single quality. The mean and variance of the loss owing to downgrades for a single bond in a particular month can be shown to be

$$\langle \text{loss} \rangle = p\mu$$
$$\sigma_{\text{loss}}^2 = p(\mu^2 + \sigma^2). \tag{14-1}$$

Figure 14-4 summarizes the model of single-bond returns. Downgrade probabilities come from the first row of Figure 14-3, and the mean and standard deviation of loss for downgraded bonds are from the "Full Year" section of Figure 14-1. The resulting statistics for a bond of a given credit quality are obtained from Equation (14-1). We see, for example, that for a typical Baa-rated security, the possibility of a downgrade over the coming year gives rise to an expected peer group underperformance of –0.74% with a standard deviation of 6.22%.

There are three possible types of rating movements: downgrade, upgrade, and no change. We have chosen to focus on the components of mean and variance that are due to downgrades. On average, of course, the mean outperformance of the peer group (averaged across the entire group) must be zero. The expected

Figure 14-4. Parameters of the Model for Downgrade Risk
Annualized

Initial Rating	Downgrade Probability (%)	Statistics of Losses Experienced by Downgraded Bonds (%)		Resulting Statistics Expected Losses on a Single Bond (%)	
		Average	Standard Deviation	Average	Standard Deviation
Aaa-Aa	8.13	−0.30	2.55	−0.02	0.73
A	5.49	−2.84	6.58	−0.16	1.68
Baa	5.70	−12.92	22.65	−0.74	6.22

underperformance owing to downgrades is offset by expected outperformance from the upgraded and unchanged bonds.[4] In terms of variance, the risk of losses owing to downgrades is of greatest concern to portfolio managers; variance of outperformance is not nearly as frightening. The isolation of risk that is due to downgrades can be considered a form of modeling downside risk as opposed to overall variance.[5] Furthermore, as shown in the next section, when the three contributions to variance are evaluated numerically, we find that the variance owing to downgrades is by far the largest component.

This analysis could be carried out on either a monthly, quarterly, or annual basis, but we have chosen to work at the annual level, the frequency at which the rating agencies typically publish transition matrices. Furthermore, quarterly data might be influenced by seasonal factors, such as the often-observed first-quarter outperformance and September/October underperformance of spread sectors.

4. This relationship gives us an estimate of the peer group outperformance that can be gained by avoiding downgrades. For example, in Figure 14-4, the 5.7% probability of being downgraded from Baa generates a peer group underperformance of −0.74%. This is offset by an equal and opposite outperformance coming from the 94.3% probability of no downgrade. The expected outperformance when downgrades are avoided is therefore 0.74% ÷ 94.3% = 0.785%.

5. For a benchmarked portfolio, it is not exactly true that there is no downside risk owing to upgrades. When index bonds not owned by the portfolio are upgraded, the portfolio underperforms. However, the nonsystematic risk owing to a particular bond is proportional to the square of the size of the overweight or underweight. Because the overweights for securities in a portfolio are typically much larger than the underweights to index bonds, the risk of downgrades to bonds in the portfolio dominates.

Figure 14-5. Average Option-Adjusted Spreads by Quality
Lehman Brothers U.S. Investment-Grade Credit and High
Yield Indices, December 31, 2001

Quality	Number of Issues	Average Option-Adjusted Spread (bp)
Aaa	186	62
Aa	636	92
A	1,585	158
Baa	1,540	234
Ba	480	449
B	493	642
Caa–C	242	2150

Alternative Model Based on the Slope of the Quality Spread Curve

In the previous analysis, we modeled the return impact of a downgrade based on the observed historical excess returns of downgraded securities. An alternative method for projecting performance consequences of any change in rating could be based on the difference between the average spread levels for the two relevant quality ratings.

Figure 14-5 shows the average spreads for bonds of different qualities in the Lehman Brothers U.S. Investment-Grade Credit and High Yield indices as of December 31, 2001. Based on the differences between the average spreads, we can project the returns associated with a particular downgrade. For example, we expect a bond suffering a downgrade from A to Baa over the course of the coming year to see its spread widen by about 75 bp (234–158) over that time. If it has a 5-year spread duration (which is about the average for the Lehman Brothers Credit Index), this will result in a return of –3.77%.

The historical likelihood of these events is reflected by the rating agencies in 1-year transition matrices. In Figure 14-3, we used these data to compute an aggregate number for overall frequency of downgrades; Figure 14-6 shows the entire transition matrix calculated by Moody's based on data from 1970 through 2001. It shows, for instance, that a bond that started a given year with a single-A rating had a 91.97% chance of remaining in single-A a year later, a 4.84% probability of being downgraded to Baa, and a 0.01% probability of defaulting within 1 year.

Combining the spread differentials from Figure 14-5 with the transition probabilities in Figure 14-6, we can build a rudimentary model of the distribution of

Figure 14-6. Moody's 1-Year Rating Transition Matrix
Adjusted for withdrawn ratings, 1970–2001

Current Rating	Rating 1 Year Forward								Total Downgrades
	Aaa	Aa	A	Baa	Ba	B	Caa-C	Default	
Aaa	91.80	7.37	0.81	0.00	0.02	0.00	0.00	0.00	8.20
Aa	1.21	90.73	7.67	0.28	0.08	0.01	0.00	0.02	8.06
A	0.05	2.49	91.97	4.84	0.51	0.12	0.01	0.01	5.49
Baa	0.05	0.26	5.45	88.54	4.72	0.72	0.09	0.16	5.70
Ba	0.02	0.04	0.51	5.57	85.42	6.71	0.45	1.28	8.44
B	0.01	0.02	0.14	0.41	6.69	83.37	2.57	6.79	9.36
Caa-C	0.00	0.00	0.00	0.62	1.59	4.12	68.04	25.63	25.63

returns. Figure 14-7 shows how this model is used to assess the risk of four hypo-thetical bonds with 5-year durations. Each column represents a bond of a differ-ent quality, whose spread is assumed equal to the average spread for its rating group. Each row in the middle part of Figure 14-7 gives the return that is achieved owing to a transition to another quality (spread change times duration). For tran-sitions straight to default, we do not assume a total loss of all invested funds, which would ignore the possibility of partial recovery through default proceed-ings and overstate the expected losses from defaults. We assume a maximum loss of –60% as a result of a downgrade or default, corresponding to an average recov-ery rate of 40%. To calculate the return statistics, we weight these conditional returns by the transition probabilities from Figure 14-6 to calculate the mean and standard deviation of returns owing to rating transitions. We see that for a Baa bond, the expected loss from rating transitions is –58 bp with a standard de-viation of 426 bp.

This result can be viewed as a measure of the extent to which the credit spread compensates investors for the risk of downgrades. The average Baa spread over Treasuries of 234 bp might be interpreted as the expected excess return of Baa credits over Treasuries under a "no change" scenario. However, even absent any systematic change in credit spreads, the effect of ratings transitions carries an expected underperformance of –58 bp. Subtracting this expected loss from the spread of 234 bp, we see that the expected excess return of a Baa bond over Trea-suries is only 176 bp. This amount should theoretically compensate investors for taking on the systematic risks of investing in Baa debt: a systematic widening of spreads, a sudden increase in the rate of downgrades, or defaults. Dividing this expected return by the standard deviation of return owing to ratings transitions

Figure 14-7. Modeled Return Impact of Rating Changes
Spreads as of December 31, 2001

Quality	Aaa	Aa	A	Baa
Initial Characteristics of Hypothetical Bonds				
Duration	5.00	5.00	5.00	5.00
Spread (bp)	62	92	158	234
Projected Returns Based on Final Rating Category (%)				
Aaa	0.00	1.52	4.83	8.60
Aa	−1.52	0.00	3.31	7.08
A	−4.83	−3.31	0.00	3.77
Baa	−8.60	−7.08	−3.77	0.00
Ba	−19.37	−17.85	−14.55	−10.78
B	−29.03	−27.51	−24.20	−20.43
C	−60.00	−60.00	−60.00	−60.00
D	−60.00	−60.00	−60.00	−60.00
Model Statistics (bp)				
Average return	−16	−28	−21	−58
Standard deviation	64	142	186	426
Expected return	46	64	137	176
Expected return/standard deviation	0.72	0.45	0.73	0.41

gives us a measure of expected return per unit of risk. Figure 14-7 shows that, by this measure, single-A securities have the highest ex ante risk-adjusted returns.

How do we compare these results with our observations of peer group under-performance? Recall that in our study of achieved performance of downgraded bonds, we compared their returns to the average return of a peer group consisting of all similar bonds in the index, including the downgraded ones. In this model, we expect the Baa portion of the index to return −58 bp owing to ratings transitions. To obtain projected returns relative to this peer group, we shift the whole column of projected returns in Figure 14-7 by this peer group return. For a Baa bond with an unchanged rating, for example, the return relative to the peer group is 0.58%, whereas a bond downgraded to Ba underperforms the peer group by −10.20% (= −10.78% − 0.58%). We can then take probability-weighted statistics over all possible downgrade events to obtain the average and standard deviation of performance relative to the peer group among downgraded securities.

For increased accuracy, the analysis illustrated in Figure 14-7 can be repeated using a finer ratings grid. The difference between the average A spread and the average Baa spread corresponds to a quality difference of a full letter grade, or three "notches." Yet, not every downgrade from A to Baa is accompanied by such a large spread movement. Most downgrades are only a single notch. To address this issue, we replace the transition matrix shown in Figure 14-6 by a finer-grained transition matrix obtained from Standard & Poor's, which includes transition probabilities among all credit notches (AA+, AA, AA−, and so on).[6] An array of average spreads for each quality notch as of December 31, 2001, replaces Figure 14-5.

Figure 14-8 illustrates the resulting calculation of return statistics relative to the peer group. This computation assumes that all ratings transitions are grouped into the three categories of upgrades, downgrades, and no change. Let us focus on the Baa column as an example. For bonds with a Baa rating, there is a 11.8% probability of a downgrade, with a resulting expected return of −832 bp over the coming year if a downgrade occurs. With 78% probability, there will be no change in rating and no return owing to ratings transitions. Upgrades have a probability of 10.2% and a conditional expected return of 225 bp for the year. Computing the weighted expected return from these three cases, we get an overall expected return of −75 bp, which we can consider the expected return of the Baa peer group.

Conditional returns for the three cases relative to the peer group can then be calculated as a simple difference. Unchanged bonds outperform the peer group by 75 bp, downgraded bonds underperform by −757 bp, and so on. Multiplying these numbers by the probabilities gives the contributions to mean relative performance: for downgrades, we have 11.8% of −757 bp, or −89 bp. The relative performance of the whole peer group must be zero, so the three contributions must cancel one another. The negative performance contributions of downgrades are offset by positive contributions to upgrades and unchanged bonds. Note that the larger of these two positive terms is due to the unchanged bulk of the peer group, which outperforms simply because the peer group return is pulled down by the downgraded bonds. The variance of the relative performance owing to downgrades also has contributions from the three possible outcomes. It is clear that here almost all of the variance of performance relative to the peer group comes from the downgraded bonds. This justifies our focus on downgrade risk as opposed to overall risk that is due to ratings transitions.

Of course, this model is very dependent on the level and slope of the credit curve, which can change dramatically over time. Figure 14-9 shows the average spreads

---

6. Because this matrix includes transitions ignored by the broader matrix (such as downgrades from AA to AA−), the probability of an unchanged rating is lower in this matrix. This effect is offset because the most common transitions are of only a single notch and thus carry smaller spread changes. The matrix used for this analysis was published by S&P in February 2002 and covers data through 2001.

Figure 14-8. Spread Differential Model

Calculating Statistics of Return Relative to the Peer Group That
Are Due to Ratings Changes (fine transition matrix, spreads as of
December 31, 2001)

Initial Rating	Aaa-Aa	A	Baa
Transition Probabilities (%)			
Upgrade	2.0	6.8	10.2
No change	86.9	81.7	78.0
Downgrade	11.1	11.5	11.8
Expected Returns Owing to Rating Transitions (bp)			
Upgrade	53	185	225
No change	0	0	0
Downgrade	−182	−342	−832
Peer group return	−19	−27	−75
Contribution to Mean Performance Relative to Peer Group			
Upgrade	1	14	31
No change	17	22	59
Downgrade	−18	−36	−89
Total	0	0	0
Contributions to Standard Deviations of Relative Performance			
Upgrade	12	67	108
No change	18	24	66
Downgrade	135	247	499
Total	136	257	515

of 10-year bullet bonds of different qualities from 1994 through 2001.[7] At the beginning of this period, spreads were quite tight on an historical basis and very stable. We can detect three different types of changes since 1998. Spreads have moved higher; they have become more volatile (particularly in 2001); and, perhaps most relevant to our model, the credit curve has steepened considerably. The spread differentials from one quality to the next have increased, giving rise to greater losses for downgraded bonds. Within the investment-grade market, the slope of the curve has been the most volatile between A and Baa; the steep transition from Baa to below investment grade shows even more variability over time.

---

7. Because this model is based on option-adjusted spreads, we do not report results prior to 1994, when our lognormal option pricing model was introduced.

Spread (bp)

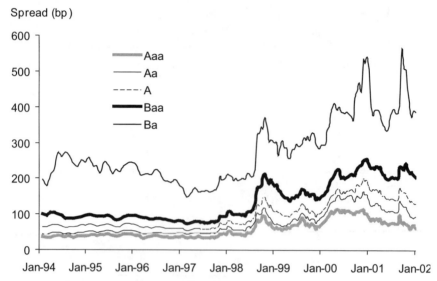

Figure 14-9. Historical 10-Year Spreads of U.S. Corporate Bonds
By Quality vs. Off-the-Run Treasury Curve

Figures 14-10 and 14-11 illustrate the model using spreads as of the end of 2001. Snapshots of the credit curve taken at different points in time would give very different results. Figure 14-10 shows the results of the spread differential model with the fine-grained transition matrix using the credit curves at the start of each year from 1994 to 2002. For example, the "2002" column was calculated using spreads as of December 31, 2001. The quantities included in this column are those shown in boldface in Figure 14-8.

Dependence on time is a major difference between the two models introduced in this section. We have studied historical returns of downgraded bonds over a long time period, and the resulting statistics reflect the net effect of events occurring in very different environments. The model built around spread differentials is based on a snapshot of the credit curve at a given point in time. To compare the two models, we take an average of the model outputs for each of the snapshots shown in Figure 14-10. These time-averaged results are compared to the results from the observed downgrade losses in Figure 14-11. We see that for single-A-rated bonds, the two models agree quite closely. However, the observed losses show greater levels of downgrade risk (both mean and standard deviation) than indicated by the spread differential model for Baa-rated bonds, and lower levels of downgrade risk for Aaa and Aa securities. When bonds are downgraded from investment grade to below investment grade, the market imposes a penalty that is greater than that implied by the spread differentials alone.

Figure 14-10. Spread Differential Model

Results depend on spread levels

Year:	1994	1995	1996	1997	1998	1999	2000	2001	2002	Average
Mean Performance of Upgraded Bonds (bp)										
Aaa-Aa	6	28	5	21	−1	66	53	75	53	34
A	51	56	49	34	55	90	83	156	185	84
Baa	182	141	170	100	84	166	120	271	225	162
Mean Performance of Downgraded Bonds (bp)										
Aaa-Aa	−62	−83	−109	−73	−103	−99	−108	−241	−182	−118
A	−172	−131	−173	−132	−129	−273	−202	−292	−342	−205
Baa	−558	−520	−651	−499	−438	−649	−670	−926	−832	−638
Contribution of Downgrades to Mean Performance (bp)										
Aaa-Aa	−6	−8	−11	−8	−11	−10	−11	−24	−18	−12
A	−18	−14	−18	−14	−14	−28	−21	−31	−36	−22
Baa	−60	−56	−70	−53	−47	−69	−71	−100	−89	−68
Standard Deviation Owing to Downgrades (bp)										
Aaa-Aa	81	86	110	97	98	123	116	159	135	112
A	172	168	191	167	161	208	204	241	247	195
Baa	369	374	421	380	360	442	467	533	499	427
Standard Deviation Overall (bp)										
Aaa-Aa	82	86	111	98	99	124	117	162	136	113
A	174	169	193	168	163	211	206	247	257	199
Baa	382	383	432	386	365	452	475	554	515	438

Figure 14-11. Comparing the Two Models of Downgrade Risk

	From Observed Downgrade Losses 1988–2001	From Credit Spread Differentials (fine transition matrix)	
		Spreads as of 12/31/01	Average 1994–2001
Average Loss (bp)			
Aaa-Aa	2	18	12
A	16	36	22
Baa	74	89	68
Standard Deviation (bp)			
Aaa-Aa	73	135	112
A	168	247	195
Baa	622	499	427

We consider the model based on historically observed losses of downgraded bonds to be our primary one, as it requires fewer assumptions and is grounded much more firmly in actual return data. As we proceed to portfolio-level modeling and optimal-structuring issues, this is the model we focus on. However, the model based on spread differentials has one key advantage. Separating the effects of transitions to different quality levels (instead of grouping all downgrades together) allows us to include the effect of rare events and create a model for the complete distribution of issue-specific returns. We therefore use this second model to calculate confidence intervals for worst-case portfolio underperformance.

PORTFOLIO DOWNGRADE RISK: ABSOLUTE AND RELATIVE TO A BENCHMARK

Let us now extend our model from a single bond to a portfolio. We prove that diversification helps reduce the standard deviation of loss and hence the chance of catastrophic losses. We start with an equally weighted portfolio of n bonds of the same credit quality and denote this portfolio's loss (underperformance of its peer group) owing to downgrades by L_n. Assume that each bond has the same probability p of a downgrade, that the size of the loss has the same distribution for all bonds, and that the results are uncorrelated. In this case, the mean loss on the portfolio is the same as for the single bond, but the variance is reduced by a factor of n :

$$\langle L_n \rangle = p\mu$$
$$\sigma_{L_n}^2 = \frac{1}{n}\sigma_{loss}^2. \tag{14-2}$$

It is important to distinguish between the absolute risk of a portfolio (standard deviation of portfolio return) and the risk relative to a benchmark (standard deviation of performance difference or tracking error). Let us assume that the benchmark for this portfolio is a broad-based index of N bonds of the same credit quality. For simplicity, the index is assumed to be equally weighted as well, but consists of a greater number of bonds ($N > n$). To analyze portfolio risk relative to the benchmark, we focus on the difference between the two returns. As the expected performance is the same for both the portfolio and the benchmark, the expected outperformance is zero. The standard deviation of the performance difference, known as tracking error (TE), is given by

$$TE^2 = \left(\frac{1}{n} - \frac{1}{N}\right)\sigma_{loss}^2. \tag{14-3}$$

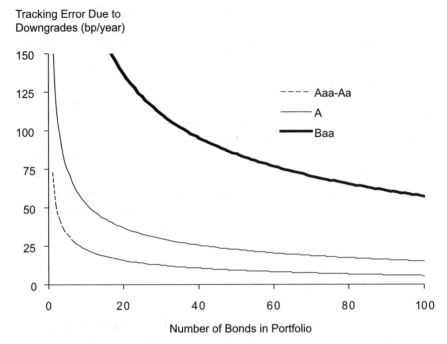

Figure 14-12. Risk Owing to Downgrades
As a Function of Portfolio Size, by Credit Quality

A comparison of the equations for absolute (14-2) and relative risk (14-3) shows that when we assume no correlations of downgrade losses among different issuers, there is very little difference between the two risk estimates until the portfolio size starts to approach that of the benchmark. In Figure 14-12, we plot portfolio risk as a function of the number of bonds in a portfolio for single-quality portfolios and benchmarks from each rating group. The graph shows the relative risk (tracking error) owing to downgrades, but would look much the same for absolute downgrade risk. This figure clearly demonstrates that because of the higher standard deviation of loss for downgrades from lower qualities, greater diversification is required to achieve a given level of risk. For example, a tracking error of 25 bp/year can be achieved by a portfolio of eight securities rated Aaa to Aa, or about forty single-A bonds, but would require well over 100 bonds in a Baa portfolio.

Correlations

Of course, downgrades of different issuers are not totally uncorrelated events. During economic downturns, many companies may simultaneously suffer financial hardship that could result in downgrades. An industry-wide slump might lead to downgrades of several companies in similar lines of business. Evaluation of the correlation between any two credits is one of the most challenging problems facing credit risk practitioners. Such practitioners understand that modeling correlations among different industries and issuers is critical and that by ignoring these correlations an asset manager can severely underestimate risk. We will see that while this is certainly true for measures of absolute risk, it is a far less important issue when evaluating risk relative to a benchmark.

When there are positive correlations among issuers, the effect of diversification is diluted, and the portfolio cannot be insulated from risk as well as Equation (14-2) implies. To illustrate this, we introduce a very simple correlation model, in which a single correlation coefficient ρ represents the correlation between the losses of any two bonds. It can be shown that the mean and variance of portfolio loss owing to downgrades under this model are given by

$$\langle L_n \rangle = p\mu$$
$$\sigma_{L_n}^2 = \sigma_{\text{loss}}^2 \left(\frac{1}{n} + \rho \, \frac{n-1}{n} \right). \tag{14-4}$$

Note that in the variance of portfolio downgrade loss expressed in Equation (14-4), there is a term $\rho\sigma_{\text{loss}}^2$ that does not disappear for a large n. To the extent that two bonds are correlated, diversification offers limited reduction of risk. In the extreme case where all bonds are perfectly correlated ($\rho = 1$), the portfolio risk is exactly the same as the risk of a single bond ($\sigma_{L_n} = \sigma_{\text{loss}}$), regardless of how many bonds are in the portfolio.

Figure 14-13 shows how the absolute risk of a Baa portfolio depends on the assumed value of the correlation coefficient ρ. While a portfolio of 100 Baa bonds has an absolute risk of downgrade loss of 62 bp in the uncorrelated case, the assumption of a positive correlation of just 5% more than doubles that risk to 152 bp. As shown in the figure, an increase in the correlations of downgrade losses among different issuers leads to an increased level of absolute risk that cannot be diversified away. However, if risk is measured vs. a benchmark, this is no longer true.

Positive correlations among the downgrade risks of different issuers essentially turn these risks into a systematic risk factor that affects the benchmark as well as the portfolio. This risk cannot be eliminated by diversification and increases the likelihood of extreme negative returns for both indices and portfolios. In fact, the increased correlations between bonds imply that the subset of index issuers held in a portfolio will be more likely to track the index closely.[8]

8. In this study, we focus on the relationship between diversification and nonsystematic risk. We implicitly assume that the portfolio matches the systematic risk exposures of the bench-

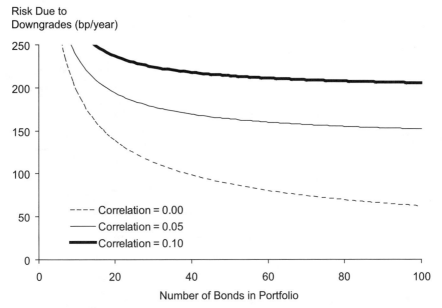

Figure 14-13. Absolute Risk
Standard Deviation of Portfolio Excess Returns Owing to Downgrades for Portfolios
Containing Different Numbers of Baa Bonds

When we revisit the calculation of relative risk with this simple constant correlation assumption, we find that the tracking error is given by

$$\sigma_{TE}^2 = \sigma_{loss}^2(1 - \rho)\left(\frac{1}{n} - \frac{1}{N}\right). \tag{14-5}$$

This function is plotted in Figure 14-14 for Baa portfolios (against a benchmark of $N = 500$ issuers), using several values of the correlation coefficient ρ. We see that increasing correlations have a much smaller (and opposite) effect on tracking error than on the absolute risk of portfolio loss. Thus, while careful estimates of correlations among the loss risks of different issuers are necessary for

---

mark. For example, a secular widening of corporate spreads will not cause underperformance as long as the portfolio has matched the benchmark's exposure to corporates. For settings in which this is not the case, such as when a portfolio uses credit against an all-government benchmark, there is indeed a systematic risk exposure. In these cases, positive correlation among different credits will certainly increase tracking error.

Tracking Error Due to
Downgrades (bp/year)

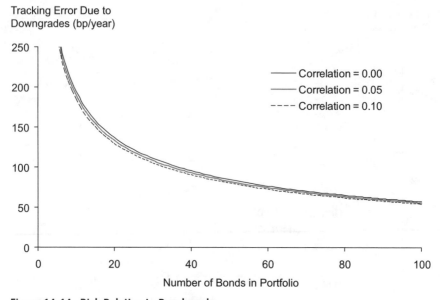

Figure 14-14. Risk Relative to Benchmark
Tracking Error Owing to Downgrades as a Function of the Number of Bonds, Baa
Portfolio vs. Baa Index (correlation matters little)

accurate measures of absolute risk, such as VaR (absolute magnitude of loss at a
given probability), they are far less critical for projecting tracking errors.[9]

Estimating Confidence Bounds

We characterized the risk owing to downgrades using the standard deviation of
either absolute or relative return. Another way of looking at risk is in terms of
worst-case returns or confidence bounds. What is the probability that the portfolio will underperform its benchmark by more than a specified amount? When
can an asset manager be 95% certain that it will not?

9. The assumption of a single correlation coefficient that relates any two credits is a gross
simplification. It is certainly conceivable that a portfolio could contain a set of bonds that are
correlated to each other much more strongly than to the index at large. This could occur, for
example, if there is a large concentration of issuers within a single industry. Once again, such a
concentration could be viewed as a systematic risk exposure. If the goal is to minimize tracking
error, the portfolio should mimic the benchmark's industry exposures to the extent possible.
If a particular sector is overweighted to express an investment view, there is always the risk that
it will result in underperformance.

Very often, such questions are addressed using the standard normal distribution. If underperformance is normally distributed with zero mean, the manager can conclude with 95% confidence that the portfolio will not underperform its benchmark by more than 1.64 times the tracking error. Yet, both of the modeling approaches detailed earlier for the single-bond case make it abundantly clear that excess returns of corporate bonds are far from normally distributed. The large negative tails of the performance distribution could lead to severe underestimates of risk if confidence bounds are based on the normal distribution.

However, if we continue to assume independence between the returns of different bonds, then the law of large numbers allows the distribution of *portfolio* performance to converge toward a normal distribution. Regardless of the underlying distribution for a single bond, an average over n independent, identically distributed variables converges to a normal distribution as n grows toward infinity. It is therefore safe to use confidence bounds based on the normal distribution for very large portfolios, but not for very small ones. To help evaluate how many bonds must be in a portfolio before the normal distribution can be used, we have to model the precise shape of the portfolio return distribution.

To approximate the complete distribution of return relative to the peer group for a single bond, we begin with our estimate of returns owing to all possible credit transitions using the spread differential model. To convert this into a continuous distribution, we include an additional source of nonsystematic risk that represents the natural spread volatility of bonds whose credit rating remains unchanged.[10] For each possible credit transition, this additional source of volatility is assumed to cause a normally distributed dispersion around the projected return shown in Figure 14-7. Owing to the discrete nature of the credit transitions, however, the overall distribution of returns for a single bond is still very different from normal. We then convolve this distribution upon itself to obtain the distribution for the average return of a portfolio of two identical, independent bonds.[11] By repeating this procedure k times, we can obtain a distribution for a portfolio of 2^k bonds of the same quality. Figure 14-15a shows the distribution obtained for a portfolio of sixteen Baa bonds. As this is a distribution of relative returns, the

---

10. This estimation is based on the observed spread volatilities of bonds that did not experience ratings changes (see Figure 14-20).

11. For any two independent random variables X and Y, the distribution of the sum $Z = X + Y$ can be obtained by the convolution of the two distributions:

$$f_Z(z) = \int_{-\infty}^{\infty} f_X(x) f_Y(z - x) dx.$$

If $f_X(x)$ is taken to be the distribution of relative return for a four-bond portfolio, for example, then this relationship can be used to numerically evaluate the distribution for an eight-bond portfolio.

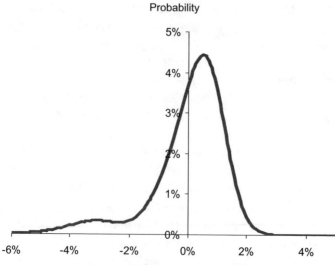

a

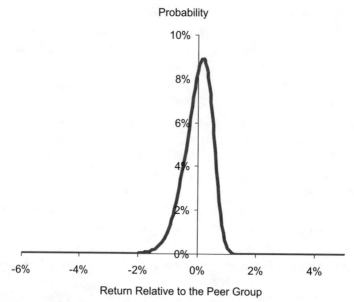

b

Figure 14-15. Modeled Distribution of Return Relative to the Peer Group for Portfolios of Baa Securities

(a) 16-Bond Baa Portfolio; (b) 128-Bond Baa Portfolio

mean is zero, yet the peak occurs at a small positive value corresponding to an un-changed rating. The distribution has a large negative tail, with a nonnegligible probability (0.34%) of underperformance by more than 500 bp. The distribution also exhibits a (much smaller) positive tail, corresponding to gains resulting from upgrades. The distribution for a 128-bond portfolio in Figure 14-15b is much more symmetrical and much closer to the normal distribution.

The distribution of portfolio returns can be used to derive confidence bounds on worst-case portfolio performance. Figure 14-16a shows that for the sixteen-bond portfolio, if a high level of confidence is desired, then the use of the normal distribution to determine the confidence bound can severely underestimate the risk of underperformance. For instance, under the normal distribution, the worst-case performance with 99% confidence is –3.08%. However, analysis of the full distribution from the model indicates that in order to have 99% confidence of achieving better than the worst-case return, the bound must be set at –4.50%. At the 95% level, the confidence bound implied by the normal distribution would be too tight by 75 bp.

For a portfolio of 128 bonds, as Figure 14-15b demonstrates, the distribution is much closer to normal, and the confidence bound drawn from the normal distribution corresponds much more closely to the one obtained from our model distribution. Combine this with the fact that the tracking error decreases as well, and we find in Figure 14-16b that even at a confidence level of 99%, the confidence bound from our model is only 19 bp worse than the one from the normal distribution.

This study makes us confident that for portfolios of moderate size, using the normal distribution to build worst-case bounds produces reasonable results. The level of confidence required determines how large a portfolio must be to justify the use of this approximation.

OPTIMAL PORTFOLIO STRUCTURE

Equipped with the foregoing model of downgrade risk, we now turn our attention to issues of portfolio structure. We look for the optimal number of bonds in various quality segments of a portfolio and the corresponding diversification constraints that should be imposed on them. We investigate several different formulations of the problem, which correspond to different investment goals. First, for a portfolio containing a given number of bonds, we show how to track an index with the least possible risk owing to downgrades. Next, to find the optimal number of bonds, we introduce a model for the value of credit research and maximize the information ratio.

To keep the focus of this study on nonsystematic risk, we limit the portfolio optimization problems to a single idealized form. We assume that the benchmark

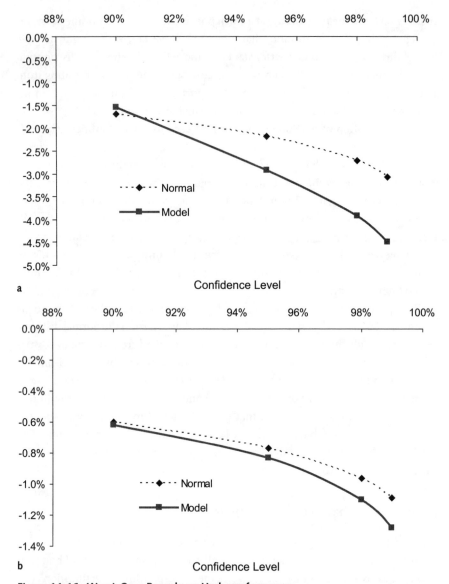

Figure 14-16. Worst-Case Bounds on Underperformance

Owing to Downgrades for Different Levels of Confidence from Model Distribution and Estimated from Normal Distribution: (a) 16-bond Baa portfolio; (b) 128-bond Baa portfolio

Figure 14-17. $1 Billion U.S. Credit Index Proxy with Equal Weights to All Securities

Quality	Percent of Index	Number of Bonds	Tracking Error Owing to Downgrades (bp/year)	Position Size	
				$ Million	Percent
Aaa-Aa	26.3	26	14	10.0	1.0
A	38.5	39	26	10.0	1.0
Baa	35.2	35	102	10.0	1.0
Total	100.0	100	38		

Worst-case boundary on underperformance owing to downgrades
(bp, 95% confidence): −62

includes all securities in the Lehman Brothers U.S. Credit Index and that the portfolio takes no systematic risks relative to the benchmark. Thus, the portfolio is assumed to match the benchmark exposures to all systematic risk factors, including yield curve, industry, and quality. Moreover, we continue to assume that both the portfolio and benchmark are equally weighted within each quality group. The only difference between the portfolio and the benchmark is that the portfolio is formed from only a subset of the index bonds within each quality group.

We illustrate the construction of an idealized $1 billion credit portfolio of 100 bonds in Figure 14-17. Partitioning the Lehman Brothers U.S. Credit Index by quality, we discover that approximately 26% of the index is concentrated in issues rated Aaa or Aa, 39% is rated A, and about 35% is rated Baa. We assume that the portfolio matches this distribution of market value. The only question is how many bonds are to be used to fill the market allotment for each quality, for example, the $350 million of Baa debt. This example simply assumes the number of bonds of each quality to be proportional to the index weight, so that a uniform position size of about $10 million is maintained across all credit qualities.

Given the number of portfolio securities in each credit quality, we use the models developed in the previous section to calculate the tracking error owing to downgrades within each quality separately. Assuming independence among the tracking errors in the different qualities, we can calculate the overall tracking error TE from the tracking errors in each quality TE_q according to the index weights w_q:

$$TE^2 = \sum_q w_q^2 TE_q^2. \tag{14-6}$$

We can see that when the portfolio is constructed using equal weights as in Figure 14-17, the tracking error in the Baa sector is much higher than in the remainder of the portfolio because of the greater risk of loss owing to downgrades.

Diversification among qualities reduces the portfolio tracking error to just 38 bp/year. This implies that in the worst case (with 95% confidence), downgrades could cause the portfolio to underperform the index by 62 bp, using the normal distribution as an approximation. However, it is clear that a smaller tracking error could be achieved by a 100-bond portfolio if the Baa portion were spread among a larger number of issuers.

Minimizing Tracking Error

Our first optimization problem can be stated as follows: for a 100-bond portfolio, how many bonds of each quality should be purchased to achieve the lowest tracking error owing to downgrades? We formulated this as an integer programming exercise and solved for the number of bonds to be allotted to each quality. The optimal allocation, shown in Figure 14-18, chooses more than twice as many Baa-rated bonds as the equal-weighted position of Figure 14-17. The size of each Baa exposure is reduced to $4.8 million, or 0.5% of the portfolio, while the Aa and Aaa exposures are allowed to grow to 4.4% each. (The total allocation to each quality continues to match that of the index.) As a result of this reallocation, we reduced the tracking error owing to the risk of downgrades of Baa securities to below investment grade from 102 to 69 bp/year. In the two higher-quality groups, where the downgrade losses are typically smaller, there are slight increases in risk because of increased concentration; the net effect is a lower overall tracking error owing to downgrades from 38 to 29 bp/year.

We repeated this exercise for portfolios of different numbers of bonds and discovered the results to be quite consistent. As shown in Figure 14-19, for portfolio sizes ranging from 50 to 500 bonds, the optimal portfolio structure is such that about 72% of the bonds are selected from Baa-rated issuers. We can demonstrate that if we relax the constraint on the number of bonds of each quality being integers, this problem can be solved in closed form. The optimal solution is such that the ratio of position sizes in different qualities is inversely proportional to the ratio of the respective volatilities of downgrade losses. The volatility of downgrade loss for Baa bonds, as seen in Figure 14-11, is 622 bp/year, about four times the volatility for single-A bonds, and about nine times that of Aa-Aaa qualities. As a result, the position sizes for single-A bonds in the optimal portfolio shown in Figure 14-18 are almost four times the Baa position size of $4.8 million, and those for Aa-Aaa are nine times as large.[12]

---

12. The ratios do not match exactly because Figure 14-18 is based on an integer number of bonds.

Figure 14-18. $1 Billion U.S. Credit Index Proxy with Optimal Allocation of Bonds to Qualities

Quality	Percent of Index	Number of Bonds	Tracking Error Owing to Downgrades (bp/year)	Position Size $ Million	Position Size Percent
Aaa-Aa	26.3	6	30	43.9	4.4
A	38.5	21	36	18.3	1.8
Baa	35.2	73	69	4.8	0.5
Total	100.0	100	29		

Worst-case boundary on underperformance owing to downgrades
(bp, 95% confidence):   −48

The implication for investment policy is clear. When a position size maximum is imposed as a diversification requirement, insisting on smaller limits for lower-quality ratings is more important. In higher qualities, where the risk of catastrophic events is smaller, larger concentrations can be tolerated.

Diversification of "Natural" Spread Volatility

The risk of downgrades, which is the main focus of this chapter, is not the only source of nonsystematic risk. Even securities that do not experience ratings changes exhibit natural spread volatility. This source of return variance may also motivate portfolio diversification. From the same data set that was used to quantify downgrade risk, we isolated a set of bonds each month whose ratings remained unchanged for at least the succeeding 6 months. We measured the standard deviation of spread changes across all the bonds within each peer group every month and averaged this quantity over time. The resulting spread volatilities are shown in Figure 14-20. This volatility tends to increase for lower-rated credits, as was the case for downgrade risk, but in a much less drastic manner. For instance, overall

Figure 14-19. Structure of Optimal Credit Index Proxies for Different Numbers of Bonds

Number of Bonds	50	100	150	200	500
Aaa-Aa	3	6	10	13	34
A	11	21	32	43	114
Baa	36	73	108	144	352
Tracking error owing to downgrades (bp/year)	42	29	23	19	10

Figure 14-20. Cross-Sectional Spread Change Volatility of Bonds with Unchanged Ratings

April 1990–December 2001

		Spread Change Volatility (bp/month)				
		Industrial	Financial	Utility	Non-U.S.	Average
Short	Aaa-Aa	16	18	15	12	15
	A	15	12	18	10	14
	Baa	19	17	19	18	19
Intermediate	Aaa-Aa	8	8	10	8	8
	A	11	9	11	9	10
	Baa	15	12	14	15	14
Long	Aaa-Aa	8	8	8	7	8
	A	9	11	9	7	9
	Baa	14	14	11	12	13

volatility in long spreads was 8 bp/month for Aaa-Aa, 9 bp/month for A, and 13 bp/month for Baa. A similar pattern holds for intermediate spreads. Spreads on short-duration bonds were more volatile and exhibited some variation from this pattern. Short spreads are relatively less stable, probably because small pricing differentials can imply relatively large spread changes for short bonds. We do not consider this to be a very significant effect.

When we add this variance to the one from downgrade risk and calculate the overall variance, we obtain a set of nonsystematic risk volatilities that are much less differentiated by quality than those from downgrade risk alone. This comparison (Figure 14-21) shows that while downgrade risk dominates in Baa, natural spread volatility may dominate in the higher qualities. The downgrade risk volatilities are obtained from Figure 14-11, using both the model based on historical returns of downgraded bonds and the one based on spread differentials. The return volatilities for "other nonsystematic risk" are obtained from Figure 14-20 as follows: The short-dated volatilities are disregarded, and the numbers from the two longer cells are averaged to obtain a monthly spread volatility per quality. We then multiply these numbers by a nominal duration of 5 to get a monthly return volatility and by $\sqrt{12}$ to annualize. The resulting annual return volatilities are displayed in the middle column of Figure 14-21 and then combined with the downgrade risk to obtain the total nonsystematic risk.

We can repeat the portfolio structuring exercise of this section to minimize overall nonsystematic risk instead of downgrade risk alone, using either one of the

Figure 14-21. Downgrade Risk vs. Other Nonsystematic Risk

	Downgrade Risk	Other Nonsystematic Risk	Total Nonsystematic Risk
From Observed Performance of Downgraded Bonds (bp)			
Aaa-Aa	73	141	159
A	168	165	236
Baa	622	231	664
Position size ratio	9:4:1		4:3:1
From Spread Differentials (bp)			
Aaa-Aa	112	141	180
A	195	165	256
Baa	427	231	486
Position size ratio	4:2:1		3:2:1

basic models for downgrade risk. The optimal ratio of A and Baa position sizes turns out to be quite stable. For either of the volatility assumptions shown, Baa position limits should be two to three times smaller than their A counterparts. The relative amount of risk in the Aaa-Aa range depends somewhat more strongly on whether we include nonsystematic risk other than downgrade risk, and on the downgrade model used. The optimal ratio of these position sizes to those in A-rated bonds ranges from more than 2 to slightly more than 1.

Maximizing Information Ratio ("When is a portfolio too diversified?")

It is apparent from the preceding discussion that as a portfolio becomes more diversified, the exposure to event risk decreases. At what point should we stop? One approach to finding the "right" number of bonds in a portfolio is to decide how much tracking error owing to downgrades can be tolerated. The number of bonds that can deliver a particular tracking error can be found in Figure 14-19.

But what about investors who do not have a preconceived limit on tracking error? Can we find the optimal amount of diversification? One possible conclusion is that a portfolio should own as many issuers as possible. However, we have seen that the benefits of increased diversification decrease as the number of bonds increases. For instance, adding fifty names to the fifty-bond portfolio shown in Figure 14-19 decreases tracking error by 13 bp/year, while adding yet another fifty bonds gives a further decline of only 6 bp/year. At the same time, there are several types of costs that are incurred by increasing the number of bonds in a portfolio.

For "fully indexed" portfolios whose goal is to passively replicate index returns, it is indeed optimal to match the index composition as closely as possible. This is the approach used by the largest index funds. In this setting, the limits to diversification are practical ones. If bond positions become so small that the transactions are considered "odd lots," there is a significant increase in transaction costs. Moreover, many older and smaller index issues are illiquid, which complicates the effort to maintain index exposures in the face of portfolio inflows and outflows. These considerations prevent all but the largest funds from pursuing the "fully indexed" approach to managing credit portfolios.

A far greater number of portfolios follow an "enhanced indexing" approach, in which the goal is to outperform the index by a modest amount while limiting the tracking error. In this setting, an increase in the number of issuers to be included in the portfolio is likely to entail an increase in the cost of credit research. In addition, a requirement to purchase a greater number of securities dilutes the value of credit research. Once the managers have purchased all highly recommended securities, further diversification is possible only by adding issuers that are considered to be trading rich or those with a neutral (or even negative) outlook. If an asset manager expects the portfolio to outperform the benchmark based on successful security picking, this outperformance tends to decrease as a greater number of bonds are added to the portfolio.

Qualitatively, then, the "right" amount of diversification is determined by the trade-off between its two main effects: risk reduction and dilution of outperformance. One way to express this goal quantitatively is to maximize the information ratio, that is, the ratio of expected outperformance to tracking error. To do this, however, we need to model the value of credit research. Such a model should estimate expected outperformance as a function of the number of bonds in a portfolio. We propose two such models.

A LINEAR MODEL FOR THE VALUE OF CREDIT RESEARCH

Our first model for the value of credit research assumes that the expected outperformance of a security is a linear function of analyst preference. Assume that the task given to the credit research team is to rank all the issuers in a particular rating group by preference. Let the variable x represent a given issuer's rank on a smooth scale where 0 represents the most recommended issuer and 100% the least. (The intuition behind this unusual convention is that if one were to buy 5% of the market, one would buy the top 5% by analyst's recommendations.) The function $f(x)$, shown in Figure 14-22a, gives expected outperformance as a function of the analyst's ranking. The favorite pick is assumed to outperform by b basis points (in this example b is 78 bp/year; the source of this assumption is discussed later with Figure 14-24); the issuer ranked lowest is assumed to underperform by the same amount; and the issuer in the middle earns the index average. Of course, there is plenty of volatility around these values, with magnitude much larger than b. But the assumption is that following the analysts' recommendations should bias the portfolio toward positive outperformance (e.g., by finding cheap valuations, predicting tightening, and avoiding downgrades).

Now let us assume that the portfolio is constructed as an equally weighted blend of bonds from the n highest-ranked issuers.[13] The expected outperformance of the resulting portfolio, as a function of the number of bonds, is shown in Figure 14-22b. Intuitively, we see that if very few bonds are used, the expected outperformance is close to b. As more and more bonds are added, the benefits of credit research are diluted. As we approach the middle of the rankings, we are adding bonds with expected outperformance close to zero; if we insist on including bonds from more than half of the issuers for diversification purposes, we are adding bonds that are expected to underperform. In the limit, when the portfolio includes all the issuers in the index ($n = N$), the risk is minimized, but the expected outperformance shrinks to zero as well.

In this model, the expected outperformance of the portfolio is a decreasing linear function of the number of issuers selected; the portfolio risk shown in Figure 14-22c also decreases with the number of bonds, but nonlinearly. If we look at the expected information ratio (expected outperformance/tracking error), we find that as we increase the number of bonds, the dominant effect at first is the decrease in risk, leading to increasing ratios. As the number of bonds grows, the risk function saturates, and eventually the steadily increasing cost of diversification starts to dominate. Any increase in the number of bonds beyond that point causes the information ratio to decrease. As seen in Figure 14-22d, the maximum information ratio occurs at about half of the issuers. For a uniform (single-quality) bond universe, it can be shown that the maximum information ratio is obtained by purchasing bonds from exactly half of the issuers in the index. This is true regardless of the value assumed for b, the expected outperformance of the most highly recommended bond.

When applied to a portfolio and index of mixed quality, we once again find that when evaluating the risk/return trade-off over different qualities simultaneously, it is optimal to diversify more in the lower qualities. For a given set of input parameters, we find the number of bonds of each quality that maximizes the information

13. In this section, we deliberately use the words "bonds" and "issuers" interchangeably. We analyze performance in terms of the number of bonds in the portfolio; yet this is compared to the number of issuers in the benchmark. The key determinant of event risk is the exposure to issuers; to maximize issuer diversity for a given number of transactions, a portfolio holds only one bond from each issuer.

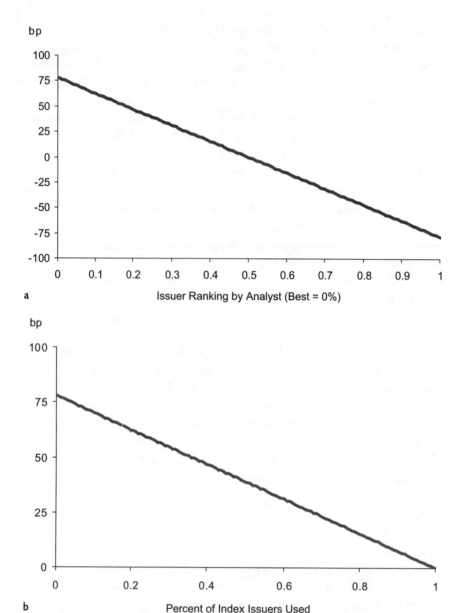

Figure 14-22. Linear Model for the Value of Credit Research
(a) Analyst Expected Return function; (b) Expected Portfolio Outperformance;
(c) Tracking Error owing to Downgrades; (d) Information Ratio

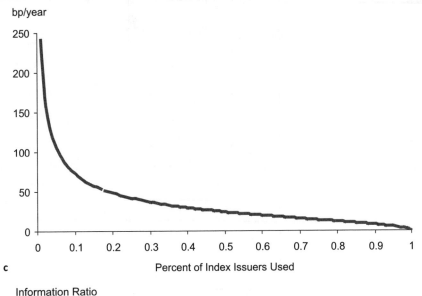

c

Percent of Index Issuers Used

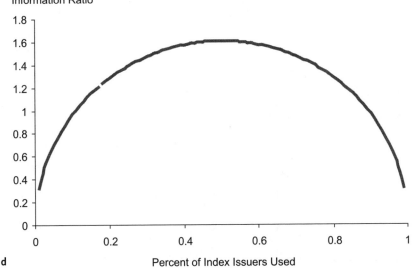

d   Percent of Index Issuers Used

Figure 14-22. (continued)

ratio. Figure 14-23 shows an example of an optimal portfolio constructed by this method. While about half of the index issuers are purchased overall, this is accomplished by using more than half of the Baa issuers and many fewer than half of the Aa and Aaa issuers. (The optimal solution would have used even more Baa bonds if the minimum position size of $1 million had not been imposed.) The ratio of position sizes is approximately 7:3:1, not too different from what we observed in tracking error minimization.

Figure 14-23. Optimal Number of Bonds According to the Linear Model

Quality	Expected Outperformance of Best Bonds (bp)	Number of Index Issuers	Number of Bonds Used	Expected Portfolio Outperformance (bp)	Tracking Error Owing to Downgrades (bp/year)	Position Size $ Million	Position Size Percent
Aaa-Aa	49	253	39	41.5	10.8	6.7	0.7
A	50	522	152	35.2	11.5	2.5	0.3
Baa	78	659	352	36.1	22.6	1.0	0.1
Total		1434	543	37.2	9.5		

These results are very sensitive to the assumed expected outperformance in each quality. The more outperformance is expected in a given quality, the steeper the performance penalty that results from the dilution of credit research. Although this quantity is not a factor in a homogeneous market (where increasing the single parameter just scales all information ratios), introducing different expectations for different qualities can drastically change our results. The more outperformance can be expected from the top picks in a given quality, the more risk in the form of larger position sizes one is willing to accept there. We can show that the optimal ratio of position sizes in different qualities is proportional to the square root of the ratio of expected outperformance.

How much outperformance can an analyst provide in each credit quality? Although this is essentially a subjective question, we investigated several different assumptions, each based on objective quantitative criteria. These assumptions, and the optimal portfolio structure for each one, are shown in Figure 14-24. The first assumption, used in Figure 14-23, is the outperformance of 49 bp in Aa, 50 bp in A, and 78 bp in Baa. These magnitudes are based on the results of our prior research on security selection using "imperfect foresight."[14] In that study, we carried out an historical simulation of security selection in which knowledge of future returns was systematically used to bias selection in favor of better-performing securities at a certain level of "skill." The outperformance levels cited earlier were achieved using the same level of skill to choose securities within the three quality groups.

In Figure 14-24, this result is compared to those obtained using several other assumptions for a $2 billion credit portfolio. The imperfect foresight assumption gives rise to an optimal position size ratio of approximately 5:2:1.[15] If we assume outperformance to be the same in all qualities, the results change very little. Another possible assumption is that the expected outperformance is proportional to volatility, under the theory that greater spread movement implies more opportunity. This assumption, which increases the performance advantage of Baa, brings the optimal position sizes closer together, for a ratio of about 4:2:1.

A fourth assumption reflects the view that the main role of credit research is to avoid downgrades. As such, we can use our empirical research on the expected peer group underperformance owing to downgrades to estimate the expected outperformance from avoiding them. If downgrades occur with probability p and have mean underperformance μ, the outperformance from avoiding downgrades

---

14. See Chapter 1. The numbers cited here are based on the data summarized there.

15. The results shown on the first line of Figure 14-24 differ from the solution of Figure 14-23 because of the difference in portfolio size. For the $2 billion portfolio of Figure 14-24, the $1 million minimum position size is not a binding constraint.

Figure 14-24. Linear Model under Different Outperformance Assumptions

	Expected Outperformance of Top Issuers (%)			Number of Bonds in Portfolio			
	Aaa-Aa	A	Baa	Aaa-Aa	A	Baa	Total
Imperfect foresight	0.49	0.50	0.78	92	363	659	1114
Equal outperformance	0.50	0.50	0.50	92	365	659	1116
Proportional to volatility	0.10	0.23	0.85	72	190	393	655
Avoid downgrades	0.03	0.16	0.78	122	194	356	672
Equal position size	0.01	0.07	1.41	243	355	325	923

is given by $-(p/1 - p)\mu$.[16] This assumption gives an estimate of expected outperformance that is more than thirty times larger in Baa than in Aa—and yet, the greater risk in Baa still makes it optimal to keep positions smaller there, with a ratio of about 2:2:1.

Just how much more performance in Baa's would we need to make a uniform position size optimal? We found that the ratio of expected outperformance would have to be 1:7:141! When we impose this assumption, our numerical optimization indeed produces a solution with equal position sizes.

Two conclusions can be drawn from Figure 14-24. First, we see that the optimal ratio of position sizes changes when we assume greater or lower potential for outperformance in various qualities. However, for all reasonable estimates of this performance advantage, it remains optimal to have a stricter diversification constraint (smaller position size) in Baa than in the higher ratings. Second, because of the nature of the linear outperformance function, for all the assumptions investigated here, the optimal overall number of issuers in the portfolio is still quite large, ranging from approximately half to all of the issuers in the index.

A PIECEWISE LINEAR MODEL

The simple linear model just described allowed us to quantify the trade-off between the costs and benefits of diversification and to demonstrate some qualitative rela-

---

16. This quantity differs by a factor of $1 - p$ from the underperformance owing to downgrades shown in Figure 14-4, which is equal to $p\mu$. For example, the expected outperformance of 0.785% of avoiding downgrades in Baa is obtained from the data in Figure 14-4 by dividing 0.74% by the 94.3% probability of no downgrade.

Resulting Position Sizes			Expected Outperformance (%)	Tracking Error Owing to Downgrades (%)	Information Ratio
Aaa-Aa	A	Baa			
5.7	2.1	1.1	0.14	0.02	5.71
5.7	2.1	1.1	0.14	0.02	5.78
7.3	4.1	1.8	0.20	0.08	2.39
4.3	4.0	2.0	0.17	0.09	1.93
2.2	2.2	2.2	0.26	0.09	2.94

tionships between our assumptions about expected outperformance and the implications for portfolio structure. However, there are some intuitively unsatisfying aspects to this model. The ranking of all issues in the universe on a smooth scale from best to worst does not correspond well to the way most research departments operate. Furthermore, the conclusion that an investor has to buy half of the issuers in the universe to achieve optimal diversification seems a bit extreme. By making a small modification to the previous model, we can remedy these two drawbacks simultaneously.

In the piecewise linear model, we continue to assume that when an issuer is researched, it is ranked on a linear scale as before, with expected outperformance b for the favorite selection and expected underperformance $-b$ for the least recommended issuer. However, we now assume that only a portion of the market is covered by credit research. Half of the covered issuers are expected to outperform and the other half to underperform; for all issuers not covered by research, the expected outperformance is zero. This middle portion of the market now offers us the opportunity to evaluate a pure diversification play. Should a portfolio contain bonds not recommended by research for the sole purpose of reducing tracking error at the expense of diluting the outperformance?

Figure 14-25 illustrates this model for outperformance in the case of a single-quality (Baa) and 20% market coverage. The expected outperformance for each bond is shown in (a). We see that zero outperformance is expected from the vast middle portion of the universe, with the top 10% expected to outperform and the bottom 10% expected to underperform. The expected portfolio outperformance for an equally weighted portfolio of the top n issuers is shown in (b). The reduction of expected portfolio outperformance is rather steep as we go from just the

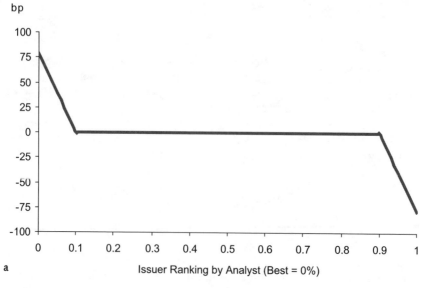

a

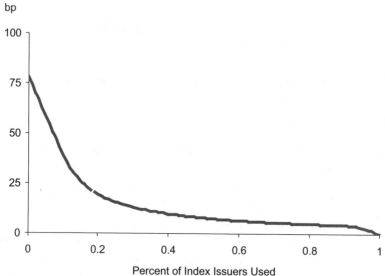

b

Figure 14-25. Piecewise Linear Model

20% Research Coverage of Market, Baa Portfolio vs. Baa Index: (a) Analyst Expected
Return Function; (b) Expected Portfolio Outperformance; (c) Tracking Error Owing to
Downgrades; (d) Information Ratio

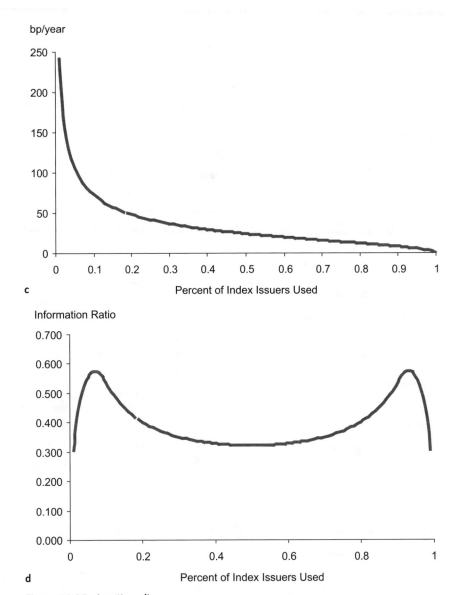

Figure 14-25. (continued)

top picks to include all recommended securities; after 10% it levels off to a slower descent, and then shoots quickly down toward zero when we start to include "sell" recommendations. The tracking error as a function of the number of bonds is repeated in (c) for comparison; it can be easily seen that it starts out with a steeper descent than the expected portfolio outperformance, but then levels off more sharply. The ratio between the two (the information ratio) is shown in (d).

It has a peak at about 7% of the issuers. The optimal information ratio is thus achieved by buying most (but not all) of the recommended bonds and none of the uncovered issues.

One interesting (and somewhat surprising) aspect of Figure 14-25d is the symmetrical shape of the information ratio function, with twin peaks at opposite ends of the spectrum. Both have information ratios of 0.57, but the portfolio using 7% of the issuers in the index achieves an expected outperformance of 51 bp and a tracking error of 88 bp, whereas the portfolio with 93% of the index has an expected outperformance of 4 bp and a tracking error of 7 bp. Clearly, the two peaks correspond to two very different investment approaches. The first portfolio is pursuing a more active strategy and the second is extremely passive. The two uses of credit research illustrated here can be referred to as "picking winners" and "avoiding losers." We can show that as long as the model for expected outperformance is symmetrical, then the information ratio is symmetrical as well, and both approaches can achieve the same range of information ratios.

The case shown in Figure 14-25, consisting of a homogeneous set of issuers from the same credit quality, with a fixed number of bonds covered by research, has a straightforward solution for the optimal number of bonds. The information ratio can easily be expressed as a function of the number of bonds in the portfolio, and we can solve for the maximum. The equation for the optimal number of bonds in this case converges to about one-third of the covered issuers (or two-thirds of the recommended bonds) when the percentage of the market covered is small and to about half of the covered issuers (almost all of the recommended bonds) when the percentage covered is large. (This corresponds well to our solution for the linear model, which is the same as the piecewise linear model with 100% market coverage.)

Having found that the optimal number of bonds in the portfolio is closely related to the percentage of the market covered by research, the next question is obvious: how much of the market should research cover? In order to make this question meaningful, though, we have to factor in the cost of research to balance against the benefit of increasing the expected portfolio outperformance. As a rough approximation, we assumed an annual research cost of $5,000 per issuer. Unlike all of the other costs and risks assessed thus far in our study, this cost is assumed to be a fixed annual amount per issuer and is not proportional to portfolio size. The performance effect of the cost of research is thus much greater on small portfolios than on large ones.

With the piecewise linear model, we look at a two-stage optimization problem. We simultaneously solve for the number of index issuers of each quality that should be covered by research as well as for the number of bonds to buy in each quality. In addition to the amount of expected outperformance from the top picks in each quality, input parameters now include the cost of research coverage and the size of the portfolio.

Figure 14-26 shows the optimal structure for a $1 billion portfolio, using an estimated annual research coverage cost of $5,000 and assuming expected annual outperformance of 49 bp, 50 bp, and 78 bp for the top picks in the Aaa-Aa, A, and Baa quality groups, respectively.[17] The cost of research is quite significant for a portfolio of this size and limits the number of issuers that can be covered. The expected annual outperformance of 44 bp is partially offset by the 16 bp spent on research coverage to achieve a net expected outperformance of 29 bp (after rounding). As we have seen before, a greater number of bonds is chosen from the Baa sector than from the higher qualities to reduce downgrade risk where it is most significant. The additional implication is that to maintain the expected out-performance, the research budget is shifted toward the Baa sector as well (although not to as great an extent).

Figure 14-27 shows the results of the model using the same parameters, but for portfolios with different total market values. As portfolio size increases, a greater number of issuers can be covered for approximately the same performance cost in basis points. Thus, for a $2 billion portfolio, we can cover twice as many issuers and purchase more than twice as many bonds as in the $1 billion portfolio, with but a very small decrease in net performance. The increased diversification results in a relatively large reduction in tracking error, and the information ratio increases accordingly.

As we move to portfolios of $5 billion and larger, we find an interesting effect that may run counter to the accepted practice. Once a certain level of diversification is reached within Baa's, the model finds it no longer cost-effective to pay for research in this sector. Rather, the maximal information ratio is achieved by switching to a strategy in which the Baa portion of the portfolio is managed totally passively against the index. This may be achieved by buying every issuer in the index or via an index swap, a strategy that does not require any credit research expenditure. All efforts at outperformance are concentrated in the higher qualities, where event risk is lower. For money managers that maintain both active and passive funds, this result suggests the strategy of using a passive Baa or high yield fund as one component of an active credit fund.

---

17. As described in our discussion of Figure 14-24, these estimates of outperformance were obtained from our study of security selection using imperfect foresight.

Figure 14-26. Optimal Number of Bonds According to the Piecewise Linear Model

Quality	Expected Outperformance of Best Bonds (bp)	Number of Index Issuers	Percent of Issuers Covered	Number of Bonds Recommended	Number of Bonds Used	Expected Portfolio Outperformance (bp)	Tracking Error Owing to Downgrades (bp/year)
Aaa-Aa	49	253	12	16	4	43	38
A	50	522	15	40	16	40	41
Baa	78	659	30	100	73	49	69
Total		1434		155	93	44	31

Figure 14-27. Piecewise Linear Model
Optimal Structure as a Function of Portfolio Size

| Portfolio Size ($ billion) | Percent of Market Covered | | | Number of Bonds in Portfolio | | | Expected Performance (bp) | | | Tracking Error (bp/year) | Information Ratio |
	Aaa-Aa	A	Baa	Aaa-Aa	A	Baa	Before Cost	Research Cost	After Cost		
0.5	6	7	15	2	8	35	44	15	29	45	0.6
1	12	15	30	4	16	73	44	16	29	31	0.9
2	26	32	64	8	36	163	43	16	27	19	1.4
5	100	100	0	54	215	659	21	8	14	4	3.3
10	100	100	0	69	272	659	19	4	15	3	4.4
20	100	100	0	78	309	659	17	2	15	3	5.0

CONCLUSION

The models we develop to represent credit risk are quite simple and similar to other transition-matrix-based models that can be found in the literature.[18] In our view, the main contribution of this study lies in the data on observed performance effects of downgrades and in our approach to portfolio structuring. The reported data provide a necessary link between the event probabilities contained in transition matrices and the actual performance implications of these events. Moreover, while the literature contains many attempts to model credit risk, we have not seen these models applied to higher-level tasks such as portfolio structuring, setting investment policy, and establishing research priorities.

One key conclusion of this work is that downgrade risk can be readily understood and managed, especially in a portfolio-vs.-benchmark setting. While the risk of events such as downgrades and defaults make the return profile of a single corporate bond far from normally distributed, managers of bond portfolios are aided by the combination of two effects. First, the law of large numbers provides that to the extent that credit events for different issuers are uncorrelated, the losses on a portfolio become closer to normal as the number of securities grows. Second, managing relative to a broad benchmark reduces the role that correlations play in diluting the diversification benefits and increasing risk because any events that affect large sections of the market impact the benchmark as well. As a result, worst-case estimates of portfolio underperformance owing to downgrades can be fairly safely constructed based on the normal distribution as long as a sufficient level of diversification has been imposed.

The conclusions of this work depend on a set of assumptions that are quite subjective in nature. We feel more comfortable estimating the volatilities of future downgrade losses based on actual market observations of past downgrade losses. Some investors may prefer to work with spread differentials, which allow risk estimates to react more quickly to changes in the marketplace. Particularly in the area of modeling outperformance due to credit research, one can suggest any number of alternative functional forms that might be more realistic, and investors may have their own views as to how much value they can add by careful security selection within different market segments. The types of portfolio optimization problems to be considered are different for active and passive investors.

---

18. Two good surveys of the literature on credit models are: Dominic O'Kane and Lutz Schlögel, "Modelling Credit: Theory and Practice," Lehman Brothers, 2001, and Duen-Li Kao, "Estimating and Pricing Credit Risk: An Overview," *Financial Analysts Journal*, vol. 56, no. 4 (July/August 2000), pp. 50–66.

Yet from any point of view, the basic message remains the same. Different credit qualities and market segments entail different amounts of nonsystematic risk, and these differences should be considered when formulating an investment strategy. The lower the quality and the greater the degree of risk, the stricter the diversification constraints that should be imposed. From the point of view of downgrade risk alone, we find that the optimal ratio of position sizes in the three quality groups studied (Aaa-Aa:A:Baa) is a rather extreme 9:4:1. In reality, of course, investors are concerned with all sources of nonsystematic risk, including the potentially significant return volatility of bonds that did not experience a rating change. This total-risk analysis produces a more realistic optimal position ratio of 4:3:1.

When considering the implications for credit research allocation, the conclusions are more dependent on the setting. In active management, the results generally follow the same pattern as for diversification: to support the selection of more securities in the lower qualities, a greater portion of the research budget should be applied. However, our research raises the possibility that in some enhanced indexing applications, it might be appropriate to allocate the bulk of the research budget to active management in the higher qualities and take a purely passive stance in the most risky portion of the market.

15. Return Performance of Investment-Grade Bonds after Distress

Given the rash of distressed bonds in the Lehman Investment-Grade Credit Index in the years 2000–2002, many investors have pondered the question of whether it makes sense to sell distressed bonds out of their portfolios. Some feel it is better to sell as soon as the issue becomes distressed because it is unlikely that it will recover. Others think that a distressed bond offers a very attractive yield and as long as the issue does not default, there is good potential for strong total and excess returns over time. The purpose of this study is to answer the following question: "Based on history, if an investment-grade issue becomes distressed, is one better off holding or selling?"

The events of the years 2000–2002 produced a large number of distressed investment-grade issues, which may indicate that today's credit markets face structural problems never seen before. However, other years also produced a significant number of distressed issues in a similarly bleak corporate environment. In fact, some may argue that the spate of distressed issues in recent years was merely the result of a vicious crisis-of-confidence cycle, with issues declining in price simply because they had declined in price. If this is the case, a dispassionate historical perspective may be helpful to portfolio managers as they decide whether to hold distressed investment-grade issues.

This study shows that distressed investment-grade bonds have performed well as a group vs. Treasuries and other corporate issues subsequent to their distress month. However, this outperformance takes time—over a year.

IDENTIFYING DISTRESSED INVESTMENT-GRADE BONDS

To answer our question we first identify those bonds in the Credit Index that become distressed and then we measure their subsequent return performance.

Based on research first published by Lehman Brothers in 2004.

410

Defining a bond as "distressed" is highly subjective. As a starting point for this analysis we define a distressed investment-grade bond as a security that: (1) is rated Baa3 or higher; (2) has a fixed coupon of at least 2%; (3) has an option-adjusted spread to U.S. Treasuries greater than or equal to 400 bp; and (4) has an index price of less than 80% of par. Of the 3951 issues in the Lehman Credit Index as of the end of August 2003, three satisfied these distress criteria. (All three had become distressed by October 31, 2002.)

At each month-end since the beginning of 1990 through August month-end 2003, we sorted through the Credit Index to generate a list of CUSIPs that satisfied the "distress" definition on that date but had not done so in the previous 12 months. We refer to the month at the end of which an issue satisfies the distress criteria for the first time in at least 12 months as the issue's "distress month." For example, if an issue was distressed at the end of June 2000 but had not been distressed at the end of the months June 1999 through May 2000, then June 2000 is its distress month. We then tracked each distressed bond over a "performance period" of up to 24 months subsequent to its distress month. We chose 24 months as the length of the performance period to give the issue a chance to resolve its credit situation one way or the other. For example, bonds whose distress month was June 2000 were tracked from July 2000 through June 2002. We found 580 issues that became distressed between January 1, 1990, and August 31, 2003.

For distressed issues that defaulted before the end of the performance period we recorded the default date (usually the Chapter 11 filing date) and, to be conservative, assumed a recovery value of zero at the end of the month in which the issue defaulted.[1] In these cases, the performance period was truncated at the end of the default month.

For distressed issues that matured or were called during the performance period we recorded the relevant date and price and assumed that the redemption occurs at the end of the month. In these cases, the performance period was truncated at the end of the month in which the issue matured or was called. For distressed issues that left the indices because they were exchanged for other issues, we assumed that the issue was exchanged as announced and the performance of the new issue was measured until the end of the performance period. The new bond's performance after the exchange was combined with the old bond's performance

---

1. This is a very conservative assumption that understates the return performance of distressed issues. Later in this chapter, we examine how the results change if we assume a default price of 20% of par rather than our previously assumed, and possibly severe, default price of zero. [For example, it was widely reported on April 14, 2003, that WorldCom debt holders will receive about $0.36 on the dollar under the proposed reorganization plan (CNN/Money website: April 14, 2003).]

Figure 15-1. All Distressed Issues: Summary Information
1990–2003, Sorted by Vintage Year

Vintage Year	Distressed Issues	Amount (Par) Outstanding		Amount (Market Value) Outstanding	
		Distressed Issues ($ million)	As Percent of Credit Index	Distressed Issues ($ million)	As Percent of Credit Index
1990	50	9,731	1.70	7,326	1.36
1991	14	1,953	0.34	1,506	0.24
1992	1	75	0.01	60	0.01
1994	1	248	0.04	192	0.03
1995	5	900	0.13	690	0.09
1996	1	100	0.01	83	0.01
1998	29	6,992	0.65	5,253	0.45
1999	10	2,375	0.20	1,840	0.16
2000	139	36,746	2.62	27,162	1.91
2001	54	17,939	1.01	13,329	0.72
2002	271	158,227	8.53	113,998	5.60
2003[a]	5	992	0.05	995	0.05
Total	580				

[a] Updated through September 30, 2003, using bonds that became distressed by August 31, 2003. Missing vintage years had no issues that satisfied distress criteria.

before the exchange to form a single distressed bond performance history. Finally, there were many bonds whose performance periods were not truncated, owing to maturity, call, or default, but for which 24 months of data were not available because they became distressed after September 2001 and our return data set ends with September 2003. For such bonds, the performance period ends with September 2003. Overall, this study accounts for all investment-grade bonds in the Credit Index that became distressed as previously defined.

If a distressed issue recovered and later became distressed again, we did not regard the two distress incidents as separate occurrences, each producing a 24-month observation unless there were 12 consecutive "nondistress" months in between. This avoided the problem of issues bouncing in and out of distress status and generating multiple observations. In our historical period, seventeen issues (from ten separate issuers, e.g., KM) became distressed, subsequently became nondistressed for at least 12 consecutive months, and then became distressed again (and therefore appear twice in our list of 580 distressed issues).

Figure 15-2. Status of Distressed Issues (up to) 24 Months after Distress Month 1990–2003[a]

Status	Number of Issues with Distress Month Prior to 2001	Number of Issues with Distress Month in 2001 or Later
Defaulted	21	60
Matured	5	0
Called	0	4
Remained distressed	42	17
Nondistressed	182	249
Total	250	330

[a]Updated through September 30, 2003, using bonds that became distressed by August 31, 2003.

Figure 15-1 presents summary data on the 580 issues in the Credit Index that met the distressed criteria from January 1990 through August 2003 and shows the number of issues and the par and market value amounts outstanding at the end of the distress month (both absolute and as a percentage of the Credit Index). Figure 15-1 aggregates the monthly results by "vintage year," with an issue's vintage year defined as the calendar year in which it became distressed (the set of bonds that became distressed in that year is called that year's "vintage") and shows that in 2002, a total of 271 investment-grade bond issues, accounting for 5.6% of the outstanding market value and 8.5% of the par value of the Credit Index, became distressed.

What eventually happens to these distressed issues? By and large they recover. As shown in Figure 15-2, of the 580 distressed issues, 431 or 74%, became nondistressed within 24 months of their distress month. This number will likely rise as the 2002 and 2003 vintages season. For issues distressed prior to 2001, approximately 75% either matured or became nondistressed within 24 months of their distress month. Of the remaining 25%, 8% defaulted and 17% remained distressed. For issues distressed in 2001 or later, approximately 75% have become nondistressed so far, 1% have been called, 18% have defaulted, and 5% remain distressed. (The percentages do not add up to 100 owing to rounding.)

TOTAL RETURN AND EXCESS RETURN PERFORMANCE OF DISTRESSED BONDS

What have been the total return and excess return performances of distressed issues subsequent to their distress month? These numbers are the most relevant to portfolio managers. Once an issue becomes distressed, does it make sense to hold it, sell it, or possibly buy more? While some of the distressed issues subsequently lost their investment-grade rating, at the end of a bond's distress month it was investment grade and eligible to remain in most investor portfolios. Many portfolio managers are allowed to continue holding an investment-grade issue that becomes distressed (although with stiffer monitoring requirements).

We measure the performance of each distressed issue for 24 months, if possible, subsequent to, but not including, its distress month. As stated earlier, for bonds that default we assume a price of zero at the end of their default month. This assumption will be relaxed later in this study.

We calculate both cumulative total returns and cumulative excess returns. Return numbers are not annualized. We calculate excess returns by measuring the difference between the 24-month cumulative total return on the distressed issue and the 24-month cumulative total return on duration-matched Treasuries.[2] This cumulative excess return calculation allows the manager to ask what his relative performance would have been if he had sold the distressed issue at the end of the distress month and invested in Treasuries with similar duration.[3]

Cumulative total returns are, of course, calculated by compounding monthly total returns. Complete time series of monthly returns that went though the normal index-pricing quality controls are available for distressed bonds that remained in one or another Lehman Brothers index during their entire performance period. Most distressed issues remained in the Credit Index or migrated to the High Yield Index during their performance period.

However, some distressed issues left the Credit Index at some point in their performance period and were no longer members of any Lehman Brothers index. For example, a distressed issue might no longer satisfy the index liquidity constraint (i.e., amount outstanding), which has increased over time. More commonly, a distressed issue might have left the index because it came within a year of its maturity date. Unfortunately, the price and return time series for distressed issues that drop out of the Lehman family of indices come to an abrupt end.

Excluding such bonds might introduce a bias into our results, so these bonds are included, and we use their known monthly return data for the months in which they remained in some index. We now discuss the methodology for calculating returns for these issues once they have left the index.

---

2. Cumulative excess returns over a multimonth period cannot be computed simply by geometrically linking the monthly excess returns (see Chapter 30).

3. Duration as a measure of price sensitivity to interest rates is of limited relevance for distressed issues. In this exercise, we wish to evaluate a strategy of selling distressed bonds for comparable duration Treasuries. Presumably, the portfolio manager would replace a distressed credit issue with a comparable duration Treasury to maintain his overall portfolio duration.

The first step is to determine the horizon price for the bond, that is, the price of the bond at the end of its performance period. The horizon price is set to 100 for matured bonds, to 0 for defaulted bonds, and to the call price for called bonds. For a bond that did not mature or default and was not called, we first look for other issues from the same issuer that have a similar maturity and rating, but satisfied the liquidity constraint and remained in the indices. We then used the bid spread of the index issue at the end of the nonindex issue's performance period to price the nonindex issue. In all but a handful of cases, distressed issues that left the indices for liquidity reasons were priced in this way using index bonds of the same issuer.[4]

We then estimated the price of the nonindex bond at every month-end between the time it left the index and the end of the performance period by interpolating linearly between the horizon price determined by our research and its price the last time it was in an index. These price data, combined with accrued interest and coupon payment information, allowed us to estimate total returns on the bond in the months when it was not in any index. We calculate excess return on the bond in a nonindex month by measuring the difference between the total return on the bond and the total return on a Treasury with a duration equal to the last reported duration of the distressed issue when it was in the indices.[5]

Figures 15-3a and b show, respectively, the cumulative total and excess returns of distressed bonds during their respective performance periods (up to 24 months after the distress month). The distressed issues are sorted by distress month, with the issues with the earliest distress month appearing at the left end of the horizontal axis and those with the latest distress month appearing at the right end. The vertical line demarks issues that became distressed before and since January 2001. Figures 15-3a and b show that total and excess returns for distressed bonds have generally been positive.

We also calculate average cumulative total and excess returns by vintage year and for the entire study period. For every vintage year we compute the cumulative total or excess returns of all bonds in the year's vintage over the bonds' respective performance periods. The unweighted average of these returns is the total or excess return for that vintage year. Total and excess returns for longer periods are calculated similarly. Figure 15-4 presents cumulative total and excess returns by vintage year. It shows that for bonds distressed prior to 2001, the 24-month total

---

4. In a handful of cases, we had to price the distressed bond that had left the indices using a comparable, but not identical, issuer. Complete details are available from the authors.

5. There may have been some distressed issues that left the index and then returned before the end of their performance period. In any case, we used this pricing methodology for all months after a distressed bond left the indices, whether or not it returned.

Cumulative Total Return (%)

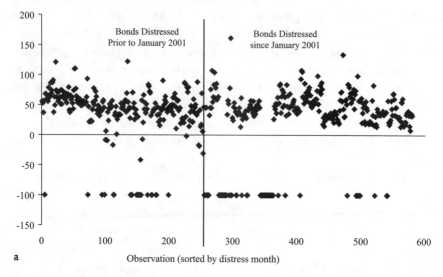

a   Observation (sorted by distress month)

Cumulative Excess Return (%)

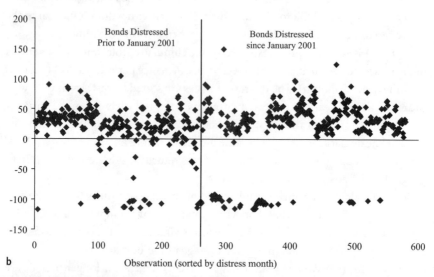

b   Observation (sorted by distress month)

Figure 15-3. Cumulative Performance of Distressed Bonds during Performance Period
Up to 24 Months after Distress Month: (a) Total Return; (b) Excess Return, January
1990–August 2003[a]

[a]Returns data through September 2003 for bonds distressed by August 2003. Prices for
defaulted bonds set to zero at end of default month.

Figure 15-4. Cumulative Total and Excess Returns vs. Duration-Matched Treasuries
24 Months (if available) after Distress Month, Results by Vintage Year: 1990–2003

Vintage Year	Observations	24-Month Cumulative Total Return (%)	24-Month Cumulative Excess Return vs. Duration-Matched Treasuries (%)
1990	50	60.36	31.58
1991	14	65.71	44.61
1992	1	54.17	24.43
1994	1	56.22	36.36
1995	5	55.11	38.63
1996	1	92.99	78.93
1998	29	25.48	21.19
1999	10	33.36	11.98
2000	139	24.34	4.82
2001	54	−7.04[a]	−17.13[a]
2002	271	25.80[a]	16.80[a]
2003[b]	5	24.60[a]	21.94[a]
Years prior to 2001	250	35.49	15.76
Years since 2001	330	20.41[a]	11.32[a]
All vintage years	580	26.91	13.24

[a]Issues of the 2001, 2002, and 2003 vintages generally do not have 24 months of returns since their distress month. Zero default recovery is assumed.
[b]Updated through September 30, 2003, using bonds that became distressed by August 31, 2003.

and excess returns have been very positive (averaging 35.49 and 15.76%, respectively). However, for bonds distressed in 2001 and thereafter, total and excess returns have been worse (averaging 20.41 and 11.32%, respectively).

The 2001 vintage stands out as the only poor performer, with an excess return of −17.13%. Even after almost 2 years it has showed little indication of full recovery. Keep in mind that this vintage is dominated by Enron issues. If we were to exclude Enron issues from the 2001 vintage, the 24-month cumulative total and excess returns as of the end of September 2003 would be 22.44 and 8.09%, respectively.

Vintage year 2002 is another story and seems to be recovering nicely, as the earlier vintages generally did (2001 notwithstanding). This vintage year was dominated by WorldCom, which became distressed in April 2002. Many more issues became distressed subsequently in 2002. By the end of September 2003, however, the vintage had cumulative total and excess returns of 25.80 and 16.80%,

Cumulative Excess Return (%)

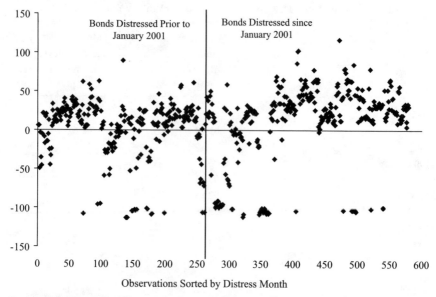

Observations Sorted by Distress Month

Figure 15-5. Cumulative Excess Return Performance of Distressed Bonds
12 Months (if available) after Distress Month, January 1990–September 2003[a]
[a]Returns data through September 2003 for bonds distressed by August 2003. Prices for defaulted bonds set to zero at end of default month.

respectively. If we were to exclude WorldCom issues from the 2002 vintage, the 24-month cumulative total and excess returns as of the end of September 2003 would be 34.75 and 25.49%, respectively.

In light of the generally strong performance of distressed issues after their distress month, we might wonder whether this strong performance begins immediately after the distress month, or perhaps these bonds continue to deteriorate for some time after the distress month only to recover later. To answer this question we examine the performance of all distressed issues in the 12-month performance period subsequent to their distress month to see if it is as good as the 24-month performance. (As before, we truncate a bond's performance period owing to maturity, default, or call or if the bond became distressed after September 2002.)

Figure 15-5 presents the performance of distressed bonds for the 12-month performance period sorted by observation, with the issues with the earliest distress month appearing to the left and those with the latest distress month appearing to the right. We have used a vertical line to mark off bonds distressed prior to 2001. We note that the distressed bonds of the 2002 and 2003 vintage years have had a relatively short time to resolve their creditworthiness, even a 12-month subsequent performance horizon may be too short to compare with other distressed issues. Figure 15-6 summarizes the 12-month total and excess returns by vintage year. For ease of comparison, this figure also repeats the 24-month total and excess returns reported in Figure 15-4.

As seen in Figures 15-5 and 15-6, for bonds distressed prior to 2001 the 12-month cumulative excess returns were significantly worse than their 24-month cumulative excess returns, indicating that distressed bonds tend to improve strongly in the second year following distress.

Although the 24-month cumulative excess returns for the 2001 vintage are better than its 12-month cumulative excess returns (−17.13 vs. −32.53%, respectively), the vintage remains a very poor performer relative to the other vintages. It seems likely that the 24-month cumulative excess return for the vintage will finish very negative—the only vintage year to do so. This vintage may have characteristics (e.g., fraud and greater leverage) that will ultimately cause its returns behavior to deviate permanently from that of the other vintages.

One might argue that the strong cumulative excess returns of distressed bonds merely reflect the outperformance of credit product in general vs. Treasuries. It is possible that credit spreads were particularly wide during years in which there were a number of distressed bonds and that the subsequent 24 months of strong excess returns may simply reflect the general recovery of credit spreads. If this is so, distressed investment-grade bonds may not have anything special to offer investors. To test this notion, we adjust the performance of a distressed bond for the performance of the credit sector by calculating the bond's excess return to corporates, defined as the bond's cumulative excess return vs. its composite credit index. We define a bond's composite credit index as the set of issues in the Lehman Credit Index (which includes any distressed issues that remain in the index) belonging to the same quality-sector bucket as the distressed bond. Long and short issues in the index are weighted so as to match the duration of the distressed bond.

Figures 15-7 and 15-8 present the cumulative excess returns of distressed bonds vs. their respective composite credit indices as defined earlier. Overall, the results show that distressed bonds tend to outperform their corporate bond counterparts. For vintage years prior to 2001, distressed investment-grade bonds outperformed their sector-quality-duration matched credit composite indices by 12.36 percentage points in the 24 months after distress. The strongly positive excess return to corporates indicates that distressed bonds do, in fact, offer higher returns than credits in general.

For vintage years 2001 and on, 24-month (if available) cumulative excess performance vs. the composite credit index was 4.02%. As with excess returns to Treasuries, the performance of the 2001 vintage, this time vs. its composite corporate index, has remained poor. The 24-month cumulative performance of the

Figure 15-6. Cumulative Total and Excess Returns vs. Duration-Matched Treasuries
24- and 12-Month Performance Periods[a]

Vintage Year	Observations	24-Month Cumulative Total Return (%)	24-Month Cumulative Excess Return vs. Duration-Matched Treasuries (%)	12-Month Cumulative Total Return (%)	12-Month Cumulative Excess Return vs. Duration-Matched Treasuries (%)
1990	50	60.36	31.58	21.80	6.67
1991	14	65.71	44.61	41.28	29.74
1992	1	54.17	24.43	32.17	17.37
1994	1	56.22	36.36	40.97	23.78
1995	5	55.11	38.63	19.22	14.21
1996	1	92.99	78.93	64.78	62.39
1998	29	25.48	21.19	10.80	13.90
1999	10	33.36	11.98	-15.65	-20.06
2000	139	24.34	4.82	9.14	-2.45
2001	54	-7.04[b]	-17.13[b]	-25.82[b]	-32.53[b]
2002	271	25.80[b]	16.80[b]	23.16[b]	15.79[b]
2003[c]	5	24.60[b]	21.94[b]	24.60[b]	21.94[b]
Vintage years prior to 2001	250	35.49	15.76	13.52	3.34
Vintage years since 2001	330	20.41[b]	11.32[b]	15.17[b]	7.98[b]
All vintage years	580	26.91[b]	13.24[b]	14.46[b]	5.98[b]

[a]Results by vintage year: 1990–2003; zero recovery assumption.
[b]Issues of the 2002 and 2003 vintages generally do not have 12 months of returns since their distress month. Issues of the 2001, 2002, and 2003 vintages generally do not have 24 months of returns since their distress month.
[c]Updated through September, 30, 2003 using bonds that became distressed by August 31, 2003.

Cumulative Excess Return vs. Composite Cedit Index

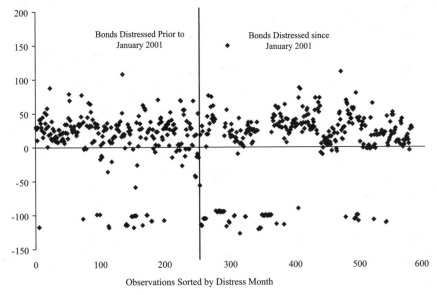

Figure 15-7. Cumulative Excess Returns vs. Quality-, Duration-, and Sector-Matched Credit Index

24-Month Performance Horizon, January 1990–September 2003[a]

[a]Returns data through September 2003 for bonds distressed by August 2003. Prices for defaulted bonds set to zero at end of default month.

2001 vintage is –20.76%, further suggesting the distinctly inferior quality of this vintage.

Figures 15-7 and 15-8 show that distressed bonds outperform their credit benchmarks. Overall, distressed issues on average outperformed a quality- and duration-matched credit portfolio by 7.61%, cumulatively over 24 months, compared with 13.24% of cumulative excess return vs. Treasuries. This indicates that the outperformance of distressed bonds vs. Treasuries is probably not due to the general tightening of corporate spreads after a period of distress. As we have seen before, there is a strong difference in performance between the pre-2001 vintages and the post-2001 vintages. Issues distressed prior to 2001 outperformed a duration-matched credit portfolio by 12.36%, on average, over the 24 months since the distress month, compared with the 15.76% cumulative 24-month excess returns vs. Treasuries for these distressed issues. Issues distressed since 2001 outperformed the Credit Index by an average of 4.02%, compared with outperforming Treasuries by 11.32%.

Figure 15-8. Cumulative Excess Returns vs. Quality- and Duration-Matched Composite Credit Index

24 Months (if available) after Distress Month[a]

Vintage Year	Number of Issues	24-Month Excess Return vs. Quality-, Duration-, and Sector-Matched Credit Index (%)
1990	50	22.16
1991	14	34.65
1992	1	22.64
1994	1	33.15
1995	5	35.71
1996	1	77.59
1998	29	10.86
1999	10	17.23
2000	139	5.02
2001	54	−20.76[b]
2002	271	8.71[b]
2003[c]	5	17.28[b]
Vintage years prior to 2001	250	12.36
Vintage years since 2001	330	4.02[b]
All vintage years	580	7.61

[a]Results by vintage year; zero recovery assumption.

[b]Issues of the 2001, 2002, and 2003 vintages do not generally have 24 months of returns since their distress month.

[c]Updated through September 30, 2003, using bonds that became distressed by August 31, 2003.

Is there any particular pattern to the cumulative excess returns (to Treasuries) of distressed issues? For example, perhaps the shorter-maturity debt of a distress issuer underperforms longer-maturity debt because the latter may have reacted more negatively during the distress month. We examine whether issues with shorter duration (as measured at the end of the distress month) have better excess return performance than longer-duration issues. Figures 15-9a (for the 1990–2000 vintages) and 15-9b (for the 2001–2003 vintages) show the relationship between a bond's duration and its cumulative 24-month (if available) excess return. We see little relationship between the two.

There does not seem to be a strong correlation between a distressed bond's duration and its cumulative 24-month excess return for either time period. This result is not surprising. When an issuer becomes distressed, all its bonds, irrespective of maturity and coupon, usually start trading at approximately the same

Cumulative Excess Return (%)

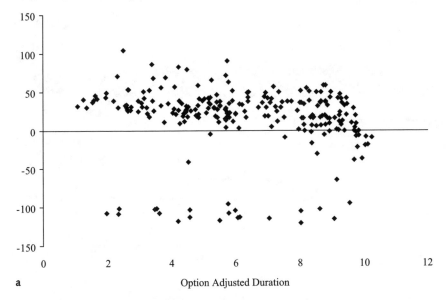

a   Option Adjusted Duration

Cumulative Excess Return (%)

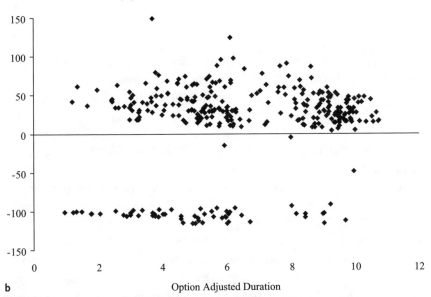

b   Option Adjusted Duration

Figure 15-9. Cumulative 24 Months (if available) Excess Returns vs. Duration
(a) 1990–2000; (b) 2001–2003 Vintage Years[a]
    [a]Prices for defaulted bonds set to zero at end of default month.

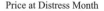

Price at Distress Month

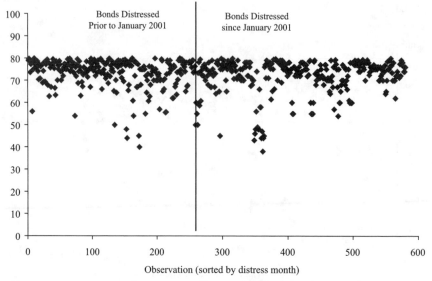

Figure 15-10. Price of Distressed Issue at End of Distress Month
January 1990–August 2003

(low) dollar price. One reason for this flat price curve is that investors seem to believe that in bankruptcy all creditors with similar claims will be treated in the same way. Since the seniority of a 3-year debenture is usually no different from that of a 30-year debenture, the holders of both can expect to receive the same recovery value (represented by the bond's dollar price). As the expected recovery value fluctuates, all issues of a given issuer will tend to have the same return irrespective of duration.

There seems to be a perception in today's corporate market that, compared to earlier years, the recent (i.e., since 2001) distressed issues have a much lower price at the end of their distress month. Figure 15-10, which plots the series of prices (at the end of the distress month), sorted by distress month, with the issues with the earliest distress month appearing at the left and those with the latest distress month appearing at the right, does not support this perception. Although there has been some recent deterioration in the price of distressed issues at the end of their distress month, it has not been large. In fact, the average distress price for the pre-2001 issues was 73.26 vs. 72.04 for the post-2001 issues.

Finally, we examine the idea of a "knife-edge" price for distressed bonds. Is there a connection between a distressed bond's price at the end of its distress month and its subsequent cumulative excess return? In other words, do bonds

Figure 15-11. Cumulative 12- and 24-Month Performance Period, Excess Returns vs. Price at End of Distress Month

1990–2003[a]

Distress Month Price Bucket	Number of Issues	12-Month Cumulative Excess Return (%)	24-Month Cumulative Excess Return (%)
1990–2003			
$80 \geq P > 70$	435	8.45	16.76
$70 \geq P > 60$	98	12.73	17.32
$60 \geq P > 50$	28	6.65	8.07
$50 \geq P$	19	−86.27	−80.80
Prior to 2001			
$80 \geq P > 70$	192	2.59	15.33
$70 \geq P > 60$	46	14.56	27.09
$60 \geq P > 50$	7	−1.64	7.91
$50 \geq P$	5	−63.77	−60.97
Since 2001			
$80 \geq P > 70$	243	13.08	17.88[b]
$70 \geq P > 60$	52	11.10	8.67[b]
$60 \geq P > 50$	21	9.41	8.13[b]
$50 \geq P$	14	−94.31	−87.88[b]

[a]Returns data through September 2003 for bonds distressed through August 2003. Prices for defaulted bonds set to zero at end of default month.

[b]Many observations since 2001 do not have a 24-month performance period.

that get hit hardest in price at the outset tend to have worse subsequent cumulative excess returns? Is there a knife-edge end-of-distress-month price below which bonds tend never to recover? Figure 15-11 shows the association between a bond's price at the end of its distress month and its subsequent cumulative excess returns (vs. Treasuries). Figure 15-12 is a graphic representation of the information in Figure 15-11. The knife-edge (for cumulative 12-month excess returns) is clearly at a price of 50 for both the before-2001 and since-2001 vintages.

RETURN PERFORMANCE ASSUMING RECOVERIES ON BONDS THAT DEFAULT

So far we have assumed a default price of zero at the default month. This is perhaps an extreme assumption, as most defaulted issues have at least some recovery

Return (%)

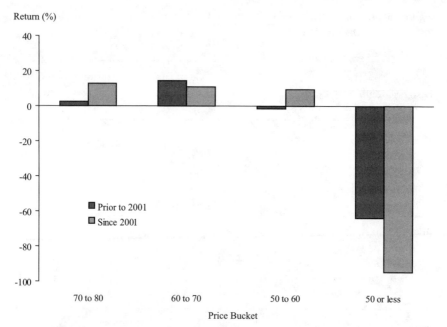

Figure 15-12. Cumulative 12-Month Excess Returns vs. Price at the End of Distress Month

Before-2001 Vintages vs. Since-2001 Vintages[a]

[a]Returns data through September 2003 for bonds distressed through August 2003. Prices for defaulted bonds set to zero at end of default month.

value. To see how sensitive our results are to the default price assumption, we reran our numbers assuming a recovery value equal to the lesser of the bond's price at the end of its default month and 20% of par. Although we label this scenario "default price = 20," in many cases we use the bond's price at the end of its default month, which was less than 20.

Figure 15-13 presents the 12- and 24-month total and excess returns for distressed bonds assuming a default price of 20. (Figure 15-13 corresponds to Figure 15-6.) As expected, the performance of distressed bonds improves, especially for the more recent vintages. The 12-month cumulative excess returns for the combined vintage years 2001–2003 increase from 7.98 to 11.71%. For vintage years prior to 2001, the improvement is from 3.34 to 5.45%. For all vintage years combined, the 12-month excess return over Treasuries for distressed bonds improves from 5.98 to 9.01%.

Figure 15-14 shows the 24-month cumulative excess returns of distressed bonds vs. a quality-, duration-, and sector-matched composite corporate index assuming

Figure 15-13. Cumulative Total Returns and Cumulative Excess Returns vs. Duration-Matched Treasuries 24 and 12 Months (if available) after Distress Month[a]

Vintage Year	Number of Issues	Default Price = $0		Default Price = Min[Price at End of Default Month, $20]	
		Twenty-Four-Month Excess Return vs. Duration-Matched UST (%)	Twelve-Month Excess Return vs. Duration-Matched UST (%)	Twenty-Four-Month Excess Return vs. Duration-Matched UST (%)	Twelve-Month Excess Return vs. Duration-Matched UST (%)
1990	50	31.58	7.67	31.67	7.67
1991	14	44.61	29.74	44.61	29.74
1992	1	24.43	17.37	24.43	17.37
1994	1	36.36	23.78	36.36	23.78
1995	5	38.63	14.21	38.63	14.21
1996	1	78.93	62.39	78.93	62.39
1998	29	21.19	13.90	24.58	17.30
1999	10	11.98	−20.06	11.98	−20.06
2000	139	4.82	−2.45	8.88	0.63
2001	54	−17.13[b]	−32.53[b]	−5.72	−26.06
2002	271	16.80[b]	15.79[b]	21.11[b]	19.05[b]
2003[c]	5	21.94[b]	21.94[b]	21.94[b]	21.94[b]
Vintage years prior to 2001	250	15.76	3.34	18.43	5.45
Vintage years since 2001	330	11.32[b]	7.98[b]	16.73[b]	11.71[b]
All vintage years	580	13.24[b]	5.98[b]	17.47[b]	9.01[b]

[a]Results by vintage year: 1990–2003. Default recovery is assumed equal to MIN (price at the end of default month, 20).
[b]Issues of the 2002 and 2003 vintages do not generally have 12 months of returns since their distress month. Issues of the 2001–2003 vintages do not have 24 months of returns since their distress month.
[c]Updated through September 30, 2003, using bonds that became distressed by August 31, 2003.

Figure 15-14. Cumulative Excess Returns vs. Quality- and Duration-Matched Credit Index
24 Months (if available) after Distress Month[a]

Vintage Year	Number of Issues	Default Price = $0 Twenty-Four-Month Excess Return vs. Duration-Matched UST (%)	Default Price = Min[price at end of default month, $20] Twenty-Four-Month Excess Return vs. Duration-Matched UST (%)
1990	50	22.16	22.26
1991	14	34.65	34.65
1992	1	22.64	22.64
1994	1	33.15	33.15
1995	5	35.71	35.71
1996	1	77.59	77.59
1998	29	10.86	14.26
1999	10	17.23	17.23
2000	139	5.02	9.08
2001	54	−20.76	−9.36
2002	271	8.71[b]	13.03[b]
2003[c]	5	17.28[b]	17.28[b]
Vintage years prior to 2001	250	12.36	15.03
Vintage years since 2001	330	4.02[b]	9.43[b]
All vintage years	580	7.61	11.84

[a]Results by vintage year. Default recovery is assumed equal to MIN (price at the end of default month, 20).

[b]Issues of the 2001, 2002, and 2003 vintages do not generally have 24 months of returns since their distress month.

[c]Updated through September 30, 2003, using bonds that became distressed by August 31, 2003.

a default price of 20. (Figure 15-14 corresponds to Figure 15-8.) For the combined vintage years 2001-2003, the 24-month performance period cumulative excess returns to corporates increase from 4.02 to 9.43%. For vintage years prior to 2001, the improvement is from 12.36 to 15.03%. Although assuming a nonzero default price improves the results, it is not the key to the story. Distressed investment-grade bonds outperform duration-matched Treasuries and quality-, duration-, and sector-matched corporates irrespective of the assumed default recovery value.

CONCLUSION

Is it better to sell or hold distressed investment grade issues? To provide some support for this portfolio decision we identified all distressed issues in the Lehman Investment-Grade Index from January 1990 to August 2003 and calculated their subsequent 24-month total and excess returns. We found that distressed bonds *as a group* have generally produced positive excess returns. This result is a bit surprising considering that we conservatively assume that recovery values for defaulted issues equals zero. We also find that distressed bonds outperform a quality- and duration-matched credit benchmark.

We show that the post-December 2000 bonds have recovered to a great extent, though it appears that the 2001 vintage itself will probably never fully recover. (The poor performance of the 2001 vintage is due to Enron.) We find little relationship between the duration of a distressed issue and its subsequent performance. In addition, we find that when an issue becomes distressed, its price at the end of its distress month has been roughly unchanged since 1990, indicating that the loss experienced by the investor up to the end of the distress month has not changed much over the years. Finally, we also show that the knife-edge price, that is, the end-of-distress-month price level below which a distressed bond is unlikely to recover, has remained at approximately 50 for both pre- and post-2001 vintages.

Other questions come to mind that we have not yet addressed. What happens to distressed bonds after the 24-month recovery period? Is their recovery sustained, or do the prices of these bonds tend to sink again? Once a bond has become distressed, are there any leading indicators that give us some idea as to whether or not the bond will recover? How applicable are these conclusions in markets outside the United States? We leave these questions for future studies.

16. Optimal Credit Allocation for Buy-and-Hold Investors

Credit by its very nature offers an asymmetric return profile. A corporate bond rewards investors with a small advantage over Treasuries (spread) during its lifetime in compensation for bearing the risk of a large loss (default) with a small probability. To a certain extent, default risk is an issuer-specific, or nonsystematic risk, and can be diminished via diversification. However, correlations among issuers make it impossible to entirely eliminate default risk through diversification. The common dependence of all issuers on general economic conditions and the common exposures of all issuers within a given industry give default risk a systematic component that cannot be diversified away.

This extremely asymmetric view of credit investing corresponds most closely to the considerations of a long-term investor who intends to buy bonds and hold them to maturity. In this case, the maximum upside is just the yield or spread earned, whereas the maximum loss is potentially the entire investment. Investors with a much shorter time frame may perceive a very different, and less asymmetric, risk/return profile. For a total return manager evaluating his investments on a monthly horizon, the dominant risks of investment-grade credit are the exposure to spread widening and the possible loss of liquidity. Yet spreads are just as likely to tighten as to widen, offering some upside to partially offset this risk. Moreover, credit degradation for investment-grade debt usually involves a sequence of downgrade events rather than direct default, so that even this component of risk is seen by total return investors primarily as downgrade risk rather than default risk.[1]

This difference in risk horizon has two main implications for buy-and-hold investors. First, the spreads at which credit trades in the market are set by the

Based on research first published by Lehman Brothers in 2004.

1. For a study of downgrade risk in investment grade credit, and the portfolio structuring implications for total return managers, see Chapter 14.

interaction between investors of all different types. High estimates of short-term spread volatility or liquidity risk on the part of total return investors can sometimes drive spreads up beyond the level justified by long-term default risk alone. For long-term credit investors, who are unaffected by these short-term risks,[2] these high spreads represent a buying opportunity. The ability to identify and exploit such opportunities is the key to their success.

Second, the asymmetric nature of the risk/return profile for long-term investors must be considered in the asset allocation process. The most common approach to asset allocation is mean-variance optimization, in which the key measure of risk is the standard deviation of asset return (or of outperformance). This approach may be suitable for total return managers, who can model the means, standard deviations, and correlations of monthly excess returns among various asset classes. However, for very asymmetric return profiles, standard deviation is not a good measure of risk. In fact, it is safe to say that no single measure of risk is universally appropriate for dealing with the extreme events at the "tail" of a probability distribution. The treatment of this "tail risk" is very subjective and must be tailored to the needs and considerations of each investor. Different approaches have been taken: downside risk measures (also known as lower partial moments) characterize the portion of the return distribution that is below some target, which can be viewed as the minimum required return. Alternatively, utility functions that incorporate risk aversion can be used to penalize negative returns more than we reward positive returns when comparing two return distributions. Asset allocation optimizations can be carried out using either of these approaches, but both of them require an explicit distribution of asset class returns. A simple characterization by mean and standard deviation is not sufficient.

As a result of these basic differences in investment objectives and risk horizons, quantitative decision-support tools for buy-and-hold managers have to analyze portfolio risk and return at a different level than those used by total return managers. Nevertheless, the management decisions in both settings can be grouped into the same two broad categories: top-down allocation among the various segments of a given market and bottom-up selection of the specific securities used to implement a desired allocation.

For total return managers, the Lehman Brothers global risk model provides a complete analysis of both systematic and nonsystematic risks over a 1-month

---

2. In reality, very few investors are entirely immune to short-term risks. Certain book value investors, for example, may be subject to downgrade risk (e.g., insurance companies with risk-based capital requirements). For the purposes of this chapter, however, we continue with the simplifying assumption that a buy-and-hold investor is concerned only with default risk. This point of view may correspond to that of a CDO manager.

horizon based on the security-level composition of a fixed-income portfolio and its benchmark.[3] For macro-level asset allocation, we have developed a risk-budgeting framework that helps translate manager views into an optimal allocation subject to various types of constraints.

For bottom-up analysis of buy-and-hold portfolios, the Lehman Brothers' Quantitative Credit Research group has developed a proprietary application known as COMPASS (Credit OptiMized Portfolio Asset Selection System), which finds the detailed security-level composition of a portfolio that minimizes the expected shortfall owing to defaults for a given average spread. Originally designed for valuation of complex credit derivatives, COMPASS uses a Monte Carlo approach with a rich set of options for modeling default correlations and tail dependence.

Here, we use a similar (but much simplified)[4] model to address the task of asset allocation among various subsets of the credit market from the viewpoint of a buy-and-hold investor. The goal is to find the optimal trade-off between the long-term payoff corresponding to current spread and the long-term risk of "unacceptably large" default losses, subjectively defined. We set out to answer the following types of questions faced by a buy-and-hold credit investor:

- How do we evaluate the trade-off between current credit spreads and expected horizon defaults? When is credit "cheap" from a buy-and-hold perspective?

- How many issuers should a portfolio contain to project a certain confidence of outperforming Treasuries over the horizon?

- How do issuer correlations affect the answers to both of the above questions?

- What is the optimal allocation between single-A and Baa credits in a portfolio for a given loss tolerance level?

This chapter does not provide definitive numerical answers to each of these questions, but rather outlines an approach to addressing them. The result of our analysis is not a single one-size-fits-all optimal allocation, but a methodology for achieving a customized solution given each investor's individual situation: the types of assets used and their spreads, views on expected default probabilities and correlations, and the precise formulation of the constraint on default risk.

---

3. A thorough discussion of multifactor risk models is contained in Chapter 26.

4. Later in the chapter, we investigate the loss of accuracy entailed in these model simplifications.

The model underlying our analysis is a well-known firm-value model originally developed by Oldrich Vasicek in 1987.[5] In its simplest form, it treats credit
markets as a homogeneous set of issuers all characterized by the same set of parameters. Correlations among issuer returns are represented by imposing identical correlations between each issuer and a single central asset return variable.
In our variation, different credit asset classes are viewed as homogeneous sub-
populations. Within each group, all issuer firms are characterized by the same
set of parameters. The parameter values change from one group to another,
but the asset returns of issuers in all groups are driven by the single common central asset return variable. The default parameters and the spread assumptions
are combined to form a return distribution for any allocation. This approach
can help investors tailor their allocation within credit to their appetite for default risk.

While the approach is broadly applicable to the task of long-term asset allocation among credit asset classes, we motivate the discussion by considering a more
specific problem often faced by insurance companies. A typical strategy is to fund
a set of projected liabilities with a higher yielding portfolio of corporate bonds.
For example, an Aa-rated insurer that purchases a portfolio of Baa-rated debt
might expect to earn the spread between typical Aa and Baa yields, minus a certain allowance for default losses. Assuming the risk of default losses in such a
strategy is considered too great, we instead seek the blend of A and Baa debt that
finds the optimum trade-off between spread pickup and default risk.

We proceed as follows: We first present a very simple model of a buy-and-hold
portfolio. We consider an equally weighted portfolio of n bonds and present a
simple approximation for the portfolio return as a function of the number of bonds
defaulting over the period. With this approximation, any distribution of the number of portfolio defaults can be transformed into a distribution of portfolio return.
The simplest one is the binomial distribution, which assumes that each issuer is
equally likely to default and that what happens to one is independent of what happens to any other. The default probability is assumed to be a constant, provided as
an input parameter. Infinitely large portfolios will always realize this default rate
exactly and thus earn a constant return. For small portfolios, this model analyzes
the random component of return owing to uncertainty in the realized portfolio
default rate. We show how this model can be used to relate the assumed default
probability, the spread, and the number of bonds in the portfolio.

5. Oldrich Vasicek, "Probability of Loss on Loan Portfolio," KMV Corporation, February
1987.

The major shortcoming of the binomial model is that it assumes a constant default rate. In reality, observed overall corporate bond default rates can vary significantly over time. This gives rise to correlations among the default probabilities of different issuers.[6] We then present a model that includes this correlation effect. As defaults are relatively rare events, it is difficult to work directly with default correlations, so this model begins by modeling the root cause of default based on the value of an issuer's assets relative to its liabilities and then models correlations among the asset returns of the various issuers. As shown by Vasicek, assuming a constant asset return correlation among all pairs of issuers is equivalent to assuming correlations with a single market variable.

The model turns out to be equivalent to using the binomial model, but with the default probability itself modeled as a random variable instead of being specified as a constant. We explore the distribution of the default probabilities in this model and how it depends on the correlation assumption. We find that as the assumed correlation increases, the shape of this distribution becomes the main driver of portfolio performance and that the number of securities in the portfolio plays a smaller role. In the limit when the portfolio contains a large number of bonds (i.e., n is large), the realized portfolio default rate follows exactly the outcome of the random market default probability. The large homogeneous portfolio (LHP) approximation, based on this assumption, allows us to broadly characterize the risk and return of a credit asset class.

We then extend this model to cover two (or more) distinct groups of credits, which could correspond to different quality ratings. Each group of issuers is homogeneous, and all issuers are linked to the same central asset return variable, but each group can have a different spread, a different expected default probability, and a different correlation. Under this set of assumptions, the LHP approximation gives us a very simple one-dimensional characterization of the return distribution of a portfolio defined as a weighted blend of these asset classes.

Given the ability to project the entire distribution of long-term returns for a given set of asset weights, we can offer several different approaches to finding the optimal allocation for a given set of risk tolerances. One can maximize expected return given a specific limit on some measure of tail risk. Tail risk can be measured

---

6. To understand the connection between time-varying default rates and default correlations, consider the effect of the overall health of the economy. In a recession, default rates increase, and the default probabilities tend to increase for all issuers. When the default probabilities for two issuers tend to rise and fall together, the two default events are correlated, and the probability of both defaulting within a given time period is higher than would be calculated under an assumption of independence.

by lower partial moments: shortfall probability, expected shortfall, or target semi-variance. Alternatively, a utility function incorporating risk aversion can be used to evaluate a given distribution as a whole.

We apply this model to the example problem of allocation between A and Baa debt, and show some numerical examples detailing the optimal allocation to Baa for different assumptions about spreads, default probabilities, correlations, and risk limits.

Finally, we take a critical look at some of the simplifying assumptions used in this analysis. The COMPASS system is used to illustrate the magnitude of the performance differences that might be expected under some more realistic assumptions about asset return distributions.

THE BINOMIAL MODEL: UNCORRELATED ANALYSIS OF SPREAD VS. DEFAULT RISK

Our analysis of the long-term risk and return of a corporate bond portfolio begins with the following simple interpretation of the buy-and-hold assumption. We choose a fixed time horizon, say, 10 years, and model the possibility of default as a single-period problem: each bond either defaults during the next 10 years or survives to maturity. Bonds that do not default are assumed to earn an annualized total return equal to their yield; bonds that default do not contribute anything to the cumulative performance beyond their recovery value. We ignore any coupon payments that might have been made before a bond defaults as well as any re-investment, essentially assuming that all defaults occur immediately at the start of the period. This makes our analysis more conservative.

Using this model, we can compare the returns on portfolios of noncallable 10-year credits to those of 10-year Treasuries. Given the current 10-year Treasury yield y_T, we can easily calculate the terminal value V_T of the portfolio for each dollar invested in Treasuries and the annualized return r_T by

$$V_T = (1 + y_T)^{10} = (1 + r_T)^{10}. \tag{16-1}$$

For riskless bonds held to maturity, the total return according to our assumptions is deterministic and equal to the yield.[7] For credit portfolios, we add an element of uncertainty—the realized portfolio default rate D. If we let s denote the average portfolio spread over Treasuries, and R the assumed recovery rate on defaulted

---

7. We have chosen to ignore the effects of reinvestment and inflation for simplicity. These factors would affect both Treasury and credit portfolios.

bonds,[8] then our simple model for the terminal value and return of the credit portfolio over 10 years is

$$V_C = (1 - D)(1 + y_T + s)^{10} + D \cdot R = (1 + r_C)^{10}. \tag{16-2}$$

A comparison between Equations (16-1) and (16-2) emphasizes the fundamental aspects of credit: the risk of default loss is offset by the additional return owing to the spread. Figure 16-1 illustrates the breakeven point between these two effects. Assuming a Treasury yield of 4% and a recovery rate of 20%, we show the maximum realized default rate that will allow the credit portfolio to at least break even with Treasuries for a given level of spread. Although Figure 16-1 is based on a Treasury yield of 4%, the results change only slightly with changes in Treasury yield. At this level, using simple annual compounding, a 10-year Treasury investment of $1 will have a terminal value of $1.48, while a credit investment with a spread of 200 bp will have a terminal value of $1.79 (if it does not default). Even assuming a very conservative 20% recovery rate,[9] Equation (16-2) tells us that a realized portfolio default rate of 19.5% would make the return on the credit portfolio equal to the Treasury return. This breakeven default rate demonstrates just how much cushion can be generated by credit spreads—with a spread of 200 bp, we can experience nine defaults in a fifty-bond portfolio and still outperform Treasuries!

The key to understanding the risk/return trade-off of credit investing is to model the likelihood of credit losses. The model given in Equation (16-2) provides a simple translation of a realized portfolio default rate to a realized portfolio return. As we proceed through different approaches to modeling the distribution of default losses, we continue to use this simple transformation to obtain corresponding distributions of portfolio return.

The first model we consider for the portfolio default rate is the binomial model. We assume that the portfolio is an equally weighted blend of n bonds with equal weights, that each bond has the same known probability of default p, and that the outcomes for all bonds are independent. The probability distribution of the number of defaulted bonds, n_{default}, is given by

$$P(n_{\text{default}} = k) = \binom{n}{k} p^k (1 - p)^{n-k}. \tag{16-3}$$

8. In reality, both the default rate and the recovery rate should be considered as random variables. For simplicity, we assume a constant recovery rate; we deal with the uncertainty in recovery rates by investigating the effect of different recovery assumptions.

9. According to Moody's, while historical recovery rates for defaulted bonds span the range from 0 to 100%, the average historical recovery rate was 41%, with a standard deviation of 28%; the median recovery rate was 35%.

Figure 16-1. Breakeven Cumulative 10-Year Portfolio Default Rates
20% Recovery

Corporate Spread (bp)	Corporate Yield (%)	Corporate Terminal Value	Breakeven Realized Defaults (%)
100	5	1.63	10.4
125	5.25	1.67	12.8
150	5.5	1.71	15.1
175	5.75	1.75	17.4
200	6	1.79	19.5
225	6.25	1.83	21.6
250	6.5	1.88	23.7
275	6.75	1.92	25.6
300	7	1.97	27.6
325	7.25	2.01	29.4
350	7.5	2.06	31.2
375	7.75	2.11	33.0
400	8	2.16	34.6
Treasury yield (%)			4
Treasury terminal value			1.48
Recovery rate (%)			20

This distribution is illustrated in Figure 16-2 for a twenty-bond portfolio with a 5% probability of default. It can be easily mapped into a return distribution by substituting $D = n_{default}/n$ in Equation (16-2). For example, if we assume a spread of 150 bp and a recovery rate of 20%, Figure 16-1 shows us that as long as realized defaults are 15.1% or less, the portfolio will outperform Treasuries. The distribution in Figure 16-2 shows that for a twenty-bond portfolio, where we can tolerate up to three defaults, the probability of outperformance is more than 98%. If the spread is only 100 bp, then realized defaults must be under 10.4% over our 10-year horizon, so only two defaults out of twenty can be absorbed. Assuming that the distribution of Figure 16-2 still applies (i.e., the same 5% default probability is assumed despite the lower spread), we see that the probability of breakeven in this case is only 92.4%.

The binomial distribution is often used to examine the role of portfolio diversification in reducing default risk. As n grows, the tails of the distribution get smaller and the distribution tends to converge around its mean. For the same set of parameters used in Figure 16-2, we can vary the number of bonds in the portfolio,

Probability

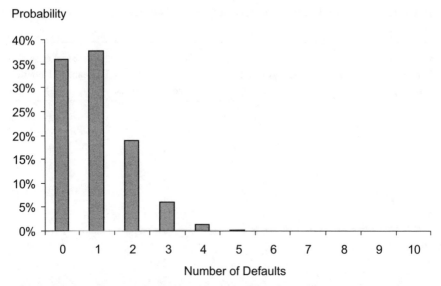

Figure 16-2. Distribution of Number of Defaulted Bonds in a Twenty-Bond Portfolio
Binomial Model, 5% Cumulative Default Probability

observe the new distribution, and recalculate the probability of outperformance. This dependence on the number of bonds is shown in Figure 16-3. We see that by increasing the number of bonds in the portfolio, we can achieve an arbitrarily high level of confidence that we will outperform Treasuries. For a 200-bond portfolio, for example, the probability of realized defaults over 10.4% is almost nil.

It is very important to exercise care in applying the binomial model in this way and interpreting the results. The model is based on the assumptions that the default probability for each issuer is a known constant and that each issuer has an independent chance of defaulting over the horizon period. The result of this combination of assumptions, as we have seen, is that as the portfolio grows, the default losses over the horizon period converge to a known deterministic amount. This clearly does not correctly reflect the reality of owning a credit portfolio. In fact, we do not know what the next 10 years have in store for the credit markets, and no amount of diversification can guarantee achieving a particular default rate.

In our interpretation, the default probability p that appears in Equation (16-3) is the realized marketwide cumulative default rate. This is the proportion of bonds in the marketplace that will default over the next 10 years, or the cohort default rate. This quantity is not yet known and must itself be treated as a random variable. The binomial model can then be used to draw conclusions about the portfolio default rate conditional on the cohort default rate. By using an appropriately

Breakeven Probability

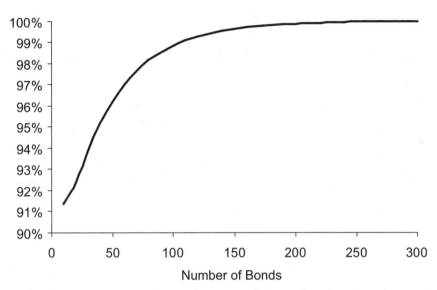

Figure 16-3. Breakeven Probability as a Function of the Number of Bonds in the Portfolio
Binomial Model, 5% Default Probability, Spread 100 bp

pessimistic "worst-case" value for p, one can gain a high level of confidence that the portfolio is sufficiently protected from default risk.

To establish these worst-case market default rates, we obtained 10-year cumulative default rates from Moody's.[10] Figure 16-4a shows such rates for two investment-grade rating categories, A and Baa, issued from 1970 through 1994 (so that the last observed 10-year time frame runs from January 1994 through December 2003). The highest 10-year default rates were observed in the period spanning the recession of the early 1990s, with peaks of 9.51% (1982 cohort) for Baa and 4.67% (1985 cohort) for A. The long-term average cumulative default rates are relatively modest at 1.56% for single-A and 4.84% for Baa. The most recent data points in this series have started to rise in response to the credit events of 2000–2002, but they are still well below the long-term average, thanks to the benefit of the placid mid-1990s experience of these cohorts.

To get a better idea of the relative magnitude of the recent credit crisis, we also looked at 3-year cumulative default rates, and these are shown in Figure 16-4b.

10. "Default & Recovery Rates of Corporate Bond Issuers," Moody's Investors Service, January 2004.

Cumulative Default Rate

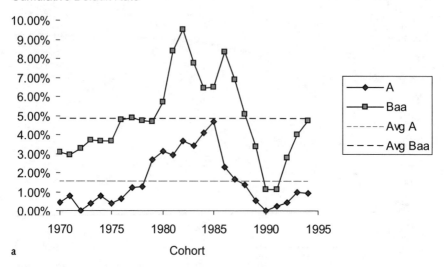

a   Cohort

Cumulative Default Rate

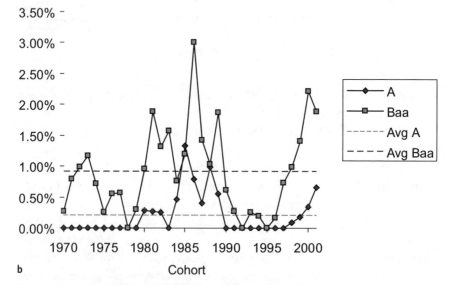

b   Cohort

Figure 16-4. Moody's Cumulative Default Rates by Annual Cohort
(a) 10-Year Cumulative Default Rates; (b) 3-Year Cumulative Default Rates

We find that the recent increase in default rates, for Baa bonds in particular, approaches the historical peaks, but remains below them. Nonetheless, the rapid rise in the 3-year rates leaves room to imagine that the worst case may exceed even the historical maximum default rate. In the next section, the effect of correlations is incorporated to help quantify the probability of such events.

INCORPORATING ISSUER CORRELATIONS

The big risk for buyers of a diversified corporate bond portfolio vs. Treasuries is that difficult economic conditions could produce a wave of defaults throughout the sector.[11] We showed in the previous section that the binomial model can be used to bound the portfolio default rate D under a worst-case assumption for the market default rate p. However, we did not offer a very rigorous process for setting this worst-case assumption. The fact that Moody's historical data over the last 30 years show a maximum 10-year cumulative default rate of under 10% certainly does not guarantee that the next 10 years will not be even worse. How can we estimate the likelihood of such an event? Clearly, if we are to consider the cohort default rate p as a random variable, we would like to have a model for its distribution. In this section, we present such a model, based on the correlated evolution of the asset values of issuing firms.[12]

An issuer is represented by the total value of its assets and liabilities. Liabilities are assumed to be constant, but asset values are subject to random fluctuations. If changes in the asset values ever bring the net worth below zero, the issuer goes into default. The key determinant of the likelihood of default is thus the relationship between the volatility of asset returns and the current net asset value of the firm.

To keep things very simple, we work with a one-period problem. That is, rather than look at the evolution of asset value over time, we just choose a horizon (say 10 years) and use a single random variable $A(i)$ to represent the cumulative asset return of issuer i over that period. We assume that this variable follows the standard normal distribution. $A(i)$ can be interpreted as a rescaling of the asset return in terms of the volatility. For example, let us say that an issuer has a current net

---

11. Note that a systematic increase in default rates may not be a very big concern for the manager of a corporate bond portfolio benchmarked to a corporate bond index. Even abysmal absolute returns can be excused when the entire asset class suffers together. The risk of high overall defaults, and thus the risk of correlated defaults, is much more harmful to a portfolio measured against a benchmark that does not share the same level of exposure to default risk. Many buy-and-hold portfolios are benchmarked against a set of liabilities that must be assumed to be default-free, and so the risk of high overall defaults poses a very real threat.

12. Dominic O'Kane and Lutz Schlogel, "Modelling Credit: Theory and Practice," Lehman Brothers, 2001.

worth of $20 billion and assume that the change in issuer asset value over the next 10 years is normally distributed with zero mean and a standard deviation of $10 billion. In this case the event $A(i) = -1$ means that the issuer suffers a one-standard-deviation loss over the period and ends with a net asset value of $10 billion. If $A(i) < -2$, the net asset value becomes negative, pushing the issuer into default. We define $C(i)$ as the return threshold, which, if crossed, results in default. In our example, $C(i) = -2$. The probability of default is then given very simply by the cumulative standard normal distribution $N(.)$:

$$p(i) = P(A(i) < C(i)) = N(C(i)). \tag{16-4}$$

Figure 16-5 gives a graphical depiction of this calculation and shows the effect of changing the threshold from -2.0 to -2.5. For our issuer that begins with $20 billion in assets (2.0 times the standard deviation of return), the ending issuer asset value is assumed to follow a normal distribution centered on this mean. This distribution is shown normalized by the $10 billion standard deviation, so that an ending value of 4.0, for example, would represent the outcome in which the issuer's asset value grows to $40 billion over the 10-year horizon. A default is triggered if the asset value becomes negative, which happens when the normalized asset return is below -2, occurring with probability 2.275%. If the issuer instead begins with $25 billion in assets, the whole distribution is shifted to the right, and a normalized return below $C(i) = -2.5$ is required to trigger a default. As seen in the figure, the shaded area under this curve is much smaller, and the default probability is reduced to 0.621%. Note that the input data describing the issuer's condition is represented by a single parameter $C(i)$, which is the negative of the number of standard deviations away from default over our selected time horizon.

In practice, when looking at asset classes such as sets of bonds with similar ratings, we do not really have a good way to determine the net asset value of a firm or the volatility of its asset values. However, we can use historical rating agency data to estimate the default probabilities and work backward from there. For example, as shown in Figure 16-4, the long-term average cumulative 10-year default rates reported by Moody's for A and Baa issuers are approximately 2 and 5%, respectively. Using the inverse of the standard normal distribution, we can obtain the values of $C(i)$ that correspond to these default probabilities. We find that $C(i)$ is -2.054 for A-rated issuers and -1.645 for Baa-rated ones. That is, a typical A-rated issuer is more than two standard deviations away from default (over a 10-year horizon), whereas a Baa-rated issuer is substantially closer to a default condition.

What happens when we apply this model to a homogeneous portfolio of n bonds? We assume that all the bonds are from firms carrying the same quality

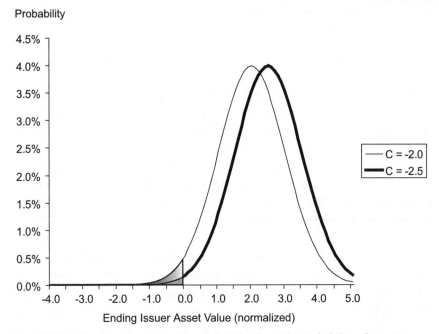

Figure 16-5. **Changing the Return Threshold (C) Affects the Probability of Negative Asset Values (i.e., Default)**

rating and therefore have the same expected default probability p and the same implied threshold C. If we further assume that the outcomes of the asset return variables $A(i)$ for all of the issuers are independent, then the default processes are independent as well, and the distribution of the number of realized defaults is given by the binomial distribution of Equation (16-3) just as in the previous section.

The usefulness of this model becomes apparent with the addition of issuer correlations. It is very difficult to work directly with default correlations,[13] owing to the fact that defaults from investment grade are rare events. In the firm value model, the correlations in the default processes are results of correlations in asset returns, which are more easily observable. The homogeneous portfolio model assumes that any two asset return variables $A(i)$ are correlated to each other with the same correlation coefficient. Vasicek showed that this set of n

---

13. The default correlation between issuers A and B relates the individual issuer default probabilities p_A and p_B to the joint default probability p_{AB}, the probability that both issuers will default over the period. It is particularly difficult to estimate these joint default probabilities.

correlated variables can be decomposed into a model with $n + 1$ independent variables as follows:

$$A(i) = \beta Z + \sqrt{1 - \beta^2} Z(i). \tag{16-5}$$

The asset return of each issuer is a weighted sum of two terms: one owing to a systematic market return Z and one to an issuer-specific return variable $Z(i)$, which is assumed to be independent of both the market return and the issuer-specific returns of all other issuers. Both Z and all of the $Z(i)$ are assumed to follow the standard normal distribution.[14] The correlations among the overall asset return variables $A(i)$ are thus due entirely to the common exposure to the market return variable. It can be easily shown from Equation (16-5) that each $A(i)$ has a correlation of β with the market return variable Z and a correlation of β^2 with the asset return $A(j)$ of any other issuer j.[15]

Returning to our homogeneous portfolio of n bonds, we find that this formulation, including issuer correlations, retains the form of the binomial distribution if we condition on the outcome of the market variable Z. That is, we analyze the probabilities of what might happen to the portfolio in two stages. In the first stage, we project the possible outcomes of the systematic variable Z, and in the second, we consider the possibility of default for each issuer. The outcome of the market variable Z determines the level of idiosyncratic asset return $Z(i)$ that will result in default. To find the conditional default probabilities, we re-express the default condition $A(i) \leq C$ in terms of the idiosyncratic asset returns, to obtain

$$p(i \mid Z) = P(A(i) \leq C \mid Z) = P\left(Z(i) \leq \frac{C - \beta Z}{\sqrt{1 - \beta^2}}\right) = N\left(\frac{C - \beta Z}{\sqrt{1 - \beta^2}}\right). \tag{16-6}$$

The quantity in the parentheses at the right of Equation (16-6) is the value of $Z(i)$ that triggers a default of issuer i, conditioned on the market return Z. Comparing this with Equation (16-4), we see that the introduction of correlations can be viewed as adjusting the default threshold C in two ways. The main adjustment, in the numerator, reflects the effect of the market return. A negative market return makes the default threshold less negative and increases the probability of

---

14. The coefficients of the two terms have been set such that if Z and $X(i)$ are independent standard normal variables (with a mean of zero and a standard deviation of one) then $A(i)$ is a standard normal variable as well, and it has a correlation of β to the market variable Z.

15. Throughout the numerical examples in this chapter, we refer to the correlations among the issuer asset returns. Thus, when we discuss a correlation of 20% between any two issuers, the underlying assumption is that each issuer's asset return $A(i)$ has a correlation of $\beta = \sqrt{0.2} = 0.447$ with the market variable Z.

default for all issuers. The second adjustment, in the denominator, scales up the magnitude of the default threshold based on the correlation. The greater the correlation with the market, the smaller the role of the idiosyncratic return in determining whether an issuer will default.

For example, assume that the correlation between any pair of assets is given by $\beta^2 = 20\%$ and the realization of the market return is $Z = -1$. A -1 standard deviation event in the market brings down the net asset value of every firm by 0.447 standard deviations. Clearly, the systematic depression of asset values increases the default probability for every issuer, as there is now a smaller cushion to protect the firms from negative returns on $Z(i)$.

Conditioned on the market return, the number of portfolio defaults follows the binomial distribution with the probability of default given by Equation (16-6). If the market return is very negative and β is positive, then the probability of default is increased for all issuers simultaneously. If the market return is positive, then all issuers have smaller default probabilities.

This two-step construction of the portfolio default distribution is illustrated in Figure 16-6 for a fifty-bond portfolio of A-rated bonds with 20% correlation. For any possible realization of the market return Z, we compute the conditional default probability using Equation (16-6). Although we start our analysis with the assumption that the ex ante 10-year cumulative default probability for A-rated debt is 2%, this can be decomposed into an average of very different default rates in different market conditions. A positive market return of $Z = 1$ results in a very low default probability of 0.26%, whereas negative market returns can result in much higher default rates: 3.62% if $Z = -1$, and 21.29% if $Z = -3$.

In each of the foregoing cases, the number of defaults in a particular fifty-bond portfolio varies around this marketwide default rate p and can be modeled using a binomial distribution parameterized by p. The binomial distributions for the three values of Z are shown in the Figure 16-6 and illustrate how this distribution changes with Z. For $Z = 1$, owing to the low market default rate, the most likely portfolio outcome by far is zero defaults (87.87% probability); there is a much smaller likelihood (11.38%) of one default, and less then a 1% chance of two or more defaults. The dominance of the zero default outcome is characteristic of the entire right-hand side of this graph. As we move over to the left, we find that the distribution of portfolio defaults moves to the right and widens. In the unlikely event of $Z = -3$, the market default rate is just over 20%, and so the number of defaults in a fifty-bond portfolio is centered on ten, with the bulk of the distribution falling between five and fifteen defaults.

We have drawn the conditional binomial distributions for three values of Z, but there is actually an infinite number of them across a continuous distribution. Assuming a standard normal distribution for the market return Z and integrating

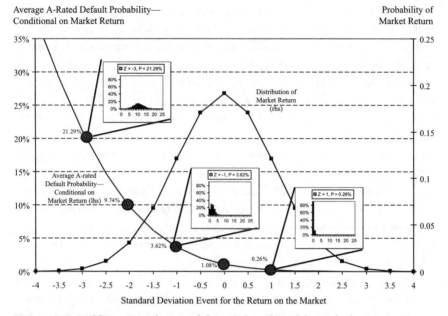

Figure 16-6. Building a Distribution of the Number of Portfolio Defaults in Two Steps
(1) Any Realization of the Market Return Variable Z Gives an Average Default Probability
P for the Market. (2) The Number of Portfolio Defaults Follows a Binomial Distribution
Conditional on P (fifty bonds, 2% default probability, 20% correlation).

numerically over these conditional binomial distributions for all possible outcomes,
we can obtain the unconditional distribution of the number of portfolio defaults.
In Figure 16-7, we plot this distribution for a fifty-bond Baa portfolio with an
expected market default rate of 5% and a correlation assumption of 20%. We
compare this distribution with those produced by the uncorrelated case (the plain
binomial distribution) using market default rates of 5 and 10%. First let us compare the correlated and uncorrelated cases using the same 5% value for the expected default rate. In this case, for a fifty-bond portfolio, the expected number of
defaults is 2.5 for both the correlated and uncorrelated cases. The binomial distribution with no correlations has its peak near this value, and a relatively short tail.
In the correlated case, the distribution shows a decreased probability of realizing
the average default rate and increased probabilities of either extremely high or
extremely low defaults.

If we increase the market default rate to 10% in the uncorrelated binomial distribution, the whole distribution shifts to the right, and the tail of the distribution
includes high probabilities that eight, nine, or ten bonds may default over the
period. This comes much closer to the tail of the correlated distribution with a 5%

Probability

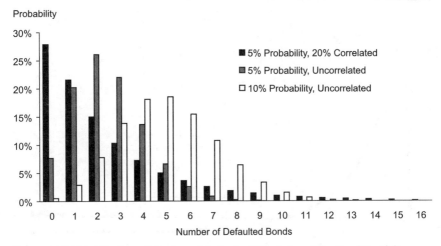

Figure 16-7. Distribution of Number of Defaulted Bonds in a Fifty-Bond Portfolio
5% Expected Default Probability with 20% Correlation, Uncorrelated Model with Market Default Rates of 5 and 10%

expected default rate. However, even in this case, the probability of eleven or more bonds defaulting is higher in the correlated model.

Figure 16-7 illustrates two methods for identifying worst-case Baa portfolio default rates. Historical data on 10-year cumulative defaults on Baa securities indicate a long-term average default rate of about 5%, with the worst observed cohort experiencing a default rate just under 10%. Using a simple binomial model, we obtain a worst case assumption for realized portfolio defaults by using the tails of the binomial distribution with the highest observed default rate of 10%. In the correlated model, we use an expected default rate of 5%, and the tails of the distribution are generated by the 20% correlation assumption.

It is also very interesting to examine the unconditional distribution of the market default rate. As shown in Figure 16-6, the realization of the market return variable Z drives the market default rate over the next 10 years according to Equation (16-6). By integrating this function over all values of Z, we can obtain the unconditional (ex ante) distribution of the market default rate. This distribution is shown in Figure 16-8 for an expected default probability of 5% and a correlation of 20%. Note that while the mean of the distribution shown in Figure 16-8 is 5%, the distribution is very asymmetric. The bulk of the distribution lies below the mean, but there is a large positive tail showing small chances of much higher default rates—as high as 25%! The higher the assumed correlation, the greater the asymmetry, and the larger the probabilities of very high market default rates.

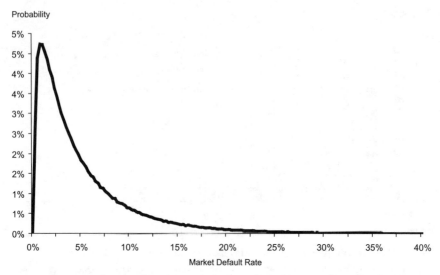

Figure 16-8. Distribution of Market Default Rate Implied by Correlation Model
Expected Cumulative Default Rate 5%, Correlation 20%

In the limit, as the number of bonds in the portfolio grows infinitely large, the realized portfolio default rate converges to the market default rate. Note that the correlation model considers the possibility of market default rates as high as 25%. According to this assumption, the overall probability of a market default rate worse than 10% is 13.6%. When we used the binomial model with a worst-case market default rate of 10%, the tail of the portfolio default distribution was due entirely to the portfolio underperforming the market owing to poor security selection in a small portfolio. We see now that the reason for the increased tail probabilities shown in Figure 16-7 is that the correlation model considers the possibility of much higher market default rates as well. This is a systematic risk that cannot be diversified away.

In Figure 16-9, we compare the worst-case realized portfolio default rates at 95 and 99% confidence levels using two different assumptions. The first is the worst-case assumption that we used in the uncorrelated case, with the market default rate assumed to take on its worst observed historical value but with no correlations. The second assumes asset correlations of 20%, with the expected default rate set to the long-term historical average. The results are shown for portfolios of twenty and fifty bonds, using default probabilities characteristic of A and Baa ratings. We find that the two sets of assumptions give quite similar results, particularly at the 95% confidence level. The most striking difference is that the assumption of 20% correlation reduces the advantage of increasing the portfolio size from

Figure 16-9. Comparing Worst-Case Realized Portfolio Default Rates

Using Historical Average 10-Year Default Rates with 20% Correlation and Worst-Case Historical Default Rates with 0% Correlation

		Number of Bonds					
		Confidence 95%			Confidence 99%		
	Correlation	20	50	100	20	50	100
A-Rated Portfolios							
Historic worst case: $p = 5\%$ (%)	0	15	10	9	20	14	11
Historic mean: $E[p] = 2\%$ (%)	20	10	8	8	20	16	14
Baa-Rated Portfolios							
Historic worst case: $p = 10\%$ (%)	0	20	18	15	30	20	18
Historic mean: $E[p] = 5\%$ (%)	20	20	18	16	30	28	26

twenty to fifty bonds. For a portfolio of Baa bonds, the worst-case realized portfolio default rate at a 99% confidence level improves from 30 to 20% as we go from twenty to fifty bonds under the uncorrelated assumption. With the 20% correlation assumption, even a fifty-bond portfolio may have a 28% default rate.

Figure 16-10 summarizes the risk/return characteristics of a fifty-bond Baa portfolio using the correlation model with expected default probability assumptions of 5, 7.5, and 10%, and correlation assumptions of 20 and 30%. A recovery rate of 20% is assumed throughout. In addition to the mean and standard deviation of the distribution of outperformance, we look at various measures of the risk in the negative tail of the distribution. The probability of outperforming Treasuries is quite high under all parameter sets considered, but the key question is how much we might underperform in a crisis. We use two additional measures of tail risk, based on a specific level of confidence: the worst-case outperformance and the expected shortfall of outperformance, which is the average outperformance conditioned on being in the tail. For example, under the assumption of 10% defaults with no correlations, there is a 95% probability of outperforming Treasuries by 0.17% or more. Over the 5% of cases in which outperformance is below this value, the expected outperformance is 0.02. Under the assumption of 5% expected default probability and 20% correlation, we obtain the same worst-case underperformance of 0.17%, but an expected shortfall of –0.48%, reflecting a worse degradation of performance beyond this point. This can be seen as well in the worst-case outperformance at the 99% level.

Figure 16-10. Risk/Return Characteristics of a Fifty-Bond Baa Portfolio under Various Assumptions for Expected Default Rate and Correlation

Corporate Yield 6.00%, Treasury Yield 4.00%, Recovery Rate 20%

Probability of default (%)	10	5	7.5	10	5	7.5	10
Correlation (%)	0	20	20	20	30	30	30
Mean outperformance (%/year)	1.01	1.50	1.24	0.97	1.49	1.22	0.95
Standard deviation of outperformance (%/year)	0.44	0.63	0.85	1.05	0.81	1.09	1.35
Information ratio	2.31	2.38	1.46	0.93	1.84	1.12	0.70
Probability of outperformance (%)	97.5	96.3	91.4	85.0	94.4	89.2	83.2
Worst-case number of defaults, 95% confidence	9	9	12	14	10	14	17
Worst-case outperformance, 95% confidence (%)	0.17	0.17	-0.51	-0.99	-0.05	-0.99	-1.74
Expected shortfall of outperformance, 95% confidence (%)	0.02	-0.48	-1.34	-1.96	-1.08	-2.28	-3.24
Worst-case number of defaults, 99% confidence	10	14	18	21	17	22	26
Worst-case outperformance, 99% confidence (%)	-0.05	-0.99	-2.01	-2.84	-1.74	-3.13	-4.37
Expected shortfall of outperformance, 99% confidence (%)	-0.18	-1.70	-2.87	-3.82	-2.91	-4.50	-5.89

With different assumptions, the correlation model allows for even more extreme predictions of portfolio default rates and shows that in the worst case corporates can underperform by a substantial amount. The most pessimistic assumptions shown combine a 10-year expected default probability of 10% with a firm value correlation of 30%. According to these assumptions, there is a 1% chance that more than half the portfolio will default. With our assumption of only 20% recovery, the resulting underperformance can be –4.37% per year or worse. Yet even according to these most pessimistic assumptions, there is compensation for taking these risks. The probability of outperformance over Treasuries is 83.2%, and the mean outperformance is 0.95% per year. Under more benevolent assumptions, the information ratio can be greater than 2. If we use the historical average default rate of 5% as the expected value of the market default rate (keeping in mind that this reflects the possibility of much higher cohort default rates, as shown in Figure 16-7), then even under an assumption of 30% correlation, the portfolio outperforms Treasuries with almost 95% confidence.

The correlation model used here takes advantage of the simplifying assumption that any two issuers are related by the same correlation coefficient. In reality, the correlations among different issuers reflect two types of factors: general macroeconomic trends that affect all issuers and industry-specific circumstances that can affect a particular sector of the market. A generally accepted market practice is to assume 30% correlation among issuers within the same industry and 15% correlation among issuers from different industries. As the model uses just a single coefficient, 20% seems like a reasonable value. While our model cannot account for industry-specific correlations,[16] these can be in large part avoided by diversification of industry exposures in the portfolio. If lack of liquidity in the market makes such diversification impossible, our breakeven default rates would have to be adjusted upward for industry correlations. Nevertheless, we believe it is feasible under most market conditions to construct a corporate portfolio of twenty or fifty names well-diversified across industries.[17]

FINDING THE OPTIMAL ALLOCATION TO TWO CREDIT QUALITIES

For a population of homogeneous issuers, we have seen that our model can be used to generate a distribution for the number of defaults over a given time horizon—

16. The model can compute portfolio loss distributions assuming a different beta for each asset. However, this would complicate the analysis without necessarily changing any of the main results.

17. While testing our risk model for total return portfolios, we found that a proxy portfolio of twenty bonds could track the Corporate Bond Index with a projected tracking error of 44 bp/year, and that this number could be reduced to 29 bp/year in a fifty-bond portfolio.

and, hence, the outperformance over Treasuries—for a portfolio of n issuers. In addition, in the limit as n gets very large, the proportion of portfolio defaults converges to the conditional probability of default given in Equation (16-6), and the overall distribution of the default rate is obtained by combining this with the standard normal distribution for Z, as illustrated in Figure 16-8.

This large homogeneous portfolio (LHP) approximation provides a characterization of a particular group of credits as an asset class that is very well suited to the task of asset allocation among the different parts of the credit market. From the point of view of the buy-and-hold investor, the distribution of returns over the holding period is the essential piece of information needed to evaluate risk and return, and to determine how much of a given asset class he should hold.

Consider an investor who plans to invest in a credit portfolio on a buy-and-hold basis over a 10-year horizon. He intends to reduce nonsystematic risk to a minimum by diversifying his positions among many issuers within each market sector selected. He assumes, broadly speaking, that securities rated Aa or better will not be able to meet his yield targets, but he is restricted to using only investment-grade credits. If we can overlook the finer distinctions within the credit market (e.g., quality tiers, industry), the asset allocation decision essentially boils down to an allocation between A-rated and Baa-rated bonds. We show how the LHP model can be used in this allocation process.

In our two-quality version of the model, we assume that instead of a single homogeneous population of issuers, there are two distinct homogeneous groups. The two groups are tied together by sharing a common exposure to the same systematic market variable Z, which we can assume relates to the overall condition of the economy. All issuers within each group are assumed to have the same correlation with the market variable and the same default threshold. The default threshold C is set to two different values for the two groups to reflect a higher probability of default for the lower-rated credits; the correlation assumptions for the two groups can be the same or different. For any outcome of Z, we can calculate the conditional default probabilities of the two qualities as

$$p_A(Z) = N\left(\frac{C_A - \beta_A Z}{\sqrt{1 - \beta_A^2}}\right) \qquad p_{Baa}(Z) = N\left(\frac{C_{Baa} - \beta_{Baa} Z}{\sqrt{1 - \beta_{Baa}^2}}\right). \tag{16-7}$$

Figure 16-11 shows these probabilities as a function of Z for parameters corresponding to A-rated and Baa-rated bonds. Based on the historical data shown in Figure 16-4, we have assumed expected 10-year cumulative default probabilities of 2% for A and 5% for Baa, with correlations of 20% for both. Figure 16-11 shows a very coarse discrete representation of the distribution of Z and is used strictly for illustration. To calculate statistics of the various distributions, we use a much

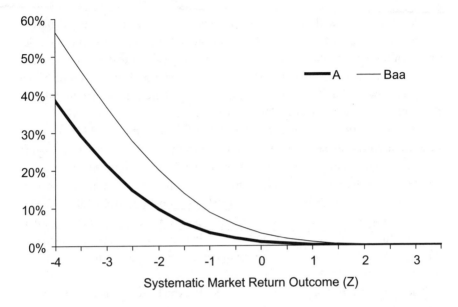

Figure 16-11. Conditional Default Probabilities for Different Qualities and Their Dependence on the Market Variable[a]

	Systematic Variable		Cumulative Probability (%)	A-Rated Bonds		Baa-Rated Bonds	
	$p(Z)$				Conditional Default Probability		Conditional Default Probability
Z	(%)			Threshold	(%)	Threshold	(%)
−4.00	0.008		0.008	−0.296	38.36	0.161	56.40
−3.50	0.049		0.057	−0.546	29.25	−0.089	46.45
−3.00	0.240		0.297	−0.796	21.30	−0.339	36.73
−2.50	0.924		1.221	−1.046	14.77	−0.589	27.79
−2.00	2.783		4.005	−1.296	9.75	−0.839	20.07
−1.50	6.559		10.564	−1.546	6.10	−1.089	13.81
−1.00	12.098		22.662	−1.796	3.62	−1.339	9.03
−0.50	17.467		40.128	−2.046	2.04	−1.589	5.60
0.00	19.741		59.870	−2.296	1.08	−1.839	3.30
0.50	17.467		77.336	−2.546	0.54	−2.089	1.84
1.00	12.098		89.434	−2.796	0.26	−2.339	0.97
1.50	6.559		95.993	−3.046	0.12	−2.589	0.48
2.00	2.783		98.776	−3.296	0.05	−2.839	0.23
2.50	0.924		99.701	−3.546	0.02	−3.089	0.10
3.00	0.240		99.941	−3.796	0.01	−3.339	0.04
3.50	0.049		99.990	−4.046	0.00	−3.589	0.02

[a]Assumptions for A-rated bonds: 2% expected cumulative default probability, 20% correlation; for Baa-rated bonds: 5% expected cumulative default probability, 20% correlation.

smaller step size. The "threshold" shown in Figure 16-11 is the quantity in parentheses in Equation (16-7). For $Z = 0$, the threshold for a single-A bond is -2.296. That is, if there is no systematic market return, a typical A-rated issuer would not default unless its idiosyncratic asset return was 2.296 standard deviations below its mean. The probability of this event, from the standard normal cumulative distribution function, is just 1.08%. However, if there is a systematic downturn of 1 standard deviation in the market ($Z = -1.0$), the default threshold is reduced in magnitude for all issuers, and now a move of only -1.796 standard deviations results in default. This carries a probability of 3.62%. It is interesting to compare how bonds of different credit qualities are affected. The same 1-standard-deviation systematic event that drove the single-A default probability from 1.08 to 3.62% raises the Baa default probability from 3.30 to 9.03%. While this systematic event increases the default probabilities for both credit qualities by approximately a factor of three, clearly the absolute change in default losses is much more severe for Baa credits.

These distributions of conditional default rates can be transformed into conditional distributions of portfolio excess return via the approximation in Equation (16-2). In addition to the default rate assumptions shown in Figure 16-11, we must provide assumptions for the spread over Treasuries and the recovery rate for each asset class. Figure 16-12 shows the conditional excess return distributions for A-rated credits, Baa-rated credits, and a 50/50 blend of the two. We see that in all three cases, a diversified credit portfolio approximately underperforms Treasuries when the systematic variable takes a value of about -2.0 or worse, which we expect to happen with a probability of about 4%. In these times of credit distress, Baa investments underperform their single-A counterparts; at all other times, they outperform. Yet it is not at all clear from Figure 16-12 how to choose which of these return distributions is better—this depends on a particular investor's goals and risk appetite.

Once we have plotted the complete return distributions as illustrated in Figure 16-12 (but, of course, at a much finer resolution), we can calculate various types of summary statistics that might drive investment decisions. Figure 16-13 compares the return distributions obtained for various blends of A and Baa securities. In addition to the expected excess return over Treasuries, we report its standard deviation, as well as several measures of tail risk.

Two types of statistics are reported on tail risk for a given confidence level. The interpretation of the value-at-risk (VaR) is that you can be 95% confident that the result you obtain will be the VaR or better. The interpretation of the expected shortfall (ExpS) is the average of all the possible outcomes that go beyond the VaR. (One can imagine two different distributions with the same VaR but with one having a much worse ExpS than the other.)

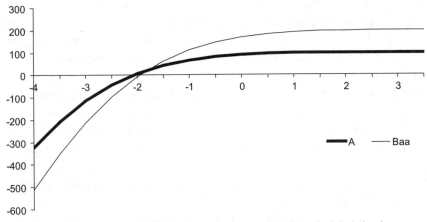

Annualized Excess Return (bp/year)

Realization of Systematic Asset Return (numbered standard deviations)

Figure 16-12. Annualized Excess Returns Realized by Bonds of Different Qualities
Conditioned on the Market Variable

Systematic Variable		Cumulative Probability	Bond Portfolio Performance (Annualized Excess Returns, bp) Conditioned on Different Outcomes of Systematic Variable Z		
Z	$p(Z)$ (%)	(%)	A	Baa	Blend
−4.00	0.008	0.008	−322	−512	−417
−3.50	0.049	0.057	−207	−349	−278
−3.00	0.240	0.297	−115	−210	−163
−2.50	0.924	1.221	−45	−96	−71
−2.00	2.783	4.005	7	−6	0
−1.50	6.559	10.564	42	62	52
−1.00	12.098	22.662	66	112	89
−0.50	17.467	40.128	81	146	114
0.00	19.741	59.870	90	169	129
0.50	17.467	77.336	95	183	139
1.00	12.098	89.434	98	191	144
1.50	6.559	95.993	99	195	147
2.00	2.783	98.776	100	198	149
2.50	0.924	99.701	100	199	149
3.00	0.240	99.941	100	200	150
3.50	0.049	99.990	100	200	150

In the example calculation shown, we use a Treasury yield of 4% and spreads of 100 bp for A and 200 bp for Baa. The achieved excess return over the 10-year horizon for A is found to have an average of 81 bp/year with a standard deviation of 26 bp,[18] but has a 1% probability of underperforming Treasuries (99% VaR) by −25 bp/year or more. For Baa, the mean outperformance is 151 bp/year with a standard deviation of 55 bp, with a 99% VaR of −63 bp/year. Assuming that the portfolio is composed of a linear blend of the two qualities gives a linear blend of the excess return numbers for every value of Z, and thus gives a linear blend of the results for all of the performance measures shown (except the information ratio).

One way to use this analysis to set the allocation is to seek to maximize the expected return subject to a specified risk limit. For example, using the data shown in Figure 16-13, an investor who requires 95% confidence that portfolio excess returns will be at least 40 bp/year would choose an allocation of 60% to Baa. As long as the maximum amount of risk that can be tolerated is known, then this method can be used to back out the blend of A and Baa bonds that will achieve that level of risk, whether specified by VaR or expected shortfall, at any confidence level.

The analysis can be modified in various ways to fit different types of long-term investment objectives. At many institutions, for example, formal risk constraints are defined in terms of VaR limits on the dollar amounts of portfolio default losses, not in terms of excess returns as illustrated earlier. In this case, the risk limit dictates a maximum exposure to Baa that does not change with fluctuating spreads. This can give rise to a two-tiered approach. First, an analysis of the portfolio loss distribution based on models of default rates, correlations, and recovery rates is used to establish a ceiling on the Baa exposure that is acceptable under the loss constraint. However, it may not always be desirable to take on this maximum exposure to Baa. A second analysis may be carried out to establish the tactical allocation, including the effect of spread levels on outperformance. At this level, the distribution of excess returns is used to compute an optimal allocation to Baa that tends to increase when spreads have widened enough to justify the additional risk. The limit on default losses places a fixed upper bound on how high this allocation is allowed to go.

An Insurance Industry Example. Consider the following credit allocation problem, typical for an insurance company portfolio. Assume that the company has an

---

18. In the absence of any defaults, the portfolio would outperform by 100 bp/year. The expected default rate of 2% over the horizon reduces this amount. From Equation (16-2), the horizon value per dollar of the corporate portfolio net default losses is $98\% \times 1.05^{10} + 2\% \times 0.20 = 1.60$, which gives an annualized return of 4.81%, outperforming the assumed 4.00%/year Treasury return by 81 bp/year.

Figure 16-13. Characteristics of Corporate Bond Portfolios Using Different Blends of A and Baa

A Weight (%)	Baa Weight (%)	Mean Annualized Excess Return (bp)	Standard Deviation Annualized Excess Return (bp)	95% VaR (%)	95% Expected Shortfall (%)	99% VaR (%)	99% Expected Shortfall (%)	Breakeven Probability (%)	Information Ratio
All A 100	0	81	26	33	−4	−25	−70	98.10	3.15
90	10	88	29	34	−6	−29	−76	98.01	3.08
80	20	95	31	36	−7	−33	−83	97.93	3.02
70	30	102	34	37	−9	−36	−89	97.86	2.97
60	40	109	37	38	−11	−40	−96	97.79	2.93
50	50	116	40	39	−13	−44	−103	97.73	2.89
40	60	123	43	40	−15	−48	−109	97.68	2.86
30	70	130	46	41	−17	−51	−116	97.63	2.83
20	80	137	49	42	−19	−55	−123	97.58	2.80
10	90	144	52	43	−21	−59	−129	97.54	2.78
0 All Baa	100	151	55	44	−23	−63	−136	97.50	2.76

Aa rating and can fund at LIBOR. It collects premiums up front against an estimated liability stream. Essentially, over the long term, the portfolio invested against
these liabilities has to outperform a default-free investment at Aa rates, and it
must ensure that the chance of underperforming is minimal.

In this case, we can modify the preceding analysis to view the credit portfolio
vs. the firm's liabilities, rather than vs. Treasuries. We repeat the analysis shown
in Figures 16-11 to 16-13, but calculate the distribution of excess returns over Aa,
rather than over Treasuries. Such an analysis is carried out in Figure 16-14 using the
following assumptions: Treasury yield 4%; spreads of 60, 80, and 130 bp for Aa, A,
and Baa, respectively; single-A expected default probability 2% with 20% issuer
correlation; Baa default probability 5% with 25% correlation; and 40% recovery
rates throughout. We see that owing to the small spread differential, A-rated
securities offer an expected return advantage over the Aa liabilities of only 4 bp/
year, with a standard deviation of 22 bp. The breakeven probability is only 75%.
For Baa securities, the larger spread cushion more than makes up for the higher
expected default rate, and thus we obtain a higher expected return as well as a
greater probability of breakeven. However, the Baa distribution has more risk in
the tails. If we seek to maximize the expected return subject to a maximum underperformance of 50 bp/year at 95% confidence, then we can allocate between 30
and 40% of the portfolio to Baa.

These results are very sensitive to the spread assumptions and, in particular,
the spread differentials from Aa to A and from A to Baa. In Figure 16-14 we assumed that A spreads were 20 bp over Aa and that Baa spreads were 50 bp wider
still; our loss constraint of 95% VaR = –50 bp led to a Baa allocation of 34%. Figure 16-15 shows how this optimal allocation would change as we vary these two
spread differentials. Naturally, an increase in the spread advantage of Baa over A
(without any adjustment of the expected default rates) increases the optimal allocation to Baa. When this advantage goes below a certain level (here shown to be
about 30 bp) the expected return is higher for A, and there is no longer any incentive to take on Baa risk.

An even larger effect can be seen as we increase the spread differential between
A and Aa. This increases the spread cushion on which the strategy rests, improving the mean excess return and the breakeven probabilities for both A and Baa
assets. This allows us to take much more risk before challenging the VaR limit
and, hence, permits much larger contributions to Baa.

ISSUER LEVEL OPTIMIZATION

The macro-level analysis presented here is based on many simplifying assumptions,
including: (1) uniform correlations (i.e., homogeneous assets); (2) asset returns

Figure 16-14. Risk and Return of Blends of A and Baa Assets vs. Aa Liabilities

A Weight (%)	Baa Weight (%)	Mean Annualized Excess Return (bp)	Standard Deviation Annualized Excess Return (bp)	95% VaR (%)	95% Expected Shortfall (%)	99% VaR (%)	99% Expected Shortfall (%)	Breakeven Probability (%)	Information Ratio
All A									
100	0	4	22	−37	−68	−86	−123	75.14	0.18
90	10	6	25	−40	−76	−96	−137	77.00	0.26
80	20	9	28	−44	−83	−106	−151	78.20	0.31
70	30	11	31	−48	−91	−117	−166	79.07	0.36
60	40	14	34	−52	−99	−127	−180	79.79	0.39
50	50	16	38	−56	−107	−137	−194	80.21	0.43
40	60	18	41	−60	−115	−147	−208	80.76	0.45
30	70	21	44	−64	−123	−158	−222	81.03	0.47
20	80	23	47	−68	−130	−168	−237	81.43	0.49
10	90	26	50	−72	−138	−178	−251	81.70	0.51
All Baa									
0	100	28	54	−76	−146	−189	−265	81.83	0.52

Optimal Allocation to Baa

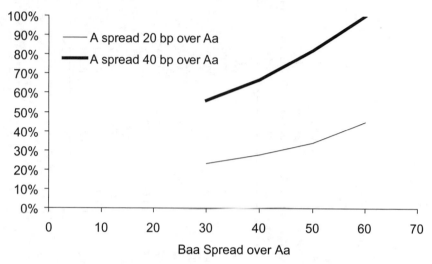

Figure 16-15. Optimal Allocation to Baa as a Function of Spread Differentials

assumed to be distributed normally; (3) constant recovery rate; and (4) issues that default are assumed to do so immediately.

When selecting specific assets for a portfolio, however, many of these simplifying assumptions should be relaxed. For example, asset returns are typically modeled as having a fat-tailed distribution, implying a greater probability of large positive and negative returns compared to a normal distribution. This also implies that the joint probability of default is underestimated when a normal distribution is assumed (so-called "tail-dependence"). Furthermore, issuer correlations are unlikely to be uniform. Issuers belonging to the same sector are more likely to have a higher default correlation with each other than with issuers belonging to different sectors. Recovery rates have been shown to be correlated with default rates, further skewing the overall loss distribution. A more realistic, nonuniform, correlation matrix might produce a more realistic joint probability distribution of default losses. Unfortunately, relaxing the assumptions of the "macro" model greatly increases its complexity.

How might the risks of various A-Baa allocations change if we were to make more realistic assumptions regarding asset return distributions? We can investigate such questions under a much broader range of assumptions using COMPASS, Lehman's portfolio simulation and optimization tool for buy-and-hold credit investors. An investor can use COMPASS to construct an optimized credit portfolio that minimizes expected shortfall while satisfying various constraints, including an expected return target. It is instructive to compare the results from the macro allocation model we presented earlier with results obtained using COMPASS, which works at the issuer level. As we show in the following, they are similar, which supports an approach for investors of first determining their macro allocation to the A and Baa sectors, and then using an optimizer such as COMPASS to select individual names for the portfolio.

COMPASS works as follows: Individual issuer default rates are mapped to historical default rates based on the issuer's credit rating. COMPASS then uses historical equity return correlations to estimate joint default correlations among issuers depending on their respective sectors. Using this information and assuming that asset return distributions are fat-tailed, COMPASS generates a joint default probability distribution for all assets in a portfolio. Using this default distribution and applying a model of recovery rates, it can generate a portfolio's loss distribution. For a given level of expected return, it generates various possible portfolio loss distributions using as inputs various combinations of the available assets. It then finds the single portfolio with the smallest expected shortfall given the level of expected return.

For Figure 16-16, we used COMPASS to examine the risks of various macro allocations when the assets come from heterogeneous sectors. We first set up all of the asset characteristics to match as closely as possible those assumed in this chapter. A-rated and Baa-rated assets are assumed to have a spread over Treasuries of 100 and 200 bp, respectively. In addition, a fixed recovery rate of 20% is assumed in both asset classes. For the first COMPASS run, we match all of the distributional assumptions of the macro model as well: a normal distribution, uniform correlations of 20%, and fixed 20% recovery rates. We find an expected loss of 2.69%, expressed as the total cumulative losses owing to defaults, net of recoveries, as a percentage of starting value. The VaR of such losses at the 99% level is 16.17%, and the expected shortfall is 19.31%. Note that performance is measured here in a somewhat different way than throughout this chapter. For the purpose of comparison, we backed out similar numbers from the results of the macro model shown in Figure 16-13. The results agree quite closely with the COMPASS results for normal returns and uniform correlations, which was expected as the underlying models are the same.

We then investigate the effect of introducing a couple of more complex assumptions. The introduction of a more fat-tailed asset return distribution (the Student-t distribution) is found to increase both VaR and ExpS by a substantial amount. However, the introduction of a nonuniform correlation matrix based on equity market sector correlations leads to a decrease in both VaR and ExpS in this example. (This is due to the combination of two factors: the 20% correlation assumption is high relative to many of the correlations found in the sector-based

Figure 16-16. Comparison of Macro Model Results with COMPASS Results
In Terms of Overall Default Loss Statistics under Various Assumptions[a]

Modeling Assumptions	Expected Loss (%)	99% VaR (%)	1% Expected Shortfall (%)
Macro model	2.86	15.13	19.25
Gaussian; uniform correlation = 0.2	2.69	16.17	19.31
Student-*t* distribution (12 degrees of freedom); uniform correlation = 0.2	2.61	20.78	25.13
Gaussian; sector-based correlation matrix	2.74	13.01	14.75
Student-*t* distribution (12 degrees of freedom); sector-based correlation matrix	2.68	17.36	20.62

[a]Assumptions: 50/50 blend of A and Baa credits; 10-year horizon; default rates 2% for A, 5% for Baa; spreads 100 and 200 bp for A and Baa, constant 20% recovery.

model, and the portfolio used in this example was well diversified in its sector exposures.) It is interesting that when we include both of these effects (Student-*t* distribution and sector-based correlations), they tend to cancel each other out, leaving the VaR and ExpS only slightly higher than in the macro model. Overall, the fact that the results from COMPASS are similar to those from the macro model supports the use of the latter for A-Baa allocation and the former for portfolio issue selection.

Even within the confines of our macro framework, there is a lot of flexibility for changing various assumptions. For example, the return approximation of Equation (16-2) assumes that defaults occur immediately, ignoring the coupon income that such bonds generate up to the default event. This conservative assumption underestimates the return advantage offered by high spreads. This is desirable when the goal is to demonstrate that credit asset classes are attractive relative to Treasuries even under the most conservative assumptions. However, in the allocation between A and Baa credits, this assumption may provide somewhat of a bias against Baa. A modified return approximation that phases in defaults over time could certainly be investigated in future research.

Similarly, we have assumed nominal 10-year default rates of 2% for A and 5% for Baa, based on Moody's long-term averages. Are these the best estimates of forward-looking default rates, regardless of current spread levels or the economic climate? Possibly not. Our goal has been to present a framework for analyzing credit allocations at the macro level; the selected horizon, expected default rates, correlation levels and spreads are inputs that can be modified to suit an investor's views.

Furthermore, the desire to include the effect of tail dependence does not require a move to a full issuer-based optimization. It has been shown that tail dependence can be incorporated into the large homogeneous portfolio (LHP) approximation without requiring simulation. Even without introducing this extra level of complexity, the tail risk of an asset class can be increased within our framework by increasing the correlation assumption.

Several notes are in order concerning the portfolio optimization criteria as well. It is widely accepted that the standard mean/variance optimization framework is not appropriate for asset classes with asymmetric return distributions, and that some adjustment is needed to reflect risk aversion. In the literature on downside risk,[19] the efficient frontier is redefined using alternative measures of risk, such as target shortfall (the mean of the distribution conditioned on it being below a specified minimum, or target, return) or target semivariance (the variance of this portion of the distribution, also called conditional variance). The expected shortfall measure used here is similar in nature to target shortfall, but is defined in terms of a confidence level rather than a fixed threshold.

An alternative approach to such optimization problems departs completely from the notion of the efficient frontier. Rather than maximize the mean of the distribution subject to a risk constraint on some other property of the distribution, a utility function is used to evaluate the value to the investor of achieving a certain return.[20] This function is characterized by a risk aversion parameter, which ensures that the penalty for a very negative return is greater than the reward for a positive return of similar magnitude. (The greater the risk aversion parameter, the greater the difference in utility.) Optimization in this framework involves finding the distribution that gives the highest expected utility. We have chosen to use explicit limits on VaR or ExpS because we have found that investors are more comfortable stating their risk limits explicitly rather than in terms of a risk aversion parameter.

We have formulated the allocation problems under the LHP approximation. This assumes that each asset class is represented in the portfolio by a large set of relatively small positions in different issuers. This may be appropriate in two situations: for investors who truly intend to maintain a low level of nonsystematic

---

19. See W. V. Harlow, "Asset Allocation in a Downside-Risk Framework," *Financial Analysts Journal*, September–October 1991.

20. The family of isoelastic utility functions takes the basic form $U(V) = 1/(1 - \alpha) \times (V^{1-\alpha} - 1)$, where V is the terminal value of a \$1 investment, and α is the risk aversion parameter. See J. Ingersoll, *Theory of Financial Decision Making*, Rowman and Littlefield, 1987.

risk or for those who wish to isolate their allocation decisions from their security selection decisions. An alternative approach, which may better suit some more active investors, is to represent the return distribution for each asset class in a manner that corresponds to the way they typically manage that asset class. That is, rather than use the default distribution for the asset class as a whole, one could use the (more skewed) default distribution for a portfolio of twenty Baa bonds, if that is the anticipated typical structure of the Baa portion of the portfolio. M. B. Wise and V. Bhansali[21] take this approach in their analysis of the optimal allocation to corporate bonds, using a utility function approach. They show that the number of bonds assumed to be in the portfolio can strongly influence the optimal allocation, but that this effect decreases as the level of assumed correlation is increased.

CONCLUSION

Credit portfolio management, whether the viewpoint is buy-and-hold or total return, is much more complicated than any of the simple abstractions considered here. First and foremost, there is no such thing as a homogeneous pool of issuers. Every issuer has its own unique financial structure and mix of businesses, with exposures to different potential risks—all of which can influence projected default probabilities and recovery rates. Correlations among the default risks of different firms can stem from shared exposures to certain industries, geographical regions, or political factors. Real portfolios cannot diversify among infinitely many issuers, nor will they have exactly the same weights in all securities. Issues related to liquidity or risk-based capital can force even an investor with a long horizon to sell positions in distressed securities.

Despite all these additional considerations, we believe there is value in the simplified models addressed in this chapter. In determining their overall allocation to credit sectors, investors must come to grips with the overall level of credit risk they are able to tolerate on a macro level. This "big picture" evaluation can be carried out using the large homogeneous portfolio approximation, leaving many of the details of portfolio construction to a later stage of the process. More complex simulation-based modeling tools such as COMPASS can incorporate more rigorous assumptions about the joint asset distributions of different issuers when implementing a desired exposure with specific positions. Taken together, we believe that these models form a flexible set of tools that can help provide illuminating insights into many more variations of the buy-hold asset allocation problem.

---

21. M. B. Wise and V. Bhansali, "Portfolio Allocation to Corporate Bonds with Correlated Defaults," *Journal of Risk,* Fall 2002.

17. A Quick Look at Index Tails

When looking at an asset class at the macro level, investors and analysts often characterize its return distribution by just two numbers: mean and standard deviation. Various forms of analysis (e.g., information ratios, Sharpe ratios, and mean-variance optimization) have been built on the assumption that the mean and standard deviation fully describe the return distribution of an asset. Often, the distribution is assumed to be normal, as this symmetric distribution is fully defined by its mean and standard deviation and because it is both relatively tractable for researchers and widely familiar to readers. However, how many times have we read footnotes and disclaimers pointing out that if the returns are not normally distributed, then all bets are off?

Yet it is widely accepted that excess returns are not normally distributed for many asset classes, notably those with embedded options or substantial credit risk. These asset classes have return distributions that are both asymmetric and fat-tailed—higher probabilities of extreme events. As we have pointed out elsewhere,[1] credit by its very nature is an extremely asymmetric investment. An investor who buys a corporate bond and holds it to maturity earns a relatively modest spread over Treasuries, with a very high probability, in return for taking the risk of a catastrophic loss (i.e., default) with a very low probability. When viewed in this framework, all of the variability in the return lies in the extreme negative tail; the up side is very limited. Since the excess return distribution is not normal, the mean and standard deviation are insufficient to fully describe the distribution. Consequently, the standard deviation of return is not an adequate risk measure for a buy-and-hold credit investor.[2]

Based on research first published by Lehman Brothers in 2004.

1. See Chapter 16.
2. If the investor's utility function were "quadratic," then the distribution's mean and standard deviation would be sufficient for the investor's financial decision making.

The situation is different for a total return investor who is concerned with monthly excess returns. For such relatively short-holding-period horizons, the excess return distribution for credit assets is much more symmetric as the bulk of the excess return is driven primarily by the widening and tightening of spreads. Viewed on a monthly basis, these returns tend to look much more balanced, with occasional large positive returns, as well as large negative returns.

In this short piece, we take a quick peek at the empirically observed monthly excess return distributions for various credit classes over the last 10 years. We attempt to address the following questions:

- How fat are the tails?

- How asymmetric is the distribution? Are the negative tails much fatter than the positive ones?

- Is there a substantial difference between investment-grade and high yield credit in this regard?

- Can we measure how this phenomenon changes with the holding-period return horizon?

In Figure 17-1, we present a summary of the last 10 years of monthly excess returns for a small set of Lehman Brothers indices. For each index shown, in addition to the mean and standard deviation of monthly excess returns, we present two measures of the degree to which the distributions are nonnormal: skewness and kurtosis. Skewness measures the extent to which a distribution is asymmetric. A perfectly symmetric distribution, like the normal, will have a skewness of zero. Negative skewness indicates that the negative tail of the distribution is larger than the positive tail—that the extreme events are more likely to be losses than gains. Kurtosis measures the fatness of the tails, both positive and negative. Positive kurtosis indicates that the distribution has fatter tails than the normal distribution (higher probability of extreme results, either positive or negative); negative kurtosis indicates a distribution with thinner tails.[3] The combination of positive kurtosis and negative skewness thus means that the tails overall are larger than normal and that the negative tail is larger than the positive one.

To help put some intuition behind these measurements, Figure 17-1 also provides some intuitive measurements of the extremes of the excess return

---

3. Technically, the normal distribution has a kurtosis of 3, and one should evaluate the relative fatness of tails by comparing the kurtosis of a given distribution to 3. In practice, it is customary to use "excess kurtosis," obtained by subtracting 3 from the kurtosis of the distribution. Here, we ignore this distinction, and use the term "kurtosis" to refer to "excess kurtosis."

Figure 17-1. Statistical Properties of the Distributions of Monthly Excess Returns
January 1994–January 2004

Index	Mean (%/month)	Standard Deviation (%/month)	Skewness	Kurtosis	Minimum (%/month)	Maximum (%/month)	Average of Worst 5%	Average of Best 5%	Average Number of Issuers
Corporates	0.03	0.70	-0.70	6.25	-2.93	2.70	-1.98	1.72	715
Consumer cyclical	0.05	1.01	-0.17	5.31	-3.89	3.71	-2.67	2.73	58
Industrials	0.02	0.80	-0.59	4.52	-2.78	2.77	-2.34	1.94	412
Energy	0.08	0.68	-1.24	7.57	-3.41	2.03	-1.89	1.67	52
Pipelines	-0.15	1.99	-5.03	41.61	-16.75	5.79	-6.26	3.01	16
High yield	0.03	2.46	-0.82	4.00	-8.85	7.38	-7.14	5.66	764
Emerging markets	0.41	4.42	-2.40	13.11	-27.88	9.01	-11.42	7.40	29

distributions. We show the minimum and maximum observed monthly excess returns for each series, as well as the averages of the worst 5% and best 5% of the observed months.[4] Last, we show an average number of issuers over the last few years for each of these indices (for the Emerging Markets Index, this is the number of countries represented).

Figure 17-2 presents histograms for several of these excess return distributions. We construct a histogram by grouping monthly excess returns that fall within a given range into one bucket, and then reporting on the vertical axis the number of monthly observations for each bucket. Each bar is placed along the horizontal axis at the midpoint of its range. For example, the bucket containing monthly observations with excess returns between –0.1 and 0.1% is placed at 0%; the bucket with excess returns between 0.1 and 0.3% is placed at 0.2%. A bucket's range of excess returns varies depending on the index.

For the Corporate Index, we see quite clearly the effect of the positive kurtosis. The return distribution is peaked in the center but has extreme events well beyond what would be expected in a normal distribution with the same mean and standard deviation (which is shown as the smooth curve in the histogram). Consistent with the relatively small negative skewness, these tail events are somewhat more extreme on the negative side, but a clear positive tail can be seen as well. The High Yield Index is similarly characterized by fat tails that are fairly symmetric. The Emerging Markets Index displays a substantially larger (negative) skewness and (positive) kurtosis, largely owing to a single huge event: the excess return of –28% in the Russian crisis of August 1998. Just for comparison, Figure 17-2d shows the distribution of excess returns over cash for the 3- to 7-year portion of the Treasury Index, with skewness and kurtosis both close to zero. This distribution can be seen to line up quite nicely with the normal.

Figure 17-3 depicts the tail symmetry of these indices. Using the average of the best 5% and the average of the worst 5% numbers from Figure 17-1, we represent each index in terms of the trade-off between upside and downside risk. The diagonal line marks the situation in which the upside gains are equal and opposite to the downside losses. We see that for the Investment-Grade Corporate Index and several of its subcomponents, the positive and negative tails are almost identical. The one glaring exception to this is the Pipelines Index, which was home to Enron at the time of its downfall. The inclusion of the Pipelines Index in this grouping is meant to illustrate the effect of nonsystematic risk.

4. For each monthly excess return series, we sorted the 121 realized return observations, then took the average of the best six monthly returns and the worst six. This corresponds roughly to an empirical version of the expected shortfall measurement at a 95% confidence level.

Probability (%)

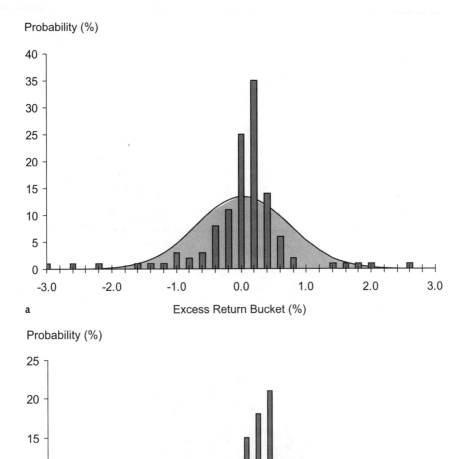

a

Excess Return Bucket (%)

Probability (%)

b

Excess Return Bucket (%)

Figure 17-2. Comparing Observed Index Excess Returns to the Normal Distribution
(a) Corporates (skewness: –0.70, kurtosis: 6.25); (b) High Yield (skewness: –0.82, kurtosis: 4.0); (c) Emerging Markets (skewness: –2.4, kurtosis: 13.1); (d) U.S. Treasuries 3–7 years, monthly excess returns over cash, August 1988–December 2003 (skewness: –0.13, kurtosis: –0.3)

(continued)

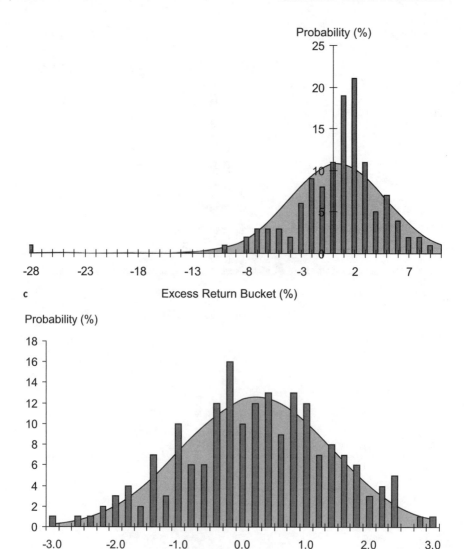

Figure 17-2. (continued)

We believe that the symmetric properties we are observing in the Corporate Index tails are due to the effect of diversification, which enables the index to avoid a huge return shock in a single month owing to default-related losses. For less diversified portfolios and indices, the risk of default threatens to bring very asymmetric losses. This relates to the observed asymmetry in the Emerging Markets returns as well. The concentration of the risk among a relatively small number of

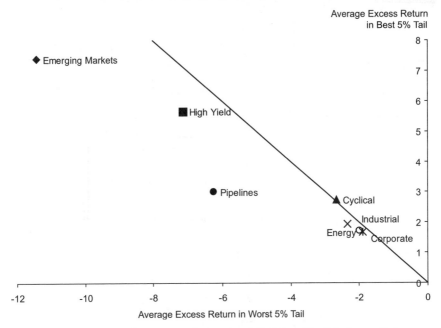

Figure 17-3. Symmetry of Positive and Negative Tails Using Monthly Excess Returns

countries in this index, coupled with the similar exposures of these countries to global economic events, creates the potential for very large negative returns. The High Yield Index, while it has a very high standard deviation of excess return, can be seen to be fairly close to the line, providing investors with the potential for large gains in return for taking the risk of large losses.

We have shown that well-diversified credit indices tend to have relatively symmetric (if fat-tailed) excess return distributions over a monthly horizon. Yes, there are fat negative tails, but they are compensated for by fat positive tails. How does this picture change as we increase the holding-period return horizon? This is a relatively tricky thing to measure, as the longer the return horizon, the fewer data points one has available. Thus, the 10-year period that we have chosen to study can provide 120 independent monthly data points, ten independent annual data points, or a single 10-year return observation. With a small number of data points, though, no robust statistical conclusions can be reached. We decided to content ourselves with a second look at the data assuming a 3-month holding-period horizon. We grouped the data into forty quarterly observations of cumulative excess returns and repeated the analysis of Figure 17-1. The results are shown in Figure 17-4. The most striking result here is that the kurtosis falls drastically for every index shown: for the Corporate Index, from 6.25 to 0.85; and for the

Figure 17-4. Statistical Properties of the Distributions of Quarterly Excess Returns 1994–2003

Index	Mean (%/month)	Standard Deviation (%/month)	Skewness	Kurtosis	Minimum (%/month)	Maximum (%/month)	Average of Worst 5%	Average of Best 5%	Average Number of Issuers
Corporates	0.08	1.34	-0.82	0.85	-3.38	2.70	-3.22	2.49	715
Consumer cyclical	0.14	1.95	-0.34	0.53	-4.44	4.41	-4.23	3.91	58
Industrials	0.06	1.59	-0.50	0.79	-3.68	3.83	-3.37	3.21	412
Energy	0.23	1.33	-1.56	3.23	-4.14	2.11	-3.66	2.10	52
Pipelines	-0.49	3.62	-3.41	14.57	-18.14	3.30	-12.98	3.30	16
High yield	0.05	4.79	-1.05	0.85	-11.07	7.73	-11.06	7.15	764
Emerging markets	1.27	8.43	-1.10	1.37	-25.51	14.73	-20.37	13.71	29

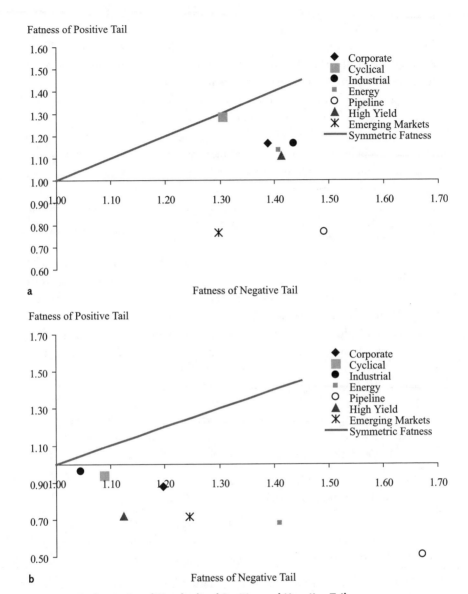

Figure 17-5. Symmetry of Standardized Positive and Negative Tails
Using Monthly (a) and Quarterly (b) Excess Returns

Emerging Markets Index, from 13.11 down to 1.37. The averaging of returns over a 3-month period smoothes out the extremes and pulls in the fat tails of the distribution. However, the skewness of the return distributions remains negative, in some cases becoming even more negative than in the monthly case.

As we go from a monthly to a quarterly horizon, what happens to the positive tail and the negative tail of the distribution? It is hard to understand this based on the skewness and kurtosis. It is also difficult to directly compare the worst 5% and best 5% results in Figures 17-1 and 17-4 as these numbers are not normalized, and it is hard to compare monthly returns with quarterly ones. To address this, we suggest the following measure of the fatness of the tails: we first normalize the worst 5% and best 5% numbers by subtracting the mean and dividing by the standard deviation; we then divide by 2.063, the average number of standard deviations in the worst 5% tail of the standard normal distribution. The result is a one-sided measure of the fatness of the positive (or negative) tail at the 95% confidence level. Numbers greater than one indicate fatter-than-normal tails, while numbers less than one indicate thinner-than-normal tails. These measures are shown in Figure 17-5a and b using monthly and quarterly data, respectively. We can see that while the monthly data tend to indicate fat tails on both the positive and negative sides of the distribution, the quarterly data indicate fat negative tails and thin positive tails for all of the asset classes shown.

We draw the following conclusions from this brief study:

1. The distributions of monthly excess returns for well-diversified credit asset classes tend to be somewhat fatter than normal, but exhibit a rough symmetry between the positive and negative tails.

2. Contrary to what might have been expected, we have found this to be true for high yield as well as investment-grade credit.

3. For the Emerging Markets Index, and potentially for any highly concentrated index or portfolio, the returns are more asymmetrically distributed, dominated by a large negative tail.

4. As we lengthen the return horizon from monthly to quarterly, we find a noticeable increase in the asymmetry of the tails. The beneficial positive tails tend to get smaller, while the negative tails remain. Presumably (although it is hard to measure), this effect increases as the return horizon increases.

18. Are Credit Markets Globally Integrated?

The Lehman Brothers Global Aggregate Index represents a highly diverse opportunity set, spanning currency, yield curve, and credit investments. Global diversification of credit holdings ensures that the index is less influenced by the idiosyncratic performance of a particular bond or issuer than traditional single-currency bond indices and allows for diversity in outperformance strategies. The opportunities offered by global credit indices include sector and name selection as well as the choice of currency in which these views are implemented. These opportunities present the investor with questions of the following type: Can one assume that different bonds from the same issuer denominated in various currencies are substitutes one for the other in the sense that movements in the spread of one are mirrored by the other? In the realm of index replication—for example, with respect to the Japanese corporate market—can one use $, €, or £ bonds from Japanese corporate issuers as a proxy? In risk management, does the holding of various issues from one issuer but in differing currencies of denomination lessen the issuer-specific risk exposure to that issuer or increase it? Can we talk in terms of global risk factors or global sector effects that are common to all bonds in those sectors, appropriately defined, irrespective of their currency of denomination? It is these types of questions that we sought to address in our study.

We report the results of an empirical study of spread performance in the Global Aggregate Index focusing on the major four currencies over a time history of 44 months. For identical issuer, sector, or quality buckets, we observe systematic differences in spread level and volatility across currencies. We measure cross-currency correlation of average spread changes for individual issuers and attempt to explain it as a function of spread level, average rating, and industry sector. Short of the conceptual framework provided by a global risk model, our results point to

Based on research first published by Lehman Brothers in 2002.

some simple investment conclusions for global credit investors. We find that as spread level increases, accompanied by volatility, the correlation between issuer LIBOR spread movements in issues denominated in different currencies rises to levels of up to 90%. Moreover, our study provides evidence that correlation has increased in recent times in tandem with the general rise in spread levels.

DATA AND DESCRIPTIVE STATISTICS

We defined our study universe by considering only liquid, noncollateralized bullet bonds, all members of the credit component of the Lehman Brothers Global Aggregate Index. This was achieved by setting a liquidity constraint of an equivalent in local currency terms of $500 million outstanding nominal and an average life between 3 and 10 years. The index from which we select our study universe is the Global Aggregate Index excluding Treasuries and collateralized securities. Our study universe captures about 47% of this index in market value terms. Figure 18-1 details the various proportions of currencies in both the index and the study universe, in terms of both market value and representation of issuers.

As can be seen immediately, while the U.S. dollar, euro, and yen are well represented, sterling is a very small proportion of both the index and our universe, reflecting the very restricted size of the £-market in comparison with the other three major currencies. Consequently, owing to the thinness of the data, we were limited in the conclusions that we could draw about correlations between currency

Figure 18-1. Summary of Study Data as of End of August 2002

	€	£	¥	$	Other
Market Value					
Percentage of Lehman Global Aggregate Index (excluding Treasuries and collateralized)	22	5	15	56	2
Percentage of study universe	25	2	18	54	0
Study universe as percentage of the index	12	1	8	26	0
Study universe as percentage of index currency allocation	55	22	55	46	0
Issuers					
Number in index	394	182	147	668	21
Number in study universe	269	48	106	354	0

Figure 18-2. Spread Summary Table

	€-£	€-¥	€-$	£-¥	£-$	¥-$
Number of issuers tested	33	34	94	10	31	48
Average OAS currency 1 (bp)	36	46	59	25	33	24
Average OAS currency 2 (bp)	30	35	69	18	48	50
Average OAS currency 1 – Average OAS currency 2	6	10	–10	7	–15	–27
Number of issuers with same sign as average at 95% confidence level	18	19	54	2	23	29

pairs involving sterling. To a lesser extent this is also true of yen-denominated data where, not only are pricing issues more challenging, but data are only available from January 2001 onward. For the above reasons our analysis focuses primarily on the €-$ results but we state results for the other currency pairs where statistically significant.

Our analysis was carried out at three levels, issuer, sector, and quality. In each case and for each currency of denomination, the study universe was divided into appropriate buckets. For example, at the issuer level all Ford €-denominated bonds formed one bucket and Ford $-denominated bonds were in another bucket. Similarly, at the sector level, $-denominated industrials were grouped together as were £-denominated financials.

At each month-end for a period spanning January 31, 1999, to August 31, 2002, the monthly changes in LIBOR spreads of bonds in a given bucket are averaged to form a time-series of average change in LIBOR spread for that bucket. Henceforth, we refer to this average as the "issuer spread," "sector spread," and so on. The correlations among these time series form the results of our study. It should be noted that all spread references in the study are with respect to the local swap curve.

Clearly, our calculations are vulnerable to inaccuracies in data. The eligibility criteria for the study universe—liquidity, the exclusion of collateralized securities, and maturity of 3–10 years—were designed to reduce the likelihood of data errors. In addition, clearly identified outliers were removed manually.

Figure 18-2 presents the average spread difference between the two currencies in each currency pair. We have also detailed the relative numbers of issuers in that combination that, at the 95% confidence level, exhibited relative spreads of the

Figure 18-3. Comparison of Systematic Volatilities

	€-£	€-¥	€-$	£-¥	£-$	¥-$
Number of issuers tested	32	33	92	10	30	48
Average volatility, currency 1 (bp/month)	9	12	18	13	14	7
Average volatility, currency 2 (bp/month)	14	8	19	7	13	13
Mean [average 1 – average 2] (bp)	–5	3	–2	5	1	–6
Number of issuers with volatility 1 – volatility 2 of same sign as mean	88	64	77	90	50	75

same sign as the averages over the appropriate time windows.[1] For example, in the case of the €-£ pair eighteen out of thirty-two issuers issuing in both currencies (with at least twelve points of comparison for OAS) produced €-spreads lower than their £-spreads in a 95% significant manner across time. The overall average spread difference across all tickers between €- and £-spreads was 5 bp—the average £-spread exceeding the €-spread by this margin.

Similarly the volatilities of the changes in LIBOR spreads were compared among currencies and the results are summarized in Figure 18-3. These statistics indicate that, all other things being equal, of the four major currencies, U.S. dollar-denominated issues exhibit the highest spread and sterling and U.S. dollar together are at the top of the volatility range with yen-denominated currencies exhibiting the lowest spreads and volatilities.

ISSUER RESULTS

The methodology and results of the study are best illustrated in the following two examples.

Example 1. European Investment Bank (EIB)

The EIB issued securities in all four of the major currencies during the period of study and, in particular, our universe, contained a total of twenty-two issues de-

---

1. Note, since only those issuers with complete pairs of data of a year or more in total were considered, the number of issuers involved is very much smaller in this sample than in the universe as a whole. It should also be noted that the average issuer spread in any given currency differs depending on the second currency in the currency pairing, as the spread is averaged over different time periods and issuers depending on the currency pairing.

Average Change in Spread (bp)

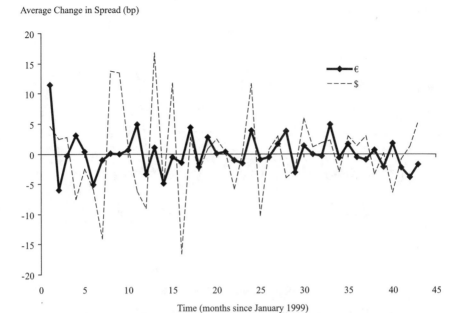

Figure 18-4. EIB Change in LIBOR Spreads over Time in € and $

nominated in euro and twenty-three in U.S. dollars. For this issuer, we were able to form the maximum-length time series of 43 months.

The average spread over the entire 44-month period of the €-denominated bonds was approximately –6 bp, and the $-denominated bonds averaged approximately –13 bp. The volatilities of changes in LIBOR spreads were seen to be 3 and 5 bp/month, respectively. At each month end we calculated the average of the changes in LIBOR spreads across all €-denominated EIB issues—the "EIB(€) issuer spread"—doing the same for the $-denominated EIB bonds. The two time series are charted in Figure 18-4. We can see that the two sets of spread behavior are only tenuously related, resulting in a low cross-currency correlation of 0.21 in LIBOR spread changes for EIB.

Example 2. Ford Capital

Ford's debt, by contrast, exhibits an entirely different relationship across currencies of denomination (Figure 18-5). (It should be noted that the scales on the Ford and EIB charts are not the same.) Over the 44-month period of the study, the euro and average spread levels were far higher at 91 and 109 bp, respectively, reflecting its A2 average credit rating. In addition, the spread volatilities were much larger, measuring 20 and 25 bp/month, respectively. The correlation between the

Average Change in Spread (bp)

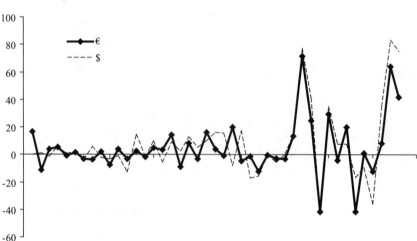

Time (months since January 1999)

Figure 18-5. Ford Change in LIBOR Spreads over Time in € and $

euro and U.S. dollar average changes in LIBOR spreads for Ford capital was measured to be 0.86, leading to rejection of the null hypothesis (of zero correlation) at high levels of significance.

It is clear from the chart that Ford's credit quality deteriorated over the period of the study; it began with an issuer spread of approximately 30 bp at a rating of A1 and ended with spreads averaging 350 bp with a rating of A3/Baa2. The correlation can be seen to increase as the spreads and volatilities rise across the time window. The figure of 0.86 is a correlation across the whole time window and mostly reflects the highly synchronized movements over the more recent time period during which spreads widened.

In our empirical analysis, we calculated correlations across all currency pairs for issuers issuing in two different currencies. In most cases the data were too scarce to draw any statistically significant conclusions. However, in a number of cases and in certain currency pairs there were sufficient data to give meaningful results. In particular, the €-$ currency pair, where the data are deepest, allowed us to gather a good deal of information. Figures 18-6 through 18-10 summarize the results in five of the six currency pairs (£-¥ being too sparsely populated to allow such a plot). The correlations summarized in the figures are all based on at least 12 months of data, but each issuer need only have had one bond at any given month end in order to allow the computation of the change in issuer spread for that month.

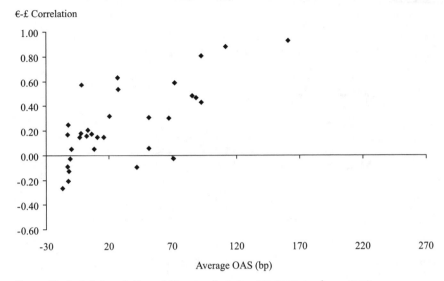

Figure 18-6. €-£ Correlation of Changes in Issuer LIBOR Spreads vs. OAS

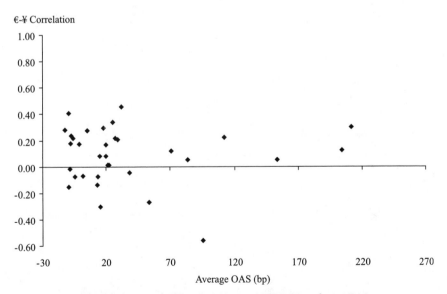

Figure 18-7. €-¥ Correlation of Changes in Issuer LIBOR Spreads vs. OAS

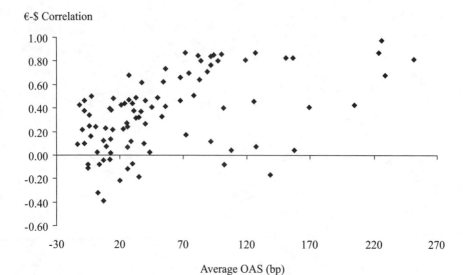

Figure 18-8. €-$ Correlation of Changes in Issuer LIBOR Spreads vs. OAS

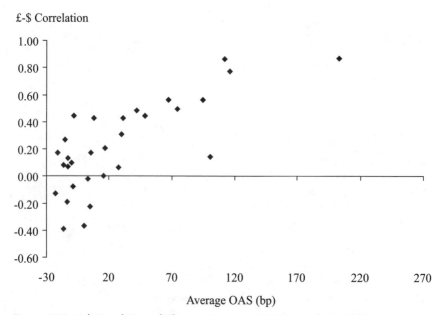

Figure 18-9. £-$ Correlation of Changes in Issuer LIBOR Spreads vs. OAS

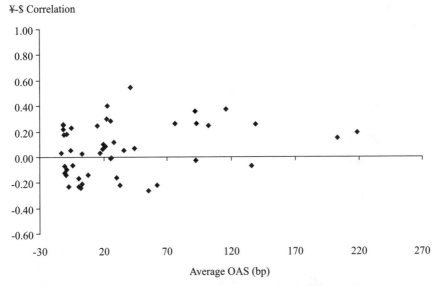

Figure 18-10. ¥-$ Correlation of Changes in Issuer LIBOR Spreads vs. OAS

In Figure 18-11, for the €-$ pair—where a good many more data were available—we also have plotted all data with at least two bonds being averaged to form the issuer spread at each month-end. The correlations plotted in the figure are based on only those issuers for which at least two bonds are available for any given month. It is evident that as the number of bonds making up the average from which the issuer spread is formed increases, the "noise" of the issue-specific behavior of any given bond is diversified away, allowing the underlying relationship between issuer spread and cross-currency correlation to be observed. As the number of bonds from which the issue spread is calculated is further increased the pattern becomes even sharper.

In Figure 18-12 we present more details for the most robust results in the €-$ currency pair, namely those of issuers having €-$ time series of at least 12 months and with at least three issues making up the average at each date in each currency. The last column, called "p value" corresponds to the p value of the null hypothesis that the cross-currency correlations under consideration is zero. The increasing correlation down the figure makes the positive relationship between spread and correlation clear.

Based on the foregoing results, we make the following observations. First, bonds denominated in Japanese yen seem to behave in an entirely different way than their counterparts in the other three currencies—this being true, in fact, across almost all issuers. Indeed, as we will see later, ¥ securities show little if any

€-$ Correlation

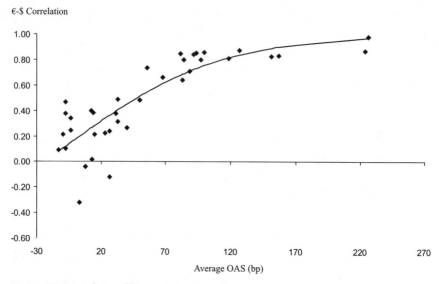

Figure 18-11. €-$ Correlation of Changes in Issuer LIBOR Spreads vs. OAS—More Robust Data

correlation with those denominated in £, $, and €, whichever way the data are bucketed. Second, for the other three currencies and their pairings, it is clear that as credit quality drops and spreads increase, correlation increases in a significant way.

To measure the key explanatory variables, both in significance and explanatory power, we simultaneously regressed the correlations on issuer spread and issuer volatility. The results of the regression are presented in Figure 18-13, which shows the R^2-values, β-coefficients, and t-statistics of the explanatory variables. For the issuer spread the t-statistic was found to be 5.5 and that of the volatility −1.1, clearly indicating that spread level was the major factor in explaining correlation. Furthermore the R^2 of 0.65 implies a high level of explanatory power of the LIBOR spread level, as this is the only statistically significant variable in the regression.

Bond-by-Bond Correlations

In addition to calculating correlations of changes in issuer spreads, we further calculated all pairwise correlations (Figure 18-14) between bonds of differing currencies and formed the average bond-by-bond correlation for that issuer in each currency pair. Thus for Ford, for example, we calculated the correlation for every pair of $- and €-denominated Ford bonds and averaged the results, which, in this case, gave an average correlation of 0.52. This figure is lower than that of the

Figure 18-12. Summary of the Most Robust €-$ Results

Issuer	Average Rating	Sector	OAS (bp)			ρ	Number of Data Points	p Value
			€	$	Average			
Landwirtschaftliche Rentenbank	Aaa	Agencies	3	23	13	0.02	21	0.93
I.B.R.D. (World Bank)	Aaa	Supranational	1	-17	-8	0.10	43	0.52
Bank Nederlandsche Gemeenten	Aaa	Finance	4	11	8	0.14	23	0.85
European Investment Bank	Aaa	Supranational	-6	-13	-10	0.21	43	0.17
General Electric Capital Corp	Aaa	Finance	5	25	15	0.21	33	0.23
ABN Amro Bank NV (Chicago)	Aa3	Finance	34	46	40	0.26	38	0.11
Rabobank Group	Aaa	Finance	-3	30	14	0.38	23	0.07
Baden Wurttemberg L-Finance NV	Aaa	Local government	5	20	12	0.40	23	0.06
Kreditanstalt für Wiederaufbau	Aaa	Agencies	-7	-8	-8	0.47	30	0.01
AIG Sunamerica Global Finance	Aa1	Finance	18	48	33	0.49	23	0.02
Daimler Chrysler North America	A2	Industrial	65	103	84	0.80	40	0.00
France Telecom SA	A3	Industrial	115	198	157	0.83	23	0.00
General Motors Accept Corp	A2	Finance	76	87	82	0.84	39	0.00
Household Finance Corp	A2	Finance	92	91	92	0.84	43	0.00
Ford Capital BV	A2	Industrial	91	109	100	0.86	43	0.00
Mexico (United Mexican States)	Baa3	Sovereign	232	215	224	0.87	29	0.00

Figure 18-13. €-$ Multifactor Regression Results

	Coefficient	t-Statistic	R^2	Number of Points
Average issuer spread level (bp)	0.005	5.52	0.65	37
Average volatility of issuer spread changes (bp/month)	−0.003	−1.07		
Intercept	0.023	0.33		

corresponding average *within* each currency (i.e., the average of all €-€ and $-$ correlations) since it does not benefit from the diversification of issue-specific performances.

The bond-by-bond correlations of individual issues in different currencies are in line with the spread and volatility statistics presented earlier (Figures 18-2 and 18-3). Dollar correlations on a bond-by-bond average basis are highest followed by sterling, indicating that the higher spread levels of these currencies has a direct implication for correlation. The matter of the relative proportion of the issue-specific and the issuer-specific volatility is central to understanding the calculation and interpretation of the correlation results. The larger the issue-specific component in comparison with the issuer-specific one, the lower the correlation tends to be.

We might expect that the issue-specific component would become less dominant as spread levels increased, since for bonds with high spread the larger spread movements would swamp the overall issue effects, whereas for lower spreads the issuer volatility is probably low and the issue-specific changes in bond spreads is more significant. Thus, in the case of El Paso, a Baa-rated issuer with average

Figure 18-14. Bond-by-Bond Correlations

Intra- vs. Intercurrency Comparison	€-£	€-¥	€-$	£-¥	£-$	¥-$
Number of issuers tested	38	37	113	10	34	57
Average intracurrency correlation	0.37	0.40	0.53	0.33	0.51	0.54
Average intercurrency correlation	0.24	0.07	0.29	0.03	0.14	0.14
Mean of (intra – inter) currency correlations	0.13	0.33	0.24	0.30	0.37	0.40

Figure 18-15. Ratios of Issue-Specific Volatility to
Issuer-Specific Volatility

	€	$
Maximum	2.11	3.93
Median	0.59	0.54
Mean	0.66	0.62
Correlation with LIBOR spread	−0.39	−0.39
t-Statistic	−3.90	−4.36

spread of 356 and 193 bp in € and $, respectively, we find that the issue-specific volatilities in € and $ are 0.16 and 0.25, respectively, times the issuer-specific volatility, whereas for BNG with an Aaa rating and average spreads of 4 and 11 bp, the corresponding ratios are 1.65 and 1.24, respectively. Figure 18-15 confirms that there is such a relationship and that spread level is a highly significant factor in explaining the ratio of issue-specific volatility to issuer-specific volatility.

However, while this is a major factor for low-spread names, where there are few issues outstanding at any given time, it should be expected that, as the number of bonds of a given issuer in a given currency increases, this issue-specific noise is diversified away, leaving only the issuer spread correlations, as explained earlier.[2] Nonetheless, the lower the issuer spread, the more issues that are necessary to accomplish this noise reduction, given the higher proportion of overall bond-level spread movement being due to issue-specific effects for lower-spread names. So for EIB, for example, where on average each month-end issuer spread is the mean of changes in LIBOR spreads from eight bonds, we would expect the issue-specific noise to have been significantly diversified leaving, to a great extent, the issuer spread. Since the EIB correlations are low (see Figure 18-12), it is clear that there are other reasons why correlations for low-spread issuers are low, aside from issue-specific factors—high issue-specific volatilities do not fully explain low correlation in low-spread securities.

The results for the average bond-by-bond correlations are presented in Figure 18-16. The correlation between average bond-by-bond correlation and spread level is a very high 0.85, underscoring the highly significant role idiosyncratic risk plays in the relative behavior of securities. It should be noted that this is only a linear correlation and that a nonlinear model is required to explain correlation accurately.

Across all currency pairs we witnessed higher averages of bond-by-bond correlations within currencies as compared with across currencies. This points to a

---

2. This assumes that issue-specific factors are uncorrelated across bonds.

Average Correlation

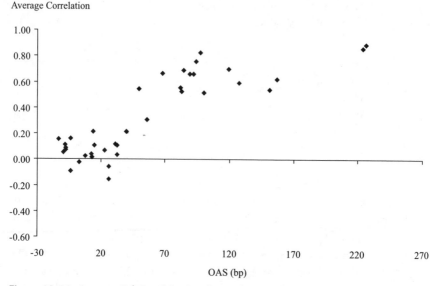

Figure 18-16. Average €-$ Bond-by-Bond Correlation by Issuer

degree of market segmentation in the investor base, which is also observed in the relative behavior of issuer and sector spreads. If investors tend to focus on one currency of denomination then we would expect issues from the same issuer to move more closely. Cross-currency movements, on the other hand, reflect differing views of a different set of investors—for example, $ and € investors—with differing risk aversions and varying familiarity with the issuing entities.

SECTOR RESULTS

We analyzed sector spread in two stages. First we looked at broad sectors such as industrials as a whole, utilities, sovereigns, and so forth; then we divided them into smaller categories such as supermarkets, banking, brokerage, automotives, and so on. The finer division did present problems of thinness of data, but we were able to obtain some useful results, for example, for the issuer-level analysis, particularly in the €-$ currency pair. In Figure 18-17 we present the results of the full study at the broader level.

Once again the first observation is that ¥-denominated issues showed no significant correlation in any bracket. However, in the other three currency pairs we see highly significant correlations in the finance and, in particular, the industrial sectors, with utilities showing very high correlation between € and $, but not between £ and $ nor € and £.

Figure 18-17. Sector Correlation Results

	Quality	Number of Issues in Universe				Average OAS (bp)	Correlation Estimate					
		€	£	¥	$		€-£	€-¥	€-$	£-¥	£-$	¥-$
Supranational	Aaa	33	27	8	76	-10	0.03	0.21	0.29	-0.07	0.12	0.13
Agencies	Aa1	138	15	219	169	-2	0.15	0.20	0.13	-0.21	0.10	-0.01
Local government	Aa2	121	6	95	42	7	NM	0.42	0.34	NM	NM	0.06
Finance	Aa3	293	37	249	436	36	0.28	0.11	0.61	0.08	0.53	-0.02
Sovereign	A2	35	3	32	102	43	NM	0.04	0.58	NM	NM	-0.11
Utilities	A1	54	9	98	101	71	0.27	0.04	0.87	0.05	0.20	0.06
Industrial	A3	239	26	90	534	77	0.59	-0.27	0.84	-0.24	0.73	-0.15

It also seems generally true to say that the correlation once again, as in the case of the issuer level, increases as we increase OAS or, equivalently, decreases quality rating. In order to examine sector cross-currency correlations more fully, we further dissect them into quality subbuckets. Figure 18-18 provides a summary of the basic statistics of this dissection. We have used the label "NM" wherever the statistic is not meaningful, having too few data points to form a time series at least 12 long or too few bonds in any bucket to make up a well-diversified bucket average.

Even though we would expect the €-$ correlations to be a function of the average spread levels in the sector concerned, nonetheless, looking at the correlations purely on a spread-level basis does not explain the variance between sectors of similar spread. For example, within the €-$ currency pair, finance A has an average OAS across the two currencies of 71 bp, similar to that of utilities A at 83 bp. However, despite the similarity of their spread levels, the correlations are quite different at 0.78 and 0.52, respectively.

Similarly, finance Aaa and agencies Aa have almost the same average OAS of 14 and 13 bp, respectively, but their correlations are 0.30 and 0.15. Agencies Aaa and supranational Aaa have average spreads of –5 and –7 bp, but correlations of 0.09 and 0.29, respectively; industrials Baa with an average OAS of 162 bp has an almost identical spread as sovereign Baa (153 bp), and yet the respective correlation estimates are 0.81 and 0.66. In general, looking through the figure, it seems that there is an ordering on the sectors with respect to correlation as follows (increasing in correlation): agencies—sovereign/local government/supranational—utilities—finance—industrial.

At the level of strict statistical significance we are less able to draw the preceding fine distinctions. Regressing the €-$ correlation on OAS and sectors, we found that only industrials gives a significant t-statistic (at the 90% level). However, upon dividing the issuers into two sectors—noncorporate credit and corporate credit—and performing a simultaneous regression of €-$ correlation on OAS and an indicator variable for these sectors, we found the noncorporate credit and corporate credit sector division to be significant at the 99% level with a t-statistic of 2.853. Clearly sector plays a part, and a finer gradation of sectors in terms of their influence on correlation is a topic for further study.

This still leaves us, however, with a question mark over the inconsistently high correlation in utilities Baa—and indeed in utilities as a whole—for the €-$ currency pair. In order to explain this we must consider the influence of rating migration on correlation. It is beyond the scope of this chapter to report on this analysis in full, but in this case it sheds valuable light on a result that, left as it is, undermines a pattern whereby utilities as a sector seems to exhibit lower correlation than industrials and finance for similar spreads.

Figure 18-18. Sector × Quality Correlation Results

	Number of Issues in Universe				Average OAS (bp)				Correlation Estimate					
	€	£	¥	$	€	£	¥	$	€-£	€-¥	€-$	£-¥	£-$	¥-$
Sovereign Aaa	7	1	9	26	0	-32	-6	-9	NM	NM	NM	NM	NM	0.24
Sovereign Aa	6	2	14	29	-12	-18	-8	-9	NM	0.54	0.22	NM	0.22	0.23
Sovereign A	14	0	7	8	28	NA	35	60	NM	0.08	0.40	NM	NM	-0.11
Sovereign Baa	20	0	9	49	122	NA	186	183	NM	0.18	0.66	NM	NM	0.05
Supranational Aaa	33	27	8	76	-3	-19	-8	-11	0.03	0.21	0.29	-0.07	0.12	0.13
Local government Aaa	59	6	42	19	1	2	-1	15	NM	0.19	0.33	NM	0.02	0.01
Local government Aa	59	0	89	15	2	NA	11	11	NM	0.20	0.28	NM	NM	-0.02
Local government A	4	0	81	8	29	NA	10	22	NM	-0.18	-0.13	NM	NM	0.24
Agencies Aaa	120	14	35	148	-2	-15	-7	-8	0.10	0.20	0.09	-0.23	0.08	-0.13
Agencies Aa	26	1	192	16	4	4	6	21	NM	0.35	0.15	NM	0.29	-0.07
Utilities Aa	21	2	98	6	29	47	8	36	NM	-0.09	0.03	NM	NM	0.01
Utilities A	33	5	0	35	63	57	NA	103	0.36	NM	0.52	NM	0.11	NM
Utilities Baa	13	3	0	66	128	111	NA	187	0.40	NM	0.95	NM	0.43	NM
Finance Aaa	61	13	6	64	6	-2	6	22	0.22	0.18	0.30	0.04	0.20	-0.18
Finance Aa	157	18	43	161	22	11	17	48	0.02	0.31	0.39	0.12	0.45	0.06
Finance A	101	7	202	221	60	89	25	81	NM	0.09	0.78	NM	0.45	-0.01
Finance Baa	6	1	28	35	138	128	73	157	NM	0.07	0.70	NM	NM	0.13
Industrial Aa	44	5	46	70	27	2	16	29	0.23	-0.14	0.42	0.12	0.16	0.14
Industrial A	136	19	31	235	70	74	28	80	0.41	-0.05	0.78	-0.01	0.45	-0.14
Industrial Baa	116	12	22	298	162	155	62	161	0.62	-0.35	0.81	-0.27	0.76	-0.28

In October 2002, 2 months after the end of the time window of this study, El Paso was downgraded to junk after a series of huge spread widenings in the months leading up to this study. These spread movements dwarfed the other more modest ones of the entire utilities sector in the €-$ currency pair. Since we would expect that events such as downgrade would carry with them very high correlations across all bonds of the issuer that is experiencing the rating migration (irrespective of the currency of denomination), the correlation of utilities $ and utilities € was "artificially" boosted to figures approaching 90%.

When the market-anticipatory spread movements leading up to this downgrade were expunged from the data set, the correlation of €-$ utilities dropped to a figure of 0.48, confirming the pattern indicated in the utilities A bracket and indeed in the €-£ and £-$ utilities figures, which, although somewhat affected by El Paso, remained at similar levels after the correction (0.24 and 0.18, respectively).[3]

HAS CORRELATION CHANGED OVER TIME?

We also divided the data along the time axis, considering data within not only the full time window of 44 months, but also for the most recent 20 months. This allowed us to examine whether correlations moved in a particular direction over time.

The pattern of the results, summarized in Figure 18-19, are unequivocal: correlations increased through time in all of the three currency pairs formed by £, $, and €. Assuming, under a null hypothesis of no change in correlation over time, that the conditional distributions are roughly symmetrical about the 44-month statistic, we find that the sector results are significant at the 90% level for the €-$ currency pair.

There are a number of reasons to account for the foregoing results: (1) The last 20 months included in the study showed particularly high volatility accompanied by a high incidence of downgrade and default, which would increase volatility and spreads. (2) Data for this latter period were probably more robust, and so some of the previous data problems that were masking the true correlation were eliminated. (3) Markets may have matured since the launch of the euro and monetary union. Moreover, the uptake of global credit indices may have served to encourage investors to view credit markets as one global market.

Figure 18-20 describes the relative correlations on a broad-quality level. Here, all monthly changes in LIBOR spreads of a given quality bracket were averaged to produce a quality spread, simulating the behavior of quality brackets as a whole.

---

3. We adopted the anticipatory periods described in Chapter 14 in selecting records pertaining to up-and-coming credit events.

Figure 18-19. Sector Correlations—Two Time Windows

	Number of Issues in Universe			Average OAS (20 months/44 months, bp)			Correlation Estimate (20 months/44 months)		
	€	£	$	€	£	$	€-£	€-$	£-$
Supranational	21	17	67	-1/-3	-8/-19	-10/-11	0.27/0.03	0.29/0.29	0.12/0.11
Agencies	93	11	147	7/2	-4/-13	5/-1	0.33/0.15	0.45/0.13	0.09/0.10
Local government	98	3	39	3/2	5/2	16/15	NM/NM	0.42/0.33	NM/NM
Finance	222	23	383	40/31	38/18	82/69	0.42/0.28	0.75/0.61	0.55/0.53
Sovereign	25	1	75	81/62	-9/-22	90/89	NM/NM	0.77/0.58	NM/NM
Utilities	51	8	101	74/61	84/68	163/146	0.32/0.27	0.97/0.87	0.31/0.20
Industrial	227	23	484	107/90	112/79	136/112	0.60/0.59	0.90/0.84	0.75/0.72

Figure 18-20. Quality Correlations—Two Time Windows

	Number of Issues in Universe				Correlation Estimate (20 months/40 months)					
	€	£	¥	$	€-£	€-¥	€-$	£-¥	£-$	¥-$
Aaa	197	37	99	304	0.22/0.14	0.38/0.36	0.39/0.28	-0.21/-0.19	0.10/0.11	-0.02/-0.05
Aa	226	18	474	252	0.26/0.12	0.02/0.02	0.61/0.45	0.21/0.21	0.44/0.41	-0.01/-0.00
A	240	27	489	441	0.59/0.49	-0.04/0.01	0.89/0.82	0.02/0.02	0.59/0.53	-0.15/-0.12
Baa	142	13	55	392	0.55/0.53	-0.35/-0.29	0.92/0.85	-0.42/-0.38	0.58/0.59	-0.28/-0.26

The results indicate that there has been no significant change in correlations within quality brackets over time (the confidence intervals around lower correlations, such as 0.45, being very wide, so that the apparent increase in the Aa sector from 0.45 to 0.61 is hard to interpret) and may serve as well to indicate the stability of the spread-correlation relationship, namely that comparable spreads are associated with similar levels of correlation irrespective of the time window employed. This merits further investigation. Furthermore, the high levels of correlation in the A and Baa brackets in particular indicate the existence of a genuine quality-based factor lying behind spread movements and its global nature.

IMPLICATIONS FOR INVESTMENT MANAGERS

The issues raised in this study have a number of immediate implications in the realm of investment strategy. In dealing with risk management, we have seen that cross-currency correlation can be explained by spread level and sector classification, with high spread levels implying higher correlation. This therefore necessitates an accounting of issuer-specific risk on a global basis, which is important to fund managers who apportion the management of global credit mandates to regional teams in the United States, Europe, and Asia, for example. If each local team chooses the same high-spread names for their part of the overall portfolio, they are increasing their overall risk exposure in comparison with a strategy of coordination, whereby different high-spread names are held in differing currencies. For low-spread instruments with stable and high-credit quality, typically agency or supranational paper, issue-specific risk is more important, and here multicurrency holdings add to its diversification. This also means that in higher-spread assets, the benefits of cross-currency diversification may not be as large as those in low-spread sectors. In the lower-spread sectors, however, it is more important to diversify the holdings among the various denominations to match the benchmark, since the U.S. dollar-denominated bonds are less of a proxy for those of the euro, for example.

In addition to the foregoing, our analysis indicates that when it really matters most, that is, when risk is high, correlations are high as well. Therefore, if a portfolio manager matches the issuer-level exposure of a benchmark he is probably not exposed to a great deal of idiosyncratic risk, even if allocation is quite different at the issue and currency levels. When correlations are low, he may be exposed to risk, but it will be of relatively small magnitude.

Concerning benchmark decisions, we note that global credit benchmarks make more sense as we cover the lower end of the credit spectrum, where the need for diversification is more acute. Our study indicates that diversification in terms of currency of denomination leads to a lowering of issuer-specific risk in low-spread names but far less so in high-spread issuers, where the cross-currency correlations are typically high. Here diversification has to be achieved through a broadening of the set of names from which the portfolio is selected rather than through cross-currency allocation techniques.

With regard to the issues of index replication, our study indicates that a strategy of representing Japanese institutional debt issued in yen by the corresponding debt in euro, U.S. dollar, or sterling has significant risks associated with it. On the other hand, a replication strategy for the yen curve in nondomestic issuers (thereby avoiding withholding tax) based on purchasing the yen-denominated debt of supranationals and agencies may have merit. The lack of correlation in high-grade debt as a whole in addition to that of the agency and supranational sectors and the low volatility of such issuers with respect to the yen swap curve would imply relatively low tracking errors with respect to the yen curve.

In regard to opportunities for outperformance, the high bond-by-bond correlation—and consequent high average hedging efficiency—for some high-spread names, provides opportunities for spread trades. For example, the debt of such an issuer has a significantly higher spread in one currency than in another, and the investor takes the view that such a relationship will persist. Then, a market-value-neutral position will benefit from the positive carry in an environment of stable spread differentials, while the high cross-currency correlation in spread changes will serve to mitigate the risk of the position. A risk-minimizing spread trade could also be constructed taking account of the relative volatilities of spread changes in the two currencies in addition to the cross-currency correlation.

CONCLUSION

We carried out an empirical study of the correlation between LIBOR spreads of credit issuers in the four major currencies, analyzing the data in several dimensions. We see a highly significant link between spread level and correlation in three of those four currencies—€, £, and $—with correlation rising steadily with spread, often to very significant levels. Moreover, we have seen evidence of sector-related effects with industrials, utilities, and finance sectors showing higher correlation than an equivalent spread level in agencies, supranationals, and other noncorporate credit.

Intuitively, spread levels can be seen as a proxy for the risk in the underlying name—the higher the spread, the higher the implied risk. This risk can be systematic (marketwide) or idiosyncratic. The greater the systematic risk, the greater the leverage (β) to the market as a whole. If spreads are high because the market sensitivity of an issuer's spread is high, then one also expects the cross-currency correlations of changes in the spread for the issuer to be high (as they are influenced significantly by overall market movements). At times of credit events we would expect the default-related component of risk to dominate, leading to very high correlations in those circumstances as well, such as have been witnessed in the cases of El Paso, WorldCom, Marconi, and the like.

Throughout the study, however, yen-denominated securities have shown no evidence of correlation at either the issuer or sector level. Here the reasons are less clear. While it is true that the yen data are much thinner and shorter, with no yen issues featuring in the study universe until September 2000, nonetheless, relatively speaking, the correlations in the most recent 20 months have been very low with only one issuer with 12 months of data showing a yen-dollar correlation in excess of 0.50. By way of explanation we note that the yen credit market exhibits certain differences from its dollar, euro, and sterling counterparts. Withholding tax, a more regional investor base, and less active secondary market trading may all make the yen credit market appear segmented from the rest of the world.

The results of the study have far-reaching ramifications for investment strategy, in particular, those involving issues of diversification and portfolio management. It implies that issuer-specific risk is diversified away by cross-currency holdings only insofar as the spread of the issuer is low, whereas correlations of debt in different denominations rise to significant levels of up to 80–90% as the credit quality of the security decreases. This is clearest in the €-$ currency pair, but our results indicate that this relationship between spread levels and correlation holds for the other two pairs, namely €-£ and £-$, as well. Furthermore, we have found support for the view that in addition to spread levels, the level of cross-currency correlation is also influenced by the sector to which an issuer belongs. For the same level of spread, issuers in the corporate credit part of our indices demonstrate higher correlations than those in the noncorporate part.

We regard the results reported in this chapter as only the beginning of an analysis of the question of cross-currency correlation. Looking ahead, we see numerous avenues for further exploration and research. The question of whether there is a significant difference at the sector level between global and local issuers—those issuing in both currencies in question and those only in one—is a key area for study, as is the comparison of downgraded issues with stable ones. Furthermore, the question of the stability of the relationship demonstrated between spread and correlation through differing market conditions is one of great interest and importance.

MANAGING MORTGAGE PORTFOLIOS

U.S. dollar mortgage-backed securities account for a large portion of total dollar public debt outstanding and of the overall global debt market, and although U.S. portfolio managers are well acquainted with MBS, many non-U.S. managers are not. As investors worldwide are moving toward global benchmarks that include a significant weighting to MBS (13% of the market value of the Lehman Brothers Global Aggregate Index as of September 2005), many non-U.S. managers face a choice: either become proficient in the MBS asset class or risk losing investment mandates to competitors.

MBS are an attractive asset class because of their high credit quality (usually Aaa) and liquid secondary market. They also have desirable risk properties in a portfolio context because their particular risks, prepayment and volatility, have low correlation with risks embedded within the government and credit components of a portfolio. MBS are often a safe haven for investors when there are marketwide concerns about credit quality, and they tend to perform well when interest rates are stable and less well when rates are rising or falling. As a result, a significant holding of MBS in a portfolio has a variance-reducing effect that improves a portfolio's overall risk-adjusted return potential. These characteristics have led many non-U.S. investors, including some official institutions, to add MBS to their portfolios even if they have not adopted a global aggregate benchmark.

Unfortunately, actively managing an MBS portfolio is a highly technical task given the uncertainty of monthly mortgage cash flows and the need for a prepayment model to guide relative value decisions. Furthermore, investors must purchase individual mortgage pools to gain cash exposure to the MBS market. The pool selection process requires additional hands-on MBS market experience and a thorough understanding of esoteric MBS terminology that many non-U. S. asset managers have not had the opportunity to develop. This complexity of MBS deters many new investors from participating in this asset class.

However, while it may be difficult for new investors to substantially out-perform an MBS benchmark, it is remarkably easy to replicate it using either MBS pools or TBAs (i.e., forward contracts to purchase MBS pools). For many investors, replicating the MBS benchmark is fully satisfactory—they can generate alpha elsewhere in their portfolio while enjoying the diversification benefits of including MBS. An investor can construct an MBS replicating portfolio by using the Lehman global multifactor risk model and optimizer to assemble a small set of highly liquid MBS securities (pools and/or TBAs) that have very low estimated tracking error volatility to the MBS benchmark.[1] Based on our experience over many years, TBA replication successfully produces a TBA portfolio having a realized tracking error of less than 4 bp/month.

In fact, not only can TBA replication successfully track an MBS benchmark, the strategy also offers a potential for modest outperformance via the occasional "specialness" of the TBA roll. Furthermore, TBA replication requires little back-office processing, which is particularly attractive for new MBS investors. The accuracy and efficiency of TBA replication enables non-U.S. portfolio managers to compete successfully for global mandates while giving them time to build in-house MBS expertise to become more active MBS managers in the future.

In contrast, for investors who aspire to actively manage an MBS index, there are many perils along the road in the search for outperformance. The first job for any portfolio manager is to thoroughly understand the MBS benchmark, and it is here that an MBS manager confronts his first challenge. MBS index rules for cal-culating prices and returns differ (for good reason) from those used by many MBS portfolio managers to monitor the price and performance of their portfolios. In particular, the index calculates prices assuming same-day settlement, whereas many portfolio managers use PSA prices that assume settlement at PSA dates. This difference in settlement assumptions can produce an index price that moves by a different amount or even in a different direction than the PSA price. More-over, the difference in settlement assumptions can also produce significant differ-ences in the pattern of daily returns within a month, as well as across months. Chapter 19 gives a brief overview of the MBS Index pricing methodology and returns calculations. Understanding the details of the MBS Index is essential for an MBS manager to be able to explain his intramonth and monthly performance relative to the benchmark. Failure to do so can produce inadvertent underperfor-mance that can erase what might have been top quartile performance.

---

1. Chapter 6 describes in detail how we use the Lehman global risk model to construct replicating MBS portfolios (using pools or TBAs). The risk model handles not only MBS pass-throughs (which make up the current MBS index), but also many other types of mortgage secu-rities: CMOs, IOs, POs, hybrid ARMs, CMBS, and mortgage-related ABS.

Another challenge confronting an active MBS manager arises from the fact that the MBS Index is composed of annual "generics," which are nontraded securities, whereas investors must purchase specific pools. How is the portfolio manager to choose among pools? While many thousands of pools "map" to the same index generic security and receive the same index price, there can be very wide variation in pool attributes (e.g., coupon, age, and loan size) and theoretical (i.e., model-derived) prices among these pools. We have analyzed this range of pool attributes and theoretical valuation and have shown that they both can be substantial. The extent to which this theoretical valuation is accurate and is not reflected in market prices reveals the potential for outperforming an MBS benchmark through individual pool selection.

Yet another challenge confronting every active MBS manager is determining the Treasury duration of an MBS position. Suppose a manager decides to over-weight MBS against Treasuries in anticipation of MBS spread tightening but does not wish to take a duration view. Which Treasuries should the manager sell? The success of this MBS basis trade depends on whether the assumed MBS duration measure accurately captures MBS interest-rate sensitivity. If the duration measure is too low, then the portfolio's actual duration will be greater than intended, and vice versa. Either way, if durations are poorly measured, movements in Treasury rates affect the success of the overweight strategy.

Chapter 20 discusses many possible MBS-duration measures and presents a methodology for evaluating their relative accuracy. We examine the relative performance of analytical (i.e., model-based) and empirical (i.e., historical) MBS duration measures *on a daily basis* since 2001. Generally, model durations have performed relatively well, and while they generally outperform empiricals, their performance deteriorates rapidly as the dollar price of the MBS exceeds 104. Empirical durations also begin to deteriorate as the price rises above 104, but at a slower rate, and they begin to strongly outperform model durations.

Many MBS investors are "long-horizon" investors, who anticipate holding MBS assets for long periods rather than actively buying and selling. These investors typically use book accounting, not mark-to-market accounting, and buy MBS for its anticipated income over the long holding period, rather than for any anticipated capital gains. Such investors face two questions: The first is how reliable is the MBS security at producing income and whether its yield at purchase is a good indicator of its potential income. Unanticipated prepayments can cause income to fall short of expectations. Credit assets, although immune from prepayment risk, also may not deliver anticipated income owing to defaults or downgrades that trigger forced sales and, consequently, realized losses. Thus, the second question is what role do MBS serve within a book portfolio containing credit assets? How well do MBS help to reduce shortfall risk of book income and do they offer any book income diversification benefits beyond helping to control shortfall risk?

In Chapter 21 we use book accounting (discussed in Chapter 9) to analyze the book income performance of both MBS and credit assets over various horizons. Although both income streams are volatile and may not deliver the income promised at purchase, credit tends to have much greater risk of severe book income underperformance (i.e., shortfall risk) compared to MBS. We find that the two asset classes have very different monthly book income distributions. We discuss how various combinations of the two assets can help manage book income shortfall risk and the variability of book income outside the tail of the portfolio's book income distribution.

High credit quality (and low "headline risk"), liquidity, and diversification potential are characteristics that ensure that MBS will remain an important asset class for global investors. The next several chapters address many MBS issues that confront portfolio managers and should help investors realize more of the potential that MBS have to offer.

19. Managing against the Lehman Brothers MBS Index: Prices and Returns

The first job for any portfolio manager is to acquire a thorough understanding of his performance benchmark. Failure to do so can result in unintended active positions with the potential for unexpected relative performance. This chapter explains and builds intuition for Lehman's MBS Index pricing methodology and describes Lehman's MBS Index returns calculations. In particular, it highlights the differing price and return dynamics that arise from the difference between the index and market settlement conventions.

Lehman Brothers maps individual MBS pools to index "annual aggregates," or "generics," according to the pool's program, coupon, and WALA. The MBS Index contains only those annual aggregates (about 400 as of the end of February 2005) with amounts outstanding that exceed a specific threshold ($250 million as of February 2005). The Lehman MBS Index has rules for calculating index prices and returns that are rather elaborate, and some investors may find them confusing. The confusion usually arises from the index's use of same-day settlement, as opposed to the market's convention of PSA settlement.

To simplify the following discussion we assume that the MBS Index contains a single premium MBS pass-through security (i.e., pool). Although the following analysis remains applicable for discounts and par-priced securities as well, some of the results may have opposite signs.

THE IMPORTANCE OF THE MBS INDEX'S SAME-DAY SETTLEMENT ASSUMPTION

Lehman MBS Index rules for calculating prices and returns differ from those used by many MBS portfolio managers to monitor the price and performance of their

Based on research first published by Lehman Brothers in 2003.

MBS portfolios. In particular, the index calculates index prices assuming same-day settlement, whereas many portfolio managers rely on PSA prices that assume settlement at their respective PSA settlement dates. This difference in settlement assumptions can produce significant differences in prices. In fact, the index price can move by different amounts or even in the opposite direction from the underlying PSA price. Moreover, the difference in settlement assumptions can also produce significant differences in the pattern of daily returns within a month, as well as in returns across months.

The same-day settlement assumption makes the Lehman MBS Index particularly useful for investors who wish to monitor their performance. PSA prices are prices for a dollar of current face for settlement at the indicated PSA date. However, the PSA settlement date can be up to a month away from the index pricing (or trade) date T. If the index were to use PSA prices, then two thorny issues would arise. First, other securities in the Lehman Global Family of Indices are priced assuming $T + 1$ settlement. If PSA settlement were used for MBS, then a broader index (e.g., the U.S. Aggregate) might contain securities with potentially very different settlement dates. Furthermore, the settlement date can jump significantly from one day to the next, which, in turn, can cause large price and valuation jumps. For example, moving from the day before to the day of the switch in the PSA settlement month (t_{sw}) causes the time until settlement for MBS to lengthen by about a month, whereas the non-MBS securities in the index would have no change in their time to settlement. The relative performance of MBS and non-MBS securities would fluctuate simply by passing over t_{sw}.

The second difficulty in using PSA settlement for the index is that settlement may not only be significantly delayed within a given month but can even occur in the following month. The owner of the MBS (i.e., the holder of record) at the end of the month is entitled to the principal paydown and full coupon to be received in the following month, whereas an investor who acquires the security on the PSA settlement date in the following month is not. At the same time, the investor who buys the security now for settlement next month has an extra month to earn some yield on the purchase price of the bond. Therefore, valuing an MBS using the PSA price for next month's settlement is inaccurate because that price does not reflect the cash flows to be received by the investor who acquires or owns the security today (and the investor's loss of interest on the purchase price). Moreover, the PSA price typically drops when the PSA settlement month changes because the net value of the following month's paydown and coupon usually exceeds the interest to be earned by holding on to the price of the security for another month. Therefore, using PSA prices to value the position tends to produce a drop in market value of the position when t_{sw} is reached.

These problems are the reasons the Lehman Index assumption of same-day settlement is so valuable. Daily index returns attempt to measure accurately the change in value of an index holding. If you bought the index position on day T and sold it on day $T + 1$, what was your market gain or loss? Suppose day T were the day before t_{sw} and PSA settlement was used. Owing to the PSA drop, there would tend to be a negative daily return. But this negative return would be due to the lengthening of the time until settlement and the fact that settlement is now taking place in the following month, not owing to any spread or term-structure movements.

Consider this problem from another angle. Imagine you bought a unit of a mutual fund that invested in a single MBS security and calculated its daily net asset value (NAV) using PSA settlement prices. You bought your unit at the NAV on day T, the day before t_{sw}. You then decide to sell the unit the following day. The NAV would tend to be lower, owing solely to the switch in the settlement month. Since the settlement month switch at t_{sw} is fully known to the market, no rational investor would invest in the fund on day T!

The index assumption of same-day settlement avoids all of these issues. The MBS Index price and market value calculation reflect the value of the position assuming you buy or sell the position on that day for cash. This feature is what makes the Lehman MBS Index so useful and logically consistent for calculating daily and month-to-date returns. Despite the usefulness of the same-day settlement assumption, however, there are some drawbacks.

First, same-day settlement is more complicated than PSA settlement and can cause confusion for investors accustomed to using PSA settlement prices for performance calculations. For example, index pricing beyond t_{sw} cannot simply use the present value of the PSA price, which assumes settlement in the following month. The index price must also be adjusted for the cash flows that the buyer today, as opposed to the buyer for settlement next month, would be entitled to receive. The adjustments needed to calculate a same-day settlement price properly can be intimidating. Much of the discussion that follows is a detailed analysis of the adjustments needed to arrive at a same-day settlement price.

A second drawback of same-day settlement is related to the first: Sometimes the cash flow adjustments must be estimated. For example, at t_{sw} the index must estimate how much of a dollar in current face today will not survive to the following month and should be priced at the present value of par and not at the present value of the PSA price for next month's settlement. Unfortunately, the paydown factor is not published by the agencies until early in the following month. As a result, the index must estimate next month's paydown factor and, hence, also next month's survival rate (the percentage of this month's current face that will survive into next month). Which of the many possible estimators for the paydown should be used? To make index pricing as model-independent as possible, the index uses last month's survival rate and then this month's actual survival rate when it becomes known (at t_f, the factor publication date) as the estimator for next month's survival rate.

While model-independent, this method of survival rate factor estimation introduces two possible distortions. The first is related to the change in index price calculation that occurs on t_{sw}, the PSA settlement switch date. Both before and after this date, the index price is designed to answer the question, "What would you pay for a dollar of current face for settlement today?" and it is impossible to answer that question without some estimate of next month's survival rate. Before t_{sw} the index implicitly uses the *market's estimate* of next month's survival rate (embedded in this month's PSA price) to calculate the index price. However, from t_{sw} on, the market PSA price for settlement next month does not implicitly incorporate the survival rate to be published next month. Consequently, the index must provide its own estimate of next month's survival rate, and it uses *last month's rate* as the estimator (since the final value of this month's rate is not yet known). In a rapidly changing interest-rate environment, the market's estimate of next month's actual survival rate (at t_{sw}) may differ significantly from last month's rate, and in that case the switch from the market's estimate to last month's survival rate causes a discrete jump in the index price that has nothing to do with market movements. The second discrete jump occurs later in the month (at t_f) when the final value of *this month's* survival rate is announced and replaces last month's rate as the index's estimator of next month's survival rate.

The use of estimated factors is unavoidable when using same-day settlement for MBS pricing, and it can lead to differences between returns calculated using PSA settlement prices and returns calculated using same-day settlement prices. However, as we discuss later, the price and return bias owing to the use of estimated factors is relatively small.

INDEX PRICES VS. PSA PRICES

Before discussing returns, it is useful to show the calculation of the index price and to highlight another difference between index same-day settlement and PSA settlement prices. Suppose today is the last day of month A, and let us assume that the PSA price is 103. (PSA settlement is for the following month, B.) What would you pay for a dollar of current face for settlement today? You know the 103 price does not reflect the paydown and full coupon you would be entitled to receive next month if you bought the security for settlement today. How would you arrive at today's same-day settlement price? You would have to provide an estimate,

$\check{S}$, of the portion of the dollar of current face that would survive into month B. The mark at the top of the symbol $\check{S}$ indicates that it is an estimate of the actual survival rate S. The value of $\check{S}$ is less than 1. In a typical market environment, $\check{S}$ might be, say, 0.96, for an MBS whose PSA price is 103. This surviving current face amount would then be priced at the present value of the PSA "dirty price" ($P^{\text{psa}} + \text{AI}^{\text{psa}}$), which equals the PSA "clean price," P^{psa}, plus accrued interest at the PSA settlement date, AI^{psa}. For a 6.5% coupon security, we might have $P^{\text{psa}} + \text{AI}^{\text{psa}} = 103.25$. The remaining nonsurviving amount, $1 - \check{S}$, would be priced at the present value of par. (The present value of this number is used because the paydown is not received until after the delay in month B.) You will also be entitled to a full month of coupon on the dollar of current face. However, since you are buying for settlement at the last day of the month, the accrued interest is roughly equal to the present value of a month of coupon, and therefore the same-day settlement *clean* price would be approximately what is shown in Equation (19-1).[1]

As of the last day of the current month:[2]

$$P^{\text{index}} \approx \check{S} \times \text{PV}[P^{\text{psa}} + \text{AI}^{\text{psa}}] + (1 - \check{S}) \times \text{PV}[100]$$
$$\approx (0.96) \times \text{PV}[103.25] + (0.04) \times \text{PV}[100] \approx 103.12. \tag{19-1}$$

Unless $\check{S}$ is unusually small or discount rates are unusually high, on the last day of the month the index price is greater than the PSA clean price. What is very important to note about the index price equation is that the index price already recognizes that only the fraction $\check{S}$ of the initial dollar in current face (or par amount) survives into the following month. Consequently, the sensitivity of the index price to changes in the PSA market price is already scaled down by the factor $\check{S}$. The market value of your position, V^{index}, is found by adding back the (approximately) full month of accrued interest (Cpn), so that on the last day of the month:

$$V^{\text{index}} = P^{\text{index}} + \text{Cpn}$$
$$\approx \check{S} \times \text{PV}[P^{\text{psa}} + \text{AI}^{\text{psa}}] + (1 - \check{S}) \times \text{PV}[100] + \text{Cpn}. \tag{19-2}$$

Now, imagine it is the first day of month B. To keep this discussion very simple, we assume that [$P^{\text{psa}} + \text{AI}^{\text{psa}}$] is unchanged since the last day of month A. How much current face do you have to sell? Answer: $\check{S}$ (still an estimate). At what price could you sell it for settlement today? Answer: $\text{PV}[P^{\text{psa}} + \text{AI}^{\text{psa}}]$. We are

---

1. The complete formulation can be found in *Managing against the Lehman MBS Index: Prices and Returns*, Lehman Brothers, November 2003.

2. We use the notation PV[.] to represent the present value of a future cashflow.

assuming that ($P^{\text{psa}} + \text{AI}^{\text{psa}}$) is unchanged, but what about P^{index}? We can easily see that the index price "jumps up." Noting that the accrued interest on the first day of the month is now zero, we have for the first day of month B:

$$P^{\text{index}} \approx \text{PV}[P^{\text{psa}} + \text{AI}^{\text{psa}}] \approx 103.25. \tag{19-3}$$

But what is the market value of your position acquired at the end month A? Ignoring the 1-day present value effect, we see from the value equation [Equation (19-4) shown later] that the market value of the index position has not changed. (Do not forget to include the paydown and coupon that you are entitled to receive later in the month!) This result is consistent with the assumption that [$P^{\text{psa}} + \text{AI}^{\text{psa}}$] is unchanged over month-end. Since the market value is unchanged, the jump up in the index price produces a price return gain that offsets the paydown loss, which is the difference between the month-end index price and par, multiplied by $1 - \check{S}$. Consequently, the index reports a negative paydown return on the first day of the month, which is offset by the positive index price return. Overall, assuming no change in the PSA price, and ignoring the 1-day present value effect, we find that the total return over month-end is zero.

On the first day of month B, the market value of the index position is determined as follows: The surviving fraction $\check{S}$ of the initial par amount is valued at the index price, P^{index}. The nonsurviving fraction, $1 - \check{S}$, of the initial par amount is valued at the present value of par. Finally, since the position was holder of record on the last day of the previous month, it is entitled to receive the full monthly coupon Cpn. So, the market value of the index position on the first day of month B is given by

$$\begin{aligned} V^{\text{index}} &\approx \check{S} \times P^{\text{index}} + (1 - \check{S}) \times \text{PV}[100] + \text{Cpn} \\ &\approx \check{S} \times \text{PV}[P^{\text{psa}} + \text{AI}^{\text{psa}}] + (1 - \check{S}) \times \text{PV}[100] + \text{Cpn}. \end{aligned} \tag{19-4}$$

Note that Equation (19-4) is identical to Equation (19-2)—ignoring the 1-day present value effect. It is important to note, however, that the par amount (i.e., current face) held in Equation (19-4) is less than the par amount held in Equation (19-2). Comparing (19-2) and (19-4) shows that total return over month-end is zero. Many index users see the reported negative index paydown return on the first day of the month. However, the total return is zero, owing to a positive index price change (assuming the PSA price is unchanged).

For investors accustomed to PSA settlement prices, seeing the same-day settlement index price jump up on the first day of the month when the PSA price is unchanged is, at first, unsettling. However, the index price now applies to units of current face that are unencumbered by this month's paydown. On the first day of the new month, the index knows that all of the surviving current face will survive to the PSA settlement date later in the month and is correctly priced at the present value of the PSA full price. This is what causes the jump in the index price.

However, the total market value of the index position is unchanged, since it was acquired at the end of the previous month and the change in value owing to price is offset by this month's paydown. Since it is market value that drives returns calculations, the daily return over month-end is zero (ignoring the one-day present value effect).

It is worth noting that while Equation (19-1), the equation for the index price at the end of the month, requires an estimate of next month's (i.e., B's) survival rate, Equation (19-3), the equation for the index price at the beginning of the month, does not explicitly use such an estimate. However, since Equation (19-3) uses the PSA price for settlement in month B the market's estimate of month C's survival rate is reflected in this PSA price because the investor who acquires the security this month will be subject to month C's paydown. Thus, the index price at the beginning of the month implicitly uses the market's estimate of the following month's S. As we pointed out earlier, the switch on this month's PSA settlement switch date from the market's estimate of next month's S to a different estimate (i.e., last month's S) can cause jumps in the index price.

An interesting implication of the value equation [Equation (19-4)] is that value does not increase with daily accrued interest. The index value is the present value of the future settlement price (i.e., the full PSA price) plus the estimated paydown and known full coupon. The *full* index price includes the value of the future coupon payments. While the index reports only a *clean* price, which subtracts off the month-to-date accrued, the index also reports a separate month-to-date accrued. The daily decrease in the clean price and daily increase in accrued cancel each other out. The only daily accrual experienced by the market value of the index position is the present value accrual that is based on 1-month LIBOR. This absence of a daily coupon accrual is discussed in the next section.

Now that we understand the difference between index and PSA prices and how the market value of an index position is calculated, it is time to turn to a discussion of returns.

INDEX RETURNS VS. PSA RETURNS

Clearly, a manager's primary concern is returns. How does a manager typically calculate total returns in the course of month B for a dollar of current face held at the end of month A? He uses the nearest PSA price to value the security. Specifically, the returns generally trace the following pattern: Until the preliminary value of the month B paydown factor is published early in month B, the manager continues to accrue coupon based on the amount of current face held at the end of month A (i.e., a dollar). As the PSA price for settlement in month B fluctuates, the manager calculates a gain or loss of market value, and thus price return, by multiplying the change in the PSA price by the dollar of current face. On t_{pub}, the day the preliminary value of the factor is published (say, the fifth business day of the month), the manager recognizes a paydown loss by marking down his current face holding by the paydown amount and simultaneously crediting his cash receivables.[3] He also writes down his month-to-date accrued interest to reflect that the position is actually accruing coupon only on S dollars of current face (where $S < 1$), not on a full dollar. When the manager recognizes the paydown, the market value of his position drops discretely (ignoring any change in the PSA price on the day). Thereafter, the manager's position accrues coupon based on the reduced current face amount and calculates a gain or loss of market value, and thus price return, by multiplying the change in the PSA price by S.

On the day that the PSA settlement month changes, t_{sw}, the manager prices his S units of current face at the new (and typically lower) PSA price. This causes the market value of his position to move discretely (assuming that the market is relatively unchanged on that day). From t_{sw} until the end of the month, the manager's position accrues coupon based on the reduced current face amount and he calculates the gain or loss of market value and, thus, price return by multiplying the change in the PSA price by S.

The manager calculates returns for a period, as does the index, simply by dividing the sum of the market value at the end of the period (plus any cash received) by the market value at the beginning of the period. At the end of the month, the manager's total monthly change in market value is the sum of three components: (1) accrued coupon on S dollars of current face; (2) the gain or loss of market value found by multiplying the change in the PSA price over the course of the month by S; and (3) the paydown loss recorded when the manager reduced his current face holding from a dollar to S units. If there is little change in the PSA price (excluding the drop on t_{sw}), then the manager's pattern of month-to-date returns (TR^{psa}) will resemble the saw-tooth-shaped dashed line in Figure 19-1. The saw-tooth shape reflects the fact that the different components of returns are recognized at different times during the month.

Month-to-date index returns (TR^{index}), using same-day settlement prices, exhibit a very different and typically smoother pattern. In Figure 19-2 we show the corresponding stylized month-to-date return dynamics for TR^{index} as we did for

---

3. Unlike the index, the manager does not wait until the final values of the paydown factors are released to use them in computing returns.

Returns

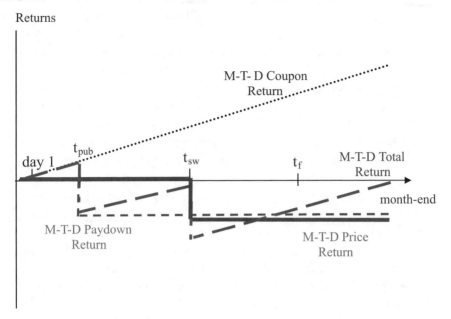

Figure 19-1. Stylized Month-to-Date PSA Return Dynamics

TR^{psa} in Figure 19-1. However, we first walk through a month and explore the dynamics of month-to-date index returns.

On the first day of the month, the index reduces its current face holding from a dollar to the estimated surviving portion $\check{S}$ [recall Equation (19-4)]. The index records a negative paydown return. However, as we discussed, there is a positive index price return so that the total return is zero. As the PSA (and, hence, the index) price fluctuates, the index records a gain or loss of market value (and, hence, returns) by multiplying the change in the index price (caused by the change in the PSA price) by $\check{S}$.

Does the surviving current face portion of the index position accrue coupon? The answer is no. The full price of a traditional (non-MBS) bond, which is priced for next-day settlement, increases daily by the bond's yield. The market convention is to subtract accrued interest, which grows daily by the coupon rate, to calculate a bond's clean price. When the yield is steady and roughly equal to the coupon rate, the bond's clean price is relatively stable. As accrued interest grows daily, the bond's full price, and hence its market value, increases.

The situation is somewhat different for MBS. The full index price is based on the full PSA price, which is the clean price plus accrued interest from the first of the month to the PSA settlement date. Since the PSA settlement date does not change from one day to the next, the full PSA price and the market value of the position does not accrue any additional daily coupon and will not do so until after the PSA settlement date. Consequently, assuming no changes in the market clean PSA price, the full PSA price is unchanged.

As discussed, the *full* index price is based on the present value of the full PSA price for forward settlement, which includes the month-to-date accrued interest as of the PSA settlement date. Consequently, assuming no changes in the market clean PSA price, the full index price is unchanged except for the present value effect, which causes the full index price to increase at the 1-month LIBOR rate. To make MBS returns similar to returns for other bonds in the Lehman Family of Indices, the index convention is to subtract month-to-date accrued interest, $AI(t)$, from the full index price. The index then reports a month-to-date accrued value. However, since the clean index price *declines* as the month-to-date accrued interest increases, when the clean price change is combined with the month-to-date accrued value, the net effect on the index position value is zero. *Ceteris paribus*, the index month-to-date position value accretes only with the present value function (i.e., 1-month LIBOR).

As discussed earlier, because of same-day settlement, there should be no *anticipated* discrete changes in market value. If there were an anticipated drop, who would buy the security the day before? For example, the publication of the preliminary paydown factor on the fifth business day of month B should not be expected to produce a discrete drop in the market value of the index position (if we neglect the present value effect and assume no change in PSA price). Why? The index fully anticipated the paydown in the *prior* month (month A). On t_{sw}, the PSA settlement switch date in month A, the index price began to incorporate three anticipated effects: (1) the estimated paydown for month B; (2) the receipt of a full month of coupon in month B; and (3) the drop in the PSA price. That is also the reason why there was no drop in the market value of the index position on t_{sw} despite the change in the PSA price on that date owing to the switch in the PSA settlement month.[4] The drop in the PSA price is offset in the value calculation by the estimated paydown and anticipated coupon.

CHANGES IN INDEX PRICES AND RETURNS ON THE PSA SWITCH DATE

On the day that the PSA settlement month changes, t_{sw}, the index prices its $\check{S}$ units of current face using the new (and typically lower) PSA price. However, in

---

4. As discussed earlier, this is not precisely correct. The index must use an estimated (i.e., last month's) paydown factor, which may differ from the market's expected factor used to price the drop.

contrast to PSA settlement pricing, the index same-day settlement assumption recognizes that only a fraction of the $\check{S}$ dollars of current face survive to the *following* month and is priced at the present value of next month's PSA price.[5] The non-surviving portion of the $\check{S}$ units of current face is priced at the present value of par. Moreover, a full month of coupon accrual for the $\check{S}$ units of current face must be added to the index price calculation. Unlike PSA returns, there is no discrete move in the month-to-date index returns due solely to the change in the PSA settlement month.

It is important to pause here. The index began the month with a dollar par amount of current face. However, the beginning-of-the-month index price fully reflected that only a fraction $\check{S}$ of the current face was expected to survive to the first day of the month. As a result, the market value change in the index position during the first week or two of the current month was driven by the change in the present value of the PSA price scaled down by $\check{S}$. After t_{sw}, however, the index must calculate a price for same-day settlement based on the PSA price for settlement the next month.

At this point, the index recognizes that not all $\check{S}$ dollars of current face are expected to survive into the next month. In fact, just as $(1 - \check{S})$ of the original $1 of current face is being paid down this month, leaving $\check{S}$ dollars of current face, the percentage of this $\check{S}$ dollars of current face that, in turn, will be paid down next month will again be $(1 - \check{S})$ (assuming an unchanged paydown rate). This leaves $\check{S} - (\check{S} \times (1 - \check{S})) = \check{S}^2$ dollars of the initial par amount that should be priced at next month's PSA price. In effect, after t_{sw}, the month-to-date market value change in the index position is driven by the change in the PSA price scaled down by $\check{S}^2$. This is a significant departure from PSA settlement returns and is a major reason why index same-day returns may differ from PSA settlement returns. In an environment of increasing PSA prices and relatively low values of $\check{S}$, index returns are likely to lag PSA-based returns.

After t_{sw} in the current month A:

$$P^{\text{index}} \approx \check{S} \times \text{PV}[P^{\text{psa}} + \text{AI}^{\text{psa}}] + (1 - \check{S}) \times \text{PV}[100] + \text{PV}[\text{Cpn}] - \text{AI}(t). \quad (19\text{-}5)$$

$$\begin{aligned} V^{\text{index}} &\approx \check{S} \times \{P^{\text{index}}\} + (1 - \check{S}) \times \text{PV}[100] + \text{PV}[\text{Cpn}] + \check{S} \times \text{AI}(t) \\ &\approx \check{S} \times \{\check{S} \times \text{PV}[P^{\text{psa}} + \text{AI}^{\text{psa}}] + (1 - \check{S}) \times \text{PV}[100_{\text{B}}] + \text{PV}[\text{Cpn}_{\text{B}}]\} \quad (19\text{-}6) \\ &+ (1 - \check{S}) \times \text{PV}[100_{\text{A}}] + \text{PV}[\text{Cpn}_{\text{A}}]. \end{aligned}$$

5. The index must estimate S (i.e., this month's survival rate) in addition to estimating the portion of S that survives into next month (next month's survival rate). The index uses the most recently published finalized survival rate as the estimator for all subsequent survival rates. On the switch date, the index price uses last month's survival rate, which is known, as the estimate of the survival rates for the current month and for next month.

As we mentioned earlier, of the $\check{S}$ units of current face that survived into this month, a portion $(1 - \check{S})$ will not survive into the next month. The index prices this $\check{S} \times (1 - \check{S})$ of nonsurviving current face at the present value of par. Of course, the $(1 - \check{S})$ units of current face that did not survive into *this* month are also priced at par. Thus, the index prices a total of $(1 - \check{S}) + \check{S} \times (1 - \check{S}) = 1 - \check{S}^2$ units of current face at par and prices only $\check{S}^2$ units of current face at the present value of the PSA price. PSA settlement returns, in contrast, price only $1 - \check{S}$ of current face at par—ignoring the paydown that will occur next month.[6]

CHANGES IN INDEX PRICES AND RETURNS ON
THE POOL FACTOR DATE

On the sixteenth business day of the month, t_f, the index collects final paydown factor data for all agency programs in the MBS Index. On that day, the index replaces the estimated values of this month's survival rates (namely last month's survival rates) with these actual values, which, in turn, are now used as estimates of next month's survival rates. In order to illustrate the two ways in which this replacement affects index returns, let us suppose that this month's actual survival rate is lower than the estimate. First of all, the current index price (and month-to-date price return)[7] will drop to reflect the fact that less current face than previously expected (at t_{sw}) survives to next month. Second, less current face survived into the current month than was previously expected. The paydown return must increase because we now know that the paydown return calculated at the beginning of the month underestimated this month's paydown rate. To correct for the reduced current face amount, the negative month-to-date paydown return is increased by the difference between the estimated and actual survival rate multiplied by the paydown loss amount. Together, these two effects reduce the index month-to-date returns on t_f. If this month's actual survival rate turns out to be higher than last month's, the opposite effects occur, and index returns are increased on t_f.

After t_f the market value of the index position accrues at the 1-month LIBOR rate. In addition, the market value records a gain or loss by multiplying the change in the index price (which is driven by the change in the PSA price scaled down by S) by the amount of current face, S. Hence, returns are driven by the change in the PSA price scaled down by $S \times S$. If we assume that there is little

---

6. Index returns may differ from PSA returns. Depending on the market environment, the return differences can accumulate and persist for many months, if not indefinitely.

7. Again, this discussion assumes an MBS generic security whose PSA price is greater than par.

Returns

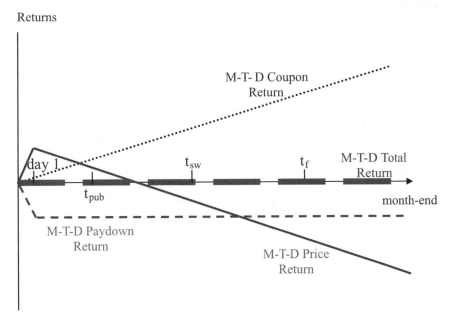

Figure 19-2. Stylized Month-to-Date Index Return Dynamics

change in the PSA price (excluding the drop on t_{sw}) and that survival rates do not differ much from one month to the next and are accurately estimated by the market, then the index's pattern of month-to-date returns look similar to the heavy dashed line in Figure 19-2. Given our assumptions, the index month-to-date total returns are very smooth, as the index accounts for the estimated paydown, a full month of coupon, and the PSA price drop simultaneously on the PSA switch date.

COMPARISON OF PSA RETURNS AND INDEX RETURNS

How does TR^{psa} compare with TR^{index}? There are two key differences. First, the two month-to-date return series exhibit different patterns over the course of the month. Figure 19-3 illustrates the month-to-date total return difference ($TR^{difference} = TR^{psa} - TR^{index}$) between PSA total returns and index total returns. Since we have made assumptions that set the month-to-date index total returns to zero, Figure 19-3 is identical to the manager return in Figure 19-1. For managers who calculate their month-to-date performance using PSA prices, Figure 19-3 shows conceptually how their performance differs from the index benchmark over the course of the month.

Second, not only does the manager's month-to-date total return performance differ from that of the index during the month, but TR^{psa} may not equal TR^{index}

Returns

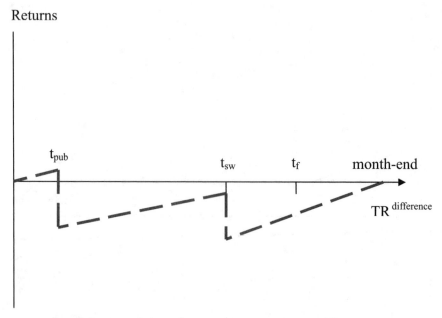

Figure 19-3. Stylized Month-to-Date Total Return Difference (TR^{difference}) Dynamics
PSA Total Return (TR^{psa}) less Index Total Return (TR^{index})

for the month as a whole. The sensitivity of monthly TR^{index} is driven by the change in the PSA price scaled by $S \times S$, whereas the sensitivity of monthly TR^{psa} is driven by the change in the PSA scaled only by S. In an environment of *rapid* paydowns (i.e., low S values) and *rising* PSA prices, TR^{psa} is likely to be greater than TR^{index}, whereas in other circumstances, TR^{psa} may be less than TR^{index}. The return differences can be significant and persist.

Figure 19-4 shows the monthly differences between returns on the MBS Index using PSA prices and returns using index prices for August 1998–May 2003. Monthly return differences can be meaningful. Depending on the market environment, the return differences can accumulate and persist for many months, if not indefinitely.

Figure 19-5 shows the 12-month cumulative total return (based on the data in Figure 19-4). As shown, the 12-month cumulative return difference can be substantial, and as of May 2003, it was almost 30 bp.

We have attempted to clarify the differences between the way the Lehman MBS Index and investment managers calculate prices and returns. The key points are as follows:

1. The same-day settlement assumption is valuable if the goal is to measure the daily change in the market value of a position. If same-day settlement were not

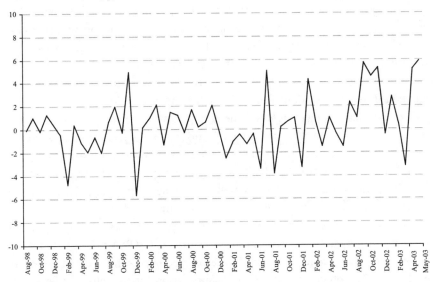

Figure 19-4. Monthly TR^{difference} for the MBS Index
August 1998–May 2003

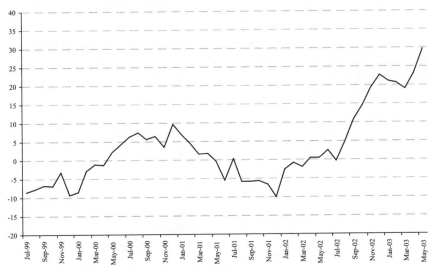

Figure 19-5. Twelve-Month Cumulative TR^{difference} for the MBS Index
July 1999–May 2003

assumed, then there would be large, fully anticipated jumps in market value on certain days every month. Such anticipated jumps are evidence that nonmarket clearing prices are being used and are inappropriate for calculating market values. This is one of the main reasons why the Lehman Brothers MBS Index uses the same-day settlement assumption to calculate index prices.

2. Same-day settlement prices can differ, move by different amounts, and move in different directions from PSA settlement prices. Moreover, month-to-date total returns using same-day settlement prices are generally much smoother than month-to-date total returns using PSA prices. At any given point in a month, there can be a large discrepancy between the two month-to-date returns.

3. The difference between PSA and same-day pricing follows a predictable monthly pattern and mostly cancels itself out over a monthly cycle. Therefore, the effect on monthly returns is not as severe as the effect on daily returns. However, the monthly effect is not negligible, and monthly returns using same-day settlement prices may not agree with monthly returns using PSA prices. One reason for this return difference is the need for estimated paydown factors in same-day settlement. The other, and more significant, reason for the return difference is that the index has a different sensitivity to changes in the market PSA price because of its recognition of next month's paydown. The index reduces the actual amount of current face outstanding in its returns portfolio on the first day of the month. Moreover, at t_{sw}, the index price recognizes a further reduction in current face owing to the change in the PSA settlement month. The net effect is that the sensitivity of monthly index returns is driven by the change in the PSA price scaled down by $S \times S$. In contrast, the sensitivity of monthly PSA returns is driven by the change in the PSA scaled down by S.

Understanding the details of the MBS Index is essential for an MBS manager to be able to explain his intramonth and monthly performance relative to the benchmark. Knowing how the index calculates prices and returns is an important step in both tracking and outperforming the benchmark.

20. Evaluating Measures of MBS Duration

Between May 2001 and February 2005, the 2-year U.S. Treasury yield declined from 4.24 to 3.60% and the 10-year yield declined from 5.29 to 4.38%. As MBS investors recall, these relatively modest declines masked more substantial changes during the intervening years. For example, between May 2001 and June 2003, the 2-year Treasury yield fell from 4.24 to 1.32%, while the 10-year yield fell from 5.29 to 3.35%. These low yields produced large increases in mortgage prepayment forecasts and large declines in MBS option-adjusted (Treasury) durations. From May 2001 to June 2003, the Lehman MBS Index OAD decreased from 3.33 to 0.58—a record low. Over this period, despite the sharp decline in Treasury rates and acceleration in forecasted (and actual) prepayments, MBS performed well. For the 14-month period, the MBS Index had a total return of 16.23% and outperformed key-rate duration (KRD) matched Treasuries by 132 bp. It was a good time to have an MBS overweight vs. Treasuries.

The success of an MBS-UST basis trade, however, depends on the assumed Treasury duration of the MBS position. Suppose a manager decides to add a 5% MBS market value overweight (against Treasuries) in anticipation of tightening in MBS spreads. Assuming the manager does not wish to take a duration position vs. the benchmark, he sells Treasuries (or some other non-MBS asset), based on the assumed MBS duration, to make room for the MBS overweight on a duration-neutral basis. The performance of the MBS basis trade depends on whether the assumed MBS duration measure accurately captures MBS interest-rate sensitivity. If the duration measure is too low, then the portfolio's actual duration will be greater than intended. Conversely, if the duration measure is too high, then the portfolio's actual duration will be less than intended. Either way, movements in Treasury rates affect the success of the overweight strategy, which is why portfolio

Based on research first published by Lehman Brothers in 2005.

managers are concerned that MBS durations accurately measure Treasury-rate sensitivity.

How well MBS durations measure Treasury-rate sensitivity is also important for managers who hold only MBS securities in their portfolios and are supposed to be duration-neutral to the MBS Index. These managers may meaningfully deviate from the MBS Index by combining different MBS positions in such a way that their portfolios have the same duration as the MBS benchmark. For example, the manager might overweight the discount and premium coupons and underweight the current coupons, while maintaining duration neutrality with respect to the benchmark. Since the Treasury manager may have overall portfolio-duration responsibility, the MBS manager wants to be sure there are no unintended duration bets in the MBS portfolio.

There are many possible MBS-duration measures. Our goal is to evaluate how well several common duration measures have performed in recent years in explaining movements in MBS prices. Investors know that MBS price returns are driven by exposure to many risk factors. In fact, the Lehman Brothers global risk model has twenty-seven risk factors for MBS consisting of six key-rate Treasury yield changes, the average yield change squared, six key-rate swap spread changes, two volatility factors, and twelve spread-risk factors depending on the MBS program, price tier, and WALA.[1] However, here we are interested in predicting MBS price returns solely on the basis of changes in Treasury yields. In effect, we are only considering a single-factor model of MBS price returns (or a six-factor model when we use KRDs). In addition, our focus is on *daily* price returns, not monthly returns, which are the basis of the risk model. Given that Treasury yields are more volatile than MBS spreads, we are assuming that over such a short time period, changes in Treasury yields are the primary driver of MBS price returns.[2] Our goal is to determine which duration measure, together with changes in the associated Treasury yield(s), best explains MBS price returns.

Our general formulation is as follows: For a given MBS, we select a duration measure and a daily UST yield change. Given the actual daily yield change, we calculate the predicted MBS percentage price return, $Ret_{predicted}$, by multiplying duration by the yield change. (In the case of KRDs, we multiply each KRD by the change in the corresponding key rate and then add up the results for all key rates.) We then compare the predicted change with the actual percentage price change, Ret_{actual}. The difference, or "error," is our measure of the accuracy of the duration

---

1. See Chapter 26 for a description of the global risk model and its uses.
2. For example, the volatility of the 10-year key-rate Treasury risk factor is 27.3 bp/month, whereas the volatility of new production, current coupon MBS spreads is approximately 6.8 bp/month.

measure. For each duration measure, we calculate an average daily root-mean-squared error (RMSE) over the past 4 years and over shorter subperiods.[3] We standardize the RMSEs by dividing each asset's RMSE over the given period by its corresponding price change volatility. We evaluate eight different duration–yield change pairs and measure their performance according to their standardized RMSEs (StdRMSE). A duration measure with a lower StdRMSE value is more accurate than one with a higher StdRMSE value.

MBS DURATION MEASURES

There are two general categories of MBS durations: "model" and "empirical." Model durations are typically calculated by shifting the UST par curve in a specific way, regenerating expected cash flows using a prepayment model in response to the rate shift, and then repricing the MBS security assuming unchanged spreads and volatilities. In contrast, empirical durations eschew prepayment models and estimate duration by regressing actual MBS percentage price changes on actual changes in UST yields. Empirical durations do not assume unchanged spreads and volatilities and, hence, reflect any correlation between UST yield movements and spread movements (or movements in any other MBS risk factor).

Both types of duration measures have their uses. Model durations are useful because they are forward looking, incorporating the latest research in prepayment modeling, and are relatively insensitive to transitory technical influences in the market that may not persist, but are nevertheless "picked-up" by empirical duration. Furthermore, model durations can be used when interest rates move outside recent interest-rate bands or when there are few relevant historical data available to estimate empirical durations (such as when a new index generic coupon enters the index). Empirical durations are useful because they incorporate any historical correlation between UST yield movements and changes in other risk factors (e.g., mortgage spreads). The idea behind the use of empirical durations is that although such correlations tend to change over time, any correlation among risk factors over the most recent short estimation period persists for at least some short time going forward. Therefore, empirical durations that exploit such correlations are likely to be more accurate than model durations that typically assume no correlation.

---

3. We do not calculate R^2, the usual measure of the success of a regression because regression analysis is not appropriate here. Regressing $\%\Delta P_{\text{actual}}$ against $\%\Delta P_{\text{predicted}}$ would mean writing $\text{Ret}_{\text{actual}} = a + b \times \text{Ret}_{\text{predicted}} + \text{Error}$ and then choosing the values of a and b that minimize the error term. We wish to write simply $\text{Ret}_{\text{actual}} = \text{Ret}_{\text{predicted}} + \text{Error}$ and measure the magnitude of the resulting error term.

In calculating $Ret_{predicted}$ we not only have to select a duration measure, but we also have to specify which UST yield change to apply. Thus each $Ret_{predicted}$ series is determined by a duration–yield change pair. It is not always obvious which yield change to use with a particular duration measure. For example, OAD measures sensitivity to a parallel shift in the fitted par UST curve. Since the UST curve does not typically move in a parallel fashion, when we calculate $Ret_{predicted}$ we must decide whether to multiply the OAD by the parallel shift component of the curve movement (however that may be defined) or by the movement in a particular point on the yield curve. KRD, on the other hand, measures the sensitivity to movements at a particular point on the par curve and, so, is paired with the yield change at that part of the curve.

Model Durations

Lehman produces two sets of MBS model durations: OAD and KRDs. To calculate OAD, the entire fitted par UST curve (often referred to as the "fitted spline curve") is shifted up and down 15 bp. For each shift, many paths of short-term interest rates are generated, each with a prepayment vector from the Lehman prepayment model. Assuming a constant OAS, a new price is calculated along each path. The average price is the assumed price change as a result of the shift in the UST curve. After a shift up and a shift down, the difference between the two calculated prices divided by the initial price level multiplied by 30 bp is the OAD measure.[4]

How can we evaluate the adequacy of OAD as a duration measure? If the par rate curve moved in a parallel fashion, and the actual percentage change in the price of the MBS equaled the OAD multiplied by the actual (parallel) change in the par curve, then OAD would be an accurate measure of the bond's sensitivity to changes in UST rates. However, the actual percentage change in the MBS price may not equal $OAD \times \Delta UST$ yield for a number of reasons. First, other MBS risk factors may change simultaneously with the change in the Treasury rate. Second, the par Treasury curve may move in a nonparallel fashion, and the actual change in price is likely to be different from the price change that would be caused by a true parallel shift. In the results section further on in this chapter, we examine the performance of OAD using two measures of yield change: changes in the

---

4. The shifted rate paths are generated using an interest rate model calibrated to current volatility data from the derivatives markets. The same rate path generation process, using the unshifted fitted par curve, is used to calculate the OAS.

10-year on-the-run UST yield and changes in the "average" UST yield calculated as the average of yield changes along the yield curve.[5] This average yield change is our measure of the "parallel" shift in the yield curve.

KRDs address the problem of nonparallel movements in yields. KRDs allow the manager to measure MBS price sensitivity to six particular par Treasury rates.[6] Each KRD is computed by shifting the corresponding rate up and down 15 bp and shifting the part of the spline curve between the adjoining key-rate points in a "hat"-shaped pattern. For each shift, multiple paths of short rates are generated, each with a prepayment vector from the prepayment model. Again, assuming a constant OAS, a new price is calculated which is the average price across all paths. After a shift up and a shift down, the difference in the two calculated prices divided by the initial price level multiplied by 30 bp is the KRD measure.

Each of the six KRDs is multiplied by the change in the corresponding key rate. The sum of the six products produces a $Ret_{predicted}$ value that is not dependent on the assumption of a parallel shift in the par rate curve. For this reason, many investors use KRDs to measure MBS interest-rate sensitivity. We might expect KRDs to do a better job of explaining MBS returns, especially when the yield curve moves in a significantly nonparallel fashion.

Empirical Durations

Both OAD and KRD are "model-dependent" duration measures since they rely on Lehman's term-structure and prepayment models. However, it is possible to generate interest-rate sensitivity measures that are model independent. One approach is to calculate "empirical" durations by measuring the historical price sensitivity of a particular MBS to changes in a particular UST yield. For example, we can regress past MBS percentage price changes on past changes in UST yields and use the resulting regression coefficient as an empirical duration measure.

There are many possible empirical duration measures.[7] For our analysis, we calculate empirical duration by regressing daily MBS percentage price changes on daily changes for the on-the-run UST 10-year yield using either 10 or 20 business days of historical price data.[8]

5. Specifically, we take the average of the changes in the six key-rate points (0.5-year, 2-year, 5-year, 10-year, 20-year, and 30-year).

6. For each MBS Index generic there are KRDs for six key-rate points (0.5-year, 2-year, 5-year, 10-year, 20-year, and 30-year).

7. We discuss only a handful of empirical duration measures commonly used by portfolio managers. There are many others.

8. We chose the 10-year UST yield because it is highly correlated with the mortgage rate that drives prepayments.

An argument in favor of empirical durations is that the marketplace reacts to changes in MBS prepayment behavior faster than modelers can update their models. As a result, if the market senses that prepayment speeds are faster or slower than model forecasts, MBS prices react to yield changes differently from what is predicted by a model-generated OAD. In addition, if rates are at levels where prepayment models have not been tested, empirical durations may offer more reliable guidance regarding sensitivity to yield changes.

Another empirical measure uses "relative coupons." For example, suppose a portfolio manager wishes to measure the duration of a GNMA 6%. Currently trading in the market are GNMA 5.5% and GNMA 6.5%, with similar seasoning profiles. The manager can then look at the prices of those two securities to esti-mate the price change for an up-and-down 50-bp change in "interest rates" from the 6% level. The total difference in prices between the outer coupons is then used as the basis for the empirical duration for GNMA 6%s.

DEFINITIONS AND DATA REQUIREMENTS OF MBS DURATION MEASURES

Data Set

Our data set contains daily index price changes for seventeen annual aggregates (or "generics") in the Lehman MBS Index, and for the index itself, for the period from June 25, 2001 to February 28, 2005. These generics were selected, first, be-cause they represented new production at the beginning of the data period and, second, because their coupons span the range of those available in the marketplace. For each generic and the index, we calculate a daily percentage (full) index price change.[9] The seventeen generics are:

* 30-year FNMAs: 5, 5.5, 6, 6.5, 7, 7.5, and 8% coupons, all of 2001 vintage
* 15-year FNMAs: 5.5, 6, 6.5, 7, and 7.5% coupons, all of 2001 vintage
* 30-year GNMAs: 6, 6.5, 7, 7.5, and 8% coupons, all of 2001 vintage

MBS Duration Measures

We examine eight duration measures (three model-based and five empirical) and associated UST yield changes to calculate predicted MBS percentage price changes.

---

9. We remove several daily observations each month from the data set. On these dates (i.e., the first day of the month, the pricing PSA-switch date, and the index factor date) the index price can change owing to the mechanics of the index price calculation and not because of any movement in UST yields or other risk factors. For a discussion of Lehman MBS Index prices and returns see Chapter 19.

Each duration–yield change pair generates a predicted daily percentage price change for each generic listed.[10] We let P_t denote the full index price of an MBS generic at the close of day t. We use $\Delta_{10}\text{yield}_t$ to denote the daily change in the 10-year on-the-run UST yield at the close of day t and $\Delta_p\text{yield}_t$ to denote the daily parallel shift, that is, the average of daily yield changes at six points on the par curve. The eight duration–yield change pairs are as follows:

Model Duration–Yield Change Pairs

(i)   OAD and ΔUST 10-year yield ("OAD(10)"),

$$\text{Ret}_{\text{predicted},t} = \text{OAD}_{t-1} \times \Delta_{10}\text{yield}_t.$$

(ii)   OAD and ΔUST parallel yield ("OAD(p)"),

$$\text{Ret}_{\text{predicted},t} = \text{OAD}_{t-1} \times \Delta_p\text{yield}_t.^{11}$$

(iii) KRD and ΔUST KRD yield ("KRD"),

$$\text{Ret}_{\text{predicted},t} = \Sigma_i (\text{KRD}_{i,\,t-1} \times \Delta_{\text{KRD}(i)}\text{yield}_t).$$

Empirical Duration–Yield Change Pairs

(iv)   "10-day" and ΔUST 10-year yield ("Emp(10,10)").

Using ten consecutive observations of percentage changes in the MBS price and changes in the on-the-run UST 10-year yield, ending with the observation on day $t - 1$, we regress percentage MBS price change against the yield change to get

$$\text{Ret}_{\text{actual},t} = \alpha + \beta_{t-1} \times \Delta_{10}\text{yield}_t + \varepsilon_t.$$

The estimated regression coefficient β_{t-1} is the empirical duration measure. Using this measure and the daily change in the on-the-run UST 10-year yield at time t, we derive the predicted daily MBS percentage price change:

$$\text{Ret}_{\text{predicted},t} = \beta_{t-1} \times \Delta_{10}\text{yield}_t.$$

The predicted return is calculated ignoring the constant term—an assumption that has negligible impact on the results.

10. Except for the relative coupon measure, which could not be used on the highest (lowest) coupon security in each program because there was no security in the program with a higher (lower) coupon. The relative coupon measure also could not be calculated for the MBS Index.

11. The "parallel" ΔUST yield, $\Delta_p\text{yield}_p$, is defined as the arithmetic average change in the 6-month, 2-year, 5-year, 10-year, 20-year, and 30-year fitted par UST yields.

(v)   "10-day" and ΔUST parallel yield ("Emp(10,p)"),

which is the same as (iv) except that the independent variable in the regression is the change in the average UST yield, $\Delta_p$yield$_t$. The estimated regression coefficient is multiplied by $\Delta_p$yield$_t$ to get the predicted percentage price change:

$$\text{Ret}_{\text{predicted},t} = \beta_{t-1} \times \Delta_p \text{yield}_t,$$

(vi)   "20-day" and ΔUST 10-year yield ("Emp(20,10)"),

which is the same as (iv) above except that the regression uses the last 20 business days of data to generate the regression coefficient.

(vii) "20-day" and ΔUST parallel yield ("Emp(20,p)"),

which is the same as (v) except that the regression uses the last 20 business days of data to generate the regression coefficient.

(viii) "Relative Coupon" and ΔUST 10-year yield ("RelC(10)").

This measure is best explained by example. To calculate the relative coupon duration for FNA06001[12] let $P6.5_t$ = Price of FNA06401, $P6.0_t$ = Price of FNA06001, and $P5.5_t$ = Price of FNA05401, all at time t. We define

$$\text{Relative coupon duration measure} \equiv \text{RDM}_{\text{FNA06001},t-1}$$
$$\equiv [P6.5_{t-1} - P5.5_{t-1}] / [P6.0_{t-1}],$$
$$\text{Ret}_{\text{predicted},t} = \text{RDM}_{\text{FNA06001},t-1} \times \Delta_{10}\text{yield}_t.$$

Results

For the seventeen generics and the MBS Index, we calculate daily actual percentage price changes over a given period. We also calculate daily predicted percentage price changes using the eight duration measures generated as of the end of the previous day multiplied by the indicated change in Treasury yield. Then, for the given period consisting of n consecutive daily observations, we calculate the RMSE as follows:

$$\text{RMSE} \equiv \sqrt{[\Sigma_{i=0,\, n-1} (\text{Ret}_{\text{predicted},t(i)} - \text{Ret}_{\text{actual},t(i)})^2/n]}.$$

12. The abbreviations for MBS index generics follow the index convention: FNA06401 represents 30-year FNMA 6.5% of 2001. Vintage is determined by the WALA of the annual aggregate.

The RMSE measures an "average" return error, in basis points, between the actual return and the predicted return.

Finally, because different generics can have very different price return volatilities, we standardize the RMSE by dividing a generic's RMSE by the volatility (i.e., standard deviation) of its actual price return for the same period:

$$StdRMSE = RMSE/Stdev(Ret_{actual}).$$

StdRMSEs can be interpreted as the percentage of price variance that is not explained by the duration measure. We compare the eight duration measures using the StdRMSE. Figure 20-1 presents StdRMSEs for the generics and index for the period from June 25, 2001 to February 28, 2005, and shows the average dollar price for each generic for the period. This information allows us to examine a commonly held view that the effectiveness of model durations degrades as the dollar price of the MBS increases.

To put the performance of the various MBS duration measures into perspective, Figure 20-1 also supplies results for some non-MBS securities and indices. Specifically, we show StdRMSE values for four agency indices (0- to 3-year duration bullets; 0- to 3-year callables; 3- to 8-year bullets; and 3- to 8-year callables), an Aa-rated corporate bond (WFC 7.55% of 6/10), and a high-coupon Treasury (9.875% of 11/15). We selected agencies because many MBS investors often compare the relative value of MBS and agencies on a duration-neutral basis. The high-quality corporate and Treasury, selected at random, are shown because most investors would expect them to have very low StdRMSEs.

Overall, the various MBS duration measures perform reasonably well. For the MBS Index, the seven duration measures (excluding the relative coupon measure) produce a StdRMSE value between 0.34 (using KRDs) and 0.42 (Emp(10,10)). In particular, even though the average dollar price for the MBS Index was 102.6 for the period, these error measures compare favorably with those for the agency bullet and callable indices and for the single corporate and Treasury bonds. For the 0- to 3-year duration bullet agency index, the OAD(10) duration measure produced a StdRMSE of 0.62, which was significantly greater than that for the MBS Index (0.35). The short callable agency index performed similarly (0.60). The OAD(10) error values for the WFC and Treasury were 0.44 and 0.27, respectively. All of the duration error measures for the corporate bond ranged between 0.44 (KRDs) and 0.49 (Emp(10,10) and Emp(10,p)), which is uniformly higher than for the MBS Index. Not surprisingly, the duration measures for the Treasury note performed best, ranging from 0.23 (KRDs) to 0.36 (Emp(10,p)).

As anticipated, KRDs usually performed better than the two OADs. However, somewhat unexpectedly, the improvement of KRDs over each of the two OADs

Figure 20-1. Predicted vs. Actual Percentage Price Change StdRMSE
June 25, 2001–February 28, 2005

	$ Price	OAD(10)	OAD(p)	KRD	Emp(10,10)	Emp(10,p)	Emp(20,10)	Emp(20,p)	RelC(10)
MBS Index	102.60	0.35	0.38	0.34	0.42	0.41	0.39	0.37	
FNA05001									
FNA05401	99.89	0.37	0.39	0.35	0.42	0.41	0.38	0.37	0.36
FNA06001	101.87	0.38	0.38	0.35	0.44	0.43	0.42	0.40	0.99
FNA06401	103.33	0.41	0.40	0.39	0.46	0.45	0.44	0.43	0.55
FNA07001	104.71	0.48	0.46	0.47	0.53	0.51	0.51	0.49	0.89
FNA07401	105.83	0.79	0.66	0.69	0.66	0.64	0.61	0.60	1.61
FNA08001	106.98	1.66	1.37	1.48	0.82	0.80	0.79	0.77	
FNC05401	102.12	0.39	0.40	0.37	0.46	0.43	0.43	0.40	0.51
FNC06001	103.52	0.43	0.43	0.42	0.49	0.46	0.46	0.44	0.58
FNC06401	104.81	0.49	0.46	0.51	0.54	0.52	0.51	0.50	0.81
FNC07001	105.69	0.90	0.74	0.81	0.65	0.63	0.61	0.59	0.97
FNC07401	106.37	1.69	1.38	1.55	0.76	0.74	0.73	0.71	
GNA06001	102.42	0.40	0.38	0.38	0.44	0.43	0.41	0.41	0.51
GNA06401	103.92	0.45	0.40	0.42	0.47	0.46	0.45	0.44	0.53
GNA07001	105.22	0.55	0.49	0.54	0.57	0.56	0.53	0.52	0.80
GNA07401	106.31	0.76	0.69	0.79	0.71	0.71	0.67	0.67	1.32
GNA08001	107.20	0.99	0.93	1.05	0.91	0.90	0.88	0.87	
0–3 Agency bullet	103.41	0.62	0.57	0.47	0.69	0.64	0.66	0.60	
0–3 Agency callables	100.52	0.60	0.57	0.56	0.65	0.61	0.62	0.59	
3–8 Agency bullet	106.87	0.34	0.38	0.29	0.39	0.37	0.36	0.33	
3–8 Agency callables	100.13	0.59	0.57	0.57	0.65	0.63	0.60	0.59	
WFC 7.55% 6/10	115.57	0.44	0.45	0.44	0.49	0.49	0.47	0.47	
T 9.875% 11/15	148.34	0.27	0.31	0.23	0.34	0.36	0.30	0.33	

was relatively small (0.34 vs. 0.35 and 0.38) for the MBS Index. Among the individual index generics, KRDs were usually, but not always, the best model-based duration measure. KRDs also generally outperformed OADs for the non-MBS issues. For the bullet agency indices and the Treasury and corporate issues, KRDs were the best model duration measure by a considerable margin, which is somewhat unexpected given the bullet nature of their cash flows. In contrast, for agency callable indices, whose constituents have significant key-rate exposure along the curve, KRDs remained the best measure, but by a much smaller margin.

For the MBS Index, empirical duration measures performed modestly worse in comparison to model durations. Empiricals produced StdRMSEs ranging from 0.37 (Emp(20,p)) to 0.42 (Emp(10,10)), which compares to the range of 0.34 to 0.38 for the model durations. Empirical durations using 20 days of data performed slightly better than their counterpart measures using only 10 days.

At the individual generic level, for coupons 7% and lower, model durations outperformed empirical durations. As an example, for FNMA 6% of 2001 (i.e., FNA06001), the eight duration measures had a StdRMSE between 0.35 (KRD) and 0.99 (RelC(10)). Model durations (OAD and KRD) handily outperformed the four empirical durations. In addition, KRDs outperformed both OAD(10) and OAD(p) and the empirical durations that used 20 days of history slightly outperformed the 10-day measures. For GNMAs and 15-year FNMAs, model durations also generally performed better than empirical durations, but to a lesser extent than for 30-year FNMAs.

Results for GNA06001 (GNMA 6% 2001) and FNC05401 (15-year FNMA 5.5% 2001) were somewhat similar to those for FNA06001. However, whereas model durations outperformed empirical durations, the performance gap for GNA06001 and FNC05401 was smaller than for FNA06001. Furthermore, KRDs performed worse for 15-year FNMAs and GNMAs than for similarly priced FNMAs.

For all duration measures, the StdRMSEs were relatively stable across price levels until the MBS price exceeded 104—at which point StdRMSEs increased rapidly. This is not surprising as higher-priced MBS typically have greater prepayment uncertainty, less liquidity, and Treasury durations shorter than their spread durations.[13] Notably, however, the increase in StdRMSE was less extreme for empirical measures than for model measures. For the individual generics, the relative performance of empirical vs. model durations depended strongly on the generic's coupon (or price level). Overall, empiricals (except RelC(10)) held up

---

13. This increases the relative influence of spread changes compared to yield changes on price movements. To the extent that empirical durations reflect all historical influences on price changes, it is reasonable to expect that empiricals for such securities would have a tendency to outperform model durations.

better than model durations as price increased. For generics with average prices less than 104, empiricals performed somewhat worse than model durations. However, for generics with prices above 104, empiricals began to perform much better. For example, for FNA07401 (average dollar price of 105.83), empirical durations (excluding RelC(10)) performed better than model durations.

Despite its popularity with investors, the relative coupon duration (RelC(10)) performed slightly worse than the other empirical measures for the lower-priced generics and performed much worse for higher-priced generics (price > 104) across all programs. For FNA07001, RelC(10) had a StdRMSE of 0.89, whereas the next largest was Emp(10,10) with a StdRMSE value of 0.53.

For the non-MBS indices and issues, the empirical measures also performed reasonably well compared to OADs. For the corporate issue, the range of its four empirical duration measures was 0.47 (Emp(20,p)) to 0.49 (Emp(10,p)) compared with 0.45 and 0.44 for OAD(p) and OAD(10), respectively. The same relative pattern between the empirical and OAD measures also held for the agency indices and the single Treasury issue. In addition, for the entire period, the empirical measures using 20 business days of data performed better than their respective counterparts using only 10 days.

Model durations performed relatively poorly for the two callable agency indices. Surprisingly, empiricals also performed poorly. For example, the 3- to 8-year agency callable index (average dollar price of 100.13) had an StdRMSE of 0.59 for OAD(10) and a value of 0.60 for Emp(20,10). The 0- to 3-year agency callable index (average dollar price of 100.52) displayed a similar pattern.

Figure 20-2 shows the relative performance, over the data period, of some duration measures as a function of a generic's average price. The duration measures displayed are: OAD(10), KRD, Emp(20,10), and RelC(10). The figure shows that Emp(20,10) performed best across most price levels, whereas the relative coupon measure generally performed worst. The performance of all duration measures began to degrade once the dollar price exceeded 104. However, the model and relative coupon duration degraded more severely than the Emp(20,10) measure.

To highlight the relative performance of MBS duration measures as a function of the MBS price, we calculated the ratio of StdRMSEs for various duration measure pairs. For the overall period, we saw that model duration performance deteriorated more rapidly than empirical performance as the MBS price increased. This pattern is clearly shown in Figure 20-3, which displays the relative StdRMSE performance of KRD model duration vs. Emp(20,10) empirical duration as a function of the MBS price. A value less than 1.0 indicates that the KRD measure performs better than the empirical measure. As the figure shows, up until a price of 104, KRD is superior. However, once the dollar price rises above 104, the KRD's relative performance deteriorates and becomes inferior to the empirical measure.

StdRMSE

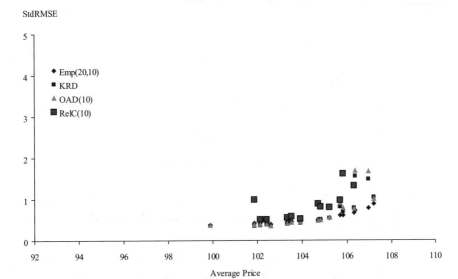

Figure 20-2. Predicted vs. Actual Percentage Price Change StdRMSE
June 25, 2001–February 28, 2005

StdRMSE Ratio

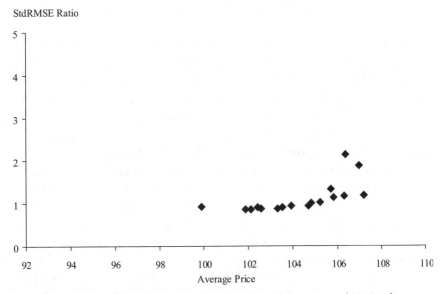

Figure 20-3. Ratio of KRD to Emp(20,10) StdRMSEs: All Generics and MBS Index
June 25, 2001–February 28, 2005

StdRMSE Ratio

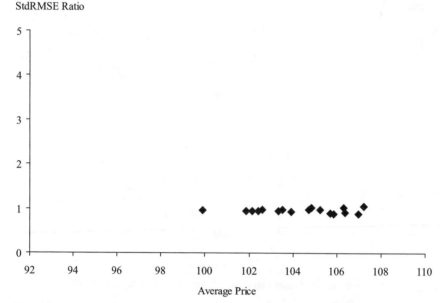

Figure 20-4. Ratio of KRD to OAD StdRMSEs: All Generics and MBS Index
June 25, 2001–February 28, 2005

In contrast, note that there is no clear indication of a price-level influence on the relative performance of KRD and OAD(10) model duration measures. This is shown in Figure 20-4.

To examine the relative performance of various durations in different interest-rate environments, we divide the data period into four subperiods (Figure 20-5). The first subperiod, June 25, 2001, to March 4, 2002, was characterized by slightly lower than average MBS prices (average dollar price equaled 102.08), relatively unchanged 10-year Treasury yield (although a heretofore new low was touched), and a 59-bp steepening of the 2–10 yield spread. The sharp reshaping of the yield curve gave KRDs an opportunity to outperform OADs during this subperiod.

The second subperiod, from March 4, 2002, to September 30, 2002, was a period of sharply and persistently declining 10-year Treasury yields (including heretofore generational lows) and little change in the 2–10 spread. Overall, the 10-year yield fell 138 bp, while the 2–10 spread increased 9 bp. Such an extreme prepayment environment was a severe test for model durations. How well did they perform compared to empiricals?

The third subperiod runs from October 7, 2002, to March 25, 2004. Although both the 10-year and the yield curve ended the period at levels with which they began it, there was a sharp market reversal (July 2003) shortly after Treasury yields

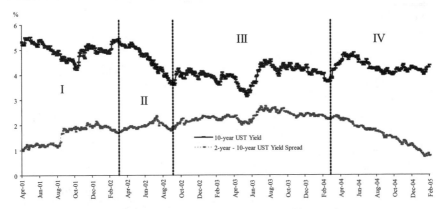

Figure 20-5. 10-Year UST Yield and 2- to 10-Year UST Yield Spread
April 30, 2001–February 28, 2005

reached new lows (the 10-year reached an all-time low of 3.07% on June 16, 2003) as fears about lower yields began to attenuate. The movement in the 10-year yield during July 2003 period was particularly large—95 bp, more than a 3-standard-deviation move. However, rates remained generally low for the entire subperiod, providing ample time for mortgage prepayment speeds to explode. The sharp market reversal may have caused empiricals to underperform model durations during the subperiod.

The final subperiod covers March 25, 2004–February 28, 2005. During this time, the 10-year yield increased 64 bp and the yield curve flattened 146 bp. Generally, this was an environment of lessened worries about prepayment risk. The considerable curve reshaping (a flattening compared to the first period's steepening) may reveal that KRDs sharply outperformed single duration measures.

Summary Statistics for the Four Subperiods

Period	Average MBS Price ($)	Change in 10-Year Yield (bp)	Range of 10-Year Yield (bp)	Change in 2–10 Spread (bp)
6/25/01–3/4/02	102.08	−13	123	+59
3/4/02–9/30/02	102.84	−138	183	+9
10/7/02–3/25/04	103.46	+12	150	+35
3/25/04–2/28/05	101.44	+64	113	−146

What was the relative performance of the various duration measures during these four very different market environments? To simplify the presentation, we focus on two model durations (KRD and OAD(10)) and two empirical durations

Emp(20,10) vs. Price

StdRMSE Ratio

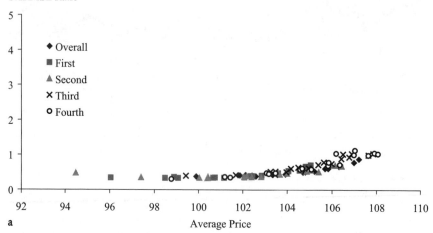

a

Average Price

OAD(10) vs. Price

StdRMSE Ratio

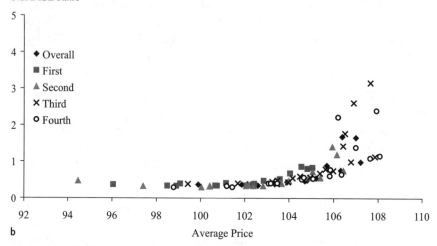

b

Average Price

Figure 20-6. Performance of Four Duration Measures across Four Subperiods and Overall Period
April 30, 2001–February 28, 2005

(Emp(20,10) and RelC(10)). Figure 20-6 shows the performance of these four duration measures for all the generics and the index, across the overall period and the four subperiods.

Across the subperiods, all four duration measures shared a tendency to deteriorate once the MBS dollar price exceeded 104. However, for prices above 104,

KRD vs. Price

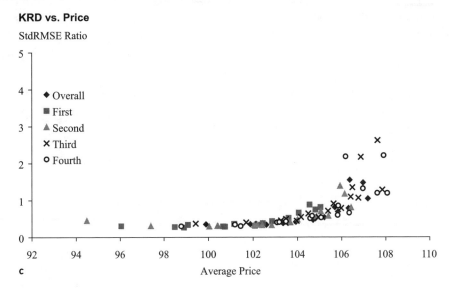

c

RelC(10) vs. Price

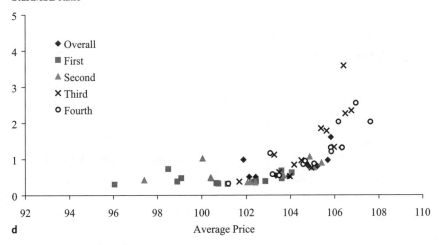

d

Figure 20-6. (continued)

although the Emp(20,10) measure performs poorly in absolute terms, it greatly outperformed the RelC(10) measure. The two model durations (OAS(10) and KRD) performed well for prices below 104, but their performance deteriorated as prices moved beyond 104.

To get a clearer picture of relative duration performance, Figure 20-7 shows the relative StdRMSE ratios across the overall period and the four subperiods for

KRD/Emp(20,10) vs. Price

StdRMSE Ratio

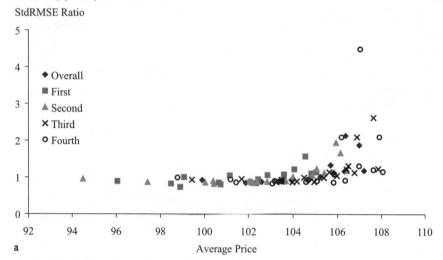

a

KRD/OAD(10) vs. Price

StdRMSE Ratio

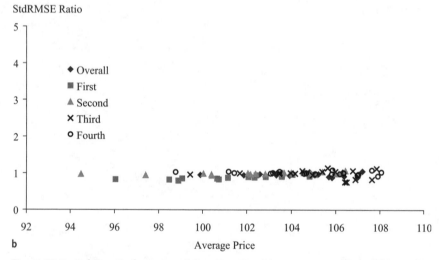

b

Figure 20-7. Relative Performance of Four Duration Measures across Four Subperiods and Overall Period

April 30, 2001–February 28, 2005

various duration pairs across all the generics and the index. The figure reveals that the patterns for the individual subperiods resemble the pattern for the overall period despite the very different market environments. Across all subperiods, Emp(20,10) underperforms KRD and OAD(10) if the MBS dollar price is less than 104. This result is shown in Figure 20-7 as the StdRMSE ratio for KRD/Emp(20,10)

Emp(20,10)/OAD(10) vs. Price

StdRMSE Ratio

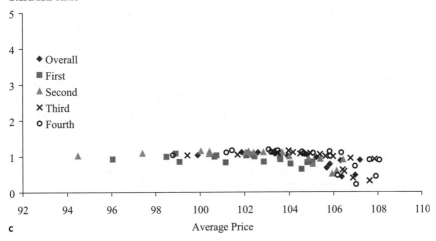

c   Average Price

Emp(20,10)/RelC(10) vs. Price

StdRMSE Ratio

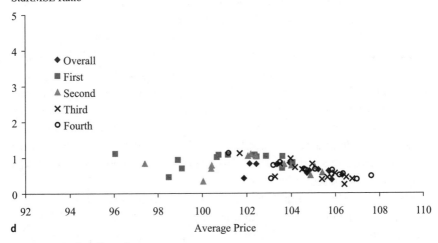

d   Average Price

Figure 20-7. (continued)

is usually less than one and the ratio for Emp(20,10)/OAD(10) is usually greater than one as long as the MBS dollar price is less than 104. However, across all four subperiods, Emp(20,10) outperforms KRD and OAD(10) when the MBS dollar price exceeds 104. This can be seen by the KRD/Emp(20,10) ratio rising and the Emp(20,10)/OAD(10) ratio falling after the 104 price is reached.

Figure 20-7 also shows that the Emp(20,10) empirical measure regularly outperforms the RelC(10) measure (i.e., the StdRMSE ratio is usually less than one). Rarely is the RelC(10) duration measure the better empirical duration. Between the two model durations, KRD typically outperforms OAD. In fact, there is no subperiod in which OAD is the better model duration.

There were, however, some notable differences across the four subperiods. In the first, a time of declining yields with the 10-year reaching a heretofore record low, empiricals performed particularly well vs. model durations as the values of the StdRMSE ratio for KRD/Emp(20,10) and Emp(20,10)/OAD(10) are noticeably above and below, respectively, the patterns for the rest of the period. In the fourth subperiod, where the 10-year yield was relatively unchanged but the curve steepened considerably, the empirical duration performed poorly compared to model durations. The sharp reshaping of the yield curve during the fourth subperiod gave KRDs an opportunity to outperform OADs. Interestingly, however, there is no perceptible KRD advantage vs. OAD during this time.

To check to see if the preceding results differed depending on the MBS program, Figure 20-8 breaks Figure 20-6 down into two MBS groups: 30-year FNMA (labeled "FNMA") and 30-year GNMA and 15-year FNMA.

Figure 20-8 shows that the pattern of duration measure performance is broadly similar across the two sets of MBS programs. However, there are some notable exceptions. First, model durations tended to perform slightly better for the FNMA set than for the GNMA and 15-year FNMA set, and this can be seen in the StdRMSE value using both OAD (10) and KRD. For a given price level, the StdRMSE value is slightly lower for the former than for the latter. Second, as the price increases above 104, the deterioration in StdRMSE is greater for the latter set than for the former. Finally, we see that both empirical measures did better for the GNMA and 15-year FNMA set than for the FNMA set.

Figure 20-9 separates Figure 20-7 into the two MBS groups and shows the relative performance of the various duration measures. The figure shows clearly that for the GNMA and 15-year FNMA set, empirical durations outperform model durations beginning with MBS price levels slightly above par. Note the StdRMSE ratio for KRD/Emp(20,10). For FNMAs, KRDs clearly outperform Emp(20,10) until the MBS price reaches above 104. In contrast, for the GNMA and 15-year FNMA set, KRDs only slightly outperform Emp(20,10) for lower price levels and begin to underperform Emp(20,10) at MBS prices of less than 104. This pattern is also visible in the Emp(20,10)/OAD(10) ratio as it begins to fall below 1.0 at a lower price level for the GNMA and 15-year FNMA set compared to the 30-year FNMA set.

GNMA and 15-yr FNMA

OAD(10) vs. Price

StdRMSE Ratio

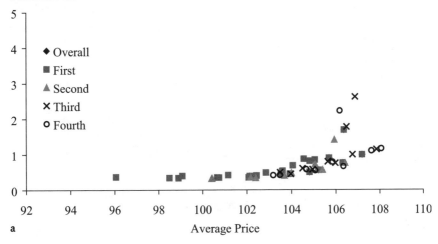

a

Average Price

Emp(20,10) vs. Price

StdRMSE Ratio

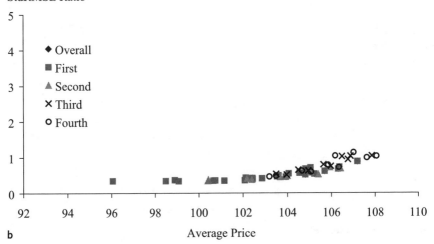

b

Average Price

Figure 20-8. Performance of Four Duration Measures across Four Subperiods and Overall Period

April 30, 2001–February 28, 2005

KRD vs. Price

StdRMSE Ratio

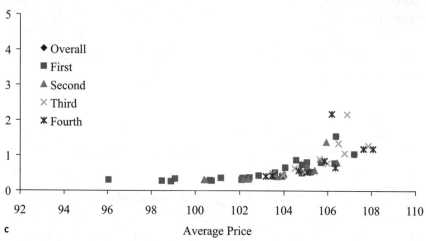

c

Average Price

RelC(10) vs. Price

StdRMSE

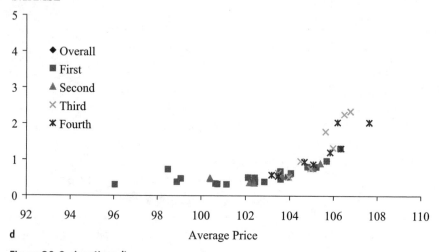

d

Average Price

Figure 20-8. (continued)

FNMA

OAD(10) vs. Price

StdRMSE Ratio

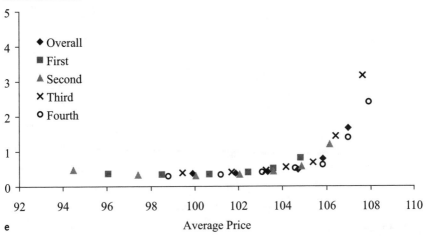

e

Emp(20,10) vs. Price

StdRMSE Ratio

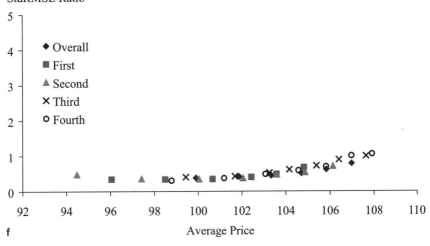

f

Figure 20-8. (continued)

KRD vs. Price

StdRMSE Ratio

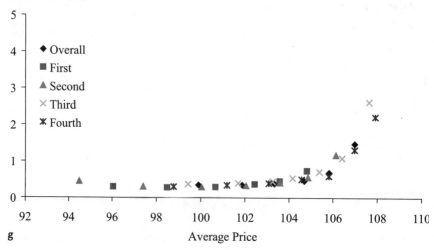

g   Average Price

RelC(10) vs. Price

StdRMSE Ratio

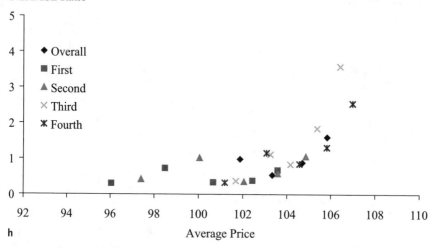

h   Average Price

Figure 20-8. (continued)

GNMA and 15-yr FNMA

KRD/Emp(20,10) vs. Price

StdRMSE Ratio

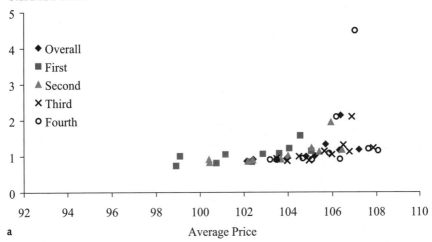

a   Average Price

KRD/OAD(10) vs. Price

StdRMSE Ratio

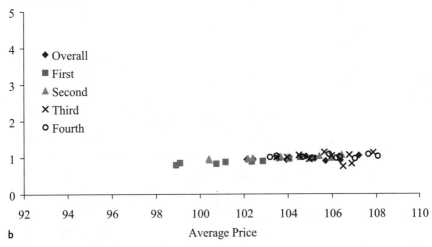

b   Average Price

Figure 20-9. Relative Performance of Four Duration Measures across Four Subperiods and Overall Period

April 30, 2001–February 28, 2005

Emp(20,10)/OAD(10) vs. Price

StdRMSE Ratio

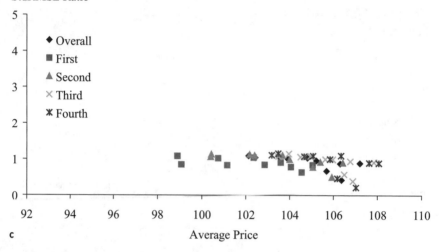

c   Average Price

Emp(20,10)/RelC(10) vs. Price

StdRMSE Ratio

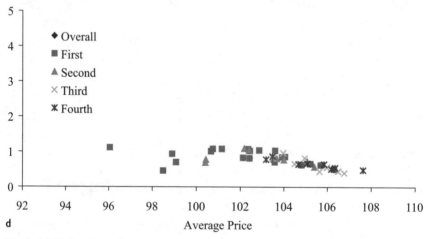

d   Average Price

Figure 20-9. (continued)

FNMA

KRD/Emp(20,10) vs. Price

StdRMSE Ratio

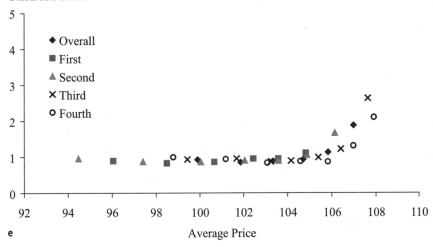

e   Average Price

KRD/OAD(10) vs. Price

StdRMSE Ratio

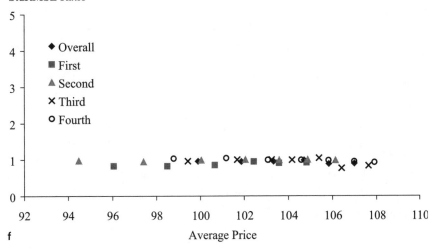

f   Average Price

Figure 20-9. (continued)

Emp(20,10)/OAD(10) vs. Price

StdRMSE Ratio

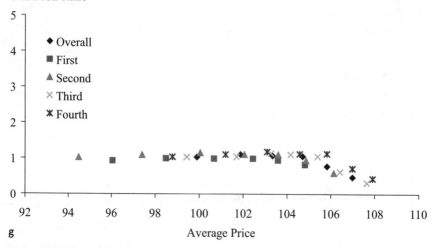

g

Average Price

Emp(20,10)/RelC(10) vs. Price

StdRMSE Ratio

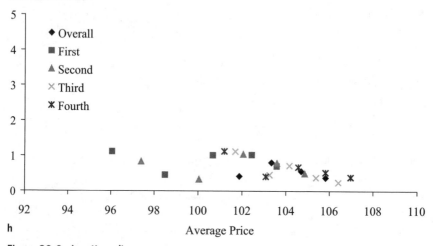

h

Average Price

Figure 20-9. (continued)

Negative Duration

A notable development during 2002 and 2003 was the prevalence of negative OADs for high-coupon MBS.[14] Negative durations imply that the MBS generic price will tend to *increase (decrease)* if UST yields *increase (decrease)*. While negative durations are common among certain MBS derivatives, they are unusual for pass-throughs. For some investors, it is a leap of faith to add securities with negative durations to their portfolios. The existence of negative durations also leads some investors to question the relevance of any MBS model duration. How well do negative OADs explain the price behavior of MBS?

We examine several 2000 vintage generics that began to have negative OADs toward year-end 2002 that persisted through June 2003. For comparison, we also examined the corresponding 2001 vintage generic having the same coupon and program but positive OADs.[15] How well did the negative model durations perform? Did they make any sense?

FNMA 8% of 2000 (FNA08000) had negative OADs from October 2002 through June 2003. Although the OADs were negative, they were only slightly so (e.g., –0.31 on October 1, 2002, and –0.29 on June 30, 2003). In contrast, the OAD for FNA08001 was significantly positive throughout the same period (e.g., 1.48 on October 1, 2002, and 1.30 on June 30, 2003).[16] FNA07400 and FNA07401 displayed a similar pattern, although the OAD for FNA07400 did become slightly positive in late 2002. FNC06400 spent most of 2003 with a negative OAD (again, only slightly negative as the OAD on June 30, 2003, was –0.16), while FNC06401 remained positive throughout, but also very close to zero. In contrast to the FNMA 7.5 and 8%s, there was little OAD difference between the 2000 and 2001

---

14. As of June 30, 2003, more than 9% of the MBS Index's market value consisted of generics with negative OADs.

15. An important reason for the OAD difference is that new mortgagors paying such high coupons in 2001, when mortgage rates were much lower, were likely to have been credit constrained and have limited prepayment possibilities.

16. Although the FNA08000 and FNA08001 generics had very different OADs, there was some similarity in their respective KRD profiles. Despite the negative OAD for FNA08000, the security had positive KRDs for the 0.5-year and 2-year key-rate points. In fact, these positive KRDs were slightly higher than the corresponding KRDs for FNA08001. The source of the negative OAD for FNA08000 and of the difference with FNA08001 lies in the longer-maturity KRD points: the 5-year, 10-year, and 20-year. FNA08000 had significantly negative KRDs at all three points. In contrast, the 5-year and the 10-year KRDs for FNA08001 were modestly positive and the 20-year KRD was close to zero. Given the large variations in price sensitivity along the curve, especially for FNA08000, OAD(10) is probably not a particularly good duration measure for either security. The StdRMSEs (using KRD) for the two annual aggregates were much closer. Nevertheless, empiricals remained the best performers.

vintages for GNMA 7.5 and 8%s for most of the time between October 2002 and June 2003.

Figure 20-10 shows the relative duration performance for these ten generics. Specifically, we compare the performance of the 2000 vintages (with very low or zero model durations) with their 2001 counterparts. Generally, for these high-coupon generics all durations, model or empirical, performed poorly. Most StdRMSE values were close to (or greater than!) one, indicating that the duration error was almost equal to the price volatility itself. In other words, assuming a duration value of zero performed almost as well (if not better) than the empirical or model duration value. Notably, the StdRMSE (OAD(10)) for FNA08001 (positive model duration) greatly exceeded that for FNA08000 (negative model duration), whereas their KRD StdRMSEs were comparable. For both generics, their empirical durations performed similarly and were much better than any of their model durations. However, given that the StdRMSEs were greater than one, assuming a duration value of zero would have resulted in a better performance. The fact that the negative model duration for FNA08000 produced a lower StdRMSE value than the positive model duration for FNA08001 most likely reflects the small absolute value of the negative duration for FNA08000 compared to the positive duration for FNA08001. The negative model durations made sense largely to the extent that their absolute values were close to zero.

If durations were truly negative, then we would expect to observe a positive relationship between changes in yields and percentage changes in prices. Figure 20-11 presents a plot of daily changes in the 10-year UST yield (horizontal axis) vs. daily percentage changes in the price of FNA08000 (with negative model OADs) for the period from October 1, 2002 to June 30, 2003. The scatter plot does show that there are many instances of a rise in 10-year yields associated with positive percentage price changes and relatively few instances of a rise in yields associated with negative price change. However, there are no instances of a comparable fall. This asymmetric relationship between yield and price changes is not fully consistent for a security with negative model duration. Although negative model durations performed reasonable well during this period, their performance owed more to their low absolute values (which closely matched empirical durations) than to the fact that the duration value was negative.

RISK MODEL EMPIRICAL DURATIONS

MBS returns are driven by many risk factors, apart from changes in UST yields, but these other factors (e.g., spreads and volatilities) are likely to be correlated with changes in UST yields. In fact, the Lehman Brothers global risk model uses monthly historical data to estimate the variances and covariances of changes in

Figure 20-10. Predicted vs. Actual Percentage Price Change StdRMSE
October 2, 2002–June 30, 2003

	$ Price	OAD10	OAD(p)	KRD	Emp(10,10)	Emp(10,p)	Emp(20,10)	Emp(20,p)	RelC10
FNA07400	106.10	1.13	1.10	1.61	0.97	0.96	0.95	0.95	
FNA07401	106.19	1.40	1.15	1.09	0.97	0.96	0.95	0.94	4.13
FNA08000	107.51	1.69	1.54	2.46	1.03	1.04	1.04	1.05	
FNA08001	107.55	2.96	2.40	2.43	1.03	1.03	1.04	1.05	
FNC06400	105.42	0.91	0.93	1.23	0.81	0.81	0.79	0.79	
FNC06401	105.51	0.74	0.73	0.89	0.81	0.81	0.79	0.79	1.55
GNA07400	106.60	0.98	0.99	1.15	0.99	0.99	0.98	0.98	
GNA07401	106.63	0.98	0.99	1.16	0.99	0.99	0.98	0.98	2.47
GNA08000	107.82	1.20	1.15	1.49	0.99	0.99	0.99	0.98	
GNA08001	107.81	1.18	1.14	1.47	0.99	0.99	0.99	0.98	

Percentage Price Change FNA08000

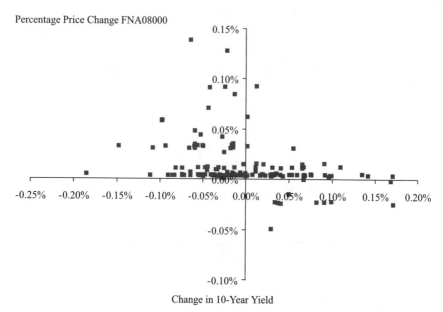

Change in 10-Year Yield

Figure 20-11. Actual Percentage FNA08000 Price Change vs. Change in UST 10-Year Yield
October 2, 2002–June 30, 2003

Treasury key rates and MBS risk factors to produce estimates of portfolio tracking error volatility vs. a benchmark. These monthly data could be used to construct MBS duration measures. Although the risk model uses monthly data to estimate the variance-covariance matrix, it would be interesting to examine how well "risk model" duration measures perform on a daily basis.

Figure 20-12 shows the estimated correlations from the global risk model (as of February 28, 2005) between changes in the 5- and 10-year par Treasury rates and some select MBS risk factors. Note that changes in most of these MBS risk factors are correlated with changes in Treasury rates—sometimes negatively correlated. For example, when the 5-year Treasury rate increases, spreads on new premium MBS tend to narrow. The global risk model's variance-covariance matrix was constructed as of November 2002 using MBS data back to May 1995 and updated each month thereafter. It is constructed in two ways. The first, called "unweighted" or "equal weighted," assigns equal weights to all historical observations and is appropriate for investors who believe that factor variances and covariances for the future are best represented by the average experience since 1995. Other investors may feel that more recently observed factor variances and covariances are more relevant for estimating factor behavior in the near future. For

Figure 20-12. Estimated Correlations among Selected MBS Risk Factors, Unweighted Covariance Matrix

February 28, 2005

MBS Risk Factor	5-Year Par UST Rate	10-Year Par UST Rate
Discount coupon/low WALA spreads	0.27	0.28
Current coupon/low WALA spreads	0.06	0.1
Premium coupon/low WALA spreads	−0.39	−0.39
Volatility (short)	−0.17	−0.16
Volatility (long)	−0.33	−0.32

them, the risk model offers a "weighted" calculation of the covariance matrix that uses an exponential time decay to weight the historical data.[17]

We can use the risk model estimated variance-covariance matrix to estimate the full response of MBS percentage price changes to changes in UST yields. For example, suppose the true model of MBS returns were as follows:

$$\%\Delta P_{\text{mbs},t} = S_{\text{yield}} \times \Delta \text{yield}_t + S_{\text{F1}} \times \Delta \text{F1}_t + S_{\text{F2}} \times \Delta \text{F2}_t + \varepsilon_t, \tag{20-1}$$

where yield_t is a Treasury rate and F1_t and F2_t are two MBS risk factors that affect MBS returns. S_j refers to the sensitivity of the MBS price return to changes in the risk factor j. For example, S_{yield} refers to the duration for the Treasury yield and S_{F1} represents the sensitivity (i.e., spread duration) of the MBS price return to changes in the spread risk factor F1.

For this study, we are concerned with how MBS price returns are related to changes in Treasury yields, either a single Treasury yield or several Treasury key rates. If changes in yield are correlated with changes in MBS risk factors, then we can generate a revised duration measure, called "risk model duration," that incorporates the changes in MBS risk factors associated with changes in yield.

To calculate the risk model duration measure, we proceed as follows. We now assume that there is a relationship between Δyield and ΔF1 and ΔF2, where F1 and F2 are risk factors that influence MBS price returns. Specifically,

$$\Delta \text{F1}_t = \gamma_{\text{F1}} \times \Delta \text{yield}_t + \xi_t,$$

$$\Delta \text{F2}_t = \gamma_{\text{F2}} \times \Delta \text{yield}_t + \varphi_t,$$

17. The speed of the time decay is fixed at a 1-year half-life, which implies that an observation of 1 year ago receives half the weight in the estimation as the most recent observations.

where ξ_t and φ_t are error terms. Using ordinary least squares,[18] we get

$$\gamma_{F1}^* = Cov_{\Delta F1, \Delta yield} / Var_{\Delta yield},$$

$$\gamma_{F2}^* = Cov_{\Delta F2, \Delta yield} / Var_{\Delta yield}.$$

Substituting into Equation (20-1), we get the following predicted value for the MBS percentage price change:

$$
\begin{aligned}
\%\Delta P_{predicted,t} \\
&= S_{yield} \times \Delta yield_t + S_{F1} \times (\gamma_{F1}^* \times \Delta yield_t) + S_{F2} \times (\gamma_{F2}^* \times \Delta yield_t) \\
&= (S_{yield} + S_{F1} \times \gamma_{F1}^* + S_{F2} \times \gamma_{F2}^*) \times \Delta yield_t \quad\quad (20\text{-}2) \\
&= (S_{yield} + S_{F1} \times Cov_{\Delta F1, \Delta yield} / Var_{\Delta yield} + S_{F2} \times Cov_{\Delta F2, \Delta yield} / Var_{\Delta yield}) \\
&\quad \times \Delta yield_t.
\end{aligned}
$$

The term in parentheses is our "risk-model duration" measure, S_{yield}^*,

$$\%\Delta P_{mbs,t} = S_{yield}^* \times \Delta yield_t.$$

This example assumes that MBS price returns are a function of a single Treasury rate. However, the MBS risk model and its covariance matrix assume that MBS price returns are a function of six Treasury key rates. Consequently, to use the risk model's factor covariance matrix, Equation (20-2) should be rewritten in terms of the six key rates:

$$\%\Delta P_{predicted,t} = \sum_i (KRD_{i,t-1} \times \Delta y_{KRD(i),t}) + \text{Effect of } \Delta y_{KRD(i),t}$$
$$\text{on other MBS risk factors.}$$

This complicates the calculation of risk model KRDs as each non-key-rate risk factor is now modeled as a function of the six key rates. For example, for spread risk factor F1 we assume

$$\Delta F1_t = \sum_i (\gamma_i \times \Delta y_{KRD(i),t}) + \tau_t.$$

Consequently, the estimators for the γ_i values involve the correlations among the six key-rate yield changes.

More generally, the risk model durations are generated as follows. If we let X represent the (6×6) covariance matrix for the six key rates, C represent the (6×20) matrix of the covariances of each of the six key rates with the twenty non-key-

---

18. For simplicity, we are ignoring the constant term. As in the preceding section, this assumption has a negligible effect on the results.

rate MBS risk factors,[19] and **S** represent the (20×1) vector of risk factor loadings, then it can be shown that the (6×1) vector of risk model durations (KRD_{RM}) is given by

$$\text{KRD}_{\text{RM}} = \text{KRD} + \mathbf{X}^{-1}\,\mathbf{CS}. \tag{20-3}$$

We construct risk model durations using both the unweighted and weighted factor covariance matrices. The performance of these durations, for December 3, 2002–February 28, 2005, is shown in Figure 20-13, which also presents results for model durations, OAD and KRD, and the empirical duration measure, Emp(20,10), for the same period.

For generics with prices under 106, both sets of risk model durations perform similarly to OAD and KRD and both tend to outperform Emp(20,10). As prices rise above 106, both risk model durations begin to deteriorate along with OAD and KRD and underperformed Emp(20,10). This result is a bit unexpected because the risk model durations are, in essence, empirical durations, and empirical measures tend to do better than analytical measures as the generic price rises. Nevertheless, for very high-dollar-priced generics, the Emp(20,10) empirical measure, calculated using daily price and yield data, does much better than the risk model durations. This result highlights a limitation of risk model durations, with their monthly sampling of price and yield data, to serve as good empirical duration measures for daily percentage price changes of high-dollar-priced generics.

CONCLUSION

The manager of an MBS portfolio or a portfolio containing some MBS securities needs confidence in MBS duration measures. For MBS, duration is relatively difficult to measure as the security's cash flows change in response to changes in rates. Managers use a number of MBS duration measures. Some, such as OAD and KRDs, are model based and rely on term-structure and prepayment models. Empirical duration measures, on the other hand, rely on historical statistical relationships between mortgage prices and selected Treasury bond yields.

In order to examine the relative accuracy of various duration measures, one must choose the Treasury yield whose change is multiplied by the duration measure to produce the predicted price return. We chose to evaluate eight duration–yield change pairs: three model durations and five empirical ones. We examined the effectiveness of these pairs in predicting the daily price movements of seventeen

---

19. See Chapter 26.

Figure 20-13. Predicted vs. Actual Percentage Price Change, Standardized RMSE, Risk Model Durations, Unweighted and Weighted
December 3, 2002–February 28, 2005

	$ Price	OAD(10)	OAD(p)	KRD	Emp(20,10)	RM$_{unweighted}$	RM$_{weighted}$
MBS Index	102.57	0.35	0.39	0.35	0.41	NA	NA
FNA06001	103.22	0.44	0.47	0.44	0.52	0.44	0.45
FNA06401	104.38	0.54	0.53	0.54	0.61	0.55	0.56
FNA07001	105.63	0.65	0.61	0.67	0.71	0.70	0.71
FNA07401	106.70	1.40	1.18	1.20	0.91	1.34	1.33
FNA08001	107.79	2.73	2.27	2.39	1.01	2.52	2.54
FNC05401	103.39	0.46	0.49	0.47	0.52	0.48	0.48
FNC06001	104.60	0.59	0.58	0.62	0.64	0.63	0.64
FNC06401	105.77	0.82	0.77	0.92	0.81	0.94	0.96
FNC07001	106.40	1.90	1.61	1.66	1.01	1.77	1.77
FNC07401	106.97	2.89	2.43	2.57	1.04	2.68	2.69
GNA06001	103.80	0.43	0.46	0.45	0.51	0.44	0.45
GNA06401	105.05	0.57	0.54	0.55	0.63	0.58	0.60
GNA07001	106.19	0.72	0.67	0.74	0.74	0.78	0.79
GNA07401	107.16	1.04	0.98	1.12	0.94	1.19	1.19
GNA08001	107.99	1.15	1.11	1.23	1.03	1.27	1.25

MBS generics and the MBS Index from June 2001 through February 2005. For the sake of comparison, we also applied these pairs to four agency indices, one Treasury, and one high-grade corporate bond.

We found that both model and empirical durations generally performed as well or better for MBS as they did for agency and corporate bonds, though, not surprisingly, they performed best for the Treasury. Empirical durations generally underperformed model durations. However, as the MBS price increased, empiricals performed better than model durations. Empiricals also tended to perform better for GNMAs and 15-year FNMAs than for 30-year FNMAs. Surprising, KRDs only slightly outperformed OAD measures, even during periods of significant curve reshaping. Finally, we found that negative model durations for very high-dollar-price MBS performed slightly better (although overall performance was poor) than durations for other high-dollar-priced MBS. However, their relative performance was likely due to the fact that their absolute values were close to zero rather than because their durations were actually negative.

21. MBS Investing over Long Horizons

Is it profitable to buy and hold MBS over long horizons? Or is MBS an "opportunistic" asset class, where the only profits come from correctly timing spread widenings and spread tightenings? Essentially, does the spread it offers more than adequately compensate investors who follow a strategy of maintaining a long-term holding of MBS?

To answer this question we consider the following MBS buy-and-hold strategy: Invest in the most recently issued 30-year FNMA MBS index generic with a price closest to par from below. Then, as a cash flow is generated it is reinvested in the new 30-year par coupon FNMA. Over time, owing to coupons and paydowns received and market movements, the portfolio will contain a range of coupons and vintages.

How should we measure the performance of such an investment strategy? For total return investors, absolute and relative performance is typically measured using mark-to-market returns. For these investors we would calculate MBS cumulative market returns and compare them to market returns for other asset classes, such as intermediate credit and agency bonds. We would then compute MBS monthly total (or, excess) return volatility and compare these "risk-adjusted" returns to those for other asset classes.[1] However, total return investors are unlikely ever

Based on research first published by Lehman Brothers in 2005.

1. Earlier studies found that MBS market excess returns, adjusted by the standard deviation of excess returns, compared unfavorably to credit and, in particular, to agency bonds. In this chapter we do not compute excess returns to Treasuries, for several reasons. First, excess returns imply that the investor wants to compare performance to a constantly shifting mix of Treasuries. For buy-and-hold investors, this is typically not the case. Assets are purchased and held (vs. liabilities) and the question for them is: "Should I buy MBS, credit, or agency bonds that are roughly similar in maturity (duration) and hold them?" Second, excess returns are very sensitive to the calculation methodology and to the quality of the duration measure. Instead, we analyze performance independent, as much as possible, of analytical sensitivity measures. Also, over long periods income return dominates performance of fixed-income securities.

to follow a buy-and-hold strategy. Their performance is measured monthly using market prices vs. an index whose performance is calculated in a similar way. For total return investors, buying and selling in anticipation of changes in spreads is their raison d'etre. Consequently, what is an appropriate performance metric for total return investors may not be appropriate for buy-and-hold investors.

Investors most likely to be interested in a buy-and-hold MBS strategy are banks, insurance companies, official institutions (foreign and domestic), and individuals who, for various regulatory, organizational, and business reasons, do not typically sell bonds after purchase. These investors seek income, not capital gains.[2] For these investors, often referred to as "buy-and-hold investors," monthly book income, not monthly total return, is the relevant return measure and the variability of book income is the relevant risk measure. As we will show, bond performance in book income space has different risk and return properties compared to performance measured in total (or excess) return space. Given that the MBS market is heavily influenced by investors who use book accounting, this may have ramifications for interpreting the relative value of various asset classes.

A bond held to maturity generates total income equal to its coupon, the difference between its purchase price and par, and any reinvestment income earned on cash flows received prior to maturity. The "promised" annual return on the bond equals its yield at purchase assuming it does not default, principal is received as anticipated at purchase, and interim cash flows are reinvested at this yield. However, a bond's book yield (and income) is not assured. Defaults, downgrades that force selling before maturity, unanticipated changes in the bond's amortization, and reinvestment at rates other than the bond's initial yield cause the bond's realized book income to differ from what was promised. This variability of a bond's book income is the risk faced by a buy-and-hold investor.

Over the life of a bond, its cumulative market return should equal its book return. However, monthly market returns are typically much more volatile than book returns. Forecasting market returns requires a different investment skill set compared to forecasting book returns. A total return investor asks: "What is the bond's likely total market return over the next month?" In contrast, the buy-and-hold investor, who is unlikely ever to sell the bond, asks: "What is the bond's likely book income over its life?" While there is some linkage between the two questions, they

---

2. There are several reasons why investors follow such a portfolio strategy. For example, insurance companies and banks have regulatory and market constraints that prevent them from recognizing gains or losses that may arise from selling bonds before maturity. Some official institutions may be reluctant to sell assets because there is the potential of sending an implied signal to the marketplace. Other investors (e.g., individuals or small pension plans) may not have the infrastructure to monitor assets for a more active management style.

reflect different risk and return assessments. As we show, assets can have market return volatilities and correlations that differ from their book return counterparts. Consequently, asset allocation conclusions reached in one risk-return framework may differ from those drawn from another risk-return framework.

The purpose of this chapter is to measure the long-term performance of MBS for buy-and-hold investors. Specifically, we address the following questions:

- What has been the long-term book income of MBS? How does MBS book income compare with credit and agency bonds?

- What has been the variability of MBS monthly book income? How does the distribution of MBS monthly book income compare to that for the other asset classes?

- What are the relationships between credit and MBS book income? Are they highly correlated? Does the presence of MBS help to reduce the volatility of book income? If so, what is the role of MBS in a credit-MBS portfolio? Does MBS have book income diversification potential beyond helping to reduce a portfolio's shortfall risk? Or, does MBS just help reduce shortfall risk?

- Do market spread (OAS) and yield levels contain information regarding MBS future relative book income performance? For example, does a wider MBS OAS level relative to credit signal an opportunity to earn additional book income, or does the spread simply compensate for the greater convexity risk that is typically realized?

MEASURING LONG-TERM PERFORMANCE: BOOK INCOME RETURN AND RISK

A buy-and-hold portfolio manager typically is striving to identify assets that produce relatively high book income (book yield) with a high degree of confidence (i.e., low default or prepayment risk) rather than anticipating monthly spread changes. This focus on book yield can often work to the advantage of the book manager. To the extent that a portion of a bond's yield reflects a risk premium to compensate total return managers for systematic spread volatility, the book manager can garner that additional spread because spread volatility does not impact the buy-and-hold manager's performance.[3]

---

3. A focus on book yield can also work to the portfolio's disadvantage. Bonds that trade at wider spreads vs. their peer group may do so because the market is assuming relatively higher default or prepayment risk. Buying bonds simply based on yield may work for a short time

Book accounting calculates a bond's book value based on its historical cost and periodically adjusts this value to fully amortize any premium or discount by the bond's anticipated maturity date. The bond's book yield is based on its yield at purchase (calculated using the bond's purchase price and expected amortization schedule) and remains relatively static until maturity irrespective of changes in market yields. Book income is calculated by multiplying the bond's current book value by its book yield and including any discrete adjustments that are due to unanticipated prepayments or credit impairment. For MBS, as prepayments occur the manager replaces expected with actual prepayments, updates the prepayment forecast, and recalculates the bond's book yield and income. Any adjustment to book value is recognized as a book gain or loss this period, which is reflected in current book income.[4] Although book income is based on a prepayment model, over time book income is adjusted to reflect actual prepayments and updated prepayment forecasts.[5]

Owing to the negative convexity of MBS, prepayments tend to accelerate when interest rates decline. Consequently, the MBS manager must reinvest principal received prematurely at lower interest rates, lowering the portfolio's book income. The portfolio's book income then starts to lag that of a portfolio that did not have negative convexity. The MBS manager may also receive paydowns when interest rates rise, offering an opportunity to increase portfolio book income. However, higher rates usually delay scheduled paydowns, causing the portfolio's book income to remain relatively static while other less negatively convex portfolios are able to reinvest more cash flow at higher yields. If rates are steady, the MBS portfolio's book income gradually increases over time, reflecting the growth in the portfolio's book value.

MBS book income fluctuates depending on the movement in interest rates. Since MBS are not vulnerable to default and downgrade risk, which can produce

---

until the bond's higher risk reveals itself through a downgrade, default, or prepayment and lower future book income. For a discussion of adjusting a buy-and-hold portfolio's book yield for embedded default risk see Chapter 9. For an empirical study on the subsequent performance of distressed investment-grade bonds see Chapter 15.

4. If prepayments are faster than expected (and/or prepayment forecasts are speeded up), then an investor in premium MBS has to mark down the book value of the holding (reducing book income) and report a lower book yield, which will also reduce book income. If prepayments are slower than expected then the investor in premium MBS has a book income gain and an increase in book yield. The opposite pattern occurs for holdings of discount MBS.

5. If different investors use different prepayment models then their MBS book incomes probably differ. Moreover, a large change to a prepayment model could produce a large change to an MBS book income in the month of the model change. In this study we updated prepayment information (realizations and forecasts) each month.

large negative shocks to book income, we would not anticipate such shocks, especially for MBS purchased close to par. If we adjust for the growth of the portfolio's book value over time, the distribution of monthly book income for an MBS portfolio should be spread around the initial book income with a bit of a negative skew. However, there should be no significant part of the distribution with large negative observations. Given the limited tail risk for MBS, the risk of long-horizon MBS investing is best measured by the volatility of book income.

The book income for a credit (bullet) bond is calculated in a similar way. Given the absence of prepayment risk, the credit manager has less reinvestment risk and may have more confidence about locking in the yield over the duration of the bond. However, instead of MBS prepayment risk, he must contend with default risk and the impact on book income. He also has downgrade risk, as many managers are required to sell credit bonds if their rating falls below some threshold (e.g., investment grade).[6] If a default or downgrade occurs, the investor no longer receives the promised income and will likely recognize a book loss (which reduces current and future book income). The investor will then reinvest the recovery proceeds at what may be higher or lower book yields than the initial bond. The buy-and-hold credit investor must worry about whether overall defaults and downgrades are greater than expected, as well as whether issuer defaults and downgrades in the portfolio are correlated. While the realized overall default rate in the market may equal the expected rate, if particular names in the portfolio default together, its default rate may exceed that of the market.[7]

The credit portfolio manager faces a very asymmetrical portfolio book income profile. Credit assets either produce their promised book income each period with some distribution around the initial book income value as cash flow is reinvested at higher and lower book yields, or they suffer a large decline in book income owing to defaults and downgrades. Given this tail risk, the risk of buy-and-hold credit investing is often measured by shortfall risk (i.e., expected shortfall), as well as by the volatility (standard deviation) of book income.

The risk to book income from agency (bullet) bonds is minimal as default and downgrade risks are very low and there is no convexity risk. The distribution of book income from agency bonds should have very little variability. As we discuss later, the absence of credit and convexity risk makes agency bonds a useful baseline against which to compare the other two asset classes.

---

6. Even if the manager is not required to sell a downgraded bond, he may have to mark the bond to market (i.e., recognize a book loss) and record book income only when coupon payments are received.

7. See Chapter 16.

To measure the historical performance of these three asset types we constructed separate book accounting indices for each of the three asset classes beginning in December 1993.[8] To make the performance measures relevant to investors we constructed indices that reflect the investment strategy of a typical buy-and-hold investor if he has an investment inflow. The indices have comparable durations and broadly reflect the asset choices facing a buy-and-hold portfolio manager. We do not make any attempt to exactly match durations (or key-rate durations) of the three investment strategies—for two reasons. First, matching durations would be very important if the goal were to compare monthly market returns, as relative performance would be heavily influenced by any duration differences in addition to monthly spread performance. However, this is not of much interest for buy-and-hold investors. Second, there is healthy skepticism about the quality of the duration number for MBS calculated long ago.[9] In general, buy-and-hold investors seek assets that match somewhat coarse maturity or duration liability buckets.

For MBS we constructed an MBS book index with an initial $1 billion investment on December 31, 1993, in a single MBS issue: the most recently issued 30-year FNMA MBS index generic with a price closest to par from below. (Note: If such a discount generic is not available, then the index buys the most recently issued 30-year FNMA whose price is closest to par.) In other words, the index buys only newly issued, slightly discounted MBS, which is typical of many buy-and-hold investors. As cash flow is generated by this portfolio, it is reinvested in the current 30-year slightly discounted FNMA index generic. Although the MBS book index begins as a single MBS generic, it gradually adds more generics as interest rates fluctuate and the current coupon MBS changes.

For credit, we constructed a credit book index by making an initial investment of $1 billion on December 31, 1993, in a modified 3- to 10-year maturity Baa-A credit index (bullets only).[10] We use this index to reflect the performance of a

---

8. Monthly book income is generated using Lehman book index (BOOKIN) software. For the three book indices we assume that bonds do not leave the book index if they have less than 1 year left to maturity or if they violate a future liquidity constraint (unlike standard Lehman total return indices). Bonds only leave a book index if they are downgraded below investment grade, mature, or prepay (for MBS).

9. We have analyzed the quality of Lehman MBS analytical durations since 2001 and found them to compare favorably to many empirical duration measures. See Chapter 20.

10. We modify the Lehman index to only include credit assets issued within the past 5 years and with a minimum amount outstanding that gradually increases over time. This restriction makes this exercise more realistic by limiting the index to buying only relatively large issues that are easily available. We also assume, unlike the standard Lehman total return indices, that bonds with less than 1 year remaining until maturity remain in the strategy portfolio until maturity.

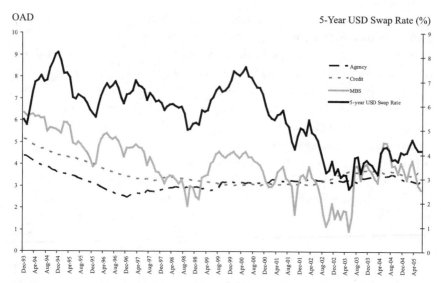

Figure 21-1. Monthly OAD for MBS, Credit, and Agency Portfolios, and 5-Year USD Swap Rate
December 1993–June 2005

purely passive buy-and-hold credit portfolio manager. Bonds that default or are downgraded below investment grade (using the Lehman index quality rating) are sold from the index, with consequences for the index's book income. As the initial index generates cash (coupons, maturities, and recoveries), we assume that the index/portfolio buys more of the current index.

Finally, we constructed an agency book index by making a similar initial investment of $1 billion on December 31, 1993, in the 3- to 10-year agency index (bullets only). As the initial index generates cash (coupons and maturities), we assume that the portfolio buys more of the current index.

The three buy-and-hold strategies receive no additional investment inflows. For each strategy (as represented by its corresponding book index) we calculate its monthly book income, book value, cash flow, book yield, market value, and market-value-weighted OAD. (For reference, the time series of each strategy's monthly OAD and the 5-year USD swap rate are shown in Figure 21-1.)

LONG-TERM PERFORMANCE OF MBS

Figure 21-2 shows the time series of monthly book income for the MBS, credit, and agency buy-and-hold investment strategies from December 1993 through June 2005. For all three strategies, book income gradually increases over time re-

Book Income ($)

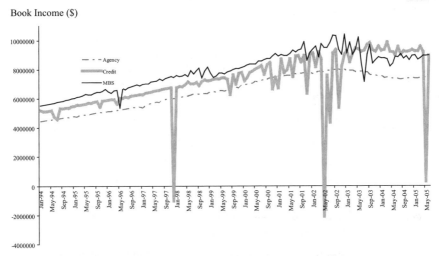

Figure 21-2. Monthly Book Income: MBS, Credit, and Agency Portfolios
December 1993–June 2005

flecting the reinvestment of coupon income. As expected, the book income pattern for the agency strategy is very smooth as there are no defaults, downgrades, or unanticipated amortizations to cause significant monthly fluctuations. The figure shows that book income gradually increased, owing to reinvestment and gradually higher yields, and then began to level off and decline slightly as market yields began to fall steadily starting in 2000.

The book income pattern for the credit strategy also displays extended periods of stability, but is occasionally interrupted by some very sharp declines in book income owing to defaults and downgrades. Not surprisingly, the periods 1997–1998, 2002–2003, and 2005 produced some large negative shocks to book income. However, note how strongly it recovered after these credit shocks as credit spreads widened, presenting an opportunity for cash flow generated by the strategy to be reinvested at higher book yields.

The mortgage strategy also displays relatively stable book income. There is an occasional drop in book income, owing to unanticipated changes in prepayments (either faster or slower), but these shocks are not nearly as severe as for credit. As interest rates fell sharply after 2000, MBS book income became more variable as prepayments surged and cash flow was unexpectedly reinvested at lower yields.

The stability of MBS book income is reflected in the monthly book return for the strategy, where book return is defined as book income this period divided by book value at the end of the prior period. Figure 21-3 plots the MBS strategy's monthly book return vs. its monthly market return. Monthly book returns fell in

Monthly Book Return

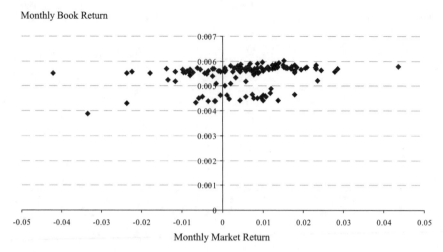

Figure 21-3. Monthly Book Return vs. Monthly Market Return: MBS Portfolio
December 1993–June 2005

a narrow band between approximately 0.40 and 0.60%, whereas monthly market returns fluctuated between approximately –4.25 and +4.50%. A buy-and-hold investor might draw very different conclusions than a total return investor regarding the risk of investing in MBS!

Figure 21-4 presents some summary information on monthly book income for the three buy-and-hold investment strategies. Over the 11.5 years, the MBS strategy produced an average monthly book income of $7.9 million with a standard deviation of $1.3 million, and the lowest figure was $5.4 million. The MBS strategy produced a range of monthly book income of $5.0 million and the average monthly book income in the worse 5% of months (i.e., 7 months) was $5.6 million.

For the credit strategy, the average monthly book income was $7.2 million with a standard deviation of $1.9 million. In sharp contrast to the MBS strategy, the lowest monthly figure for the credit strategy was –$2.1 million. The credit strategy also produced a wide range of monthly book income, a whopping $11.9 million, and the average monthly book income in the 5% tail was $2.3 million.

The agency strategy performed as expected. While average monthly book income ($6.5 million) was less than that for the MBS strategy, the standard deviation was also less at $1.1 million. The agency strategy produced a relatively narrow range ($3.5 million) and its 5% shortfall value, $4.5 million, indicates very little tail risk.

How is monthly book income correlated between MBS and credit? Is there a tendency for the book income for the two strategies to fluctuate together? To highlight the monthly variability of book income we detrend MBS and credit

Figure 21-4. Monthly Book Income Summary Information
MBS, Credit, and Agency Portfolios, December 1993–June 2005

	MBS	Credit	Agency
Mean ($)	7,907,649	7,189,929	6,525,134
Standard deviation ($)	1,260,784	1,902,635	1,145,248
Maximum ($)	10,395,557	9,840,480	7,995,244
Minimum ($)	5,352,440	(2,105,668)	4,459,097
Range ($)	5,043,117	11,946,148	3,536,147
Shortfall (5%) ($)	5,573,724	2,282,657	4,533,466

monthly book income by subtracting the monthly book income for the agency strategy, which is akin to looking at excess book income (à la excess market returns). These net book income values can also be interpreted at net book income for a high-quality financial institution that funds its asset purchases at levels comparable to that of the agencies.

The time series of "net" monthly book income for the MBS and credit strategies are shown in Figure 21-5 and summary information is presented in Figure 21-6. Given the limited occurrence of negative net book income months for the MBS strategy (compared to the credit strategy), adding MBS to a credit portfolio can help reduce the portfolio's overall shortfall risk. For institutions sensitive to the potential for negative book income (net of funding), an MBS allocation can help the institution target a shortfall level that meets its risk profile.

By inspection, the fluctuations in net monthly book income seem uncorrelated and, in fact, the sample correlation coefficient shows that the two series are slightly negatively correlated (–0.08). Out of curiosity, what is the corresponding correlation of monthly market returns? We calculated monthly market total returns for the MBS and credit strategies and subtracted from each the corresponding monthly agency strategy market return to make the returns comparable to the net book income returns. Over the same period, the correlation of MBS and credit net market returns was 0.41.

Note how the two asset classes behave differently in a book accounting world compared to total return. Credit net market returns are less volatile than MBS (standard deviation of monthly net total returns of 41 and 49 bp, respectively), which is quite contrary to the book income world. Credit still underperforms MBS, and we should not expect much of a difference with the book income world, as eventually book income and market returns should converge over the life of the investment. However, the monthly volatility of book income and market returns can be significantly different.

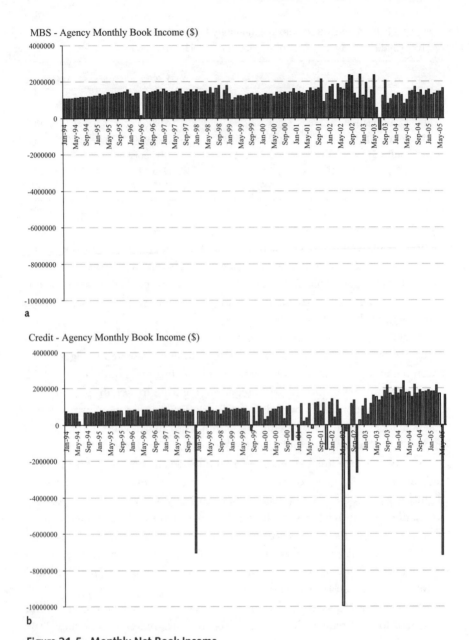

Figure 21-5. Monthly Net Book Income

MBS and Credit (net of agency) Portfolios, December 1993–June 2005

**Figure 21-6. Monthly Net Book Income and Market Returns
Summary Information**

MBS and Credit (net of agency) Portfolios, December 1993–June 2005

	MBS Strategy	Credit Strategy
Monthly Net Book Income		
Mean ($)	1,382,515	664,795
Standard deviation ($)	349,450	1,522,513
Maximum ($)	2,400,313	2,398,497
Minimum ($)	(623,739)	(9,945,674)
Range ($)	3,024,052	12,344,170
Shortfall (5%) ($)	503,741	(4,648,138)
Correlation	−0.08	
Monthly Net Market Returns		
Mean (bp)	5	4
Standard deviation (bp)	49	41
Correlation	0.41	

Why is credit less volatile than MBS when expressed in terms of market returns? Monthly mark-to-market requires credit investors to recognize the market impact of gradual credit deterioration as it occurs each month. In contrast, the book investor reports the cumulative impact of credit deterioration only in the month when the bond is declared credit impaired.[11] Again, cumulative book return should approximately equal cumulative market return over a bond's life. However, in a book accounting framework, the fact that credit securities can experience more extreme monthly negative tails increases the relative portfolio benefit of including MBS to control the portfolio's shortfall risk.

The vulnerability of the credit strategy to shocks is most apparent if we remove the worst 7 months (5% of all months) from the 138 months of the strategy's history. As shown in Figure 21-7, without the 7 worst net book income credit months the average monthly net book income for credit would have been $0.9 million with a standard deviation of $0.5 million. Most notable is the reduction of tail risk, as the book income of the worst month would have been only –$0.8 million (compared to –$9.9 million before) and a range of $3.2 million. Both of these

---

11. For the MBS book income calculation we update the prepayment forecast each month. Some book accounting investors may not do this. Instead they may update, for example, only quarterly. If so, the MBS mortgage book income values may appear smoother in our presentation compared to that experienced by some buy-and-hold investors.

**Figure 21-7. Monthly Net Book Income and Market Returns
Summary Information**

MBS and Credit (net of agency) Portfolios, Excluding the Worst 7 Months for
Credit Strategy, December 1993–June 2005

	MBS Strategy	Credit Strategy
Monthly Net Book Income		
Mean ($)	1,378,920	948,693
Standard deviation ($)	352,308	544,895
Maximum ($)	2,400,313	2,398,497
Minimum ($)	(623,739)	(810,487)
Range ($)	3,024,052	3,208,984
Shortfall (5%) ($)	521,059	(210,512)
Correlation	−0.01	
Monthly Net Market Returns		
Mean (bp)	5	4
Standard deviation (bp)	51	39
Correlation	0.41	

values are somewhat more comparable to the MBS strategy. However, some tail risk remains for the credit strategy as the (5%) shortfall value is –$0.2 million, which, while much less than before (–$4.6 million), is still considerably lower than the shortfall for the MBS strategy. Also notable in Figure 21-7 is that the low correlation of monthly net book income remains even after removing the worst 5% of book income months for the credit strategy. This supports the idea that MBS have a diversification potential in buy-and-hold portfolios beyond their ability to reduce a portfolio's overall tail risk.

CONSTRUCTING BUY-AND-HOLD PORTFOLIOS: ALLOCATION TO MBS AND CREDIT

The historical record suggests that MBS have performed well, that the asset class has little tail risk, and that its monthly book income has low correlation with that for credit, even after removing the negative credit tail event months. Given this diversification potential for MBS, what was the "optimal" historical allocation for an MBS-credit buy-and-hold portfolio over the 1993–2005 period? While the record shows that the MBS strategy outperformed credit and agency strategies from a book income perspective, there are no assurances that this income out-performance will continue. So we focus instead on the risk attributes of MBS in a

Net Book Income

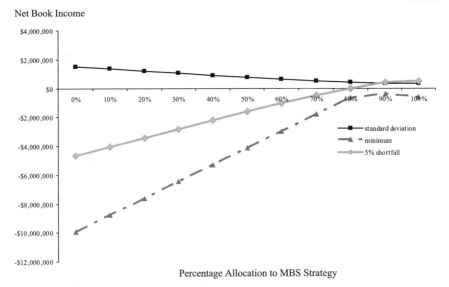

Percentage Allocation to MBS Strategy

Figure 21-8. Monthly Net Book Income Summary Information
MBS and Credit (net of agency) Portfolios, December 1993–June 2005

buy-and-hold portfolio, which are likely to be longer lasting. In other words, how did the book income risk of the portfolio vary depending on the portfolio's percentage allocation to MBS?

Figure 21-8 shows the monthly standard deviation of net book income as well as the minimum monthly book income and shortfall (5% tail, i.e., the average book income in the worst 7 months) for various asset allocations to MBS and credit. For example, with a 0% allocation to the MBS strategy, Figure 21-8 shows the same results as Figure 21-6. As the allocation to MBS is increased (in 10% increments), the standard deviation, minimum, and (5%) shortfall of monthly book income improve steadily. Although the standard deviation declines until the MBS allocation equals 100%, the minimum and (5%) shortfall reach a minimum at a 90% allocation to MBS. If the goal is to obtain a (5%) shortfall greater than zero (i.e., always generate more income than funding cost), this is achieved with an 80% allocation to the MBS strategy. Figure 21-8 highlights the significant risk reduction potential offered by MBS in a buy-and-hold portfolio.

Even after excluding the 5% of months when the credit strategy had the worst net book income, MBS continues to offer substantial risk reduction potential. Figure 21-9 is the same as Figure 21-8 except that the months associated with the worst seven (5%) net book income months for the credit strategy have been removed from the time series. Figure 21-9 shows that MBS continues to offer substantial risk reduction potential even after much of the tail risk has been removed from

Net Book Income

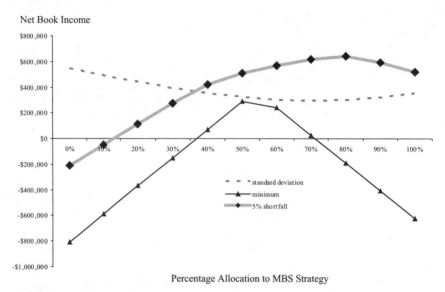

Percentage Allocation to MBS Strategy

Figure 21-9. Monthly Net Book Income Summary Information
MBS and Credit (net of agency) Portfolios, Excluding Worst Seven Months for Credit
Strategy, December 1993–June 2005

the credit strategy. The standard deviation of portfolio net book income is minimized with a 70% allocation to the MBS strategy and the minimum monthly book
income is maximized with a 50% allocation. The (5%) shortfall now achieves a
level greater than zero with a 20% allocation to the MBS strategy.

Even without introducing the superior book income performance of MBS for
buy-and-hold portfolios, we see that MBS offers meaningful diversification
benefits. For institutions worried about shortfall risk (especially net book income less than zero), MBS plays an important role in reducing the shortfall risk to
book income of a credit portfolio. Somewhat surprisingly, even without the negative credit tail event months, MBS continues to offer a risk reduction benefit to
portfolios.

SENSITIVITY TO INITIAL INVESTMENT MONTH FOR CREDIT
AND MBS BUY-AND-HOLD STRATEGIES

The previous section discussed the long-term performance of the MBS and credit
strategies assuming that a buy-and-hold investment was made at the end of 1993.
However, the performance of each strategy may have been sensitive to the choice
of the initial starting month as the portfolio's book income was, of course, influenced by the market yield at the time of the initial investment. How sensitive are

our results to the initial investment month? It would also be informative to explore whether there are more opportune times to invest in the MBS or credit strategies. For example, does investing in the credit strategy when the MBS-credit OAS spread (or yield ratio) is below average produce relatively higher net book income or is its relative OAS advantage offset by subsequent higher defaults and downgrades? Conversely, does investing in the MBS strategy when the MBS-credit OAS spread is above average produce higher net book income or does its relative OAS advantage fully reflect higher likelihood of prepayment surprises?

To answer these questions, we constructed new buy-and-hold MBS and credit strategy portfolios at 3-month intervals beginning in December 1993. We then examined each strategy's subsequent 5-year book income performance. Although these 5-year periods are overlapping and are not independent observations, they do give an indication of what the long-run (i.e., 5-year) performance of an investment in MBS and credit would have been at quarterly intervals over the past 11.5 years. We can also see if the relative performance of MBS vs. credit was related to the ratio of MBS yields to credit yields, or relative OAS spreads, at the beginning of each quarterly period.

First, what is the relationship between a strategy's initial book yield and its subsequent average book income performance? Figure 21-10 shows the initial book yield for each strategy and the subsequent average monthly book income over the following 5 years for each starting calendar quarter. For all three strategies there is a strong linear relationship between the initial yield and the subsequent average monthly book income. In particular, for the agency strategy the relationship is very strong, with a sample correlation equal to 0.98. Not surprisingly, the relationship is less strong for MBS and credit, as unexpected prepayments and credit impairments cause the realized book income to deviate from what was "promised" by the initial book yield. The correlation coefficient for the credit strategy was 0.89, which was greater than that for the MBS strategy at 0.82.

However, while the observed strong linear relationship between initial yield and subsequent income is reassuring to buy-and-hold investors, the relationship does not address whether the level of book income is commensurate with each strategy's book yield. For example, does the level of book income reflect the strategy's initial yield or is there a persistent underproduction of book income from a particular strategy? Furthermore, what is the distribution of monthly book yield during the subsequent 5 years?

To answer these questions, we calculate the *net* (vs. agency) book income performance over the following 5 years and report the mean, standard deviation, minimum, and range for both the MBS and credit strategies (Figure 21-11). (Again, net book income can be interpreted as book income net of funding costs for highly rated institutions.) We also report the shortfall of each strategy measured

MBS Strategy ($)

Average Monthly Book Income

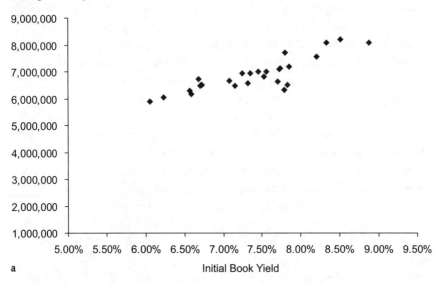

a   Initial Book Yield

Credit Strategy ($)

Average Monthly Book Income

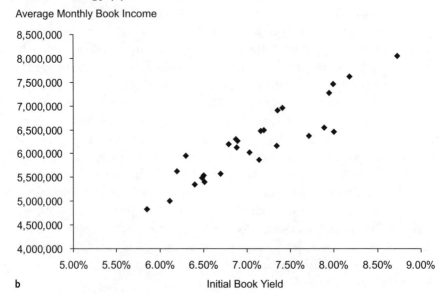

b   Initial Book Yield

Figure 21-10. Initial Book Yield and Subsequent 5-Year Average Monthly Book Income Performance

MBS, Credit, and Agency Portfolios, Quarterly Starting Periods, December 1993–June 2005

Agency Strategy ($)

Average Monthly Book Income

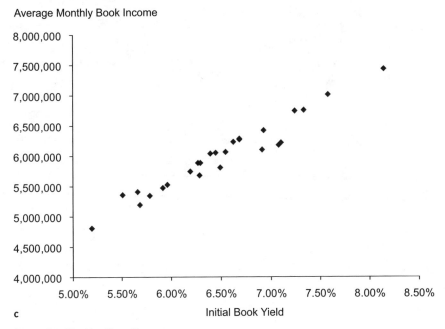

c   Initial Book Yield

Figure 21-10. (continued)

by the net book income for the worst 3 months (i.e., 5% of the months) over the following 5-year period.[12] For example, assuming an investment at the end of June 1998, the average monthly net book income for the MBS and credit strategies was $938,002 and $950, respectively. The standard deviation of net book income for the MBS and credit strategies was $191,207 and $1,473,199, respectively. In addition, MBS had a minimum monthly net book income of $682,127 and a range of $803,493 compared to credit's minimum of –$8,771,326 and range of $10,040,564. Finally, the worst 3 months (5% of all 60 months in a 5-year period) produced an average net book income of $518,487 and –$7,421,970 for the MBS and credit strategies, respectively.

Figure 21-11 shows that the MBS strategy enjoyed higher average monthly net book income with a lower standard deviation compared to the credit strategy for just about any 5-year period since December 1993. The MBS strategy started to underperform the credit strategy in 2000, as the subsequent unexpected very

---

12. Given that we are assuming 5-year investment periods, our last observation is for strategies that commence at the end of June 2000.

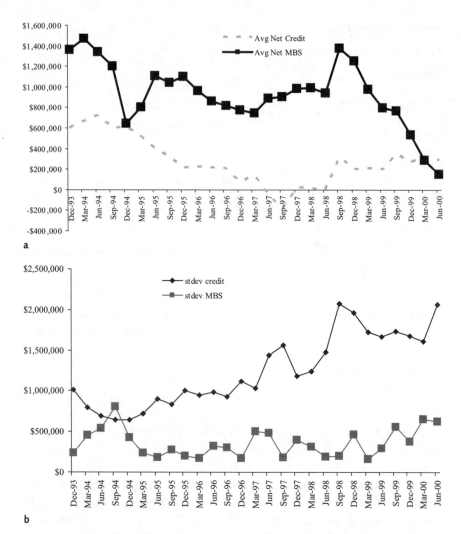

Figure 21-11. Five-Year-Horizon MBS and Credit Portfolios: Average, Standard Deviation, Minimum, Range and 5% Shortfall of Net Monthly Book Income
(a) Average Monthly Net Book Income; (b) Standard Deviation Monthly Net Book Income; (c) Minimum Monthly Net Book Income; (d) Range of Monthly Net Book Income; (e) 5% Shortfall of Monthly Net Book Income, Quarterly Starting Periods, December 1993–June 2005

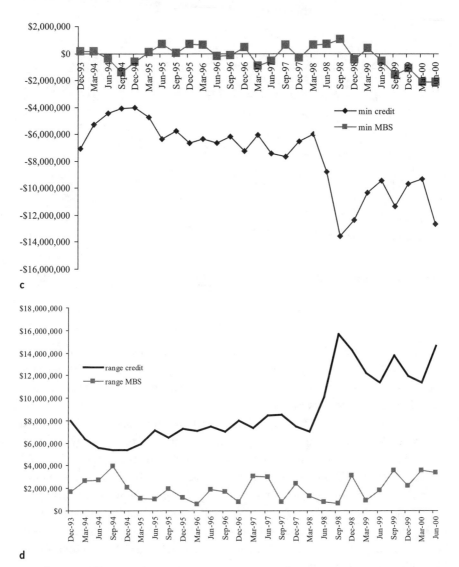

Figure 21-11. (continued)

fast prepayment speeds and low market yields caused MBS book income to drop sharply. Most noticeably, however, the minimum, range, and (5%) shortfall of monthly book income for the MBS strategy are relatively stable over time and reflect very little tail risk compared to the credit strategy. The figure shows that the MBS strategy generally produces greater net book income than the credit strategy, but there are months in which MBS relative performance is stronger or weaker.

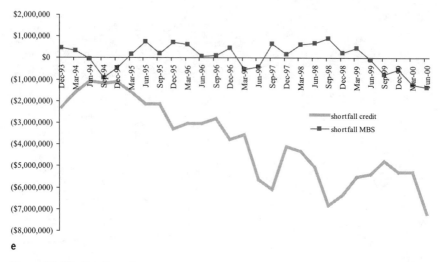

e

Figure 21-11. (continued)

Are there any indications at the beginning of the strategy, such as MBS-credit relative yield or OAS, that would help forecast the relative performance of the MBS and credit strategies and assist buy-and-hold investors to make asset allocation decisions for new investment inflows?

To investigate this, at the beginning of each quarterly period, we calculated the ratio of the MBS strategy book yield to that for the credit strategy and then plotted (Figure 21-12) the subsequent difference between the average net book incomes for the two strategies. Figure 21-12 suggests that there is only a moderate positive relationship (sample correlation is equal to 0.50) between the MBS yield advantage at the beginning of the 5-year holding period and its subsequent net book income performance relative to the credit strategy. However, there does seem to be some basis for buy-and-hold investors to use relative yields as a basis for allocating new cash between MBS and credit. In other words, a sector's relative yield advantage does not appear to have been completely squandered by subsequent credit or prepayment events.

Another potential relative performance indicator is the difference in OAS between MBS and credit. We calculated the OAS difference of the two strategies at the beginning of each quarter and plotted (Figure 21-13) the subsequent difference between the average net book incomes for the two strategies. While the relationship is positive (sample correlation is equal to 0.36), the relationship is weaker than for relative yields.

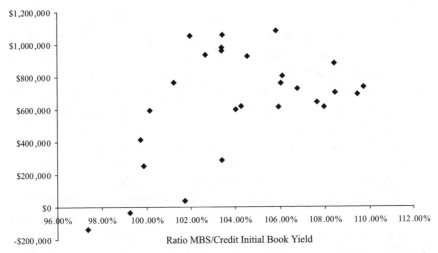

Average Net Book Income MBS - Average Net Book Income Credit

Figure 21-12. Initial Relative Yields and Subsequent 5-Year Average Relative Net Book Income Performance

MBS and Credit Portfolios, Quarterly Starting Periods, December 1993–June 2005

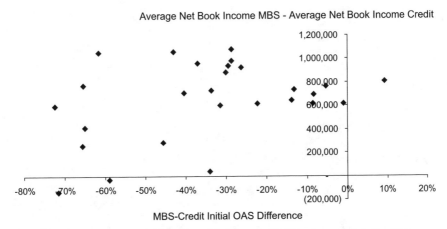

Average Net Book Income MBS - Average Net Book Income Credit

MBS-Credit Initial OAS Difference

Figure 21-13. Initial OAS Difference and Subsequent 5-Year Average Relative Net Book Income Performance

MBS and Credit Portfolios, Quarterly Starting Periods, December 1993–June 2005

CONCLUSION

This chapter uses book accounting measures (book income and book return) to evaluate the long-term performance of a buy-and-hold investment in MBS. These are the same measures used by significant participants in the MBS market. By constructing buy-and-hold investment strategies over the period from 1994 to 2005, we compared the long-term book income performance of various asset classes (MBS, credit, and agency). We showed that in comparison to an investment in credit, an investment in MBS offers superior book income with lower volatility and tail risk. Moreover, MBS monthly book income has low correlation with credit book income, making it a good portfolio diversifier and warranting significant MBS allocations. These results also hold when we analyze MBS buy-and-hold performance and risk profile over shorter, 5-year, holding periods. Finally, there seems to be moderate correlation between relative MBS-credit market yields (and OAS differences) and subsequent relative MBS book income performance.

MANAGING CENTRAL BANK RESERVES

Why does the subject of central bank reserve management warrant a separate discussion? Collectively, central banks hold a high percentage of the U.S. government debt (28.5% as of June 2005) and an increasing percentage of other fixed-income asset classes. The size of their investments and the potential market influence of their transactions make it important for every fixed-income investor to understand central banks' constraints and objectives. Likewise, it is important for central bank reserve managers to keep up with the best practices of fixed-income asset managers, some of which are presented in this book. While reserve managers represent a special group benchmarked to highly customized indices in a buy-and-hold or total return framework, they are nevertheless similar to other institutional fixed-income investors in many ways. Moreover, most central banks share similar portfolio management objectives and constraints, so that a strategy followed by one of them is likely to be of interest to others.

Traditionally, reserve portfolios have been invested in short-duration Treasury securities denominated in USD, euro (or deutschemark prior to EMU), and Japanese yen. The main function of the reserve portfolio is to provide liquidity for a possible currency intervention. The structure of the reserve portfolio has been traditionally determined by the liquidity and capital preservation constraints and, to a lesser degree, by the return maximization objective. Lately, a number of long-term factors have shifted this balance from constraint-driven portfolios toward total return maximization. In Chapter 22, we discuss these factors in some detail, but the two major ones have been the creation of the ECB Reserve Portfolio in Europe and the rapid growth of reserve portfolios at several Asian central banks. In fact, some central banks' reserves have reached a size at which total return management becomes impossible, and the buy-and-hold approach becomes a practical imperative. In such cases, the reserves may be separated into a large buy-and-hold portfolio and a smaller alpha portfolio. This separation of the reserve

portfolio by investment objectives is gradually replacing the traditional partitioning into liquidity and investment portfolios.

The degree of central bank reserve managers' risk taking is regulated by self-
imposed (or, for EMU member banks, mandated by ECB) benchmarks. For most
banks, the actual portfolio holdings are never meant to match the benchmark
composition, but rather reflect security selection and the macro views of the
manager. For some, however, the benchmark represents a neutral portfolio that
the manager will own in the absence of active views on the market. In either case,
most of these benchmarks reflect the duration target and asset mix consistent with
the bank's tolerance for losses and return objective. Most are highly customized
benchmarks that are marked to market monthly. Managers of the largest portfolios are also increasingly interested in the book accounting indices described
in Chapter 9. In Chapter 22, we discuss methodologies for defining total return
benchmarks for a typical reserve portfolio.

As reserve portfolios expand beyond Treasury securities, many of the concepts
we introduce in this book for commercial asset managers become relevant to reserve managers as well. These include sufficient diversification of issuer-specific
credit risk, index replication techniques for spread product (including MBS), swap
indices, and book accounting indices. The usual transition of a central bank toward assuming risks other than yield curve risk is to expand into U.S. agencies
first, followed by sovereign and supranational debt, bank credit, ABS, corporate
bonds, and MBS. Central banks are always looking to minimize "headline risk"
inherent in corporate debt and are increasingly interested in understanding the
highly technical U.S. MBS market.

Chapter 22 presents a quantitative framework developed to address two major
issues in designing a central bank benchmark: setting the benchmark's target
duration and determining its allocation (if any) to non-Treasury spread assets. To
assist with the all-important decision on the benchmark duration, we developed
a framework we call the "no-view Treasury portfolio optimization." This strategy
maximizes the expected return under an unchanged yield curve assumption
(hence, "no-view"), subject to shortfall constraints that are typically quite tight,
reflecting the essential central bank consideration of capital preservation.

If invoked infrequently (e.g., once a year), no-view optimization can be used to
set benchmark duration targets. When used more frequently (e.g., monthly), it
can be used as a tool that enhances performance by dynamically allocating positions along the yield curve. This method has been shown to consistently produce
respectable information ratios. It is also easily customized for a particular benchmark definition, risk tolerance, and required minimum return.

Chapter 22 also deals with techniques for setting an allocation to non-Treasury
asset classes, relying on historical correlations between such asset classes and

Treasuries. When such correlations are low, adding spread assets to a Treasury benchmark may actually reduce the overall volatility while enhancing the expected return. For example, a modest allocation to corporate bonds can reduce the return volatility of a Treasury portfolio. Various candidate asset classes are examined for their long-term diversification benefits vs. Treasuries, risk and return characteristics, and the degree of diversification required to get to acceptably low levels of event risk.

Today, liquidity portfolios of central banks continue to have relatively short-duration targets. In Chapter 23, we examine conditions in which positive annual total returns of short-term (1–3 years) Treasury indices cannot be taken for granted. We show that, conceivably, the timing of yield changes and the steepness of the curve may work together to push the annual total return into the negative. In this chapter we shed some light on the likelihood of this event and present a framework for analyzing such conditions. Although the study was performed several years ago, the proposed approach is relevant whenever the yield curve is low and flat.

We are confident that in the foreseeable future, central bank reserve holdings will continue to represent a significant share of fixed-income assets, and that central banks' actions will be carefully followed by all market participants. Reserve portfolios will look increasingly like other institutional fixed-income pools of assets, covering an increasing segment of the global bond market, including fixed-income derivatives. Quantitative methodologies for benchmark design and portfolio engineering will be shared among asset managers and reserve managers for the mutual benefit of both groups.

22. Total Return Management of Central Bank Reserves

Several events over the past decade have led central banks and other national wealth managers to re-examine their portfolio investment strategies. Perhaps the most important factor was the decline in the supply of U.S. Treasuries over much of the 1990s. This asset class has historically comprised a substantial percentage of dollar reserves held by non-U.S. official institutions. As of September 2004, non-U.S. official institutions' holdings of marketable U.S. government debt comprised 29% of outstanding marketable supply.[1] Figure 22-1 shows the dramatic decline in the supply of U.S. Treasuries between 1997 and early 2002. The drop in the supply of U.S. Treasuries was truly remarkable, in terms of both magnitude and suddenness. No one had anticipated such a dramatic turn of events. This down trend has reversed to some extent since the beginning of 2002, in response to the U.S. slowdown, tax cuts, and increased spending for national security. However, the supply of U.S. Treasuries currently available is still substantially lower than it was in the mid-1990s.

Figure 22-2 illustrates the effect of the change in the supply of U.S. Treasuries on the composition of the Lehman Brothers U.S. Aggregate Index. As of December 2001, Treasuries made up only 22% of the index, compared with 46% at the beginning of the 1990s. Despite the subsequent reversal in the supply of U.S. Treasuries since 2002, their share of the Aggregate Index has increased only slightly. In contrast, the share of credit assets in the index increased from 19% in 1998 to 27% by early 2003. As of the beginning of September 2004, the market shares of Treasuries and credit were about even at 24% each, well behind the 36% share for mortgage-backed securities.

Based on research first published by Lehman Brothers in 2002.

1. Federal Reserve Board of Governors, Flow of Funds Accounts of the United States, Z.1 Release, Second Quarter 2004 and U.S. Treasury Monthly Statement of the Public Debt of the United States, August 31, 2004.

Figure 22-1. Market Value of Outstanding Supply of U.S. Treasuries
All Maturities, December 1991–August 2004

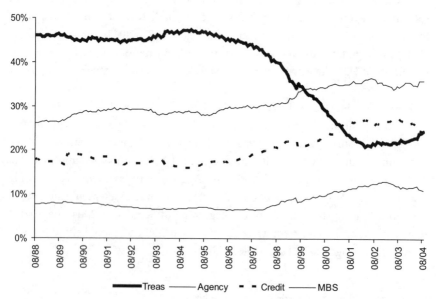

Figure 22-2. Asset Class Composition of the U.S. Aggregate
August 1988–August 2004

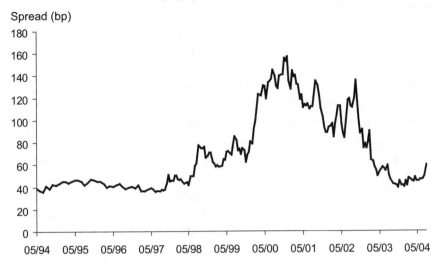

Figure 22-3. Ten-Year Aa-Rated Industrial Corporate Spreads to Off-the-Run U.S. Treasuries
May 1994–August 2004

The large shift in the relative supply of Treasuries and spread product has contributed to the repricing of spread assets. Figure 22-3 shows the spread to off-the-run Treasuries of 10-year Aa-rated industrial corporate bonds since May 1994. Note that corporate spreads began to widen after it became apparent that the absolute Treasury supply was declining. Corporate spreads continued to widen as the economy cooled and investors' perceptions of default risk increased. Following the reversal in the supply of U.S. Treasuries in 2002, corporate spreads tightened dramatically, reaching a level of 40–60 bp.

National reserve managers responded in several ways to the reduction in Treasury supply and the increased relative attractiveness of spread product. First, many institutions expanded their investments in other asset classes that had long been acceptable, such as Aaa-rated sovereign and U.S. agency debt (including both debentures and, in rare instances, mortgage pass-through securities). Others began to explore new asset classes such as Aaa-rated asset-backed securities with stable cash flows. Over the years, official institutions have conducted research and have developed their back-office and trading capabilities in these asset classes. These particular assets have several attributes that make them a reasonable substitute for a portion of official U.S. Treasury holdings. First, they are all Aaa-rated, which allows institutions to add these assets without having to staff a large credit analysis operation. Second, these assets involve very little "headline," or "C-1," risk.[2] Official institutions have long been sensitive to the potential political problems of holding debt securities of an entity that is receiving unfavorable public scrutiny. Simply holding the entity's debt could give the appearance of endorsing its behavior.

Another response to reduced Treasury supply and the headline risk attached to specific credit assets has been consideration of interest rate swaps as a source of credit spread exposure. As the supply of swaps is potentially unlimited and does not depend on a single issuer, the swaps market avoids many of the idiosyncratic risks that accompany the U.S. Treasury and credit markets. Official institutions can invest cash in short-term bank and corporate assets and increase their spread duration by receiving the fixed-rate leg of an interest-rate swap.

The second major event of the past decade to influence reserve management practices was the emergence of the euro. The sharing of a single currency permits better reserves efficiency, allowing EMU member countries to pool their foreign currency reserves. Instead of each national central bank (NCB) holding significant reserves to buffer balance-of-payment and exchange-rate fluctuations both within Euroland and with other countries, the ECB can meet the same requirements on behalf of all members with much smaller reserves overall. Consequently, the ECB has unshackled a significant amount of NCB reserves from the need to provide immediate liquidity. While it is still a possibility that NCBs may be called on to support the ECB in a major foreign exchange crisis, the ECB has given the NCBs the opportunity to manage their reserves with more of a total return objective. Instead of considering reserves solely as a liquidity reservoir, reserves (or some portion thereof) can be viewed as a national asset and maximizing its total risk-adjusted rate of return as a national priority.

A related event in the 1990s was a reconsideration of the efficacy of foreign exchange intervention on a massive scale. Previously, central banks felt that they needed vast sums in dollars available at a moment's notice to challenge speculators whom they believed were destabilizing the currency. However, as massive intervention did not always accomplish its goal, they began to search for other ways to bolster their credibility in order to defend their currency. The increased use of joint intervention among several central banks and a willingness to intervene on a smaller, but much more sustained, scale have given central banks much-needed time when combating destabilizing currency movements. Central banks no longer have to manage their dollar reserves with the possibility that they would have to liquidate a substantial portion of reserves on short notice. Instead, they can credibly and effectively defend their currencies by demonstrating a commitment to

---

2. "C-1" risk refers to an event that figures prominently on the front page of the Money & Investing section (page C-1) of the *Wall Street Journal*.

liquidate dollar holdings as needed over time. This change in intervention think-ing also allows central banks to manage their dollar reserves with more of a total return and less of a liquidity objective.

The emergence and deepening of the euro credit market has been another event over the decade that has caused central banks and other national wealth managers to re-examine their investment strategies. In the past, if an official institution wanted to invest in a credit product, it could do so only in dollars. This limitation was a major disincentive for official investors to expend the time and resources to develop credit expertise. Today, there exists a thriving euro credit market that is expected to grow significantly in the future. The potential rewards of credit analy-sis are now much greater and can be applied to the management of all national financial assets.

Also recent is the willingness of central banks to gradually sell portions of their gold holdings. While this activity will have little short-term impact, the long-run implications for reserve management are substantial. It is reasonable to expect that some proceeds from gold sales will be redeployed in higher yielding fixed-income assets. Consequently, fixed-income assets are likely to grow from this activity, and there will be a need to find attractive ways to invest these assets.

All of these events have caused central banks to review the investment strategies for their reserve portfolios. In some cases, particularly for the NCBs in EMU mem-ber countries, the new circumstances may allow currency allocations to change significantly, possibly including a portion in the institution's domestic currency. Even when relieved of the burden of supporting the currency, however, central banks must consider many factors in setting their currency allocations besides to-tal return maximization (e.g., balance of trade and liability matching). This deci-sion is a complex one, and the primary considerations vary from one country to the next. For these reasons, the details of the currency allocation decision are out-side the scope of this chapter, which focuses on total return management.

Within each currency, central banks and other official institutions are now thinking more like traditional portfolio managers in the private sector. As a result of this shift in investment strategy, institutions are encountering two questions commonly faced by traditional asset managers:

1. How do they set the portfolio's duration target?

2. How much of the portfolio (if any) should be allocated to various non-Treasury asset classes?

We devote a separate section of this chapter to each of the two questions and show how quantitative portfolio techniques can be used to address them.

NO-VIEW OPTIMIZATION AS A METHOD FOR SETTING THE PORTFOLIO DURATION TARGET

If an institution manages its reserves to maximize risk-adjusted returns, what should be the duration target of its portfolio? Extending the duration or the interest-rate sensitivity of a portfolio tends to increase the portfolio's expected returns but at the cost of increased market value volatility. Generally, portfolio managers have no incentive to extend the portfolio's duration unless they expect to be compensated sufficiently for the increase in risk. One traditional approach to duration target setting is to select the duration value that historically has produced the best risk-adjusted performance or the greatest return per unit of risk (Sharpe ratio).

One objection to using historical Sharpe ratios for portfolio duration targeting is that realized returns can vary widely from one year to the next. In contrast, volatilities are much less variable. Consequently, historical Sharpe ratios fluctuate significantly depending on the time period selected. Using the Sharpe ratio may be appropriate for an organization that plans to change its portfolio's duration target relatively infrequently.

Moreover, the Sharpe ratio alone does not accurately represent the approach to risk and reward typical of official institutions such as central banks. The implicit message of such a ratio is that any risk may be acceptable as long as it carries the promise of sufficient expected returns. This may be reasonable for a long-term total return manager, but does not reflect the constraints under which reserves managers must operate. In many cases, the prime directive given by a reserves board to its managers resembles the doctor's oath: "First, do no harm." In other words, the goal is to achieve the highest possible returns while maintaining liquidity and minimizing the probability of negative total returns over the course of a review period.

Limitations of the Sharpe ratio maximization approach became particularly apparent to managers of U.S. dollar-denominated reserves in 1994. This was a year of significant interest-rate tightening by the Federal Open Market Committee of the U.S. Federal Reserve Board that saw 3-month Treasury bill yields rise from 3.08 to 5.69%. Returns for many fixed-income assets were close to zero for the year, including assets in the 1- to 3-year maturity bucket traditionally preferred by central banks and often selected by the Sharpe ratio approach. Relying on short-duration assets, with their typical low yields, is no guarantee of positive total returns!

Investors in short-duration Treasuries faced a similar situation at the end of October 2004 when the yield on the Lehman 1- to 3-Year Treasury Index dropped to 2.48%, one of the lowest levels on record. This low yield level provided relatively thin protection against the prospect of a negative total return over the next

12 months. The small safety margin against negative returns was particularly troublesome given the steepness of the yield curve and its implications for future yield increases and negative price returns. Investors in this part of the curve might have been concerned that an unexpectedly strong and fast economic recovery could result in the first negative annual return for 1- to 3-year Treasuries.

In light of these events, many institutions have sought a quantitative mechanism for setting the portfolio's duration under a "no loss" requirement. One response is to use historical data to answer the following question: What fixed combination of Treasury assets of various maturities would have maximized the long-term average total return subject to the constraint that the total return in every review period was positive? As one would expect, the answer differs depending on the portfolio review period. To guarantee no negative returns over any given monthly review period requires an extremely conservative portfolio duration. Guaranteeing nonnegative returns for longer review periods (e.g., a quarter, half-year, or full year) allows for progressively longer durations.

There are other drawbacks to this type of analysis. Essentially, it assumes that an allocation based on historical data that never had a negative return over a given review period is unlikely to have one in the future. Yet this is not foolproof. An allocation having a constraint of no negative annual return based on data before 1994 would have had a negative return in 1994. (As a result, the same analysis repeated 1 year later would indicate a shorter duration—but only after the fact.) However, duration targets based on shorter review periods would have succeeded in avoiding negative returns for 1994.

Another drawback of this static approach is that it assumes a single target duration held constant over time. In fact, this decision is often reviewed periodically, based on the current level and slope of the yield curve. Higher yields mean that a larger rise in rates can be absorbed without experiencing a loss, so a steeper yield curve provides a bigger incentive to extend along the curve. Each time the target duration is revisited, the decision should therefore consider the current market environment, as well as the requirement to achieve a minimum return (e.g., zero) over the review period.

To improve on the static approach and at the request of several central banks, we developed the Lehman Brothers no-view (NVO) Treasury optimization strategy. This dynamic strategy imposes a minimum return requirement (e.g., zero), but allows the target duration to change periodically in response to market conditions. In this method, historical returns are used to determine the risk of various points on the yield curve, but not to project their expected returns. To estimate expected returns, the investment manager is assumed to have "no view" on the movement in interest rates. He simply assumes that the current yield curve will be the yield curve at the end of his review period. Given the current yield curve and the review period (say, one quarter), expected returns and standard deviations of returns can be calculated for various maturity points. The minimum return requirement, at a given level of confidence, specifies the allowable amount of risk. With expected returns and a minimum return requirement we can construct the portfolio with the highest expected return for this given amount of risk. The duration of this portfolio can then be considered to be the optimal target duration.

NVO is designed to boost portfolio performance while meeting institutional requirements for liquidity and capital preservation. It can be used for two important portfolio management applications. The first is to determine the portfolio's target duration, as described earlier. While the optimization produces an optimal portfolio allocation to a given set of assets, the key output in this application is the target duration. This process is repeated on a fairly infrequent basis, perhaps annually. Later, we present an example of using NVO to determine a portfolio's target duration.

The second application of NVO uses the optimization as a portfolio strategy tool to help outperform a benchmark. In this case, the optimization is carried out frequently (e.g., monthly), and the portfolio is rebalanced to match the optimal allocation along the yield curve. Later we discuss and present an example of this second application of NVO. Throughout this section, we provide illustrations of the strategy's behavior based on data through the end of 2001.

Application 1. Using No-View Optimization to Determine a Portfolio's Target Duration

The key feature of NVO is that there is no attempt to predict future interest rates. Instead, we assume that the current par yield curve remains unchanged over the review period. In essence, this is a naïve yield curve model that maintains the constant prediction of no change in the yield curve. In practice, weekly and monthly changes are extremely hard to predict. Few sophisticated yield curve forecasting models offer better forecasts than the naïve model. Rather than having portfolio allocations driven by imprecise estimates of yield curve changes, NVO sets the expected return for the upcoming period equal to current yield plus rolldown plus a convexity correction.[3] The procedure employs statistical optimization to select assets offering the highest expected return for a given amount of risk using historical

---

3. For two assets of the same duration, the one with greater positive convexity will outperform in an extreme yield curve shift in either direction. The convexity term reflects this as an advantage in expected return. The convexity correction is $(\frac{1}{2}) \times$ convexity $\times$ (volatility)^2. This correction increases the expected return of longer duration (i.e., more convex) assets so that expected returns of all assets in the investment set can be compared on a convexity neutral basis.

return volatilities (usually computed by taking the standard deviation of realized total returns over, say, the last 60 months).

NVO chooses portfolio asset weights (and, hence, the portfolio's duration) to maximize expected return subject to risk constraints. The optimization has three basic parameters that can be adjusted to reflect the risk tolerance of a particular institution: the length of the review period, the minimum allowable return, r_{min}, and the level of confidence, n, in achieving the minimum return. The length of the review period is defined as the performance interval for the strategy. For example, if the strategy is required to produce a specific minimum return each quarter, then the length of the review period is 3 months. For very short review periods, the strategy is forced to select a very-short-duration portfolio, as a small rise in yields can easily offset the yield earned on the portfolio. However, lengthening the review period generally allows the strategy to take more risk (i.e., by increasing the portfolio's duration), as the portfolio has additional time to earn a yield to offset any adverse price movement.

The minimum return threshold specifies the minimum critical return value, which the portfolio is allowed to violate only a certain percentage of the time, depending on n. In other words, the expected return on the portfolio over the review period must be at least n standard deviations above the worst-case return, r_{min}. Together, r_{min} and n determine the statistical frequency that the portfolio's return may fail to achieve a return equal to r_{min}. As explained more fully later, a given review period, minimum return threshold, and confidence level determine the set of allowable portfolios, each with its own expected return, $E[r_{portfolio}]$ and risk, $\sigma_{portfolio}$.

Figure 22-4, which shows a stylized distribution function of a portfolio's total return, presents a graphic description of a portfolio that satisfies the risk constraint. For example, if the review period is quarterly, the minimum return threshold is 1%, and the confidence level is one standard deviation, the optimization procedure looks for the portfolio with the highest expected return whose expected return and standard deviation of returns satisfy the risk constraint. In this example, a portfolio whose standard deviation of returns, $\sigma_{portfolio}$, equals 50 bp and whose quarterly expected return is at least 1.50% satisfies the risk constraint. The amount of risk the strategy can take can be increased by lengthening the review period, by lowering the minimum return threshold, or by reducing the confidence level. Moving any parameter in the opposite direction makes the strategy more conservative.

It is important to note that a portfolio that satisfies the risk constraint (ex ante) may sometimes violate the minimum return threshold (ex post). There is always the possibility that some extraordinary event will cause yields to rise faster than ever before. However, if the volatility of future yield changes is assumed to be

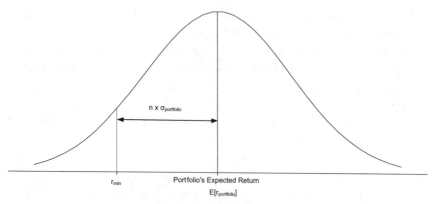

Figure 22-4. No-View Optimization, Risk Constraint Schematic

similar to the historical volatility, then the probability of losses beyond the confidence interval is relatively small and is known in a statistical sense. If returns are normally distributed, then for $n = 1$, the probability that returns will violate the minimum return threshold is 15.9%.[4] If a higher level of confidence is required, a greater value of n should be used. If $n = 2$ standard deviations, the probability that returns will violate the minimum return threshold falls to 2.3%. As the value of n increases, the optimization selects a less volatile (i.e., shorter-duration) portfolio in order to reduce the chance that portfolio returns will violate the minimum return threshold.

In mathematical terms, NVO finds the asset weights, w_i, for all assets eligible to be included in the portfolio (i.e., the investment set) that solve the following linear programming problem:[5]

Maximize $\sum_i w_i E[r_i]$ such that

$$\sum_i w_i (E[r_i] - n \times \sigma_i) = r_{min}, \tag{22-1}$$

and $w_i \geq 0$ for all i (i.e., no short sales allowed), where $E[r_i]$ is the expected return of the ith security in the investable set; n is the number of standard deviations used to determine the confidence level; σ_i is the return volatility of the ith security

---

4. If portfolio returns are normally distributed, then the probability that returns are within 1 standard deviation from the mean is 68.3%. Consequently, the probability that returns are less than 1 standard deviation below the mean is 15.9% [$= \frac{1}{2} \times (1 - 0.683)$].

5. Results are similar whether one uses a quadratic procedure to calculate portfolio risk or a linear procedure that simply assumes that all Treasury returns are perfectly correlated. To err on the side of conservatism, our procedure assumes that Treasury returns are perfectly correlated in the risk constraint, implying that all points on the yield curve experience their worst-case returns simultaneously.

Figure 22-5. Portfolio Duration Targeting: No-View Optimization Inputs
June 30, 2001

U.S. Treasury Maturity	6/30/2001 Yield (%)	Quarterly Expected Return (%)	Standard Deviation of Quarterly Returns (%)
3-month	3.65	0.89	0.07
6-month	3.63	0.89	0.15
1-year	3.63	0.89	0.33
2-year	4.26	1.05	0.77
3-year	4.60	1.13	1.16
4-year	4.89	1.21	1.54
5-year	4.95	1.23	1.96
7-year	5.27	1.32	2.53
10-year	5.40	1.38	3.31
20-year	5.91	1.54	3.85
30-year	5.81	1.56	4.90

in the investable set; and r_{min} is the minimum return threshold for the review period. The following example shows how NVO can be used to set a portfolio's target duration. Assume that the manager's review period is one quarter, the minimum return threshold is 25 bp/quarter, and the confidence level is 1 standard deviation. Based on the yield curve as of June 30, 2001, and the historical volatilities of quarterly asset returns over the preceding 5 years, the inputs for the optimization are presented in Figure 22-5.

Figure 22-6 displays the information in Figure 22-5 graphically. The solid black line shows the expected return as a function of the maturity of the Treasury security. The dotted line represents the minimum return threshold of 25 bp/quarter. For each maturity, quarterly expected return equals the current yield plus rolldown plus a convexity adjustment, assuming that the yield curve remains unchanged over the review period. The vertical bars at each maturity represent 1 standard deviation around the expected return value. For example, for the 2-year Treasury, the quarterly expected return is 1.05%, and a 1-standard-deviation interval around the expected return is given by 1.05% – 0.77% to 1.05% + 0.77%, or 0.28 to 1.82%. Note that the 2-year Treasury delivers the required minimum return in the worst case but all longer maturity Treasuries do not.

NVO then finds the best combination of issues to maximize expected returns subject to the risk constraint. Figure 22-7 presents the portfolio produced by NVO. The portfolio contains a 33% weighting in the 3-month Treasury bill and a 67% weighting in the 3-year Treasury note. By buying some of the low-risk asset

Expected Return (%)

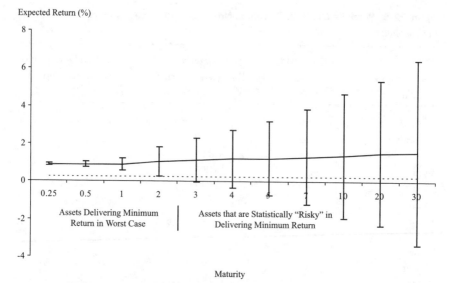

Figure 22-6. No-View Optimization Expected Returns of U.S. Treasury Assets with
1-Standard-Deviation Intervals
June 30, 2001

(i.e., the 3-month Treasury bill) the optimization is able to buy some riskier assets (i.e., the 3-year Treasury note) to obtain a higher expected return. The portfolio's target duration is given by the duration of the portfolio found by the optimization: 1.85 years. As will be shown later, concentration constraints can be
imposed so that NVO will not recommend too high a concentration in a single
position.

There are several ways to use the output of the optimization to form a performance benchmark. An investment manager can use the optimal portfolio (with
its precise asset weights) as a performance benchmark. Alternatively, the duration
of the optimal portfolio can be used strictly to determine the target duration for
the portfolio. It is then possible to define a performance benchmark with this tar-

Figure 22-7. Portfolio Duration Targeting, No-View Optimization Results
June 30, 2001

U.S. Treasury Issue	Percent Market Value in Portfolio	Duration
3-month	33	0.24
3-year	67	2.64
	100	1.85 = Target duration

get duration but with asset weights determined using other methods that might better reflect a manager's investment restrictions. One example would be to subdivide the Lehman Treasury Index into a short-duration and a long-duration subindex, and then weight the two subindices so that benchmark duration equals the NVO target duration.

As discussed, NVO uses the current yield curve as of the analysis date to set the target duration. However, this target may become "stale" as the yield curve changes over time. If left unchanged for too long, it could drift away from the current optimal target duration. On the other hand, if the portfolio's target duration is recomputed too frequently, portfolio duration and risk properties may become highly variable. A reasonable compromise is to recompute the target duration whenever the yield curve moves significantly. Perhaps the easiest way to determine staleness is to set recomputation triggers based on the cumulative change in the steepness and level of the Treasury curve.

Application 2. Using No-View Optimization to Outperform an Established Performance Benchmark

NVO is also helpful when trying to outperform a prespecified benchmark. For this application, the risk parameters r_{min} and n can be set based on the institution's overall risk constraint or set to match the benchmark's risk profile. In addition to the main risk constraint, the procedure may also contain a concentration constraint (discussed later) that limits exposure to any single asset. Investors can then employ NVO to search for a portfolio that has a higher expected return than the benchmark but satisfies the risk constraint.

As an example, suppose an investor's performance benchmark is a 3-year maturity U.S. Treasury note. Assuming a quarterly performance horizon, we express expected returns, return volatility, and the minimum allowable return in terms of percentage per quarter. Let us initially suppose that the minimum allowable return is a fixed *negative* 25 bp/quarter (r_{min} = –0.25) and the confidence level is set to 1 standard deviation ($n = 1$). The investment set consists of 3-month, 6-month, 12-month, 2-year, 3-year, 5-year, 7-year, 10-year, 20-year, and 30-year Treasuries.

NVO seeks to maximize expected return subject to the risk constraint. If the investment set contains only securities with maturities of 3 years or less, the procedure would choose a 100% investment in the 3-year note because the 3-year note offers the highest expected return and does not violate the risk constraint. In one particular case (in April 1996), the portfolio's expected return was 1.61% (per quarter).

However, with the actual investment set, the procedure improves on a 100% investment in the 3-year note by placing 60% of asset value in the 2-year note and

40% in the 7-year note. The very small decrease in expected return that comes from moving assets from the 3-year to the 2-year note moves the portfolio further away from its risk constraint. The optimization procedure then finds that it can allocate this "unused" portion of the risk constraint to a position in the 7-year note and achieve a pickup in portfolio expected return of 6 bp/quarter (= 1.67% – 1.61%) while still satisfying the risk constraint.

In this example, the risk constraint had a static minimum return threshold. However, this threshold could be made variable and customized to reflect the performance benchmark. The next section illustrates some possible enhancements to the risk constraint.

Setting the Minimum Return Threshold

The minimum return threshold can be defined in a variety of ways. The simplest is to set the minimum return to be a fixed constant as was shown earlier (e.g., r_{min} = –25 bp/quarter). However, floating thresholds and relative thresholds are also possible. A *floating* minimum return threshold ties the minimum worst-case return to the expected return of the benchmark portfolio. One example of a floating threshold would be to set the threshold to the expected return on the benchmark less 50 bp (quarterly). In other words, the floating threshold would be:

$$r_{min} = E[r_{bench}] - 50 \text{ bp},$$

where $E[r_{bench}]$ is the expected return on the benchmark. In this case, as interest rates and the expected return of the benchmark rise, the worst-case return rises as well.

A *relative* minimum return threshold ties the minimum worst-case return to the minimum worst-case return of the benchmark. In other words, a relative minimum return threshold uses an equation of the form

$$r_{min} = E[r_{bench}] - n \times \sigma_{bench},$$

where $E[r_{bench}]$ is the expected return on the benchmark; σ_{bench} is the benchmark's return volatility; and n is the number of standard deviations used in the risk constraint [Equation (22-1)].

In general, a relative threshold tends to produce a portfolio with a risk similar to that of the benchmark. How so? The risk constraint requires that

$$E[r_{portfolio}] - r_{min} = n \times \sigma_{portfolio}.$$

Substituting $E[r_{bench}] - n \times \sigma_{bench}$ for r_{min}, we have

$$E[r_{portfolio}] - E[r_{bench}] = n \times (\sigma_{portfolio} - \sigma_{bench}).$$

If the expected returns on the portfolio and the benchmark are close, then $\sigma_{portfolio}$ will be close to σ_{bench}.

In the case of a relative minimum return threshold, changes in the investor's value of n have little effect on the portfolio's volatility. To see this, step through the changes in the risk constraint as n increases. If the investor increases his value of n, the minimum return threshold (r_{min}) decreases. Holding everything else unchanged, the lower threshold permits selection of a portfolio with higher expected return and risk since the minimum return threshold is now further away from the portfolio's expected return. However, this effect is immediately offset because the increase in the confidence level implies that the investor wishes to reduce the probability that his portfolio's return violates the now-lower minimum return threshold. In other words, the effect on portfolio risk ($\sigma_{portfolio}$) of the reduction in r_{min} is offset by the demand for greater confidence that the portfolio's return does not fall short of r_{min}. Consequently, changes in the investor's value of n tend to have little effect on $\sigma_{portfolio}$.

The relative threshold tries to keep the worst-case return for the portfolio close to the worst-case return for the benchmark. This allows the optimization procedure to create a portfolio that is expected to outperform the benchmark at no additional risk.

We now turn to some advanced features of NVO.

Inversion Detection

NVO is based on the assumption of a positive risk-return trade-off. When the yield curve is inverted, the assumption of an unchanging yield curve is not tenable because it implies that short-maturity bonds have both lower risk and higher expected returns than long-maturity bonds. In order to avoid using the unchanging yield curve assumption during such periods, an inversion detection procedure can be invoked that requires buying the benchmark during inversions.

One detects yield curve inversion as follows:

1. Divide assets in the investment set into a short bloc (3-month to 2-year) and a long bloc (3-year to 10-year).

2. Calculate the average expected return for each bloc.

3. If the expected return on the long bloc is less than the expected return on the short bloc, then the yield curve is inverted and inversion detection requires investment in the benchmark.

If the yield curve was inverted in the previous period, then the quarterly expected return on the long bloc this period has to be at least 5 bp higher than the short bloc for the procedure to declare that inversion has ended. This 5-bp buffer provides stability during periods in which the yield curve is on the cusp of inversion.

Dynamic Adjustment of the Minimum Return Threshold

Investors can also implement NVO with a dynamic adjustment feature that automatically varies the risk constraint depending on year-to-date performance. Specifically, if the portfolio has underperformed the benchmark beyond a certain limit, then dynamic adjustment tightens the minimum return threshold (i.e., increases r_{min}). Conversely, if the portfolio has outperformed, then the minimum return threshold is loosened. (We represent the change in the minimum return threshold owing to the dynamic adjusted feature by the term Δ_{dyn}.)

The dynamic adjustment feature is very flexible. Dynamic adjustment can be used with different types of minimum return thresholds (e.g., absolute and relative). The rule can be uniform throughout the year or it can change in ways most suitable for the investor. For example, some investors may choose to set dynamic adjustment (Δ_{dyn}) equal to zero in the fourth quarter irrespective of the level of year-to-date outperformance. This feature helps to protect earlier gains as the portfolio nears the end of its annual review period. We use this feature in the example that follows.

To use dynamic adjustment, the investment manager specifies a maximum amount of *annual* underperformance to be tolerated *relative to the performance target*. If the manager is using an absolute minimum return threshold, then the minimum annual return is the performance target. If he is using a relative minimum return threshold, then the benchmark is the performance target. Once he specifies an annual underperformance limit, the following two quantities can be defined:

Pro rata limit = Annual underperformance limit
$\times$ Fraction of a year since January 1,

and

Excess underperformance = MAX[realized YTD underperformance
– *Pro rata* limit, 0].

If year-to-date underperformance is less than the pro rata limit, then the risk constraint is left unchanged. However, if the year-to-date underperformance is greater than the pro rata limit, then the risk constraint is tightened by the amount of the excess underperformance. The risk constraint can be tightened until the portfolio is forced to hold cash (i.e., duration = 0). In the case of year-to-date outperformance, dynamic adjustment loosens the risk constraint by the amount of realized year-to-date outperformance. In summary, dynamic adjustment equals excess underperformance or year-to-date actual outperformance (or is equal to 0 in the fourth quarter).

For example, if an absolute minimum return threshold is used and the portfolio underperforms this target, then dynamic adjustment tightens the risk constraint (raises r_{min}), which shortens the portfolio's duration. The shorter duration reduces the risk that the portfolio will further underperform its target and also gives the portfolio a chance to recover a portion of its absolute underperformance via earnings on its short-duration assets.

Dynamic adjustment works in much the same way if the investor uses a relative minimum return threshold. The effect of dynamic adjustment on the relative minimum return threshold is as follows:

$$r_{min} = E[r_{bench}] - n \times \sigma_{bench} - \Delta_{dyn}.$$

To illustrate dynamic adjustment, consider the case in which the annual underperformance limit is set to 200 bp, implying a quarterly pro rata limit of 50 bp. At the start of the year, the amount of dynamic adjustment equals zero. If first-quarter realized underperformance exceeds 50 bp, then the risk constraint tightens by the amount of the underperformance in excess of 50 bp. If the amount of underperformance is less than 50 bp, then dynamic adjustment equals zero. Figure 22-8 illustrates the dynamic adjustment function at the end of the first quarter.

If year-to-date underperformance exceeds 100 bp at the end of the second quarter, then the minimum return threshold is increased by the amount of the underperformance in excess of 100 bp. If it is less than 100 bp at that point, then the dynamic adjustment equals zero. Figure 22-9 illustrates the dynamic adjustment function at the end of the second quarter.

In each period, if the portfolio has year-to-date outperformance, then dynamic adjustment loosens the risk constraint by the full amount of year-to-date outperformance. However, in an effort to safeguard year-to-date gains going into the fourth quarter, the amount of dynamic adjustment equals zero at the start of the fourth quarter irrespective of the amount of year-to-date outperformance.

Depending on year-to-date performance, dynamic adjustment moderates the aggressiveness of NVO in its search for excess returns while still meeting the yearly risk constraint. Figure 22-10 shows how dynamic adjustment can alter the risk of the portfolio. In this example, the portfolio has outperformed, producing a positive

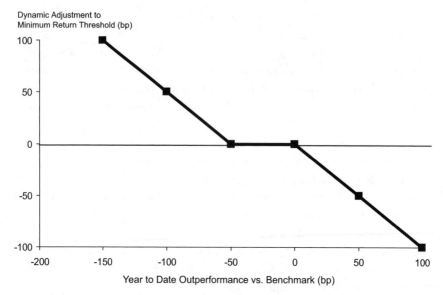

Figure 22-8. Dynamic Adjustment Function at the End of the First Quarter

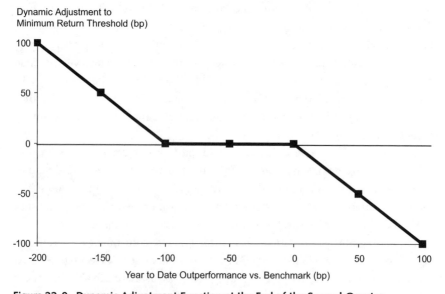

Figure 22-9. Dynamic Adjustment Function at the End of the Second Quarter

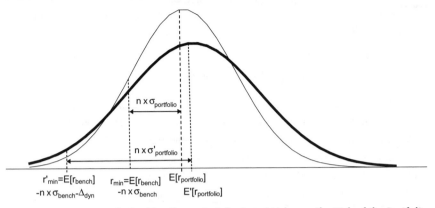

Figure 22-10. Impact of a Positive Dynamic Adjustment Value on the Risk of the Portfolio

dynamic adjustment value. In turn, the minimum return threshold is reduced by the dynamic adjustment value. Assuming that the investor leaves his confidence level, n, unchanged, the optimization selects a riskier (i.e., $\sigma'_{portfolio} > \sigma_{portfolio}$) portfolio if it will produce greater expected returns while still meeting the new risk constraint, r'_{min}.

Conversely, if the portfolio had underperformed, it would have produced a negative dynamic adjustment value equal to the excess underperformance. Consequently, the minimum return threshold is increased by the dynamic adjustment value (Figure 22-11). Assuming that the investor leaves n unchanged, the optimization now selects a less risky (i.e., $\sigma''_{portfolio} < \sigma_{portfolio}$) portfolio to maximize expected returns while meeting the new risk constraint (r''_{min}). It is important to

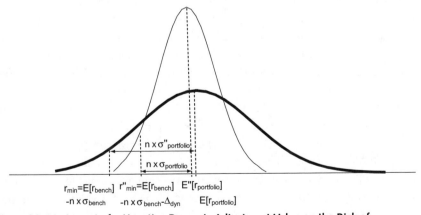

Figure 22-11. Impact of a Negative Dynamic Adjustment Value on the Risk of the Portfolio

note that the new portfolio is less risky in an absolute sense (i.e., lower duration), not necessarily in a relative sense (i.e., duration closer to that of the benchmark).

Other Advanced Features of No-View Optimization

NVO seeks to maximize expected return subject to the risk constraint. Depending on the shape of the yield curve and historical volatilities, NVO may select a portfolio with a duration very different from the benchmark duration. This may make some managers uncomfortable, despite the fact that the portfolio should not violate the minimum return threshold at the stated confidence level.

To further reduce the possibility of violating the minimum return threshold, NVO allows the user to specify constraints on the maximum and minimum portfolio duration (the *duration constraint*). Typically, duration constraints are set to keep portfolio duration within a symmetric band around the benchmark duration. It also allows the user to set the maximum portfolio percentage allocation to any single security (the *concentration constraint*). This feature allows investors to reduce the potential for peculiar movements at points along the yield curve to affect relative performance.

Later in this section, we present data on the effects of these two constraints on the performance of the portfolio.

Evaluating the Performance of No-View Optimization

It is instructive to examine in detail the performance of the NVO strategy. When is the strategy likely to outperform and underperform the benchmark?

To illustrate the ability of NVO to outperform a benchmark, we simulated the performance of the strategy over a 15-year period. The investment set consisted of 3-month, 6-month, 12-month, 2-year, 3-year, 5-year, 7-year, 10-year, 20-year, and 30-year Treasuries. The performance benchmark was a 3-year duration Treasury Index and the portfolio was rebalanced at the end of each month according to the optimization solution. The performance horizon was quarterly. We used a relative minimum return threshold and inversion detection, and we set the confidence level equal to one. The concentration constraint was set to 60% and the dynamic adjustment mechanism allowed a 50-bp shortfall per quarter (i.e., a 200-bp annual underperformance limit) before any tightening of the risk constraint.

Quarterly results for three different settings of the duration constraint are shown in Figure 22-12. The first set of columns contains results for a very loose duration constraint (0 to 10 years). The second requires the portfolio's duration to be within 1 year of the benchmark's duration. The last set imposes a very tight duration constraint, forcing the portfolio's duration to be within 0.5 year of the

Figure 22-12. Performance of No-View Optimization: Impact of the Duration Constraint

Performance Benchmark—3-Year Duration U.S. Treasury Index, 1986–2000

| | | Duration Constraint | | | | | | | | |
| | | 0–10 Years | | | 2–4 Years | | | 2.5–3.5 Years | | |
Year	Benchmark Return (%)	Return (%)	Difference (%)	Duration	Return (%)	Difference (%)	Duration	Return (%)	Difference (%)	Duration
1986	12.80	12.10	-0.68	4.89	14.60	1.80	4.00	13.50	0.68	3.50
1987	2.32	2.88	0.56	3.06	2.88	0.56	3.06	2.88	0.56	3.06
1988	6.27	6.46	0.19	2.80	6.46	0.19	2.80	6.45	0.19	2.80
1989	12.80	13.50	0.69	3.17	13.50	0.71	3.14	13.50	0.74	3.10
1990	9.23	9.24	0.01	3.03	9.24	0.01	3.03	9.24	0.01	3.03
1991	12.90	16.10	3.28	3.44	14.70	1.88	3.26	14.30	1.42	3.14
1992	6.13	6.48	0.35	4.41	6.72	0.59	3.42	6.63	0.50	3.21
1993	7.54	13.50	5.95	7.71	9.00	1.46	3.89	8.36	0.83	3.46
1994	-0.80	-1.04	-0.25	3.03	-1.04	-0.25	3.03	-1.04	-0.25	3.03
1995	13.70	21.90	8.18	7.16	15.70	2.04	3.94	14.70	1.02	3.49
1996	3.83	3.65	-0.18	3.63	3.54	-0.29	3.44	3.48	-0.35	3.40
1997	7.82	8.31	0.49	3.89	9.06	1.24	3.75	8.44	0.63	3.46
1998	8.23	8.64	0.41	3.83	8.76	0.53	3.51	8.84	0.61	3.28
1999	0.43	0.27	-0.16	3.24	0.27	-0.16	3.24	0.27	-0.16	3.22
2000	9.96	8.75	-1.21	2.92	8.75	-1.21	2.92	9.30	-0.67	2.97
Average	7.54	8.72	1.18	4.01	8.15	0.61	3.36	7.93	0.38	3.21
Standard deviation			2.61			0.93			0.57	
Information ratio			0.45			0.65			0.67	

benchmark's duration. We discuss the results for the optimization with the widest duration constraint (i.e., 0 to 10 years) in detail. The wide duration constraint helps to magnify the performance of the strategy and highlights those environments in which the strategy is likely to outperform or underperform.

In an effort to maximize expected returns, in a positive yield curve environment NVO has a tendency to produce a portfolio with a duration longer than the benchmark. Since a positively sloped yield curve is the usual situation, NVO is typically long its benchmark. Note that the relative duration of the portfolio is likely to be only loosely related to the degree of curve steepness. The optimization tries to maximize expected returns and does so in all positively sloped curve environments. Even if the curve is only moderately steep, the optimization tries just as hard to add duration as it would if the curve were particularly steep. In contrast, the relative duration of the portfolio is likely to be more closely related to the looseness of the risk constraint. As the risk constraint is loosened, the optimization maximizes expected returns with more latitude to increase portfolio volatility (i.e., duration).

Figure 22-13 shows the monthly relative duration of the optimized portfolio vs. the benchmark since January 1986. Note that the relative duration is typically greater than 1.0, indicating that the portfolio generally has a longer duration than the benchmark.

Since the strategy usually begins with a relatively long duration, it initially outperforms in a given year if rates decline. This outperformance, in turn, loosens the risk constraint (via dynamic adjustment), which allows the strategy to increase its relative duration for the next month. If the market continues to rally, the strategy's outperformance increases, which further loosens the risk constraint and permits further relative duration extension. Consequently, in a trending and rallying market, this strategy will likely perform well.

If, instead of continuing to rally, rates increase, the strategy begins to underperform. Depending on the magnitude of the underperformance, the risk constraint is tightened, which tends to reduce the portfolio's duration. If the market continues to sell off, the portfolio's relative underperformance likely continues (although at a diminished rate), which produces a further tightening of the risk constraint (and duration reduction).

This duration reduction from the tightening risk constraint serves two purposes. First, if the portfolio's duration was initially greater than the benchmark's, it brings it closer, which tends to slow down any further relative underperformance. Second, the duration reduction serves to protect the portfolio's absolute return. If the rising-interest-rate trend continues, the portfolio's absolute duration declines further (i.e., relative duration less than 1.0) and tends to "lock in" the portfolio's absolute performance for the year. However, it is important to note

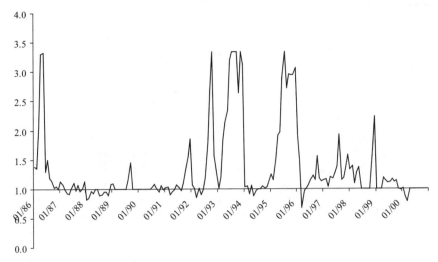

Figure 22-13. Ratio of No-View Optimization Portfolio Duration to Benchmark Duration
3-Year Duration Benchmark, Relative Minimum Return Threshold, Quarterly Review
Period, Monthly, January 1986–December 2000

that the portfolio's relative performance is not locked in. In fact, if rates continue
to rise, the portfolio (whose duration has been shortened relative to the benchmark) may begin to outperform the benchmark.

In a "choppy" market, the strategy's performance will likely stay close to the
benchmark's, depending on the monthly pattern of rate movements. If the market initially rallies, the strategy outperforms and its relative duration extends as
described earlier. If the market then sells off, the strategy gives up some of (perhaps exceeding) its prior month's gain, producing a possible tightening of its risk
constraint. Consequently, as the market bounces around, the strategy produces
small gains and losses.

To better understand how NVO performs, let us examine actual annual performance of the strategy. Figure 22-14 shows the performance of NVO for the
years 1990 through 2000. Note that in every year but one (1994), the strategy had
positive absolute returns.

Figure 22-15 shows the slope (10-year vs. 2-year) of the U.S. Treasury curve for
the years 1990 through June 2004. Inversion detection occurred in early 1990,
mid-1998, early 1999, and for most of 2000. The figure also shows the yield of the
5-year Treasury note. As discussed earlier, we would expect NVO to perform well,
both absolutely and relatively, in a trending and a rallying market. Based on Figure 22-15, Figure 22-16 lists the years in which the level of yields declined somewhat steadily throughout much of the year. How well did the strategy perform?

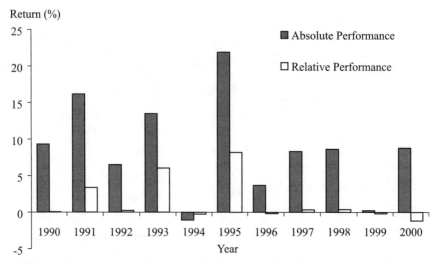

Figure 22-14. No-View Optimization Annual Performance
Absolute and Relative Returns, 3-Year Duration Benchmark, Relative Minimum Return
Threshold, Quarterly Review Period, 1990–2000

The answer is that it performed extremely well, both absolutely and relatively,
in 4 of these 5 years. As the market rallied, the portfolio, with its relatively long-
duration position, outperformed the benchmark. As the portfolio outperformed,
the risk constraint was loosened, allowing the portfolio to lengthen further, producing additional outperformance as the market steadily rallied.

It is informative to compare performance in the years 1993 and 1995. Although yields declined in both years, they fell only in the second half of 1993,
whereas they fell continuously throughout 1995. In addition, rates fell more than
twice as much in 1995 as they did in 1993. As a result, 1995 was able to profit
more from the relaxation of the risk constraint and achieve greater absolute and
relative outperformance compared with 1993.

Note, however, the peculiarly poor performance in 2000. Rates rose early in
the year, producing underperformance. Although rates fell sharply in the second
half of the year, inversion detection kicked in, which prevented the strategy from
going long-duration vs. the benchmark as the market rallied. Instead, inversion
detection required that the portfolio invest in the benchmark, locking in its relative losses from the first half of the year. However, the portfolio and the benchmark were able to enjoy some respectable absolute returns for the year.

As Figure 22-15 shows, interest rates increased steadily during most, if not
all, of the following three years: 1994, 1996, and 1999. Figure 22-17 reveals that
the strategy underperformed its benchmark in each of these 3 years. However, the

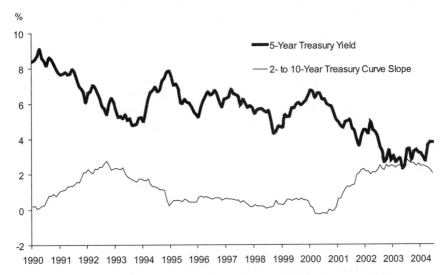

Figure 22-15. Two- to 10-Year Treasury Curve Slope and 5-Year Treasury Yield
1990–2004

underperformance was relatively small. As discussed earlier, the increase in yields caused the relatively long-duration portfolio to underperform the benchmark. As rates continued to rise, the underperformance persisted, but was mitigated by the tightening of the risk constraint.

Note the performance in 1996: relative performance of –0.18%, but an absolute performance of 3.65%. In this year, rates rose in the first half but declined in the second, with a small overall increase for the year. As rates initially rose, the strategy underperformed relative to the benchmark, causing its duration to drift

Figure 22-16. No-View Optimization in Years of Generally Falling Yields
3-Year Duration Benchmark, Relative Minimum Return Threshold, Quarterly Review Period, Absolute and Relative Performance

Year	Inversion Detection during Year?	Portfolio's Average Duration	Portfolio's Relative Performance (%)	Portfolio's Absolute Performance (%)
1991	No	3.44	3.28	16.14
1993	No	7.71	5.95	13.49
1995	No	7.16	8.18	21.87
1998	Yes	3.83	0.41	8.64
2000	Yes	2.92	–1.21	8.75

Figure 22-17. No-View Optimization in Years of Generally Rising Yields
3-Year Duration Benchmark, Relative Minimum Return Threshold, Quarterly Review
Period, Absolute and Relative Performance

Year	Inversion Detection During Year?	Portfolio's Average Duration	Portfolio's Relative Performance (%)	Portfolio's Absolute Performance (%)
1994	No	3.03	−0.25	−1.04
1996	No	3.63	−0.18	3.65
1999	Yes	3.24	−0.16	0.27

toward that of the benchmark. As rates subsequently fell, the portfolio's absolute performance improved but its relative underperformance persisted.

The strategy managed to outperform in 1997 both absolutely (+8.31%) and relatively (+0.49%), despite the rise in yields in the first third of the year, because it was able to maintain a long-relative-duration position as yields rallied for the remainder of the year.

The years 1990 and 1992 were roughly neutral relative performance years. In 1990, rates rose initially, producing underperformance. However, they rallied strongly in the second half of the year, allowing the strategy to perform in line with the benchmark. In 1992, rates rose initially, then rallied for most of the year allowing the portfolio to outperform and extend duration. Unfortunately, rates rose strongly in the last 4 months of the year and erased much of its earlier relative outperformance.

In general, the strategy produces good relative performance in years in which interest rates trend downward. However, the downward trend must occur before any market sell-off causes the dynamic adjustment mechanism to constrain its relative and absolute duration position. The danger for the strategy is if interest rates rise sharply, causing underperformance and a tightening of the risk constraint that limits potential for relative and absolute market gains if rates were to fall subsequently. After a period of rising rates, investors may be tempted to remove the dynamic adjustment feature. However, this feature protected the portfolio nicely during some of the most difficult market environments in which rates continued rising. Overall, the strategy follows the successful trader's maxim: "Let your profits run, but cut your losses early."

Is there a particularly good time to begin this strategy? As discussed, the strategy has a bias to be long-duration vs. the benchmark. Should investors implement the strategy when the curve is particularly flat (but not inverted) or steep? Con-

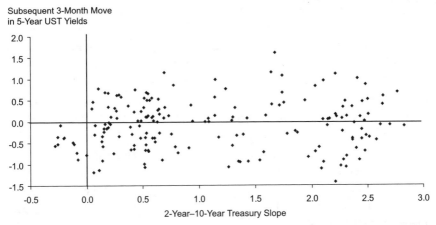

Figure 22-18. Two- to 10-Year Treasury Curve Slope vs. Subsequent 3-Month Move in 5-Year Treasury Yield
June 1989–June 2004

ventional wisdom suggests that when the curve is steep, it is a signal that economic recovery may begin soon, causing interest rates to rise. Conversely, when the curve is flat, it is a signal of an impending economic slowdown, leading to lower interest rates. If conventional wisdom holds, then it may be better to implement this strategy when the curve is relatively flat rather than when it is steep.

However, conventional wisdom may not be a good guide. Figure 22-18 plots the 2- to 10-year Treasury spread and the subsequent 3-month move in 5-year Treasury yields. It shows that the current slope of the yield curve is not a clear indicator of subsequent moves in the 5-year Treasury. Interestingly, the figure shows that when the yield curve is inverted, the 5-year Treasury yield declines over the next 3 months. This empirical result may persuade some investors to go long-duration vs. the benchmark. However, NVO with inversion detection requires investing in the benchmark when the curve is inverted. If inversion detection were disabled, the inverted curve would cause the optimization to produce a relatively short-duration portfolio. Consequently, some investors may decide not to implement NVO if the curve is inverted. In general, there is no particularly good or bad time to implement NVO. Investors can rely on the dynamic adjustment feature to limit losses if they happen to begin the strategy at an inopportune time.

Evaluating Variants of No-View Optimization

Figure 22-12, shown earlier, presented simulation results for three different settings of the duration constraint and revealed the following pattern: As the duration constraint is tightened both average outperformance and the volatility of out-performance decrease. A tighter duration constraint forces the portfolio to replicate the benchmark more closely, diminishing the strategy's potential outperformance. However, the figure also showed that tightening the duration constraint increases the strategy's information ratio.[6]

Which duration constraint to use? It is preferable to use a moderate duration constraint because it gives the portfolio a chance for greater absolute outperfor-mance for roughly the same information ratio. Against a 3-year constant dura-tion benchmark, this would point to the 2- to 4-year duration constraint. This strategy achieved an average outperformance of 61 bp/year. The volatility of outperformance was 93 bp/year, producing an information ratio of 0.65.

To examine the effect of the concentration constraint, Figure 22-19 compares the results of two optimizations that are identical in every respect except for the concentration constraint. The first (called "standard") has the concentration con-straint set to 60%, whereas the second has no concentration constraint. Both have the duration constraint set to within 1 year of benchmark duration, as well as inversion detection and dynamic adjustment of the minimum return threshold.

The concentration constraint has a minor effect on realized performance, in-creasing average outperformance by 4 bp (from 57 to 61 bp) but also increasing the volatility of outperformance by 10 bp (from 83 to 93 bp). Overall, the concen-tration constraint slightly reduces the strategy's information ratio from 0.69 to 0.65. However, commonsense notions of diversification argue for avoiding highly concentrated investments in a portfolio. In this case, the investor would want to weigh the analytical cost of the concentration constraint against its intuitive benefits.

Figure 22-20 compares the "standard" analysis to two variants of the strategy in order to investigate the effects of (1) dynamic adjustment and (2) inversion de-tection. The first variant does not use dynamic adjustment of the minimum return threshold. The second does not use inversion detection, so it does not invest in the benchmark during inversions. All other parameter settings are identical. Fig-ure 22-20 shows that dynamic adjustment allows the optimization to be more aggressive, returning 21 bp of additional average outperformance (0.61 vs. 0.40 bp) and 19 bp of increased outperformance volatility. Overall, the inclusion of the dynamic threshold adjustment increased the information ratio from 0.54 to 0.65.

---

6. Information ratio is average outperformance relative to the performance benchmark divided by the volatility of the outperformance. The information ratio and the Sharpe ratio are closely related. The Sharpe ratio measures an asset's risk and return vs. cash, whereas the infor-mation ratio measures a portfolio's risk and return vs. the portfolio's benchmark. If the bench-mark is cash, then the Sharpe ratio and information ratio are identical.

Figure 22-19. Performance of No-View Optimization: Impact of the Concentration Constraint 1986–2000

Year	Benchmark Return (%)	"Standard" Case 60% Concentration Constraint			No Concentration Constraint		
		Return (%)	Difference (%)	Duration	Return (%)	Difference (%)	Duration
1986	12.80	14.60	1.80	4.00	14.50	1.71	4.00
1987	2.32	2.88	0.56	3.06	2.99	0.67	3.06
1988	6.27	6.46	0.19	2.80	6.87	0.60	2.93
1989	12.80	13.50	0.71	3.14	13.50	0.70	3.15
1990	9.23	9.24	0.01	3.03	9.18	-0.05	3.04
1991	12.90	14.70	1.88	3.26	14.40	1.57	3.25
1992	6.13	6.72	0.59	3.42	6.41	0.28	3.37
1993	7.54	9.00	1.46	3.89	9.00	1.46	3.88
1994	-0.80	-1.04	-0.25	3.03	-1.04	-0.24	3.02
1995	13.70	15.70	2.04	3.94	15.30	1.56	3.76
1996	3.83	3.54	-0.29	3.44	3.64	-0.19	3.37
1997	7.82	9.06	1.24	3.75	9.00	1.18	3.75
1998	8.23	8.76	0.53	3.51	8.79	0.56	3.54
1999	0.43	0.27	-0.16	3.24	0.28	-0.15	3.27
2000	9.96	8.75	-1.21	2.92	8.84	-1.12	2.93
Average	7.54	8.15	0.61	3.36	8.11	0.57	3.35
Standard deviation			0.93			0.83	
Information ratio			0.65			0.69	

Figure 22-20. Performance of No-View Optimization: Impact of Dynamic Adjustment and Inversion Detection 1986–2000

Year	Benchmark Return (%)	"Standard" Case Dynamic Adjustment + Inversion Detection			No Dynamic Adjustment			No Inversion Detection		
		Return (%)	Difference (%)	Duration	Return (%)	Difference (%)	Duration	Return (%)	Difference (%)	Duration
1986	12.80	14.60	1.80	4.00	14.40	1.60	3.55	14.60	1.80	4.00
1987	2.32	2.88	0.56	3.06	3.06	0.74	2.77	2.88	0.56	3.06
1988	6.27	6.46	0.19	2.80	6.52	0.25	2.79	6.46	0.19	2.80
1989	12.80	13.50	0.71	3.14	13.70	0.86	3.05	12.80	-0.01	3.41
1990	9.23	9.24	0.01	3.03	9.22	-0.02	3.02	8.83	-0.41	3.07
1991	12.90	14.70	1.88	3.26	13.50	0.63	2.93	14.70	1.88	3.26
1992	6.13	6.72	0.59	3.42	6.59	0.47	3.10	6.72	0.59	3.42
1993	7.54	9.00	1.46	3.89	8.12	0.58	3.23	9.00	1.46	3.89
1994	-0.80	-1.04	-0.25	3.03	-0.93	-0.13	3.00	-1.04	-0.25	3.03
1995	13.70	15.70	2.04	3.94	15.50	1.78	3.91	15.70	2.04	3.94
1996	3.83	3.54	-0.29	3.44	2.99	-0.84	3.59	3.54	-0.29	3.44
1997	7.82	9.06	1.24	3.75	8.32	0.51	3.40	9.06	1.24	3.75
1998	8.23	8.76	0.53	3.51	8.76	0.53	3.51	8.29	0.06	3.93
1999	0.43	0.27	-0.16	3.24	0.39	-0.04	3.14	0.22	-0.21	3.39
2000	9.96	8.75	-1.21	2.92	9.09	-0.87	3.00	9.44	-0.52	3.00
Average	7.54	8.15	0.61	3.36	7.94	0.40	3.20	8.08	0.54	3.43
Standard deviation			0.93			0.74			0.91	
Information ratio			0.65			0.54			0.60	

Inversion detection also improved average outperformance. Figure 22-20 shows that inversion detection increased average outperformance by 7 bp (0.61 vs. 0.54 bp) at a negligible 2-bp increase in outperformance volatility. Inversion detection improved the strategy's information ratio from 0.60 to 0.65.

Overall, in this example, we find that the best NVO strategy is one with a moderate duration constraint (within 1 year of the benchmark), a 60% concentration constraint, inversion detection, and dynamic adjustment of the minimum return threshold. This variant of the strategy produced an average annual outperformance of 61 bp to the 3-year duration benchmark, with an information ratio of 0.65.

No-view Treasury optimization has demonstrated an ability to outperform a short Treasury performance benchmark while meeting a central bank's need for safety and liquidity. In addition, it can be used to set a portfolio's duration target.

METHODS FOR DETERMINING THE PORTFOLIO'S ALLOCATION TO NON-TREASURY ASSETS

The Investment Case for Non-Treasury Assets

As discussed earlier, some central banks are considering managing their dollar reserves with more emphasis on liquidity and are contemplating the possibility of adding non-Treasury securities to their dollar portfolios. Naturally, a relevant question is whether the non-Treasury market is liquid enough for participation by official institutions. Most portfolio managers, especially since the various traumatic economic events of the late 1990s, desire liquidity. Issuers, acting in their own self-interest, have responded by issuing debt in larger and larger issue sizes. For example, in response to the Treasury buyback announcement in 2000, Fannie Mae and Freddie Mac expanded their benchmark and reference note programs with their large issue sizes and regular issuance intervals.[7] The intention of these programs is to reduce debt cost by directly satisfying the liquidity demands of investment managers. Other issuers have responded similarly, dramatically increasing the average issue size over the decade, as shown in Figure 22-21. The net effect is that the growth in average issue size has increased the liquidity of credit issues, allowing official institutions to participate effectively.

Adding non-Treasury assets to a portfolio may still raise questions regarding liquidity. While many highly rated non-Treasury assets are relatively liquid, they are not as liquid as U.S. Treasuries. It is useful to note, however, that a very strict

---

7. Average agency new issue size also spiked in 2000 because the inverted yield curve discouraged issuance of callable agency debt, which is typically smaller in size. Once the yield curve became positively sloped, callable issuance resumed and the average new issue size dropped from the high 2000 level.

Issue Size ($ million)

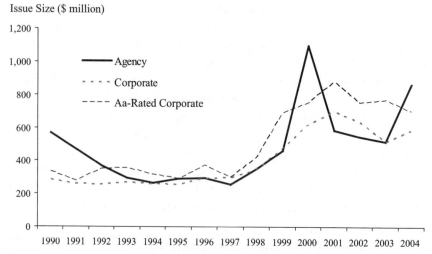

Figure 22-21. Average New Issue Size in the U.S. Agency and Credit Markets
All Issues with at Least $150 Million Outstanding, 1990–2004

liquidity requirement for a portfolio containing non-Treasury assets can be satisfied by the use of derivatives. For example, suppose a central bank wishes to have
a relatively high exposure to the credit sector but is worried about liquidity. Instead of constraining the benchmark to hold a smaller-than-desired percentage in
credit assets, the central bank can allow the use of futures, swaps, and structured
products to replicate a portion of the desired credit exposure. As these derivatives
are liquid instruments (more so than many individual corporate names), a central
bank can accomplish a higher benchmark weighting to the credit sector while
satisfying its liquidity requirement.[8]

One way to measure the investment potential of non-Treasury assets is to
examine their historical duration-matched performance vs. Treasuries. Figure
22-22 presents mean excess returns over duration-matched Treasuries for the four
spread asset classes for the period from August 1988 through June 2004. The figure also shows the volatility of these excess returns as well as the information ratio, which is defined as the mean excess return divided by the standard deviation.
For the period, agencies had the highest information ratio—a result of having
both the highest average excess return and the lowest standard deviation of excess
returns. Supranationals had the next highest information ratio, followed by cor-

8. See Chapter 4. For example, a portfolio of swaps and CDX replicated the U.S. Credit Index with a tracking error volatility of 29 bp/month during August 2002–September 2004.

Figure 22-22. Monthly Excess Returns over Duration-Matched Treasuries
August 1988–June 2004

	Average (bp)	Standard Deviation (bp)	Annualized Information Ratio
Agencies	3.5	18.8	0.65
Sovereigns	1.3	55.2	0.08
Supranationals	3.3	25.8	0.45
Corporates	4.0	47.6	0.29

porates and sovereigns. Figure 22-23 displays the cumulative time series of annualized information ratios for the four asset classes.

Figure 22-24 offers correlations among the asset classes for both total returns and excess returns over duration-matched Treasuries for the period from August 1988 to June 2004. Correlations of total returns are relatively high, reflecting the exposure to the term structure of interest rates shared by all five asset classes. Correlations of excess returns (which strip out the common influence of Treasury returns) highlight the potential for the four spread asset classes to move independently of each other.

We have shown that spread assets offer long-term investment advantages over similar duration Treasuries. However, over short holding periods, investing in spread product involves the risk of underperforming similar duration Treasuries.

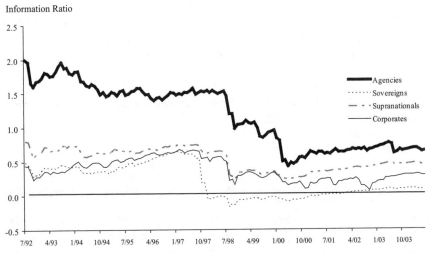

Figure 22-23. Cumulative Information Ratios vs. Treasuries for Various Asset Classes
July 1992–June 2004, Using Data since August 1988

Figure 22-24. Correlations of Total Returns and Excess Returns for Various Asset Classes
August 1988–June 2004

	Total Returns				
	Treasuries	Agencies	Sovereigns	Supranationals	Corporates
Treasuries	1.00				
Agencies	0.97	1.00			
Sovereigns	0.92	0.91	1.00		
Supranationals	0.94	0.95	0.96	1.00	
Corporates	0.93	0.94	0.92	0.94	1.00

	Excess Returns			
	Agencies	Sovereigns	Supranationals	Corporates
Agencies	1.00			
Sovereigns	0.34	1.00		
Supranationals	0.54	0.62	1.00	
Corporates	0.38	0.43	0.56	1.00

Since August 1988, what has been the magnitude of this "shortfall" risk? For each of the four spread asset classes, Figure 22-25 presents the *worst* excess return for various holding periods since 1988. For example, the figure shows that the worst 1-year excess return for agencies was –1.94%, whereas for sovereigns, it was –10.68%.

Another way to examine the shortfall potential of investing in spread assets is to ask what was the worst total return for various holding periods as a function of the percentage of spread assets in a Treasury portfolio. For example, Figure 22-26 illustrates that the worst 1-year total return for a portfolio containing 40% agen-

Figure 22-25. Shortfall Risk—Worst Excess Return (nonannualized) over Duration-Matched Treasuries for Various Holding Periods
August 1988–June 2004

	Holding Period						
	1 Month	3 Months	6 Months	1 Year	5 Years	10 Years	Full Period
Agencies	–1.04	–1.60	–1.84	–1.94	–0.57	4.11	22.92
Sovereigns	–3.88	–7.26	–8.09	–10.68	–9.72	–11.29	8.39
Supranationals	–1.71	–2.45	–2.81	–2.84	–1.84	3.82	23.13
Corporates	–2.09	–2.75	–3.37	–3.43	–4.17	0.90	27.53

Figure 22-26. Shortfall Risk—Worst Holding Period Total Return (nonannualized) for Various Allocations to Spread Assets
August 1988–June 2004

	Holding Period			
	6 Months	1 Year	1.5 Years	2 Years
100% Treasuries	−4.47	−4.46	−0.60	5.18
Agencies				
20%	−4.69	−4.82	−0.71	4.79
40%	−4.90	−5.17	−0.82	4.39
100%	−5.55	−6.23	−1.76	3.21
Sovereigns				
20%	−5.12	−5.25	−1.19	5.14
40%	−5.77	−6.03	−1.77	5.09
100%	−7.69	−8.34	−3.52	2.91
Supranationals				
20%	−4.87	−4.94	−0.86	5.14
40%	−5.27	−5.42	−1.12	5.09
100%	−6.48	−6.83	−1.91	4.95
Corporates				
20%	−4.58	−4.55	−0.64	5.09
40%	−4.69	−4.63	−0.67	5.00
100%	−5.01	−4.87	−1.35	4.28

cies and 60% Treasuries was −5.17%. This compares to the worst 1-year total return of −4.46% for a portfolio of 100% Treasuries. For a portfolio containing 20% sovereigns, the worst 1.5-year period total return (nonannualized) was −1.19%. Noticeably, for a 2-year holding period, no portfolio had a worst-case total return that was negative, irrespective of the percentage of spread assets.

Determining the Proper Weighting

While the possibility of adding highly rated non-Treasury asset classes is appealing, how much weight should non-Treasury assets have in the portfolio? As a first step, it is useful to look at the market value percentage of available supply. For example, as of August 2004, the Lehman U.S. Aggregate Index has a 24% market value weight in the credit sector. Is this market weighting appropriate for the

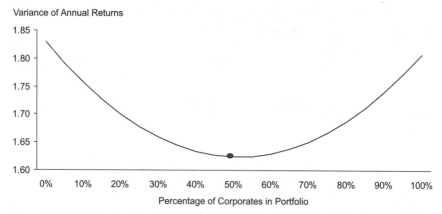

Figure 22-27. Variance of Portfolio Returns for Different Combinations of Treasuries and Duration-Matched Corporates
March 1989–June 2004

portfolio of an official institution? An advantage of using the percentage of avail-able supply as the portfolio weight is that the exposure to the sector gradually changes over time along with the market, allowing the portfolio to track the over-all sector availability in the marketplace. However, using the percentage of avail-able supply does not address the level of risk introduced into the portfolio and whether this level of risk is appropriate.

The advantage of adding non-Treasury asset classes to a portfolio is that their returns may not be perfectly correlated with returns on traditional Treasury secu-rities. Consequently, adding a new asset class may reduce overall portfolio risk for a given level of expected return. One way to show the benefit of diversification is to plot the total return variance for various portfolios containing different com-binations of U.S. Treasuries and the new asset class. For example, Figure 22-27 shows the total return variance for portfolios with different combinations of U.S. Treasuries and U.S. corporate bonds (represented by the U.S. Credit Index) for the period from March 1989 to June 2004.

Figure 22-27 is constructed as follows. For a given U.S. Treasury portfolio, we substitute a duration-matched corporate portfolio for a portion of the U.S. Trea-sury portfolio. That portion is shown as a percentage along the horizontal axis. As a result of this substitution, what would have been the variance in total returns for the Treasury plus corporate portfolio for the entire period? This exercise is repeated for various degrees of substitution: from 0 to 100%. As the percentage of corpo-rates rises above zero, the overall variance of the portfolio decreases. This is the result of the less-than-perfect correlation in total returns between Treasuries and corporates. The decline in portfolio volatility continues up to a point and then begins to increase as the higher volatility of the corporate component of the portfolio begins to outweigh the diversification effect. The results show that a portfolio composed of roughly equal shares of corporates and U.S. Treasuries would have produced the minimum variance portfolio over the entire 15-year period.

Finding the minimum variance portfolio allocation is one way to determine the proper weighting of nongovernment assets in the portfolio. A similar method is to calculate the Sharpe ratio (i.e., mean excess return over riskless rate divided by excess return volatility) for various allocations. An advantage of the minimum variance method is that variances are less volatile than mean excess returns over time, which may produce results more suitable for organizations that plan to change their allocations infrequently.

CONCLUSION

We are in the midst of an exciting transformation in reserve management of central banks, from the traditional "liquidity first" focus to a more balanced objective that includes total return maximization and risk diversification considerations. The long-term forces driving this transformation may well be permanent. Even if some of the original motivations have lost their urgency (e.g., the demise of the U.S. Treasury asset class no longer looms on the horizon), the momentum has shifted. Almost every member of the global official institution community is revising benchmarks (or put differently—long-term asset allocation decisions). Institutions managing the national wealth of countries are leading the way, with central bank reserve managers following closely behind.

To be sure, the considerations driving such revisions are different for central banks than for pure institutional asset managers, with principal preservation, liquidity preference, and "headline" credit risk remaining major concerns. However, this process, once started, will inevitably lead to a significant broadening of the investment opportunity set and the resulting improvement in long-term risk-adjusted returns.

We have addressed two of the important portfolio management issues currently facing many official institutions: how to set the portfolio's duration target and how much of the portfolio (if any) should be allocated to non-Treasury asset classes. We offered quantitative techniques to help answer these questions. For duration targeting, we reviewed the use of Sharpe ratios, which are based on historical returns, and no-view optimization (NVO), which is based on an agnostic assessment of the current market environment. We also demonstrated how NVO can be used to outperform an established benchmark. Finally, we presented evidence supporting the case for non-Treasury assets in a portfolio, based on risk-adjusted returns and diversification benefits.

With a broader set of asset classes to consider, reserve managers will get an opportunity for diversification of portfolio management style. Instead of only timing duration or curve movements, they will be able to engage in the top-down style of sector rotation or the bottom-up style of security selection, especially in credit products. Duration and curve timing, in turn, may be achieved by combining subjective views of investment committees and portfolio managers with model-driven approaches (such as NVO) offering a disciplined objective alternative.

Asset classes to enter the traditional mix of reserve portfolios will probably expand over time from Aaa-rated fixed cash-flow instruments such as U.S. agency bullet debentures, supranational and sovereign debt, and ABS to the high-grade credit securities. In time, there may even be interest in achieving additional return by assuming the prepayment risk of U.S. MBS securities, which represent a very liquid and deep market (about 36 and 14% of the market value of the Lehman U.S. Aggregate and Global Aggregate indices, respectively, as of August 2004). The highly technical nature of this market creates unavoidable complexities in any attempt to outperform it, but it is fairly easy to replicate with minimal back-office requirements.[9] The day may even come when a small portion of the reserves is invested in high-yield securities, as in "core-plus" strategies of institutional investment managers.

Swaps may also emerge as an important total return instrument in central banks' reserve portfolios. Unlike many credit sectors, swaps offer tremendous liquidity benefits, as well as virtually no idiosyncratic event risk. Swaps have offered total returns that are comparable with other spread assets and can provide useful portfolio diversification benefits because of their relatively low correlation with other asset classes.

The shift in asset allocation of reserve portfolios that we began to see in the late 1990s, from short-dated Treasury securities to a more diversified mix of assets, may, in fact, be one of the most interesting developments in the world of fixed-income securities over the next decade.

9. See Chapter 6.

23. The Prospects of Negative Annual Total Returns in Short-Duration Treasury Benchmarks

The 1- to 3-year Treasury Index has never experienced a negative 12-month total return in the Lehman data history. Many users of that index seek capital preservation and have found comfort in its unbroken streak of positive annual returns. However, short-duration assets are no guarantee of positive total returns, especially in an environment of low yields and a very steep yield curve. The purpose of this chapter is to present a framework for analyzing the magnitude, likelihood, and timing of a Treasury curve backup that may cause negative annual returns for the 1- to 3-year Treasury Index and the 2-year on-the-run Treasury note.

One might be tempted to use the following standard duration-based approximation for returns,

$$(y \times \Delta t) - (D \times \Delta y), \tag{23-1}$$

to assess the yield increase required for the index to experience negative returns. At the end of September 2001,[1] index duration was 1.70 years. With this number and a yield of 2.79%, Equation (23-1) finds that a 164-bp increase in index yield would be sufficient to push twelve returns to zero, and any increase in yields beyond this level would result in negative cumulative returns.

Equation (23-1) is accurate only for short holding periods in which both yield changes (Δy) and time changes (Δt) are small. Moreover, it assumes that time return is unaffected by the yield change. Suppose the increase in yield occurred halfway into the 12-month investment period. Then, in 6 months, the index would suffer a similar negative price return of roughly $[-(1.7) \times (1.64)] = -2.79\%$ at the moment of the yield increase.[2] However, index yield would rise to 4.43% for

Based on research first published by Lehman Brothers in 2001.

1. This study used as an example the yield curve at the end of September 2001. The on-the-run yields were as follows: 6-month: 2.35%; 2-year: 2.82%; 5-year: 3.80%; 10-year: 4.59%; 30-year: 5.42%.

2. Owing to monthly rebalancing, one would expect index duration in 6 months to remain close to unchanged.

Figure 23-1. Yield Increase Required for Negative Total Return
October 1, 2001

	Required Yield Increase (bp)	
Timing of Increases	6-Month Holding Period	12-Month Holding Period
Immediately	109	356
At a constant rate	94	225
At the end	82	164

the second 6 months of the investment horizon. The resulting increase in time return would boost the index's 12-month cumulative return by roughly 82 bp and result in a positive total 12-month return of roughly 0.82%.

Timing is crucial. If the increase in yields occurs immediately, then the index benefits from the higher time return for the entire 12 months. On the other hand, if the yield change occurs at the end of the investment period, the increase in index yield causes the index to have an adverse price return with no accompanying increase in time return over the 12-month horizon. Figure 23-1 reports the yield increases required for the 1- to 3-year Treasury Index to experience negative 12-month total returns under three scenarios: (1) all increases in yield occur immediately, (2) yield increases occur at a constant rate over time, and (3) all yield increases occur at the end of the investment period.

ROLLDOWN AND EXPECTED FUTURE YIELD CURVE SHIFTS

The shape of the yield curve may provide important information about likely yield changes. One important factor influencing future index yield is the change in index yield that comes from rolling down the current yield curve. Rolldown effects were approximated from the shape of the off-the-run spline. The current yield curve is quite steep and offers a 5.2-bp decrease in yield at each month's rebalancing. Over 6 months, this translates into a decline of 31 bp. Over a year, it comes to a 62-bp drop. These rolldown yield changes must be combined with the numbers from Figure 23-1 to obtain the yield curve shift that would result in a negative realized return.

Figure 23-2 shows that the short end of the yield curve would have to shift up by more than 125 bp to result in a negative 6-month total return. A negative 12-month holding period return would require the short end of the curve to shift up by more than 287 bp. Both of the numbers are under the "constant rate increase" scenario.

Figure 23-2. Rolldown Effects and Curve Shift Required for Negative Returns
October 1, 2001

Timing of Increases	6-Month Holding Period			12-Month Holding Period		
	Breakeven Index Yield Increase (bp)	Rolldown (bp)	Breakeven Curve Increase (bp)	Breakeven Index Yield Increase (bp)	Rolldown (bp)	Breakeven Curve Increase (bp)
Immediately	109	31	140	356	62	418
At a constant rate	94	31	125	225	62	287
At the end	82	31	113	164	62	226

YIELD CURVE STEEPNESS

Yield curve steepness tends to be mean reverting. Abnormally steep yield curves eventually revert to normal steepness. Similarly, abnormally flat or inverted yield curves can also be expected to revert to normal steepness. As one moves down the end-of-September yield curve from the point that matches current index duration to the point 12 months farther out on the spline, yields increase by 59 bp. Typically, the point 12 months farther out on the Treasury spline from the spot that matches the duration of 1- to 3-year Treasuries has 20 bp of additional yield. It would be reasonable to expect this 38 bp of abnormal slope to be erased over some future time horizon.

Of course, it is not clear how much of this 38-bp move, if any, will occur over the next 12 months. Moreover, it is not clear how much of the movement will result in an increase in 1- to 3-year yields, rather than a decrease in 2- to 4-year yields. However, once the economy hits bottom, one can be confident that interest-rate movements will be uniformly in the upward direction.

Regardless of how one allocates the 38 bp of abnormal steepness in this part of the curve, it clearly cannot be more than a minor factor relative to the 287-bp yield shift required to put 1- to 3-year Treasuries into negative annual return territory. For 6-month returns, the abnormal steepness is 20 bp, once again falling far short of what would be required to generate negative 6-month holding period returns.

Figure 23-3 incorporates rolldown and yield curve steepness effects to estimate the unanticipated shift in the Treasury curve required to push total returns negative. If yield increases occur at a constant rate, the Treasury curve must increase by 287 bp to result in negative total returns (Figure 23-2). Current yield curve steepness suggests that the market anticipates a 38-bp increase, implying that 249 bp of unanticipated yield curve increases will lead to breakeven total returns for the year. The analysis estimates that anything more than this will lead to negative total returns over the upcoming 12-month holding period.

TWO-YEAR ON-THE-RUN TREASURY NOTES

As noted earlier, the 2-year on-the-run Treasury note has rewarded investors with positive total returns over every 12-month interval in our data history dating back to 1985. At the end of September, the 2-year on-the-run had a yield of 2.82% and a 1.84-year duration. If we were to pursue breakeven analysis by applying these numbers to the standard duration-based approximation [Equation (23-1)], the prediction obtained would be that a 153-bp increase in yield would be sufficient to cause negative 12-month returns.

Figure 23-3. Steepness Effects and Curve Shift Required for Negative Returns
October 1, 2001

Timing of Increases:	6-Month Holding Period			12-Month Holding Period		
	At the Start	Constant Rate	At the End	At the Start	Constant Rate	At the End
Breakeven index yield increase (bp)	109	94	82	356	225	164
Rolldown (bp)	31	31	31	62	62	62
Abnormal steepness (bp)	20	20	20	38	38	38
Breakeven unanticipated curve increase (bp)	120	105	93	380	249	188

However, we have already seen that the standard duration-based approximation for returns can be misleading. This is particularly the case for the 2-year on-the-run. A precise calculation shows that a 365-bp shift in the Treasury curve is required to send 12-month returns on the 2-year note to zero. For holding periods with nontrivial length, it is important to apply the complete quadratic approximation for realized return:

$$(y \times \Delta t) - (D \times \Delta y) + \frac{1}{2} \times C \times (\Delta y)^2 + \frac{1}{2} \times y^2 \times (\Delta t)^2 \\ + (1 - y \times D) \times \Delta t \times \Delta y, \tag{23-2}$$

where D is duration and C is convexity. For short-maturity indices such as the 1- to 3-year Treasury Index, convexity is quite small, allowing us to ignore the third term. Similarly, y^2 is a very small number $(0.0282)^2$, implying that the fourth term in Equation (23-2) can also be safely ignored. However, the last term in Equation (23-2) is significant. $(1 - y \times D)$ is close to 1, and Δt equals 1 for an annual investment horizon.[3] Therefore, the last term is on the order of Δy and is important in determining the breakeven yield change.

Applying the end-of-September index numbers to Equation (23-2) estimates the breakeven yield change required for a negative 12-month total return on the 2-year on-the-run to be 316 bp. Adding rolldown effects brings the estimated yield curve increase required for negative 12-month returns to be 378 bp, reasonably close to the precise calculation, which is based on complete repricing.

THE HOLD-TO-MATURITY EFFECT

The 1- to 3-year Treasury Index and the 2-year on-the-run offer comparable yields (2.79% for the 1- to 3-year index, 2.82% for the 2-year note), and the 2-year note has a slightly longer duration: 1.84 vs. 1.70 years for the index. Yet the 2-year note provides more protection against a negative 12-month return. The key factor behind this is that the index rebalances each month to maintain an approximately constant duration of 1.7 years, whereas the duration of the 2-year note gradually declines from 1.84 to 0.90 years. The time-averaged duration of the 1- to 3-year index is roughly 1.63 years, compared with 1.37 years for the 2-year note. While the current duration of the 2-year note is longer than the current duration

---

3. The last term in Equation (23-2) can be safely ignored for investment strategies like the 1- to 3-Year Treasury Index that rebalance monthly. The proper way to apply Equation (23-2) to assess annual returns with monthly rebalancing is to set Δt to $(\frac{1}{12})$ and then compound the results. Setting Δt to $(\frac{1}{12})$ reduces the importance of the last term in Equation (23-2) by a factor of 12 relative to the importance of the standard duration term.

of the 1- to 3-year index, the time-averaged duration of the index is much longer than the time-averaged duration of the note over the following 12-month period (1.63 vs. 1.37).

Alternatively, this can be thought of as a "hold-until-maturity" effect. The 2-year note will certainly return its 2.82% yield if held for 2 years, regardless of any interim yield changes. A 12-month holding period for a 2-year note is sufficiently close to the security's total life that a partial "hold-until-maturity" effect, represented by the last term in Equation (23-2), greatly increases the yield change required for negative cumulative returns.

YIELD CURVE VOLATILITY

Although the current abnormally steep yield curve may not have much impact on expected interest-rate movements, one might be concerned that they are an indicator of an abnormally volatile interest-rate environment. Swaption volatilities can be used to assess current volatility. Swaption volatilities are typically quoted in terms of "yield volatilities," which are at an all-time high for short-tenor, short-maturity swaptions. For instance a 1-month option on a 2-year swap has a record implied yield volatility of 35.10% per year, more than twice its historical average of 17.25%.

However, the volatilities relevant for our analysis are basis point volatilities. Basis point volatility is yield volatility multiplied by yield level. Currently, the combination of extremely low yield levels and extremely high yield volatilities has caused basis point volatilities to be near their average levels. Basis point volatility on the 1-month, 2-year swaption mentioned earlier is 121 bp per year, slightly above its typical level (101 bp). On the basis of this implied swaption volatility, an unanticipated 249-bp increase in rates would be slightly more than a 2-sigma event for a 1-year horizon and clearly cannot be dismissed.

WHAT TO DO?

Investors who cannot tolerate negative annual returns may wish to shorten portfolio duration; 12-month bills always provide 100% safety against negative annual returns. Of course, it is not necessary to go that far. Our analysis of a buy-and-hold position on a 2-year note showed that a position with a time-averaged duration of 1.37 requires the yield curve to increase by more than 365 bp for negative 12-month returns to be realized. The current duration of the 1- to 3-year Treasury Index is 1.70. Moving portfolio duration from this range down to the vicinity of 1.3 years should provide solid protection. Currently, the 1-year part of the Treasury curve is rich, offering yields below both the 6-month and 2-year regions. Thus, moving to 1-year maturity assets will adversely affect yield. An alternative

Figure 23-4. Yield Increase Required for Negative Total Return
Constant Increase Scenario

	Required Yield Increase (bp)	
	6-Month Holding Period	12-Month Holding Period
1- to 3-year U.S. Treasuries	94	225
1- to 3-year U.S. agencies	105	258
2-year swap (rebalanced monthly)	97	230

would be to invest in 3- and 6-month bills, but this approach is likely to cause investors to reinvest at lower rates should the Fed continue to ease.

In addition to shortening duration, investors may wish to consider shifting to high-grade spread product. At the end of September, the yield of the 1- to 3-year Agency Index was 3.13%, offering investors a somewhat larger cushion against the prospect of negative annual returns. One- to 3-year agencies also had a slightly shorter duration (1.67 vs. 1.70). Figure 23-4 reports the yield increase required for negative 12-month returns for 1- to 3-year U.S. Treasuries, 1- to 3-year agencies, and investment in the 2-year swap (rebalanced monthly). All numbers assume a gradual rise in yields. Compared to Treasuries, 1- to 3-year agencies required an additional 33-bp increase in rates before suffering negative 12-month returns.

PART II

Portfolio Management Tools

OPTIMAL RISK BUDGETING WITH SKILL

In all but the most passive portfolios, the main role of a portfolio manager is to generate outperformance via active strategies, subject to a set of constraints designed to limit risk or reflect investment policy preferences. In order to do this, the manager integrates information from various sources and decides on the portfolio's exposures to all macro-level risks as well as its allocation to specific issuers and securities.

The manager relies on many sources: specific forecasts and recommendations from analysts within his organization, outputs of quantitative models, published research from sell-side firms or in the public domain, news, and personal intuition. Each of these inputs may come to bear on his major decisions: currency exposures, yield curve positioning, sector allocation, and issuer selection, all of which are usually backed by rigorous bottom-up procedures that build confidence in their correctness.

Yet in the key task of integrating all these views into a final portfolio, the manager is often left to his own devices, with no clear guidance on how to weigh one view vs. another. Certainly, most investors have access to some sort of asset allocation software that can help guide the allocation process. However, we have found that most managers place very little confidence in the results of such portfolio optimization, in large part because there is a disconnect between the problem addressed by the optimizer and the manager's view of the investment process. In most cases, the optimizer operates in the space of *asset classes*. To feed strategic views into the optimization process, the manager may have to assign precise forecasts of excess return to all asset classes under consideration. Yet his views often take a different form—they are usually expressed as *strategies* as opposed to asset classes and they are often directional, with no specific associated magnitude. For example, a manager might be quite confident that the yield curve will steepen, but be reluctant to guess about exactly what returns to expect for the 1- to 3-year or 5- to 10-year segments of the Treasury market. Hence, the optimizer's dependence on the specific forecasts of asset class returns can undermine the manager's confidence in its results. Consequently, many managers take a less rigorous approach to top-down management. They prefer to make subjective calls on a directional basis and implement these views ad hoc, with the sizing of particular exposures treated as more of an art than a science.

In the wake of our "imperfect foresight" studies of manager skill at different investment styles (Chapters 1 and 2), we received a number of inquiries as to how to best allocate risk to different strategies. We responded by proposing and developing a framework we call optimal risk budgeting with skill (ORBS), a formal quantitative approach to top-down portfolio management, based on directional views and skill. Importantly, ORBS allows the inputs to the optimization problem to be stated in the most intuitive manner.

In Chapters 1 and 2, we investigated how different strategies contribute to portfolio performance, given certain assumptions about the skill at forming views behind these strategies. We found that performance can be improved by increasing the skill, by diversifying the portfolio's risk among a mix of several strategies, and by selecting a set of strategies that are not highly correlated. Toward the end of Chapter 2, we addressed the optimal mix of two correlated strategies and presented an analytical solution for a highly simplified two-strategy optimization problem.

For the more general case of multiple correlated strategies with arbitrary constraints, the optimal solution cannot be written out in closed form. However, we can formulate an optimization problem to solve for it numerically. The fundamental approach is laid out in Chapters 24 and 25; the key concept is that the expected return of a given strategy is not directly specified as an explicit input to the model, but rather backed out from the combination of the strategy's estimated risk, the stated directional view, and the skill associated with that view.

We have seen great investor interest in customized implementations of this decision-making framework, in which the set of strategies to be considered by the model is tailored to match the investment process already in place for a given portfolio. This approach allows the introduction of a more rigorous top-down risk budgeting without requiring any changes in the rest of the management process. This appeals to managers who are confident in the rigorous quantitative processes they have set up for bottom-up strategy formation, but who currently use ad hoc methods to integrate these strategies and establish the portfolio's positions. The risk-budgeting framework is schematically illustrated in Figure 1.

The middle part of the diagram depicts the main components of the risk-budgeting framework that have to be customized to the management process of a particular portfolio. The construction of the model requires detailed information about how the portfolio is managed. A thorough review of the investment process

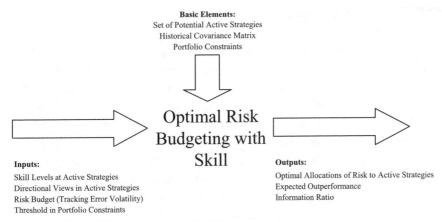

Basic Elements:
Set of Potential Active Strategies
Historical Covariance Matrix
Portfolio Constraints

Optimal Risk Budgeting with Skill

Inputs:
Skill Levels at Active Strategies
Directional Views in Active Strategies
Risk Budget (Tracking Error Volatility)
Threshold in Portfolio Constraints

Outputs:
Optimal Allocations of Risk to Active Strategies
Expected Outperformance
Information Ratio

Figure 1. Optimal Risk Budgeting with Skill

is carried out to abstract the alpha-generation strategies down to a specific set of active strategies on which a view will be formed periodically (e.g., each month). Some examples of the many questions, both general and very specific, that we ask investors at this stage are:

- What are the key strategies used for alpha generation?

- How do you implement steepening and flattening views on the yield curve? (Are there several such trades you might use in different circumstances?)

- For an overweight to credit, is the interest-rate exposure hedged with Treasuries? Swaps? Futures?

- Are there explicit limits on duration deviation from the benchmark, sector allocations, futures position sizes, portfolio turnover, out-of-benchmark allocations?

- Is leverage allowed? Up to what limit? Are short positions allowed in some or all asset classes?

This detailed review of the management process is used to translate a high-level description of the portfolio's active exposures (e.g., long duration by 0.5 year, overweight credit by 1 year of spread duration, and so on) into a more detailed picture of how such views are implemented in practice. This allows the optimization framework to accurately model the risk of a given position and to ensure that the portfolio satisfies all the constraints. For example, as discussed in Chapter 2, if a portfolio is not permitted to take short positions in Treasuries or to use futures, it may not be feasible to implement a long-duration view without also taking a flattening view. Such constraints may not allow the implementation of strategies that are otherwise optimal.

This framework requires a mechanism for measuring risk. At the heart of the model is a covariance matrix that can be used to project the risk of any combination of active strategies. The best way to implement this depends on the specifics of the portfolio; we have used three distinct methods so far. First, one can directly model the risk of each active strategy and the correlations among them to form a strategy covariance matrix. Second, the implementation viewpoint can be used to estimate the risk of the portfolio based on a covariance matrix of *asset class returns*. Third, an existing factor-based risk model (Chapter 26) can be used as the basis for risk measurement; this requires mapping each strategy onto the corresponding set of risk factor loadings.

The actual use of the framework, once it has been constructed, is depicted from left to right along the bottom of the diagram in Figure 1. For each of the included active strategies, the investor specifies a directional view (e.g., long or short, overweight or underweight), as well as an assumed skill level in developing that view. In addition, the investor specifies the threshold levels for each constraint under which the portfolio must operate, as well as the overall risk budget. The optimization process then computes the allocation of risk to active strategies that maximizes alpha—defined here as the expected outperformance based on the specified views—subject to the risk budget and all the additional constraints. While maximizing alpha, the optimizer prefers high-skill strategies that are relatively uncorrelated with each other. Skill determines the portion of risk translated into outperformance, so alpha is directly proportional to skill. The low correlation allows giving more risk to each of the strategies without spending significantly more of the overall risk budget.

Figures 2 and 3 present a highly simplified example based on an actual implementation of the ORBS framework. Figure 2 shows the directional views, with associated skill levels, that comprise the key inputs to the optimization process. In a portfolio benchmarked to the Lehman Brothers U.S. Aggregate Index, the manager wants to shorten duration, overweight investment-grade credit and underweight MBS relative to governments, and invest in two out-of-benchmark ("core-plus") asset classes: high yield and emerging markets. Additional input panels, not shown, specify the details of various constraints, as well as the assumptions concerning the idiosyncratic tracking error and alpha within each asset class. The overall risk budget (tracking error volatility) is 100 bp/year.

Figure 3 presents the results of the optimization. Systematic risk exposures, corresponding to implementation of the macro views, consume most of the risk budget (97.5 bp/year) and generate most of the expected alpha (49.1 bp). Idiosyncratic effects, owing to the active management of issuer exposures within each

Figure 2. Optimal Risk Budgeting with Skill: Example Inputs

Strategy	Skill	View
Yield Curve Strategies		
Duration	10	Short
0–2 slope	10	Neutral
2–5 slope	10	Neutral
5–10 slope	10	Neutral
10–30 slope	10	Neutral
Core Strategies		
IG credit vs. government	10	Long
MBS vs. government	10	Short
ABS/CMBS vs. government	10	Neutral
Core-Plus Strategies		
High yield vs. government	5	Long
EMD vs. government	5	Long
Overall Risk Budget (bp/yr)	100	

sector, in accordance with the input assumptions, contribute smaller amounts to both risk and expected return. Because these risks are assumed to be uncorrelated with the systematic risks, the impact of the nonsystematic exposure on the overall risk is quite small, although the expected alphas are assumed to be additive.

Additional tables within Figure 3 show the optimal portfolio from different viewpoints: the allocation of risk to strategies is kept distinct from the implementation in terms of cash allocations to asset classes. The active risk exposures panel shows the risk exposures that the optimizer has determined should be taken (in terms of the portfolio market value percentages). The magnitudes of the short positions along the curve reflect the curve allocation of the benchmark (duration is shortened in a curve-neutral fashion). The actual positions panel lists the ultimate portfolio composition and its differences from the benchmark. The Treasury allocations displayed here are different from those shown in the active risk exposures because they reflect the Treasury positions used to hedge the interest-rate exposures of the active positions in other asset classes, such as credit and MBS. It is these implementation-level weights that are compared with the constraints to make sure a particular combination of strategies is feasible. We see that allocations to favored strategies can be limited by different considerations. The long position to credit and the short position in MBS are limited by constraints on the

Figure 3. Optimal Risk Budgeting with Skill: Example Output Report

Performance Summary		Active Risk Exposures (%)	
Total Portfolio TE (bp/yr)	100.0	USD Curve: 2 yr	−3.24
Systematic	97.5	USD Curve: 5 yr	−2.33
Nonsystematic	22.3	USD Curve: 10 yr	−1.25
Portfolio Alpha (bp)	64.7	USD Curve: 30 yr	−1.71
Systematic	49.1	IG Credit vs. government	15.71
Nonsystematic	15.6	MBS vs. government	−34.43
Information Ratio	0.65	HY vs. government	2.97
		EMD vs. government	3.01

Actual Positions	Benchmark MV (%)	Portfolio MV (%)	Difference (%)	Maximum Allocation Constraint (%)
Cash	—	8.53	8.53	20.00
USD government 2 yr	13.93	7.95	−5.98	
USD government 5 yr	9.98	25.99	16.01	100.0
USD government 10 yr	5.39	6.72	1.34	
USD government 30 yr	7.33	0.18	−7.15	
Investment grade credit	24.29	40.00	15.71	40.00
MBS	34.43	0.00	−34.43	50.00
ABS/CMBS	4.66	4.66	0.00	10.00
High yield	—	2.97	2.97	5.00
Emerging markets	—	3.01	3.01	5.00
Total	100.00	100.00	0.00	

Strategy	Contribution to Variance (%)	Systematic Alpha (bp)	Nonsystematic Alpha (bp)
Cash			2.1
Duration		12.3	
0–2 slope		0.0	
2–5 slope	22.0	0.0	
5–10 slope		0.0	
10–30 slope		0.0	
IG credit vs. government	24.40	11.4	10.0
MBS vs. government	4.30	14.1	0.0
ABS/CMBS vs. government	0.00	0.0	0.5
High yield vs. government	18.84	4.0	1.5
EMD vs. government	30.50	7.4	1.5
Total	100.0	49.1	15.6

portfolio allocations. Conversely, the long positions in the two volatile core-plus assets, high yield and emerging markets, fall well within their constraints and are limited by the overall risk budget. Finally, the last panel details each strategy's contribution to the overall risk as a percentage of variance, as well as the contributions to expected outperformance, or alpha, from both the systematic and non-systematic exposures.

The ORBS framework can be used in two distinct ways. In typical day-to-day use, all of the strategic inputs on the left side of the diagram are held relatively stable, except for the directional views. The optimizer is then used to rebalance the portfolio each time there is a significant change in the set of views.

The ORBS model has been found useful in longer-term planning as well. It is an ideal platform for evaluating changes in the investment process. Portfolio managers face constraints that can have a meaningful impact on investment performance. The model can quantify the performance costs of specific constraints. In this mode of operation, the set of views is held constant, and the portfolio constraints are changed. How much higher could the information ratio be if we increased the allowed allocation to high yield or allowed some leverage? To maximize the usefulness of the framework in evaluating potential changes to the investment policy, or the introduction of new asset classes or alpha-generation strategies, it is important to include these capabilities from the outset. At the construction stage, the framework should be designed to handle the broadest range of products and strategies that might be considered for inclusion in the future. They can easily be excluded from optimizations of the current portfolio by the use of constraints; but once they are available within the framework, it is easy to investigate how the further diversification of the strategy mix can improve the portfolio's performance.

In a similar application, the framework can be used to evaluate the fairness of an alpha target. A common complaint from asset managers is that plan sponsors expect alpha targets that are unrealistically high given the risk limits and constraints imposed on their mandates. How much alpha can reasonably be expected from a manager in a given setting? Within the risk-budgeting framework, one can back out the skill level that must be assumed for each active strategy in order to produce a certain alpha given a fixed set of active strategies, views, risk budget, and portfolio constraints. If the required skill levels are unrealistically high, one could make the case that either the alpha target has to be lowered or that some of the portfolio constraints have to be relaxed.

What is the right level of skill to assume? The specified skill levels play a critical role in determining the output of the optimization. The higher the skill levels specified, the higher the expected return; as a result, if skill levels are assumed to be higher for certain strategies, these strategies will be favored in the optimization.

Ideally, the skill levels that are specified for each strategy should be based on a long-term track record. As described in Chapter 1, we define skill based on the probability of a directional view being correct; likewise, it can be measured from a historical sequence of stated directional views and subsequent market movements. The percentage of time that the view on a particular strategy turns out to be correct can be used to estimate the skill at that strategy. However, the accuracy of such historical estimates grows with the length of the track record, as discussed in Chapter 2. (Certainly, if an analyst expressed a view on a given strategy only once and happened to be right, we would not be ready to assume a skill level of 100%!) Most portfolio managers rarely achieve information ratios above 1. The empirical studies in Chapters 1 and 2 link levels of skill with the achieved information ratios, showing that, for a single strategy, skill of 20% produces information ratios in the vicinity of 0.6. In a portfolio with multiple strategies the information ratio is higher, which points to 20% as the realistic maximum skill level.

Another way to measure the skill of different strategies based on historical performance is to use the results of a performance attribution model. As described in Chapter 27, performance attribution evaluates the contributions of different strategies to portfolio outperformance. If such a model has been in place for a sufficiently long period of time, then the track record of historical outperformance for each strategy can be used as a basis for estimating skill.

Unfortunately, in many cases long track records of strategy performance are simply not available in any form, either because an analyst has only recently started expressing views on a particular strategy or because records of the past views and their performance have not been maintained. In such cases, we must rely on ad hoc methods to specify the initial skill levels assumed for each strategy. We usually recommend that the same skill level be assumed for all strategies. This ensures that the risk budget allocation is driven by the combination of the views expressed and the correlations among the various strategies.

When we first developed our risk-budgeting framework, it dealt exclusively with the allocation of risk to macro strategies. However, we soon realized that even in a top-down view of portfolio management, we have to recognize the contributions of security selection strategies to both alpha and risk. Security selection is not just an implementation detail that comes up when filling the allocation to credit. Key management decisions revolve around the question of how to determine the right balance between systematic and issuer-specific risk in a portfolio. Here we find ourselves facing the same questions that came up in our discussion of investment styles in Chapter 1 and in our investigation of sufficient diversification in Chapter 14. Should alpha generation focus more on sector timing or on issuer selection? How should this affect the allocation of the research budget?

Our next two chapters discuss two different ways to address the interaction between asset allocation and security selection within the context of a risk-budgeting framework. First, in Chapter 24, we continue to allocate risk to macro strategies, but have the optimization take into account the characteristic idiosyncratic risk and return of each asset class. For example, when a manager makes a top-down allocation to credit, he knows to allow for a certain amount of nonsystematic risk within the credit portfolio; he also counts on achieving some additional outperformance if the team is skilled in name selection. The expected idiosyncratic risk and security selection alpha that are specified for each asset class do not reflect just the objective characteristics of an asset class, but also the bottom-up style used to manage that asset class within the portfolio.

The recognition of idiosyncratic risk is necessary to make sure that the portfolio stays within the overall risk budget. In addition, the ability to specify idiosyncratic alpha enables the framework to model the following frequently observed phenomenon. Many managers have a bias toward being overweight credit, even when their view on the asset class is neutral. This can be represented in the risk-budgeting framework by assigning a high ratio of assumed idiosyncratic alpha to idiosyncratic risk. This gives the optimizer two legitimate reasons to overweight credit: to take advantage of a positive view on the asset class as a whole, or just to put more resources at the disposal of the security selection team.

This approach is most appropriate for a hierarchical management structure, in which the top-level manager allocates the portfolio resources among a set of sector-specific funds, but does not directly control the management of the sector funds. The manager of a global aggregate mandate, for example, might buy shares in funds that invest in U.S. MBS or euro credit, managed by a different team within the organization. The investment style of those funds and the amount of risk they each take relative to their sector benchmarks cannot be modified by the global manager, but can and should be taken into account as he sets the allocations. (This approach was taken in the ORBS example discussed earlier.)

What about the situation in which the CIO has control over all aspects of the management process? Say the CIO is trying to establish research priorities between focusing on a diversified set of macro strategies and building up security selection skills. Should alpha generation focus more on sector timing or on issuer selection? How should this affect the allocation of the research budget? Should he hire credit analysts or yield curve experts?

In Chapter 25, we explore different ways to address problems of this type within our skill-based risk-budgeting methodology. First, in the setting of a highly simplified example, we take a top-down view in which security selection is modeled in the abstract, without views on specific issuers. Rather, as we establish our position in a particular sector, we specify not just the percentage allocation, but also the number of issuers that will represent this sector. The smaller the number of issuers, the greater the issuer-specific risk.

The second approach is more concrete, incorporating explicit directional views on individual issuers, in addition to the macro views at the sector level. This method, which we call "credit ORBS" uses credit derivatives to manage the trade-off between systematic and idiosyncratic risk. A set of pure systematic risk exposures can be constructed to express macro views with credit portfolio products such as CDX and iTraxx contracts and their sector-specific variants. Alternatively, the risk budget can be focused on issuer-specific exposures, by going long the favored issuers and short the negatively viewed issuers via single-name CDS. The ability to blend these very different types of strategies according to the manager's views and skills provides a very flexible and powerful optimization framework.

Chapters 24 and 25 take two mutually exclusive views of issuer-specific risk. In Chapter 24, idiosyncratic risk and the resulting alpha in each sector are inputs. We then address their impact on sector allocation. In contrast, in Chapter 25, the extent of diversification can vary and is determined by the optimization. Security selection as a strategy competes for the risk budget with sector views and other macro strategies. Most investors find themselves in one of the two situations, but not in both. To allow the reader a choice of proceeding directly to the relevant chapter, we provide a brief introduction to ORBS in both chapters.

24. Effect of Security Selection Skill on Optimal Sector Allocation

Risk budgeting is a quantitative method for finding the optimal allocation of risk to different investor views. At the macro level, portfolio management consists of translating the views of many analysts into portfolio exposures to various risk factors. The fundamental decisions in a fixed-income portfolio revolve around interest rates, sector allocation, exchange rates, and volatility. Beneath these macro-level decisions lies the domain of security selection, where asset class allocations become holdings in specific bonds and issuers. Very often, the macro-level asset allocation problem is addressed independently of security selection. However, it is the combination of the two that ultimately determines both the risk and the return of the portfolio. In this short piece, we use a simple example to illustrate how consideration of security selection can influence the asset allocation or risk-budgeting process.

As an example, we consider a portfolio benchmarked to a global Treasury index that is allowed to hold credit as a noncore position. Typically, a view that credit will outperform Treasuries would be the reason for taking a position in this asset class. But is an allocation to credit appropriate when one does not expect credit to have a positive excess return? Many would say no, because credit is not included in the benchmark. Why include a credit position that will increase tracking error volatility with no expected benefit in terms of outperformance? The reason could be security selection.

Credit allocation decisions often involve multiple views. Typically, a strategist has an opinion on the relative future performance of various sectors or asset classes; credit analysts have views on individual names within their respective sectors. In our global Treasury mandate example, we would forgo the value of name selection skill if we let the strategist determine the optimal credit allocation and set it to zero in the absence of a bullish view on the asset class. In fact, even when

Based on research first published by Lehman Brothers in 2004.

the asset class is not expected to perform well, holding small allocations to our most favored security selection picks may be justified. Yet to make a credit allocation worthwhile despite the neutral sector view, the expected alpha from security selection must compensate for both the systematic risk of the sector exposure and the idiosyncratic risk from the individual issuer exposures. We need a model to determine the optimal allocation.

The Lehman Brothers optimal risk budgeting with skill (ORBS) model provides a setting in which we can examine such issues. Prompted by our research on the value of skill at different portfolio management styles,[1] we developed this model for finding the optimal allocation of portfolio risk exposures. Owing to the differences in portfolio management styles, benchmarks, allowed asset classes, and investment constraints, this has been a highly customized effort, with a separate implementation for each investor portfolio considered.

THE MODEL

Our risk-budgeting model[2] is based on investment skill and builds on published conceptual work by Grinold and Kahn, as well as on our empirical studies of skill in fixed-income portfolios.[3]

The information ratio of an investment strategy is defined as the ratio of portfolio outperformance over tracking error volatility or active risk:

$$IR = \frac{\alpha}{TE} \tag{24-1}$$

Grinold and Kahn have shown that the information ratio of a strategy is essentially determined by two things: skill and breadth. Skill can be measured as the "information coefficient," that is, the correlation between investment forecasts and the realized market movements. Breadth refers to the number of independent decisions that the strategy implements and is a function of two factors: how often the strategy is executed (e.g., weekly, monthly) and how many independent decisions are made at each execution. The information ratio achieved by a strategy should roughly follow the law

$$IR = Skill \cdot \sqrt{Breadth}. \tag{24-2}$$

---

1. See Chapter 2.

2. This chapter is relevant where the degree of issuer diversification is given. In Chapter 25, the degree of issuer concentration is allowed to vary.

3. Richard C. Grinold and Ronald N. Kahn, *Active Portfolio Management*, McGraw-Hill, 1999.

Putting these two equations together yields the following formulation for the portfolio alpha:

$$\alpha = \text{TE} \cdot \text{IR} = \text{TE} \cdot \text{Skill} \cdot \sqrt{\text{Breadth}}. \tag{24-3}$$

That is, the expected active return of a portfolio is a function of active risk, investment skill, and the diversity of positions that it implements. A key implication of this is that a risk-budgeting framework can make allocation decisions based on directional views without requiring strategists to specify precise basis point forecasts of market movements. At first glance, this may seem odd: how can we assume that outperformance is proportional to tracking error volatility? Does merely taking a risk guarantee that it will pay off? The answer is that in the presence of skill, risk eventually translates into outperformance. So the alpha in our equations should be understood as the expected long-term payoff for assigning risk budget to a certain strategy or strategist. The information ratio, projected based on skill (from historical track record or some other estimation method), tells us the magnitude of outperformance to expect per unit of risk when following this strategist's directional views.

The Equation (24-3) is very simple. It assumes that there is only one active strategy implemented in the portfolio or that all active bets benefit from a uniform investment skill and generate identical contributions to tracking error volatility. In practice, the investment process consolidates different strategies supported by different sets of skills. For example, a global portfolio could rely on the distinct skills of a macro strategist, duration managers in several major markets, a currency overlay manager, and several credit research teams. Individual strategies related to each of these risk dimensions combine to generate the active risk and return of the overall portfolio.

The portfolio outperformance is the sum of contributions of individual strategies and reflects the information ratio of each active strategy on a stand-alone basis, as well as the risk budget allocated to it:

$$\alpha_p = \sum_i \text{IR}_i \cdot \text{TE}_i. \tag{24-4}$$

The portfolio active risk, or tracking error volatility, TE, combines the tracking errors generated by each individual strategy but reflects the correlation structure between the payoffs of individual strategies.

Although the alpha contributions of the different strategies add up to the portfolio alpha, the tracking error volatility contributions do not combine in a simple additive way, owing to the benefit of diversification. If we assume independence among the payoffs of individual strategies, then the tracking error volatility contributions combine according to a simple sum-of-squares equation:

$$\mathrm{TE}_P^2 = \sum_i \mathrm{TE}_i^2. \qquad (24\text{-}5)$$

A more comprehensive approach considers the correlations among the different strategies. In this case, the tracking error volatility is calculated by multiplying the vector of risk exposures from different strategies by the covariance matrix representing the risks of all strategies and the correlations among them:

$$\mathrm{TE}_P^2 = T' \cdot \Omega \cdot T. \qquad (24\text{-}6)$$

We can optimize the mix of active strategies in much the same way as one would optimize a static asset portfolio. However, in contrast to traditional mean-variance optimization, the optimal allocation is not defined strictly in terms of market value weights to asset classes. Rather, we find the optimal allocation of active risk to a set of individual alpha-generation strategies. This allocation is then translated into a market value allocation.

The objective of the optimization is always to achieve the best trade-off between risk and return, but this can be formulated in several different ways. One approach is to minimize tracking error variance for a given expected outperformance. (One can repeat this exercise for a number of different alpha levels to trace out an efficient frontier.) Another is to find the allocation that gives the highest information ratio. Yet another is to generate the highest possible alpha subject to the constraint that the portfolio tracking error volatility stays within the risk budget. While all these are very closely related, we have found that the formulation that uses the notion of the risk budget constraint corresponds better to the way most portfolio managers view their role.

A SIMPLE EXAMPLE

Within the context of this risk-budgeting framework, we have attempted to construct the simplest possible example to address the question of how skill at security selection within an asset class affects the macro-allocation decision. We look at a global Treasury portfolio and assume that just three strategies underlie the portfolio performance: timing of credit allocation, security selection within the credit market, and all other active strategies together. For each of these strategies, we make some arbitrary assumptions about investment skill and breadth and derive information ratios. Figure 24-1 summarizes the main characteristics of these three strategies evaluated on an isolated basis.

Figure 24-1. Arbitrary Assumptions about the Three Active Strategies Considered

	Credit Allocation	Security Selection in the Credit Market	All Other Active Strategies
Skill (%)	10	2	10
Breadth	12	120	60
Information ratio	0.35	0.22	0.78

The skill of each strategy is the correlation between the view expressed by the investor and the market realization. For simple directional views, a zero skill assumes that the investor does no better than a coin toss and anticipates the market direction correctly only 50% of the time; a 10% skill implies that he is right 55% of the time. The breadth reflects an assumption about the number of independent decisions that a strategy can implement each year. In our example, we assume that all strategies are rebalanced monthly. The breadth of the strategy is then twelve times the number of independent decisions made each month. We assume that one credit allocation and ten security selection decisions are made each month. The third column is a catch-all category that represents all other active strategies that might be available to the fund manager. For example, it could include active bets on exchange rates and duration and curve reshaping in several currencies. This category is assumed to comprise on average five such alpha-generation bets each month, all mutually independent. We have arbitrarily assumed that skill at security selection is much smaller than skill at credit allocation or other macro decisions. The information ratios at the bottom of Figure 24-1 highlight the differences among strategies, the security selection one being the least attractive.

Note that this study does not address the issue of which type of strategy is likely to generate the best results; by assuming greater skill or breadth, we could have easily shown security selection to be the most efficient strategy. Similarly, none of the "optimal" allocations to credit discussed in this chapter should be construed as a practical recommendation: the precise levels of the allocations are driven by the set of arbitrary assumptions in Figure 24-1. Our goal is to illustrate the interaction among various views relating to a common asset class and to explain how the optimal asset allocation is formed to best exploit these views.

Our example assumes that credit investments must be fully funded and ignores the possibility of hedging systematic credit risk through basket products such as CDX or iTraxx. This assumption, together with our assumption that security selection involves a ten-bond portfolio each month, implies that there is no ability to take on systematic credit risk independently of idiosyncratic credit risk. The exposures to credit allocation and credit security selection are forced to be

identical. At the same time, we also assume that the other active strategies implemented in the portfolio—essentially interest rate and FX-related strategies—can
be implemented with futures and swaps and, therefore, do not interfere with any
allocation to the credit market.

Although Figure 24-1 provides information ratios that we expect to observe on
average over some significant time period, we are concerned with the risk allocation at a particular point in time, namely when the strategist's macro view on
credit might be neutral. In that case, the information ratio associated with credit
sector allocation is nil; an asset allocation decision to overweight the credit market is not expected to contribute any return. However, it certainly contributes to
risk because there is no credit allocation in the benchmark. So any credit allocation has to be supported by views and skill in security selection. The combination
of a neutral view on credit allocation and positive views on selected names yields
a risk that reflects both the overweighting of the asset class and the concentration
in a small set of selected names.

In general, the highest information ratio is achieved by diversifying risk among
a set of independent active strategies. The benefits of risk diversification can be
diluted by correlations among the strategies that stem from two distinct sources.
The correlations between the returns of different asset classes (e.g., governments
and corporates) are one major source; the other is the correlation of views that
can arise within a given organization. For most of this study, we assume for simplicity that all strategies are independent. At the end, we briefly explore the role of
correlations among the returns of the active strategies.

RESULTS

Figure 24-2 answers our original question according to our simple model. With a
neutral view on the credit sector and a positive view on certain credit securities,
there is indeed justification for a significant allocation to credit. In particular,
under the assumptions presented in Figure 24-1, we find it optimal to invest 13.9%
of the portfolio in credit against our all-government benchmark. To accommodate the additional risks of this exposure, both systematic and nonsystematic, and
still stay within our 100-bp overall risk budget, we scale down our exposures to all
other sources of risk by a factor of 98.1%.

It is readily apparent that there is a one-to-one correspondence in Figure 24-2
between the active weights and the isolated tracking error volatility contributions,
in which a 1% change in active weight corresponds to a 1-bp change in tracking
error volatility. This is not true in general, but is rather the result of some assumptions that we have made here to simplify the relationship between market value
exposures and risk contributions. We have assumed that each strategy is formu-

Figure 24-2. Optimal Risk Allocation under a Neutral Credit Sector View and Positive Security Selection View

Versus an All-Government Benchmark

	Credit Allocation	Security Selection in the Credit Market	All Other Active Views	Overall Portfolio
Active weight (%)	13.9	13.9	98.1	
Alpha contribution (bp)	0.0	3.0	76.0	79.0
Tracking error volatility contribution (bp/year)	13.9	13.9	98.1	100.0
Isolated information ratio	0.00	0.22	0.78	0.79

lated so that a 100% allocation to that strategy would result in exactly 100 bp/year of tracking error volatility.

Assuming that a full exposure to credit creates 100 bp of systematic tracking error volatility with respect to a global Treasury benchmark is certainly a bit simplistic, but not at all unrealistic. We used our multifactor risk model to calculate and attribute the tracking error volatility of the Global Credit Index with respect to the Global Treasury Index and obtained a systematic tracking error volatility of 121 bp/year, not that far from our naïve assumption. Similarly, the assumption that a full allocation to security selection would create an isolated tracking error volatility of 100 bp/year is consistent with a set of ten overweight positions with a 5-year spread duration and 18 bp/month of idiosyncratic spread volatility. Data from our multifactor risk model indicate that such idiosyncratic spread volatility is typical for many A-Baa-rated corporate issuers. The "other active views" category can be seen as a set of long-short positions that apply to the entire portfolio; we assume that a 100% allocation to that category represents the maximum risk allocation allowed. We believe that a 100-bp/year tracking error volatility budget is consistent with the typical risk target of a moderately conservative fixed-income portfolio. These assumptions should be revisited when applying the model to any particular portfolio. To arrive at the optimal positioning for a particular portfolio, many different types of factors must be considered simultaneously. These can include constraints on market value allocation, duration, and the like, as well as considerations of risk exposures, active views, market volatilities, and correlations. A multifactor risk model akin to the one discussed in Chapter 26 can quantify the active risk associated with typical portfolio structures and specific views.

Let us continue with our example of a global Treasury portfolio contemplating credit investment as a noncore allocation. We can modify the investment parameters to form different sets of active views. Figure 24-3 presents different combinations of views on the credit asset class as a whole and on security selection. When we are neutral on the credit asset class and have no strong issuer views, then the intuitive result is to take no credit position. When we are neutral on the asset class but have a strong security selection view, as we saw earlier, the optimal credit allocation is 13.9%. Conversely, if we are bullish on the asset class but neutral on individual names, we obtain an optimal sector weight of 21.3%. This is true despite the fact that we have to account for the unwanted risk that the assumed small number of credit bonds creates in the portfolio. (As noted earlier, the fact that the credit allocation for the sector-driven view is higher is only a reflection of the arbitrary parameters that we have selected for this example in Figure 24-1. There is no fundamental reason to believe that a macro-based credit strategy should perform better than security selection; in fact, our research would support the opposite conclusion.)[4]

Figure 24-3 also illustrates the case in which one is bullish on the credit asset class and has outperformance views on individual securities with respect to the asset class. When both the systematic risk and the idiosyncratic risk of the credit position reflect views that can drive up expected outperformance, the asset class deserves a larger share of the overall risk budget—now 32.4%—and the exposures to all other risks are reduced even further (down to 88.9%) to make room in the risk budget.

Finally, the rightmost column of Figure 24-3 shows the optimal credit allocation when one is bullish on the asset class and able to avoid security-specific risk. For example, we can get very close to this ideal if we use well-diversified basket products to implement our view. In this case, the portfolio combination that maximizes the information ratio has a larger allocation to credit, almost double the one we obtain when we have to cope with limited diversification and security-specific risk.

Up to this point, we have considered allocation to an out-of-benchmark asset class. How does the interaction between sector allocation and security selection change if the selected sector is part of the benchmark? To address this issue, we now assume that our portfolio's performance is measured against a benchmark composed of 80% governments and 20% credit.

---

4. See, e.g., Chapter 1. We found that security selection offers much higher information ratios than macro strategies, but that work assumed a higher level of diversification than the ten securities considered here.

Figure 24-3. Portfolio Risk Allocations and Expected Outperformance under Different Combinations of Views
Versus an All-Government Benchmark

Macro-Credit View	Neutral	Neutral	Positive	Positive	Positive
Security-Specific View	Neutral	Active	Neutral	Active	Neutral No Security-Specific Risk
Active Weight					
Credit allocation (%)	0.0	13.9	21.3	32.4	40.8
Security selection (%)	0.0	13.9	21.3	32.4	40.8
Other active strategies (%)	100.0	98.1	95.3	88.9	91.3
Alpha Contribution					
Credit allocation (bp)	0.0	0.0	7.4	11.2	14.1
Security selection (bp)	0.0	3.0	0.0	7.1	0.0
Other active strategies (bp)	77.5	76.0	73.9	68.8	70.7
Portfolio alpha (bp)	77.5	79.0	81.2	87.2	84.9
Portfolio tracking error volatility (bp/year)	100.0	100.0	100.0	100.0	100.0
Portfolio information ratio	0.78	0.79	0.81	0.87	0.85

The key difference in our analysis is that the risk exposures to the sector allocation and security selection strategies are no longer the same. If, for example, our portfolio has a 30% allocation to credit split among ten securities, then we still have a 30% allocation to our security selection strategy, but the exposure to credit sector allocation strategy reflects only the 10% overweight to the asset class.

Comparing the results of Figure 24-4 with those in Figure 24-3, we find that this theme continues throughout. In each case, the optimal overall allocation to credit (shown as the active weight to security selection) is greater than it was against an all-government benchmark, but the optimal overweight (shown as the allocation to credit allocation) is lower. As a result, the risk allocations and the alpha contributions are now higher for the security selection strategy and lower for the credit sector allocation strategy. For example, when we are neutral on the asset class and credit investment is driven by the security selection view, we are still overweight credit, but by a much smaller 3.7%. Yet because we are able to capitalize on these views using the total credit allocation of 23.7%, the alpha contribution from security selection increases from 3.0 to 5.2 bp. When the overweight is driven by a sector view, we again see a smaller overweight, owing to the additional security selection risk and a smaller contribution to alpha as a result. When we are positive on both the asset class and the security selection, we again see that more of the outperformance is due to the security selection strategy, owing to its larger exposure, even though we assumed in Figure 24-1 that the credit allocation strategy is inherently more efficient.

An interesting effect can be observed in the first column of Figure 24-4. We see that if in a given month we have no particularly strong views on either the credit sector or specific securities, the optimal solution is not to stay neutral with respect to credit, as would seem intuitive, but rather to underweight the asset class by 10%. The active risk exposure to all our other alpha-generation strategies is scaled down somewhat to make room in the risk budget for an active sector underweight that is not expected to generate any alpha. Why? The answer is: to reduce the idiosyncratic risk in the credit portion of the portfolio. This stems from our assumption that the credit portion of the portfolio is always represented by a portfolio of ten names.[5]

The rightmost column of Figure 24-4 once again represents the case where a positive view on credit is implemented using diversified basket products. As

---

5. If instead we made the assumption that the credit portion of the portfolio could track the index very closely, we would obtain the intuitive result that a neutral view requires a neutral position. This would clearly be preferable when there is no strong view on security selection and could be achieved by increasing the number of names in the portfolio. However, this is not always practical. At any rate, the search for the "right" number of names in the portfolio is a separate topic beyond the scope of this chapter. See Chapter 14.

Figure 24-4. Portfolio Risk Allocations and Expected Outperformance under Different Combinations of Views

The Benchmark Including 20% Credit

Macro-Credit View	Neutral	Neutral	Positive	Positive	Negative	Positive
Security-Specific View	Neutral	Active	Neutral	Active	Active	Neutral No Security-Specific Risk
Active Weight						
Credit allocation (%)	-10.0	3.7	11.1	22.1	-20.0	40.8
Security selection (%)	10.0	23.7	31.1	42.1	0.0	60.8
Other active strategies (%)	99.0	97.1	94.4	88.0	98.0	91.3
Alpha Contribution						
Credit allocation (bp)	0.0	0.0	3.8	7.7	6.9	14.1
Security selection (bp)	0.0	5.2	0.0	9.2	0.0	0.0
Other active strategies (bp)	76.7	75.2	73.1	68.1	75.9	70.7
Portfolio alpha (bp)	76.7	80.4	77.0	85.0	82.8	84.9
Portfolio tracking error volatility (bp/year)	100	100	100	100	100	100
Portfolio information ratio	0.77	0.80	0.77	0.85	0.83	0.85

mentioned before, we assume that such products can track the index perfectly and that the idiosyncratic risk is zero. As a result, we show the same results as vs. the all-government benchmark: the portfolio overweights credit by 40.8% and adds 14.1 bp of alpha as a result. However, this assumption is certainly imprecise. A credit basket product such as CDX or iTraxx has two significant sources of risk in tracking a credit index: (1) the idiosyncratic risk between the set of equally weighted issuer exposures in the basket and the (usually market-weighted) exposures of the index, and (2) the basis risk between the CDS in the basket vs. the cash bonds in the index. This risk, when considered more carefully, would have different implications depending on whether the benchmark includes credit.

We have seen that when dealing with an asset class that is part of the benchmark, the security selection view takes on more importance since it is reflected even in the part of the allocation that is neutral to the benchmark weight. However, the inclusion of the asset class in the benchmark has another important implication for the sector allocation strategy: it allows for the possibility of an underweight to capitalize on a negative view on the asset class. For out-of-benchmark assets, the inability to underweight the asset class may negate half the value of the strategist's effort because we are able to generate alpha only in months when the view is positive (and results in a long position). The interaction between sector allocation and security selection should work to our advantage when the view on the asset class is short and the security selection view is neutral; by underweighting the asset class, we simultaneously take the desired active view and reduce the unwanted idiosyncratic exposure. In the fifth column of Figure 24-4, we see that under a negative view on the credit asset class and no strong security selection view, we find it optimal to bring the corporate exposure down to zero, resulting in a total expected alpha of 82.8 bp.

CORRELATION OF VIEWS

So far, our analysis has assumed that the payoffs of the three active strategies are independent of each other. This assumption fits the framework of our global risk model, where idiosyncratic credit spread risk is by definition orthogonal to systematic factors (including credit spreads) that typically describe macro-allocation decisions.[6] We could argue, however, that strategy payoffs are different from market risks because they result from taking active views and are a function of the

---

6. Systematic views are, of course, subject to market correlations, and real-life ORBS implementations reflect that. In this study, though, we ignore the correlation between the credit view and the fuzzy catch-all "other strategies" view.

Credit Allocation

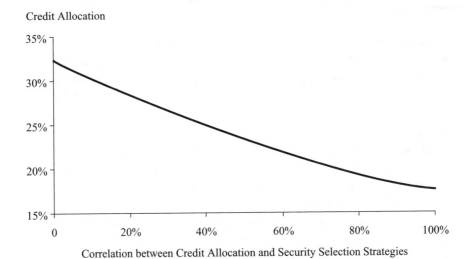

Correlation between Credit Allocation and Security Selection Strategies

Figure 24-5. Effect of Correlation between Credit Allocation and Security Selection Strategies

direction of such views. Indeed, the payoff of a permanently long position in the credit asset class as a whole is independent of the incremental payoff of a permanently long position in a few individual names relative to their peer group. Yet it is debatable whether active and changing positions deliver independent returns. It is quite likely that significant correlations may exist between active strategies if some commonality underlies the view creation process within an organization. For example, a macro economist potentially influences both macro strategists and fundamental analysts, who strive to express views consistent with their in-house global economic scenario. Consensual decision-making processes also have the potential to reinforce a common scenario.

Correlation of strategy payoffs requires that we adapt our model. We can no longer represent the portfolio active risk as a sum of individual risk contributions, but must now include a covariance matrix in our aggregation of risk. We can still assume that the two credit strategies are independent of the catch-all "other strategies" group, but now introduce a positive correlation between the payoffs of the credit allocation and security selection strategies. Using different correlation assumptions, we repeat the optimization shown in the fourth column of Figure 24-3, in which views are positive on both the credit asset class and a set of specific securities vs. an all-government benchmark. Figure 24-3 showed that with no correlation between these views, the optimal allocation to credit is 32.4%. In Figure 24-5, we see that in the presence of a positive correlation between these views, the optimal allocation to credit can be significantly lower.

CONCLUSION

In this chapter, we have formulated a simple model to examine the interaction between the views and risk exposures at the levels of asset allocation and security selection. We have shown that when determining the macro-level allocation to an asset class, it is important to consider how the allocation is likely to be implemented at the security level, and how much security-selection risk and outperformance can be expected as a result.

In the simple example illustrated here, this trade-off was considered for just a single asset class: investment-grade credit as a whole. In a more general asset allocation setting, these security-level implementation issues must be considered for each asset class in the model.

We have developed the Lehman ORBS model to assist in tactical risk allocation based on directional views, using a highly customized approach tailored to each individual portfolio. One aspect of ORBS featured here is the recognition that every macro allocation to an asset class must consider the idiosyncratic exposures that are entailed as well.

25. Risk Budget Allocation to Issuer and Sector Views

Active portfolio managers seek to enhance return of their portfolios by taking on risk exposures of various types in accordance with their market views. Very often, managers have clear directional views on different market segments, along with clear ideas of what trades to execute in order to reflect those views in their portfolios. They might go long 10-year U.S. Treasury note futures to reflect a bullish view on U.S. interest rates, or long EUR vs. GBP to reflect an FX outlook, or long corporate bonds vs. swaps to reflect a bullish view on credit. Our model for optimal risk budgeting with skill (ORBS) helps managers allocate risk among such macro strategies. Risk projections for each strategy are based on historical volatilities and correlations, whereas return projections are based on the manager's directional views and stated skill levels.

Yet portfolio exposures are not limited to macro factors. Subjective views on specific issuers can be a major driver of outperformance, especially in credit portfolios. Recent developments in credit markets have created liquid markets in many types of credit derivatives, which makes the implementation of issuer-specific and macro strategies much more similar. For example, one could take an exposure to credit as a whole using a portfolio product such as CDX or iTraxx, or to a particular sector using the sector-specific versions of these contracts, or to a specific issuer using single-name credit default swaps (CDS). Any of these strategies can be used to take either a long-credit exposure by selling protection or a short-credit exposure by buying protection; and all three markets are quite liquid. For market participants who may use them, these products offer great flexibility to implement strategies that would have been impractical using "cash" bonds alone.

Given the ease with which they can implement either a sector or an issuer view, some credit managers have begun to consider them on an equal level. Given a set of long and short views on specific issuers as well as on various sectors, what is the right level of risk to assign to the implementation of each such view? This

Based on research first published by Lehman Brothers in 2004.

question motivated the creation of "credit ORBS," which combines directional views on both issuers and credit sectors to construct the optimal portfolio.

In the following section, we review the ORBS model for macro-level allocation of risk to various strategies, based on directional views and skill. Next, we discuss the various approaches we have taken to incorporate security selection effects into this framework. We then describe in detail the credit ORBS model, which uses specific issuer views and allows various types of long-short trading strategies. An example of the model's output illustrates the trade-off between macro and micro strategies as well as the effect of leverage.

THE ORBS MODEL

The ORBS model was developed as the culmination of a sequence of historical simulation studies of investment style carried out over the past several years. The skill-based approach underlying this effort was described in Chapter 1. In Chapter 2, we applied this methodology to the task of managing a global fixed-income portfolio using a combination of macro strategies, including views on interest rates and foreign exchange rates in multiple currencies, as well as global views on various spread sectors, from agencies and investment-grade credit to high yield and emerging markets. We found that for all core strategies for which the manager could express a view in either direction, similar information ratios are produced for a given level of skill.

This key observation—that the achieved information ratio is essentially determined by the skill level—is consistent with the "fundamental law of active management" as proposed by Grinold and Kahn.[1] They show that the information ratio, IR, is a function of skill and strategy breadth:

$$IR \cong Skill \cdot \sqrt{Breadth}. \qquad (25\text{-}1)$$

The breadth is the number of independent decisions made each period, and the skill is represented by the information coefficient, which is defined as the correlation between forecasts and actual outcomes. Our skill parameter is equivalent to Grinold and Kahn's information coefficient if we limit ourselves to directional decisions and directional outcomes.

Our study on global macro strategies also dealt with combinations of strategies. Obviously, it is advantageous for managers to focus their efforts on the strategies in which they have the most skill. However, there is a diversification benefit to splitting the portfolio's risk among several different alpha-generation strategies,

---

1. Richard C. Grinold and Ronald N. Kahn, *Active Portfolio Management*, McGraw-Hill, 1999.

rather than concentrating on a single one. We showed, for example, that even if the skill at timing global duration is higher than that at timing high yield spreads, the right combination of the two strategies can produce a higher information ratio than either strategy alone.

After conclusion of that study, the challenge was to apply the model to a forward-looking optimal allocation of risk to strategies. We soon realized that the definition of skill based on the probability of a correct call can provide a good fit for managers who feel more comfortable making directional calls than precise basis point forecasts. The risk allocation problem faced by many managers can be formulated as follows: Given a set of directional views on a diverse set of strategies, find the optimal allocation of risk among these strategies so as to maximize the expected outperformance subject to an overall limit on portfolio tracking error volatility (i.e., the risk budget). Assuming that we can model the risk associated with each proposed trade, as well as the correlations between these positions, the main quantity that remains to be specified is the expected return for each such exposure.

In ORBS, we back out the strategy expected returns from the fundamental law cited earlier. The information ratio of an investment strategy is defined as the ratio of portfolio outperformance over tracking error volatility or active risk:

$$IR = \frac{\alpha}{TE}. \tag{25-2}$$

Combining Equations (25-1) and (25-2), we obtain the following expression for α:

$$\alpha = TE \cdot IR \cong TE \cdot Skill \cdot \sqrt{Breadth}. \tag{25-3}$$

That is, the active return of a strategy is a function of active risk, investment skill, and the diversity of bets that it implements. A key implication here is that a risk-budgeting framework can help make allocation decisions based on directional views without requiring strategists to make precise basis point forecasts of market movements. Indeed, in the presence of skill, risk eventually translates into outperformance.

Equation (25-3) describes only one active strategy implemented in the portfolio, or assumes that all active bets benefit from a uniform investment skill and all generate identical contributions to tracking error volatility. In practice, the investment process includes different strategies supported by different sets of skills. The expected portfolio outperformance is the sum of contributions of individual strategies and reflects the information ratio of, and the risk budget allocated to, each active strategy on a stand-alone basis:

$$\alpha_P = \sum_i TE_i \cdot IR_i = \sum_i TE_i \cdot Skill \cdot \sqrt{Breadth}. \tag{25-4}$$

The portfolio active risk combines the tracking errors generated by each individual strategy, but reflects the correlation structure among the payoffs of different strategies. In various ORBS implementations, we have used two distinct methods to measure strategy risk. In the direct method, we simulate the historical returns of all strategies and compute their historical volatilities and correlations. Suppose, for example, that a strategy expresses a view on credit spreads vs. swaps. The risk of this strategy would be measured based on the time series of excess returns of credit over duration-matched swaps. In an alternative method, we compute the risk exposures of each strategy to the standard set of risk factors in our global risk model and use the model to calculate the strategy volatilities and correlations.

We can optimize the mix of active strategies in much the same way one would optimize a static asset portfolio. However, in contrast to traditional mean-variance optimization, the optimal allocation is not defined in terms of market value weights to individual assets. Rather, we find the optimal allocation of active risk to a set of individual alpha-generating strategies. This allocation is then translated into position amounts. Thus, instead of making a detailed forecast of the magnitudes of changes in market variables, the investor identifies those trades that are expected to perform well and provides assumptions of skill at timing such trades.

The effect of strategy correlations on the optimal risk allocation depends on the directionality of the stated views. For example, spreads on investment-grade credit and high yield credit have a strong positive correlation. As a result, if the views on both of these asset classes are positive, the risks of implementing the two views simultaneously are largely additive, and the optimal allocation limits the positions to relatively small sizes. However, if the view is to go long investment-grade and short high yield (or vice versa), the risks of the two positions are partially offsetting, and position sizes of larger magnitudes are allowed in the two trades.

ORBS has been used across a broad range of portfolio management applications and markets. We have worked with individual managers to form suites of strategies that correspond to their particular styles. Strategies have included views on global interest rates (at various levels of detail), spread sectors, high yield and emerging markets, FX rates, and equities. We have taken great care to model implementation constraints so that the model provides practical solutions to the allocation problem.

ORBS can be used in different ways throughout the portfolio management process. Portfolio managers use it as described earlier to help find the risk allocation that most efficiently implements their subjective views. CIOs can rely on it to answer more abstract questions about their management process. When planning the research effort, where will an increase in skill have the greatest impact on performance? How much would an additional strategy or the relaxation of a particular constraint improve the expected performance of the portfolio? What levels of skill are needed in a given set of strategies in order to achieve a target alpha while remaining within the risk budget? The answers to these questions, which may be obtained by running ORBS with different sets of inputs, can help make the case for investment policy changes. These could include, for example, the addition of a new asset class or strategy, a change in the target alpha or the risk budget, or a loosening of some of the constraints under which the manager must operate.

MODELING SECURITY SELECTION WITHIN THE ASSET ALLOCATION PROCESS

Risk budgeting is essentially a top-down process, so one can view security selection strictly as an implementation issue, to be treated independently. For example, the Lehman Brothers global risk model reports separately on systematic risk from exposures to macro factors and idiosyncratic risk from issuer concentrations. One could conceivably set up separate risk limits to deal with each type of risk: issuer risk might be controlled via an overall limit on idiosyncratic tracking error volatility and/or by explicit limits on issuer exposures, whereas systematic risk could be controlled by a cap on systematic tracking error volatility. In this framework, risk budgeting could apply to the systematic portion alone to determine the optimal set of systematic risk exposures given the manager's macro views.

However, this strict separation between macro allocation and security selection does not always give the best results. First, how do we decide upon an a priori allocation between systematic and idiosyncratic risk? Second, this approach ignores the various types of interactions that may exist between top-down and bottom-up effects in portfolios and is likely to result in a suboptimal overall risk allocation or an underutilization of the overall risk budget.

There are several ways to incorporate security selection effects in a risk-budgeting framework. One can view these as different ways to find the right balance between a pure macro-level allocation model and a pure security-level optimization.

Macro Allocation with Consideration of Security Selection Issues

The first, and simplest, approach involves a modification of the macro-level risk-budgeting model to recognize the fact that we must leave room within the overall risk budget for idiosyncratic risk, and that depending on the macro allocation, different amounts of idiosyncratic risk can be assumed. If a primary view is to go long Baa credit, we must recognize that this position is liable to entail much more issuer risk than, for example, a long view on the Treasury curve. In the latter

Figure 25-1. Example Specification of Risk and Reward for Issuer Selection within Different Market Sectors

Asset Class	Idiosyncratic Volatility (bp/year)	Idiosyncratic Alpha (bp/year)
Governments	5	0
Agencies	20	10
Investment-grade corporates	50	30
High yield corporates	100	50

case, we might allow for a greater amount of systematic risk within the overall risk budget.

The next step is to recognize that a portfolio's exposure to specific issuers brings not only risk, but also a potential reward for superior security selection. The expected outperformance from security selection may be very different from one asset class to another. For example, an allocation to credit obviously offers more potential for security selection outperformance than an allocation to agencies. By specifying how much alpha can be expected from security selection for each asset class, we can consider these factors when maximizing outperformance within the risk budget. In Chapter 24, we showed how this approach can be used to model a bias toward a certain sector. For example, some managers tend to be long credit even when their macro view on credit is neutral because they are confident in their ability to generate outperformance via issuer selection. Reducing the allocation to credit in an all-cash setting would reduce the potential for alpha generation from security selection.

In several ORBS implementations, we have adopted this view of the allocation process. It requires from the portfolio manager only one more set of inputs, the idiosyncratic excess return volatility and expected alpha within each asset class, as illustrated in Figure 25-1. It is important to note that these parameters are not necessarily characteristic of the asset class as a whole, but rather of how an allocation to this asset class is likely to be managed within a given portfolio. Highly diversified portfolios would generate little issuer-specific risk and little security selection alpha. The opposite should be true of concentrated portfolios.

In this framework, the issuer selection style within each sector is an input and influences macro-allocation decisions. For example, a money manager may allocate a portion of a particular mandate to an internal high yield fund that is known to be managed with a certain style and risk level. This information will be considered when setting the allocation to high yield. In this approach, the idiosyncratic risk and return expected from each asset class are allowed to influence the allocation process. However, it remains essentially a top-down process; the only decision variables in the optimization are the allocations to each macro strategy.

Choosing the Issuer Selection Style

Another approach is to allow the risk-budgeting process more control over the underlying investments within each asset class. That is, not only should it determine how large a risk exposure to take in corporates, but also how to structure this portion of the portfolio—how concentrated or diversified this portion should be. In this approach, the model has much more freedom to trade off systematic and idiosyncratic risk against each other. The overall risk budget can be spent by taking on large active sector exposures using highly diversified portfolios within each sector, focusing on macro views to generate alpha and minimizing the idiosyncratic risk. Alternatively, managers might choose to focus their alpha-generation efforts on security selection. In this case, the portfolio may have relatively small sector exposures, with most of the risk budget dedicated to the idiosyncratic risk from issuer concentrations.

There are a number of questions that have to be answered in this setting. How much idiosyncratic risk should be taken within each sector? How should the overall risk budget be divided among systematic and idiosyncratic risk? To what extent should this allocation depend on the level of idiosyncratic risk in the marketplace?

To address these issues in the simplest possible way, we formulate a simple risk-budgeting exercise consisting of just three sectors: Treasuries, A financials, and Baa industrials. The only systematic views considered are long or short the two corporate sectors and long or short duration. In addition, there is room for additional risk and return from security selection within the two corporate sectors. Given a fixed overall risk budget, a set of systematic views, and skill parameters corresponding to each strategy, we seek to optimize the outperformance vs. a simple benchmark.

We assume that the benchmark contains a 40% allocation to Treasuries and 30% to each of the corporate sectors, with a 5-year duration in each sector. The portfolio optimization problem is to set five parameters in order to maximize alpha, subject to a fixed risk budget: (1) duration, (2) allocation to A financials, (3) allocation to Baa industrials, (4) number of bonds in A financials, and (5) number of bonds in Baa industrials.

We assume that the corporate sectors of the portfolio match the 5-year index duration, so that the allocation uniquely determines the spread duration exposure; the duration decision is independent of the allocation to the corporate sectors and is assumed to be implemented either within the Treasury portion of the portfolio

Figure 25-2. The Simple Three-Factor Risk Model to Measure Systematic Risk

	Factor Volatility (bp/month)	Correlation Matrix		
		10-Year	Finance A	Industrials Baa
10-year yield	30	1.0	−0.2	−0.3
Finance A spreads	10	−0.2	1.0	0.5
Industrials Baa spreads	15	−0.3	0.5	1.0

or using a futures overlay. The Treasury allocation is just 100% minus the allocations to the two corporate sectors and is constrained to be nonnegative.

Systematic risk is determined within this framework using a simple risk model with three factors: changes to Treasury yields, A financial spreads, and Baa industrial spreads. The three are assumed to be characterized by the arbitrarily specified factor volatilities and correlations shown in Figure 25-2. We have assumed that the two spread factors are positively correlated and that each of the spread factors is negatively correlated with the yield factor. These properties, although not necessarily the precise numbers, are consistent with historical experience.

We measure nonsystematic risk by assuming that the holdings of both the index and the portfolio within a given sector are composed of an equally weighted mix of bonds, except that the index has 100 bonds in each sector and the portfolio has the number determined in the optimization. Within each sector, based on the allocation, the number of bonds, and the assumed 5-year spread duration,[2] we can calculate the size of the spread duration mismatch between the portfolio and benchmark for each of the bonds held in the portfolio (typically overweights) and for each of the benchmark bonds not held in the portfolio (underweights). We then characterize each sector by the level of idiosyncratic spread volatility typical for an issuer in that sector. Our base case assumption is 15 bp/month for A financial issuers and 30 bp/month for Baa industrials. We assume here that the Treasury portion of the portfolio has no idiosyncratic risk or alpha. The overall risk of the portfolio is then calculated assuming that the risks of all idiosyncratic exposures are not correlated with each other or with the systematic risk.

In our risk-budgeting framework, the expected outperformance from implementing a view is proportional to the risks taken, with the proportionality factor determined by the assumed level of skill associated with the view and the breadth

---

2. As with the systematic risk exposures, the exposure to idiosyncratic issuer spread change is measured by contributions to spread duration. For simplicity, we assume that every credit bond has a spread duration of 5 years.

Alpha (bp/month)

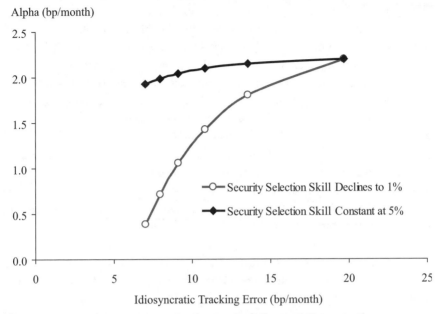

Idiosyncratic Tracking Error (bp/month)

Figure 25-3. Idiosyncratic Risk and Return under Different Skill Assumptions

of the strategy. For each systematic view, we assume a skill level of 10% and a breadth of one decision per month.

For projecting the alpha owing to security selection, we assume that the number of bonds selected affects the calculation in several different ways simultaneously. First, as already discussed, the number of portfolio bonds in a given sector determines the spread duration exposure for each bond in the portfolio and thus determines the nonsystematic tracking error volatility. Second, the number of bonds is used as the breadth of the strategy. Third, the skill level for security selection within a sector is itself considered to be a function of the number of bonds. We cannot assume that even highly skilled analysts with solid track records can maintain the same level of skill as we ask them to consider more and more bonds. Therefore, we specify security selection skill on a sliding scale. Our base case assumption is that, within each sector, analysts can select either five bonds with 5% skill or thirty bonds with 1% skill. Between these two values, skill is a linear function of the number of bonds chosen.

Figure 25-3 shows the results of this model for idiosyncratic alpha as we vary the number of bonds from five to thirty. At the maximum-risk point on the graph, there are five bonds in the portfolio, and the skill level is 5% according to both assumptions. As we increase the number of bonds, tracking error volatility decreases, and we start moving left along the graph. If we assume that security selection skill is constant regardless of how many bonds are chosen, the reduction in tracking error volatility is almost exactly offset by the increase in breadth, and the alpha remains almost unchanged. In this case, one can find little justification for portfolio concentrations of any kind: the optimal solution will always be to diversify as much as possible. When we link increasing diversification with declining skill, we obtain a much more interesting and realistic trade-off between the costs and benefits of expressing security selection views. This particular set of assumptions represents a rather steep decline in alpha with increasing diversification. Various other functional forms can be suggested to model this dependence. The best representation for this function depends on the approach to credit research within a given organization.

To carry out an optimal risk-budgeting example, we must specify a set of views. We take a systematic view to go long industrial Baa spreads (at 10% skill), with neutral views on the other two systematic factors. The main risk trade-off in this case is just how much of the risk to place on an overweight to Baa industrials vs. concentrations in selected names. Figure 25-4 shows results for two different assumptions about the level of security selection skill.

In the first case, we assume that security selection skill is relatively high: 5% if we choose just five bonds per sector, down to 1% if we choose thirty bonds. In this case, the tracking error volatility is dominated by nonsystematic risk. Positions in each credit bond are about 4% of the portfolio. The overweight to industrials comes mostly at the expense of Treasuries, and the position in financials contributes to security selection outperformance. Despite the neutral view on interest rates, the portfolio is long duration, which results in a small reduction in overall risk, owing to the negative correlation between rates and credit spreads.

When security selection skill is weak, ranging from a high of only 2% down to 1%, the results are very different. The overweight to industrials is even larger, and more of it comes at the expense of financials; the positive correlation between financial and industrial sector spreads makes a long-short sector strategy an attractive outperformance bet. In this situation, the sector view dominates portfolio performance, and the balance of risk allocation tilts in favor of systematic risk.

In Figure 25-5, we repeat this exercise for different levels of security selection skill. In each case, the skill level shown is for the most concentrated case allowed, that is, five securities per sector. The skill for thirty bonds per sector is set at 1% in every case. We see the trend described earlier continued. At very low skill levels, the sector view is translated into a straight sector spread trade, overweighting the favored industrials vs. the correlated financial sector. At a skill level of about 6%, the financial allocation is neutral; outperformance is generated by overweighting industrials vs. Treasuries and by security selection. At very high idiosyncratic skill levels, we end up with slight overweights not only to industrials but also to

Figure 25-4. Example Optimization Results. Systematic Views
Long Industrial Baa, Neutral on Duration and Finance A: (a) Security Selection Skill:
5% for 5 Bonds, to 1% for 30 Bonds; (b) Security Selection Skill: 2% for Five Bonds,
to 1% for Thirty Bonds

(a)
Composition of Portfolio and Benchmark

	Benchmark Weight	Portfolio Weight	Difference	Number of Bonds	Position Size
Treasuries	40%	24%	−16%		
Finance A	30%	27%	−3%	6	4.30%
Industrials Baa	30%	50%	20%	13	3.80%
Duration	5.00	5.14	0.14		

	Alpha (bp/month)	Tracking Error Volatility (bp/month)	Information Ratio (annualized)
Systematic	1.5	13.4	0.4
Idiosyncratic	3.6	21.1	0.6
Total	5.0	25.0	0.7

(b)
Composition of Portfolio and Benchmark

	Benchmark Weight	Portfolio Weight	Difference	Number of Bonds	Position Size
Treasuries	40%	26%	−14%		
Finance A	30%	15%	−15%	8	2.00%
Industrials Baa	30%	59%	29%	24	2.40%
Duration	5.0	5.2	0.2		

	Alpha (bp/month)	Tracking Error Volatility (bp/month)	Information Ratio (annualized)
Systematic	2.2	18.5	0.4
Idiosyncratic	1.2	16.8	0.3
Total	3.4	25.0	0.5

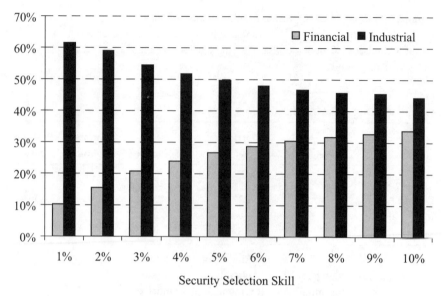

Figure 25-5. Credit Sector Allocations as a Function of Security Selection Skill

financials, as the prospect of security-specific return proves to be the main driver of performance.

Figure 25-6 shows the effect of changing the overall risk budget. We assume the low level of security selection skill, shown in Figure 25-4b, with only 2% skill for the most favored bets. As we raise the risk budget, the size of the overweight to the favored industrial sector grows steadily. We observe that the allocation to the financial sector, on which we are neutral, drops to zero when the overall risk budget reaches 35 bp/month. From this point on, additional risk is exercised by further increasing the overweight to industrials at the expense of Treasuries.

When the same exercise is carried out assuming that security selection skill goes up to 5%, the systematic allocations (not shown) are very different. The overweight to industrials comes largely at the expense of Treasuries, with the allocation to financials maintained at index level until the Treasury allocation has been reduced to zero at a risk budget of 45 bp/month. Only then do we begin to reduce the position in financials, giving up the opportunity for security selection outperformance in that sector.

How does the allocation between systematic and idiosyncratic risk depend on the current environment? Investors have wondered how they should adjust their portfolio management style during times of low idiosyncratic spread volatility. Should they increase issuer concentrations at such times in an effort to add alpha? Should they rather focus on systematic views?

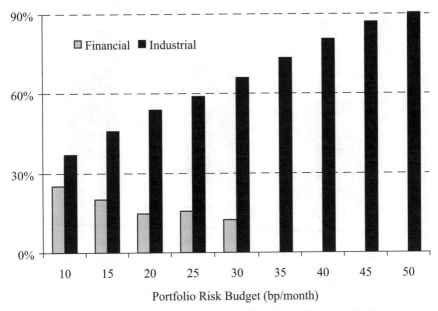

Figure 25-6. Credit Sector Allocations as a Function of Overall Risk Budget

Using the simple model presented here (with a maximum security selection skill of 5%), we perturbed our base case assumptions for idiosyncratic volatility (15 bp/month for financials and 30 bp/month for industrials) up and down by one third—to 10 and 20 bp/month in the low-volatility case and to 20 and 40 bp in the high-volatility case. The results are shown in Figure 25-7. In part (a), we see the predictable effect on the number of securities. As the idiosyncratic spread volatilities increase, we increase the number of bonds in the portfolio, diversifying further to keep risk within limits; when volatilities decline, we are free to take bigger concentrations in the portfolio. Part (b) shows a less obvious effect; the smaller number of bonds in the portfolio in the low-volatility case does not fully offset the decrease in volatility. As a result, the idiosyncratic tracking error volatility is lower overall despite the greater concentration; this, in turn, allows an increase in systematic risk and a better balance between systematic and nonsystematic tracking error volatility. The opposite observations can be made in the high-volatility case.

Credit ORBS: Equal Treatment of Macro and Issuer Views

Both Chapter 24, which describes how security selection considerations can impact macro allocation, and the analysis of investment style in the previous section

Number of Bonds

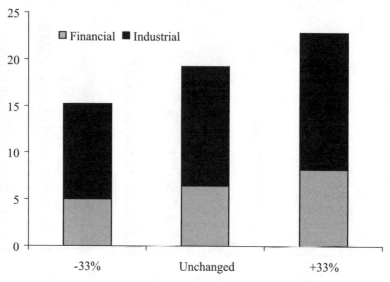

a   Change in Issuer-Specific Spread Volatility from Base Case

Tracking Error Components (bp/month)

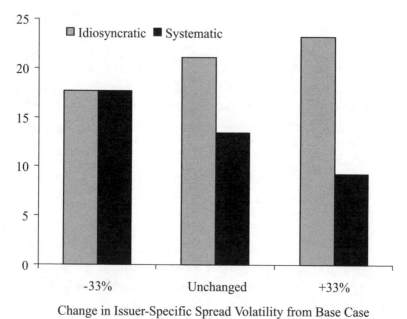

b   Change in Issuer-Specific Spread Volatility from Base Case

Figure 25-7. Effect of Changes in Idiosyncratic Spread Volatility on Optimal Portfolio Allocations

(a) Number of Credit Bonds; (b) Allocation between Idiosyncratic and Systematic Risk

treat security selection in the abstract. We have characterized the security selection return we can achieve within a sector by a small set of parameters—selection skill, number of bonds, and spread volatility—and investigated how this affects the overall asset allocation. However, managers who are about to rebalance their portfolios to reflect current views see things in much more concrete terms. They usually have clear views on particular sectors relative to corporates overall, as well as on specific issuers that they would like to include in their portfolios. How much risk should be assigned to each view?

One possible approach would be to drop the macro orientation of our risk-budgeting framework entirely and carry out a full-blown portfolio optimization at the level of issuers or even bonds. However, the additional complexity of such a model has a price in terms of computational issues, ease of use, and transparency of results. In addition, we may end up missing the forest for the trees. How would such an optimizer determine exactly how much risk to allocate to each macro view? How much of a duration exposure should the portfolio have to reflect a bullish view on rates?

To address these issues, we have developed the credit ORBS model, which stakes out a middle ground between the pure macro allocation of ORBS and a true issuer-level optimization. The model is designed in a hierarchical fashion that mimics the way credit is approached at many institutions. Within each sector, an analyst ranks a set of covered issuers into a set of discrete categories. The number of categories used and their specific descriptions vary from one institution to another. The available set of categories may be {long, short, neutral} or {outperform, underperform, market perform}, and there may be more than one level of positive or negative views. In addition, investment teams may follow different definitions of sectors and different strategies for implementing sector views. Nevertheless, this general approach of expressing issuer views by ranking them into several categories within each sector is quite prevalent in the industry.

In credit ORBS, we form a set of issuers upon which a positive view has been expressed (the "longs") and a set of issuers for which the view is negative (the "shorts") within each sector. We use these sets as the basic building blocks from which the portfolio is to be composed. We assume that a long exposure to a specific set of issuers may be implemented with a portfolio of either bonds or CDS; a short exposure would be assumed to be implemented with CDS. These baskets of specifically selected issuers are used to build bottom-up strategies for outperformance. In addition, they may be augmented by credit portfolio products such as CDX and iTraxx contracts to help implement top-down views with much less idiosyncratic risk or to help hedge out the systematic exposures in an issuer selection trade.

	Sector Rotation			Implement with:			Security Selection	Num. issuers	
	Skill		Strategy	CDX/iTraxx [Flip all]	Longs [Flip all]	Shorts [Flip all]	Skill	Long	Short
Overall Credit Allocation	15		Long						
EUR		Banking/Finance	Neutral	☐	☑	☐	5	22	20
		Basic Industry	Long	☐	☑	☐	5	8	14
		Cyclical	Neutral	☐	☑	☐	5	8	8
	10	Non-Cyclical	Short	☐	☑	☐	5	6	0
		Communication	Neutral	☐	☑	☐	5	4	7
		Utility	Neutral	☐	☑	☐	5	10	11
		High Yield	Neutral	☐	☑	☐	5	9	3
USD		Banking/Finance	Neutral	☑	☐	☐	5	22	25
		Basic Industry	Neutral	☑	☑	☐	5	22	18
		Cyclical	Neutral	☑	☐	☑	5	6	6
	10	Non-Cyclical	Neutral	☐	☑	☑	5	10	19
		Communication	Neutral	☑	☑	☑	6	14	14
		Utility	Neutral	☐	☑	☐	5	20	17
		High Yield	Neutral	☐	☑	☐	5	10	7

Figure 25-8. Credit ORBS Example: Specification of Macro Views and Implementation Choices

The credit ORBS formulation allows these simple building blocks to be combined in different ways to offer an extremely versatile set of strategies. A sample implementation is shown in Figure 25-8. For each sector, the manager specifies a directional view as well as the combination of products within that sector. In most portfolios, the set of implementation choices is likely to be the same for most sectors; in this example, we have tried to illustrate the different types of strategies that can be implemented.

Within the various sectors of the EUR credit market, the check boxes indicate that the sector allocations can be filled only by going long the selected basket of favored issuers. This corresponds to an all-cash portfolio in which the position in a sector is implemented by taking long positions in selected bonds.

Within the USD credit sectors, we have checked off a different implementation strategy for each sector. For banking/finance, we express a pure macro view on the sector, with as little idiosyncratic risk as possible. This can be accomplished with the appropriate CDX sector contract, either alone or against the overall CDX contract. In basic industry, we have selected both the CDX sector contract and the long-issuer basket. This enables us to go long our basket of favored issuers and short the CDX sector contract, to hedge out as much of the systematic exposure as possible and leave a pure issuer exposure. In the cyclical sector, we turn this around, specifying a combination of CDX contracts and short positions in the basket of issuers for which we have bearish views (buy protection on this set of names). This allows the expression of negative views on specific issuers relative to their industry peer group. In the noncyclical sector, we do not use the CDX contract, but choose a long-short strategy in which we go long certain issuers and short others within the sector. In the communications sector, all three boxes are checked, to allow the full flexibility to mix and match these strategies within the specified limits on tracking error volatility and leverage.

We have seen that this simple structure, in which the portfolio's position within a sector is built with three prespecified baskets of credits (the traded contract, the set of "longs," and the set of "shorts"), can express a wide range of strategies. Still, might the portfolio's flexibility be somewhat limited by its inability to diversify further into issuers on which the view is neutral? We are confident that this is not the case. In prior research on credit diversification,[3] we found that, given an analyst's positive and negative views on a subset of the issuers in the market, the highest information ratio can be achieved by either of two very different strategies, which can be thought of as "picking winners" and "avoiding losers." In the former, the portfolio should contain only names on which the outlook is positive and none of the securities for which the outlook is negative or neutral. In the latter, the portfolio diversifies as much as possible, while excluding the issuers for which the outlook is negative. Both of these strategies can be easily implemented using the three-basket approach of credit ORBS.

Modeling Risk and Return in Credit ORBS

The issuer selection process is implemented as follows. First, the manager specifies the universe of issuers covered by the fund's credit research. Then, for every covered name, the manager can express a view—positive (long), neutral, or negative (short). The model then gathers all the issuers for which the manager has specified a positive view within a given sector and forms an equally weighted set of these issuers. The risk of this basket of bonds is calculated based on data from the Lehman Brothers global risk model.[4]

The idiosyncratic risk is estimated by mapping each security with a nonneutral view onto one of the idiosyncratic "shelves" defined in the risk model. These shelves are peer groups organized by currency-sector-quality, for example, USD-industrial-Baa. All issuers in the same peer group are assumed to have identical

---

3. See Chapter 14.
4. See Chapter 26.

idiosyncratic spread volatility. By definition, residuals are assumed to be uncorre-lated with each other. Consequently, the larger the number of bonds within a sector on which the manager has a view, the lower the idiosyncratic volatility of the basket. The alpha associated with the selection of a particular issuer is assumed to be proportional to both the issuer selection skill and the idiosyncratic volatility of the issuer, in accordance with Equation (25-3). However, the idiosyncratic alpha within a sector is not directly affected by the number of selected issuers because, other things being equal, a larger number of issuers simply means smaller alloca-tions to each. The specific set of issuers selected within a given sector affects the assumption for idiosyncratic alpha primarily through the quality distribution of the chosen issuers—lower quality names are modeled as having greater risk and, therefore, greater opportunity for alpha.

The systematic risk is also estimated with the help of the global risk model. Each trading strategy—long a CDX sector contract, long a basket of positive-view issuers, short a basket of negative-view issuers—is mapped onto a vector of sys-tematic risk factors (exposures to industry × quality cells). This allows us to use the risk model covariance matrix to quantify the systematic risk of the portfolio exposures.[5] Once again, the systematic alpha assumed for each strategy is based on the amount of risk taken, the stated directional view, and the assumed level of skill.

To implement a long view in a particular sector, the model can consider two distinct options: the sector contract and the basket of positive-view issuers. Both should provide similar systematic risk and alpha, but very different idiosyncratic behavior—close to zero idiosyncratic risk and alpha for the sector contract and much more significant issuer selection risk and alpha for the basket of issuers.

Because issuer selection is a distinct source of outperformance, the assumed skill levels for this task are considered independent of those assigned to sector rotation decisions. In fact, although there is one skill level for sector rotation (in a particular currency), name selection skills in different sectors need not be the same. Indeed, larger institutions tend to have teams of credit analysts who spe-cialize by sectors.

Example Optimization

To illustrate the model's implementation, we present the following example with two systematic views: long communications and short cyclical; we also labeled

---

5. Just as in the risk model, the manager may choose to measure risk based on historical data that is equally weighted over a long time period or use a weighted approach that emphasizes recent history.

five issuers with a positive view and five issuers with a negative view within each global credit sector.[6] The skill at sector allocation was assumed to be 10% and that at security selection 5%. Note that this example does not correspond to the inputs shown in Figure 25-4. We ran the model in the most flexible setting, allowing it to use both CDX and iTraxx contracts and baskets of single-issuer CDS on a long and short basis (i.e., both selling and buying protection).[7] Leverage was permitted up to a limit of 100% of market value; this was defined by a constraint that the sum of the notional values of all the long and short positions, respectively, may not exceed 200 and 100% of portfolio market value. The risk budget was set to 25 bp/month. The results of the optimal risk budgeting are shown in Figure 25-9.

We see that the model utilizes leverage to capitalize on both sector and issuer views. The net exposure to communication is +99.6% of portfolio market value, while the net exposure to cyclicals is –47.4%. This systematic exposure is implemented in the issuer-specific portion of the portfolio using a combination of the "long" and "short" issuer baskets and augmented by an overlay of CDX and iTraxx sector contracts that push this exposure even further. It is interesting that despite this sector view, the model still allocates some weight to long positions in the favored cyclical issuers and short positions in the lowest-ranked communications issuers. In sectors with a neutral systematic view, such as basic industry, the tendency is to play the long issuers against the short with a minimal net exposure to the sector. The portfolio achieves a fairly even balance of the systematic and idiosyncratic risk; the expected outperformance is also well balanced, with just a bit more coming from the more highly diversified issuer-specific views.

The relatively high information ratio of 1.94 (annualized) might be achieved because of several assumptions that may not be appropriate for every portfolio. First, we assumed quite an active issuer selection program. We specified five positive and five negative issuer views within each of the six sectors, for a total of 60 issuer-specific views; despite this rather prolific generation of trade ideas, we assumed a relatively high skill level of 5%. Second, we allowed the portfolio to be leveraged up by 100%, facilitating the use of long-short strategies to magnify the issuer positions while hedging the sector exposures. If we limit the portfolio to long positions only, using just the baskets of positive-view issuers, the information ratio falls to 1.04.

---

6. The model actually distinguishes between the sector views in different currencies as well as the allocations by sector within each currency; we have combined these here for simplicity of presentation.

7. This corresponds to checking all of the check boxes shown in Figure 25-8, as was illustrated there for the USD communications sector.

Figure 25-9. Example Risk Budget Allocation for a Global Long/Short Credit Portfolio

Risk Budget 25 bp/month, Leverage Limit 100%

Risk/Reward Summary

Total portfolio tracking error (bp/month)	25.0
Systematic (bp/month)	17.6
Idiosyncratic (bp/month)	17.8
Portfolio alpha (bp/month)	14.0
Systematic (bp/month)	6.0
Idiosyncratic (bp/month)	8.0
Information ratio (annualized)	1.94

Position Summary (% of Portfolio MV)

	Long	Short	Net
CDX/iTraxx contracts	41.7	-32.7	8.9
Bonds/CDS	132.2	-67.2	65.0
Cash	26.1	0.0	26.1
Total	200.0	-100.0	100.0

Sector Exposures (% of Portfolio MV)

	CDX/iTraxx Contracts (% of Portfolio MV)	Specific Issuer Exposures (% of Portfolio MV)			Alpha (bp/month)	
		Longs	Shorts	Net	Systematic	Idiosyncratic
Banking/finance	0.0	14.8	-10.8	3.9	0.0	0.8
Basic industry	1.7	17.6	-16.2	3.0	0.0	1.2
Cyclical	-32.7	3.2	-17.8	-47.4	1.9	1.2
Noncyclical	0.0	16.6	-6.6	10.0	0.0	0.8
Communication	40.0	60.5	-1.0	99.6	4.1	3.1
Utility	0.0	19.6	-14.8	4.8	0.0	0.9
Total	8.9	132.2	-67.2	73.9	6.0	8.0

CONCLUSION

The ORBS model provides managers with the ability to allocate risk among multiple macro strategies, based on skilled directional views and historically derived risk measures. Several different approaches may be taken to incorporate issuer views into this optimization framework. The interaction between sector allocation and security selection is quite complex and far beyond the scope of this short chapter. We have not discussed the effect of several key practical issues, from unequal issuer weights in the benchmark to correlations at the issuer level.

There are two main points that we would like to emphasize. The first is that in order to address the trade-off between systematic and nonsystematic risk, it is imperative to model the effect of diversification on security selection outperformance. The second is how to manage these two aspects of risk. Is it a one-step process in which we simultaneously decide on the systematic risk allocations and the issuer-level structure of the portfolio within each sector? Or is it a two-step process: first establish a preferred level of issuer diversification within each sector and then optimize sector allocations to fit the macro views, keeping in mind the assumed levels of idiosyncratic risk and return within each sector?

The problem with the one-step approach is that in most portfolios, it is not practical to change the level of diversification on a regular basis. The problem with the two-step approach is even more basic: if we are going to fix the level of diversification for good, we had better get it right! On what basis is this determination made?

An integrated model that combines both approaches can ensure that the joint decisions are consistent and appropriately reflect the respective levels of skill and market volatility of the macro allocation and security selection decision processes.

Credit ORBS incorporates specific issuer views into the risk allocation process by summarizing them at the sector level. Along with the use of credit derivatives, this allows for an extremely flexible analysis of the allocation of risk between sector and issuer views.

MULTIFACTOR RISK MODELING
AND PERFORMANCE ATTRIBUTION

For a portfolio manager whose performance is measured relative to a benchmark, the difference between the portfolio and benchmark returns becomes a single, most important metric. Analytics systems and models are deployed to help managers control, monitor, and understand this difference. The models discussed in the next two chapters are designed to illuminate the sources of return differentials, both expected and realized. Risk analysis highlights potential return differences that may arise in the coming period (e.g., next month), while performance attribution explains the differences in the actual returns over a past period. In both cases, a detailed bottom-up analysis of the composition of the portfolio and the benchmark forms the basis for a calculation of the macro-level risk exposures and their return implications.

Conceptually, the portfolio management cycle proceeds as follows. At the start of a review period, managers express their views on macro-level market factors as well as on specific issuers and securities. These views largely determine the kinds and magnitudes of risk exposures built into the portfolio. Ideally, some formal risk-budgeting process such as the one described in the previous section is used to finalize the mix of portfolio exposures. The views are implemented via transactions, with a host of factors, such as risk limits, transaction costs, availability of securities, and pricing levels, affecting the final outcome. A risk model should be used throughout this stage to monitor the risk exposures, ensuring that no unintended bets are creeping in, that sufficient risk is allocated to each active view, and that the overall portfolio risk is within limits and in line with the alpha objective.

At the end of the review period, performance is analyzed with the same set of active views in mind, to determine outperformance owing to each macro call or issuer selection. (Over the long term, a performance record can be built for each strategy, allowing objective measurement of skill levels required for the optimal risk budgeting.)

Although risk analysis and performance attribution complement each other as ex ante and ex post views of the portfolio's performance, the challenges faced by the two models are quite different. Risk analysis has to consider the full range of possible market events and model the probability distribution of portfolio performance. Performance attribution, on the other hand, deals with known events, and the challenge is to untangle the combined effects of all market- and issuer-level events on outperformance, to map all these events onto the strategic decisions made at the outset, and to quantify the contribution of each decision to the overall result. Sometimes, to best explain an unexpected outcome in a given period, it is helpful to view the portfolio allocations in a way that highlights the exposure to a particular event. This reverse-engineering process often requires a level of detail and customization not feasible (nor necessary) in a risk model. As a result, despite the close functional relationship between the two models, we have developed them independently, each according to its own set of requirements.

Chapter 26 offers a comprehensive account of the risk model developed at Lehman Brothers and the broad scope of its portfolio management applications. The model was originally designed for the day-to-day management of portfolio risk exposures, as described earlier. However, the power of the model in summarizing the dynamics of return generation across fixed-income markets has made it extremely useful in many other ways, from the generation of scenarios consistent with history to portfolio optimization.

The fundamental influence of the risk model on our research manifests itself throughout this book. In our studies of index replication in Chapters 4 through 8, the risk model was used to corroborate the results of historical simulations of various replication strategies. When we implemented the risk-budgeting concepts of Chapters 24 and 25, we used risk model data to derive systematic factor covariances and to characterize nonsystematic risk in different sectors. In our work on empirical hedge ratios—of Bunds vs. Treasuries in Chapter 32 or of high yield bonds in Chapter 33—we cross-checked our results with those implied by the risk model.

Chapter 27 describes a "hybrid" performance attribution model with a focus on the risk exposures of a portfolio. Like the risk model, it recognizes that every security carries exposures to different types of risks that are likely to be managed separately. To analyze the return impact of management decisions, the model first splits the return of every security into different components and then attributes performance separately for each component, based on the relevant risk profile. For example, outperformance owing to yield changes is explained based on allocations to key-rate durations, just as in the risk model. Spread outperformance is analyzed based on allocations to different segments of the credit market. However, in the attribution of spread return based on sector allocations, the model departs from the fixed sector-quality partition of the risk model and allows much more flexibility in defining the market partition along which the portfolio is managed. As a result, the model is similar enough to the risk model to enable their complementary use within the portfolio management cycle, as described earlier; yet it allows a much higher degree of customization, so that it can reflect a manager's decisions as accurately as possible.

Performance attribution is carried out for different reasons and for different target audiences. A portfolio manager may use attribution to monitor and assess how his various market strategies have impacted performance in an ongoing effort to optimize the decision-making process. Alternatively, attribution may be performed to give a plan sponsor some color on the sources of portfolio outperformance. The head of a large management team might use attribution to assess the contributions of different team members to the overall portfolio performance. Clearly, these three settings present very different requirements for an attribution report. When the manager produces reports for his own use, the primary objective is to match the actual decision process as closely as possible; for investors, a less detailed, easier-to-follow view might be preferable; for team management, objective fairness is paramount. The ability to customize the analysis is thus critical.

One interesting difference between risk analysis and performance attribution, which has practical implications, concerns the data requirements of the two models. The calibration and maintenance of the risk model is extremely data intensive; the model is based on the realized monthly returns of tens of thousands of securities over the course of many years. However, to run a portfolio through the model one has to know only the composition of the portfolio and the benchmark at the time of the analysis. The data dependence in the attribution model runs in the other direction. No historical data from before the start of the review period is necessary. However, to achieve the most precise analysis possible, the model requires accurate daily pricing of every security in both the portfolio and the benchmark for every day in the return period, as well as a precise record of all portfolio transactions with the associated trade prices. This need for comprehensive portfolio pricing data is largely responsible for the following paradox: while predicting what might happen next is fundamentally a much more complex problem than explaining what happened in the past, it is widely acknowledged that performance attribution is more difficult to implement than risk analysis.

26. The Global Risk Model: A Portfolio Manager's Guide

Managing a fixed-income portfolio was once a reasonably simple endeavor. Total return portfolio managers generally kept their portfolios overweight in spread sector assets, in the form of a well-diversified group of issuers, and occasionally took modest duration bets. Moreover, up until the early 1980s, homeowners had yet to use repeated mortgage refinancing to supplement monthly income—so that mortgage prepayments were reasonably predictable and durations relatively stable. Of course there was market volatility and an occasional credit horror story, but by and large life for the portfolio manager was not so bad.

In such an environment, quantifying the risk of a fixed-income portfolio was not a major preoccupation for most managers or plan sponsors. An intuitive feel for how much a duration or sector over- or underweight could go "wrong" in a month was usually enough to measure the portfolio's overall risk. However, for several reasons, this intuitive approach to risk is no longer sufficient.

First, after the 2000–2002 equity market rout, there was a renewed understanding that even long-horizon investors had to be concerned with fluctuations in portfolio valuations. Companies, states, and municipalities have considerable future pension obligations and analysts (both equity and debt) are giving increasing attention to fluctuations in the funded status of pension plans. Consequently, as a liability-management tool, fixed-income securities are regaining some of the popularity they lost during the equity market boom. The increased attention and asset allocation to fixed income has been accompanied by very strong demand for better risk measurement from consultants, investors, and plan sponsors. Investors have learned the hard way that return must be adjusted for the risk exposure.

Second, with the poor equity returns in 2000–2002 and forecasts of only modest future equity returns over the balance of this decade, sponsors are paying

Based on research first published by Lehman Brothers in 2005.

increasing attention to returns on fixed-income assets. In a world of lower annual
equity returns, excellent fixed-income returns are, more than ever, integral to
a portfolio's overall performance. Fixed-income returns are too important to ignore. Underperforming a fixed-income benchmark by 100 bp, for example, is a
serious issue for the overall portfolio and must be explained and justified. Was
such underperformance the result of a well-calculated bet that at least offered the
possibility of good risk-adjusted performance, or did the manager just make a
major mistake? Plan sponsors and consultants now demand a full explanation.

Third, the array and complexity of fixed-income products increased substantially. Moreover, this occurred during a period in which the world economy
changed, and old, long-term relationships now seem less reliable. Imagine a corporate portfolio manager who took a sabbatical from the business in 1996 and
returned in 2004. In 1996, Ford (A-rated), Deutsche Telekom (Aa-rated), PG&E
(A-rated), AT&T (Aa-rated), J. C. Penney (A-rated), and the highly regarded
pipeline company Enron (Baa2-BBB+) were considered solid credits. An overweight to these names and sectors was considered an unremarkable, low-risk
credit portfolio. In 2004, an equivalent overweight to these names (if available)
would cause even the most experienced credit portfolio manager some anxiety. In
addition, what do recent developments such as credit derivatives, equity volatility,
correlated defaults, and "leveraged" capital imply about credit sector volatilities and
correlations?

Fourth, the growth of financial leverage (e.g., via hedge funds) has transformed
the marketplace, even for investors in Treasuries and highly rated credit debt. As
we learned during the 1998 collapse of Long-Term Capital Management, leverage
(especially the rapid unwinding of leverage) can exacerbate spread volatility.
Ironically, sponsors who prohibited their asset managers from using leverage
nevertheless suffered during this period. Measuring risk is everyone's priority.

Fifth, portfolios have become increasingly globalized. Plan sponsors and their
managers have learned the importance of having a range of less correlated bets in
a portfolio as a way to improve risk-adjusted performance. Consequently, many
plan sponsors have adopted highly diversified benchmarks such as the Lehman
Global Aggregate Index, which allows managers to express a wide range of low-
correlation views. However, moving to a global benchmark raises a number of
new questions. In particular, should the plan sponsor hire individual managers
for each currency market or hire global managers? Global managers have argued
that a single manager can allocate assets across markets to take better advantage
of investment opportunities and to track overall portfolio risk better. How can the
traditional domestic fixed-income manager compete in a world moving toward
more global benchmarks?

For a fixed-income portfolio, all these developments imply more varied risk exposure, less predictable volatilities and cross-market correlations, less reliance on intuition, and increased demand for more objective risk quantification. The increased attention to the quantification of risk has generated considerable interest in risk models—tools for estimating either the total return volatility of a portfolio or the volatility of the relative return of a portfolio vs. an index over a particular holding period. The risk model development effort at Lehman Brothers began in the mid-1980s and culminated in the launch of its first fixed-income risk model in 1991. Over subsequent years, as new asset classes (e.g., ABS and CMBS) emerged in the marketplace, they were added to the risk model. As new security analytics were developed, new modeling techniques were incorporated as well.

The job of a risk model is to quantify the sources of risks within a portfolio, reflecting the interrelationships among different exposures. For example, a mortgage portfolio manager generally knows that his portfolio contains many active positions vs. the benchmark. He may describe the portfolio as overweight duration, short spread duration, less negatively convex than the benchmark, and overweight both 15-year vs. 30-year and GNMAs vs. conventionals. However, how much risk is the portfolio taking? While many experienced portfolio managers have an intuitive idea as to what a single, active position, in isolation, means in terms of possible under- or outperformance, intuition reaches its limit when there are many simultaneous active decisions in the portfolio. Some active positions offset each other and reduce overall portfolio risk, whereas others can compound and increase risk. A risk model quantifies how these various risks are interrelated and adds real value by giving the portfolio manager a complete picture of the portfolio's risk exposure.

Consider the case of a corporate bond manager who has an undesired underweight exposure to the consumer cyclical sector. He has an opportunity to buy more of a cyclical issuer, such as Toyota. However, while this purchase would eliminate the sector underweight, it might produce an overweight in the issuer's name within the portfolio relative to the benchmark. Does the elimination of the sector-specific systematic risk more than offset the increase in idiosyncratic risk owing to the overweight in the issuer? Without a sophisticated risk model, any manager would be hard pressed to answer such a question.

These questions become more difficult as the scope of the portfolio and benchmark increase. For a portfolio benchmarked to the U.S. Aggregate Index, how does an MBS sector overweight relate to an agency sector underweight? Do these positions largely offset each other? If so, does this remain true if the MBS portfolio contains an overweight to GNMA premiums? The situation becomes even more complicated for a global manager using the Global Aggregate Index. What are the interrelationships for all of the various risk exposures in a global portfolio? If the manager is overweight euro cyclical corporates and decides to short yen vs. the dollar, has the manager increased or decreased the tracking error risk of the portfolio vs. the benchmark?

Plan sponsors can also use a risk model in their investment decision-making process. Many investment guidelines are structured by considering the allowable risks in isolation. For example, a manager must have the portfolio's duration within 0.5 year of the benchmark. Separately, the manager may only have an MBS sector overweight/underweight of at most 10% of the portfolio's market value. Some guidelines may specify a minimum percentage holding of GNMAs, but most are silent on the permissible convexity deviation vs. the benchmark. How much risk is the plan sponsor allowing the investment manager to take? A risk model can help answer such key questions.

The definition of risk varies depending on an investor's objectives. For a buy-and-hold investor with a long investment horizon and a stream of liabilities, the main sources of risk are the default risk of credit holdings and the re-investment risk of interim cash flows. For a total return investor benchmarked to a market index, risk is usually defined in terms of performance relative to the benchmark.

The Lehman Brothers global multifactor risk model focuses on the second definition of risk. It was developed to help investors benchmarked to one of the Lehman bond indices quantify the expected monthly volatility of the return difference between the portfolio and the benchmark. The model is based on the historical returns of individual securities in the Lehman indices, in many instances dating back to the late 1980s. Over time, with the accumulation of longer time series and further methodological improvements, the quality of the risk model should continue to improve.

The model derives historical magnitudes of different market risk factors and the relationships among them. It then measures current mismatches between portfolio and benchmark sensitivities to these risks and multiplies these mismatches by historical risk factor volatilities and correlations (covariance matrix) to produce its key output—monthly tracking error volatility. Tracking error volatility (sometimes simply referred to as "tracking error") is an important ingredient in the fixed-income manager's portfolio management process.

Tracking error volatility (TEV) is defined as the projected standard deviation of the monthly return differential between the portfolio and the benchmark. Although a measure of volatility, TEV can be used to forecast the likely distribution of a portfolio's future returns relative to its benchmark. For example, assuming return differences are normally distributed, we would expect a portfolio with a

TEV (i.e., 1 standard deviation) of 25 bp/month to have a return within ±25 bp/month of the benchmark's return[1] approximately two-thirds of the time (and underperformance of worse than −25 bp about one-sixth of the time). The risk model offers detailed analyses of sources of the TEV, their relative contribution to the total risk, and their interdependence.

Since the early 1990s, we have developed and shared a number of versions of this proprietary risk model with investors. In the new global risk model (released in November 2003), we have retained our time-tested approach to analyzing all sources of bond returns, have revised all asset-class-specific risk models, and have expanded security coverage to include global investment-grade, inflation-linked, USD and euro high yield and emerging market securities. This new model also handles out-of-index instruments such as interest-rate futures, swaps, caps, and floors.

Consistent with past practice, our risk model considers all sources of performance differential between a portfolio and a benchmark. Market risk falls into two broad categories: risk resulting from the differences between the sensitivities of the portfolio and the benchmark to common market risk factors (such sensitivities are, e.g., yield curve durations, spread durations, sector allocations) and diversification risk (i.e., security selection) that is present in the portfolio even when all the portfolio's common market sensitivities match the benchmark. The first category is called systematic risk, the second is security-specific or idiosyncratic risk, and the risk model considers both. Furthermore, for securities rated Baa or lower, the model goes one step further and includes default risk, which is translated into units of return volatility.

Default risk is part of systematic spread risk and idiosyncratic risk. However, when a bond goes into default, multiplying the spread duration of the promised cash flows (which will not be paid in full) by the spread volatility of its peer group is an extremely imprecise measure of risk. We have found that substantially greater accuracy can be obtained for "default-risky" bonds by including a set of default risk factors that account for the difference between the bond's promised cash flow and the likely recovery rate in the event of default. We also include the effect of default correlations among issuers, which represents the systematic risk of an overall increase in default rates.

The risk model covers all twenty-three (as of March 2005) currencies in the Lehman Global Aggregate Index and a wide spectrum of spread asset classes. The expansion beyond the U.S. dollar increased the complexity of the model and

---

1. More precisely, TEV measures the volatility of the uncertain part of the return difference between the portfolio and the benchmark around the expected difference in their returns.

required developing new techniques for dealing with historical time series of uneven length in different currencies. For example, historical return time series for euro-denominated assets starts in 1999, whereas the Lehman U.S. Credit Index returns go back to 1987. The risk model attempts to use the maximum-length time series in all instances. With the model's globalization came the need to compute risk for out-of-index instruments included in nearly every global portfolio (e.g., interest-rate futures, currency forwards, and interest-rate swaps). The model handles a wide variety of such instruments, mostly by mapping their risk exposures on appropriate risk factors in the cash markets.

The main purpose of the risk model is to help a manager structure a portfolio with a desired set of risk exposures ("bets") relative to the benchmark. (The benchmark can be a generic Lehman index, a custom investor-specific index, or another portfolio.) The model is not intended just for ex post analysis of a manager's positions, but rather as an ex ante tool for portfolio structuring. Construction of portfolios with a desired level of active risk is crucial for asset managers who aim to generate a target alpha. For example, most "long-only" practitioners consider a realized information ratio (alpha divided by TEV) of 0.5–1.0 to be at the high end of an achievable range (of course, hedge funds strive for considerably higher results). This means that a manager with an expected alpha of 50 bp/year has to run a risk of deviation from the benchmark of 50–100 bp/year. Should the projected TEV be much lower, achieving the target alpha is very unlikely. Active managers can use the risk model to ensure that the expected gain from a given exposure is sufficient to justify the risk to the portfolio from that exposure.

Risk budgeting has become an increasingly important portfolio management discipline to allocate risk optimally within a portfolio. The appropriate quantification and budgeting of active risks is a multidimensional task that is difficult to accomplish without the aid of tools such as a risk model. In particular, the correlations among the different active exposures make the measurement of net risk quite complex. However, TEV offers a common unit (return volatility relative to the benchmark) for diverse sources of risk ranging from FX exposure to credit sector overweights to issuer concentrations. For risk budgeting, the common unit facilitates comparing views along different market dimensions and the allocation of total risk to these views. After the manager's ex ante views have been reflected as active exposures in the portfolio, ex post performance attribution analysis is often performed along the same views. The objective is to find out whether these ex ante views paid off as expected.

The risk model uses historical data, which, admittedly, has limitations. However, there are few alternatives to a history-based approach to the construction of a robust risk model. In this chapter, we review some of these alternatives, such as scenario analysis or path simulation, and point out the pros and cons of each. Even when the objective is to stress test a portfolio relative to an index in an extreme scenario, historical magnitudes of market risks and the relationships among them are required to generate either extreme or historically consistent scenarios.

The model can construct index-replicating (proxy) portfolios by rebalancing a portfolio so that it has a very low TEV, using a number of optimization algorithms to find the necessary portfolio position trades given various market constraints. It helps investors structure active or replicating portfolios, rebalance portfolios to changing objectives with minimum turnover, and optimize risk budget allocations. The chapter is organized as follows.

The first section describes our approach to risk modeling. We discuss some of the difficulties and criticisms of our method, as well as some alternative approaches. On balance, however, we argue that our approach, which utilizes Lehman Brothers' extensive database of bond-level returns, offers portfolio managers two important benefits: robust model calibration and intuitive specification of portfolio risk exposures. In other words, a manager can not only use the model with a high level of confidence, but he can also translate its output into specific market actions to achieve a specific goal.

When using the risk model to analyze a portfolio, a manager receives an extensive and objective analysis of the portfolio's risk both in absolute terms and relative to the benchmark. One of the key outputs of the model is the portfolio's expected TEV vs. its benchmark. However, the model offers considerably more detailed risk analysis, delivered in the form of a risk report, which is described in the second section. After reviewing the report, a portfolio manager is able to answer the following questions: How risky is the portfolio? What are the sources of this risk? What is the portfolio's sensitivity to risk factors? To what degree are the portfolio's risk exposures correlated? What are the portfolio's security and issuer-specific risk?

The specific contents of the risk report vary depending on the underlying portfolio and benchmark. For example, a portfolio containing only USD assets managed against the Lehman U.S. Aggregate Index will not show risk exposures to non-U.S. currencies, euro or sterling credit risk factors, and so on. Similarly, a sterling-only portfolio managed against the Sterling Aggregate Index will not show risk exposures to the USD or euro or USD credit spread risk factors, and so forth. While the contents of the report may vary from portfolio to portfolio, its general format is invariant. The second section describes the risk report for a USD portfolio vs. the U.S. Aggregate Index.

As noted earlier, the risk model is best used by portfolio managers as an ex ante trade or portfolio evaluator, not as an ex post portfolio reporting system. The power of the model is that it gives the manager a set of optimal choices based on his experience and assessment of market conditions. The third section illustrates (with examples) many of the portfolio applications of the risk model:

- Structuring an Efficient Active Portfolio: A portfolio manager can use the risk model to structure portfolios finely tailored to reflect his market views.

- Evaluating Portfolio Trades: The risk model can be readily used to analyze the risk impact of a proposed trade.

- Optimizing a Portfolio: The risk model has a built-in optimizer that allows the manager to select from an eligible list of bonds those that will help reduce his portfolio's TEV to the desired level.

- Constructing Proxy Portfolios: The risk model and optimizer can be combined to construct a "proxy" portfolio containing relatively few issues that is designed to track a broader index.

- Scenario Analysis: The risk model can be used to help the manager specify scenarios, as well as the probabilities of the scenarios, that are internally consistent with broad market history (i.e., "maximum likelihood" scenarios).

- Risk Budgeting: A manager (and the plan sponsor) can use the risk model to monitor the portfolio's adherence to its risk budget allocation and to compare different types of risk on the same grounds.

The fourth section offers details of the structure of the risk model. The first step in the modeling is to decompose a bond's random total returns into various components. The first component is the systematic component of total return, which is the result of exposure to risk factors that affect the returns of all bonds in a given peer group (i.e., systematic risk factors). The other component of returns is the idiosyncratic return, which is driven by factors specific to the bond's issuer.

Once returns are split into their various components, what are the risk factors that influence these returns? Specifically, what are the systematic risk factors? How do we measure a portfolio's sensitivity to these factors? How does the risk model measure idiosyncratic risk? How does it handle default risk (including correlated defaults)? Answers to these questions depend on a bond's asset class. For example, a euro corporate bond and a USD corporate bond have different systematic risk factors. The fourth section of this chapter provides some detail on how the risk model handles "return splitting" and how the risk factors and sensitivities are specified for each asset class. (Readers who have little familiarity with risk models can refer to Appendix A for a brief tutorial. Appendix B reviews basic risk model mathematics.)

The fifth section provides evidence on the predictive power of our multifactor risk modeling approach to estimate a portfolio's ex post risk. We perform various tests to examine whether the risk model does a good job of estimating volatilities. This section shows that the model produces good estimates of total return and tracking error volatilities, validating our risk-modeling methodology.

The risk model is one of several portfolio risk measurement tools available to a manager. As described in the sixth section, these other tools include scenario analysis, value-at-risk, Monte Carlo simulation, performance attribution, and traditional mean-variance analysis. Because all tools have their particular strengths and weaknesses, these are often best used in a complementary fashion. For example, scenario analysis allows a manager to examine the portfolio's performance in extreme scenarios—so-called stress testing. The limitation of scenario analysis, as we discuss, is the difficulty in defining multisector scenarios that are consistent with market behavior.

Simulation allows a manager to examine the performance of his portfolio (usually in absolute terms) in a set of worst-case environments (i.e., "tail risk"). The potential advantage of simulation is that it can model the behavior of the portfolio's performance with few restrictions on the underlying distribution of returns. Generally, simulation uses the actual shape of the distribution of historical returns to generate a distribution of potential portfolio returns. In contrast, the risk model uses only the mean and standard deviation of historical returns to generate the future portfolio return distribution. The limitation of simulation is the vast complexity of the exercise, especially for global portfolios. This section discusses several other risk management tools and how they compare with the risk model.

We conclude with a brief discussion of future directions for the Lehman Brothers global risk model that have arisen from our interaction with portfolio managers, plan sponsors, consultants, and academics.

MOTIVATION FOR USING THE LEHMAN BROTHERS RISK MODEL

In the absence of a risk model, the standard approach to risk estimation is to compare a portfolio vs. its benchmark along relevant dimensions (e.g., duration buckets, credit sectors, MBS pricing tiers). We call this comparison a "market structure" report. Figure 26-1 shows an example of such a report for a portfolio [Aggregate-active (2)] vs. a benchmark (the Lehman U.S. Aggregate Index). The manager verifies that the exposures in every significant cell reflect his views in both sign and magnitude. This is always a valid and necessary step in portfolio

Figure 26-1. Simple Market Structure Report, USD Portfolio vs. U.S. Aggregate Index
December 31, 2004

	Total	Treasury	Agency	Credit	MBS	ABS	CMBS	Cash
Market Value								
Aggregate-active(2)	$2,900,741,606	$711,620,565	$190,349,958	$983,590,537	$687,361,815	$116,194,013	$112,838,348	$98,786,371
OA Duration								
Aggregate-active(2)	4.52	6.01	5.66	5.38	2.57	1.97	4.08	0
U.S. Aggregate	4.34	5.35	3.79	5.74	2.86	2.58	4.59	
Difference	0.18	0.66	1.87	−0.36	−0.29	−0.61	−0.51	
OA Spread Duration								
Aggregate-active(2)	4.64	5.93	5.68	5.34	3.23	1.97	4.08	0
U.S. Aggregate	4.49	5.30	3.72	5.71	3.35	2.58	4.59	
Difference	0.15	0.63	1.96	−0.37	−0.12	−0.61	−0.51	
Market Value (%)								
Aggregate-active(2)	100	24.53	6.56	33.91	23.70	4.01	3.89	3.41
U.S. Aggregate	100	24.68	11.01	24.8	35.08	1.37	3.06	
Difference	0	−0.15	−4.45	9.11	−11.38	2.64	0.83	3.41
Contribution to OASD								
Aggregate-active(2)	4.52	1.45	0.37	1.82	0.61	0.08	0.16	0
U.S. Aggregate	4.34	1.31	0.41	1.42	1.00	0.04	0.14	0
Difference	0.18	0.15	−0.04	0.40	−0.39	0.04	0.02	0

construction. These cells are essentially common market risk factors that the manager feels are relevant to a specific portfolio.

However, while useful, the market structure approach has significant shortcomings that the risk model addresses. First, even along the same axis, cells differ in risk terms. For example, does the −0.61 spread duration mismatch in ABS entail much more risk than the −0.12 mismatch in MBS? Second, some mismatches offset one another to a significant degree (e.g., a market value underweight to agencies and overweight to ABS). The model takes the extra steps of determining which risk factors, or "cells," best explain the return volatility of each asset class by quantifying their historical variances and correlations. This allows these differences in cell allocations (risk sensitivities) to be properly translated into total risk. In both the market structure and risk model approaches, it is also usual to examine issuer concentration reports. The risk model concentration report not only gives a sense for the over- or underweight in a given issuer, but also quantifies the associated contribution to TEV.

We certainly do not advocate reliance on the risk model output to the exclusion of the market structure report. The risk model is driven by historical relationships among risk factors, which can lose predictive power temporarily (e.g., during extreme market liquidity crises). Such crises are usually short-lived and are followed by a reversion to more historically typical behavior. Nevertheless, a cell-by-cell comparison between the benchmark and the portfolio constructed with the help of the risk model can ensure that no extreme cell exposures are taken because of overreliance on historical correlations. On the other hand, exclusive reliance on cell comparisons can lead to an insufficient risk budget and low alpha, misplaced views, and wrong magnitudes of exposures.

The Historical-Parametric Approach to Risk Modeling

We derive risk measures using variances and correlations calculated from historical returns. Critics of this history-based approach might cite the instability of correlations among market risk factors or the dependence of their volatilities on the interest-rate cycle. Another objection to this approach is the sole reliance on the means and standard deviations. In reality, many returns distributions are characterized by "fat tails," where the risk of extreme events is inadequately captured by the standard deviation.

A further objection to the historical-parametric approach is the difficulty of dealing with historical time series of unequal length. For example, there may be 10 years worth of corporate bond data but only 5 years of ABS data. How can this approach calculate a correlation between these two sectors of the market without curtailing the longer time series? Given the growth of new markets (e.g., CMBS, inflation-linked notes, and euro corporates) and the relatively recent emergence of returns data for other asset classes (e.g., smaller European countries), the problem of dealing with unequal time series is a limitation. Although there are statistical techniques to deal with this problem in a consistent way while preserving the valuable historical information embedded in the longer historical time series, it remains a target for criticism. Our confidence in our approach derives from the relative stability of long-term correlations among asset returns. While correlations may deviate for a month or two from their normal long-term values, they tend to be mean reverting. We feel that the value of using as much of the available time series as possible, in order to capture asset return behavior in as wide an assortment of market environments as possible, greatly outweighs the difficulty of working with uneven time series.

An alternative approach to risk modeling is "forward simulation" or "scenario analysis." Instead of relying on historical variances and correlations, the manager analyzes the relative performance of the portfolio and benchmark under many possible future market environments. For securities whose returns are driven mostly by term-structure risk, such as Treasuries or MBS, one can generate a set of likely or extreme yield curve scenarios. "Extreme" term-structure scenarios can be derived from implied interest-rate volatilities (in the option or swaption markets) rather than from history.

However, for multisector portfolios with allocations to credit (with default risk), such scenario simulation is a daunting task. The portfolio manager must simulate not only the term structure, but movements in credit spreads as well. Furthermore, the manager's simulations must be consistent. In other words, simulated movements in the term structure, combined with movements in credit spreads must have some foundation in reality—not only in both the absolute and relative magnitude and direction of the movements, but also in the probability. This foundation can only come from historical observations.

Reliance on "implied" volatilities and correlations for scenario analysis is not feasible as there is not enough market-based information on implied credit spread volatility and correlations of spreads with interest rates. Moreover, the dimensionality of a scenario definition for credit is extremely high; there are many credit sectors, credit ratings, and individual issuers. As many portfolio managers will attest, a complete simulation of possible scenarios for a multisector portfolio is a very complex and time-consuming task. While scenario analysis is very useful for examining possible extreme market movements, its practicality for measuring risk in normal market environments is very limited.

We have examined many of the concerns raised by our historical-parametric risk-modeling approach. In some cases we have used them to help improve the risk model. One example is the concern over the potential instability of asset return correlations. In response, the risk model defines the spread risk factors as movements in spreads vs. the local swap curve, as opposed to the Treasury curve. In particular, our procedure is to divide spreads over Treasuries into swap spreads and spreads over swap rates. What do we gain with this decomposition?

First, the decomposition allows us to consider the volatility of swap rates as a separate source of risk. It is statistically and economically meaningful to single out this risk factor. The decomposition also makes it easier to identify the different sources of correlation instability. We argue that much of the instability of the correlations among spread specific risk factors when defined against the Treasury curve over the last few years is in fact embedded in swap spreads and not in the specific factors. When these two factors (i.e., spreads to swaps and swap spreads) are bundled together, we get an impression of instability that may be false. Once the source of instability—namely swap spreads—is removed, that impression is largely reduced. Therefore, the decomposition delivers a more accurate picture of the different sources of risk and the nature of their relationship. The result is that the correlations across the spread risk factors to the swap curve are, in fact, much more stable.

To illustrate this point, let us look at the correlation among changes in spreads for major U.S. indices. We begin by constructing two series of changes of OAS for each index: one with OAS defined over the Treasury curve and the other over the swap curve. We divide the sample period—January 1992 to September 2003—in two: January 1992 to July 1998 and August 1998 to September 2003. We choose this division to highlight the latter period, when swap spreads were relatively volatile. Finally, we focus on four USD asset classes: corporates, MBS, ABS, and agencies.

Figure 26-2 presents the correlation matrices for each asset class pair. The differences in correlations between swap (SWP)-based and Treasury (TSY)-based spreads are clear once the two subperiods are analyzed. For instance, over the first subperiod the corporate/agency correlations under SWP and TSY are quite different, 0.62 and 0.34, respectively. Over the second subperiod these numbers for the agency/MBS are also quite dissimilar, 0.32 and 0.72, respectively.

Compare the correlations across the two periods for each of the two spread definitions. Figure 26-2 shows that swap-based spread correlations are quite stable across the two subperiods. The only exception is the corporate/agency pair, but this was due to the rash of significant credit shocks throughout the second period. However, correlations change significantly across periods when we look at Treasury-based spreads.

Moreover, one can see that all correlations are equal or (significantly) higher over the second period for Treasury-based spreads. This means that using the data from the first period would significantly underestimate the correlation of the

Figure 26-2. Correlation of Swap- and Treasury-Based Spread Changes

1992–2003

	CRP	AGY	MBS	ABS
CRP		0.34	0.27	0.62
AGY	0.31		0.28	0.52
MBS	0.33	0.44		0.33
ABS	0.60	0.42	0.37	

TSY spreads · SWP spreads

1992–1998

	CRP	AGY	MBS	ABS
CRP		0.62	0.40	0.65
AGY	0.34		0.27	0.55
MBS	0.30	0.10		0.35
ABS	0.44	0.29	0.21	

1998–2003

	CRP	AGY	MBS	ABS
CRP		0.31	0.28	0.65
AGY	0.34		0.32	0.57
MBS	0.40	0.72		0.34
ABS	0.66	0.49	0.48	

factors over the second period. This seems to justify the concerns about the stability of correlations referred to earlier, but the same is not true for the swap-based spreads. There is no apparent systematic bias in any particular direction for the latter. The exception again is for the corporate class, for which the correlations are generally lower in the second period.

Overall, the evidence seems to suggest significant stability in the correlation matrix for the swap-based spread definition used in the new global risk model. This result supports our historical-parametric approach to risk model design and the usefulness of the risk model as a tool for forward-looking risk measurement.

Weighting Historical Observations

As discussed earlier, use of historical data to compute the volatility and correlation parameters often runs into the problem of short or uneven time series, owing to the inclusion of new asset classes (e.g., euro credit) or the lack of long stationary time series for established asset classes (e.g., MBS). But even when this is not an issue, we have to ask how many of the available historical observations should be used when estimating the risk model's parameters? Should the model use all available history with equal weights or give greater weight to more recent observations? While there is no obvious right or wrong answer to this question, it is useful to consider some of the arguments on both sides.

There are two strong arguments in favor of weighting historical observations unevenly. First, the risk characteristics of some asset classes evolve over time. Consequently, giving more weight to recent historical observations may be reasonable. For USD MBS, for example, prepayment efficiency has increased so dramatically over the last decade that the prepayment history of the late 1980s and early 1990s is no longer applicable. Whenever such evolution occurs, we should limit historical observations used in calibrating the model to the relevant time period.

Second, during times of rapidly rising market volatility, an equal-weighted series of historical observations would underestimate the near-term risk of a portfolio. An example is the rise in issuer-specific volatility in the USD credit markets in 2001–2002. During such times, the risk model has to incorporate recent experience "faster" in order to give more realistic risk projections. This can be achieved by giving greater weight to more recent observations of market behavior and less weight to older historical experience. However, in calm markets, this "time decay" approach to the use of historical observations could lead to underestimation of risk because of the low weight given to past market crises.

In contrast, the advantage of giving equal weight to all historical observations is that the risk model incorporates risks about which market participants may have become complacent. For example, the spike in volatility in 1997 and 1998 followed a relatively long tranquil period in the fixed-income markets. During the tranquil period, the model overestimated risk because it "remembered" the volatility experienced in the late 1980s and early 1990s. Consequently, the volatility experienced in 1997 and 1998 was not inconsistent with the risk model's expectations. Our recommended answer to the historical weighting question is to run the risk model under both assumptions and use the higher result as a conservative risk estimate.

Why a Multifactor Model and Not an Asset Volatility Model?

Why resort to a factor analysis of bond returns that decomposes returns into components driven by common market variables (e.g., yield curve movement, sector spread changes, volatility changes)? Why not just study historical volatilities and correlations of asset classes (or sectors) present in the portfolio and the benchmark and multiply them by portfolio overweights or underweights to each one? Or, alternatively, why not study historical behavior of individual issuers (issues) in the portfolio and the benchmark and derive risk estimates from over- or underexposure of the portfolio to individual holdings?

The traditional approach to evaluating risk in a multisector portfolio does indeed rely on volatilities and correlations among different asset classes. The active view relative to a benchmark becomes simply the weight differential between the portfolio weight and the benchmark weight in a particular asset class. These weight differentials (active exposures) are then multiplied by a matrix of volatilities of each asset class and their correlations to get the projected tracking error.

This approach has two main shortcomings. First, the dominance of interest rates in driving the returns of all fixed-income instruments creates very high correlations among asset classes. This makes it very difficult to measure (and optimize) the risk owing to sector allocations properly. This issue can be partly addressed either by subdividing markets by maturity or duration or by viewing spread asset classes in terms of excess returns, but each of these approaches brings issues of its own.

Second, the asset class representation ignores diversification risk. Assume that the portfolio allocation to a given asset class is achieved by holding few securities and that the benchmark allocation is well diversified. The asset volatility approach shows no risk as long as these two allocations have identical weights. Resorting to historical analysis of correlations among specific issuers (or issues) solves this problem, but creates many others. How does one evaluate the risk of a new issuer with no established market history? As a practical matter, how can one derive correlations among thousands of issuer (or issue) return time series from the limited set of available observations?

Risk factor decomposition of security returns provides a viable solution for both of these problems. First, our model selects a fairly small number of common risk factors for each market sector, which leads to a manageable number of correlations to be estimated from history. Then, we conduct historical calibration at the individual security level, leaving us with the part of bond returns unexplained by changes in all common market risk factors combined. We use these residuals to quantify security-specific risk by category of issuer (or issue) and compute the diversification risk in a portfolio.

Methodological Advantages

As discussed earlier, it is our belief that the historical-parametric approach to multifactor risk modeling offers an objective and realistic tool for forward-looking risk measurement. Moreover, our particular risk model implementation offers two distinct benefits to portfolio managers: accurate model calibration and intuitive specification of the exposures to the risk factors. There are several reasons why we are able to deliver these benefits to users of our risk model.

Lehman Brothers has been a provider of fixed-income market indices for over 30 years. Over these decades, the trader-sourced pricing and analytics data in our indices have been assiduously monitored by many investors benchmarked to these indices. We, therefore, have high-quality historical information *at the individual security level* that we use to calibrate the risk model.

Second, our modeling approach has always been attuned to designing tools that are intuitive to portfolio managers. It is important for the manager to be able to easily translate the output from the risk model into specific market actions to achieve a desired goal. To maintain an intuitive set of risk factors, we use a larger set of correlated factors instead of the smallest possible set of independent factors, which are often referred to as "principal components" of market movement.

To understand the importance of this modeling orientation, consider that risk measures are a product of current risk sensitivities and the historical volatilities and correlations of risk factors. For a portfolio manager, the risk sensitivity of a bond is a duration-type measure (i.e., the price of the bond will change by a certain percentage amount given a specified change in interest rates). Moreover, a portfolio manager usually interprets risk factors as changes in rates, spreads, or volatilities.

The risk model was designed with this intuition in mind. It also relies on state-of-the art modeling efforts in interest rates, prepayments, and volatilities to generate risk sensitivity measures (key-rate-durations, spread durations, and vegas) for individual bonds. The same models are used to produce risk sensitivities for both portfolios and indices, which enables an "apples-to-apples" comparison. When we fit bond returns to the risk factor model, we use these sensitivity measures, with which managers are very familiar, as the independent variables (i.e., we impose risk sensitivities). The regression coefficients are then risk factors (i.e., we "back out" the factor realizations), which can be readily interpreted as changes in rates, spreads, and volatilities. Although our method may be contrary to the conventional approach to risk modeling, a portfolio manager will find our model much easier to use.

For example, the uncertain part of the excess return of a corporate bond (over key-rate duration-matched Treasuries) is modeled as its spread duration (risk sensitivity) times an unknown quantity (risk factor), plus an unexplained residual. Since returns are in percentage units, and spread duration is in units of percentage/bp, the risk factor is in basis points and can easily be interpreted as the average spread change for the bond's credit sector. If the manager wishes to reduce his risk exposure to this factor, he can rely on spread duration matching to build a trade.

This is in contrast to a modeling approach that represents excess return as the average spread change across a given sector (the independent variable) times an unknown sensitivity of a particular bond to this change, which is estimated as the fitted regression coefficient. As this fitted sensitivity measure may be greater or less than the standard spread duration measure, how readily can the portfolio manager know what trade to execute to reduce his risk exposure?

Finally, the risk model quantifies security-specific risk by analyzing historical returns of individual securities. Diversification risk is very high on the investor's agenda, especially in credit portfolios. The idiosyncratic risk model uses the absolute value of the residual returns of individual securities unexplained by a combination of all the systematic risks. Later we provide much more detail on the structure of the risk model, but first we describe and discuss its output and illustrate its many practical applications.

THE ANNOTATED RISK REPORT

The key output of the risk model is the risk report. While the specific content of the risk report varies depending on the underlying portfolio and benchmark, its general format stays the same. This section provides a detailed description of the risk report.[2] The report is extensive, with a summary page and many supporting pages of detail, and is organized around the following questions:

---

2. The benchmark in the risk model may be an index, custom index, or portfolio. Consequently, the model may be used to run risk reports for one index against another, or one portfolio against another, or a portfolio vs. cash.

1. How risky is the portfolio (in absolute terms and versus its benchmark)?

2. What are the sources of this risk?

3. What is the portfolio's sensitivity to risk factors?

4. To what degree are the portfolio's risk exposures correlated?

5. What are the portfolio's security and issuer specific risks?

After reviewing the risk report, a portfolio manager will not only know the answers to these questions but will be able to use the optimizer embedded in the risk model to identify portfolio trades that could adjust his portfolio's risk to the desired level.

Consider the following $2.9 billion fixed-income portfolio (the same portfolio introduced in the previous section). The benchmark is the U.S. Aggregate Index. For this portfolio, the manager's investment style is to take modest duration bets (up to 0.5 year) and to overweight/underweight sectors (e.g., underweight MBS vs. credit). The portfolio does take active corporate sector and name selection positions, but the corporate portfolio is generally well diversified. For the MBS/ABS/CMBS portfolios, the manager tries to track the respective indices using liquid names.

Using the simple market structure report in Figure 26-1, we see that as of December 31, 2004, the portfolio (containing ninety-nine positions, including a small amount of cash) was positioned as follows vs. the benchmark:

- Duration overweight of 0.18 year.

- Underweight MBS (both in terms of market value and contribution to spread duration).

- Probably, as a result of the MBS underweight, less negatively convex than the benchmark (not shown in Figure 26-1).

- Overweight credit (both in terms of market value and contribution to spread duration).

- Modest market value overweights to ABS and CMBS.

In terms of contribution to spread duration, the portfolio has a credit and government (Treasury and agency) overweight of 0.40 year and 0.11 year, respectively. It also has small overweights, in terms of contribution to spread duration, to both the ABS and CMBS sectors. In regard to MBS, the portfolio has a contribution to spread duration underweight of 0.39 year.

How is the portfolio positioned within each sector? The credit portion of the portfolio has a shorter duration (5.38) than the credit portion of the Aggregate, as does the CMBS portion of the portfolio. There may also be other significant differences between the portfolio and benchmark within each sector. For example, what are the relative exposures to the various credit quality categories on industry sectors? Since the credit portion of the portfolio probably holds many fewer names than the benchmark, the portfolio probably has a moderate amount of idiosyncratic (i.e., "name") risk relative to the benchmark.

The government portion of the portfolio has much longer duration (6.01 for Treasuries and 5.66 for agencies) than the government sector in the Aggregate, possibly implying an overweight (underweight) at the long (short) end of the government curve. In contrast, the MBS and ABS portions of the portfolio are shorter than their respective indices in the Aggregate Index.

In summary, the portfolio has many active positions vs. the benchmark: duration overweight, credit/ABS/CMBS overweight, MBS underweight, and convexity underweight—plus subsector and security-level active positions within each subportfolio vs. its respective sector index.

What is the risk of the portfolio performing differently from its Aggregate benchmark? As a very rough approximation, assuming that Treasury interest rates have a monthly standard deviation of about 25 bp, then the 0.2-year-duration overweight implies a monthly TEV of about 5 bp. How does the credit overweight interact with the duration exposure: does it increase or decrease the portfolio's tracking error arising from the duration exposure? The same question applies to the MBS underweight. Similarly, how do any subsector credit or MBS positions affect the overall tracking error number for the portfolio? To understand how the various risk exposures interact, we have to know how the various risk factors are correlated—and this is the job of the risk model.

When running the risk model, the portfolio manager must specify how much weight the model should give to historical observations when estimating the risk factor covariances. The risk model gives the manager two choices: equal weighting or exponential time weighting with a rate of time decay equal to a 1-year half-life (i.e., an observation that is 1 year old has one-half the weight of the most recent observation). When invoking the risk model, the manager will be prompted to select a weighting scheme. For our example, we use equal weighting for systematic and nonsystematic risks and for credit default rates. The first page of the risk model report summarizes the manager's estimation choices (Figure 26-3).

The risk report is designed to answer several important questions regarding the risk of the manager's portfolio.

Figure 26-3. User Defined Parameters, U.S. Aggregate Portfolio

Parameter	Value
Base currency	USD
Portfolio	Aggregate-active(2)
Benchmark	U.S. Aggregate
Time-weighting of historical data in covariance matrix:	
For systematic risk	No
For nonsystematic risk	No
Time-weighting of credit default rates	No
(Implicit) currency hedging for portfolio	No
(Implicit) currency hedging for benchmark	No
Number of lines displayed in issue-specific and credit tickers reports	100

How Risky Is the Portfolio?

The next page of the risk report is the portfolio/benchmark comparison report (shown in Figure 26-4). This report, which provides information similar to the market structure report, shows the portfolio's 0.18-long-duration position, as well as its less negative convex position (0.34). This implies that the portfolio's performance is less susceptible than the Aggregate Index to an increase in realized volatility. The portfolio's OAS is modestly higher than the benchmark, probably owing to the market value underweight to the government and MBS sectors and the large overweight to credit. Other factors may be at work here, which we will try to uncover. The report shows that the portfolio has an overweight to spread duration. Consequently, given its overweight to credit/ABS/CMBS and under-weight to MBS, a tightening of credit/ABS/CMBS spreads and/or a widening of MBS spreads is likely to help the portfolio outperform the benchmark.

The comparison report provides an estimated TEV in terms of basis points per month. As of December 31, 2004, the portfolio had an estimated TEV of approx-imately 29 bp/month—quite a bit larger than our back-of-the-envelope 5-bp/month calculation based solely on exposure to Treasury curve risk (i.e., duration). We examine the details of this 29-bp/month TEV number later.

The report also includes systematic, default, and nonsystematic volatilities for both the portfolio and the benchmark. These values indicate the expected vari-ability of the portfolio owing to exposure to the systematic risk factors, exposure to default risk, and exposure to nonsystematic risk factors. We discuss each of these in turn.

Figure 26-4. Portfolio/Benchmark Comparison Report, U.S. Aggregate Portfolio
December 31, 2004

Parameter	Portfolio	Benchmark	Difference
	Aggregate-active(2)	U.S. Aggregate	
Positions	99	5836	
Issuers	38	614	
Currencies	1	1	
Number of positions processed	99	5831	
Number of positions excluded	0	5	
Percentage of MV processed	100.0	100.0	
Percentage of MV excluded	0.0	0.0	
Market value (USD)	2,900,747,874	8,215,148,923	
Coupon (%)	5.66	5.24	0.42
Average life (years)	6.99	6.87	0.12
Yield to worst (%)	4.31	4.38	−0.07
ISMA yield (%)	4.2	4.15	0.05
OAS (bp)	40	33	7
OAD (years)	4.51	4.33	0.18
ISMA duration (years)	5.29	5.26	0.03
Duration to maturity (years)	5.06	5.05	0.01
Vega	−0.04	−0.05	0.02
OA spread duration (years)	4.64	4.49	0.15
OA convexity (years^2/100)	−0.15	−0.49	0.34
Total tracking error volatility (bp/month)			28.8
Systematic volatility (bp/month)	106.69	108.42	
Nonsystematic volatility (bp/month)	19.72	2.47	
Default volatility (bp/month)	7.07	3.27	
Total volatility (bp/month)	108.73	108.5	
Portfolio beta			0.967

The total return on the portfolio has an estimated systematic volatility of approximately 106.7 bp/month, arising from the portfolio's exposure to the volatility of systematic risk factors (i.e., risk factors that are common to many issues such as changes in Treasury key rates). In other words, the portfolio is expected to have a standard deviation of returns of approximately 106.7 bp/month around its expected return. In contrast, the benchmark has an expected systematic volatility of approximately 108.4 bp/month.

For the index, the default volatility is 3.3 bp/month (the risk model only models default risk for bonds rated Baa and below). In contrast, the portfolio has 7.1 bp/month of default volatility, indicating that the portfolio has a lower-quality credit profile than the index. This relative exposure arises in large part from a 0.72% position in FirstEnergy Corp. 5.5%s of 11/06, rated Ba1, and a 1.26% position in AT&T 9.75% of 11/31, also rated Ba1. The possibility of default adds to total return volatility even if there are no changes in the systematic and nonsystematic (i.e., nondefault) risk factors. As we explain later, given a default probability, a recovery value assumption, correlation of defaults with other issuers rated Baa or lower (if there were any) in the portfolio, and a market value weight of the bond in the overall portfolio, we can estimate the expected volatility to portfolio returns owing to the possibility of defaults.

Finally, nonsystematic, or idiosyncratic, volatility arises from (nondefault) issuer-specific risks. For a portfolio, nonsystematic volatility generally decreases as the number of issuers increases. For the index, with a large number of issuers, nonsystematic volatility is relatively low at 2.5 bp/month. For our portfolio with ninety-nine issues, nonsystematic volatility is higher at 19.7 bp/month. We disclose the source of the portfolio's relatively high nonsystematic volatility later in our discussion of the risk report.

For the risk model, the three components of portfolio volatility are assumed to be independent of each other. Consequently, total portfolio volatility equals:

$$\text{Total volatility} = \sqrt{[(\text{Sys. vol.})^2 + (\text{Default vol.})^2 + (\text{Idio. vol.})^2]}$$
$$= 108.7 \text{ bp/month.}$$

The portfolio beta, 0.97, is the expected change in the portfolio's value in basis points, given a 1-bp change in the value of the benchmark arising from the benchmark's systematic risk exposures. For example, if a change in systematic risk factors produces a 10-bp increase in the benchmark's total return, then the same change in risk factors would be expected to produce a 9.7-bp increase in the portfolio's return.

The systematic, default, and nonsystematic volatilities are calculated separately for the portfolio and the benchmark. The TEV, on the other hand, represents the volatility of the return difference between the portfolio and the benchmark around the expected difference in their returns. Although both the benchmark and portfolio have total volatilities of approximately 110 bp/month, the TEV between the two is only 29 bp/month. Obviously, returns on the benchmark and the portfolio are highly correlated, and the small difference between the two is driven by their relative exposures to risk factors. This raises the next important question.

Figure 26-5. Tracking Error Report, U.S. Aggregate Portfolio
December 31, 2004

Global Risk Factor	Isolated TEV (bp)	Cumulative TEV (bp)	Difference in Cumulative (bp)	Percentage of Tracking Error Variance	Systematic Beta
Yield curve	7.27	7.27	7.27	6.66	1.03
Swap spreads	1.12	7.17	-0.10	-0.03	1.02
Volatility	1.48	7.63	0.45	-0.12	0.66
Investment-grade spreads	5.96	9.46	1.83	9.60	1.12
Treasury spreads	0.27	7.67	0.04	0.04	1.08
Credit and agency spreads	5.52	9.22	1.55	9.38	1.29
MBS/securitized	2.53	9.39	0.17	-0.14	0.66
CMBS/ABS	0.35	9.46	0.07	0.33	1.27
High yield spreads	13.83	18.68	9.23	30.26	3.91
Emerging markets spreads	4.94	21.08	2.40	7.23	0.97
Systematic risk	21.08	21.08	0.00	53.60	
Idiosyncratic risk	19.09	28.44	7.36	43.94	
Credit default risk	4.51	28.80	0.36	2.46	
Total risk		28.80	0.00	100.00	
Portfolio volatility (bp/month)				108.73	
Benchmark volatility (bp/month)				108.50	

What Are the Sources of Risk?

What are the sources of risk in this portfolio relative to its benchmark? The tracking error report in Figure 26-5 shows how the overall tracking error number (28.8 bp/month) can be broken down by relative exposures to broad categories of risk factors (systematic, default, and nonsystematic). For example, the report shows that relative exposures of the portfolio and benchmark to the seven yield curve risk factors (i.e., six key-rate factors and a convexity factor) account, in isolation, for 7.3 bp/month of overall tracking error. Recall that the portfolio is 0.18 year longer in duration than the benchmark. As we will see shortly, the various key-rate factors have an average volatility of approximately 26.3 bp/month. As a rough approximation, we should expect about 0.18×26.3 bp/month ≈ 4.7 bp/month of tracking error owing to relative exposures to the yield curve risk factors. The difference between 7.3 and 4.7 bp/month is largely explained by convexity. Recall that the portfolio is 0.34 year less negatively convex than the benchmark. This implies that the duration difference alone underestimates the return difference between the portfolio and benchmark owing solely to changes in the yield curve.

The report then shows how much tracking error is due to the relative exposure to swap spreads. As we discuss later, an asset's spread return is split into components that are due, respectively, to changes in par swap spreads and changes in sector spreads to swaps and other risk factors particular to the asset's peer group. Considering changes in swap spreads by themselves (i.e., ignoring their correlation with changes in other risk factors), we see that relative exposure to the six par swap rates produces only 1.1 bp/month of tracking error. This value is shown in the column "isolated TEV." Why so low? As we will see in the next report, compared with the benchmark, the portfolio has only a modest overweight in exposure to swap spreads. Furthermore, par swap spreads are not very volatile (about 7.6 bp/month, on average), so the portfolio's exposure to par swap spreads relative to the benchmark, in isolation, produces little tracking error.

Since changes in swap spreads have low correlation with changes in Treasury rates (e.g., the correlation of changes in the 10-year swap spread with changes in the 10-year Treasury key rate is 0.08), the portfolio's modest long exposure to changes in swap spreads (shown in Figure 26-6) helps offset the portfolio's long exposure to changes in Treasury yields. Moreover, since changes in swap spreads have low volatility, the long-swap-spread exposure adds little to the overall tracking error, which is shown in the "cumulative TEV" column. The combined relative exposures to Treasury rates and swap spreads produce a TEV of 7.17 bp/month, which is slightly lower than the isolated exposure to Treasury rates alone (7.27 bp/month).

The tracking error report continues in this fashion: It lists the next group of risk factors and reports the TEV resulting from active exposures to those factors in isolation ("isolated TEV") and then in combination with all preceding groups of risk factors ("cumulative TEV"). Note that the cumulative TEV does not increase by the isolated TEV amount, owing to less than perfect correlations among the risk factors. In fact, as we just saw, it may even decrease from inclusion of a risk category with low correlation to the preceding risk categories.

The pattern of the cumulative TEV as we move down the column depends on the ordering of the risk factors. The particular order used in the risk report reflects the relative importance of the risk factors for a typical fixed-income portfolio. While a different ordering will still produce the same overall TEV, the levels and changes in the cumulative (but not in the isolated) TEV may vary.

For the USD market, there are six volatility factors, grouped under "volatility" in the tracking error report. There is a single volatility factor for each of the following sectors: Treasury, agency, investment-grade credit, and high yield. In addition, there are two volatility factors for the MBS sector: a long (expiry) and a short (expiry) volatility factor. The exposure of a portfolio or benchmark to changes in a volatility risk factor is measured by its volatility duration, which is related to the portfolio's vega. From the portfolio/benchmark comparison report, we know that our portfolio has slightly less vega exposure than the index (probably owing to the portfolio's MBS underweight). The combination of small relative volatility exposure and level of volatility of changes in implied volatility itself produces a low isolated TEV (1.5 bp/month).

The investment-grade spread factors include all risk factors pertaining to the spread sectors (e.g., agency, credit, MBS, ABS, and CMBS), as well as some pertaining to the Treasury market beyond exposure to changes in key rates and convexity (such as spread slope and liquidity). Exposure to these spread factors is measured by a bond's option-adjusted spread duration (OASD). As we see in the portfolio/benchmark comparison report, the portfolio has longer OASD than the benchmark by 0.15 year, implying that the portfolio will underperform if spreads generally widen. Overall, owing to the relative spread exposure, the portfolio has an isolated TEV from spread risk factors of 6.0 bp/month—the third-largest source of isolated systematic TEV in the portfolio. However, since spread changes have low (or negative) correlation with changes in yield curve risk factors, the cumulative TEV increases only 1.9 bp/month, from 7.6 to 9.5 bp/month.

The tracking error report then divides the investment-grade spread risk into four investment-grade market segments: Treasury, credit and agency, MBS (including any structured MBS), and CMBS/ABS. As shown in Figure 26-5, the exposure to credit and agency spread risk factors produces an isolated TEV of 5.5 bp/month, whereas the relative exposure to the MBS spread risk factors produces an isolated TEV of 2.5 bp/month. This may surprise investors. Recall that at the outset, the portfolio had a credit-and-agency overweight (4.7% in market value and 0.36 year in contribution to spread duration), compared with an MBS underweight (11.4% in market value and 0.39 year in contribution to spread duration). The MBS active position seems larger than the credit-and-agency position, so why is the isolated TEV for credit and agency so much larger than for MBS? As we will see in the full factor exposure report (Figure 26-6), the spread factors for credit and agency are generally more volatile.

Next in the tracking error report is TEV owing to exposure to high yield spread factors. (More details on the high yield risk model are provided later.) The Aggregate (Statistics) Index, by definition,[3] contains no exposure to high yield risk factors. The portfolio, however, has two high yield bonds with a combined portfolio market value weight of 1.98% and a contribution to spread duration of 0.15 year. This exposure, given the relatively high volatility of high yield spread risk factors, produces an isolated TEV of 13.8 bp/month.

Finally, the portfolio and benchmark have exposure to bonds from issuers in emerging countries. In particular, our portfolio has both a PEMEX and an UMS issue. As of December 2004, Mexico was rated Baa3, so Mexican issuers were part of the EM index. In addition, investment-grade dollar issuers (such as PEMEX and UMS) belonged to the Aggregate Index. Consequently, both the portfolio and benchmark have exposure to EM risk factors (discussed later). On a net basis, the relative EM exposures produce a TEV of 4.9 bp/month.

Overall, our portfolio has an estimated systematic TEV of 21.1 bp/month vs. the Aggregate Index. There are two other components in the total TEV: Nonsystematic (i.e., idiosyncratic) TEV and credit default TEV. Idiosyncratic TEV measures the risk owing to concentrations in a particular bond or issuer. For a given bond, the portion of its normal (i.e., nondefault related) return not explained by the systematic risk factors is defined as its idiosyncratic return. For a well-diversified portfolio or index, idiosyncratic risk is typically small, as the exposure to it is spread across many small exposures to independent sources of issuer-specific risk. Although the level of a portfolio's idiosyncratic risk generally declines with the number of issues, a single large position in a particularly risky asset can create significant nonsystematic risk. As discussed earlier, the level of idiosyncratic volatility in the portfolio and index was 19.7 and 2.5 bp/month, respectively.

Idiosyncratic TEV is driven by the relative exposures to specific bonds and issuers. For example, if the portfolio and benchmark each have a 0.5% market value exposure to the Ford 7.5s of 8/26, then the contribution of this issue to the

---

3. If the benchmark is the Aggregate Index (returns universe), then there may be exposure to high yield risk factors, as downgraded bonds are not removed from the index until the end of the month.

portfolio's idiosyncratic TEV is zero. However, if the portfolio has a 0.5% market value weight to this issue, while the benchmark has only a 0.1% weight, then the net exposure to the issue is 0.4%, which would contribute to the portfolio's idiosyncratic TEV. The calculation of the portfolio's idiosyncratic TEV begins once all the issue-level positions have been netted.

Idiosyncratic tracking error variance (i.e., the square of idiosyncratic TEV) is the weighted sum of the individual issuer-level idiosyncratic tracking error variances (i.e., issuer-level idiosyncratic risks are assumed to be independent). However, in the risk model, to arrive at issuer-level idiosyncratic tracking error variance, net issue-level exposures of opposite sign for a given issuer do not fully offset each other. The degree of this offset is an increasing function of the issuer's spread level. In other words, the degree of issue-level offset is larger for high-spread issuers compared with low-spread issuers.[4] Although this relationship has been supported empirically, the underlying intuition is that higher-spread issuers are more susceptible to event risk, which would produce similar spread changes for all of the issuer's bonds.

For example, suppose a portfolio and benchmark each have a 0.5% exposure to Ford, but the portfolio's exposure is only to the Ford 7.5s of 8/26, whereas that of the benchmark is only to the Ford 7.125s of 11/25. The two Ford issues are very similar (e.g., similar exposures to the key rate, swap spread, and corporate risk factors), and they have similar idiosyncratic risk (267 and 273 bp/month for the 7.5s and 7.125s, respectively). Because the spread level for Ford is (currently) relatively high (about +250 to Treasuries), the risk model offsets a significant amount of the idiosyncratic risk when calculating the portfolio's idiosyncratic TEV. In this example, the portfolio's idiosyncratic TEV arising from the Ford exposure would be only 0.55 bp/month.

Contrast this result with an issuer with lower spreads. Suppose a portfolio and benchmark each have a 0.5% exposure to Wells Fargo. However, the portfolio's exposure is only to the WFC 4.95s of 10/13, whereas that of the benchmark is only to the WFC 4.625s of 4/14. The two WFC issues are very similar (e.g., similar exposures to the key rate, swap spread, and corporate risk factors), and they have similar idiosyncratic risk (107 and 112 bp/month for the 4.95s and 4.625s, respectively). However, because the spread level for WFC is (currently) relatively low (about +65 to Treasuries), the risk model offsets less of the idiosyncratic risk when calculating this issuer's contribution to portfolio's idiosyncratic TEV. In this example, the portfolio's idiosyncratic TEV arising from the WFC exposure is 0.58 bp/month, which, despite the shorter spread duration and lower idiosyn-

---

4. For more details, refer to Chapter 18.

cratic risk for the WFC issues compared with the F issues, is larger than the 0.55 bp/month of idiosyncratic TEV arising from the Ford issues.

In short, one can think of idiosyncratic risk as having two components: issuer-specific risk and issue-specific (or bond-specific) risk. As the credit-worthiness of an entity decreases (and its spread widens), the former dominates the latter. For highly rated issues (e.g., Aaa-rated supranationals), the issue-specific risk, typically associated with liquidity risk, outweighs any fundamental credit concerns.

Generally, a portfolio has greater weights in a smaller set of issues, whereas the benchmark has smaller weights to many more bonds. As a result, the most domi-nant active weights are usually driven by the portfolio weights, and a portfolio's idiosyncratic TEV is generally close to the portfolio's idiosyncratic volatility. For our portfolio, the idiosyncratic TEV is 19.1 bp/month, close to the portfolio's idiosyncratic volatility of 19.7 bp/month.

By assumption, idiosyncratic risk is independent of systematic risk. As a result, the cumulative TEV is simply:

$$\text{Cumulative TEV} = \sqrt{[(\text{Isolated systematic TEV})^2 + (\text{Isolated idiosyncratic TEV})^2]}.$$

For our manager's portfolio, we have

$$\text{Cumulative TEV} = \sqrt{[21.08^2 + 19.09^2]} = 28.44 \text{ bp/month.}[5]$$

Finally, the credit default TEV arises from exposure to the default risk of bonds rated Baa or lower. (The tracking error due to defaults of higher-rated bonds is not modeled explicitly. Owing to its extreme rarity and sparseness of data, default risk for such bonds is captured in the idiosyncratic risk term.) TEV arising from default risk is 4.5 bp/month. Again, in our model, the default TEV is assumed to be independent of both the idiosyncratic and the systematic TEV. Consequently, total TEV is defined as

$$\text{Total TEV} = \sqrt{[(\text{Isolated systematic TEV})^2 + (\text{Isolated idiosyncratic TEV})^2 + (\text{Default TEV})^2]} = 28.8 \text{ bp/month.}$$

---

5. Assuming zero autocorrelation of the monthly tracking errors, an annual tracking error volatility number can be calculated by multiplying the monthly tracking error volatility number by $\sqrt{12}$. In this example, $\sqrt{12} \times 28.4$ bp/month = 98.4 bp/year.

Figure 26-6. Factor Exposure Report—Full Details, U.S. Aggregate Portfolio
December 31, 2004

Factor Name	Sensitivity/Exposure	Portfolio Exposure	Benchmark Exposure
Currency			
USD Currency	MW%	100.0	100.0
Key Rates and Convexity			
USD 6-month key rate	KRD (years)	0.151	0.145
USD 2-year key rate	KRD (years)	0.377	0.655
USD 5-year key rate	KRD (years)	0.967	1.151
USD 10-year key rate	KRD (years)	1.671	1.239
USD 20-year key rate	KRD (years)	0.971	0.8
USD 30-year key rate	KRD (years)	0.381	0.349
USD convexity	OAC (years^2/100)	−0.155	−0.493
Swap Spreads			
USD 6-month swap spread	SSKRD (years)	0.17	0.15
USD 2-year swap spread	SSKRD (years)	0.412	0.527
USD 5-year swap spread	SSKRD (years)	0.907	0.918
USD 10-year swap spread	SSKRD (years)	0.79	0.88
USD 20-year swap spread	SSKRD (years)	0.525	0.434
USD 30-year swap spread	SSKRD (years)	0.382	0.269
Treasury Spread and Volatility			
USD Treasury volatility	Volatility duration	0.0	0.0
USD Treasury spread	OASD (years)	1.455	1.309
USD Treasury spread slope	OASD × (TTM − AvgTTM) (years^2)	10.983	8.447
USD Treasury liquidity	OASD × (OAS − AvgOAS) (years × %)	0.0070	−0.0070
Agency Spread and Volatility			
USD agency volatility	Volatility duration	0.0	0.0010
Farm	OASD (years)	0.0	0.0040
FHLB	OASD (years)	0.152	0.068
FHLMC	OASD (years)	0.014	0.131
FNMA	OASD (years)	0.159	0.17
Other agencies	OASD (years)	0.048	0.036
USD agency LIBOR spread slope	OASD × (TTM − AvgTTM) (years^2)	1.155	2.076
USD agency liquidity	OASD × (OAS − AvgOAS) (years × %)	0.049	0.0090

Net Exposure	Factor Volatility	TE Impact of an Isolated 1 Standard Deviation Up Change (bp)	TE Impact of a Correlated 1 Standard Deviation Up Change (bp)	Marginal Contribution to TEV (bp)	Percentage of TE Variance
–0.0	0.0	–0.0		0.0	–0.0
0.0060	24.01	–0.14	8.3	–6.922	–0.14
–0.278	29.53	8.2	8.73	–8.949	8.63
–0.184	30.82	5.68	6.7	–7.167	4.59
0.432	27.43	–11.86	3.78	–3.603	–5.41
0.172	23.47	–4.03	1.91	–1.554	–0.93
0.032	22.44	–0.73	1.47	–1.144	–0.13
0.338	4.75	1.61	0.2	0.033	0.04
0.021	11.38	–0.23	0.49	–0.195	–0.01
–0.115	5.76	0.66	0.93	–0.186	0.07
–0.011	5.78	0.06	1.21	–0.243	0.01
–0.09	6.78	0.61	1.41	–0.331	0.1
0.091	7.95	–0.72	1.15	–0.318	–0.1
0.112	7.76	–0.87	0.96	–0.258	–0.1
–0.0	112.81	0.01	–2.26	8.842	–0.0
0.146	1.4	–0.2	–0.56	0.027	0.01
2.536	0.04	–0.11	2.62	0.0040	–0.04
0.014	14.46	–0.21	–2.59	1.3	0.06
–0.0010	117.57	0.13	–2.36	9.633	–0.04
–0.0040	5.28	0.02	–2.23	0.41	–0.01
0.084	5.28	–0.44	–1.71	0.314	0.09
–0.117	5.3	0.62	–0.83	0.153	–0.06
–0.011	4.02	0.05	–2.24	0.313	–0.01
0.012	4.83	–0.06	–1.48	0.249	0.01
–0.92	0.34	0.31	0.6	–0.0070	0.02
0.04	18.37	–0.73	–2.89	1.846	0.25

(continued)

Figure 26-6. (continued)

Factor Name	Sensitivity/Exposure	Portfolio Exposure	Benchmark Exposure
Credit IG Spread and Volatility			
USD corporate volatility	Volatility duration	0.0	0.0010
USD banking Aaa-Aa	OASD (years)	0.017	0.029
USD banking A	OASD (years)	0.344	0.212
USD banking Baa	OASD (years)	0.0	0.016
USD basic industry Aaa-Aa	OASD (years)	0.0	0.0090
USD basic industry A	OASD (years)	0.0	0.039
USD basic industry Baa	OASD (years)	0.03	0.066
USD cyclical Aaa-Aa	OASD (years)	0.0	0.01
USD cyclical A	OASD (years)	0.0	0.018
USD cyclical Baa	OASD (years)	0.238	0.128
USD communication Aaa-Aa	OASD (years)	0.0	0.0
USD communication A	OASD (years)	0.276	0.083
USD communication Baa	OASD (years)	0.21	0.116
USD energy Aaa-Aa	OASD (years)	0.0	0.0060
USD energy A	OASD (years)	0.0	0.024
USD energy Baa	OASD (years)	0.0	0.076
USD financial Aaa-Aa	OASD (years)	0.087	0.039
USD financial A	OASD (years)	0.048	0.064
USD financial Baa	OASD (years)	0.0	0.039
USD noncyclical Aaa-Aa	OASD (years)	0.0	0.022
USD noncyclical A	OASD (years)	0.0	0.05
USD noncyclical Baa	OASD (years)	0.042	0.054
USD noncorporate Aaa–Aa	OASD (years)	0.046	0.118
USD noncorporate A	OASD (years)	0.0	0.032
USD noncorporate Baa	OASD (years)	0.0	0.011
USD utility Aaa–Aa	OASD (years)	0.0	0.0
USD utility A	OASD (years)	0.01	0.026
USD utility Baa	OASD (years)	0.143	0.081
USD corporate spread slope	OASD × (TTM – AvgTTM) (year^2)	13.337	10.964
USD corporate liquidity	OASD × (OAS – AvgOAS) (years × %)	0.402	0.222
USD foreign corporates Aaa-Aa	OASD (years)	0.033	0.067
USD foreign corporates A	OASD (years)	0.0	0.095
USD foreign corporates Baa	OASD (years)	0.0	0.103

Net Exposure	Factor Volatility	TE Impact of an Isolated 1 Standard Deviation Up Change (bp)	TE Impact of a Correlated 1 Standard Deviation Up Change (bp)	Marginal Contribution to TEV (bp)	Percentage of TE Variance
−0.0010	101.24	0.08	−1.89	6.661	−0.02
−0.012	8.38	0.1	−9.68	2.816	−0.12
0.133	9.22	−1.22	−12.75	4.083	1.88
−0.016	19.58	0.31	−10.73	7.297	−0.41
−0.0090	6.48	0.06	−7.88	1.774	−0.05
−0.039	7.44	0.29	−10.76	2.778	−0.37
−0.037	9.84	0.36	−12.28	4.194	−0.54
−0.01	6.37	0.07	−8.9	1.968	−0.07
−0.018	9.88	0.17	−11.63	3.99	−0.25
0.11	21.58	−2.36	−12.66	9.492	3.61
−0.0	8.56	0.0	−10.16	3.018	−0.0
0.193	9.37	−1.81	−12.38	4.026	2.69
0.094	15.93	−1.5	−13.12	7.256	2.37
−0.0060	7.34	0.05	−7.84	1.999	−0.04
−0.024	7.67	0.19	−10.8	2.875	−0.24
−0.076	10.12	0.77	−12.1	4.251	−1.13
0.048	7.57	−0.37	−11.84	3.113	0.52
−0.016	10.28	0.17	−12.82	4.576	−0.26
−0.039	12.92	0.5	−10.24	4.592	−0.62
−0.022	6.75	0.15	−9.24	2.166	−0.17
−0.05	6.93	0.34	−9.87	2.376	−0.41
−0.012	9.05	0.11	−10.85	3.412	−0.14
−0.073	5.52	0.4	−6.26	1.199	−0.3
−0.032	7.99	0.26	−10.93	3.033	−0.34
−0.011	16.98	0.19	−10.29	6.07	−0.23
−0.0	8.18	0.0	−8.71	2.473	−0.0
−0.017	8.15	0.13	−11.03	3.121	−0.18
0.062	14.72	−0.91	−11.71	5.984	1.28
2.373	0.22	−0.53	2.49	−0.019	−0.16
0.18	7.48	−1.35	−13.71	3.563	2.23
−0.034	3.46	0.12	0.41	−0.05	0.01
−0.095	4.23	0.4	5.06	−0.743	0.25
−0.103	5.82	0.6	3.78	−0.763	0.27

(continued)

Figure 26-6. (continued)

Factor Name	Sensitivity/Exposure	Portfolio Exposure	Benchmark Exposure
Credit High Yield Spread and Volatility			
High yield communication	OASD (years)	0.134	0.0
High yield utility	OASD (years)	0.013	0.0
High yield spread slope	OASD × (TTM – AvgTTM) (years²)	2.539	0.0
High yield liquidity	OASD × (OAS – AvgOAS) (years × %)	0.064	0.0
Emerging Markets Spread			
Global EM investment grade	OASD (years)	0.173	0.045
Global EM nondistressed slope	OASD × (TTM – AvgTTM) (years²)	1.054	0.414
Global EM nondistressed liquidity	OASD × (OAS – AvgOAS) (years × %)	0.066	0.02
MBS Spread and Volatility			
USD MBS short volatility	Volatility duration	0.011	0.013
USD MBS long/derivative volatility	Volatility duration	0.02	0.033
USD MBS new discount	OASD (years)	0.019	0.05
USD MBS new current	OASD (years)	0.336	0.568
USD MBS new premium	OASD (years)	0.297	0.388
USD MBS seasoned current	OASD (years)	0.0020	0.012
USD MBS seasoned premium	OASD (years)	0.113	0.158
USD MBS GNMA 30-year	OASD (years)	0.12	0.136
USD MBS conventional 15-year	OASD (years)	0.199	0.273
USD MBS GNMA 15-year	OASD (years)	0.0	0.0080
USD MBS conventional balloon	OASD (years)	0.0	0.015
CMBS Spread			
USD CMBS Aaa	OASD (years)	0.141	0.129
USD CMBS Aa	OASD (years)	0.018	0.0060
USD CMBS A	OASD (years)	0.0	0.0040
USD CMBS Baa	OASD (years)	0.0	0.0010
USD CMBS principal payment window	OASD × WIN (years)	0.073	0.049
USD CMBS average life slope	OASD × (AL – AvgAL) (years²)	0.121	0.247

Net Exposure	Factor Volatility	TE Impact of an Isolated 1 Standard Deviation Up Change (bp)	TE Impact of a Correlated 1 Standard Deviation Up Change (bp)	Marginal Contribution to TEV (bp)	Percentage of TE Variance
0.134	102.01	−13.68	−18.05	63.922	29.77
0.013	76.51	−0.98	−13.71	36.413	1.62
2.539	0.53	−1.34	12.22	−0.224	−1.98
0.064	7.98	−0.51	−13.72	3.804	0.85
0.128	38.27	−4.88	−12.11	16.093	7.13
0.639	1.46	−0.93	6.74	−0.342	−0.76
0.046	14.47	−0.67	−10.61	5.332	0.85
−0.0020	112.41	0.22	0.14	−0.552	0.0
−0.014	84.45	1.17	−0.44	1.304	−0.06
−0.031	8.3	0.26	−0.28	0.082	−0.01
−0.232	6.84	1.59	0.9	−0.213	0.17
−0.092	8.88	0.81	−0.28	0.086	−0.03
−0.011	10.78	0.11	1.9	−0.711	0.03
−0.045	10.41	0.47	−2.95	1.067	−0.17
−0.016	3.94	0.06	−2.32	0.318	−0.02
−0.073	3.91	0.29	−1.79	0.243	−0.06
−0.0080	5.85	0.04	−1.75	0.356	−0.01
−0.015	8.25	0.13	−3.2	0.918	−0.05
0.012	5.79	−0.07	−6.85	1.377	0.06
0.012	6.68	−0.08	−5.26	1.221	0.05
−0.0040	7.77	0.03	−5.59	1.508	−0.02
−0.0010	10.75	0.01	−5.27	1.97	−0.01
0.024	2.12	−0.05	1.33	−0.098	−0.01
−0.126	0.66	0.08	3.02	−0.069	0.03

(*continued*)

Figure 26-6. (continued)

Factor Name	Sensitivity/Exposure	Portfolio Exposure	Benchmark Exposure
USD CMBS liquidity	OASD × (OAS – AvgOAS) (years × %)	0.0020	0.0020
USD CMBS age	OASD × (AGE – AvgAGE) (years^2)	0.21	0.054
USD CMBS price current pay Aaa	OASD × (Price – AvgPrice) (years × $)	0.041	−0.016
USD CMBS price noncurrent pay Aaa	OASD × (Price – AvgPrice) (years × $)	0.368	0.197
USD CMBS price non-Aaa	OASD × (Price – AvgPrice) (years × $)	0.134	0.022
ABS Spread			
USD ABS auto	OASD (years)	0.0050	0.0060
USD ABS card	OASD (years)	0.021	0.014
USD ABS home equity loans	OASD (years)	0.01	0.0070
USD ABS manufactured housing	OASD (years)	0.0	0.0030
USD ABS utilities	OASD (years)	0.043	0.0070
USD ABS non-Aaa	OASD (years)	0.0	0.0050
USD ABS average life slope	OASD × (AL – AvgAL) (years^2)	0.016	0.043
USD ABS liquidity	OASD × (OAS – AvgOAS) (years × %)	−0.0	0.0030
USD ABS price	OASD × (Price – AvgPrice) (years × $)	0.0040	−0.0040
USD ABS auto WALA	OASD × (WALA – AvgWALA) (years^2)	0.0020	0.0
USD ABS home equity loans WALA	OASD × (WALA – AvgWALA) (years^2)	0.017	0.0
USD ABS manufactured housing WALA	OASD × (WALA – AvgWALA) (years^2)	0.0	−0.0020

Net Exposure	Factor Volatility	TE Impact of an Isolated 1 Standard Deviation Up Change (bp)	TE Impact of a Correlated 1 Standard Deviation Up Change (bp)	Marginal Contribution to TEV (bp)	Percentage of TE Variance
−0.0	5.79	0.0	−2.25	0.452	−0.0
0.156	0.6	−0.09	4.42	−0.092	−0.05
0.057	0.81	−0.05	−3.34	0.094	0.02
0.17	0.41	−0.07	−2.8	0.04	0.02
0.112	0.29	−0.03	−3.51	0.035	0.01
−0.0010	7.83	0.01	−8.84	2.404	−0.01
0.0070	5.56	−0.04	−7.71	1.489	0.04
0.0030	10.79	−0.04	−5.81	2.179	0.03
−0.0030	25.36	0.06	−3.37	2.968	−0.03
0.036	5.31	−0.19	−6.49	1.196	0.15
−0.0050	6.74	0.03	1.35	−0.317	0.01
−0.027	1.11	0.03	2.64	−0.101	0.01
−0.0030	9.15	0.02	−1.78	0.566	−0.01
0.0070	0.71	−0.01	0.05	−0.0010	−0.0
0.0010	5.81	−0.01	−5.95	1.2	0.01
0.016	2.41	−0.04	−5.57	0.466	0.03
0.0020	2.64	−0.0	0.16	−0.014	−0.0

The tracking error report shows the isolated TEV for the various risk factor groups. However, owing to correlations among the risk factors, the isolated TEV does not necessarily represent the contribution of the set of risk factors to the portfolio's overall TEV. To gain a sense of the relative importance of the various factor groups, the risk model calculates the tracking error variance (i.e., TEV^2) produced by each set of risk factors (taking into account the risk factors' own volatility and correlations to all other risk factors) and expresses it as a percentage of the portfolio's total TEV^2. For the portfolio, we see that idiosyncratic risk and exposure to high-yield spreads account for more than two-thirds of the total tracking error (TE) variance.

The risk report has now answered the questions: How risky is the portfolio? And what are the sources of this risk? Next, the portfolio manager will want to know more detail regarding the sources of risk. For example, the portfolio has 5.5 bp of isolated TEV owing to exposure to credit spreads. Which sectors of the credit market are responsible for this risk in the portfolio? For this level of information, we have to identify the individual risk factors, the net exposure of the bonds in the portfolio to these risk factors (relative to the benchmarks), and the volatilities and correlations of the risk factors.

What Is the Portfolio's Sensitivity to Risk Factors, and How Are They Correlated?

Figure 26-6, which reproduces the factor exposure report, gives a detailed breakdown of TEV. This report lists all of the relevant risk factors, the portfolio's and benchmark's exposure to each, and the net exposure and the volatility of the risk factor.

For example, the portfolio has a 10-year key-rate duration (KRD) of 1.67 years, whereas the index has a 10-year KRD of 1.24 years. The net exposure is 0.43, as shown. The volatility of the 10-year par Treasury rate risk factor is reported as 27.4 bp/month. Consequently, if the 10-year par Treasury rate moved up by 1 standard deviation (i.e., 27.4 bp), and if all other risk factors were unchanged, then the portfolio would underperform the benchmark by 11.9 bp (= 0.43 × 27.4 bp). This value is shown in the column labeled "TE impact of an isolated 1-standard-deviation up change."

Based on historical data, a 1-standard-deviation move in the 10-year par Treasury rate is usually associated with movement in other risk factors. Based on this historical factor correlation, if the 10-year par Treasury rate moves by 1 standard deviation and all other risk factors move, in turn, according to the historical factor correlation matrix, then what would be the effect on the portfolio's return vs. the index? This value is shown in the next column "TE impact of a correlated

1-standard-deviation up change." As Figure 26-6 shows, a 27.4-bp increase in the 10-year par Treasury rate produces portfolio outperformance of 3.8 bp, not underperformance of 11.9 bp. This is because, for example, some of our largest contributions to risk are due to short positions to other key rates and to long positions in credit whose spreads are negatively correlated with rates and would typically be expected to tighten if rates increased.

Note that the "isolated impact" reflects only the exposure to the specific factor. Thus, since this portfolio is overweight the 10-year and underweight the 5-year, we find that the effect of an upward move in rates is negative at the 10-year point but positive at the 5-year point. By contrast, the "correlated impact" column considers the full set of portfolio exposures; the overall long-duration credit exposures, coupled with the high correlations among different points on the curve and negative correlation with credit spreads, make the effect of a rate rise positive all along the curve, even at the 10-year point.

The column labeled "marginal contribution to TEV" measures how a small increase in exposure to the risk factor affects the portfolio's systematic TEV. In other words, the marginal contribution to TEV equals the partial derivative of TEV with respect to the risk factor. For example, Figure 26-6 shows that the marginal contribution to TEV for the 10-year key-rate risk factor is –3.6. This means that if the portfolio's exposure to the 10-year key-rate point were to increase by 1.0, holding all other risk exposures unchanged, then its TEV would decrease by 3.6 bp/month.[6] This change incorporates all of the correlations of the 10-year key-rate risk factor with all other risk factors. Generally, a positive value for the "marginal contribution to TEV" indicates that the portfolio has a positive view (i.e., an overweight) on the risk factor, whereas a negative value indicates a negative view (i.e., an underweight). However, as our portfolio shows, this is not always the case. Consider the marginal contribution to TEV for the 10-year key-rate risk factor. Although it is negative (i.e., = –3.6), the portfolio has a positive exposure to this risk factor (= +0.43). An increase in exposure to the 10-year key-rate risk factor decreases the portfolio's overall TEV once we consider the correlations with all other risk factors. Recall that the portfolio is overall long duration and credit vs. the benchmark. Given that the key-rate risk factors are highly correlated and rates and credit are negatively correlated, an increase in exposure to the 10-year key-rate factor causes the portfolio's overall TEV to decrease despite the overweight exposure to the risk factor. This is because the effect of moving the net exposure to the 10-year key-rate factor further away from zero is more than offset

6. This calculation assumes that the increase in exposure to the risk factor is accomplished by changing cash. In effect, net exposures to all other risk factors are unchanged.

by the increased extent to which the 10-year key-rate exposure offsets some of the long credit exposures.

As described earlier, the last column, "percentage of TE variance," measures how much the portfolio's current net exposure to a given risk factor contributes to the overall systematic TEV^2, taking into account the risk factor's own volatility as well as the correlations with all other risk factors. In Figure 26-6, the portfolio's net exposure to the 2-year key-rate risk factor (= –0.28) accounts for 8.6% of the portfolio's TEV^2. This value incorporates the contribution of the portfolio's net exposure to the 2-year key-rate risk factor as well as the portfolio's net exposures to all the other risk factors with which it is correlated. In contrast, the portfolio's net exposure to the 10-year key-rate factor (= 0.43) accounts for –5.4% of its TEV^2. In other words, the current exposure reduces the portfolio's TEV^2. The total percentage of TE variance measures (across all risk factors) sums to 100%, and the values are independent of the order in which they are displayed.[7]

While the factor exposure report gives details on the systematic risk factor exposures, it does not identify the sources of idiosyncratic risk. We now turn to identifying those sources.

What Are the Portfolio's Security and Issuer-Specific Risks?

The next report is the portfolio issue-specific risk report (Figure 26-7), which measures each issue's weight in the portfolio, net market value issue weight (vs. the benchmark), net market value issuer weight, marginal systematic TE variance, and systematic, idiosyncratic, and issuer idiosyncratic TEV. The issues are sorted in descending order of each issue's percentage market value weight in the portfolio.

For example, the portfolio contains a 3.4% market value holding in 30-year FNMA 6% MBS. The marginal systematic TE variance of this position answers the following question: If I were to increase my position in this issue slightly, what would be the effect on the portfolio's overall TE variance given the other positions in the portfolio? In other words, this value is the partial derivative of the portfolio's TE variance with respect to the net market value of the position. Portfolio managers can use this value to gauge where they can make small changes in their portfolio to reduce systematic TE variance. In this particular case, since the portfolio has a large underweight to MBS, increasing the holding of FNA060QG at the margin would reduce the portfolio's systematic TE variance.

An issue's systematic TEV measures the consequences of the portfolio's net exposure to the issue (i.e., net of the benchmark's exposure) with respect to all of

---

7. This is not the case for the TEV.

the systematic risk factors. This value is calculated by first subtracting the benchmark's percentage holding from the portfolio's holding to produce the issue's net factor loading, which is then applied to the systematic risk factor variance-covariance matrix to arrive at this issue's overall systematic TEV. This TEV value treats the portfolio's net exposure to this issue in isolation from all other portfolio issues.

An issue's idiosyncratic TEV measures the level of idiosyncratic TEV produced by the portfolio's net exposure to the issue without regard to other issues held. The idiosyncratic TEV produced by the portfolio's 1.88% holding in the Ford 7.375s of 10/09 is 2.0 bp/month. This value is calculated by multiplying the 1.81% net exposure of the portfolio to this issue (subtracting the issue's 0.07% weight in the Aggregate Index) by the idiosyncratic risk of the issue's sector (26.8 bp/month for Baa3) and by the issue's OASD (= 4.12).

An issuer's idiosyncratic TEV is presented in the credit tickers report (Figure 26-8), which provides a list of the top 100 credit issuers (in terms of idiosyncratic risk) in the portfolio, as well as the portfolio's issuer-level net market value exposure and the net contribution to OASD vs. the benchmark. In addition, the report shows the systematic TEV of the net exposure in isolation. The idiosyncratic TEV presents the idiosyncratic risk of the net position. It is fair to argue that the order of this report should reflect the credit preferences of the portfolio manager.

The risk model assumes that an issuer's idiosyncratic risk is independent of all other risk factors in the risk model. This name-specific risk is determined by the idiosyncratic risk (i.e., risk not explained by all of the systematic risk factors) of the issuer's quality-sector bucket. For example, as of December 31, 2004, Ford Capital belongs to the Baa3-automotive bucket, so its idiosyncratic volatility equals the unexplained variation of all bonds belonging to the Baa3-automotive bucket. For our portfolio, there are two Ford Capital issues with a combined market value issuer weight of 2.77% vs. a benchmark issuer weight of 0.67%. The portfolio's net exposure to Ford produces an idiosyncratic TEV of 3.8 bp/month.

The biggest source of idiosyncratic risk in our portfolio is the 1.26% holding in the AT&T Corp. bond—a bond with a very long spread duration (10.65) and a Ba1 rating, in the volatile wirelines sector (idiosyncratic sector volatility = 130.4 bp/month). This single issue produces 17.5 bp/month of idiosyncratic TEV and is the dominant source of idiosyncratic (and total) risk for the portfolio.

As we explained earlier, the issuer's idiosyncratic risk in the portfolio is calculated by examining the weights and spread durations of the issuer's various bonds in the portfolio vs. those in the benchmark. The idiosyncratic risk model incorporates the less-than-perfect correlation in the idiosyncratic returns between two issues of the same issuer. Thus, for example, if the portfolio had the same market value weight and spread duration in Ford Capital as did the benchmark,

Figure 26-7. Portfolio Issue-Specific Risk Report, U.S. Aggregate Portfolio
December 31, 2004

Identifier	Ticker	Description	Currency	Coupon (%)	Maturity
912828AS	US/T	U.S. Treasury notes	USD	1.62	1/31/2005
912810DY	US/T	U.S. Treasury bonds	USD	8.75	5/15/2017
FNA060QG	FNMA	FNMA conventional long-term 30-year	USD	6.0	
FNA054QG	FNMA	FNMA conventional long-term 30-year	USD	5.5	
FNA050QG	FNMA	FNMA conventional long-term 30-year	USD	5.0	
912810DX	US/T	U.S. Treasury bonds	USD	7.5	11/15/2006
FNA064QG	FNMA	FNMA long-term 30-year	USD	6.5	
912810DV	US/T	U.S. Treasury bonds	USD	9.25	2/15/2016
912810EH	US/T	U.S Treasury bonds	USD	7.88	2/15/2021
FNC054QG	FNMA	FNMA conventional intermediate 15-year	USD	5.5	
FNC050QG	FNMA	FNMA conventional intermediate 15-year	USD	5.0	
345397SM	F	Ford Motor credit—global	USD	7.38	10/28/2009
912810EM	US/T	U.S. Treasury bonds	USD	7.25	8/15/2022
FNC044QG	FNMA	FNMA conventional intermediate 15-year	USD	4.5	
92344GAK	VZ	Verizon Global Funding Corp-GL	USD	6.75	12/1/2005
36962GA4	GE	General Electric Capital—global	USD	2.85	1/30/2006
500769AN	KFW	Kredit fuer Wiederaufbau—global	USD	2.38	9/25/2006
001957BD	T	AT&T Corp—global	USD	9.75	11/15/2031
31359MHK	FNMA	FNMA	USD	5.5	3/15/2011

but different issue weights, the portfolio would still have some idiosyncratic TEV arising from the issuer.

RISK MODEL APPLICATIONS

The risk model is best used by a portfolio manager as an objective way to rank portfolio alternatives under consideration. In other words, the risk model is an ex ante trade or portfolio evaluator. While a risk manager can also use it as an ex post portfolio reporting system, the utility and power of the model lies in its ability to

Current OAS (bp)	MV Issue Weight (%)	MV Issue Net Weight (%)	MV Issuer Net Weight (%)	Marginal Systematic TEV (bp)	Systematic TEV (bp)	Idiosyncratic TEV (bp)	Issuer Idiosyncratic TEV (bp)
−47.3	7.3	7.3	7.3	−0.0077	0.14	0.01	0.01
0.8	5.82	5.6	5.6	−0.3978	12.38	0.45	0.45
11.3	3.41	3.41	1.17	−0.1623	1.87	0.47	0.15
18.0	2.98	2.98	−1.83	−0.2379	2.59	0.35	0.23
20.3	2.85	2.85	−0.2	−0.3184	3.6	0.44	0.07
−0.4	2.67	2.41	2.41	−0.4017	5.36	0.19	0.19
31.6	2.45	2.45	1.39	−0.1021	0.99	0.39	0.21
−0.4	2.29	2.21	2.21	−0.3917	4.5	0.16	0.16
0.6	2.28	2.13	2.13	−0.3651	5.36	0.2	0.2
14.3	1.93	1.93	1.37	−0.1725	0.98	0.28	0.2
17.2	1.92	1.92	1.92	−0.2528	1.56	0.24	0.24
193.0	1.88	1.81	2.1	0.2669	2.46	2.0	3.78
0.2	1.7	1.57	1.57	−0.3422	4.14	0.16	0.16
23.5	1.68	1.68	0.23	−0.3077	1.77	0.26	0.08
35.0	1.43	1.43	1.99	−0.0546	0.33	0.19	1.53
27.7	1.39	1.37	1.79	−0.0771	0.36	0.11	0.5
11.7	1.37	1.33	1.1	−0.1829	0.64	0.18	0.17
306.7	1.26	1.26	1.26	8.6374	12.51	17.49	17.49
38.4	1.23	1.17	1.17	−0.4425	1.81	0.28	0.28

offer optimal risk choices rather than simply monitor choices that have already been made.

In this section, we present six important portfolio management applications of the risk model:

1. Structuring an Efficient Active Portfolio: A portfolio manager can use the risk model to structure a portfolio that is finely tailored to reflect his market views. He may have a view on credit spreads, and by using the model, he can make sure that the portfolio does not have any unintentional market exposures.

Figure 26-8. Credit Tickers Report, U.S. Aggregate Portfolio

December 31, 2004

Ticker	Name	Sector	Rating	Currency
T	AT&T Corp—global	Wirelines	Ba1	USD
F	Ford Capital B.V.	Transportation-services	Baa3 Baa2	USD
MEX	United Mex States—global	Sovereigns	Baa3	USD
FON	Sprint Capital Corp.	Wireless	Baa3	USD
PEMEX	Pemex Finance Ltd.	Foreign-agencies	Baa1 Aaa Baa3	USD
IBM	International Business Machines	Technology	A1	USD
CMCSA	Comcast Cable Communication	Media-cable	Baa3	USD
TXU	Oncor Electric Delivery	Electric	Baa2 Baa3	USD
VZ	GTE Corp.	Wirelines	A3 A1 A2 Baa2 Baa1	USD
NI	Columbia Energy Group	Electric	Baa2 Baa3	USD
GS	Goldman Sachs Group—global	Brokerage	A1 A3	USD
C	Commercial Credit	Banking	Aa3 A1 A2	USD
FE	Cleveland Electric Illumination	Electric	Baa3 Baa1 Ba1	USD
WFC	Wells Fargo & Co.—global	Noncaptive consumer	Aa3 A1 A2	USD
GM	General Motors Acceptance Corp.	Automotive	Baa3	USD
LEH	Lehman Brothers Holdings, Inc.	Brokerage	A2	USD
KFT	Nabisco	Food and beverage	A3 Baa1	USD
WMI	WMX Technologies	Environmental	Baa3	USD
GE	General Electric Capital Services	Multiple	Aaa A3	USD
TWX	Time Warner Inc.	Media-cable	Baa1	USD
JPM	Bank One National Illinois— global	Banking	Aa3 A2 A3 A1	USD
DCX	Chrysler	Automotive	Baa2	USD

2. Evaluating Portfolio Trades: The risk model can readily be used to analyze the risk impact of a proposed trade. Does the trade introduce any unexpected and unwanted risk exposures?

3. Optimizing a Portfolio: The risk model has a built-in optimizer, which allows the manager to select from an eligible list of bonds those that would help reduce the portfolio's TEV to a desired level. We describe how the optimizer works and highlight its key features.

4. Constructing Proxy Portfolios: The risk model and optimizer can be combined to construct a "proxy" portfolio containing relatively few

Number of Issues in Portfolio	Portfolio Weight (%)	Benchmark Weight (%)	Net Weight (%)	Contribution to OASD (years)	Systematic TEV (bp)	Idiosyncratic TEV (bp)
1	1.26	0.0	1.26	0.134	12.51	17.49
2	2.77	0.67	2.1	0.142	4.57	3.78
1	1.22	0.48	0.74	0.077	3.26	2.99
1	0.95	0.2	0.75	0.1	2.63	2.34
1	1.2	0.16	1.04	0.056	2.52	2.18
1	1.1	0.13	0.96	0.143	3.35	2.17
1	0.96	0.25	0.71	0.08	2.14	1.91
1	0.8	0.06	0.74	0.078	2.08	1.8
2	2.29	0.3	1.99	0.103	2.34	1.53
2	1.44	0.04	1.41	0.058	1.57	1.29
1	0.73	0.36	0.37	0.072	1.71	1.17
2	2.12	0.5	1.62	0.073	1.88	1.14
1	0.72	0.01	0.7	0.012	0.86	1.0
1	1.17	0.24	0.93	0.053	1.49	0.86
2	1.78	0.62	1.16	0.028	0.89	0.76
1	1.04	0.2	0.84	0.047	1.34	0.74
1	0.74	0.12	0.61	0.036	1.01	0.67
1	0.77	0.06	0.7	0.025	0.74	0.54
2	2.51	0.72	1.79	0.048	1.27	0.5
0	0.0	0.26	−0.26	−0.022	0.6	0.49
1	0.99	0.53	0.47	0.011	0.39	0.36
0	0.0	0.26	−0.26	−0.014	0.4	0.3

issues designed to track a broader index with minimum expected TEV. We work through a detailed example of proxy portfolio construction using the optimizer.

5. Scenario Analysis: Many portfolio managers supplement their risk analysis by stress testing their portfolios using scenario analysis. However, fully specifying scenarios is difficult. Given a hypothetical movement in the term structure, what happens to spreads in the various market sectors? To volatility? To currencies? It is unrealistic to assume that these other risk factors remain unchanged when the term structure moves. The risk model can be used to help the manager specify scenarios,

and probabilities of those scenarios, that are internally consistent with broad market history.

6. Risk Budgeting: Not only can the risk model be used to measure risk, it can also be used to control risk allocation. An increasing number of managers operate within a prespecified "risk budget." In other words, the manager is required to take market positions so that the portfolio's expected TEV remains within a certain limit. A manager (and the plan sponsor) can use the risk model to monitor the portfolio's adherence to its risk budget and to compare different types of risk on the same footing.

Structuring an Efficient Active Portfolio

Consider the following everyday investment process: a portfolio manager with views on expected movements in rates, spreads, and volatilities wishes to create a portfolio that reflects those views. Generally, he will take an existing portfolio and make provisional trades until the portfolio has the desired exposures, but there are many possible ways to structure a portfolio to reflect a particular view. Some trades may introduce unintentional exposures to other risk factors. Perhaps buying long credit bonds has introduced an undesired exposure to credit spreads, or perhaps a lightening of the MBS portfolio has left the portfolio underweighted to the premium MBS sector. Since a given bond has exposure to many different risk factors, transactions within a portfolio can easily produce some unintended risk exposures. This is particularly true for portfolios benchmarked against broad-based indices such as the U.S. Aggregate or the Global Aggregate.

By running the portfolio, with provisional trades, through the risk model, the manager can quickly identify any unexpected active exposures. As a simple example, consider a manager who has decided to be long-duration in anticipation of a decline in long Treasury yields. By examining the factor exposure report discussed earlier, the manager may discover that the portfolio has a large relative exposure to Baa-rated cyclicals arising from a position in long auto bonds. The manager's overall position to cyclicals may be neutral in market value terms, but he has a net portfolio exposure to changes in the spreads of Baa-rated cyclicals. This exposure is probably making the portfolio's tracking error larger than if the portfolio did not have this sector exposure. If the manager has no particular view on cyclical spreads, removing this exposure will help reduce undesired tracking error.[8]

---

8. There is a feature in the risk model optimizer that allows a manager to freeze exposures on certain risk factors and reduce tracking error arising from exposure to all other risk factors.

Using the risk model to examine a portfolio and any proposed trades is also useful when a portfolio is managed by a group of portfolio managers. In such a setting, it is not unusual for the chief investment officer or senior portfolio manager to set the tone for the overall portfolio (e.g., "the Fed is expected to ease and we expect rates to decline with a general recovery in spreads"). The sector portfolio managers are then free to structure their sector portfolios with this top-down view in mind. However, a problem can develop if all the portfolio managers incorporate the same view in their own individual portfolios. For example, the MBS manager may underweight MBS overall, and current coupons and premiums in particular, if rates are expected to decline. Perhaps he will invest cash from any dollar rolls in lower-rated spread assets. The corporate manager may overweight the long end of the corporate spread curve and increase exposure to lower-rated names. So, too, for the ABS and CMBS managers. How do all these portfolios fit together, and how do their risks interrelate? Although each individual portfolio conforms to the CIO's worldview, is the overall portfolio taking too much risk owing to a compounding of active exposures? Perhaps there are too many proposed trades? Running the portfolio and the proposed trades through the risk model is a useful check for excessive or unintentional risk exposures.

As we described earlier, the risk report is extensive: relative exposures to all of the risk factors; estimated TEVs arising from various sets of risk factors including an overall portfolio TEV; and estimated tracking error arising from idiosyncratic risk exposures. While all of this information is helpful, the overall tracking error number usually receives the most attention. The estimated TEV is the model's estimate of the standard deviation of the total return difference between the portfolio and the benchmark.[9] This estimated TEV is based, in part, on the historical relationship of the risk factors captured by the historical variance-covariance matrix of the realized risk factors.

All of the foregoing presupposes that historical volatilities and correlations are a good guide to the future, and as we noted earlier there is some evidence to support this assertion. Nonetheless, the near-term future may differ from the historical experience used to estimate the variance-covariance matrix. This possibility may cause managers to have low confidence in the estimated tracking error number. However, even a skeptic in these matters should note that when structuring and evaluating different portfolios what is important is relative TEV—in other words, how does the TEV of the original portfolio compare to the proposed portfolio? Managers should have much more confidence in relative tracking errors

---

9. If return differences are assumed to be normally distributed, then a familiar confidence interval can be constructed: The return difference will be within $\pm 1.96 \times$ TEV of the mean return difference 95% of the time.

since both TEVs are calculated using the same variance-covariance matrix. If portfolio A has a tracking error of 30 bp/month and portfolio B has a tracking error of 20 bp/month, then there is high confidence that portfolio A is 50% riskier than portfolio B. Whereas risk factor volatilities may fluctuate over time, the correlations of risk factors are more stable. Consequently, comparing tracking errors of portfolios at a given time is a realistic ranking of their relative risks.

All of the foregoing implies that portfolio managers can confidently leverage the power of the risk model to add significant value in the portfolio-structuring process, helping them to implement only those views that they wish to express, with a careful eye toward the risk embedded in the portfolio.

Evaluating Proposed Trades

Not only is the risk model useful for evaluating a portfolio structured around a particular market view, it can also provide valuable insight when considering individual proposed trades, such as a modest duration extension, sector overweight, or a one-on-one bond swap. Does such a proposed trade produce any unexpected risk exposures? Another important question is whether a proposed trade produces an expected return pickup that would justify any potential increase in tracking error. Alternatively, a proposed trade may offer both an expected return pickup, as well as a reduction in expected tracking error. As an example of how to use the risk model to evaluate proposed trades, consider the U.S. Aggregate portfolio discussed in the previous section.

Suppose the portfolio manager is considering adding to the portfolio's corporate exposure because he expects either tighter corporate spreads or unchanged spreads and would like to increase the carry on the portfolio. He is considering selling $37 million of the UST 7.25 of 8/22 and buying $48.3 million (which would be market value neutral) of the Sprint Capital 6.875% of 11/28. The Sprint bonds are Baa-rated and have an OAS of +124 bp. The proposed trade would be approximately 1.5% of the overall market value of the portfolio.

The portfolio manager can enter the proposed trade into the portfolio and then examine how the revised portfolio compares to the benchmark. The effect of the trade is shown below:

	Pretrade	Post-Trade	Benchmark
OAD	4.51	4.56	4.33
Contribution to credit OASD	1.82	2.03	1.42
Yield (%)	4.31	4.34	4.38
OAS (bp)	40	42	33
TEV (bp/month)	28.8	31.6	

The proposed trade would certainly have the anticipated effect on the portfolio. While the overall duration would be little changed, the contribution to credit spread duration would increase from 1.82 to 2.03, and the portfolio yield and OAS would increase from 4.31% and 40 bp, to 4.34% and 42 bp, respectively.

Is this yield pickup and increased spread exposure worth the risk? Using the risk model, we see that the portfolio's estimated TEV has increased from 28.8 to 31.6 bp/month. This 3-bp/month increase is approximately 10 bp/year. Is the 3 bp in portfolio yield worth the increase in portfolio risk? Without a risk model, the manager would have had difficulty formulating the portfolio management question so precisely.

Optimizing a Portfolio

The risk model does a good job of identifying and measuring the relative risk exposures of a portfolio vs. its benchmark. However, suppose the manager wants to reduce the estimated TEV. Which bonds should be sold and bought? Since a bond has exposure to many risk factors, selling a particular bond and buying another to reduce one risk exposure may introduce other active risk exposures that could partially frustrate the effort to reduce overall TEV. The large number of risk dimensions makes it difficult for a portfolio manager to move efficiently toward a desired TEV target without the aid of an optimizer.

Built within the risk model is an optimizer that minimizes a portfolio's estimated tracking error by suggesting trades from among the existing bonds in the portfolio and a set of eligible bonds provided by the portfolio manager. When invoked, the optimizer uses an algorithm known as "gradient descent" to suggest a list of portfolio bonds to sell (or buy). This list is sorted by the impact that the sale of the bond, at the margin, will have on the TEV. The portfolio manager can then select a bond from the list, and the optimizer will provide a list of the best bonds to buy, *given the selected sale.* Although the optimizer provides a "best sell candidate" and an associated "best buy candidate," it is important to note that the portfolio manager is at liberty to select any bond in each list. This essential feature allows the manager to bring his intuition and market knowledge to bear on the optimization process, both to identify bonds that can be realistically bought and sold and to select credits on which he has a positive outlook.

The optimization can be constrained so as not to disturb a desired portfolio exposure. For example, if the manager is happy with the portfolio's exposure to the MBS risk factors, then he can instruct the optimizer to keep the exposure on the mortgage portion of the portfolio, and it will recommend trades that will reduce the overall TEV subject to keeping the active portfolio exposures to the MBS risk factors.

Alternatively, the optimization can be modified so as to ignore the portfolio exposure to a certain set of risk factors. To see the usefulness of this feature, recall that exposure to yield curve risk factors is a major source of portfolio TEV. Consider a manager who is currently overall duration-neutral to the benchmark. However, the duration of his credit sector holdings is much longer than that of the benchmark's credit sector. If he wanted to balance his credit sector mismatches, the optimizer would be reluctant to shorten the duration of his credit sector, since doing so would introduce an overall portfolio duration bet that would tend to increase TEV. The manager can tell the optimizer to ignore exposure on the yield curve and it will suggest trades to move the portfolio's credit sector exposure closer to that of the benchmark without regard to the resulting yield curve exposure ramifications. Once the credit sectors are aligned, the manager can then remove the "ignore" feature on the yield curve and let the optimizer suggest trades (most likely Treasury trades) to match up yield curve exposures.

Another example of an application of this "ignore" feature is the case of a credit manager whose performance is measured in excess return space. This manager assumes that any yield curve exposure generated by the credit portfolio will be hedged away by the duration manager. Consequently, the credit manager can disregard yield curve exposures when structuring the credit portfolio. The important risk measure for this manager is the TEV excluding the term-structure risk factors, and the "ignore" feature allows this to be minimized.

The risk model and optimizer can be used in several other portfolio applications, such as constructing proxy portfolios, scenario analysis, and risk budgeting. We now turn to a discussion of these other applications.

Constructing Proxy Portfolios

The risk model and optimizer can also be used to construct efficient proxy portfolios from cash. A proxy portfolio is designed to track an index with minimum realized tracking error. A "passive" manager may construct proxy portfolios to fill a mandate for a low-tracking-error portfolio. An "active" manager may use a proxy portfolio to hold an influx of new cash, or when he is very defensive vs. the benchmark, or as a core portfolio to express portfolio views.

Without the use of a risk model, a passive portfolio is typically constructed using stratified sampling. However, because stratification does not allow risk in one dimension to help offset risk in another dimension, proxy portfolios constructed in this fashion tend to contain a relatively large number of issues as it becomes necessary to populate all of the "buckets." While this may be feasible for very large passive portfolios, it is an inefficient strategy for smaller ones.

Given the interrelationship of risks captured in the risk model, a low-tracking-error portfolio may not necessarily have issues populating each "bucket." Instead, the risk model realizes that a bond contributes to many dimensions of a portfolio's risk, so it may choose to leave a bucket empty if the exposures arising from that bucket are matched by bonds in other highly correlated buckets. As a result, a proxy portfolio constructed using the risk model and optimizer is typically smaller. Given the transaction costs for small lots and the difficulty of finding particular bonds to populate specific buckets for a stratified sample, a proxy portfolio constructed using the risk model can be executed more quickly and more cost efficiently.

Investors have successfully used the risk model and optimizer for many years to construct proxy portfolios. Typically, realized tracking errors have been somewhat less than estimated tracking errors. For example, proxy MBS and government portfolios have been built and run for many years with realized tracking errors very rarely exceeding 1 standard deviation (TEV = 5 bp/month). The reason for the success of such portfolios is the lack of idiosyncratic risk in these bond instruments. A distinctive feature of proxy portfolios is that they contain relatively few bonds, whereas the underlying benchmark usually holds hundreds of positions. (For example, an MBS proxy portfolio may contain twelve bonds, whereas the MBS Index contains almost 410 generics.) Consequently, a bond in the proxy portfolio may comprise a 5% market value weight, compared with a 0.5% weight in the index. This is a very large relative overweight, which exposes the proxy portfolio to event risk. Generally, MBS and government bond issues have very little idiosyncratic (or, event) risk, which greatly increases the probability that the proxy will closely track the benchmark.

However, this is not the case for corporate bonds or for any other asset class with a relatively large amount of idiosyncratic risk. A distinguishing characteristic of the Lehman risk model is that it explicitly incorporates a bond's idiosyncratic risk into the measurement of overall tracking error. To reduce idiosyncratic risk (and, hence, overall TEV) to a reasonable level, a proxy corporate portfolio must contain a fairly large number of bonds. Although the systematic component of TEV can be lowered with a relatively small number of bonds, idiosyncratic risk can only be effectively reduced by adding to the number of bonds in the proxy.

Figure 26-9 graphs the relationship between the number of bonds in a U.S. Aggregate proxy portfolio and the estimated TEV. The proxy portfolio begins with a single corporate bullet bond with its duration matched to the Aggregate Index (HFC $4\frac{1}{8}$s of 12/2008, belonging to the A-rated financial credit sector), which produces a TEV of approximately 81 bp/month. The systematic (43 bp/month) and idiosyncratic (70 bp/month) components of TEV are also shown. Note that the idiosyncratic risk is a substantial portion of the overall TEV. We then let the

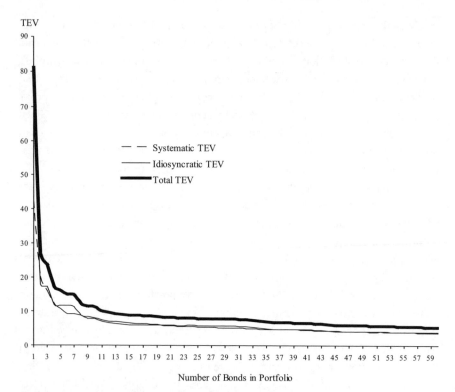

Figure 26-9. Proxy Portfolios: TEV as a Function of the Number of Bonds
U.S. Aggregate Proxy Portfolio, December 31, 2004

optimizer recommend sells and buys to bring down the TEV.[10] Figure 26-9 shows what happens to the systematic, idiosyncratic, and overall TEV as bonds are added to the proxy portfolio.

By the time the proxy portfolio contains five bonds, the overall TEV has already fallen by over 80% to 16 bp/month. The systematic TEV has declined to 11 bp/month, whereas the idiosyncratic TEV has fallen from 70 to 12 bp/month.

What did the optimizer do to bring TEV down so quickly? Before giving the answer, let us first build some intuition. The initial TEV is 81 bp/month. What are the components of TEV? Figure 26-10 presents the risk sector components of TEV. For the initial one bond proxy portfolio, risk from yield curve exposure is 30 bp/month. Although the bond matches the overall duration of the benchmark, there is substantial KRD exposure (i.e., a large overweight to 5-year Treasury key-rate and large underweight to all other key rates). Risk from agency-credit spreads

10. We limit the set of bonds eligible for portfolio inclusion to issues in the U.S. Aggregate Index that were issued within the prior 3 years and have at least $500 million outstanding.

TEV

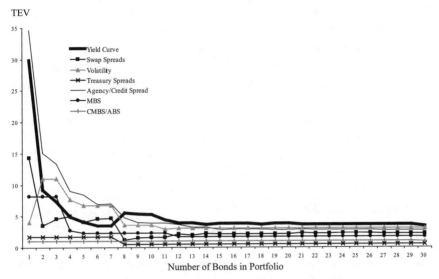

Figure 26-10. Proxy Portfolios: TEV Sector Components as a Function of the Number of Bonds

U.S. Aggregate Portfolio, December 31, 2004

is relatively large at 35 bp/month. This risk arises solely from exposure to credit risk factors, as the portfolio is 100% invested in credit. The third largest component of systematic risk is the 14-bp/month exposure to swap spreads. Again, the single-bond portfolio is a bullet with a concentrated positive exposure to 5-year swap spreads and large underweight to all other key-rate swap spreads.

Intuition tells us that the portfolio needs exposure to other parts of the Treasury curve and other swap spreads, and should reduce credit sector exposure. In fact, this is what the optimizer recommends with a single trade.

First Trade Recommended by the Optimizer

- Sell: 89% portfolio position in HFC corporate bond.

- Buy: 89% portfolio position in FNMA 51/2s 7/2012 callable at 7/2005.

The Fannie Mae callable debenture gives the portfolio exposure to many points along the Treasury and swap spread curve. In addition, it gives the portfolio large exposure to a different, and less volatile (factor volatility of 4.1 bp/month), part of the agency-credit sector, while substantially reducing exposure to the A-rated financial sector (factor volatility of 10.7 bp/month).

This first trade reduces the overall TEV to 27 bp/month from 81 bp/month. Note what happens to the components of the TEV: TEV that is due to yield curve exposure falls from 30 to 9 bp/month; swap spread exposure from 14 to 4 bp/

month, and agency-credit spread exposure from 35 to 15 bp/month. The movements in the TEV components can be seen in Figure 26-10.

Although most of the TEV components decreased with the first trade, the observant investor will note that the TEV owing to volatility exposure increased! This is because the callable FNMA bond is much more negatively convex than both the credit bond that was sold and the benchmark. As a result, the portfolio TEV exposure owing to volatility has increased from 4 to 11 bp/month. However, the increase in the exposure to volatility is more than offset by the reduction in the other systematic risk exposures. The optimizer allows an increase in some risk exposures, provided that the reduction in others produces an overall TEV reduction.

Idiosyncratic risk also drops sharply with the introduction of the second bond in the portfolio—for two reasons. First, for bonds that belong to different issuers, the risk model assumes that their idiosyncratic risks are uncorrelated. Consequently, adding bonds to the portfolio reduces idiosyncratic risk through diversification. Second, the FNMA bond has much lower idiosyncratic risk (18 bp/month) than the HFC bond, whose position was reduced (70 bp/month).

Once the portfolio contains fifteen bonds, its TEV is 8.8 bp/month with systematic TEV at 6 bp/month and idiosyncratic TEV at 6.5 bp/month. Note also that the components of the TEV begin to flatten out (Figure 26-9). Adding more bonds to the portfolio improves TEV, both systematic and idiosyncratic, but only very gradually. By the fiftieth bond, the overall TEV is 5.8 bp/month, with systematic TEV at 4 bp/month and idiosyncratic TEV at 4.1 bp/month.[11]

The large spurt of idiosyncratic risk in 2001 and 2002 prompted a new feature in the Lehman risk models. Since idiosyncratic risk is "episodic," if it is averaged over long periods of time, the magnitude of idiosyncratic risk may seem small, although, over short periods, it can dominate. The risk model measures idiosyncratic risk historically, but the user has the choice of specifying how much weight to give to recent, as opposed to more distant, history. For example, if the manager feels that a recent period of high idiosyncratic risk is likely to persist, he can ask the model to give more weight to recent periods when measuring the magnitude of idiosyncratic risk. This choice increases the TEV penalty for holding too few bond issuers and encourages the proxy portfolio builder to add more names. How-

---

11. It is important to note that the TEV measures "normal market" volatility. A portfolio containing relatively few bonds managed against the U.S. Aggregate Index remains vulnerable, as the particular credit issues selected may experience unusual volatility (i.e., downgrades or defaults) not fully captured by historical volatilities. Portfolio managers have to determine whether there is sufficient diversification in their credit portfolio beyond the reported TEV number. For details, see Chapter 14.

ever, if the manager has a forecast of low idiosyncratic risk, he may wish to use a level of idiosyncratic risk measured over a long historical period, which will typically be low. Generally, it is wise to err on the conservative side, running the risk model using both assumptions for idiosyncratic risk and taking the higher of the two estimated TEVs.

Although the risk model allows calibration of idiosyncratic risk to match a manager's near-term forecast more closely, idiosyncratic risk is still measured historically. As such, it cannot capture any new event risk that may affect a particular issuer.

Scenario Analysis

The tracking error number from a risk model is just one way of measuring a portfolio's risk vs. its benchmark. To supplement their risk analysis, many investors also perform scenario analysis.

Scenario analysis involves specifying various possible future market environments and measuring how the portfolio performs in each. For example, a common set of scenarios is to examine the portfolio assuming that the UST yield curve shifts in a parallel fashion ±50, ±100, and ±200 bp over a relevant holding period horizon (say, 12 months). Both the portfolio and benchmark are repriced at the horizon with the new UST curve, and the relative performance is calculated.

The difficulty with scenario analysis is the specification of the scenarios. Portfolio managers must guard against specifying scenarios that conform only to their market forecasts, and scenarios must be internally consistent. If a manager specifies movements in the UST curve, how should the other risk factors change commensurately? Is it realistic to specify a +100-bp shift in the UST curve and hold credit spreads unchanged? In other words, for each of the UST curve scenarios what should happen to spreads? To volatility? To the slope of the UST curve? To the slope of the various spread sector curves?

The risk model can be used to help the portfolio manager construct realistic scenarios. It is important that he construct scenarios, both "favorable" and "adverse," in a fashion that is internally consistent with realistic market behavior. For example, suppose a manager specifies a –100-bp shift in the UST curve along with a 50-bp tightening of credit spreads. The historical experience is that UST yield changes and spread changes tend to be negatively correlated. Therefore, the manager's scenario is very unlikely and probably adds very little relevant information regarding the risk of his portfolio. Alternatively, he may assume that the UST curve is unchanged but wants to examine the portfolio given a 20-bp widening of industrial sector spreads. What should he assume about spread movements in other sectors? Is it a realistic scenario to assume that all other sector spreads remain unchanged?

The data contained in the risk model can be very helpful in constructing scenarios. Many managers may want to examine how the portfolio performs assuming various UST yield curve shifts, but may not have views on changes in sector spread or volatility. In this case, a manager may simply want the scenario to reflect the assumed yield curve move and the most likely concomitant move in the other risk factors. Given a manager's specified shift in some risk factor(s), the risk model can use the historical risk factor variance-covariance matrix to generate the expected shift in all other risk factors.

Using the risk model to construct realistic scenarios increases the value of the scenario analysis to the portfolio manager. He can specify a shift in some set of risk factors, and, in turn, the risk model will shift all the other risk factors in a way that makes the scenario most likely.

Risk Budgeting

We have described many uses of the risk model to measure risk. However, it can also be used to control risk. This feature is particularly attractive to a plan sponsor or a chief investment officer who wishes to limit the ex ante risk of an investment manager.

Most investment management agreements specify risk guidelines. Similarly, internal investment company policies limit the risk that an individual manager may take. However, these guidelines are generally written in terms of permitted portfolio deviations from a target level or benchmark. For example, some guidelines state that a portfolio's duration must remain within a value of 5 ± 0.5. Presumably, this tolerance band was specified to limit the total return volatility of the portfolio. However, when was the tolerance band established? Was it during a period of low interest-rate volatility so that a 0.5-duration deviation implied a relatively modest total return deviation? Or was it during a high-volatility period so that the plan sponsor fully expected more extreme portfolio return deviations? Depending on when the guidelines were written, the permitted duration deviation could imply very different portfolio return deviations.

This issue becomes more complicated when the risk guidelines involve many constraints. For example, apart from a duration constraint, risk guidelines may also specify permitted sector overweights (in market value terms) such as "the portfolio's weighting in the corporate sector may not deviate by more than 5 percentage points from the benchmark weight." The guidelines may also specify a permitted over- or underweight in the various quality sectors (e.g., the portfolio may not contain more than 10% in bonds rated Baa or worse).

The problem with risk guidelines specified in such a manner is that the constraints are piecemeal. It is difficult to determine the overall level of risk permitted in the portfolio, which is, presumably, what the plan sponsor is trying to articulate. As the market environment changes, the same constraints could imply very different portfolio risk levels. Furthermore, how do the various risk constraints interact? A duration overweight with a 10% MBS overweight could imply a different portfolio risk level than the same duration overweight with a 10% MBS underweight, although both positions would be permissible.

The underlying goal of the plan sponsor or chief investment officer is to limit the overall risk of the portfolio. In effect, the intent is to constrain the volatility or the tracking error of the portfolio vs. a benchmark. Ideally, the guidelines should be specified in terms of tracking error limits (i.e., a risk budget), and the portfolio manager should have discretion as to where to take risk, provided the portfolio stays within the risk budget.

The risk model can enable a manager to operate within a risk budget. Rather than specify individual limits (e.g., duration deviation must be within 0.5 year and Baa's must be less than 10% of the overall portfolio), the sponsor may specify that the manager may take no more than 50 bp/year of expected tracking error. The manager is then free to take active exposures anywhere in the portfolio provided, of course, that the portfolio's overall estimated tracking error remains less than 50 bp. The risk model can be used as an objective monitor of the portfolio manager's activities.

MODEL OVERVIEW BY ASSET CLASS

Moving from a theoretical concept of a risk model to a practical portfolio management tool requires the specification and estimation of the risk factors. So far, we have only spoken of the systematic risk factors in the abstract. What are the systematic risk factors? Where do they come from? How do we estimate their values?

The risk model construction process begins by decomposing bond returns into various parts. This exercise is often referred to as "return splitting." For each bond in the Lehman index database, we break down a bond's monthly return into the following components:[12]

$$\text{TotalRet} = \text{CurrencyRet} + \text{CarryRet} + \text{YieldCurveRet} + \text{VolatilityRet} \\ + \text{SwapSpreadRet} + \text{SpreadRet.}$$

First, for bonds that are in a different currency than the base currency, there is a stochastic CurrencyRet component to total returns. The risk model currently contains twenty-two currency risk factors covering twenty-three currencies.[13]

---

12. We simply outline the return splitting process here. Details are beyond the scope of this chapter.

13. One currency is the base currency for calculating FX rates and volatility. Hence, there are twenty-two currency risk factors.

The CarryRet component is deterministic (i.e., known at the beginning of each month), and is simply the bond's monthly coupon return plus any return arising simply from the passage of time.

The four remaining return components are stochastic (i.e., unknown at the beginning of the month). Each of these components of return is modeled separately and is assumed to be driven by its own set of risk factors. The YieldCurveRet component represents that portion of a bond's total return that is due to the movement of the currency's benchmark curve. For example, the YieldCurveRet for a USD bond is modeled as the sum of the bond's Treasury KRDs multiplied by the change in the appropriate key rate.[14] (This is discussed in more detail later.) Similarly, the VolatilityRet is modeled as the sum of a bond's volatility duration multiplied by the change in the corresponding implied volatility. The SwapSpreadRet component is modeled as the sum of a bond's swap spread KRDs multiplied by the change in the appropriate key-rate swap spreads.

The YieldCurveRet, VolatilityRet, and SwapSpreadRet return component models are relatively straightforward and are similar across different asset classes within a currency market. In other words, all U.S. securities have the same YieldCurveRet model (and, hence, potential exposure to the same set of key-rate risk factors). Moreover, the YieldCurveRet models are also similar across currency markets. For example, the USD and euro models both have similar sets of six key-rate risk factors—specific, of course, to their own benchmark yield curve.

The last component of return is SpreadRet, which is the portion of a bond's total return that is not explained by carry, changes in the yield curve, changes in volatility, and changes in swap spreads. Treatment of this component of a bond's return depends heavily on the characteristics of the bond's asset sector. Consequently, each major asset sector of a given currency market has its own SpreadRet model and its own set of risk factors. The USD credit SpreadRet model is very different structurally from the USD MBS SpreadRet model. The credit SpreadRet model has changes in various credit sector spreads as the main risk factors—exactly what a credit portfolio manager's intuition would indicate. In contrast, the MBS SpreadRet model has changes in spreads for discount/current/premium price mortgages as the main risk factors—exactly what an MBS portfolio manager's intuition would indicate. This difference in model specification reflects the different drivers of spread return in the various asset sector markets.

Moreover, there may be differences in models for the same sector but in different currency markets. As a result, while the USD credit SpreadRet model shares similar characteristics with that of euro credit, there are some differences. For ex-

---

14. There is also a convexity factor in the YieldCurveRet model.

ample, the USD model has nine credit sectors, whereas the euro model has seven. Differences in model specification reflect different market sector structures.

In summary, the total return for each bond is split into several components. Each component, in turn, is then modeled as a linear combination of systematic risk factors. Each month, across all bonds in the index, each component of total return is regressed on the factor loadings for each of the component's risk factors. (Note, the YieldCurveRet and Swap SpreadRet components are modeled using observed factors.) These factor loadings are calculated from the cash flows of each bond. The realized monthly value for the risk factor is the estimate produced by the regression. The residuals from each component regression (i.e., the portion of returns not explained by the systematic risk factors) are aggregated and used in the model for the bond's nonsystematic (i.e., idiosyncratic) risk.

We now discuss the four main systematic components of a bond's returns: YieldCurveRet, SwapSpreadRet, VolatilityRet, and SpreadRet. For each of these model components we provide a brief description of the model's specification. Where significant, we highlight how the model's specification varies depending on the particular currency or sector. Much of the section describes the SpreadRet models, where there is a great deal of variety in the model specifications.

Yield Curve Return Models

Over the past decade, the local swap curve—not the Treasury curve—has become the benchmark curve for many asset classes. For asset classes that continue to quote bond spreads relative to the Treasury curve, an increasing number of investors also examine the spread to the swap curve. There are two main reasons for this development. First, there has been rapid growth in assets managed by investors who fund themselves at LIBOR (i.e., swap rates). For this influential class of investors, their relative value decision is based, in part, on a bond's spread to the swap curve. Second, during the latter part of the 1990s, there was growing concern (now passed) regarding the scarcity of USD Treasury securities. As a result, U.S. investors and traders began to hedge their positions using swaps and to view swaps as a more relevant benchmark.

The risk model recognizes the swap curve as the benchmark curve for all assets. In other words, movement in the swap curve is the systematic component of return that is common to all assets. However, for the four major currency markets (USD, euro, sterling, and yen) the risk model splits changes in the swap curve into two pieces: changes in the local Treasury yield curve and changes in local swap *spreads* (i.e., spreads of the swap curve to the Treasury curve in each currency). Consequently, every spread sector bond in these four currency markets has components of total return that are due, respectively, to changes in the Treasury curve and changes in swap spreads. In the risk model, each component of a bond's return is modeled separately with its own set of risk factors: Treasury curve risk factors (changes in Treasury key rates) for the YieldCurveRet model and swap spread risk factors (i.e., changes in swap spreads) for the SwapSpreadRet model. We first discuss the YieldCurveRet model, then the SwapSpreadRet model (applicable to the four major currency markets).

Movements in the local Treasury or swap yield curve will clearly have a major effect on almost any fixed-income security. By considering the effect of the reshaping of the yield curve during the course of a month, holding all else constant, we calculate the return of a given security owing to that movement—the YieldCurveRet component of a bond's total return. To model this component of return, we consider the movement of a few key points on the par curve. These key rates, along with the sensitivity of the security to them—KRDs—allow us to explain over 95% of the yield curve return. With the inclusion of a convexity term, we explain close to 100%.

For each month, we collate these key-rate factors, obtaining historical monthly realizations for all of our factors going back as far as January 1990. By way of illustration, a sample time series of the USD 6-month key-rate movements follows:

Month	Movement of USD 6-Month Key Rate (%)
Jan-90	0.151
Feb-90	−0.087
Mar-90	0.270
Apr-90	0.089
May-90	−0.381
. . .	. . .
Apr-03	0.011
May-03	−0.086
Jun-03	−0.142
Jul-03	0.121
Aug-03	0.005
Sep-03	−0.042

Risk factor time series data are then used to generate the covariance matrix. As data for each additional month become available, the risk factor database and covariance matrix are updated.

While structurally similar, there are some differences in the YieldCurveRet models for the various currency markets. The U.S. dollar, euro, sterling, Norwe-

Figure 26-11. Systematic Risk Factors, YieldCurveRet Models

Market	Yield Curve Risk Factors
USD, EUR, and GBP	6-month; 2-year; 5-year; 10-year; 20-year; and 30-year Treasury key rates
JPY	6-month; 2-year; 5-year; 7-year; 10-year; 20-year; and 30-year Treasury key rates
CAD	6-month; 2-year; 5-year; 10-year; and 30-year swap key rates
SEK and NOK	6-month; 2-year; 5-year; and 10-year swap key rates
CHF	6-month; 2-year; 5-year; 10-year; and 20-year swap key rates
DKK	6-month; 2-year; 5-year; 10-year; 20-year; and 30-year swap key rates

gian kroner, Swedish krona, Danish krone, Canadian dollar, Swiss franc, and yen YieldCurveRet models have the key-rate risk factors shown in Figure 26-11.

The factor loading for each key rate is the bond's KRD for that key rate. Note the presence of the 7-year key rate for the yen market, reflecting the importance of that point of the curve for the yen yield curve. Each of the four major currency models (USD, euro, sterling, and yen) also includes a convexity risk factor, which is defined as the square of the average change in all of the key rates in the relevant market.

The YieldCurveRet model for other markets (i.e., Australia, New Zealand, Hungary, Korea, Poland, Slovakia, Thailand, Czech Republic, South Africa, and Singapore) is a single factor, the average change in their respective Treasury market's par yield, and a bond's loading on that risk factor is the bond's modified duration.

Swap Spread Return Models

Having first stripped away the deterministic component of return—coupon and rolldown—and the local Treasury yield curve return as described earlier, we then identify the component of a bond's total return owing to movement in swap spreads. This applies to the four major currency markets where the yield curve risk factors are Treasury key rates.

The SwapSpreadRet model estimates a bond's return owing to swap spread changes as the sum of the changes in several key swaps, each multiplied by the bond's appropriate swap spread KRD. The SwapSpreadRet model is similar to the

Figure 26-12. Systematic Risk Factors, SwapSpreadRet Models

Market	Swap Spread Risk Factors
USD	6-month; 2-year; 5-year; 10-year; 20-year; and 30-year swap spreads
EUR and GBP	2-year; 5-year; 10-year; and 30-year swap spreads
JPY	6-month; 2-year; 5-year; 7-year; 10-year; 20-year; and 30-year swap spreads

YieldCurveRet model, except that changes in key swap spreads replace changes in Treasury key rates and swap spread KRDs replace Treasury KRDs.

Again, while structurally similar, there are some differences in the SwapSpread-Ret models for the various currency markets. The swap spread risk factors for the U.S. dollar, euro, sterling, and yen SwapSpreadRet models are shown in Figure 26-12. For bonds outside of these markets (e.g., Australia, New Zealand, and Singapore), changes in swap spreads are not used as risk factors.

As discussed earlier, the introduction of swap spread risk factors is a notable change from the previous U.S. risk model. This change was driven by changes in the marketplace over the intervening period and the broadening of the risk model coverage to include markets and assets for which the swap curve has long been used as a pricing benchmark. We discuss the empirical significance of swap spreads as a risk factor in the next section.

Volatility Return Models

After the yield curve and swap spread components of return are stripped away, a portion of the total return for bonds with embedded options (e.g., callable corporates and MBS) is driven by changes in implied volatilities. The risk model has a single estimated volatility risk factor each for USD agencies, USD Treasuries, USD investment-grade corporates, and USD high yield, and two estimated volatility risk factors for MBS (a short-expiry factor and a long-expiry factor). The EUR and GBP markets, having few bonds with optionality, have as their volatility factor the observed change in the 5×5 swaption volatility. The risk exposure to the volatility risk factor is measured by the bond's "volatility duration," which is calculated by dividing the bond's vega by its full price.[15]

---

15. For USD MBS, a bond's overall volatility duration is partitioned into a short-expiry and long-expiry volatility duration based on the bond's option-adjusted duration.

Spread Return Models

The foregoing risk factors—movements of key points on par curves, changes in swap spreads, and some volatilities—are all "observable." In other words, we can read their values off a market data screen and maintain them in a database. The final systematic component of return—those owing to spread movements—is, however, more challenging and must be modeled in a different way.

The SpreadRet component of a bond's total return refers to that portion of return remaining after all other systematic return components have been accounted for and stripped away. SpreadRet is, in turn, made up of two distinct parts: systematic, which is modeled, and nonsystematic, which is whatever is left unexplained. Both parts of SpreadRet are vital in quantifying the volatility of a given security's total return and, hence, the total return volatility of a portfolio. We now discuss the systematic SpreadRet model. The estimation of idiosyncratic risk is discussed toward the end of this section.

To build intuition for modeling the systematic component of a bond's Spread-Ret we discuss the approach for credit bonds briefly. However, the analysis also applies to all bonds that trade with a spread: for example, agencies, USD MBS, and pfandbriefes.

Consider a security that belongs to the USD A-rated-financial sector of the credit market. In any given month, this security's total return is driven by a series of market factors. We have already discussed several of these systematic factors: currency (CurrencyRet), yield curve movements (YieldCurveRet), changes in swap spreads (SwapSpreadRet), and changes in volatility (VolatilityRet). These systematic factors generally account for a large part of the bond's total return. However, a significant portion of total return remains unexplained. This remaining portion of return is usually driven by spread movements within the bond's asset sector. It seems reasonable that the return of this particular A-rated-financial bond will, to some extent, reflect spread movements in the A-rated-financial sector as a whole. This is a sector or peer group effect on total return that is common (i.e., systematic) to all bonds belonging to that credit sector. The risk model treats this sector factor (i.e., changes in the average spread for bonds in a sector) as a systematic risk factor. Credit bonds have exposure only to the sector risk factor of their sector.

In addition to sector risk, there are other systematic risk factors that drive SpreadRet. Bonds that belong to the same sector may have differential returns owing to their relative spread level and relative maturity. For example, some A-rated-financial bonds may trade at a wider OAS compared with other A-rated-financial bonds. This wider spread level may reflect a relative lack of liquidity (i.e., a liquidity premium) or perhaps there is a "subsector" within the A-rated-financial sector that naturally trades at a somewhat wider spread. Fluctuations in this liquidity premium or "subsector" premium contribute to the SpreadRet for bonds with wider or narrower spreads than their peer group average. Consequently, the risk model treats this OAS level factor as a systematic risk factor.

A similar argument also applies to the relative maturities of bonds in a given sector. In other words, there may be a spread slope so that longer-maturity bonds in a sector trade differently than shorter-maturity bonds. Fluctuations in the slope of the spread curve contribute to a bond's SpreadRet beyond the sector and spread-level effects. Consequently, the risk model treats relative maturity (i.e., a slope factor) as a systematic risk factor. Finally, the risk model applies a geographical factor that explains the additional component of return that corresponds to potential return differential, arising from market segmentation effects, between U.S. and non-U.S. domiciled credit issuers.

Using this type of market analysis and intuition, we identify potential systematic spread risk factors and build the SpreadRet model corresponding to these market effects. Having decided on the form that the systematic risk factors will take, we fit the historical data to the model. Depending on the asset class and currency market, the SpreadRet model can vary considerably. We use robust statistical techniques to explain as much of the spread return of a security as possible by systematic spread risk factors. In this way, we produce a set of risk factors for each of the major asset classes in each currency market. By leveraging the vast quantity of data at our disposal—historical returns at the individual bond level going back more than a decade in many cases—we are able to form both systematic and non-systematic risk factors of considerable explanatory power, robustness, and intuitive interpretation. As of this publication, there are 152 spread risk factors for bonds in the Global Aggregate Index (75 USD, 37 euro, 24 sterling, 12 yen, 1 Canadian dollar, and 3 global emerging markets). In addition, the risk model includes complete SpreadRet models for USD and euro high yield, inflation-linked, and emerging market securities. We now discuss SpreadRet models for several of the major asset classes in more detail.

SPREAD RETURN MODELS FOR AGENCY AND CREDIT

The market spread return risk models for agency and credit are primarily based on issuer, industry, and rating. The first step is to partition each subindex into different "peer groups" or buckets."

1. For USD agency, we partition the index into five buckets based on issuer. There are four major issuers in the U.S. Agency Index: Fannie Mae (FNMA), Freddie Mac (FHLMC), Federal Home Loan Bank (FHLB), and Farmer Mac (FARM). The remaining bonds, from smaller issuers, are lumped together into a residual bucket (other).

2. For USD credit, including both investment grade and high yield, the partition is based on industry and rating. We group investment-grade bonds into twenty-seven buckets by intersecting nine industries (banking, basic industry, cyclical, communication, energy, financial, noncyclical, noncorporate, and utility) and three ratings (Aaa-Aa, A, and Baa). USD high yield bonds rated B and above are grouped into eleven industry buckets: basic industry, capital goods, media, communication, cyclical, noncyclical, energy, technology, transportation, utility, and financial. We place all high yield bonds rated Caa and below into a single "distressed group" bucket. A fuller description of the risk model for high-yield assets—incorporating default risk—is presented later in this section.

3. The partitions for euro, sterling, and yen investment-grade credit are slightly different from those of USD credit. For euro and sterling, we have twenty-one buckets across different ratings (Aaa-Aa, A, and Baa) and industries (banking, finance, basic industry, cyclical, noncyclical, communication, utility, and noncorporate) for each subindex. For Japan, we have nine buckets across different ratings and industries (agency, banking/financial, industrial, utility, and noncorporate). Euro high yield bonds follow the same partitioning scheme as USD high yield.

For each bucket, we have a spread risk factor for which the risk exposures are the spread durations of individual bonds. Since the spread return for an individual bond can be approximated by the product of its spread duration and change in OAS during the period, the risk factor can be interpreted as *average* OAS change for all bonds in the corresponding bucket. The only exception is the "distressed" bucket for USD and euro high yield, where the risk exposure is simply unit, that is, not weighted by anything. The corresponding "distressed" factor is then the *average* excess return for all bonds rated at Caa and below. We make such a model choice because change of OAS is no longer a small number for bonds trading at Caa and below, and the first-order approximation of spread return no longer holds. Moreover, market experience suggests that this asset class does not trade on spread but rather on price.

Beyond those bucket-specific factors, we include other systematic spread factors to capture different characteristics of individual bonds. For instance, we have a "slope" factor and an "OAS-level" factor for each subindex (USD agency; USD investment grade and high yield credit; euro investment grade and high yield credit; sterling credit; and yen credit). The long and short bonds load with opposite signs for the slope factors, whereas the high- and low-spread bonds load with opposite signs for "OAS" factors.

For USD investment-grade credit, we have three nondomestic issuer risk factors for each market corresponding to the three rating groups (Aaa-Aa, A, and

Baa) and just one for euro and sterling. These nondomestic risk factors account for different spread behaviors of bonds issued by nondomestic entities compared to domestic issuers. For USD and euro high yield, we also have two additional risk factors for the distressed sector: a leverage factor and a subordinated type factor (USD only). The leverage factor captures the market's fluctuating treatment of high-leveraged firms relative to low-leveraged firms. A bond's "loading" on the leverage risk factor is its relative leverage ratio with respect to its peers. This factor is designed to capture the common variation among highly leveraged firms. The subordinated factor is designed to capture the common movement for subordinated bonds, all of which have unit loadings for this factor; all other bonds have zero loading.

Credit bonds issued in currencies apart from the dollar, euro, sterling, and yen have their SpreadRet modeled with reference to the major market that most closely resembles their own, as explained later. Figure 26-13 summarizes the SpreadRet model risk factors for the agency and credit asset classes.[16]

SPREAD SECTOR RETURN MODELS FOR MBS, CMBS, AND ABS

The securitized sectors of the Global Aggregate currently comprise approximately 20% of the index's total market value. The three major securitized asset classes in the Global Aggregate Index are USD agency mortgage-backed securities (MBS), commercial mortgage-backed securities (CMBS), and asset-backed securities (ABS). There are also other securitized asset classes in other currencies [e.g., pfandbriefes (euro)]. Each securitized asset class has exposure to its currency's systematic yield curve and swap spread risk factors, but for the SpreadRet component each has exposure to risk factors that are unique to its respective market. We now discuss the three main securitized asset classes in the Global Aggregate Index and their particular spread risk factors.

USD MBS. Although the agency-MBS holder is not exposed to credit risk, the holder is exposed to the risk that the underlying mortgage loan will be prepaid by the homeowner. This risk, called prepayment risk, involves either an earlier-than-expected return of principal when rates are low or a later-than-expected return of principal when rates are high. Either of these events would be detrimental to the total return for the MBS holder. Prepayment risk is a function of many variables, including implied interest-rate volatility, the price of the MBS, and the age [or weighted average loan age (WALA)] of the MBS. As interest rates are the key driver of mortgage prepayments, a prepayment model is used to estimate this effect when calculating the option-adjusted KRDs used to measure interest-rate

---

16. Credit assets in CHF, DKK, NOK, and SEK have as their systematic spread risk factor the average change in swap spreads in their respective markets.

risk. Changes in mortgage prices not predicted by the prepayment model can be due to any of the other factors listed earlier. Consequently, MBS returns are sensitive to changes in risk factors that influence prepayment risk: changes in implied volatility; changes in spreads for various price tiers of the MBS market (i.e., discount, current-coupon, and premium); and changes in spreads for various age cohorts of the MBS market (i.e., new vs. seasoned). An MBS security's exposure to changes in spread for a given price and age tier is measured by its OASD.

An MBS security is defined by its underlying particular mortgage-underwriting program. Depending on the program and market environment, an MBS security may have more or less prepayment risk compared to other MBS securities. Since relative MBS total returns are influenced by the nature of the underlying mortgage program, the MBS SpreadRet model includes risk factors that correspond to the main MBS programs (i.e., 15-year and 30-year GNMAs and conventionals, and balloons). An MBS security's exposure to these program risk factors is also given by the MBS OASD. A summary of the ten MBS SpreadRet model risk factors (apart from the yield curve, swap spread, and volatility risk factors) is provided in Figure 26-14.

While CMOs (collateralized mortgage obligations) are not part of the Lehman indices, they are ubiquitous in investor portfolios. The risk model accommodates agency and nonagency CMOs, hybrid ARMs, and IOs/POs. Lehman MBS analytics identifies the MBS collateral underlying a CMO and analyzes the CMO cash-flow structure. Based on this analysis, option-adjusted KRDs are calculated for the CMO tranche along with an OASD value. The CMO sensitivity to prepayments relative to the sensitivity of the underlying MBS securities is measured as well. This measure is then used to adjust the CMO OASD to better reflect the CMO sensitivity to the MBS prepayment risk factors in the SpreadRet model. For example, a well-structured PAC generally has less sensitivity to prepayment risks than the underlying collateral. To reflect this, the risk model adjusts the CMO OASD downward for the purposes of loading the CMO exposure onto the MBS risk factors.

USD CMBS. Although commercial mortgages are mortgage-backed securities, the nature of the underlying collateral and the structure of the security itself expose CMBS investors to risks not present in agency MBS.

CMBS do not carry an agency guarantee and, therefore, involve credit risk. To mitigate this risk, overcollateralization is often used to improve credit rating. Consequently, the first set of risk factors measures exposures to changes in spread associated with particular credit qualities. CMBS returns may also differ depending on their "window" to receive principal payments. Some CMBS are current-pay bonds whereas others may be locked out for a period of time. Depending on the market environment, locked-out bonds may enjoy a return advantage over

Figure 26-13. Systematic Spread Risk Factors, USD, Euro, Sterling, and Yen
Agency and Credit

Market	Asset Class	SpreadRet Risk Factors
USD	Agency	Five issuer factors (FARM, FHLMC, FNMA, FHLB, and others)
		One spread-slope factor
		One spread-level factor
	Credit—investment grade	Twenty-seven sector factors: three qualities (Aaa-Aa, A, Baa) × nine sectors (banking, finance, basic, energy, cyclical, noncyclical, communication, utility, and noncorporate)
		One spread-slope factor
		One spread-level factor
		Three geographic factors (Aaa-Aa, A, and Baa)
	Credit—high yield	Twelve sector factors:
		11:1 quality (Ba/B) × 11 sectors (financial, basic industry, energy, media, cyclical, noncyclical, technology, transportation, communication, utility, and capital goods)
		1: distressed (i.e., quality less than B)
		Two slope factors for Ba-B and for distressed
		Two level factors for Ba-B and for distressed
		One leverage factor for distressed
		One subordination factor for distressed
EUR	Agency—Pan Euro	Two issuer factors (Aaa and Aa-A-Baa)
		One spread-slope factor
		One spread-level factor

Credit—investment grade	Seventeen sector factors: three qualities (Aaa-Aa, A, Baa) × seven sectors (banking, finance, basic, cyclical, noncyclical, communication, utility)[a]
	Four noncorporate sector factors (Aaa, Aa, A, and Baa)
	One spread-slope factor
	One spread-level factor
	One factor for U.S. issuers in euro
Credit—high yield	Twelve sector factors:
	11:1 quality (Ba-B) × 11 sectors (financial, basic industry, energy, media, cyclical, noncyclical, technology, transportation, communication, utility, and capital goods)
	1: distressed (i.e., quality less than B)
	Two slope factors for Ba-B and for distressed
	Two level factors for Ba-B and for distressed
	One leverage factor for distressed
GBP	
Credit—investment grade	Seventeen sector factors: three qualities (Aaa-Aa, A, Baa) × seven sectors (banking, finance, basic industry, cyclical, noncyclical, communication, utility)[a]
	Four noncorporate sector factors (Aaa, Aa, A, and Baa)
	One spread-slope factor
	One spread-level factor
	One factor for U.S. issuers in sterling
JPY	
Agency	One sector factor (A-Baa)
Credit—investment grade	Five sector factors: two qualities (Aaa-Aa and A-Baa) × three sectors (banking/financial, industrial, and utility)
	Two noncorporate sector factors (Aaa-Aa, and A-Baa)
	One spread-slope factor
	One spread-level factor

[a]In some cases, two or more sparsely populated cells have been merged.

Figure 26-14. SpreadRet Models, USD MBS Systematic Risk Factors

Asset Class	MBS Risk Factors
MBS	Six price-WALA factors (discount/new, discount/seasoned, current/new, current/seasoned, premium/new, and premium/seasoned).
	Four sector factors (GNMA 15-year and 30-year; conventional 15-year; and balloon). There is no explicit 30-year conventional sector factor. Consequently, the four sector risk factors are interpreted as changes in spread relative to the 30-year conventional sector.

current-pay bonds. Consequently, CMBS are exposed to changes in spreads for bonds with varying payment "windows."

Third, CMBS can experience spread changes that depend on their average life. This is basically spread curve exposure. Investors' appetite for long-average-life assets depends on the market environment. Therefore the model includes a risk factor that reflects changes in this appetite and is loaded by average life.

A fourth factor influencing CMBS returns is the age of the commercial loans underlying the bond. Seasoned loans may have more or less prepayment risk and more or less default risk. As a result, market conditions may cause low-WALA bonds to trade differently than high ones. A fifth risk factor is related to the price level of the bond as higher-price bonds may have more prepayment risk and different total return performance than discount-priced bonds. Finally, owing to structural or issuer characteristics, a CMBS may trade at a different spread than otherwise similar bonds. For example, a particular loan originator associated with a bond may be viewed as less diligent than other loan originators. The twelve CMBS risk factors (apart from the term structure risk factors) are shown in Figure 26-15.

USD ABS and Non-USD Securitized Assets. In addition to the term-structure risk factors, an ABS bond is exposed to systematic risk factors that depend on the underlying collateral (i.e., auto, credit card, manufactured housing, home equity, utility-rate reduction, and all others) and on the quality of the bond (i.e., Aaa-rated vs. non-Aaa-rated). Thus, the total return of a credit card ABS is driven by the change in credit card sector spreads weighted by the bond's OASD.

The total return on an ABS bond is also driven by changes in spreads for bonds depending on: (1) the average life of the bond; (2) whether the bond is at a premium or discount; (3) whether the assets underlying the ABS bond are seasoned or new (applicable to prepayment-sensitive ABS only: home equity, manufactured housing, and auto loans); and (4) whether the ABS is trading at a wider or narrower spread owing to particular structural or issuer characteristics. The thir-

Figure 26-15. SpreadRet Models, USD CMBS Systematic Risk Factors

Asset Class	CMBS Risk Factors
CMBS	Four quality factors: Aaa, Aa, A, and Baa
	One payment "window" factor (current pay vs. noncurrent pay)
	Three price factors—one each for current pay, noncurrent pay, and non-Aaa bonds
	One average life factor
	One age (WALA) factor
	One OAS spread level factor
	One CMBS IO factor

teen USD ABS SpreadRet risk factors (apart from the term-structure risk factors) are summarized in Figure 26-16.

There are other mortgage-related securitized assets in other currency markets (e.g., pfandbriefes). For these asset classes (euro and sterling only), the risk model uses only a single SpreadRet factor and the bond's exposure to this risk factor is the bond's OASD.

DEFAULT RISK MODEL FOR USD AND EURO BAA AND HIGH YIELD ASSETS

In this section, we discuss the default risk model for Baa and high yield securities. In general, the broad concept of credit risk includes market spread risk and default risk. Market spread risk results from the fluctuation in the level of credit spread

Figure 26-16. SpreadRet Models, USD ABS and Non-USD Securitized Assets Systematic Risk Factors

Market	Asset Class	ABS Spread Risk Factors
USD	ABS	Six sector factors: auto, credit card, manufactured housing, home equity loan, utility, and "all others" representing collateral that does not belong to the other five categories
		One quality factor: non-Aaa-rated bonds
		Three age (i.e., WALA) factors—one each for auto, home equity loan, and manufactured housing
		One average life factor
		One OAS spread level factor
		One price level factor
EUR	Securitized	One factor
GBP	Securitized	One factor

with an implicit assumption that the issuer will not default in the given period (spreads include a penalty owing to the prospect of default). So far, we have focused on this source of risk. On the other hand, default risk is the risk that the issuer will fail to meet its contractual obligation in a given period of time. While the default risk is relatively unimportant for investment-grade issues rated A or better, owing to small default probabilities, it is a significant source of risk for Baa and high yield issues. Our risk model provides a unified framework to quantify both risks.

In our model, the default risk for a single issue depends on its default probability and expected recovery rate upon default. The default probability is calibrated ex ante using historical default data and the expected recovery rate is a function of the bond's seniority. Both the default and recovery rates are estimated using both long-term and 12-month trailing historical data. To convert default risk into units of return volatility, the standard units of the risk model, we multiply the square root of the issuer's default probability by one minus the recovery rate upon default. Furthermore, when portfolio effects are calculated, we have to take default correlation into account. It is widely acknowledged that, like market spread risk, default risk is also a type of systematic risk. Empirical evidence shows that aggregate default rates are related to general macroeconomic factors and business cycle indicators. The financial distress of one firm can directly trigger distress of other firms. Hence, defaults are correlated and we have to account for that in our model.

Our setup for default correlation follows a structural framework based on the value of the firm, along the lines developed by Robert Merton in 1974.[17] In this approach, a default event is triggered whenever the firm's asset value falls below a threshold defined by the firm's liabilities. Hence, dependence of the default of one firm on the default of other firms can be modeled through the correlation among firms' asset value fluctuations. Because we cannot directly observe a firm's asset value, we use equity correlation as a proxy for asset correlation. Our model uses a t-dependence correlation structure under which extreme movements and co-movements are more likely. Using such a structural framework, we are able to generate realistic default correlations. So for both the USD and euro high yield risk model, we estimate two correlation matrices: the systematic risk factor matrix and the issuer default correlation matrix.

17. Robert Merton, "On the Pricing of Corporate Debt: The Risk Structure of Interest Rates, *Journal of Finance*, 1974, vol. 29.

SPREAD RETURN MODEL FOR INFLATION-LINKED SECURITIES

The risk model includes a completely integrated model for inflation-linked securities. Inflation linkers raise an interesting modeling question: What is the spread component of return for a linker? In other words, we seek to perform return splits for inflation linkers and isolate a spread return that contains not only country-related spread factors, as already exist in the risk model, but also a spread return arising from the inflation-linked nature of the security. To do this we have to estimate sensitivities to both the nominal curve and the spread movements.

The uncertainty with regard to the cash flows of an inflation-linked bond is not the same as for a nonlinked credit asset. For the latter, the uncertainty is a matter of whether the promised cash flows will be paid. For a linker, however, the uncertainty is related to the size of the payment, which depends on the announced level of a particular index at some point in the future. (A credit bond that is also inflation-linked is subject to both types of uncertainty.) Nonetheless, despite these differences, the analytical approach taken in handling credit securities can also be adapted to our purpose.

For a credit security the uncertainty in the cash flows is reflected in its option-adjusted spread. We assume that the cash flows as given by the cash-flow schedule at the time of evaluation are certain, and we solve the pricing equation to obtain a fixed spread above the discount curve that prices those cash flows correctly. The spread captures the risk of uncertainty (along with any other sources of discount) and allows us to calculate analytics and performance attribution in a relatively simple manner. In terms of the pricing equation we write:

$$PV = \sum_i \frac{CF_i}{(1 + y_i)^i (1 + s)^i}. \tag{26-1}$$

For inflation-linked securities we can adopt a similar approach that allows us to look at these bonds as simple variations on bullet bonds with an appropriate spread. This translates into the following pricing equation:

$$PV = \sum_i \frac{CF_i(1 + \pi)^i}{(1 + y_i)^i}. \tag{26-2}$$

The equivalence can then be expressed mathematically as

$$1 + \pi = \frac{1}{1 + s} \Rightarrow s = \frac{-\pi}{1 + \pi}. \tag{26-3}$$

The essential insight here is that the risk of default for a credit bond reduces the expected value of a given cash flow, leading to a positive spread. In contrast, the effect of index linking is to increase the expected value of a linker (from that of the real coupon), resulting in a negative spread. This thought process leads us to identify a corresponding spread for a linker in the same way as for a credit security. It will be a negative spread of the order of inflation expectations out to the maturity of the bond, but the similarity in terms of risk modeling is clear.

Thus, we have cast the inflation-linked security into a familiar form: that of a bullet credit bond with the associated spread. We then identify spread risk factors specific to the linkers markets and model the spread return of this asset class along with the other sources of return over and above those that they have in common with nominal securities (i.e., the effect of realized inflation).

In our model, the monthly spread return (i.e., total return less CarryRet and YieldCurveRet) is modeled as being driven by two sets of risk factors: (1) changes in realized inflation during the month, and (2) changes in breakeven inflation (i.e., inflation expectations). There is a short (5-year) and a long (20-year) inflation expectations risk factor.

The sensitivity of a linker to the realized inflation factor is the fraction of its market value that is represented by the unknown cash flows. The risk factor is the return of the inflation index ratio. (We use the latest ratio available at the time of calibration, not the official one used for price quotations in the marketplace.)

For the modeling of inflation expectations, expressed in the pricing of the bond via the breakeven spread, we model (in each currency market separately) the behavior of the term-structure breakeven inflation rates along the same lines as we do for the yield curve. In other words, we use a few constant maturity points along the curve that capture the bulk of the movements of breakeven inflation spreads of all securities in the marketplace. A bond's sensitivity to inflation expectations is its OASD, which is apportioned across the two inflation expectations factors depending on the bond's maturity.

In summary, an inflation-linked bond loads on nominal curve risk factors with a sensitivity equal to its analytical OAD, as well as inflation-specific factors, namely those reflecting the risk in realized and expected inflation movements.

SPREAD RETURN MODEL FOR EMERGING MARKETS SECURITIES

The risk model covers emerging markets (EM) securities, both investment grade and high yield. The EM spread return risk model framework mirrors that for investment-grade and high yield credit bonds. In these models, spread return risk has two components: market spread risk driven by exposure to sectors of the marketplace and default risk. For investment-grade credit, sectors in the market spread risk model are based on country, industry, and rating. For high yield (rated Ba-B), credit bonds are grouped based on industry. For distressed high yield (rated Caa and lower), a different strategy is used as all bonds are pulled

Figure 26-17. Systematic Spread Risk Factors, Emerging Markets Securities (USD)

Asset Class	SpreadRet Risk Factors
Investment grade	One sector factor, one spread-slope factor, and one spread-level (liquidity) factor
High yield, nondistressed	Ten sector factors (EM America, Argentina, Brazil, Mexico, and Venezuela; EM Asia, Philippines; EM Europe, Russia, and Turkey) One spread-slope factor, and one spread level (liquidity) factor
High yield, distressed	One sector factor, one spread-slope factor, and one price-level factor

together independently of country or industry. For purposes of modeling market spread risk for EM bonds, which approach should we use?

Emerging markets debt is defined as bonds from countries with sovereign ratings of Baa3 or below. The model covers debt denominated in all major currencies: EUR, GBP, JPY, and USD. We first group the bonds into three major geographical regions—Latin America, Europe, and Asia (including the Middle East and Africa)—and three rating buckets (investment grade, Ba-B, and distressed). However, owing to the limited number of investment-grade and distressed bonds in some regions, we merge the three investment-grade buckets and the three distressed buckets into two respective all-regions buckets.

For high yield nondistressed bonds, the bulk of the EM debt, there are sufficient data to estimate individual factors for the three regions, and it is wise to do so, as there have been several episodes in which their behaviors differed substantially. In fact, we went further with this exercise and estimated individual country factors. This should be reassuring to portfolio managers with exposures centered on a small set of emerging market countries, who may worry that the country-specific risk their portfolios are exposed to is being washed away by the aggregation within blocs. To avoid this dilution we estimate individual factors for countries that are major issuers in the EM. In summary, we partition EM issues into twelve sectors (see Figure 26-17).

We investigated whether to model sovereign and nonsovereign debt differently. The data indicated similar volatility behavior for these two types of bonds, so we decided not to model their spread risk separately yet differentiate their default treatment. Finally, some of the bonds from EM are "Brady bonds"—bonds whose collateral is partially guaranteed, usually by U.S. government bonds. The existence of these guarantees distorts the usual bond analytics. Taking that into account, we use the corrected ("stripped") analytics for these bonds whenever needed.

We model EM default risk in a similar fashion as the Lehman high yield risk model. However, we treat the recovery process for EM bonds differently. The experience with defaults in EM is significantly different than that from the developed countries. The number of defaults is also much smaller, so we cannot model them with a partition as is done in the high yield risk model. Instead, we set recovery rates for EM bonds using a major established fact about EM defaults: recovery rates for sovereign bonds tend to be higher than their corporate counterparts. In particular, we set the recovery rates to 25% for EM sovereign bonds and 10% for EM nonsovereign bonds. These numbers are conservative estimates.

Idiosyncratic Return Model

The systematic factors explain about 30–65% of the time variability of spread returns.[18] The variance that cannot be explained by systematic factors is called idiosyncratic variance, and this risk is especially important for portfolios with few bonds. We assume that the idiosyncratic variance is issuer specific: only bonds from the same issuer have correlated idiosyncratic risks. For example, the idiosyncratic risk of a bond issued by Ford is independent of the idiosyncratic risk of a bond issued by GMAC; however, it is correlated with the idiosyncratic risk of another Ford bond even if the two are issued in different currencies. An exception to this idiosyncratic correlation structure is the USD agency sector. Because we partition the Agency Index by issuer in the systematic model, the issuer effect for USD agency has already been captured by those five bucket factors; hence, all idiosyncratic risks for USD agency bonds are assumed to be independent. A similar model exists for euro Treasuries (e.g., Italy and Spain), which have designated factors in their domestic currencies.

The volatilities for the idiosyncratic risks are estimated using the residuals from the systematic model: the error terms that cannot be explained by systematic factors. The same industry-rating-issuer buckets used for systematic risks are also used to estimate idiosyncratic volatilities. Therefore, all the bonds in a given bucket share the same (spread) idiosyncratic volatility. Such a methodology allows us to quantify the idiosyncratic volatility for securities from new issuers as they come into the market.

The idiosyncratic correlation among bonds from the same issuer depends on the average spread of all this issuer's bonds. The correlation structure applies across

---

18. Of course, the overall explanatory power using all risk factors (e.g., the yield curve) is much higher for total returns.

different currencies and sectors. We assign one correlation for all pairs, regardless of their currencies and sectors. In general, empirical studies show that the higher the spread, the higher the correlation.[19]

Putting Asset Class Models Together

The calibration of any risk model has to overcome certain practical hurdles. Frequently the lengths of history for different factors are unequal—often highly unequal—which presents the problem of measuring relationships among different pairs of market factors over different periods of time. To compare USD credit and yield curve factors may mean looking at data going back 13 years, whereas a similar comparison of USD credit and euro credit can only cover the period from January 1999 onward, given the relatively recent emergence of a euro bond market. To simply use the data as such would be to compare apples and oranges— credit volatility has increased dramatically over the last 23 years, and we would expect both volatilities and correlations to have increased over such a period. In the early 1990s, interest-rate volatility was high in comparison to recent years. To combine these mismatched time series would be to use the relationship of USD credit with USD rates over the last 13 years and that with euro credit over only 5 years. This inconsistency is clearly highly undesirable. Moreover, using mismatched histories removes the guarantee of "positive-definiteness"—the TEV can no longer be guaranteed to always be a positive number. Negative volatilities are obviously meaningless, and the covariance matrix, describing the relationships among all the factors, must give rise to sensible TEV estimates.

These issues are not new. Techniques for dealing with missing data are well known and have been deployed. The new challenge was the new scale on which we seek to model global risk. We have moved from a model with approximately seventy-five factors in a single currency framework to one approaching 300 factors covering global fixed-income markets. Back-filling is less of an option on this extended scale.

Furthermore, with so many factors and their mutual relationships to calibrate, we begin to run into problems of dimensionality. In other words, we have more factors than we have data to estimate with in a stable and robust way. At most we have 13 years—156 months of factor realizations—often much less, and yet we seek to estimate covariances among almost 300 different factors. To deal with both of these issues, we have developed a methodology that allows us to reduce the scale of the problem, stabilizing the covariance matrices and enabling us to impute missing data with confidence.

19. For more details, see Chapter 18.

The core factor approach postulates that across asset class correlations among market factors are driven by a smaller set of fundamental factors. Each individual local factor—one of the 300 or so—is driven in part by its sensitivity to its relevant core factors. The supposition of the core factor methodology is that the core-driven part of each factor captures the commonality of behavior among factors from differing asset classes. Thus, the correlation between the 5-year point of the U.S. Treasury par curve and the corresponding 2-year point on the sterling par curve is captured by the relationship between the three core yield curve factors in each market: shift, twist, and butterfly, one set of these three for each market. Insofar as the 5-year USD curve point and the 2-year sterling rate are sensitive to their respective shift, twist, and butterfly core factors, so will the covariance of the USD 5-year and GBP 2-year rates be a function of the $3 \times 3 = 9$ resulting cross-market covariances of these $3 + 3 = 6$ core factors.

This is the technique that we have adopted and our results have verified the veracity of the underlying hypothesis of the explanatory power of the core factors. Within asset blocs—USD credit, euro volatility, sterling swap spreads, yen credit, and so on—the covariances are in keeping with the sample covariances (i.e., the observed relationship among the factors). Covariances across asset blocs are driven by the core factors.

Finally, in seeking to cover currencies outside the four major markets, we have had to address the issue of how to model the smaller markets—Asia ex-yen, Scandinavia, Switzerland, and Canada. The approach chosen was, where appropriate, to map a given market to one of the four major markets. We cannot identify a Swedish krona communications Baa market factor, but we can make the approximation that it will move in a fashion closely related to its euro equivalent. CAD-denominated securities are approximated by drawing from the USD market, while Switzerland and Scandinavia map to the euro factors. Each of these markets has its curve risk—generally the major component of systematic TEV—modeled with respect to its local swap or Treasury curve, and only the spread factors are "proxied" by other closely related markets.

Australia, New Zealand, Thailand, Singapore, and Korea are less clear. Our decision was to incorporate more general market information from the USD market and not to map directly to detailed systematic factors as was done with Scandinavia, Switzerland, and Canada. Again, each has curve risk modeled locally.

PREDICTIVE POWER OF THE MODEL

Testing Model Performance

What is the ability of the risk model to predict the ex post risk of a portfolio? To assess the predictive ability of our risk model methodology, we performed unit

Figure 26-18. Total Return and Tracking Error Volatilities Model
Long-Term and Out-of-Sample

Portfolio 1	Portfolio 2	Model Volatility (December 2002) (bp/month)		
		Portfolio 1	Portfolio 2	TEV (1–2)
Global Aggregate	U.S. Aggregate	146.3	88.2	115.0
U.S. Credit	Euro Credit (USD)	136.4	293.1	286.2
Euro Aggregate	Asian Aggregate (EUR)	103.1	311.5	315.8

Portfolio 1	Portfolio 2	Long-Term Volatility (January 1990–February 2005) (bp/month)		
		Portfolio 1	Portfolio 2	TEV (1–2)
Global Aggregate	U.S. Aggregate	150.8	[112.6]	102.7
U.S. Credit	Euro Credit (USD)	139.5	318.1	273.6
Euro Aggregate	Asian Aggregate (EUR)	90.4	297.0	323.6

Portfolio 1	Portfolio 2	January 2003–February 2005 Volatility (bp/month)		
		Portfolio 1	Portfolio 2	TEV (1-2)
Global Aggregate	U.S. Aggregate	[184.1]	[128.5]	117.3
U.S. Credit	Euro Credit (USD)	168.2	313.7	254.4
Euro Aggregate	Asian Aggregate (EUR)	88.8	254.8	274.3

variance tests for several index pairs. Using the risk model (equal time weighting), we produced estimates (as of December 2002) of the total return volatilities for several indices and the TEVs of one index vs. another. We used risk parameters available at the beginning of that month: covariance matrix between systematic risk factors and estimates of idiosyncratic spread volatility across market sectors.

We then calculated the actual long-term volatilities of monthly total return and tracking errors for the period from January 1990 through February 2005, as well as out-of-sample volatilities for the period from January 2003 through February 2005. The data are presented in Figure 26-18.

If the risk model is doing a good job of estimating volatilities, then we would expect the ratio of the model volatility to the actual volatility to be close to one. Our test was therefore a variance ratio test of the model volatilities vs. both the long-term and the out-of-sample volatilities. All but three of the tests (shown in brackets in Figure 26-18) rejected the alternative hypothesis that the variance ratio is not equal to one.[20] These tests clearly support our claim that the risk model produces good estimates of total return and tracking error volatilities and validate our risk-modeling methodology.

Relevance of Changes in Swap Spreads as a Risk Factor

The decomposition of Treasury spreads into swap spreads and spreads over swap rates seems to identify different sources of volatility. As seen earlier, this is useful for the stabilization of risk factor correlations. However, we must still check whether this separation is relevant for the different asset classes. That is, do we really need two risk factors to explain the changes in the spreads over Treasuries of a particular asset class? If the true underlying risk is well captured by a single factor, the decomposition may be redundant.

To focus on the value added from the inclusion of swap spreads as a risk factor, we isolate the part of a bond's return, r_t^i, that is not explained by Treasury-rate movements. Then, we run the following regression:

$$r_t^i = \beta_0 + \beta_1 F_t^{SS} + \beta_2 F_t^{Si} + v_{it}, \tag{26-4}$$

where F_t^{SS} is the swap spread risk factor and F_t^{Si} is the asset class specific factor. Moreover, to understand the individual contribution of each of the factors, we also separately fit the non-Treasury component of a bond's return to the swap spread factor and to the asset-class-specific factor.

Figure 26-19 presents the results of these regressions for several USD asset classes. It suggests that, in general, the remaining risk factors do explain a significant part of the variance of returns not accounted for by changes in the Treasury rates. The R^2's are high—recall that this explanatory power is in addition to any that may be related to Treasury factors—ranging from 33 to 67% when both risk factors are considered. Moreover, one can see that swap spreads are an important independent source of risk. The coefficient β_1 is always significant at the 1% confidence level.

The same is not necessarily true for the asset-class-specific factor. In particular, the results suggest that for both the agency and ABS this factor does not explain much about the returns left unexplained by Treasuries. The results seem to indicate that there is no role in these asset classes for an asset-specific risk factor. Alternatively, we believe that the result is due to the fact that we are looking at

---

20. The duration of the U.S. Aggregate around December 2002 was at historical lows, which may explain the underestimation of its longer-term volatility.

Figure 26-19. Regression Results by Asset Class

Asset Class	1990–2003		
	β_1 (swaps)	β_2 (asset specific)	$\bar{R}^2$ (%)
Agency	-2.69^a	1.81^a	33
	-1.85^a		20
		0.33^a	0
Corporate	-5.68^a	4.94^a	63
	-3.65^a		14
		3.78^a	31
MBS[b]	-3.71^a	2.78^a	39
	-2.87^a		18
		1.88^a	9
CMBS[c]	-4.80^a	2.94^a	67
	-3.87^a		42
		1.58^d	6
ABS[c]	-2.69^a	1.56^a	42
	-1.66^a		18
		0.60^a	3

[a]Significant at the 1% level.
[b]From January 1995.
[c]From August 1999.
[d]Significant at the 5% level.

highly aggregated asset classes. The heterogeneities within each asset class are specifically considered in the risk model, but are absent in this analysis.

In this regard, the results are interesting only if we hold portfolios highly correlated with the indexes for the overall asset class. With this in mind, we briefly analyze the results for each asset class separately. Swap spreads are the important independent source of risk for agencies: this confirms the popular notion that agencies are a "swap product." We also find that the remaining classwide specific systematic risk is very small and highly correlated with swap spreads. The analysis of the ABS sector follows the same lines. However, data are available only for the period beginning in August 1999, when swap spreads were extremely high. For this period, we fail to identify an important asset-class-specific factor. The variance in returns is mainly driven by swap rates. Once again, the correlation between the two risk factors is relatively strong, approximately −0.50.

In regard to corporates, the results suggest that both factors explain a significant portion of the variance in excess returns over Treasuries. For this asset class, the factors represent two important and relatively independent sources of risk. In particular, the results suggest that portfolios of corporate bonds that hedge their exposure to swap spreads continue to be exposed to significant (credit) risk.

The same happens with MBS. The returns from this asset class over the full sample are driven by two relatively independent sources of risk. However, the increase in the swap spread volatility after 1998 gave prominence to this factor as the explanatory variable (results not shown). The evidence suggests that a well-diversified MBS portfolio hedged with respect to swap spreads may have been exposed to only minimal risk during the last 5 years. The recent decrease in swap spread volatility may reshift the relative importance of the two risk factors to the pre-1998 scenario. The results from the CMBS follow the same pattern (again recall that data are available only after 1998).

Overall, the results show that swap spreads and asset-class-specific factors are relatively independent and important in explaining returns for several asset classes. Therefore, their separation delivers a better characterization of the nature of returns variability for those asset classes. In conjunction with the evidence discussed earlier, these results strongly support the decomposition of Treasury spreads into swap spreads and spreads over swaps as introduced in the new global risk model.

RELATIONSHIP WITH OTHER MODELS

Scenario Analysis

A manager has several tools at his disposal for analyzing portfolio risk on a forward-looking basis that complement each other in several ways. The simplest approach, conceptually, is scenario analysis (discussed earlier). The manager projects what will happen to the market over a given horizon, in as much or as little detail as desired, and asks the question, "What will my performance be if this happens?"

The problem is that there is an infinite number of market scenarios that could drive returns. Yields can change in parallel along the curve or can exhibit a complex combination of twists and curvature changes. Changes in credit spreads can affect the market as a whole or focus on a particular industry or issuer. How much of this detail can a manager specify in a scenario definition? With a very simple scenario specification, there are many market events that cannot be properly represented. Moreover, the output of the analysis is largely determined by a set of implicit assumptions rather than by the scenario specification itself. With a more detailed specification, more work is required just to produce a single scenario, and an extremely large number of scenarios would be required to "cover all the bases." Furthermore, with so many interrelated parameters to specify, a scenario that seems plausible may in fact be largely self-contradictory (i.e., it may specify a combination of events that is extremely unlikely given the historical correlations).

The risk model approaches the exercise of projecting portfolio returns on a forward-looking basis from a totally different viewpoint. Imagine the set of all possible market outcomes. Scenario analysis seeks to identify a single outcome within this set and calculates portfolio performance at that point. The risk model takes a step back and tries to characterize the distribution of returns across the entire set of outcomes. Without explicitly evaluating a precise return number for even a single scenario, the risk model effectively calculates the standard deviation of returns over all possible scenarios using a joint probability distribution consistent with historical observations.

To get a complete picture of risk, a manager may wish to combine the strengths of both of these models. The risk model provides an overview of all the different categories of risk to which a portfolio is exposed, showing the relative magnitudes of risk in each category, and details the key exposures that drive portfolio risk within each one. To further flesh out an understanding of the risks, a portfolio manager might use this information to build scenarios that are tailored to stress the most significant of these exposures. For example, if the risk report shows a mismatch in the KRD profile, an asset manager might use scenarios to see just how much underperformance would result from specific nonparallel yield curve changes. Similarly, sector spread risk exposures might be complemented by looking at total returns under different sector spread change scenarios.

The synergy between the two models can work in the other direction as well. In addition to using scenarios to support and augment risk analysis, we can use the risk model as part of the scenario design process. When specifying complex scenarios on many market parameters at once, a portfolio manager can easily generate scenarios that are inconsistent with historical correlations, or at least are extremely unlikely. The risk model's covariance matrix can be used to form a measure of the historical likelihood of a scenario. This can be used to aid in the specification of scenarios by allowing a manager to specify partial information about a scenario and fill in the missing sections in a way that is most consistent (maximum likelihood) with the specified information.

Value-at-Risk and Monte Carlo Simulation

It is a well-known problem in modeling risk in corporate securities and portfolios that the bell-shaped normal distribution fails to reflect the chance of extreme losses or gains that are occasionally noted in this asset class—known as "tail risk." A related concept, value-at-risk (VaR), is designed to identify the worst-case performance over a given time horizon for a given probability. VaR is usually used in

a somewhat different context—to measure the risk of absolute losses for an institution as a whole, rather than portfolio returns relative to a benchmark. Moreover, VaR is typically assessed over a shorter time scale, from daily to biweekly
rather than monthly. For example, an institution might define VaR as the amount
$x such that they are 99% confident of not losing more than $x over 2 weeks.
Thus, it might be that the chance of losing $100 million over the next 2 weeks is
estimated to be 1%. The 99% VaR statistic would then be $100 million.

There are a number of approaches commonly taken in forecasting VaR. The
parametric approach takes a distribution (typically a normal distribution) generated from an historic mean and standard deviation. A VaR calculated as a percentage of market value, at the 16.6% confidence level (i.e., 1 standard deviation
from the mean), over a 1-month time horizon, is similar to our TEV (assuming that
return differences between the portfolio and the benchmark are normally distributed). Simulation-based methods are also often used to calculate VaR. Essentially,
a simulation approach attempts to approximate the distribution of projected returns by analyzing a large number of correlated, randomly generated scenarios.
The key to the accuracy of such an approach is in the generation of these random
scenarios. What kind of distribution should be used and with how many degrees
of freedom? Is there an accurate model for the extent of the correlation and the
tail dependence among all the different factors?

In theory, the simulation approach is more general than the risk model. For
example, a manager could design a simulation procedure based on the risk model
(and making the same assumptions about risk factor distributions) that would
produce results consistent with the model. He could then change some of the
distributional assumptions in the simulation to obtain results that could not be
obtained from the model itself.

In practice, simulation methods are generally not used for such high-dimensional
challenges as the management of global bond portfolios. The complexity of the
problem presents two main challenges. First, when we simulate many sources of
risk at once, the number of simulated scenarios required to get a good estimate
of the distribution (and particularly its tail) becomes very large. This method is,
therefore, much more computationally intensive than the multifactor approach.
Second, the complexity of the scenario-generation process, and the many assumptions required along the way, particularly about the interdependence of the outcomes of different risk factors, can raise many questions about the reliability and
accuracy of the simulation process. For this reason, simulation-based approaches
tend to be much more focused in nature. For example, detailed simulations of
individual issuer defaults are used to analyze credit risk, and detailed simulations
of the evolution of the Treasury yield curve evolution are used in the analysis of
MBS portfolio performance.

Performance Attribution

Scenarios and simulations, like the risk model, are forward-looking (ex ante) tools for analyzing how a given investment strategy might fare (whether in terms of returns or risk) over some future time period. Performance attribution, by contrast, is an ex post tool that seeks to explain the sources of realized returns and, specifically, the performance of a portfolio relative to its benchmark. This backward-looking analysis of the single course of events that actually transpired might seem to be a simple exercise in accounting, having little in common with the complex forward-looking models that must consider the probabilities of every possible outcome. Yet the relationship between these two types of models is very close. Portfolio managers take risks only in order to generate rewards. The same portfolio attributes and exposures that the risk model uses in its forward-looking projections of TEV should ultimately determine whether, and by how much, the portfolio will outperform its benchmark.

Lehman Brothers has developed a new version of its performance attribution model—a "hybrid" model, in which each security's return is first split into the currency, yield curve, volatility, and spread components. Each component of portfolio-level outperformance is then analyzed separately, using an approach that mirrors that of the risk model. Outperformance in yield curve returns is explained in terms of KRD exposures and spread return outperformance in terms of spread duration contributions to different market cells.

Why not take the foregoing arguments even further and develop a pure "risk-based" attribution model, in which realized performance is analyzed entirely based on the set of factor exposures from the risk model? We have not adopted this approach because the structure of the performance attribution exercise may differ from manager to manager. There are many possible ways to do a performance attribution, and none of them can be deemed "correct." Rather, for each manager, the best attribution is the one that corresponds most closely to his decision process. For this reason, we have placed a premium on making our attribution module highly customizable, rather than insisting on a perfect one-for-one correspondence with risk factors.

Asset Allocation

The standard approach to portfolio asset allocation today is the mean-variance optimization model developed by Harry Markowitz.[21] Such models seek the "efficient frontier"—the set of allocations that can provide a given amount of

---

21. Harry Markowitz, "Portfolio Selection," *Journal of Finance*, 1952, vol. 7.

expected return for the smallest amount of risk. A central element of these models is the covariance matrix of asset class returns, which is used to generate the risk estimate to be minimized. In this sense, these models are quite similar to our risk model: a tracking error is computed based on differences between portfolio and benchmark allocations and a covariance matrix built from historical data.

The two big differences lie in the construction of the covariance matrix and in the level of detail of the analysis. Typically, asset allocation models take a macro view of a portfolio and a benchmark. The market is carved up into a set of broad asset classes, and the analysis seeks the optimal allocation among these asset classes. The implementation of these allocations in terms of individual securities is outside the scope of the model, as are the additional risks that might be incurred as a result. The risk model, by contrast, is concerned with portfolio allocation within a single macro-asset class (i.e., fixed income) and evaluates the risk of the portfolio down to the specific set of industry and issuer exposures within the asset class. Similarly, the covariance matrix in asset allocation models is formed from historical total returns of entire asset classes. For a fixed-income risk model, however, a covariance matrix of total returns can display extremely high correlation among fixed-income assets. This can be partially addressed by using excess returns over Treasuries for spread asset classes. In our risk model, the risk of every asset class is decomposed into exposures to a set of systematic risk factors, each of which can affect multiple asset classes where appropriate. This better reflects the hierarchical nature of the market, in which common risk factors exist at several levels. For example, our model has features that address interest rates, swap spreads, corporate spreads in general, and industry-specific and even issuer-specific spreads.

CONCLUSION

Lehman Brothers has provided investors with fixed-income risk models based on the historical-parametric approach since the early 1990s. We believe that this method of multifactor risk modeling offers portfolio managers several distinct benefits. Our modeling approach stresses the use of an intuitive set of risk factors. Although the risk factors we use are not always independent and do not make up the smallest possible set of risk factors, they are easily interpretable by portfolio managers as, for example, changes in rates, spreads, or volatilities. This ease of interpretation greatly facilitates understanding portfolio risks and managing them.

Second, our approach (which may be contrary to the conventional one) imposes risk factor sensitivities (e.g., OASD) and then estimates the risk factor volatilities. This offers two key advantages. Lehman uses state-of-the art modeling efforts in interest rates, prepayments, and volatilities to generate risk sensitivity measures (KRDs, spread durations, and vegas) for individual bonds. The same models are used to produce risk sensitivities for both portfolios and indices, which enables an "apples-to-apples" comparison. When we fit bond returns to the risk factor model, we use these sensitivity measures. We then estimate the risk factors that can be readily interpreted as changes in rates, spreads, and volatilities. If a manager wishes to reduce his risk exposure to a particular risk factor, he can rely on a well-understood risk factor sensitivity (e.g., OASD) to build a trade. Finally, since the Lehman risk model works with bond-level returns data, it can quantify security-specific risk. Diversification risk (especially credit risk) is very high on the investor's agenda.

The risk model covers all assets and currencies in the Lehman Global Aggregate Index. It also handles several other asset classes including floating-rate bonds, interest-rate and bond futures, interest-rate and cross-currency swaps, several classes of derivatives, and an array of structured securities. Global investors can incorporate currency hedges in the analysis.

Over the years, our modeling choices have evolved as fixed-income markets have changed. First, swaps have achieved a prominent role as a reference asset class. Investors are increasingly using swap-based indicators of relative value, such as LIBOR-OAS and asset swap spreads. Active managers are increasingly making bets on swap spreads and evaluating excess returns to the swap curve. In our own analyses, we find correlations of spreads to the swap curve to be more stable over time than correlations of spreads to the local Treasury curve. As a result, we have modified the risk model and introduced swap spreads as a risk factor.

For high yield securities, modeling of credit has been expanded to incorporate default and recovery considerations in addition to changes in market prices and spreads. We find that explicit consideration of default leads to improved estimates of tracking error. Furthermore, we have noted the historical clustering of defaults across firms and can capture it using models of default correlation. These methods are identical to the models developed by Lehman to price CDOs and other structured credit transactions based on a portfolio of collateral. As a consequence, we now decompose the total TEV into three components: systematic market risk, idiosyncratic risk, and default risk.

With expanded asset coverage, we were faced with the problem of relatively short data history for several asset classes. The Lehman indices provide us with a large proprietary database of bond-level price data on many asset classes going back to the 1970s. However, for other classes such as ABS and CMBS, the available history is shorter. The currency unification in Europe in 1999 presented a similar problem. We have developed and used sophisticated estimation procedures to obtain stable and reliable covariance matrices. As always, our access to index data allows us to estimate risk factors using individual bond prices rather than industry averages and leads to reliable quantification of nonsystematic risk and the penalty for insufficient diversification.

In addition to the risk model, we support investors with tools that help construct low-tracking-error portfolios (portfolio optimizer), asset allocation that accounts for relative risks and expected returns (risk budgeting), and evaluation of the impact of large market events (scenario analysis). Lehman Brothers fixed-income research uses the risk model on a regular basis to help investors structure active or replicating portfolios, rebalance to changing objectives with minimum turnover, and optimize risk budget allocation.

Risk may be measured in many ways, and we plan to introduce alternative measures of risk geared more toward longer-horizon investors, such as expected performance shortfall, probability of extreme losses, value on default, and the properties of loss distributions as measured by historical simulations. For some time now we have been exploring the possibility of forward-looking measures of risk, such as implied volatility, as well as time-varying models of volatility, such as GARCH models. As our research leads to better estimators of TEV, we will introduce these models into our suite of tools.

The most exciting projected developments are tools for enhanced portfolio structuring and analyses that take advantage of the risk model. We plan to combine scenario and total return analysis for portfolios with the risk model for scenario optimization, that is, maximizing the portfolio expected return over a set of scenarios with a constraint on TEV. We expect the next generation of tools to consist of global constrained optimizers and enhanced methods for risk budgeting.

APPENDIX A: RISK AND RETURN OF A FIXED-INCOME SECURITY

Imagine that your fixed-income portfolio contains a single bond: the Wells Fargo (WFC)-global 5% of 11/15/2014. This is a bullet bond issued by a strong U.S. superregional bank. The issue is rated Aa2/A+ (i.e., Lehman index rating of A) and has roughly 10 years remaining to maturity. Assume that the bond is trading at a 78-bp spread to the on-the-run 10-year Treasury for a yield-to-maturity of 4.555% and a dollar price of 103-23.

What determines the 1-month holding period return for this bond?[22] Most investors would say that the return on the WFC bond depends on the change in the 10-year UST yield (weighted by WFC's duration), the change in the spread for WFC's "peer group" A-rated banking sector (weighted by WFC's spread duration), and any WFC company-specific event that would cause WFC's spread to

---

22. For this discussion, we are ignoring the deterministic (or carry) component of return.

move differently than its sector (weighted by WFC's spread duration). In other words,[23]

$$\text{Return}_{\text{WFC}} \approx - (\text{OAD}_{\text{WFC}} \times \Delta\text{yield}_{\text{10-yearUST}})$$
$$- (\text{OASD}_{\text{WFC}} \times \Delta\text{Sector\_ spreads}_{\text{A/banking}}) \tag{A1}$$
$$- (\text{OASD}_{\text{WFC}} \times \Delta\text{idioWFC\_spread}).$$

The term ΔidioWFC_spread refers to the change in the WFC bond's spread, *net* of the change in spreads for the A-rated banking sector.

What is the risk of holding this bond? Here we are discussing absolute risk, not the risk of outperforming some other asset such as cash, a Treasury bond, or an index. In other words, over a reasonably short holding period (say, 1 month), what are the factors that will cause the total 1-month holding-period return on this bond to fluctuate? Given the return equation (A1), it is clear that the volatility of returns (i.e., the risk) for this bond is driven by three risks: (1) volatility of changes in 10-year UST yields; (2) volatility of changes in sector spreads; and (3) volatility of changes in the idioWFC spread. So, the risk of the bond's price return can be summarized as in Equation (A2):

$$\sigma_{\text{WFCpr\_ret}} = f(\text{OAD}_{\text{WFC}} \times \sigma_{\text{USTyield}}, \text{OASD}_{\text{WFC}} \times \sigma_{\text{A/banking}},$$
$$\text{OASD}_{\text{WFC}} \times \sigma_{\text{idioWFC\_spread}}). \tag{A2}$$

The volatility of the UST yield is often referred to as interest-rate risk, the volatility of sector spread changes as sector spread risk, and the volatility of isolated WFC events as security-specific (or idiosyncratic) risk. For the WFC position, how much return volatility can be ascribed to each of these three sources of risk?

INTEREST-RATE RISK

The return on the WFC bond fluctuates with the yield on the underlying 10-year Treasury note, holding the bond's spread constant. Currently, the on-the-run Treasury is the 4% of 2/2015 with a yield of 3.775%. Given the duration of the WFC bond, if the yield on the Treasury were to increase to 3.875% at the same spread of 78 bp, the price of the WFC bond would decline to 102-28, producing a negative price return of approximately 81 bp.

This is an example of a realized return effect of a known change in the Treasury yield. However, when we talk about "risk" we are referring to the potential variability (i.e., standard deviation) in the WFC bond's return owing to changes

23. Note the negative sign in front of each term: an increase in rates or spreads causes returns to fall. Furthermore, the risk model would model the WFC bond's exposure to the six key-rate points, not to a single point on the yield curve.

in the Treasury yield. To measure the standard deviation of these WFC returns, we simply have to know the standard deviation of the 10-year Treasury yield change over the specified holding period and the sensitivity (i.e., duration) of the WFC bond to changes in the Treasury yield. In other words:

$$\sigma_{WFC(interest\_rate\_risk)} = OAD_{WFC} \times \sigma_{USTyield}.$$

The duration for the WFC bond is 8.45 and the monthly standard deviation of changes in the 10-year Treasury yield is approximately 27.25 bp.[24] Consequently, the interest-rate risk of the WFC is roughly 230 bp/month (= 8.45 × 27.25 bp).[25]

SECTOR SPREAD RISK

The return on the WFC bond also fluctuates with its spread to its "parent" Treasury bond (i.e., the on-the-run 10-year), holding the Treasury's yield constant. Currently, the spread is 78 bp. Given the spread duration of the WFC bond, if the bond's spread were to increase to 85 bp, holding the Treasury's yield constant, the price of the WFC bond would decline to 103-4, producing a negative price return of approximately 57 bp.

To measure the standard deviation of WFC returns owing to changes in its spread we simply have to know the standard deviation of spread changes for the bond over a specified holding period and the bond's sensitivity (i.e., spread duration) to changes in its spread. The change in WFC's spread has two components: a portion that is common for all A-rated banking sector bonds (i.e., WFC's peer group) and another portion that is specific to Wells Fargo. The latter component of spread change we assign to the WFC-specific category (i.e., idiosyncratic risk), which is described later. For measuring spread risk, we are concerned with the spread risk for the bond's sector. In other words, the price risk of the WFC bond arising from sector spread risk is

$$\sigma_{WFCspread\_risk} = OASD_{WFC} \times \sigma_{A/banking}.$$

---

24. To estimate the risk of holding the bond, we would ideally want to know what the standard deviation will be during the forthcoming holding period. Unfortunately, this value is not known and must be estimated. The Lehman risk model uses historical data to estimate the standard deviations and correlations of risk factors. See the first section for a discussion of the historical-parametric risk model approach.

25. We have not made any distributional assumptions about changes in the 10-year Treasury yield. If one were to assume that monthly yield changes are distributed normally, then a confidence interval could be constructed for the price return on the WFC bond owing to interest-rate risk. For example, a 95% confidence interval would be ±1.96 × $\sigma_{WFCpr\text{-}ret}$ about the mean return difference.

The spread duration for the WFC bond is 8.23, and the monthly standard deviation of changes in OAS for the A-rated banking credit sector is approximately 9.4 bp. Thus, the spread sector risk of the WFC bond is roughly 77 bp/month (= 8.23 × 9.4 bp). These first two risks are common to many other bonds besides our WFC bond (e.g., a 10-year BAC bond), which is why we refer to interest-rate and spread risk as "systematic" risks. In other words, the WFC bond contains two systematic risks: 10-year UST yields (i.e., interest-rate risk) and A-rated banking sector spreads (i.e., sector spread risk). What is the overall systematic risk of the bond? It is unlikely to be the sum of the two risks as interest-rate and spread changes will not be perfectly correlated. In general, the risk of a portfolio containing two risks, A and B, is given by

$$\sigma_{(A+B)} = \sqrt{(\sigma_A^2 + \sigma_B^2 + 2 \times \rho_{A,B} \times \sigma_A \times \sigma_B)}. \tag{A3}$$

If interest-rate and spread changes are perfectly correlated (i.e., $\rho_{A,B} = 1$), then $\sigma_{(A+B)} = (\sigma_A + \sigma_B)$. However, if $\rho_{A,B} < 1$, then $\sigma_{(A+B)} < (\sigma_A + \sigma_B)$.

Using historical data for 10-year Treasury yield changes and A-rated banking sector spread changes, we find that the correlation coefficient, ρ, is −0.35. Thus, the systematic risk of our position is

$$\sigma_{\text{WFCsystematic\_risk}} = \sqrt{[(230 \text{ bp})^2 + (77 \text{ bp})^2 + 2 \times (-0.35) \times 230 \text{ bp} \times 77 \text{ bp}]}$$
$$= 215 \text{ bp/month}.$$

Note that the total systematic risk of 215 bp is less than the sum of the two individual systematic risks (230 bp + 77 bp). In this particular case, the total systematic risk is less than the interest-rate risk by itself. The explanation, of course, is that the two risk factors have relatively high negative correlation. In other words, when the 10-year UST yield rises, producing a negative total return, there is a tendency for sector spreads to tighten, which helps to offset some of the loss owing to rising rates.

An investor knows that the WFC bond may not strictly follow movements in the 10-year UST yield or spread changes in the A-rated banking sector. In fact, WFC bonds may have their own specific risk (also known as idiosyncratic or nonsystematic risk), which is assumed to be *independent* of the systematic risk factors. Together, systematic risk and idiosyncratic risk account for the entire risk of holding the WFC bond. How is the idiosyncratic risk measured?

WFC-SPECIFIC RISK

The return on the WFC bond also fluctuates if its spread moves independently of the systematic risk factors. For example, all A-rated banking bonds may have widened 5 bp over the month, whereas WFC issues tightened 3 bp because of a favorable litigation result. Given both this idiosyncratic WFC spread move of 8 bp and the spread duration of the bond, holding the Treasury's yield and A-rated banking spreads constant, the price of the WFC bond would rise to 104-13, producing a positive price return of approximately 67 bp.

To measure the standard deviation of WFC returns owing to idiosyncratic changes in its spread, we simply need an estimate for the volatility of these changes for the bond and the bond's sensitivity (i.e., spread duration) to them.[26] We have already described how the risk model estimates a bond's idiosyncratic spread volatility by measuring that of the bond's peer group. In this case, the relevant sector is A-rated banking and the risk model estimates this sector's idiosyncratic spread volatility to be 14.8 bp/month. Therefore, the price risk of the WFC bond arising from idiosyncratic spread risk is

$$\sigma_{WFCidio\_risk} = OASD_{WFC} \times \sigma_{idioWFC},$$

$$\sigma_{WFCidio\_risk} = 8.23 \times 14.8 \text{ bp/month} = 122 \text{ bp/month}.$$

The idiosyncratic risk for WFC bonds is measured by multiplying the monthly idiosyncratic spread volatility of 14.8 bp by the 8.23 spread duration, to produce a monthly idiosyncratic risk of 122 bp.

Thus, the systematic risk of the WFC bond is 215 bp/month, and the idiosyncratic risk is 122 bp/month. What is the total risk for a holder of the bond? Since the systematic and idiosyncratic risks are assumed to be independent of each other ($\rho_{systematic, idiosyncratic} = 0$), the total risk of the bond is as follows:

$$\sigma_{WFCtotal\_risk} = \sqrt{(\sigma_{WFCsystematic}^2 + \sigma_{WFCidiosyncratic}^2)}$$
$$= \sqrt{(215^2 + 122^2)}$$
$$= 247 \text{ bp/month}.$$

We began this discussion by asking, what are the total return risks of holding this WFC bond? Most investors would respond by saying that the biggest factors in the fluctuations of the returns on this bond are changes in the 10-year UST yield, changes in spreads for the A-rated banking sector, and any company event that is specific to WFC. Using the historical volatility of these risk factors, the correlations among these risk factors, and the sensitivity (i.e., duration) of the bond

---

26. Estimation of a bond's idiosyncratic risk requires a history of prices for *individual* bonds that the risk model obtains from the extensive database of the Lehman Brothers Family of Indices.

to these risk factors, we were able to estimate the standard deviation of the WFC bond's monthly total returns to be 247 bp.[27]

This is exactly how a linear multifactor risk model operates. It specifies the appropriate risk factors, estimates their volatilities and correlations, calculates each bond's sensitivity to those factors, and produces an estimate of the total return volatility for each bond. Generally, a risk model identifies more than just two risk factors. For example, the Lehman risk model assumes that the WFC bond is exposed to several points along the UST curve (not just the 10-year), depending on the bond's KRD profile. Moreover, the risk model assumes that the bond is exposed to a "convexity risk factor," a "liquidity risk factor," and a corporate "spread slope risk factor." The foregoing example was designed to be relatively simple to highlight the basic mechanics of a risk model.

APPENDIX B. BASIC RISK MODEL MATHEMATICS

OVERVIEW

The primary goal of the risk model is to project how well a portfolio is likely to track its benchmark over the coming month. To accomplish this, the model establishes a relationship between individual security returns and a set of risk factors that drives them. This relationship forms the bridge by which market experience in the form of past returns can be applied to characterize the expected distribution of future returns. In this appendix, the model is viewed as a probabilistic model for future returns. The difference between portfolio and benchmark returns over the coming period is represented by a random variable, and we characterize its distribution in terms of the distribution of the risk factors.

The model's basic assumption is that the covariance matrix, composed of volatilities and correlations of historical risk factor realizations, is a reasonable characterization of the risk factor distribution for the coming period. The model extrapolates only these second-moment statistics. It does not attempt to project expected values of portfolio return or outperformance (alpha) based on historical returns.

MODELING RETURNS

Let us assume that our investment universe consists of a finite set of N securities. The performance of the entire universe over the coming month can then be represented by an $N \times 1$ random vector, r, of (unknown) individual security total

---

27. According to the Lehman Brothers risk model, which takes into account several additional risk factors, the WFC bond has an expected monthly total return volatility of 254 bp.

returns. The multifactor model attempts to explain the return r_i on any bond i in terms of broader market movements. A set of M risk factors ($M \ll N$) is chosen to represent the primary sources of risk (and return) to which a portfolio may be exposed. The extent to which bond i is exposed to a particular risk factor j is modeled by a fixed factor loading f_{ij}. The $1 \times M$ row vector f_i thus characterizes the exposure of security i to systematic risk.

The return of any bond i can be expressed in terms of the $M \times 1$ random factor vector x by

$$r_i = \sum_{j=1}^{M} f_{ij} x_j + \varepsilon_i = f_i x + \varepsilon_i, \tag{B1}$$

where $f_i = \{f_{ij}\}$ is the known vector of factor loadings that characterizes bond i, and ε is the nonsystematic random error. That is, ε_i is the portion of the return r_i that is not explained by the systematic risk model. This reflects the possibility of events specific to a given issue or issuer, such as a sudden demand for a particular Treasury security or a takeover announcement by a particular corporate issuer.

If we let F be the $N \times M$ matrix containing one row for the factor-loading vector of each of the N bonds in our universe and denote by ε the $N \times 1$ vector of nonsystematic random errors, we can restate Equation (B1) in matrix form:

$$r = Fx + \varepsilon. \tag{B2}$$

It then becomes clear that (to the extent that the nonsystematic error vector is small, or $\varepsilon \ll r$) the factor vector x summarizes the holding period performance of our universe.

The distribution of possible returns on individual securities and portfolios can thus be expressed in terms of the distributions of values of the random factor vector x and the random error vector ε. Specifically, the systematic risk can be expressed in terms of the $M \times M$ covariance matrix $\Omega = \{\Omega_{jk}\}$, where $\Omega_{jk} = \mathrm{Cov}(x_j, x_k)$. (On the diagonal, $\Omega_{jj} = \mathrm{Var}[x_j]$.)

APPLICATION TO PORTFOLIO MANAGEMENT

We can represent a given portfolio p by a $1 \times N$ allocation vector q_p, which states the proportion of the market value of the portfolio allocated to each of the N securities in our universe. The portfolio return, r_p, is then given by

$$r_p = q_p r = q_p F x + q_p \varepsilon = f_p x + q_p \varepsilon, \tag{B3}$$

where $f_p = q_p F$ is the factor-loading vector that summarizes the systematic risk exposure of a portfolio as a weighted sum of the exposures of its constituent securities.

Of primary importance in assessing portfolio risk are the second-moment statistics—the return volatilities. The variances σ_p^2 and σ_b^2 of the portfolio and benchmark returns, r_p and r_b, may be expressed as

$$\sigma^2 r_p = VAR(r_p) = f_p \Omega f_p^T + q_p \Gamma q_p^T,$$
$$\sigma^2 r_b = VAR(r_b) = f_b \Omega f_b^T + q_b \Gamma q_b^T, \tag{B4}$$

where the covariance matrix Ω is the $M \times M$ matrix described earlier that contains the covariances of the systematic risk factors, and Γ is a sparse $N \times N$ matrix that contains the covariances of the security-specific residual risk terms, $\Gamma_{ij} = \text{Cov}(\varepsilon_i, \varepsilon_j)$. The portfolio variance can be seen to be composed of one term due to systematic risk and another due to security-specific risk. There are no cross terms, owing to our assumptions that the error vector ε and the systematic factor vector x are uncorrelated ($E[\varepsilon_i x_j] = 0$ for all i, j), and that the errors have mean zero ($E[\varepsilon_i] = 0$ for all i).

In the context of portfolio/benchmark comparison, we report the return volatilities, σ_p and σ_b, of the portfolio and benchmark, respectively, as given by Equation (B4). In addition, we report the tracking error σ_{TE} and the β given by

$$\sigma_{TE}^2 = VAR(r_p - r_b) = (f_p - f_b)\Omega(f_p - f_b)^T + (q_p - q_b)\Gamma(q_p - q_b)^T$$
$$\beta = \frac{COV(r_p, r_b)}{VAR(r_b)} = \frac{1}{\sigma_b^2}(f_p \Omega f_b^T + q_p \Gamma q_b^T). \tag{B5}$$

The tracking error measures the dispersion between portfolio and benchmark returns. The β measures the sensitivity of the portfolio return to changes in the benchmark return. From the definition of tracking error, it is obvious that the smaller the value of σ_{TE}, the closer the portfolio tracks the benchmark. If the portfolio and the benchmark are identically composed ($q_p = q_b$), then r_p is identical to r_b under all random outcomes, and we have $\sigma_{TE} = 0$ and $\beta = 1$. This is the only way that a zero tracking error can be achieved; however, other portfolios might achieve $\beta = 1$.

The β is closely related to both the tracking error σ_{TE} and the correlation coefficient ρ between portfolio and benchmark returns. These relationships can be expressed as

$$\rho = \frac{COV(r_p, r_b)}{\sigma_p \sigma_b} = \frac{\sigma_b}{\sigma_p}\beta, \tag{B6}$$
$$\sigma_{TE}^2 = \sigma_p^2 + \sigma_b^2 - 2\rho\sigma_p\sigma_b = \sigma_p^2 + \sigma_b^2 - 2\beta\sigma_b^2.$$

Thus, when $\beta = 1$, the variance of outperformance, σ^2_{TE}, reduces to a difference between the variances of the returns of the portfolio and the benchmark; at the other extreme, when $\beta = 0$, the tracking error becomes the sum of these variances. The correlation coefficient measures the extent to which portfolio and benchmark returns move in the same direction. It may take values from -1 to $+1$, and is unaffected by the relative magnitudes of the portfolio and benchmark risk. Although the risk model does not report this quantity, it can be easily calculated from the reported β using Equation (B6).

APPENDIX C. RISK MODEL TERMINOLOGY

Risk Model: A tool designed to quantify portfolio risk and determine its sources. The risk is defined as the expected volatility of portfolio returns (usually relative to a benchmark).

Benchmark: Portfolio (or index) against which the portfolio's performance is measured.

Risk Factor: A market change that affects returns of all securities in a certain market segment (e.g., changes in interest rates, sector spreads, volatility of interest rates). In the Lehman global risk model, some risk factors, such as the 10-year Treasury par rate, are directly observed in the financial markets. Others, such as the sector spread of financial Aa or better-rated bonds, are not measured directly but are estimated using cross-sectional regression.

Tracking Error (TE): The difference between portfolio and benchmark returns.

Tracking Error Variance (TE Variance): The projected monthly variance of the difference between portfolio and benchmark returns. It is estimated from historical return data and from portfolio and benchmark characteristics. It can be decomposed into three sources: systematic, idiosyncratic, and default.

Tracking Error Volatility (TEV): Monthly standard deviation of the difference between portfolio and benchmark returns; the square root of the TE variance.

Systematic (Market) Risk: Risk owing to the effect of risk factors of the Lehman Brothers risk model. Systematic risk can be measured at the security or portfolio level.

Idiosyncratic (Nonsystematic) Risk: Risk not explained by the combination of all risk or default factors. Represents risk owing to nondefault events that affect only the individual issuer or bond. Idiosyncratic risk can be diversified by increasing the number of bonds and issuers in the portfolio.

Default Risk (Bonds Rated Baa and Lower): Risk that is due to an obligor's failure to meet its contractual obligation. This risk can be reduced by diversification, but cannot be eliminated entirely, owing to default correlations. We only model default risk for issues rated Baa and below.

Time Weighting: Calibration of the model to historical data. It can be specified separately for the three different components of the model: systematic, idiosyncratic, and default. The two choices in each case are: (1) *No weighting*—The statistics (variances, correlations, and default rates) are calculated from historical data using an equally weighted methodology. The same weight is given to all historical observations. (2) *Time decay*—The statistics are calculated using a time-weighted (exponential) methodology (1-year half-life). Recent observations are assigned a greater weight in the calculations. In particular, every observation has about 6% more weight than the one from the preceding month.

Systematic Volatility: The portion of the TEV attributable to the risk factors.

Default Volatility: The portion of TEV explained by the default risk of the portfolio. It is zero for portfolios not holding securities rated Baa and below. The risk model assumes that the correlation between default risk and the systematic risk factors is zero. In practice this correlation is very close to zero.

Nonsystematic Volatility: The portion of TEV attributable to the idiosyncratic risk. It is independent of the other sources of TEV.

Total Volatility: The expected total volatility of the portfolio (and benchmark) return. This is a measure of the total risk of the portfolio (compared to TEV, which measures the risk of the portfolio relative to the benchmark).

Portfolio Beta: The sensitivity of the portfolio's return to benchmark return. If beta is 0.9, then the model projects that if the return for the benchmark over a given period is 100 bp, the return for the portfolio will be 90 bp.

Isolated TEV: Monthly TEV owing to a single group of risk factors in isolation; no other forms of risk are considered. It is independent of the order of presentation. The tracking error that the portfolio would have if the net exposure to the other factors were zero.

Cumulative TEV: Monthly TEV owing to the cumulative effect of several groups of risk factors. Used sequentially to calculate the incremental impact on the TEV as a result of incorporating an additional risk factor into a set of risk factors already considered. It is therefore dependent on the sequence in which risk factors are accounted for. The addition of a risk factor could cause the cumulative TEV to drop should the added factor have a low enough correlation with previous factors.

Percentage of Tracking Error Variance: Contribution, in percentage terms, of each set of factors to the variance of the portfolio return over the benchmark (the square of the TEV). This includes the effect of the variance of that factor as well as the covariance with each of the other factors.[28]

---

28. The distribution is made accordingly to the following reasoning. Suppose we only have two factors, F_1 and F_2. Then the total variance from these factors is $\text{Var}(F_1 + F_2) = \text{Var}(F_1) + \text{Var}(F_2) + 2 \times \text{Cov}(F_1, F_2)$. The percentage of TE variance from factor 1 ($\%F_1$) is defined as: $\% F_1 = [\text{Var}(F_1) + \text{Cov}(F_1, F_2)]/\text{Var}(F_1 + F_2)$.

Systematic Beta (by Risk Factor Group): The sensitivity of the portfolio's return to the component of the benchmark's return corresponding to a particular set of risk factors. See Figure 26-5 on page 704 for an example.

Sensitivity (Factor Loading): Sensitivity of a given security (or portfolio) to a particular risk factor (e.g., KRD, option adjusted convexity, option adjusted spread duration, or vega). It also describes the units in which the loadings (sensitivities) are expressed and any normalization performed. [*Note:* By default, the sensitivities are presented in units (e.g., durations are in years). However, there are some exceptions, owing to the nature of the factors or for a better interpretation of some of the statistics (e.g., marginal contribution to the TEV).]

Exposure: Market-value-weighted factor loading for a portfolio, a benchmark, or the difference between a portfolio and a benchmark with respect to a given risk factor. The exposure determines the portfolio's return sensitivity to changes in the risk factors.

Factor Volatility: Monthly standard deviation of a particular risk factor, estimated from historical data. [*Note:* By default, the units for the factor volatility are presented in basis points. However, there are exceptions: the units for factor volatility are adjusted to keep factor volatility times exposure in basis points. Example: the currency exposures are multiplied by 100 (they are presented in percentage points, e.g., 34%, instead of the default units –0.34). Therefore, the factor volatility is displayed divided by 100 (presented in percentage points instead of basis points, e.g., 1 instead of 100). Without the normalization, the product of loading times volatility is $0.34 \times 100 = 34$ bp. With the normalization we also have $34\% \times 1\% = 34$ bp.]

TE Impact of an Isolated 1-Standard-Deviation Change: The product of exposure (the difference between the benchmark and the portfolio) and factor volatility for a given risk factor. It indicates the return difference between the portfolio and the benchmark given a 1-standard-deviation increase for the given factor, assuming that all other risk factors remain unchanged. [*Note:* The relationship between factor and return movements is usually negative: for example, if net exposure to key rates is positive, we expect a negative impact on returns from an increase in the key rates. The three exceptions are the currency, convexity, and high yield distressed factors. These three groups of factors have a positive relation with returns: for example, if the portfolio has a positive net exposure to EUR, then we expect positive returns from its appreciation.

TE Impact of a Correlated-Standard-Deviation Change: The return difference between the portfolio and the benchmark given a 1-standard-deviation change for the given risk factor, assuming all other risk factors change according to the correlations implied by the covariance matrix.

Marginal Contribution to TEV: The effect on TEV of an increase in the exposure to a particular factor. This number should be read with the exposure units of the respective factor in mind. Suppose this field is 2.4 for the EUR currency. Recall that the currency factors are expressed in percentage points. Therefore, if we increase the exposure to EUR by 1 percentage point, the TEV will increase by 2.4 bp. [This example also shows why normalizing the sensitivities is useful, as without it the previous example would read: TEV would increase by 240 bp when exposure to the EUR increases by 100 percentage points—clearly a less intuitive reading.]

Idiosyncratic TEV (Isolated): The contribution of an issue to the idiosyncratic TEV, ignoring the correlations with the idiosyncratic error of issues from the same issuer.

Issuer Idiosyncratic TEV: The contribution of the issuer to the portfolio idiosyncratic TEV. As idiosyncratic errors are uncorrelated across issuers, the sum of squares of all issuer's idiosyncratic TEV equals the portfolio idiosyncratic variance.

APPENDIX D. RISK MODEL FACTOR DESCRIPTIONS

In this appendix, we detail the meaning of each risk factor, describe its units, and provide examples of its interpretation. The numbers are given for explanatory purposes only. For simplicity, we interpret them as if the benchmark chosen is cash, meaning that the net loadings are also the portfolio exposures.

The factors and variables in this description are found in the factor exposure-full details report. In particular, the columns "portfolio exposure," "benchmark exposure," and "net exposure" are in the same units as "sensitivity/exposure"; "factor volatility" is in the same units as "factor value."

The definitions of these units are such that the product of exposures and factor volatilities is interpreted as returns in basis points (e.g., the "TE impact" columns have precisely this interpretation: a value of 3.5 means that returns are expected to increase by 3.5 bp). Figure 26-D1 presents a summary of the units used.

Figure 26-D1. Summary of Units

Factor	Exposure Units	Factor Volatility Units	Exposure × Factor
All market-weighted loaded factors (e.g., currency)	Percentage points (pp)	Percentage points (pp)	Basis points (bp)
Convexity	Units/100	Basis points × 100 (100th bp)	Basis points (bp)
Liquidity	Percentage points (pp)	Percentage points (pp)	Basis points (bp)
All other factors	Units	Basis points (bp)	Basis points (bp)

NOTES

1. In what follows, we present factor blocks for a particular currency. The corresponding factor blocks for other currencies have similar interpretations and are presented in the same units.

2. Factor and factor volatilities have the same units.

BLOCK 1: CURRENCY

These factors measure the exposure of the portfolio to the different currencies and therefore to the different exchange-rate risks (should the portfolio have holdings in other than the base currency). Currency exposures of both portfolio and benchmark are assumed to be 100% in the base currency if the "both benchmark and portfolio are implicitly hedged" option is selected.

Example: EUR Currency		Units	Value
Factor captures:	Percentage change in the EUR/(base currency) exchange rate	pp	2.92
Loading is:	Percentage of portfolio's market value [MV(%)]	pp	31.65
Interpretation:	The portfolio has 31.65% of its market value in EUR, including cash, securities, and hedge transactions. The typical monthly change in the EUR/USD exchange rate is 2.92%. Therefore, if the EUR appreciates by 2.92%, we expect returns to go up by 2.92% × 31.65% = 92.56 bp.		

BLOCK 2: KEY RATES AND CONVEXITY

This block measures the exposure of the portfolio to shifts in the treasury yield curve for the different currencies. For each currency, this exposure is measured by two types of factors: those related to durations for the different points on the yield curve and one related to the portfolio's convexity.

Example 1: EUR 6-Month Key Rate		Units	Value
Factor captures:	Change in the 6-month Treasury par yield	bp	24.37

Loading is:	Duration, in years, to the 6-month Treasury par yield key rate [KRD (years)]	Unit	0.073

Interpretation:	The portfolio's duration to the EUR 6-month key rate is 0.073 year. The typical change in the EUR 6-month key rate is 24.37 bp. Therefore, if this key rate goes up by 24.37 bp, we expect returns to change by -0.073×24.37 bp $= -1.78$ bp.

Example 2: EUR Convexity		**Units**	**Value**
Factor captures:	Squared average change of the six key rates ($\times 0.5$)	bp $\times 100$	3.96
Loading is:	Normalized portfolio's convexity [OAC (year^2/100)]	Unit/100	-0.161
Interpretation:	The (normalized) portfolio's convexity is -0.161. Half of the typical squared average change in the six key rates considered is 0.0396 percentage points (e.g., the typical average change is 0.2814 percentage points). Therefore, in a typical month, we expect the change in return owing to convexity to be 3.96 bp $\times (-0.161) = -0.64$ bp.		

BLOCK 3: SWAP SPREADS

Similar to the previous block, this one measures the exposure of the portfolio to shifts in swap spreads for the different currencies. However, this time the exposure is measured only by one type of factor: the swap spread durations for the points along the swap spread curve. Swap spreads are attributed to the different points along the curve based on the distribution of KRDs.

Example: JPY 6M Swap Spread		**Units**	**Value**
Factor captures:	Change in the 6M JPY swap spread	bp	12.08
Loading is:	Duration, in years, to the 6M swap spread [SSKRD (years)]	Unit	0.097

Interpretation: The portfolio's duration to the JPY 6-month swap spread is 0.097 year. The typical change in this swap spread is 12.08 bp. Therefore, if this swap spread goes up by 12.08 bp, we expect returns to change by -0.097×12.08 bp $= -1.17$ bp.

BLOCK 4: VOLATILITY (NON-USD)

This block captures the exposure of the portfolio to shifts in the volatility of non-USD bonds (USD-denominated bonds' volatility is treated separately—see details in what follows). The risk model has two independent non-USD volatilities, one for EUR and the other for GBP. Their factor realization is proxied by swaption volatilities and their sensitivities by the volatility durations. Therefore, EUR- or GBP-denominated bonds with embedded options will load on this factor.

BLOCK 5: TREASURY SPREAD AND VOLATILITY

This block is the first of the asset-class-specific blocks. Its goal is to measure the exposure of the portfolio to shifts in spreads over the yield curve (usually this asset class does not load on the swap spreads block). As with the other asset classes, we capture the sensitivity of returns to changes in spreads with four different types of factors. The first factor captures the return owing to changes in volatility. The second looks at the return owing to the average change in spread of the overall Treasury class. The third captures the potential shift in the slope of the spread curve, for example, if spreads widen more for longer maturities. Finally, some bonds trade systematically with spreads different from their peers. The level of this systematic difference shifts constantly. The return that is due to this shift is captured by the fourth factor.

In particular, the asset-class-specific return owing to changes in spreads is modeled as:

$$R_{spread} = -OASD \times (Change\_OAS) = -OASD \times (F_{spread i} + \beta_s F_{slope} + \beta_o F_{oas}),$$

where i indicates that we may want to calculate F_{spread}—the average change in spread—for different subgroups (e.g., different industries in the corporate block).

Example 1: USD Treasury Volatility	Units	Value
Factor captures: Change in US Treasury Volatility	bp	94
Loading is: Volatility duration of the portfolio	Unit	0.000001
Interpretation: The volatility duration indicates how much the market value of the portfolio changes if volatilities change by 1 percentage point. In our case, the duration is equal to 0.01 bp. The typical change in the Treasury's volatility is 94 bp. Therefore, if volatility increases by 94 bp, we expect returns to change by -0.000001×94 bp $= -0.000094$ bp.		

Example 2: USD Treasury Spread	Units	Value
Factor captures: Average OAS change for all Treasury spreads	bps	1.44
Loading is: The OASD from the portfolio [OASD(year)]	Unit	0.532
Interpretation: The portfolio's return sensitivity to the change in the Treasury's spreads (over the fitted Treasury spline curve) is 0.532 year. The typical change in Treasury spreads is 1.44 bp. Therefore, if spreads increase by 1.44 bp, we expect returns to change by -0.532×1.44 bp $= -0.77$ bp.		

Example 3: USD Treasury Spread Slope	Units	Value
Factor captures: Change in the slope of the Treasury's spread	bp	0.0428
Loading is: $OASD \times \beta_{slope} = OASD \times$ (Time to maturity – Median time to maturity) [(year^2)]	Unit	3.4
Interpretation: The loading units should be interpreted as follows: this factor captures the extra change in OAS—above that accounted for by the previous factor—that comes from a twist in the spread curve. We then multiply this extra change by the OASD to go from changes in OAS to returns. Suppose the		

OASD of the portfolio is 3.4 years and (TTM – MedianTTM) = 1. This means that our portfolio is relatively long in maturity. If the spread curve flattens, our portfolio benefits, and it would benefit more if the mismatch in maturity were larger. Thus, if the slope decreases by 0.0428 bp, we expect returns to change by -3.4×-0.0428 bp = 0.15 bp.

Example 4: USD Treasury Liquidity		Units	Value
Factor captures:	Change of TSY "liquidity premium" (or OAS difference)	pp	14.32
Loading is:	$OASD \times \beta_{slope} = OASD \times (OAS - MedianOAS)$ (year $\times$ pp)	pp	−0.007
Interpretation:	Again, we begin by interpreting the loading: it captures the extra return that comes from the fact that systematic differences in OAS among similar bonds change. Suppose the OASD of the portfolio is 1 year but our portfolio has spreads that are on average smaller than the typical Treasury portfolio (e.g., the median OAS is 5 bp, whereas our portfolio's average is only 4.3 bp). In effect, we are paying a liquidity premium to hold this portfolio. If this premium decreases (i.e., a negative factor realization), our portfolio will register an extra positive return. Suppose the "liquidity premium" increases by 14.32%: we would expect returns to change by $-0.007\% \times 14.32\% = -0.10$ bp.		

BLOCK 6: AGENCY SPREAD AND VOLATILITY

This block uses the same kind of factors described in the previous block, with two differences. The first is that spreads are defined against the swap curve. The second is that we have several factors to capture the average change in spreads. Each will capture this average for a particular subgroup. Specifically, we use five subgroups for the agency block. The loadings and factors from this block have similar interpretations as those from the Treasury block, so we do not extend the analysis here.

BLOCK 7: INVESTMENT-GRADE CREDIT SPREAD AND VOLATILITY

This block uses the same kind of factors described in block 5. Note that as in block 6, spreads are defined against the swap curve. Moreover, several factors are used to capture average change in spreads across different industries. In addition, an extra series of factors is used to capture additional changes in the OAS for bonds with different qualities issued by nonlocal firms (for non-USD we have three such factors, whereas we have only one for the EUR and GBP credit blocks). In particular, these factor loadings and definitions are similar to the other corporate spread factors

Example: GBP U.S. Issuers		**Units**
Factor captures:	Changes in average spreads for U.S. issuers	PP
Loading is:	OASD (years)	PP
Interpretation:	See "USD Treasury Spread" example.	

BLOCK 8: HIGH YIELD CREDIT SPREAD AND VOLATILITY

This block uses the same kind of factors described in the previous block. The differences arise from the fact that bonds are divided into distressed and nondistressed. The model for the nondistressed follows the IG model closely. However, the return from spreads for the distressed bonds is modeled directly:

$$R_{\text{spread\_distressed}} = F_{\text{return}i} + \beta_s F_{\text{slope}} + \beta_p F_{\text{price}} + \beta_L F_{\text{leverage}} + \beta_{\text{sub}} F_{\text{subordinated}}.$$

The liquidity factor is replaced by the price factor. The distress return is explained by two extra factors: one that controls for leverage and the other for the collateral type underlying the security.

Example: Distressed Subordinated		**Units**
Factor captures:	Average extra return from high yield subordinated issues	PP
Loading is:	Unit (×100)	PP
Interpretation:	Additional average return for subordinated bonds.	

BLOCK 9: MBS SPREAD AND VOLATILITY

This block uses the same kind of factors described in block 7. However, MBS risk is modeled taking into account two volatilities—short and long term. Moreover, the average change in spreads is calculated for several (nondisjoint subgroups) based on type, term, government agency, age, and price.

BLOCK 10: CMBS SPREAD AND VOLATILITY

This block closely follows the previous one, with the following differences: The slope factor is based on average life—not maturity—and the model also uses three other factors:

Example 1: USD CMBS Principal Payment Window		Units
Factor captures:	Additional average spread change for issues at or near principal payment	bp
Loading is:	OASD×WINDOW (year^2)	Unit
Interpretation:	Extra return for issues at or near principal payment. These bonds are more sensitive to prepayment risk.	

Example 2: USD CMBS Age		Units
Factor captures:	Additional spread changes for issues with different WALAs	bp
Loading is:	OASD $\times$ (AGE – MedianAGE) (year^2/100)	Unit
Interpretation:	Extra change in OAS per extra year of WALA of the portfolio. "Older" bonds have different prepayment or default probabilities than "younger" bonds.	

Example 3: USD CMBS Price Current Pay Aaa		Units
Factor captures:	Additional (normalized) spread change for issues at premium/discount	bp
Loading is:	OASD $\times$ (Price – MedianPrice) (years $\times$ \$)	Unit
Interpretation:	Extra change in OAS per extra dollar of average price. Proxies for sensitivity to prepayment risk: premium bonds are more sensitive to prepayments.	

BLOCK 11: ABS SPREAD AND VOLATILITY

This block closely follows the previous one. Here, however, we apply an extra factor to capture the extra change in OAS for a non-Aaa rated bond. The treatment of this factor is the same as any of the spread factors shown previously.

Example: USD ABS Non-Aaa		**Units**
Factor captures:	Additional spread change for non-Aaa issues	bp
Loading is:	OASD × Indicator (years)	Unit
Interpretation:	Extra average change in OAS for non-Aaa issues.	

27. The Hybrid Performance Attribution Model

Active portfolio management involves forming views on various aspects of financial markets and expressing these views as portfolio risk exposures. To achieve the best possible performance per unit of risk, managers try to diversify their exposures among a set of uncorrelated strategies at which they are highly skilled. Fixed-income managers, in particular, may employ strategies involving currency exchange rates, interest rates, volatilities, and credit spreads—either by sector or by issuer.

At the end of a review period, managers analyze their portfolio's performance to see which strategies proved to be the most effective. Ideally, performance should be broken down into the effects of the specific views that were reflected in the portfolio. For example, an investor would be delighted to hear that, in a given month, he outperformed the benchmark by 10 bp owing to the decision to go long-duration; gained another 5 bp by the decision to short credit; and yet another 4 bp from the overweight to a particular issuer. The next step in this analysis might be to compare the achieved results with the amount of risk that had been taken for each of these portfolio exposures. Over the longer term, the (risk-adjusted) track record achieved by a manager in various strategies can be used to estimate skill at each strategy. Going forward, this skill measurement mechanism can form a key component of the risk-budgeting process used to decide how much risk to take in each dimension.

Yet, while the goals of performance attribution are clear, many fixed-income practitioners have found that achieving a satisfactory result at this task is much harder than it might seem, for several reasons. First, it can be very difficult to cleanly separate the effects of different strategies, because they can interact with each other in many ways. A single transaction can affect the portfolio's exposures

Based on research first published by Lehman Brothers in 2005.

to interest rates, sectors, volatility, and so on. Second, exposures do not stay constant over the course of a review period, but change continually as a result of both transactions and market shifts. Third, it can be difficult to find the right balance between the two main objectives of a good attribution scheme: intuitive clarity and analytical precision.

Our solution to this complex problem builds on our prior experience with two very different approaches to attribution, designed to answer different types of questions about achieved returns. Each of these two models has its strengths and weaknesses.

The first approach focuses on the sources of absolute returns. How can we explain the return of a given security by various market changes? How much return is due to the carry earned with the passage of time and how much to changes in yield, volatility, and spread? Once we perform this analysis for every security in the universe, the results can be aggregated to answer these questions about a given portfolio or an index.

In the second approach, we explain the performance of a portfolio relative to its benchmark in terms of overweights and underweights to different market segments. The focus is on the differences in the *composition* of the portfolio and the benchmark; the total return of each security is treated as an atomic unit.

In this chapter, we introduce our new "hybrid" performance attribution model, which combines the best features of each of these approaches. First, the return of each security is split into separate components owing to foreign exchange, yield curve, volatility, and spread. Each of these components is further subdivided into a carry portion and a spread change portion. Second, the performance of a portfolio relative to its benchmark is addressed separately for each return component, using an appropriate form of analysis for each component. Outperformance owing to yield curve positioning is modeled in terms of key-rate duration (KRD) exposures and changes in key rates, making the model consistent with our global risk model.[1] Outperformance owing to sector allocation is analyzed in terms of overweights and underweights along a flexible partition, so that it can be tailored to fit the specific management process used for each portfolio. Allocations by market weight explain the outperformance owing to carry (spread); outperformance that is due to spread change is explained in terms of contributions to spread duration.[2]

1. See Chapter 26.

2. Contributions to spread duration represent sensitivities to a parallel shift in spreads within a given market cell. If one would instead prefer to use sensitivities to proportional spread changes, outperformance would be attributed based on contributions to duration times spread (DTS). See Chapter 34.

In the following section, we review the basic mathematics of three classic approaches to attribution. Then, we show how we combined these approaches to achieve a model that is flexible, intuitive, and precise.

THE BASICS OF ATTRIBUTION

The successive valuation technique splits the absolute return of a given bond into separate components, for example, those that are due to carry, yield change, and spread change. Partition-based attribution analyzes sector allocations to attribute the outperformance of a portfolio relative to its benchmark to such decisions as sector allocation and security selection. The third approach, which traces returns to exposures to common risk factors that drive market returns, shares aspects of both return splitting and partition-based attribution.

Return Splitting by Successive Valuation

In the successive valuation method, we work with a pricing model that explains the price of a security at a given point in time as a function of a set of inputs. For example, assume that the price of bond i is given by the function

$$P(i) = f(i, t, y, \sigma, s), \tag{27-1}$$

where i represents the indicative characteristics of the bond, t the time at which we are pricing the bond, y the yield curve environment, σ the volatility, and s the spread. (Each of these can be a vector or a complex specification.)

When pricing the portfolio at the start and end of a review period, we fit a risk-free yield curve to the Treasury or swaps market and a volatility surface to data from the derivatives markets; we then use the pricing equation to back out the option-adjusted spread of bond i from the market price, defining s_i^{beg} and s_i^{end} as the spreads that satisfy the following:

$$\begin{aligned} P_i^{\text{beg}} &= f(i, t^{\text{beg}}, y^{\text{beg}}, \sigma^{\text{beg}}, s_i^{\text{beg}}) \\ P_i^{\text{end}} &= f(i, t^{\text{end}}, y^{\text{end}}, \sigma^{\text{end}}, s_i^{\text{end}}). \end{aligned} \tag{27-2}$$

We can then decompose the return over the period into components owing to the passage of time, changes in the yield curve, and changes in volatility and spread by repeating the OAS-based valuations under various scenarios, changing just one element of the pricing environment at a time, as follows:

$$\begin{aligned} P_i^{\text{unch}} &= f(i, t^{\text{end}}, y^{\text{beg}}, \sigma^{\text{beg}}, s_i^{\text{beg}}) \\ P_i^{\text{yldchg}} &= f(i, t^{\text{end}}, y^{\text{end}}, \sigma^{\text{beg}}, s_i^{\text{beg}}) \\ P_i^{\text{volchg}} &= f(i, t^{\text{end}}, y^{\text{end}}, \sigma^{\text{end}}, s_i^{\text{beg}}). \end{aligned} \tag{27-3}$$

This creates a sequence of hypothetical prices for security i as of the end of the review period: P_i^{unch} assuming unchanged yields, volatilities, and spreads; P_i^{yldchg} if we factor in changes to the yield curve as well; and P_i^{volchg} if we add in the effect of changes in volatility, still holding spreads constant. (Once we include the ending spread as well, we arrive at the ending price just shown.) This allows us to break the return into additive components corresponding to the passage of time, changes to the yield curve, changes in volatility, and change in spread:

$$
\begin{aligned}
R_i &= \frac{P_i^{\text{end}} - P_i^{\text{beg}}}{P_i^{\text{beg}}} \\
&= \frac{(P_i^{\text{end}} - P_i^{\text{volchg}}) + (P_i^{\text{volchg}} - P_i^{\text{yldchg}}) + (P_i^{\text{yldchg}} - P_i^{\text{unch}}) + (P_i^{\text{unch}} - P_i^{\text{beg}})}{P_i^{\text{beg}}}. \\
&= R_i^{\text{sprchg}} + R_i^{\text{volchg}} + R_i^{\text{yldchg}} + R_i^{\text{time}}
\end{aligned}
\tag{27-4}
$$

This approach can be extended to obtain an even finer breakdown of return by including additional intermediate valuations. For example, in our first model, based on absolute returns, we subdivided the monthly return owing to yield curve change into components that are due to shift, twist, and butterfly movements of the curve.

Partition-Based Attribution

The attribution of relative performance, targeted at managers whose performance is measured against an index, addresses a different set of key issues. First, the quantity to be explained is not the portfolio return itself, but the performance differential between the portfolio and the benchmark. Second, there is less emphasis on which market events drove outperformance and more on attributing performance to specific managerial decisions, such as sector allocation and security selection.

Let us express the returns of a portfolio, P, and a benchmark, B, over a given time period in terms of the market weights, w, assigned to various market segments and the sector returns, r, earned within each sector, as follows:

$$
R^P = \sum_i w_i^P r_i^P, \qquad R^B = \sum_i w_i^B r_i^B.
\tag{27-5}
$$

This representation allows us to identify two key drivers of performance differences between the portfolio and the benchmark: the differences in the sector allocations, w_p, and the differences in the returns, r_i, earned within each sector. To distinguish between the performance contributions of these two effects, we introduce a hypothetical position that follows the sector weighting of the portfolio, but earns the return of the benchmark within each sector. The outperformance earned by this simple reweighting of the benchmark is considered to be the outperformance owing to asset allocation; the outperformance that is due to the intrasector return differences can be regarded as the effect of security selection:[3]

$$R^P - R^B = \sum_i (w_i^P r_i^P - w_i^P r_i^B + w_i^P r_i^B - w_i^B r_i^B)$$

$$= \sum_i w_i^P (r_i^P - r_i^B) + \sum_i (w_i^P - w_i^B) r_i^B \qquad (27\text{-}6)$$

$$= \text{Outp}_{\text{selection}} + \text{Outp}_{\text{allocation}}.$$

If we take advantage of the fact that both portfolio and benchmark weights must sum to one, we can refine the expression for outperformance owing to asset allocation as follows:

$$\text{Outp}_{\text{allocation}} = \sum_i (w_i^P - w_i^B) r_i^B$$

$$= \sum_i (w_i^P - w_i^B) r_i^B - R^B + R^B$$

$$= \sum_i (w_i^P - w_i^B) r_i^B - \sum_i w_i^P R^B + \sum_i w_i^B R^B \qquad (27\text{-}7)$$

$$= \sum_i (w_i^P - w_i^B)(r_i^B - R^B)$$

$$= \sum_i (\text{sector } i \text{ overnight}) \times (\text{sector } i \text{ relative performance}).$$

Note that the top and the bottom expressions in this sequence sum to the same overall outperformance, but differ in their allocation of this outperformance to different sectors. The bottom expression gives a very intuitive attribution of outperformance to each allocation decision: the allocation to sector i generates a positive contribution to outperformance if it is either an overweight to a sector that outperforms the benchmark or an underweight to an underperforming sector.

3. In some attribution models, in addition to asset allocation and security selection, there is an additional term to capture the interaction between them. Just as the calculation of outperformance owing to asset allocation assumes that the only difference between the portfolio and the benchmark is the market weights, a pure security selection return can be modeled under the assumption that no change has been made to the benchmark market weights. This approach is described in G. P. Brinson, L. R. Hood, and G. L. Breebower, "Determinants of Portfolio Performance," *Financial Analysts' Journal*, January–February 1995. In our definition of security selection return, security selection is considered to take place within the context of the portfolio asset allocation weights. As a result, our security selection effect can be seen to include the "interaction" term in addition to the pure security selection return of the Brinson model, as follows:

$$\text{Outp}_{\text{selection}} = \sum_i w_i^P (r_i^P - r_i^B)$$

$$= \sum_i w_i^B (r_i^P - r_i^B) + \sum_i (w_i^P - w_i^B)(r_i^P - r_i^B).$$

$$= \text{Outp}_{\text{pure\_selection}} + \text{Outp}_{\text{interaction}}$$

Risk-Based Attribution

In the factor-based approach, the return of a bond over a given time period is represented as the sum of return components owing to changes in a preselected set of risk factors. Each factor return is the product of a factor loading, or exposure, and the realization of that factor:

$$R_i = R_i^{\text{syst}} + R_i^{\text{nonsyst}} = \sum_j f_{ij} x_j + \varepsilon_i, \qquad (27\text{-}8)$$

where x_j is the realization of risk factor, j (a market event that affects returns of an entire market segment), f_{ij} is the exposure of bond i to factor j (factor loading), and ε_i is the nonsystematic return on bond i (issuer and individual issue effects).

Very often, portfolio weights are managed in terms of exposures to risk factors, rather than by market weights. For example, yield curve exposures might be expressed in terms of KRDs; sector weights might be expressed as contributions to spread duration, which are exposures to parallel shifts in spread throughout a sector. In such cases, risk-based attribution can explain realized returns in terms of the risk exposures that were taken.

Risk-based attribution can be used both for return splitting and for performance attribution. Equation (27-9) makes it clear that the return of each bond is broken down into subcomponents owing to each risk factor. Nevertheless, the focus on finding common factors of risk and return makes it easy to analyze the relative performance of a portfolio against a benchmark based on risk factor overweights and underweights. Let the total portfolio exposure to risk factor j be given by $f_j^P = \sum_i w_i^P f_{ij}$, and similarly define the benchmark risk exposures, f_j^B; the performance difference between the two can be easily expressed in terms of the active exposures to risk factors and the risk factor realizations, as follows:

$$R_i^P - R_i^B = \sum_j (f_j^P - f_j^B) x_j + \sum_i (w_i^P - w_i^B) \varepsilon_i. \qquad (27\text{-}9)$$

The first sum in Equation (27-9) gives components of outperformance that are due to active exposures to systematic risk factors, and the second gives outperformance owing to security selection.

Comparison of the Three Attribution Models

As we have seen, several different approaches can be taken to modeling fixed-income attribution. No single model can be objectively selected as the "best"—this is a subjective evaluation that depends on the specific portfolio, the strategies used to manage it, and the intended audience for and use of the attribution analysis. For a portfolio manager interested in understanding the results of various decisions on the portfolio's performance, the best attribution analysis is the one that best matches the decision process. From this viewpoint, let us examine the strengths and weaknesses of these attribution models.

The return-splitting technique allows the most precise analysis of yield curve positioning. In our first, absolute returns-based, attribution model, we use the successive valuation approach shown in Equations (27-2) through (27-4), with more scenarios to further break down yield curve returns into return components that are due to parallel shift, twist, and butterfly movements of the curve. Returns owing to time passage were divided into accretion of interest and the effect of rolling down the yield curve. This model was very successful at explaining returns owing to interest-rate movements and is well suited to the needs of a Treasury portfolio manager whose primary emphasis is on yield curve positioning. However, it leaves all spread-related return in a single category and does not directly address the effects of sector allocation and security selection.

The risk-based model addresses this issue. In addition to the risk factors that measure exposures to interest rates (in the case of our model, KRDs are used to measure exposures to six points along the curve in each major currency), there are factors that measure exposures to systematic changes in swap spreads, credit sector spreads, volatility, and the like. For a manager who relies heavily on a particular risk model and expresses all allocation decisions in terms of risk factor exposures, an attribution model matched to that model would be ideal. However, a single risk model with a fixed choice of risk factors cannot be expected to represent exactly the decision process used to manage every portfolio, from broad global funds to specialized sector mandates.

In the partition-based approach, we use repeated applications of Equation (27-7) to attribute portfolio outperformance to yield curve allocation, sector allocation, and security selection. A first partition, by duration or maturity, is used to attribute outperformance owing to yield curve positioning. The second and third levels of the partition, nested within each duration or maturity cell, serve to determine outperformance owing to sector allocation. The difference between the returns of the portfolio and the benchmark within each cell at the finest level of the partition constitutes outperformance that is due to security selection and can be attributed to the performance of each portfolio holding relative to its peer group in the index.

The fundamental advantage of the partition-based attribution methodology is its flexibility. The ability to analyze portfolio allocations along an arbitrarily specified market partition makes it possible to customize this model to fit many different types of portfolios and management styles. The sector partition can be coarse for a very broadly based portfolio (e.g. Treasuries, agencies, corporates, mortgages) or use a fine industry grid for a corporate portfolio.

The main disadvantage of this approach is that it forces us to analyze yield curve and spread returns within the same partition-based framework. Partitioning the portfolio in terms of market weights to specified duration cells does not give the most precise results for yield curve allocation. If the cells are defined too coarsely (e.g., into three duration cells: short, medium, and long), then significant differences could arise between the portfolio and benchmark duration within each cell, and the allocations analyzed would not appropriately reflect the true portfolio yield curve exposure. To avoid this problem, one could use a finer grid for duration cell allocation—for example, half-year duration cells—but then the analysis would lose its intuitive value, as it would no longer correspond to the way managers think of the allocation process.

Furthermore, relative value allocations to spread sectors are often made on an excess return basis, independently of the yield curve positioning. The emphasis is exclusively on choosing the right sectors and/or issuers. Interest-rate exposures are decided upon separately and manipulated either using the Treasury part of the portfolio or with an overlay of futures or swaps. To a manager who views the market in this way, the notion of separately examining the sector allocations within each duration cell would seem very artificial and counterintuitive. If yield curve positioning is carried out separately from the sector allocation, then the attribution method that would best match the decision process must similarly analyze the two allocations separately.

THE HYBRID MODEL

The hybrid model combines all three of the foregoing approaches to allow fixed-income portfolio managers to achieve the best match to their decision processes. The model offers enhanced flexibility in defining arbitrary hierarchical partitions along which sector allocation decisions are expressed. However, before the analysis of sector allocations even begins, returns that stem from exposures to common market factors (interest rates, foreign exchange, and volatility) are stripped out and analyzed separately.

The model consists of two basic steps: return splitting and performance attribution. We first split returns into several components by successive valuation, as in Equation (27-4), and then separately attribute outperformance that is due to each return component using a different form of analysis, as appropriate. A schematic view of the model is given in Figure 27-1.

The return-splitting algorithm divides each day's return for every security into components owing to currency, yield curve, volatility, and spread, and attribution analysis begins with these return components. Outperformance owing to currency allocation is analyzed in terms of the active weights in different currencies,

Figure 27-1. Schematic View of the Hybrid Model

Choosing the Appropriate Attribution Mechanism to Explain Each Return Component

Return Category	Return Split Components	Attribution Mechanism
Currency return	Cost of hedge (deposit rate differentials) FX change	Market value allocations by currency
Yield curve return	Term premium over cash (carry) Yield change	Contributions to KRDs
Volatility return	Change in volatility	Volatility sensitivities (vega contributions)
Spread return	Spread carry Spread change	Allocations along customized partition by market value (for carry) and by spread duration (for spread change)

including the effect of all hedges. As discussed later, this analysis includes both the carry advantage from differences in interest rates in different currencies, as well as any outperformance from changes in foreign exchange rates. Outperformance owing to yield curve positioning within each currency is analyzed using the risk-based approach. Following our global risk model, it uses the exposures to six key-rate durations to characterize both the portfolio and the benchmark and explain the yield curve returns of each. Outperformance owing to volatility is attributed based on the volatility sensitivities of the portfolio and the benchmark in different sectors.

Finally, the outperformance in the spread-related portion of the return is broken down into sector allocation and security selection by applying the flexible partition approach of Equation (27-7). At this stage, there is one more enhancement to the model that is inspired by the risk-based approach. The primary credit risk factors in our risk model are changes in spreads within various sector × quality cells. As a result, the risk model views active sector allocation exposures in terms of contributions to spread duration, not market value. When considering the allocation to different spread sectors, the hybrid model considers both market value allocations and contributions to spread duration. Market value overweights and underweights are used to allocate outperformance to spread carry; overweights and underweights in terms of contributions to spread duration are used to allocate outperformance owing to spread changes. This is true when explaining both sector allocation outperformance in terms of sector weights and security selection returns in terms of exposures to specific bonds or issuers.

Figure 27-2. Outperformance Summary for Sample Baa Portfolio vs. Baa Index

March 2005

Total unhedged portfolio return (USD)	–112.9
Total unhedged benchmark return (USD)	–189.4
Total unhedged outperformance (USD)	76.5
Hedging	0.0
Total hedged outperformance (USD)	76.5
FX allocation	0.0
FX cross-term	0.0
Local allocation	0.0
Local management	76.5
Owing to yield curve	–2.6
Owing to volatility	–0.1
Owing to spread duration mismatch	26.3
Owing to asset allocation	29.7
Owing to security selection	24.4
Trading and market timing	0.0
From excluded positions	0.0
Local residual	–1.2
FX hedge local outperformance	0.0

Sample Attribution Analysis: Baa Credit Portfolio

To illustrate the model, we examine the analysis produced for a sample portfolio. The portfolio consists of an equally weighted blend of twenty-five Baa-rated corporate bonds, benchmarked against the Lehman Brothers U.S. Corporate Baa Index. The analysis is shown for March 2005, a month characterized by a large widening in credit spreads. Figure 27-2 shows the top-level summary of the month's performance. While both the portfolio and the benchmark turn in negative absolute returns, the portfolio outperforms by 76.5 bp. The performance advantage is quite clearly due to the credit positioning. The model attributes 26.3 bp to an overall underweight in spread duration, 29.7 bp to asset allocation, and 24.4 bp to security selection. The yield curve exposures of the portfolio contribute a slight underperformance of 2.6 bp. Each of these numbers is supported by a more detailed report.

Although it is but a minor contributor to outperformance in this particular example, we begin with the outperformance owing to yield curve exposure. Figure 27-3 gives a complete accounting of the yield curve exposures of the portfolio and the resulting underperformance. The first line compares the overall duration of the portfolio and the benchmark. We see that the portfolio duration is shorter

Figure 27-3. Yield Curve Allocation

| | Yield | | Exposure (duration) | | | | | Outperformance (bp) | | |
| | Initial Level (%) | Change (bp) | Average | | Portfolio – Benchmark | | | | | |
			Portfolio	Benchmark	Mean	Minimum	Maximum	Carry	Change	Total
Parallel Shift										
Average	4.168	11.8	5.33	6.36	-1.03	-1.08	-0.99	0.0	13.0	13.0
Key Rates and Cash										
Cash	2.579	33.1	0.00	0.00	0.00	0.00	0.00	-0.1	0.0	-0.1
6-month	2.964	14.4	0.01	0.06	-0.05	-0.05	-0.04	1.5	0.1	1.6
2-year	3.586	20.9	0.42	0.43	-0.01	-0.01	0.00	0.0	0.1	0.1
5-year	4.001	15.7	2.54	1.71	0.83	0.82	0.83	-1.2	-3.2	-4.4
10-year	4.454	12.3	2.36	1.69	0.68	0.65	0.70	0.0	-0.4	-0.4
20-year	4.837	7.3	0.00	1.27	-1.27	-1.30	-1.25	-0.2	-5.5	-5.7
30-year	4.659	6.8	0.00	1.21	-1.21	-1.24	-1.17	-0.1	-6.0	-6.1
Rest of curve and convexity								0.0	-0.7	-0.7
Total Treasury curve levels and shifts								-0.1	-2.6	-2.6

than that of the benchmark by an average of 1.03 years over the course of the month. As yields rose on average by 11.8 bp, a simple linear approximation, applied daily, gives us an outperformance of 13.0 bp for this duration underweight.[4]

However, the average duration only measures the exposure to a parallel shift in yield. When yield change is not parallel, as in our example, the actual yield curve return can be very different. In this particular month, the yield curve rose and flattened. The portfolio, with a strong concentration in the 5- to 10-year part of the curve, is hurt by the flattening move. It is overweight the 5-year point, where rates rose by more than the 11.8-bp average, and underweight the 20- to 30-year part of the curve, where rates rose by considerably less. At the 5-year point, for example, the portfolio was long-duration by 0.83 years on average, and the yield rose by 15.7 bp, exceeding the parallel shift by 3.9 bp. This gives a return contribution of $-3.9 \times 0.83 = -3.2$ bp as an adjustment to the parallel shift return. The total underperformance owing to nonparallel yield curve movement overshadows the parallel shift outperformance from the duration underweight, giving a total underperformance of -2.6 bp from yield curve movement.

The second-to-last line of Figure 27-3 gives the outperformance that is due to the "rest of curve" and convexity. This component summarizes the difference between the outperformance explained by this analysis of KRD exposures and the exact calculation of yield curve return from our return split by successive valuation. We would expect to see a significant contribution here when there is a convexity mismatch and a large change in yields; otherwise, this number tends to be quite small, and can be a result of yield curve movement that is not linear between key-rate points.

Now let us turn to the spread-related outperformance. Figure 27-4 summarizes the various spread-related components and details the analysis of the overall spread duration exposure. The portfolio is underweight spread duration by an average of 1.03 years. With an average benchmark spread widening of 26 bp, this results in 26.4 bp of outperformance.

The breakdown of the remaining spread return into components owing to asset allocation and security selection is somewhat subjective. For a pure bottom-up manager, it may be that there is no explicit sector allocation decision, and the

---

4. A careful reader will notice that there seems to be a small discrepancy in the numbers. An active duration exposure of -1.03 years, multiplied by a parallel shift of 11.8 bp, should give us an outperformance of 12.2 bp, not 13.0 bp. However, this simple multiplication, while correct for each single-day attribution, is not valid unless the active exposure remains constant throughout the review period. To give some insight into the dynamics of each exposure during the review period, Figure 27-3 shows not only that the active duration exposure averaged -1.03, but that it ranged from -1.08 to -0.99. Similar columns are included in all of our model's reports, although they have been trimmed from the other figures in this chapter to reduce clutter.

Figure 27-4. Summary of Outperformance Owing to Spread Exposures
Sample Baa Portfolio

Spread Component Summary	
Spread contribution to outperformance	80.7 bp
Owing to spread duration mismatch	26.4 bp
Owing to asset allocation	29.8 bp
Market weight allocation	−1.1 bp
Spread duration allocation	31.0 bp
Owing to security selection	24.3 bp

Spread Duration Mismatch

Spread Duration (years)				
Portfolio	Benchmark	Portfolio – Benchmark	Benchmark Spread Change (bp)	Outperformance (bp)
5.39	6.42	−1.03	26.0	26.4

portfolio composition is determined purely by a combination of issuer views. In that case, the entire corporate sector can be included as a single cell in a simple broad partition of, say, governments vs. corporates. Other managers may employ complex top-down schemes involving multiple levels of partitions: sector, quality, subordination, callability, and so forth. Typically, a more detailed partition scheme results in more homogeneous cells at the finest partition level and attributes more of the outperformance to allocation and less to security selection. The division between asset allocation and security selection is therefore clearly subjective. The goal is to allocate return to the different stages of the decision process—yet there is no way for a model to examine the contents of a portfolio and deduce the sequence of decisions by which the manager arrived at his current portfolio composition. Therefore, it is critical for the model to allow the manager to specify as closely as possible the nature of the sector allocation scheme that underlies his decision process. The specific details of the sector partition thus constitute an important input to the model.

In Figure 27-5, we show the allocations of our Baa portfolio along a one-dimensional industry partition. The allocation by market weights is used to attribute outperformance owing to spread carry and the allocation by contributions to spread duration is used to attribute outperformance from spread change. We find that the largest single contribution to sector allocation outperformance is a

21-bp outperformance from consumer cyclicals. Benchmark spreads in this sector widened by 69.6 bp, 43.6 bp more than the average widening of 26.0 bp for the benchmark as a whole. The portfolio is underweight this sector by a spread duration contribution of −0.70, but we must not use this number directly; we have already credited the benchmark with an outperformance owing to an overall underweight in spread duration, and we do not want to analyze that same decision again. Rather, we view the underweight in terms of relative spread duration allocations. The portfolio's 0.64 year of spread duration in consumer cyclicals represents 11.9% of its total spread duration, whereas the benchmark has 20.9% of its exposure in this sector. The resulting spread duration underweight is −9.0% of the portfolio spread duration of 5.38, or −0.48 year. Multiplying this by the relative spread widening of 43.6 bp, we obtain a 21-bp outperformance owing to this spread duration allocation.

The primary driver of sector allocation returns over the short term is usually spread change. However, we must also consider the effect of holding securities that yield more or less than the benchmark. The extra carry earned by higher-spread securities can give portfolios that are overweight credit a steady return advantage that can become significant if spreads remain stable over long periods of time. In this example, the net underweight to credit gives rise to a small under-performance. The most noticeable component of this is again in consumer cyclicals, a high-spread sector where the portfolio has a market value underweight of 10.75%. The spread carry advantage of consumer cyclicals relative to the index changes throughout the month, but can be approximated using an average spread level that is the beginning spread plus half the spread change, or roughly 208 bp for cyclicals and 118 bp for the index. One month of carry advantage is approximately one-twelfth of the 90-bp difference, or 7.5 bp; the portfolio's underweight of 10.75% thus gives rise to an underperformance of 0.8 bp.

Figure 27-6 shows the calculation of outperformance owing to security selection within a single sector. This is the difference in the overall return of the portfolio that stems from the differences between the specific holdings of the portfolio and the benchmark within each sector. First, we look at the differences in the relative issuer weights of the portfolio and the benchmark, both by market weight and by percentage of spread duration, to get the outperformance owing to issuer allocation. Then, we look at the effect of the security selection decisions used to implement each issuer exposure.

In this example, the portfolio is represented in the consumer cyclical sector by an equally weighted portfolio of three bonds from three issuers; bonds from these issuers represent only 29.6% of the benchmark's allocation to this sector. The portfolio's relative allocation to Ford (F) within the sector is similar to that of the

Figure 27-5. Outperformance Owing to Sector Allocation by Industry
Sample Baa Portfolio

	Benchmark OAS (bp)		Market Weight (%)		
Industry Group	Initial Level	Change	Portfolio	Benchmark	Difference
Banking/brokerage	81.5	11.8	7.98	3.65	4.33
Other financials	90.4	13.0	11.85	7.91	3.93
Basic industry	74.3	13.7	15.90	10.78	5.12
Consumer cyclical	172.8	69.6	11.88	22.62	−10.75
Consumer noncyclical	75.8	12.7	11.96	10.33	1.62
Energy and transportation	93.7	12.9	15.92	11.06	4.85
Technology and communication	93.8	18.9	11.99	19.28	−7.29
Utilities	79.7	12.6	11.94	13.99	−2.05
Others	70.1	7.6	0.60	0.36	0.24
Total	105.1	26.0	100.00	100.00	0.00

benchmark; it is a slight overweight in terms of market value and a slight underweight in terms of contribution to spread duration. As a result, the outperformance from issuer allocation to Ford is quite small. A more significant issuer exposure can be seen to Disney (DIS), which represents 35.6% of the portfolio's spread duration allocation of 0.64 year within the sector but only 3.1% of the benchmark's allocation. As the Disney portion of the benchmark widened by only 11.4 bp,

Figure 27-6. Outperformance Owing to Security Selection (excerpt)
Sample Baa Portfolio, Advanced Aspects of the Model[a]

	Average OAS (bp)			OAS Change (bp)			Average Relative Market Weight (%)		
Ticker	Portfolio	Bench	Difference	Portfolio	Bench	Difference	Portfolio	Bench	Difference
F	210	299	−89	114	77	38	33.3	25.1	8.2
DIS	59	69	−10	22	11	10	33.5	3.7	29.7
LEA	133	197	−64	59	92	−34	33.3	0.8	32.5
Not in portfolio		231			68			70.4	−70.4
Total	134	242	−108		69		100.0	100.0	

[a]Consumer cyclicals—portfolio weight: 11.88%; portfolio contribution to duration: 0.64 year; benchmark carry return: 16.5 bp; benchmark OAS change: 69.6 bp.

Contribution to Spread Duration (years)			Percentage of Spread Duration			Outperformance (bp)		
Portfolio	Benchmark	Difference	Portfolio	Benchmark	Difference	Market Weight	Spread Duration	Total
0.42	0.18	0.24	7.8	2.8	5.0	−0.1	3.8	3.7
0.78	0.45	0.33	14.5	7.0	7.5	−0.1	5.2	5.2
0.94	0.73	0.20	17.5	11.4	6.1	−0.2	3.9	3.8
0.64	1.34	−0.70	11.9	20.9	−9.0	−0.8	21.0	20.2
0.71	0.61	0.10	13.2	9.5	3.7	0.0	2.7	2.6
0.87	0.84	0.04	16.2	13.1	3.1	−0.1	2.2	2.2
0.52	1.34	−0.82	9.7	20.9	−11.2	0.1	−4.2	−4.1
0.50	0.92	−0.42	9.3	14.3	−5.0	0.1	−3.5	−3.5
0.00	0.01	−0.01	0.0	0.2	−0.2	0.0	−0.2	−0.2
5.38	6.42	−1.04	100.0	100.0	0.0	−1.1	30.8	29.8

compared to 68.8 bp for the sector overall, the impact of this overweight on the portfolio's performance is −32.5% × 0.64 × (11.4 − 68.8) = 11.9 bp.

To achieve this outperformance and the corresponding spread carry term based on market value allocations, the portfolio would have to implement the issuer allocation by purchasing all benchmark bonds from that issuer, in index proportions. In our example, this is far from the case; the portfolio contains just one

Average Relative OASD Contribution (%)			Outperformance from Issuer Allocation		Outperformance from Security Selection		Total Outperformance
Portfolio	Bench	Difference	Market Value	Spread Duration	Market Value	Spread Duration	
19.5	24.4	−4.9	0.0	0.3	−0.3	−4.7	−4.7
35.6	3.1	32.5	−0.4	11.9	0.0	−2.3	9.1
44.8	0.6	44.2	−0.2	−6.7	−0.2	9.7	2.7
	71.8	−71.8	0.1	−0.2			−0.1
100.00	100.0		−0.5	5.3	−0.5	2.7	7.0

bond from each issuer. The outperformance owing to security selection reflects the differences between the spread levels and the spread changes observed within each issuer between the specific bonds in the portfolio and the average across all benchmark bonds from a given issuer. For example, while we saw that the issuer allocation to Ford was fairly passive, there is a significant underperformance owing to the specific Ford bond chosen, which widened by 114.4 bp, compared to an average of 76.9 bp for the issuer as a whole. As this issuer accounts for 19.5% of the portfolio's spread duration contribution of 0.64 in the sector, this generates a contribution to underperformance of $-19.5\% \times 0.64 \times (114.4 - 76.9) = -4.7$ bp.

A full detailed specification of the model is beyond the scope of this chapter. We have tried to focus on the fundamental two-stage design of the model and on the flexible framework, which allows the attribution analysis to be customized to a portfolio manager's decision process. For the sake of clarity, we have consciously glossed over some of the more intricate details of the model's design. We have presented equations and example reports only for a simple single-currency example, with no transactions during the return period, with sector allocation analyzed over a simple, one-dimensional industry partition. Before we conclude, however, we touch briefly on several important topics: the handling of portfolio transactions, multicurrency attribution, hierarchical partitions, and some practical implementation issues.

TRANSACTIONS AND TIME VARIATION

In many portfolio analytics systems, the fundamental representation of a portfolio is a snapshot of its precise security-level composition: a list of security identifiers and par values. This is sufficient for forward-looking analysis as of a particular date, including comparison of portfolio and benchmark statistics, risk modeling, scenario analysis, and the like. However, this approach cannot support a proper analysis of holding-period returns. It cannot even calculate the correct return for the portfolio, and certainly cannot properly credit the role played by intramonth transactions in timing shifts in yield curve or sector allocations.

To support portfolio attribution with intramonth transactions, a portfolio must be represented as a dynamic entity characterized by a sequence of transactions, rather than a flat listing of securities and par values. This allows the model to keep track of how a portfolio's contents and its positioning relative to the benchmark change over time.

In our new hybrid model, the entire attribution analysis is carried out on a daily time step. The positioning of the portfolio relative to the benchmark—in terms of exposures to FX, yield curves, sectors, and securities—is re-evaluated as of the start of each trading day, and the outperformance for that day is calculated accordingly. A linking algorithm is used to calculate the various return components over the entire holding period based on the daily results.[5]

When the active position of the portfolio is modified significantly in the middle of the review period, it becomes much more difficult to present the analysis of the sources of return. For example, assume that a portfolio is long-duration by 1 year for the first half of the month and then short-duration by 1 year for the second half. If yields rally by 10 bp in the first half of the month and then rise 10 bp in the second half, the successful yield curve timing trade produces 20 bp of outperformance. Our summary of outperformance indicates this 20 bp of yield curve return correctly, but the analysis of the sources of yield curve returns seeks to explain it in terms of the month-to-date yield change, which is zero. In cases like this, where intramonth transactions are used to impose substantive shifts in the portfolio's exposures, a manager might gain additional insight into the portfolio's performance by dividing the return period into two or more subperiods corresponding to significant trade dates.

MULTICURRENCY PORTFOLIOS, FX RETURNS, AND HEDGING

The manager of a multicurrency portfolio has to make two separate allocation decisions, and the two need not be linked. In the asset or market allocation decision, he chooses the currency denominations of the securities in the portfolio and, hence, the currency profile of the portfolio's yield curve and spread exposures. A separate decision concerns the currency allocation of the portfolio—to which exchange rates the portfolio will be most sensitive. Hedging transactions of various kinds—futures, forwards, swaps, and more—can be used to transfer FX exposures from one currency to another. In many investment institutions, these two sets of decisions are made independently, and their effects on portfolio performance should be evaluated separately.

In a landmark paper, Brian Singer and Denis Karnosky laid down a general framework for multicurrency attribution.[6] The key principle is that there are two distinct components of outperformance owing to global allocation effects: (1) a market allocation effect defined in terms of allocations to assets denominated in

---

5. The exact nature of the algorithm that should be used to link the results of a multiperiod attribution has been the subject of intense debate in the performance attribution literature. The entire Fall 2002 issue of the *Journal of Performance Measurement* was devoted to this topic. The linking algorithm presently used in our model is roughly similar to that described in Andrew S. B. Frongello, "Linking Single Period Attribution Results," *Journal of Performance Measurement,* Spring 2002.

6. Brian D. Singer, and Denis S. Karnosky, "The General Framework for Global Investment Management and Performance Attribution," *Journal of Portfolio Management,* Winter 1995.

different currencies, and (2) a currency allocation effect defined in terms of exposures to foreign exchange rates. For unhedged portfolios, these two types of allocations go hand in hand, but for hedged portfolios, they can be entirely different. Furthermore, the outperformance that is due to currency allocation should always include two components: one that is due to changes in exchange rates and one owing to the differences in short-term deposit rates in different currencies. This is intuitively clear for unhedged portfolios, but the role of hedging is a bit harder to understand. If a fund benchmarked against U.S. Treasury bill returns purchases short-term Brazilian debt on an unhedged basis, it will clearly benefit from higher yields in addition to taking on the risk of changes in the U.S. dollar–Brazilian real exchange rates. However, if the position is taken on a currency-hedged basis, then not only does the investor reduce his exposure to changes in exchange rates, but he also essentially gives up the yield advantage as well, since the cost of the hedge is proportional to the difference in deposit rates in the two currencies. As a result, the carry return that the portfolio earns over time is largely determined by the currency exposure of the portfolio, including all hedges. Allocation return should be analyzed only in terms of the return over cash that every security earns within its own currency.

In the hybrid performance attribution model, for a multicurrency portfolio, we first analyze the currency-related returns owing to the allocation differences between the portfolio and the benchmark. As seen in Figure 27-2, we report an outperformance component owing to local market allocation (to different currency denominations) and on one resulting from FX allocation (exposure to FX rates, including all hedge transactions). Then, a local market outperformance summary report shows how much outperformance was generated within each local market and, of that, how much was from the yield curve, sector allocation, security selection, and so on. A full set of reports as shown in Figures 27-3 through 27-6 is then provided to detail the sources of outperformance within each local currency market.

RETURN COMPONENTS UNIQUE TO SPECIFIC ASSET CLASSES

Some asset classes have unique characteristics that give rise to return components that do not fall neatly into the four categories sketched out in Figure 27-1. For example, for U.S. mortgage-backed securities, prepayment experience can be a major driver of performance. When appropriate, we have extended our return-splitting model to break out additional return components for specific types of securities. For mortgages, this allows us to attribute outperformance to expected prepayments and prepayment surprise. Similarly, for inflation-protected securities, we break out two additional return components for realized inflation and for changes in market-implied expectations of future inflation.

HIERARCHICAL PARTITIONS

Whenever we wish to attribute returns to an allocation scheme with more than one dimension (e.g., currency and duration or sector and quality), we have to make sure that we correctly represent the way these dimensions interact in the decision process. There are several possibilities. First, we can flatten out the partition and treat is as if it were one-dimensional. For example, a partition of four sectors by three credit qualities can be flattened out to a one-dimensional partition with twelve sector × quality cells, without giving preferential treatment to either sector or quality.

Alternatively, we can build the partition up in a hierarchical fashion. For example, the first level of the partition can be allocation to sectors, and then quality allocation is a secondary decision within each sector. In the hierarchical approach, the decisions made at any level must be viewed subject to the decisions already made at a higher level.

To illustrate what we mean by this, let us take a close look at the equation for attributing return owing to spread change. We continue with the factor-based notation of Equation (27-9), understanding that in this case the factor loadings f_i^P and f_i^B represent the contributions to spread duration in sector i for the portfolio and the benchmark, and x_i^B represents the benchmark spread change in sector i. [The portfolio spread change is not relevant to this portion of the analysis. Analogous to Equation (27-6), only benchmark spread changes are used when evaluating the outperformance owing to allocation to sectors where spreads tighten more compared to the benchmark spread. The difference between portfolio and benchmark spread change within sector i is analyzed either as the next level down in the hierarchical analysis, i.e., allocation to subsets of sector I, or as security selection.] The overall spread duration of the portfolio is simply the sum of the sector contributions, $f^P = \Sigma f_i^P$ (and similarly for the benchmark), but the overall benchmark spread change is defined as the duration-weighted spread change, given by $x^B = \Sigma_i f_i^B x_i^B / f^B$. With this in mind, the following equation shows how we can develop two very different views of the spread sector allocations and how they each impact outperformance:

$$
\begin{aligned}
\text{Outperf}_{\text{SprChangeAlloc}} &= \sum_i (f_i^P - f_i^B) x_i^B \\
&= \sum_i (f_i^P - f_i^B) x^B + \sum_i (f_i^P - f_i^B)(x_i^B - x^B) \\
&= (f^P - f^B) x^B + \sum_i \left(f_i^P - \frac{f^P}{f^B} f_i^B \right)(x_i^B - x^B) \\
&\quad + \sum_i \left(\frac{f^P}{f^B} f_i^B - f_i^B \right)(x_i^B - x^B) \\
&= (f^P - f^B) x^B - f^P \sum_i \left(\frac{f_i^P}{f^P} - \frac{f_i^B}{f^B} \right)(x_i^B - x^B).
\end{aligned}
$$

(27-10)

The first line of Equation (27-10) views the allocations to sectors as a set of independent decisions. The manager who wishes to remain neutral matches benchmark exposures to all sectors; if there is an overweight to sector i, it will be credited with a proportional contribution to outperformance if spreads tighten and to underperformance if they widen.

While this intuitive view corresponds well to the approach of some managers, there are others who prefer to explicitly incorporate an overall view on credit into their allocation process. In this case, two adjustments to the Equation (27-10) are called for. First, in the second line, we pull the overall duration difference out into a separate term that gives the exposure to overall benchmark spread change and adjust the sector-specific terms accordingly. Each sector overweight now measures the outperformance owing to the spread change in that sector being greater or less than the spread change of the benchmark as a whole. This is consistent with the similar adjustment that we showed in Equation (27-7).

However, the third and fourth lines of Equation (27-10) show an additional step, which is important in dealing with a systematic overweight or underweight to credit as a whole. Assume that the main decision made by the manager in a given month was to be long-credit overall, while remaining neutral on the sector allocation within credit. The vector of sector exposures shows that he has a proportionally long position in every sector. The analysis on the second line of Equation (27-10) shows (in addition to the main outperformance owing to the overall duration exposure) a set of secondary allocation terms assigning outperformance to each sector: positive contributions for all better-than-average index sectors and negative contributions for all worse-than-average index sectors. Although these contributions sum to zero, they are reporting performance results of a set of individual decisions that this manager did not make! If he has indicated an overall overweight to credit, then that should imply a proportional overweight to each sector. If we wish to further analyze sector composition conditioned on this overweight, we should focus on the differences between the actual portfolio allocation and the benchmark allocation scaled up to reflect this overweight. That is, we should adjust the analysis to compare the relative allocations of spread duration to sectors in the portfolio and the benchmark. This adjustment is carried out in the last two lines of Equation (27-10)[7]; a review of Figures 27-4 and 27-5 will show that we have used this analysis of relative allocations of spread duration to produce our example reports.

In a hierarchical partition, were we to further attribute outperformance within sector i to allocations to subgroups of sector i, we would use this same relative

---

7. To obtain the last line of Equation (27-10), we note that the last term on the third line is zero. This result depends on the definition of x^B as the duration-weighted average spread change.

approach. While the contributions to sector i spread duration may be different for the portfolio and the benchmark, we have already accounted for that difference at this level. At the next level down in the analysis, we compare the percentage allocations of these durations to the different subgroups in the partition.

Implementation Issues

The model described in this chapter is very demanding from the implementation viewpoint. All the securities in both the portfolio and the benchmark must be priced on each day during the review period.[8] We then compute numerous quantities that require option-adjusted calculations, which are used throughout the analysis. These include option-adjusted spread (OAS), option-adjusted duration (OAD), key-rate durations (KRDs), option-adjusted spread duration (OASD), and volatility sensitivity (vega). Option-adjusted calculations are also used to calculate and store the return splits for each day's total return for each security.

CONCLUSION

Fixed-income portfolio managers have at their disposal a wide variety of financial instruments and risk management tools to help them manage a multidimensional set of risk exposures according to their subjective views. The decisions on how to position the portfolio with respect to interest rates, foreign exchange, volatility, sector allocations, and specific issuers can be made independently by different groups of people. In such a setting, performance attribution methods that are limited to simple partitioning of the portfolio by market value are woefully inadequate.

   If our key concern is to express outperformance in terms of exposures to common market risks, why not link the attribution model directly to the risk model? Using the approach of Equation (27-9), we could have built an attribution model that calculates a component of outperformance corresponding exactly to each risk factor in our global risk model. However, we believe that our hybrid model is better because of the additional flexibility it offers, compared to the fixed set of risk factors that is required by the risk model. First, different investors view their allocations differently, and one of the most important aspects of an attribution analysis is that it matches the decision process as closely as possible. Second, a manager may change the way he views sector allocations from month to month,

---

   8. Interpolation techniques can be used to fill in missing prices for illiquid securities. However, this can reduce the accuracy of the attribution. It is most important for all securities to be accurately priced as of the beginning and end of the review period, as well as on significant transaction dates.

according to market conditions. In one month, the most important factor in explaining credit performance might be the allocation to the automotive sector; in another, it might be the allocation to tobacco. Both of these effects would be beneath the level of detail in our risk model, which would view these industry groups as subsets of consumer cyclicals and consumer noncyclicals, respectively.

The hybrid performance attribution model analyzes the returns of the portfolio and the benchmark each day and explains them in terms of sensitivities to common factors: foreign exchange rates, interest rates, volatility, and spreads. The spread component is broken down further along a flexibly defined hierarchical partition that represents the sector allocation decisions of the portfolio manager. This partition of spread returns is used to distinguish between outperformance owing to sector allocation and security selection. To correctly reflect the impact of transactions, the analysis is repeated for each day in the review period after adjusting all risk sensitivities to reflect the day's trades and market movements; outperformance in each category is compounded up to the full period, using a specially designed linking algorithm. The result is a model that is both flexible enough to express the strategic decisions of most managers and precise enough to report the performance implications of every decision accurately.

PORTFOLIO AND INDEX ANALYTICS

The tools of the trade in the bond industry are based on complex mathematics. Modern models of yield curve movements, credit risk, and stochastic volatility go far beyond the simple price-yield relationship we studied in Bond Math 101. As new mathematical models become available, investors integrate them into their management processes and work to understand and interpret their results. Yet these models do not replace managers' intuitive feel for the market, but augment it. No matter how sophisticated the arsenal of quantitative tools they have at their disposal, managers want their resulting portfolios to "make sense." By this, they mean that risk exposures and returns should tie in with their intuitive view of the market or with some simple back-of-the-envelope calculations.

A handful of simple linear relationships forms a sound basis for an intuitive view of fixed-income portfolio management. If interest rates rally, the resulting returns should be roughly duration times the yield change. (If the yield change is large enough, one might include a simple correction based on convexity.) Excess returns are proportional to spread duration times spread change. Carry returns are proportional to yield multiplied by elapsed time. Hedge ratios can be used to express any duration exposure in terms of "10-year equivalents."

While we are all aware that these relationships are only first-order approximations to the truth, they tend to work quite well most of the time. Occasionally, however, portfolio or index performance may seem to violate these simple rules. As providers of analytics for portfolios and indices, we have received many inquiries regarding paradoxical portfolio behavior. For example, an investor might wonder how it is possible that they were long-duration in a month when interest rates rallied and still underperformed the index.

Most of the topics included in this section were spurred by investor questions of this sort. Why did a particular back-of-the-envelope calculation fail to explain the behavior of the portfolio or the benchmark this month? Under what circumstances are given approximations valid? Do all of the approximations that apply to a single bond apply equally well to a portfolio or an index? When they do not, how can we modify them to obtain simple linear relationships that work better? The key to successfully applying an intuitive view of portfolio management is to understand when these simple and practical rules of thumb apply and when they break down.

Chapter 28 deals with the relationship between duration and convexity. We all know that duration is closely related to the derivative of price with respect to yield and that convexity is associated with the second derivative. As a result, it is commonly conceived that convexity is a good measure of the sensitivity of duration to changes in yield. In this chapter, we examine this relationship closely to see how these two quantities should be interpreted at the portfolio and index level.

In Chapter 29 we take a look at even more fundamental definitions of portfolio statistics. It is standard practice to publish market-weighted yields and durations for market indices. However, if both yields and durations are market weighted, then some of the simple relationships that we expect to hold between them are not necessarily true. The yield of a bond can alternatively be interpreted as the carry return it delivers over the short term or as the internal rate of return considering all of its cash flows. When we calculate the market-weighted average yield of a portfolio, can it still be interpreted in these ways? Similarly, the duration of a bond represents a sensitivity to the change in its yield. Is the market-weighted average duration of an index its sensitivity to yield change? To what yield change exactly?

In Chapter 30, we turn our attention to excess returns and address similar questions. At issue is the precise methodology to be used for calculating the excess returns of spread securities over duration-matched Treasuries. A method based on key-rate durations is put forth here as superior to a method based on the returns of duration cells of the Treasury Index. Both of these methods are compared to an intuitive linear model that includes a carry component proportional to spread level and a spread change component given by the product of spread change and spread duration. Here, too, we discuss how this approximation is best applied and understood at a portfolio level. We show that the market-weighted average spread duration of a portfolio is a sensitivity to the duration-weighted average spread change.

Another type of simple linear rule that traders and managers find immensely practical is the notion of hedge ratios. How much of asset A is needed to offset the exposure of asset B to a particular market risk? Hedge ratios may be based on analytical measures such as option-adjusted durations or on empirical analyses of historical data. In Chapter 20, for example, we discussed the merits of hedging the yield curve risk of mortgage-backed securities using either option-adjusted or empirical durations. In this section, we address several further issues related to hedging for which investors have sought guidance from empirical studies.

Chapter 31 deals with what may seem to be the most straightforward of hedging applications: currency hedging. For an investor who wishes to invest in USD-denominated securities without taking exposure to USD exchange rates, it is clear that every dollar invested must be hedged back to the base currency. This is typically done using currency forwards. However, we must recognize the limits of this simplified approach and understand that hedging can never entirely eliminate currency risk because fluctuations in local market value can change the size of the currency exposure. This risk can be limited by rebalancing the hedge more frequently—perhaps even daily—at the expense of increased transaction costs. Conversely, for a portfolio managed against a broad global benchmark on a currency-hedged basis, the need to maintain a stable currency exposure over a relatively long time frame might encourage a manager to reduce hedging costs by using longer-dated forwards. In addition to the increased currency exposure that comes with less frequent rebalancing, the manager must also consider the interest-rate exposure that is entailed in such hedging transactions.

One more aspect of managing a portfolio against a currency-hedged benchmark must be considered as well. Given that the benchmark hedge position is rebalanced only on a monthly basis, a large market movement can give rise to nonnegligible currency exposures, and hence currency returns, in the benchmark. The manager in such a case has a clear choice. Is the goal of his hedge position to keep the portfolio currency returns as close to zero as possible or as close to those of the benchmark as possible? In other words, is the goal to minimize the volatility of currency return or tracking error? If we maintain our view that risk is defined relative to the benchmark, then we arrive at the somewhat paradoxical conclusion: the risk-minimizing hedge position is not the one that brings the currency exposures to zero, but the one that matches the currency exposures of the benchmark.

The ability to hedge out currency risk enables managers to engage in strategies that key on the relative performance of one interest-rate market vs. another. Chapter 32 deals with a specific example of this type of strategy: how do we set up, or analyze, an exposure to USD interest rates vs. euro rates? This is not an issue just for managers of global portfolios. Many single-currency portfolios use hedged exposures to non-base-currency assets to build a diversified mix of alpha strategies. A common expression of such a strategy, for example, would be for a USD-based investor to go short the U.S. 10-year Treasury note and long the 10-year Bund hedged into USD.

Frequently, the trade is established based on roughly equal market values or roughly equal duration contributions in each of the two legs of the trade, so as to be neutral with respect to global duration. The intuition behind this is that the trade expresses a view on the spread between the interest rates in the two currencies, not on the direction of rates in general; by remaining neutral in global duration, we do not gain or lose in parallel shift in either direction. The problem with this approach is that, while interest rates in the United States and Europe have been historically positively correlated, they do not tend to move in parallel at all. Rather, a change in USD rates is likely to be accompanied by a change in euro rates that is in the same direction, but smaller in size. This indicates that if the goal is to create an exposure to spread change that is not directionally sensitive to overall rate changes, it would be better to size the euro leg of the trade such that its duration exposure is roughly half that of the USD exposure, not equal to it.

The final three chapters in this section deal with the sensitivities of credit securities to three types of market events: changes in Treasury yields, changes in credit spreads, and equity returns.

Chapter 33 addresses the interest-rate exposure of credit securities, and particularly that of high yield bonds. For most high yield managers, duration plays a minor role in the management process. Bonds often trade on price, rather than at a spread over Treasuries, and the major focus of portfolio construction is issuer selection and the modeling of future defaults. However, for managers of investment-grade portfolios who include high yield as a core-plus investment, it is important to understand how the high yield investment affects the portfolio's interest-rate exposure. The reported portfolio duration typically averages in the cash-flow duration of the high yield portion on a market-weighted basis; this can result in an overstatement of the portfolio's true exposure to rate changes.

Consider, for example, an investment-grade benchmark with a duration of 4.5 years, and a portfolio invested 80% in investment-grade and 20% in high yield, with a duration of 5.0 years within each segment. If we choose to ignore the duration of high yield, the portfolio's duration is 4.0; if we include it fully, the portfolio duration is 5.0. This creates a huge uncertainty regarding the true yield curve positioning of the portfolio; by varying the amount of high yield duration that we take into account from 0 to 100%, we change our measure of yield curve exposure from short half a year to long half a year. In Chapter 33, we investigate the correct hedge ratios to use in this situation, based on evidence from both our risk model and empirical studies; we analyze the dependence of these empirical durations on credit quality and spread.

In the investment-grade credit arena, the primary focus is on changes in spreads, on either an industrywide or issuer-specific basis. To measure exposures to such spread changes, managers often look at portfolio and benchmark contributions to spread duration, which measure sensitivities to parallel shifts in spreads across an industry group. In Chapter 34, we present an alternative approach to measuring spread exposure, based on the idea of relative spread change as opposed to parallel shifts in spread across all spread levels. That is, if there is a systematic widening of credit spreads and a bond whose spread was 100 widens to 110, we would expect a spread of 200 to widen by the same 10% to 220, rather than a parallel shift to 210. Exposures to this sort of market change can be measured using contributions to duration times spread (DTS), which is shown to be an excellent predictor of excess return volatility, superior to spread duration.

Another view of credit securities sees them as a blend of fixed income and equity. To what extent can a corporate bond be hedged, or replicated, by combining a Treasury bond with a position in the issuer's equity? How should we set the hedge ratio that determines how much equity to buy in such a scheme? Two very different approaches can be taken to constructing debt-to-equity hedge ratios: an empirical approach based on historical data or a theoretical approach based on modeling the financial structure of the issuer, as first proposed by Merton.[1] In Chapter 35, we investigate the effectiveness of hedging debt exposures using equity positions, employing both empirical and structural models. One of the key results of this empirical study is that there is a systematic difference between the behavior of corporate bonds and that of equities, and the hedge can therefore be improved by including an exposure to the corporate bond market as a whole.

---

1. R. Merton, "On the Pricing of Corporate Debt: The Risk Structure of Interest Rates," *Journal of Finance*, May 1974; *Continuous-Time Finance*, Blackwell, 1990.

28. Insights on Duration and Convexity

. . . .

The extreme volatility of bond markets in the late 1990s has led to heightened awareness of the significance of sound risk management practices for bond portfolios. One important aspect of bond portfolio risk management is monitoring duration exposure and understanding how it is affected by shifts in important market parameters such as yield. Duration and convexity pertain to relative price changes (price returns), not absolute price changes, which complicates their relationship. This short chapter is designed to elucidate some of these complexities and describe the relationship between convexity and the sensitivity of duration to changes in yield. We focus on these relationships as they apply to bullet securities, so this discussion is more relevant to the corporate market than to mortgages.

CONVEXITY AND THE SENSITIVITY OF DURATION TO YIELD

Consider the standard two-term approximation for expressing changes in bond value as a function of yield:

$$P(y + \Delta_y) - P(y) \approx P'(y)\Delta_y + (1/2) P''(y)\Delta_y^2, \tag{28-1}$$

where $P(y)$ is the bond value expressed as a function of yield and Δ_y is the change in bond yield. Equation (28-1) expresses the change in bond value as a function of the change in bond yield. Portfolio managers in bond markets generally find it more useful to express bond performance in terms of returns rather than profit and loss. By dividing both sides of Equation (28-1) by price, we can re-express Equation (28-1) in terms of return,

$$\frac{P(y + \Delta_y) - P(y)}{P(y)} \approx \frac{1}{P(y)} P'(y)\Delta_y + (1/2) \frac{1}{P(y)} P''(y)\Delta_y^2, \tag{28-2}$$

Based on research first published by Lehman Brothers in 2000.

which yields the following relationship:

$$\text{Return} \approx -\text{Duration } \Delta_y + (1/2) \text{ Convexity } \Delta_y^2, \qquad (28\text{-}3a)$$

with the equations[1]

$$\text{Duration} = -\frac{1}{P(y)} P'(y), \qquad (28\text{-}3b)$$

$$\text{Convexity} = \frac{1}{P(y)} P''(y). \qquad (28\text{-}3c)$$

In Equation (28-3a) duration and convexity are in positions parallel to $P'(y)$ and $P''(y)$ in Equation (28-1). Just as $P''(y)$ is the sensitivity of $P'(y)$ to changes in bond yield, it is tempting to think that convexity is the sensitivity of duration to changes in bond yield. However, the latter turns out to be quite different. As is shown in the following, the actual equation is

$$D'(y) = D^2 - C, \qquad (28\text{-}4)$$

where D is duration and C is convexity. To see the magnitude of the potential discrepancies, consider the current 30-year on-the-run Treasury. As of the close of trading on April 6, 2000, its duration was 13.644 and its convexity was 288. The true sensitivity of duration to yield changes was $(13.64)^2 - 288 = -102$, which is strikingly different from -288, the result obtained if one ignores the duration term in Equation (28-4). A 100 bp increase in bond yield reduces duration by approximately 1.02, not 2.88.

Given the parallel structure of Equations (28-1) and (28-3a), why is convexity not the sensitivity of duration to yield changes? The answer comes from the fact that Equation (28-1) is written in terms of bond *values,* whereas the duration and convexity approximation is written in terms of bond *returns.* Duration is the sensitivity of price *return* to changes in yield. A comparison of Equations (28-1) and (28-2) shows that expressing performance in terms of returns rather than values causes the duration equation to be $1/P(y)$ times $-P'(y)$ rather than $-P'(y)$ alone. The magnitude of $1/P(y)$ is increasing in yield whereas the magnitude of $P'(y)$ is decreasing in yield. Without further analysis, it is not clear whether duration should increase or decrease as a result of an increase in bond yield.

1. Throughout, duration refers to modified duration. The return in Equation (28-3) is the instantaneous return owing to the change in yield. Because this equation is the instantaneous return, the time return is zero.

The extra $1/P(y)$ in the duration equation requires use of the product rule to determine the derivative of duration with respect to yield:

$$D'(y) = \frac{1}{P(y)^2}(P'(y))^2 - \frac{1}{P(y)}P''(y). \tag{28-5}$$

The second term on the right-hand side of the Equation (28-5) is convexity. The first term on that side arises from the fact that $1/P(y)$ is increasing in yield, and it is equivalent to D^2. As described earlier, the two effects work in opposite directions, causing them to enter into the $D'(y)$ equation with opposite signs. Despite the fact that yield changes push $1/P(y)$ and $P'(y)$ in opposite directions, it can be shown that duration for bullet bonds is always decreasing in yield (see the appendix).[2]

While convexity is not the sensitivity of duration to changes in yield, it is the case that dollar convexity is the magnitude of the sensitivity of dollar duration to bond yield. Dollar duration is bond value times duration, which reduces to $-P'(y)$. Dollar convexity is bond value times convexity, which reduces to $P''(y)$.

Figure 28-1 graphs value per dollar par value for a 30-year, 6% coupon bond as a function of its yield. This graph has the familiar downward sloping, convex shape. The slope of this curve is the change in bond value per unit change in yield $P'(y)$, not return per unit change in yield. The convex shape of the graph of price as a function of yield implies that the magnitude of $-P'(y)$ is decreasing in yield. But it does not directly imply anything about duration—the sensitivity of return to increases in yield.

By plotting $-P'(y)$ and duration on the same graph, Figure 28-2 brings the distinction between $-P'(y)$ and duration into sharper focus. The figure graphs $-P'(y)$, the slope of the bond value curve, against the right-hand axis and the duration of the same 30-year, 6% bond against the left-hand axis.[3]

Note that the duration graph is much closer to linear than the one for $-P'(y)$. The flatness of the duration graph relative to the $-P'(y)$ graph is a general property. Duration multiplies $-P'(y)$ by $1/P(y)$. Since the bond value function $P(y)$ is convex, the magnitude of $P'(y)$ is decreasing in bond yield. However, $P(y)$ is also decreasing in bond yield. Thus for low yields, the magnitude of $P'(y)$ is large, but $P(y)$ is also large, causing duration to be moderate. On the other hand, when yields are high, the magnitude of $P'(y)$ is small, but $P(y)$ is also small, once again causing duration to be moderate. Thus, changes in duration per unit change in

2. While Equations (28-3a,b,c) and (28-4) hold for nonbullets, $D^2 - C$ does not have to be negative for callable bonds or mortgages.

3. For small yield changes, the duration graph can be linearly rescaled to provide the return graph per unit yield change for small changes in bond yield.

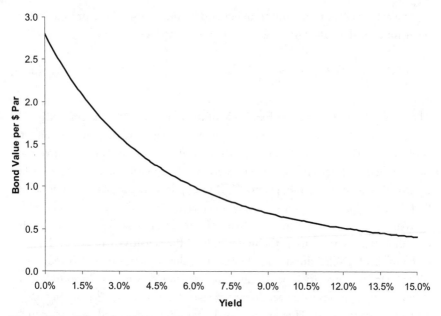

Figure 28-1. Value of a 30-Year, 6% Coupon Bond as a Function of Yield

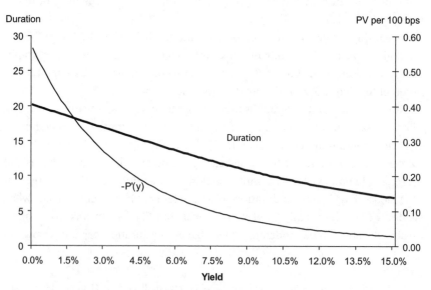

Figure 28-2. Duration vs. Change in Price per Change in Yield
30-Year, 6% Bond

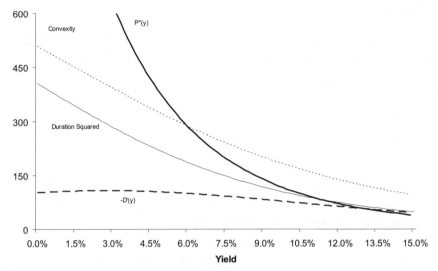

Figure 28-3. Sensitivity of Duration to Yield
30-Year, 6% Bond

yield are much less extreme than changes in $-P'(y)$ per unit change in yield, as can be seen in Figure 28-3.

$P''(y)$ is the slope of the $P'(y)$ graph. Of the various lines plotted in Figure 28-3, $P''(y)$ has, by far, the most variability. For example, when the bond yield is 3%, $P''(y)$ is 632. This drops to 71 for a yield of 12%. The dashed line in the figure is convexity. Note that convexity is more moderate and flatter than the $P''(y)$ curve, the reason being the same as the reason that the graph of duration is more moderate than the graph of $-P'(y)$. Convexity is $P''(y)$ multiplied by $1/P(y)$, and both $P''(y)$ and $P(y)$ are large when bond yields are low and low when bond yields are high.

From Figure 28-3, we also see that, while the variability in convexity may be much more moderate than the variability in $P''(y)$, it is still quite large relative to the variability in $-D'(y)$, the magnitude of the slope of the duration curve. Figure 28-3 demonstrates the importance of using the correct equation for the sensitivity of duration to yield curve changes: $D^2 - C$. For a long bond, such as the 30-year bond graphed in the figure, both D^2 and C are very large numbers. Each has a magnitude several times larger than $-D'(y)$. Using $-C$ alone leads to large-magnitude errors in one's assessment of the sensitivity of duration to bond yield.

EXAMPLE

Consider the $6\frac{1}{8}$%, August 2029 U.S. Treasury that had the following statistics at the close of trading on April 6, 2000:

Full Price:	102.844
Yield:	5.919%
Modified Duration:	13.644
Convexity:	288.4

Consider an increase in bond yields of 25 bp. The duration-convexity equation approximates the return on the bond owing to this yield shift to be $-(13.644)(0.0025) + (1/2)(288.4)(0.0025)^2 = -0.0332$ or -3.32%.

Most risk managers prefer to renormalize yield and return units so that 1.00 denotes a 1% return, rather than a 100% return. In this case, the 25-bp increase would be denoted 0.25, rather than 0.0025. With these units, the convexity number must be divided by 100 and enter the duration/convexity approximation as 2.884.[4] For these units, the duration/convexity return approximation is written as follows: $-(13.644)(0.25) + (1/2)(2.884)(0.25)^2 = -3.32$, which corresponds to a bond return of -3.32%. In general, these units are easier to work with and provide the motivation behind a convention of reporting convexity in hundreds.

Alternatively, we can assume a 25-bp increase in bond yields. With this shifted Treasury curve, the new bond price is 99.397, implying that a 25-bp increase in yield would lead to a -3.35% bond return: $(99.397 - 102.844)/102.844 = -3.35$%, which is reasonably close to the predicted -3.32% return from the duration/convexity approximation.

---

4. Let r and y be return and yield, respectively, measured such that 1.00 represents a return or yield of 100%. The standard duration/convexity approximation is

$$r \approx -D\Delta_y + (1/2)\text{Convexity}\,(\Delta_y)^2.$$

Multiplying both sides by 100,

$$100r \approx -D(100\Delta_y) + (1/2)\text{Convexity}(100)(\Delta_y)^2$$

$$100r \approx -D(100\Delta_y) + (1/2)(\text{Convexity}/100)(100\Delta_y)^2$$

Let $R = 100r$ and $Y = 100y$. In units of R and Y, 1 corresponds to 1%, rather than 100%.

$$R \approx -D(\Delta_Y) + (1/2)(\text{Convexity}/100)(\Delta_Y)^2.$$

Note that with these units, duration is unchanged, but the original convexity number must be divided by 100.

We can apply the equation for the sensitivity of duration to yield changes, $D'(y) = D^2 - C$, to the current example, with duration of 13.644 and convexity of 288.4. Thus, $D'(y) = (13.644)^2 - 288.4 = -102.2$. The duration sensitivity equation predicts that duration will fall by 1.022 per 100-bp increase in yield.

We can check the accuracy of this prediction by re-evaluating the duration of this bond at a 25-bp increase and decrease in yields. A 25-bp increase results in a modified duration of 13.389. For a 25-bp decrease, the bond duration is 13.900. The realized change in bond duration per unit change in bond yield was (13.389 – 13.900)/(0.5%) = –102.2, an exact match to the number predicted by the term $D^2 - C$.

CONCLUSION

Duration and convexity are among the most important tools available to managers of bond portfolios. This chapter examined some of their intricacies. Duration is the sensitivity of return, not price, to yield shift. For this reason, duration sensitivity to yield shift is not given by convexity but comes rather from the expression provided in Equation (28-4). Dollar convexity, on the other hand, is the sensitivity of dollar duration to a shift in yield.

APPENDIX

This appendix establishes that duration is strictly decreasing in yield for bullet bonds. From Equation (28-4) , the sensitivity of duration to yield change is

$$D'(y) = D^2 - C. \tag{A1}$$

Let

$$w_i = \frac{1}{P} \frac{\text{Bond cashflow at time } t_i}{(1 + (y/2))^{2t_i}},$$

where w_i is the proportion of bond value coming from the ith cash flow.

From the definitions of modified duration and convexity for bullets,

$$D = \frac{1}{(1 + (y/2))} \sum_i w_i t_i, \tag{A2}$$

$$C = \frac{1}{(1 + (y/2))^2} \sum_i w_i (t_i^2 + t_i) = \frac{1}{(1 + (y/2))^2} \sum_i w_i t_i^2 + \frac{1}{(1 + (y/2))} D. \tag{A3}$$

Since the weights w_i are all nonnegative and sum to one, Jensen's inequality implies

$$\sum_i w_i t_i^2 \geq \left(\sum_i w_i t_i \right)^2.$$

Therefore, from Equation (A2),

$$\frac{1}{(1 + (y/2))^2} \sum_i w_i t_i^2 \geq D^2.$$

Combining this result with Equations (A1) and (A3) yields

$$D'(y) = D^2 - C \leq - \frac{1}{(1 + (y/2))} D < 0.$$

For bullet bonds, since $D'(y)$ is always negative, duration is strictly decreasing in yield.

29. Portfolio Yields and Durations

....

Many investors regularly monitor the average yield of their portfolios. For short-term investors, yield might be used to project horizon expected return under an "unchanged yield" assumption; for longer-horizon investors, it measures portfolio value on a held-to-maturity basis. Investors often expect the yields of their portfolios to behave just like the yields of individual bonds. Yet, there is more than one valid way to define the yield of a portfolio, and it may be that different approaches should be used in different applications.

Typically, the yield of a portfolio or an index is calculated as a market-value-weighted average of the yields of individual securities. Can a portfolio yield computed in this way be used both to project the carry return of the portfolio and to approximate its internal rate of return? Similarly, it is conventional to report the market-weighted average duration of a portfolio. If this duration is to be viewed as a sensitivity to yield change, how exactly should we interpret it—as a sensitivity to a change in what portfolio yield?

This chapter explores the properties of various measures of portfolio yield and duration. In particular, we examine market-weighted averages of security durations, market-weighted averages of security yields, and dollar-duration-weighted averages of security yields and their relation to portfolio internal rate of return. We show that:

- The market-weighted average of security yields provides the expected return of a portfolio over the coming period under the assumption of no change in security yields.
- The market-weighted average of security durations is the sensitivity of portfolio return to changes in the dollar-duration-weighted average of security yield changes.

Based on research first published by Lehman Brothers in 2000.

- The dollar-duration-weighted average of security yields provides a first-order approximation to portfolio internal rate of return.

- This approximation holds with the greatest precision when intraportfolio yield variations and security convexities are small.

Intraportfolio yield variations are likely to be large whenever either: (1) the yield curve is steeply sloped, generating large yield variations across maturities; or (2) credit spreads are wide. We provide a second-order approximation for portfolio internal rate of return based on the dollar-duration-weighted average of security yields that is appropriate in these situations or for portfolios with extreme convexity securities.

The ability to approximate internal rate of return as a dollar-duration-weighted average of the yields of component cash flows can also be used to interpret the meaning of internal rate of return for securities and portfolios generating interim cash flows.

The market-weighted average of security yields will be closest to the portfolio's internal rate of return in situations where rolldown returns are trivial. Generally, this occurs when the yield curve and term structure of spreads are flat and/or the portfolio's cash-flow profile is heavily back loaded. However, the magnitude of credit spreads does not affect the closeness of the market-weighted average of security yields to the portfolio's internal rate of return, provided that the term structure of these spreads is flat.

PORTFOLIO YIELD TO MATURITY AND TIME RETURN

To maintain focus on the essential issues, the analysis considers a zero volatility environment in which all changes in bond yields are perfectly predictable.[1] The current yield curve can have any shape and can change over time but all such changes are completely deterministic.

Notation

The current market values of the portfolio and the portfolio's holdings of the ith bond are, respectively, V_{port} and V_i. Let $w_i = V_i / V_{\text{port}}$, where w_i is the portfolio weight of bond i. y_i is the continuously compounded yield to maturity of bond i at time t, and is the internal rate of return for bond i defined from the following equation:

---

1. The appendix treats stochastic bond yields.

$$V_i = \sum_j e^{-y_i[t_j-t]} c_{t_j}^i, \tag{29-1}$$

where $c_{t_j}^i$ is the cash flow that arrives at time t_j from the portfolio's holdings in security i and $t_j - t$ is the number of years until date t_j. Similarly, y_{IRR} is the internal rate of return of the portfolio's cash flows at time t defined from

$$V_{port} = \sum_j e^{-y_{IRR}[t_j-t]} c_{t_j}^{port}, \tag{29-2}$$

where $c_{t_j}^{port}$ is the portfolio cash flow that arrives at time t_j. In addition, define

$$D_{IRR} = \frac{-1}{V_{port}} \frac{dV_{port}}{dy_{IRR}},$$

where D_{IRR} is the sensitivity of the portfolio's return to changes in its internal rate of return.

Expected Returns and Yields

The yield to maturity of an individual security is often used as a gauge of the expected return from holding the security to maturity. For a risk-free zero coupon bullet bond, yield to maturity does indeed provide the exact return from holding the security to maturity. For coupon-paying bonds, the issue becomes more complicated. One approach is to view the coupon-paying bond as a portfolio of zero coupon bonds, where each coupon and principal payment is treated as a separate entity. In this case the original bond's yield to maturity can be viewed as an amalgamation of the expected holding period returns of the zero coupon bonds in this equivalent portfolio. In general, a bond's yield to maturity is a nonlinear combination of the yields of its component cash flows. However, continuing to view a bond as an equivalent portfolio of zero coupon bonds, we can interpret yield to maturity as being, to a first-order approximation, the dollar-duration-weighted average of the yields of the bond's component cash flows.

Alternatively, one can view yield to maturity as providing expected return from holding the bond to maturity subject to the assumption that one will be able to reinvest interim coupons at the bond's current yield to maturity. However, this assumption is typically untenable, particularly when the yield curve exhibits substantial volatility or slope.

The interpretation of internal rate of return becomes especially troublesome for portfolios, which generally contain bonds that mature at different times. By design, the cash-flow stream generated by a bond portfolio (coupon and principal repayments) is often relatively smooth over time. Thus the typical time profile of a portfolio's cash flows is very different from the time profile of a zero coupon bond's cash flow. These differences exacerbate the problems that the interim cash flows create for the interpretation of portfolio internal rate of return as a measure of the expected return for holding a portfolio until its "maturity."

Moreover, a portfolio may contain bonds with a wide variety of credit qualities. Unless each bond is replaced at maturity with a bond that trades at a similar credit spread, portfolio internal rate of return may be dramatically affected by the maturity schedule of the bonds in the portfolio. Similarly, unless the yield curve is flat, a portfolio's internal rate of return will be affected by any changes in the overall time profile of its cash flows caused by the manager's policy of reinvesting coupon and principal payments received. These issues diminish the usefulness of interpreting portfolio internal rate of return as an expected return for holding a portfolio's assets until maturity. Instead the ability to approximate a portfolio's internal rate of return by the dollar-duration-weighted average of the yields of its component bonds is particularly relevant for imparting meaning to yield to maturity in a portfolio context.

Portfolio internal rate of return can be used to calculate expected returns over short horizons. The portfolio's expected return over the next instant in time is given by

$$y_{IRR} - D_{IRR} dy_{IRR} \tag{29-3}$$

Recall that D_{IRR} is the sensitivity of the portfolio's return to changes in its internal rate of return, and dy_{IRR} is the (expected) change in its internal rate of return.[2] The expected portfolio return is the sum of two components: the static portfolio yield (IRR) plus the return from the expected capital gain or loss in portfolio value owing to the change in the portfolio's IRR yield.

However, Equation (29-3) is rarely used in practice. Generally, it is simpler to assess a portfolio's expected return over short horizons using an equation based on the market-weighted average of the yields of the portfolio's component securities. Here the analysis starts from the following expression for the expected return of an individual bond (bond i) over the next instant in time:

$$y_i - D_i dy_i, \tag{29-4}$$

where D_i is the duration of bond i $(-1/V_i)(dV_i/dy_i)$. Since a portfolio's expected return is the market-weighted average of the expected returns of its component securities, its expected return over the next instant can also be expressed as

---

2. Since we are working in an environment in which all yield changes are known in advance, dy_{IRR} is also equal to the realized yield change. All yields are continuously compounded.

$$\sum_i w_i y_i - \sum_i w_i D_i dy_i. \tag{29-5}$$

The portfolio's expected return is equal to the sum of the market-weighted averages of: (1) the individual security yields, and (2) the expected capital gain or loss return of the individual securities.

At this point, we introduce the following notation:

Let

$$y_{mw} = \sum_i w_i y_i,$$

where y_{mw} is the market-weighted average of the individual security yields; let

$$D_{mw} = \sum_i w_i D_i,$$

where D_{mw} is the market-weighted average of the individual security durations; and let

$$dy_{\$dur} = \frac{\sum_i w_i D_i dy_i}{D_{mw}},$$

where $dy_{\$dur}$ is the dollar-duration-weighted average of the expected yield changes of the portfolio's component securities.

Equation (29-5) can be re-expressed as follows: The portfolio's instantaneous expected return at time t is[3]

$$y_{mw} - D_{mw} \, dy_{\$dur}. \tag{29-6}$$

From Equation (29-6) the portfolio's expected return can alternatively be expressed as the sum of: (1) the market-weighted average of the individual security yields and (2) the (market-weighted) portfolio duration multiplied by the dollar-duration-weighted average of the expected individual security yield changes.

If we make the simplifying assumption that the yields of all bonds in the portfolio will remain unchanged over the coming month, then Equation (29-6) shows that the instantaneous return per unit time is given by the market-weighted yield.

---

3. If we consider discrete rather than infinitesimal yield changes, then the second-order approximation of the expected portfolio return is $y_{mw} - D_{mw} \Delta y_{\$dur} + (1/2) C_{mw} (\Delta y)^2_{\$dur}$, where $\Delta y_{\$dur}$ is the expected change in the dollar-duration-weighted average of the yields of the portfolio's component securities; $(\Delta y)^2_{\$dur}$ is the dollar-duration-weighted average of the squared of the expected yield changes of the portfolio's component securities; and C_{mw} is the market-weighted average of the convexities of the portfolio's component securities.

This is not true for the IRR; even if we assume that all security yields remain unchanged, the portfolio IRR can change as portfolio composition changes, owing to coupon payments and maturities.

More surprisingly, Equation (29-6) shows that D_{mw}, the market-weighted average of security durations, is the sensitivity of portfolio return to changes in the dollar-duration-weighted average of individual bond yields.[4]

PORTFOLIO INTERNAL RATE OF RETURN AND THE DOLLAR-DURATION-WEIGHTED AVERAGE OF ASSET YIELDS

We have just seen that D_{IRR} is the sensitivity of portfolio return to shifts in the portfolio's internal rate of return, whereas the market-weighted average of security durations D_{mw} is the sensitivity of portfolio return to changes in the dollar-duration-weighted average of individual bond yields. In general, these two sensitivities are not identical.

In this section, we show that, to a first-order approximation, the dollar-duration-weighted average of security yields is the same as the portfolio's internal rate of return. Thus while D_{mw} and D_{IRR} are generally not identical, to a first-order approximation they are sensitivities to the same variable. In situations where this first-order approximation holds with greatest precision, they have very similar values.

Let $V_i(y)$ be the present value of the cash flows that the portfolio receives from its investment in security i discounted at yield y. Recall that y_i is the observed yield to maturity of bond i; $V_i(y_i)$ is the current market value of the portfolio's holdings in security i.

Let

$$y_{\$dur} = \frac{\sum_i w_i D_i y_i}{D_{mw}},$$

where $y_{\$dur}$ is the dollar-duration-weighted average of the yields of the portfolio's component securities.

Consider a portfolio of n securities. By the definition of portfolio yield to maturity, the value y_{IRR} that solves the equation

$$V_{port}(y_{IRR}) = V_1(y_{IRR}) + V_2(y_{IRR}) + \ldots + V_n(y_{IRR}) \tag{29-7}$$

---

4. In this zero volatility environment, Equation (29-6) provides the portfolio's realized instantaneous return, as well as its expected return, and $dy_{\$dur}$ is both the expected and realized change in the dollar-duration-weighted average of security yields.

is the portfolio's internal rate of return. Note that $V_i(y_{IRR})$ is not equal to the value of the portfolio's holdings of bond i. Instead, it is equal to the present value of the cash flows from the portfolio's investment in the ith bond discounted at yield y_{IRR}.

From the standard first-order duration approximation,

$$\frac{V_i(y_{IRR}) - V_i(y_i)}{V_i(y_i)} \approx -D_i(y_{IRR} - y_i)$$

or

$$V_i(y_{IRR}) \approx V_i(y_i) - V_i(y_i)D_i(y_{IRR} - y_i), \qquad (29\text{-}8)$$

where $V_i(y_i)$ is simply V_i, the current market value of the portfolio's holdings in bond i.

From Equations (29-7) and (29-8),

$$V_{port}(y_{IRR}) \approx [V_1 - V_1 D_1(y_{IRR} - y_1)] + \ldots + [V_n - V_n D_n(y_{IRR} - y_n)]$$

or

$$V_{port}(y_{IRR}) \approx [V_1 + V_2 + \ldots + V_n] - [V_1 D_1(y_{IRR} - y_1)$$
$$+ \ldots + V_n D_n(y_{IRR} - y_n)]. \qquad (29\text{-}9)$$

Note that $V_{port}(y_{IRR}) = [V_1 + V_2 + \ldots + V_n]$; the market value of a portfolio equals the sum of the market values of its component assets. Substituting this into Equation (29-9) gives

$$V_1 D_1(y_{IRR} - y_1) + V_2 D_2(y_{IRR} - y_2) + \ldots + V_n D_n(y_{IRR} - y_n) \approx 0. \qquad (29\text{-}10)$$

In Equation (29-10), we assume that the analyst knows all prices, durations, and yields for individual securities, and the only unknown is the portfolio yield. Solving for y_{IRR}, we get

$$y_{IRR} \approx \frac{V_1 D_1 y_1 + V_2 D_2 y_2 + \ldots + V_n D_n y_n}{V_1 D_1 + V_2 D_2 + \ldots + V_n D_n} = y_{\$dur}. \qquad (29\text{-}11)$$

From Equation (29-11), the dollar-duration-weighted average of bond yields provides the first-order approximation of the portfolio's internal rate of return. To first order, D_{mw} and D_{IRR} provide return sensitivities to the same entity.

THE ACCURACY OF THE FIRST-ORDER APPROXIMATION OF PORTFOLIO IRR

Equation (29-11) is based on the first-order duration approximation of bond return. It holds with the greatest precision in situations where the first-order duration approximation is most accurate. For the current application these conditions are: (1) intraportfolio variations in yield are small ($y_{IRR} - y_i$ is small for all i) and (2) security convexities are close to zero.

First we consider the effect of intraportfolio yield variations on the tightness of the match between the dollar-duration-weighted average of security yields and the portfolio internal rate of return. Figure 29-1 considers two portfolios. The first consists of all bullet bonds in the Lehman Gov/Corp Index, and the second has 50% of its holdings in the bullet bonds in the Lehman Gov/Corp Index with the remaining 50% in the bullet bonds in the Lehman High Yield Index. The mixed gov/corp, high yield portfolio can be expected to have significantly more intraportfolio yield variation than the gov/corp-only portfolio. The figure presents results for August 31, 1993, and September 30, 1998, dates on which intraportfolio yield variation was generally especially high. The Treasury curve was particularly steep in August 1993, generating substantial yield differentials between long- and short-maturity assets, and the spread sector crash in early fall of 1998 led to wide yield differentials across credit qualities in late September 1998.

The dollar-duration-weighted average and portfolio internal rate of return match quite closely for the Gov/Corp Index at each date. The match is substantially worse for the mixed gov/corp, high yield portfolio. The market-weighted average of portfolio yields proved to be a very poor indicator of portfolio internal rate of return in all cases presented in the figure.

The second-order duration/convexity approximation,

$$V_i(y_{IRR}) \approx V_i(y_i) - V_i(y_i)D_i(y_{IRR} - y_i) + (1/2)V_i(y_i)C_i(y_{IRR} - y_i)^2,$$

can be used to show that to a second-order approximation,[5]

$$y_{IRR} \approx y_{\$dur} + \frac{1}{2} \sum_i \frac{w_i C_i}{D_{mw}} (y_{IRR} - y_i)^2. \tag{29-12}$$

---

5. It can be shown that when one replaces Equation (29-8) with a second-order duration/convexity approximation, Equation 29-10 becomes

$$V_1 D_1(y_{IRR} - y_1) + \ldots + V_n D_n(y_{IRR} - y_n) \approx (1/2)V_1 C_1(y_{IRR} - y_1)^2 + \ldots$$
$$+ (1/2)V_n C_n(y_{IRR} - y_n)^2.$$

Equation (29-12) follows immediately.

Figure 29-1. Effect of Intraportfolio Yield Variation on Dollar-Duration Yield and Portfolio IRR

Date	Portfolio	Internal Rate of Return (%)	Dollar-Duration Yield (%)	Market-Weighted Yield (%)
8/31/1993	Gov/corp bullets	5.73	5.70	5.07
	50% gov/corp, 50% high yield (bullets)	7.30	7.18	6.74
9/30/1998	Gov/corp bullets	5.23	5.22	4.97
	50% gov/corp, 50% high yield (bullets)	6.69	6.54	6.46

From Equation (29-12), the ratio of the market-weighted average of security convexities divided by the portfolio's market-weighted duration, D_{mw}, provides a measure of the extent to which the dollar-duration-weighted average of the portfolio's security yields is likely to be appreciably different from the portfolio's internal rate of return.

If all securities in the portfolio have nonnegative durations and convexities, then the fraction on the right-hand side of Equation (29-12) is nonnegative. For securities with nonnegative durations and convexities, the dollar-duration-weighted average of individual security yields is never greater than the portfolio IRR, provided terms beyond second order are trivial.

Figure 29-2 considers low- and high-convexity/duration subsets of the two portfolios considered in Figure 29-1. The former consists of maturities of 5 years or less and the latter of maturities of 25 years or more.

As indicated in Equation (29-12), the dollar-duration-weighted yields are always less than or equal to the portfolio internal rates of return in Figures 29-1 and 29-2, and the dollar-duration yields match the portfolio internal rates of return in Figure 29-2 more closely for the short-maturity portfolios than for those of long maturity. The market-weighted yields seem to do a better job approximating portfolio internal rates of return for high-convexity portfolios. Convexity poses a particular problem for the use of dollar-duration-weighted averages as approximations of portfolio IRR, but do not appear to be an important factor determining the accuracy of market-weighted yields as an approximation of portfolio IRR.

SECOND-ORDER APPROXIMATION OF PORTFOLIO IRR

While market-weighted averages worked well for the high-convexity portfolios considered in Figure 29-2, one cannot generally rely on them to be good

Figure 29-2. Effect of Portfolio Convexity on Dollar-Duration Yield and Portfolio IRR

Date	Portfolio	Maturity	Convexity/ Duration	Internal Rate of Return	Dollar-Duration Yield	Market-Weighted Yield
8/31/1993	Gov/corp bullets	Short (≤5 years)	3.50	4.38	4.37	4.21
		Long (≥25 years)	18.90	6.40	6.39	6.39
	50% gov/corp, 50% high yield (bullets)	Short (≤5 years)	3.60	6.31	6.21	5.88
		Long (≥25 years)	17.70	7.80	7.61	7.82
9/30/1998	Gov/corp bullets	Short (≤5 years)	3.60	4.66	4.66	4.65
		Long (≥25 years)	20.30	5.72	5.65	5.70
	50% gov/corp, 50% high yield (bullets)	Short (≤5 years)	3.40	6.38	6.29	6.23
		Long (≥25 years)	19.10	7.23	6.97	7.19

Figure 29-3. Accuracy of Second-Order Approximation of Portfolio Internal Rate of Return

Date	Portfolio	Maturity	Internal Rate of Return	Dollar-Duration Yield	y_{IRR}^{so}
8/31/1993	Mixed gov/corp high yield	All	7.3	7.18	7.31
		Short	6.31	6.21	6.31
		Long	7.8	7.61	7.79
9/30/1998	Mixed gov/corp high yield	All	6.69	6.54	6.69
		Short	6.38	6.29	6.39
		Long	7.23	6.97	7.22

approximations of portfolio internal rate of return. For portfolios containing high-convexity assets, the more prudent procedure is to solve explicitly for the portfolio's internal rate of return directly from its cash flows.

Failing this, Equation (29-12) provides a mechanism for generating the second-order approximation. Setting Equation (29-12) to equality creates a quadratic equation that can be solved in closed form. The solution, y_{IRR}^{so}, is the second-order approximation to portfolio IRR. Alternatively, one can approximate the solution by replacing y_{IRR} with $y_{\$dur}$ on the right-hand side of Equation (29-12). Figure 29-3 uses this shortcut to approximate portfolio IRR for the portfolios in Figures 29-1 and 29-2, in which dollar-duration-weighted yields differed noticeably from portfolio IRR. The second-order approximations shown in Figure 29-3 match the portfolio internal rates of return quite well.

PORTFOLIO INTERNAL RATE OF RETURN AND THE MARKET-WEIGHTED AVERAGE OF SECURITY YIELDS

We can use Equations (29-3) and (29-6) to understand the relationship between the market-weighted average of the yields of the portfolio's constituent securities and the portfolio's internal rate of return. Setting the right-hand sides of these two equations equal to each other, we obtain

$$y_{mw} - y_{IRR} = D_{mw}\, dy_{\$dur} - D_{IRR}\, dy_{IRR}. \qquad (29\text{-}13)$$

Recall that $dy_{\$dur}$ and dy_{IRR} refer to the expected changes in portfolio yield per unit time. These changes tend to be greatest when the yield curve or term structure of credit spreads is highly positively or negatively sloped. Equation (29-13) suggests that the differential between portfolio internal rates of return and market-

Figure 29-4. Accuracy of Market-Weighted Yield as an Approximation to Portfolio IRR

Date	Portfolio	Maturity	Internal Rate of Return	Market-Weighted Yield	Difference (bp)
8/31/1993	Gov/corp	All	5.73	5.07	66
		Short	4.38	4.21	17
	Mixed gov/corp high yield	All	7.30	6.74	56
		Short	6.31	5.88	43
9/30/1998	Gov/corp	All	5.23	4.97	26
		Short	4.66	4.65	1
	Mixed gov/corp high yield	All	6.69	6.46	23
		Short	6.38	6.23	15

weighted yields will be greater during periods like August 1993, when the yield curve was steeply sloped, rather than September 1998, when the yield curve was relatively flat. This is confirmed in Figure 29-4. The September 1998 market-weighted yields performed much better than the August 1993 in matching their respective portfolios internal rate of return, despite the erratic nature of credit spreads in the early fall of 1998.

The expected change in portfolio yield per unit time ($dy_{\$dur}$ or dy_{IRR}) will invariably be much lower for long-maturity assets than for those of short maturity. For instance the Lehman Treasury spline for 9/30/98 showed no difference in fitted yields between 20 and 25 years. The difference between the 5-year yield and the 1-month yield from the same 9/30/98 spline was 32 bp.[6] The difference in magnitude of $dy_{\$dur}$ or dy_{IRR} for long-maturity vs. short-maturity portfolios is much greater than the magnitude of the differences in portfolio duration. Therefore, from Equation (29-13), one would expect market-weighted yields to much more closely approximate portfolio internal rates of return for very-long-maturity portfolios rather than for short-maturity portfolios. Figure 29-2 confirms this. In all cases the market-weighted yield closely approximates portfolio IRR for the long-maturity portfolios but is a very poor approximation for those of short maturity.

In July 2000, the fixed-income market was experiencing a very flat yield curve and very wide credit spreads (see Figure 29-5). The wide credit spreads imply that differences between portfolio internal rate of return and dollar-duration-weighted

---

6. For 8/31/93 the corresponding numbers for 25-year yield minus the 20-year yield was 13 bp and the 5-year yield minus the 1-month yields was 139 bp.

Figure 29-5. Dollar-Duration Yield, Market-Weighted Yield, and Portfolio IRR.
July 31, 2000

Portfolio	Maturity	Convexity/ Duration	Internal Rate of Return	Dollar-Duration Yield	Market-Weighted Yield	$y_{\text{IRR}}^{\text{so}}$
Gov/corp bullets	All	11.0	6.79	6.75	6.81	6.79
	Short (≤5 years)	3.3	6.84	6.84	6.79	6.79
	Long (≥25 years)	18.9	6.76	6.68	6.74	6.76
50% gov/corp	All	9.4	8.81	8.52	8.68	8.81
50% high yield (bullets)	Short (≤5 years)	3.3	9.11	8.92	8.72	9.12
	Long (≥25 years)	17.7	9.31	8.43	9.23	9.01

yields should be particularly large, whereas the flat yield curve implies that market-weighted averages should come relatively close to portfolio internal rates of return.

The market-weighted yields outperform dollar-duration yields in terms of their ability to approximate portfolio internal rates of return for all portfolios other those with short maturities. In fact, the market-weighted average is able to provide a better IRR approximation than the second-order approximation based on Equation (29-12) in the long-maturity, high-intraportfolio yield variation case.

PORTFOLIO DURATION

The portfolio duration,

$$D_{IRR} = \frac{-1}{V_{port}} \frac{dV_{port}}{dy_{IRR}},$$

contains a derivative with respect to shifts in the portfolio's internal rate of return, whereas individual security durations $(-1/V_i)(dV_i/dy_i)$ contain derivatives with respect to the individual security yields. Since a portfolio IRR is not a linear function of the yields of the individual securities in the portfolio, it follows that in general D_{IRR} cannot equal D_{mw}.

Modified adjusted duration measures the sensitivity of a bond's return to a parallel shift in the Treasury par curve, holding spreads and volatility parameters constant. Modified adjusted duration can be expressed as $(-1/V_{port})$ $(\partial V_{port}/\partial y_{par})$ for a portfolio and as $(-1/V_i)(\partial V_i/\partial y_{par})$ for an individual security, where dy_{par} is a unit change in the Treasury par curve.[7] In both cases the derivative is with respect to the same entity. Therefore, the modified adjusted duration of a portfolio is exactly equal to the market-weighted average of the modified adjusted durations of the portfolio's constituent securities.

As shown in Chapter 28, the sensitivity of security duration to shifts in security yield is always given by $D_i'(y_i) = D_i^2 - C_i$. In order to discuss the sensitivity of portfolio duration to changes in portfolio yield, one must identify the specific form of portfolio duration and yield under consideration. The derivative of D_{IRR} with respect to the portfolio's internal rate of return is given by the analogous equation: $D^2_{IRR} - C_{IRR}$, where C_{IRR} is the convexity calculated directly from the portfolio's cash flows. However, there is no simple equation for the derivative of D_{mw} with respect to shifts in y_{mw} unless one restricts attention to parallel shifts in

---

7. Since the dy_{par} is multidimensional, dV_i/dy_{par} and dV_{port}/dy_{par} are gradients. However, linearity is maintained.

the yield curve, where $dy_i = dy_{IRR} = dy_{mw}$. Here one can treat all of these yield differentials interchangeably and the equation $D' = D^2 - C$ holds for all forms of portfolio duration.

CONCLUSION

When comparing portfolio and benchmark yields at the start of a given month, the traditional yield measure is the market-value-weighted yield that gives a crude estimate of short-term expected returns under a simple "no-change-in-yields" scenario. Internal rate of return gives a measure of the long-term increase in portfolio wealth to be expected in a held-to-maturity context, but is problematic for portfolios with relatively smooth cash-flow profiles over time. Portfolio internal rate of return is most often used in applications like dedication, where a portfolio is purchased to match a set of liabilities. For a given liability stream, the portfolio with the highest internal rate of return also has the lowest cost.

The closeness of fit of the dollar-duration-weighted average of security yields to portfolio internal rate of return depends on security convexities and the cross-sectional variation in yield. This variation is driven by credit spreads and the distribution of constituent securities across the yield curve. On the other hand, the closeness of fit of the market-weighted average of security yields to portfolio internal rate of return is determined by the rate at which portfolio yields are expected to change over time. This effect is largely captured by the slope of the relevant parts of the yield curve and the term-structure of credit spreads.

We further show that:

- The market-weighted average of security durations is the sensitivity of portfolio return to changes in the dollar-duration-weighted average of security yield changes.

- The dollar-duration-weighted average of security yields provides a first-order approximation to portfolio internal rate of return.

We also provide a simple second-order approximation of portfolio internal rate of return based on the dollar-duration-weighted average of security yields

APPENDIX. STOCHASTIC BOND YIELDS

In this appendix we derive the analog to Equation (29-13) for the case in which there are stochastic bond yields. Actual interest-rate processes are more complicated than those considered here, and actual yields evolve stochastically over time.

Let μ_i be the expected change in the yield of bond i at time t. Similarly, let σ_i be the volatility of the yield process for bond i at time t. The portfolio's expected return over the next instant in time is given by

$$y_{IRR} - D_{IRR}\mu_{IRR} + \frac{1}{2}C_{IRR}\sigma^2_{IRR},$$ (A1)

where μ_{IRR} is the instantaneous expected change in the portfolio's internal rate of return; y_{IRR} (denoted dy_{IRR} in the section that treated zero volatility interest-rate environments); σ^2_{IRR} is the instantaneous volatility of the portfolio's internal rate of return; and

$$C_{IRR} = \frac{1}{V_{port}}\frac{d^2V_{port}}{dy^2_{IRR}}.$$

Equation (A1) replaces Equation (29-3) under stochastic yields.

Similarly, the expected return on bond i over the next instant in time is:[8]

$$y_i - D_i\mu_i + \frac{1}{2}C_i\sigma^2_i.$$ (A2)

With stochastic yields, Equation (29-5) is replaced by the following expression for the portfolio's expected return over the next instant in time:

$$\sum_i w_i y_i - \sum_i w_i D_i \mu_i + \sum_i w_i \frac{1}{2}C_i\sigma^2_i.$$ (A3)

8. More formally, let the total change in the yield of security i, dy_i, come from the diffusion $dy_i = \mu_i dt + \sigma_i dz_i$, where μ_i and σ_i may be functions of time and current and past yields. The innovation driving the shock to the ith bond, dz_i, may have arbitrary correlation with the innovations driving the yield shocks of other bonds in the portfolio. Note that the yield for each bond is modeled directly, rather than the instantaneous risk-free rate and spread. However, since μ_i and σ_i are allowed to be arbitrary functions of time and yield history, this form is completely general (except for the exclusion of jump processes). Ito's lemma implies

$$\frac{dV_i}{dt} = \frac{\partial V_i}{\partial t} + \frac{\partial V_i}{\partial y_i}\frac{\partial y_i}{\partial t} + \frac{1}{2}\frac{\partial^2 V_i}{\partial y_i^2}\sigma^2_i,$$

which results in

$$\frac{dV_i}{dt} = V_i y_i - V_i D_i\frac{\partial y_i}{\partial t} + \frac{1}{2}V_i C_i\sigma^2_i.$$

Equation (A2) follows.

Let $C_{mw} = \Sigma_i w_i C_i$, where C_{mw} is the market-weighted average of the individual security convexities. Let

$$\sigma^2_{\$cvx} = \frac{\sum_i w_i C_i \sigma_i^2}{C_{mw}}$$

be the dollar-convexity-weighted average of the squared yield volatilities of the individual securities, and

$$\mu_{\$dur} = \frac{\sum_i w_i D_i \mu_i}{D_{mw}},$$

the dollar-duration-weighted average of the expected yield changes of the portfolio's component securities.

Equation (A3) can be re-expressed as follows: the portfolio's expected return over the next instant in time is

$$y_{mw} - D_{mw}\mu_{\$dur} + \frac{1}{2}C_{mw}\sigma^2_{\$cvx}. \tag{A4}$$

Note that the market-weighted average of security durations continues to provide the sensitivity of portfolio returns to changes in the dollar-duration-weighted average of the expected changes in the yields of the portfolio's component securities. Here the convexity correction involves multiplying the market-weighted average of individual security convexities by the dollar-duration-weighted average of the volatilities of the individual security yields.

By setting Equations (A1) and (A4) equal to each other, we obtain

$$y_{mw} - y_{IRR} = [D_{mw}\mu_{\$dur} - D_{IRR}\mu_{IRR}] + \frac{1}{2}[C_{IRR}\sigma^2_{IRR} - C_{mw}\sigma^2_{\$cvx}]. \tag{A5}$$

Equation (A5) replaces Equation (29-13) in the presence of stochastic yields. Incorporating the effects of stochastic yields tends to increase the difference between the portfolio's internal rate of return and the market-weighted average yield. Owing to diversification effects, if all bonds in the portfolio do not have perfectly correlated yields, σ^2_{IRR} will be less than the dollar-duration-weighted average value of σ_i^2. All else equal, the second term on the right-hand side of Equation (A5) will tend to be positive.

30. Computing Excess Return of Spread Securities

Bond investors often gain insight and gauge the efficacy of their portfolio practices by measuring the performance of spread asset classes relative to Treasuries. This practice, which can be conducted in any currency that has both spread products and government-issued debt, requires the calculation of excess returns of spread securities over those of "equivalent" Treasury securities.

The notion of excess return has a long history. Intuitively, and initially through the simple observation of nominal return differentials, asset managers expect performance compensation for holding risky assets. For an individual security, a portfolio, or an entire asset class, excess returns offer a purer measure of this compensation than nominal returns. However, there are many different excess return calculation methodologies—the differences mainly reflecting various mechanisms for defining an equivalent Treasury position.

The simplest technique compares a spread sector bond's return to the nearest Treasury on-the-run. More precise methods require that the equivalent Treasury position match the duration of the spread security. The duration-bucket approach calculates an equivalent Treasury return for each duration neighborhood, based on the average returns on Treasuries and spread sectors, partitioned into semiannual duration cells.

A security's duration does not fully reflect its yield curve exposure, particularly for securities with embedded optionality, such as callable bonds or MBS. A more precise method is to fully characterize each security's exposure along the curve by a set of key-rate durations (KRDs). Then its return can be compared with that of an all-Treasury portfolio with the same KRD profile.

In what follows, we describe how KRDs are calculated and used to construct equivalent Treasury positions and compute excess returns. The results of the KRD-

Based on research first published by Lehman Brothers in 2000.

based method are then compared with the duration-cell technique. An intuitive approximation for excess return based on option-adjusted spread (OAS) helps compare the two methods. A detailed analysis of this approximation explains how to properly weight portfolio spreads and spread changes to allow portfolio-level quantities to be used in the excess return calculations. Finally, we discuss how to annualize periodic (e.g., monthly) excess return numbers correctly.

KEY-RATE DURATIONS AND EXCESS RETURNS

The U.S. Treasury off-the-run yield curve is modeled by fitting a smooth discount curve to the prices of U.S. Treasury securities. In addition, a term structure of volatility is fitted to a selected set of caps and swaptions. These fitted curves serve as the basis for our OAS models: a lognormal tree model for government and corporate securities and a Monte Carlo simulation model for MBS. In both models, sensitivities to changes in interest rates are measured by shocking the yield curve by a fixed amount, keeping volatility constant, and repricing each security at a constant OAS. This mechanism is used to calculate option-adjusted durations as sensitivities to a parallel shift in the Treasury par curve.

KRDs are sensitivities to the movement of specific parts of the par yield curve. We have selected six key points along the curve: 0.5, 2, 5, 10, 20, and 30 years to maturity. The movements of the par yields at these six points are assumed to capture the overall movement of the yield curve. Sensitivities of a bond to these six yields summarize its exposure to yield curve movements. To compute these sensitivities, the yield curve is perturbed by applying a change in the par yield curve around each of these points one at a time, and the bond is repriced at a constant OAS. The sum of the six KRDs is approximately equal to the option-adjusted duration. The distribution of the bond's duration among the six KRDs gives a more detailed view of how it will respond to different types of yield curve movements.

To calculate excess returns using KRDs, we proceed as follows. At the start of each month, we construct a set of six hypothetical par-coupon Treasuries corresponding exactly to the maturities of the six KRDs. Each of these bonds is priced exactly off the curve (at zero OAS). To this set, a riskless 1-month cash security is added. We can find a combination of these seven securities that matches the KRD profile and market value of any security at the beginning of the period. This combination constitutes the equivalent Treasury position to which the security's return is compared. At the end of the period (e.g., month), each of the hypothetical securities is repriced at zero OAS off the end-of-month Treasury curve, and its total return for the month is calculated. An excess return for the security is then calculated as the difference between its total return and that of the equivalent Treasury position.

**Figure 30-1. Excess Returns for Selected Components of the U.S.
Aggregate Index by KRD-Based and Duration Cell Methods**
September 2000

	Excess Returns (%)	
Index	KRD-Based	Duration-Cell-Based
Agency	0.54	0.48
Intermediate	0.42	0.35
Long	1.15	1.14
Callable	0.36	0.26
Credit	0.25	0.19
Intermediate	0.26	0.20
Long	0.23	0.17
Callable	0.12	0.02
Government/credit	0.18	0.15
Long utilities	−0.08	−0.22
MBS	0.44	0.12

Figure 30-1 compares the excess returns computed for various Lehman indices in September 2000 using the KRD-based and the duration-cell methods. The two models produce similar results for the Gov/Credit Index, but show greater differences for sectors with more callable bonds. The largest discrepancy between the two is for the MBS Index, for which the KRD-based excess return is 44 bp, as opposed to the 12 bp produced by the duration-cell approach.

Figure 30-2 compares historical excess returns obtained by the two models for the U.S. Credit Index over a 9-month period. For the most part, the two models produce similar results. In 3 months out of 9, however, the differences between the models were 9 bp or greater.

APPROXIMATING EXCESS RETURNS FROM OAS

As discussed earlier, no excess return methodology has been standardized. To evaluate excess returns produced by the two models, we calculated excess returns on the Credit Index using a third method—a simple intuitive approximation based on the sources of excess return for spread product. Securities considered

Figure 30-2. Monthly Excess Returns for the Lehman Brothers Credit Index
Comparison of the Two Methods

	Dec-99	Jan-00	Feb-00	Mar-00	Apr-00	May-00	Jun-00	Jul-00	Aug-00
Duration-cell excess return (bp)	0.27	-0.43	-0.50	-1.34	-0.49	-0.58	0.69	0.28	-0.22
KRD-based excess return (bp)	0.14	-0.44	-0.59	-1.31	-0.46	-0.60	0.70	0.19	-0.21
Difference (bp)	0.13	0.01	0.09	-0.03	-0.03	0.02	-0.01	0.09	-0.01

more risky than Treasuries usually earn a spread over Treasury yields; when a spread remains unchanged, the excess return should be approximately equal to the spread itself. The risk of such securities is realized when spreads do change. In this case, the additional (positive or negative) excess return is given by the change in spread multiplied by the spread duration.

Let ER_i denote the excess return of bond i; s_i is its OAS; Δs_i is the monthly change in OAS; and D_i is its spread duration. Our simple first-order approximation for monthly excess return is given by

$$ER_i \approx \frac{s_i}{12} - D_i \Delta s_i. \tag{30-1}$$

The charming simplicity of this approximation might lead one to ask why this should not be adopted as the standard definition of excess return. However, this simple model does not cover all possible sources of return differences between Treasuries and spread product. For example, callable bonds may experience excess returns owing to volatility changes, even with unchanged OAS. Returns on mortgage-backed securities are affected by prepayment surprises and volatility changes in addition to changes in spread. Therefore, it is important to retain a model that works in return space by subtracting an equivalent Treasury return from each security's total return.

Although the OAS-based approximation of excess return given in Equation (30-1) may not be rigorously correct for volatility-sensitive instruments, we feel that it gives intuitive results for a largely noncallable index such as the U.S. Credit Index. As shown in Figure 30-3, OAS-approximated excess returns for the Credit Index agree quite closely with the KRD-based approach. In particular, in the 3 months in which the KRD-based and duration-cell methods disagree (December, February, and July), the OAS-based approximation is much closer to the KRD-based numbers. This supports our claim that the KRD method is superior to the duration-bucket approach.

AVERAGING PORTFOLIO SPREADS AND SPREAD CHANGES

In the application of the OAS-based estimate to portfolio or index excess returns, one detail merits a closer look. It is important to pay attention to the weighting mechanism used to compute portfolio averages. We show that while the spread levels should be weighted by market value, the changes in spreads should be weighted by dollar duration (the product of market value and spread duration). A failure to do so can lead to inaccuracy when the term structure of spreads changes.

Figure 30-3. Monthly Excess Returns for the Lehman Brothers Credit Index

Comparison with OAS-Based Approximation

	Dec-99	Jan-00	Feb-00	Mar-00	Apr-00	May-00	Jun-00	Jul-00	Aug-00
Duration-cell excess return (bp)	0.27	-0.43	-0.50	-1.34	-0.49	-0.58	0.69	0.28	-0.22
KRD-based excess return (bp)	0.14	-0.44	-0.59	-1.31	-0.46	-0.60	0.70	0.19	-0.21
OAS-based estimate (bp)	0.14	-0.42	-0.56	-1.33	-0.53	-0.62	0.70	0.18	-0.20

For a portfolio, let w_i represent the percentage of portfolio market value in security i. The portfolio excess return (for 1 month) is then the weighted sum of component securities' returns:

$$ER_P = \sum_i w_i ER_i \approx \frac{\sum_i w_i s_i}{12} - \sum_i w_i D_i \Delta s_i. \tag{30-2}$$

Let us look at how this calculation can be expressed in terms of portfolio-level quantities. We define the following portfolio averages for spread duration, spread, and spread change:

$$D_P^{MW} = \sum_i w_i D_i$$

$$s_P^{MW} = \sum_i w_i s_i$$

$$\Delta s_P^{DDW} = \frac{\sum_i w_i D_i \Delta s_i}{\sum_i w_i D_i}, \tag{30-3}$$

where the superscripts MW and DDW refer to a market-weighted portfolio average and a dollar-duration-weighted average, respectively. The quantity D_P^{MW} is the market-weighted average portfolio spread duration; s_P^{MW} is the market-weighted average portfolio OAS; and Δs_P^{DDW} is the dollar-duration-weighted average portfolio OAS change.

We can see that the approximation for portfolio excess return in Equation (30-2) can be rewritten as

$$ER_P \approx \frac{s_P^{MW}}{12} - D_P^{MW} \Delta s_P^{DDW}. \tag{30-4}$$

The first term of Equation (30-2) is given by the market-weighted spread. In the second term, the duration cancels out the denominator of the duration-weighted spread, leaving an expression identical to that found in the equation.

This weighting scheme is in accordance with our intuitive understanding. The first component corresponds to the return that is earned by a security if its spread remains unchanged. This spread should be weighted by market value, as are returns. The second term represents the return impact of spread changes. Spread changes in longer-duration securities have a greater effect and should be given greater weight.

Is this overly complex for a back-of-the-envelope calculation like this one? It would certainly be simpler just to use all market-weighted quantities in Equation (30-4). One might wonder how much of a difference it could make. The answer is clear from Figure 30-4, which compares the results of our approximation using both market and dollar-duration weights with the excess returns from the KRD-based methodology. The dollar-duration-weighted estimate agrees quite well with the KRD-based approach. The use of market-weighted spread change leads to inaccuracies of 14 bp or more in either direction in 5 out of the 9 months shown.

Why is the dollar-duration-weighted approximation consistently accurate, whereas the market-weighted method results vary? What is the difference between July 2000, when the market-weighted approximation was as good as the dollar-duration-weighted one, and April 2000, when the market-weighted approximation was significantly off? Figure 30-5 provides some clues.

In July 2000, spread movements were consistently small across the yield curve. In March there was a significant widening, but it was relatively consistent across the curve. On the other hand, the April widening was uneven, its level varying greatly depending upon the duration bucket. Whenever there are systematic changes in the shape of the spread curve, a market-weighted change in spreads gives a distorted estimate of the effect on returns.

ANNUALIZING EXCESS RETURNS

Portfolio managers using excess returns often present their results on an annual basis. Although annualizing total returns is a trivial compounding exercise, excess returns are arithmetic differences between two numbers and, as such, should not be compounded.

The "right" approach to annualizing excess returns depends on whether one is dealing with a cash portfolio of bonds, whose size changes every month, or with a constant-size hedging setting in which the credit portfolio is the long position and the term-structure-matched Treasuries is the short one. In the hedging context, the initial outlay is zero, return measures are undefined, and excess return is essentially a profit-and-loss number. In this context, the reasonable procedure for annualizing excess returns is simply to add them. In fact, many portfolio managers add monthly excess returns even in the traditional cash portfolio setting, to avoid the obviously flawed direct compounding.

Nevertheless, the compounding effect is undoubtedly present when a cash portfolio invests in assets that, for example, consistently outperform Treasuries. The challenge is to find a way to capture this effect correctly. We suggest a procedure for annualizing excess returns on indices and portfolios that we believe is both computationally valid and intuitively appealing. Let us assume that in a particular month we compute both total and excess returns for a portfolio. Now, what is the meaning of the difference between these two numbers? We can say that it is the total return on an implied term-structure-matched Treasury portfolio. But total

Figure 30-4. OAS-Based Approximation of Excess Returns for the Lehman Brothers Credit Index

Comparing Market and Dollar-Duration Weighting of Spread Changes

	Dec-99	Jan-00	Feb-00	Mar-00	Apr-00	May-00	Jun-00	Jul-00	Aug-00
KRD-based excess return (bp)	0.14	-0.44	-0.59	-1.31	-0.46	-0.60	0.70	0.19	-0.21
OAS-based estimate (DDW) (bp)	0.14	-0.42	-0.56	-1.33	-0.53	-0.62	0.70	0.18	-0.20
OAS-based estimate (MW) (bp)	0.16	-0.26	-0.32	-1.24	-0.78	-0.43	0.56	0.20	-0.10
Error (DDW) (bp)	0.00	0.02	0.03	-0.02	-0.07	-0.02	0.00	-0.01	0.01
Error (MW) (bp)	0.02	0.18	0.27	0.07	-0.32	0.17	-0.14	0.01	0.11

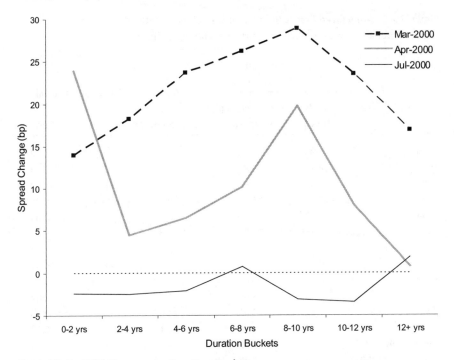

Figure 30-5. OAS Changes per Duration Bucket

returns can be compounded. Thus if every month we compute total returns on these implied Treasury portfolios, then we can annualize them at the end of the year and subtract the resulting annual return from the corresponding annual return on the cash portfolio. The result is the annualized excess return.

Let us explain the technique using a simple example of two-period compounding for the Lehman Credit Index. We denote the total return of the implied term-structure-matched Treasury portfolio as ImpliedTreas. The two-month total return for the Credit Index is

$$\text{TwoMonths\_CreditTR} = (1 + \text{Month1\_CreditTR}) \\ * (1 + \text{Month2\_CreditTR}) - 1.$$

Similarly, the 2-month total return for the implied Treasury portfolio is

$$\text{TwoMonths\_ImpliedTreasTR} = (1 + \text{Month1\_ImpliedTreasTR}) \\ * (1 + \text{Month2\_ImpliedTreasTR}) - 1.$$

Then, the compounded 2-month excess return is simply

$$\text{TwoMonths\_CreditTR} - \text{TwoMonths\_ImpliedTreasTR}.$$

Figure 30-6. Annualized Excess Returns for the Lehman Brothers Credit Index
Compounding Using an Implied Treasury Portfolio vs. Addition

| | Annualized Total Return (%) | | Annualized Excess Return (%) | | |
	Credit Index	KRD-Matched Treasuries	Compounded	Added	Difference
1990	7.06	8.95	−1.89	−1.77	0.12
1991	18.52	15.84	2.68	2.30	−0.38
1992	8.69	7.65	1.04	0.96	−0.09
1993	12.16	11.25	0.91	0.82	−0.09
1994	−3.93	−4.46	0.53	0.57	0.04
1995	22.25	20.89	1.36	1.13	−0.23
1996	3.28	2.03	1.25	1.22	−0.03
1997	10.23	10.54	−0.30	−0.28	0.02
1998	8.57	10.95	−2.38	−2.20	0.18
1999	−1.95	−3.65	1.70	1.74	0.04
2000	9.39	14.01	−4.63	−4.17	0.46
2001[a]	12.14	11.01	1.13	1.03	−0.10
Mean (1990–1995)	10.79	10.02	0.77	0.67	−0.10
Mean (1996–2001)	6.94	7.48	−0.54	−0.44	0.09
Mean (1990–2001)	8.87	8.75	0.12	0.11	0.00

[a]Through October 31, 2001.

We applied this technique to about 12 years worth of monthly excess returns of the Lehman Credit Index. In Figure 30-6, we show annualized excess returns obtained by the suggested compounding procedure, as well as by simple addition. While the average difference between the two happens to be almost zero over the whole period, this is no more than a chance. By breaking the time span into two parts, we highlight the magnifying effect of compounding. In the early 1990s, credit product generally outperformed Treasuries. The positive differences are captured more strongly by the compounded annualized excess returns than by the added ones (average of 77 vs. 67 bp/year for 1990–1995). The general lagging of credit in the late 1990s is likewise magnified by the compounded aggregation (average of −54 vs. −44 bp/year for 1996–2001).

CONCLUSION

The use of KRDs to calculate excess returns leads to more accurate results, particularly for volatility-sensitive securities such as callable bonds and MBS. A simple approximation of excess return based on OAS and changes in OAS supports the KRD-based methodology. When this approximation is used, the portfolio-level spread change should be calculated as a dollar-duration-weighted average of the security-level spread changes.

For most unleveraged bond portfolios, the compounding effect of excess returns is real and should be captured. We believe that many portfolio managers looking for the proper way to aggregate excess returns will find the foregoing simple technique helpful and easy to implement.

31. Currency-Hedged Returns in Fixed-Income Indices

Portfolio managers typically minimize currency exposure in bond portfolios with the use of foreign-exchange forward transactions (forwards). However, the use of forwards cannot entirely eliminate currency volatility, since fluctuations in underlying asset values will lead the portfolio to be either over- or underhedged. Moreover, the use of forwards changes portfolio interest-rate exposures. In this chapter, we discuss the currency volatility and interest-rate exposures of currency-hedged securities and portfolios and the risk introduced against hedged indices by not replicating index hedges. We also discuss the effect of exchange-rate fluctuations on the relative country allocations of portfolios managed against hedged benchmarks. We discuss the methods that investors can use to minimize risk vs. hedged benchmarks.

RISK EXPOSURES IN CURRENCY HEDGES

The Interest-Rate Exposure

The exchange rate at which a forward is struck (forward rate) is the spot exchange rate adjusted for the interest-rate differential between the two currencies (forward points). This is a necessary no-arbitrage condition, illustrated in Figure 31-1. In the example shown in the figure, the forward rate is mispriced, as it does not reflect the interest-rate differential between the two currencies, so an investor can buy euros forward too cheaply. As the interest-rate differential between two currencies changes, so does the forward rate, eliminating arbitrage opportunities.

Consider another investor, who holds a 10-year U.S. Treasury yielding 4.2% and hedges the USD exposure into euros with a 1-year forward. As the differential between euro and U.S. interest rates fluctuates, so will the pricing of the forward points. This investor is effectively long 1-year euro interest rates and short 1-year

Based on research first published by Lehman Brothers in 2003.

Figure 31-1. Covered Interest Arbitrage Example

USD/EUR spot rate:	1.1	Today	
USD/EUR 1-year forward rate:	1.08	Borrow 100 EUR for 1 year at 2%	
		Sell 100 EUR for USD and invest at 1%	
1-year deposit rate		Sell $110 × (1.01) 1 year forward	
EUR	2.00%		
USD	1.00%	1 year later	
		Repay the EUR loan	(EUR 102)
		Receive EUR from forward	EUR 102.87
		(= 110 × 1.01/1.08)	
		Profit	EUR 0.87

USD rates. The currency hedge, therefore, has an effect on the duration exposure of the investor's euro and USD portfolios. Accordingly, an investor who chooses a different tenor of hedge from a currency-hedged index is assuming active interest-rate risk.

This example demonstrates another effect of currency hedging on a portfolio. The yield on the portfolio has also changed. Assuming that the forward rate is now correctly priced and using the same deposit rates, the yield on the hedged 10-year Treasury is now 5.2%, reflecting the interest-rate differential. More generally, the hedged yield on a security can be expressed approximately as follows:

$$\text{Hedged yield} \approx \text{Bond yield} + (\text{Base currency interest rate} - \text{Local interest rate}). \quad (31\text{-}1)$$

The duration of a hedged instrument can be expressed approximately as

$$\text{Hedged-bond duration} = \text{Bond duration} - \text{Tenor of bond hedge}. \quad (31\text{-}2)$$

The duration decrease in local currency is offset by a corresponding increase in base-currency duration.

The Exchange-Rate Exposure

An investor typically calculates the amount of local currency to be sold forward to hedge a security's foreign exchange exposure in one of two ways—using either the expected future value of the security at the forward date or the current market value of the security.[1] Since the end-of-period market value of the security

---

1. Some managers prefer to hedge current rather than future values, entering into currency swaps (a spot purchase and forward sale of currency) when purchasing new securities.

being hedged is not known, unless this period is equal to the security's maturity, this hedge is not perfect (see an exception later). If, for example, a euro-based investor hedges a USD bond with a market value of $1,000 through the sale of a forward of equal magnitude and the bond rises to $1,100, the investor has an exposure of $100 to the USD/EUR exchange rate. In practice, many investors periodically rehedge their portfolios to reduce currency exposures, though as we shall see, this may introduce tracking error vs. a hedged index. Investors who use longer tenors for currency hedges without periodical rehedging tend to have larger currency exposures and currency return volatilities.[2]

A foreign security with predictable cash flows may be perfectly currency hedged if the bond is held to maturity and each future cash flow is separately hedged back into base currency. As seen from the previous example, as the pricing of the forwards reflects the interest-rate differential between the two currencies, this transaction would exchange the interest-rate risk of the foreign security for base-currency interest-rate risk. This would defeat the purpose of owning the foreign security, unless the purpose is to create a new "synthetic" base-currency bond, cheaper than a "conventional" substitute.[3]

The size of the index currency hedge is effectively established at the beginning of each month, when the expected future value of all non-base-currency exposures is hedged for 1 month. The index is not rehedged until the end of the month and, therefore, to the extent that bond markets move away from their expected month-end values, will be exposed in part to currency movements. The non-deterministic portion of the currency returns for a given country's hedged bond market index is given by

(Local bond market return − Expected bond market return)
× (FX appreciation).   (31-3)

The historical volatility and return of the currency component for a selection of hedged indices are show in Figure 31-2b.

This analysis suggests that currency volatility has a limited effect on the overall volatility of currency-hedged indices; nevertheless, it should not be ignored, especially for single-country bond portfolios hedged into the base currency. Furthermore, there is a marked tendency for spikes in bond market volatility to accompany spikes in currency volatility, increasing the overall volatility of currency

---

2. For example, a euro-based investor hedging the U.S. component of the Lehman Global Aggregate with a 3-month hedge, with no intraperiod adjustment, incurred a currency loss equal to 0.11% for the 3 months ending June 30, 2003.

3. In practice, the arbitrage advantage of a synthetic bond has to be significant to offset its substantially reduced liquidity.

Figure 31-2. Volatility of Currency-Hedged Bond Indices
3 Years Ending June 30, 2003

	Base Currency	Annual Return (%)	Annual Standard Deviation (%)
(a) Total Return			
Lehman Global Aggregate	USD	7.74	2.74
Lehman U.S. Aggregate	EUR	10.57	3.23
Lehman U.S. Aggregate	JPY	6.72	3.28
(b) Currency Return			
Lehman Global Aggregate	USD	0.05	0.05
Lehman U.S. Aggregate	EUR	−0.11	0.12
Lehman U.S. Aggregate	JPY	−0.02	0.09
(c) Total Return Less Currency Return			
Lehman Global Aggregate	USD	7.69	2.73
Lehman U.S. Aggregate	EUR	10.69	3.28
Lehman U.S. Aggregate	JPY	6.74	3.27

returns [this can be seen from Equation (31-3), in which both bracketed terms would increase]. For example, in December 2002 and May 2003, a substantial return on the U.S. Aggregate was accompanied by a large fall in the dollar, leading to an average currency loss for euro-hedged investors of 9 bp/month.

Figure 31-2c suggests that investors who wish to minimize overall portfolio risk should not be overly concerned about the volatility of the hedged currency return. Eliminating currency risk entirely can actually increase portfolio risk, as one source of portfolio diversification (at least at these low effective concentrations) is removed.

THE IMPLEMENTATION OF CURRENCY HEDGES

The Timing

Investors incur tracking errors vs. hedged indices to the extent that their hedging methods differ from the treatment of hedges in indices. In particular, hedgers may choose to establish and roll over their hedges at a different time of the month. This may be unavoidable in the middle of the month if the investor establishes a portfolio or receives a large cash flow. Such an investor is now faced with two choices—the most obvious being to hedge the current or future expected currency exposure. However, the index will itself be partially unhedged, owing to bond market fluctuations away from month-end expected values. The currency volatility of the hedged indices given earlier provides a guide to the potential tracking error such a choice would introduce. Therefore, some investors prefer the second choice: match the index method and leave part of the currency exposure unhedged. To replicate the index return midmonth, the investor has to sell the expected forward value of all local currency bonds, computed as at the beginning of the month, for month-end value. Our analytic systems (detailed later) enable users to obtain these values for each bond, as well as aggregate values for each currency.

The Tenor

Some investors choose to use forwards longer (or shorter) than the 1-month tenor used by the indices. We established that implementing a long-horizon hedging strategy represented a view on the direction of relative interest rates between the hedging and base currencies. Investors face a trade-off between increased tracking error and potential increased return. A longer-tenor hedging strategy can, depending on the relative shapes of the yield curves, increase carry return relative to a shorter tenor. Moreover, such a strategy leads to modestly reduced transaction costs, as forwards are "rolled" less frequently. An empirical study of various hedging tenors concluded that longer-horizon hedging strategies (up to 6 months), designed to maximize carry return, have delivered positive information ratios. In that study, we examined the performance of hedging strategies independent of the performance of the underlying bond portfolio. In practice, managers utilizing longer-tenor hedges would likely adjust hedges periodically, as movements in bond values create unintended currency exposures.

The Effect of Currency Fluctuations on Index Weights

All Lehman Brothers indices used in the computation of reported returns (the returns universes) are reconstituted every month according to the market capitalization of the underlying securities that compose the index. For global indices, market values are all converted to the base currency. Accordingly, the changes in index country weights from month to month depend on, among other factors, monthly fluctuations in exchange rates. Country weights for hedged indices are set to be equal to unhedged indices. Therefore, an investor with a perfect index-replicating multicurrency-hedged portfolio has to make adjustments to country weights at month-end to preserve the integrity of the replication.

For example, following the euro's 5.4% rise against the dollar in May 2003, the euro component of the Global Aggregate rose by 1.5%. An investor would have to

Figure 31-3. Currency Composition of the Lehman Brothers Global Aggregate Index in 2003

	Composition (%)						
	12/31	1/31	2/28	3/31	4/30	5/31	6/30
USD	45.4	44.8	44.7	44.6	44.2	43.1	43.3
EUR	28.4	29.2	29.3	29.4	29.6	31.1	31.0
JPY	18.5	18.2	18.3	18.3	18.3	17.7	17.7
GBS	3.8	3.9	3.7	3.7	3.8	3.8	3.8
CAD	1.6	1.7	1.7	1.7	1.8	1.9	1.8
Other	2.3	2.3	2.3	2.3	2.3	2.5	2.5

make portfolio adjustments to reflect changes in index composition anyway, owing to bonds entering and exiting the index, but currency volatility is likely to be the largest contributor to changes in country composition. Figure 31-3 shows the changes in the currency composition of the Global Aggregate Index for the year to date.

Minimizing the Tracking Error Effect of Currency Exposure for Hedged Indices

We have shown that investors can replicate the currency exposure of hedged bond indices by matching the tenor and timing of currency hedges. A final potential source of tracking error can arise from executing hedging transactions at prices different from those used for index calculations. Although these price differences may be small, their large portfolio weight can cause a meaningful performance shortfall. This is especially true for portfolios composed largely of non-base-currency bonds.

Managing and Calculating the Currency Exposure for Hedged Indices

The following offers a practical outline of the steps needed to replicate the performance of currency-hedged indices, including descriptions of fields that will be available shortly in index analytics. Using a single bond as an example, Figure 31-4 provides these calculations.

The index hedges at 4 PM on the last business day of every month, using a 1-month forward. The amount of the hedge is given by RUMVHedgeB. Managers who wish to replicate the bond fully have to replicate the foreign exchange exposure of the bond, RUFXExpsr. This arises from the mismatch between the

Figure 31-4. Currency-Hedging Example

Bond CUSIP: 69352BAC
Index Base Currency: Euro

	Field	06/30/03	07/17/03
Price (% of par)		115.623	114.121
Accrued (% of par)		4.427	0.396
Par value	RUOutLoc	314,202	295,221
EUR/USD spot rate		0.870815	0.894174
EUR/USD forward rate		0.871569	0.894501
Market value bonds—local currency		377,200	338,078
Market value bonds—base currency	RUMVSecry	328,471	302,301
Market value cash—local currency	RUMVCashL	0	32,968
Market value cash—base currency	RUMVCash	0	29,479
Market value bonds + cash—local[a]		377,200	371,046
Market value bonds + cash—base		328,471	331,780
Market value of hedge			
Forward sale USD—local	RUMVHedgeB	379,104	379,104
Forward sale USD—base		−329,913	−338,886
Forward purchase—EUR		329,913	329,913
Profit on hedge—base	RUHedgePL		−8,694
Total market value of hedged bond			
Total value—local	RUMVTotLc	377,200	371,046
Total value—base	RUMVTotal	328,471	323,086
Currency exposure—local	RUFXExpsr[b]	−1,905	−8,058

[a]The hedge amount is calculated at the beginning of the month from the expected value of the bond as at month-end. This amount includes any expected security cash flows.

[b]Since the size of the hedge is based on the month-end expected value of the security, it will be slightly larger than the current market value, creating a small currency exposure.

current (local) market value of securities and the expected month-end value (representing the amount of the hedge).

RUMVTotLc is the market value of a bond in local currency, including cash generated from that security during the month:

$$RUMVTotLc = (Price + Accrued\ Interest) \times (RUOutLoc/100)$$
$$+ RUMVCashL.$$

RUMVTotal is the market value of a local bond hedged into base currency. This comprises the market value of the security (in base-currency terms) and the unrealized profit/loss on the forward foreign exchange contract (the sale of local currency back into base):

RUMVTotal = RUMVSecry + RUMVCash + RUHedgePL (see next).

RUHedgePL is the unrealized profit/loss on the outstanding forward contract. For the returns universe, the size of the forward (in local currency) is computed at the beginning of each month, shown as RUMVHedgeB:

$$RUHedgePL = RUMVHedgeB \times (Fwd\ RateEnd_{local/base} - Fwd\ Rate\ Begin_{local/base}),$$

where $Rate_{local/base}$ is equal to the number of local currency units per unit of base currency. RUFXExpsr is the amount by which a bond is not fully hedged owing to fluctuations in its value (including cash) away from the predicted month-end value. This amount can be aggregated to give the total currency exposure for each index currency:

RUFXExpsr = RUMVTotLc – RUMVHedgeB.

CONCLUSION

It is not possible to entirely eliminate absolute currency volatility from foreign bond portfolios, but this is neither desirable nor necessary. One can imagine an extreme dynamic hedging strategy in which all currency risk would be eliminated as soon as it arose. Every fluctuation of a bond away from its expected value would give rise to a currency transaction to eliminate the resulting currency risk. Such an exercise would be time consuming and costly and, in our analysis, would increase both absolute and relative volatility. Index replication of currency-hedged indices is possible, given transparent index methodology and analytic systems. Moreover, active managers can use currency hedges as an additional alpha-generation tool because a hedge has both a yield and a duration effect on portfolio exposures.

32. The Bund-Treasury Trade in Portfolios

In recent months, investors have been looking closely at the U.S. to euro zone bond trade. Accelerating U.S. economic growth alongside anemic growth in the euro zone and a runaway U.S. budget deficit suggest to many investors that U.S. yields are likely to rise relative to European yields. At the same time, a widening U.S. current account deficit raises the possibility of further euro currency gains. For U.S. managers putting on the trade opportunistically or for global managers establishing the trade strategically, the questions are the same: How risky is the trade? In what ratio should the trade be executed? For an unhedged position, what portion of the risk comes from currency exposure? How does the trade affect overall portfolio risk given exposures to other risk factors? In this chapter, we provide some answers to these questions. Although the chapter was written from the perspective of a manager who wishes to express a specific view (that Bunds will outperform Treasuries), the analysis and conclusions are generally valid for most cross-currency bond trades.

STRUCTURING THE TRADE

For investors who make use of derivatives or the repo market, expressing a view on the Bund-Treasury spread is relatively straightforward. Either sell Treasury futures and buy Bund futures or sell Treasury cash instruments short and purchase Bunds. A similar view can also be expressed through the swaps market. The key question for these trades would be the appropriate hedge ratio (see later).

For investors who do not or cannot use derivative instruments, the trade may be more problematic. For a U.S. or a global manager with a centralized decision-making process, existing portfolio holdings determine which bond will be sold.

Based on research first published by Lehman Brothers in 2003.

Many managers have only small holdings in Treasury securities, and these may not be in maturities in which the manager would desire to put on the spread trade. If there is a maturity mismatch between the Treasury sold and the Bund purchased, then the trade is exposed to yield curve risk as well as spread risk. Alternatively, other assets (e.g., agencies) may be sold. A decentralized global manager whose portfolios are managed by regional teams faces an added challenge. For such a manager, the view on the United States vs. Europe is likely to be expressed by allocating more to the euro team and less to the U.S. team. If the Global Aggregate is the benchmark, simply taking 5% out of the European portfolio and putting it into the U.S. portfolio changes many more exposures than just the exposure to the Bund-Treasury spread.

A HEDGED BOND TRADE

A manager who wishes to express a view on the Treasury-Bund spread typically hedges currency exposure using foreign exchange forwards. Frequently asset managers express a view on the spread by selling 10-year U.S. Treasuries for 10-year euro government bonds (unless otherwise indicated, we assume the trade is executed through the sale of 10-year U.S. Treasuries and a purchase of Bunds). The most obvious way of executing the trade is by dollar-duration matching, but that does not make it the right way. Duration is a measure of price sensitivity with respect to yield. The problem in this case is that for U.S. Treasuries and Bunds, duration measures the sensitivity with respect to U.S. yields and Bund yields, respectively.[1] What we need instead is a measure of the sensitivity of a change in Bund prices with respect to Treasury yields.[2] Fortunately, we do not have to invent one: beta-weighted duration performs admirably in this respect. If

$$\beta_{\epsilon,\$} = \frac{\text{Cov}(\Delta y_\epsilon, \Delta y_\$)}{\text{Var}(\Delta y_\$)}, \tag{32-1}$$

where $\beta_{\epsilon,\$}$ = Beta of euro bond relative to U.S. bond; Δy_ϵ = Change in euro bond yield; $\Delta y_\$$ = Change in dollar bond yield. Then,

$$\beta\text{-adjusted } Mkt.\ val_\$ = Mkt.val_{\epsilon,\$terms} * \frac{\text{Dur}_\epsilon}{\text{Dur}_\$} * \beta_{\epsilon,\$}.$$

---

1. It is for this reason that many global managers ignore average portfolio duration as a statistic, since this measure combines sensitivities to shifts of different yield curves.

2. Using euro bonds as the "base," we could also compute beta-weighted durations of U.S. Treasuries with respect to Bund yields.

Figure 32-1. Betas, Volatilities, and Correlations for Same-Maturity Treasuries and Bunds
Weekly Data Beginning January 1, 2000 (betas shown in bold)

Yield Volatilities (bp/week)		USD 2-year	USD 5-year	USD 10-year	USD 30-year	EUR 2-year	EUR 5-year	EUR 10-year	EUR 30-year
15.6	USD 2-year	1				**0.57**			
16.1	USD 5-year	0.93	1				**0.56**		
14.9	USD 10-year	0.82	0.94	1				**0.51**	
12.3	USD 30-year	0.63	0.78	0.92	1				**0.53**
12.0	EUR 2-year	0.74	0.74	0.68	0.55	1			
11.7	EUR 5-year	0.73	0.78	0.77	0.68	0.91	1		
9.5	EUR 10-year	0.66	0.75	0.79	0.76	0.78	0.93	1	
8.9	EUR 30-year	0.47	0.57	0.67	0.74	0.53	0.73	0.89	1

Figure 32-1 shows betas for various maturities of Treasuries and Bunds using on-the-run yields, as well as volatilities and correlations. For example, for a sale of 10-year Treasuries for 10-year Bunds, the beta is 0.51, so a purchase of a $1 million value (in U.S. dollar terms) 7-year-duration Bund would be funded with the sale of a $510,000 equal-duration U.S. Treasury.

The usefulness of beta as a measure can be seen in Figure 32-2, which demonstrates that over the past 4 years, the movement of the Bund-Treasury spread has been highly correlated with absolute movements in U.S. Treasury yields. Over this period, more than 60% of the movements in the Bund-Treasury spread were explained by absolute movements in U.S. 10-year yields. Thus, historically, a manager who established a Bund-Treasury trade on a duration-weighted basis was essentially expressing a U.S.-interest-rate view. If U.S. yields declined, the U.S. yield spread to Bunds tended to narrow, whereas if U.S. yields rose, the yield spread widened. The chart suggests that the spread narrowed by around 5 bp for every 10-bp fall in U.S. yields (a beta of 0.5). Perhaps managers have often put on this trade out of a desire to express a view on U.S. yields alongside the direction of the spread. However, we believe that at least some managers would want to be able to establish the trade without having a view on U.S. bond yields. Beta weighting the trade largely eliminates the effective U.S.-interest-rate exposure, leaving the performance of the trade dependent upon the fundamentals (and technicals) of the Bund market.

Estimates of betas do change over time, as volatilities and correlations change. Over the past 4 years, for example, the 10-year/10-year beta has varied between 0.42 and 0.60. In our view, far from invalidating the use of beta, this suggests that

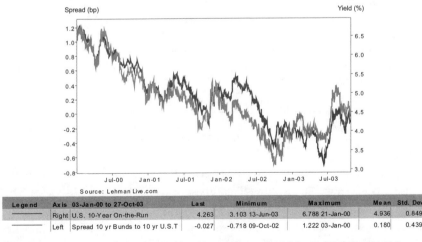

Figure 32-2. Movements in the 10-Year Treasury over Bund Spread Relative to U.S. 10-Year Yield

Figure 32-3. Output of the Global Risk Model for Bund-Treasury 10-Year Trade
(a) Duration-Weighted Hedge; (b) Beta-Weighted Trade

Factor Name	Sensitivity/ Exposure	Portfolio Exposure	Benchmark Exposure	Net Exposure
(a) Key Rates				
USD 6-month KRD	KRD	0.0	0.0010	−0.0010
USD 2-year KRD	KRD	0.0	−0.0060	0.0060
USD 5-year KRD	KRD	0.0	0.933	−0.933
USD 10-year KRD	KRD	0.0	6.788	−6.788
USD convexity	OAC	0.0	0.723	−0.723
EUR 6-month KRD	KRD	0.0030	0.0	0.0030
EUR 2-year KRD	KRD	−0.152	0.0	−0.152
EUR 5-year KRD	KRD	0.561	0.0	0.561
EUR 10-year KRD	KRD	7.158	0.0	7.158
EUR 30-year KRD	KRD	−0.168	0.0	−0.168
EUR convexity	OAC	0.677	0.0	0.677
(b) Key Rates				
USD 6-month KRD	KRD	0.0	0.0	−0.0
USD 2-year KRD	KRD	0.0	−0.0030	0.0030
USD 5-year KRD	KRD	0.0	0.484	−0.484
USD 10-year KRD	KRD	0.0	3.518	−3.518
USD convexity	OAC	0.0	0.375	−0.375
EUR 6-month KRD	KRD	0.0030	0.0	0.0030
EUR 2-year KRD	KRD	−0.152	0.0	−0.152
EUR 5-year KRD	KRD	0.561	0.0	0.561
EUR 10-year KRD	KRD	7.158	0.0	7.158
EUR 30-year KRD	KRD	−0.168	0.0	−0.168
EUR convexity	OAC	0.677	0.0	0.677

duration weighting the trade (essentially fixing the beta at 1) is the least appropriate approach.

We would emphasize that in using beta, we are attempting to eliminate the sensitivity of changes in the Bund-Treasury spread to a change in U.S. yields. This is not the same, however, as minimizing the overall volatility of the position. Moreover, the beta we measure here is the sensitivity relative to U.S. yields. To measure the beta relative to Bund yields (i.e., weight the trade to eliminate sensitivity to Bund yields), we would have to substitute the variance of the change in Bund yields in the denominator of Equation (32-1).

Factor Volatility (bp/month)	TE Impact of an Isolated 1-Standard-Deviation Up Change (bp/month)	TE Impact of a Correlated 1-Standard-Deviation Up Change (bp/month)	Marginal Contribution to TEV (bp/month)	Percent Contribution to TEV
24.73	0.02	33.46	−0.033	0.0
33.75	−0.22	112.68	−0.149	−0.1
34.94	32.62	122.27	−0.168	15.66
28.74	195.06	114.01	−0.129	87.35
3.5	−2.53	6.48	0.0010	−0.06
17.66	−0.05	63.17	−0.044	−0.01
25.3	3.85	61.74	−0.061	0.93
22.79	−12.78	30.81	−0.028	−1.55
20.54	−147.05	7.78	−0.0060	−4.49
17.53	2.95	12.39	−0.0090	0.14
1.81	1.22	−11.48	−0.0010	−0.06
24.73	0.01	1.71	−0.0040	0.0
33.75	−0.11	18.43	−0.053	−0.02
34.94	16.91	16.43	−0.048	2.35
28.74	101.11	5.7	−0.014	4.87
3.5	−1.31	12.85	0.0040	−0.14
17.66	−0.05	7.67	−0.011	−0.0
25.3	3.85	−18.27	0.039	−0.59
22.79	−12.78	−54.31	0.105	5.86
20.54	−147.05	−69.7	0.121	86.55
17.53	2.95	−59.62	0.088	−1.48
1.81	1.22	11.21	0.0020	0.12

Our global risk model[3] allows us to examine how the choice of duration weighting or beta weighting changes both the sensitivity of a Bund-Treasury trade to U.S. yields and the overall risk of the position.

Figure 32-3 shows some output from the model, where we have established a one-bond portfolio (10-year hedged Bund), benchmarked against a one-Treasury portfolio (10-year Treasury with cash to match duration or beta as appropriate).

3. See Chapter 26.

Figure 32-4. Monthly Data for 7- to 10-Year Government Bond Indices
5 years ending October 31, 2003

	Duration Weighted	Beta Weighted
Standard deviation (%)	1.25	0.85
Correlation to U.S. Treasuries	−0.75	−0.07
Correlation to Bunds	−0.19	0.55

All data are expressed in basis points per month. In (a), the position is established with equal duration weights. Some 87% of the variance of the overall position comes from the variance of the U.S. 10-year key rate. In (b), the position is established with beta-adjusted weights. An identical 87% proportion of the variance is now due to the euro key rate. Furthermore, the "TE impact of a correlated 1-standard-deviation up change" column shows that the sensitivity of both portfolios to a movement in key rates in the United States and Europe changes dramatically. Beta weighting makes the performance of the spread trade dependent on movements in euro rates rather than in U.S. rates. Using the risk model, a manager could establish what weighting would balance the relative influences of U.S. and euro key rates on movements in the spread.

What difference would the two weighting options have made historically to the performance of a Bund-Treasury trade? In Figure 32-4, we examine the historical volatility of trades that were established with 1-month time horizons, using the 7- to 10-year U.S. Treasury and 7- to 10-year German Government (USD-hedged) constituents of the Lehman Global Treasury Index. Duration-weighted ratios are calculated using beginning-of-month durations and beta-weighted ratios using trailing 5 years of monthly data. The figure illustrates both the substantially reduced volatility of the beta-hedged position, as well as the greatly reduced sensitivity of the trade with respect to movements in U.S. Treasuries, compared with duration weights. Moreover, there is a notable change in the correlation of the trade with movements in Bund yields. A duration-weighted trade is negatively correlated with Bunds. That is, a purchase of Bunds vs. Treasuries would actually lose when Bunds rally. The beta-weighted trade, on the other hand, is positively correlated with Bunds (and negatively correlated with Treasuries), as perhaps it should be.

Many times, managers choose to express bond and currency trades separately, for example, by using foreign exchange forwards to express a relative spread view on bond markets, or by using short-term bonds or money market securities to express a currency view. A manager who expresses both views together will be exposed to movements in the bond spread as well as to movements in the euro (and

Figure 32-5. Volatility of Duration-Weighted vs. Beta-Weighted Bund-Treasury Trades

Weighting Scheme	FX Exposure	Volatility (bp/month)	Volatility from Currency (%)
Duration	Hedged	160	0.0
Beta	Hedged	109	0.0
Duration	Unhedged	335	69.5
Beta	Unhedged	289	83.6

their co-movements). In Figure 32-5, using our risk model, we examine what proportion of the volatility of the return on an unhedged 10-year Bund was due to currency exposure. Compared to the hedged position, the volatility is twice to nearly three times as great for an unhedged position, depending on the weighting method used. Overall, currency volatility comprises 70–84% of the total position. The overall risk of the beta-weighted position is lower, given its lower sensitivity to more volatile U.S. yields, and therefore the proportion of risk from currency volatility is proportionately greater.

MEASURING THE IMPACT OF THE TRADE ON OVERALL PORTFOLIO RISK

Gauging the impact of a Bund-Treasury trade (particularly if it is unhedged) on portfolio risk is not a trivial exercise. Exchange-rate exposures are correlated with spread exposures, as well as with yield curve exposures. It is even harder for decentralized Global Aggregate managers because for such managers, a view on the Bund-Treasury spread is likely to be expressed through a reallocation from the U.S. team to the European team. The trade then becomes a long position in the Euro Aggregate and an effective short position in the U.S. Aggregate. How can this trade be correctly sized to take duration differences between the two regional indices into account? How does one allow for the correlations among the various sectors of the U.S. and euro portions of the Global Aggregate? What is needed is a global risk model that can consider the impact of such a trade on total portfolio risk relative to benchmark, taking into account the correlations among all portfolio risk exposures.

We have already noted that the Bund-Treasury trade should be beta adjusted in order not to change the portfolio's sensitivity to U.S. interest-rate movements. The impact of the trade on total portfolio risk, as well as sensitivity to other risk exposures can be gauged by examining the output of a report generated from the global risk model before and after the Bund-Treasury trade. The impact of the trade on all portfolio sensitivities can be gauged in two ways. First, the report displays the impact on relative portfolio performance of a 1-standard-deviation move in a specific risk factor (Figure 32-3). If this number changes before and after the trade, we know that the portfolio's exposure to that risk factor would be changed by the Bund-Treasury trade. Second, the marginal contribution to tracking error (MCTE) examines the impact on portfolio risk of a 1% increase in exposure to that risk factor. If the MCTE from a given risk factor would fall as a result of the trade, the portfolio would become less sensitive to that factor.

CONCLUSION

A manager who expresses a view on the Bund-Treasury spread must be careful to avoid unintended changes in portfolio exposures to the U.S. or euro yields and credit spreads. In particular, a duration-weighted switch out of Treasuries into Bunds is as much an expression of a view with respect to the direction of U.S. yields as it is a view on the movement of the Bund-Treasury spread. A similar argument can be made for other cross-market trades. Where correlations between markets are high, beta-weighted switches can allow for spread views to be expressed in isolation from yield curve views. Where correlations between markets are low (e.g., JGBs vs. Europe or the United States), spread trades are effectively two independent trades. So a JGB to Europe trade is effectively two independent trades: a short JGB position and a long euro bond position.

When cross-country trades are made on an unhedged basis, the impact on portfolio risk becomes less intuitive because currency risk is itself correlated with the cross-market spread. It is also correlated with other portfolio exposures (e.g., credit), though these relationships tend to be less stable, given the instability of foreign exchange volatilities. Gauging the impact of cross-currency trades becomes even more problematic for the Global Aggregate manager. The global risk model, our portfolio and index analysis tool, allows investors to measure directly the contribution of hedged and unhedged cross-currency exposures to total portfolio risk, taking into account correlations with other existing portfolio exposures.

33. Empirical Duration of Credit Securities

Many portfolio managers with investment-grade benchmarks are allowed out-of-benchmark ("core-plus") allocations to high yield debt. As with any other asset class, they must understand the effect that such allocations have on the overall portfolio duration.

Portfolio analytics will, of course, dutifully turn out analytical duration numbers for high yield bonds, based, as they are for all other bonds, on their promised cash flows. Yet it is widely acknowledged that the interest-rate sensitivity of high yield securities is not necessarily what their stated cash flows imply; many claim that high yield debt exhibits rather equity-like behavior.

There is a wide range of opinion on this issue among portfolio managers. At one extreme are the managers who account for the full analytical duration of the high yield component, and, at the other, are those who ignore the duration contribution of high yield entirely and base their assumed exposure to interest rates solely on investment-grade instruments. The majority, in between, usually have some heuristic rule of thumb—for example, to consider 25% of the analytical duration for high yield bonds.

Not infrequently, the attitude is that the duration assigned to high yield bonds is not particularly important because the interest-rate risk of a high yield investment pales in comparison to the credit and default risks involved. When one is prepared to accept such major risks, should one worry about a bit more or a bit less interest-rate exposure?

In fact, uncertainty about the interest-rate sensitivity of high yield bonds can severely affect the ability of portfolio managers to express their views on rates accurately. Assume, for example, that a portfolio and its benchmark both have duration of 5 and that the manager shifts 10% of the portfolio into high yield, also

Based on research first published by Lehman Brothers in 2004.

with (analytical) duration of 5. Depending on one's opinion, the "true" duration of the portfolio is anywhere between 4.5 and 5.0—a tremendous range for many managers used to tweaking duration in much smaller increments when expressing their views on rates. If the portfolio target duration is 4.80 and the manager is prepared to adjust the Treasury component of the portfolio to hit this target, does he have to add duration or subtract it?

The first part of this chapter is devoted to the sensitivity of high yield securities to changes in interest rates. The results, based both on an empirical study of asset class data and on our risk model, corroborate the market perception that the observed yield curve sensitivity of high yield securities is much lower than is indicated by their reported analytical duration. For Ba-rated debt, the ratio between the two was found to be roughly a quarter. Lower-quality investments, such as those rated B and C, exhibit close to zero, or even negative, interest-rate sensitivity.

We find that the very low interest-rate sensitivity of high yield debt is largely due to the negative correlation between interest rates and credit spreads. If a change in interest rates is likely to be accompanied by an opposing change in spread, then the rate change will have a smaller net effect on prices and returns. As we move to lower-rated asset classes with higher spreads and higher spread volatilities, the magnitude of this opposing spread change effect continues to grow until it is comparable to that of the rate change itself. This interaction gives rise to an empirical duration that, depending on the time period and other factors, hovers around zero.

In the second part of the chapter we look at the variation in empirical duration over time. We find that even within a given credit rating, the empirical duration varies widely in response to changes in spread levels and spread volatility. In the current low-spread, low-volatility environment, this means that empirical durations can be expected to be significantly higher than the long-term average results.

ANALYSIS OF EMPIRICAL DURATION

To find the empirical duration of high yield (and investment-grade) bonds in different credit-rating categories, we use historical index data and several different approaches. First, we regress daily price returns of whole-letter-grade components of the Lehman Investment-Grade and High Yield Credit indices against daily changes in the 10-year U.S. Treasury yield. The (negative of the) regression coefficients can be interpreted as empirical durations, that is, the return realized per unit of yield change. These are plotted in Figure 33-1a alongside the average analytical durations (OAD) for each index over the same period: August 1998–September 2004. We see that in higher qualities, the empirical durations are almost

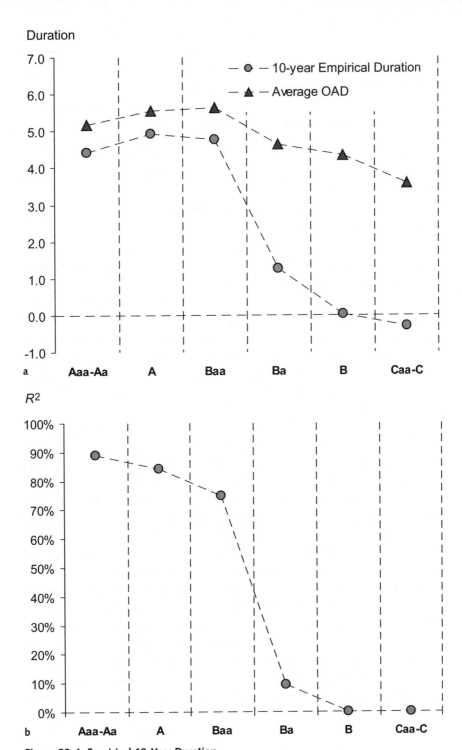

Figure 33-1. Empirical 10-Year Duration
(a) vs. OAD, (b) R^2, Daily Observations, August 1998–September 2004

identical to OAD; for the Baa rating, the gap increases somewhat; and for high yield the empirical durations plummet to near zero.

The R^2 of the regressions (Figure 33-1b) confirm a common market perception: changes in interest rates explain most of what happens to investment-grade debt and very little of what happens to high yield. Nevertheless, a distinction can be drawn between the Ba category, where interest rates explain 9.4% of return variance, and the two lower-rated categories for which the explanatory power is zero.

As far as the duration levels themselves, we find that for the Ba-rating category the empirical duration is 1.27, or 24.4% of the analytical OAD of 5.21. For B-rated debt, the empirical duration is effectively zero, and for securities rated Caa and below duration actually becomes negative, indicating that this asset class tends to have positive returns when interest rates rise.

One possible explanation for the pattern in Figure 33-1 is the negative correlation generally observed between interest rates and credit spreads. This is what causes the total return volatility of investment-grade credit indices to be lower than that of Treasuries; here it shows itself as a decrease in empirical duration as the exposure to credit spread risk grows. The lower the credit quality, the more pronounced this effect becomes. In the extreme, the exposure to credit spread becomes high enough to create negative durations.

To corroborate these results, we turned to our global risk model.[1] For each of the letter-grade credit indices, we performed the following experiment. We calculated the key-rate durations (KRDs) of the index (the full analytical values) and then constructed an all-Treasury portfolio with the same KRD profile. We then used the risk model to analyze one against the other, using the all-Treasury portfolio as the benchmark and the credit index as the portfolio. Among other things, the risk model calculates beta of the portfolio relative to the index, defined as the ratio of the covariance of portfolio and benchmark returns to the benchmark return variance. For a unit of the benchmark return, beta gives the expected portfolio return. Beta can also be viewed as a hedge ratio. In this particular case, where the benchmark represents pure term-structure risk, a beta of 1 means that the expected response of the portfolio to a change in rates is exactly in line with what is implied by its KRD profile. A beta less than 1 means that the KRDs taken alone overstate the exposure to term-structure risk and that once the model takes into account the correlation between term-structure factors and all other risk factors, the effective sensitivity to changes in rates is just a fraction of what is implied by the KRDs alone.

---

1. For details on our global risk model see Chapter 26.

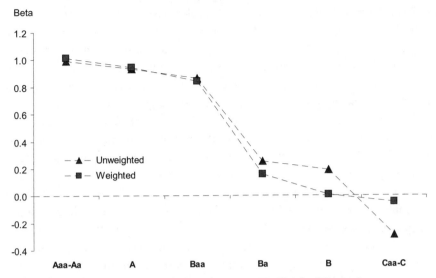

Figure 33-2. Risk Model Betas: Credit Indices vs. KRD-Matched Treasuries
As of September 30, 2004

Figure 33-2 shows the risk model betas obtained for different credit ratings. Two sets of results are shown, reflecting two different methods of calibrating the model covariance matrix from historical data. The "unweighted" mode uses all of the available historical data and is thus based on about 15 years worth of monthly bond market history. The "weighted" mode uses exponential time decay with a half-life of 1 year to ensure a much stronger influence by the most recent historical data.

The results from the two calibration methods are very similar. Consistent with Figure 33-1, we see a beta of 1 for credits rated Aa and better and a small decrease from this value as we move to the A and Baa ratings. A sudden drop occurs as we cross into high yield, with the betas for Ba near 0.2 and those for lower-rated credits near zero.

The close agreement between Figure 33-1 and the two results in Figure 33-2 is quite remarkable, especially considering the different data sets that were used in the analysis. The regressions of Figure 33-1 used 6 years of daily data, whereas the two risk model results of Figure 33-2 are based on monthly data histories that are either longer (in the unweighted case) or shorter (weighted) than the daily data set. The largest disagreement among the three results is in the lowest-rated portion of the High Yield Index. The longer data series points to a significant negative empirical duration for Caa and lower (beta of –0.29); the estimates based on more recent history indicate a beta closer to zero. Similarly, for B-rated credits, the long-term beta is 0.19, but the more recent estimate is closer to zero.

In the Ba rating category, the unweighted risk model results dovetail quite nicely with the daily regressions, with both showing the empirical duration of about 25% of the analytical duration. These results seem to justify certain popular practices. A rule of thumb to recognize 25% of analytical duration might indeed be called for when the high yield investment consists largely of Ba-rated securities, but 0% might be more appropriate for lower-rated high yield investments.

Just how much of an effect on portfolio performance might this have? Do these relatively modest duration adjustments matter at all compared with the volatility of high yield investments? We investigate using an historical simulation of a simple high yield core-plus strategy. To a portfolio benchmarked against Lehman U.S. Gov/Credit Index, we add a 10% out-of-benchmark allocation to Ba Credit. To implement this, we shift assets out of the investment-grade credit portion of the portfolio. We then address the duration mismatch between the resulting portfolio and the gov/credit benchmark by adjusting the Treasury component (re-weighting between its long and intermediate parts, above and below 10 years, respectively). This duration-hedging adjustment is carried out under several different assumptions of how much of the analytical duration of the Ba component should be counted in the portfolio duration.

Figure 33-3 shows the results of an historical simulation of these different hedging approaches from January 1996 through September 2004, using monthly rebalancing and monthly returns. We first looked at the standard deviation of strategy outperformance over time, or tracking error volatility (TEV). In this regard, the results were mixed. Relative to the 100% case, the hedging strategies that recognize only a part of the high yield duration contribution (and hence add duration in Treasuries to prevent an unintended duration underweight) do show a decrease in TEV. Ignoring the duration of Ba credit entirely causes duration overhedge and leads to an even higher TEV (the 0% case). However, the decreases in TEV in the partial-hedging cases are relatively small compared to the total amount of risk, from 14.8 bp/month down to a minimum of 13.8 bp/month. Moreover, if minimizing TEV is the goal, the best hedge ratio seems to be 50%, and not 25% as indicated by our empirical studies.

We should bear in mind, though, that the main goal of the strategy is to express a view on the Ba asset class while remaining neutral on interest rates. To test how well this was accomplished, we measured the correlation of the strategy's outperformance with the total return of the U.S. Treasury Index. Here, once again, we see that this is best accomplished with the 25% hedging rule. When the full duration of the Ba component is included in our portfolio duration, the outperformance series has a correlation of –0.53 with the Treasury Index, a clear indication of a duration underweight (whenever the Treasury Index does well, the portfolio underperforms). When the Treasury hedge is increased because 0% contribution

Figure 33-3. Effect of Assumed Duration Hedge Ratio, vs. Gov/Credit Index
10% Core-Plus Position in Ba Credit, January 1996–September 2004

Assumed duration contribution of high yield (% of OAD)	100	50	25	0
Realized TEV (bp/month)	14.8	13.8	14.2	15.1
Correlation of outperformance with Treasury Index return	−0.53	−0.20	−0.01	0.16

of the Ba duration is assumed, we cross over to a positive correlation, indicating a duration overweight. The crossover point at which the correlation becomes zero is at a beta of almost exactly 25%.

THE RELATIONSHIP BETWEEN HIGH YIELD RETURNS AND EQUITY MARKETS

If interest rates do not drive high yield returns, what does? It is widely perceived that high yield returns follow the equity market, so our next step was to regress the monthly price returns of the letter-grade credit indices on the returns of broad equity market indices. The results were fairly disappointing. As can be seen in Figure 33-4b, the R^2 for the S&P 500 Index did not exceed 30% for bonds of any credit rating.[2] We then replaced the broad market index by customized equity indices matched to each bond index. These "matched-equity" indices consist only of the equity of the issuers in the particular bond index, with weights determined by the issuer market value weights within the bond index. Regressions of letter-grade credit indices against their matched-equity indices showed much higher explanatory power for the high yield returns, with R^2 as high as 61% for B-rated credit. The important message here is that the assumption that high yield returns strongly follow equity returns is only true at the level of a single firm. While a particular high yield bond might be best hedged by the equity of the issuing firm (see Chapter 35), equity market as a whole does not explain high yield returns.

We have attempted to measure the empirical duration of high yield bonds via simple empirical methods. We have seen that their empirical duration is much shorter than their analytical duration, and surmise that this is due to the negative

---

2. Figure 33-4 shows the results for the S&P 500 Index over a relatively short period. We repeated this regression over a much longer period (January 1989–September 2004), as well as for two broader equity indices—the Russell 2000 and the Wilshire 5000. None of these other regressions achieved an R^2 above 30%.

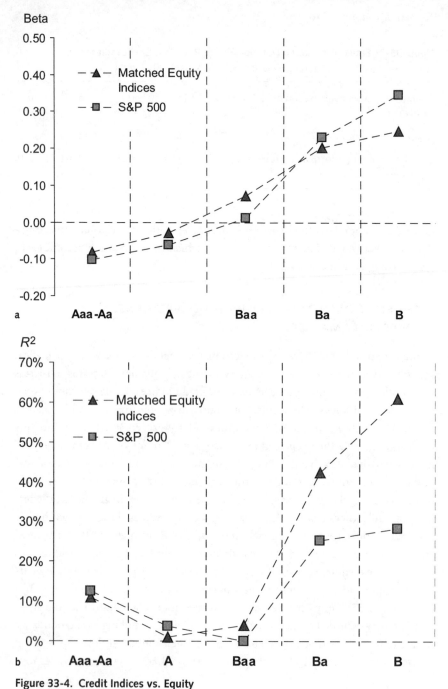

Figure 33-4. Credit Indices vs. Equity
(a) Regression Betas, (b) Regression R^2, Monthly Observations, November 2000–
September 2004

Figure 33-5. A Deeper Look: Results of a Multivariate Regression
Monthly Observations, November 2000–September 2004

	Aaa-Aa	A	Baa	Ba	B	Caa-C
Coefficients						
Intercept	0.05	−0.06	−0.12	−0.26	−0.42	−0.69
Matched equity	0.03	0.01	0.06	0.15	0.16	0.18
Investment-grade credit OAS change	−0.97	−4.58	−6.96	−8.91	−9.5	−11.47
10-year yield change	−4.65	−5.19	−5.67	−2.92	−2.66	−1.79
R^2 (%)	97	96	96	73	71	64
t-Statistics						
Intercept	1.28	−1.32	−2.13	−1.46	−1.6	−1.47
Matched equity	2.55	0.86	3.88	3.94	4.61	4.55
Investment-grade credit OAS change	−2.51	−8.77	−12.12	−5.13	−3.58	−2.44
10-year yield change	−32.53	−31.52	−28.86	−4.71	−3.04	−1.13

correlation between Treasury yields and credit spreads. Partly to test this theory and partly to separate the direct effect of interest-rate movement from the indirect effect of other correlated factors, we carried out one more set of regressions to explain monthly high yield returns. This time, we used three variables: the matched-equity indices discussed earlier, the 10-year Treasury yield change, and the monthly change in the OAS of the U.S. Investment-Grade Credit Index.

The results of these regressions are shown in Figure 33-5. We found them interesting in several ways. First, this combination of factors does a good job of explaining index returns across the credit spectrum, with high R^2 down through high yield. As expected, the key explanatory factor (the one with the high t-statistics) for investment-grade credit is the 10-year yield change. We were particularly intrigued by the fact that all three factors were statistically significant (t-statistics with absolute value greater than 2) from Baa through B. The equity component is significant even at the Baa level (and somewhat improbably for Aa), and the interest-rate sensitivity remains significant down to the B level. When we looked at the single-variable regression against Treasury yields, we found little or no sensitivity for B-rated credits, owing to the correlations with credit spreads and equities. When these other exposures are adequately hedged, the remaining return does retain an interest-rate component—roughly equivalent to half of its analytical duration.

The regression coefficients for the OAS change variable confirm our earlier conclusions. As we go down the credit spectrum, the sensitivity to the spread factor continues to increase. In a sense, it seems as if high yield represents an amplified exposure to investment-grade credit spreads. This increased exposure, combined with the negative correlation of this factor with interest rates (−0.23 for the period July 1989–September 2004), causes the steep decrease in empirical duration seen in Figures 33-1 and 33-2.

SPREAD DEPENDENCE OF EMPIRICAL DURATION

Are the results presented so far typical of every period? If not, how much variation do empirical durations exhibit over time? In particular, are empirical durations affected by changes in spread levels and spread volatility? We investigated this possibility and found strong evidence that empirical durations do, indeed, depend on spreads.

To gain a better understanding of the relationship between empirical duration and spread level, we first look at the contemporaneous changes in empirical duration and spread level. Figure 33-6 plots the time series of 90-day trailing empirical duration between December 1998 and January 2005 alongside the average spread during that period for the Ba Credit Index. The figure illustrates two issues. First, there is considerable variation in empirical duration, which ranges in the sample between −1.8 and +3.0. Second, empirical duration is negatively correlated to spread. Empirical duration rises when spreads fall and vice versa.

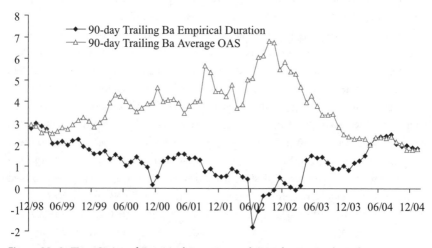

Figure 33-6. Time Series of Empirical Duration and OAS for Ba Credit Index
Based on 90-Day Trailing Observations, December 1998–January 2005

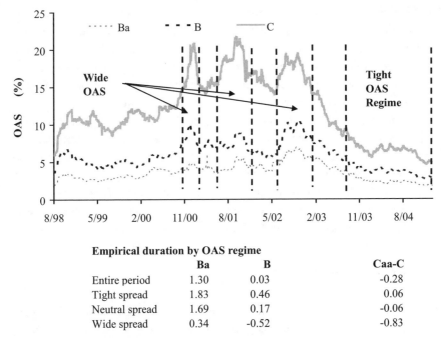

Empirical duration by OAS regime

	Ba	B	Caa-C
Entire period	1.30	0.03	-0.28
Tight spread	1.83	0.46	0.06
Neutral spread	1.69	0.17	-0.06
Wide spread	0.34	-0.52	-0.83

Figure 33-7. Empirical Duration in Various Spread Regimes
Daily Observations, August 1998–February 2005

Are the findings in Figure 33-6 applicable to the lower end of the high yield credit universe as well? In order to answer this question, we divided the sample period into three spread regimes: wide, neutral, and tight. Wide and tight OAS regimes are defined as periods in which the average OAS of the three credit quality groups (Ba, B, and Caa-C) is above and below the seventy-fifth and twenty-fifth percentiles, respectively.[3] Figure 33-7 plots the three daily spread time series classified by regime between August 1998 and February 2005. Not surprisingly, the persistent decrease in spreads since the end of 2002 resulted in the period since August 2003 being classified as a tight-spread regime. The period between November 2000 and February 2003 includes three separate subperiods classified as a wide regime. The rest of the observations in that time period and those before November 2000 fall into the neutral category.

Figure 33-7 reports empirical duration figures by quality and regime (i.e., three separate calculations are performed for each credit quality, with duration calculated

---

3. We take the average spread of the three credit qualities in order to get a more stable classification of the observations into regimes. The results do not change substantially if we repeat the analysis with separate bounds for each credit quality.

as the sensitivity of daily price returns to daily changes in the 10-year yield). The results demonstrate a striking difference in the empirical duration in the three different regimes. Whereas empirical duration figures during the neutral spread period are similar to those previously reported for the entire period, the figures for the tight and wide regimes are significantly different: it is higher than average in tight-spread periods and lower than average in wide-spread periods.

Figures 33-6 and 33-7 illustrate that empirical duration is correlated with the level of spread. To quantify the effect of a change in spread level on empirical duration explicitly, we regress the index price change of both investment-grade and high yield credit between August 1998 and February 2005 against two explanatory variables. The first variable is simply the daily yield change of the 10-year Treasury, and the second is the product of the 10-year yield change and spread level (OAS).[4] The results of this regression form a simple linear approximation for the empirical duration of each quality group as a function of spread:

$$D_j^{\mathrm{emp}}(S) = \beta_j + \gamma_j S. \tag{33-1}$$

The first coefficient, β_j, gives an upper limit to the empirical duration that might be expected for a given quality as spreads approach zero; the second coefficient, γ_j, which tends to be negative, describes the reduction in empirical duration as spreads widen. Since the unrealistic zero-spread case is not represented in the data, it is more meaningful to restate this relationship by centering around the mean spread, $\bar{s}_j$:

$$D_j^{\mathrm{emp}}(S) = (\beta_j + \gamma_j \bar{S}_j) + \gamma_j(S - \bar{S}_j) = D_{j,\mathrm{avg}}^{\mathrm{emp}} + \gamma_j(S - \bar{S}_j). \tag{33-2}$$

The first term in Equation (33-2) is the empirical duration at the average spread; the second term gives an upward or downward adjustment for spreads that are tighter or wider than average.

The regression estimates for the coefficients of empirical duration, β_j, and spread slope, γ_j, are shown in Figure 33-8. The spread slope coefficient is negative and significant for all qualities except Aaa-Aa, which confirms the assertion that duration has a significant spread-dependent component even for investment-grade

---

4. Specifically, we estimated the following regression:

$$\left(\frac{\Delta P}{P}\right)_{j,t} = -\left(\Delta Y_t \times \sum_j I_{j,t}\beta_j + \Delta Y_t S_{j,t}\sum_j I_{j,t}\gamma_j\right) + \varepsilon_{j,t} \quad j \in \{\mathrm{Aaa/Aa, A, Baa, Ba, B, Caa - C}\},$$

where Y is the 10-year Treasury yield, S is the option-adjusted spread, and I_j is a dummy variable that equals 1 if the return is on the j quality group and zero otherwise. Pooling all observations instead of estimating six separate regressions is more efficient but still allows for separate estimates of the coefficients by quality.

Figure 33-8. Regression Estimates of Empirical Duration with Spread Dependence
Daily Data, August 7, 1998–February 10, 2005; Adjusted R^2 = 0.38

	Aaa-Aa	A	Baa	Ba	B	Caa-C
Empirical duration (limit)	4.40	5.85	6.34	3.20	1.15	0.82
t-Statistic	12.38	16.46	17.24	9.19	3.14	2.55
Spread coefficient	0.02	–0.72	–0.78	–0.50	–0.19	–0.09
t-Statistic	0.03	–2.68	–4.42	–5.75	–3.23	–3.66
OAS range						
Minimum	0.32	0.59	1.08	1.71	2.53	4.60
Mean	0.73	1.23	1.93	3.62	5.82	11.91
Maximum	1.22	2.30	3.74	7.01	10.44	21.71
Empirical duration at						
Minimum OAS	4.41	5.43	5.50	2.35	0.67	0.41
Mean OAS	4.41	4.96	4.83	1.39	0.04	–0.25
Maximum OAS	4.42	4.20	3.42	–0.31	–0.83	–1.13
Long-term empirical duration (no spread dependence)	4.41	4.95	4.78	1.30	0.03	–0.28

bonds. For all qualities, duration increases as spreads tighten. To see the effect of changes in OAS on duration, the figure shows the average, minimum, and maximum OAS levels over the period and the associated empirical durations. For example, the empirical duration of Ba ranges between –0.31 and +2.35, with a value of 1.39 at the average OAS level of 362 bp. For comparison, Figure 33-8 also shows the long-term empirical durations that are obtained for the entire time period if the spread dependence is ignored. We find that by using the spread-adjusted method, our duration estimates are somewhat longer than the long-term numbers, even for mean OAS levels, and significantly longer when spreads are tighter than average, as is currently the case.

A potential criticism of the regression results reported in Figure 33-8 is that they fail to control for fundamental changes in index duration that affect both analytical and empirical durations. Such changes can arise from a decline in yields (i.e., simply moving on the price-yield curve) or as a natural result of index turnover (e.g., an increase in supply at the long end of the curve). To control for all such effects, we re-estimate the regression after making a simple modification. The two explanatory variables are multiplied by the OAD, so that our regression yields an estimate of the hedge ratio directly (empirical duration divided by OAD),

Figure 33-9. Direct Estimation of Hedge Ratios

Daily Data, August 7, 1998–February 10, 2005, Adjusted $R^2 = 0.38$

	Aaa-Aa	A	Baa	Ba	B	Caa-C
Empirical hedge ratio (limit)	0.92	0.97	1.00	0.64	0.26	0.21
t-Statistic	12.21	15.27	16.52	8.94	3.22	2.77
Spread slope	−0.04	−0.09	−0.11	−0.10	−0.04	−0.02
t-Statistic	−0.44	−1.83	−3.87	−5.52	−3.29	−3.79
Hedge Ratio Calculated at:						
Minimum OAS	0.91	0.91	0.88	0.47	0.15	0.11
Mean OAS	0.89	0.86	0.78	0.28	0.02	−0.06
Maximum OAS	0.87	0.76	0.58	−0.06	−0.18	−0.28

as opposed to an estimate of the empirical duration. The results in Figure 33-9 illustrate once again that the hedge ratios are spread dependent, except for Aaa-Aa, and that the spread effect is stronger for high yield than for investment-grade credit, as reflected in the higher *t*-statistics and in the wider variation of hedge ratios across the observed range of spreads. For Ba-rated debt, in particular, the empirical hedge ratio can be anywhere from −0.1 to 0.5, depending on spreads.

Based on the results in Figure 33-9, we can express the empirical hedge ratio as a linear function of spread, much as we did in Equation (33-2) for empirical duration:

$$H_j^{\text{emp}}(S) = H_{j,\text{avg}}^{\text{emp}} + Slope_j(S - \bar{S}_j), \tag{33-3}$$

where $H_{j,\text{avg}}^{\text{emp}}$ denotes the hedge ratio that would be expected at average spread levels, and the slope is the rate at which this hedge ratio would change with widening spreads. Figure 33-10 plots this linear function, separately for each quality, across the range of OAS levels observed during our sample period (August 1998–February 2005). There is a striking amount of overlap among the hedge ratios for different quality groups, especially considering that each line segment shown was estimated independently. The empirical duration of a C-rated bond at a period when spreads are tight can be the same as that of a B-rated bond when spreads are wider. It seems that the three investment-grade qualities could fit quite well to a single model for empirical duration as a function of spread; the three high yield quality groups could be combined as well. However, there does seem to be a significant gap between the behavior of high yield and investment-grade assets. Baa-rated assets with a spread of 200–300 bp have exhibited hedge ratios between 0.6

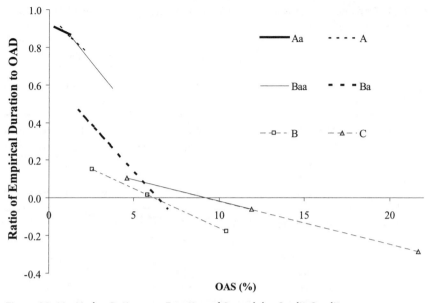

Figure 33-10. Hedge Ratios as a Function of Spread, by Credit Quality

and 0.8, whereas Ba-rated assets in the same range have hedge ratios closer to 0.3 or 0.4.

This fundamental difference between investment-grade and high yield bonds is primarily the role of default risk. When the likelihood of default is perceived as high, the primary determinant of a bond's value is the assumed rate of recovery upon default. In extreme cases, this may cause all bonds of a given issuer (at the same seniority level) to be marked at the same dollar price, regardless of maturity. Clearly, such a valuation would be little influenced by changes in Treasury yields. In situations such as this, the perceived negative correlation between Treasury yields and spreads is just an artifact of an improperly specified model, in which the bond's price is related to the discounted value of cash flows that the market assumes will never arrive.

Even in less extreme situations, the pricing of credit-risky securities is influenced by the probabilities that the issuer will default at different points in time and the assumptions investors make about what the recovery rate would be should this occur. Including the possibility of a recovery event in which we receive a principal payment smaller than the full amount, but earlier in time, lessens the sensitivity of the pricing model to changes in Treasury rates.

Would the gap between investment grade and high yield in Figure 33-10 disappear if we could screen out bonds trading to a default assumption? To investigate this possibility, we repeated the regressions shown in Figures 33-9 and 33-10

Figure 33-11. Empirical Durations and Hedge Ratios Estimated Using Different Approaches
As of February 10, 2005

		Aaa-Aa	A	Baa	Ba	B	Caa-C
OAS (%)		0.33	0.59	1.10	1.74	2.73	4.86
OAD		4.80	5.83	6.52	5.32	4.34	4.19
Empirical durations	90-day trailing estimate	4.16	5.22	5.47	1.94	0.22	−0.02
	Estimated as a function of spread—from Equation (33-2)	4.40	5.43	5.48	2.32	0.64	0.38
	Long-term average	4.41	4.95	4.78	1.30	0.03	−0.28
Empirical hedge ratios	90-day trailing estimate	0.87	0.90	0.84	0.36	0.05	0.00
	Estimated as a function of spread—from Equation (33-3)	0.91	0.91	0.88	0.47	0.14	0.10
	Long-term average	0.89	0.86	0.78	0.26	0.01	−0.06

after screening our database to remove all bonds with a dollar price of 80 or less. To our surprise, we found that the results hardly change. The large difference between investment grade and high yield persists, with substantially lower hedge ratios for high yield bonds than for investment-grade bonds at similar spreads. This suggests that the difference between the interest-rate sensitivities in the two markets may not be entirely due to considerations of default and recovery, but rather might be due to market segmentation effects. It is typical for investors in investment-grade credit to measure their performance in terms of excess returns over Treasuries (or swaps), whereas high yield performance is usually measured in terms of total return. This difference in approach (and the hedging practices that result from it) could well be an additional factor that mitigates the effect of interest-rate movements on high yield valuations.

So where do we stand today? In the current low-spread environment, how should one hedge the duration of a high yield investment? Figure 33-11 offers several answers to this question. First, we present simple estimates of empirical duration calculated over the most recently observed 90 business days and divide by the OAD to obtain the corresponding estimate of the hedge ratio. Second, using the linear estimates we have developed for empirical durations and hedge ratios as functions of spread, we plug in the current spread levels. We then compare these results with the long-term averages, with no adjustment for spread level. We find agreement between these two approaches that the current hedge ratio should be higher than the historical long-term average; however, our spread-dependent estimate gives values that are even higher than those indicated by the most recent empirical tests. For example, our estimate suggests that the Ba hedge ratio should be 0.47 based on the current spread level; the observed 90-day trailing result of 0.36 is about halfway between this value and the long-run ratio of 0.26.

CONCLUSION

This chapter endeavors to shed light on a very practical issue of hedging interest-rate exposure of credit investments. The sheer number of opinions on the subject that we have encountered, as well as the ad hoc nature of many practices adopted by various managers, show that this is still very much an open question. Our empirical results corroborate one of the more prevalent practices for high yield: hedging a quarter of the duration. We derive additional confidence from the fact that different methods, applied over different time periods, seem to indicate the same "magical" number of 0.25. The necessary caveat, though, is that this hedge ratio applies only to the Ba part of the high yield market. Lower-quality investments, such as B and Caa, exhibit essentially no interest-rate sensitivity and do not require additional hedging when added to investment-grade portfolios.

As with all empirical findings based on historical data, caution is in order. Empirical durations vary significantly from one time period to another. We demonstrate that the empirical duration of credit securities varies over time in response to changes in the spread environment; in particular, it increases as spreads tighten. The interest-rate sensitivity of Ba credit, for example, can be anywhere between 0 and 50% of its OAD, a wide range around the long-term mean of 25%. This relationship is not confined to high yield credit but is evident in investment grade as well. In light of the current tight-spread environment, our results stress that the interest-rate sensitivity of high yield bonds should not be overlooked.

In the course of this study, we also obtained a deeper insight into why these lower-quality bonds seem to have zero duration. Additional regressions using equity returns, as well as the multivariate regression described just prior to this conclusion, convinced us that sensitivity of the cash flows of high yield bonds to interest rates does not just disappear, or get replaced somehow with sensitivity to equity market moves. The main reason behind the apparently nonexistent duration is that credit spread sensitivity reaches a level where its magnitude is comparable to rates sensitivity. The negative correlation between the two (a well-known phenomenon in itself) then produces duration that, depending on the time period and other factors, hovers around zero.

34. Duration Times Spread: A New Measure of Spread Risk for Credit Securities

The standard presentation of the asset allocation in a portfolio or a benchmark is in terms of percentage of market value. It is widely recognized that this is not sufficient for fixed-income portfolios, where differences in duration can cause two portfolios with the same allocation of market weights to have very different exposures to macro-level risks. As a result, many fixed-income portfolio managers have become accustomed to expressing their allocations in terms of contributions to duration—the product of the percentage of portfolio market value represented by a given market cell and the average duration of securities comprising that cell. This represents the sensitivity of the portfolio to a parallel shift in yields across all securities within this market cell. For credit portfolios in particular, the corresponding measure would be contributions to spread duration, measuring the sensitivity to a parallel shift in spreads. Determining the set of active spread duration contributions (the differences between the exposures of the portfolio and the benchmark) to market cells and/or issuers is one of the primary decisions taken by credit portfolio managers.

Yet all spread durations were not created equal. Just as one can create a portfolio that matches the benchmark exactly by market weights, but clearly takes more credit risk (e.g., by investing in the longest-duration credits within each cell), one can match the benchmark exactly by spread duration contributions and still take more credit risk—by choosing the credits with the widest spreads within each cell. These credits presumably trade wider than their peer groups for a reason; that is, the market consensus has determined that they are more risky, and they are often referred to as "high-beta" credits because their spreads tend to react more strongly than the rest of the market to any systematic shock. Portfolio managers are well

Based on research first published by Lehman Brothers in 2005.

aware of this, but many of them tend to treat it as a secondary effect, rather than as an intrinsic part of the allocation process.

To reflect the view that higher-spread credits represent greater exposures to sector-specific risks, we propose a simple risk-sensitivity measure that utilizes spreads as a fundamental part of the credit portfolio management process. We represent sector exposures by contributions to duration times spread (DTS), computed as the product of market weight, spread duration, and spread. An overweight of 5% to a market cell implemented by purchasing bonds with a spread of 80 bp and a spread duration of 3 years is considered to be of the same magnitude as an overweight of 3% using bonds with an average spread of 50 bp and a spread duration of 8 years ($0.05 \times 0.80 \times 3 = 0.03 \times 0.50 \times 8 = 0.12$).

How does this make sense? As mentioned above, a portfolio's contribution to spread duration within a given market cell is its sensitivity to a parallel shift in spreads across all the bonds in that cell. What is the intuition behind the new measure we propose?

In fact, the intuition is very clear. Let us look at a simple expression for the return of a given bond owing strictly to change in spread R_{spread}. Let D denote the spread duration of the bond and s its spread; the spread change return[1] is then given by

$$R_{spread} = -D \cdot \Delta s. \tag{34-1}$$

It is quite easy to see that this equation is equivalent to

$$R_{spread} = -D \cdot s \cdot \frac{\Delta s}{s}. \tag{34-2}$$

That is, just as spread duration is the sensitivity to an absolute change in spread (e.g., spreads widen by 5 bp), DTS is the sensitivity to a relative change in spread (e.g., spreads increase by 5% of their current levels). Note that this notion of relative spread change provides for a formal expression of the rough idea discussed earlier—that credits with wider spreads are riskier since they tend to experience greater spread changes.

Given that the two foregoing representations are equivalent, why should one be preferred over the other? The advantage of the second approach, based on relative spread changes, is due to the stability of the associated volatility estimates.

---

1. Spread change return is closely related to excess return, the return advantage of a corporate bond over duration-matched Treasuries. Excess return can be approximated by the sum of the spread change return and an additional component owing to spread carry.

In the absolute spread change approach [Equation (34-1)] we can see that the volatility of excess returns can be approximated by

$$\sigma_{return} \cong D \cdot \sigma_{spread}^{absolute}, \tag{34-3}$$

while in the relative spread change approach of Equation (34-2), excess return volatility follows

$$\sigma_{return} \cong D \cdot s \cdot \sigma_{spread}^{relative}. \tag{34-4}$$

Using a large sample with more than 450,000 observations spanning the period September 1989–January 2005, we demonstrated that the volatility of spread changes (both systematic and idiosyncratic) is indeed linearly proportional to spread level. This relation holds irrespective of the sector duration or time period. This explains why relative spread volatilities of spread asset classes are much more stable than absolute spread volatilities, across both different sectors and credit quality tiers, as well as over time.

The paradigm shift we advocate has many implications for portfolio managers, in terms of both the way they manage exposures to industry and quality factors (systematic risk) and their approach to issuer exposures (nonsystematic risk). Throughout the chapter, we present evidence that the relative spread change approach offers increased insight into both of these sources of risk.

The chapter is divided into two parts. First, we examine the behavior of spread changes of corporate bonds and establish that absolute spread volatility is proportional to spread—at both the sector and the issuer levels. These results apply to both investment-grade and high yield credit. Second, we look at what our findings imply for the management of a portfolio's excess return volatility. We start by showing that portfolios with very different spreads and spread durations but with similar product of the two exhibit the same excess return volatility. We then demonstrate that modeling spread changes in relative rather than absolute terms generates improved forward-looking estimates of excess return volatility. Finally, in a controlled index replication experiment, we show that matching index sector-quality allocations in terms of contributions to DTS can track the credit index more closely than matching the contributions to duration. We conclude with a discussion of the various implications of this research for portfolio managers.

ANALYSIS OF SPREAD BEHAVIOR OF CORPORATE BONDS

How can we get a good feeling for the amount of risk associated with a particular market sector? Most typically, for lack of any better estimate, the historical volatility of a particular sector over some prior time period is used to estimate its volatility

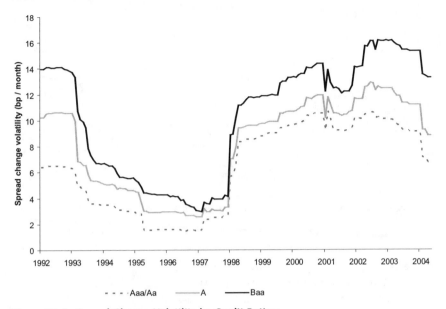

Figure 34-1. Spread Change Volatility by Credit Rating
Trailing 36 Months, September 1992–January 2005[a]
[a]Based on all bonds comprising the Lehman Corporate Index.

for the coming period.[2] For this approach to be reliable, we would like to find that these volatilities are fairly stable. Unfortunately, this is not always the case.

As an example, Figure 34-1 shows the 36-month trailing volatility of spread changes for various credit ratings comprising the Lehman Corporate Index between September 1992 and January 2005. It is clear that spread change volatility decreased substantially until 1998 and then increased significantly from 1998 through 2005. The dramatic rise in spread volatility since 1998 was only partially a response to the Russian crisis and the Long-Term Capital Management debacle, as volatility has not reverted to its pre-1998 level.

One explanation for the large variation in volatility during this time period is that spreads increased significantly for all credit asset classes. If the investment-

---

2. This practice leads to perennial questions about how much history should be used in such estimation. A longer time period leads to more stable estimates of volatility; a shorter time period (or a weighting scheme that gives more weight to recent observations) makes the estimate less stable, but better able to adapt to fundamental changes in the marketplace. In either case, the large swings in volatility that the market can experience mean that we are always trying to catch up to market events, and there will always be some amount of lag between the time of a volatility change and the time that it is first reflected in our estimates.

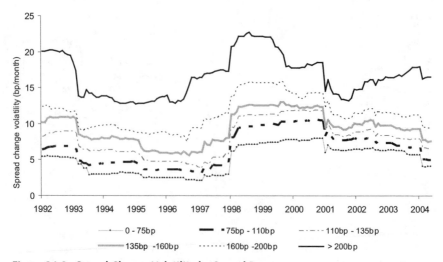

Figure 34-2. Spread Change Volatility by Spread Range
Trailing 36 Months, September 1992–January 2005[a]
  [a]Based on all bonds comprising the Lehman Corporate Index.

grade corporate universe is partitioned by spread levels, the volatilities of the resulting spread buckets are considerably more stable, as seen in Figure 34-2. After an initial shock in 1998, the volatilities within each spread bucket reverted almost exactly to their pre-1998 level (beginning in August 2001, exactly 36 months after the Russian crisis). In this respect, one could relate the results of Figure 34-1 to an increase in spreads—both across the market and within each quality group.

As suggested by Equation (34-4), our proposed remedy to the volatility instability problem is to approximate the absolute spread volatility (in bp/month) by multiplying the historically observed relative spread volatility (in percent/month) by the current spread (in bp). This can help stabilize the process if relative spread volatility is more stable than absolute spread volatility. The results in Figure 34-2 point in this direction, as they show a clear relationship between spread level and volatility.

Figure 34-3 plots the volatility of absolute and relative spread changes of all the bonds in the Lehman Corporate Index rated Baa side by side. (Relative spread changes are calculated simply as the ratio of spread change to the beginning-of-month spread level.) The comparison illustrates that a modest stability advantage is gained by measuring the volatility of relative spread changes; however, the improvement is not as great as we might have hoped, and the figure seems to show that even relative spread changes are quite unstable. This apparent instability, how-

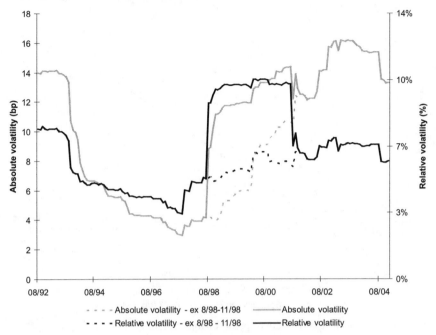

Figure 34-3. Absolute and Relative Spread Change Volatility of Baa Credit
Trailing 36 Months (September 1992–January 2005)

ever, is due solely to the dramatic events that took place in the second half of 1998. We recompute the two time series excluding the four observations representing the period August 1998–November 1998 and plot the two modified volatility time series alongside the two original time series. The difference between the modified time series is striking. From a low of 3 bp/month in mid-1997, absolute spread volatility increased steadily through a high of 15 bp/month in 2002–2003, growing by a factor of five. However, once we remove the effect of those few months in 1998, we find that relative spread volatility increases much more modestly over the same time period, from 3 to 7% a month.

Another demonstration of the enhanced stability of relative spreads is seen when we compare the volatilities of various market segments over distinct time periods. We have already identified 1998 as a critical turning point for the credit markets, owing to the combined effect of the Russian default and the Long-Term Capital Management crisis. To what extent is volatility information prior to 1998 relevant in the post-1998 period? In Figure 34-4, we plot pre-1998 volatility on the x-axis, and post-1998 volatility on the y-axis. We do this for two different measures of

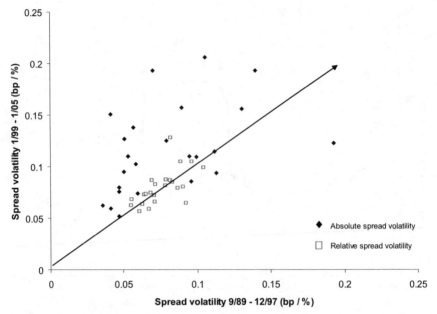

Figure 34-4. Absolute and Relative Spread Change Volatility
Before and after 1998[a]

[a]Based on a partition of the corporate investment-grade universe of eight sectors ×
three credit ratings.

volatility: absolute and relative spread volatility.[3] Each point shown on the graph
represents a particular sector × quality cell of our Investment-Grade Corporate
Index, which we have divided into eight industry groups and three quality cells.[4]
Points along the diagonal line indicate that the volatilities are the same over the
two time periods.

Two clear phenomena can be observed here. First, most of the observations
representing absolute spread volatilities are located quite far above the line, pointing to an increase in volatility in the second period of the sample, despite the fact
that the events of 1998 are not reflected in the data. In contrast, relative spread
volatilities are quite stable with almost all observations located on the 45° line or

3. To enable the two to be shown on the same set of axes, both absolute and relative spread
volatility are expressed in units with similar magnitudes. However, the interpretation is different: an absolute spread change of 0.1 represents a 10-bp parallel shift across a sector, whereas
a relative spread change of 0.1 means that all spreads in the sector move by 10% of their current
values (e.g., from 50 to 55, from 200 to 220).
4. The sector breakdown is: banking, finance, basic industry, consumer cyclical, consumer
noncyclical, communications, energy, and utility.

very close to it. This is because the pick-up in volatility in the second period was accompanied by a similar increase in spreads. Second, relative spread volatilities of various sectors are quite tightly clustered, ranging from 5% to a bit over 10%, whereas the range of absolute volatilities is much wider, ranging from 5 bp/month to more than 20 bp/month.

The results presented so far clearly indicate that absolute spread volatility is highly unstable and tends to rise with increasing spread, but computing volatilities based on relative spread change generates a more stable time series. These findings have important implications for the appropriate way of measuring excess return volatility and demonstrate the need to better understand the behavior of spread changes.

To analyze the behavior of spread changes we first examined the dynamics of month-to-month changes in spreads of individual bonds. When spreads widen or tighten across a sector, do they tend to follow a pattern of parallel shift or one in which spread changes are proportional to spread? This key issue should determine how we measure exposures to systematic spread changes.

As a next step, we looked at systematic spread volatility. If spreads change in a relative fashion then the volatility of systematic spread changes across a given sector of the market should be proportional to the average spread of that sector. This is true when comparing the risk of different sectors at a given point in time or when examining the volatility of a given sector at different points in time.

To complete our analysis we also examined nonsystematic spread volatility, or issuer risk. The dispersion of spread changes among the various issuers within a given market cell, or the extent by which the spread changes of individual issuers can deviate from those of the rest of the sector, also tends to be proportional to spread.

We investigated each of these issues using monthly spread data from the Lehman Brothers Corporate Bond Index historical database. The data set spans more than 15 years, from September 1989 through January 2005, and contains monthly spreads, spread changes, durations, and excess returns for all the bonds in the Corporate Bond Index. For the sections of our study that include high yield bonds as well as investment grade, we augment the data set with historical data from the Lehman High Yield Index. A more detailed description of the data set can be found in the appendix.

The Dynamics of Spread Change

In order to understand why absolute spread volatility is so unstable, we first have to examine how spreads of individual securities change in a given month at a more fundamental level. One basic formulation of the change in spread of some bond i

at time t is that the overall change is simply the sum of two parts—systematic and idiosyncratic:

$$\Delta s_{i,t} = \Delta s_{J,t} + \Delta s_{i,t}^{\text{idiosyncratic}} \quad i \in J, \tag{34-5}$$

where J denotes some peer group of bonds with similar risk characteristics (i.e., such as financials rated Baa with duration of up to 5 years). This formulation is equivalent to assuming that spreads change in a parallel fashion across all securities in a given market cell J (captured by $\Delta s_{J,t}$).

Alternatively, if changes in spreads are proportional to spread level then we have (omitting the subscript t for simplicity):

$$\frac{\Delta s_i}{s_i} = \frac{\Delta s_J}{s_J} + \frac{\Delta s_i^{\text{idio}}}{s_i} \quad \text{or} \quad \Delta s_i = s_i \cdot \frac{\Delta s_J}{s_J} + \Delta s_i^{\text{idio}}. \tag{34-6}$$

Equation (34-6) reflects the idea that systematic spread changes are proportional to the current (systematic) spread level and that the sensitivity of each security to a systematic spread change depends on its level of spread. Higher-spread securities are riskier in that they are more affected by a widening or tightening of spreads than lower-spread securities with similar characteristics.

In order to analyze the behavior of spread changes across different periods and market segments we use Equations (34-5) and (34-6) as the basis of two regression models that we estimate. The first corresponds to the parallel shift approach shown in Equation (34-5):

$$\Delta s_{i,t} = \alpha_{J,t} + \varepsilon_{i,t}. \tag{34-7}$$

The second model reflects the notion of a proportional shift in spreads as in Equation (34-6):

$$\Delta s_{i,t} = \beta_{J,t} \cdot s_{i,t} + \varepsilon_{i,t}. \tag{34-8}$$

Comparing Equations (34-8) and (34-6) shows that the slope coefficient $\beta_{J,t}$ we estimate corresponds to the proportional systematic spread change $\Delta s_{J,t}/s_{J,t}$. These two models are nested in a more general model that allows for both proportional and parallel spread changes to take place simultaneously:

$$\Delta s_{i,t} = \alpha_{J,t} + \beta_{J,t} \cdot s_{i,t} + \varepsilon_{i,t}. \tag{34-9}$$

Before we proceed with a full-scale estimation of the three models, we illustrate the idea with a specific example. Figure 34-5 shows changes in spreads experienced by large issuers that make up the communications sector of the Lehman

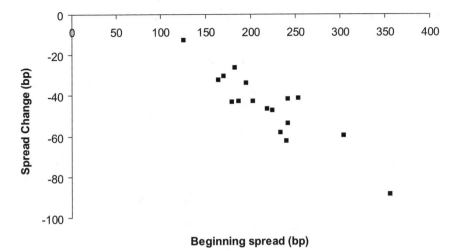

Figure 34-5. Average Spreads and Spread Changes for Large Issuers in the Communications Sector
As of January 2001

Corporate Index against their beginning-of-month spreads for January 2001.[5] It is clear that this sectorwide rally was not characterized by a purely parallel shift; rather issuers with wider spreads tightened by more.

Figure 34-6 shows the regression results when the three general models of spread change are fitted to the data in this specific example. The results verify that spreads in the communication sector in January 2001 changed in a proportional fashion. The slope estimate is highly significant and the high R^2 (97.1%) indicates that the model fits the data well.[6] The combined model, which allows for a simultaneous parallel shift, achieves only a slightly better fit (97.7%) and yields a somewhat unintuitive result: it shows that the sector widens by a parallel shift of 16 bp and simultaneously tightens by a relative spread change of –28%. We therefore estimate a fourth model, which is essentially a variant of the "combined" model:

$$\Delta s_{i,t} = \tilde{\alpha}_{J,t} + \beta_{J,t} \cdot (s_{i,t} - \bar{s}_{J,t}) + \varepsilon_{i,t}. \tag{34-10}$$

5. "Large issuers" refers to issuers that have outstanding issues with market value in excess of 1% of the sector aggregate market value. There are a total of seventeen issuers that represent 216 outstanding issues.

6. Note that since we compare models with and without an intercept, Figure 34-6 reports uncentered R^2 calculated using the total sum of squares (without subtracting the average spread change) rather than centered R^2.

Figure 34-6. Regression Estimates of Various Models of Spread Change

Based on Data for Large Issuers in the Communications Sector as of January 2001

| Model | Equation | Coefficients | | t-Statistics | | R^2 (%) |
		Shift (bp)	Slope (%)	Shift	Slope	
Parallel	(35-7)	−45		−10.9		88.20
Relative	(35-8)		−21		−23.2	97.10
Combined	(35-9)	16	−28	2	−7.9	97.70
Combined with normalized spread	(35-10)	−45	−28	−24.1	−7.9	97.70

Normalizing spreads by subtracting the average spread level in Equation (34-10) yields identical slope coefficients and R^2 to those generated by the "combined model," but now the intercept $\bar{\alpha}_{J,t}$ represents the average spread change in the sample. This model expresses the month's events as a parallel tightening of −45 bp coupled with an additional relative shift, with a slope of −28%, that defines how much more spreads move for issuers with above-average spreads and how much less they move for issuers with below-average spreads.

We conducted a similar analysis to the one presented in Figure 34-6 using individual bond data in all eight sectors and 185 months included in the sample. Our hypothesis that the relative model provides a generally accurate description of the dynamic of spread changes has several testable implications. First, the overall R^2 for the relative model should be significantly better than that of the parallel model and almost as good as that of the combined model. Second, we would like to find that the slope factor is statistically significant (as indicated by the t-statistic) in most months and sectors. Third, the realizations of the slope and the parallel shift factor in the combined model with normalized spread should be in the same direction, especially whenever the market experiences a large move. That is, in all significant spread changes, issues with wider spreads experience larger moves in the same direction.

We find support for all three implications. Figure 34-7 shows the aggregate R^2 for these regressions across all sectors and months. The relative model explains much more of the spread movement in the market than the parallel shift model and almost as much as the less restrictive combined model.

With respect to the second empirical implication, we found that the slope factor was statistically significant 73% of the time. The fact that we found a clear

**Figure 34-7. Aggregate Fit of Various
Models of Spread Change**
Based on 1480 Individual Regressions
(185 months × 8 sectors)

Regression Model	Aggregate R^2 (%)
Combined	35.20
Relative	33.00
Parallel	16.90

linear relationship between the shift and slope factors in the combined model with normalized spreads serves as an additional validation of the relative model. The relatively low R^2 results shown in Figure 34-7 are due to the fact that in many months, there is little systematic change in spreads, and spread changes are largely idiosyncratic. Figure 34-8 shows that large spread changes are accompanied by slope changes in the same direction (the correlation between the two is 80%). That is, bonds that trade at wider spreads widen by more in a widening and tighten by more in a rally. There are essentially no examples of large parallel spread movements in which the slope factor moves in the opposite direction.

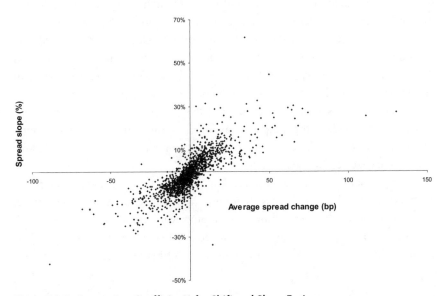

Figure 34-8. Regression Coefficients for Shift and Slope Factors
Based on 1480 Individual Regressions (185 months × 8 sectors)

Systematic Spread Volatility

The security-level analysis established (via the slope coefficient β) that systematic changes in spreads are proportional to the systematic level of spread consistent with Equation (34-6). We now take it a step further and examine the relationship between systematic spread volatility and the level of spreads. To do this, we would like to partition our data set by spread level, separately measure the volatility of each spread bucket, and examine the relationship between spread level and spread volatility.

However, the nature of the data set presents several challenges. First, it is far from homogeneous—it contains bonds from different industries, credit qualities, and maturities. Second, the spreads of corporate bonds changed quite substantially during the course of the period studied, so the populations of any fixed-spread buckets vary substantially from one time period to another. Our goal was to design a partition fine enough that the bonds in each cell share similar risk characteristics, yet coarse enough so that our cells are sufficiently well populated over the course of the time period to give statistically meaningful results.

We have chosen to partition the corporate bond market rather coarsely by sector and duration, and then to subdivide each of these sector × duration cells by spread. We use three sectors (financials, industrials, and utilities) and three duration cells (short, medium, and long). To ensure that each of these cells is well populated each month, the division into three duration groups is not done on the basis of prespecified duration levels, but rather by dividing each sector cell each month into three equally populated groups by duration.[7] Then, bonds in each sector × duration cell are further divided by spread level. To allow a detailed partitioning of the entire spread range while minimizing the number of months in which a bucket is scarcely populated, the spread breakpoints differ from sector to sector. In addition, the financial and industrial sectors are divided into six spread buckets, whereas the utilities sector has only five spread buckets. Hence, based on this partition, bonds in the sample are assigned to one of fifty-one buckets. Further details on the precise definition of the partition and the sample populations assigned to each cell can be found in the appendix.

The systematic spread change in cell *J* in month *t* can be represented simply as the average spread change across all bonds in that bucket in month *t*. Therefore, for each of the cells in the partition, we compute every month the median spread, the average spread change, and the cross-sectional standard deviation of spread change. This procedure produces fifty-one distinct time series data sets; each con-

---

7. Our analysis shows that the distribution of spread duration varies significantly across time and therefore does not allow for a partition based on constant spread duration values.

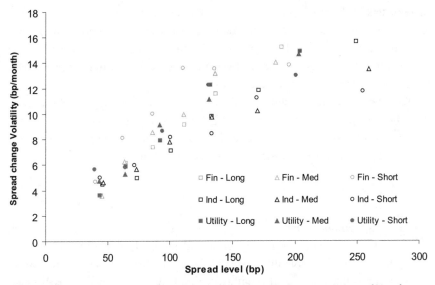

Figure 34-9. Time Series Volatility of Systematic Spread Changes vs. Spread Level
Based on Investment-Grade Credit Data and Monthly Observations, September 1989–
January 2005

sisting of a fairly homogeneous set of bonds for which we have monthly data on
spreads and spread changes. We then calculate the average spread for each group
over time and the time series volatility of these systematic spread changes.[8]

Some caution is in order when using spread data. Spread figures are model
driven and can exhibit extreme values (especially since our modeling of option-
adjusted spreads has changed during the sample period). To mitigate the effect of
outliers, observations that reflect extreme spread changes are excluded.[9] Similarly, the spread level for bucket J is calculated as the time-series average of the
monthly median spread rather than the average spread.

The relation between the volatility of systematic spread changes and spread
level is plotted in Figure 34-9, where each observation represents one of the fifty-

8. Despite our efforts to ensure uniform cell populations, some cells are very sparsely populated (or even empty) in some months. Months in which a cell is populated by fewer than twenty
bonds are not used in the analysis. As a robustness check, we repeat the analysis using the entire
available time series of systematic spread changes and a weighted volatility estimate (where the
number of observations in each month is used as the weighing factor). The results are essentially
unchanged.

9. The entire data set is filtered to exclude observations where changes in spread fall above
the ninety-ninth percentile or below the first percentile. As a result, monthly spread changes
included in our analysis range from –60 to +78 bp.

one buckets in the partition. Figure 34-9 illustrates a clear relationship between spread volatility and spread level. Higher spreads are accompanied by higher volatilities for all sector × duration cells. The duration cells do not seem to have any significant systematic effect; relatively minor differences can be seen between industrials and the other two broad sectors.

Nonetheless, the results shown in Figure 34-9 do not perfectly corroborate our hypothesis of proportional spread volatility, which would predict that all of our observations (or at least all observations within a given sector) should lie along a diagonal line that passes through the origin, of the form

$$\sigma_{\text{spread}}^{\text{absolute}}(s) \cong \theta \cdot s. \tag{34-11}$$

Although the points at the left side of Figure 34-9 seem to fit this description, those to the right, representing higher spread levels, do not seem to continue along this line. Rather, volatility seems to flatten out beyond the 200- to 250-bp range. Is it possible that spread volatility does not continue to grow linearly when spreads increase beyond a certain point?

Before we reject our hypothesis, we should question the significance of these few highest-spread observations. This region of 200–300 bp spreads lies right on the boundary between investment grade and high yield. For a good part of the time period of our study, these spread cells were very lightly populated by our investment-grade bond sample. Owing to our policy of excluding any cell with fewer than twenty bonds, the summary results for these cells may be less robust than desired.

To further examine the relationship between systematic spread change volatility and spread level beyond the 200-bp level, we repeat the analysis including all bonds rated Ba and B during the same time period. This increases the sample size by roughly 34% from 416,783 to 565,602 observations. We use the same sector × duration × spread partition, with the addition of a few more spread buckets to accommodate the widening of the spread range. This expanded partition is shown in Figure 34-10, with the new spread buckets shaded.

Figure 34-11 plots the relationship between systematic spread volatility and spread level using both investment-grade and high yield data. We now find that the linear relationship we were looking for extends out through spreads of 400 bp. As before, the three observations that represent the highest spread bucket in industrials (circled) have somewhat lower than expected spread volatility. Once again, we suspect the statistical relevance of these most extreme data points. The simple linear model of Equation (34-11) provides an excellent fit to the data shown in Figure 34-11, with θ equal to 9.1% if we use all the data points or 9.4% if we exclude the three circled outliers. Thus, our data show that the historical volatility

Figure 34-10. Corporate Investment-Grade and High Yield Universe Partition by Sector and Spread
September 1989–January 2005[a]

Bucket	Spread (bp)								
	1	2	3	4	5	6	7	8	9
Financials	<50	50–75	75–100	100–125	125–150	150–200	>200		
Industrials	<60	60–85	85–120	120–150	150–200	200–275	275–350	350–500	>500
Utilities	<55	55–75	75–115	115–150	150–250	>250			

[a]Spread breakpoints are determined based on population of all bonds rated Aaa–B.

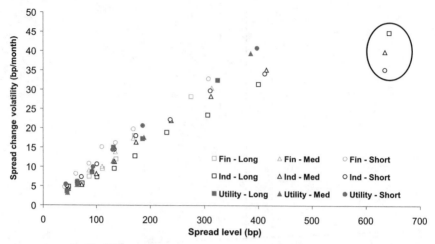

Figure 34-11. Systematic Spread Change Volatility vs. Spread Level Including High Yield Credit
Monthly Observations for All Bonds Rated Aaa-B, September 1989–January 2005

of systematic spread movements can be expressed quite compactly, with only minor dependence on sector or maturity, in terms of a relative spread change volatility of about 9% per month. That is, spread volatility for a market segment trading at 50 bp should be about 4.5 bp/month, whereas that of a market segment at 200 bp should be about 18 bp/month.

Idiosyncratic Spread Changes

To study the spread dependence of idiosyncratic spread volatility, we employ the same sector × duration × spread partition we used for the study of systematic spread volatility. Instead of the average spread change experienced within a given cell in a given month, we now examine the dispersion of spread changes across each cell. Define the idiosyncratic spread change of bond i in market cell J at time t as the difference between its spread change and the average spread change for the cell in that month:

$$\Delta s_{i,t}^{\text{idio}} = \Delta s_{i,t} - \Delta s_{J,t}. \tag{34-12}$$

The volatility of idiosyncratic spread changes is then exactly equal to the cross-sectional standard deviation of total spread changes.[10] Figure 34-12 shows a scatter

10. In order to be consistent with our modeling of relative spread change as in Equation (34-6), we should assume that the effect of the systematic spread change of bond i is propor-

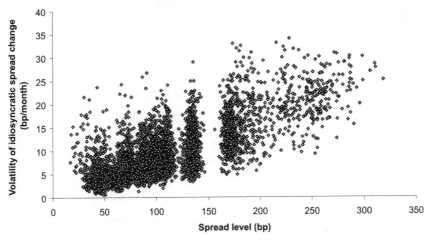

Figure 34-12. Volatility of Idiosyncratic Spread Change vs. Spread Level
September 1989–January 2005[a]

[a] Monthly calculations, computed separately by sector, duration, and spread bucket
($N = 5035$).

plot of the cross-sectional volatility from all months and spread buckets. This plot clearly shows the general pattern of volatilities increasing with spread, as well as the relative paucity of data at the higher spread levels.

Next, we aggregate these data over time to obtain a single measure of idiosyncratic spread volatility for each market cell. We pool all observations of idiosyncratic risk within a given market cell J over all bonds and all months and calculate their standard deviation. This pooled measure of idiosyncratic spread volatility per market cell is plotted in Figure 34-13 against the median spread of the cell.

In Figure 34-13, the linear relationship between spread and spread volatility is strikingly clear. A regression fit against these data shows it to be consistent with Equation (34-11). Moreover, unlike our results for the systematic spread volatility solely within investment-grade data (Figure 34-9), the intercept of this regression is not significantly different from zero.

As before, we extend the analysis to include bonds rated Ba and B. To conserve space we only present the pooled cross-sectional volatility results (Figure 34-14), which clearly illustrate that observations that represent buckets populated almost exclusively by high yield bonds seem to follow the same pattern as buckets

---

tional to its spread, and define idiosyncratic spread change as $\Delta s_{i,t}^{\text{idio}} = \Delta s_{i,t} - (s_{i,t}/s_{J,t}) \cdot \Delta s_{J,t}$. However, as we are carrying out this test over relatively narrow spread buckets, there is very little difference in practice between the two definitions.

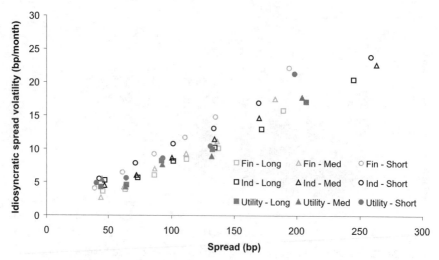

Figure 34-13. Pooled Idiosyncratic Spread Volatility vs. Spread Level[a]

[a]Each observation represents the standard deviation of idiosyncratic spread changes aggregated across all sample months separately by sector, duration, and spread bucket ($N = 51$).

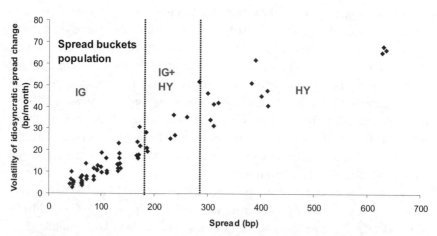

Figure 34-14. Pooled Idiosyncratic Spread Volatility vs. Spread Level Including High Yield Credit

September 1989–January 2005[a]

[a]Computed separately by sector, duration, and spread bucket; sample includes monthly observations for all bonds rated Aaa-B.

populated mostly by investment-grade bonds. However, observations representing the former exhibit more variation than those representing the latter. Once again, the regression results indicate a zero intercept, but the estimated slope coefficient (the relative volatility of idiosyncratic yield change) is somewhat larger than estimated previously, 11.5 vs. 9.6%.

Stability of Spread Behavior

We have established that spreads change in a relative fashion, so that spread volatility (systematic and idiosyncratic) is linearly related to the level of spread. On average, a 100-bp rise in spreads leads to pickups in systematic and idiosyncratic volatility of roughly 9.0 and 11.5 bp/month, respectively. However, except in Figure 34-4 we did not directly address the issue of stability. How much variation do these figures exhibit across sectors and time?

To examine the magnitude of variation across time, we compute (in the sector × duration × spread partition) the yearly systematic spread volatility and corresponding average spread level (i.e., using 12 months of average spread change) for each bucket. Depending on the sample composition and population, this procedure generates between 38 and 66 observations a year.[11] We then regress these estimates of systematic spread volatility against an intercept and a spread slope factor. We do the same for idiosyncratic spread volatility—except that we use the monthly cross-sectional volatility estimates—which results in 300–500 observations in each yearly regression.

Parts (a) and (b) of Figure 34-15 show the yearly spread slope estimates and corresponding adjusted R^2. The results are plotted for investment-grade credit and separately when high yield securities are included as well. The estimated coefficients are all highly significant, with t-statistics ranging between 15 and 30 for both systematic and idiosyncratic spread volatility. Not surprisingly, Figure 34-15 reveals that including high yield data generally increases the spread estimate for both systematic and idiosyncratic volatility. The spike in volatility caused by the 1998 Russian crisis is evident in the large estimate of spread slope in 1998 (except for the case of idiosyncratic volatility with high yield). Excluding 1998, the spread slope estimates are remarkably stable in light of the small number of observations used in the estimation.

---

11. When high yield securities are included in the sample, the partition has a total of sixty-six buckets. Only observations that represent buckets that were populated with a minimum of twenty securities during the entire year are included in the analysis.

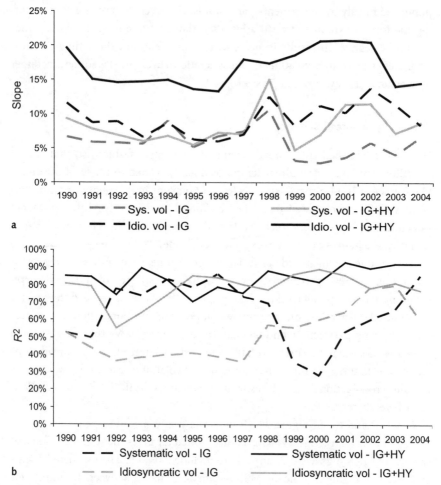

Figure 34-15. Yearly Regression of Spread Volatility against Spread Level
January 1990–December 2004[a]

[a] Monthly observations, using all U.S. corporate bonds rated Aaa-Baa and separately including high yield bonds rated Ba-B.

Figure 34-15b reveals that the explanatory power of the regressions is higher and more stable when high yield securities are included. When we analyze investment-grade data only, the R^2 of our regressions goes as low as 40% for systematic volatility and 30% for idiosyncratic volatility. When we include high yield data as well, the regression results are much better, achieving R^2 values consistently over 70% for systematic volatility and 60% for idiosyncratic volatility. Overall, this pattern

Figure 34-16. Regression of Spread Volatility against Spread Level with an Adjustable Slope

Using All U.S. Corporate Bonds Rated Aaa-B, September 1989–January 2005

		Systematic Volatility		Idiosyncratic Volatility	
		Investment-Grade	Investment-Grade + High Yield	Investment Grade	Investment-Grade + High Yield
	Spread slope (%)	8.1	10.7	9.9	14.7
	t-Statistic	18.98	52.98	35.88	24.42
	Adjusted R^2 (%)	90.0	96.6	94.4	97.7
	N^a	48	63	51	66
		Adjustments (t-statistic reported below estimates)			
Sector	Financials (%)	0.8	0.3	0.5	0.2
		1.73	1.15	1.50	0.28
	Industrials (%)	−0.9	−1.5	0.1	−2.0
		−1.90	−7.22	0.31	−3.50
Duration	Medium (%)	−0.2	−0.7	−1.6	−2.1
		−0.49	−3.35	−5.71	−3.97
	Long (%)	−0.3	−1.2	−2.1	−2.3
		−0.63	−5.61	−7.62	−4.24

[a] The number of observations in the regression is equal to the number of buckets in the partition by sector × duration × spread. Three buckets were excluded from the regression of systematic volatility since they were sparsely populated.

confirms that relative spread changes characterize both investment-grade and high yield credit.

To analyze the variation in the relation between spread volatility and level owing to sector, duration, and credit quality, we conducted a similar analysis with one major difference: instead of estimating a common spread coefficient, we estimated an unconstrained model in which the spread slope coefficient can vary by sector and duration (a single spread volatility estimate per bucket is now calculated across all periods).

The estimation results for systematic and idiosyncratic spread volatility are presented in Figure 34-16, with separate columns for the case of investment-grade credit alone and for the one that includes high yield securities as well. The row titled "spread slope" represents the change in spread volatility owing to a 1-bp change in spread for short-duration utilities and serves as a benchmark.[12] The coefficients reported at the bottom of the figure represent marginal adjustment to the spread slope owing to sector (financials, industrial) and duration (medium, long). The t-statistics indicate whether the marginal adjustments are statistically significant. For example, looking at systematic spread volatility with investment grade only, none of the adjustments is significant, implying that the same spread slope of 8.1% can be applied uniformly. When high yield securities are included, the spread slope estimate changes to 10.7%, but the slope of long industrials is hardly changed after it is adjusted downward by 2.7% (1.5% + 1.2%), to 8%.

Overall, the results confirm that relative spread volatility is not restricted to a single sector or maturity, but characterizes the entire market. They suggest that some adjustments by sector/maturity have to be made, but that all spread coefficients (except in the last column reflecting idiosyncratic volatility with high yield) have the same magnitude of roughly 9 bp/month pickup in volatility for every 100-bp increase in spread over time.

A NEW RISK MEASURE OF EXCESS RETURN VOLATILITY

So far we have established that both systematic and idiosyncratic spread changes are proportional to the level of spread. We now illustrate the implications of this relationship with respect to excess return volatility. Specifically, we show that the appropriate risk measure for credit securities is DTS rather than spread duration.

We first show that portfolios with very different spreads and spread durations but with similar DTS exhibit the same excess return volatility. For example, a portfolio with a weighted spread of 200 bp and spread duration of 2 years is as risky as a portfolio with a spread of 100 bp and spread duration of 4 years. Next, we examine excess return volatility forecasts generated using two risk measures: spread duration and DTS. The results suggest that using DTS provides more accurate forecasts with fewer instances of extreme excess return realizations.

We also compare the efficacy of spread duration and DTS in the context of constructing portfolios with minimal tracking errors. We show that a replication strategy based on matching contributions to DTS tracks better than one based on matching contributions to spread duration.

---

12. Specifically, we estimate the following regression:

$$\sigma(\Delta s)_{i,d,s} = s_{i,d,s} \times (\beta + \beta_{Fin} \cdot I_{Fin} + \beta_{Ind} \cdot I_{Ind} + \beta_{Med} \cdot I_{Med} + \beta_{Long} \cdot I_{Long}) + \varepsilon_{i,d,s},$$

where i, d, and s denote the sector-duration-spread combination of each observation. I_{Fin} and I_{Ind} are dummy variables equal to 1 if i = financials or industrials, respectively, and zero otherwise. Similarly, I_{Med} and I_{Long} are equal 1 if d = medium or long, respectively, and zero otherwise.

DTS, Spread Duration, and Excess Returns

In the first part of the chapter, we established that the volatility of both systematic and idiosyncratic spread changes is proportional to the level of spread. Consequently, the volatility of excess returns over a given time period should be linearly related to DTS, with the proportionality factor equal to the volatility of relative spread changes over the same period.

To examine this prediction, each month bonds are assigned to quintiles based on DTS. Each of these quintiles is further subdivided into six buckets based on spread. Every month the average excess returns and median DTS are calculated, and then the time-series volatility of excess returns and average DTS are calculated separately for each bucket.[13]

Our formulation yields two empirical predictions:

1. Excess return volatility should increase linearly with DTS, where the ratio of the two (or slope) represents the volatility of relative spread changes we previously estimated.

2. The level of excess return volatility should be approximately equal across spread buckets with a similar DTS characteristic.

The results of the analysis, presented in Figure 34-17, support both empirical predictions. First, it is clear that excess return volatility increases with the level of DTS and that a straight line through the origin provides an excellent fit. This is indeed confirmed by a regression of the excess return volatility on average DTS, which finds a fit of 98% and an insignificant intercept. The slope estimate is 8.8%, which is in line with the estimated slope from the analysis of systematic spread volatility. Second, consistent with prediction (2), observations representing the same DTS quintile but with differing spread levels exhibit very similar excess return volatilities. The one exception to this is in the highest DTS quintile, where the subdivision by spread causes wide variations in DTS as well. As a result, the points no longer form a tight cluster, but they continue to follow the same general relationship between DTS and volatility.

To fully appreciate the significance of the second result, Figure 34-18 reports the average spread and spread duration for each of the thirty buckets. The figure illustrates the extent of the differences among the spreads and corresponding spread durations of buckets with almost identical DTS. For example, the top and

---

13. Note that based on previous findings that did not detect a significant industry effect, we do not explicitly control for industry. This allows us to use a finer DTS partition and also makes our results more robust.

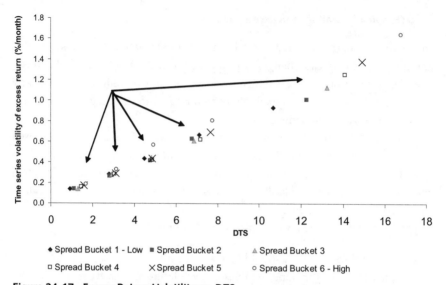

Figure 34-17. Excess Return Volatility vs. DTS
Based on Monthly Observations of All Investment-Grade Bonds, September 1989–
January 2005[a]

   [a]Bonds are first divided into DTS quintiles and then further subdivided into six
buckets by spread.

bottom spread buckets, which are part of the second DTS quintile 2 (shown in
bold) exhibit almost identical DTS values of 296 and 321, respectively. Yet, they
have very different spread and spread duration characteristics: bonds comprising
the top bucket have average spread duration of 5.48 and trade at a spread of 54 bp,
whereas bonds in the bottom cell have spread duration of 2.53 and a spread of
127 bp. Hence, a portfolio of high-spread bonds with short duration can be as
risky as one comprised of low-spread bonds with long duration.

   To verify that the results are not driven by our specific partition, Figure 34-19
presents the results of the analysis using a 10 × 3 partition that has the same number of points as before, but allows a more detailed look at the relationship between
excess return volatility and DTS. The results in Figure 34-19 are very similar to
those in Figure 34-17 with respect to the slope estimate (8.9 vs. 8.8%) and the
overlapping of observations representing different spread buckets within the same
DTS bucket.

A Comparison of Excess Return Volatility Forecasts

A natural step to extend our analysis is to examine which approach provides a
better forecast of the excess return volatility of a portfolio:

Figure 34-18. Summary Statistics by DTS and Spread Buckets

Based on Monthly Observations of All Investment-Grade Bonds, September 1989–January 2005[a]

(a) Spread

Spread subbuckets	DTS Buckets				
	Low	2	3	4	High
Low	41	**54**	64	77	97
2	52	68	79	94	116
3	60	78	88	106	135
4	69	87	98	118	156
5	79	99	112	135	184
High	100	**127**	143	172	246

(b) Spread Duration

Spread subbuckets	DTS Buckets				
	Low	2	3	4	High
Low	2.38	**5.48**	7.20	9.53	11.15
2	2.19	4.24	6.12	7.17	10.62
3	2.17	3.80	5.50	6.51	9.78
4	2.17	3.54	4.96	6.09	9.09
5	2.09	3.25	4.43	5.72	8.23
High	1.65	**2.53**	3.52	4.53	6.91

[a]Bonds are first assigned to DTS quintiles and then further subdivided into six buckets by spread.

1. Spread duration × historical volatility of absolute spread change.

2. DTS × historical volatility of relative spread change.

To better understand the conditions under which the volatility forecasts generated by the two measures differ, we write the expression for the ratio of the two measures at month t for some bucket J explicitly:

$$\text{Vol ratio}_{J,t} = \frac{\sigma\left(\frac{\Delta s_{J,t}}{s_{J,t}}\right) \times \sum_{i \in J} D_{i,t} \times s_{i,t}}{\sigma(\Delta s_{j,t}) \times \sum_{i \in J} D_{i,t}} \cong \frac{\theta \times \sum_{i \in J} D_{i,t} \times s_{i,t}}{\theta \times \bar{s}_{J,t} \times D_{J,t}}$$

$$\cong \frac{\sum_{i \in J} D_{i,t} \times (s_{J,t} + s_{i,t}^{\text{idio}})}{\bar{s}_{J,t} \times D_{J,t}} \cong \frac{s_{J,t} \times D_{J,t}}{\bar{s}_{J,t} \times D_{J,t}} = \frac{s_{J,t}}{\bar{s}_{J,t}}. \tag{34-13}$$

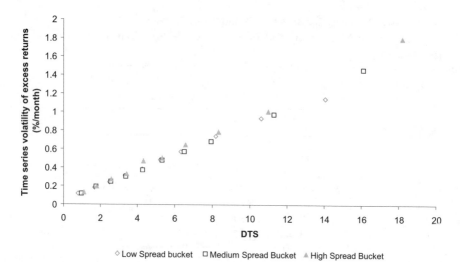

◇ Low Spread bucket   □ Medium Spread Bucket   ▲ High Spread Bucket

Figure 34-19. Excess Return Volatility vs. DTS

September 1989–January 2005[a]

[a]Based on monthly observations of all investment-grade bonds. Bonds are first partitioned into ten DTS buckets and then further subdivided to three spread buckets.

Looking at Equation (34-13), we see that the volatility measure based on relative spread changes reflects the current spread level of bucket J, while the volatility measure based on absolute spread changes reflects the time-weighted average spread the bucket has exhibited over the volatility estimation period (denoted $\bar{s}_{J,t}$).

If, for example, the systematic spread level of bucket J over the estimation period was unchanged, the ratio would be equal to one. Otherwise, the ratio would be above or below one, depending on whether the current spread is above or below the historical average. Using a shorter period for estimating spread change volatility will not necessarily reduce the difference between the two measures, if the long-term historical spread is a better reflection of the current spread environment than the recent past.

Figure 34-20 plots the time series of volatility ratio using the same partition we used to construct Figure 34-4 (eight sectors × three credit qualities). Every month, two forecasts of excess return volatility are calculated using all available history at that time, based on absolute and relative spread changes. The volatility ratios computed separately for every bucket are then averaged to yield a representative volatility ratio for each month.

As we can expect, the volatility ratio tracks the index spread very closely. In the period between September 1992 and May 1998, spreads were relatively tight and the volatility ratio was below one, indicating that using spread duration and ab-

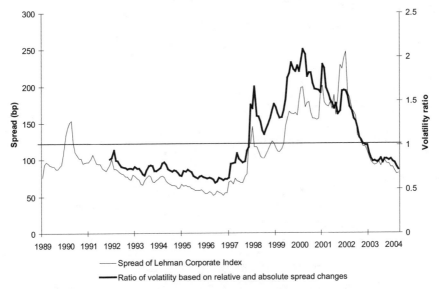

Figure 34-20. Ratio of Conditional Volatility Estimates and Spread on the Lehman Corporate Index[a]

[a] Based on absolute and relative spread changes calculated using the entire available history since September 1989.

solute spread change volatility would have generated an upward biased volatility estimate. In contrast, the Russian crisis in late 1998 and periods of dramatic widening of spreads since have raised the volatility ratio to between 1.5 and 2.0. Hence, the relative spread change volatility measure reacted in a more timely manner to the change in spread environment than the measure based on absolute spread change.

To compare the forecasting accuracy of the two measures directly, we conducted the following test: In addition to the two volatility forecasts, each month we calculated the realized excess return of the twenty-four buckets. The carry component (spread/12) is stripped from the realized excess return, and the random part is then divided by one of the two forecasts of excess return volatility.[14] If the projected excess return volatility is an unbiased estimate of the "true" volatility, then the time-series volatility of these standardized excess return realizations should be very close to one.

14. Although the carry component is time varying, we analyze each month's excess return conditioned on the beginning-of-month spread. We can therefore treat the carry component as deterministic.

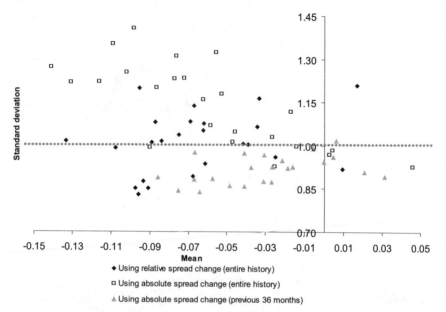

Figure 34-21. Mean and Standard Deviation of Normalized Excess Return Realizations
September 1989–January 2005[a]

[a] Conditional volatility estimates are computed monthly by sector and credit quality based on the entire available history or previous 36 months using monthly spread change observations.

Our premise is that relative spread change volatility is a more timely measure than absolute spread change volatility, since it can react almost instantaneously to a change in market conditions. Hence we expect the sample time series standard deviation of excess returns to be closer to 1 when using (2) than when using (1). Second, a volatility measure that is quicker to adjust for changing market conditions generates less extreme realizations (i.e., realizations that fall above/below 2 or 3 standard deviations) relative to a measure that is slower to react.

Figure 34-21 shows the mean and standard deviation of the time series of normalized residuals (each observation represents one of the twenty-four buckets). The normalized residuals are generated using the two volatility measures taking the entire available history for each month into account. In addition, Figure 34-21 shows the mean and standard deviation of normalized residuals when the absolute spread change volatility is calculated over the previous 36 months.

Comparing the three sets of observations reveals that using absolute spread changes produces estimates of volatility that are downward (upward) biased when using the entire available history (previous 36 months). As a result the average standard deviation of normalized excess returns using the entire and partial history is above and below 1 (1.14 and 0.92, respectively). In contrast the observations generated using relative spread changes are evenly spread around 1 and the average standard deviation of standardized excess returns is 1.01 (Figure 34-22 provides a detailed comparison by sector and credit rating).

These findings support our empirical prediction and are also consistent with the analysis of the ratio of the two volatility measures. Excess return volatility estimates based on absolute spread changes are very sensitive to the length of the estimation period: they may show overreaction when using too few data points and can be slow to adjust when using a long history. The optimal length of the estimation period is not clear ex ante when using absolute spread changes. In contrast, a longer estimation period is always desired when using proportional spread changes since it improves the accuracy of the proportionality factor, while at the same time the volatility estimate adjusts instantaneously because of the multiplication by the current spread level.[15]

The second empirical prediction states that the percentage of extreme realizations (positive or negative) should be lower when using relative rather than absolute spread change volatility. Figure 34-23 plots a histogram of the standardized excess return realizations for all sector × quality cells based on the two volatility measures. For comparison, the standard normal distribution is also displayed.

Not surprisingly, the histogram reveals that both volatility estimators generate distributions that are negatively skewed (−2.67 and −1.35 using the relative and absolute spread-change-based volatility measures). With respect to the percentage of outliers, 7.06% of the observations in the distribution based on absolute spread changes are located beyond 2 standard deviations from the mean. In the case of the distribution based on relative spread changes, the same figure is just more than half, at 4.03%.

Index Replication by Stratified Sampling

As a final comparison between spread duration and DTS, we examine which of the two can replicate an index with a smaller tracking error. As before, we use the 8 × 3 partition of the investment-grade credit universe to construct a market-weighted index and calculate the aggregate excess return, spread duration, DTS, and spread each month. The replicating portfolio is constructed using one or two bonds from every bucket. In both cases the idea is similar: the replicating portfolio is not designed to match multiple index characteristics, but only the aggregate

---

15. A longer estimation period is always desired, as long as the proportionality factor is stable across periods, which we found to be the case.

Figure 34-22. Standard Deviation of Standardized Excess Returns Using Various Volatility Measures

Using Monthly Observations, September 1992–January 2005

Market Cell		Absolute Spread Change		Relative Spread Change
Sector	Credit Rating	Entire Available History	Previous 36 Months	Entire Available History
Average		1.14	0.92	1.01
Banking	Aaa-Aa	0.93	0.92	1.20
	A	0.98	0.91	1.16
	Baa	0.93	0.91	1.21
Basic industries	Aaa-Aa	1.32	0.94	1.06
	A	1.23	0.93	1.08
	Baa	1.01	0.95	1.00
Cyclicals	Aaa-Aa	1.03	0.99	1.14
	A	1.27	0.89	1.02
	Baa	1.07	0.92	1.01
Communications	Aaa-Aa	1.41	0.86	0.87
	A	1.22	0.84	0.85
	Baa	1.31	0.87	1.08
Energy	Aaa-Aa	1.22	0.84	0.85
	A	1.16	0.92	1.05
	Baa	1.00	1.02	0.96
Financials	Aaa-Aa	1.12	0.96	1.01
	A	1.05	0.87	0.94
	Baa	0.97	0.89	0.92
Noncyclicals	Aaa-Aa	1.18	0.97	1.04
	A	1.20	0.97	1.01
	Baa	0.99	0.98	0.99
Utilities	Aaa-Aa	1.25	0.88	0.83
	A	1.23	0.86	0.89
	Baa	1.35	0.88	1.08

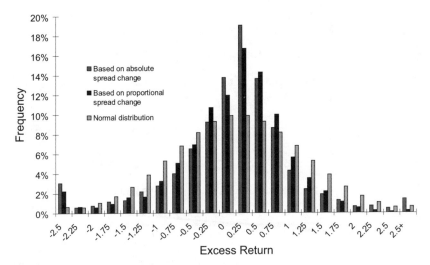

Figure 34-23. Distribution of Standardized Excess Returns
September 1992–January 2005[a]

[a] Based on observations from all sectors and credit ratings.

spread duration or DTS. *Hence, the intention is not to create an "optimal" replication, but rather to focus on the relative efficacy of one measure against the other.*

Replication Algorithms

Single-Bond Replication. The algorithm selects the bond from each bucket that best matches the aggregate spread duration or DTS and allocates the entire bucket weight in the index to that bond. Although the replication is not exact, the bonds that are selected typically match their respective bucket aggregate characteristic very closely. One caveat, however, is that the two bonds selected to represent a bucket under the two matching criteria are almost always different. As a result, the variation in tracking errors may reflect not only the difference between the two systematic risk measures, but also different levels of idiosyncratic risk.

Two-Bond Replication. This replication is more complex but has two main advantages over the single-bond replication. First, the same two bonds are used to match each cell's spread duration or DTS (with different weights), which addresses the issue of different idiosyncratic risk. Second, based on the matching criteria, the algorithm exactly matches either the bucket spread duration or DTS. Furthermore, in order to magnify the difference between the two competing risk measures, the two bonds selected from each bucket possess very different spread duration and DTS characteristics. As a result, the weights allocated to the two bonds within each cell are very different under the two matching criteria.

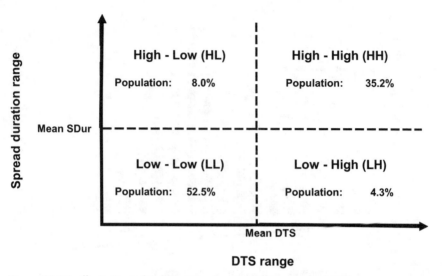

DTS range

Figure 34-24. Illustration of Cell Partition by Spread Duration and DTS
September 1989–January 2005[a]

   [a] Based on monthly observations from all sectors and credit quality ratings.

The replicating portfolio is constructed as follows: every month, all bonds in each bucket are assigned to one of four quadrants. The quadrants are defined using a 2×2 grid based on the market-weighted spread duration and DTS (Figure 34-24). Bonds with spread duration and DTS above the weighted mean are allocated to the upper-right quadrant denoted "HH." Similarly, bonds with spread duration above the mean but DTS below the mean are allocated to the upper-left quadrant ("HL") and so on.

The algorithm selects one bond from each of the HL and LH quadrants and calculates two sets of weights such that the two bonds exactly match either the spread duration or the DTS of the cell. Since, by construction, there is always one bond with spread duration or DTS above the bucket mean and a second bond with the same characteristic below the bucket mean, we are guaranteed to get exact replication with both bonds having positive weights.

The specific bonds that comprise the replicating portfolio are selected based on one of several criteria, such as market value, spread, spread duration, or DTS. Based on the first criterion, for example, the algorithm would select the largest bonds in the two quadrants. If, instead, the selection criterion is spread duration or DTS, the algorithm searches for the two bonds with the largest mismatch with respect to the selected characteristic. To achieve this, if the selection criterion is spread duration (DTS), the algorithm selects the bond with the highest (lowest) and lowest (highest) spread duration (DTS) from the HL and LH quadrants, respectively. Thus, this algorithm not only ensures that the weights of both bonds are positive, but also attempts to magnify the bond weight differential under the two matching criteria.

Since spread duration and DTS are highly correlated, the bond population within a bucket is not evenly divided among the quadrants. In fact, as Figure 34-24 shows, the HL and LH population account for only 12.3% on average of a bucket population. This, in turn, implies that at least one of the HL or LH quadrants is not populated in about 25% of the more than 4300 period-cell pairs. Whenever the algorithm is unable to find a bond in either the HL or LH quadrant, it selects two bonds from the HH and LL quadrants instead.[16]

Results

The replication results using both algorithms are presented in Figure 34-25. The figure shows the monthly tracking error, as well as the average mismatch in overall spread and DTS relative to the index, for the matched spread-duration replication. The same statistics are given for the second replication except that the spread-duration mismatch is reported instead. For the two-bond replication, the figure also shows the average absolute difference in weights assigned to the same bond under the two matching criteria (the column titled "bucket" gives the difference within each bucket, whereas the column titled "overall index" weights the difference by the bucket weight in the index).

The first two rows report the results of the three replications that use a single bond from each cell. Matching the index market value of each cell using the largest issue results in a tracking error of 25.9 bp/month, partly because of overexposures both in terms of spread duration (long 0.82 on average) and DTS (long 1.01). By choosing the single bond in each cell that best matches spread duration instead, the tracking error is reduced to 17.5 bp/month; matching DTS does even better, bringing the tracking error down to 14.7 bp/month.

The two-bond-per-cell replications exhibit similar results. Choosing the bond with the highest market value in each selected cell quadrant and then blending them together to match the cell's market value as well as spread duration brings the tracking error down to 13.2 bp/month; blending the same two bonds to match cell market value and DTS improves the tracking error to 11.9 bp/month. To help make our results more robust, we tried several different methods for selecting the two bonds in each cell. Different criteria change the result somewhat, but in most

---

16. If the selection criterion is spread duration, then the algorithm selects the highest- and lowest-spread-duration bonds from the HH and LL quadrants, respectively. Alternatively, if the selection criterion is DTS, then the algorithm selects the lowest and highest DTS bonds from the LL and HH quadrants, respectively.

Figure 34-25. Replication Results Using Various Algorithms
September 1989–January 2005[a]

Bond Selection Criteria	Duration Matched Replication			Weight Differential (%)		DTS Matched Replication		
	Tracking Error (bp/month)	Mean Mismatch				Tracking Error (bp/month)	Mean Mismatch	
		DTS	Spread (bp)	Bucket	Overall Index		Duration	Spread (bp)
Largest issue	25.9	1.01	3.6	NA	NA	NA	0.82	NA
Single bond	17.5	-0.18	2.3	NA	NA	14.7	0.27	4.9
Two bond								
Market value	13.2	0.28	13.3	29.0	1.4	11.9	0.14	6.4
Duration	14.6	-0.10	4.0	33.8	1.5	12.9	0.00	6.4
DTS	16.7	0.81	19.5	25.8	1.2	14.8	-0.06	8.1
Minimum spread	14.3	-0.29	2.3	26.5	1.1	14.2	0.28	4.9
Maximum spread	14.5	0.77	21.9	26.2	1.1	14.9	-0.08	10.5

[a] Replication of the Aggregate Index is performed through matching the spread or DTS characteristic of each of the twenty-four cells in the partition (eight sectors × three credit quality ratings). Based on monthly observations.

cases the better tracking error is achieved by matching DTS rather than spread duration. The one exception was the case in which the bond with the largest spread was chosen within each cell quadrant, where the DTS replication had a slightly higher tracking error (14.9 vs. 14.5 bp/month for the duration-matched approach).

The differences between the two replication techniques are somewhat masked by the amount of idiosyncratic risk inherent in tracking the credit index with a portfolio of twenty-four or forty-eight bonds. A more extensive study of this variety might involve replication with a larger number of bonds, or simulation using some randomized mechanism for bond selection within a cell. Nevertheless, we feel that the results of this experiment confirm that matching DTS contributions provides better replication results than matching contributions to duration.

THE SCOPE OF DTS

Spread Volatility as Spreads Approach Zero

Perhaps the most fundamental empirical regularity we established is that absolute spread volatility is linearly proportional to spread level. The results were not confined to investment-grade credit. When the analysis was extended to include high yield securities, we found that the same relationship holds up to spreads of 450 bp.

What do these findings imply for the level of spread volatility as spreads approach zero? Taking our results at face value suggests that there is no lower bound for volatility and that spread volatility should decline to almost zero for very-low-spread securities. Spread volatility, however, is not driven solely by changes in risk but also by non-risk-based factors. Non-risk-based spread changes can result from "noise" (e.g., pricing errors), demand/supply imbalance (e.g., when securities enter/exit the Lehman Brothers Corporate Index), and other factors.

Spread volatility (systematic or idiosyncratic) can therefore be expressed as the sum of two terms: a constant that reflects non-risk-based spread volatility and a second term that represents spread volatility owing to changes in risk (which may be approximated by a linear function of spread) as follows:

$$\sigma(\Delta s) = \sqrt{\sigma^2_{\text{non-risk}} + \theta^2 \cdot s^2}. \tag{34-14}$$

Equation (34-14) makes it clear that for sufficiently high spreads, the second term dominates the first, and spread volatility can be well approximated by a linear function of spread, as we find for corporates. As spreads tighten and approach zero, the first term dominates, and spread volatility should converge to some minimum "structural" level.

A natural place to examine Equation (34-14) is to look at the relationship between spread volatility and spread level in agency debentures. Because of market

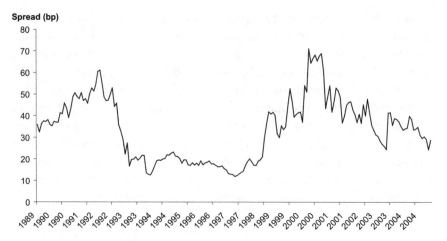

Figure 34-26. Median of Agency Spread Distribution
Monthly Observations (September 1989–April 2005)[a]
  [a]Based on all Aaa-rated, noncallable debentures in the Lehman Agency Index.

perception that securities issued by the three main agencies are backed by the U.S. government, these securities typically trade at very low spreads. Figure 34-26 presents the median spread for agency debentures between September 1989 and April 2005. The figure illustrates that except for a few distinct months, the median spread at which agencies traded ranged between 20 and 50 bp.

We studied the relationship between spread volatility and spread level as we did for corporates. Each month, bonds were partitioned based on beginning-of-month spread level. Average spread change and median spread level were computed separately for each bucket. We then examined the relationship between the time-series volatility and average (median) spread level of each bucket.

The sample spans roughly the same time period as for corporates (September 1989–April 2005) and includes all Aaa rated, noncallable debentures from the Lehman Brothers Agency Index.[17] As before, extreme observations (which reside in either the top or bottom percentile of the spread distribution) are discarded. Since the total number of observations (73,000) is about 17% of the corporate sample size, we use only eight spread buckets.

The results are presented in Figure 34-27. To guarantee that our results are not driven by outliers, volatility is calculated in two ways: filtered (equal weighting ex-

---

17. Including publicly issued debt of U.S. government agencies, quasi-federal corporations, and corporate or foreign debt guaranteed by the U.S. government (such as USAID securities).

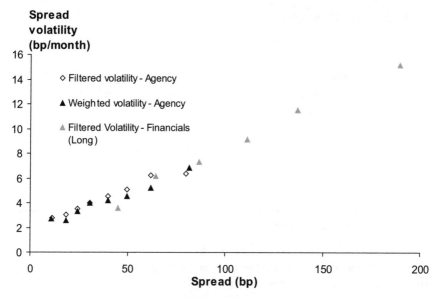

Figure 34-27. Systematic Spread Volatility vs. Spread Level
Monthly Observations, September 1989–April 2005[a]
    [a] Based on all Aaa-rated, noncallable debentures in the Lehman Agency Index.

cluding months with fewer than twenty bonds) and weighted (all months weighted by the number of issues). For comparison, Figure 34-27 also presents the spread volatility of long-duration financials we computed previously, which possess many of the same characteristics as agencies.

The plot in Figure 34-27 illustrates that spread volatility is roughly constant for spreads below 20 bp, and the level of "structural" systematic volatility is about 2.5–3.0 bp/month. Above 20 bp, the relation takes the usual linear shape and fits nicely with that of long financials. A regression of spread volatility against spread level reveals a flatter slope than we estimated for corporates (5.7 vs. 9%), consistent with Equation (34-14).[18]

Figure 34-28 shows the pooled cross-sectional spread volatility when individual idiosyncratic spread changes are aggregated across all periods. The results suggest that idiosyncratic volatility increases moderately as spreads increase from 20 to 80 bp and indicate a "structural" volatility level of 4.0–4.5 bp/month. The fact that idiosyncratic "structural" volatility is higher than the corresponding systematic

18. The results were unchanged when issues with a market value below $300 million were excluded or when non-U.S. agencies were excluded.

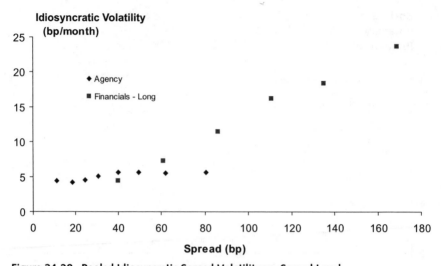

Figure 34-28. Pooled Idiosyncratic Spread Volatility vs. Spread Level
Monthly Observations, September 1989–April 2005[a]

[a]Based on all Aaa-rated, noncallable debentures in the Lehman Agency Index.

level is to be expected, as pricing noise should be more pronounced for individual securities.

To complete the analysis, the sample is partitioned into twelve DTS buckets and the excess return volatility of each bucket is plotted against its DTS (Figure 34-29). Similar to corporates, the results indicate that excess return volatility increases linearly with DTS (the estimated slope from the regression is 9.8%, vs. 8.8% for corporates). As the DTS approaches zero, however, there is a clear flattening of the relationship, and volatility does not decline further. Indeed, the regression yields a significant intercept of 3 bp, which is consistent with our previous estimate of "structural" systemic volatility.

DTS in the Euro Corporate Market

Is the proportionality of spread changes unique to the U.S. corporate market or is it a broader phenomenon? If we consider our results in the framework of a log-normal model in which a security spread reflects all the current information about its risk, then we can expect our findings to apply to corporate bonds in general and not just in the United States.

We conduct an analysis similar to the one we performed using U.S. data for the euro corporate market, except for changes stemming from differences between the markets: First, the euro sample spans a much shorter period, from Jan-

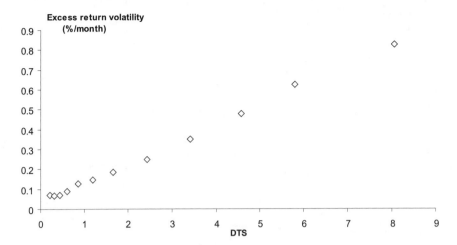

Figure 34-29. Excess Return Volatility vs. DTS
Monthly Observations Using All Aaa-Rated, Noncallable Debentures in the Lehman
Agency Index, September 1989–April 2005[a]
  [a]Bonds are assigned to one of twelve buckets based on DTS.

uary 2000 to May 2005, and is therefore more limited in size (roughly 48,000 observations).[19] Second, the overall credit quality of bonds in the euro market is
higher than in the United States, which leads to a much narrower range of spreads.

In order to analyze spread volatility, the sample is divided into nine spread
buckets (based on the results for U.S. corporates, we do not control for sector or
duration). The results for both systematic and pooled idiosyncratic spread volatility are plotted in Figure 34-30 and illustrate two key points: First, spread volatility
in the euro market exhibits the same patterns as in the U.S. market. Both systematic and idiosyncratic spread volatility are proportional to the level of spread. Second, the generally higher quality of issuers in the euro market results in a large
number of observations with low spreads, which also allows us to examine the behavior of spread volatility in the limit. Consistent with the results we have found
for agencies, spread volatility seems to stabilize around 20–30 bp. Furthermore,
the level of "structural" volatility is similar as well: the systematic spread volatilities of euro corporates and agencies are 2.5 and 2.0 bp/month, respectively; idiosyncratic spread volatilities are 6.0 and 5.2 bp/month.

The similarity between the U.S. and euro markets is also evident in Figure
34-31, which plots excess return volatility for twenty-four buckets against their

19. We decided not to use any data prior to January 2000 in order to allow a 1-year window
following the introduction of the new currency.

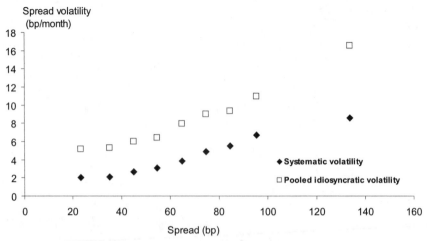

Figure 34-30. Spread Volatility vs. Spread Level in the Euro Corporate Market
January 2000–April 2005[a]

[a] Based on monthly observations using all investment-grade euro bonds classified as financials, industrials, or utilities.

respective DTS level. Buckets are populated monthly by first splitting the sample into DTS sextiles and then dividing each sextile into spread quartiles. Figure 34-31 illustrates that excess return volatility increases linearly with DTS. (A regression of excess return volatility against DTS yields a significant intercept of 3.3 bp and a slope of 5.8% with an R^2 of 95%.) Buckets with similar DTS and different spreads tend to overlap quite nicely, although not as well as we have seen with U.S. data.

SUMMARY AND IMPLICATIONS FOR PORTFOLIO MANAGEMENT

This chapter presents a detailed analysis of the behavior of spread changes. Using our extensive corporate bonds database, which spans 15 years and contains well over 400,000 observations, we demonstrated that spread changes are proportional to the level of spread. Systematic changes in spread across a sector tend to follow a pattern of relative spread change, in which bonds trading at wider spreads experience larger spread changes. The systematic spread volatility of a given sector (if viewed in terms of absolute spread changes) is proportional to the median spread in the sector; the nonsystematic spread volatility of a particular bond or issuer is proportional to its spread as well. Those findings hold irrespective of sector-duration or time period.

In a sense, these results are not altogether surprising. The lognormal models typically used to represent changes in interest rates assume that changes in yield

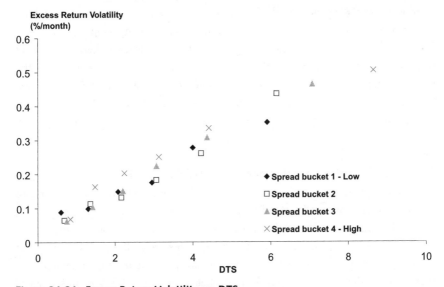

Figure 34-31. Excess Return Volatility vs. DTS
Based on Monthly Observations (January 2000–April 2005) Using All Investment-Grade Euro Corporates[a]
[a]Each month, bonds are assigned to DTS sextiles and then further divided into spread quartiles.

are proportional to current yield levels. Models for pricing credit derivatives have used a similar lognormal model to describe changes in credit spreads.[20] An assumption of lognormal spread changes would imply two things: that spread changes are proportional to spreads and that the relative spread changes are normally distributed. Our results can be seen as providing empirical evidence to support the first of these assumptions, but not necessarily the second.

For a portfolio manager who wishes to act on these results, there are many implications. First, the best measure of exposure to a systematic change in spread within a given sector or industry is not the contribution to spread duration, but the contribution to DTS. At many management firms, the targeted active exposures for a portfolio relative to its benchmark are expressed as contribution-to-duration overweights and underweights along a sector by quality grid—and reports on the actual portfolio follow the same format. In the relative spread change paradigm, managers would express their targeted overweights and underweights in terms of contributions to DTS instead.

20. For example, see Philipp Schönbucher, "A LIBOR Market Model with Default Risk," working paper, University of Bonn, 1999.

If we take this approach to the limit, we can arrive at an even more radical departure from current practice. In the sector by quality management grid discussed earlier, the macro views of the manager are often expressed largely in terms of sectors or industries, and the role of the quality dimension is to control for the level of risk taken in implementing each view. If contributions to DTS are used to express industry exposures on a risk-weighted basis, then a further partition by quality may no longer be necessary. Instead, managers may view this as an opportunity to express more focused views and slice the credit markets into a more finely grained partition by industry.

Second, our conclusion that nonsystematic spread volatility is proportional to spread (and hence that the volatility of nonsystematic return is proportional to DTS) suggests another way of defining issuer limits in a portfolio. In Chapter 14, we focused on the return implications of credit-rating downgrades and emphasized that to reduce portfolio risk from downgrades, issuer limits should be much tighter for lower-rated issuers. For example, an investment policy might specify that no more than 1% of the portfolio market value can be invested in securities of any single Baa-rated issuer, no more than 2% in any A-rated issuer, and no more than 4% in any Aa-rated issuer. Our current research addresses exposures to overall nonsystematic returns, not specifically those connected with ratings transitions—yet it offers an even simpler mechanism for defining an issuer limit policy that enforces smaller positions in more risky credits. We can simply set a limit on the overall contribution to DTS for any single issuer. For example, say the product of market weight × spread × duration must be 5 or less. Then, a position in issuer A, with a spread of 100 bp and a duration of 5 years, could be up to 1% of portfolio market value, while a position in issuer B, with a spread of 150 and an average duration of 10 years, would be limited to 0.33%.

Establishing issuer limits based on spreads has advantages and disadvantages relative to a ratings-based approach. One advantage, as described earlier, is the simplicity of specifying a single uniform limit that requires increasing diversification with increasing risk. The key difference between the two approaches, though, concerns the frequency at which issuer limits are adjusted. In a ratings-based framework, bond positions that are within policy on the date of purchase tend to remain in policy unless they are downgraded. A spread-based constraint, by contrast, is by its very nature continuously adjusted as spreads change. One possible result is that as spreads widen, a position that was in policy when purchased can drift over the allowable DTS limit. Strict enforcement of this policy, requiring forced sales to keep all issuer exposures within the limit, could become very distracting to managers and incur excessive transaction costs as spreads trade up and down. One possible solution would be to specify one threshold for new purchases and a higher one at which forced sales would be triggered. This could provide a mechanism that adapts to market events more quickly than the rating agencies without introducing undue instability. Another possible disadvantage of the DTS-based issuer caps is that it allows for large positions in low-spread issuers and exposes the portfolio to "credit torpedoes." This, too, would argue for using the DTS-based approach in conjunction with caps on market weights.

Third, there could be hedging implications. Say a hedge fund manager has a view on the relative performance of two issuers within the same industry and would like to capitalize on this view by going long issuer A and short issuer B in a market-neutral manner. How do we define market neutrality? A typical approach might be to match the dollar durations of the two bonds, or to go long and short CDS of the same maturities with the same notional amounts. However, if issuer A trades at a wider spread than issuer B, our results would indicate that a better hedge against marketwide spread changes would be obtained by using more of issuer B, so as to match the contributions to DTS on the two sides of the trade.

Our investigation of the relationship between DTS and excess return volatility in this chapter has focused almost entirely on investment-grade credit in the United States and in Europe. However, there is good reason to believe that it carries over to other asset classes as well. We have included in this study some results from high yield credit that show that the paradigm of proportional spread changes carries through to high yield as well. Indeed, we believe that perhaps one of the most useful applications of DTS will be in the management of core-plus portfolios that combine both investment-grade and high yield assets. It might be typical to manage investment-grade credit portfolios based on contributions to duration and high yield portfolios based on market-value weights; using contributions to DTS across both markets could help unify this process. Skeptics may point out that in high yield markets, especially when moving toward the distressed segment, neither durations nor spreads are particularly meaningful, and the market tends to trade on price, based on an estimated recovery value. A useful property of DTS in that context is that in the case of distressed issuers, where shorter-duration securities tend to have artificially high spreads, DTS is fairly constant across the maturity spectrum, so that managing issuer contributions to DTS becomes roughly equivalent to managing issuer market weights.

The phenomenon of proportional spread volatility may extend beyond credit-risky securities. An analysis of agency debentures revealed that this pattern holds for spreads above 20–30 bp. The fundamental idea that the mechanism by which spreads change is via a multiplicative factor rather than a parallel shift could apply equally well to other spread sectors, such as mortgage-backed securities and other collateralized sectors. A preliminary investigation of the MBS sector indicates that this may indeed be the case; more research is required.

Should portfolio management tools such as risk analysis and performance attribution be modified to view sector exposures in terms of DTS contributions and sector spread changes in relative terms? For performance attribution, the answer is clear, because a key goal for attribution models is to match the allocation process as closely as possible. If and when a manager starts to state his allocation decisions in terms of DTS exposures, performance attribution should follow suit. For risk analysis, which is based largely on the results of regressions against individual bond returns similar to those discussed at the beginning of the chapter, there is certainly room to question whether a more extensive use of DTS can improve the model.[21]

One practical difficulty that may arise in the implementation of DTS-based models is an increased vulnerability to pricing noise. For the most part, models of portfolio risk and reporting of active portfolio weights rely largely on structural information. Small discrepancies in asset pricing give rise to small discrepancies in market values, but potentially larger variations in spreads. Managers who rely heavily on contribution-to-DTS exposures have to implement strict quality controls on pricing.

We believe that the DTS paradigm accurately represents the impact of spread changes on excess returns, and that its acceptance of this result could have wide-ranging effects on portfolio management practice throughout the industry. We anticipate a continued research in this area on several fronts, including extension to other asset classes, and implementation of DTS-based features into portfolio analytics offerings.

APPENDIX

The data set used in the empirical analysis spans the period between September 1989 and January 2005 (a total of 185 months). The sample includes all the bonds that comprise the Lehman Corporate Index excluding (1) zero-coupon bonds, (2) callable bonds, and (3) bonds with nonpositive spreads. The final data set contains a total of 416,783 observations (see Figure 34-A1 for a breakdown of the sample by sector and year). We also extend the analysis to include high yield

---

21. The Lehman risk model currently includes factors representing parallel shifts in spread along a 9×3 sector $\times$ quality partition, and a single credit slope factor similar to the one in Equation (34-10), representing a further marketwide increase in wider-than-average spreads. Chapter 26 provides a complete description of the model.

Number of bonds

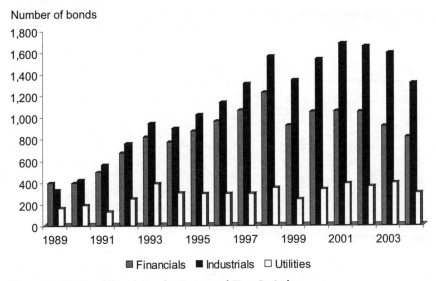

Figure 34-A1. Bond Population by Sector and Time Period
Sample Includes Investment-Grade Bonds Only; Number of Bonds as of December of
Each Year

bonds rated Ba and B,[22] which increases the number of observations by roughly
35% (from 416,783 to 565,602).

Figure 34-A2 outlines the exact breakdown into spread buckets by industry
and maturity that we employ in analyzing the relation between spread volatility
and spread level. A careful look reveals that because of the general tendency of
spread to rise with maturity, the population of the short-maturity bucket is concentrated in the lowest-spread bucket (denoted by 1), whereas the opposite holds
for the long-maturity bucket. Figure 34-A2 also reports the percentage of months
during the sample period in which the bond population exceeds twenty for each
bucket. This statistic is of interest since months with less than twenty observations are filtered out of any volatility calculation. The percentage of months with
a sufficient number of observations varies between 30 and 50% for utilities and
50 to 80% for financials and industrials.

22. We include bonds rated Ba or B only if their price is above 80 in order to screen potential default effects.

Figure 34-A2. Sample Partition by Sector, Duration, and Spread[a]

Sector/	Spread Bucket/Breakpoints					
Maturity	1	2	3	4	5	6
Financials	<0.50	0.50–0.75	0.75–1.00	1.00–1.25	1.25–1.50	>1.5
Short	16,881	13,201	9,351	5,296	2,677	4,004
	(50.8%)	(82.7%)	(64.9%)	(46.5%)	(30.8%)	(37.3%)
Medium	5,839	14,838	11,156	8,173	5,133	6,904
	(28.6%)	(65.4%)	(73.5%)	(61.6%)	(44.3%)	(48.1%)
Long	2,183	12,875	10,743	8,174	6,130	11,993
	(18.9%)	(54.6%)	(81.1%)	(73.0%)	(58.9%)	(55.1%)
Industrials	<0.60	0.60–0.85	0.85–1.20	1.20–1.50	1.50–2.00	>2.00
Short	22,794	13,705	12,172	7,670	6,277	6,167
	(84.9%)	(97.8%)	(78.9%)	(54.6%)	(48.6%)	(30.8%)
Medium	12,814	14,621	14,424	9,109	9,300	9,131
	(70.3%)	(85.4%)	(96.2%)	(65.4%)	(54.6%)	(43.2%)
Long	9,212	13,961	16,248	10,088	11,010	8,940
	(68.1%)	(81.6%)	(94.6%)	(69.7%)	(53.5%)	(40.5%)
Utilities	<0.55	0.55–0.75	0.75–1.15	1.15–1.50	>1.50	
Short	5,017	3,233	4,443	2,388	2,350	
	(46.5%)	(35.7%)	(48.6%)	(22.2%)	(16.8%)	
Medium	3,430	3,552	4,484	2,699	3,889	
	(41.1%)	(38.9%)	(41.1%)	(32.4%)	(23.2%)	
Long	3,030	3,199	4,457	2,653	2,350	
	(32.4%)	(40.5%)	(52.4%)	(25.4%)	(29.2%)	

[a]Sample includes investment-grade bonds only, between September 1989 and January 2005. Breakdown into spread buckets, number of bonds in each cell, and the percentage of months during which a bucket is populated by more than twenty bonds.

35. Hedging Debt with Equity

∙∙

With the growth and improved liquidity of the corporate and credit derivatives market, capital structure arbitrage and debt-equity relative value trading have recently become popular. Credit hedge funds and banks have become active in such trading. An important consideration in such trades is the degree to which a debt position can be hedged with a position in the issuer's equity. One needs to have a good estimate of the hedge ratio of debt with respect to equity. This in turn necessitates a good understanding of the co-movement between debt and equity. The objective of this chapter is to empirically investigate the effectiveness of hedging debt with equity and to provide estimates of the appropriate hedge ratios.

In theory, hedging debt with equity should not be difficult. In a frictionless world, all financial securities such as debt and equity can be regarded as contingent claims on the same underlying, namely the firm's assets. Indeed, in the world of R. Merton,[1] a firm's equity is simply a call option on the firm's assets with the strike price being the face value of the debt. The debt is equivalent to a long position in a riskless bond combined with a short position in a put option with the same strike price as the equity. The movements in firm value drive all the uncertainty in the model and debt can be perfectly hedged with equity.

Variations of Merton's model (such as Moody's KMV™ and Creditgrades™) are, in fact, being used by many investors in structuring debt-equity trades. It is tempting to use these models at face value, in the same way as the Black-Scholes model is being used for options.[2] In practice, however, there are several reasons to believe that the relationship between debt and equity is not as tight as the Merton

Based on research first published by Lehman Brothers in 2003.

1. R. Merton, "On the Pricing of Corporate Debt: The Risk Structure of Interest Rates," *Journal of Finance*, May 1974; *Continuous-Time Finance*, Blackwell Publishing, 1990.

2. F. Black and M. S. Scholes, "The Pricing of Options and Corporate Liabilities," *Journal of Political Economy*, 1973, vol. 81, no. 3, pp. 637–654.

model would suggest. Given that fund managers typically specialize in investing either in fixed-income markets or in equity markets (but rarely in both), it is conceivable that the two markets are segmented and that there is only a limited amount of capital allocated to arbitraging any discrepancies between debt and equity markets. The rebalancing and transaction costs in implementing debt-equity trades can also be considerable, given the difficulty in shorting debt instruments. It is also the case that the informational cost of implementing debt-equity trades using Merton-type models can be high because of the difficulty in obtaining accurate volatility forecasts and capital structure leverage data. It is, therefore, important to investigate the empirical performance of equity-based hedges of debt positions and to compare the performance of empirically derived and model-based hedging strategies.

We present and compare two methodologies for determining hedge ratios of debt with respect to equity. The first methodology is the CAESAR empirical hedging methodology, which uses a regression analysis of bond excess returns on equity returns. This approach is useful in investigating the historical performance of equity-based hedges of debt positions and estimating the debt-equity hedge ratios. The second methodology is based on the ORION model, a new equity-based model of credit valuation that overcomes some of the shortcomings of the Merton approach by directly modeling the observed equity value instead of the unobserved firm value. We use the model to determine the delta (hedge ratio) of debt with respect to equity in much the same way as option-pricing models are used to compute deltas of derivatives with respect to the underlying asset.

In addition to the foregoing methodologies, we also present a scenario analysis approach of looking at debt-equity trades. Investors can stress test a median scenario, their intuitions, and predictions by varying the assumptions on spread and equity returns. It is a less systematic approach, but it can prove useful in the implementation of a debt-equity hedging trade.

Our main conclusions are the following. Our empirical estimates (based on CAESAR) of the hedge ratios of debt with respect to equity are in the range of 2–4% for A- and Baa-rated issuers and in the range of 12–20% for high yield issuers. The reduction in the volatility of the position by hedging with the issuers' equity is in the range of only 7–15% for A- and Baa-rated issuers. This implies the presence of a large residual in bond excess returns after removing the effect of equity. This residual is strongly correlated with the performance of the credit market as a whole for investment-grade debt. The reduction in volatility by hedging with the issuer's equity and the credit market is in the range of 50–71% for A- and Baa-rated issuers, which emphasizes the importance of a close monitoring of the credit market exposure of debt-equity trades. The effect of overall market movement is reduced in the high yield market, where a pure equity-based hedge performs reasonably well. The reduction in volatility by hedging only with the issuer's equity is in the range of 15–22% for high yield issuers. This reduction hardly changes (14–20%) when we hedge high yield issuers with their equity and the credit market.

The chapter is structured as follows: first, we present the CAESAR empirical hedging methodology for estimating the hedge ratios between debt and equity and for investigating the historical performance of equity-based hedged debt positions. Next, we briefly introduce the ORION model and present a similar hedging analysis using the hedge ratios derived from ORION. Then, we turn to the scenario analysis approach to look at the performance of debt-equity trades. We conclude with a comparison of our findings across the different methodologies.

HEDGING ANALYSIS WITH CAESAR

In this section, we investigate the empirical delta hedging of debt with equity by using a bond-level regression analysis. We call our regression model CAESAR (credit and equity statistical arbitrage model). The empirical betas resulting from the regressions are then used to hedge the debt against the equity movement. We perform three sets of regressions: a single-variable regression with equity, a two-variable regression with equity and a corporate index, and a three-variable regression with equity, a corporate index, and an equity index. For each of these experiments, we estimate the empirical hedge ratios of debt with respect to equity and report the averages of these hedge ratios by rating and sector. We also quantify the reduction in volatility obtained by implementing the hedging strategies corresponding to the three experiments.

We use monthly bond data from the Lehman Brothers U.S. Investment-Grade and High Yield Corporate indices from January 1990 to August 2003, the Lehman Brothers Euro High Yield and Investment-Grade Corporate indices from January 1999 to August 2003. For our analysis, we consider a subset of these corporate indices—more than 4500 noncallable, nonputable bonds in USD and around 1200 bonds in euro. All the bonds we consider have listed equity. The bond excess returns are monthly excess returns over duration-matched Treasuries; the equity returns are monthly total returns.

Hedging with Issuers' Equity Alone: CAESAR I

In this experiment, we regress bond excess returns on 1-month equity returns using a 24-month rolling window. At the beginning of the month, for each bond, we compute the beta coefficient of the regression of the bond excess return on the equity return of the issuer using observations in the past 24 months. The estimated beta is an estimate of the hedge ratio for bonds with respect to the issuer's equity. A hedged debt-equity position in our analysis would go long the bond (hedged by duration-matched Treasuries) and go short beta times the bond market value of equity.

In Figure 35-1, we present the average betas and average regression R^2 for the different rating categories in USD for the full sample for 1990–2003 and 1999–2003. The average betas reported in this figure are computed as follows. First, the beta for a particular month for a given rating is computed as the cross-sectional average (par-weighted) of the individual bond betas for the given rating from the foregoing regressions. Then we compute the time-series average of these cross-sectional average betas by ratings and investment-grade sectors and for different sample periods. Figure 35-1 shows these time-series averages. We also report t-statistics corresponding to these time-series averages. The t-statistics are adjusted for autocorrelation in the series according to the Newey-West procedure. A beta of 0.028 means that one needs $28,000 of stock to hedge $1,000,000 of bond.

Figure 35-1 shows that the betas increase as we go down the rating spectrum. In the full sample, they range from 0.02 for A-rated bonds to 0.22 for Caa-rated bonds. This observation is consistent with Merton-type models if we consider rating as a proxy for leverage. The lower the leverage, the more the equity is in-the-money and the debt out-of-the-money, thus less sensitive to equity price movements. In the 1999–2003 sample for USD, the betas and R^2 are usually higher: ranging from 0.020 to 0.299 and from 11.0 to 32.5%, respectively, reflecting a higher debt-equity correlation in the past few years.

Figure 35-1 also gives the results for euro-denominated bonds. As in the USD case, the betas usually increase as we go down the rating spectrum (0.01 for A-rated bonds to 0.32 for Caa-rated bonds). The investment-grade betas for euro Aa, A, and Baa are smaller than the U.S. betas for the same rating categories. The high yield betas for euro follow a different pattern, and are higher than their USD counterparts by more than half.

In Figure 35-2, we present the betas and R^2 for the different investment-grade sectors in USD for the entire sample (1990–2003) and for the more recent period of 1999–2003 and in EUR for 1999–2003. For USD, in the full sample, the betas range from 0.011 for utilities to 0.042 for cyclicals. The average beta is also relatively high for the banking sector; the betas for the other sectors are distributed in a narrow range between 0.018 and 0.020. Since 1999, the betas have increased most dramatically in the telecoms sector (116% higher than in the full sample), financial sector (42%), basic industries sector (39%), and cyclical sector (38%).

The betas in euro are on average around half the USD betas in magnitude. The beta for utilities in EUR is 0.006 compared with 0.011 in USD; for noncyclicals, it is 0.009 in euro compared with 0.019 in USD. The most extreme example is for

Figure 35-1. Average Beta, R^2, and t-Statistics of the Betas by Rating

U.S. and Euro Corporate Indices

Rating	USD: 1990–2003			USD: 1999–2003			EUR: 1999–2003		
	Average Beta (equity)	R^2 (%)	t-Statistic (average beta)[a]	Average Beta (equity)	R^2 (%)	t-Statistic (average beta)[a]	Average Beta (equity)	R^2 (%)	t-Statistic (average beta)[a]
Aa	0.012	10.1	3.68	0.02	11.0	6.23	0.003	5.5	1.73
A	0.019	11.2	4.87	0.027	12.3	3.66	0.014	8.9	1.79
Baa	0.031	10.5	4.97	0.04	11.5	2.50	0.029	12.0	2.04
Ba	0.066	11.5	4.56	0.083	15.8	2.87	0.116	20.1	6.18
B	0.105	16.9	4.51	0.143	23.6	4.09	0.164	24.4	1.88
Caa	0.217	19.8	3.14	0.299	32.5	8.17	0.323	41.1	7.81
Ca	0.123	22.5	2.07	0.061	25.0	0.39	0.32	36.1	6.14

[a] The t-statistics correspond to the time-series averages of betas. They are adjusted for autocorrelation in the series according to the Newey-West procedure.

Figure 35-2. Average Beta and R^2 by Investment-Grade Sector
U.S. and Euro Corporate Indices

Sector	USD: 1990–2003		USD: 1999–2003		EUR: 1999–2003	
	Average Beta (equity)	R^2 (%)	Average Beta (equity)	R^2 (%)	Average Beta (equity)	R^2 (%)
Banking	0.027	15.6	0.029	16.1	0.005	6.3
Basic industries	0.018	7.9	0.025	8.4	0.018	8.9
Communications	0.019	8.6	0.041	11.0	0.029	12.5
Cyclicals	0.042	13.9	0.058	18.5	0.017	12.6
Energy	0.020	8.4	0.024	9.2	0.021	8.1
Financials	0.019	11.2	0.027	9.3	0.013	6.3
Noncyclicals	0.019	8.6	0.018	6.5	0.009	7.1
Utilities	0.011	6.5	0.012	7.1	0.006	7.0

banking, where the beta for EUR is 0.005, compared with 0.027 for USD. In the basic industries, telecom, and energy sectors, the betas are more comparable, although smaller than their USD counterparts; R^2 is also the highest for cyclicals and telecoms and the lowest for banking and financials.

Hedging with Issuers' Equity and the Corporate Index: CAESAR II

In this experiment, we regress bond excess returns on 1-month equity returns and the corporate market factor (MKT) using a 24-month rolling window. We calculate a different corporate market factor for each rating by taking the excess return of a par-weighted portfolio of all bonds in our sample in that rating category. In other words, the excess return of an A-rated bond is regressed on the equity of the issuer and the A-rated corporate market factor. For this reason, the betas against the credit market factors are not comparable across ratings. The beta (equity) and beta (MKT) give the hedge ratios of the debt with respect to the equity and the corporate market factor, respectively. In Figure 35-3, we present the results for U.S. corporate bonds over the entire sample period. A striking result is the change in the equity betas. The magnitudes of the new betas are now, on average, half those of the previous betas (without a corporate index factor). Among investment-grade bonds, the average equity beta for A-rated bonds is 0.008, compared with 0.019 without the index. Among high yield bonds, the average beta for Ba-rated bonds is 0.034 compared with 0.066 without the index.

Figure 35-3. Average Beta and R^2 by Rating
U.S. and Euro Corporate Indices

	USD: 1990–2003			EUR: 1999–2003		
Rating	Average Beta (equity)	Average Beta (MKT)	R^2 (%)	Average Beta (equity)	Average Beta (MKT)	R^2 (%)
Aa	0.005^a	0.698^a	39.6	0.000	0.890^a	23.1
A	0.008^a	0.827^a	42.7	0.003	0.701^a	27.4
Baa	0.015^a	0.828^a	37.8	0.016^a	0.599^a	25.0
Ba	0.034^a	0.949^a	32.2	0.081^a	0.557^a	30.5
B	0.059^a	0.779^a	38.3	0.150	0.146^a	30.9
Caa	0.149^a	0.988	29.2	0.254^a	0.530^a	51.1
Ca	0.041	0.414	29.9	0.320^a	−0.033	38.2

[a] Corresponds to t-statistics in excess of 2. The t-statistics are for the time-series averages of betas and are adjusted for autocorrelation in the series according to the Newey-West procedure.

There is a substantial increase in the R^2 when the corporate market factor is included—almost threefold for investment-grade bonds compared with those in CAESAR I. This means that a hedging strategy based purely on issuers' equity leaves a significant residual that is strongly correlated with the credit market as a whole. These results are consistent with those documented by Collin-Dufresne et al.[3] The importance of the market factor is less for high yield bonds, where the increase in R^2 is about 1.5 times.

The beta on the corporate index of the same rating is also interesting—around 0.8 for A, Baa, and B corporate bonds and close to 1 for Ba and Caa-rated bonds. This variation reflects the weight of the systematic component relative to the idiosyncratic component as captured by the equity. Figure 35-3 shows a similar drop in equity beta values for euro-denominated bonds. The beta for A-rated bonds is 0.003—79% less than the beta without an A-rated corporate index. The beta for Baa-rated bonds is 0.016—45% less than the beta without a Baa-rated corporate index. Among high yield bonds, the beta for Ba-rated bonds is 0.081—30% less than the beta without a Ba-rated corporate index. Relative to the USD equity betas, the EUR-based betas follow a pattern similar to that seen when no corporate index is used: they are lower for A-rated bonds and higher for Baa-rated and high yield bonds.

3. P. Collin-Dufresne, R. S. Goldstein, and S. J. Martin, "The Determinants of Credit Spread Changes," *Journal of Finance*, 2001, vol. 56, no. 6, pp. 2177–2207.

Figure 35-4. Average Beta and R^2 by Investment-Grade Sector
U.S. and Euro Corporate Indices

Sector	USD: 1990–2003			EUR: 1999–2003		
	Average Beta (equity)	Average Beta (MKT)	R^2 (%)	Average Beta (equity)	Average Beta (MKT)	R^2 (%)
Banking	0.012	0.943	48.7	−0.001	0.880	25.0
Basic industries	0.008	0.818	35.5	0.008	0.569	23.1
Communications	0.007	0.802	34.7	0.015	1.025	32.2
Cyclicals	0.017	0.997	44.7	0.007	0.464	24.2
Energy	0.009	0.802	37.0	0.009	0.671	22.6
Financials	0.009	0.799	45.7	0.006	1.134	23.5
Noncyclicals	0.011	0.711	33.5	0.007	0.617	25.6
Utilities	0.008	0.577	34.2	0.000	0.592	26.5

In Figure 35-4, we report the results for investment-grade U.S. corporate bonds over the full sample by sector. Consistent with the results by rating categories, the equity betas are smaller when a corporate index is included. The drop is the largest for telecoms (–63%) and the smallest for utilities (–27%). We also note a large improvement in R^2 across all sectors.

We present the same results for investment-grade EUR corporate bonds by sector. We also see a drop in the equity betas. The drop is the largest for banking (–120%) and utilities (–100%) and the smallest is for noncyclicals (–22%). This means that hedging banking and utilities debt in euro is not efficiently done with equity, but should rather be done with a corporate index. As for USD bonds, we observe a large improvement in R^2 across all sectors.

Hedging with Issuers' Equity, and Corporate and Equity Indices: CAESAR III

In this experiment, we regress bond excess returns on 1-month equity returns, the credit market factor (of the same rating, as defined in the previous section) and the Equity Mirrored Index (EQMKT) using a 24-month rolling window. The EQMKT factor mirrors the corporate index of the same rating and is constructed as the equity return on a par-weighted portfolio of the equity of issuers of that particular rating category. The betas from the regression give the hedge ratios with respect to the issuers' equity, the credit market factor (of that rating), and the equity market factor.

Figure 35-5. Average Betas and R^2 by Rating
U.S. and Euro Corporate Indices

	USD: 1990–2003				EUR: 1999–2003			
Rating	Average Beta (equity)	Average Beta (MKT)	Average Beta (EQMKT)	R^2 (%)	Average Beta (equity)	Average Beta (MKT)	Average Beta (EQMKT)	R^2 (%)
Aa	0.005[a]	0.699[a]	−0.001	42.9	−0.003[a]	0.903[a]	0.002	27.5
A	0.009[a]	0.830[a]	−0.003	46.3	0.007	0.761[a]	−0.014[a]	31.1
Baa	0.015[a]	0.850[a]	−0.008	41.5	0.021	0.739[a]	−0.028[a]	30.2
Ba	0.039[a]	1.038[a]	−0.049[a]	36.2	0.115[a]	1.123[a]	−0.204[a]	41.4
B	0.085[a]	0.921[a]	−0.100[a]	41.4	0.192[a]	0.516[a]	−0.198[a]	37.1
Caa	0.184[a]	1.031[a]	−0.079	31.6	0.317[a]	0.759[a]	−0.236[a]	53.4
Ca	0.315[a]	0.642[a]	−0.325[a]	41.5	0.324[a]	0.067[a]	−0.081	41.0

[a]Corresponds to t-statistics in excess of 2. The t-statistics are for the time-series averages of betas and are adjusted for autocorrelation in the series according to the Newey-West procedure.

In Figure 35-5, we present the results for U.S. corporate bonds over the full sample. The equity betas for Aa-, A-, Baa-, and Ba-rated bonds are not very different from the equity betas when an equity index is not included. Interestingly, the betas on equity indices have a negative sign, which points to a significant correlation in the idiosyncratic components of bond excess returns and equity returns. The R^2's tend to improve marginally, except for Ca-rated bonds, where there is a larger improvement. The pattern is similar in euro-denominated bonds.

In Figure 35-6, we report the results for U.S. corporate bonds by investment-grade sectors over the full sample. There is a slight improvement in the R^2, and overall the beta coefficients on the issuer equity and the Credit Index have the same order of magnitude as in CAESAR II. A similar pattern exists for euro-denominated bonds.

Effectiveness of Hedging with Equity, Credit, and Equity Indices

In this section, we investigate the effectiveness of hedging debt positions using the empirical hedge ratios given by CAESAR I, II, and III. For this purpose, we compute the volatility of the hedged and unhedged excess returns for different currencies, ratings, and sectors. We also report the percentage reduction in volatility obtained using hedging strategies corresponding to the three foregoing experiments.

In Figure 35-7, we present the results by rating for U.S. corporate bonds for the 1990–2003 period. The figure shows the volatility of monthly excess returns

Figure 35-6. Average Beta and R^2 by Investment-Grade Sector
U.S. and Euro Corporate Indices

Sector	USD: 1990–2003				EUR: 1999–2003			
	Average Beta (equity)	Average Beta (MKT)	Average Beta (EQMKT)	R^2 (%)	Average Beta (equity)	Average Beta (MKT)	Average Beta (EQMKT)	R^2 (%)
Banking	0.009	0.897	0.010	52.1	−0.001	0.905	−0.003	29.1
Basic industries	0.008	0.847	−0.006	38.9	0.014	0.697	−0.026	27.6
Communications	0.108	0.845	−0.015	38.8	0.018	1.097	−0.021	35.8
Cyclicals	0.011	1.037	−0.003	48.1	0.013	0.560	−0.022	30.1
Energy	0.011	0.827	−0.008	40.6	0.009	0.720	−0.007	26.0
Financials	0.009	0.787	0.000	49.1	0.006	1.162	−0.006	28.8
Noncyclicals	0.006	0.765	−0.004	37.8	0.009	0.684	−0.013	29.4
Utilities	0.010	0.596	−0.011	38.4	0.001	0.634	−0.003	29.8

Figure 35-7. Average Volatility and Volatility Reduction by Rating
U.S. Corporate Index, 1990–2003

| | Unhedged | CAESAR I | | CAESAR II | | CAESAR III | |
	Volatility	Volatility	% Reduction	Volatility	% Reduction	Volatility	% Reduction
Rating							
Aa	0.37	0.35	3.3	0.12	67.3	0.12	67.8
A	0.46	0.43	7.3	0.13	71.4	0.12	73.5
Baa	0.85	0.73	14.1	0.36	57.3	0.37	56.8
Ba	1.72	1.35	21.4	1.08	37.3	1.08	37.2
B	2.92	2.32	20.5	2.05	29.9	2.01	31.3
Caa	8.77	7.09	19.1	7.84	10.6	7.85	10.4
Ca	12.51	13.98	−11.7	13.31	−6.4	14.76	−17.9

on bonds in our sample (the unhedged volatility), as well as the volatility of returns on hedged positions in bonds. The hedged positions are created according to the three experiments described above using the regression-based hedge ratios. Results corresponding to CAESAR I relate to the case in which bond positions in any month are hedged with issuers' equity alone, with the hedge ratios given by betas estimated over the previous 24 months. Results for CAESAR II and III are for the case in which the hedge includes the Corporate Index (CAESAR II) and both Corporate and Equity indices (CAESAR III). Since our starting point is always excess bond returns, all positions are always hedged against interest-rate risk.

Hedging only with the equity of the issuer with CAESAR I reduces volatility from an average of 21% for Ba-rated bonds to 7% for A-rated bonds and even increases volatility for Ca-rated bonds. The inclusion of a corporate index of the same rating as a hedging instrument improves the hedging performance dramatically for investment-grade bonds. There is a 71% reduction in volatility for A-rated bonds in CAESAR II, compared with only 7% in CAESAR I, and 57% for Baa-rated bonds in CAESAR II, compared with 14% in CAESAR I. The drop in hedging volatility is also significant in the high yield universe for Ba- and B-rated bonds. The hedging volatility increases for Caa- and Ca-rated corporate bonds. CAESAR III, which incorporates an equity index, does not significantly reduce the volatility of hedged returns beyond CAESAR II.

In Figure 35-8, we report the same results for EUR corporate bonds for the 1999–2003 period. Hedging only with the equity of the issuer with CAESAR I reduces volatility from an average of 15.1% for A-rated bonds to 2.6% for Aa-rated bonds and even increases volatility for Caa-rated bonds. As in the USD case, the inclusion of a corporate index of bonds of the same rating in CAESAR II also improves the hedging dramatically for investment-grade bonds. There is a 74.3% reduction in volatility for A-rated bonds, compared with 15.1%, and 35.2% for Baa-rated bonds, compared with 10.5%. Hedging volatility does not fall in the high yield universe except for B-rated bonds. Interestingly, CAESAR III, which incorporates an equity index, improves on the hedging volatility only for Baa-rated bonds, decreasing volatility by 50.5 instead of 35.2%.

In Figure 35-9, we present the results by investment-grade sector for USD corporate bonds for the 1990–2003 period. Hedging only with the equity of the issuer with CAESAR I reduces volatility from an average of 23.2% for cyclical sector bonds to 1.8% for noncyclical sector bonds. As for ratings, the inclusion of the Corporate Bond Index of the same rating in CAESAR II also improves the hedging dramatically for investment-grade bonds, from 64.4 to 21.9%. We also see that CAESAR III (hedging including the equity index) does not seem to improve the hedging significantly.

Figure 35-8. Average Volatility and Volatility Reduction by Rating
Euro Corporate Index, 1999–2003

Rating	Unhedged Volatility	CAESAR I Volatility	CAESAR I % Reduction	CAESAR II Volatility	CAESAR II % Reduction	CAESAR III Volatility	CAESAR III % Reduction
Aa	0.11	0.10	2.6	0.05	52.5	0.05	54.6
A	0.37	0.31	15.1	0.09	74.3	0.09	74.6
Baa	0.89	0.80	10.5	0.58	35.2	0.44	50.5
Ba	4.25	3.66	13.8	5.06	–19.2	6.34	–49.2
B	14.95	14.37	3.9	14.49	3.1	14.32	4.2
Caa	14.01	14.88	–6.2	15.48	–10.5	15.93	–13.7
Ca	12.25	11.73	4.3	12.40	–1.2	12.76	–4.1

Figure 35-9. Average Volatility and Volatility Reduction by Sector
U.S. Corporate Index, 1990–2003

	Unhedged	CAESAR I		CAESAR II		CAESAR III	
Sector	Volatility	Volatility	% Reduction	Volatility	% Reduction	Volatility	% Reduction
Banking	0.42	0.40	4.0	0.24	42.6	0.24	43.2
Basic Industries	0.58	0.55	4.5	0.32	44.0	0.33	42.8
Communications	0.84	0.72	13.5	0.33	60.3	0.31	63.3
Cyclicals	1.00	0.77	23.2	0.36	64.4	0.35	64.6
Energy	0.63	0.60	5.6	0.34	46.0	0.35	45.4
Financials	0.61	0.57	6.7	0.32	48.3	0.32	47.3
Noncyclicals	0.46	0.45	1.8	0.30	35.4	0.30	35.0
Utilities	1.05	0.94	10.1	0.82	21.9	0.81	22.5

In Figure 35-10, we report the equivalent results by sector for euro corporate bonds for the 1999–2003 period. Hedging only with the equity of the issuer with CAESAR I reduces volatility from an average of 16.1% for basic industries sector bonds to 8.6% for cyclical sector bonds. There is even an increase in volatility with noncyclical sector bonds. As in the USD case, the inclusion of the Corporate Index of same rating in CAESAR II also improves the hedging dramatically for investment-grade bonds, from 55.1% for telecom bonds to 11.3% for noncyclicals. Finally, CAESAR III seems to improve the hedging for basic industries and cyclical sector bonds and marginally for energy, financial, noncyclical, and utilities sector bonds.

HEDGING ANALYSIS WITH ORION

The second hedging methodology is based on our equity-based credit valuation model, ORION. The structural approach of the model benefits from explicit modeling assumptions and parameter calibration. Its main drawback is model risk, especially if an important variable is not present in the model. In this section, we first describe the ORION model and its implications for hedge ratios. We then look at the performance of equity-based hedging of debt with hedge ratios given by the model.

The ORION Model

The ORION model is an equity-based credit valuation model. It uses equity price as its main driving variable and spread information to determine the level of a default barrier. It avoids the complication of Merton-type models by taking the equity value as the fundamental driving variable instead of the value of the firm's assets. For this reason, ORION does not have to use accounting leverage data—which may not always be reliably available—explicitly. With a stochastic barrier perfectly correlated across issuers, ORION can also capture a systematic credit market factor that is not usually modeled in structural credit models.

In the ORION model:

- The firm defaults when the stock price, $S(t)$, falls below the default barrier, $B(t)$.

- The default barrier evolves stochastically over time.

The barrier $B(t)$ (in comparison to the equity price) can be thought of as a summary measure of the strength of all possible factors that might lead to a credit

Figure 35-10. Average Volatility and Volatility Reduction by Sector
Euro Corporate Index, 1999–2003

Sector	Unhedged	CAESAR I		CAESAR II		CAESAR III	
	Volatility	Volatility	% Reduction	Volatility	% Reduction	Volatility	% Reduction
Banking	0.14	0.13	11.5	0.08	47.8	0.08	41.6
Basic industries	0.99	0.83	16.1	0.75	23.6	0.57	42.2
Communications	0.94	0.82	12.7	0.42	55.1	0.45	52.4
Cyclicals	0.49	0.45	8.6	0.38	22.3	0.29	40.2
Energy	0.45	0.38	15.4	0.27	39.1	0.27	40.1
Financials	0.45	0.41	10.7	0.31	32.5	0.30	34.2
Noncyclicals	0.45	0.46	-1.2	0.40	11.3	0.40	12.0
Utilities	0.44	0.39	11.6	0.32	26.5	0.32	28.5

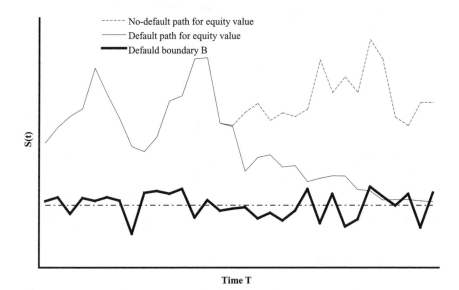

Figure 35-11. The Equity Value and Default Boundary Are Both Stochastic[a]
[a]Default can be caused by the equity value moving below the default boundary.

event (e.g., liquidity shortage, reduction in the ability to service long-term debt, or even marketwide financial distress). The barriers could be correlated across firms to reflect a systematic credit market risk factor.

The ORION model assumes that S_t, the stock price of a firm, follows a log-normal Brownian motion:

$$dS_t = S_t(r - \delta_t)dt - \sigma S_t dW_t, \tag{35-1}$$

where r is the default-free interest rate, δ is the dividend pay-out ratio, σ is the volatility of the equity return process, and dW_t is an increment of standard Brownian motion with zero mean and variance dt.

The stochastic barrier follows a diffusion process:

$$dB_t = \sigma_B \cdot B_t dW_{Bt}. \tag{35-2}$$

The initial barrier level is assumed to be B_0. Default occurs if the equity price falls below the default barrier. Figure 35-11 illustrates two possible sample paths of the firm's equity.

Given the foregoing assumption, we can value securities whose cash flows are contingent on default, such as credit bonds and default swaps. Using these valuation equations, we can also compute the model-implied hedge ratios (or deltas) of credit securities with respect to the issuers' equity.

Pricing of Corporate Debt in ORION

The simple ORION framework allows us to compute the values of the firm's liabilities. For example, the value of a bond is simply the discounted sum of coupons and principal payment weighted by the survival probabilities:

$$D(0, T) = \sum_{j=1}^{n} C(T_j)Z(0, T_j)P(\Gamma > T_j \mid \Gamma > 0) + RG(T_n), \tag{35-3}$$

where G is the present value of receiving 1 euro if default occurs over the interval $[0,T]$, $C(T_j)$ is the coupon paid at time T_j, $Z(0, T_j)$ is the discount rate between time zero and time T_j, $P(\Gamma > T_j \mid \Gamma > 0)$ is the survival probability, and R is the bond recovery value.

Derivation of the Hedge Ratios: Bond/CDS-Equity

The model-implied hedge ratio, $\Delta(t)$, is given by the partial derivative of the bond-pricing equation with respect to $S(t)$. (Both the survival probability and the present value of receiving 1 euro if default occurs are functions of the equity price.) For hedging a long debt position worth \$M, one needs to go short the issuer's equity worth \$$M\Delta(t)S(t)/D(t)$, where $S(t)$ is the market value of equity per share and $D(t)$ is the market value per unit of debt.

We compare the hedging results obtained using the empirical methodology (CAESAR) and the model-based methodology (based on ORION). For the model-based hedging, we compute the delta hedge every month after calibration of the model to the equity price, the equity volatility, and the spread curve of the issuer. We then go long the bond (hedged by duration-matched Treasuries) and short sell the appropriate amount of issuer's equity. We compute the returns of the hedged position a month later. We repeat this hedging exercise every month and report the average volatility of the hedged and unhedged excess returns and the percentage reduction in the volatility.

In Figure 35-12, we present the average hedge ratios (or equity betas) for the top 100 USD issuers (by par amount outstanding) by rating categories for the 1999–2003 period. The model-based hedge ratios are larger than the empirical betas across all the ratings from Aa to B. Since our model assumes credit spreads reflect only default risk, and not any non-default-related risk such as illiquidity, the model may overestimate the risk of default and, consequently, the correlation of equity and debt values.

In the same figure, we also present the average equity betas for the top 100 euro issuers by rating categories. The model-based betas are larger than empirical betas

Figure 35-12. Average Betas by Rating
Top 100 U.S. and Euro Corporate Issuers

	Top 100 USD Issuers: 1999–2003		Top 100 EUR Issuers: 1999–2003	
	Empirical Hedging with Equity	Model-Based Hedging with Equity	Empirical Hedging with Equity	Model-Based Hedging with Equity
Rating	Average Beta (equity)	Average Beta (equity)	Average Beta (equity)	Average Beta (equity)
Aa	0.029	0.145	0.006	0.068
A	0.034	0.176	0.019	0.099
Baa	0.053	0.194	0.035	0.143
Ba	0.082	0.243	0.215	0.212
B	0.200	0.256	0.144	0.148

for investment-grade bonds and, interestingly, are close to empirical betas for Ba- and B-rated bonds.

In Figure 35-13, we report the average volatility reduction owing to empirical and model-based hedging for the top 100 USD issuers by rating categories for the 1999–2003 period. The model-based hedging performs slightly worse than empirical hedging except for B-rated bonds.

In Figure 35-14, we show the average volatility reduction owing to hedging for the top 100 EUR issuers by rating categories. Despite the difference in the magnitudes of the hedge ratios, model-based hedging performs better than the empirical hedging for A-, Baa-, Ba-, and B-rating categories. On average, the volatility

Figure 35-13. Average Volatility and Volatility Reduction by Rating
Top 100 USD Issuers by Par Amount Outstanding, 1999–2003

	Unhedged	Empirical Hedging with Equity		Model-Based Hedging with Equity	
Rating	Volatility	Volatility	% Reduction	Volatility	% Reduction
Aa	0.67	0.61	9.0	0.74	−11.3
A	0.93	0.76	19.1	0.88	6.2
Baa	1.74	1.26	27.6	1.33	23.6
Ba	4.01	3.13	22.0	3.35	16.5
B	10.65	8.62	19.1	7.95	25.4

Figure 35-14. Average Volatility and Volatility Reduction by Rating
Top 100 EUR Issuers by Par Amount Outstanding, 1999–2003

Rating	Unhedged Volatility	Empirical Hedging with Equity		Model-Based Hedging with Equity	
		Volatility	% Reduction	Volatility	% Reduction
Aa	0.29	0.27	6.6	0.34	−16.8
A	0.63	0.54	14.1	0.39	37.6
Baa	1.76	1.55	11.9	1.15	34.8
Ba	6.02	4.51	25.1	4.48	25.6
B	2.66	2.84	−6.9	2.30	13.6

drops by a third when an equity hedge is used. It is clearly not a perfect hedge as two-thirds of the volatility remains.

Finally, it may be noted that the default barrier is also stochastic in ORION: hedging with equity alone is insufficient to completely immunize a bond or a CDS portfolio. If we make the additional assumption that the barriers across all the assets are perfectly correlated because the Brownian term is shared and represents a measure of liquidity or systematic risk, the hedging strategy would consist of the issuer's equity as well as a credit market index hedge.

SCENARIO ANALYSIS

As shown earlier, hedging investment-grade debt with equity produces mixed results unless wider market factors are taken into account. This section presents a scenario-based approach for analyzing such trades. At the single-issuer level, debt-equity trades are highly idiosyncratic in nature. For this reason, the debt-equity relationship is complex and difficult to model accurately. Unpredictable co-movements of debt and equity can have a significant effect on the performance of a debt-equity trade, so care must be taken to understand the range of possible outcomes. To illustrate how to do this, we present the following example.

Example: Long Bond, Short Equity

Consider an investor who is long €1 million face value of a 5.25% November 08 bond (5-year maturity) with a full price of 100.37, and short 15,000 of the issuer's equity shares with a share price at €10. For valuation purposes, suppose that the

Figure 35-15. Mark-to-Market Variation of a Long-Bond, Short-Equity Trade

Share Price Varies across Columns and CDS Spreads Vary Down Rows

Trade MTM	(€, 000s)	Stock Price								
		8.0	8.5	9.0	9.5	10.0	10.5	11.0	11.5	12.0
CDS spread	100	+80	+72	+65	+57	+50	+42	+35	+27	+20
	150	+57	+50	+42	+35	+27	+20	+12	+5	−3
	200	+35	+28	+20	+13	+5	−2	−10	−17	−25
	250	+14	+7	−1	−8	−16	−23	−31	−38	−46
	300	−6	−14	−21	−29	−36	−44	−51	−59	−66

LIBOR term structure is flat at 3% and the CDS credit curve is flat at 200 bp, with an assumed 40% recovery. The bond is funded at LIBOR flat.

Figure 35-15 shows the mark-to-market (MTM) of this trade at a 3-month horizon as a function of the spread and stock price on that future horizon date. In this figure, we have allowed the spreads to move in the range of 100–300 bp while the share price moves between €8 and €12. Moreover, we have used CDS spreads to characterize the state of the debt market in the future, assuming that bonds and default swaps are consistently priced.

Consider what happens if the share price rallies from €10 to €11 and the CDS spread tightens from 200 to 150 bp. First, the MTM of the short equity position is €(11 − 10) × (−15,000) = − €15,000. If the CDS spread tightens to 150 bp, then the corresponding model-implied full bond price is 103.82, which means that the long bond position has a positive MTM of €(103.82 − 100.37) × 1 million = €34,500. The cost of funding the bond over this period is 3% × 0.25 × 100.37 × €1 million = €7,500. The net MTM of the trade (ignoring interest on any short equity proceeds) in this case is therefore a positive €12,000.

Figure 35-15 shows the wide range of values that the trade MTM can take, depending on the states of the debt and equity markets at the horizon date. If the markets remain static, then the trade accrues carry net of funding, which is shown in the figure as the intersection of the shaded row and column. However, as the figure shows, this number could vary between +€80,000 and −€66,000, depending on the joint realization of spreads and equity prices. Of course, the extreme outcomes are relatively less likely and we should attempt to assign some likelihood to them.

Further, this trade is exposed to default risk, and the VOD (value on default) depends strongly on the realized recovery rate, as shown in Figure 35-16. For example, if the issuer defaults with 30% recovery, then the loss on the bond is €(30.00

Figure 35-16. Value on Default (VOD) as a Function of Realized Recovery Rate

Recovery (%)	10	20	30	40	50	60	70	80	90
VOD (€1,000)	−754	−654	−554	−454	−354	−254	−154	−54	+46

− 100.37) × 1 million = −€703,700. Assuming conservatively that the equity is worthless after default, we see that the gain on the short equity position is −€10.00 × (−15,000) = + €150,000. The net effect is a negative value on default of −€553,700. Figure 35-16 summarizes various outcomes.

This example demonstrates the necessity of stress testing a debt-equity hedge. A model-based or empirically determined hedge ratio implicitly contains a view on the co-movement of debt and equity markets in the future. If the realized outcomes differ from this view, the MTM of the hedge could deviate significantly from zero. In the remainder of this section, we analyze a specific debt-equity hedge within the foregoing framework.

Example: Long Ahold 5.875% May 08 vs. Short Equity

Consider an investor who goes long €1 million of the Ahold 5.875% 08 bond, paying a full price of 102.52, corresponding to a CDS spread of 200 bp, and hedges this by selling Ahold shares. The share price is €8.02. The 5-year Euro swap rate is 3.75%. Suppose the investor has a 3-month horizon.

The equity hedge implied by the ORION model for this bond is to go short 24.4% of the market value of the bond. This corresponds to selling 31,200 shares at the current price. Figure 35-17 shows a sample of how the MTM of this hedge can behave. The hedge is effective within a certain range of realizations, which represents the implicit view on how the debt-equity relationship is expected to evolve. Outside of this range, the hedge can turn out to be a strong bullish or bearish trade. Corporate events such as nationalization, rights issue, share buy-back, merger, or a takeover can create unexpected co-movements. As in the previous example, this trade too is exposed to significant default risk, which depends on the realized recovery rate following a credit event.

In summary, the contemporaneous relationship between debt and equity is complex and generating robust hedges consisting only of issuers' equity is difficult. For this reason, scenario analysis is a useful approach for investigating how different outcomes of the market might affect the performance of a given debt-equity trade.

Figure 35-17. Sample MTM of the Debt-Equity Hedge

Share Price Varies across Rows and CDS Spreads Vary Down Columns

MTM	(€, 000s)	Stock Price						
		5.0	6.0	7.0	8.0	9.0	10.0	11.0
CDS Spread	50	+160	+129	+98	+67	+36	+4	−27
	75	+150	+119	+87	+56	+25	−6	−37
	100	+139	+108	+77	+46	+15	−17	−48
	125	+129	+98	+67	+36	+4	−27	−58
	150	+119	+88	+57	+26	−6	−37	−68
	175	+109	+78	+47	+16	−16	−47	−78
	200	+100	+68	+37	+6	−25	−56	−88
	225	+90	+59	+28	−4	−35	−66	−97
	250	+81	+49	+18	−13	−44	−75	−107
	275	+71	+40	+9	−22	−53	−85	−116
	300	+62	+31	−0	−31	−62	−94	−125
	325	+53	+22	−9	−40	−71	−103	−134
	350	+45	+13	−18	−49	−80	−111	−143

CONCLUSION

In this study, we have used two different methodologies to hedge debt with equity: (1) the empirical hedging methodology based on a regression analysis using the CAESAR model and (2) model-based hedging using the equity-based credit valuation model ORION. We have also introduced a scenario-based analysis for special situations. We presented an empirical investigation of the performance of CAESAR and ORION and discussed the use of scenario analysis of hedging strategies. One important conclusion is that pure-investment-grade debt-equity hedging needs a credit index hedge to perform reasonably well because the equity and credit markets may not be completely integrated: the credit market is subject to a systematic risk factor not directly related to equity. The effect of this overall market factor is smaller for high yield and crossover bonds. The pure equity-based hedging results are better for high yield and crossover bonds with both CAESAR and ORION. It is possible to achieve a reduction in volatility by hedging with equity, more so with high yield and crossover bonds, but it is far from perfect. Debt-equity hedging should be complemented by a better understanding of systematic market effects and through the use of scenario analysis.

INDEX

Page numbers followed by *f* indicate figures; those followed by *n* indicate notes.